FIRST CANADIAN EDITION

Contemporary
Financial Management

DON CYR
Brock University

ALFRED L. KAHL
University of Ottawa

WILLIAM F. RENTZ
University of Ottawa

R. CHARLES MOYER
Babcock Graduate School of Management
Wake Forest University

JAMES R. McGUIGAN
JRM Investments

WILLIAM J. KRETLOW
University of Houston

THOMSON
NELSON

Australia   Canada   Mexico   Singapore   Spain   United Kingdom   United States

THOMSON
─────✦─────™
NELSON

Contemporary Financial Management,
First Canadian Edition

by Don Cyr, Alfred L. Kahl, William F. Rentz,
R. Charles Moyer, James R. McGuigan, William J. Kretlow

Editorial Director and Publisher:
Evelyn Veitch

Executive Editors:
Veronica Visentin & Ric Kitowski

Executive Marketing Manager:
Don Thompson

Developmental Editor:
Eliza Marciniak

Photo Researcher:
Paula Joiner

Permissions Coordinator:
Paula Joiner

Production Editor:
Natalia Denesiuk

Copy Editor:
Joan Rawlin

Proofreader:
June Trusty

Indexer:
Jin Tan

Senior Production Coordinator:
Hedy Sellers

Creative Director:
Angela Cluer

Interior Design:
Christy Carr

Design Modifications for This Edition:
Tammy Gay

Cover Design:
Ken Phipps

Cover Images:
Top: ©Macduff Everton/Iconica
Bottom: ©Paul Simcock/Iconica
Background: ©Grego
Schuster/Iconica

Compositor:
Gerry Dunn

Printer:
Transcontinental

National Library of Canada Cataloguing in Publication

Contemporary financial management / Don Cyr...[et al.]. — 1st Canadian ed.

Includes bibliographical references and index.
ISBN 0-17-616992-X

1. Corporations—Finance. 2. Business enterprises—Finance. I. Cyr, Donald A., 1957–

HG4026.C58 2004   658.15
C2003-907168-5

To Lola
ALK

To Claudette
WFR

To Sally, Craig, and Laura
RCM

To the memory of my mother and father
JRM

To Cindy, John, and Jim
WJK

About the Authors

Don Cyr

is the Associate Dean and an Associate Professor of Finance in the Faculty of Business at Brock University. Previously he taught at the University of Saskatchewan and the University of Northern British Columbia. He earned his B.Sc. from Concordia University, his M.B.A from the University of Saskatchewan, and his M.A. and Ph.D. from the University of Alberta.

In addition to coauthoring *Contemporary Financial Management,* First Canadian Edition, he has also presented several papers at professional society meetings and has published a number of articles in academic and professional journals, including the *Journal of Futures Markets* and the *International Review of Economics and Finance.* He has also authored and provided several training programs for the investment industry and has consulted for a number of firms.

Professor Cyr has received teaching excellence awards at both the University of Saskatchewan and at Brock University.

Alfred L. Kahl

is Adjunct Professor of Finance at the School of Management of the University of Ottawa. Previously he taught at Minnesota State University–Mankato, the University of Georgia, and the University of Tunis.

He has been a visiting professor at the University of Lethbridge, the Universidad Internacional de las Americas in Costa Rica, the Sorbonne in France, the Riga Business School in Latvia, the Academy of Economic Studies in Romania, and at Xian-Jiaotong University in China. He has taught online for the University of Maryland and Florida Institute of Technology.

He earned his B.A. at the University of Maryland, his M.B.A. at the University of Pittsburgh, and his Ph.D. in Business and Economics from the University of Florida.

Professor Kahl is a Chartered Financial Management Analyst (CFMA), a Certified Computer Professional (CCP), and a Certified E-commerce Consultant (CEC).

In addition to coauthoring *Contemporary Financial Management,* First Canadian Edition, he has also coauthored *Canadian Financial Management,* Fourth Edition (Dryden, 1994), *Introduction aux Affaires,* (Morin, 1993), and *Spreadsheet Applications in Engineering Economics* (West, 1992), as well as *Engineering Economics* (McGraw-Hill Ryerson, 1986). Professor Kahl has published extensively in leading academic and professional journals, including *Journal of Finance, Journal of Business Finance and Accounting, Accounting and Business Research, International Journal of Accounting, Journal of Public and International Affairs, Financial Review, American Economic Review, Decision Science, Management Science, Management International Review,* and many others.

William F. Rentz

is Associate Professor of Finance and Business Economics at the School of Management of the University of Ottawa. Previously he taught at Northwestern University and at the University of Texas at Austin.

He has been a visiting professor at the Universidad Internacional de las Americas in Costa Rica; the University of Florida, the State University of New York at Binghampton, and Stanford University in the United States; and the University of Basel in Switzerland.

He earned his S.B. in electrical engineering from the Massachusetts Institute of Technology, and his A.M. and Ph.D. in Economics from the University of Rochester.

In addition to coauthoring *Contemporary Financial Management*, First Canadian Edition, he has also coauthored *Canadian Financial Management*, Fourth Edition (Dryden, 1994), *Spreadsheet Applications in Engineering Economics* (West, 1992) and *Engineering Economics* (McGraw-Hill Ryerson, 1986). Professor Rentz has published extensively in leading academic and professional journals, including *Journal of Finance, Journal of Business Finance and Accounting, Journal of Risk and Insurance, Financial Review, American Economic Review, Management Science,* and many others.

R. Charles Moyer

holds the GMAC Insurance Chair in Finance and is Dean of the Babcock Graduate School of Management, Wake Forest University. Previously he taught at Texas Tech University, the University of Houston, Lehigh University, and the University of New Mexico. He earned his B.A. in economics (*cum laude*) from Howard University. He received his M.B.A. and Ph.D. in Business from the University of Pittsburgh.

Professor Moyer has been a productive scholar. In addition to coauthoring *Contemporary Financial Management*, Ninth Edition (South-Western, 2003), he has also coauthored *Managerial Economics*, Ninth Edition (South-Western, 2002), and *Financial Management with Lotus 1-2-3* (West, 1986). Professor Moyer has published extensively in leading finance and economic journals, including *Financial Management, Journal of Financial and Quantitative Analysis, Journal of Finance, Financial Review, Journal of Financial Research, International Journal of Forecasting, Journal of Economics and Business, Journal of Industrial Organization,* and many others.

Professor Moyer has received teaching excellence awards both at the University of New Mexico and at Wake Forest University.

James R. McGuigan

currently owns and operates his own numismatic investment firm. Previously, he was Associate Professor of Finance and Business Economics in the School of Business Administration at Wayne State University, where he taught for 10 years. He also has taught at the University of Pittsburgh and Point Park College.

Dr. McGuigan received his undergraduate degree from Carnegie-Mellon University, his M.B.A. from the University of Chicago, and his Ph.D. from the University of Pittsburgh.

He has published articles dealing with his research on options in the *Journal of Financial and Quantitative Analysis*. In addition to coauthoring *Contemporary Financial Management*, Ninth Edition (South-Western, 2003), Dr. McGuigan has coauthored books in managerial economics, including *Managerial Economics,* Ninth Edition (South-Western, 2002), which he coauthored with R. Charles Moyer and Frederick Harris.

William J. Kretlow

is an Associate Professor of Finance at the University of Houston. He earned his B.S. from the University of Michigan, his M.B.A. from the University of Houston and his Ph.D. from Purdue University. He has also been part-time Associate Professor of Economics at Rice University.

Professor Kretlow has received several teaching awards, including the University of Houston Teaching Excellence Award and the College of Business Administration Excellence in Teaching Award. He also is recipient of Rice University's *Magna Cum Laude* Teaching Excellence Award.

In addition to coauthoring *Contemporary Financial Management*, Ninth Edition (South-Western, 2003), Professor Kretlow has published numerous articles and presented papers at professional society meetings. His research deals with the capital asset pricing model, dividend policy, bond ratings, and financial planning models.

Brief Contents

Contents

Preface

The financial management field continues to experience exciting change and growth. Financial practitioners are increasingly employing new financial management techniques and sophisticated computer resources to aid in their decision making. "Financial engineers" have created new derivative financial instruments and transactions, such as options, financial futures contracts, foreign currency swaps, and interest rate swaps, to help managers manage risk and increase shareholder wealth. Many domestic industries have been restructured because of the pressures of foreign competition. Leveraged buyout transactions also have forced managers to make more careful use of their firm's resources. Corporate reformers have focused attention on the structure of corporate governance relationships and the impact of alternative managerial compensation packages on performance.

Access to and content of the Internet have greatly expanded, making timely financial information increasingly available to customers, investors, and managers. The Internet is transforming the way securities are bought and sold and the way companies access new capital. At the same time, financial researchers have made important advances in valuation, cost of capital, capital structure theory and practice, option valuation (including "real" options associated with capital investments), hedging strategies, and dividend policy.

The future promises to be an even more exiting time for finance professionals. Financial managers have refocused their attention on the basic objective of maximizing shareholder wealth. Managers who act contrary to the interests of shareholders face the prospect of an unfriendly takeover, a corporate restructuring, pressure from foreign competitors, or pressures from shareholder groups and institutional investors. Firms increasingly must find operating savings necessary to remain competitive, as managers continue to struggle to find the optimal capital structure of their firm. The central importance of cash flows in the financial management of a firm has never been more apparent. Firms carrying significantly more debt than in the past faced new challenges during the recession of 2001–2002. With the economic unification of Europe and the rise of capitalism in Eastern Europe, the former Soviet Union, and China, contemporary financial managers must possess greater knowledge of the important aspects of doing business in a global marketplace. In addition, the standards of ethical behaviour adopted by managers of business enterprises becomes ever more important. Finally, the impact of the Internet on all areas of business practice continues to revolutionize the financial arena due to the lifting of barriers to timely information access and the increase of competitive pressures on business managers.

Contemporary Financial Management, First Canadian Edition, incorporates these changes—the increased focus on shareholder wealth maximization and cash flow management, an emphasis on the global aspects of financial management, a concern for ethical behaviour of managers, and the new information available on the Internet—into a textbook designed for an introductory course in financial management. The book is also suitable for management development programs.

We recognize that students enter the introductory course with a wide variety of backgrounds in accounting, economics, mathematics, and statistics.

Organization and Intended Use

The book is organized in seven major parts. Part One defines the finance function, examines the goals of the firm, considers the role of the financial manager, reviews the structure and functioning of the domestic and global financial marketplaces, and reviews accounting fundamentals, including the forecasting and evaluation of financial performance. The role of investment dealers/bankers in the issuance of securities is discussed. The importance of tax considerations to the practice of financial management is also analyzed. The basic concepts of shareholder wealth maximization, cash flows, and net present value are presented. Part Two develops the theory of valuation, including a comprehensive treatment of time value of money concepts, the valuation of fixed income securities, and the valuation of equity securities. Risk and return analysis concepts are presented. Part Three covers the firm's cost of capital and its capital investment decisions. Both the theoretical and the practical aspects of capital budgeting are emphasized, including the role played by real options in the capital budgeting process. Part Four deals with the capital structure and dividend policy decisions, including the determinants of the optimal capital structure of the firm. Part Five considers working capital management decisions in the management and financing of the current assets—cash, marketable securities, accounts receivable and inventories—and the sources of short- and intermediate-term funds. Part Six covers the important aspects of domestic and international financial risk management. Part Seven covers leasing and corporate restructuring.

Instructors who wish to cover topics in an order different than that provided in the book will find it very easy to do so. The book is designed for use in a one-term introductory course in financial management. Typically, within the constraints of this time limit, it is very often not possible to fully cover all of the topics. The book is organized to make it very flexible. Instructors will find it easy to defer more advanced or specialized topics to a later course.

Distinctive Features

Contemporary Financial Management, First Canadian Edition, has been carefully designed to assist the student in learning and to stimulate student interest. Distinctive pedagogical features include:

- **Foundation Concepts** These important concepts are introduced early in the book and are highlighted.

- **Learning Objectives** Each chapter begins with a listing of learning objectives.

- **Financial Challenges** Each chapter begins with a real-life financial management problem. These challenges are revisited at the end of each chapter.

- **International Issues** To emphasize and reinforce the global nature of financial decision making, we have included "International Issues" sections throughout the book. In these sections, the global issues in financial decision making are illustrated.

- **Ethical Issues** "Ethical Issues" sections are integrated throughout the book to present some of the ethical dilemmas facing financial managers and raise sensitivities to these issues.

- **Entrepreneurial Issues** In recognition of the important role of small and medium-sized enterprises in the contemporary Canadian business environment, we have included "Entrepreneurial Issues" sections throughout the book to emphasize unique financial problems and concerns of entrepreneurs.

- **Calculator Application Illustrations** Many chapters have easy-to-follow, step-by-step calculator keystrokes to solve many of the time value of money examples in the book. These sections are set up in a generic manner and can be used with virtually any financial calculator.

- **Spreadsheets** In addition to spreadsheets in selected chapters, some chapters have appendices that explain how spreadsheets can be used to help solve financial problems. MS Excel templates to solve many of the problems in the book are available on the book's Web site.

http://cyr.nelson.com

- **Internet Applications** There are numerous references throughout the book to Internet resources, and more are available on the book's Web site.

- **Problem Sets** The end-of-chapter problem sets have been organized into three degrees of difficulty: basic, intermediate, and challenge. The problem sets provide students and instructors with a greater breadth and depth of problem coverage than is the case with many competing textbooks. Even more problems are available on the book's Web site.

- **Self-Test Problems** Each chapter includes end-of-chapter self-test problems that students can use for practice and enhanced understanding of the concepts developed in the chapters. Detailed solutions to these problems appear at the back of the book.

- **Check Answers** In addition, there are check answers to selected problems at the back of the book so students can see if they have correctly solved the selected problems in the problem sets.

Organizational Design

Contemporary Financial Management is organized around the objective of maximizing the value of the firm for its shareholders. This objective is introduced early in the book, and each major financial decision is linked to the impact it has on the value of the firm. The distinctive content features are designed to complement this objective:

1. **Emphasis on the fundamental concepts of cash flow, net present value, and risk-return relationships** There are three concepts that are central to a complete understanding of most financial management decisions:

   - The importance of cash flows as the relevant source of value to a firm

   - The significance of the net present value rule for valuing cash flows

   - The relationship between risk and return in the valuation process

2. **Unique treatment of problems of international financial management** In a business world that is increasingly global, it is important that finance students be aware of the most important dimensions of international finance. Important international finance relationships, including the operation of foreign currency markets, exchange rate determination, and the role of multinational firms in the global economy, are covered in Chapter 2 ("The Domestic and Global Financial Marketplace"). More advanced international topics, such as international parity relationships, the management of foreign exchange risk, and hedging exchange rate risk are introduced in Chapter 18, "Managing International Risk." In addition, international viewpoints are covered in other chapters where appropriate. This treatment of the international dimensions of financial management is consistent with the AACSB's recommendations for coverage of these issues.

3. **Comprehensive and integrated coverage of ethical issues facing financial managers** Financial managers seeking to maximize shareholder wealth must also confront difficult ethical dilemmas. "Ethical Issues" sections are integrated throughout and present some of the ethical dilemmas facing financial managers. This treatment of the ethical dimensions of financial management is consistent with the AACSB's recommendations for coverage of these issues.

4. **Attention to unique problems of financial management in entrepreneurial finance** In recognition of the important and growing role of small- and medium-sized firms in the Canadian business environment, "Entrepreneurial Finance Issues" sections emphasize unique finance-related problems and concerns of entrepreneurs (small businesses).

5. **Early coverage of institutional characteristics and valuation models for financial instruments** We have provided separate chapters (Chapters 5 and 6) to deal with the valuation of fixed-income securities and common shares. These chapters also define all of the important characteristics of each of these security types and cover the institutional aspects of the markets for these securities, including the reading and understanding of security transaction information from sources like *The Globe and Mail*.

6. **Early coverage of time value of money concepts** Time value of money concepts are covered in depth in Chapter 4. This treatment provides students with the exposure needed to fully understand the valuation process that is central to the goal of shareholder wealth maximization. In addition, coverage of the time value of money involves students in useful practical applications early on in the course, setting an early tone of relevance for the course.

7. **The importance of cash flow analysis is introduced early and re-emphasized throughout the text** Chapter 1 introduces students to the importance of the cash flow concept. This concept is then applied extensively in the context of evaluating and forecasting financial performance (Chapter 3), valuation (Chapters 5 and 6), capital budgeting (Chapters 9, 10 and 11), dividend policy (Chapter 14), working capital management (Chapter 15), and corporate restructuring (Chapter 20).

8. **Extensive development of the cash flow estimation process in capital budgeting** Perhaps the most important step in the capital budgeting process is the estimation of cash flows for potential projects. An entire chapter (Chapter 9) is devoted to this topic and the effects of the Canadian capital cost allowance (CCA) system. The US modified accelerated cost recovery system (MACRS) is profiled in the "International Issues" section of the chapter.

9. **A detailed discussion of real options that are embedded in many capital investment projects** Finance scholars and practitioners have increasingly focused attention on "embedded options" in capital investment projects, such as the option to abandon, the option to expand, and the option to defer investments. These options add value to an investment project, above that normally identified in a net present value calculation. Chapter 10 includes an extensive and intuitive discussion of real options in capital budgeting.

10. **Coverage of the newest financial analysis and performance appraisal concepts** The increased attention given to the objective of shareholder wealth maximization has brought about the development of new performance appraisal models that can be used to judge a firm's performance and motivate managers to create value. The "market value added" and "economic value added" concepts, developed by Stern-Stewart, are covered in detail in Chapter 3 ("Evaluating and Forecasting Financial Performance") along with the Standard & Poor's core earnings concept.

11. **Integrated treatment of working capital management** For many small and medium-sized companies, the management of working capital can present more challenges than any other area of financial management.

12. **Introduction to new financial instruments and strategies** Financial futures contracts, options, interest rate swaps, corporate restructuring, and leveraged buyouts, to name but a few, have become increasingly important to contemporary financial managers. These topics are introduced in an applied context that illustrates their value to financial managers.

13. **Frequent coverage of the impact of agency relationships in financial management** The impact of principal-agent relationships on decisions in the areas of goal setting, valuation, capital structure, dividend policy, and corporate restructuring are presented throughout the book.

Ancillary Materials for the Student

- *The Study Guide* contains detailed chapter outlines, multiple-choice questions, true/false questions, a large number of solved numerical problems, and more.

- *Microsoft® Excel* templates, available on the text Web site, are designed to solve a wide variety of financial management problems. Problems in the text that can be solved using these templates are indicated with an Excel logo next to the problem. The templates require absolutely no prior knowledge of Excel. All of the templates are designed so they can be used to solve actual business financial analysis problems, not just simplified textbook examples.

- A *Microsoft® PowerPoint®* slide presentation package is offered to enhance lecture materials, and presents the key topics in each chapter in an electronic format. This is available on the text Web site for both instructors and students.

- *CTV video* segments bring the "real world" right to your desktop. The CTV video exercises on the text Web site help to illustrate how finance is an important part of your daily life.

- http://cyr.nelson.com is the address of the Web site that supports this book. The site provides student resources, Internet application links, interactive quizzes, an interactive "Ask the Author" section, links to relevant finance sites, and many more features.

Ancillary Materials for the Instructor

A complete set of ancillary materials is available to instructors:

- An *Instructor's Resource Manual* (IRM) is available to instructors. It contains detailed solutions to the end-of-chapter questions and problems, and documentation for the Excel templates is included in the back of the manual. The solutions to text questions and problems have been thoroughly checked to assure their accuracy. In addition, topical categories of the end-of-chapter questions and problems are listed in a new appendix. The IRM is available to instructors on the text Web site.

- An extensive *Test Bank,* offers over 1,500 multiple-choice questions and problems. This unique test bank is designed with the instructor in mind. Approximately 60 percent of the questions are "fact" questions, taken directly from the discussion in the text. Approximately 20 percent of the questions are "elementary problem" questions that closely parallel problem examples developed in the chapter and basic problems at the end of the chapter. Approximately 20 percent of the questions are "challenging problems" that require the student to apply concepts developed in the chapter to new problem situations.

  - Following each "fact" question, the instructor is provided with (1) the correct answer and (2) an identification of the question topic (that is, a reference to the major heading or subheading in the text where the correct answer is found).
  - Following each "elementary problem" and "challenging problem," the instructor is provided with (1) the correct answer, (2) an identification of the question topic (that is, a reference to the major heading and subheading in the text where the procedure for calculating the correct answer is found), and (3) a detailed solution to the problem.

- A *Microsoft® PowerPoint®* slide presentation package is offered to enhance lecture materials, and presents the key topics in each chapter in an electronic format. This is available on the text Web site for both instructors and students.

- *http://cyr.nelson.com* is the address of the Web site that supports this book. The site provides instructor resources, student resources, Internet application links, interactive quizzes, an interactive "Ask the Author" section, links to relevant finance sites, and many more features.

Acknowledgments

The authors wish to acknowledge the careful reviews and suggestions made by the following professors and professionals:

Ben Amoako-Adu, Wilfrid Laurier University
Dorothee Feils, University of Alberta
Gerald Garvey, University of British Columbia
J. Terry Gordon, British Columbia Institute of Technology
Greg Hebb, Dalhousie University
Sean M. Hennessey, University of Prince Edward Island
Nobuhiko Hibara, University of Saskatchewan
Kai Li, University of British Columbia
Wendy Rotenberg, University of Toronto
Don Rowlatt, University of Victoria
David Stangeland, University of Manitoba
Lorne N. Switzer, Concordia University
Khalil M. Torabzadeh, University of Lethbridge
Eric Wang, Athabasca University
Semih Yildirim, University of Saskatchewan
Ayse Yuce, Ryerson University
Pierre Rostan, Montreal Exchange

Part One

Foundations

1 The Role and Objective of Financial Management

2 The Domestic and Global Financial Marketplace

3 Evaluating and Forecasting Financial Performance

Part One provides an overview of the field of financial management. Chapter 1 discusses the role of financial management in the firm and the alternative forms of business organization. It also identifies the primary goal of the firm as the maximization of shareholder wealth. The foundation concepts of cash flow and net present value are introduced. The chapter also considers the organization of the financial management function and the relationship between finance and other business disciplines. Chapter 2 presents key elements of the global financial marketplace and the role of stock exchanges. Also included is an introduction to the various types of financial derivative securities. The last part of the chapter contains an introduction to international financial management, including multinational enterprises and the foreign currency markets and exchange rates. Chapter 3 deals with the tools of financial statement analysis used to forecast and evaluate a firm's financial performance. An appendix introduces spreadsheets.

The Role and Objective of Financial Management

Learning Objectives

After studying this chapter you should

1. Understand that the most important forms of business organization are the sole proprietorship, the partnership, and the corporation

2. Understand that corporations have the advantages of limited liability for owners, potential perpetual life, and the ability to raise large amounts of capital

3. Understand that shareholder wealth is defined as the present value of expected future returns to the owners of the firm. It is measured by the market value of the common shares

4. Understand that the primary normative goal of the firm is to maximize shareholder wealth

5. Understand that the achievement of the shareholder wealth maximization goal is often constrained by social responsibility concerns and problems arising out of agency relationships

6. Understand that the market value of a firm's common shares is determined by the magnitude, timing, and risk of the cash flows the firm is expected to generate. Managers can take a variety of actions to influence the magnitude, timing, and risk of the firm's cash flows. These actions are often classified as investment, financing, and dividend decisions

7. Understand that cash flow is a fundamental concept in finance and a focus of financial managers who are concerned with raising cash to invest in assets that will generate future cash flows for the firm and its owners

8. Understand that the *net present value rule* is the primary decision-making rule used throughout the practice of financial management. The net present value of an investment is equal to the present value of future returns minus the required initial investment outlay. The net present value of an investment made by a firm represents the contribution of that investment to the value of the firm and, accordingly, to the wealth of shareholders

9. Understand that ethical standards of performance are an increasingly important dimension of the decision-making process of managers

10. Understand that the finance function of a firm is usually headed by a vice president or chief financial officer (CFO). Financial management responsibilities are often divided between the controller and the treasurer. The controller normally has responsibility for all activities related to accounting. The treasurer is normally concerned with the acquisition, custody, and expenditure of funds

Financial Management Questions

■ Maximizing shareholder wealth is the primary normative goal of the firm. How does Canada's largest telecommunications company, BCE, achieve this goal?

■ Why do companies, such as AT&T Canada (restructured in April 2003 as an independent company and renamed Allstream) and others, take large "one-time" restructuring charges? AT&T Canada wrote off $2.7 billion in the second quarter of 2002.

■ Suncor Energy Inc. is a growing Canadian integrated energy company with $8 billion in assets. In January 2003, it announced that its capital investment in the northern Alberta oil sands would be $1.05 billion in 2004. Why is Suncor proceeding with this investment while other firms are not?

■ Why does the Canadian tobacco firm Rothmans pay a generous annual dividend while other companies, such as the Canadian computer video card maker ATI Technologies, do not?

■ In 2001, Canada 3000 Airlines filed for bankruptcy protection. It had previously grown rapidly, acquiring another airline, Royal, as it grew. Now both are no longer flying. What factors led to these financial crises?

Each of these situations has implications for financial decision making. Financial management decisions made within enterprises—small or large, international or local, profit-seeking or not-for-profit—help to determine the kinds of products and services we consume and their prices, availability, and quality. Financial decisions can also affect the risk of a firm and the success of that firm in maximizing shareholder wealth. In short, financial decision making has effects that are felt daily throughout the entire economy.

The situations described above pose important questions for financial managers. The financial concepts and tools needed to deal with problems such as these and to make you a more effective decision maker are the subject matter of this book and will be covered in later chapters.

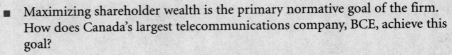

COURTESY OF SUNCOR ENERGY INC.

Yahoo! maintains a finance portal site for a wide range of data, tools, financial analysis, and commentary at
http://finance.yahoo.ca

Introduction

Financial managers have the primary responsibility for acquiring funds (cash) needed by a firm and for directing those funds into projects that will maximize the value of the firm for its owners. The field of financial management[1] is an exciting and challenging one with a wide range of rewarding career opportunities in the fields of corporate financial management, investment banking, investment analysis and management, portfolio management, commercial banking, real estate, insurance, wealth management, and the public sector—to name only a few broad areas.

Articles appear regularly in major business periodicals, such as *The Globe and Mail, Canadian Business,* and *The Wall Street Journal,* describing financial managers' involvement in important and challenging tasks. Consider, for example, the alternatives facing Fording management and shareholders in late 2002 when they were deciding whether to accept the takeover offer of Sherritt International or to convert into an income trust. The seventh proposal, the end result of many months of negotiations, was announced on January 14, 2003. The new Fording Trust, worth $1.83 billion, merges all of western Canada's metallurgical coal operations of Fording, Sherritt International, and Teck Cominco into one firm that accounts for about 20 percent of global output in this industry. Fording is now number two in the world behind Australia's BHP Billiton, which has about 30 percent of the world market.

Think about the challenges facing airline executives in the aftermath of the September 11, 2001, terrorist attacks on New York and Washington. In the face of falling passenger load factors, should an airline cut service—as Air Canada and most of the other major airlines in the world did—or should the airline view this as an opportunity to expand and gain market share—as the financially strong but much smaller WestJet did?

Any business has important financial concerns, and its success or failure depends largely on the quality of its financial decisions. Every key decision made by a firm's managers has important financial implications. Daily, managers face questions like the following:

- Will a particular investment be successful?

- Where will the funds come from to finance the investment?

- Does the firm have adequate cash or access to cash—through bank borrowing agreements, for example—to meet its daily operating needs?

- Which customers should be offered credit, and how much should they be offered?

- How much inventory should be held?

- Is a merger or acquisition advisable?

- How should cash flows be used or distributed? That is, what is the optimal dividend policy?

- In trying to arrive at the best financial management decisions, how should risk and return be balanced?

- Are there "intangible" benefits (e.g., real option aspects) from an investment project that the firm is considering that will affect the accept/reject decision emerging from traditional quantitative analysis procedures?

This textbook presents an introduction to the theory, institutional background, and analytical tools essential for proper decision making in these and related areas. As a

---

[1] The terms financial management, managerial finance, corporate finance, and business finance are virtually synonymous and are used interchangeably. Most financial managers, however, seem to prefer either financial management or managerial finance. For more information visit **www.infotrac-college.com** and **http://finance.swcollege.com** and search for these keywords.

prospective manager, you will be introduced to the financial management process of typical firms. By learning how the financial management process works, you will establish one of the key building blocks for a successful management career.

Forms of Business Organization

Most businesses are organized as a sole proprietorship, a partnership, or a corporation.

Sole Proprietorship

Sole Proprietorship
A business owned by one person. The owner of a sole proprietorship has unlimited liability for debts incurred by the business.

A **sole proprietorship** is a business owned by one person. One of the major advantages of the sole proprietorship business form is that it is easy and inexpensive to establish. A major disadvantage of a sole proprietorship is that the owner of the firm has *unlimited personal liability* for all debts and other obligations incurred by the firm. Unlimited personal liability means that the sole proprietor is personally responsible for paying all debts and obligations of the proprietorship. Examples of obligations include wages, salaries, rent, leases, and taxes.

Sole proprietorships have another disadvantage in that their owners often have difficulty raising funds to finance growth. Thus, sole proprietorships are generally small. Sole proprietorships are especially important in the retail trade, service, construction, and agriculture industries.

Partnership

Partnership
A business organization in which two or more persons form a business with the intention of making a profit.

A **partnership** is a business organization in which two or more co-owners form a business, normally with the intention of making a profit. Each partner agrees to provide a certain percentage of the funds necessary to run the business and/or agrees to do some portion of the necessary work. In return, the partners share in the profits (or losses) of the business.

General Partnership
In a *general partnership,* each partner has unlimited liability for the debts of the firm.

Partnerships may be either general or limited. In a **general partnership,** each partner, like a sole proprietor, has unlimited liability for all of the obligations of the business. Thus, general partnerships have the same major disadvantage as sole proprietorships. Even so, most partnerships are of this type.

Limited Partnership
Limited partnerships allow one or more partners to have limited liability.

A **limited partnership** usually involves one or more general partners and one or more limited partners. Although the limited partners may limit their liability, the extent of this liability can vary and is set forth in the partnership agreement. In other words, the losses of a limited partner are limited to the capital that such a partner provides or to an amount specified in the partnership agreement. Limited partnerships are common in real estate ventures.

Partnerships have been relatively important in the agriculture, mining, oil and gas, finance, insurance, real estate, and services industries. Partnerships are relatively easy to form, but they must be re-formed when there is a change in the makeup of the general partners. Partnerships have a greater capacity to raise capital than sole proprietorships, but they lack the tremendous capital-attraction ability of corporations.

Corporation

Corporation
A business organization that is created as a "legal person" separate and distinct from the individual or individuals who own the firm's shares. The primary characteristics and advantages of incorporating include limited liability for the firm's owners, permanency, and flexibility with respect to making changes in ownership.

A **corporation** is a "legal person" composed of one or more actual individuals or legal entities. It is considered separate and distinct from those individuals or entities. Money contributed to start a corporation is called *capital stock* and is divided into *shares.* The owners of the corporation are called *shareholders.*

Even though only approximately 45 percent of all business firms in Canada are corporations, they make about 95 percent of all sales.

The corporate form of business organization has four major advantages over both sole proprietorships and partnerships.

- **Limited Liability** Once shareholders have paid for their shares, they are not liable for any obligations or debts the corporation may incur. They are liable only to the extent of their investment in the shares.

- **Permanency** The legal existence of a corporation is not affected by whether shareholders sell their shares or die, which makes it a more permanent form of business organization.

- **Flexibility** A change of ownership within a corporation is easily accomplished when one individual merely sells shares to another. Even when shares are sold, the corporation continues to exist in its original form.

- **Ability to Raise Capital** Due to the limited liability of its owners and the easy marketability of its shares of ownership, a corporation is able to raise large amounts of capital, which makes large-scale growth possible.

However, the ability to raise capital comes with a cost. In the typical large corporation, ownership is separated from management. This gives rise to potential conflicts of goals and certain costs, called agency costs, which will be discussed later. However, the ability to raise large amounts of capital at relatively low cost is such a large advantage of the corporate form over sole proprietorships and partnerships that a certain level of agency costs is tolerated.

As a "legal person," a corporation can purchase and own assets, borrow money, sue, and be sued. Its officers are considered to be agents of the corporation and are authorized to act on the corporation's behalf. For example, only an officer, such as the treasurer, can sign an agreement to repay a bank loan for the corporation.

Corporate Organization and Governance In most corporations, the shareholders elect a board of directors, which, in theory, is responsible for managing the corporation. In practice, however, the board of directors usually deals only with broad policy matters, leaving the day-to-day operations of the business to the officers, who are elected by the board. Corporate officers normally include a chairman of the board, chief executive officer (CEO), chief operating officer (COO), chief financial officer (CFO), president, vice president(s), treasurer, and secretary. In some corporations, one person holds more than one office. For instance, many small corporations have a person who serves as secretary-treasurer. In most corporations, the president and various other officers are also members of the board of directors. These officers are called "inside" board members, whereas other board members, such as the company's attorney or banker, are called "outside" board members. A corporation's board of directors usually contains at least three members. The inside board members are the top managers of the firm. Since these managers may not individually own very many shares, an important question arises: How can the owners minimize the cost of having someone else (the managers who are their agents) make decisions that affect them as well as the other stakeholders? The answer to these agency problems involves

1. Creating incentives, constraints, and punishments
2. Establishing reasonable monitoring methods
3. Using contracts that minimize possible conflicts of interest

Corporate Securities In return for the use of their funds, investors in a corporation are issued certificates, or securities. Corporate securities represent claims against the assets and future earnings of the firm.

There are two types of corporate securities. Investors who lend money to the corporation are issued debt securities. These investors expect periodic interest payments, as well as the eventual return of their principal. Owners of the corporation are issued

Major corporations today maintain extensive Web sites, displaying their histories, products, services, financial statements, and much more. Check out the Web sites of Alcan and Nortel Networks, for example, and explore a few of their many links at **www.alcan.com** and **www.nortel.com** In addition, information about corporate securities of Canadian firms can be found at **www.sedar.com** (Canadian Securities Administrators) and also at **www.sec.gov/edgar.shtml** for Canadian firms traded in the United States.

equity securities. Equity securities take the form of either common shares or preferred shares. Common shares are a residual form of ownership. That is, the claims of common shareholders on the firm's earnings and assets are considered only after all other claims—such as those of the government, debt holders, and preferred shareholders—have been met. Common shareholders are considered to be true owners of the corporation. Common shareholders possess certain rights or claims, including dividend rights, asset rights, voting rights, and pre-emptive rights.[2] In Chapters 5 and 6 we illustrate how to obtain information about a company's debt securities and common shares from such sources as *The Globe and Mail* and the *National Post*.

Preferred shareholders have priority over common shareholders with regard to the firm's earnings and assets. They are paid cash dividends before common shareholders. In addition, if a corporation enters bankruptcy, is reorganized, or is dissolved, preferred shareholders have priority over common shareholders in the distribution of the corporation's assets. However, preferred shareholders are behind the firm's creditors.

Because of the advantages of limited liability, permanency, and flexibility, shares in corporations tend to be more liquid (and hence relatively more valuable) than ownership interests in proprietorships and partnerships. Thus, it is easy to see why the majority of business conducted in Canada, Mexico, and the United States, as well as in many other countries, is done under the corporate form of organization.

Foundation Concept

Maximizing Shareholder Wealth as the Primary Goal

Effective financial decision making requires an understanding of the goal(s) of the firm. What objective(s) *should* guide business decision making—that is, what should management try to achieve for the owners of the firm? The most widely accepted objective of the firm is to maximize the value of the firm for its owners, that is, to *maximize shareholder wealth*. **Shareholder wealth** is represented by the market price of a firm's common shares.

Warren Buffett, the famous value investor and CEO of Berkshire Hathaway, an outspoken advocate of the shareholder wealth maximization objective, says it this way:

> Our long-term economic goal . . . is to maximize the average annual rate of gain in intrinsic business value on a per-share basis. We do not measure the economic significance or performance of Berkshire by its size; we measure by per-share progress.[3]

The shareholder wealth maximization goal states that management should seek to maximize the present value of the expected future returns to the owners (that is, shareholders) of the firm. These returns can take the form of periodic dividend payments or capital gains to the shareholders from the sale of their common shares. **Present value** is defined as the value today of some future payment or stream of payments, evaluated at an appropriate discount rate. This present value is an **intrinsic value**. A value investor attempts to find shares whose current prices are below their respective estimated intrinsic values. In a well-functioning stock market, of course, it should not be easy to find such bargains, but Buffett has frequently done so. The appropriate **discount rate** to evaluate any payment or payment stream takes into account the returns that are available from alternative investment opportunities during a specific (future) time period. As we shall see in Chapter 6, the longer it takes to receive a benefit, such as a cash dividend or price appreciation of the firm's shares, the lower the value investors place on that ben-

Shareholder Wealth
Present value of the expected future returns to the owners (that is, shareholders) of the firm. It is equal to the market value (price) per common share times the number of shares outstanding.

Present Value
The value today of a future payment (or a series of future payments) evaluated at the appropriate discount rate.

Intrinsic Value
The value of a share determined by the discounted cash flow method.

Discount Rate
The rate of interest used in the process of finding present values, also called the required rate of return.

---

[2] Shareholder rights are discussed in greater detail in Chapter 6.

[3] Berkshire Hathaway, Inc. Annual Report (2001). See also the owner's manual at **www.berkshirehathaway.com**

Risk
The possibility that actual future returns will deviate from expected returns; the variability of returns.

Market Value (of a security)
The price at which a security trades in the financial marketplace.

efit. In addition, the greater the **risk** associated with receiving a future benefit, the lower the value investors place on that benefit. Share prices, the measure of shareholder wealth, reflect the magnitude, timing, and risk associated with future benefits expected to be received by shareholders.

Shareholder wealth is measured by the market value of their shares. **Market value** is defined as the price at which the shares trade in the marketplace, such as on the Toronto Stock Exchange. Thus, total shareholder wealth equals the number of shares outstanding times the market price per share.

The objective of shareholder wealth maximization has a number of distinct advantages. First, this objective explicitly considers the timing and the risk of the benefits expected to be received from share ownership. Similarly, managers must consider the elements of timing and risk as they make important financial decisions, such as capital expenditures. In this way, managers can make decisions that will contribute to increasing shareholder wealth.

Second, it is conceptually possible to determine whether a particular financial decision is consistent with this objective. If a decision made by a firm has the effect of increasing the market price of the firm's shares, it is a good decision. If it appears that an action will not achieve this result, the action should not be taken (at least not voluntarily).

Third, shareholder wealth maximization is an impersonal objective. Shareholders who object to a firm's policies are free to sell their shares under more favourable terms (that is, at a higher price) than are available under any other strategy and invest their funds elsewhere. Thus, the shareholder wealth maximization objective is the primary goal in financial management. However, concerns for the social responsibilities of business, the existence of other objectives pursued by some managers, and problems that arise from agency relationships may cause some departures from pure wealth-maximizing behaviour by owners and managers. (These issues are discussed later.) Nevertheless, the shareholder wealth maximization goal provides the standard against which actual decisions can be judged and, as such, is the objective assumed in financial management analysis.

Social Responsibility Concerns

Stakeholders
The constituent groups in a firm, including shareholders, bondholders, suppliers, customers, employees, community neighbours, and creditors, as well as governments.

Most firms now recognize the importance of the interests of all their constituent groups, or **stakeholders**—customers, employees, suppliers, and the communities in which they operate—and not just the interests of shareholders. For example, Barrick Gold Corporation—one of Canada's multinational firms—recognizes responsibilities to its various constituencies around the world. Its policy is to donate 1 percent of annual pretax income to community causes in the areas of the world where it operates. It also provides post-secondary scholarships for children of employees and is a recognized leader in environmental leadership among mining companies.[4] Barrick sees no conflict between being a good citizen and running a successful business.

A wide diversity of opinion exists as to what corporate social responsibility actually entails. The concept is somewhat subjective and is neither perceived nor applied uniformly by all firms. As yet, no satisfactory mechanism has been suggested that specifies how these social responsibility commitments can be balanced with the interests of the owners of the firm. However, in most instances, a manager who takes an appropriate long-term perspective in decision making, rather than focusing only on short-term accounting profits, will recognize responsibility to all of a firm's constituencies and will help lead the company to the maximization of value for shareholders.

---

[4] Barrick Gold Corporation, Annual Report (2001): 20–23. For more information visit **www.barrick.com**

Divergent Objectives

The goal of shareholder wealth maximization specifies how financial decisions should be made. In practice, however, not all management decisions are consistent with this objective. For example, Joel Stern and Bennett Stewart have developed an index of managerial performance that measures the success of managers in achieving the goal of shareholder wealth maximization.[5] Their performance measure, called **economic value added (EVA)**, is the difference between a firm's annual after-tax operating profit and its total annual cost of capital. Many North American corporations, including such Canadian firms as the Bank of Montreal, have used the concept. The poor performances of other firms may be due, in part, to a lack of attention to shareholder interests and the pursuit of goals more in the interests of managers.

In other words, there often may be a divergence between the shareholder wealth maximization goal and the actual goals pursued by management. The primary reason for this divergence has been attributed to separation of ownership and control (management) in corporations.

Separation of ownership and control has permitted managers to pursue goals more consistent with their own self-interests as long as they satisfy shareholders sufficiently to maintain control of the corporation. Instead of seeking to maximize some objective (such as shareholder wealth), managers "satisfice," or seek acceptable levels of performance, while maximizing their own welfare.

Maximization of their own personal welfare (or utility) may lead managers to be concerned with long-run survival (job security). The concern for long-run survival may lead managers to minimize (or limit) the amount of risk incurred by the firm, since unfavourable outcomes can lead to their dismissal or possible bankruptcy for the firm. Likewise, the desire for job security is cited as one reason why management often opposes takeover offers (mergers) by other companies. Giving senior managers appropriate "golden parachute" contracts to compensate them if they lose their positions as the result of a merger is one approach designed to help ensure that they will act in the interests of shareholders in merger decisions, rather than in their own interests.

Some firms expect top managers and directors to have a significant ownership stake in the firm. Many other firms, such as Nortel, provide key managers with significant stock options that increase in value with improvements in the firm's performance, in an attempt to align their interests more closely with those of shareholders.

Agency Problems

The existence of divergent objectives between owners and managers is one example of a class of problems arising from agency relationships. **Agency relationships** occur when one or more individuals (the **principals**) hire another individual (the **agent**) to perform a service on behalf of the principals. In an agency relationship, principals often delegate decision-making authority to the agent. In the context of finance, two of the most important agency relationships are the relationship between shareholders (owners) and managers and the relationship between shareholders and creditors.

Shareholders and Managers Inefficiencies that arise because of agency relationships have been called agency problems. These problems occur because parties to a transaction are assumed to act in their own respective best interests. The example cited earlier—the concern by management for long-run survival (job security) rather than shareholder wealth maximization—is an agency problem. Another example is the consumption of on-the-job perquisites (such as the use of company airplanes, limousines, and luxurious offices) by managers who have no (or only a partial) ownership interest in the firm.

---

[5] J. M. Stern, J. S. Shiely, I. Ross, *The EVA Challenge* (New York: Wiley, 2001). For more recent information visit **www.sternstewart.com**

Economic Value Added (EVA)
The difference between operating profits after tax and the cost of capital that indicates a firm's success in creating value for shareholders.

Agency Relationships
Occur when one (or more) person (principal) hires another person (agent) to perform a service on the principal's behalf. Agency relationships often lead to agency problems and costs. Two of the most important agency relationships are those between owners (shareholders) and managers and between owners and creditors.

Principal
In an agency relationship, the party who employs someone else, the agent, to perform service on behalf of the principal.

Agent
The person who acts on behalf of the principal and has a legal responsibility to act in the best interests of the principal in an agency relationship.

In June of 2002, the board of directors of Hydro One Inc. terminated the employment of Eleanor Clitheroe as president and CEO of the firm. Among the improper things she was accused of were using service providers retained by the firm to perform renovations to her personal residence, using the company credit card for personal expenses, and using company-provided transportation (limousine companies) for personal purposes despite being provided with a vehicle and an allowance for operating it. She was also paid a six-figure salary. She denies any wrongdoing and will sue the company. Shirking by managers (not doing their share of the work) is also an agency-related problem.

These agency problems give rise to a number of **agency costs**, which are incurred by shareholders to minimize agency problems. Examples of agency costs include

Agency Costs
Costs incurred by owners of a firm when the firm is managed by others, including monitoring costs, bonding costs, and any losses that cannot be eliminated economically by monitoring and bonding.

1. Expenditures to structure the organization in such a way as to minimize the incentives for management to take actions contrary to shareholder interests, such as providing a portion of management's compensation in the form of shares in the corporation

2. Expenditures to monitor management's actions, such as paying for audits of managerial performance and internal audits of the firm's expenditures

3. Bonding expenditures to protect the owners from managerial dishonesty

4. The opportunity cost of lost profits arising from complex organizational structures that prevent management from making timely responses to opportunities

Of course, if no expenditures (zero agency costs) are made to affect management behaviour, shareholders undoubtedly will suffer some loss of shareholder wealth due to inappropriate behaviour. Thus, in theory, agency costs should be incurred only up to the point where the last dollar of agency costs generates at least one more dollar of shareholder wealth.

Managerial motivations to act in the interests of shareholders include the structure of their compensation package, the threat of dismissal, and the threat of takeover by a new group of owners. Financial theory has shown that agency problems and their associated costs can be greatly reduced if the financial markets operate efficiently. Some agency problems can be reduced by the use of complex financial contracts. Remaining agency problems give rise to costs that show up as a reduction in the value of the firm's shares in the marketplace.

Shareholders and Creditors   Another potential agency conflict arises from the relationship between a firm's owners and its creditors. Creditors have a fixed financial claim on the firm's resources in the form of long-term debt, bank loans, commercial paper, leases, accounts payable, wages payable, taxes payable, and so on. Because the returns offered to creditors are fixed whereas the returns to shareholders are variable, conflicts may arise between creditors and owners. For example, owners may attempt to increase the riskiness of the company's investments in hopes of receiving greater returns. When this occurs, bondholders suffer because they do not have an opportunity to share in these higher returns. The issue of bondholder rights remains controversial, however.

In order to protect their interests, creditors often insist on certain protective covenants in a company's bond indentures.[6] These covenants take many forms, such as limitations on dividend payments, limitations on the type of investments (and divestitures) the company can undertake, poison puts,[7] and limitations on the issuance of new debt. The constraints on the owner-managers may reduce the potential market value of

---

[6] Protective covenants are discussed in more detail in Chapters 5 and 15.

[7] A poison put is an option contained in a bond indenture that permits the bondholder to sell the bond back to the issuing firm at face value under certain circumstances, such as a leveraged buyout that raises the risk for existing debt holders.

Chapter 1   The Role and Objective of Financial Management

the firm. In addition to these constraints, bondholders may also demand a higher fixed return to compensate for risks not adequately covered by bond indenture restrictions.

Maximization of Shareholder Wealth: Managerial Strategies

If the managers of a firm accept the goal of maximizing shareholder wealth, how should they achieve this objective? One might be tempted to argue that managers will maximize shareholder wealth if they maximize the profits of the firm. After all, profit maximization is the predominant objective that emerges from static microeconomic models of the firm. Unfortunately, the profit maximization objective has too many shortcomings to provide consistent guidance to the practicing manager.

Before discussing some of these shortcomings, it is useful to highlight one important managerial decision rule that emerges from the microeconomic profit maximization model. In order to maximize profits, we learned in microeconomics that a firm should expand output to the point where the marginal (additional) cost (MC) of the last unit produced and sold just equals the marginal revenue (MR) received. To move beyond that output level will result in greater additional costs than additional revenues and hence lower profits. Failing to produce up to the point where MC = MR results in a lower level of total profits than is possible by following the rule. This fundamental rule, that an economic action should be continued up to the point where the marginal revenue (benefit) just equals the marginal cost, offers excellent guidance for financial managers dealing with a wide range of problems. For example, we shall see that the basic capital expenditure analysis model is simply an adaptation of the MC = MR rule. Other applications appear in the working capital management and capital structure areas.

Despite the insights it offers financial managers, the profit maximization model is not useful as the central decision-making model for the firm for several reasons. First, the standard microeconomic model of profit maximization is static. That is, it lacks a time dimension. Profit maximization as a goal offers no explicit basis for comparing long-term and short-term profits. Major decisions made by financial managers must reflect the time dimension. For example, capital expenditure decisions, which are central to the finance function, have a long-term impact on the performance of the firm. Financial managers must make trade-offs between short-run and long-run returns in conjunction with capital investment decisions.

The second limitation of the profit maximization objective has to do with the definition of profit. Generally accepted accounting principles (as discussed in Chapter 3) result in literally hundreds of definitions of profit for a firm because of the latitude permitted in recognizing and accounting for costs and revenues. Even if we could agree on the appropriate accounting definition of profit, it is not clear whether a firm should attempt to maximize total profit, the rate of profit, or earnings per share.

Suppose a firm with 10 million shares outstanding currently earns a profit of $10 million after tax. If the firm sells an additional 1 million shares and invests the proceeds to earn $100,000 per year, the total profit of the firm will increase from $10 million to $10.1 million. However, are shareholders better off? Prior to the sale, earnings per share are $1 ($10 million profit divided by 10 million shares). After the sale, earnings per share decline to $0.92 ($10.1 million in earnings divided by 11 million shares). Although total profit has increased, earnings per share have declined. Shareholders are not better off as a result of this action.

This example might lead one to conclude that managers should seek to maximize earnings per share (for a given number of shares outstanding). This, too, can result in misleading actions. For example, consider a firm with total assets at the start of the year of $10 million. The firm is financed entirely with stock (1 million shares outstanding) and has no debt. After-tax earnings are $1 million, resulting in a return on shareholders' equity of 10 percent ($1 million in earnings divided by $10 million in shareholders' equity), and earnings per share are $1. The company decides to retain one-half of this year's earnings (increasing assets and equity to $10.5 million) and pay out the balance in shareholders' dividends. Next year the company's earnings total $1.029 million, resulting in earnings per share of $1.029. Are shareholders better off because of the decision by managers to reinvest $500,000 in the firm? In this example, a strong argument can be made that the position of shareholders has deteriorated. Although earnings per share have increased from $1 per share to $1.029 per share, the realized return on shareholders' equity has actually declined, from 10 percent to 9.8 percent ($1.029 million divided by $10.5 million of shareholders' equity). In essence, the company's managers have reinvested $500,000 of shareholders' money to earn a return of only 5.8 percent ($0.029 million of additional earnings divided by $0.5 million of additional investment). This type of investment is not likely to result in maximum shareholder wealth because shareholders probably have better investment alternatives.

The third major problem associated with the profit maximization objective is that it provides no direct way for financial managers to consider the risk associated with alternative decisions. For example, two projects generating identical future expected cash flows and requiring identical outlays may be vastly different with respect to the risk of the expected cash flows. Similarly, a firm can often increase its earnings per share (EPS) by increasing the proportion of debt financing (leverage) used in the firm's capital structure. However, leverage-induced increases in EPS come at the cost of increased financial risk. The financial marketplace will recognize the increased risk of financial distress that accompanies increases in debt financing and will value the resulting EPS accordingly.

Determinants of Value

If the profit maximization objective does not provide the proper guidance to managers seeking to maximize shareholder wealth, what rules should these managers follow? First, it is important to recognize that the maximization of shareholder wealth is a market concept, not an accounting concept. Managers should attempt to maximize the *market value* of the company's shares, not the accounting or **book value** per share. The book value reflects the historic cost of assets, not the earning capacity of those assets. Also, the book value does not consider the risk associated with the assets.

Three major factors determine the market value of a company's shares: the amount of the cash flows expected to be generated for the benefit of shareholders, the timing of these cash flows, and the risk of the cash flows.

Cash Flow   Throughout the book we stress the importance of cash flows in the practice of financial management. **Cash flow** relates to the actual cash generated or paid by the firm. In contrast, the accounting system focuses primarily on a matching over time of the historic, cost-based revenues and expenses of a company, resulting in a bottom-line earnings figure. But accounting earnings are often misleading because they do not reflect the actual cash inflows and outflows of the firm.

Timing of Cash Flows   The market value of a share is influenced not only by the amount of the cash flows it is expected to produce but also by the timing of those cash flows. If faced with the alternatives of receiving $100 today or $100 three years from today, you would surely choose the $100 today because you could invest that $100 for three years and accumulate the interest. Thus, financial managers must consider both the magnitude of the cash flows they expect to generate and the timing of these cash flows because shareholders will reflect these dimensions of return in their valuation of the firm.

Risk   Finally, the market value of a share of stock is influenced by the perceived risk of the cash flows it is expected to generate. The relationship between risk and required

Book Value

The accounting value of an asset or a corporation. The book value per common share is equal to the total book value of the firm, or shareholders' equity, divided by the total number of common shares outstanding.

Cash Flow

The actual amount of cash collected and paid out by a firm.

return is an important concept in financial management and is discussed in detail in Chapter 7. In general, the greater the perceived risk associated with an expected cash flow, the greater the rate of return required by investors and managers. Thus, financial managers must also consider the risk of the cash flows expected to be generated by the firm because investors will reflect this risk in their valuation of the enterprise.

Managerial Actions to Influence Value

How can managers influence the magnitude, timing, and risk of the cash flows expected to be generated by the firm in order to maximize shareholder wealth? Many factors ultimately influence the magnitude, timing, and risk of a firm's cash flows and thus the price of the firm's shares. Some of these factors are related to the external economic environment and are largely outside the direct control of managers. Other factors can be directly manipulated by the managers. Figure 1.1 illustrates the factors affecting share prices. The top panel enumerates some of the factors in the economic

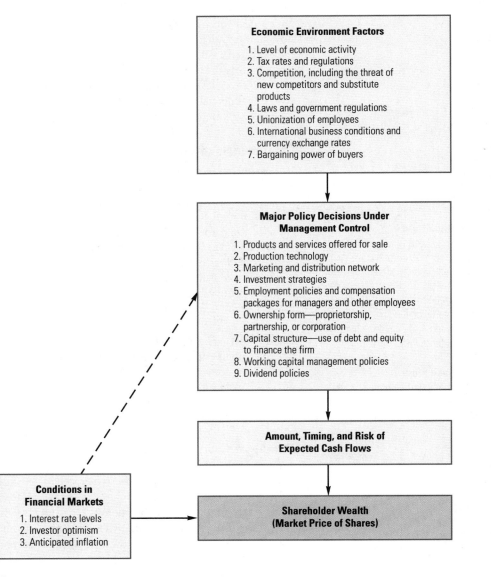

Figure 1.1
Factors Affecting Share Prices

environment that have an impact on the strategic decisions managers can make. Even though economic environment factors are largely outside the direct control of managers, managers must be aware of how these factors affect the policy decisions under the control of management.

In this context, it is useful to consider a competitive strategy framework developed initially by Michael E. Porter[8] and developed further by Alfred Rappaport.[9] Porter and Rappaport recommend that managers formulate an overall competitive strategy analyzing five competitive forces that can influence an industry's structure and can thereby, in turn, ultimately affect the market prices of shares of individual companies in a particular industry. The five competitive forces are

1. The threat of new entrants
2. The threat of substitute products
3. The bargaining power of buyers
4. The bargaining power of suppliers
5. The rivalry among current competitors

By making policy decisions using such a competitive framework, managers can be in a position to create value for shareholders.

Accordingly, the focus of this book is on making financial decisions that can improve the amount, timing, or risk profile of a firm's cash flow stream, thus leading to increases in shareholder wealth and value. Financial managers are not only responsible for measuring value, but also for creating value.

The next section defines the cash flow concept and establishes why cash flows are the relevant source of value in finance.

Cash Flow

The concept of *cash flow* is one of the central elements of financial analysis, planning, and resource allocation decisions. Cash flows are important because the financial health of a firm depends on its ability to generate sufficient amounts of cash to pay its creditors, employees, suppliers, and owners. Only cash can be spent. You cannot spend net income because net income does not reflect the actual cash inflows and outflows of the firm. For example, an accountant records depreciation expense in an attempt to recognize the decline in value of an asset over its life. However, depreciation expense requires no cash outlay, because the entire cash outflow occurred at the time the asset was purchased.[10]

The Cash Flow Generation Process

Financial managers are concerned primarily with raising funds (cash) for use by the firm and investing those funds in assets that can be converted into a stream of cash flows accruing to the firm and its owners. If the value today of the stream of cash flows generated by the assets of a firm exceeds the cost of those assets, the investments undertaken by the firm add value to the firm. When financial managers perform this primary function of acquiring funds and directing the investment of those funds into value-maximizing projects, they must balance the risk (variability) and timing of the expected cash

---

[8] Michael E. Porter, *Competitive Advantage* (New York: Free Press, 1985), Chapter 1. Visit his Web site at **www.isc.hbs.edu/index.html** for more information.

[9] Alfred Rappaport, *Creating Shareholder Value*, 2nd ed. (New York: Free Press, 1998), Chapters 4 and 5.

[10] Because depreciation is used in computing a firm's tax liability, it can affect after-tax cash flows. This concept is discussed further in Chapters 3 and 9.

flow stream against the magnitude of the expected returns. The cash flow generation process for a firm is illustrated in Figure 1.2.

A firm can raise funds by issuing different types of financial securities, including both debt and equity types.[11] Financing decisions such as these are summarized on the liabilities and owners' equity side of the balance sheet. In addition to selling securities, a firm can raise cash by borrowing from a lender such as a chartered bank. Funds can also be raised by generating cash flow internally. Internal cash flows include cash generated from operations and cash generated by the sale of assets.

Once cash is available, a decision must be made to invest it in one or more assets. The acquisition of the best long-term assets is crucial, because, of course, they impact the firm for a long time. Long-term assets can be sold if necessary, but, sometimes, only at a significant loss. Current assets, or working capital, such as cash, accounts receivable, and inventory are held for operating purposes and generally offer little or no explicit return. If current asset balances are kept too high, shareholder wealth is sacrificed due to the opportunity cost of funds, that is, the returns that could be earned if these funds had been invested elsewhere. On the other hand, if current asset balances are too low, the risk of the firm increases because the firm may encounter difficulty in meeting its current financial obligations. In addition, low current asset balances (particularly inventories and accounts receivable) may prevent a firm from responding to the needs of prospective customers in a timely and profitable way.

Eventually, all assets are transformed into a cash flow. Plant and equipment generate a product or service. Inventory is gradually sold and generates cash sales or accounts receivable. Cash flow is generated as accounts receivable are collected. Then, the firm must decide how much of its cash flow to use to acquire additional assets, pay off creditors, and distribute to its owners.

Importance of Cash Flows

The valuation of debt and equity securities is based on the present value of the cash flows that these securities are expected to provide to investors.[12] Similarly, the value of

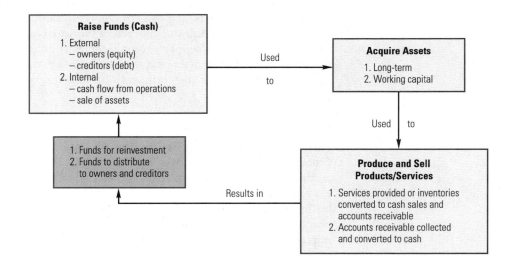

Figure 1.2
A Firm's Cash Flow Generation Process

---

[11] Chapter 5 discusses various types of debt securities and preferred shares. Chapter 6 discusses common shares.

[12] The present value concept is discussed in detail in Chapter 4.

a capital expenditure is equal to the present value of the cash flows that the asset is expected to produce for the firm. In addition, cash flows are central to the prosperity and survival of a firm. For example, rapidly expanding firms often grow faster than their ability to generate internally the cash flows needed to meet operating and financial commitments. As a result, these firms may be faced with difficult financial decisions regarding the external sources of funds needed to sustain rapid growth. On the one hand, increases in debt to support expansion result in an increase in the firm's financial risk. On the other hand, if new shares are sold, ownership in the firm may be diluted more than is desired by the firm's controlling group of owners. Therefore, managers need to pay close attention to the projected cash flows associated with investment and firm expansion strategies.

Generally accepted accounting principles (GAAP) provide considerable latitude in the determination of the net income. As a consequence, GAAP concepts of net income do not provide a clear indication of the economic performance of a firm. Cash flow concepts are unambiguous and provide the necessary insight for managers making a wide range of financial resource allocation decisions. Investors also find that cash flow concepts provide a clear measure of performance. Accordingly, the concept of cash flow assumes great importance in the analysis of a firm's performance and the management of its resources.

Cash Flows and Shareholder Wealth

In spite of the close tie between cash flow concepts and the objective of shareholder wealth maximization, many managers do not seem to place enough emphasis on this concept. Some managers focus on alternative performance measures, including accounting net income, accounting profit ratios (such as the return on equity or the return on assets), the sales growth rate, and market share. The focus on these accounting-based measures of performance may detract from the long-term performance of the company, because performance measures that are not based on cash flows are subject to short-term manipulation by managers.

By emphasizing cash flows rather than accounting-based measures of performance when making decisions, a manager is more likely to achieve the objective of shareholder wealth maximization. A firm that takes actions to maximize the present value of expected future cash flows will achieve a record of financial performance that will be reflected both in the company's financial statements and in the market value of its shares.

Foundation Concept

Net Present Value (NPV)
The present value of the stream of net cash flows resulting from a project, discounted at the appropriate discount rate (usually the firm's cost of capital), minus the project's net investment. It is used to evaluate, rank, and select from among various investment projects according to the contribution of an investment to shareholders' wealth.

Net Present Value (NPV) Rule

To achieve the objective of shareholder wealth maximization, a set of appropriate decision rules must be specified. Earlier in this chapter we saw that the decision rule of setting *marginal cost equal to marginal revenue* (MC = MR) provides a framework for making many important resource allocation decisions. The MC = MR rule is best suited for situations when the costs and benefits occur at approximately the same time. Many financial decisions, however, require that costs be incurred immediately but result in a stream of benefits over several future time periods. In these cases, the **net present value (NPV)** rule provides appropriate guidance for decision makers. Indeed, the NPV rule is central to the practice of financial management. You will find this rule constantly applied throughout your study of finance.

The net present value of an investment is equal to the present value of the expected future cash flows generated by the investment minus the initial outlay of cash, or

(1.1) NPV = Present value of future cash flows minus initial outlay

The net present value of an investment made by a firm represents the contribution of that investment to the value of the firm and, accordingly, to the wealth of shareholders. For example, if MDG Computers expects a new line of personal computers to have a positive net present value, the value of MDG's common shares can be expected to increase.

The net present value concept provides a framework for evaluating future cash flows from an investment or a firm. Thus, the net present value concept can be viewed as the bridge between cash flows and the goal of shareholder wealth maximization.

Organization of the Financial Management Function

Many firms divide the decision-making responsibilities of management among several different officers, which often include those in manufacturing, marketing, finance, personnel, and engineering. A sample organization chart emphasizing the finance function is shown in Figure 1.3. The finance function is usually headed by a vice president of finance, or *chief financial officer* (CFO), who reports to the president. In some corporations the CFO may also be a member of the board of directors. In addition to overseeing the accounting, treasury, tax, and audit functions, today's CFO often has responsibility

ETHICAL ISSUES

The Practice of Financial Management

Webster's dictionary defines ethics as "the discipline dealing with what is good or bad, right or wrong, or with moral duty and obligation."

Ethical considerations impact all kinds of business and financial management decisions. Some financial decisions with important ethical dimensions, such as loan policies of financial institutions, command national attention. Financial managers encounter other decision situations on a day-to-day basis. For example, as a loan officer, should you recommend approval of a loan to a long-time friend, even though she does not quite meet the normal standards? As an account executive at a brokerage firm, should you recommend to your clients the securities of firms that have poor environmental management records? Should you tell your father-in-law that your firm is likely to become a takeover candidate before this becomes public knowledge? As a division manager being evaluated on return on assets, should you

lease assets to keep them out of the asset base for evaluation purposes? Should your firm aggressively use allowable accounting practices to mask a deteriorating level of performance? Should you move your factory to Mexico to save on labour costs?

This brief sampling of the ethical dimensions of some decisions provides a feel for the breadth of ethical issues facing financial managers. Actual decision making is very complex and involves many trade-offs among parties with competing interests. However, explicitly recognizing the costs and benefits associated with each of these decisions and making the decision in an atmosphere of balanced objectivity and fairness can help financial managers avoid apparent or real breaches of their ethical trust.

Throughout the text, we will highlight ethical issues that confront financial managers as they make important decisions. Our objective is to raise your consciousness of these issues.

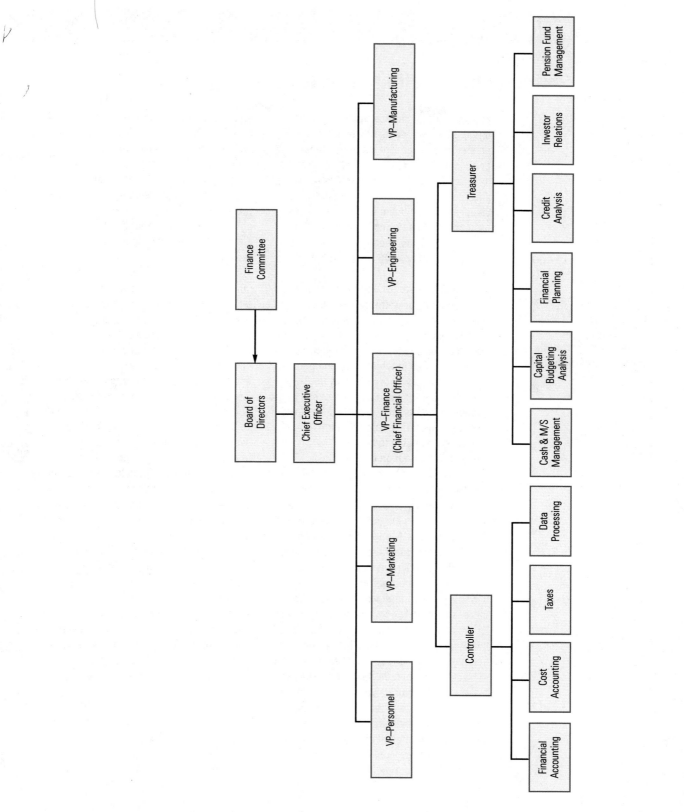

Figure 1.3
Sample Organization Chart

Shareholder Wealth Maximization

For more information on small business visit the SME centre at **www.cga-canada.org/ eng/sme/default.htm**

Entrepreneurial finance deals with the financial issues facing small businesses— an important sector of the North American economy. Small business firms may be organized as sole proprietorships, partnerships, or corporations. In Canada, almost 98 percent of all business firms are considered small. These firms account for the majority of private sector employment and nearly all of the recent net growth in new jobs.

It is difficult to arrive at a precise definition of a small, or entrepreneurial, business. However, the characteristics of small business firms can be identified. In general, small businesses are not the dominant firms in the industries in which they compete, and they tend to grow more rapidly than larger firms. Small firms have limited access to the financial markets, and they often do not have the depth of specialized managerial resources available to larger firms. Small firms also have a high failure rate.

In our discussion of the goals of the firm, we concluded that the predominant goal of financial managers is to maximize shareholder wealth, as measured by the price of the firm's shares. Many entrepreneurial corporations are closely held, and their shares trade infrequently, if ever. Other entrepreneurial firms are organized as sole proprietorships or partnerships. In these cases, there is no readily accessible external measure of performance. Consequently, these firms often rely more heavily on accounting-based measures of performance to track their progress. Accounting-based measures of performance are discussed in Chapter 3. In spite of the lack of an objective, readily available measure of performance, the fundamental decisions made by entrepreneurs are unaltered. That is, the firm should invest resources in projects expected to earn a rate of return at least

equal to the required return on those projects, considering the project's risk. However, because many entrepreneurs are poorly diversified with respect to their personal wealth (that is, they have a large proportion of their personal wealth tied up in the firm), these owners are often more concerned about avoiding risks that could lead to financial ruin than are managers of public corporations.

As discussed earlier, in the large modern corporation, there is a concern that a firm's managers may not always act in the interests of the owners (the agency problem). This problem is less severe in many entrepreneurial businesses because managers and owners are one and the same. An entrepreneur who consumes "excessive" perks is merely reducing his or her ability to withdraw profits from the firm. To the extent that the manager is the owner, there is no owner-manager agency problem. Of course, the potential for agency-related conflicts between entrepreneurs and lenders still exists and may be greater in the closely held firm. As a consequence, many small firms find it difficult to acquire capital from lenders without also giving the lender an option on a part of the ownership of the firm or having the entrepreneur personally guarantee the loan.

Throughout this book we will identify situations where the entrepreneurial financial management of small businesses poses special challenges. In general, we find that small firms often lack the depth of managerial talent needed to apply sophisticated financial planning techniques. Also, because significant economies of scale are often associated with using sophisticated financial management techniques, these techniques are frequently not justified on a cost-benefit analysis basis in many entrepreneurial companies.

for strategic planning, monitoring and trading foreign currencies, managing the risk from volatile interest rates, and monitoring production and inventory levels. CFOs also must be able to communicate effectively with the investment community concerning the financial performance of the company.

The chief financial officer often distributes the financial management responsibilities between the *controller* and the *treasurer*. The controller normally has responsibility for all accounting-related activities. These include such functions as

- **Financial Accounting** This function involves the preparation of the financial statements for the firm, such as the balance sheet, income statement, and the cash flow statement.

- **Cost Accounting** This department often has responsibility for preparing the firm's operating budgets and monitoring the performance of the departments and divisions within the firm.

- **Taxes** This unit prepares the reports that the company must file with the various government agencies (local, provincial, and federal, as well as foreign).

- **Data Processing** Given its responsibilities involving corporate accounting and payroll activities, the controller may also have management responsibility for the company's data processing operations.

The treasurer is normally concerned with the acquisition, custody, and expenditure of funds. These duties often include

- **Cash and Marketable Securities Management** This group monitors the firm's short-term finances—forecasting its cash needs, obtaining funds from bankers and other sources when needed, and investing any excess funds in short-term interest-earning securities.

- **Capital Budgeting Analysis** This department is responsible for analyzing capital expenditures—that is, the purchase of long-term assets, such as new facilities and equipment.

- **Financial Planning** This department is responsible for analyzing the alternative sources of long-term funds, such as the issuance of bonds or common shares that the firm will need to maintain and expand its operations.

- **Credit Analysis** Most companies have a department that is responsible for determining the amount of credit that the firm will extend to each of its customers. Although this group is responsible for performing financial analysis, it may sometimes be located in the marketing area of the firm because of its close relationship to sales.

- **Investor Relations** Many large companies have a unit responsible for working with institutional investors (for example, mutual fund management firms), bond rating agencies, shareholders, and the general financial community.

- **Pension Fund Management** The treasurer may also have responsibility for the investment of employee pension fund contributions. The investment analysis and portfolio management functions may be performed either within the firm or through outside investment advisors.

It should be emphasized that the specific functions of the controller and treasurer shown in Figure 1.3 are illustrative only and that the actual functions performed vary from company to company. For example, in some companies, the treasurer may have responsibility for tax matters. Also, as shown in Figure 1.3, the board of directors of the company may establish a finance committee, consisting of a number of directors and officers of the firm with substantial financial expertise, to make recommendations on broad financial policy issues.

The Cost of Capital for Multinational Companies

Many Canadian firms export much of their output. Since Canada has adverse weather conditions much of the time, it is necessary to import some types of food that cannot be grown in Canada. Some other items not produced in Canada are also imported. Canada is a small open economy.

In 2001, Canada's merchandise exports totalled $414.6 billion and merchandise imports totalled $350.6 billion. The difference between merchandise exports and imports is the *merchandise trade balance*. In 2001, Canada had a *merchandise trade surplus* of approximately $64 billion, representing an increase from the previous year. A weak Canadian dollar during 2001 made exports of our goods relatively inexpensive for many foreigners, especially our biggest customer, the United States.

Many Canadian firms have become

multinationals as they have expanded their operations around the world to secure raw materials or new markets. For example, Bombardier, a well-known Canadian firm, earned 94 percent of its 2002 revenues outside of Canada. It still has 35 percent of its workforce in Canada (27,000 jobs across the country) and it pays them $1.7 billion annually in salaries and benefits.

Bombardier has more than 5,600 suppliers also generating wealth and jobs for Canadians. In addition to its Canadian factories, Bombardier also has factories in the United States, the United Kingdom, Germany, and Austria. Bombardier's exports have returned $35 billion to the Canadian economy over the five-year period ending in 2001. Bombardier's exports were nearly 2 percent of Canada's total exports during those years.

Financial Management and Other Disciplines

As you pursue your study of financial management, you should keep in mind that financial management is not a totally independent area in business administration. Instead, it draws heavily on related disciplines and fields of study. The most important of these are *accounting* and *economics*. In the latter discipline, both *macroeconomics* and *microeconomics* are significant. *Marketing, production, human resources management,* and the study of *quantitative methods* also have an impact on the financial management field. Each of these is discussed below.

Accounting

Financial managers are responsible for managing a firm's financial and real assets and securing the funding needed to support these assets. Examples of financial assets are cash and marketable securities, such as government bonds. Examples of real assets are property, plant, and equipment. Accountants are the firm's scorekeepers. Financial managers often turn to accounting data to assist them in making decisions. Generally a company's accountants are responsible for developing financial reports and measures that assist its managers in assessing the past performance and future direction of the firm and in meeting certain legal obligations, such as the payment of taxes. The accountant's role includes the development of financial statements, such as the *balance sheet*, the *income statement*, and the *cash flow statement*. These financial statements are discussed in Chapter 3.

Financial managers are primarily concerned with a firm's cash flows, because they often determine the feasibility of certain investment and financing decisions. The financial manager refers to accounting data when making future resource allocation decisions concerning long-term investments, when managing current investments in working capital, and when making a number of other financial decisions. Determining the most appropriate capital structure or relative amounts of long-term debt and equity financing is an example of such a decision. Another is identifying the best and most timely sources of funds needed to support the firm's investment programs.

In many small and medium-sized firms, the accounting function and the financial management function may be handled by the same person or group of persons. In such cases, the distinctions just identified may become blurred.

Economics

For up-to-date information on business disciplines consult the BizTech Network portal at **www.brint.com**

There are two areas of economics with which the financial manager must be familiar: *microeconomics* and *macroeconomics*. Microeconomics deals with the economic decisions of individuals, households, and firms, whereas macroeconomics looks at the economy as a whole.

The typical firm is heavily influenced by the overall performance of the economy and is dependent on the money and capital markets for investment funds. Thus, financial managers should recognize and understand how monetary policies affect the cost of funds and the availability of credit. Financial managers should also be versed in fiscal policy and how it affects the economy. What the economy can be expected to do in the future is a crucial factor in generating sales forecasts as well as other types of forecasts.

The financial manager uses microeconomics when developing decision models that are likely to lead to the most efficient and successful modes of operation within the firm. Specifically, financial managers use the microeconomic concept of setting marginal cost equal to marginal revenue when making long-term investment decisions (*capital budgeting*) and when managing cash, inventories, and accounts receivable (*working capital management*).

Marketing, Production, Quantitative Methods, and Human Resources Management

Figure 1.4 depicts the relationship between financial management and its supportive disciplines. In addition to the primary supportive disciplines of accounting and economics (both macro and micro), marketing, production, quantitative methods, and

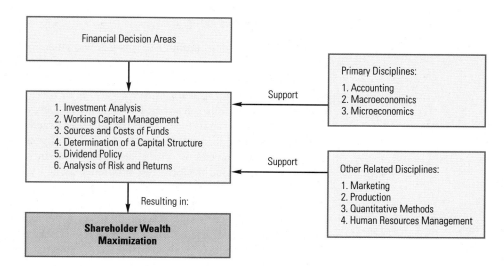

Figure 1.4
Impact of Other Disciplines on Financial Management

The Web site maintained by *Canadian Business* magazine provides articles on many financial issues you will encounter in this course: **www.canadianbusiness. com** Similarly, *The Globe and Mail*'s Web site is a rich source of information and examples of issues central to this course: **www. globeandmail.com**

Looking for a job? Soon to be looking for a job? See this web portal (one of many job search Web sites): **www.allstarjobs.ca/jobs**

human resources management are related to the key day-to-day decisions made by financial managers.

For example, marketing must provide accurate sales forecasts to enable the firm to have good cash and marketable securities management. As well, financial managers performing capital budgeting analysis should consider the impact of new product development and promotion plans made in the marketing area because these plans will require capital outlays and have an impact on the firm's projected cash flows. Similarly, changes in the production process may necessitate capital expenditures, which the firm's financial managers must evaluate and then finance. The tools of analysis developed in the quantitative methods area are frequently helpful in analyzing complex financial management problems. Compensation policies not only affect cash management but may impact the extent of agency problems in a firm and shareholder wealth maximization.

Career Opportunities in Finance

The finance profession offers a number of exciting career opportunities. As illustrated in the organization chart in Figure 1.3, the corporate finance function encompasses a wide range of activities involved with acquisition and expenditure of the firm's resources. In addition to careers in corporate finance, opportunities are available in the financial services sector. The financial services sector includes such businesses as chartered banks, securities brokers, investment dealers, mutual fund and pension fund management firms, real estate companies, and insurance companies. One should keep in mind that organizational structures differ significantly among various companies and that the specific responsibilities and duties for a given position may vary considerably among companies.

Organization of the Text

This text provides an introduction to both analytical tools and descriptive materials that are useful in financial management. Because this is an *introductory*-level text, however, it does *not* attempt to make the reader an expert in every aspect of financial decision making. Instead, it is intended to do the following:

■ Acquaint the reader with the types of decisions faced by financial managers

■ Develop a framework for analyzing these decisions in a systematic manner

■ Provide the reader with the background necessary to pursue more advanced readings and courses in financial management

Although the subject matter in this text is divided into distinct parts, in reality and practice, the various types of financial decisions are interrelated and should not be considered in isolation from one another.

Each chapter begins with a preview listing of the major learning objectives of the chapter. This is usually followed by a financial challenge faced by a real firm(s) and is related to the material in the chapter. At the end of each chapter the financial challenge is revisited. In addition, there is a point-by-point summary of the chapter and extensive sets of discussion questions. Except for some of the introductory chapters, all chapters have problems, including "Self-Test Problems," which you can use to test your understanding of the text material. Detailed solutions to the "Self-Test Problems" appear at the back of the book. The regular problems are divided into basic, intermediate, and challenge levels of difficulty categories. "Check" answers to selected regular problems also appear at the back of the book. As well, a glossary of key terms is provided there. MS Excel spreadsheet *templates* are available for solving many of the chapter problems at the book's Web site. Special sections on *International Issues, Ethical Issues,* and *Entrepreneurial Issues* are integrated throughout the book where appropriate.

Parts of the Text

Part One: Foundations   Chapter 2 reviews the major elements of the Canadian and global financial marketplaces. It includes a discussion of the structure of the Canadian financial system and the role of stock exchanges and investment dealers. Also included are brief introductions to international financial management (including foreign exchange rates and markets) and the financial management aspects of income taxes. Chapter 3 considers the major financial statements and ratios that can be used to evaluate the financial performance of a firm. It also includes a brief appendix on spreadsheets for financial statement analysis.

Part Two: Valuation of Cash Flows   Valuation is a central theme of the book. Chapter 4 develops the concept of the time value of money (cash flows). This concept is used in the valuation of securities and the evaluation of investment projects expected to provide benefits over a number of years. Chapter 5 applies the basic valuation model to fixed income securities, such as bonds and preferred shares. Chapter 6 deals with the valuation of common shares. Chapter 7 provides a comprehensive introduction to the concept of risk in finance and the relationship between risk, required return, and the shareholder wealth maximization goal of the firm.

Part Three: Capital Investment Decisions   This portion of the text focuses on capital expenditure decisions—that is, investments in long-term assets. Chapter 8 illustrates the principles of measuring a firm's cost of capital. The cost of funds to the firm is an important input in the capital budgeting process. Chapters 9 and 10 present the fundamentals of capital budgeting, namely, the process of investing in long-term assets. Chapter 9 deals with the measurement of the cash flows (benefits and costs) associated with long-term investment projects. Chapter 10 considers various decision-making criteria that can be used when choosing projects that will maximize shareholder wealth. Chapter 11 extends the concepts developed in Chapter 10 by considering some of the decision-making techniques that attempt to deal with the problem of the risk associated with a specific project's cash flow.

Part Four: Capital Structure and Dividend Policy Decisions   Chapters 12 and 13 address the relationship of the cost of capital to the firm's capital structure. Chapter 14 discusses the factors that influence the choice of a dividend policy and the impact of various dividend policies on the value of a firm.

Part Five: Working Capital Management Decisions   Chapters 15 and 16 examine the management of a firm's current asset and liability accounts—that is, net working capital. Chapter 15 provides an overview of working capital management, with emphasis on the risk-return trade-offs involved in working capital decision making. It also discusses the management of secured and unsecured short-term and intermediate-term credit. Chapter 16 deals primarily with the management of cash, marketable securities, accounts receivable, and inventories.

Part Six: Risk Management   Chapter 17 deals with the management of domestic risk. Chapter 18 focuses on the management of international risk. Chapter 17 focuses on derivative security-related financial risk management activities, including the use of convertible securities, warrants, options, and swaps. Chapter 18 discusses the factors that affect exchange rates and foreign exchange risk. The chapter also discusses the methods financial managers can use to manage foreign exchange risk.

Part Seven: Advanced Capital Investment and Structure Decisions   Chapter 19 deals with leasing. Chapter 20 examines corporate restructuring decisions, including mergers and acquisitions, bankruptcy, and reorganization.

The questions posed in the financial challenge for this chapter are discussed later in the appropriate chapters of the book.

The risk-return trade-off in the context of maximizing shareholder wealth is examined for BCE in Chapter 7. One-time restructuring charges, such as those of AT&T Canada (restructured and renamed Allstream), are discussed in Chapter 3. Capital investment projects, such as those of Suncor, are discussed in Chapters 9 to 11 inclusive. Dividend policy, such as that of Rothmans, is discussed in Chapter 14. The factors that led Canada 3000 Airlines and others into bankruptcy are discussed in Chapter 20.

Summary

- The three primary forms of business organization are the *sole proprietorship,* the *partnership,* and the *corporation.* Corporations have certain advantages over the other two forms of business organization, especially for large businesses.

- A corporation is defined as a "legal person" composed of one or more actual individuals or legal entities. The owners of a corporation are called *shareholders.* The shareholders elect a *board of directors* that usually deals with broad policy matters, whereas the day-to-day operations are supervised by the corporate *officers.*

- Corporations issue *debt securities* to investors who lend money to the corporation and *equity securities* to investors who become owners.

- The optimal form of organization for a business enterprise is influenced by such factors as cost, complexity, owner liability, business continuity, the need for raising capital, the owners' desire to maintain decision-making authority, and tax considerations.

- The primary normative goal of financial management decision making is the *maximization of shareholder wealth* as measured by the price of the firm's common shares.

- *Agency relationships,* such as the relationship between shareholders and managers and the relationship between owners and lenders, give rise to certain agency problems and costs that can have an important impact on firm performance.

- The amount, timing, and risk of the cash flows generated by a firm are, in large part, determined by key financial management decisions, including investment decisions, dividend decisions, financing decisions, and ownership structure decisions. These decisions must be made in the context of factors in the broader economic environment.

- The cash flow concept is a fundamental concept in finance. Financial managers focus on raising cash to invest in assets that will, in turn, generate future cash flows for the firm and its owners.

- The net present value (NPV) rule is central to financial analysis. The net present value of an investment is equal to the present value of future returns minus the initial outlay. Future outlays are discounted back to the present at a required rate of return that reflects the perceived risk of the investment.

- The net present value of an investment made by a firm represents the contribution of the investment to the value of the firm and, accordingly, to the wealth of shareholders.

- The finance function is usually headed by a vice president or *chief financial officer (CFO).* The financial management responsibilities are often divided between the *controller* and the *treasurer.* The controller normally has responsibility for all accounting-related activities. The treasurer is normally concerned with the acquisition, custody, and expenditure of funds.

■ Financial management is closely related to other areas of business decision making, particularly accounting and economics.

■ The finance profession offers a number of exciting career opportunities both within the corporate finance function and in the financial services sector.

Questions and Topics for Discussion

1. Define *shareholder wealth*. Explain how it is measured.

2. What are the differences between shareholder wealth maximization and profit maximization? If a firm chooses to pursue the objective of shareholder wealth maximization, does this preclude the use of profit maximization decision-making rules? Explain.

3. Which type of corporation is more likely to be a shareholder wealth maximizer— one with wide ownership and no owners directly involved in the firm's management or one that is closely held? Why?

4. Is the shareholder wealth maximization goal a short- or long-term goal? Explain your answer.

5. It has been argued that shareholder wealth maximization is not a realistic normative goal for the firm, given the social responsibility activities that the firm is "expected" to engage in (such as contributing to the arts, education, etc.). Explain why these social responsibility activities are not necessarily inconsistent with shareholder wealth maximization.

6. Explain why management may tend to pursue goals other than shareholder wealth maximization.

7. Explain what is meant by *agency relationships* and *agency costs*.

8. Give some examples of agency costs incurred by shareholders in the agency relationship between the shareholders (owners) and management of a firm.

9. What is the source of potential agency conflicts between owners and bondholders? Who is the agent and who is the principal in this relationship?

10. Explain the differences in the responsibilities of the treasurer and the controller in a large corporation.

11. Explain the relationship between financial management and (a) microeconomics and (b) macroeconomics.

12. Why is earnings per share not a consistently good measure of a firm's performance?

13. What are the major factors that determine the value of a firm's shares?

14. What is the relationship between the concepts of net present value and shareholder wealth maximization?

15. How can the adherence to high standards of ethical business practice contribute to the goal of shareholder wealth maximization?

16. Compare the potential for agency problems in sole proprietorships, partnerships, and corporations. In light of your analysis, why is the corporate form of organization so popular?

Other Practice Materials and Resources

For interactive quizzes, Internet exercises, crossword puzzles, CTV videos, and more, go to the *Contemporary Financial Management* Web site at **http://cyr.nelson.com**

The Domestic and Global Financial Marketplace

Learning Objectives

After studying this second introductory chapter you should

1. Understand that in the Canadian financial system, as well as any other financial system, funds flow from net savers (such as households) to net investors (such as businesses) through investment dealers and financial intermediaries

   a. Investment dealers facilitate the direct transfer of funds to corporations, governments, and other organizations that issue new securities

   b. Financial intermediaries include chartered banks, trust companies, credit unions and caisses populaires, insurance companies, pension fund management firms, and investment companies. Financial intermediaries facilitate the indirect transfer of funds among ultimate borrowers and lenders. Their activities are influenced by the Bank of Canada

   c. Financial assets include money, debt securities, equity securities, and derivative securities

2. Understand that financial markets for debt securities and equity securities are classified as money or capital markets and primary or secondary markets

   a. Short-term securities with maturities of one year or less are traded in money markets

   b. Long-term securities have maturities of more than one year and are traded in capital markets

   c. New securities are traded in the primary markets

   d. Existing securities are traded in the secondary markets, such as the Toronto Stock Exchange, the New York Stock Exchange, the NASDAQ market, and the over-the-counter (OTC) market

   e. Derivative securities are usually traded in their own specialized financial markets, such as the Montreal Exchange

3. Understand that many Canadian companies are regularly engaged in international financial transactions. They face political and exchange rate risks in addition to the risks encountered in domestic transactions. Financial assets, such as forward contracts, futures contracts, and options on currencies are types of derivative securities that help firms manage exchange rate risks

4. Understand that most financial decisions are affected by taxes. Thus, it is important to know the basic features of the Canadian taxation system

Ritchie Bros. Auctioneers Inc. (NYSE: RBA)
The little company that could—a Canadian success story

RBA's Web site at
www.rbauction.com
can be used by customers
who read English, French,
Spanish, and German.

The three Ritchie brothers started their family business in 1958 by selling off some used equipment to pay off a loan. Like the little engine that could, their business grew and grew. Today, their company is the world's leading auctioneer of industrial equipment, operating through 90 offices in 21 countries around the world. RBA conducts 140 unreserved public auctions every year, with an average of over 1,000 bidders participating in each auction, either in person or over the Internet. The headquarters of this multinational firm are located in Richmond, BC.

When the company decided to go public in 1998, it consulted with investment dealers in Canada as well as in the United States. The company does only one-sixth of its business in Canada and two-thirds in the United States, with the balance in Europe and Asia. RBA considered the costs and benefits of listing its shares on the Toronto Stock Exchange (TSX) as well as on the New York Stock Exchange (NYSE). The company decided that it would list only on the NYSE. It is the first Canadian firm to make this decision, but it is highly unlikely that it will be alone for long. Another 33 Canadian firms are not listed in Canada and are listed only on a US exchange other than the NYSE. In addition, there are 184 Canadian companies that are interlisted on both the TSX and a US exchange as well. Currently, about 60 percent of the trading of the interlisted shares occurs in Canada, with the rest of the transactions in the United States.

For the financial managers of most of the larger Canadian firms, the financial marketplace includes both Canada and the United States. Many Canadian firms, like RBA, do most of their business outside of Canada and publish their annual reports denominated in US dollars, although they use Canadian GAAP (generally accepted accounting principles). Many Canadian firms export to the United States and receive substantial sales revenues in US dollars. However, if they manufacture only in Canada, most of their expenses are denominated in Canadian dollars. Thus, they are obliged to make foreign exchange transactions.

Introduction

This chapter provides a look at the domestic and international financial marketplaces within which Canadian business firms operate. These financial marketplaces serve the role of allocating scarce resources from saving units (such as individuals) to investing units (such as firms).

We provide an overview of the operation of the Canadian and international financial systems, distinguishing between the money and capital markets. The major financial intermediaries are discussed, and the operation and structure of secondary security markets are presented.

One important element of the financial marketplace is the structure of corporate and personal taxation. The existence of corporate and personal income taxes has important implications for financial managers. Because so many financial decisions are based on after-tax cash flows, finance and business professionals must have a basic understanding of tax matters. Thus, this chapter closes with an overview of some important elements of Canadian tax laws.

Central Banking

For more information on the Bank of Canada see **www.bankofcanada.ca/en** Click on the Research and Publications button for detailed studies or click on the Rates link for interest rate and currency exchange rate information.

Canada's central bank, the Bank of Canada, was created in 1934 for the purposes of

- Controlling the growth of the money supply
- Acting as banker for the Government of Canada
- Acting as banker for the Canadian chartered banks
- Acting as lender of last resort
- Administering the Bank Act
- Administering and regulating the orderly buying and selling of Canadian dollars in the foreign exchange market

Bank Reserves

To enable the Bank of Canada to carry out its functions, the Bank Act requires the chartered banks to maintain primary reserves at the Bank of Canada. The Bank Act specifies what kind of cash and cash-like assets may be used as reserve assets. The Bank of Canada is also empowered by the Bank Act to require chartered banks to hold secondary reserves if this is deemed to be necessary by the Bank of Canada to carry out its functions.

The chartered banks do not receive interest on their reserve assets so, for them, the reserves they maintain with the Bank of Canada are similar to the cash maintained by nonfinancial firms in their chequing accounts (also known as **demand deposits**) with the chartered banks.

Demand Deposits
Money deposited in chequing accounts.

Monetary Policy

The chartered banks may increase their assets by lending up to the limit allowed them by the reserve requirement. This process is called fractional reserve banking. With a 10 percent reserve requirement, for example, the chartered banks could collectively expand by 10 times the amount of additional demand deposits they receive.

The Bank of Canada can affect bank deposits by open market purchase and sale operations in bonds and/or Treasury bills. If the Bank of Canada buys bonds or bills, for example, it will pay the sellers of those assets. The sellers will most likely deposit the funds in a bank account, thus increasing bank deposits and allowing the banks to lend more. Conversely, the Bank of Canada may sell bonds or bills to purchasers of those assets. The purchasers will probably pay by writing cheques on their bank accounts, thereby reducing bank deposits. If bank deposits are reduced, the chartered banks must either (1) reduce their lending operations, (2) sell off some of their investments to raise money to lend, (3) increase deposits by offering higher interest rates to their customers, or (4) borrow from other chartered banks or the Bank of Canada.

If the Bank of Canada wishes to discourage the chartered banks from borrowing from the central bank it can raise its own lending rate, the **bank rate**. This is the rate that usually applies to loans made by the Bank of Canada to the chartered banks in its lender of last resort role. The Bank of Canada can also affect the **overnight rate**. This is the rate that applies to transactions between the chartered banks that regularly borrow from and lend to each other to cover the settlement of their electronic transactions in the **Large Value Transfer System (LVTS)**. The overnight rate is usually slightly lower than the bank rate although both are within an operating band. For example, the operating band might be 4.25 to 4.75 percent, so the overnight rate target rate would be 4.50 and the bank rate would be 4.75. Since the overnight rate is lower, the banks have an incentive to deal with each other rather than directly with the Bank of Canada.

The overnight rate serves as the base rate of interest in the economy because it is the opportunity cost of chartered bank borrowing, so the chartered banks usually use it as the basis for setting their own **prime rate**, which is the interest rate they usually charge their best customers. The prime rate is normally higher than the bank rate to allow the banks to earn enough to cover their expenses. Other lending rates are higher than the prime rate according to the risks perceived by the lenders.

Sometimes, however, new funds coming into the chartered banks will more or less offset the funds going out. In this case, the individual banks may be unaffected by the Bank of Canada's monetary policy actions. The Bank of Canada must, therefore, have other means of achieving its objectives. One possibility is to change the secondary reserve requirement. Another possibility is to shift some of the Government of Canada deposits. The switching of the Government of Canada deposits from the chartered banks to the Bank of Canada or vice versa is probably the most widely used technique of Canadian monetary policy. The Bank of Canada can do this because it is also the government's banker and as such it can manage the government's cash balances. Keeping these government deposits with the chartered banks is a way for the government to compensate the banks for the cashing of government cheques. The switching of government deposits as a monetary policy tool has an important advantage over open market operations. This is because it affects bank deposits, but it does not affect market rates of interest on financial instruments as open market operations would.

Thus, with all the tools of monetary policy, governments can essentially control the supply of money by having the central bank control the reserves of the nation's banking system. This controlling of the money supply may be sufficient to control the growth of the economy by attenuating the fluctuations of the business cycle. Monetary policy works best when it is also supplemented by a complementary fiscal (tax and government expenditure) policy.

In Canada, exercising practical control over the nation's money supply is much more difficult than might be expected due to our proximity to the United States and the interconnectedness of the North American economy. In international terms, the Canadian economy is a small open economy that must, therefore, react to international economic forces. Most of Canada's exports go to the United States, and much of our imports come from there. International trade must be financed, of course. If there is a trade deficit for any country, there will be an outflow of funds from the country unless there are countervailing capital movements. For example, capital is also free to come in or go out at will in response to changes in interest rates, both here and elsewhere. Usually, therefore, the Bank of Canada keeps interest rates higher in Canada than they are elsewhere in the world so that money will not flow out of Canada. The outflow of funds would cause the value of the Canadian dollar to decline, as sellers of the Canadian dollar would outnumber buyers. As the value of the Canadian dollar goes down, our imports

Bank Rate
The rate of interest charged to banks that borrow from the Bank of Canada.

Overnight Rate
The interest rate charged on loans from one chartered bank to another.

Large Value Transfer System (LVTS)
An electronic transfer method for settling transactions between and among Canadian chartered banks.

Prime Rate
The lowest rate normally charged by banks on loans made to their most creditworthy business customers.

become more expensive. This is because more Canadian dollars must be exchanged for the foreign currency required to pay for the imports. However, the lower value of the Canadian dollar makes our exports cheaper for others to buy as well. Thus, there are advantages as well as disadvantages to be considered in analyzing the decline in external value of any country's currency.

The Bank of Canada has responsibility for managing the exchange value of the Canadian dollar. Our dollar had been in a general downtrend against most of the world's major currencies since 1975 but in early 2003 our dollar rose against the US dollar. The Bank of Canada manages the exchange value of the Canadian dollar by buying Canadian dollars when everyone else wants to sell them and vice versa, borrowing from other central banks if necessary. The real object of this kind of control of the exchange rate is to keep the fluctuations small and gradual, rather than to maintain a strictly fixed exchange rate. The governmental and central bank control of the money supply has been only very briefly described here. It is the subject matter of money and banking and macroeconomics courses. More detailed coverage of monetary policy is therefore beyond the scope of this book.

Fiscal Policy

Fiscal policy affects the financial system in at least two major ways. The stabilization function of fiscal policy, which is intended to attenuate the business cycle, affects also the level of interest rates in the economy. The federal government is the best borrower in the economy. It has a monopoly on money, so it can print money if necessary. There is no doubt that the federal government can pay its debts. If there is a recession, federal revenues will go down. However, spending will go up since the government will be obliged to spend more for employment insurance and other benefits. If this causes a federal government deficit, the government will borrow in the financial markets, squeezing out other borrowers of lower quality. Thus, the other borrowers (firms and individuals) will have to pay more for the money that is available or they will have to go without. If the government chooses not to borrow, it will have to either raise taxes or print money. The revenue aspects of fiscal policy affect the after-tax income of the financial institutions. If tax rates are raised, deductions are reduced, or new taxes imposed, the capital of the financial institutions will be adversely affected. Earnings after taxes will be reduced. Therefore, less earnings will be available to pay shareholder dividends and to be reinvested in the business. If profits are insufficient, the financial institutions will be unable to grow as quickly as desired. Economic growth of the economy will also be slower. This is because financial institutions will have less money to lend to those who wish to make the productive investments that create jobs.

An Overview of the Canadian Financial System

For more information see **www.fcac-acfc.gc.ca/ eng/financialservices/ facts.asp** This Web site of the Financial Consumer Agency of Canada has a great deal of financial information for consumers, such as mortgage payment, bank fee, and credit card fee calculators, which can be very useful for consumers in need of financial services.

The Canadian financial system is an important sector of the Canadian economy. It employs more than half a million Canadians and supports another half a million jobs indirectly through purchases of supplies, equipment, and services. It provides a yearly payroll of over $22 billion, pays over $9 billion in tax revenue to all levels of government, and exports approximately $50 billion worth of services annually. All of this activity represents approximately 5 percent of Canada's gross domestic product, a proportion exceeded only by the manufacturing sector. Canada's financial sector ranks fifth in the world in international competitiveness and is widely acknowledged as one of the safest and healthiest in the world.

The Canadian financial system serves an important function in the efficient operation of the economy. The financial system is the vehicle that channels funds from saving units (savers) to investing units. The rates of return that investing units must pay for the capital supplied by savers are determined competitively in financial markets. As we shall

Investment Dealer (Banker)

A financial institution that underwrites and sells new securities. Investment dealers help firms to obtain new financing.

Direct Transfer

The transfer of funds directly from lenders to borrowers, usually facilitated by investment dealers.

Financial Intermediaries

Include chartered banks, trust companies, credit unions and caisses populaires, insurance companies, pension fund firms, and investment companies. These firms facilitate indirect transfers of funds among ultimate lenders and borrowers.

Indirect Transfer

The transfer of funds from savers to investors through financial intermediaries, such as banks.

Interest Rate Spread

Financial intermediaries are usually compensated for their services by an interest rate spread. Banks, for example, borrow by paying depositors 4% or less and lend by charging borrowers 7% or more. The difference between these rates is the spread. The spread must cover their costs of operation plus their profit.

For more information on investment dealers see **www.ida.ca**

see later in the book, investment activity undertaken by firms is influenced by the rate of return (cost of capital) the firms must pay to attract resources from savers. Accordingly, it is important for financial managers to understand the elements and functioning of the financial marketplace so that capital costs can be minimized for any set of investments a firm undertakes.

In considering any economy as a whole, the actual savings for a given period of time must equal the actual investments. This phenomenon is called the *saving-investment cycle.*

The saving-investment cycle depends on net savers, or *surplus spending units,* and net investors, or *deficit spending units.* The cycle is completed when the surplus spending units transfer funds to the deficit spending units. The main purpose of the Canadian financial system—including the financial markets and all financial institutions—is to facilitate this transfer of funds. Figure 2.1 graphically depicts this continual flow.

Funds flow from surplus spending units, such as households, to deficit spending units, such as businesses, through investment dealers and financial intermediaries. **Investment dealers** (also known as **investment bankers** in some other countries) facilitate the **direct transfer** of funds from surplus spending units to corporations, governments, and other organizations that issue new securities. These securities are called *primary claims,* because they are sold directly by the ultimate borrowers and bought directly by the ultimate lenders.

Financial intermediaries include chartered banks, trust companies, credit unions and caisses populaires, insurance companies, pension fund management firms, and investment companies. They differ from investment dealers in that they issue *secondary claims* to the ultimate lenders instead of primary claims. (A bank savings account is an example of a secondary claim.) A financial intermediary may lend money to a corporation, even though there is a small chance that the corporation will default on its loan. In general, individuals or households are unwilling to lend funds to a corporation under these circumstances. However, they will allow a chartered bank to use their funds, because the bank can guarantee them both liquidity and safety.

Thus, financial intermediaries facilitate the **indirect transfer** of funds among ultimate borrowers and lenders. They are compensated for their services by an **interest rate spread.** For example, a bank might loan money to a business at an average of 7 percent

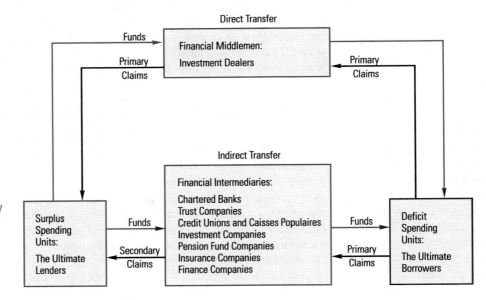

Figure 2.1
Flow-of-Funds Diagram

interest, pay depositors an average of 4 percent interest, and use the 3 percent difference to pay employee salaries and other expenses, as well as to provide a return to their shareholders. The various financial intermediaries are examined in greater detail later in this section.

Financial Assets

Although money is the most obvious financial asset, there are others as well, including **debt securities** and **equity securities**. Both debt and equity securities represent claims against the assets and future earnings of the corporation. Debt and equity securities are financial assets of the investors who own them, and, at the same time, these securities appear on the *liabilities and shareholders' equity* side of the issuing company's balance sheet.

Derivative securities are financial assets that derive their values from other assets. Forward contracts, futures contracts, and options on currencies are examples of derivative securities that are discussed later in this chapter.

Financial Markets

Financial markets are the vehicles through which financial assets are bought, sold, and traded. Financial markets are generally classified as money or capital markets and primary or secondary markets.

Money and Capital Markets
Money markets deal in short-term securities having maturities of one year or less. Capital markets deal in long-term securities having maturities greater than one year. (In both cases, the one-year break point is somewhat arbitrary.)

Most large corporations participate in the money markets, especially when they have more cash on hand than needed to run their businesses. For example, Magna International Inc., the Canadian auto parts company, had over US$890 million in cash and short-term investments at the end of 2001—approximately 25 percent of its current assets and 11 percent of its total assets. By investing in money market securities, the company earned interest rather than leaving its funds in non-interest-bearing chartered bank chequing accounts. Magna uses the US dollar as its functional currency because most of its sales and purchases are in US dollars. For this reason Magna and many other Canadian companies publish their financial statements denominated in US dollars. (In 2002, 14.6 percent of the Canadian companies listed in the *Report on Business Top 1000* reported in US dollars.)

Corporations enter the capital markets to obtain long-term funds, either debt or equity. Many corporations are unable to generate enough funds *internally* to satisfy their needs. Hence, they raise additional funds *externally* in the capital markets, as Magna does. In 1999, Magna borrowed 100 million euros by selling debentures in Europe. In 2000, Magna borrowed US$90 million by selling debentures in the United States. (Debentures and other fixed income securities are discussed in more detail in Chapter 5.) Magna also raises equity capital in these markets. (Common shares are discussed in more detail in Chapter 6.)

Primary and Secondary Markets
Anyone who purchases new securities is participating in a **primary market**. Net proceeds from the sale of new securities go directly to the issuing company. On virtually any given business day, the financial press contains announcements about the issuance of new debt and equity securities. (These are called tombstones because of their resemblance to epitaphs.)

Anyone who resells existing securities is participating in a **secondary market**. Secondary markets are well established in North America, where shares can be traded on the "floor" of a security exchange, such as the Toronto Stock Exchange (TSX) or

Debt Securities
Financial assets that represent debt transactions.

Equity Securities
Financial assets that represent ownership transactions.

Financial Assets
Financial assets include money as well as debt, equity, and derivative securities owned by investors.

Financial Markets
Places where financial securities (debt, equity, and derivative) can be exchanged between buyers and sellers.

For more information see
http://top1000.robmagazine. com

Primary Markets
Markets where new securities are sold, with the funds going directly to the issuing firms.

Secondary Markets
Financial markets in which existing securities are offered for resale. The Toronto Stock Exchange (TSX) is a secondary market.

the New York Stock Exchange (NYSE) or on the NASDAQ market or in the over-the-counter (OTC) markets. In addition to their role in primary markets, investment dealers function as brokers in these secondary markets. Brokers bring together buyers and sellers of existing securities. The structure and operation of the secondary markets is discussed in greater detail in the following sections. The operation of the primary markets is examined later in The Securities Offering Process section of this chapter.

Derivative Securities Markets   Derivative securities usually are traded in specialized financial markets, such as the Montreal Exchange (ME). Appropriate use of derivative securities helps a firm to manage risks. Later in this chapter, we introduce several derivative securities that a firm can use to manage exchange rate risk in international financial transactions. In Chapter 18, we show how such derivative securities can actually be used to manage exchange rate risk. Of course, exchange rate risk is not the only risk that firms face. In Chapter 17, we introduce other derivative securities to manage various domestic risks.

Financial Intermediaries

A variety of different financial intermediaries exists to facilitate the flow of funds between surplus spending units and deficit spending units. These different financial intermediaries specialize in the types of deposits they accept (sources of funds) and the types of investments they make (uses of funds). The Office of the Superintendent of Financial Institutions (**OSFI**) regulates federally chartered financial institutions and federally administered pension plans.

OSFI
Office of the Superintendent of Financial Institutions. The OSFI regulates federally chartered financial institutions and federally administered pension plans.

For more information see
www.osfi-bsif.gc.ca

Term Loan
A debt obligation having an initial maturity (i.e., maturity at the time of issue) between 1 and 10 years. Term loans are usually repaid in instalments over the life of the loan. This often is referred to as intermediate-term credit.

Chartered Banks   Chartered banks accept both demand deposits (in the form of chequing accounts) and term deposits (in the form of savings accounts and guaranteed investment certificates) from individual and other savers who temporarily have surplus funds that they lend to the bank. The bank then lends these funds to individuals, businesses, and governments. Chartered banks are an important source of short-term loans. Seasonal businesses, such as some retailers, certain manufacturers (for example, those who deal in leisure products), some food processors, and builders often require short-term financing to help them through peak periods. Many other types of businesses have a more or less continuing need for short-term financing and make prior arrangements with their banks to borrow on short notice. Banks provide significant amounts of both temporary "operating" and more "permanent" short-term financing for businesses.

Banks are also a major source of **term loans**, which have initial maturities between 1 and 10 years and are usually repaid in instalments over the life of the loan. The proceeds from term loans can be used to finance current assets, such as inventory or accounts receivable, and to finance the purchase of fixed plant facilities and equipment, as well as to repay other debts. Term loans are discussed in more detail in Chapter 15.

In 2003, the Canadian banking industry included 13 domestic banks, 34 foreign bank subsidiaries, and 11 foreign bank branches operating in Canada. Banks held approximately 70 percent of the total domestic assets of the financial services sector. The six major domestic banks (Royal Bank of Canada, Canadian Imperial Bank of Commerce, Bank of Montreal, Bank of Nova Scotia, Toronto-Dominion Bank, and the National Bank of Canada—the Big Six) held over 90 percent of the assets of the banking industry. They operated an extensive network of about 8,000 branches and 17,000 automated banking machines all across Canada. The six major Canadian banks are multinational firms active in the United States, Mexico, Latin America, and the Caribbean. Their international operations generated approximately half of the net revenue of the Big Six in 2000.

For more information see
www.cba.ca

Canada has one of the most concentrated banking sectors of any industrial country with the top three banks holding 54 percent of the industry's assets compared, for example, with the United States, where the top three banks hold only 18 percent of the industry's assets. Both economic theory and most of the empirical evidence suggest that such a high level of concentration would make it more difficult for smaller firms to obtain bank financing. However, a World Bank study found that the level of difficulty in obtaining bank credit was lower in Canada than in most countries, with only Sweden presenting its firms with better access.[1]

Trust Companies   Trust companies serve savers and make loans. They also serve as fiduciary money managers for trusts, estates, and registered investment plans. Anyone can create a trust by transferring assets to a trustee (the trust company) to be managed for the benefit of a beneficiary. Trusts can be created by a living person or as a result of the provisions of a will (estate). The beneficiary could be an infirm relative, a spouse, or a child. Thus, a trust might provide the income necessary for a student while in university or college. A Registered Educational Savings Plan (RESP) can also accomplish this objective. Similarly, a trust might be used to provide income for a surviving spouse. An alternative would be a Registered Retirement Savings Plan (RRSP). Although trust companies were once one of the main "pillars" of the Canadian financial system, there are now only a few independent trust companies because most of the trust companies have become subsidiaries of chartered banks.

For more information on credit unions see
www.cucentral.ca

Credit Unions and Caisses Populaires   Credit unions and caisses populaires are co-operative financial institutions that are owned by their members. Their mission is to promote thriftiness and provide user-friendly savings institutions for individuals. Because the banks originally served only businesses and wealthy people, ordinary people had no financial institution to call their own. The credit unions and caisses populaires met this need. These institutions now accept both demand and term deposits and invest most of their funds in home mortgages and consumer loans. They have gradually become more and more like banks and now also serve small businesses. Many of them, especially the caisses populaires in Quebec, are located in small towns where they may be the only local financial institution. In 2001, there were 703 credit unions and 1,069 caisses populaires in Canada. Canada has the world's highest per capita membership in the credit union movement, with over 10 million members, or about one-third of the Canadian population.

For more information see
www.ific.ca

Investment Companies   Investment companies, such as mutual fund management companies, pool the funds of many savers and invest these funds in various types of assets. Mutual fund management firms invest in specific financial assets—such as debt and equity securities of corporations or money market instruments—according to the objectives of the fund. The main types of mutual funds are money market funds, bond funds, equity funds, dividend funds, mortgage funds, and real estate funds. Mutual fund companies attempt to achieve superior performance through diversification and professional investment management. In 2002, there were 80 mutual fund management companies operating in Canada, with the top 10 holding over 70 percent of the assets of the industry. The 80 fund management companies provided about 1,800 different mutual funds to their 50 million account holders. Note that this number exceeds the population of Canada because many investors in mutual funds diversify their portfolios by holding several types of mutual funds.

---

[1] Thorsten Beck, Asli Demirguc-Kunt, and Vojislav Maksimovic, "Bank Competition, Financing Obstacles, and Access to Credit," working paper 2996 (2003) World Bank, Washington, DC.

For more information see
www.piacweb.org

Pension Fund Companies   Private pension fund management companies pool the contributions of employees (and/or employers) and invest these funds in various types of financial assets, such as corporate securities, or real assets, such as real estate. Pension funds are often managed by trust companies, life insurance companies, or investment counsellors. Pension funds are of two basic types: defined benefit and defined contribution. Defined benefit pension plans promise to pay pensioners a monthly benefit for life that is determined according to a formula, such as 2 percent per year of service times the highest five-year average salary. Thus, a pensioner with 35 years of service would receive up to 70 percent of the prior working salary in retirement. Defined contribution plans promise to pay pensioners during retirement only the income that the assets in the pension plan can generate. Thus, a pensioner's income in retirement is likely to fluctuate.

For more information on life insurance companies see
www.loma.org

Insurance Companies   Insurance companies receive periodic or lump-sum premium payments from individuals or organizations in exchange for agreeing to make certain future contractual payments if specified insured events occur. Life insurance companies make payments to a beneficiary based on the death or disability of the insured party. Property and casualty insurance companies make payments when a financial loss occurs due to such events as fire, theft, accident, or illness. The premiums received are used to build reserves to pay future claims. These reserves are invested in various types of assets, such as corporate securities. There are hundreds of insurance companies in Canada. Many of the larger firms also operate outside of Canada. Like the banks, they generate about half of their premium income from their foreign operations.

The Structure and Operation of Security Markets

As discussed above, capital markets are usually classified as either *primary* or *secondary* markets. New securities are issued in the *primary* markets, and the firms issuing these securities receive the proceeds from their sale, thus raising new capital. Outstanding securities are traded in the *secondary* markets, where owners of these securities may sell them to other investors, usually aided by investment dealers acting as brokers. The corporations whose securities are traded in the secondary markets do not share in the proceeds from these sales.

Although primary and secondary markets are separate, they are closely related. Smoothly functioning secondary markets aid the primary markets, because investors tend to be more willing to purchase new securities when they know they can sell them in the secondary market. In fact, the potential liquidity available in the secondary markets may make investors more willing to accept slightly lower returns on their investments, thereby lowering the cost companies have to pay for their funds.

Secondary Markets and Stock Market Indexes

Security Exchanges
Operate at designated places of business and have requirements governing the types of financial securities they can list and trade.

Secondary markets can be classified as security exchanges, formal virtual markets, and informal over-the-counter (OTC) markets. **Security exchanges** operate at designated places of business and have requirements governing the types of securities they can list and trade. **Formal virtual markets**, such as the NASDAQ, have listing requirements like security exchanges but do not operate at designated places of business. The **OTC security markets** are informal markets that do not have centralized places of business.

Formal Virtual Markets
Secondary securities markets that have listing requirements but no physical place of business, such as NASDAQ.

Over-the-Counter (OTC) Securities Markets
A network of security dealers connected by a communications system of telephones and computer terminals that provides price quotations on individual securities.

Security Exchanges   The Toronto Stock Exchange (which also includes the TSX Venture Exchange) is Canada's only stock exchange, with approximately 1,300 issues listed. The volume of share trading activity on the TSX is only about 2 percent of the world total (about the same size as the national stock exchanges in Holland, Italy, and Switzerland). This is too small for many Canadian firms, which are listed also in the

United States and Europe. CHC Helicopter Corporation of St. John's, Newfoundland, for example, is listed on both the Toronto and the New York stock exchanges.

Some Canadian firms do not even bother to list their shares in Canada and are listed only in the United States. For example, Vancouver-based Ritchie Bros. Auctioneers, which does two-thirds of its business in the United States, is listed only on the NYSE. It is one of about three dozen Canadian firms listed only on a US exchange.

Similarly, some of the smaller US firms are listed only on the TSX Venture Exchange rather than on any of the US stock exchanges. Security exchanges typically charge listing fees to listed firms.

For more information see
www.tsx.ca
www.me.org
www.wce.ca

In the past, Canadian stocks were traded on exchanges located in Alberta as well as Montreal, Toronto, and Vancouver. In 1999, the four exchanges decided to reorganize the industry so that all of the shares would be traded on the TSX and TSX Venture Exchanges while the Montreal Exchange (ME) became the derivatives exchange for the country. There is also the Winnipeg Commodities Exchange (WCE), where contracts on agricultural commodities are traded.

For more information see
www.nyse.com

The New York Stock Exchange is the largest stock exchange in the United States and the most important in the world. Over 2,000 common and preferred shares and over 800 bonds are listed on the NYSE. For a company's shares to be listed and traded on the NYSE, the firm must meet certain minimum requirements with regard to the number of shares outstanding, the number of shareholders, the geographical distribution of shareholders, the value of assets, the market value of shares, and the net income level. As a result, the NYSE tends to list only the larger firms. In 2002, Nortel Networks was in danger of losing its coveted listing on the NYSE because the price of its common shares slipped below the minimum required level of US$1 per share for a few weeks.

The NYSE, as well as the TSX, is composed largely of security firms that purchase memberships, or *seats*. The cost of these seats varies, depending on the securities industry outlook.

For more information see
www.amex.com

Another important exchange for Canadian firms is the American Stock Exchange, which, like the NYSE, is located in New York City. The companies listed on the AMEX are smaller on average than those listed on the NYSE. The AMEX has less stringent listing requirements than the NYSE.

Formal Virtual Markets   The NASDAQ market is the largest formal virtual market in the world. Shares of many firms are traded in the NASDAQ market, which has no single physical place of business and conducts operations through an electronic communications network. The NASDAQ is actually larger than the NYSE in terms of the volume of trades. Many large companies, such as Microsoft and Intel, prefer to have their shares listed on NASDAQ. Like the security exchanges, NASDAQ charges listing fees to the listed firms.

For more information see
www.nasdaq.com

Over-the-Counter Markets   Securities not listed on any of the exchanges or formal virtual markets are said to be traded "over the counter." In general, these include stocks of small and relatively unknown companies and some corporate bonds and preferred shares. In addition, most government bonds are traded in OTC markets. (Canada Savings bonds are not marketable, so they are not traded in OTC markets.) Security firms that deal in OTC securities and actually carry inventories in certain securities play an important role in the smooth functioning of OTC markets. These dealers are said to "make a market" in the securities they inventory. Since there is no formal list of companies that may be traded, companies are not charged any listing fees, and the OTC markets are considered to be unlisted or informal markets.

Stock Market Indexes   Stock market indexes give a broad indication of how the stock market or a segment of it performed during a particular day. The most frequently quoted stock market index in Canada is the S&P/TSX Composite Index. When a news announcer says, "The market was up five points today," the announcer means the stock market index was up five points. Although the index may have gone up, any individual stock may have gone down on the same day.

The most frequently quoted stock market index in the world is the Dow Jones Industrial Average (DJIA), which is based on the share prices of 30 large, well-established industrial corporations. The DJIA is calculated by adding the prices of the 30 stocks and dividing by a number that reflects prior stock dividends and splits. (Stock dividends and splits are discussed in Chapter 14.)

The NASDAQ Index is usually also reported in Canada, along with the S&P/TSX and DJIA. In the United States, the Standard & Poor's 500 Stock Price Index (S&P 500) is another frequently quoted stock market index. It is significantly broader than the DJIA. It is compiled from the share prices of 400 leading industrial firms, 20 transportation firms, 40 utilities, and 40 financial institutions. The S&P 500, like the S&P/TSX Composite Index and the NASDAQ Index, is a *market value–weighted index*. This means, for example, that a share whose total market value is $2 billion influences the index twice as much as a share whose total market value is $1 billion. Unlike the S&P 500, however, the number of stocks in the S&P/TSX Composite and NASDAQ indices may change somewhat over time. In January 2003, the S&P/TSX Composite Index contained less than 300 stocks and the NASDAQ Index contained approximately 4,100 stocks, of which 85 were Canadian stocks.

Regulation of the Security Markets

In Canada, the 10 provinces and 3 territories regulate the securities markets located within their borders because the Canadian Constitution assigns that power to them. The Canadian Securities Administrators (CSA) organization includes the 13 securities regulators of Canada. The mission of the CSA is to give Canada a national harmonized securities regulatory system (the Canadian Securities Regulatory System: CSRS) that protects investors from unfair, fraudulent practices and fosters fair, efficient, and vibrant capital markets. The CSA mandates full disclosure of information to investors, educates investors about the risks and responsibilities of investing, authorizes persons to provide investment services to the public, and supervises market intermediaries. The CSA sometimes has a difficult time getting the 13 member securities commissions to agree.

The two largest provincial securities commissions, the Ontario Securities Commission and the Quebec Securities Commission, are usually considered the leaders because they have the most investors and companies within their jurisdictions.

In the United States, both the federal government and the individual states regulate the securities business. Each of the 50 states (with the exception of Delaware) has passed so-called blue sky laws. The term *blue sky* came about when some risky securities were called nothing more than "pieces of blue sky." In spite of these state laws, many investors received incomplete and even fraudulent security information during the 1920s. This fact, combined with the 1929 stock market crash and the general reform spirit of the 1930s, led to the enactment of two principal pieces of security legislation—the Securities Act of 1933 and the Securities Exchange Act of 1934—and the establishment of the Securities and Exchange Commission (SEC). This federal legislation has been aimed primarily at ensuring full disclosure of security information. Notwithstanding these two federal laws, many investors once again received incomplete and even fraudulent information about securities in the 1990s and early 2000s that led to calls for further reforms. One result of these calls is the Sarbanes-Oxley Act of 2002.

Because so many Canadian firms have raised money in the United States, they are subject to all of the US regulations, including the Sarbanes-Oxley Act of 2002. This law requires CEOs and CFOs to personally certify the accuracy and completeness of their firms' financial statements. When it went into effect on August 29, 2002, it applied to

For more information see
www.tsx.ca and
www.wsj.com

For more information see
www.csa-acvm.ca

For more information see
www.osc.gov.on.ca and
**www.cvmq.com/
index_en.asp**

For more information see
www.sec.gov

ETHICAL ISSUES

Insider Trading

In 2002, a Canadian actress, Kathryn Gannon, was convicted in the United States of profiting from insider information that she received from a Wall Street executive. She was sentenced to three months in prison. She stated, "I did a lot of wrong things, but I'm an adventurous Aries and a Canadian."

Her co-conspirator, James McDermott, was a $4 million a year executive known for his appearances on TV investment programs. He admitted giving stock tips to Gannon. He was sentenced to five months in jail.

Gannon expects that a movie will be made about her life story. She is "happy to pay the time for the crime" because she thinks that her time in jail will promote the movie. Watch for it.

Do you agree that insider trading is a victimless crime? Who should be considered an insider for purposes of enforcing such a rule? Can you think of any reasons why insider trading should be permitted?

Source: Associated Press online, Wednesday, October 23, 2002.

503 non-US companies. Thus, it is not prudent for Canadian financial managers to ignore the SEC and the US laws that apply to Canadian firms.

Of course, if Canadian firms raise money in other countries, such as England or France, they also become subject to the laws and rules of those countries and their securities exchanges.

In addition to regulating the disclosure of information in new securities offerings and setting disclosure requirements for nearly all firms whose shares trade publicly, securities regulators also regulate "insider" trading. Any time a director, officer, or major shareholder—that is, an "insider"—of a large corporation trades in that corporation's securities, the trade must be reported to the relevant securities regulators. This information is available to the public and is used by some investors in deciding which shares to buy or sell. This reporting requirement attempts to prevent insiders from trading securities secretly on the basis of private information.

The Securities Offering Process

Investment dealers/investment bankers are financial middlemen who bring together suppliers and users of long-term funds in the capital markets and thereby play a key role in the security offering process.

Whenever a large corporation is considering raising funds in the capital markets, whether as debt or equity, it almost always enlists the services of an investment dealer. In fact, most large industrial corporations have ongoing relationships with their investment dealers.

Investment dealers assist client corporations in the offering process in a variety of ways, including the following:

- Long-range financial planning
- The timing of security issues
- The purchase of securities
- The marketing of securities

Public Cash Offering
The sale of securities to investors, also called an initial public offering.

Private Placement
The sale of an entire security offering to one or more institutional investors rather than the general public. This also is termed a direct placement.

Rights Offering
The sale of new common shares by distributing stock purchase rights to a firm's existing shareholders. This also is termed a *privileged subscription*.

Bought Deal
A firm commitment underwriting by investment dealers who agree to buy all of the securities issued by a firm. The underwriters then take the risk that they will be able to sell the securities.

Initial Public Offering (IPO)
The first public sale of a firm's shares to the public.

Competitive Bidding
The process of selling a new security offering to the highest bidding underwriting syndicate of investment dealers.

Negotiated Underwriting
A process whereby a firm wishing to sell new securities to the public negotiates the terms of the underwriting with the investment dealers.

Underwriter
An investment dealer firm or group that agrees to buy all of an issue of securities from a corporation that wants to raise money. The underwriter then takes the risk that it may not be able to resell the issue to retail investors at a higher price than it paid the firm.

- The arrangement of private loans and leases
- The negotiation of mergers

In summary, the investment dealer is an important source of financial market expertise and an important part of the security offering process. The role of an investment dealer in the security offering process is called investment banking, even in Canada.

How Securities Are Sold

Firms can sell securities in the primary capital markets in one of three ways:

1. By selling securities through investment dealers to the public in a **public cash offering**
2. By placing a debt or share issue with one or more large investors in a **private**, or **direct, placement**
3. By selling common shares to existing shareholders through a **rights offering**

Investment dealers usually assist firms in all three methods of sale. Figure 2.2 outlines the various methods and steps for the sale of corporate securities.

Public Cash Offerings   Normally, when a corporation wishes to issue new securities and sell them to the public, it makes an arrangement with an investment dealer who agrees to purchase the entire issue at a set price. This is called a **bought deal** or *firm commitment underwriting*. The investment dealer then resells the issue to the public at a higher price.

Hemosol Inc. (HML) raised $15 million that it needed to fund ongoing clinical trials of its major product in a bought deal with a syndicate of underwriters co-led by Sprott Securities Inc. and Yorkton Securities Inc. in early 2002. In addition to their commissions, the underwriters were given an option to purchase an additional $5 million worth of shares. Hemosol was already known to the investment community and is listed on the TSX.

When a firm sells shares to the public for the first time, it makes an **initial public offering (IPO)**. The Hockey Company, a Montreal holding company that owns the CCM, Koho, and Jofa brands, announced a $73 million IPO on April 9, 2003, while the hockey playoffs were in progress.

Underwriting can be accomplished either through *negotiations* between the underwriter and the issuing company or by **competitive bidding**. A **negotiated underwriting** is simply an arrangement between the issuing firm and its investment dealers. Most large industrial corporations turn to investment dealers with whom they have had ongoing relationships. In competitive bidding, the firm sells the securities to the **underwriter** (usually a group) that bids the highest price. Many regulated companies are required to sell new security issues in this way.

Security issues sold to the public through underwriters normally exceed $25 million in size. Amounts totalling several hundred million dollars (particularly bond issues) are not uncommon. Due to the size of these issues, individual investment dealers usually do not want to underwrite an entire issue by themselves. Normally, a group of underwriters, called a **syndicate**, agrees to underwrite the issue in order to spread the risk.[2] Sometimes the underwriting syndicate can sell an entire issue to large institutional investors.[3] This is often true with high-quality debt issues. On other occasions—particularly with large debt issues or equity issues—the underwriters organize a **selling group**

---

[2] In most cases, one to three underwriters agree to manage an issue, handling all legal matters, advertising, and so on. These firms are the *managing underwriters*.

[3] Institutional investors include life insurance companies, pension fund and mutual fund management companies, and chartered banks.

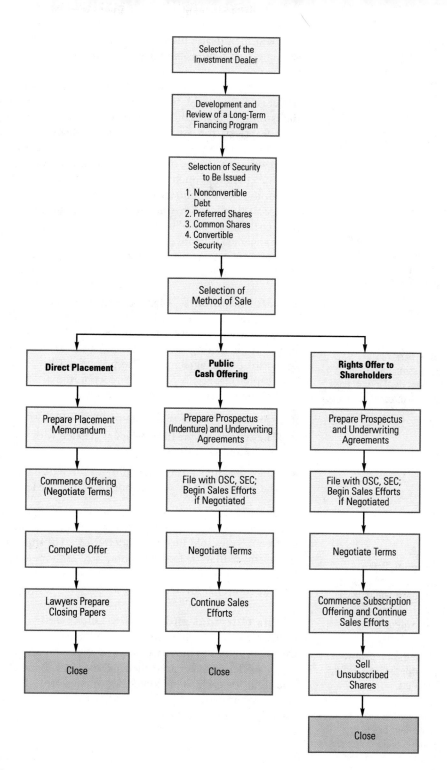

Figure 2.2
How Securities Are Sold

of investment dealer firms to market the issue to the public. It is not uncommon for a selling group responsible for marketing a large issue to number over 100 firms around the world.

An important part of the negotiations between the issuing firm and the investment dealer is the determination of the security's selling price. It is in the best interests of both the issuing firm and the underwriter to have the security "fairly priced." If the security is underpriced, the issuing firm will not raise the amount of capital it could have, and the underwriter may lose future business from the firm. If the security is overpriced, the underwriter may have difficulty selling the issue. Furthermore, investors who discover that they paid too much may choose not to purchase the next issue offered by either the corporation or the underwriter.

Occasionally, with smaller company issues, the investment dealer agrees to help market the issue on a "**best-efforts**" basis rather than underwriting it. Under this type of arrangement, the investment dealer has no further obligation to the issuing company if some of the securities cannot be sold. The investment banking firm functions as a *dealer* in an underwriting situation and as a *broker* in a best-efforts situation.

Private Placements   Many industrial companies choose to *directly,* or *privately, place* debt or preferred share issues with one or more institutional investors instead of having them underwritten and sold to the public. In these cases, investment dealers who act on behalf of the issuing company receive a **finder's fee** for finding a buyer and negotiating the terms of the agreement. The private market is an important source of long-term debt capital, especially for smaller corporations.

Private security placements have a number of advantages:

- They can save on flotation costs by eliminating underwriting costs.

- They can avoid the time delays associated with the preparation of registration statements and with the waiting period.

- They can offer greater flexibility in the writing of the terms of the contract (called the *indenture*) between the borrower and the lender.

An offsetting disadvantage is that, as a very general rule, interest rates for private placements are about one-eighth of a percentage point *higher* than they are for debt and preferred issues sold through underwriters. For small debt and preferred share issues—that is, those that are less than about $20 million—the percentage cost of underwriting becomes fairly large. Because of this, these smaller issues are frequently placed privately with institutional investors.

Rights Offerings and Standby Underwritings   Firms may sell their common shares directly to their existing shareholders through the issuance of rights, which entitle the shareholders to purchase new shares at a **subscription price** below the market price. (Rights offerings also are called **privileged subscriptions**.) Each shareholder receives one right for each share owned. In other words, if a firm has 100 million shares outstanding and wishes to sell an additional 10 million shares through a rights offering, each right entitles the holder to purchase 0.1 shares. Hence, it takes 10 rights to purchase one share.[4]

When selling shares through a rights offering, companies usually enlist the services of investment dealers, who urge rights holders to purchase the shares. In an arrangement called a **standby underwriting**, the investment dealer agrees to purchase—at the subscription price—any shares that are not sold to rights holders. The investment dealer then resells the shares. In a standby underwriting, the investment dealer bears risk and is compensated by an underwriting fee.

---

[4] Rights and rights offerings are discussed in greater detail in Chapter 17.

During 2002, Indigo Books & Music raised funds both by private placement and by a rights offering. Rights offerings have declined in popularity as a method of raising equity capital in North America. However, in the United Kingdom, rights offerings are more common. In October 1992, British Aerospace attempted an underwritten rights offering totalling $732 million (£432 million). The offering price was 380 pence per share. Unfortunately, the price of British Aerospace stock declined to 363 pence during the period of the offering and only a small portion (4.9%) of the offering was purchased by rights holders. The underwriters were forced to take large losses on the offering when they were stuck with the balance of the issue.[5]

Direct Issuance Costs   An investment dealer who agrees to underwrite a security issue assumes a certain amount of risk and, in turn, requires compensation in the form of an *underwriting discount* or underwriting spread, computed as follows:

(2.1)   Underwriting spread = Selling price to public – Proceeds to company

It is difficult to compare underwriting spreads for negotiated and competitive offerings because rarely are two offerings brought to market at the same time that differ only in the ways in which they are underwritten. Generally, underwriters receive lower spreads for competitively bid issues than for negotiated offers. This may be due to differences in the level of risk of individual firms.

In addition to the underwriting spread, other direct costs of security offerings include legal and accounting fees, taxes, registration fees with the appropriate Canadian provincial and US securities commissions, and printing costs. For equity offerings in Canada, these direct costs may exceed 8 percent of the gross proceeds from the offering, on average.[6]

Generally, direct issuance costs are higher for common share than preferred share issues, and direct issuance costs of preferred shares are higher than those of debt issues. One reason for this is the amount of risk each type of issue involves. Common shares usually involve more risk for underwriters than preferred shares, and preferred shares involve more risk than debt. Share prices are subject to wider price movements than debt prices. Another reason for these differences in direct issuance costs is that investment dealers usually incur greater marketing expenses for common shares than for preferred share or debt issues. Common shares are customarily sold to a large number of individual investors, whereas debt securities are frequently purchased by a much smaller number of institutional investors.

Direct issuance costs also depend on the quality of the issue. Low-quality debt issues, for example, tend to have higher percentage direct issuance costs than high-quality issues. This occurs because underwriters bear more risk with low-quality issues and therefore require greater compensation. Finally, direct issuance costs are dependent on the size of the issue. That is, costs tend to be a higher percentage of small issues, all other things being equal, because underwriters have various fixed expenses (such as advertising expenses, legal fees, registration statement costs, and so on) that are incurred regardless of the issue's size.

Other Issuance Costs   In addition to direct costs, there are significant other costs associated with new security offerings, including

1. The *cost of management time* in preparing the offering
2. The *cost of underpricing* a new (initial) equity offering below the correct market value.

---

[5] "British Aerospace Lesson: How Not to Sell Issues," *The Wall Street Journal* (October 30, 1992): C1.

[6] Vijay Jog, "The Climate for Canadian Initial Public Offerings," in *Financing Growth in Canada*, ed. P. J. Halpern (University of Calgary Press, 1997): 357–401.

Registration Statement
An information disclosure document required of firms that issue securities.

Prospectus
A document that contains information about a company's legal, operational, and financial position. It is prepared for the benefit of prospective investors in a new security issued by the firm.

Multijurisdictional Disclosure System (MJDS)
A joint Canada-US system that allows issuing firms to use the registration statements and prospectuses of their home country for sales of their securities in the other country.

For more information on filings see **www.sedar.com** and **www.sec.gov/edgar.shtml**

For a sample final shelf registration prospectus, navigate to the company profile for BCE Inc. on the **www.sedar.com** Web site and view the August 1, 2002, link.

Shelf Registration
A method whereby large firms can issue securities over a period of time with the same registration statement and prospectus. In Canada this is called the **POP (Prompt Offering Prospectus) System**.

Underpricing occurs because of the uncertainty associated with the value of initial public offerings and a desire to ensure that the offering is a success. For example, the initial public offering for Krispy Kreme Doughnuts in April 2000 was priced at $21. After the first day of trading it closed at $38.37, or a gain of 82.7%, and by the end of the year 2000 it closed at $83, or a gain of 295%. Examples such as this and many Internet company shares in the late 1990s are extreme, although not uncommon, examples of the underpricing associated with many initial public offerings

3. The *cost of share price declines* for offerings by firms whose shares are already outstanding—so-called seasoned offerings. The announcement of new share issues by a firm whose shares are already outstanding causes a price decline averaging about 3 percent for the outstanding shares

4. The *cost of other incentives* provided to the investment dealer, including the over-allotment or "Green Shoe" option. This option, often contained in underwriting contracts, gives the investment dealers the right to buy up to 15 percent more new shares than the initial offering amount at a price equal to the offering price. The option is designed to allow investment dealers to handle oversubscriptions. This option normally lasts for 30 days.

These indirect costs can, in aggregate, constitute a very significant expense associated with security offerings (especially for common equity). Estimates of these costs in Canada indicate that they may be as high as 10 percent of the gross proceeds of the issue, making the total costs about 18 percent. In the United States, these costs are even higher.[7]

Registration Requirements   Any firm offering *new* securities to the public must make a complete disclosure of all pertinent facts regarding these securities. This is a legal requirement. In addition, trading in *existing* securities also must be disclosed. The various governments have created securities commissions (as discussed earlier) that are responsible for administering the legislation. These laws make no judgements regarding the quality of securities issues. They simply require full disclosure of the facts.

Any company that plans to sell a large security issue is required to register the issue with the appropriate regulatory bodies. The procedure involves the preparation of a **registration statement** and a **prospectus**. The registration statement contains a vast amount of information about the company's legal, operational, and financial position. The prospectus summarizes the information contained in the registration statement and is intended for the use of potential investors. Since 1991, when Canada and the United States implemented **the Multijurisdictional Disclosure System (MJDS)**, Canadian firms can file their Canadian disclosure documents with the US SEC. This system greatly reduced the registration costs for interlisted firms and encouraged more Canadian firms to raise funds in the United States.

After a company has filed a registration statement and prospectus, there is normally a waiting period before the appropriate securities commission approves the issue and the company can begin selling the securities. During the waiting period, the company may use a preliminary prospectus in connection with the anticipated sale of securities. This preliminary prospectus is often called a "red herring" because it contains a statement, usually marked in red, saying that the prospectus is "not an offer to sell." All buyers of the new securities must be provided with a final copy of the prospectus.

Shelf Registration—the POP (Prompt Offering Prospectus) System   Since 1983, **shelf registration** of debt and equity securities has been permitted for larger firms with a high (*investment grade*) rating. Under the shelf registration procedure, a firm files a *master registration* statement with the appropriate securities commission. The

---

[7] See T. Loughran, J. R. Ritter, and K. Rydqvist, "Initial Public Offerings: International Insights," *Pacific Basin Financial Journal* (May 1994): 165–199.

Export Financing

Most of the developed countries have an export credit agency to promote exports. In Canada, the federal government has created a Crown corporation, Export Development Canada (EDC) to act as a bridge between the support provided by the banks and what Canadian exporters need to succeed in export markets. EDC provides financial and insurance services to exporters, especially smaller firms. EDC's services include credit insurance, political risk insurance, direct loans to buyers, and lines of credit in other countries to encourage buyers to "buy Canadian." Exports are crucial for Canada because exports account for one in three jobs. EDC helps Canadian exporters get paid.

Approximately 85 percent of Canadian exports go to the US.

In January 2003, EDC announced that it had extended $3.8 billion in trade finance and risk management services to finance or insure export sales by 27 Canadian companies in the aerospace sector during 2002. This compares with $3.4 billion in 2001. The majority of EDC exposure in the aerospace sector is secured by mortgages on aircraft operated by 26 of the world's leading airlines and their regional affiliates. Exports aided by EDC have enabled the Canadian aerospace industry to become the third largest in the world, employing more than 85,000 Canadians in 400 companies across the country.

For more information see
www.edc.ca

company is then free to sell small increments of the offering over an extended time period (two years) merely by filing a brief *short-form statement* with the commission only hours before the actual offering. By placing its new securities "on the shelf" awaiting an opportune time for issuance, the company has the capability to time its issuance with the specific financing needs of the firm and to take advantage of perceived favourable pricing windows in the market. There is some evidence that the shelf registration procedure is less costly than traditional underwriting for equity offerings. In Canada, this shelf registration procedure is properly called the **Prompt Offering Prospectus (POP) System** and the firms using it are called POP issuers. However, most investors, their investment dealers, and the issuing firms usually refer to it as shelf registration, as this is the internationally accepted terminology.

The Global Economy and Multinational Enterprises

As mentioned in Chapter 1, the importance of understanding the global economy can be seen in the volume of Canadian exports and imports. In 2002, merchandise exports totalled $410.3 billion and merchandise imports totalled $356.1 billion. The difference between merchandise exports and imports is the *merchandise trade balance*. In 2002, Canada had a *merchandise trade surplus* of approximately $54.2 billion, which was a decrease from the surplus of $64 billion for 2001.

Business enterprises participate in the global marketplace in a wide variety of ways. Some firms simply *export* finished goods for sale in another country and/or *import* raw materials or products from another country for use in their domestic operations. At the other end of the spectrum are *multinational enterprises*. A **multinational corporation** has direct investments in manufacturing and/or distribution facilities in more than one country. Often, these foreign operations are structured to be relatively freestanding subsidiaries. Among the Canadian multinational firms are Abitibi Consolidated, Alcan,

Multinational Corporation
A firm with direct investments in more than one country.

Barrick, Bombardier, Canfor, Domtar, Inco, George Weston, Magna International, Nortel Networks, Onex, and TransCanada Pipelines. Many foreign-based multinationals are active in Canada, including ABB, Ford, DaimlerChrysler, General Motors, IBM, Microsoft, Nokia, Toyota, Royal Dutch/Shell, and Unilever.

ABB is one of the non-North American multinational firms that reports all of its financial results in US dollars and also uses English as the official language of the firm in all of its worldwide operations. The headquarters of the firm are located in Zurich, Switzerland, and many of its top executives are Swedish.

The rise of the multinational firm has drastically changed the way business is done around the world. The multinational organization makes it relatively easy for firms to use the key factors of production—land, labour, and capital—in the location where they can be most productive. This represents a dramatic change from the time when the factors of production were thought to be immobile and only goods and services could be moved easily across borders. As a result, the process of resource allocation and business decision making has become more complex. At the same time, multinational firms have the opportunity to benefit from imperfections that arise in various national markets for capital and other factors of production. Furthermore, whether or not a firm is engaged in international transactions, the decline of trade barriers and the increasing ease of moving assets to those countries where they will be the most productive add a new element of competition for all firms. It is no longer possible for a Canadian firm to worry about just its domestic competitors. Competition is now global.

All firms engaged in international business transactions face unique problems and risks not encountered by firms that operate in only one country. First, there are difficulties associated with doing business in different currencies. Financial transactions between Canadian firms and firms (or individuals) in foreign countries normally involve foreign currency that ultimately has to be converted into dollars. Therefore, firms that do business internationally are concerned with the *exchange rate* between dollars and foreign currencies. Second, problems arise because of different government regulations, tax laws, business practices, and political environments in foreign countries.

Foreign Currency Markets and Exchange Rates

Whenever a Canadian firm purchases goods or services from a firm in another country, two currencies normally are involved. For example, when a Canadian company purchases materials from a British supplier, the British firm usually prefers payment in British pounds, whereas the Canadian company prefers to make payment in Canadian or US dollars. If the sales agreement requires that payment be made in pounds, the Canadian company will have to exchange (that is, *sell*) dollars to obtain the required number of pounds. The exact amount of dollars the Canadian company will have to sell depends on the **exchange rate** between the two currencies.

Exchange Rate
The rate at which a currency can be converted into another currency.

Suppose, for example, that the exchange rate at the time of the transaction is CDN\$2.38 per pound, £. Furthermore, assume that the British supplier and the Canadian firm have agreed on a price of £2 million for the materials. Therefore, the Canadian firm will have to exchange CDN\$4.76 million (that is, £2,000,000 × \$2.38/pound) to obtain the British currency to pay for the purchase.

Foreign currency needed for international financial transactions can be exchanged for domestic currency in most countries either at banks or at a central bank operated by the government. The volume of foreign currency transactions is very large. For example, the Bank for International Settlements estimates that daily, worldwide foreign currency trading exceeds US\$1.5 trillion. Of this amount, nearly 60 percent is between international banks; about 25 percent is between banks within a country; and the balance is with foreign currency dealers and other banking customers. The most important foreign currency trading centers are in New York, Tokyo, Hong Kong, Sydney, Singapore, Bahrain, Frankfurt, Zurich, London, San Francisco, Chicago, and Toronto.

The Eurocurrency Market

Eurocurrency
A currency that is deposited in a bank outside of the country of origin.

A **Eurocurrency** is a currency that is deposited in a bank located outside the country of origin. Eurodollars are created when, for example, a multinational firm transfers US dollars from a bank in the United States to a bank outside the United States. When these US dollars are deposited in a bank outside the United States, they become **Eurodollars**. The bank outside the US may, for example, be either a non-US bank, such as Deutsche Bank, or a foreign branch of a US bank, such as Citibank. Other important Eurocurrencies include Euroyen and Eurosterling (Japanese yen and British pounds), deposited outside their country of origin. (There are also Eurocanadiandollars, although the market for them is not very large.) The gross size of the Eurocurrency market is in excess of US$8 trillion. About two-thirds of the Eurocurrencies outstanding are US dollar-denominated. The typical Eurocurrency deposit is a nonnegotiable time deposit with a fixed term to maturity. Maturities range from overnight to as long as five years.

Eurodollars
US dollars deposited in banks outside the United States.

The Eurocurrency market provides an important alternative to domestic sources of funds for multinational firms. For example, in Canada, large, well-established firms can borrow funds in the Canadian financial market, in the US financial market, or in the international financial marketplace, such as the Eurocurrency market. If Magna International chooses to borrow in the Eurodollar market it might receive a Eurodollar loan from a foreign bank, such as Barclays Bank in London or Deutsche Bank in Frankfurt. The interest rate in the Eurodollar market is usually related to the *London Interbank Offer Rate,* or *LIBOR*. **LIBOR** is the interest rate at which banks in the Eurocurrency market lend to each other. The cost to borrow in the Eurocurrency market is usually stated as a margin above LIBOR. Typically, Eurodollar borrowing rates are between 0.5 percent and 3 percent over LIBOR, with a median of about 1.5 percent. Eurocurrency loans range in maturity up to 10 years for the best-quality borrowers.

London Interbank Offer Rate (LIBOR)
The interest rate at which banks in the Eurocurrency market lend to each other.

The Euro: A Common European Currency

On January 4, 1999, 11 countries of the European Union (EU) turned over control of their monetary policies to the new European Central Bank and the single European currency, the **euro**, was born. During a transition period, the euro was being used only for paperless transactions. However, on January 1, 2002, euro bills and coins began circulation and six months later, the national currencies of these 11 countries ceased to exist. This move toward a single European currency is the logical outgrowth of the development of a single European market, where goods, services, and people flow freely across national borders. The use of a common currency eliminates exchange costs associated with converting from one currency to another and also eliminates the uncertainty of exchange rate fluctuations among these countries. The euro initially traded in the foreign currency marketplace at a rate of about US$1.17 per €. By late 2001, however, the value of the euro declined to about US$0.88 because of a number of factors, including the relative strength of the U.S. and European economies. In August of 2002, the euro traded at US$0.98 and by mid-May 2003 was trading at US$1.1543. Regardless of its short-term performance, the euro is sure to become a major international currency, rivalling the US dollar in importance.

Euro
The European single currency that went into circulation in 2002.

Direct and Indirect Quotes

Exchange rates can be expressed as either *direct quotes* or *indirect quotes*. A **direct quote** is the home currency price of one unit of foreign currency. For example, from the perspective of a North American firm like Canada's Magna International, whose **functional currency** (the currency in which it does most of its business operations) is the US dollar, a quote of US$1.1543 per euro is a direct quote. An **indirect quote** is the foreign currency price of one unit of the home currency. Thus, a quote of €0.8663 per US$ would be an indirect quote from the perspective of a North American firm whose functional currency is the US dollar. Direct quotes and indirect quotes have a reciprocal

Direct Quote
The home currency price of one unit of a foreign currency.

Functional Currency
The currency in which the majority of a firm's transactions are denominated. The US dollar is the functional currency for many Canadian firms.

Indirect Quote
The foreign currency price of one unit of the home currency.

Some exchange rates can be found in *The Globe and Mail* and on its Web site at **www.globeandmail.com** A more comprehensive site is **www.x-rates.com**

Spot Rate
The rate of exchange between two currencies being bought and sold for immediate delivery.

Forward Rate
The rate of exchange between two currencies being bought and sold for delivery at a future date.

Forward Contract
A contract calling for the delivery of a specified amount of some item at a future point in time at a price set at the present time. Compared to futures contracts, forward contracts are not liquid, can be customized with regard to the date or amount, and carry performance risk.

relationship. Accordingly, the indirect quote was derived by taking the reciprocal (1/$1.1543/€) of the direct quote. For a Canadian firm whose functional currency is the Canadian dollar, CDN$1.5776 would be the direct quote for the euro and €0.6339 would be the indirect quote.

Spot Rates

Exchange rates between Canadian and US dollars and the currencies of most countries are reported daily in *The Globe and Mail*. Table 2.1 shows the Canadian and US dollar exchange rates on May 16, 2003. **Spot rates** represent the rate of exchange for currencies being bought and sold for immediate delivery. Spot rates were used in the examples in the preceding paragraph.

Banks profit from their foreign currency transactions by buying currencies at one rate (*bid*) and selling them at another, higher rate (*ask* or *offer*). For example, a bank may quote the euro at US$1.0822 bid, and US$1.0832 offer. This quote is often written simply as 1.0822 32.

Forward Rates

In addition to spot transactions, currencies can also be bought and sold today for delivery at some future time, usually 30, 90, or 180 days from today. In these cases, **forward rates** are used, rather than spot rates. Forward exchange rates between Canadian and US dollars and the currencies of several of the major industrial countries are also reported daily in the financial press. Table 2.2 shows some example exchange rates relative to the Canadian and US dollars on May 16, 2003.

As shown later in Chapter 18, firms engaged in international transactions can use the forward foreign exchange market to hedge against the risk of adverse fluctuations in exchange rates.

Foreign Currency Futures

A foreign currency *futures contract* is similar to a *forward contract*. Both call for the delivery of a specified amount of some item, such as a foreign currency, at a future point in time at a price set at the present time. A **forward contract** is normally a contract between two parties that are known to each other, such as an importer and a bank. Performance of the contract by the seller and the buyer depends on the character and capacity of the parties. Because these contracts are negotiated between the parties, forward contracts can be established for any future time period and for any quantity of any item that is agreeable to the two parties. Forward contracts are not liquid. That is, it is difficult or impossible for either party to transfer its interest in the contract to another party once the contract has been agreed to. The seller of the contract must deliver the promised item at the agreed time and the buyer must pay for it and accept delivery.

Table 2.1	Canadian and US Dollar Exchange Rates	
	US$1 in CDN$ =	**CDN$1 in US$ =**
Spot	1.3667	0.7317
1 mo. Forward	1.3690	0.7305
3 mo. Forward	1.3740	0.7278
6 mo. Forward	1.3820	0.7236
1 yr. Forward	1.3981	0.7153
3 yrs. Forward	1.4462	0.6915
5 yrs. Forward	1.4787	0.6763

Source: The Globe & Mail (May 17, 2003): B8. Based on the mid-market rates in Toronto on May 16, 2003. Prepared by BMO Nesbitt Burns Capital Markets.

Table 2.2 Foreign Exchange Rates

Currency	CDN$ per unit	US$ per unit
British Pound (£) Spot	2.2198	1.6242
British Pound 1 mo. Forward	2.2190	1.6209
British Pound 3 mo. Forward	2.2185	1.6146
British Pound 6 mo. Forward	2.2184	1.6052
British Pound 1 yr. Forward	2.2195	1.5875
European Euro (€) Spot	1.5776	1.1543
European Euro 1 mo. Forward	1.5786	1.1531
European Euro 3 mo. Forward	1.5815	1.1510
European Euro 6 mo. Forward	1.5866	1.1480
European Euro 1 yr. Forward	1.5978	1.1428
Japanese Yen (¥) Spot	0.011780	0.008619
Japanese Yen 1 mo. Forward	0.011814	0.008630
Japanese Yen 3 mo. Forward	0.011882	0.008648
Japanese Yen 6 mo. Forward	0.011986	0.008673
Japanese Yen 1 yr. Forward	0.012199	0.008725

Source: *The Globe & Mail* (May 17, 2003): B8. Based on the mid-market rates in Toronto on May 16, 2003. Prepared by BMO Nesbitt Burns Capital Markets.

Futures Contract
A contract calling for the delivery of a standardized quantity and quality of some item, such as a foreign currency, crude oil, or securities, at a future point in time at a price set at the present time.

Option
A contract (often in the form of a security) that gives its holder the right but not the obligation to buy (call) or sell (put) an asset at a set price during a specified time period.

Call Option
A contract that gives the holder the right but not the obligation to *buy* an asset at a set price. Also referred to as a *call*.

Put Option
A contract that gives the holder the right but not the obligation to sell an asset at a set price during a specified period of time. Also referred to as a put.

In contrast to a forward contract, a **futures contract** is an *exchange traded agreement* that calls for the delivery of a *standardized amount* of an item (such as 125,000 euros) at a *standardized maturity date*. The most important currency futures market in North America is the Chicago Mercantile Exchange (CME). Contracts traded on the CME mature on the third Wednesday of the contract month, with the last trading day being two days prior to that. Unlike forward contracts, there is virtually no performance risk in a futures contract. Rather than the buyer and seller of the contract dealing directly with each other, the exchange clearinghouse acts as the buyer and seller of all contracts. Buyers and sellers of futures contracts must post collateral (as their performance bond). Each day the value of the contract is "marked to market," with all gains and losses being paid between the parties in cash. If payment is not made, the contract is sold by the clearinghouse and the performance bond of the defaulting party is charged for any losses. In essence, one can think of a futures contract as a series of forward contracts that are settled each day. Only about 5 percent of currency futures contracts are settled by means of delivery of the underlying currency from the seller to the buyer. More commonly, the parties will offset their position prior to expiration by making a transaction opposite to the original one. For example, a buyer of a contract for 125,000 euros with delivery in March usually sells an identical contract prior to expiration. The sale of an identical contract by an initial buyer of the same contract fully offsets the position from the perspective of the clearinghouse.

Foreign Currency Options

Whereas forward and future currency contracts reflect an *obligation* to either buy or sell a currency at a future date, currency **options** are contracts that give the option buyer the *right, but not the obligation,* to either buy or sell a fixed amount of a currency at a fixed price at a time up to, or at, the expiration date of the option. There are two fundamental types of options. A **call option** is an option to buy something, such as currency, and a **put option** is an option to sell. Options may also differ in their exercise privilege. For example, an *American option* gives the holder the right to buy (call) or sell (put) the underlying asset, such as a currency, at any time prior to or on the expiry date. In contrast, a *European option* gives the holder the right to buy or sell the underlying asset only on the expiry date. Large banks offer customized options for all major currencies with exercise periods of up to a year. In addition, currency options are also traded on the Chicago Mercantile Exchange. Financial assets such as currency options as well as forward and futures contracts are types of derivative securities that help firms manage their foreign exchange risk. (This topic is discussed further in Chapter 18.)

Income Taxes and Financial Management

Knowledge of tax laws and regulations is essential in making a wide variety of business decisions that affect shareholder wealth, such as what form of business organization to select, what types of securities to issue, and what investment projects to undertake. Some specific provisions of the Canadian tax system are discussed later in this chapter. First, we present an overview of some important managerial implications of the tax system. Then we discuss some of the more important specific topics.

Implications of Income Taxes for Financial Managers

Although the effect of income taxes on financial decisions is discussed in detail where appropriate throughout the book, a brief review of some of the critical areas of concern is provided in this section.

Capital Budgeting   *Capital expenditure decisions* are also influenced by corporate income taxes. Capital expenditures require an outlay of *after-tax* dollars to acquire the needed assets. The assets are expected to generate a stream of operating income that is subject to tax. A *tax-deductible expense* associated with many capital expenditures is *depreciation*. **Depreciation** provides a tax deduction equal to a part of the original cost of a depreciable asset, such as machinery or buildings. The tax code details the methods that may be used to depreciate assets. Because depreciation is a noncash expense (the cash outlay was made when the asset was purchased), it simply reduces taxable income and hence reduces the amount of taxes that must be paid. Changes in the tax code that speed up (slow down) the depreciation rate increase (decrease) the present value of the cash flows from the investment project and make the project a more (less) desirable investment. (More details on the capital cost allowance (CCA) system of depreciation for tax purposes are provided in Chapter 9.) Therefore, financial managers must pay close attention to expected tax law changes.

Depreciation
The systematic allocation of the cost of an asset over its expected economic life or some other period of time.

Capital Structure Policy   An optimal capital structure policy determines the relative amounts of debt and equity financing that maximize shareholder wealth. Taxes have important implications for capital structure policy. The interest payments associated with debt financing are deductible from earnings when computing a firm's income tax liability, whereas common share dividends and preferred share dividends are not deductible. In other words, for a firm with positive pretax earnings and a 40 percent income tax rate, a new debt issue that increases interest expenses by $1,000,000 per year would cost the company (i.e., reduce after-tax income) only $600,000—$1,000,000 interest expense less $400,000 tax savings (.40 × $1,000,000). This tax advantage of debt is a prime reason for leveraged buyouts and financial restructurings.

Dividend Policy   A firm's dividend policy may be influenced by personal income taxes. When dividends are paid to common shareholders, these dividends are taxed immediately as income to the shareholder. Although the gross-up and tax credit system (discussed later in this chapter) causes dividends to be taxed at a lower rate than other income, some tax must be paid when the dividends are received. If, instead of paying dividends, a firm retains and reinvests its earnings, the price of the share can be expected to increase. Personal taxes owed on common share appreciation are deferred until the shares are sold. At that time, capital gains tax will be payable, but the investor may be in a lower tax bracket than now. The ability to defer personal taxes on retained earnings causes some investors (e.g., those in high marginal tax brackets) to prefer retention and reinvestment and ultimately capital gains rather than immediate dividend payments. This investor preference can have an impact on corporate dividend policy, particularly in small, closely held companies.

Leasing   The decision to lease or buy an asset is often motivated by its tax effects. If the lessee (asset user) is losing money or not subject to taxation (a nonprofit enterprise), leasing may be advantageous because the lessor (asset owner) can reflect the tax benefits of ownership in the lease rate charged to the lessee.

These and other tax effects of financial decisions will be encountered throughout the text and in the practice of financial management. Capital expenditure decisions are discussed in Chapters 9, 10, and 11. Capital structure decisions are discussed in Chapters 12 and 13. Dividend decisions are discussed in Chapter 14. Leasing is discussed in Chapter 19. Corporate restructuring is discussed in Chapter 20.

Tax Rate Used in the Text

Canadian federal and provincial tax laws impose progressive tax rates on corporate and personal income—the larger the income, the higher the tax rate. In 2003, the highest combined federal and provincial marginal tax rate (i.e., tax rate on the next dollar of income) was 41.12 percent for the largest corporations in Saskatchewan. There are deductions for certain types of business income and provincial rates differ, so most firms may actually pay less than this. Throughout the text, however, we usually use an *assumed* marginal tax rate of 40 percent rather than the *actual* tax rate. There are two reasons for doing this. First, it simplifies many of the calculations. Second, a 40 percent rate is a good approximation of the combined federal and provincial income tax rates faced by most firms because the average of the applicable rates in 2003 was 38.07 percent.

Canadian Income Taxation

Introduction

Both individuals and businesses must pay taxes on their incomes. The type and rates of taxation that businesses must pay depends on how they are organized. Generally, when organized as a corporation, business income is taxed at corporate rates, whereas business income of sole proprietorships and partnerships is taxed at the rates of the individual owners or partners. Since corporations are the dominant form of business organization (in terms of sales), we focus primarily on corporate income taxes.

Corporate Income Taxes

In general, the taxable income of a corporation is calculated by subtracting business expenses from revenues in accordance with generally accepted accounting principles (GAAP). Tax-deductible business expenses normally include the cost of goods sold, selling and administrative expenses, and interest expenses. In Canada, there is only one method for determining depreciation for tax purposes, the capital cost allowance (CCA) system. Federal income taxes are computed on the resulting taxable income. For the tax year 2003, the top combined federal and provincial income tax rates imposed on corporations are shown in Table 2.3. Although taxes can and usually are changed in each government budget, sometimes tax reductions are scheduled in advance. The 2000 federal budget announced a five-year tax reduction plan. Thus, corporate tax rates were expected to be reduced each year until 2006.

Table 2.3 Combined Top 2003 Corporate Marginal Tax Rates on Active Income

Jurisdiction	General		CCPC** Small	
	Non-M&P* Income	M&P Income	Business Income Lower Bracket	Business Income Upper Bracket
Federal	24.12%	22.12%	13.12%	22.12%
Alberta	36.62%	34.62%	17.12%	28.12%
British Columbia	37.62%	35.62%	17.62%	26.62%
Manitoba	40.12%	38.12%	18.12%	29.12%
Newfoundland	38.12%	27.12%	18.12%	36.12%
New Brunswick	37.12%	35.12%	16.12%	27.12%
Nova Scotia	40.12%	38.12%	18.12%	38.12%
Ontario	36.62%	33.12%	18.62%	29.62%
Prince Edward Island	40.12%	29.62%	20.62%	38.12%
Quebec	33.16%	31.16%	22.16%	31.16%
Saskatchewan	41.12%	32.12%	19.12%	28.12%
Average	38.07%	33.47%	18.57%	31.22%

*M&P is Manufacturing & Processing.
**CCPC is Canadian Controlled Private Corporation.

Average Tax Rate
The average tax rate is calculated by dividing the total amount of taxes payable by the taxable income.

Marginal Tax Rate
The tax rate on the next dollar of taxable income earned by a taxpayer.

Capital Gain
Profit on the sale of a capital asset.

Capital Loss
Loss on the sale of a capital asset.

The **average tax rate** of a corporation is calculated by dividing the total tax by taxable income. The **marginal tax rate** of a corporation is defined as the tax rate on the next dollar of taxable income. For large corporations, the maximum effective marginal and average tax rates will be equal to approximately 40 percent, depending on the provincial tax rate. There are reduced tax rates for manufacturing and processing income and for small businesses.

In addition to paying taxes on *operating* or *ordinary income,* corporations must also pay taxes on *capital gains. Dividend income* may or may not be taxable (see below).

Capital Gains   Corporate **capital gains** are currently (2003) taxed at 50 percent of the marginal tax rate of ordinary income. Corporate **capital losses** are deductible only against capital gains. Net capital losses may be carried back and applied against net gains in the prior three years. Any remaining net capital loss may be carried forward until fully applied against capital gains.

Dividend Income   Dividends received by a Canadian corporation from another Canadian corporation are *excluded* from taxable income. Dividends received by a Canadian corporation from a non-Canadian firm are taxed as ordinary income.

Loss Carrybacks and Carryforwards   Corporations that sustain net operating losses during a particular year are permitted by tax laws to apply the losses against any taxable income in other years, thereby lowering the taxes owed in those years. If such a loss is applied against a previous year, it is called a *loss carryback.* If it is applied against a succeeding year, it is called a *loss carryforward.*

The tax laws currently (2003) specify that a corporation's net operating loss may be carried back three years and forward seven years to offset taxable income in those years. For example, suppose the NOL Corporation incurs a net operating loss totalling $200,000 in 20X6. This loss may be carried back three years to 20X3. If the NOL Corporation had 20X3 taxable income of $125,000, for example, it could receive a tax refund equal to the taxes it paid for that year. The remaining $75,000 portion of the 20X6 net operating loss next could be carried back to 20X4.

Tax information is available at **www.ccra.gc.ca**

Proprietorship, Partnership, and Personal Income Taxes

Individuals pay taxes on their profits from proprietorships and partnerships as well as on any employment income (wages and salaries) and investment income (dividends, interest, and capital gains). Personal income taxes are the largest expense for most individual Canadians. For the tax year 2003 the top combined marginal tax rates imposed on individuals are shown in Table 2.4. The federal five-year tax reduction plan announced in the 2000 budget scheduled annual reductions in individual tax rates. Since this plan may have been changed by the time you read this, it is wise to check with the Canada Customs and Revenue Agency (CCRA) for the latest tax information.

Capital Gains   Individual capital gains, like corporate capital gains, are currently (2003) given preferential tax treatment. Only half of the net capital gains amount is included in taxable income. Thus, many individuals prefer this type of income. Individual capital losses are deductible only against capital gains. Net capital losses may be carried back and applied against net gains in the prior three years. Any remaining net capital loss may be carried forward until fully applied against capital gains.

Dividend Income   Individual dividend income is also given preferential tax treatment. Individual residents of Canada who receive dividends from a Canadian corporation must first gross-up (increase) the amount of the dividends by 25 percent and include this grossed-up amount in taxable income. Thus, if an individual investor received a cash dividend of $100, the grossed-up amount of $125 would be reported as dividend income and the tax liability would be calculated on the $125 amount. Then, a dividend tax credit of 13.33 percent of this grossed-up amount is allowed against taxable income. The 25 percent dividend gross-up and the 13.33 dividend tax credit are the 2003 rates. The government has changed these rates by legislation on several occasions. This **dividend gross-up and tax credit** system reduces the overall tax burden on dividends because the corporation, of course, has already paid income tax on its income before it paid dividends to the shareholders. Thus, there is double taxation of this income. The tax credit partially compensates the investor for the taxes already paid by the corporation.[8] However, dividends received from a non-Canadian firm are taxed as ordinary income. This provision of the law encourages Canadian investors to invest in Canadian firms.

Dividend Gross-Up and Tax Credit
A method used in Canada to partially compensate investors for the taxes already paid by the corporation. According to the tax rules in effect in 2003, the cash dividend received by the investor is grossed-up by 25% and the investor is allowed a tax credit (reduction) of 13.33% of the grossed-up amount.

Table 2.4	Combined Top 2003 Personal Marginal Tax Rates		
Jurisdiction	**Ordinary**	**Dividends**	**Capital Gains**
Federal	29%	19.58%	14.5%
Alberta	39%	24.08%	19.5%
British Columbia	43.7%	31.58%	21.85%
Manitoba	46.4%	35.08%	23.2%
Newfoundland	48.64%	37.32%	24.32%
New Brunswick	46.84%	32.38%	23.42%
Nova Scotia	47.34%	31.91%	23.67%
Ontario	46.41%	31.33%	23.2%
Prince Edward Island	47.37%	31.96%	23.69%
Quebec	48.22%	32.81%	24.11%
Saskatchewan	44%	28.33%	22%
Average	45.75%	31.48%	22.89%

[8] For a firm with a 40 percent marginal corporate tax rate, a 66.67 percent gross-up with a 40 percent dividend tax credit would fully compensate the investor for the taxes already paid by the corporation.

Small Business Corporations

For more information see
www.bdc.ca

The federal Income Tax Act allows a small business reduction equal to 16 percent of the first $200,000 of active business income earned by a Canadian controlled private corporation (CCPC). The deduction is 7 percent on income between $200,001 and $300,000. In addition, the provinces also allow a similar small business tax rate reduction. Thus, in 2003, the lowest combined tax rate on the first $200,000 of active business income was 16.12 percent in New Brunswick and the highest rate was 22.16 percent in Quebec. Since small businesses are very dynamic and create many jobs, the federal and provincial governments encourage them.

In addition to special tax provisions, there is a special financial institution for small businesses: the federal Business Development Bank. The BDC plays a leadership role in delivering financial and consulting services to Canadian small business, with a particular focus on technology and exporting. The BDC now fulfils a complementary role to other commercial financial institutions and is attempting to increase its activity in smaller loans and also First Nations businesses.

Loss Carrybacks and Carryforwards   Individuals can also carry back or carry forward any net operating losses from their business ventures, just like corporations.

Interest Income   Individuals pay tax on interest income at the same rate as on ordinary employment income. This high rate of taxation discourages many investors from investing in securities that pay interest.

Financial Challenge Revisited

Ritchie Bros. Auctioneers was listed on the NYSE in March 1998. Its share price at that time was $21. In mid-January 2003, its share price was $33.50. One of the advantages of the listing of shares on a major exchange is that the firm gets free publicity because its price is in the financial press every day and there are more frequent articles about the firm. This increased interest on the part of investors and potential investors is widely believed to lead to higher share prices, which is the goal of financial management. When the BC government decided to sell its three Fast Cat ferry boats, whom did it choose? Ritchie Bros. Auctioneers!

Summary

- The main purpose of any economy's financial system is to facilitate the transfer of funds from *surplus spending units* to *deficit spending units*. *Investment dealers* bring together the surplus and deficit spending units in the capital markets so that funds can be directly transferred. *Financial intermediaries,* such as chartered banks, facilitate indirect transfers of funds among the ultimate borrowers and lenders.

- *Financial assets* include *money, debt securities, equity securities,* and *derivative securities.*

- Financial markets are the vehicles through which financial assets are bought and sold. They include *money* or *capital markets* and *primary* or *secondary markets,* as well as derivative securities markets. Money markets deal in securities with maturities of approximately one year or less, while capital markets deal in securities with maturities greater than one year. Primary markets are those in which *new* securities are issued. Secondary markets are those in which *existing* securities are traded. Secondary markets may be classified as *security exchanges,* such as the TSX, *formal virtual markets,* such as the NASDAQ, and the informal *over-the-counter (OTC) markets.* Derivative securities are usually traded in their own specialized financial markets, such as the Montreal Exchange.

- Investment dealers assist firms in the securities offering process by providing advice on a wide range of corporate financial transactions, including the timing and structure of new securities offerings. Their role in the process is called investment banking. New corporate securities are sold through *public cash offerings, private placements,* and *rights offerings.*

- Issuance costs for sales of common equity are normally significantly greater than those for corporate debt or preferred shares. There are significant economies of scale associated with security offerings.

- A *Eurocurrency* is a currency deposited in a bank located outside the country of origin. The Eurocurrency market is an important alternative to domestic sources of financing for multinational firms. The interest rate charged for Eurocurrency loans is tied to LIBOR, the London Interbank Offer Rate.

- The *exchange rate* is the rate at which one currency can be converted into another. A *direct quote* is the home currency price of one unit of foreign currency. An *indirect quote* is the foreign currency price of one unit of the home currency. The *spot rate* is the rate of exchange for currencies being bought and sold for *immediate delivery today.* The *forward rate* is the rate of exchange between currencies to be delivered at a future point in time—usually 30, 90, and 180 days from today.

- Financial assets, such as *forward contracts, futures contracts,* and *options* on currencies, are types of derivative securities that help firms manage exchange rate risk.

- Taxes affect most financial decisions. Thus, it is important for managers to know the basic features of the tax system.

Questions and Topics for Discussion

1. Describe and discuss the saving-investment cycle (flow of funds).
2. What roles do investment dealers and financial intermediaries play in the operation of the Canadian financial system? How do the two differ?
3. How do money and capital markets differ?
4. Describe the various types of financial intermediaries, including the sources of their funds and the types of investments they make.

5. What factors need to be considered when determining the optimal form of organization for a business enterprise?

6. How do primary and secondary financial markets differ?

7. What are the differences among security exchanges, formal virtual markets, and the over-the-counter markets?

8. What are the differences between a public cash offering, a private placement, and a rights offering of securities?

9. Identify the major issuance costs associated with a securities offering.

10. Define the following terms:
   a. Multinational corporation
   b. Spot exchange rate
   c. Forward exchange rate
   d. Direct quote versus indirect quote
   e. LIBOR
   f. Euro

11. Suppose you own 100 common shares of BCE and the firm just earned $6 per share. Suppose further that BCE can either pay all its earnings out in dividends (in which case you would receive $600) or retain the earnings in the business, buying more assets and causing the share price to go up by $6 per share (in which case the value of your shares would rise by $600).
   a. How do the tax laws influence what you, as a typical shareholder, want the firm to do?
   b. Is your choice influenced by how much other income you have?
   c. How might the corporation's dividend policy decision influence the price of its shares?

12. Explain how the income tax structure affects the choice of financing (debt versus equity) used by business firms.

13. For someone planning to start a new business, is the average or the marginal tax rate more relevant?

Self-Test Problems

ST1. The OFF Corporation of Brandon, Manitoba, has an income of $250,000 from operations in 2003 after all operating costs but before (a) interest charges of $30,000, (b) dividends of $25,000 to be paid, and (c) income taxes. What is the firm's tax bill?

ST2. The NST Corporation of Peggy's Cove, Nova Scotia, has made $200,000 before taxes for each of the last eight years. However, it incurred a loss of $1,000,000 in 2003 because of a decline in the number of US tourists due to the strengthening Canadian dollar. The firm will claim a tax credit on its 2003 tax return and receive a cheque from the government. Show how it will calculate this credit and indicate what effects, if any, will apply to future years.

ST3. Using the data in Table 2.2, find the direct and indirect quotes for the Japanese yen for a firm whose functional currency is the Canadian dollar.

Problems*

1. Canadian National Railway sold 10 million shares to the public at $30 per share. The firm received net proceeds from its underwriters of $287,506,114. What was the underwriting spread on this offering?

2. The ON Corporation of Sudbury, Ontario, has an income of $200,000 from operations after all operating costs but before (a) interest charges of $10,000, (b) dividends of $20,000 to be paid, and (c) income taxes. What is the firm's income tax bill?

3. The BC Corporation of Surry, BC, has made $200,000 before taxes for each of the last 10 years, and it expects to make the same amount in the future. However, it incurred a loss of $1,200,000 in 2002. The firm will claim a tax credit on its 2002 tax return and will receive a cheque from the government. Show how it will calculate this credit and indicate what effects, if any, will apply to future years.

4. Solve Self-Test Problem ST1 for a company in your province. (If your province is Manitoba or Ontario, do this problem for Saskatchewan.)

5. Solve Self-Test Problem ST2 for a company in your province. (If your province is Nova Scotia or British Columbia, do this problem for New Brunswick.)

6. Redo Self-Test Problem ST3 for a Canadian multinational company whose functional currency is the US dollar.

*Coloured numbers and letters denote problems that have "check" answers provided at the back of the book.

Other Practice Materials and Resources

For interactive quizzes, Internet exercises, crossword puzzles, CTV videos, and more, go to the *Contemporary Financial Management* Web site at **http://cyr.nelson.com**

Evaluating and Forecasting Financial Performance

3

Learning Objectives

After studying this chapter you should be able to

1. Understand that the evaluation of financial performance involves a series of techniques that can be used to help identify the strengths and weaknesses of a firm

2. Calculate financial ratios, which use data from a firm's balance sheet, income statement, cash flow statement, and certain market data that are often used when evaluating the financial performance of a firm. These ratios are usually categorized as follows

   a. *Liquidity ratios* indicate a firm's ability to meet its short-term financial obligations

   b. *Asset management ratios* indicate how efficiently a firm is using its assets to generate sales

   c. *Financial leverage management ratios* indicate a firm's capacity to meet short- and long-term debt obligations

   d. *Profitability ratios* measure how effectively a firm's management generates profits

   e. *Market-based ratios* reflect the financial market's assessment of a company's performance

   f. *Dividend policy ratios* indicate the dividend practices of a firm.

3. Utilize common-size financial statements that express financial items as

percentages (rather than dollar amounts) to evaluate financial performance

4. Utilize trend analysis to evaluate a firm's performance over time as well as comparative analysis to evaluate a firm's performance relative to other firms

5. Understand that when evaluating a firm's performance based on its financial statements and financial ratios, a good financial analyst must be aware of the accounting techniques used by the firm and mindful of the quality of the firm's earnings and its balance sheet

6. Understand that by using the relationship of "margin" and "turnover" to return on investment, DuPont analysis can indicate if deficient profitability of a firm is caused by one or the other or both components. Corrective action can then be taken if needed

7. Understand that the percentage of sales forecasting method is usually used in estimating the amount of additional financing that a firm will need for a given increase in sales, based on assumptions about the relationship between sales and the various asset and liability accounts

8. Understand that market value added (MVA) is the market's assessment of the accumulated value from a firm's past and anticipated capital investment projects

9. Understand that economic value added (EVA) is a yearly measure of the operating performance of a firm, considering investors' return requirements

10. Understand that cash flows are the ultimate source of financial value. Therefore, cash flow analysis and forecasting are important parts of a firm's financial plans

11. Understand that after-tax cash flow is equal to earnings after tax plus noncash charges.

12. Understand that the cash flow statement shows the effects of a firm's operating, investing, and financing activities on its cash balance. Pro forma cash flow statements can be used to forecast additional financing that a firm may need

13. Understand that a cash budget is the projection of a firm's cash receipts and disbursements over a future time period and is useful in determining the amount of short-term funds that a firm may need to borrow

14. Understand the usefulness and limitations of computerized financial planning models

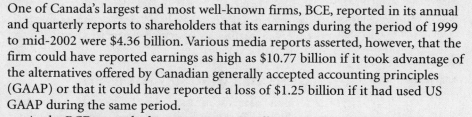

Financial Challenge

Earnings Management and Financial Performance Measurement

© CHRIS COLLINS/CORBIS/MAGMA

One of Canada's largest and most well-known firms, BCE, reported in its annual and quarterly reports to shareholders that its earnings during the period of 1999 to mid-2002 were $4.36 billion. Various media reports asserted, however, that the firm could have reported earnings as high as $10.77 billion if it took advantage of the alternatives offered by Canadian generally accepted accounting principles (GAAP) or that it could have reported a loss of $1.25 billion if it had used US GAAP during the same period.

As the BCE example demonstrates, generally accepted accounting principles provide companies with considerable latitude in the preparation of key financial statements used to measure performance. Some firms take advantage of this latitude and choose financial reporting methods that do not provide a fair reflection of ongoing performance. As a consequence, it is important for financial managers and analysts to have a solid understanding of financial statement analysis so that it is possible to make a balanced assessment of the true performance of a company.

The earnings management tricks that have been used by some companies include

1. Timing store openings or asset sales in a way that keeps earnings growing at a smooth rate

2. Accelerating (or delaying) shipments at the end of a quarterly reporting period to either increase sales in a weak quarter or defer sales into the next quarter when the current quarter's numbers are especially strong

3. Capitalizing normal operating expenses. Without this accounting treatment, a firm may report losses instead of profits

4. Taking "big bath" write-offs and using "spin" control for bad earnings. Many companies have found that if they take large so-called one-time write-offs, it will be easier to meet earnings objectives in future years

5. Increasing reserves in good times and drawing down on them in bad times. Many firms create reserves for product returns, bad loans, retirement benefits, and insurance losses. In good years these reserve allocations can be overfunded so that, in bad years, they can be drawn against while protecting reported earnings. Banks, with their loan-loss reserves, are especially able to use these practices to manage earnings, but other types of firms are not supposed to do so

This chapter introduces financial statement analysis techniques that can be used in the evaluation of a company's true performance and for forecasting its future performance. Good financial analysts need to have a strong understanding of the interpretation of financial statements—including their associated notes, which often provide excellent clues regarding potential problems and hidden sources of value. Conclusions about a company's financial performance derived from its financial statements should be regarded with caution and considered only as a sign of the company's strengths and weaknesses. Some of the shortcomings of financial statement analysis as a performance measure can be overcome by considering alternative measures of performance derived directly from the financial marketplace. These market measures of performance are also discussed in this chapter.

Many of the major search engines maintain a finance area with extensive financial information as well as links to hundreds of different financial sites. Begin by looking at the Yahoo! Web site **www.yahoo.com** and then follow the links to its financial information/data. (Yahoo! also has pages for Canada and Mexico as well as many other countries.)

Financial Analysis
The utilization of a group of analytical techniques, including financial ratio analysis, to determine the strengths, weaknesses, and direction of a firm's performance.

Financial Ratio
A statistical yardstick that relates two numbers generally taken from a firm's income statement, balance sheet, or both at a specific point in time.

For more information on MDG and IBM see **www.mdg.ca** and **www.ibm.ca**

Introduction

This chapter reviews the basic accounting statements and concepts. It also deals with the evaluation of financial performance using financial statement analysis. A carefully executed financial statement analysis can assist financial managers in assessing the current financial condition of a firm. Trend analysis and common-size financial statements can assist financial managers in detecting changes in a firm's financial performance over time. The chapter also discusses financial forecasting and cash budgets.

Uses of Financial Analysis

A **financial analysis** assists in identifying the major strengths and weaknesses of a business enterprise. It indicates whether a firm has (1) enough cash to meet obligations; (2) a reasonable accounts receivable collection period; (3) an efficient inventory management policy; (4) sufficient plant, property, and equipment; and (5) an adequate capital structure. All of these are necessary if a firm is to achieve the goal of maximizing shareholder wealth. Financial analysis can also be used to assess a firm's viability as an ongoing enterprise and to determine whether a satisfactory return is being earned for the risks taken.

When performing a financial analysis, an analyst may discover specific problem areas in time for remedial action. For example, an analyst may find that a firm has unused borrowing power that could finance additional income-producing assets. The results of a financial analysis may indicate facts and trends that can aid the financial manager in planning and implementing a course of action consistent with the goal of maximizing shareholder wealth.

Financial analyses are also used by persons other than financial managers. For example, credit managers may examine basic financial ratios of a prospective customer when deciding whether to extend credit. Security analysts use financial analysis to help assess the investment worth of different securities. Bankers use the tools of financial analysis when deciding whether to grant loans. Financial ratios have been used successfully to forecast such financial events as impending bankruptcy. Unions refer to financial ratios when evaluating the bargaining positions of certain employers. Finally, students and other job hunters may perform financial analyses of potential employers to determine career opportunities.

Interpreting Financial Ratios

A **financial ratio** is a relationship that indicates something about a firm's activities, such as the ratio between current assets and current liabilities or between its accounts receivable and its annual sales. Financial ratios enable an analyst to make a comparison of a firm's financial condition over time or in relation to other firms. For example, the total profits of IBM normally are many times those of MDG Computers, because IBM is a much larger firm. By computing a ratio such as net profits divided by total assets, the relative performance of the two firms can be assessed more accurately.

Successful financial ratio analysis requires that an analyst keep in mind the following points:

- Any discussion of financial ratios is likely to include only a representative sample of possible ratios. Many other ratios can be developed to provide additional insights. In some industries, such as banking, analysts use special ratios unique to the activities of the firms in those industries.

- Financial ratios are only "flags" indicating potential areas of strength or weakness. A thorough analysis requires the examination of other data as well.

- Frequently, a financial ratio must be dissected to discover its true meaning. For example, a low ratio may be caused by either a low numerator or a high denominator. Good financial analysts examine both the numerator and the denominator before drawing any conclusions.

- A financial ratio is meaningful only when it is compared with some standard, such as an industry average ratio, a ratio trend for the specific firm being analyzed, or a stated management objective.

- When financial ratios are used to compare one firm with another, it is important to remember that differences in accounting techniques may result in substantial differences in financial ratios. Failure to consider this may lead to incorrect conclusions.

Basic Classifications of Financial Ratios

Because different groups inside and outside a company have varying objectives and expectations, they approach financial analysis from different perspectives. For example, suppliers and short-term creditors are likely to be most concerned with a firm's current liquidity and near-term cash-generating capacity. Bondholders and holders of preferred shares, who have long-term claims on a company's earnings and assets, focus on the firm's cash-generating ability over the long run and on the claims other investors have on the firm's **cash flows**. Common shareholders and potential investors are especially interested in measures of profitability and risk. This is because common share prices are dependent on the amount and stability of a firm's future earnings and dividends. Management is concerned not only with maximizing shareholder wealth but also with all other aspects of running the firm. Therefore, it conducts financial analysis on both a short- and a long-term basis. It is responsible for conducting the firm's day-to-day operations and earning a competitive rate of return for risks taken.

No single financial ratio can begin to answer all of these analytical needs. In fact, six different groups of ratios have been developed:

1. *Liquidity ratios* indicate a firm's ability to meet short-term financial obligations.
2. *Asset management ratios* indicate how efficiently a firm is using its assets to generate sales.
3. *Financial leverage management ratios* indicate a firm's capacity to meet short- and long-term debt obligations.
4. *Profitability ratios* measure how effectively a firm's management generates profits on sales, assets, and shareholders' investments.
5. *Market-based ratios* measure the financial market's evaluation of a firm's performance.
6. *Dividend policy ratios* indicate the dividend practices of a firm.

Each type is discussed in detail in this chapter.

Key Financial Statements

The financial statements of the Maple Manufacturing Company (MMC), a medium-sized firm that produces various replacement components for the lawn equipment industry, will be examined to illustrate how ratios are used in financial analysis. Data will be used from MMC's *balance sheet* for the years ending December 31, 20X6 and 20X5, and from its *income statement* for the year 20X6.

Cash Flows
The actual amounts of cash collected and paid out by a firm during some period of time, such as a year.

Balance Sheet
A financial statement that lists a firm's assets, liabilities, and shareholders' equity at a point in time.

Shareholders' Equity
The total of a firm's common shares, contributed capital (if any), and retained earnings (if any) accounts from the balance sheet. It sometimes is called the *book value* of the firm, *owners' equity, stockholders' equity,* or *net worth.*

Income Statement
A financial statement that indicates how a firm performed during a period of time.

Earnings after Taxes (EAT)
A firm's earnings after taxes is the amount available for dividends to shareholders or for reinvestment in the firm.

The Balance Sheet   The **balance sheet** shown in Table 3.1 contains information on MMC's *assets, liabilities,* and *shareholders' equity.* The figures provide a "snapshot" view of the firm's financial health on December 31, 20X6, and December 31, 20X5. MMC's assets (cash, marketable securities, accounts receivable, inventories, and plant and equipment) are recorded on the balance sheet at the price the firm paid for them (that is, at historic cost). The balance sheet is sometimes presented in side-by-side format. The left-hand side lists the assets while the right-hand side lists the liabilities and shareholders' equity accounts. The liabilities (accounts payable, notes payable, accrued taxes payable, other current liabilities, the current portion of long-term debt, and the long-term debt) are amounts the firm owes its creditors. The **shareholders' equity** (also termed *net worth* or *owners' equity*) is the difference between total assets and total liabilities. The shareholders' equity accounts in Table 3.1 are (1) common shares ($10 par value), (2) contributed capital, and (3) retained earnings. (Only some provincially chartered firms have shares with par value, so most Canadian firms do not have such complex shareholders' equity accounts.)

The Income Statement   The **income statement** in Table 3.2 indicates MMC's performance during the year ended December 31, 20X6. The *cost of sales, operating expenses, interest expenses,* and *taxes* are deducted from the revenues generated or *net sales,* to arrive at the firm's *net income,* or **earnings after taxes (EAT).** The statement in Table 3.2 also shows how the firm's earnings are distributed between dividend payments to shareholders and earnings reinvested in the firm.

Table 3.1	Maple Manufacturing Company Balance Sheet (in Thousands of Dollars)			
		December 31, 20X6		December 31, 20X5
ASSETS				
Cash		$ 2,540		$ 2,081
Marketable securities		1,800		1,625
Accounts receivable, net		18,320		16,850
Inventories		27,530		26,470
Total current assets		$50,190		$47,026
Plant and equipment	$43,100		$39,500	
Less: Accumulated depreciation	11,400		9,500	
Net plant and equipment		$31,700		$30,000
Total assets		$81,890		$77,026
LIABILITIES AND SHAREHOLDERS' EQUITY				
Accounts payable		$ 9,721		$ 8,340
Notes payable—bank (10%)		8,500		5,635
Accrued taxes payable		3,200		3,150
Other current liabilities		2,102		1,750
Current portion of long-term debt		2,000		2,000
Total current liabilities		$25,523		$20,875
Long-term debt ($9\frac{5}{8}$% mortgage bonds)*		$22,000		$24,000
Total liabilities		$47,523		$44,875
Common shares ($10 par value)	$13,000		$13,000	
Contributed capital in excess of par	10,000		10,000	
Retained earnings	11,367		9,151	
Total shareholders' equity		$34,367		$32,151
Total liabilities and shareholders' equity		$81,890		$77,026

*Mortgage bonds require a $2,000(000) annual payment to a sinking fund.

Table 3.2 Maple Manufacturing Company Income Statement (in Thousands of Dollars)

For the Year Ended December 31, 20X6

Net sales		$112,760
Cost of sales		85,300
Gross margin		$ 27,460
Operating expenses:		
Selling	$6,540	
General and administrative*	9,400	
Total operating expenses		15,940
Earnings before interest and taxes (EBIT)		$ 11,520
Interest charges:		
Interest on bank notes	$ 850	
Interest on mortgage bonds	2,310	
Total interest charges		3,160
Earnings before taxes (EBT)		$ 8,360
Federal and provincial income taxes at a combined 40% rate		3,344
Earnings after taxes (EAT) and available for common shareholders		$ 5,016
OTHER INFORMATION		
Dividends paid on common shares		$ 2,800
Earnings retained in the firm		$ 2,216
Shares outstanding (000)		1,300
Market price per share		$ 24
Book value per share		$ 26.44
Earnings per share		$ 3.86
Dividends per share		$ 2.15

*Includes $150(000) in annual lease payments.

Cash Flow Statement
A financial statement showing the effects of a firm's operating, investing, and financing activities on its cash balance.

The Cash Flow Statement The **cash flow statement** is useful in financial analysis, too. It indicates how a firm generated cash flows from its operations, how it used cash in investing activities, and how it obtained cash from financing activities. The cash flow statement is analyzed later in this chapter.

Liquidity Ratios

Liquidity Ratios
Financial ratios that indicate a firm's ability to meet short-term financial obligations.

A firm that intends to remain a viable business entity must have enough cash on hand to pay its bills as they come due. In other words, the firm must remain *liquid*. One way to determine whether this is the case is to examine the relationship between a firm's current assets and approaching obligations. **Liquidity ratios** are quick measures of a firm's ability to provide sufficient cash to conduct business over the next few months. *Cash budgets* provide the best assessment of a firm's liquidity position. They are discussed later in this chapter.

This section discusses two different liquidity ratios—the *current ratio* and the *quick ratio*.

Current Ratio
A measure of liquidity that is calculated as current assets divided by current liabilities.

Current Ratio The **current ratio** is defined as follows:

$$(3.1) \qquad CR = \frac{CA}{CL}$$

where CA = Current Assets, and CL = Current Liabilities.

Current assets include the cash a firm already has on hand and in the bank plus any assets that can be converted into cash within a "normal" operating period of 12 months, such as marketable securities held as short-term investments, accounts receivable, inventories, and prepayments. Current liabilities include any financial obligations expected to fall due within the next year, such as accounts payable, notes payable, the current portion of long-term debt due, other payables, and various accruals such as taxes and wages due.

Using data from Table 3.1, MMC's current ratio at year-end 20X6 can be calculated as \$50,190/\$25,523 = 1.97, or about 2:1. Or, it can be said that MMC's current assets *cover* its current liabilities about two times.

The ratio is interpreted to mean that to satisfy the claims of short-term creditors exclusively from existing current assets, MMC must be able to convert each dollar of current assets into at least \$1.00/1.97 = \$0.51 of cash. The *industry average* for the current ratio is 2.40 times,[1] meaning that the average firm in the industry must convert only \$1.00/2.40 = \$0.42 of each dollar of current assets into cash to meet short-term obligations.

The fact that MMC's current ratio is below the industry average does *not* mean that the firm would consider closing its doors voluntarily to meet the demands of short-term creditors. Nor does it mean that MMC's creditors are any less well protected than the creditors of competing firms, because no two firms—even those in the same industry—are identical. In fact, ratios that suggest the presence of a problem in one firm may be quite satisfactory for another firm.[2] MMC's current ratio provides only *one* standard for measuring liquidity. The financial analyst must dissect, or go behind, the ratio to discover why it differs from the industry average and determine whether a serious problem exists.

Quick Ratio

A liquidity ratio calculated as current assets minus inventories divided by current liabilities.

Quick Ratio   The **quick ratio** is defined as follows:

$$(3.2) \qquad QR = \frac{CA - Inv}{CL}$$

where CA = Current Assets, Inv = Inventories, and CL = Current Liabilities.

This ratio, sometimes called the "acid test," is a more stringent measure of liquidity than the current ratio. By subtracting inventories from current assets, this ratio recognizes that a firm's inventories are often one of its least-liquid current assets.[3] Inventories, especially work-in-process, are very difficult to liquidate quickly at or near their book value. Referring to the figures on MMC's balance sheet (Table 3.1), the firm's quick ratio at year-end 20X6 is calculated as follows:

$$QR = \frac{\$50,190 - \$27,530}{\$25,523} = \frac{\$22,660}{\$25,523} = 0.89 \text{ times}$$

The industry average is 0.92 times; MMC's quick ratio is nearly equal to that.

The quick ratio is interpreted to mean that MMC's cash and other current assets one step removed from cash—that is, marketable securities and accounts receivable—are equal to 89 percent of the current liabilities. The crucial assumption behind the quick ratio is that a firm's accounts receivable may be converted into cash within the "normal"

---

[1] Industry averages are obtained from various sources. The Sources of Comparative Financial Data section later in this chapter discusses a number of such sources.

[2] Many practitioners view a current ratio of 1.5 times (1.5X) as satisfactory for industrial firms. A financial analyst must be very cautious when using any rules of thumb. The safe level of a current ratio is a function of how fast the firm's current assets and liabilities turn over. In the case of a public utility, the accounts receivable turn over on a monthly basis—much faster than in the typical industrial firm. Thus, public utilities are able to safely sustain lower current ratios than industrial firms.

[3] Some analysts also subtract prepaid expenses from current assets in the calculation of the quick ratio because prepayments are difficult to convert back to cash.

collection period (and with little "shrinkage") or within the period of time for which credit was initially granted.

An analyst who doubts the liquidity of a firm's receivables may wish to prepare an *ageing schedule*. The following one lists MMC's accounts receivable as of December 31, 20X6:

Days Outstanding	Amount Outstanding (in Thousands of Dollars)	Percentage of Total
Less than 30	$9,450	51.6%
30–59	5,161	28.2%
60–89	2,750	15.0%
90 and more	959	5.2%
Total accounts receivable	$18,320	100.0%

Unfortunately, the data required to prepare an ageing schedule are not normally available to outside analysts. Hence, the ageing schedule is useful primarily for internal analysis.

To evaluate the figures contained in an ageing schedule, an analyst would need to consider MMC's selling terms. If, for example, MMC's customers are expected to pay within 40 days (which, in fact, they are), then the ageing schedule indicates that many accounts are past due. However, because only 5.2 percent of the firm's receivables have been outstanding over 90 days, the major problem appears to be with slow-paying rather than uncollectable accounts. Some analysts adjust the quick ratio *downward* if a significant percentage of a firm's receivables are long past due and have not been written off as losses. However, since MMC's accounts outstanding over 90 days are very small, the difference between the quick ratio, 0.89 times, and the adjusted ratio, 0.85 times, is probably insignificant. Therefore, even if MMC's accounts over 90 days old were considered uncollectable, this alone would not indicate any real problem for the firm.

Asset Management Ratios

One objective of financial management is to determine how a firm's resources can be best distributed among the various asset accounts. If a proper mix of cash, receivables, inventories, plant, property, and equipment can be achieved, the firm's asset structure will be more effective in generating sales revenue.

Asset management ratios indicate how much a firm has invested in a particular type of asset (or group of assets) relative to the revenue the asset is producing. By comparing asset management ratios for the various asset accounts of a firm with established industry norms, the analyst can determine how efficiently the firm is allocating its resources.

This section discusses several types of asset management ratios, including the *average collection period*, the *inventory turnover ratio*, the *fixed-asset turnover ratio*, and the *total asset turnover ratio*.

Average Collection Period   The **average collection period** is the average number of days an account receivable remains outstanding. It is usually determined by dividing a company's year-end receivables balance by the average daily credit sales (based on a 365-day year).[4]

Asset Management Ratios
Financial ratios that indicate how efficiently a firm is using its assets.

Average Collection Period
The average number of days between when a credit sale is made and when the customer's payment is received.

---

[4] When credit sales figures are not available (which is frequently the case), total sales figures are customarily used in calculating the ratio, resulting in an *overstatement* of the average daily credit sales and an *understatement* of the average collection period. When firms have seasonal sales, an analyst should calculate an average of the end-of-month receivables balances. When comparing average collection period ratios with industry norms, the analyst must make sure the industry ratios have been computed in the same manner as the particular firm's ratios.

$$(3.3) \qquad ACP = \frac{AR}{ACS/365}$$

where AR = Accounts Receivable, and ACS = Annual Credit Sales.

Using figures from both MMC's balance sheet (Table 3.1) and the income statement (Table 3.2), the average collection period at year-end 20X6 can be calculated as $18,320/($112,760/365) = $18,320/$308.93 = 59.3 days. Because the industry average for this ratio is 47 days, MMC's ratio is substantially above the average.

MMC's credit terms call for payment within 40 days. The ratio calculations show that 59.3 days of sales are tied up in receivables, meaning that a significant portion of MMC's customers are not paying bills on time. (This is also indicated by the ageing schedule of the firm's accounts receivable.) The analyst interprets this ratio to mean that MMC has allocated a greater proportion of total resources to receivables than the average firm in the industry. If the company implemented a more vigorous collection program and reduced the collection period to the industry norm of 47 days, some of these funds would be released for investment elsewhere or for debt reduction. The released funds of (59.3 days – 47 days) × $308.93 per day = $3,800 could be invested in other assets that might contribute more significantly to profitability.[5]

An average collection period substantially above the industry norm is usually not desirable and may indicate too liberal a credit policy. Ultimately, a firm's managers must determine if the liberal credit policy generates enough incremental sales and profits to justify the incremental cost.[6] In contrast, an average collection period far *below* the industry norm may indicate that the firm's credit terms are too stringent and are hurting sales by restricting credit to the very best customers. Although moderate- to slow-paying customers may seem troublesome individually, they can be profitable as a group, and a credit policy that is too tight may drive them to competing firms.

Some analysts also use the **receivables turnover ratio**. It can be calculated by dividing 365 by the ACP. It can also be calculated directly by dividing annual credit sales by accounts receivable. For MMC, the receivables turnover is 365/59.3 = 6.16 times per year.

Inventory Turnover Ratio The inventory turnover ratio is defined as follows:

$$(3.4) \qquad IT = \frac{COS}{Avg\ Inv}$$

where COS = Cost of Sales, and Avg Inv = Average Inventory.

Although the cost of sales is usually listed on a firm's income statement, the average inventory has to be calculated. This can be done in a number of ways. For example, if a firm has been experiencing a significant and continuing rate of growth in sales, the average inventory may be computed by adding the figures for the beginning and ending inventories for the year and dividing by 2. If sales are seasonal or otherwise subject to wide fluctuations, however, it would be better to add the month-end inventory balances for the entire year and divide by 12.

Some analysts calculate inventory turnover as simply the ratio of annual sales to ending inventory. Although the *sales-to-inventory ratio* is technically inferior and gives different results than more commonly used ratios, it may be satisfactory if used consistently when making comparisons between one firm and the industry as a whole. However, the problem with this ratio is that it tends to differ from one firm to another, depending on policies regarding mark-ups on the cost of sales.

Receivables Turnover Ratio
An asset management ratio calculated by dividing 365 by the average collection period that indicates how fast a firm is collecting its accounts receivable.

---

[5] Recall that the analysis for MMC is being done in terms of thousands of dollars. Hence, the actual released funds total approximately $3.8 million.

[6] Chapter 16 contains an example of this type of incremental analysis.

Because MMC's sales are spread evenly over the year and its growth rate has been fairly moderate, the average inventory can be calculated by taking the average of the beginning and ending inventory balances ($27,530 + $26,470)/2 = $27,000. Dividing the cost of sales by this figure, $85,300/$27,000, gives an inventory turnover ratio of 3.16 times. This is considerably below the industry norm of 3.9 times, indicating that MMC has a larger investment in inventory relative to the sales being generated than the average firm. If the company could increase its inventory turns up to the industry average of 3.9 times, its average inventory investment in 20X6 would be $21,872 ($85,300/3.9). The released funds, $27,000 − $21,872 = $5,128, could be used either for investment in other, potentially more profitable assets or possibly for debt reduction.[7]

Two factors may be responsible for MMC's apparently excessive amount of inventory:

- The firm may be attempting to carry all possible types of replacement parts so that every order can be filled immediately. MMC should carefully examine this policy to determine whether the incremental cost of carrying large stocks of inventory is justified by the incremental profits earned on additional sales.[8]

- Some of MMC's inventory may be damaged, obsolete, or slow moving. Inventory falling into these categories has questionable liquidity and should be recorded at a value more reflective of the realizable market value.

If a firm's inventory turnover ratio is too high, it may mean that the firm is frequently running out of certain items in stock and losing sales to competitors. For inventory to contribute fully to profitability, the firm has to maintain a reasonable balance of inventory levels.

Fixed-Asset Turnover Ratio
An asset management ratio calculated by dividing sales by net fixed assets that shows how well a firm is using its fixed assets to generate sales.

Fixed-Asset Turnover Ratio The **fixed-asset turnover ratio** is defined as follows:

$$(3.5) \qquad \text{FAT} = \frac{\text{S}}{\text{NFA}}$$

where S = Sales, and NFA = Net Fixed Assets.

This ratio indicates the extent to which a firm is using existing property, plant, and equipment to generate sales.

The balance sheet figures that indicate how much a firm has invested in property, plant, and equipment are affected by several factors, including the following:

- The cost of the assets when acquired

- The length of time since acquisition

- The depreciation policies adopted by the firm

- The extent to which fixed assets are leased rather than owned

Because of these factors, it is possible for firms with virtually identical plants to have significantly different fixed-asset turnover ratios. Thus, the ratio should be used primarily for year-to-year comparisons within the same firm, rather than for intercompany comparisons.

MMC's fixed-asset turnover ratio is $112,760/$31,700 = 3.56 times, considerably below the industry average of 4.6 times. However, a financial analyst should acknowledge the shortcomings of the ratio and perform further analyses before concluding that the company makes inefficient use of its property, plant, and equipment.

---

[7] Recall that the analysis for MMC is being done in terms of thousands of dollars. Hence, the actual released funds total approximately $5.128 million.

[8] The management of inventory is discussed in Chapter 16.

Total Asset Turnover Ratio   The total asset turnover ratio is defined as follows:

$$(3.6) \qquad \qquad \text{TAT} = \frac{\text{S}}{\text{TA}}$$

where S = Sales, and TA = Total Assets.

It indicates how effectively a firm uses its total resources to generate sales and is a summary measure influenced by each of the asset management ratios previously discussed.

MMC's total asset turnover ratio is $112,760/$81,890 = 1.38 times, whereas the industry average is 1.82 times. In view of MMC's other asset turnover ratios, the firm's relatively poor showing with regard to this ratio is not surprising. Each of MMC's major asset investment programs—accounts receivable, inventory, and property, plant, and equipment—has been found apparently lacking. The analyst could look at these various ratios and conclude that MMC is not generating the same level of sales from its assets as other firms in the industry.

Financial Leverage Management Ratios

Financial Leverage Management Ratios

Financial ratios that measure the degree to which a firm is financing its assets with fixed-charge sources of funds such as debt, preferred shares, or leases.

Whenever a company finances a portion of assets with any type of fixed-charge financing—such as debt, preferred shares, or leases—the firm is said to be using *financial leverage*. **Financial leverage management ratios** measure the degree to which a company is employing financial leverage and, as such, are of interest to creditors and owners alike.

Both long- and short-term creditors are concerned with the amount of leverage a company employs because it indicates the firm's risk exposure in meeting debt service charges (that is, interest and principal repayment). A firm that is heavily financed by debt offers creditors less protection in the event of bankruptcy. For example, if a firm's assets are financed with 85 percent debt, the value of the assets can decline by only 15 percent before creditors' funds are endangered. In contrast, if only 15 percent of a company's assets are debt financed, asset values can drop by 85 percent before jeopardizing the creditors.

Owners are interested in financial leverage because it influences the rate of return they can expect to realize on their investment and the degree of risk involved. For example, if a firm is able to borrow funds at 9 percent and employ them at 12 percent, the owners earn the 3 percent difference and are likely to view financial leverage favourably. On the other hand, if the firm can earn only 3 percent on the borrowed funds, the –6 percent difference (3% – 9%) will result in a lower rate of return to the owners.[9]

Either balance sheet or income statement data can be used to measure a firm's use of financial leverage. The balance sheet approach gives a *static* measure of financial leverage at a specific point in time and emphasizes *total* amounts of debt, whereas the income statement approach provides a more *dynamic* measure and relates required interest payments on debt to the firm's ability to pay. Both approaches are employed widely in practice.

There are several types of financial leverage management ratios, including the *debt ratio*, the *debt-to-equity ratio*, the *times interest earned ratio*, and the *fixed-charge coverage ratio*.

Debt Ratio

A leverage ratio calculated by dividing total debt by total assets that indicates how much of the firm's assets were financed with debt.

Debt Ratio   The **debt ratio** is defined as follows:

$$(3.7) \qquad \qquad \text{DR} = \frac{\text{TD}}{\text{TA}}$$

where TD = Total Debt, and TA = Total Assets.

---

[9] The trade-off between risk and return resulting from the use of financial leverage is discussed in Chapters 12 and 13.

It measures the proportion of a firm's total assets that is financed with creditors' funds. As used here, the term *debt* encompasses all short-term liabilities and long-term borrowings.

Bondholders and other long-term creditors are among those likely to be interested in a firm's debt ratio. They tend to prefer a low debt ratio because it provides more protection in the event of liquidation or some other major financial problem. As the debt ratio increases, so do a firm's fixed-interest charges. If the debt ratio becomes too high, the cash flows a firm generates during economic recessions may not be sufficient to meet interest payments. Thus, a firm's ability to market new debt obligations when it needs to raise new funds is crucially affected by the size of the debt ratio and by investors' perceptions about the risk implied by the level of the ratio.

Debt ratios are stated in terms of percentages. MMC's debt ratio as of year-end 20X6 is ($25,523 + $22,000)/$81,890 = $47,523/$81,890 = 0.58, or 58 percent. The ratio is interpreted to mean that MMC's creditors are financing 58 percent of the firm's total assets. This figure is considerably higher than the 47 percent industry average, indicating that MMC has less unused borrowing capacity than the average firm in the industry.

A high debt ratio implies a low *proportionate equity base,* that is, the percentage of assets financed with equity funds. As the proportionate equity base declines, investors are more hesitant to acquire a firm's debt obligations. Whether MMC can continue to finance its assets with 58 percent of "outsider" money largely depends on the growth and stability of future earnings and cash flows.

Debt-to-Equity Ratio   The debt-to-equity ratio is defined as follows:

$$(3.8) \qquad\qquad DE = \frac{TD}{TE}$$

where TD = Total Debt, and TE = Total Equity.

It is similar to the debt ratio and relates the amount of a firm's debt financing to the amount of equity financing. The debt-to-equity ratio, in actuality, is not really a new ratio. It is simply the debt ratio in a different format.

The debt-to-equity ratio is also stated as a percentage. MMC's debt-to-equity ratio at year-end 20X6 is $47,523/$34,367 = 1.38, or 138 percent. Because the industry average is 88.7 percent, MMC's ratio indicates that the firm uses more than the usual amount of borrowed funds to finance its activities. Specifically, it raises nearly $1.38 from creditors for each dollar invested by shareholders, which is interpreted to mean that the firm's debt suppliers have a lower margin of safety than is common in the industry. In addition, MMC has a greater potential for financial distress if earnings do not exceed the cost of borrowed funds.

Because most interest costs are incurred on long-term borrowed funds (greater than one year to maturity) and because long-term borrowing places multiyear, fixed financial obligations on a firm, some analysts also consider the ratio of *long-term debt-to-total assets,* or *long-term debt-to-equity.* Another modification that is sometimes made in these ratios is to include the capitalized value of noncancellable financial leases (discussed in Chapter 19) in the numerator. Some analysts also include a firm's preferred shares with its debt when computing these ratios because preferred share dividends, like interest requirements, are usually fixed.

Earnings Before Interest and Taxes (EBIT)
A firm's earnings before payment of interest and taxes (also called *operating earnings*).

Times Interest Earned Ratio   The times interest earned ratio is defined as follows:

$$(3.9) \qquad\qquad TIE = \frac{EBIT}{IC}$$

where **EBIT** = Earnings Before Interest and Taxes, and IC = Interest Charges.

Often referred to as simply *interest coverage,* this ratio employs income statement data to measure a firm's use of financial leverage. It tells an analyst the extent to which the firm's current earnings are able to meet current interest payments. The EBIT figures are used because the firm makes interest payments out of operating income, or EBIT. When the times interest earned ratio falls below 1.0, the continued viability of the enterprise is threatened because the failure to make interest payments when due can lead to bankruptcy.

MMC's times interest earned ratio is $11,520/$3,160 = 3.65 times. In other words, it covers annual interest payments 3.65 times; this figure is considerably below the industry norm of 6.7 times. This ratio is further evidence that the company makes extensive use of creditors' funds to finance its operations.

Fixed-Charge Coverage Ratio The fixed-charge coverage ratio is defined as follows:

$$(3.10) \qquad FCC = \frac{EBIT + LP}{IC + LP + PDBT + SFBT}$$

where EBIT = Earnings Before Interest and Taxes, LP = Lease Payments, IC = Interest Charges, PDBT = Preferred Share Dividends Before Tax, and SFBT = Sinking Fund Payments Before Tax.

It measures the number of times a firm is able to cover total *fixed charges,* which include (in addition to interest payments) preferred dividends and payments required under long-term lease contracts. Many companies are also required to make *sinking fund* payments on bond issues, which are annual payments aimed at either retiring a portion of the bond obligation each year or providing for the ultimate redemption of bonds at maturity. Under most sinking fund provisions, the firm either may make these payments to the bondholders' representative (the *trustee*), who determines through a lottery process which of the outstanding bonds will be retired, or may deliver to the trustee the required number of bonds purchased by the firm in the open market. Either way, the firm's outstanding indebtedness is reduced.

In calculating the fixed-charge coverage ratio, an analyst must consider each of the firm's obligations on a *pretax* basis. However, because sinking fund payments and preferred share dividends are not tax-deductible and therefore must be paid out of after-tax earnings, a mathematical adjustment has to be made. After-tax payments must be divided by $(1 - T)$, where T is the marginal tax rate. This effectively converts such payments to a pretax basis, or one that is comparable to the EBIT.[10] As well, since lease payments are deducted in arriving at the EBIT, they must be added back into the numerator of the ratio because the fixed charges (in the denominator) also include lease payments.

The fixed-charge coverage ratio is a more severe measure of a company's ability to meet fixed financial obligations. Using figures from MMC's income statement for 20X6,[11] the fixed-charge coverage ratio can be calculated as follows:

$$\frac{\$11,520 + \$150}{\$3,160 + \$150 + \$2,000/(1 - 0.4)} = \frac{\$11,670}{\$6,643} = 1.76 \text{ times}$$

---

[10] The rationale for this computation is as follows:

$$\text{Earnings after taxes} = \text{Earnings before taxes} - \text{Taxes}$$
$$= \text{Earnings before taxes} - \text{Earnings before taxes} \times T$$
$$= \text{Earnings before taxes} (1 - T)$$
$$\text{Earnings after taxes}/(1 - T) = \text{Earnings before taxes}$$

[11] Some analysts exclude preferred dividend payments when computing the fixed-charge coverage ratio. In the calculation in the text, the $150 represents annual long-term lease payments and the $2,000 represents sinking fund obligations.

Because the industry average is 4.5 times, once again it is apparent that MMC provides creditors with a smaller margin of safety—that is, a higher level of risk—than the average firm in the industry. As a result, MMC is probably straining its relations with creditors. If a tight money situation developed in the economy, MMC's high debt and low coverage ratios would most likely limit the firm's access to new credit sources, and MMC might be forced to curtail operations or borrow on prohibitively expensive and restrictive terms.

Profitability Ratios

More than any other accounting measure, a firm's *profits*[12] demonstrate how well its management is making investment and financing decisions. If a firm is unable to provide adequate returns in the form of dividends and share price appreciation to investors, it may be unable to maintain, let alone increase, its asset base. **Profitability ratios** measure how effectively a firm's management is generating profits on sales, total assets, and, most importantly, shareholders' investment. Therefore, anyone whose economic interests are tied to the long-run survival of a firm will be interested in profitability ratios.

Profitability Ratios
Financial ratios that measure the total effectiveness of a company's management in generating profits.

There are several types of profitability ratios, including the *gross profit margin ratio,* the *net profit margin ratio,* the *return on investment ratio,* and the *return on total equity ratio.*

Gross Profit Margin Ratio   The **gross profit margin ratio** is defined as follows:

Gross Profit Margin Ratio
A profitability ratio calculated by dividing sales minus cost of sales by sales that indicates how efficiently the firm is managing the production process.

$$(3.11) \qquad \mathrm{GPM} = \frac{S - COS}{S}$$

where S = Sales, and COS = Cost of Sales.

It measures the relative profitability of a firm's sales after the cost of sales has been deducted, thus revealing how effectively the firm's management is making decisions regarding pricing and the control of production costs.

MMC's gross profit margin ratio is $27,460/$112,760 = 24.4%, just slightly below the industry average of 25.6 percent. This percentage indicates that either MMC's pricing policies or its production methods are not quite as effective as those of the average firm in the industry. Differences in inventory accounting methods (and, to a lesser extent, depreciation methods) used by MMC and the firms included in the industry average also influence the cost of sales and, by extension, the gross profit margin.

Net Profit Margin Ratio   The **net profit margin ratio** is defined as follows:

Net Profit Margin Ratio
A profitability ratio calculated by dividing earnings after tax by sales.

$$(3.12) \qquad \mathrm{NPM} = \frac{EAT}{S}$$

where EAT = Earnings After Taxes, and S = Sales.

It measures how profitable a firm's sales are after all expenses, including taxes and interest, have been deducted.

Some analysts also compare an *operating profit margin ratio,* defined as EBIT/sales. It measures the profitability of a firm's operations before considering the effects of financing decisions. Because the operating profit margin is computed before considering interest charges, this ratio is often more suitable for comparing the profit performance of different firms.

MMC's net profit margin ratio is $5,016/$112,760 = 4.45%, which is below the industry average of 5.1 percent and is interpreted to mean that the firm is earning 0.65

---

[12] The terms *profits, earnings,* and *net income* are used interchangeably in this discussion.

percent less on each dollar of sales than the average firm in the industry. This percentage indicates that MMC may be having difficulty controlling either total expenses (including interest, operating expenses, and the cost of sales) or the prices of its products. In this case, the former is probably more accurate, because MMC's financial structure contains a greater proportion of debt, resulting in more interest charges.

Return on Investment Ratio
A profitability ratio calculated by dividing earnings after tax by total assets that indicates how profitably the firm uses its assets.

Return on Investment (Total Assets) Ratio   The **return on investment ratio** is defined as follows:

$$(3.13) \qquad ROI = \frac{EAT}{TA}$$

where EAT = Earnings After Taxes, and TA = Total Assets.

It measures a firm's net income in relation to the total asset investment.

MMC's return on investment ratio, $5,016/$81,890, is 6.13 percent, which is considerably below the industry average of 9.28 percent and is a direct result of the firm's low asset management ratios and low profit margins.

Some analysts also like to compute the ratio of EBIT/Total Assets. This measures the operating profit rate of return for a firm or its *basic earning power*. This ratio is computed before interest charges and may be more suitable when comparing the operating performance of two or more firms that are financed differently.

Return on Total Equity Ratio
A profitability ratio calculated by dividing earnings after tax by total equity that indicates how profitably the firm uses its assets that were financed by equity.

Return on Total Equity Ratio   The **return on total equity ratio** is defined as follows:

$$(3.14) \qquad ROE = \frac{EAT}{TE}$$

where EAT = Earnings After Taxes, and TE = Total Equity.

It measures the rate of return that the firm earns on total equity. Because only the total equity appears in the denominator, the ratio is influenced directly by the amount of debt a firm is using to finance assets.

MMC's return on total equity ratio is $5,016/$34,367 = 14.6%. Again, MMC's ratio is below the industry average of 17.54 percent. The firm's low asset management ratios and low profit margins result in profitability ratios inferior to the industry norms, even after the effects of debt financing (financial leverage) are considered. When a firm has preferred shares in its capital structure, one may wish to calculate the return on common equity. This return is:

$$(3.15) \qquad ROCE = \frac{(EAT - PD)}{TCE}$$

where PD = Preferred Share Dividends and TCE = Total Common Equity.

Market-Based Ratios

Market-Based Ratios
These ratios reflect the financial market's assessment of a firm's performance.

The financial ratios discussed in the previous four groups are all derived from accounting income statement and balance sheet information provided by the firm. Analysts and investors are also interested in the financial market's assessment of the performance of a firm. The **market-based ratios** for a firm should parallel the accounting ratios of that firm. For example, if the accounting ratios of a firm suggest that the firm has more risk than the average firm in the industry and has lower profit prospects, this information should be reflected in a lower market price of that firm's shares.

Price-to-Earnings (P/E) Ratio

The **price-to-earnings ratio** is defined as follows:

$$(3.16) \qquad P/E = \frac{MPS}{EPS}$$

where MPS = Market Price per Share, and EPS = Earnings per Share.

(Some analysts use next year's projected earnings per share in the denominator. There is nothing wrong with this alternative definition as long as comparisons between firms are done on the same basis.)

In general, *the lower the firm's risk, the higher its P/E ratio* should be. In addition, *the better the growth prospects of its earnings, the greater is the P/E multiple.*

MMC's current (20X6) earnings per share are $3.86 (earnings of $5,016 divided by 1,300 shares). If MMC's current market price is $24 per share, its P/E ratio is 6.22 times. This is below the industry average of 8.0 times, and indicates that MMC has either higher risk than the average firm, lower growth prospects, or both.

As a supplement to the price-to-earnings ratio, financial analysts sometimes also examine a firm's *share price-to-free cash flow ratio*. **Free cash flow** (discussed further in Chapters 13 and 20) represents the portion of a firm's total cash flow available to service additional debt, to pay common share dividends, and to invest in other projects (e.g., capital expenditures and/or acquisition of other firms). Free cash flow is often viewed as a better measure of the financial soundness of a firm than earnings. Earnings data can sometimes be misleading because accounting rules give firms discretion in such areas as the recognition of revenues that have not been received and the allocation of costs over different time periods.[13] For example, some companies have had positive earnings but negative cash flow and were forced into bankruptcy.

Market Price-to-Book Value (P/BV) Ratio

The **market price-to-book value ratio** (often called simply the market-to-book ratio) is defined as follows:

$$(3.17) \qquad P/BV = \frac{MPS}{BVPS}$$

where MPS = Market Price per Share, and BVPS = Book Value per Share.

Generally, the higher the rate of return a firm is earning on its common equity relative to the return required by investors (the cost of common equity), the higher will be the P/BV ratio.

The book value per share is determined by dividing the total common shareholders' equity for a firm by the number of shares outstanding. In the case of MMC at year-end 20X6, the book value per share is equal to $26.44 (shareholders' equity of $34,367 divided by 1,300 shares outstanding). With a market price per share of $24, the market-to-book ratio for MMC is 0.91. This compares unfavourably with the industry average of 1.13.

It should be noted that, because the market-to-book ratio contains the book value of the common shareholders' equity in the denominator, it is affected by the accounting treatments used by a firm in such crucial areas as inventory valuation and depreciation. For this reason, comparisons between firms can often be misleading.

Dividend Policy Ratios

The two primary dividend policy ratios, the payout ratio and the dividend yield, give insights regarding a firm's dividend strategies and its future growth prospects.

Payout Ratio   The **payout ratio** indicates the percentage of a firm's earnings that are paid out as dividends. It is defined as:

---

[13] The issue of earnings quality is discussed in more detail later in the chapter.

$$(3.18) \qquad\qquad PR = \frac{DPS}{EPS}$$

where DPS = Dividends per Share, and EPS = Earnings per Share.

In the case of MMC, the payout ratio is equal to 55.7 percent ($2.15 annual 20X6 dividends ÷ $3.86 annual 20X6 earnings per share). As discussed in Chapter 14, companies are extremely reluctant to cut their dividends because of the negative signal such an action transmits to the financial marketplace. Accordingly, firms with stable earnings are more likely to pay out a greater proportion of their earnings as dividends than are companies with more volatile earnings. Also, firms with a large, continuing number of high-return investment projects are less likely to pay out a high proportion of earnings as dividends because of their need for the capital to finance these projects.

Dividend Yield
The annual dividend payment divided by the market price of the share.

Dividend Yield A share's **dividend yield** is the expected yearly dividend divided by the current share price, or:

$$(3.19) \qquad\qquad DY = \frac{DPS}{P}$$

where DPS = Expected Dividend per Share, and P = Price of the share.

The current dividend yield for MMC is 8.96 percent ($2.15 dividend divided by the $24 share price). As discussed in Chapter 6, the returns received by an investor in common shares are the sum of the dividend yield and expected growth in the firm's earnings, dividends, and ultimately its share price. Shares with a low dividend yield may indicate high expected future growth. High dividend yields may be indicators of low future growth prospects. *Very* high dividend yields often signal a company facing financial difficulty that the market expects to be accompanied by future cuts in the dividend amount.

Summary of Financial Ratio Analysis

Table 3.3 lists all the financial ratios calculated for the Maple Manufacturing Company, summarizing the comparative financial ratio analysis undertaken for the firm.

The assessment column to the right of the table contains an evaluation of each of MMC's ratios in comparison with the industry averages. For example, the firm's liquidity position is rated fair to satisfactory. Although its current ratio is somewhat below the industry norm, its quick ratio is satisfactory, indicating that MMC probably has sufficient liquidity to meet maturing obligations. The firm's asset structure is not generating sufficient sales revenues, however. MMC's asset management ratios indicate that the firm is investing too much in receivables and inventories, as well as property, plant, and equipment, relative to the sales volume being generated. Thus, MMC should consider implementing more stringent credit and collection policies as well as better inventory controls. The firm should also evaluate its investment in property, plant, and equipment to determine whether reductions could be made without impairing operations.

MMC's financial leverage ratios indicate that the firm is using significantly more debt to finance operations than the average firm in the industry. Because of its poor coverage ratios, the firm may have difficulty obtaining debt financing for further asset additions. In the event of an economic slowdown, MMC's creditors would probably re-evaluate the firm's borrowing capacity and make less funds available to it. If MMC wants to restore its borrowing capacity, it should take steps to increase its equity base. The market-based ratios confirm the analysis performed using MMC's financial statements, and the dividend policy ratios indicate that the firm may have low growth prospects.

Table 3.3 Ratio Analysis Summary for the Maple Manufacturing Company

Ratio	Definition
LIQUIDITY	
1. Current ratio	$\dfrac{\text{Current assets}}{\text{Current liabilities}}$
2. Quick ratio (acid test)	$\dfrac{\text{Current assets} - \text{Inventories}}{\text{Current liabilities}}$
ASSET MANAGEMENT	
3. Average collection period	$\dfrac{\text{Accounts receivable}}{\text{Credit sales/365}}$
4. Inventory turnover	$\dfrac{\text{Cost of sales}}{\text{Average inventory}}$
5. Fixed-asset turnover	$\dfrac{\text{Sales}}{\text{Fixed assets}}$
6. Total asset turnover	$\dfrac{\text{Sales}}{\text{Total assets}}$
FINANCIAL LEVERAGE MANAGEMENT	
7. Debt ratio	$\dfrac{\text{Total debt}}{\text{Total assets}}$
8. Debt-to-equity	$\dfrac{\text{Total debt}}{\text{Total equity}}$
9. Times interest earned	$\dfrac{\text{Earnings before interest and taxes (EBIT)}}{\text{Interest charges}}$
10. Times fixed charges earned	$\dfrac{\text{EBIT} + \text{Lease Payments}}{\text{Interest} + \text{Lease payments} + \text{Before-tax sinking fund} + \text{Preferred share dividends before tax}}$
PROFITABILITY	
11. Gross profit margin	$\dfrac{\text{Sales} - \text{Cost of sales}}{\text{Sales}}$
12. Net profit margin	$\dfrac{\text{Earnings after taxes (EAT)}}{\text{Sales}}$
13. Return on investment	$\dfrac{\text{Earnings after taxes (EAT)}}{\text{Total assets}}$
14. Return on total equity	$\dfrac{\text{Earnings after taxes (EAT)}}{\text{Total equity}}$
MARKET-BASED	
15. Price-to-earnings ratio	$\dfrac{\text{Market price per share}}{\text{Current earnings per share}}$
16. Market-to-book ratio	$\dfrac{\text{Market price per share}}{\text{Book value per share}}$
DIVIDEND POLICY	
17. Payout ratio	$\dfrac{\text{Dividends per share}}{\text{Earnings per share}}$
18. Dividend yield	$\dfrac{\text{Expected dividend per share}}{\text{Share price}}$

Table 3.3 *continued*

Calculation	Industry Average	Assessment
$\dfrac{\$50,190}{\$25,523} = 1.97$ times	2.40 times	Fair
$\dfrac{\$22,660}{\$25,523} = 0.89$ times	0.92 times	Satisfactory
$\dfrac{\$18,320}{\$112,760/365} = 59.3$ days	47 days	Unsatisfactory
$\dfrac{\$85,300}{(\$27,530 + \$26,470)/2} = 3.16$ times	3.9 times	Unsatisfactory
$\dfrac{\$112,760}{\$31,700} = 3.56$ times	4.6 times	Poor
$\dfrac{\$112,760}{\$81,890} = 1.38$ times	1.82 times	Poor
$\dfrac{\$47,523}{\$81,890} = 58$ percent	47 percent	Poor
$\dfrac{\$47,523}{\$34,367} = 138.3$ percent	88.7 percent	Poor
$\dfrac{\$11,520}{\$3,160} = 3.65$ times	6.7 times	Poor
$\dfrac{\$11,520 + \$150}{\$3,160 + \$150 + \$2,000/(1 - 0.4)} = 1.76$ times	4.5 times	Poor
$\dfrac{\$27,460}{\$112,760} = 24.4$ percent	25.6 percent	Fair
$\dfrac{\$5,016}{\$112,760} = 4.45$ percent	5.10 percent	Unsatisfactory
$\dfrac{\$5,016}{\$81,890} = 6.13$ percent	9.28 percent	Poor
$\dfrac{\$5,016}{\$34,367} = 14.60$ percent	17.54 percent	Poor
$\dfrac{\$24}{\$3.86} = 6.22$ times	8.0 times	Poor
$\dfrac{\$24}{\$26.44} = 0.91$	1.13	Poor
$\dfrac{\$2.15}{\$3.86} = 55.7$ percent	28 percent	High, implying low growth prospects or lower earnings risk
$\dfrac{\$2.15}{\$24} = 8.96$ percent	4.2 percent	High, implying low growth prospects

It should be emphasized that the ratios discussed in this analysis are interrelated. For example, MMC is using more debt and investing more in receivables and inventories than the average firm in the industry. If the company could reduce its investment in receivables and inventories and use the released funds to lower debt, *both* the asset management ratios and the financial leverage ratios would be closer to the industry averages.

Common-Size Analysis

Common-Size Balance Sheet
A balance sheet in which a firm's assets and liabilities are expressed as a percentage of total assets, rather than as dollar amounts.

Common-Size Income Statement
An income statement in which a firm's income and expense items are expressed as a percentage of net sales, rather than as dollar amounts.

Common-size financial statements are also helpful in financial analysis. A **common-size balance sheet** shows the firm's assets and liabilities and shareholders' equity as a percentage of total assets, rather than in dollar amounts. Table 3.4 shows MMC's common-size balance sheet on December 31, 20X6, and December 31, 20X5.

A **common-size income statement** lists the firm's income and expense items as a percentage of net sales, rather than in dollar amounts. Table 3.5 contains MMC's common-size income statement for the year ended December 31, 20X6. Common-size financial statements allow trends in financial performance to be detected and monitored more easily than with financial statements showing only dollar amounts.

Table 3.4	Maple Manufacturing Company Common-Size Balance Sheet	
	December 31, 20X6	December 31, 20X5
ASSETS		
Cash	3.1%	2.7%
Marketable securities	2.2	2.1
Accounts receivable, net	22.4	21.9
Inventories	33.6	34.4
Total current assets	61.3%	61.1%
Net plant and equipment	38.7	38.9
Total assets	100.0%	100.0%
LIABILITIES AND SHAREHOLDERS' EQUITY		
Current liabilities	31.2%	27.1%
Long-term debt ($9\frac{5}{8}$% mortgage bonds)	26.8	31.2
Total liabilities	58.0%	58.3%
Shareholders' equity	42.0	41.7
Total liabilities and shareholders' equity	100.0%	100.0%

Table 3.5	Maple Manufacturing Company Common-Size Income Statement
For the Year Ended December 31, 20X6	
Net sales	100.0%
Cost of sales	75.7
Gross margin	24.3%
Operating expenses	14.1
Earnings before interest and taxes (EBIT)	10.2%
Interest charges	2.8
Earnings before taxes (EBT)	7.4%
Federal and provincial income taxes at a combined 40% rate	3.0
Earnings after taxes (EAT) and available for common shareholders	4.4%

Trend Analysis

Trend Analysis
An examination of a firm's performance over time. It is frequently based on one or more financial ratios.

Thus far, the analysis of the MMC has focused solely on the year 20X6. This has provided a fairly complete, if rather static, picture of the firm's situation at that particular point in time in comparison with industry standards. To gain insight into the direction the firm is moving, however, a trend analysis should be performed. A **trend analysis** indicates a firm's performance *over time* and reveals whether its position is improving or deteriorating relative to other firms in the industry.

A trend analysis requires that a number of different ratios be calculated over several years and plotted to yield a graphic representation of the firm's performance. Figure 3.1 depicts a trend analysis for MMC for the years 20X0 to 20X6 and indicates the direction the firm has been taking for the past several years. Each of the first four different categories of financial ratios is represented in the figure. For example, it is evident that the firm's liquidity position—as measured by the quick ratio—has declined gradually over the seven-year period, falling to slightly below the industry average in 20X6. Unless this downward trend continues, however, liquidity should not be a major problem for the firm.

The trend analysis tells another story about the firm's leverage and profitability. MMC's use of debt has exceeded the industry average since 20X2. The asset management ratios—the total asset turnover ratio and the average collection period ratio—indicate that the firm has used much of this new debt to finance additional assets, including a buildup in receivables. Unfortunately, the new assets have not produced offsetting increases in profits. As a result, returns on investment have dropped below the industry standards by increasing amounts over the past seven years. Trend analysis can also be performed on common-size financial statements.

In summary, the comparative financial ratio analysis, common-size analysis, and trend analysis combined provide a fairly clear picture of MMC's performance. As is evident from the analysis, MMC has employed excessive debt to finance asset additions that have not been sufficiently productive in generating sales revenues. The result is returns on investment and shareholders' equity that are significantly lower than the industry average. If the firm intends to reverse these trends, it will have to make more effective use of assets and reduce the use of creditors' funds. These steps will enable the firm to improve relations with creditors and potentially increase profitability and reduce risk for its owners.

DuPont Analysis of Profitability: Return on Investment

The preceding discussion of ratios indicates that a firm's return on investment (ROI) is defined as the ratio of earnings after taxes (EAT) to total assets. The ROI ratio can be examined more closely to provide additional insights into its significance.

The ROI can also be viewed as a function of the net profit margin times the total asset turnover because the net profit margin ratio = EAT/sales and the total asset turnover ratio = sales/total assets:

$$(3.20) \qquad \text{ROI} = \frac{\text{EAT}}{\text{TA}} = \frac{\text{EAT}}{\text{S}} \times \frac{\text{S}}{\text{TA}}$$

where EAT = Earnings After Tax, TA = Total Assets, and S = Sales.

It is important to examine a firm's ROI in terms of "margin" and "turnover," because each plays a major role in contributing to profitability. Margin measures the profit earned per dollar of sales but ignores the amount of assets used to generate sales. The ROI relationship brings these two components together and shows that a deficiency in either one will lower a firm's return on investment.

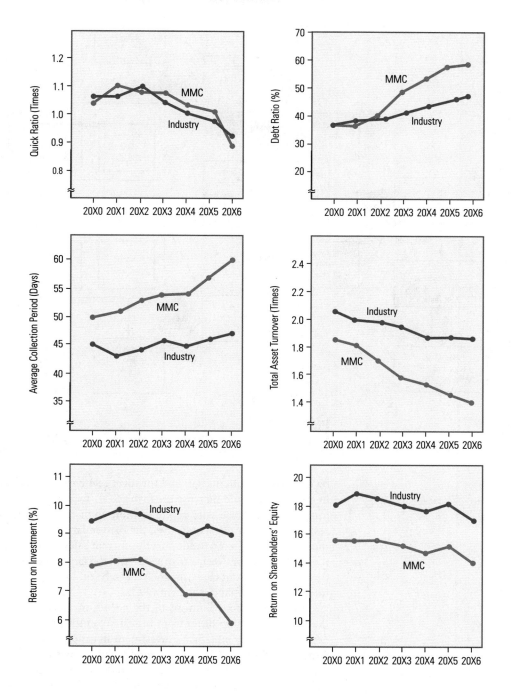

Figure 3.1
Trend Analysis of the Financial Ratios for the Maple Manufacturing Company from 20X0 to 20X6

Using the figures from the net profit margin ratio and total asset turnover ratio calculated previously for MMC, the firm's ROI for 20X6 can be computed as 4.45% × 1.38 = 6.14%, which differs slightly from the previous result of 6.13% due to roundoff error. Figure 3.2, called a *modified DuPont chart* because it was developed and is used by the DuPont Corporation, illustrates this relationship. For purposes of comparison, the industry average ROI = 5.10% × 1.82 = 9.28%. The ROI relationship shows MMC to

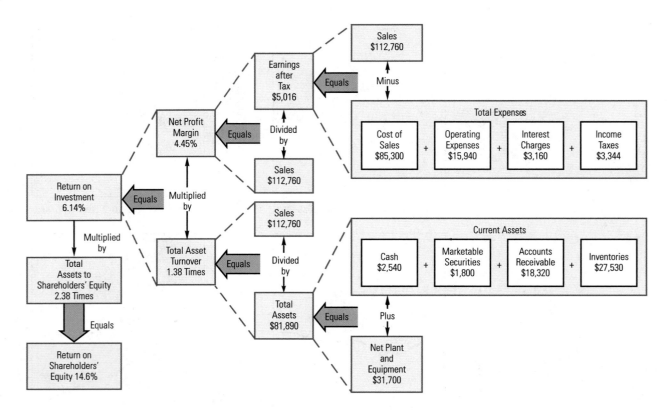

Figure 3.2
Modified DuPont Analysis for the Maple Manufacturing Company, 20X6

be deficient in both margin and turnover relative to the industry average. Improvement in either area would increase the firm's ROI. To improve its *margin,* for example, MMC must either increase sales revenues more than costs or decrease costs more than sales revenues. To improve its *turnover,* the firm must either increase sales revenue or reduce the asset level required to support the current sales volume. The DuPont chart illustrates the relationship between a firm's ROI and the factors that determine it. By working back through the DuPont chart, an analyst can begin to pinpoint potential areas for improvement that will enhance the firm's ROI.

The relative contributions of the net profit margin and the asset turnover ratio in the ROI relationship differ from industry to industry. Specifically, the turnover ratio is dependent largely on a firm's investment in property, plant, and equipment. Firms with large investments in fixed assets tend to have low turnover ratios; public utilities, railroads, and large industrial firms fall into this category. If these companies are to succeed, their relatively low turnover ratios must be offset by correspondingly high margins to produce competitive ROIs. For example, electric and gas utilities typically have net profit margins of 10 to 15 percent. In contrast, other industries require much lower investments in fixed assets, resulting in higher turnover ratios. A typical example is the retail grocery chain industry, which has margins of only 1 or 2 percent. Firms in this industry often achieve turnovers of 10 times or more. If a grocery chain had a lower turnover, its ROI probably would not be sufficient to attract investors.

Analyzing Profitability Through Return on Equity

Figure 3.2 also shows MMC's return on equity, which is computed as 14.6 percent. If the firm were financed solely with common equity (shares), the return on equity would equal the return on investment. MMC's shareholders have supplied only about 42 percent of the firm's total capital, whereas creditors have supplied the remaining 58 percent. Because the entire 6.14 percent return on investment belongs to the shareholders (even though they supplied only 42 percent of the total capital), MMC's return on common equity is higher than its return on investment.

To clarify how the return on equity is determined, a new ratio, the *equity multiplier ratio,* is defined as follows:

$$(3.21) \qquad EM = \frac{TA}{TE}$$

where TA = Total Assets and TE = Total Equity.

MMC's equity multiplier ratio is computed from figures found in Table 3.1 as $81,890/$34,367 = 2.38 times. The industry average for the ratio is 1.89 times. Once again, it can be seen that MMC has financed a greater proportion of assets with debt than the average firm in the industry.

The equity multiplier ratio may be used to show how a firm's use of debt to finance assets affects the return on equity, as follows:

$$(3.22) \quad ROE = \text{Net profit margin} \times \text{Total asset turnover} \times \text{Equity multiplier}$$

$$ROE = \frac{EAT}{S} \times \frac{S}{TA} \times \frac{TA}{TE}$$

In MMC's case the return on total equity is 4.45% × 1.38 × 2.38 = 14.6%.

Although this figure is the same as the return on equity computed directly by dividing earnings after tax by total equity, the calculations shown illustrate more clearly how MMC managed to magnify a 6.14 percent return on total investment into a 14.6 percent return on total equity by making more extensive use of debt financing than did the average firm in the industry. This increased use of debt has improved MMC's return on equity but has also increased its risk—more likely resulting in a decline in MMC's share price relative to other, similar firms.

Using Financial Ratios to Forecast Bankruptcy

One of the primary limitations of traditional financial ratio analysis is that it looks at only one ratio at a time and then relies on the analyst to form a judgement about the overall financial profile of the firm. Recently, more powerful statistical techniques have been applied to assist analysts in making judgements about the financial condition of the firm.

Discriminant Analysis
A statistical technique designed to classify observations (firms) into two or more predetermined groups based on certain characteristics (such as financial ratios) of the observations.

Discriminant analysis is a statistical technique that helps the analyst classify firms into two or more predetermined groups based on certain characteristics of the observation. In the context of financial statement analysis, the characteristics typically are financial ratios.

One early application of discriminant analysis in finance was a model developed by Edward Altman to predict bankruptcy of firms.[14] Altman identified five financial ratios that contributed significantly to the predictive accuracy of his Zeta model, whose formula is:

---

[14] Edward I. Altman, "Financial Ratios, Discriminant Analysis and the Prediction of Corporate Bankruptcy," *Journal of Finance,* vol. 23 (September 1968): 589–609.

$$Z = 0.012X_1 + 0.014X_2 + 0.033X_3 + 0.006X_4 + 0.999X_5$$

where

$X_1 =$ Net working capital/Total assets

$X_2 =$ Retained earnings/Total assets

$X_3 =$ EBIT/Total assets

$X_4 =$ Market value of total equity (common and preferred)/Book value of total debt

$X_5 =$ Sales/Total assets

For more about bankruptcy research see Professor Altman's Web site at **www.stern.nyu/~ealtman** Financial data on firms (financial statements, ratio analyses, histories, products, profit projections, etc.) are available at hundreds of different Web sites. Some of them are free, and others charge a fee. Here are just a few of the "comprehensive" Web sites: **www.globeinvestor.com www.hoovers.com www.bloomberg.com**

Altman's basic model was developed from a sample of 66 manufacturing firms—half of which went bankrupt. On the basis of the analysis, he established a guideline cut-off score of 2.675, which could be used to classify firms as either financially sound or headed toward bankruptcy. The lower the score, the greater the probability of bankruptcy. The higher the score, the lower the probability of bankruptcy. In other words, the lower the values of the five ratios just listed, in general, the greater the probability of bankruptcy.

More recent refinements of Altman's bankruptcy forecasting model have made it applicable to retailing as well as manufacturing firms.[15] The newer model is about 70 percent accurate as much as five years prior to bankruptcy.

Altman and Mario Lavallée studied a sample of Canadian firms and came up with a somewhat different model.[16] The Canadian equation is:

$$Z = -1.6180 + 0.23414X_1 + 0.62096X_2 + 0.89075X_3 + 0.65779X_4 + 0.50355X_5$$

where

$X_1 =$ Sales/Total assets

$X_2 =$ Net profit/Total assets

$X_3 =$ Current ratio

$X_4 =$ Net profit/Total debt

$X_5 =$ Growth rate of equity less growth rate of total assets

Sources of Comparative Financial Data

An analyst may refer to a number of sources of financial data when preparing a comparative financial analysis, including the following:

Dun & Bradstreet Dun & Bradstreet (D&B) prepares a series of 14 key business ratios for 800 different lines of business. These ratios are based on the financial statements of some 500,000 companies in North America. D&B reports three values for each ratio—the *median,* the *upper quartile,* and the *lower quartile.* The median is the figure that falls in the middle when individual ratios of sampled firms are arranged by size. The figure halfway between the median and the ratio with the highest value is the upper quartile, and the figure halfway between the median and the ratio with the lowest value is the lower quartile. By reporting three values for each ratio, D&B enables the analyst to compare a particular firm with the "average" (median) firm, as well as with the

For more information see **www.dnb.ca**

---

[15] E.I. Altman, R.G. Haldeman, and P. Narayanan, "Zeta Analysis: A New Model to Identify Bankruptcy Risk of Corporations," *Journal of Banking and Finance,* vol.1 (June 1977): 29–54.

[16] Edward Altman and Mario Lavallée, "Un modèle discriminant de prediction des faillites au Canada," *Finance,* vol.1, part 1(1980): 74–81.

Information about the Financial Post data can be found at **www.financialpost.com**. For Moody's data see **www.mergent.com**. For Standard & Poor's data see **www.standardandpoors.com**

For more information see **www.sedar.com**

For more information see **www.sec.gov/edgar.shtml**

For more information see **www.valueline.com** See **http://finance.swcollege.com** for synopses of recent articles on financial statement analysis.

Generally Accepted Accounting Principles (GAAP)

A broad set of accounting rules followed in preparing financial statements.

For more accounting information see **www.cica.ca www.cga-canada.org www.fasb.org www.iasc.org.uk**

"typical" firms in the top and bottom halves of the sample. The D&B publication containing the data is entitled *Industry Norms and Key Business Ratios*.

Financial Post, Moody's, or Standard & Poor's (S&P) Publications   These contain a large amount of financial statement data, as well as other relevant information about a firm. *Financial Post* and Standard & Poor's also publish industry surveys using the new Global Industry Classification Standard (GICS) that provides data on the firms that compose the industry as defined by S&P. The GICS is also used for the S&P/TSX Composite Index.

Annual Reports   Most corporations publish annual reports containing income statement and balance sheet data, along with other information of interest. These reports can usually be downloaded from the company's Web site or from the SEDAR Web site.

10K Reports   Every widely held firm that raises capital in the United States (including Canadian firms) is required to file a 10K report each year with the SEC. These reports contain income statement and balance sheet data, plus a wide range of other relevant information dealing with the firm's past and current performance and expected future prospects. These reports include data not normally disclosed in Canada, so this is an important source of information on the Canadian firms that are subject to the SEC rules.

Trade Journals   These are published by trade associations and contain a great deal of financial and other types of information on member firms.

Computerized Data Sources   A number of computerized databases are also available to assist in financial analysis. The *Financial Post* database of 500 Canadian companies can usually be accessed from libraries at little or no cost, or it may be purchased from the FP Data Group. The *Compustat* database is available for a fee from Standard & Poor's. It contains complete balance sheet, income statement, share price, and dividend information for several thousand companies, covering a period of up to 20 years. *Value Line* provides summary financial data and forecasts of future performance for over 1,700 firms. The *Value Line* database is available in both hard copy and on the Internet. Both of these databases include Canadian firms traded in the United States as well as their US competitors.

A Word of Caution about Financial Ratio Analysis

Throughout the analysis of MMC, we emphasized that an analyst must exercise caution when evaluating a firm's financial ratios. Although ratios can provide valuable information, they can also be misleading for a number of reasons.

First, ratios are only as reliable as the accounting data on which they are based. The financial statements of most firms are prepared in accordance with **generally accepted accounting principles (GAAP)**. In Canada, the Canadian Institute of Chartered Accountants' *Handbook* is the definitive reference source for GAAP. In the United States, the Financial Accounting Standards Board issues *Statements of Financial Accounting Standards* (SFAS), which describe accounting rules that firms must follow. Internationally, the International Accounting Standards Committee (IASC) publishes a *Framework for the Presentation of Financial Statements*, which is the world GAAP. Both Canada and the United States, as well as Mexico, are members of the IASC. Although there are some national differences, it is expected that gradually the various GAAP standards will converge. The Certified General Accountants-Canada association publishes annually a *GAAP Guide*, which explains the similarities and differences between and among the US, Canadian, and International GAAP.

Even though careful financial analysis can provide excellent insights into the direction and relative strength of the firm, the financial analyst must keep in mind that GAAP gives firms considerable latitude in reporting their financial positions, as is evident in this chapter's Financial Challenge. Different firms follow different accounting procedures for inventory valuation, depreciation, pension fund contributions, and mergers and acquisitions, to name just a few. These, in turn, affect reported earnings, assets, and owners' investments. Unless the analyst makes adjustments for accounting reporting differences, ratio comparisons between individual companies and with various industry norms cannot be viewed as definitive.

Second, with the exception of disclosing upper and lower quartile values, firms that compile industry norms often do not report information about the *dispersion,* or distribution, of the individual values around the mean ratio. If the reported ratios are dispersed widely, the industry average will be of questionable value because it may not reflect the so-called typical firm in the industry. Furthermore, the standard of comparison probably should not be the "typical" firm but rather the better-performing firms in the industry. Without some measure of dispersion, however, ratios for these better-performing firms cannot be determined.

Comparative Analysis
An examination of a firm's performance based on one or more financial ratios, which are compared with the financial ratios of competitive firms or with an industry standard or benchmark.

Third, valid **comparative analysis** depends on the availability of data for appropriately defined industries. Some industry classifications are either too broad or too narrow to be reliable sources of comparative data when an analyst is evaluating a particular firm. Most firms operate in more than one industry, which makes analysis more difficult.

Fourth, it is important to remember that financial ratios provide a *historic* record of the performance and financial condition of a firm. Further analysis is required before this historic record can be used as a basis for future projections.

Finally, comparisons of a firm's ratios with industry norms may not always be what they seem. Ratios comparing unfavourably with industry norms should be construed as red flags indicating the need for further investigation—not signals of impending doom. On the other hand, even if a firm's ratios compare favourably with those of the better-performing firms in the industry, it does not necessarily mean the firm is performing adequately. If, for example, the industry itself is experiencing a declining demand for its goods and services, favourable ratio comparisons may simply indicate that a firm is not decaying as rapidly as the typical firm in the industry. Thus, comparisons of selected ratios—particularly those relating to profitability—must be made with *national* industry averages in order to determine whether a particular firm in a particular industry is justified in making further investments.

In summary, ratios should not be viewed as substitutes for sound business judgement. Instead, they are simply tools that can help management make better decisions.

Earnings and Balance Sheet Quality and Financial Analysis

When performing a financial analysis of a firm, an analyst must be mindful of the *quality of the earnings* reported by a firm, as well as the *quality of the firm's balance sheet.* These two dimensions of financial analysis can have a critical impact on the final assessment of the firm's financial condition.

Earnings Quality

When considering the quality of a firm's earnings, two key factors should be kept in mind. First, high-quality earnings tend to be cash earnings. The proportion of a firm's earnings that can be viewed as cash earnings is greatly influenced by the firm's procedures with respect to sales revenue recognition. For example, a firm may recognize a sale at the time a contract is signed, a down payment is made, or when the full proceeds from

Financial Analysis of Multinational Corporations

The tools of financial analysis developed in this chapter are useful in evaluating the financial performance of purely North American firms as well as firms with small international operations. However, assessing the financial performance and condition of a firm with sizable international operations is generally more complicated than analyzing a firm whose operations are largely domestic.

Part of the complication involves the translation of foreign operating results from the host country's currency to dollars. To illustrate, suppose Harvey's European Union operations show net earnings of 200 million euros. Harvey's reports its results to shareholders denominated in dollars. Therefore the euro income must be translated into dollars. The *dollar* amount of Harvey's euro earnings depends on the exchange rate between dollars and euros. If this exchange rate is 1.2 euros per dollar, the dollar earnings from 200 million euros are reported as $166.67 million (200 million euros/1.2 euros per dollar). But if the exchange rate changes to 1.5 euros/dollar, the dollar value of 200 million euros drops to $133.33 million. Thus, the earnings reported by a Canadian-based company with sizable foreign operations depend not only on the local currency earnings but also on the exchange rate between the dollar and the local currency. When the dollar is relatively strong against a foreign

currency—that is, when the dollar will buy more euros, for example—foreign earnings translate into fewer dollars than when the dollar is relatively weak.

An additional complication in financial analysis of multinational firms arises because of fluctuating exchange rates. What happens to the *dollar* value on the parent firm's balance sheet of its European assets and liabilities as the exchange rate between euros and dollars changes? Assets and liabilities are normally translated at the exchange rate in effect on the balance sheet date. However, any gains or losses resulting from the translation of asset and liability accounts are not reflected on the income statement and therefore also are not included in the retained earnings figure on the balance sheet. Instead, gains and losses from foreign translation are reported separately on the balance sheet as a part of shareholders' equity, usually under a heading such as "Currency translation adjustment." For example, during 2001, Magna reported a decrease of US$158 million in its translation adjustment account. This decrease did not affect Magna's 2001 earnings, but it did change shareholders' equity on its balance sheet.

Financial managers and analysts will have to be knowledgeable about the complex international aspects of financial statement analysis.

the sale are actually collected as cash. Generally, the closer the recognition of a sale is to the time the full proceeds from that sale are collected, the higher is the quality of the firm's reported earnings.

Although there is frequently a close correlation between a firm's earnings and its cash flows over time, generally accepted accounting principles give companies substantial latitude in the reporting of earnings. Distortions in earnings can arise from such issues as the time of revenue recognition, the establishment of reserves for such items as loan loss provisions in banking, the amortization of intangible assets, and the like.

In times of business downturns earnings often plummet while cash balances soar. For example, in the first quarter of 2002, Nortel Networks saw its sales fall more than

For more information see
www.nortel.com

ETHICAL ISSUES

Security Analysts and Their Reports to the Public

Many, if not most, individual investors rely on the buy, hold, or sell recommendations of the analysts that are employed by the investment dealers with which they deal. In recent years, some security analysts' public reports have been criticized because the individual analysts recommended to the public that a particular security be bought while at the same time recommending the opposite to their friends and relatives. Is this ethical behaviour?

Investment dealers sometimes act as underwriters in the original issue of shares to the public. Later, they act as brokers for individual investors who are interested in buying or selling the shares.

In January 2003, the Ontario and Quebec securities commissions punished CIBC World Markets, the investment dealer of the CIBC bank. CIBC had acted as the lead underwriter in the initial public offering (IPO) of Shoppers Drug Mart shares and still owned 7,450,000 shares. Furthermore, Shoppers Drug Mart owed $67.4 million to the CIBC. CIBC World Markets failed to adequately inform investors of these material facts during 2001 and 2002 in five published reports that recommended that investors buy Shoppers Drug Mart shares. This action was not only unethical, it was also illegal.

50 percent relative to the same quarter in 2001. It lost US$463 million, compared with a loss of only US$277 million a year earlier. Yet cash balances soared above US$6.6 billion, due to cuts in capital spending and reductions in inventory.

Another area of earnings reporting abuse is so-called "pro forma" profitability measures. They are computed by firms "as if" certain ordinary expenses did not exist. In one particularly abusive example, Waste Management Inc. treated the cost of painting its trucks as an extraordinary one-time expense and thus excluded this expense from pro forma earnings calculations.

A firm's earnings can be viewed as high quality if a greater proportion of those earnings is derived from regularly recurring transactions. To the extent that reported earnings reflect the impact of nonrecurring transactions, the quality of those earnings is reduced. Nonrecurring gains can emerge when a firm repurchases its debt on the open market at a price lower than the face value of that debt. Also, a firm may change its accounting treatment of inventories and record a significant gain from this transaction. Another example of a nonrecurring transaction from which gains can occur involves lowering the reported depreciation expense on a company's existing assets. Examples such as this can be found almost any week in the financial press. The lesson from these examples is simple: The quality of a firm's earnings decreases in direct proportion to the increase in nonrecurring items reported in its earnings figures.

Another quality of earnings problem is pension plan deficits. Many firms have defined benefit pension plans that promise to pay retirees a monthly pension for life when they retire. Actuaries calculate the value of assets that are needed now to allow the firm to pay the promised pensions in the future based on assumptions about the length of time retirees will live and the expected returns on invested assets between now and the time the payments must be made. The firms then make payments each year into the pension plan to be invested until the pensions are required to be paid. The legislation governing such pension plans usually requires the sponsoring firms to make increased payments into the pension plan if the actuaries discover that the assets are insufficient.

For more on OPS see
www.stockdiagnostics.com

For more information about Professor Sunder see
www.som.yale.edu/faculty/sunder

A 2003 *Financial Post* survey found that 43 of the S&P/TSX 60 Index firms had pension deficits totalling $16 billion. Thus, if the stock market does not go up soon, these large companies will have to make contributions to their pension plans instead of paying dividends to their shareholders.[17]

In 2002, Standard & Poor's announced a new measure of corporate earnings, called *core earnings*.[18] Core earnings will be used as the new standard in S&P publications, including the *Compustat* database. The definition of **core earnings** *includes* employee stock option grant expenses and pension costs and *excludes* gains on pension funds, reversals of prior-year charges and provisions, and litigation or insurance settlements and proceeds.

In 2003, StockDiagnostics.com proposed another alternative measure called **operational cash flow per share (OPS)**, which is calculated by dividing a firm's cash flow from operations by the number of shares outstanding.

Balance Sheet Quality

The quality of a firm's balance sheet should also be of concern to a financial analyst. If the assets on a firm's balance sheet have a market value equal to or greater than the book value at which they are being carried, this enhances the quality of the firm's balance sheet. In contrast, if a significant portion of the assets of a firm has a market value substantially below book value, the quality of the firm's balance sheet is reduced. Over the last decade, we have seen many firms in the so-called "smokestack" industries record large losses as significant portions of their assets are abandoned and written off as losses. Banks regularly write off a portion of their loan portfolios when it becomes clear that particular loans will not be repaid. These actions greatly reduce a firm's equity ratios. Similarly, if a firm has significant amounts of inventory that cannot be moved, the quality of the balance sheet is reduced until the firm charges off this low-quality inventory.

In addition to asset quality issues, an analyst should also be aware of hidden liabilities. These liabilities may take the form of such things as uninsured losses arising from pending lawsuits. When large potential liabilities exist, an analyst must be quite careful before drawing conclusions about the adequacy of a firm's capital structure, based on an analysis of its reported balance sheet.

In contrast, some firms have significant hidden assets. These assets may be physical assets, such as real property that has appreciated in value but is carried on the firm's books at cost, or securities that are carried on the books at cost even though the market value of these securities has increased above the original cost. These hidden assets may also consist of intangibles, such as valuable patents or brand names.

This list of balance sheet and earnings quality issues is not all-inclusive, but it does give an indication of the extent to which a surface analysis of a firm's financial statements can lead to misleading conclusions about the financial condition of that firm. As Professor Shyam Sunder of Yale has said, "Off-balance sheet financing is a nice, gentlemanly label given to misrepresentation." Good financial analysts develop an eye for this type of deception.

Inflation and Financial Statement Analysis

Inflation can cause a number of problems for a financial analyst who is trying to assess the performance of a firm over time and in comparison with other firms in the industry. In particular, *inventory profits*—short-lived increased profits that occur as a result of the timing of price increases—can make a significant difference in a firm's reported earnings from year to year.

---

[17] Derek DeCloet, "There Is a Real Problem Here," *National Post* (May 9, 2003).

[18] Standard & Poor's, *Standard & Poor's Core Earnings Technical Bulletin* (October 24, 2002): 1–5.

For example, consider a supply company that buys equipment parts wholesale from the manufacturer for $4.00 each and sells them at a retail price of $5.00 each, realizing a profit of $1.00 per unit. Suppose the manufacturer announces a price increase of $0.50 per unit to $4.50, effective on the first of next month. If the supply company passes the increase on to customers and announces a price increase of its own to $5.50, also effective on the first of next month, it will realize a gross profit of $1.50 on every unit sold that originally cost $4.00. In other words, the firm will make additional profit on the units already in inventory *prior to the price increase*. Once it begins purchasing parts from the manufacturer at the new price of $4.50 per unit, it will revert to its original $1.00 profit. In the meantime, however, the timing of the price increase will allow the company to enjoy short-lived increased profits, or inventory profits.

The *last-in, first-out* (**LIFO**) inventory valuation method assumes that the items a firm uses from inventory are those that were acquired most recently. Thus, they can be *priced out* of the inventory based on the most recent inventory acquisition costs. In contrast, the *first-in, first-out* (**FIFO**) method of inventory valuation, which assumes that the items a firm uses from inventory are the oldest items in inventory, results in the firm's having to show a higher profit.

The accounting method used for inventory will affect a firm's profits and its balance sheet. Hence, any financial ratio that contains balance sheet inventory figures (for example, the total asset turnover ratio) or net income will vary from one firm to another, depending on the firm's accounting treatment of inventory. Another effect of inflation on financial statements is the tendency for the value of fixed assets to be understated. Also, to the extent that inflation causes a rise in interest rates, the value of long-term debt outstanding will decline. Thus, a firm will appear to be more financially leveraged in an inflationary period than is actually the case.

Inventory profits and inflation are only two factors that can affect a firm's reported earnings. Differences in the reporting of earnings, the recognition of sales, and other factors can also make comparisons between firms somewhat misleading. Again, a good financial analyst will always "go behind" the figures stated on a firm's income statement or balance sheet to find out what is actually occurring within a company.

Market Value Added: An Alternative Measure of Performance

As already discussed, traditional financial analysis focuses on a set of financial ratios derived primarily from accounting information. Using an approach such as DuPont analysis, a firm's financial performance can be dissected into its component elements. The ultimate measure of firm performance is the return on common equity. Although insights can be gained from this type of analysis, traditional financial analysis suffers from weaknesses inherent in reported accounting information, and it does not directly consider risk in the measure of performance. The greatest shortcoming of traditional financial analysis is the lack of a direct tie between performance, as measured using financial ratios, and shareholder wealth, as measured by the market price of a firm's shares.

A number of alternative performance measures are available. These include *The Globe and Mail Report on Business 1000* (which ranks firms according to their profit after tax in the most recent fiscal year), the *Financial Post 500* (which ranks firms according to their revenues), and the *Canadian Business Investor 500* (which ranks firms according to their market value).

The Market Value Added Concept

The *Stern Stewart Performance 1000* (for the United States) and *300* (Canada) are based on the concept of **market value added (MVA).** MVA is defined as the market value of

---

LIFO

The acronym for the *last-in, first-out* inventory valuation method. The method assumes that a firm uses the most recently acquired items in the inventory first. Thus, they are *priced out* of the inventory based on the most recent inventory acquisition costs rather than the oldest.

FIFO

The acronym for the *first-in, first-out* inventory valuation method. The method assumes that a firm uses the oldest items in the inventory first. Thus, they are *priced out* of the inventory based on the oldest inventory acquisition costs rather than the most recent.

For more information see **http://top1000. robmagazine.com www.infomart.ca/fp/fp/ fp_product.php** and **www.canadianbusiness. com/i500**

Market Value Added (MVA)

MVA is defined as the market value of debt, preferred equity, and common equity capitalization, less capital (all the cash raised from investors or retained from earnings to fund new investments in the business since the firm's inception).

debt, preferred equity, and common equity capitalization, less capital. Capital is a measure of all of the cash raised from investors or retained from earnings to fund new investments in the business since the company's inception.

$$(3.23) \qquad \text{MVA} = \text{Market value} - \text{Capital}$$

MVA is the capital market's assessment of the accumulated net present value (NPV) of all of the firm's past and projected investment projects. NPV was introduced in Chapter 1 and is discussed in more detail in Chapter 10. For example, in 1999, Bombardier had MVA of $16,141,707,000, according to Stern Stewart.[19]

Economic Value Added

Stern Stewart & Co. has a comprehensive Web site on EVA issues at **www.sternstewart.com** or at **www.eva.com**

Economic value added (EVA®) is defined as:

$$(3.24) \quad \text{EVA} = [\text{Return on total capital } (r) - \text{Cost of capital } (k)] \times \text{Capital}$$

where r = net operating profits after tax divided by beginning of year capital, and k = weighted after-tax cost of capital, discussed in Chapter 8. For example, Bombardier had EVA of $340,059,000 in 1999 with $r = 14.2\%$ and $k = 9.5\%$, according to Stern Stewart.

Using this relationship, it can be seen that a firm's managers can increase EVA by

1. Increasing operating efficiency and thereby increasing r

2. Committing new resources to the enterprise that promise a return in excess of the firm's weighted (and risk-adjusted) cost of capital

3. Redirecting resources from projects that do not earn adequate returns (relative to the cost of capital) and show little promise of doing so in the future, to more productive uses. This includes the payment of dividends and reduction of debt levels if no adequate-return projects are present

4. Making prudent use of the tax benefits of debt financing to create value, while considering risk versus return trade-offs

Firms that consistently earn returns in excess of their cost of capital will have positive EVA. This is likely to enhance the MVA of the enterprise. For example, Bombardier's 1999 EVA mentioned above shows that the firm was likely adding to shareholder wealth during that year. (Investors may have anticipated this EVA and their wealth could then reflect this EVA before it occurred.)

In contrast, firms that earn less than their cost of capital will have negative EVA. Consistent negative EVA likely will result in a decline in a firm's MVA. For example, in 1999 Nortel Networks had EVA of *negative* $130,953,000. (Its share price subsequently dropped.)

One important implication of the MVA and EVA concepts is that growth in earnings does not necessarily add to the value of an enterprise (MVA) unless it is achieved by making (and managing) investments such that they earn a return in excess of the cost of capital (positive EVA). Another implication is that increasing the rate of return on investment will not necessarily increase MVA because it is necessary to link the return earned with the market-required rate of return (weighted cost of capital). Finally, a company's dividend policy, discussed in Chapter 14, has no direct impact on MVA since the payment of dividends equally reduces both the book and the market value of capital. Only if dividend payments provide credible signals to the capital markets about future prospects (for EVA) will dividend payment patterns have an impact on value.

---

[19] Irwin Ross, "The Stern Stewart Performance 1000," *Bank of America Journal of Applied Corporate Finance* (Winter 1999): 122–34.

The EVA and MVA concepts used in the construction of the *Stern Stewart Performance* indexes provide a useful alternative way to focus on the performance of an enterprise in the context of the objective of maximizing the value of the enterprise. This way of looking at financial analysis is appealing because it explicitly ties together the investment decisions with measures of firm performance. As such, financial managers and analysts may find this approach to firm performance analysis a useful complement to more traditional approaches. [20]

Financial Forecasting

Financial forecasting allows a firm to estimate the amount of additional financing it will require in an upcoming period. While it is possible to extrapolate trends into the future, this section presents an overview of the more precise percentage of sales financial forecasting process, with emphasis on the important role of pro forma financial statements. **Pro forma financial statements,** showing the results of some *assumed* event, rather than an *actual* event, are usually an integral part of a financial forecast. Pro forma statements and financial ratios can be used to forecast future financial performance.

Percentage of Sales Forecasting Method

The **percentage of sales forecasting method** permits a company to forecast the amount of financing it will need for a given increase in sales. This method is simple and can provide information useful in preparing pro forma financial statements and in estimating future funds needs. The method assumes that (1) present asset levels are optimal with respect to present sales; (2) most items on the balance sheet increase in proportion to sales increases; and (3) the firm's profit margin on sales (EAT/Sales) remains constant. The use of this method is illustrated with the following example of the Industrial Supply Company (ISC), a key MMC supplier.

It is extremely important to MMC that ISC be a reliable supplier. So, MMC has alerted ISC that MMC expects to increase sales and hence its purchases from ISC by 25 percent next year. ISC has checked with its other customers and has concluded that its own sales will increase by 25 percent overall, or by $3,750,000 next year to total $18,750,000. The present (20X6) ISC balance sheet and income statement are shown in Table 3.6.

One of management's primary concerns is the amount of funds (cash) needed to finance this sales growth. Until now, the firm has financed its growth by using both internally and externally generated funds. The firm has reinvested most of its past earnings into additional inventory. The firm has also used external financing in the form of short-term borrowings from its bank.

To determine the amount of additional financing necessary to reach the expected sales level, management has made the following observations about the firm's various assets and liabilities:

1. **Cash** Management feels that the company's cash balances are generally adequate for the present sales level and would have to increase proportionately as sales increase.

2. **Accounts Receivable** The firm's present average collection period is about 49 days. Management feels that the firm's present credit policies are appropriate for its type of business. Thus, they feel that the average collection period will remain approximately constant and that accounts receivable will increase proportionately as sales increase.

3. **Inventory** Management feels that the company's inventory is properly managed at present. Therefore, they feel inventory would have to increase proportionately for sales to increase.

Financial Forecasting
The projection and estimation of a firm's future financial statements.

Pro Forma Financial Statements
Financial statements that project the results of some *assumed* event, rather than an *actual* event.

Percentage of Sales Forecasting Method
A method of estimating the additional financing that will be needed to support a given future sales level.

---

[20] For a discussion of Canadian value-creating firms, see Vijay Jog, "Value Creation and the Credibility of Financial Reporting in Canada," *Canadian Investment Review* (Fall 2002): 12–20.

Table 3.6 Industrial Supply Company Financial Statements

Balance Sheet as of December 31, 20X6

Assets		Liabilities and Equity	
Cash	$ 500,000	Accounts payable	$1,500,000
Accounts receivable	2,000,000	Notes payable	1,000,000
Inventories	4,000,000	Total current liabilities	$2,500,000
Total current assets	$6,500,000	Long-term debt	500,000
Fixed assets, net	1,000,000	Shareholders' equity	4,500,000
Total assets	$7,500,000	Total liabilities and equity	$7,500,000

Income Statement for the Year Ended December 31, 20X6

Sales	$15,000,000
Expenses, including interest and taxes	14,250,000
Earnings after taxes	$ 750,000
Dividends paid	$ 250,000

Selected Financial Ratios

Current ratio	2.60 times
Debt ratio	40%
Return on stockholders' equity	16.7%
Net profit margin on sales (EAT/Sales)	5.0%

4. **Fixed Assets** Because the firm's fixed assets *are being used at nearly full capacity,* management feels that fixed assets will have to increase as sales grow. For financial planning purposes, management is willing to assume that the *net* fixed asset figure on the balance sheet will increase proportionately as sales increase.

5. **Accounts Payable** The firm now maintains good relations with its suppliers. As the company purchases more inventory, its accounts payable balance will increase proportionately as sales increase.

6. **Notes Payable and Long-Term Debt** Notes payable and long-term debt do not necessarily have a direct relationship to the sales level. For example, a portion of the firm's future cash flows may be used to pay off the present debt.

In summary, as the firm's sales increase, its assets will increase proportionately to support the new sales. In addition, the current liabilities that vary directly with sales, namely accounts payable, will also increase. The difference between the forecasted asset increase and the forecasted current liability increase is equal to the total financing needed (TFN) by the company. This relationship can be expressed in equation form as follows:

$$(3.25) \qquad \text{TFN} = \frac{A}{S}(\Delta S) - \frac{CL^*}{S}(\Delta S)$$

where A is the company's present level of assets *that vary proportionately with sales,* S is the company's present sales, CL^* is the company's present level of liabilities *that vary proportionately with sales* (e.g., accounts payable), and ΔS is the forecasted sales increase.[21]

A portion of the total financing needed can be generated internally from increased retained earnings (IRE). Specifically, the increased retained earnings generated during the time period when sales increase from S to S + ΔS can be expressed in equation form as follows:

---

[21] Current liabilities, such as accounts payable, that automatically expand (contract) as the volume of business increases (decreases) are often referred to as "spontaneous" sources of financing. Chapter 15 contains a more detailed discussion of short-term sources of funds.

$$(3.26) \qquad\qquad IRE = EAT - D$$

where EAT = Earnings After Tax, and D = Dividends.

The additional financing needed (AFN) can be calculated by subtracting the increased retained earnings from the total financing needed:

$$(3.27) \qquad AFN = \left[\frac{A}{S}(\Delta S) - \frac{CL^*}{S}(\Delta S) \right] - [EAT - D]$$

Referring back to the ISC example, the additional financing needed to support a sales increase of $3,750,000 up to the $18,750,000 level can now be calculated. Assume that management forecasts expenses to be $17,750,000 and EAT to be $1,000,000 during the coming year. Assume further that the firm plans to maintain its dividend payments at the same level in 20X7 as in 20X6. Substituting this data into Equation 3.27 yields

$$AFN = \left[\frac{\$7,500,000}{\$15,000,000}(\$3,750,000) - \frac{\$1,500,000}{\$15,000,000}(\$3,750,000) \right] -$$
$$[\$1,000,000 - \$250,000]$$
$$= \$750,000$$

The approximate amount of additional financing that will be needed to finance the forecasted growth in sales from $15,000,000 to $18,750,000 is $750,000.[22] Even though the financing will be needed gradually as sales increase, ISC management has to decide whether to (1) borrow on a short-term basis, (2) borrow on a long-term basis, (3) sell additional common shares, or (4) cut dividends. The factors that influence the debt versus equity decision are discussed in Chapter 12, the factors that influence the short-term versus long-term debt decision are discussed in Chapter 15, and the factors that influence the dividend decision are discussed in Chapter 14. As this example illustrates, *the investment, financing, and dividend decisions of the firm are interdependent.*

Table 3.7 shows ISC's pro forma financial statements for 20X7, *assuming* that all of the additional financing needed is in the form of short-term notes payable. Examination of the selected financial ratios in Tables 3.6 and 3.7 shows that this financing plan will increase return on shareholders' equity from 16.7 percent in 20X6 to 19.0 percent in 20X7. However, it also reduces the firm's current ratio (measure of liquidity) from 2.60 to 2.24 times and increases its debt ratio (measure of leverage) from 40 percent to 44 percent. ISC management would have to analyze these factors to determine the optimal way to obtain the $750,000 of additional financing needed. The percentage of sales forecasting method for calculating financing needs is a useful and convenient forecasting technique. However, as with all analytical techniques, the application of this method should be supplemented by any additional factors that are unique to the particular situation.

One such factor is *economies of scale.* Economies of scale may result in nonlinear relationships between sales and certain types of assets. In other words, the relationships may not be strictly proportional, as assumed in the model. For example, a 10 percent increase in sales may require only a 5 percent increase in fixed assets or inventories. Another factor in some industries is that capacity can be added only in *discrete* or *"lumpy" increments.* Once output reaches the capacity of an existing production facility, expansion requires building another facility. This causes fixed assets to increase in a stepwise manner as sales are increased, rather than increasing proportionately.

---

[22] The $750,000 figure assumes that none of the present notes payable or long-term debt will have to be repaid during the year. Note that the AFN calculation ignores additional interest or dividends paid on the AFN.

Table 3.7 Industrial Supply Company Pro Forma Financial Statements

Pro Forma Balance Sheet as of December 31, 20X7

Assets		Liabilities and Equity	
Cash	$ 625,000	Accounts payable	$1,875,000
Accounts receivable	2,500,000	Notes payable	1,750,000
Inventories	$5,000,000	Total current liabilities	$3,625,000
Total current assets	$8,125,000	Long-term debt	500,000
Fixed assets, net	$1,250,000	Shareholders' equity	5,250,000
Total assets	$9,375,000	Total liabilities and equity	$9,375,000

Pro Forma Income Statement for the Year Ending December 31, 20X7

Sales	$18,750,000
Expenses, including interest and taxes	17,750,000
Earnings after taxes	$ 1,000,000
Dividends	250,000
Retained earnings	$ 750,000

Selected Pro Forma Financial Ratios

Current ratio	2.24 times
Debt ratio	44%
Return on shareholders' equity	19.0%

Cash Flow Analysis

Foundation Concept

Traditional financial ratio analysis can be a useful tool to an analyst trying to evaluate a firm's performance. However, many of the key performance measures, such as return on sales, assets, and equity, rely on accounting income concepts. Accounting income is not the relevant source of value in a firm—cash flow is. Only cash can be spent. Accounting income, in contrast, does not reflect the actual cash inflows and outflows in a firm. Consequently, in this section we illustrate and define further the cash flow concept you encountered in Chapter 1, and introduce the cash flow statement.

The Cash Flow Concept

After-Tax Cash Flow (ATCF)
Earnings after tax plus noncash charges, such as depreciation and future tax liabilities.

Earlier we encountered the income statement for MMC (Table 3.2). The income statement can be modified to provide a quick measure of the **after-tax cash flow** (ATCF) that is available from current operations to make capital expenditures, pay dividends, and repay debt. Accordingly, the ATCF is generally a more important number than the net income (EAT) figure. One shortcoming of the ATCF is that it does not consider additional cash tied up in (or released from) net working capital. ATCF adds back noncash charges to EAT.

$$(3.28) \qquad \text{ATCF} = \text{EAT} + \text{Noncash charges}$$

The most common examples of noncash charges are depreciation and future tax liabilities (formerly called deferred taxes).

Depreciation *Depreciation* is defined as the systematic allocation of the cost of an asset over more than one year. The annual depreciation expense recorded for a particular asset is an allocation of its original cost and does not represent a cash outlay. As a result, a firm's annual depreciation expense is added to earnings after taxes in calculating after-tax cash flow. For example, in 2001, Magna International had earnings after taxes

Financial Forecasting:
Sustainable Growth and Ownership Control

Sustainable growth rate
The rate at which a firm can grow without being required to sell more equity securities.

Small, closely held firms often find it difficult to sell new shares. Furthermore, even if the owners could find new shareholders, the owners may be reluctant to sell more shares because of worries about losing control of the firm. Thus, an important question for such entrepreneurs is: How fast can the firm grow without having to sell new shares? To find this **sustainable growth rate** (g^*), assume that sales (S) as well as all assets (A) grow at this rate (g^*) and the firm's net profit margin ratio (NPM), debt-to-equity ratio (D/E), and retention rate (r) (additions to retained earnings/EAT) remain constant.

The sustainable growth rate (g^*) is the solution to Equation 3N.1:

(3N.1)   Outside equity financing = 0 = Increase in total assets
− Additions to retained earnings − Increase in total liabilities

$$= Ag^* - [NPM \times S \times r(1 + g^*)] - [NPM \times S \times r(1 + g^*)\, D/E]$$

Solving Equation 3N.1 for g^* and then doing some algebraic rearranging yields

(3N.2) $$g^* = [ROE \times r]/[1 - (ROE \times r)]$$

where ROE is return on equity.

If a firm has no debt, the sustainable growth formula simplifies to

(3N.3) $$g^*_{\text{no debt}} = [ROI \times r]/[1 - (ROI \times r)]$$

where ROI = Earnings after taxes/Total assets.

This is because ROI = ROE when a firm has no debt. Sometimes this simplified expression has been used even for firms with debt and referred to as the *internal growth rate* that requires *no* external financing. In this case, the firm's debt-to-equity ratio would be declining over time. It is hard to imagine that a firm's profit margin would remain constant (a model assumption) as interest charges become a declining percentage of sales. Hence, we recommend using this simplified formula only for firms with no debt.

Below are the simplified balance sheet and income statement for 20X6 of the LaGrange Furniture Store, a small family-owned business.

LaGrange Furniture Store Balance Sheet for the Year Ended December 31, 20X6
(in Thousands of Dollars)

Assets		Liabilities and Equity	
Current assets	$300	Current liabilities	$200
Net fixed assets	600	Long-term debt	100
		Shareholders' equity	600
Total assets	$900	Total liabilities and equity	$900

LaGrange Furniture Store Income Statement for the Year Ended December 31, 20X6
(in Thousands of Dollars)

Sales	$1,200
Expenses*	1,020
Earnings after taxes	$ 180
Dividends	$ 60
Additions to retained earnings	$ 120

* Expenses include cost of sales, selling and administrative expenses, interest expense, depreciation, and taxes.

We can calculate the firm's return on shareholders' equity and retention rate from its balance sheet and income statement as

$$\text{ROE} = \$180{,}000/\$600{,}000 = 0.30 \text{ or } 30\% \text{ and } r = \$120{,}000/\$180{,}000 = \tfrac{2}{3}$$

Substituting into Equation 3N.2 yields the firm's sustainable growth rate:

$$g^* = [0.30 \times (\tfrac{2}{3})]/[1 - \{0.30 \times (\tfrac{2}{3})\}] = 0.20/.80 = 0.25 \text{ or } 25\%$$

Note also that the net profit margin ratio and debt-to-equity ratio for this firm are

$$\text{NPM} = \$180{,}000/\$1{,}200{,}000 = 0.15 \text{ or } 15\%$$

$$\text{D/E} = (\$200{,}000 + \$100{,}000)/\$600{,}000 = 0.50$$

To see that g^* is the sustainable growth rate, examine the firm's pro forma balance sheet and income statements for 20X7. These statements were generated by growing all balance sheet and income statement items by the firm's sustainable growth rate of 25%.

LaGrange Furniture Store Balance Sheet for the Year Ended December 31, 20X7
(in Thousands of Dollars)

Assets		Liabilities and Equity	
Current assets	$ 375	Current liabilities	$ 250
Net fixed assets	750	Long-term debt	125
		Shareholders' equity	750
Total assets	$1,125	Total liabilities and equity	$1,125

LaGrange Furniture Store Income Statement For the Year Ended December 31, 20X7
(in Thousands of Dollars)

Sales	$1,500
Expenses*	1,275
Earnings after taxes	$ 225
Dividends	$ 75
Additions to retained earnings	$ 150

*Expenses include cost of sales, selling and administrative expenses, interest expense, depreciation, and taxes.

cont'd

Clearly, the values of NPM = $225,000/$1,500,000 = 0.15, D/E = ($250,000 + $125,000) /$750,000 = 0.50, and r = $150,000/$225,000 = 2/3 have remained constant. Furthermore, the additions to retained earnings of $150,000 for 20X7 matches the *change* in share-holders' equity of ($750,000 – $600,000) = $150,000 between the years 20X7 and 20X6.

If the firm tried to grow at any rate greater than this sustainable growth rate, it would find that the required change in shareholders' equity would exceed the additions to retained earnings. In other words, it would need to sell some additional common shares to obtain outside equity.

For more information on Magna see **www.magna.com**

of US$580 million. Its 2001 depreciation expense of US$399 million must be added to the earnings after taxes amount in calculating Magna's 2001 ATCF.[23]

Future Tax Liabilities   After-tax cash flow also differs from earnings after taxes by the amount of a company's *future tax liabilities (deferred taxes)*. In accordance with gen-erally accepted accounting principles, a firm usually reports a different income tax expense amount to its shareholders than it actually pays in cash during that year. Frequently, the income tax amount shown on the firm's income statement is larger than the income tax amount paid. The difference between the tax amount reported to share-holders and the cash amount actually paid is referred to as a *future tax liability (deferred tax)* because it is due to be paid by the firm sometime in the future.

Future tax liabilities generally occur because of temporary differences in the stated amounts of assets and liabilities *for financial reporting purposes* and for tax purposes. Specifically, some of the more common differences between financial reporting and tax methods relate to accounting for depreciation, inventories, and pensions. Many compa-nies use the straight-line depreciation method to calculate the income they report to their shareholders and an accelerated depreciation method to calculate taxable income. This practice usually results in the taxes currently owed being less than they would be if the firm used straight-line depreciation methods for tax purposes. The company effec-tively can continue to defer payment of these taxes as long as it continues to purchase a sufficient amount of new fixed assets. When it ceases purchasing such assets or pur-chases fewer of them, it will have to pay the future tax liabilities.

Thus, if a firm's only noncash charges are depreciation and future tax liabilities, the after-tax cash flow can be calculated using Equation 3.29, as follows:

(3.29)   ATCF = Earnings after taxes + Depreciation + Future tax liabilities

Table 3.8 derives ATCF for MMC by taking earnings after tax from MMC's publicly reported income statement and adding back noncash charges: MMC has noncash charges of $2,000 ($1,900 from depreciation and $100 from future tax liabilities). Hence, for MMC the ATCF is

$$ATCF = \$5,016 + \$1,900 + \$100$$
$$= \$7,016$$

The Cash Flow Statement
The cash flow statement, together with the balance sheet and the income statement, constitute a major portion of a firm's financial statements. The *cash flow statement*

---

[23] Magna, *Annual Report 2001* (Aurora, ON: Magna, 2002): 43.

Table 3.8	Maple Manufacturing Company: After-Tax Cash Flow Calculation (in Thousands of Dollars) for the Year Ended December 31, 20X6	
Net sales		$112,760
Cost of sales		85,300
Gross margin		$ 27,460
Operating expenses		15,940
Earnings before interest and taxes (EBIT)		$ 11,520
Interest charges		3,160
Earnings before taxes (EBT)		$ 8,360
Federal and provincial income taxes at a combined 40% rate		3,344
Earnings after taxes (EAT) and available for common shareholders		$ 5,016
Plus noncash expenses		
Depreciation		1,900
Deferred income taxes		100
After-tax cash flow (ATCF)		$ 7,016

shows the effects of a firm's *operating, investing,* and *financing* activities on its cash balance. The principal purpose of the cash flow statement is to provide relevant information about a company's cash receipts and cash payments during a particular accounting period. The cash flow statement provides a more complete indication of the sources (and the uses) of a firm's cash resources over time.

The procedures for preparing the cash flow statement are presented in CICA *Handbook* Section 1540. It requires companies to include a cash flow statement when issuing a complete set of financial statements for annual reports. It encourages companies to prepare their cash flow statements using the *direct* method of presenting cash flows from operating activities.

Cash Flow Statement: Direct Method Table 3.9 shows an example of a cash flow statement using the direct method for the Summit Furniture Company (SFC), a recently acquired subsidiary of MMC. During the year, SFC's "cash flows from operating activities" totalled $14,600 ($142,000 cash received from customers, plus $600 of interest received, less $120,000 paid to suppliers and employees, less $2,000 interest paid, less $6,000 of income taxes paid). SFC's investing activities used net cash of $18,000. The firm spent $19,000 on capital expenditures and received $1,000 in proceeds from the sale of an asset. During the year the net cash provided by financing activities equalled $3,600. The $3,600 is calculated as the difference between financing activities that require cash outflows and those that result in cash inflows. SFC had financing cash outflows totalling $3,100 ($2,600 repayment of long-term debt and $500 of dividends paid out) and financing cash inflows totalling $6,700 (bank borrowing of $1,000 plus proceeds from the issuance of long-term debt of $4,000 plus proceeds from the issuance of common shares of $1,700). The overall change in cash is calculated as follows:

(3.30) Net cash increase (decrease) = Net cash provided (used) by operating activities

+ Net cash provided (used) by investing activities

+ Net cash provided (used) by financing activities

Net cash increase (decrease) = $14,600 + $18,000 + $3,600

= $200

Table 3.9	Summit Furniture Company Cash Flow Statement for the Year Ended December 31, 20X6

Increase (Decrease) in Cash and Cash Equivalents* (000)

Cash Flows from Operating Activities:		
Cash received from customers	$ 142,000	
Cash paid to suppliers and employees	(120,000)	
Interest received	600	
Interest paid (net of amount capitalized)	(2,000)	
Income taxes paid	(6,000)	
Net cash provided (used) by operating activities		$14,600
Cash Flows from Investing Activities:		
Proceeds from sale of asset	1,000	
Capital expenditures	(19,000)	
Net cash provided (used) by investing activities		(18,000)
Cash Flows from Financing Activities:		
Net borrowings under bank line-of-credit agreement	1,000	
Repayments of long-term debt	(2,600)	
Proceeds from issuance of long-term debt	4,000	
Proceeds from issuance of common shares	1,700	
Dividends paid	(500)	
Net cash provided (used) by financing activities		3,600
Net Increase (Decrease) in Cash and Cash Equivalents		200
Cash and Cash Equivalents at Beginning of Year		5,000
Cash and Cash Equivalents at End of Year		$ 5,200

*Cash and cash equivalents include currency on hand, bank deposits and similar accounts, and short-term (maturities less than three months), highly liquid investments.

The cash flow statement presented in Table 3.9 provides SFC's management, investors, and creditors with a summary of its cash flows for the year. In particular, SFC's operations provided net cash of $14,600. However, the firm used a total of $18,000 in its investing activities. As a result, if SFC wanted to keep its cash balance at about $5,000, the firm's financing activities would have to provide $3,400 of net cash ($18,000 − $14,600). In fact, SFC's financing activities actually did provide $3,600, causing the ending cash balance to be $5,200, or $200 above the beginning $5,000.

Cash Flow Statement: Indirect Method   Some companies use the indirect, or reconciliation, method to report the net cash flow from operating activities. The *indirect method* involves adjusting net income to reconcile it to net cash flow from operating activities plus adjusting net income from the accrual method (required by GAAP) to the cash amount by showing increases and decreases in its various current asset and liability accounts. This method gives the same result as the direct method. As previously noted, CICA *Handbook* Section 1540 encourages companies to use the direct method.

Cash Budgeting

Even though the cash flow statement is a useful tool that can provide insights regarding financing needs, *cash budgets* can estimate more precisely *both* the *amount* of financing needed by a firm and the *timing* of those financing needs. Cash budgeting plays an important role in the firm's financial forecasting process. Effective cash budgeting can help management identify potential cash flow problems. Usually, cash flow problems are easier to solve when they are anticipated. In addition to a detailed discussion of cash budgets, this section contains a brief overview of budgeting.

An Overview of Budgeting   *Budgets* are simply pro forma financial statements that show how the firm's cash will be spent on labour, materials, and capital goods and indicate how cash will be obtained.

Budgets are used to *plan, coordinate,* and *control* a firm's operations. They are essential to *planning* because they represent the company's objectives in numerical terms, such as dollars of sales, units of production, pounds of raw materials, and dollars of financing required from the capital markets. Once a firm has made financial plans, it refers to the budgets when *coordinating* its overall activities. For example, the purchasing department examines the budgets when deciding how best to integrate purchasing activities with monthly production requirements to ensure the availability of sufficient raw materials. The production and marketing departments then work together to guarantee that sufficient finished goods inventories are on hand. Finally, the finance department coordinates the company's need for funds with the requirements of the purchasing, production, and marketing departments.

The projected figures in a firm's budgets are also used as a *control* device against which actual figures are compared; this ensures that the various departments and divisions are functioning properly and working together toward the objectives developed in the planning phase.

A firm's budgets are based on the *assumption* of certain future sales and production levels. As pro forma financial statements, budgets predict *what* a company's financial statements will look like *if* specific plans are realized.

Cash Budget

A projection of a firm's cash receipts and disbursements over some future time period.

Cash Budgets   A **cash budget** is the projection of a firm's cash receipts and disbursements over some future period of time. Typically, a cash budget is prepared on an annual basis and subdivided into months. However, more detailed and refined cash budgeting is done on a weekly or even daily basis by some companies that employ good ongoing cash management procedures.

Cash budgets are useful in determining the amount of short-term funds the firm may need to borrow to cover any projected cash shortages. Short-term borrowed funds are almost always easier to obtain when the need for them is anticipated. In addition to planning for any cash shortages, the cash budget also indicates the periods when the firm may have cash surpluses. This information is helpful in managing the firm's marketable securities investments. Thus, the cash budget is one of the most important short-range financial forecasting tools. In addition, cash budgets can be useful for control and coordination purposes.

To explore actual cash budgeting procedures, the MMC Central Division will be examined. Table 3.10 illustrates a cash budget worksheet for that division for the first quarter of 20X6. Table 3.11 is an actual cash budget for the time period.

The first step in cash budget preparation is the estimation of cash receipts, which results directly from the sales forecast. MMC has found that, on the average, about 10 percent of total sales in any given month are cash sales. The remaining 90 percent are credit sales.[24]

About 30 percent of the company's credit sales are collected during the month in which the sale is made, and all of the remaining 70 percent are collected during the following month. Thus, the total accounts receivable the company can expect to collect during January are equal to 70 percent of the forecasted December credit sales plus 30 percent of the forecasted January credit sales.

$$(0.70 \times \$486,000) + (0.30 \times \$450,000) = \$340,200 + \$135,000$$
$$= \$475,200$$

The forecasted cash receipts for February and March are calculated the same way.

---

[24] Estimated December credit sales are 90 percent of estimated December sales. That is, $0.90 \times \$540,000 = \$486,000$.

Chapter 3   Evaluating and Forecasting Financial Performance

Table 3.10 Cash Budget Worksheet—Maple Manufacturing Company

Maple Manufacturing Company—Central Division
Cash Budget Worksheet
First Quarter, 20X6

	December	January	February	March
Budget of Receipts from Sales				
Estimated sales	$540,000	$500,000	$550,000	$620,000
Estimated credit sales	486,000	450,000	495,000	558,000
Estimated receipts:				
Cash sales		$ 50,000	$ 55,000	$ 62,000
Collections of accounts receivable:				
70% of last month's credit sales		$340,200	$315,000	$346,500
30% of current month's credit sales		135,000	148,500	167,400
Total accounts receivable collections		$475,200	$463,500	$513,900
Budget of Payments for Purchases				
Estimated purchases*	$275,000	$302,500	$341,000	
Estimated payments of accounts payable†		$275,000	$302,500	$341,000

*Purchases are estimated at 55 percent of next month's sales.
†Payments are estimated to lag purchases by one month.

Table 3.11 Cash Budget—Maple Manufacturing Company

Maple Manufacturing Company—Central Division
Cash Budget*
First Quarter, 20X6

	December	January	February	March
Sales	$540,000	$500,000	$550,000	$620,000
Projected cash balance, beginning of month		$ 61,000	$ 50,700	$ 50,000
Receipts:				
Cash sales		50,000	55,000	62,000
Collection of accounts receivable		475,200	463,500	513,900
Total cash available		$586,200	$569,200	$625,900
Disbursements:				
Payment of accounts payable		$275,000	$302,500	$341,000
Wages and salaries		158,000	154,500	145,500
Rent		17,000	17,000	17,000
Other expenses		4,500	7,000	8,000
Taxes		81,000	—	—
Dividends on common shares		—	—	30,000
Purchase of new equipment (capital budget)		—	70,000	—
Total disbursements		$535,500	$551,000	$541,500
Excess of available cash over disbursements		$ 50,700	$ 18,200	$ 84,400
Cash loans needed to maintain balance of $50,000		—	31,800	—
Loan repayment		—	—	(31,800)
Projected cash balance, end of month		$ 50,700	$ 50,000	$ 52,600

*Prepared December 15, 20X5.

The next step in cash budgeting is the scheduling of *disbursements,* or payments the firm must make to others. Many of these items remain relatively constant from month to month and thus are relatively easy to budget. Others, however, such as the payment of accounts payable for purchases of merchandise, raw materials, and supplies, are more complicated. The key determinants of a firm's schedule of payables are the level of purchases per period and the terms given by suppliers.

Frequently, accounts payable become due before goods are sold and cash is received; this can lead to temporary cash shortages. In fact, many companies experience cash difficulties immediately after a good sales period. Inventories are depleted and must be replenished, but cash is low because collections from the good sales period have not yet been received. MMC's purchases generally are estimated to be 55 percent of next month's sales. This percentage is based on the company's past experience and can vary considerably among industries and companies. (Note that depreciation does not appear as a disbursement in the cash budget, because it is a noncash charge.)

After cash receipts and disbursements have been estimated, the next step in the cash budgeting process is the determination of a desired cash balance at the beginning of each month. This minimum cash balance figure is usually a function of several factors, depending on the nature of the business. Table 3.11 lists the firm's projected cash balances for the beginnings of January, February, and March. Note that the projected cash balance at the *beginning* of each month is equal to the projected cash balance at the *end* of the previous month. In this example, $50,000 is assumed to be the most appropriate minimum cash balance for the first quarter of 20X6.[25]

Table 3.11 shows that the firm expects to need a short-term loan of $31,800 in February to maintain a minimum cash balance of $50,000 because the company expects a decrease in the collection of accounts receivable in February, brought about by slightly lower than normal sales expected in January. In addition, the company plans to purchase new equipment in February, which will cost $70,000. This also contributes to the expected need for a short-term loan.

If the company planned to spend much more money than this on new equipment, it might decide to secure longer-term financing at this time, instead of the short-term loan. The proceeds from longer-term financing could be budgeted as a separate cash receipt in February, permitting the company to separate short-term and long-term cash needs.

After projecting the need for a short-term loan in February, the cash budget in Table 3.11 shows that the loan can probably be paid at the end of March because the available cash balance of $84,400 will still be above $50,000 after repayment of $31,800. The company has indicated the repayment on the cash budget by adding another side caption: Loan repayment.[26]

Most companies follow this same general format for cash budgeting, yet few companies use *exactly* the same format. A company's actual cash budgeting system will depend on its business and its accounting procedures. Computerized financial spreadsheet models are useful in constructing and analyzing cash budgets.

Pro Forma Cash Flow Statement

The cash flow statement can also be used to determine how much additional financing a firm will need in some future period. Suppose SFC, whose cash flow statement for 20X6 was shown earlier in Table 3.9, is preparing a cash flow forecast for 20X7. In the fall of 20X6, the firm's management tentatively decides to spend $25,000 in 20X7 for capital expenditures. Also, SFC's financial manager estimates that the firm's 20X7

---

[25] Cash management is discussed further in Chapter 16.

[26] Note that the cash budget does not include any interest payments on this loan (or interest earned on investments of excess cash). These items generally have a relatively small impact on cash flows. However, they can be added to the cash budget if necessary.

operating activities will *provide* approximately $21,000 of net cash. This forecast is detailed in MMC's pro forma cash flow statement, which is shown in Table 3.12.

Next, SFC's financial manager must estimate whether the firm's financing activities will need to provide cash in order to maintain its desired cash balance. Because the net cash expected to be *used* by investing activities is greater than the net cash expected to be *provided* by operating activities, the firm's financing activities will need to *provide* net cash to maintain the present cash balance. In addition, SFC feels that its cash balance needs to be increased by approximately $1,500. As a result, SFC's financing activities in 20X7 must *provide* net cash of $5,500 (–$21,000 + $25,000 + $1,500). The pro forma cash flow statement details how SFC expects to achieve $5,500 of net cash provided by financing activities.

Computerized Financial Forecasting and Planning Models

In recent years, many firms have spent considerable amounts of time and money developing models to represent various aspects of their financial planning process, as well as cash flow forecasting. Today, these representations are usually computerized and are generally called **financial planning models.** A detailed discussion of these models is beyond the scope of this text because it requires a familiarity with a number of quantitative techniques, such as regression analysis and linear programming—topics not covered here. A brief general introduction to the topic is provided for informational purposes, however.

Financial planning models are often classified according to whether they are *deterministic* or *probabilistic* and whether they attempt to *optimize* (that is, achieve the most desirable level of) the value of some objective function, such as net income or share price.

Financial Planning Model
A computerized representation of some aspect of a firm's financial planning process.

Table 3.12	Pro Forma Cash Flow Statement for the Year Ending December 31, 20X7—Summit Furniture Company	
Increase (Decrease) in Cash and Cash Equivalents* (000)		
Cash Flows Expected from Operating Activities:		
Cash received from customers	$170,000	
Cash paid to suppliers and employees	(140,000)	
Interest received	500	
Interest paid (net of amount capitalized)	(2,500)	
Income taxes paid	(7,000)	
Expected net cash provided (used) by operating activities		$21,000
Cash Flows Expected from Investing Activities:		
Proceeds from sale of assets	—	
Capital expenditures	(25,000)	
Expected net cash provided (used) by investing activities		(25,000)
Cash Flows Expected from Financing Activities:		
Net borrowings under bank line-of-credit agreement	2,000	
Repayment of long-term debt	(3,000)	
Proceeds from issuance of long-term debt	7,000	
Proceeds from issuance of common shares	—	
Dividends paid	(500)	
Expected net cash provided (used) by financing activities		5,500
Expected Net Increase (Decrease) in Cash and Cash Equivalents		1,500
Cash and Cash Equivalents at Beginning of Year		5,200
Expected Cash and Cash Equivalents at End of Year		$ 6,700

*Cash and cash equivalents include currency on hand, bank deposits and similar accounts, and short-term (maturities less than three months), highly liquid investments.

Deterministic Model
A financial planning model that projects single-number estimates of a financial variable or variables without specifying their probability of occurrence.

Sensitivity Analysis
A method of analysis in which a financial planning model is rerun to determine the effect on the output variable(s) (for example, profit) of given changes in the input variable(s) (for example, sales). Sensitivity analysis is sometimes called *what-if* analysis.

Scenario Analysis
A procedure used to evaluate the change in some objective, such as net present value, to simultaneous changes in several variables influencing that objective, such as price, unit sales volume, and operating costs.

Probabilistic Model
A financial planning model that uses probability distributions as inputs and generates a probability distribution for financial variables as output.

Optimization Model
A financial planning model that determines the values of financial decision variables that maximize (or minimize) some objective function such as profits (or costs).

A **deterministic model** gives a single-number forecast of a financial variable or variables without stating anything about its probability of occurrence. An example of a deterministic model is a computerized representation of a firm's operating budget, or a *budget simulator.* Companies that employ budget simulators enter estimated future revenues and expenses into the computer and receive as output an estimate of various financial variables, such as net income and earnings per share. The model tells the firm nothing about the chances of achieving these estimates, nor does it indicate whether the company will be able to manage its resources in such a way as to attain higher levels of these variables.

The main advantage of deterministic models is that they allow the user to perform *sensitivity analyses* quickly and easily. A **sensitivity analysis** essentially consists of rerunning the model to determine the effect on the output variables of changes in the input variables. For example, a firm may want to know *what* its net income will be *if* it discontinues some product line. Thus, sensitivity analysis is also called *what-if* analysis.

Some companies prepare different budgets to reflect different assumptions about the type of year they expect to have. For instance, a firm may compile three separate budgets to reflect *pessimistic, realistic,* and *optimistic* assumptions about the coming year. Whereas these **scenario analysis** models are essentially deterministic, they represent a first step toward the use of probabilistic models.

Probabilistic models are becoming increasingly popular because they often provide financial decision makers with more useful information than other models. Whereas deterministic models yield single-point estimates, probabilistic models yield more general probability distributions using simulation. To illustrate, suppose a firm is planning to build a new plant. Instead of estimating a single sales figure, the firm's planners might estimate a 25 percent chance that the firm's sales will be $2 million, a 50 percent chance that they will be $3 million, and a 25 percent chance that they will be $4 million. The use of a probabilistic planning model yields output in the form of a probability distribution, which gives the firm's planners more useful information than a deterministic model would. In the case of complex probabilistic models, more input is necessary.[27]

Optimization models determine the values of financial decision variables that optimize (that is, maximize or minimize) some objective function such as profits or costs. For example, consider an oil refinery whose capacity and production costs are known. By combining these known figures with estimates of the sales prices for gasoline and heating fuel, it is possible, with the use of an optimization model, to specify what output product mix will achieve an optimal level of operating income. Optimization models are not used widely in finance, even though various applications have been proposed in the financial literature.

---

[27] Sensitivity analysis, scenario analysis, and simulation are further discussed in Chapter 11 in the context of capital budgeting.

After studying this chapter, you should now be much more aware of the possible problems in the interpretation of financial statements and the ratios that are based on the numbers in those statements. In evaluating the performance of the firm that you work for, or the firm that you intend to work for, the quality of earnings is very important. Economic value added is a useful indicator of whether or not the firm is adding value to shareholders' wealth. It is also important to be aware of changes to the generally accepted accounting principles that are announced from time to time.

Summary

- Financial ratios fall into six categories:
  1. *Liquidity ratios,* which measure a firm's ability to meet its maturing obligations
  2. *Asset management ratios,* which measure how efficiently a firm is using resources to generate sales
  3. *Financial leverage management ratios,* which indicate a firm's capacity to meet short- and long-term debt obligations
  4. *Profitability ratios,* which measure the firm's ability to generate profits on sales, assets, and owners' investment
  5. *Market-based ratios,* which measure the market's (investors') perceptions of a firm's performance and risk
  6. *Dividend policy ratios,* which indicate the dividend practices of a firm

- *Common-size financial statements,* which express financial items in percentages, are helpful in detecting and monitoring financial trends.

- *Trend analysis* introduces the element of time into financial ratio analysis. It gives the analyst a more dynamic view of a company's situation than does a pure comparative financial ratio analysis alone.

- The DuPont analysis relationship of the return on investment (ROI) to *margin* and *turnover* can be used to determine if one or both are deficient in contributing to the profitability of a firm.

- To gain further insight into the relative financial position of a firm, the analyst must compare the financial ratios with *industry averages.* The more diversified the firm, the more difficult it will be to make such a comparison.

- Financial statements of multinational firms are influenced by fluctuating foreign exchange rates.

- The *market value added* concept is the market's assessment of the *accumulated* value created from a firm's past and projected investment projects.

- *Economic value added* is a *yearly* measure of the operating performance of a firm, considering investor return requirements.

- After-tax cash flow is equal to earnings after tax plus noncash charges. Depreciation and future tax liabilities are examples of noncash charges.

- Financial forecasting involves the projection and estimation of a firm's future cash needs. The percentage of sales method, cash flow statement, cash budgets, and computerized financial planning models can be used in financial forecasting.

- The *percentage of sales* method can be used to estimate the amount of additional financing that will be needed to support a given future sales level.

- The *cash flow statement* is a major financial statement showing the effects of a firm's operating, investing, and financing activities on its cash balance. Pro forma cash flow statements can be used to forecast additional financing that a firm may need. *Pro forma financial statements* show the results of some *assumed* rather than *actual* events.

- *Cash budgets* are projections of cash receipts and disbursements over some future time period. The steps involved in preparing a cash budget include
  1. Estimating cash receipts based on historical data about the collection of accounts receivable
  2. Scheduling disbursements
  3. Determining a minimum cash balance
  4. Calculating the amount of loans required to cover any cash shortages

- A *financial planning model* is a computerized representation of some aspect of a firm's financial planning process. Financial planning models are usually classified according to whether they are *deterministic* or *probabilistic* and whether they seek to *optimize* the value of some objective function.

Questions and Topics for Discussion

1. What are the primary limitations of ratio analysis as a technique of financial statement analysis?

2. What is the major limitation of the current ratio as a measure of a firm's liquidity? How may this limitation be overcome?

3. What problems may be indicated by an average collection period that is substantially above or below the industry average?

4. What problems may be indicated by an inventory turnover ratio that is substantially above or below the industry average?

5. What factors limit the use of the fixed-asset turnover ratio in comparative analyses?

6. What are the three most important determinants of a firm's return on shareholders' equity?

7. What specific effects can the use of alternative accounting procedures have on the validity of comparative financial analyses?

8. How can inflation affect the comparability of financial ratios between firms?

9. What is the relationship between a firm's P/E multiple and that firm's risk and growth potential?

10. Discuss the general factors that influence the quality of a company's reported earnings and its balance sheet.

11. Why would you anticipate a lower P/E ratio for a typical natural gas utility than for a computer technology firm, such as MDG Computers?

12. Recently, many large corporations, such as BCE, have written off large amounts of their nonperforming (or poorly performing) assets as they have shrunk their operations. What is the impact of these asset write-offs on the future return on assets, future return on common equity, and future financial leverage ratios? What impact would you expect these write-offs to have on the market value of the firm's equity securities? Why?

13. The Western Farmers Bank recently has been earning an above-average (compared to the overall banking industry) return on total assets of 1.50 percent. The bank's return on common equity is only 12 percent, compared with an industry average of 15 percent.

a. What reasons can you give for the bank's low return on common equity?

b. What impact do you think this performance by the bank is having on the value of its debt and equity securities?

14. What are *future tax liabilities*, and how do they come into being?

15. What is the relationship between EVA and MVA?

16. What are *pro forma financial statements*?

17. What is the *percentage of sales forecasting method*? What are some of the limitations of which financial analysts should be aware in applying this method?

18. What is a *cash budget*? What are the usual steps involved in preparing a cash budget?

19. Illustrate how the cash flow statement can be used as a financial planning technique.

20. Explain the difference between deterministic and probabilistic financial planning models.

Self-Test Problems

The following data for the Fremont Corporation are to be used in the first six self-test problems.

Fremont Corporation Balance Sheet ($000)			
Assets		**Liabilities and Stockholders' Equity**	
Cash	$ 1,500	Accounts payable	$12,500
Marketable securities	2,500	Notes payable	12,500
Accounts receivable	15,000	Total current liabilities	$25,000
Inventory	33,000	Long-term debt	22,000
Total current assets	$52,000	Total liabilities	$47,000
Fixed assets (net)	35,000	Common shares	23,000
Total assets	$87,000	Retained earnings	17,000
		Total shareholders' equity	$40,000
		Total liabilities and shareholders' equity	$87,000

Fremont Corporation Income Statement ($000)	
Sales (all on credit)	$130,000
Cost of sales	103,000
Gross margin	$ 27,000
Operating expenses*	16,000
Earnings before interest and taxes	$ 11,000
Interest expense	3,000
Earnings before taxes	$ 8,000
Income tax	3,000
Earnings after taxes	$ 5,000

*Includes $200 (000) in lease payments.

Other Information	
Share price	$9.50
Book value/share	$8.00
Number of shares	5,000 (000)

ST1. Calculate the following liquidity ratios:

a. Current ratio

b. Quick ratio

ST2. Calculate the following asset management ratios:

    a. Average collection period

    b. Inventory turnover

    c. Fixed asset turnover

    d. Total asset turnover

ST3. Calculate the following financial leverage management ratios:

    a. Debt ratio

    b. Debt-to-equity ratio

    c. Times interest earned ratio

    d. Fixed-charge coverage ratio

ST4. Calculate the following profitability ratios:

    a. Gross profit margin

    b. Net profit margin

    c. Return on investment

    d. Return on total equity

ST5. Calculate the following market-based ratios:

    a. Price-to-earnings ratio

    b. Market price-to-book value ratio

ST6. Express the return on total equity ratio as a function of the net profit margin, total asset turnover, and equity multiplier ratios.

ST7. Janjic Properties Ltd. had gross fixed assets of $1,000 at the end of 20X8. By the end of 20X9, these had grown to $1,100. Accumulated depreciation at the end of 20X8 was $500, and it was $575 at the end of 20X9. The firm has no interest expenses. The firm expected sales during 20X9 to total $500. Operating expenses (exclusive of depreciation) were forecasted to be $125. The firm's marginal tax rate is 40 percent.

    a. What was the firm's 20X9 depreciation expense?

    b. What were the firm's 20X9 earnings after taxes (EAT)?

    c. What was the firm's 20X9 after-tax cash flow using Equation 3.25?

    d. Show that EAT less the increase in *net* fixed assets is equivalent to after-tax cash flow less the increase in *gross* fixed assets.

ST8. Laurentian Products Ltd. has current sales of $60 million. Sales are expected to grow to $80 million next year. The firm currently has accounts receivable of $9 million, inventories of $15 million, and net fixed assets of $21 million. These assets are expected to grow at the same rate as sales over the next year. Accounts payable are expected to increase from their current level of $15 million to a new level of $19 million next year. The firm wants to increase its cash balance at the end of next year by $3 million over its current cash balance. Earnings after taxes next year are forecasted to be $12 million. The firm plans to pay a $2 million dividend. The firm's marginal tax rate is 40 percent.

    How much external financing is required next year by the firm?

ST9. Use the percentage of sales forecasting method to compute the additional financing needed by Lambrechts Specialty Shoppes, Ltd. if sales are expected to increase from a current level of $20 million to a new level of $25 million over the coming year. The firm expects earnings after taxes to equal $1 million over the next year (2005). The firm intends to pay a $300,000 dividend next year. The current-year balance sheet is as follows:

Lambrechts Specialty Shoppes, Ltd. Balance Sheet as of December 31, 2004			
Cash	$ 1,000,000	Accounts payable	$ 3,000,000
Accounts receivable	1,500,000	Notes payable	3,000,000
Inventories	6,000,000	Long-term debt	2,000,000
Net fixed assets	3,000,000	Shareholders' equity	3,500,000
Total assets	$11,500,000	Total liabilities and equity	$11,500,000

All assets, except cash, are expected to vary proportionately with sales. Of total liabilities and equity, only accounts payable is expected to vary proportionately with sales.

Problems*

BASIC

1. Vanier Press, Ltd. has annual credit sales of $1,600,000 and a gross profit margin of 35%.
   a. If the firm wishes to maintain an average collection period of 50 days, what level of accounts receivable should it carry? (Assume a 365-day year.)
   b. The inventory turnover for this industry averages six times. If all of the firm's sales are on credit, what average level of inventory should the firm maintain to achieve the same inventory turnover figure as the industry?

2. Pacifica Fixtures Ltd. lists the following accounts as part of its balance sheet:

Total assets	$10,000,000
Accounts payable	2,000,000
Notes payable (8%)	1,000,000
Bonds (10%)	3,000,000
Common shares	1,500,000
Retained earnings	2,500,000
Total liabilities and shareholders' equity	$10,000,000

   Compute the return on shareholders' equity if the firm has sales of $20 million and the following net profit margin:
   a. 3%
   b. 5%

3. Luba Industries Ltd. had sales in 20X4 of $40 million, 20% of which were cash. If the firm normally carries 45 days of credit sales in accounts receivable, what are its average accounts receivable balances? (Assume a 365-day year.)

4. Waterton Oil Company had a return on shareholders' equity of 18% during 20X4. Its total asset turnover was 1.0 times, and its equity multiplier was 2.0 times. Calculate the firm's net profit margin.

5. The shares of Bouchard Corporation, a metals producer, are currently selling for $50. The book value per share is $125. In contrast, the share price of Datangelo is $40, compared to a book value per share of $10. Datangelo is a software developer. Why do these two firms have such dramatically different market-to-book ratios?

6. Last year, Deer Lake Mines, Inc. had earnings after tax of $650,000. Included in its expenses were depreciation of $400,000 and future tax liabilities of $100,000. The firm also purchased new capital equipment for $300,000. Calculate the firm's after-tax cash flow for last year.

7. Refer to the SFC example (Table 3.9). Recalculate the cash and cash equivalents at the end of 20X6 assuming that (1) the company had 20X6 capital expenditures of $22,000; (2) it paid dividends of $800; and (3) it did not issue any common shares.

*Coloured numbers and letters denote problems that have "check" answers provided at the back of the book.

www.smallbusinessbc.ca/ibp

Assume that the firm's other cash flows are the same as those shown in Table 3.9.

8. Examine the Interactive Business Planner at the Small Business Web site. How can you use a tool such as this as the manager of an existing firm or a new start-up enterprise? Also examine the tutorials on this Web site. Prepare a memo to your instructor summarizing what you found.

INTERMEDIATE

9. Trudeau Furniture Company is planning to establish a wholly owned subsidiary to manufacture upholstery fabrics. The firm expects to earn $1 million after taxes on the venture during the first year. The president of the firm wants to know what the subsidiary's balance sheet would look like. The president believes that it would be advisable to begin the new venture with ratios that are similar to the industry average.

The firm plans to make all sales on credit. All calculations assume a 365-day year. In your computations, you should round all numbers to the nearest $1,000.

Based on the industry average financial ratios presented here, complete the projected balance sheet for the firm's upholstery subsidiary.

Industry Averages	
Current ratio	2:1
Quick ratio	1:1
Net profit margin ratio	5%
Average collection period	20 days
Debt ratio	40%
Total asset turnover ratio	2 times
Current liabilities/shareholders' equity	20%

Forecasted Upholstery Subsidiary Balance Sheet			
Cash	_____	Total current liabilities	_____
Accounts receivable	_____	Long-term debt	_____
Inventory	_____	Total debt	_____
Total current assets	_____	Shareholders' equity	_____
Net fixed assets	_____		_____
Total assets	_____	Total liabilities and shareholders' equity	_____

10. The Scotia Schooner Company has total assets of $100 million. Of this total, $40 million was financed with common equity and $60 million with debt (both long- and short-term). Its average accounts receivable balance is $20 million, and this represents an 80-day average collection period. The firm believes it can reduce its average collection period from 80 days to 60 days without affecting sales or the dollar amount of net income after taxes (currently $5 million). What will be the effect of this action on the firm's return on investment and its return on shareholders' equity if the funds received by reducing the average collection period are used to buy back its common shares at book value? What impact will this action have on the firm's debt ratio?

11. The Juneau Corporation has current assets of $3.0 million. Of this total, $1.0 million is inventory, $0.5 million is cash, $1.0 million is accounts receivable, and the balance is marketable securities. The firm has $1.5 million in current liabilities.

   a. What are the firm's current and quick ratios?

   b. If the firm takes $0.25 million in cash and pays off $0.25 million of current liabilities, what happens to its current and quick ratios? What happens to its real liquidity?

c. If the firm sells $0.5 million of its accounts receivable to a bank and uses the proceeds to pay off short-term debt obligations, what happens to its current and quick ratios?

d. If the firm sells $1.0 million in new shares and places the proceeds in marketable securities, what happens to its current and quick ratios?

e. What do these examples illustrate about the current and quick ratios?

12. Ghiz Controls Ltd. has a net profit margin of 10% and earnings after taxes of $600,000. Its current balance sheet follows:

Ghiz Controls Ltd. Balance Sheet as of December 31, 20X7			
Current assets	$1,800,000	Current liabilities	$600,000
Fixed assets	2,200,000	Long-term debt	1,000,000
Total assets	$4,000,000	Retained earnings	2,400,000
		Total liabilities and	
		shareholders' equity	$4,000,000

a. Calculate the firm's return on shareholders' equity.

b. The industry average ratios are as follows:

Net profit margin	6%
Total asset turnover	2.5 times
Equity multiplier	1.4 times

Compare the firm with the average firm in the industry. What is the source of the major differences between the firm and the industry average ratios?

13. Given the following data for Profiteers Ltd. and the corresponding industry averages, perform a trend analysis of the return on investment and the return on shareholders' equity. Plot the data and discuss any trends that are apparent. Also, discuss the underlying causes of these trends.

Profiteers Ltd. Years	20X1	20X2	20X3	20X4	20X5
Net profit margin	14%	12%	11%	9%	10%
Asset turnover	1.26X	1.22X	1.20X	1.19X	1.21X
Equity multiplier	1.34X	1.40X	1.61X	1.65X	1.63X

Industry Averages Years	20X1	20X2	20X3	20X4	20X5
Net profit margin	12%	11%	11%	10%	10%
Asset turnover	1.25X	1.27X	1.30X	1.31X	1.34X
Equity multiplier	1.42X	1.45X	1.47X	1.51X	1.53X

14. Key Resources Ltd. has a net profit margin of 8% and earnings after taxes of $2 million. Its current balance sheet is as follows:

Key Resources Ltd. Balance Sheet as of December 31, 20X7			
Current assets	$6,000,000	Current liabilities	$3,500,000
Fixed assets	10,000,000	Long-term debt	5,500,000
Total assets	$16,000,000	Retained earnings	7,000,000
		Total liabilities and	
		shareholders' equity	$16,000,000

a. Calculate the firm's return on shareholders' equity.

b. Industry average ratios are

Net profit margin	10%
Total asset turnover	2.0 times
Equity multiplier	1.5 times

What does a comparison of the firm to these averages indicate about the firm's strengths and weaknesses?

c. The firm has inventories of $3.2 million. Compute the firm's quick ratio.

15. Palmer Chocolates Ltd., a maker of chocolates that specializes in Easter candy, had the following inventories over the past year:

Month	Inventory Amount	Month	Inventory Amount
January	$25,000,000	July	$25,000,000
February	60,000,000	August	38,000,000
March	90,000,000	September	50,000,000
April	30,000,000	October	60,000,000
May	20,000,000	November	70,000,000
June	22,000,000	December	30,000,000

The firm had sales of $290 million over the past year. Cost of sales constituted 50% of sales. Calculate the firm's inventory turnover using beginning of year inventory, end of year inventory, and a monthly average inventory. Which method do you feel is most appropriate? Why?

16. Fill in the balance sheet for the Jamais Company presented below based on the following data (assume a 365-day year):

Sales = $3,650,000

Total asset turnover = 4X

Current ratio = 3:1

Quick ratio = 2:1

Current liabilities to net worth = 30%

Average collection period = 20 days

Total debt to total assets = 0.4

Jamais Company Balance Sheet			
Cash	_____	Accounts payable	_____
Accounts receivable	_____	Total current liabilities	_____
Inventory	_____	Long-term debt	_____
Total current assets	_____	Total debt	_____
Net fixed assets	_____	Shareholders' equity	_____
Total assets	_____	Total liabilities and shareholders' equity	_____

17. Armbrust Corporation is the maker of fine fitness equipment. Armbrust's bank has been pressuring the firm to improve its liquidity. Which of the following actions proposed by the CFO do you believe will actually achieve this objective? Why or why not?

a. Sell new equity and use the proceeds to purchase a new plant site.

b. Use cash and marketable securities to pay off short-term bank borrowings and accounts payable.

c. Borrow long term and use the proceeds to pay off short-term debt.

d. Sell surplus fixed assets and invest the proceeds in marketable securities.

18. Consider the Inuit Supply Company data below. Assume that the company plans to maintain its dividend payments at the same level in 2007 as in 2006. Also assume that all of the additional financing needed is in the form of short-term notes payable. Determine the amount of additional financing needed and pro forma financial statements (that is, balance sheet, income statement, and selected financial ratios) for 2007 under each of the following conditions:

	Increase in Sales	Increase in Expenses
a.	$3,750,000	$3,750,000
b.	$3,000,000	$2,800,000
c.	$4,500,000	$4,000,000

Inuit Supply Company Balance Sheet as of December 31, 2006

Assets		Liabilities and Equity	
Cash	$ 500,000	Accounts payable	$1,500,000
Accounts receivable	2,000,000	Notes payable	1,000,000
Inventories	4,000,000	Total current liabilities	$2,500,000
Total current assets	$6,500,000	Long-term debt	500,000
Net fixed assets	1,000,000	Shareholders' equity	4,500,000
Total assets	$7,500,000	Total liabilities and equity	$7,500,000

Inuit Supply Company Income Statement for the Year Ended December 31, 2006

Sales	$15,000,000
Expenses, including interest and taxes	14,250,000
Earnings after taxes	750,000
Dividends paid	250,000

Inuit Supply Company Selected Financial Ratios

Current ratio	2.60 times
Debt ratio	40%
Return on shareholders' equity	16.7%
Net profit margin on sales (EAT/Sales)	5.0%

19. Consider again the Inuit Supply Company data above where it was assumed that the firm's fixed assets were being used at nearly full capacity and that net fixed assets would have to increase proportionately as sales increased. Now suppose that the firm has excess fixed assets and that *no increase* in net fixed assets is required as sales are increased. Assume that the firm plans to maintain its dividend payments at the same level in 2007 as in 2006. Determine the amount of additional financing needed for 2007 under each of the following conditions:

	Increase in Sales	Increase in Expenses
a.	$3,750,000	$3,750,000
b.	$3,000,000	$2,800,000
c.	$4,500,000	$4,000,000

20. Rocky Mountain Registers Ltd. has current sales of $50 million. Sales are expected to grow to $75 million next year. The firm currently has accounts receivable of $10 million, inventories of $15 million, and net fixed assets of $20 million. These assets are expected to grow at the same rate as sales over the next year. Accounts payable are expected to increase from their current level of $10 million to a new level of $13 million next year. The firm wants to increase its cash balance at the end of next year by $2 million over its current cash balance, which averages $4 million. Earnings after taxes next year are forecasted to be $10 million. Next year, the firm plans to pay dividends of $1 million, up from $500,000 this year. The firm's marginal tax rate is 34%.

How much external financing is required by the firm next year?

21. Berea Resources is planning a $75 million capital expenditure program for the coming year. Next year, Berea expects to report to the Canada Customs and Revenue Agency (CCRA) earnings of $40 million after interest and taxes. The firm presently has 20 million common shares issued and outstanding. Dividend payments are expected to increase from the present level of $10 million to $12 million. The firm expects its current asset needs to increase from a current level of $25 million to $30 million. Current liabilities, excluding short-term bank borrowings, are expected to increase from $15 million to $17 million. Interest payments are $5 million next year, and long-term debt retirement obligations are $8 million next year. Depreciation next year is expected to be $15 million on the firm's financial statements, but the firm will report depreciation of $18 million for tax purposes.

How much external financing is required by Berea for the coming year?

CHALLENGE

22. Using the data below for a number of firms in the same industry, do the following:
    a. Compute the total asset turnover, the net profit margin, the equity multiplier, and the return on equity for each firm.
    b. Evaluate each firm's performance by comparing the firms with one another. Which firm or firms appear to be having problems? What corrective action would you suggest the poorer performing firms take? Finally, what additional data would you want to have on hand when conducting your analyses?

(in Millions of $)	Firm A	Firm B	Firm C	Firm D
Sales	$20	$10	$15	$25
Net income after tax	3	0.5	2.25	3
Total assets	15	7.5	15	24
Shareholders' equity	10	5.0	14	10

23. Using the data on page 118 for Jacques Products Company:
    a. Evaluate the liquidity position of the firm relative to that of the average firm in the industry. Consider the current ratio, the quick ratio, and the net working capital (current assets minus current liabilities). What problems, if any, are suggested by this analysis?
    b. Evaluate the firm's performance by looking at key asset management ratios. Are any problems apparent from this analysis?
    c. Evaluate the firm's financial risk by examining its times interest earned ratio and its equity multiplier ratio relative to the same industry average ratios.
    d. Evaluate the firm's profitability relative to that of the average firm in its industry.
    e. Give an overall evaluation of the firm's performance relative to other firms in its industry.
    f. Perform a DuPont analysis for the firm. What areas appear to have the greatest need for improvement?
    g. The firm's current P/E ratio is 7 times. What factor(s) are most likely to account for this ratio relative to the higher industry average ratio?

Jacques Products Company's Balance Sheet, December 31, 20X1			
Cash	$240,000	Accounts payable	$ 380,000
Accounts receivable	320,000	Notes payable (9%)	420,000
Inventory	1,040,000	Other current liabilities	50,000
Total current assets	$1,600,000	Total current liabilities	$ 850,000
Net fixed assets	800,000	Long-term debt (10%)	800,000
Total assets	$2,400,000	Shareholders' equity	750,000
		Total liabilities and	
		shareholders' equity	$2,400,000

24. If a company sells additional common shares and uses the proceeds to increase its inventory level and to increase its cash balances, what is the near-term (immediate) impact (increase, decrease, no change) of this transaction on the following ratios?

   a. Current ratio
   b. Return on shareholders' equity
   c. Quick ratio
   d. Debt to total assets
   e. Total asset turnover

25. Harper Paper Company, a profitable distributor of stationery and office supplies, has an agreement with its banks that allows it to borrow money on a short-term basis to finance its inventories and accounts receivable. The agreement states that the firm must maintain a current ratio of 1.5 or higher *and* a debt ratio of 50% or lower. Given the following balance sheet, determine how much additional money it could borrow at this time to invest in inventory and accounts receivable without violating the terms of its borrowing agreement.

Harper Paper Company Balance Sheet			
Cash	$ 50,000	Current liabilities	$ 200,000
Accounts receivable	150,000	Long-term debt	300,000
Inventory	250,000	Shareholders' equity	630,000
Fixed assets	680,000	Total liabilities and	
Total assets	$1,130,000	shareholders' equity	$1,130,000

26. Sun Minerals Ltd. is considering issuing additional long-term debt to finance an expansion. At the present time, the firm has $50 million in 10% debt outstanding. Its after-tax net income is $12 million, and the firm's tax rate is 40%. The firm is required by the debt holders to maintain its times interest earned ratio at 3.5 or greater.

   a. What is the present coverage (times interest earned) ratio?
   b. How much additional 10% debt can the firm issue now and maintain its times interest earned ratio at 3.5? (Assume for this calculation that earnings before interest and taxes remain at their present level.)
   c. If the interest rate on additional debt is 12%, how much unused debt capacity does the firm have?

27. The balance sheet and income statement of Eastland Products Ltd. are as follows:

Eastland Products Ltd. Balance Sheet, December 31, 20X1 (in $millions)			
Current assets	$ 40	Current liabilities	$30
Net fixed assets	110	Long-term debt	40
		Common shares	25
		Retained earnings	55
Total assets	$150	Total liabilities and shareholders' equity	$150

Eastland Products Ltd. Income Statement for Year Ended December 31, 20X1
(in $millions)

Sales	$120
Cost of sales	80
EBIT	$40
Interest	5
EBT	35
Taxes (40%)	14
Net income (EAT)	$ 21

Additional Information

Total dividends	$10 million
Market price of a common share	$32 a share
Number of common shares issued	5 million

Using these data, determine the following:

a. Earnings per share
b. Price-to-earnings ratio
c. Book value per share
d. Market-to-book ratio
e. How much of the retained earnings total was added during 20X1?
f. Show the firm's new balance sheet after the company sells 1 million new common shares in early 20X2 to net $30 a share. Part of the proceeds, $10 million, is used to reduce current liabilities, and the remainder is temporarily deposited in the firm's bank account. Later, this remaining amount (along with additional long-term debt financing) will be invested in new manufacturing facilities.

28. Thomson Electronics Ltd. is presently 100% equity financed and has assets of $100 million. The firm's present net income is $9 million, and the firm's marginal and average tax rates are 40%. In addition, the firm has 4 million common shares outstanding, and its current annual dividend is $0.75 a share. At the present time, the firm is able to borrow 10% *perpetual* debt, that is, debt that has no maturity date. What amount of 10% perpetual debt would the firm have to borrow in order to increase its return on total equity to 15%?

29. The Southwick Company has the following balance sheet ($000):

Southwick Company's Balance Sheet, December 31, 20X1

Cash	$500	Accounts payable	$1,750
Marketable securities	750	Notes payable	1,250
Accounts receivable	2,000	Total current liabilities	$3,000
Inventory	2,500	Long-term debt	1,750
Total current assets	$5,750	Total liabilities	$4,750
Net fixed assets	5,000	Common shares	3,000
		Retained earnings	3,000
		Total shareholders' equity	6,000
Total assets	$10,750	Total liabilities and shareholders' equity	$10,750

Financial Ratios

Current ratio	1.92
Quick ratio	1.08
Debt-to-equity ratio	0.79

Evaluate the impact of each of the following (independent) financial decisions on the firm's current, quick, and debt-to-equity ratios:

a. The firm reduces its inventories by $500,000 through more efficient inventory management procedures and invests the proceeds in marketable securities.

b. The firm decides to purchase 20 new delivery trucks for a total of $500,000 and pays for them by selling marketable securities.

c. The firm borrows $500,000 from its bank through a short-term loan (seasonal financing) and invests the proceeds in inventory.

d. The firm borrows $2,000,000 from its bank through a five-year loan (interest due annually, principal due at maturity) and uses the proceeds to expand its plant.

e. The firm sells $2,000,000 (net) in common shares and uses the proceeds to expand its plant.

30. Prepare a cash budget for Atlas Products Ltd. for the first quarter of 2006, based on the following information.

The budgeting section of the corporate finance department of the firm has received the following sales estimates from the marketing department:

	Total Sales	Credit Sales
December 2005	$825,000	$770,000
January 2006	730,000	690,000
February 2006	840,000	780,000
March 2006	920,000	855,000

The firm has found that, on average, about 25% of its credit sales are collected during the month when the sale is made, and the remaining 75% of credit sales are collected during the month following the sale. As a result, the firm uses these figures for budgeting.

The firm estimates its purchases at 60% of next month's sales, and payments for those purchases are budgeted to lag the purchases by one month.

Various disbursements have been estimated as follows:

	January	February	March
Wages and salaries	$250,000	$290,000	$290,000
Rent	27,000	27,000	27,000
Other expenses	10,000	12,000	14,000

In addition, a tax payment of $105,000 is due on January 15, and $40,000 in dividends will be declared in January and paid in March. Also, the firm has ordered a $75,000 piece of equipment. Delivery is scheduled for early January, and payment will be due in February.

The firm's projected cash balance at the beginning of January is $100,000, and the firm desires to maintain a balance of $100,000 at the end of each month.

31. Prepare a cash budget for Elmwood Manufacturing Company for the first three months of 20X7 based on the following information:

Month	Estimated Sales	Estimated Factory Overhead	Estimated Selling and Administrative Expenses
December	$ 4,600,000	$640,000	$1,250,000
January	6,400,000	650,000	1,275,000
February	11,200,000	670,000	1,285,000
March	8,400,000	670,000	1,310,000
April	7,000,000	680,000	1,300,000

The firm has found that approximately 40% of sales is collected during the month the sale is made and the remaining 60% is collected during the month following the sale. Material purchases are 30% of next month's estimated sales, and payments lag these purchases by one month. Labour costs are 35% of next month's sales and are paid during the month incurred. Factory overhead and selling and administrative expenses are paid during the month incurred. In addition, a payment for new equipment of $1.5 million is due in February. Also, a tax payment of $1.6 million and a dividend payment of $650,000 are due in March.

The firm's projected cash balance at the beginning of January is $1.5 million. Furthermore, the firm desires to maintain a $750,000 cash balance at the end of each month.

32. The Podrasky Corporation is considering a $200 million expansion (capital expenditure) program next year. The firm wants to know approximately how much additional financing (if any) will be required if it decides to go through with the expansion program. The firm presently has $400 million in net fixed assets. Next year, the firm expects to earn $80 million after interest and taxes. The firm also expects to maintain its present level of dividends, which is $15 million. If the expansion program is accepted, the firm expects its inventory and accounts receivable each to increase by approximately $20 million next year. Long-term debt retirement obligations total $10 million for next year, and depreciation is expected to be $80 million. The firm does not expect to sell any fixed assets next year. The firm maintains a cash balance of $5 million, which is sufficient for its present operations. If the expansion is accepted, the firm feels it should increase its year-end cash balance to $8 million because of the increased level of activities. For planning purposes, assume no other cash flow changes for next year.

33. Hudon Produits Ltée anticipates reaching a sales level of $6 million in one year. The firm expects earnings after taxes during the next year to equal $400,000. During the past several years, the firm has been paying $50,000 in dividends to its shareholders. The firm expects to continue this policy for at least the next year. The firm's actual balance sheet at the end of 2008 and its income statement during 2008 follow:

Hudon Produits Ltée Balance Sheet as of December 31, 2008

Cash	$ 200,000	Accounts payable	$ 600,000
Accounts receivable	400,000	Notes payable	500,000
Inventories	1,200,000	Long-term debt	200,000
Fixed assets, net	500,000	Shareholders' equity	1,000,000
Total assets	$2,300,000	Total liabilities and equity	$2,300,000

Hudon Produits Ltée Income Statement for the Year Ending December 31, 2008

Sales	$4,000,000
Expenses, including interest and taxes	3,700,000
Earnings after taxes	$ 300,000

a. Using the percentage of sales method, calculate the additional financing the firm will need over the next year at the $6 million sales level. Show the pro forma balance sheet for the company as of December 31, 2009, assuming that a sales level of $6 million is reached. Assume that the additional financing needed is obtained in the form of additional notes payable.

b. Suppose that the firm's management feels that the average collection period on its additional sales—that is, sales over $4 million—will be 60 days, instead of the current level. By what amount will this increase in the average collection period increase the financing needed by the firm over the next year?

c. If the firm's banker requires the company to maintain a current ratio equal to 1.6 or greater, what is the maximum amount of additional financing that can be in the form of bank borrowings (notes payable)? What other potential sources of financing are available to the firm?

Other Practice Materials and Resources

For interactive quizzes, Internet exercises, crossword puzzles, CTV videos, and more, go to the *Contemporary Financial Management* Web site **http://cyr.nelson.com**

APPENDIX 3A: SPREADSHEET ANALYSIS OF FINANCIAL RATIOS

Electronic Spreadsheets

Electronic spreadsheet software replaces columnar paper, pencils, erasers, and calculators in performing repetitive calculations of the type needed in financial ratio analysis. The most popular electronic spreadsheet software is MS Excel. There are also several others, including some free clones of Excel. To supplement this book, spreadsheets are available on the book's Web site.

Spreadsheets are organized in rows and columns and each cell at the intersection of a row and column can contain data or a formula to display the result of a calculation. It is recommended to use a portion of the top part of the spreadsheet for input data, such as interest and tax rates, that can be reused in the formulas within the cells below. Hence, for the ratios spreadsheet that accompanies this chapter, there is an input section followed by calculations of the various ratios described in this chapter. The cells have been programmed with the formulas contained in the chapter. The spreadsheet template *ratios.xls* also contains some explanatory comments. To use the template, simply type in the appropriate data from the financial statements and the ratios will be calculated and displayed in the lower section of the spreadsheet. This will aid you in doing the homework problems. There are other spreadsheet templates on the book Web site for use with other chapters. In the next chapter, which deals with the time value of money, we explain how to use calculators to solve time value of money problems, and also include a simplified spreadsheet. For more extensive information on how to use spreadsheets, see Conrad Carlberg, *Business Analysis with Microsoft Excel*, 2nd edition (Indianapolis, IN: 2002).

Financial Ratios for Molson Inc.

Balance Sheet Items	Enter Data?	Year 2002	Year 2001	Year 2000
Cash and Marketable Securities	Yes	$71	$70	$62
Accounts Receivable	Yes	$192	$102	$154
Inventories	Yes	$184	$139	$132
Other Current Assets	Yes	$64	$121	$106
Total Current Assets	No	$510	$432	$452
Total Net Fixed Assets	Yes	$1,187	$915	$777
Other Assets	Yes	$2,824	$1,934	$1,883
Total Assets	No	$4,521	$3,281	$3,112
Total Current Liabilities	Yes	$876	$618	$599
Total Long-Term Liabilities	Yes	$2,472	$1,867	$1,487
Total Liabilities	No	$3,347	$2,485	$2,086
Total Equity	No	$1,174	$795	$1,026
Total Liabilities and Equity	No	$4,521	$3,281	$3,112
Income Statement Items	No	2002	2001	2000
Sales	Yes	$2,102	$1,857	$1,754
− Cost of Sales	Yes	$1,726	$1,506	$1,658
Gross Profit	No	$376	$352	$96
+ Other Revenues	Yes	$0	$0	$0
− Other Expenses Except Interest	Yes	$55	$88	$91
Earnings before Interest & Taxes	No	$322	$264	$4
− Interest	Yes	$66	$69	$73
Earnings before Taxes	No	$256	$195	($68)
− Taxes	Yes	$81	$58	($3)
Earnings after Taxes	No	$176	$137	($66)
+ Depreciation	Yes	$55	$49	$57
Net Cash Flow	No	$230	$187	($9)
Liquidity Ratios	No	2002	2001	2000
Current Ratio	No	0.58	0.70	0.76
Quick Ratio	No	0.37	0.47	0.54
Asset Management Ratios	No	2002	2001	2000
Average Collection Period	No	33.35	20.11	31.97
Inventory Turnover	No	11.46	13.37	13.33
Receivables Turnover	No	10.94	18.15	11.42
Fixed Asset Turnover	No	1.77	2.03	2.26
Total Asset Turnover	No	0.47	0.57	0.56
Leverage Management Ratios	No	2002	2001	2000
Debt Ratio	No	0.74	0.76	0.67
Debt-to-Equity Ratio	No	2.85	3.13	2.03
Times Interest Earned Ratio	No	4.91	3.84	0.06
Profitability Ratios	No	2002	2001	2000
Gross Profit Margin Ratio	No	17.90%	18.93%	5.45%
Net Profit Margin Ratio	No	8.35%	7.39%	−3.75%
Return on Investment (Total Assets) Ratio	No	3.88%	4.18%	−2.11%
Return on Total Equity	No	14.96%	17.25%	−6.42%

Note: All input financial statement figures are in $ millions.

Part Two

Determinants of Valuation

The primary objective of financial management is to maximize the value of the firm's common shares. This part discusses the valuation process in detail. Chapter 4 deals with discounting cash flows and the time value of money. This is essential for any serious analysis of important financial decisions that impact an enterprise over a number of years. Chapters 5 and 6 build valuation models for a firm's securities. Chapter 5 focuses on the valuation of fixed-income securities—namely, bonds and preferred shares. Chapter 6 deals with the valuation of common shares. These chapters are important because valuation is the dominant theme carried throughout the text and related to all financial decisions. Chapter 7 explores the determinants of risk and relates risk to the valuation process.

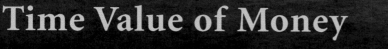

Time Value of Money

Learning Objectives

After studying this chapter you should be able to

1. Understand the concept of interest
   a. Simple interest is paid on the principal sum only
   b. Compound interest is paid both on the initial principal amount and on any interest earned but not withdrawn during earlier periods

2. Perform future (compound) value calculations to determine the value at some future time of X dollars invested today, earning some compound rate of interest, *i*, per period

3. Perform present value calculations to determine the value today (present value) of some amount to be received in the future

4. Understand that an annuity is a series of equal periodic payments
   a. Ordinary annuity payments are made at the end of each period
   b. Annuity due payments are made at the beginning of each period
   c. A perpetuity is an ordinary annuity that lasts forever

5. Perform future value of an annuity calculations to determine the future value of an annuity stream of cash flows

6. Perform present value of an annuity calculations to determine the present value of an annuity stream of cash flows

7. Understand other important topics
   a. Compounding frequency
   b. Present value of perpetuities
   c. Present value of uneven cash flow streams
   d. Present value of deferred annuities
   e. Present value of growth annuities and growth perpetuities

Powerball Opportunity

Unlike major Canadian lotteries that pay only lump-sum prizes, the multistate Powerball Lottery in the United States gives its winners a choice. During the summer of 2001 the Powerball jackpot reached US$294.8 million. Many Canadians live close enough to the border that they could participate in this lottery and many of them crossed the border to buy tickets. Unfortunately, none of them won. For this particular draw, four winning tickets were sold, with each winning ticket entitled to one-fourth of the total jackpot, or $73.7 million. Each of the four winners had two choices concerning payment of the prize:

1. Receive an immediate lump-sum payment of $41.4 million.

2. Receive $73.7 million paid out over 25 years—that is, $2.948 million at the beginning of each year for the next 25 years.

Suppose you are a financial advisor to one of the winning ticket holders. How should the ticket holder go about choosing between the two alternatives? Obviously, the rate of return your client could expect to earn from investments is an important variable in making an informed decision.

Many decisions that managers encounter involve streams of cash flows that are paid out over time. To make informed decisions, a manager needs a working knowledge of the time value of money—the topic of this chapter. Later in the chapter, we provide a solution to the decision of whether to take the lump-sum payment or the 25 annual payments. (Note: Although lottery winnings are tax-free in Canada, they are taxable in the United States. So, if a Canadian won, this winner would have to pay income taxes on the lottery prize to the United States on this US source income. Nevertheless, we will ignore taxes in the analysis.)

Introduction

Understanding the time value of money is crucial to effective financial management. In fact, anyone who is involved with money should have some comprehension of the time value of money. Consider the following examples:

- A banker who makes loans and other investments
- A financial officer whose job includes the consideration of various alternative sources of funds in terms of their cost
- A corporate planner who must choose among various alternative investment projects
- A securities analyst who evaluates the securities that a firm sells to investors
- An individual who is confronted with a host of daily financial problems ranging from personal credit account management to deciding how to finance a new-home purchase

Each of these individuals makes frequent use of the time value of money. Many people fear that a working knowledge of the time value of money concept might be too difficult to master. However, the availability of interest tables and financial calculators makes the subject readily accessible.

Although an understanding of the time value of money is useful in and of itself, it is also a necessary prelude to the following topics:

- Valuation of securities and other assets
- Capital budgeting (the analysis of investment projects)
- The cost of capital and capital structure
- Working capital (short-term asset and liability) management
- Lease analysis

This chapter introduces the concepts and skills necessary to understand the time value of money and its applications.

The analysis in this chapter assumes that you will use a financial calculator, the Microsoft Excel spreadsheet program, or the interest tables (Tables I through IV) at the back of the book to solve problems. Calculator and spreadsheet solutions are presented for many of the examples in this chapter. *These solutions are shown to the nearest penny, in contrast to table solutions that are usually rounded to the nearest dollar.* The most important point, however, is that you learn the principles of the time value of money.

A Word about Notation

A brief discussion of financial notation is in order before we begin our time value of money discussion. In finance, as a general rule, lowercase letters are used to denote percentage rates and lengths of time, whereas capital letters are used to denote money or dollar amounts. For example, we use i to denote the interest rate, n to denote the number of periods, PMT to denote cash payments, PV to denote the present value dollar amount, and FV to denote the future value dollar amount. One important exception in this text is that we use T to denote the tax rate instead of t. Lowercase t denotes time. Our use of i to denote the interest rate is similar to the notation used on most financial calculators, although some calculators use uppercase letters such as I, I/Y, or I%YR. Later in the text (for example in Chapter 5) when the interest rate becomes a specific required rate of return, we use k to denote required return. This is the custom used by many financial analysts.

Try typing "time value of money" into the search engine at **www.google.ca** and watch how many millions of hits you get. Then take a look at the different kinds of hits (calculators, etc.). You will probably agree that time value of money is indeed a cornerstone of business theory and practice.

Click on the Investment Analysis Calculator button at **http://finance.swcollege. com** for an interactive financial calculator.

Interest

Money can be thought of as having a time value. In other words, an amount of money received today is worth more than the same dollar amount would be if it were received a year from now.[1] The primary reason that a dollar today is worth more than a dollar to be received sometime in the future is that the current dollar can be invested to earn a rate of return. (This holds true even if risk and inflation are not considerations.) Suppose, for example, that you had $100 and decided to put it into a savings account for a year. By doing this, you would temporarily give up, or forego, (1) spending the $100 as you wished, (2) earning the return that the $100 might earn from some alternative investment, or (3) paying an additional $100 on your mortgage. Similarly, a bank that loans money to a firm foregoes the opportunity to earn a return on some alternative investment.

Interest is the return earned by or the amount paid to someone who has foregone current consumption or alternative investment opportunities and "rented" money in a creditor relationship.[2] The **principal** is the amount of money borrowed or invested. The **term of a loan** is the length of time or number of time periods during which the borrower can use the principal. The rate of interest is the percentage on the principal that the borrower pays the lender per time period as compensation for foregoing other investment or consumption opportunities.

Interest
The return earned by or the amount paid to an investor who foregoes current consumption or alternative investments and "rents" money to a business, a bank, an individual, the government.

Principal
An amount of money that has been borrowed or invested.

Term of a Loan
The length of time or number of periods during which the borrower can use the principal.

Simple Interest
Interest paid or earned on the principal only.

Simple Interest

Simple interest is the interest paid (in the case of borrowed money) or earned (in the case of invested money) on the principal only. The amount of simple interest is equal to the product of the principal times the rate per time period times the number of time periods:

$$(4.1) \qquad I = PV_0 \times i \times n$$

where I = the simple interest in dollars; PV_0 = the principal amount at time 0, or the present value; i = the interest rate per time period; and n = the number of time periods. The following problems illustrate the use of Equation 4.1.

1. What is the simple interest on $100 at 10 percent per annum for six months? Substituting $100 for PV_0, 10 percent (0.10) for i, and 6/12 (0.5) for n yields the following:

$$I = \$100 \times 0.10 \times 0.5 = \$5$$

2. If Isaiah Williams borrowed $30,000 at a 10 percent annual interest rate, what would be his first month's interest payment? Substituting $30,000 for PV_0, 10 percent (0.10) for i, and 1/12 for n yields the following:

$$I = \$30,000 \times 0.10 \times 1/12 = \$250$$

3. Mary Schiller receives $30 every three months from a bank account that pays a 6 percent annual interest rate. How much is invested in the account? Because PV_0 is the unknown in this example, Equation 4.1 is rearranged:

$$(4.2) \qquad PV_0 = \frac{I}{i \times n}$$

---

[1] The terms amount of money, cash flow, and payment are used interchangeably throughout the chapter.

[2] Although other forms of returns are dealt with throughout the text, this discussion is limited to borrowing-lending situations.

Substituting $30 for I, 0.06 for i, and 1/4 (0.25) for n yields the following:

$$PV_0 = \frac{\$30}{0.06 \times 0.25} = \$2,000$$

It also is useful to be able to calculate the amount of funds a person can expect to receive at some point in the future. In financial mathematics, the terminal, or future, value of an investment is called FV_n and denotes the principal plus interest accumulated at the end of n years. It is written as follows:

(4.3)
$$FV_n = PV_0 + I$$

4. Raymond Gomez borrows $1,000 for nine months at a rate of 8 percent per annum. How much will he have to repay at the end of the nine-month period? Combining Equations 4.1 and 4.3 to solve for FV_n results in the following new equation:

(4.4)
$$FV_n = PV_0 + (PV_0 \times i \times n)$$

Substituting $1,000 for PV_0, 0.08 for i, and 3/4 (9 months = 3/4 of 1 year) for n yields the following:

$$FV_{3/4} = \$1,000 + (1,000 \times 0.08 \times 3/4) = \$1,060$$

This problem can be illustrated using the following timeline:

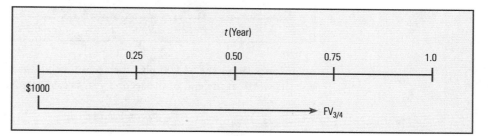

5. Marie Comeau agrees to invest $1,000 in a venture that promises to pay 10 percent simple interest each year for two years. How much money will she have at the end of the second year? Using Equation 4.4 and assuming two 10 percent simple interest payments, the future value of Marie's investment at the end of two years is computed as follows:

$$FV_2 = PV_0 + (PV_0 \times i \times 2)$$
$$= \$1,000 + (\$1,000 \times 0.10 \times 2)$$
$$= \$1,200$$

This problem can be illustrated using the following timeline:

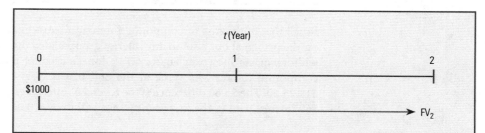

In general, in the case of simple interest, the future, or terminal, value (FV_n) at the end of n years is given by Equation 4.4.

Compound Interest and Future Value

Compound Interest
Interest that is paid not only on the principal but also on any interest earned but not withdrawn during earlier periods.

Future (Compound) Value
The value at some future point in time of a present payment (or a series of payments) evaluated at the appropriate interest (growth) rate.

Compound interest is interest that is paid not only on the principal but also on any interest earned but not withdrawn during earlier periods. For example, if Jerry Jones deposits $1,000 in a savings account paying 6 percent interest compounded annually, the **future (compound) value** of his account at the end of one year (FV_1) is calculated as follows:

$$(4.5) \qquad FV_1 = PV_0(1 + i)$$
$$= \$1,000(1 + 0.06)$$
$$= \$1,060$$

This problem can be illustrated using the following timeline:

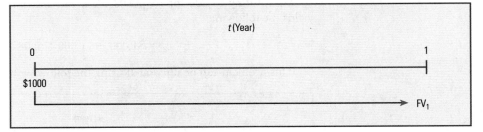

If Jones leaves the $1,000 plus the accumulated interest in the account for another year, its worth at the end of the second year is calculated as follows:

$$(4.6) \qquad FV_2 = FV_1(1 + i)$$
$$= \$1,060(1 + 0.06)$$
$$= \$1,123.60$$

This problem can be illustrated using the following timeline:

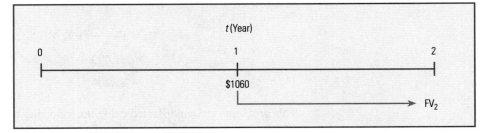

Recall that in the case of compound interest, interest in each period is earned not only on the principal but also on any interest accumulated during previous periods and not withdrawn. As shown in Figure 4.1, if Jones's account paid simple interest instead of compound interest, its value at the end of two years would be $1,120 instead of $1,123.60. The $3.60 difference is the 6 percent interest earned in the second year on the $60 interest paid in the first year but not withdrawn, $0.06 \times \$60$.

If Jones makes no withdrawals from the account for another year, it will total the following at the end of the third year:

(4.7)
$$FV_3 = FV_2(1 + i)$$
$$= \$1,123.60(1 + 0.06)$$
$$= \$1,191.02$$

This problem can be illustrated using the following timeline:

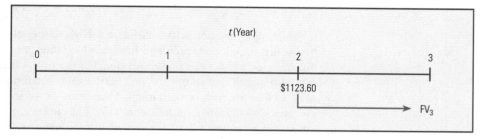

Figure 4.1 illustrates that if the account paid only simple interest, it would be worth only $1,180 at the end of three years. The $11.02 difference (i.e., $1,191.02 − $1,180) is the interest on the first and second years' interest, $0.06 \times (\$60 + \$123.60)$.

A general formula for computing future values can be developed by combining Equations 4.5, 4.6, and 4.7. Substituting Equation 4.6 into Equation 4.7 yields the following equation:

$$FV_3 = FV_1(1 + i)(1 + i)$$

or

(4.8)
$$FV_3 = FV_1(1 + i)^2$$

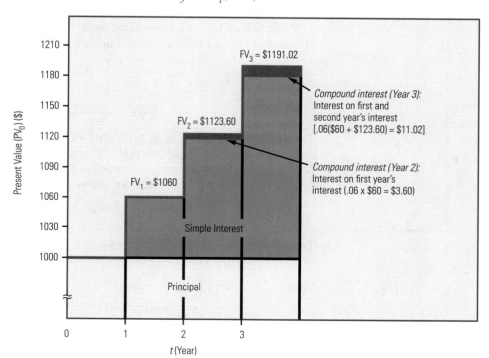

Figure 4.1
Simple versus Compound Interest

Substituting Equation 4.5 into Equation 4.8 yields the following:

$$FV_3 = PV_0(1 + i)(1 + i)^2$$

or

(4.9)
$$FV_3 = PV_0(1 + i)^3$$

This equation can be further generalized to calculate the future value at the end of period n for any payment compounded at interest rate i:

(4.10)
$$FV_n = PV_0(1 + i)^n$$

Although Equation 4.10 is useful for solving future value problems, it is rather tedious to use this equation for problems involving long time periods unless your calculator has a function key for y^x, i.e., a power function. For example, solving for 20 years into the future would require calculating $(1 + i)^{20}$. Future value interest factors (FVIFs) are commonly used to simplify such computations. Thus, even someone using the most basic calculator can quickly calculate a future value. Table I at the back of the book provides a listing of future value interest factors for various interest rates covering up to 60 periods (years or other time periods). Because each future value interest factor is defined as

(4.11)
$$FVIF_{i,n} = (1 + i)^n$$

Equation 4.10 may be rewritten as follows:

(4.12)
$$FV_n = PV_0(FVIF_{i,n})$$

where i = the effective interest rate per period and n = the number of periods.

To better understand Table I, it is helpful to think of each factor as the result of investing or lending \$1 for a given number of periods, n, at interest rate i. The solution for any amount other than \$1 is the product of that principal amount times the factor for a \$1 principal amount.

A portion of Table I is reproduced as Table 4.1. Table 4.1 can be used to determine the value of \$1,000 compounded at 6 percent for 20 years:

$$FV_{20} = PV_0(FVIF_{0.06,20})$$
$$= \$1,000(3.207)$$
$$= \$3,207$$

The 3.207 figure is arrived at by reading down the 6 percent, or 0.06, column and across the 20 row under the "End of Period (n)" heading to where the row and column meet. Note also that the 3.207 figure is rounded to four digits in Table 4.1. Thus, one can find the future value only to four significant digits, which is the nearest dollar in *this* example.

The future value amount can also be computed using a financial calculator. For example, the above problem can be solved as follows:

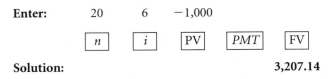

Calculator Solution

Enter: 20   6   −1,000

| n | i | PV | PMT | FV |

Solution: 3,207.14

Note: When no value appears above a "key box," such as *PMT* in this example, it is not necessary to enter any value to solve the problem. However, it is possible for data from a previous calculation to remain in the memory. To be safe, it is wise to enter zero for *PMT*. On most financial calculators, the PV of −1,000 is entered as 1000 [+/−]. Most financial calculators come with a default of compounding interest 12 times a year. Unless compounding frequency is specifically mentioned, all calculator examples in this text assume that the compounding frequency has been changed to once per year.

* Students who are planning to use a financial calculator should become familiar with the keystrokes needed to solve time value of money problems. The manual accompanying your financial calculator explains the basic operations required to solve the examples and problems.

Table 4.1 Future Value Interest Factors (FVIFs) for $1 at Interest Rate *i* for *n* Periods*

End of Period (*n*)	Interest Rate (*i*)				
	1%	5%	6%	8%	10%
1	1.010	1.050	1.060	1.080	1.100
2	1.020	1.102	1.124	1.166	1.210
3	1.030	1.158	1.191	1.260	1.331
4	1.041	1.216	1.262	1.360	1.464
5	1.051	1.276	1.338	1.469	1.611
8	1.083	1.477	1.594	1.851	2.144
9	1.094	1.551	1.689	1.999	2.358
10	1.105	1.629	1.791	2.159	2.594
20	1.220	2.653	3.207	4.661	6.728
25	1.282	3.386	4.292	6.848	10.835

*The values in this and similar tables in this text have been rounded off to three places. When large sums of money are involved, more accurate tables or financial calculators should be used.

The solution can be computed with a spreadsheet as follows:

Spreadsheet Solution

	A	B	C	
1	TVM	INPUTS	SOLUTION	
2	Periods, n	20		
3	Rate, i	6.00%		
4	PV	1000		
5	PMT			
6	FV		$3,207.14	

To construct a spreadsheet, begin by putting labels for the three column headings in row 1 in cells A1, B1, and C1, respectively. Then in column A, starting with cell A2, enter the labels for five time value of money variables in the same order as they appear on most calculators. Next, enter the data inputs in column B. First, enter the number of periods, 20, in cell B2. Then, enter the interest rate (we first used the percentage format for that cell), 6, in cell B3. Then, enter the present value, 1000, in cell B4. Then, enter the formula for Equation 4.11: **=B4*(1+B3)^B2** in cell C6, and the future value $3,207.14 will appear (if the cell is formatted for currency). This type of spreadsheet format can be reused for other calculations just by changing the input values.

However, it is even easier to use the built-in Excel function wizard. To do so, first change the PV to a *negative* number in cell B4. In contrast to a financial calculator that uses 1000 [+/−], in Excel, you enter −1000. Then, with the cursor in cell C6, click on the function wizard button on the menu that is usually next to the Σ button. The drop-down function menu will appear. If FV appears, choose it. If FV does not appear, you may have to sequentially choose up to two submenus such as Other Functions and Financial before choosing FV. Then, enter the appropriate cell numbers for the data inputs in the appropriate boxes of the FV function drop-down menu and the value $3,207.14 should appear. The formula: **=FV(B3,B2,,B4)** will be entered into cell C6 by the function wizard.

Solving for the Interest Rate

In some compound value problems, the present value (PV_0) and future value (FV_n) are given and the objective is to determine the interest rate (i) that solves Equation 4.10. For example, the future value interest factor for an investment requiring an initial outlay of $1,000 and promising a $1,629 return after 10 years is as follows:

$$FVIF_{i,10} = FV_{10}/PV_0 = 1.629$$

Reading across the 10-year row in Table 4.1, 1.629 is found in the 5 percent column. Thus, the investment yields a 5 percent compound rate of return.

Calculator Solution

The interest rate can also be computed using a financial calculator. For example, the above problem can be solved as follows:

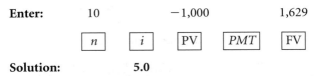

Enter:	10		−1,000		1,629
	n	i	PV	PMT	FV

Solution: 5.0

Spreadsheet Solution

The solution can also be computed with a spreadsheet as follows:

	A	B	C	
1	TVM	INPUTS	SOLUTION	
2	Periods, n	10		
3	Rate, i		5.00%	
4	PV	−1000		
5	PMT			
6	FV	1629		

Enter the appropriate data inputs in column B. Choose the RATE function for cell C3. The wizard will help you create the appropriate formula =**RATE(B2,,B4,B6)** and display the solution.

Solving for the Number of Compounding Periods

The future value interest factor tables can also be used to determine the number of annual compounding periods (n). For example, to determine how long it would take for $1,000 invested at 8 percent to double, search the 8 percent column to locate a future value interest factor of 2.000. The closest value to this figure is 1.999. Reading to the left of this figure, it can be seen that the original $1,000 would be worth nearly $2,000 in nine years. This problem can also be solved algebraically:

$$FV_n = PV_0(FVIF_{0.08, n})$$

$$FVIF_{0.08, n} = FV_n/PV_0 = 2.000$$

Referring to Table 4.1, the closest value to FVIF = 2.000 under the 8 percent column is 1.999, which occurs at approximately nine years.[3]

Calculator Solution

The number of periods can also be computed using a financial calculator. For example, the above problem can be solved as follows:

Enter:	8	−1		2
n	i	PV	PMT	FV

Solution: 9.01

The number of periods can also be computed with a spreadsheet as follows:

Spreadsheet Solution

	A	B	C	
1	TVM	INPUTS	SOLUTION	
2	Periods, n		9.01	
3	Rate, i	8.00%		
4	PV	−1		
5	PMT			
6	FV	2		

Enter the appropriate data inputs in column B. Choose the NPER function for cell C2. The wizard will create the appropriate formula **=NPER(B3,,B4,B6)** and display the solution.

Compounding can also be illustrated graphically. Figure 4.2 shows the effects of time, n, and interest rate, i, on the growth of a $100 investment. As the figure shows, the higher the compound interest rate, the faster the growth rate of the value of the initial principal. The notion that an interest rate may be thought of as a growth rate will be useful during later discussions of valuation and cost of capital.

---

[3] In a shortcut solution to this type of problem known as the "Rule of 72," the number 72 is divided by the interest rate to determine the number of years it would take for a sum of money to double. In this case, 72/8% = 9. The Rule of 72 can also be used to determine the interest rate required for a sum of money to double in a given number of years: 72/9 = 8%. The Rule of 72 does not yield exact figures, but it can be used to calculate good approximations.

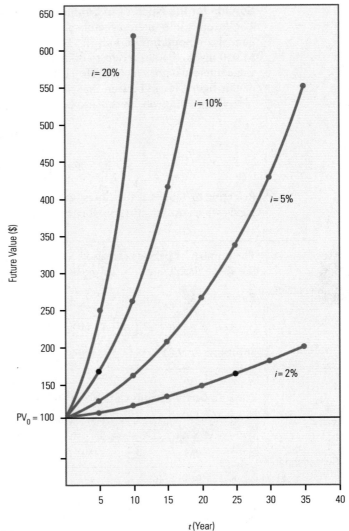

Figure 4.2
Growth of a $100 Investment at Various Compound Interest Rates

Present Value

The compound, or future, value calculations answer the question: What will be the future value of X dollars invested today, compounded at some rate of interest, i? The financial decision maker, however, is often faced with another type of problem: Given some future value, FV_n, what is its equivalent value today? That is, what is its **present value**, PV_0? The solution requires present value calculations, which are used to determine the dollar amount today, PV_0, that is equivalent to some promised future dollar amount, FV_n. The equivalence depends on the rate of interest (return) that can be earned on investments during the time period under consideration.

The relationship between compound value and present value can be shown by rewriting Equation 4.10 to solve for PV_0:

$$FV_n = PV_0(1 + i)^n$$

or

(4.13)
$$PV_0 = FV_n\left[\frac{1}{(1 + i)^n}\right]$$

Present Value
The value today of a future payment, or stream of payments, discounted at the appropriate rate.

where $1/(1 + i)^n$ is the reciprocal of the compound interest factor. The process of finding present values is frequently called discounting. Equation 4.13 is the basic discounting formula.

To illustrate the use of Equation 4.13, suppose your banker offers to pay you $255.20 in five years if you deposit X dollars today at an annual 5 percent interest rate. Whether the investment would be worthwhile depends on how much money you must deposit, or the present value of the X dollars. FVIF tables, such as Table 4.1 presented earlier, can be used to solve the problem as follows:

$$PV_0 = FV_5 \left(\frac{1}{FVIF_{0.05,5}} \right)$$

$$\$255.20(1/1.276) = \$200$$

This problem can be illustrated with the following timeline:

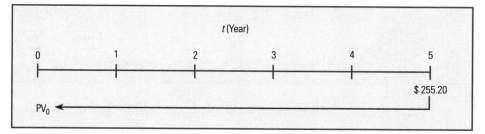

Thus, an investment of $200 today would yield a return of $55.20 in five years.

Because determining the reciprocals of the compound value interest factors, $1/(1 + i)^n$, can be a tedious process, present value interest factors (PVIFs) commonly are used to simplify such computations. Defining each present value interest factor as

(4.14)
$$PVIF_{i,n} = \frac{1}{(1+i)^n}$$

Equation 4.13 can be written in the following form:

(4.15)
$$PV_0 = FV_n(PVIF_{i,n})$$

Table II at the end of the book provides a number of present value interest factors. A portion of Table II is reproduced here as Table 4.2.

Table 4.2	Present Value Interest Factors (PVIFs) for $1 at Interest Rate i for n Periods					
	Interest Rate (i)					
End of Period (n)	1%	5%	6%	8%	10%	13%
1	0.990	0.952	0.943	0.926	0.909	0.885
2	0.980	0.907	0.890	0.857	0.826	0.783
3	0.971	0.864	0.840	0.794	0.751	0.693
4	0.961	0.823	0.792	0.735	0.683	0.613
5	0.951	0.784	0.747	0.681	0.621	0.543
8	0.923	0.677	0.627	0.540	0.467	0.376
10	0.905	0.614	0.558	0.463	0.386	0.295
20	0.820	0.377	0.312	0.215	0.149	0.087
25	0.780	0.295	0.233	0.146	0.092	0.047

For example, Table 4.2 can be used to determine the present value of $1,000 received 20 years in the future discounted at 10 percent:

$$PV_0 = FV_{20}(PVIF_{0.10,\ 20})$$
$$= \$1,000(0.149)$$
$$= \$149$$

Thus, $149 invested today at 10 percent interest compounded annually for 20 years would be worth $1,000 at the end of the period. (Since there are only three significant digits in the factors in Table 4.2, one can find the present value to only three significant digits, which is the nearest dollar in *this* example.) Conversely, the promise of $1,000 in 20 years is worth $149 today, given a 10 percent interest rate.

Calculator Solution

Enter: 20   10   −1,000

| n | | i | | PV | | PMT | | FV |

Solution: 148.64

The solution can also be computed with a spreadsheet as follows:

Spreadsheet Solution

	A	B	C	
1	TVM	INPUTS	SOLUTION	
2	Periods, n	20		
3	Rate, i	10.00%		
4	PV		$148.64	
5	PMT	78		
6	FV	−1000		

Enter the data in column B and use the formula wizard to select the PV function for cell C4. It will create the appropriate formula and display the solution.

Solving for Interest and Growth Rates

Present value interest factors as well as future value interest factors can be used to solve for interest rates. For example, suppose you wish to borrow $5,000 today from an associate. The associate is willing to loan you the money if you promise to pay back $6,250 four years from today. The compound interest rate your associate is charging can be determined as follows:

$$PV_0 = FV_4(PVIF_{i,\ 4})$$
$$\$5,000 = \$6,250(PVIF_{i,\ 4})$$
$$(PVIF_{i,\ 4}) = \$5,000/\$6,250 = 0.800$$

Reading across the four-year row in Table 4.2, 0.800 is found between the 5 percent (0.823) and 6 percent (0.792) columns. Interpolating between these two values yields

$$i = 5\% + \frac{.823 - .800}{.823 - .792}(1\%) = 5.74\%$$

Thus, the effective interest rate on the loan is 5.74 percent per year, compounded annually.

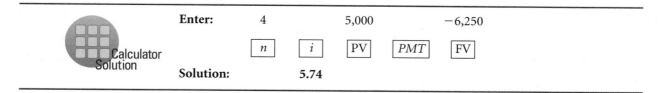

Enter: 4   5,000   −6,250

n i PV   PMT   FV

Solution: **5.74**

The solution can also be computed with a spreadsheet as follows:

	A	B	C
1	TVM	INPUTS	SOLUTION
2	Periods, n	4	
3	Rate, i		5.74%
4	PV	5000	
5	PMT		
6	FV	−6250	

Enter the appropriate data inputs in column B and choose the RATE function for cell C3.

Another common present value application is the calculation of the compound rate of growth of an earnings or dividend stream. For example, B & N had earnings of $0.93 per share in 1997. Suppose these earnings grow to $2.04 at the end of 2002. Over this five-year period, what is the compound annual rate of growth in B & N's earnings? The answer to this problem can be obtained by solving for the present value interest factor over the five-year period as follows:

$$\$0.93 = \$2.04(\text{PVIF}_{i,\,5})$$

$$\text{PVIF}_{i,\,5} = 0.456$$

From Table II, we find this present value interest factor in the five-year row under the 17 percent interest, or growth rate, column. Hence the compound annual rate of growth in B & N's earnings per share has been 17 percent.

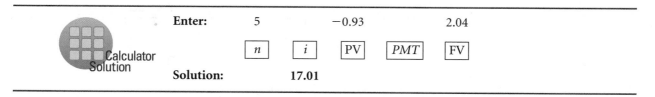

Enter: 5   −0.93   2.04

n i PV   PMT   FV

Solution: **17.01**

The solution can also be computed with a spreadsheet as follows:

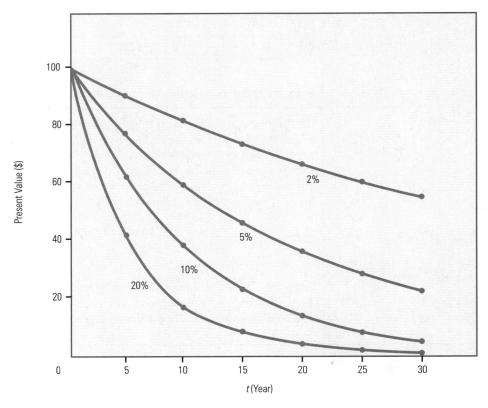

Spreadsheet Solution

	A	B	C	
1	TVM	INPUTS	SOLUTION	
2	Periods, n	5		
3	Rate, i		17.01%	
4	PV	−0.93		
5	PMT			
6	FV	2.04		

Enter the appropriate data inputs in column B and choose the RATE function for cell C3.

The discounting process can also be illustrated graphically. Figure 4.3 shows the effects of time, n, and interest rate, i, on the present value of a $100 investment. As the figure shows, the higher the discount rate, the lower the present value of the $100.

Clearly, present value interest factors could also be used to solve for the number of compounding periods as we did previously with future value interest factors.

Figure 4.3
Present Value of $100 at Various Discount Rates

Annuities

An **annuity** is the payment or receipt of equal cash flows per period for a specified amount of time.[4] An **ordinary annuity** is one in which the payments or receipts occur at the end of each period, as shown in Figure 4.4. Typically, payments on consumer loans are ordinary annuities. An **annuity due** is one in which payments or receipts occur at the beginning of each period, as shown in Figure 4.5. Insurance premiums and most lease payments, such as apartment rentals, are annuities due.

In a four-year ordinary annuity, the last payment is made at the end of the fourth year. In a four-year annuity due, the last payment is made at the end of the third year (the beginning of the fourth year).

Future Value of an Ordinary Annuity

A future value of an ordinary annuity ($FVAN_n$) problem asks the question: If PMT dollars are deposited in an account at the end of each year for n years and if the deposits earn interest rate i compounded annually, what will be the value of the account at the end of n years? To illustrate, suppose Marci MacDonald receives a three-year ordinary annuity of $1,000 per year and deposits the money in a savings account at the end of each year. The account earns interest at a rate of 6 percent compounded annually. How much will her account be worth at the end of the three-year period? Figure 4.6 illustrates this concept.

The problem involves the calculation of future values. The last deposit, PMT_3, made at the end of year 3, will earn no interest. Thus, its future value is as follows:

$$FV_{3rd} = PMT_3(1 + 0.06)^0$$
$$= \$1,000(1)$$
$$= \$1,000$$

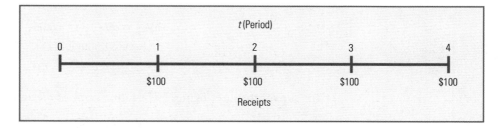

Figure 4.4
Timeline of an Ordinary Annuity of $100 per Period for Four Periods

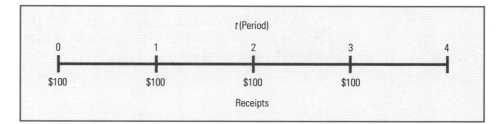

Figure 4.5
Timeline of an Annuity Due of $100 per Period for Four Periods

---

[4] This discussion focuses primarily on periods of one year.

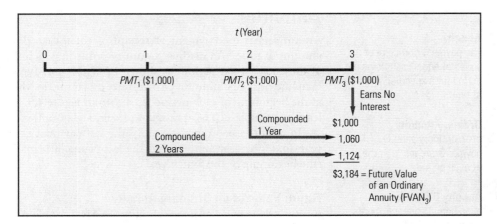

Figure 4.6
Timeline of the Future Value of an Ordinary Annuity ($PMT = \$1,000$; $i = 6\%$; $n = 3$)

The second deposit, PMT_2, made at the end of year 2, will be in the account for one full year before the end of the three-year period, and it will earn interest. Thus, its future value is as follows:

$$
\begin{aligned}
\text{FV}_{2\text{nd}} &= PMT_2(1 + 0.06)^1 \\
&= \$1,000(1.06) \\
&= \$1,060
\end{aligned}
$$

The first deposit, PMT_1, made at the end of year 1, will be in the account earning interest for two full years before the end of the three-year period. Therefore its future value is the following:

$$
\begin{aligned}
\text{FV}_{1\text{st}} &= PMT_1(1 + 0.06)^2 \\
&= \$1,000(1.124) \\
&= \$1,124
\end{aligned}
$$

The sum of the three figures is the future value of the annuity:

$$
\begin{aligned}
\text{FVAN}_3 &= \text{FV}_{3\text{rd}} + \text{FV}_{2\text{nd}} + \text{FV}_{1\text{st}} \\
&= \$1,000 + \$1,060 + \$1,124 \\
&= \$3,184
\end{aligned}
$$

The future value of an annuity interest factor (FVIFA) is the sum of the future value interest factors presented in Table I. In this example, the future value of an annuity interest factor is calculated as

$$
\begin{aligned}
\text{FVIFA}_{0.06,\,3} &= \text{FVIF}_{0.06,\,2} + \text{FVIF}_{0.06,\,1} + \text{FVIF}_{0.06,\,0} \\
&= 1.124 + 1.060 + 1.000 \\
&= 3.184
\end{aligned}
$$

Tables of the future value of an ordinary annuity interest factors are available to simplify computations. Table III at the back of the book provides a number of future value of an annuity interest factors. A portion of Table III is reproduced here as Table 4.3.

Table 4.3 Future Value of an Ordinary Annuity Interest Factors (FVIFA) for $1 per Period at Interest Rate i for n Periods

End of Period (n)	Interest Rate (i)			
	1%	5%	6%	10%
1	1.000	1.000	1.000	1.000
2	2.010	2.050	2.060	2.100
3	3.030	3.152	3.184	3.310
4	4.060	4.310	4.375	4.641
5	5.101	5.526	5.637	6.105
10	10.462	12.578	13.181	15.937
20	22.019	33.066	36.786	57.275
25	28.243	47.727	54.865	98.347

FVIFAs can also be computed as follows:

$$(4.16) \qquad \text{FVIFA}_{i,n} = \frac{(1+i)^n - 1}{i}$$

This formula can be used when you do not have access to interest tables with the appropriate values of i and n or to a financial calculator.

The future value of an ordinary annuity (FVAN_n) may be calculated by multiplying the annuity payment, PMT, by the appropriate interest factor, $\text{FVIFA}_{i, n}$:

$$(4.17) \qquad \text{FVAN}_n = PMT(\text{FVIFA}_{i, n})$$

Table 4.3 can be used to solve the problem involving Marci MacDonald's annuity. Because $PMT = \$1,000$ and the interest factor for $n = 3$ years and $i = 6\%$ is 3.184, the future value of an ordinary annuity can be calculated as follows:

$$\begin{aligned} \text{FVAN}_3 &= PMT(\text{FVIFA}_{0.06, 3}) \\ &= \$1,000(3.184) \\ &= \$3,184 \end{aligned}$$

Calculator Solution

Enter:	3	6		−1,000	
	n	i	PV	PMT	FV

Solution: 3,183.60

The solution can also be computed with a spreadsheet as follows:

Spreadsheet Solution

	A	B	C
1	TVM	INPUTS	SOLUTION
2	Periods, n	3	
3	Rate, i	6.00%	
4	PV		
5	PMT	−1000	
6	FV		$3,183.60

Enter the appropriate data inputs in column B and choose the FV function for cell C6.

Sinking Fund

An annuity amount that must be invested each period (year) to produce a future value.

Sinking Fund Problem Future value of an annuity interest factors can also be used to find the annuity amount that must be invested each year to produce a future value. This type of problem is sometimes called a **sinking fund** problem. Suppose the Omega Graphics Company wishes to set aside an equal, annual, end-of-year amount in a "sinking fund account" earning 9.5 percent per annum over the next five years. The firm wants to have $5 million in the account at the end of five years to retire (pay off) $5 million in outstanding bonds. How much must be deposited in the account at the end of each year?

This problem can be solved using either Equation 4.17 or a financial calculator. Substituting $n = 5$, $\text{FVAN}_5 = \$5{,}000{,}000$, and $i = 0.095$ into Equation 4.17 yields

$$\$5{,}000{,}000 = PMT(\text{FVIFA}_{0.095,\,5})$$

Since the interest rate of 9.5 percent is not in Table III, you must use Equation 4.16 to determine $\text{FVIFA}_{0.095,\,5}$.

$$\$5{,}000{,}000 = PMT\left(\frac{(1 + 0.095)^5 - 1}{0.095}\right)$$

$$PMT = \$827{,}182.09$$

By depositing $827,182.09 at the end of each of the next five years in the account earning 9.5 percent per annum, Omega will accumulate the $5 million needed to retire the bonds.

Calculator Solution

Enter:	5	9.5		−5,000,000	
	n	i	PV	PMT	FV

Solution: 827,182.09

The solution can also be computed with a spreadsheet as follows:

Spreadsheet Solution

	A	B	C	
1	TVM	INPUTS	SOLUTION	
2	Periods, n	5		
3	Rate, i	9.5%		
4	PV			
5	PMT		$827,182.09	
6	FV	−5000000		

Enter the appropriate data inputs in column B and choose the PMT function for cell C5.

Future Value of an Annuity Due

Table III at the end of the book (future value of an annuity interest factors) assumes ordinary (end-of-period) annuities. For an annuity due, in which payments are made at the beginning of each period, the interest factors in Table III must be modified.

Consider the case of Marci MacDonald cited earlier. If she deposits $1,000 in a savings account at the beginning of each year for the next three years and the account earns 6 percent interest, compounded annually, how much will be in the account at the end of three years? (Recall that when the deposits were made at the end of each year, the account totalled approximately $3,184 at the end of three years.)

Figure 4.7 illustrates this problem as an annuity due. PMT_1 is compounded for three years, PMT_2 for two years, and PMT_3 for one year. The correct annuity due interest factor may be obtained from Table III by multiplying the FVIFA for three years and 6 percent (3.184) by 1 plus the interest rate (1 + 0.06). This yields a FVIFA for an annuity due of 3.375, and the future value of the annuity due ($FVAND_n$) is calculated as follows:

$$(4.18) \qquad FVAND_n = PMT[FVIFA_{i, n}(1 + i)]$$

$$FVAND_3 = \$1,000(3.375)$$

$$= \$3,375$$

Calculator
Solution

This problem must be solved with the calculator in the *beginning of period* payment mode.

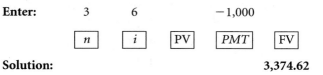

Enter: 3   6   −1,000

$\boxed{n}$ $\boxed{i}$ $\boxed{PV}$ $\boxed{PMT}$ $\boxed{FV}$

Solution: **3,374.62**

Note: This amount is larger than the $3,183.60 obtained in the ordinary annuity example given previously by an amount equal to 1 + *i*, or 1.06 in this particular example.

The solution can also be computed with a spreadsheet as follows:

Spreadsheet
Solution

	A	B	C	
1	TVM	INPUTS	SOLUTION	
2	Periods, n	3		
3	Rate, i	6.00%		
4	PV			
5	PMT	−1000		
6	FV		$3,374.62	
7	Type	1		

Enter the appropriate data inputs in column B and choose the FV function for cell C6. In Excel, the *beginning of period payment* mode is indicated by the *Type* of annuity input. Thus, type 0 = ordinary annuity and type 1= annuity due. If type is not specified, the default is zero.

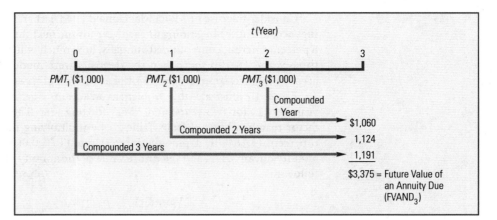

Figure 4.7
Timeline of the Future Value of an Annuity Due (PMT = $1,000; i = 6%; n = 3)

Present Value of an Ordinary Annuity

The present value of an ordinary annuity ($PVAN_0$) is the sum of the present value of a series of equal periodic payments.[5] For example, to find the present value of an ordinary $1,000 annuity received at the end of each year for five years discounted at a 6 percent rate, the sum of the individual present values would be determined as follows:

$$
\begin{aligned}
PVAN_0 &= \$1,000(PVIF_{0.06,\,1}) + \$1,000(PVIF_{0.06,\,2}) \\
&\quad + \$1,000(PVIF_{0.06,\,3}) + \$1,000(PVIF_{0.06,\,4}) \\
&\quad + \$1,000(PVIF_{0.06,\,5}) \\
&= \$1,000(0.943) + \$1,000(0.890) + \$1,000(0.840) \\
&\quad + \$1,000(0.792) + \$1,000(0.747) \\
&= \$1,000(0.943 + 0.890 + 0.840 + 0.792 + 0.747) \\
&= \$4,212
\end{aligned}
$$

Figure 4.8 illustrates this concept.

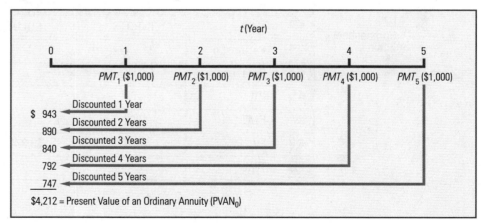

Figure 4.8
Timeline of a Present Value of an Ordinary Annuity (PMT = $1,000; i = 6%; n = 5)

Tables of the present value of an ordinary annuity interest factors (PVIFA) are available to simplify computations. Table IV at the back of the book provides a number of the present

---

[5] This discussion focuses primarily on annual payments.

value of an annuity interest factors. A portion of Table IV is reproduced here as Table 4.4.

PVIFAs can also be computed as follows:

$$(4.19) \qquad \text{PVIFA}_{i,\,n} = \frac{\left[1 - \dfrac{1}{(1 + i)^n} \right]}{i}$$

This formula is useful when one does not have access to interest tables with the appropriate values of i and n or a financial calculator.

The present value of an annuity can be determined by multiplying the annuity payment, PMT, by the appropriate interest factor, $\text{PVIFA}_{i,\,n}$:

$$(4.20) \qquad \text{PVAN}_0 = PMT(\text{PVIFA}_{i,\,n})$$

Referring to Table 4.4 to determine the interest factor for $i = 6\%$ and $n = 5$, the present value of an annuity in the previous problem can be calculated as follows:

$$\text{PVAN}_0 = PMT(\text{PVIFA}_{0.06,\,5})$$
$$= \$1,000(4.212)$$
$$= \$4,212$$

Table 4.4	Present Value of an Ordinary Annuity Interest Factors (PVIFA) for \$1 per Period at Interest Rate i for n Periods			
		Interest Rate (i)		
End of Period (n)	**1%**	**5%**	**6%**	**10%**
1	0.990	0.952	0.943	0.909
2	1.970	1.859	1.833	1.736
3	2.941	2.723	2.673	2.487
4	3.902	3.546	3.465	3.170
5	4.853	4.329	4.212	3.791
10	9.471	7.722	7.360	6.145
20	18.046	12.462	11.470	8.514
25	22.023	14.094	12.783	9.077

Calculator Solution

Enter: 5   6   −1,000

[n] [i] [PV] [PMT] [FV]

Solution: 4,212.36

The solution can also be computed with a spreadsheet as follows:

Spreadsheet Solution

	A	B	C
1	TVM	INPUTS	SOLUTION
2	Periods, n	5	
3	Rate, i	6.00%	
4	PV		\$4,212.36
5	PMT	−1000	
6	FV		

Enter the appropriate data inputs in column B and choose the PV function for cell C4.

Solving for the Interest Rate   Present value of an annuity interest factors can also be used to solve for the rate of return expected from an investment.[6] Suppose BCE purchases a machine for $100,000. This machine is expected to generate annual cash flows of $23,742 to the firm over the next five years. What is the expected rate of return from this investment?

Using Equation 4.20, we can determine the expected rate of return in this example as follows:

$$PVAN_0 = PMT(PVIFA_{i,\,5})$$

$$\$100,000 = \$23,742(PVIFA_{i,\,5})$$

$$PVIFA_{i,\,5} = 4.212$$

From the five-year row in Table 4.4 or Table IV, we see that a PVIFA of 4.212 occurs in the 6 percent column.[7] Hence, this investment offers a 6 percent expected rate of return.

Calculator Solution

Enter:	5		$-100,000$	23,742	
	n	i	PV	PMT	FV
Solution:		6.00			

The solution can also be computed with a spreadsheet as follows:

Spreadsheet Solution

	A	B	C	
1	TVM	INPUTS	SOLUTION	
2	Periods, n	5		
3	Rate, i		6.00%	
4	PV	−100000		
5	PMT	23742		
6	FV			

Enter the appropriate data inputs in column B and choose the RATE function for cell C3.

Loan Amortization
The liquidation of a loan on an instalment basis, with periodic payments that include both interest and principal.

Loan Amortization and Capital Recovery Problems   Present value of an annuity interest factors can be used to solve a **loan amortization** problem, where the objective is to determine the payments necessary to pay off, or amortize, a loan.

For example, suppose you borrowed $10,000 from a bank. The loan is for a period of four years at an interest rate of 10.5 percent. It requires that you make four equal, annual, end-of-year payments that include both principal and interest on the outstanding balance.[8] This problem can be solved using either Equation 4.20 or a financial calculator.

---

[6] This interest rate, or rate of return, is referred to by various names in finance, depending on the type of investment under consideration. When evaluating a bond (fixed-income security), this rate is referred to as the *yield-to-maturity* (YTM) (see Chapter 5). In the analysis of capital expenditure decisions, this rate is known as the *internal rate of return* (IRR) (see Chapter 10). Finally, when calculating the cost of bank loans and other types of credit, this rate is known as the *effective annual rate* (EAR) (see Chapter 15).

[7] Interpolation can be used to find the approximate interest rate when the PVIFA falls between two values in the table. See the example discussed earlier involving PVIFs for an illustration of this technique.

[8] Loan repayment schedules other than equal periodic payments are discussed in Chapter 15.

Substituting $n = 4$, $\text{PVAN}_0 = \$10,000$, and $i = 0.105$ into Equation 4.20 yields:

$$\$10,000 = PMT(\text{PVIFA}_{0.105,\, 4})$$

Since the interest rate (i) of 10.5 percent is not in Table IV, you must use Equation 4.19 to determine $\text{PVIFA}_{0.105,\, 4}$:

$$\$10,000 = PMT\left(\dfrac{1 - \dfrac{1}{(1 + 0.105)^4}}{0.105}\right)$$

$$PMT = \$3,188.92$$

Calculator Solution

Enter:	4	10.5	$-10,000$		
	n	i	PV	PMT	FV

Solution: 3,188.92

The solution also can be computed with a spreadsheet as follows:

Spreadsheet Solution

	A	B	C	
1	TVM	INPUTS	SOLUTION	
2	Periods, n	4		
3	Rate, i	10.5%		
4	PV	−10000		
5	PMT		$3,188.92	
6	FV			

Enter the appropriate data inputs in column B and choose the PMT function for cell C5.

By making four annual, end-of-year payments to the bank of $3,188.92 each, you will completely pay off your loan, plus provide the bank with its 10.5 percent interest return. This can be seen in the loan amortization schedule developed in Table 4.5. At the end of each year, you pay the bank $3,188.92. During the first year, $1,050 of this payment is interest (0.105 × $10,000 remaining balance), and the rest ($2,138.92) is applied against the principal balance owed at the beginning of the year. Hence, after the first payment, you owe $7,861.08 ($10,000 − $2,138.92). Similar calculations are done for years 2, 3, and 4. Note that the last payment in *this* example would be one penny less to exactly amortize the loan. Later in this chapter we present such a spreadsheet for a mortgage.

Table 4.5	Loan Amortization Schedule			
End of Year	**Payment**	**Interest (10.5%)**	**Principal Reduction**	**Remaining Balance**
0	—	—	—	$10,000.00
1	$3,188.92	$1050.00	2,138.92	7,861.08
2	3,188.92	825.41	2,363.51	5,497.57
3	3,188.92	577.24	2,611.68	2,885.89
4	3,188.91	303.02	2,885.89	0

Capital Recovery
An annuity amount necessary
to recover a capital
investment.

Present value of an annuity interest factors can also be used to find the annuity amount necessary to recover a capital investment, given a required rate of return on that investment. This type of problem is called a **capital recovery** problem.

Present Value of an Annuity Due

Annuity due calculations are also important when dealing with the present value of an annuity problem. In these cases, the interest factors in Table IV must be modified.

Consider the case of a five-year annuity of $1,000 each year, discounted at 6 percent. What is the present value of this annuity if each payment is received at the beginning of each year? (Recall the example presented earlier, illustrating the concept of the present value of an ordinary annuity, in which each payment was received at the end of each year and the present value was approximately $4,212.) Figure 4.9 illustrates this problem.

The first payment received at the beginning of year 1 (end of year 0) is already in its present value form and therefore requires no discounting. PMT_2 is discounted for one period, PMT_3 is discounted for two periods, PMT_4 is discounted for three periods, and PMT_5 is discounted for four periods.

The correct annuity due interest factor for this problem may be obtained from Table IV by multiplying the present value of an ordinary annuity interest factor for five years and 6 percent (4.212) by 1 plus the interest rate $(1 + 0.06)$. This yields a PVIFA for an annuity due of 4.465, and the present value of this annuity due ($PVAND_0$) is calculated as follows:

$$(4.21) \qquad PVAND_0 = PMT[PVIFA_{i,\,n}(1 + i)]$$
$$PVAND_0 = \$1{,}000(4.465)$$
$$= \$4{,}465$$

Calculator Solution

This problem must be solved with the calculator in the beginning of period payment mode.

Enter: 5 6 −1,000

| n | i | PV | PMT | FV |

Solution: 4,465.11

Note: This amount is larger than the $4,212.36 obtained in the ordinary annuity example presented previously by an amount equal to $1 + i$, or 1.06 in this particular example.

The solution can also be computed with a spreadsheet as follows:

Spreadsheet Solution

	A	B	C	
1	TVM	INPUTS	SOLUTION	
2	Periods, n	5		
3	Rate, i	6.00%		
4	PV		$4,465.11	
5	PMT	−1000		
6	FV			
7	Type	1		

Enter the appropriate data in column B and choose the PV function for cell C4. Make sure you include the type variable, as this is necessary to switch the spreadsheet into annuity due mode.

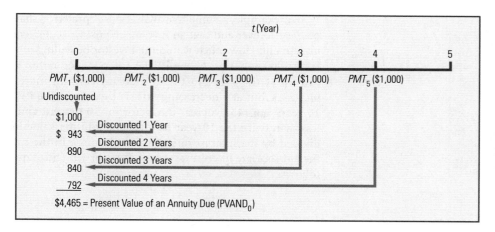

Figure 4.9
Timeline of a Present Value of an Annuity Due ($PMT = \$1,000$; $i = 6\%$; $n = 5$)

Annuity due calculations are especially important when dealing with rental or lease contracts because it is common for these contracts to require that payments be made at the beginning of each period.

Present Value: Some Additional Cash Flow Patterns

The discussion of present value thus far has focused on two cash flow patterns: single payments and annuities. The present value of three additional types of cash flow streams are examined in this section: namely, perpetuities, uneven cash flows, and deferred annuities. Examples of these types of cash flows are encountered in many different areas of financial decision making.

Perpetuities

Perpetuity
A financial instrument that pays an equal cash flow per period into the indefinite future (that is, infinity).

A **perpetuity** is a financial instrument that promises to pay an equal cash flow at the end of each period forever. That is, a perpetuity is an ordinary annuity with an infinite series of payments. Some bonds (and some preferred shares) take the form of a perpetuity because these special securities never mature. That is, there is no obligation on the part of the issuer to redeem these bonds at their face value at any time in the future. A financial instrument such as this provides the holder with a series of equal, periodic payments into the indefinite future.

Consider, for example, a financial instrument that promises to pay an infinite stream of equal, annual payments (cash flows) of $PMT_t = PMT$ for $t = 1, 2, 3, \ldots$ years; that is, $PMT_1 = PMT_2 = PMT_3 = \ldots = PMT$. If we wish to find the present value ($PVPER_0$) of this financial instrument, it can be represented as follows:

$$PVPER_0 = \frac{PMT}{(1 + i)} + \frac{PMT}{(1 + i)^2} + \frac{PMT}{(1 + i)^3} + \ldots$$

or, using summation notation, as

(4.22)
$$PVPER_0 = \sum_{t = 1}^{\infty} \frac{PMT}{(1 + i)^t}$$

where i equals the rate of return required by an investor in this financial instrument. It should be apparent that Equation 4.22 represents a special type of annuity, where the number of periods for the annuity equals infinity. This type of problem cannot be solved using Table IV.

For example, assume that BCE series X preferred shares promise payments of $4.50 per year forever and that an investor requires a 10 percent rate of return on this type of investment. How much would the investor be willing to pay for this security?

An examination of the PVIFA interest factors for 10 percent (in Table IV) indicates that the value in the 10 percent column increases as the number of years increases, but at a decreasing rate. For example, the PVIFA factor for 10 percent and 10 years is 6.145, whereas the factor for 10 percent and 20 years is only 8.514 (much less than twice the 10-year factor). The limiting value in any column of Table IV is 1 divided by the interest rate of that column, i. In the case of a 10 percent perpetuity, the appropriate interest factor is 1/0.10, or 10. Thus Equation 4.22 can be rewritten as follows:

$$(4.23) \qquad \text{PVPER}_0 = \frac{PMT}{i}$$

In this example, the value of a $4.50 perpetuity at a 10 percent required rate of return is given as

$$\text{PVPER}_0 = \$4.50/0.10 = \$45$$

In Chapter 5 the concept of a perpetuity is examined in more detail in the specific cases of preferred shares and perpetual bonds.

Present Value of an Uneven Payment Stream

Many problems in finance—particularly in the area of capital budgeting—cannot be solved according to the simplified format of the present value of an annuity because the periodic cash flows are not equal. Consider an investment that is expected to produce a series of unequal payments (cash flows), PMT_1, PMT_2, PMT_3, . . , PMT_n, over the next n periods. The present value of this uneven payment stream is equal to the sum of the present values of the individual payments (cash flows). Algebraically, the present value can be represented as

$$PV_0 = \frac{PMT_1}{(1 + i)} + \frac{PMT_2}{(1 + i)^2} + \frac{PMT_3}{(1 + i)^3} + \ldots + \frac{PMT_n}{(1 + i)^n}$$

or, using summation notation, as

$$(4.24) \qquad PV_0 = \sum_{t=1}^{n} \frac{PMT_t}{(1 + i)^t}$$

$$(4.25) \qquad = \sum_{t=1}^{n} PMT_t(\text{PVIF}_{i,t})$$

where i is the interest rate (that is, required rate of return) on this investment and $\text{PVIF}_{i,t}$ is the appropriate interest factor from Table II. It should be noted that the payments can be either positive (cash inflows) or negative (outflows).

Consider the following example. Suppose the Gilet Company is evaluating an investment in new equipment that will be used to manufacture a new product it has developed. The equipment is expected to have a useful life of five years and yield the following stream of cash flows (payments) over the five-year period:

End of Year t	Cash Flow PMT_t
1	+ $100,000
2	+ 150,000
3	− 50,000
4	+ 200,000
5	+ 100,000

Note that in year 3, the cash flow is negative. (This is due to a new law that requires the company to purchase and install pollution abatement equipment.) The present value of these cash flows, assuming an interest rate (required rate of return) of 10 percent, is calculated using Equation 4.25 as follows:

$$PV_0 = \$100,000(PVIF_{0.10,\ 1}) + \$150,000(PVIF_{0.10,\ 2})$$
$$- \$50,000(PVIF_{0.10,\ 3}) + \$200,000(PVIF_{0.10,\ 4})$$
$$+ \$100,000(PVIF_{0.10,\ 5})$$
$$= \$100,000(0.909) + \$150,000(0.826)$$
$$- \$50,000(0.751) + \$200,000(0.683) + \$100,000(0.621)$$
$$= \$375,950$$

Figure 4.10 illustrates a timeline for this investment. The present value of the cash flows ($375,950) would be compared with the initial cash outlay (that is, net investment in year 0) in deciding whether to purchase the equipment and manufacture the product. Thus, if the firm had to invest less than $375,950, the investment would be worthwhile. Suppose, for example, that the initial outlay were only $300,000. In that case, the net present value would be $375,950 − $300,000 = $75,950. When the net present value is positive the firm should invest. If the net present value is negative, however, the firm should not invest. Suppose, for example, that the initial outlay were $400,000. In that case, the net present value would be $375,950 − $400,000 = −$24,050. In the first example the investment adds $75,950 to the value of the firm, but in the second example the investment reduces the value of the firm by $24,050.

As will be seen later in the text, during the discussion of capital budgeting, calculations of this type are extremely important when making decisions to accept or reject investment projects.

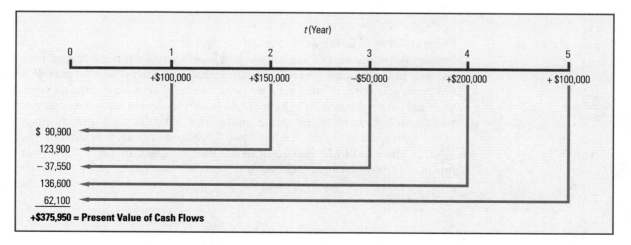

Figure 4.10
Timeline of a Present Value of Unequal Payments ($i = 10\%$, $n = 5$)

Enter: 10   100,000 150,000 −50,000 200,000 100,000

| i | CF1 | CF2 | CF3 | CF4 | CF5 | NPV |

Solution: **376,005.12**

We have not shown the cash flow at time zero. To net the initial outlay from the present value of the five future cash flows, enter 300000 [+/−] into CF0 to obtain $76,005.12 or enter 400000 [+/−] to obtain −$23,994.88.

Better financial calculators have uneven cash flow menus that handle this type of problem. However, the keystrokes differ somewhat among brands and sometimes differ even among different models of the same brand. So, it is best to consult your calculator manual. In particular, one should pay careful attention to how to enter the interest rate for uneven cash flow problems. Usually, the 10 must be entered on the [i] key that is part of the NPV menu, instead of the [i] key that is part of the TVM keys or menu.

The solution to this type of problem can also be found with a spreadsheet using the net present value or NPV function appropriately modified as follows:

	A	B	C	D	E	F	G
1	Rate, i	10.00%					
2	Time	0	1	2	3	4	5
3	Cash Flows		100000	150000	−50000	200000	100000
4	NPV	$376,005.12					

Enter the rate *i* as 10% in cell B1 and enter the five future cash flows in cells C3 through G3, respectively. The Excel function wizard could be used to enter the NPV function in cell B4. The NPV function in Excel, however, calculates only the PV of future cash flows. *Suppose that we want to calculate the PV of future cash flows* net *of the initial outlay. This is the definition of NPV in finance!* In cell B4, type in the formula **=B3+NPV(B1,C3:G3)**. Then we can calculate the NPV of $76,005.12 if we input −300000 in cell B3, or the NPV of −$23,994.88 if we input −400000 in cell B3.

Present Value of Deferred Annuities

Frequently, in finance, one encounters problems where an annuity begins more than one year in the future. For example, suppose that your parents wish to provide for the university education of your younger sister. She will begin university five years from now, and your parents wish to have $15,000 available for her at the beginning of each year during her schooling. How much must be invested today at a 12 percent annual rate of return in order to provide the four-year, $15,000 annuity for your sister?

This problem can be illustrated in the timeline given in Figure 4.11. Four payments of $15,000 each are required at the end of years 5, 6, 7, and 8. Of course, this problem could be solved by finding the sum of the present values of each of the payments as follows:

Year t	Payment PMT_t	$PVIF_{.12,t}$	Present Value
5	$15,000	0.567	$ 8,505
6	$15,000	0.507	$ 7,605
7	$15,000	0.452	$ 6,780
8	$15,000	0.404	$ 6,060
		Present Value of Deferred Annuity =	$28,950

It should be apparent that this would be an extremely tedious method of calculation in the case of a 10-year-deferred annuity, for example. Figure 4.11 illustrates one alternative means of solving this problem. First, you can calculate the present value of the four-year annuity, evaluated at the end of year 4 (remember that this is the same as the beginning of year 5). This calculation is made by multiplying the annuity amount ($15,000) by the PVIFA for a four-year, 12 percent annuity. This factor is 3.037 and can be obtained from Table IV. Next the present value of the annuity ($45,555), evaluated at the end of year 4 $(PVAN_4)$, must be discounted back to the present time (PV_0). Hence, we multiply $45,555 by a PVIF for 12 percent and four years. This factor, obtained from Table II, is equal to 0.636. The present value of the **deferred annuity** is $28,973. (This differs from the amount calculated earlier due to rounding in the tables. No difference will exist if this problem is solved with a calculator or tables that are carried out to more decimal places.)[9]

Deferred Annuity
An annuity that begins sometime in the future.

If you have $28,973 today and invest it in an account earning 12 percent per year, there will be exactly enough money in the account to permit your sister to withdraw $15,000 at the beginning of each year in school. After the last withdrawal, the account balance will be zero.

Present Value of a Growth Annuity

Growth Annuity
In a growth annuity each succeeding payment grows by a constant percentage of the preceding payment.

Previously, we calculated the present value of $4,212 for an ordinary annuity $(PVAN_0)$ of $1,000 received at the end of each year for five years with a required rate of return of 6 percent. Suppose now that we wish to calculate the present value of a growth annuity $(PVGAN_0)$. In a **growth annuity**, each succeeding payment grows by a constant percentage of the preceding payment.

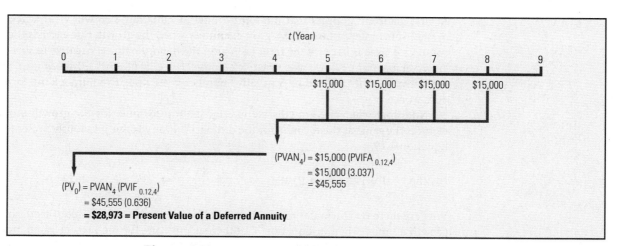

Figure 4.11
Timeline of a Deferred Four-Year Annuity ($i = 12\%$)

[9] Another way to solve this problem is to multiply the annuity payment ($15,000) by the difference between $(PVIFA_{.12,8})$ and $(PVIFA_{.12,4})$. By subtracting $(PVIFA_{.12,4})$ from $(PVIFA_{.12,8})$ you are viewing this problem as an eight-year annuity that has no payments during the first four years. In this case, the calculation yields $PV_0 = \$15,000(4.968 - 3.037) = \$28,965$. (The slight difference from the amount calculated earlier is due to rounding in Table IV.)

For example, suppose that the $1,000 payment at the end of the first year grows by 4 percent per year for the next four years. The present value of this growth annuity at a 6 percent discount rate is determined as follows:

$$
\begin{aligned}
\text{PVGAN}_0 &= \$1{,}000(\text{PVIF}_{0.06,\,1}) + \$1{,}000(\text{FVIF}_{0.04,\,1})(\text{PVIF}_{0.06,\,2}) \\
&\quad + \$1{,}000(\text{FVIF}_{0.04,\,2})(\text{PVIF}_{0.06,\,3}) + \$1{,}000(\text{FVIF}_{0.04,\,3})(\text{PVIF}_{0.06,\,4}) \\
&\quad + \$1{,}000(\text{FVIF}_{0.04,\,4})(\text{PVIF}_{0.06,\,5}) \\
&= \$1{,}000(0.943) + \$1{,}000(1.040)(0.890) + \$1{,}000(1.082)(0.840) \\
&\quad + \$1{,}000(1.125)(0.792) + \$1{,}000(1.170)(0.747) \\
&= \$1{,}000(0.943 + 0.926 + 0.909 + 0.891 + 0.874) \\
&= \$4{,}543
\end{aligned}
$$

As expected, the present value of $4,543 for this growth annuity exceeds the previously calculated present value of $4,212 for the ordinary annuity of $1,000 at the end of each year for five years that also had a required rate of return of 6 percent. This is because the payments received under the growth annuity exceed the payments under the ordinary annuity for every year after the first year, with equal payments only in the first year.

Equation 4.19 previously gave a formula for the present value of an ordinary annuity factor ($\text{PVIFA}_{i,n}$). Is there a generalization of this formula for the growth annuity factor ($\text{PVIFGA}_{i,g,n}$)? Yes, there is, as shown in the two formulas below comprising Equation 4.26.

$$
(4.26) \quad \text{PVIFGA}_{i,g,n} =
\begin{cases}
\dfrac{\left[1 - \dfrac{(1+g)^n}{(1+i)^n}\right]}{(i-g)}, & \infty > i > -1,\ \infty > g \geq -1,\ i \neq g \\[4ex]
\dfrac{n}{(1+i)}, & \infty > i = g > -1
\end{cases}
$$

At first glance, it appears that the top formula in Equation 4.26 will yield a negative present value interest factor for a growth annuity when the growth rate exceeds the discount rate. This is because the term $(i - g)$ in the denominator is negative in this case. However, the numerator is also negative because $(1 + g)^n / (1 + i)^n > 1$ when $g > i$. Since a negative number divided by a negative number gives a positive number, the formula does work for $g > i$.

Note that when the growth rate is zero, the top formula for the growth annuity factor is the same as the formula for the ordinary annuity factor previously presented in Equation 4.19.

$$
(4.26a) \quad \text{PVIFGA}_{i,0,n} = \text{PVIFA}_{i,n} = \dfrac{\left[1 - \dfrac{1}{(1+i)^n}\right]}{i}, \quad \infty > i > -1,\ i \neq 0
$$

Why are there two formulas in Equation 4.26 for the present value interest factor of the growth annuity when in Equation 4.19 there is only one for the present value interest factor of the ordinary annuity factor? Actually, there are also two formulas for the ordinary annuity factor. Note that Equation 4.26a is valid only for permissible interest rates that are different from zero. From the bottom formula of Equation 4.26, we can derive the second equation for the ordinary annuity factor by setting the interest rate (which equals the growth rate) equal to zero.

$$
(4.26b) \quad \text{PVIFGA}_{0,0,n} = \text{PVIFA}_{0,n} = n
$$

In practice, interest rates are almost always positive finite values, which we were implicitly assuming in Equation 4.19. From Equation 4.26a, we now see that the ordinary annuity factor is also valid for interest rates between zero and −100%. However, for a zero interest rate, Equation 4.26b must be used. Most financial calculators have both Equations 4.26a and 4.26b programmed into them for the present value interest factor for an annuity, along with logic that appropriately switches between the two formulas. Furthermore, if you try to enter an interest rate that is −100% or smaller such as −200%, then the calculator will display an error message.

Now let us use the first formula of Equation 4.26 to find the present value of the growth annuity example.

$$PVGAN_0 = \$1,000(PVIFGA_{0.06,\,0.04,\,5})$$

$$= \$1,000\left(\frac{1 - \dfrac{1.04^5}{1.06^5}}{(.06 - .04)}\right)$$

$$= \$1,000(4.54231)$$

$$= \$4,542.31$$

The factor 4.54231 was obtained by using a scientific calculator, not by using table values that are rounded to three decimals. Thus, the result differs slightly from the previous result of $4,543 obtained by using table values.

So far, we have shown how to calculate the present value of a growth annuity by a tedious process using table values and by using a formula and a scientific calculator. Is there any way to use the standard financial functions that are built into an inexpensive financial calculator? Yes, we can replace the growth annuity by an equivalent ordinary annuity with payments PMT^* given by Equation 4.27 and a discount rate i^* given by Equation 4.28, where PMT in Equation 4.27 is the first payment of the growth annuity.

(4.27)
$$PMT^* = \frac{PMT}{(1 + g)}, \infty > g > -1$$

(4.28)
$$i^* = \frac{(i - g)}{(1 + g)}, \infty > i > -1, \infty > g > -1$$

Substituting the values for our growth annuity example in Equations 4.27 and 4.28 yields the following equivalent annuity payments and discount rate:

$$PMT^* = \frac{\$1,000}{1.04} = \$961.54$$

$$i^* = \frac{(.06 - .04)}{1.04} = 0.01923077 = 1.923077\%$$

Following is the calculator solution based on these equivalent ordinary annuity payments and discount rate.

Calculator Solution

Enter:	5	1.923077%		−961.54	
	n	i	PV	PMT	FV

Solution: 4,542.32

Note that this financial calculator result differs by only a penny from our previous result using the first formula of Equation 4.26. If PMT^* were rounded to the nearest 1/10 of a cent (which is \$961.538) instead of to the nearest penny, then the previous result of \$4,542.31 would be obtained.

The solution can also be computed with a spreadsheet as follows:

Spreadsheet Solution

	A	B	C	
1	TVM	INPUTS	SOLUTION	
2	Periods, n	5		
3	Rate, i	1.923077%		
4	PV		\$4,542.32	
5	PMT	−961.54		
6	FV			

Enter the appropriate data inputs in column B and choose the PV function for cell C4.

The concept of a growth annuity will be used in Chapter 6 to value a finite stream of dividends that are growing at a rate that is different from a future perpetual growth rate for dividends.

Present Value of a Growth Perpetuity

Growth Perpetuity
A growth annuity that lasts forever.

Suppose that the growth annuity lasts forever. That is, it is a **growth perpetuity**. If the growth rate equals or exceeds the discount rate, then the present value of each succeeding payment is at least as large as the preceding payment. Since there are an infinite number of payments in a growth perpetuity, such a growth perpetuity (if you could find one) should have an infinite value for any finite permissible discount rate. Since we don't see infinitely valued assets trading in financial markets, we restrict our attention to growth perpetuities with the growth rate less than the discount rate. In this case, the present value of a growth perpetuity ($PVGPER_0$) is as follows:

$$(4.29) \qquad PVGPER_0 = \frac{PMT}{(i - g)}, \infty > i > g \geq -1$$

When the growth rate equals zero, the growth perpetuity becomes an ordinary perpetuity and Equation 4.29 simplifies to Equation 4.23 for a perpetuity. Note from Equation 4.29 that not only must the discount rate for this ordinary perpetuity be finite, but it must also be positive. This is because the discount rate must exceed the growth rate, which is zero for an ordinary perpetuity.

Previously, we used Equation 4.23 to calculate a present value of \$45 for a perpetuity with annual payments of \$4.50 and a discount rate or required rate of return of 10 percent. With no other changes of assumptions, suppose each succeeding payment were 2 percent greater than the preceding payment. This growth perpetuity should have a greater present value than the perpetuity with the same first payment and discount rate. To see this, substitute into Equation 4.29 to obtain

$$PVGPER_0 = \frac{\$4.50}{(.10 - .02)} = \$56.25$$

However, if the growth rate were *negative* 2 percent, then the growth perpetuity would have lower present value than the comparable ordinary perpetuity.

$$PVGPER_0 = \frac{\$4.50}{(.10 + .02)} = \$37.50$$

The above results are general ones. Since ordinary perpetuities valued by Equation 4.23 must have a finite positive discount rate, any growth perpetuity with a permissible positive growth rate (i.e., $\infty > i > g > 0$) will have higher value than the ordinary perpetuity. Similarly, any growth perpetuity with a permissible negative growth rate (i.e., $\infty > i > 0 > g \geq -1$) will have a lower value than the ordinary perpetuity.

In Chapter 6, the concept of a growth perpetuity is used to value the price of a common share of stock. We shall also use the growth perpetuity in Chapter 9, albeit with a negative growth rate, to obtain the present value of the tax savings generated by capital cost allowance (CCA).

Compounding Periods and Effective Interest Rates

The frequency with which interest rates are compounded (for example, annually, semiannually, quarterly, and so on) affects both the present and future values of cash flows as well as the effective interest rates being earned or charged.

Effect of Compounding Periods on Present and Future Values

Thus far, it has been assumed that compounding (and discounting) occur annually. Recall the general compound interest Equation 4.10:

$$FV_n = PV_0(1 + i)^n$$

where PV_0 is the initial deposit, i is the effective annual interest rate, n is the number of years, and FV_n is the future value that will accumulate from the annual compounding of PV_0.

Effective Annual Rate (EAR)
The effective annual rate of interest paid by the borrower or earned by the lender.

Annual Percentage Rate (APR)
The simple, annual percentage interest rate for a loan.

In the remainder of this section, this **effective annual rate (EAR)** will be designated i_{eff} to differentiate it from the stated or quoted annual interest i_{nom}. The stated rate is also called the **annual percentage rate (APR)**. Most financial calculators, however, refer to this rate as the nominal rate, which is why we often use i_{nom} in most equations. Similarly, the effective annual rate is often denoted as EAR in the equations of many financial textbooks, but we usually follow the financial calculator usage of i_{eff} in our equations. When compounding is done annually, $i_{eff} = i_{nom}$. This is why we made no distinction before and simply used i.

In some circumstances, interest on an account is compounded semiannually instead of annually. That is, half of the nominal annual interest rate, $i_{nom}/2$, is earned at the end of every six months. In calculating interest compounded semiannually, Equation 4.10 is rewritten as follows:

$$FV_n = PV_0\left(1 + \frac{i_{nom}}{2}\right)^{2n}$$

The same logic applies to interest compounded quarterly:

$$FV_n = PV_0\left(1 + \frac{i_{nom}}{4}\right)^{4n}$$

In general, the compound interest for any number of periods during a year may be computed by means of the following equation:

$$(4.30) \qquad FV_n = PV_0 \left(1 + \frac{i_{nom}}{m}\right)^{mn}$$

where m is the number of times during the year the interest is compounded and n is the number of years. (The limiting case of continuous compounding and discounting is discussed in Appendix 4A.)

Table 4.6 contains the future value, FV_1, of $1,000 earning a nominal interest of 10 percent for several different compounding frequencies. For example, the future value (FV_1) of $1,000 compounded semiannually $(m = 2)$ at a nominal interest rate (i_{nom}) of 10 percent per year by Equation 4.30 is

$$FV_1 = \$1,000\left(1 + \frac{0.10}{2}\right)^{2 \times 1} = \$1,102.50$$

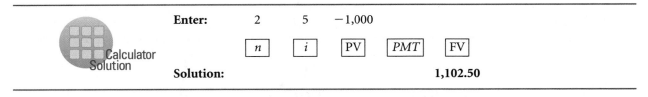

Calculator Solution

Enter:	2	5	−1,000		
	n	i	PV	PMT	FV
Solution:					1,102.50

The solution can also be computed with a spreadsheet as follows:

Spreadsheet Solution

	A	B	C	
1	TVM	INPUTS	SOLUTION	
2	Periods, n	2		
3	Rate, i	5.00%		
4	PV	−1000		
5	PMT			
6	FV		$1,102.50	

Enter the appropriate data inputs in column B and choose the FV function for cell C6.

Table 4.6	Effects of Different Compounding Frequencies on Future Values of $1,000 at a 10 Percent Interest Rate	
Initial Amount	**Compounding Frequency**	**Future Value, FV_1 (End of Year 1)**
$1,000	Yearly	$1,100.00
1,000	Semiannually	1,102.50
1,000	Quarterly	1,103.81
1,000	Monthly	1,104.71
1,000	Daily	1,105.16
1,000	Continuously*	1,105.17

*For advanced applications, it is useful to know that continuous compounding is obtained by letting m approach infinity in $FV_n = PV_0 (1 + i/m)^{mn}$. In this case, $\lim_{m \to \infty} (1 + i/m)^m = e^i$, and the compound value expression becomes $FV_n = PV_0 (e)^{in}$, where e is the exponential number having the approximate value of 2.71828. See Appendix 4A for a complete discussion of continuous compounding and discounting.

As Table 4.6 shows, the more frequent the compounding, the greater the future value of the deposit and the greater the effective interest rate. Effective interest, in contrast to nominal interest, is the rate of interest earned by the lender and is generally the most economically relevant definition of interest rates.

The relationship between present values and compound values suggests that present values will also be affected by the frequency of compounding. In general, the present value of a sum to be received at the end of year n, discounted at the rate of i_{nom} percent and compounded m times per year, is as follows:

$$(4.31) \qquad PV_0 = \frac{FV_n}{\left(1 + \frac{i_{nom}}{m}\right)^{mn}}$$

Table 4.7 contains a number of present values, PV_0, for $1,000 received one year in the future discounted at a nominal interest rate of 10 percent with several different compounding frequencies. For example, the present value (PV_0) of $1,000 compounded quarterly ($m = 4$) at a nominal interest rate (i_{nom}) of 10 percent per year by Equation 4.31 is

$$PV_0 = \frac{\$1,000}{\left(1 + \frac{0.10}{4}\right)^{4 \times 1}} = \$905.95$$

As shown in Table 4.7, the more frequent the compounding, the smaller the present value of a future amount.

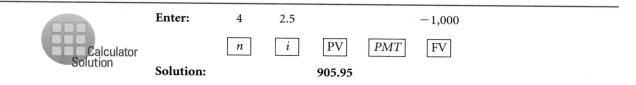

Enter: 4   2.5 $-1,000$

$\boxed{n}$ $\boxed{i}$ $\boxed{PV}$ $\boxed{PMT}$ $\boxed{FV}$

Solution: **905.95**

Note: If the compounding frequency is changed from once per year to four times per year, then the nominal annual rate of 10 percent can be entered for [i].

The solution can also be computed with a spreadsheet as follows:

	A	B	C	
1	TVM	INPUTS	SOLUTION	
2	Periods, n	4		
3	Rate, i	2.5%		
4	PV		$905.95	
5	PMT			
6	FV	-1000		

Enter the appropriate data inputs in column B and choose the PV function for cell C4.

Throughout the text, much of the analysis assumes annual compounding instead of compounding for more frequent periods because it simplifies matters and because the differences between the two are small. Similarly, unless otherwise stated, cash flows from

Table 4.7	Effects of Different Compounding Frequencies on Present Values of $1,000 at a 10 Percent Interest Rate	
Amount	Compounding Frequency	Present Value, PV_0
$1,000	Yearly	$909.09
1,000	Semiannually	907.03
1,000	Quarterly	905.95
1,000	Monthly	905.21
1,000	Daily	904.85
1,000	Continuously	904.84

a security or investment project are assumed to be received in a lump sum at the beginning or end of each period. More frequent compounding periods require more extensive tables or the use of a financial calculator.

Regardless of the frequency of compounding, it is important to recognize that effective rates of interest are the relevant rates to use for financial and economic analysis. The next section considers the calculation of effective interest rates in more detail for those cases where compounding is done more than one time per year.

Effective Rate Calculations

The previous section illustrated the fact that the more frequently a nominal annual rate of interest is compounded, the greater is the effective rate of interest being earned or charged. Thus, if you were given the choice of receiving (1) interest on an investment, where the interest is compounded annually at a 10 percent rate, or (2) interest on an investment, where the interest is compounded semiannually at a 5 percent rate every six months, you would choose the second alternative, because it would yield a higher effective rate of interest.

Given the nominal annual rate of interest (i_{nom}), the effective annual rate of interest (i_{eff}) can be calculated as follows:

(4.32)
$$i_{eff} = \left(1 + \frac{i_{nom}}{m}\right)^m - 1$$

where m is the number of compounding intervals per year.

For example, suppose a bank offers you a loan at a nominal annual interest rate of 12 percent compounded quarterly. What effective annual interest rate (EAR) is the bank charging you? Substituting $i_{nom} = 0.12$ and $m = 4$ into Equation 4.32 yields

$$i_{eff} = \left(1 + \frac{0.12}{4}\right)^4 - 1 = 0.1255$$

or 12.55 percent.

Now suppose the bank again quotes an interest rate of 12 percent but compounding is done monthly. What effect does this have on the EAR? To see the effect, we simply change m from 4 to 12 in two places in our previous calculation.

$$i_{eff} = \left(1 + \frac{0.12}{12}\right)^{12} - 1 = 0.1268$$

Thus, we see that the EAR *increases* from 12.55 percent to 12.68 percent for the *same* quoted interest rate of 12 percent as the compounding frequency *increases* from 4 times to 12 times per year.

There are also situations in finance where one is interested in determining the interest rate during each compounding period that will provide a given annual effective rate of interest. Let the rate of interest per period or effective periodic rate be denoted by i_p, where p is the frequency of compounding per year. Equation 4.33 determines this effective periodic rate that will result in an effective annual rate of interest, i_{eff}, if compounding occurs p times per year.

$$(4.33) \qquad\qquad i_p = (1 + i_{eff})^{(1/p)} - 1$$

Note that once the effective annual interest rate is obtained from Equation 4.32 by using the quoted compounding frequency m, Equation 4.33 is valid for *any* positive finite compounding frequency p (including even compounding less than once per year).

Let us illustrate the point that compounding frequency p need not be the quoted compounding frequency m originally used to calculate the EAR. Suppose that the quoted interest rate is 20 percent with annual compounding. Of course in the case of annual compounding for the quoted rate, the effective rate simply equals the quoted rate of 20 percent. Nevertheless, Equation 4.32 could be used even for this trivial case. Suppose one now wants to know an effective quarterly rate that will compound to the same effective annual rate of 20 percent. From Equation 4.33, we can find this effective quarterly rate.[10]

$$i_p = (1 + 0.20)^{0.25} - 1$$
$$= (1.04663514) - 1$$
$$= 0.04663514 \text{ or } 4.663514\%$$

Thus, if you earn 4.663514 percent per period and compounding occurs four times per year, the effective annual rate earned will be 20 percent. We have calculated the effective periodic interest rate here to 6 decimal places in percentage form, which is the practice of some Canadian financial institutions. We have not used as many decimal places before, but we wanted the reader to be introduced to this practice before the next section on Canadian mortgages.

Suppose that you wanted to know the effective monthly interest rate that also compounded to an EAR of 20 percent. Again, Equation 4.33 can be used.

$$i_p = (1 + 0.20)^{(1/12)} - 1$$
$$= (1.01530947) - 1$$
$$= 0.01530947 \text{ or } 1.530947\%$$

Thus, an annual effective periodic rate of 20 percent, a quarterly effective periodic rate of 4.663514 percent, and a monthly effective periodic rate of 1.530947 percent all compound to a 20 percent effective annual rate. One can confirm this by using Equation 4.32, with i_p replacing i_{nom}/m as the effective periodic rate.

Another way to view this is that a quoted interest rate of 20 percent with annual compounding, a quoted interest rate of $(4)(4.663514\%) = 18.654056$ percent with quarterly compounding, and a quoted interest rate of $(12)(1.530947\%) = 18.371364$ percent with monthly compounding all have the same EAR of 20 percent. One can conclude that for the *same* EAR, the quoted interest rate *declines* as the frequency of compounding *increases*. This is consistent with the previous result that the EAR *increases* for the *same* quoted interest rate as the frequency of compounding *increases*.

---

[10] Finding the 1/4 or 0.25 root of $(1 + 0.20)$ can be done easily with any financial or scientific calculator using the power function on the calculator.

Canadian Mortgages

Canadian mortgages are unique. The law requires that interest be compounded semi-annually and payments are often made monthly. This is different from the method used in the United States that is normally preprogrammed into financial calculators, where both compounding and payments on loans and mortgages are normally made monthly.

The following example integrates the calculation of an effective annual rate i_{eff} via Equation 4.32 with the calculation of an effective periodic rate i_p via Equation 4.33. Suppose a bank offers to lend you $200,000 to buy a house at a quoted interest rate i_{nom} of 6%, compounded semiannually. What is the effective annual rate, i_{eff}, that the bank is charging you?

Substituting into Equation 4.32 gives

$$i_{eff} = \left(1 + \frac{.06}{2}\right)^2 - 1 = 1.0609 - 1 = 1.0609$$

Now suppose that you want to make monthly payments to amortize the loan over 25 years. What is the effective monthly rate that the bank is charging?

Substituting into Equation 4.33 gives

$$i_p = (1.0609)^{1/12} - 1 = 1.00493862 - 1 = 0.00493862$$
$$\text{or } 0.493862\%$$

Clearly, both a quoted interest rate of 6 percent with semiannual compounding and a quoted rate of $(12)(0.493862\%) = 5.926344$ percent with monthly compounding give the same EAR of 6.09 percent. The Bank Act, however, requires the bank's quoted interest rate or annual percentage rate (APR) to be based on semiannual compounding. Thus, the 5.926344 percent rate can be viewed as an **implied APR** based on compounding at the payment frequency of 12 times per year rather than the quoted semiannual compounding frequency.

Implied APR
The APR calculated based on monthly, rather than semi-annual, compounding.

To find the monthly payment, first substitute into Equation 4.19 to obtain the PVIFA for the interest rate i_p for the number of months ($12 \times 25 = 300$) in 25 years.

$$PVIFA_{0.00493862,300} = \frac{1 - \dfrac{1}{(1.00493862)^{300}}}{.00493862}$$
$$= 156.2973$$

Finally, solve Equation 4.20 for the monthly payment.

$$PMT = \$200,000/156.2973 = \$1,279.61$$

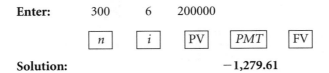

Calculator Solution

Some financial calculators, such as the Texas Instruments BAII+, allow you to independently set the frequency of payments per year [P/Y] from the frequency of compounding per year [C/Y]. Set [P/Y] = 12 and [C/Y] = 2 for monthly payments and semiannual compounding, then

Enter: 300   6   200000

[n]   [i]   [PV]   [PMT]   [FV]

Solution: −1,279.61

If your calculator does not have this ability, then you should leave the compounding per "year" at 1 and enter the effective monthly rate of 0.493862 percent in [i]. (The calculator is really compounding per period and the period becomes a month in this example when the effective monthly rate is used.)

Let us now illustrate how a spreadsheet can be used to calculate a loan amortization schedule. Start by downloading and saving the spreadsheet Loan Amortization.xls from the Web site for this book. In cells B6 through B11, input the relevant data for this mortgage problem. See Table 4.8.

Note that we set the term of the loan to be 0.5 years which is six months. Why might you want only a six-month term? If you feel that interest rates will be lower in six months, you might want the flexibility then to lower monthly payments and/or shorten the amortization period. Alternatively, if you expect an improvement in your financial position in six months with no change in interest rates, you might want the flexibility then to increase monthly payments to shorten the amortization period.

In addition to the data entered in cells B6 through B11, we changed the label in cell B1 from Loan Amortization.xls to Mortgage Amortization Schedule.xls. Then we used the Save As button instead of the Save button so that we could rename the spreadsheet. This allows us to reuse the original Loan Amortization.xls spreadsheet for other amortization problems without overwriting this mortgage example.

Although we have shown a mortgage example with monthly payments, you can usually arrange with your financial institution when you apply for a mortgage to have more frequent payments. Typically, you can match the frequency of mortgage payments with the frequency of your wage payments. Thus, in addition to monthly payments, twice-a-month, biweekly (once every 2 weeks), and weekly payments are available in Canada.

Canadian banks have mortgage calculators at their Web sites. For example, see **www.bmo.com/mortgage** Click on WHAT WILL MY MORTGAGE PAYMENTS BE?

Table 4.8 — Loan Amortization Schedule

INPUT DATA

$200,000.00	$= PV =$ Loan amount or present value
6.00000000%	$= i_{nom} =$ Quoted interest rate or annual percentage rate (APR)
2	$= m = $ # of compounding periods per year
12	$= p = $ # of payment periods per year
25	$= n = $ Amortization in years
0.5	$= t = $ Loan term in years, $t <$ or $= n$

OUTPUT DATA

$1,279.61	$= PMT =$ Payment per period
$198,226.92	$= BAL =$ Balance remaining at end of loan term
$7,677.66	$= PAY =$ Total payments during loan term
$5,904.58	$= INT =$ Total interest paid during term
$1,773.08	$= PRN =$ Total principal paid during term
3.00000000%	$= i_m = i_{nom}/m =$ Effective compounding period rate
6.09000000%	$= i_{eff} = (1 + i_m)^m - 1 =$ Effective annual rate
0.49386220%	$= i_p = (1 + i_{eff})^{1/p} - 1 =$ Effective payment period rate
5.926346%	$= i_{nom}* = pi_p =$ Equivalent or implied APR based on the payment frequency p
300	$= N = np = $ # of payment periods to amortize the loan
6	$= T = tp = $ # of payment periods during term of the loan (not to exceed 360)

PAYMENT PERIOD	TOTAL PAYMENT	INTEREST PAYMENT	PRINCIPAL PAYMENT	REMAINING BALANCE
0	$0.00	$0.00	$0.00	$200,000.00
1	$1,279.61	$987.72	$291.89	$199,708.11
2	$1,279.61	$986.28	$293.33	$199,414.78
3	$1,279.61	$984.83	$294.78	$199,120.00
4	$1,279.61	$983.38	$296.23	$198,823.77
5	$1,279.61	$981.92	$297.69	$198,526.08
6	$1,279.61	$980.45	$299.16	$198,226.92

Financial Challenge Revisited

Recall from the Financial Challenge at the beginning of this chapter that a lottery winner needs to decide which alternative payoff from the Powerball Lottery is the best option. The winning ticket holder has two choices:

1. A lump-sum payment today of $41.4 million
2. Twenty-five beginning-of-the-year payments of $2.948 million each

Based on a careful study of the material in this chapter, you have decided to compute the rate of return that will make the winner indifferent between the two options. You set up the following problem using the present value of an annuity due formula (Equation 4.21):

$$\$41,400,000 = \$2,948,000(\text{PVIFA}_{i,25})(1 + i)$$

This problem can be solved best with the help of a financial calculator, yielding an indifference rate of return of 5.59 percent.

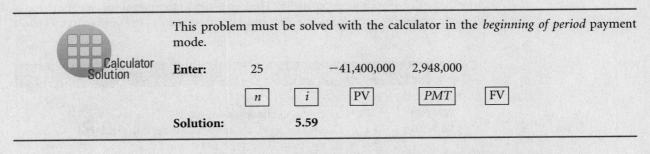

Calculator Solution

This problem must be solved with the calculator in the *beginning of period* payment mode.

Enter:	25		−41,400,000	2,948,000	
	n	i	PV	PMT	FV

Solution: **5.59**

Spreadsheet Solution

The solution can also be computed with a spreadsheet as follows:

	A	B	C	
1	TVM	INPUTS	SOLUTION	
2	Periods, n	25		
3	Rate, i		5.59%	
4	PV	−41400000		
5	PMT	2948000		
6	FV			
7	Type	1		

Enter the appropriate data inputs in column B and choose the RATE function in cell C3. Make sure you include the type variable, as this is necessary to switch the spreadsheet into annuity due mode.

This indifference rate of return can now be compared with the investment opportunity rate of return for investments of similar risk. Because the payment stream from the Lottery Board is virtually risk-free, you believe it is appropriate to compare the 5.59 percent indifference rate of return with the return on 25-year government bonds. These bonds are also considered to be free of default risk. If the winner can earn a return greater than 5.59 percent on the government bonds, the winner should take the lump-sum payment and invest it in government bonds. That is, the present value ($41.4 million) of the bonds will exceed the present value of the 25-year annuity payments at this higher government bond rate of return. On the other hand, if the rate of return on the government bonds is less 5.59 percent, the winner would be better off taking the stream of annuity payments.

Summary

- An understanding of interest is crucial to sound financial management. *Simple interest* is interest earned or paid on the principal only. *Compound interest* is interest paid not only on the principal but also on any interest earned but not withdrawn during earlier periods.

- An *annuity* is the payment or receipt of a series of equal cash flows per period for a specified number of periods. In an *ordinary annuity*, the cash flows occur at the end of each period. In an *annuity due*, the cash flows occur at the beginning of each period. A *deferred annuity* is an ordinary annuity that starts in a later period. A *perpetuity* is an ordinary annuity that lasts forever. A *growth annuity (perpetuity)* is a generalization of the ordinary annuity (perpetuity).

- Table 4.9 summarizes the equations used to compute the future and present values of the various cash flow streams.

- In solving financial mathematics problems, it is necessary to answer two questions:

  1. Do we need a future value or a present value?

  2. Are we dealing with a single payment or an annuity?

  Once these questions have been successfully answered, the following table can be used to select the appropriate table of interest factors:

	Future Value	Present Value
Single Payment	Table I	Table II
Annuity	Table III	Table IV

- *Sinking fund* problems determine the annuity amount that must be invested each year to produce a future value.

- *Capital recovery* problems determine the annuity amount necessary to recover some initial investment.

- The more frequently compounding occurs during a given period, the higher the *effective* interest rate on an investment. More frequent compounding results in higher future values and lower present values than less frequent compounding at the same interest rate.

- The appropriate compounding or discount rate to use in a particular problem depends on the general level of interest rates in the economy, the time frame used for analysis, and the risk of the investment being considered.

Table 4.9 Summary of Future and Present Value Equations

Type of Calculation	Equation	Interest Factor Table	Equation Number
Future value of a single payment	$FV_n = PV_0(FVIF_{i,n})$	Table I	4.12
Future value of an (ordinary) annuity	$FVAN_n = PMT(FVIFA_{i,n})$	Table III	4.17
Future value of an annuity due	$FVAND_n = PMT[FVIFA_{i,n}(1 + i)]$	Table III	4.18
Present value of a single payment	$PV_0 = FV_n(PVIF_{i,n})$	Table II	4.15
Present value of an (ordinary) annuity	$PVAN_0 = PMT(PVIFA_{i,n})$	Table IV	4.20
Present value of an annuity due	$PVAND_0 = PMT[PVIFA_{i,n}(1 + i)]$	Table IV	4.21
Present value of an uneven payment stream	$PV_0 = \sum_{t=1}^{n} PMT_t(PVIF_{i,t})$	Table II	4.25
Present value of a (ordinary) perpetuity	$PVPER_0 = \dfrac{PMT}{i}$	—	4.23

Definitions:
n = number of time periods of discounting or compounding (usually years).
i = annual rate of interest (i.e., annual nominal interest rate).
PMT = annuity cash flow (i.e., amount of cash flow paid or received for a specified number of years or forever in the case of a perpetuity). In an ordinary annuity, the cash flows are received at the end of each year. In an annuity due, the cash flows are received at the beginning of each year.
PMT_t = payment (cash flow) in period t.

Questions and Topics for Discussion

1. Which would you rather receive: the proceeds from a two-year investment paying 5 percent simple interest per year or from one paying 5 percent compound interest? Why?

2. Which is greater: the future value interest factor (FVIF) for 10 percent and two years or the present value interest factor (PVIF) for 10 percent and two years?

3. What happens to the present value of an annuity as the interest rate increases? What happens to the future value of an annuity as the interest rate increases?

4. Which would you prefer to invest in: a savings account paying 6 percent compounded annually or a savings account paying 6 percent compounded daily? Why?

5. What type of contract might require the use of annuity due computations?

6. What effect does more frequent compounding have on present values?

7. Why should each of the following be familiar with compounding and present value concepts?
   a. A marketing manager
   b. A personnel manager

8. Explain what is meant by the "Rule of 72." How can it be used in finance applications? (See Footnote 3.)

9. What is the relationship between present value and future value?

10. What is the difference between an ordinary annuity and an annuity due? Give examples of each.

11. If the required rate of return decreases, what is the impact on the following?
    a. A present value of an annuity
    b. A future value of an annuity

12. Explain how future value of an annuity interest factors can be used to solve a sinking fund problem.

13. Describe how to set up a loan amortization schedule.

14. Give an example of a perpetuity. How does a perpetuity differ from an annuity?

15. Explain how to determine the present value of an uneven cash flow stream.

16. Evaluate the following statement: "The development of powerful, inexpensive microcomputers has made the hand calculator as obsolete as the slide rule."

Self-Test Problems

ST1. Calculate the value in five years of $1,000 deposited in a savings account today if the account pays interest at a rate of
   a. 8% per year, compounded annually
   b. 8% per year, compounded quarterly

ST2. A business is considering purchasing a machine that is projected to yield cash savings of $1,000 per year over a 10-year period. Using a 12% discount rate, calculate the present value of the savings. (Assume that the cash savings occur at the end of each year.)

ST3. Simpson Peripherals earned $0.90 per share in 1998 and $1.52 in 2003. Calculate the annual growth rate in earnings per share over this period.

ST4. You own a small business that is for sale. You have been offered $2,000 per year for five years, with the first receipt at the end of four years. Calculate the present value of this offer, using a 14% discount rate.

ST5. Yolanda Williams is 35 years old today and is beginning to plan for her retirement. She wants to set aside an equal amount at the end of each of the next 25 years so that she can retire at age 60. She expects to live to an age of 80 and wants to be able to withdraw $50,000 per year from the account on her 61st through 80th birthdays. The account is expected to earn 10% per year for the entire period of time. Determine the size of the annual deposits that she must make.

Problems*

BASIC

1. How much will $1,000 deposited in a savings account earning a compound annual interest rate of 6% be worth at the end of the following number of years?
   a. 3 years
   b. 5 years
   c. 10 years

2. If you require a 9% return on your investments, which would you prefer?
   a. $5,000 today
   b. $15,000 five years from today
   c. $1,000 per year for 15 years

*Coloured numbers and letters denote problems that have "check" answers provided at the back of the book.

3. The Lancer Company has agreed to lease a hydraulic trencher to the Russo Company for $20,000 per year over the next eight years. Lease payments are to be made at the beginning of each year. Assuming that Lancer invests these payments at an annual rate of 9%, how much will it have accumulated by the end of the eighth year?

4. The Mutual Life Assurance Company is offering an insurance policy under either of the following two terms:

   a. Make a series of twelve $1,200 payments at the beginning of each of the next 12 years (the first payment being made today)

   b. Make a single lump-sum payment today of $10,000 and receive coverage for the next 12 years

   If you had investment opportunities offering an 8% annual return, which alternative would you prefer?

5. How much must you deposit at the end of each year in an account that pays a compound annual rate of 20% if, at the end of five years, you want $10,000 in the account?

6. A leading broker has advertised money multiplier certificates that will triple your money in nine years. That is, if you buy one for $333.33 today, it will pay you $1,000 at the end of nine years. What rate of return will you earn on these money multiplier certificates?

7. What is the present value of $800 to be received at the end of eight years, assuming the following nominal annual interest rate?

   a. 4%, discounted annually

   b. 8%, discounted annually

   c. 20%, discounted quarterly

   d. 0%

 Excel

8. Gaston Benoit bought a building for $60,000, payable on the following terms: a $10,000 down payment and 25 equal annual instalment payments to include principal and interest of 10% per annum. Calculate the amount of the instalment payments. How much of the first year's payment goes toward reducing the principal amount?

9. A firm purchases 100 hectares of land for $200,000 and agrees to remit 20 equal annual end-of-year instalments of $41,067 each. What is the true annual interest rate on this loan?

10. Suzanne Robineau is planning for her retirement. She is 30 years old today and would like to have $600,000 when she turns 55. She estimates that she will be able to earn a 9% rate of return on her retirement investments over time. She wants to set aside a constant amount of money every year (at the end of the year) to help achieve her objective. How much money must she invest at the end of each of the next 25 years to realize her goal of $600,000 at the end of that time?

11. A life insurance company offers loans to its policy holders against the cash value of their policies at a nominal annual interest rate of 8%, compounded quarterly. Determine the effective annual percentage interest rate on these loans.

12. Two investment opportunities are open to you: Investment 1 and Investment 2. Each has an initial cost of $10,000. Assuming that you desire a 10% return on your initial investment, compute the net present value of the two alternatives and evaluate their relative attractiveness:

Investment 1		Investment 2	
Cash Flows	Year	Cash Flows	Year
$5,000	1	$8,000	1
$6,000	2	$7,000	2
$7,000	3	$6,000	3
$8,000	4	$5,000	4

13. Your great-uncle Claude is 82 years old. Over the years, he has accumulated savings of $80,000. He estimates that he will live another 10 years at the most and wants to spend his savings by then. (If he lives longer than that, he figures you will be happy to take care of him.)

Uncle Claude places his $80,000 into an account earning 10% annually and sets it up in such a way that he will be making 10 equal annual withdrawals—the first one occurring one year from now—such that his account balance will be zero at the end of 10 years. How much will he be able to withdraw each year?

14. Strikler, Inc. has issued a $10 million, 10-year bond issue. The bonds require Strikler to establish a sinking fund and make 10 equal, end-of-year deposits into the fund. These deposits will earn 8% annually, and the sinking fund should have enough accumulated in it at the end of 10 years to retire the $10 million of bonds. What are the annual sinking fund payments?

 Excel

15. Construct a loan amortization schedule for a three-year, 11% loan of $30,000. The loan requires three equal, end-of-year payments. (The last payment may differ slightly to exactly amortize the loan.)

16. On retirement, your goal is to spend five years travelling around the world. To travel in the style to which you are accustomed will require $250,000 per year at the beginning of each year. If you plan to retire in 30 years, what are the equal, annual, end-of-year payments necessary to achieve this goal? The funds in the retirement account will compound at 10% annually.

17. Determine the value at the end of three years of a $10,000 investment (today) in a guaranteed investment certificate (GIC) that pays a nominal annual interest rate of 8%, compounded
    a. Semiannually
    b. Quarterly
    c. Monthly

18. An investment requires an outlay of $100,000 today. Cash inflows from the investment are expected to be $40,000 per year at the end of years 4, 5, 6, 7, and 8. If you require a 20% rate of return on this type of investment, should the investment be undertaken?

19. An investment of $100,000 is expected to generate cash inflows of $60,000 in one year and $79,350 in two years. Calculate the expected rate of return on this investment to the nearest whole percentage.

20. Try using one of the many Internet calculators to calculate your time-value problems. If you have not yet visited **www.moneyadvisor.com** you should start there.
    a. Suppose you wanted to borrow $100,000 for 25 years at an 8% annual nominal interest rate with monthly compounding. Using an Internet calculator, find your monthly payment.
    b. Using an Internet calculator, find how much $2,000 saved at the end of each of the next 30 years will grow to be, assuming it earns a constant 10% nominal annual interest rate with monthly compounding.

21. Using an Internet calculator, amortize a $100,000 loan over 10 years at a 9% nominal annual interest rate with monthly compounding. What is the remaining balance after the fifth monthly payment?

INTERMEDIATE

22. What would you be willing to pay for a $1,000 bond paying $70 interest at the end of each year and maturing in 25 years if you wanted the bond to yield the following rates of return?

    a. 5%

    b. 7%

    c. 12%

    (Note: At maturity, the bond will be retired and the holder will receive $1,000 in cash in addition to the $70 interest for that year. Bonds are typically issued with $1,000 face, or par, values. The actual market value at any point in time will tend to rise as interest rates fall and fall as interest rates rise.)

23. You decide to purchase a building for $30,000 by paying $5,000 down and assuming a mortgage of $25,000. The seller offers you a 15-year mortgage requiring annual end-of-year payments of $3,188 each. The seller also requires you to pay a 3% loan origination fee, which will reduce the effective amount lent to you. Compute the effective annual percentage rate of interest on this loan.

24. An investment promises to pay $6,000 at the end of each year for the next five years and $4,000 at the end of each year for years 6 through 10.

    a. If you require a 12% rate of return on an investment of this sort, what is the maximum amount you would pay for this investment?

    b. Assuming that the payments are received at the beginning of each year, what is the maximum amount you would pay for this investment, given a 12% required rate of return?

25. Mitchell Investments has offered you the following investment opportunity:

    ■ $6,000 at the end of each year for the first five years, plus

    ■ $3,000 at the end of each year from years 6 through 10, plus

    ■ $2,000 at the end of each year from years 11 through 20

    a. How much would you be willing to pay for this investment if you required a 15% rate of return?

    b. If the payments were received at the beginning of each year, what would you be willing to pay for this investment?

26. You deposit $4,500 per year at the end of each of the next 25 years into an account that pays 10% compounded annually. How much could you withdraw at the end of each of the 20 years following your last deposit? (The 25th and last deposit is made at the beginning of the 20-year period. The first withdrawal is made at the end of the first year in the 20-year period.)

27. You deposit $10,000 at the end of each of the next four years into an account that pays 14% annually. What is the account balance at the end of 10 years?

28. An investment offers the following year-end cash flows:

End of Year	Cash Flow
1	$20,000
2	$30,000
3	$15,000

Using a 15% interest rate, convert this series of irregular cash flows to an equivalent (in present value terms) three-year annuity.

29. How much must you deposit at the end of each quarter in an account that pays a nominal interest rate of 20%, compounded quarterly, if at the end of five years you want $10,000 in the account? (Hint: In working with the compound interest tables when solving this problem, you need to adjust the interest rate and the number of compounding periods to reflect quarterly, rather than annual, compounding.)

30. Steven White is considering taking early retirement, having saved $400,000. He desires to determine how many years the savings will last if $40,000 per year is withdrawn at the end of each year. He feels the savings can earn 10% per year.

 Excel

31. A bank has offered you a $1,000,000 five-year loan at an interest rate of 11.25%, requiring equal annual end-of-year payments that include both principal and interest on the unpaid balance. Develop an amortization schedule for this loan. (The last payment may differ slightly to exactly amortize the loan.)

CHALLENGE

32. A small corporation is considering investing in a bond that matures 20 years from now. It pays an annual end-of-year coupon rate of interest of 8.75%, or $87.50 per year. The bond currently sells for $919. The firm's marginal income tax rate (applied to interest payments) is 28%. Capital gains are taxed at half the rate of ordinary income for corporations. What is the firm's after-tax rate of return if it buys this bond today and holds it until maturity?

33. Your parents have discovered a $1,000 bond at the bottom of their safety deposit box. The bond was given to you by your late great-aunt Hilda on your second birthday. The bond pays interest at a rate of 5% per annum, compounded annually. Interest accumulates and is paid at the time the bond is redeemed. You are now 27 years old. What is the current worth of the bond (principal plus interest)?

34. Your mother is planning to retire this year. Her firm has offered her a lump-sum retirement payment of $50,000 or a $6,000 lifetime annuity—whichever she chooses. Your mother is in reasonably good health and expects to live for at least 15 more years. Which option should she choose, assuming that an 8% interest rate is appropriate to evaluate the annuity?

35. James Street's son, Harold, is 10 years old today. Harold, a studious young fellow, is already making plans to go to college on his 18th birthday, and his father wants to start putting money away now for that purpose. Street estimates that Harold will need $18,000, $19,000, $20,000, and $21,000 for his first, second, third, and fourth years, respectively. He plans on making these amounts available to Harold at the beginning of each of these years.

Street would like to make eight annual deposits (the first of which would be made on Harold's 11th birthday, one year from now, and the last on his 18th birthday, the day he leaves for college) in an account earning 10% annually. He wants the account to eventually be worth enough to just pay for Harold's college expenses. Any balances remaining in the account will continue to earn the 10%.

How much will Street have to deposit in this "planning" account each year to provide for Harold's education?

36. RIA Investments develops retirement programs for individuals. You are 30 years old and plan to retire on your 60th birthday. You want to establish a plan with RIA that will require a series of equal, annual, end-of-year deposits into the retirement account. The first deposit will be made one year from today on your 31st birthday. The final payment on the account will be made on your 60th birthday. The retirement plan will allow you to withdraw $120,000 per year for 15 years,

with the first withdrawal on your 61st birthday. Also, at the end of the 15th year, you wish to withdraw an additional $250,000. The retirement account promises to earn 8% annually.

What periodic payment must be made into the account to achieve your retirement objective?

37. You have just had your 30th birthday. You have two children. One will go to college 10 years from now and require four beginning-of-year payments for college expenses of $10,000, $11,000, $12,000, and $13,000. The second child will go to college 15 years from now and require four beginning-of-year payments for college expenses of $15,000, $16,000, $17,000, and $18,000. In addition, you plan to retire in 30 years. You want to be able to withdraw $50,000 per year (at the end of each year) from an account throughout your retirement. You expect to live 20 years beyond retirement. The first withdrawal will occur on your 61st birthday.

What equal, annual, end-of-year amount must you save for each of the next 30 years to meet these goals, if all savings earn a 13% annual rate of return?

38. You are currently 30 years of age. You intend to retire at age 60 and you want to be able to receive a 20-year, $100,000 beginning-of-year annuity, with the first payment to be received on your 60th birthday. You would like to save enough money over the next 15 years to achieve your objective. That is, you want to accumulate the necessary funds by your 45th birthday.

    a. If you expect your investments to earn 12% per year over the next 15 years and 10% per year thereafter, how much must you accumulate by the time you reach age 45?

    b. What equal, annual amount must you save at the end of each of the next 15 years to achieve your objective, assuming that you currently have $10,000 available to meet your goal? Assume the conditions stated in part a.

39. Suppose today is July 1, 2003, and you deposit $2,000 into an account today. Then you deposit $1,000 into the same account on each July 1, beginning in 2004 and continuing until the last $1,000 deposit is made on July 1, 2009. Also, assume that you withdraw $3,000 on July 1, 2011. Assuming a 7% annual compound interest rate, what will be the balance in the account at the close of business on July 1, 2013?

40. Your son, Charlie, has just turned 15. Charlie plans to go to college to study electronics on his 18th birthday. College is expected to cost Charlie $15,000, $16,000, $17,000, and $18,000 for each of his four years in school. You want these funds to be available to him at the beginning of each year in college. In addition, you want to give Charlie a $25,000 graduation gift on his 22nd birthday so that he can get a start on his career or on graduate school.

You currently have $8,000 to meet these obligations. You want to save an equal amount at the end of each of the next six years to meet the remaining obligations. If your investments earn 10% pretax and your marginal tax rate is 30%, how much must you save at the end of each of the next six years?

41. Frank Chang is planning for the day when his child, Laura, will go to college. Laura has just turned eight and plans to enter college on her 18th birthday. She will need $25,000 at the beginning of each year in school. Frank plans to give Laura a Mercedes-Benz as a combination graduation and 22nd birthday present. The Mercedes is expected to cost $55,000. Frank currently has $10,000 saved for Laura. Also, Frank expects to inherit $25,000 nine years from now that will be used for Laura's education. Frank expects to be able to earn 7% after tax on any investments. How much must Frank save at the end of each of the next 10 years in order to provide for Laura's education and the Mercedes?

42. Ted Gardiner has just turned 30 years old. He has currently accumulated $35,000 toward his planned retirement at age 60. He wants to accumulate enough money over the next 30 years to provide for a 20-year retirement annuity of $100,000 at the beginning of each year, starting with his 60th birthday. He plans to save $5,000 at the end of each of the next 10 years. What equal amount must he save at the end of years 11 through 30 to meet this objective? The interest rate for the first 10 years will be 5%. After that time, the interest rate is expected to be 7%.

43. Torbet Fish Packing Company wants to accumulate enough money over the next 10 years to pay for the expected replacement of its digitalized, automated scaling machine. The new machine is expected to cost $200,000 in 10 years. Torbet currently has $10,000 that it plans to invest over the next 10 years to help pay for the new machine. Torbet wants to put away an equal, end-of-year amount into a sinking fund investment account at the end of each of the next 10 years. Earnings on all of the investments are expected to be 7% for the first five years and 9% thereafter. What equal, end-of-year amount must Torbet save each year over the next 10 years to meet these needs?

44. Garrett Erdle has just turned 26 years of age. Although Garrett currently has a negative net worth, he expects to pay off all of his financial obligations within four years and then to embark on an aggressive plan to save for retirement. He wishes to be able to withdraw $100,000 per year during the first 10 years of retirement (the first withdrawal coming on his 61st birthday) and $150,000 during the next 10 years of retirement. As a precaution against unexpected longevity, he would like to have a net worth of $500,000 after the withdrawal on his 80th birthday. Garrett expects the after-tax return on his investments to be 6% until he turns age 50, and 7% thereafter. What equal annual amount must Garrett save at the end of each year (the first deposit will occur on his 31st birthday and the last deposit will occur on his 60th birthday) to meet these retirement goals?

45. Bobbi Proctor does not want to gamble on the CPP taking care of her in her old age. Hence she wants to begin to plan now for retirement. She has enlisted the services of Hackney Financial Planning to assist her in meeting her goals. Proctor has determined that she would like to have a retirement annuity of $200,000 per year, with the first payment to be received 36 years from now at the end of her first year of retirement. She plans a long, enjoyable retirement of about 25 years. Proctor wishes to save $5,000 at the end of each of the next 15 years, and an unknown, equal end-of-period amount for the remaining 20 years before she begins her retirement. Hackney has advised Proctor that she can safely assume that all savings will earn 12% per annum until she retires, but only 8% thereafter. How much must Proctor save per year during the 20 years preceding retirement?

46. You have decided to start planning for your retirement by analyzing different retirement plans. You have been offered a plan that requires you to deposit $5,000 at the beginning of each of the next 30 years. The retirement plan guarantees a 10% annual compounding rate over the 30-year time period. When you retire at the end of the 30th year, the interest earned on the money in the account is guaranteed to increase to a 12% annual rate. If you plan on making 20 equal withdrawals at the beginning of each year from the account (with the first withdrawal made at the end of the 30th year—the first year of retirement), how much can you withdraw?

Time Value of Money

Assume that you are 30 years old today and expect to retire when you reach age 65. If you were to retire today, you would like a fixed (pretax) income of $60,000 per year (in addition to CPP) for a period of 15 years (your approximate life expectancy at age 65). However, you realize that price inflation will erode the purchasing power of the dollar over the next 35 years and you want to adjust your desired retirement income at age 65 to reflect the decline in the purchasing power of the dollar. In addition to the fixed annual income, payable at the beginning of each year starting at age 65, you want to have assets (i.e., securities investments) of $1,000,000, either for your own needs or to donate to heirs, when you reach 80 years of age.

Empirical studies have estimated the average compound rate of price inflation and returns on shares and bonds over the past 70 years to be approximately:

	Compound Rate (%)
Inflation	3
Common shares	11
Corporate bonds	6
Equally weighted portfolio (50% common shares, 50% bonds)	8.5

Assume that these rates will remain the same over the next 50 years and that you can earn these rates of return, after transactions costs, by investing in stock and/or bond index mutual funds. Also assume that contributions to your retirement fund are made at the end of each year. Finally, assume that income taxes on the returns from any retirement investments (e.g., RRSP plans) can be deferred until you withdraw the funds beginning at age 65.

1. Determine your required inflation-adjusted annual (pretax) income at age 65. Assume that this annual amount remains constant from age 65 to age 80.

2. Determine the amount you must accumulate by age 65 to meet your retirement goal, assuming that you invest in
   a. Common shares
   b. Corporate bonds
   c. Equally weighted portfolio (50 percent common shares, 50 percent bonds)

3. Determine the annual investment in common shares required to accumulate the funds determined in question 2, assuming that the first payment is made at age
   a. 30
   b. 40
   c. 50

4. Determine the annual investment in corporate bonds required to accumulate the funds determined in question 2, assuming that the first payment is made at age
   a. 30
   b. 40
   c. 50

5. Determine the annual investment in an equally weighted portfolio (50% common shares, 50% bonds) required to accumulate the funds determined in question 2, assuming that the first payment is made at age
   a. 30
   b. 40
   c. 50

6. What conclusions can be drawn from the answers to questions 3, 4, and 5?

Other Practice Materials and Resources

For interactive quizzes, Internet exercises, crossword puzzles, CTV videos, and more, go to the *Contemporary Financial Management* Web site at **http://cyr.nelson.com**

APPENDIX 4A: CONTINUOUS COMPOUNDING AND DISCOUNTING

Continuous Compounding

In Chapter 4 we assumed that interest was received (or growth in a stream of payments occurred) at discrete points in time, such as at the end of each year, semiannually, quarterly, and so forth. It was shown that a nominal rate of i_{nom} percent per year results in a greater than i_{nom} percent effective rate per year if compounding occurs more frequently than one time per year. Specifically, the future value (FV_n) of some initial amount (PV_0) is given by Equation 4.30:

$$FV_n = PV_0 \left(1 + \frac{i_{nom}}{m} \right)^{mn}$$

where i_{nom} is the nominal annual rate of interest or growth, m is the number of times per year that compounding occurs, and n is the number of years compounding occurs.

As is shown in Table 4.6, the more often the compounding takes place each year, the greater will be the future value of some present amount. Another way of looking at this is to indicate that the more often compounding takes place each year, the greater is the effective rate of interest (or growth) compared to the stated nominal annual rate.

At the limit, we could accrue, or compound, interest continuously. In this limiting case, the future value equation for continuous compounding becomes

(4A.1) $$FV_n = PV_0 (e)^{i_{nom} n}$$

where e is approximately equal to the value 2.71828. (This value is the base number in natural logarithms.) If you have a financial or scientific calculator, the value of $e^{i_{nom} n}$ normally can be found by multiplying the nominal rate i by the number of years n and then punching the e^x key.

For example, if $1,000 is invested for one year at a nominal rate of 10 percent compounded continuously, the future value at the end of that year is given as follows:

$$FV_1 = \$1,000(e)^{0.10(1)} = \$1,000(2.71828)^{0.10}$$
$$= \$1,105.17$$

In the case where the $1,000 is invested at a nominal rate of 10 percent for three years, the future value, assuming continuous compounding, is equal to

$$FV_3 = \$1000(e)^{0.10(3)} = \$1,000(2.71828)^{0.30}$$
$$= \$1,349.86$$

Continuous Discounting

Equation 4A.1 can also be modified to reflect continuous discounting. At the limit where compounding takes place continuously, present values can be computed as follows:

(4A.2) $$PV_0 = \frac{FV_n}{e^{i_{nom} n}}$$

or equivalently

(4A.3)
$$PV_0 = FV_n(e)^{-i_{nom}n}$$

For example, if $1,349.86 is to be received three years from now at the continuously compounded rate of 10 percent, the present value can be computed as follows:

$$PV_0 = \frac{\$1,349.86}{(2.71828)^{0.10(3)}} = \$1,000$$

Effective Rate Calculations

When a nominal annual rate, i_{nom}, of interest (or growth) is known and compounding occurs continuously, it is easy to compute the effective annual rate using the following expression:[11]

(4A.4)
$$i_{eff} = e^{i_{nom}} - 1$$

For example, if the nominal annual rate is 20 percent and compounding occurs continuously, the effective annual rate is computed as follows:

$$i_{eff} = 2.71828^{(0.2)} - 1$$
$$= 1.2214 - 1$$
$$= 0.2214 \text{ or } 22.14\%$$

The effective rate is higher than the nominal rate because, with continuous compounding, the money is working harder. That is, interest is being accumulated more frequently (continuously), and this accumulated interest is available to earn its own interest on an ongoing (continuous) basis.

Self-Test Problems: Appendix 4A

ST1. What is the future value of $1,000 invested for seven years at a nominal interest rate of 10% compounded continuously?

ST2. What is the present value of receiving $5,000 eight years from now if the nominal discount rate is 9%, discounted continuously?

ST3. Calculate the effective annual rate if the nominal annual rate is 12%, compounded continuously.

Problems: Appendix 4A*

BASIC

1. What is the future value of $10,000 invested for two years at a nominal interest rate of 12%, compounded continuously?

---

[11] Equation 4A.4 is obtained from Equation 4.32 by letting m approach infinity:

$$i_{eff} = \lim_{m \to \infty} \left(1 + \frac{i_{nom}}{m}\right)^m - 1 = e^{i_{nom}} - 1$$

*Coloured numbers and letters denote problems that have "check" answers provided at the back of the book.

2. You expect to receive $5,000 in five years. What is the present value of this future receipt at the continuously discounted rate of 8%?

3. The nominal rate of interest on a GIC is 8%. If compounding occurs continuously, what is the effective annual rate?

4. Given a nominal annual interest rate of 20%, determine the effective annual rate with
   a. Annual compounding
   b. Quarterly compounding
   c. Monthly compounding
   d. Continuous compounding

5. What is the future value of $1,000 invested for 10 years at a nominal interest rate of 10% compounded continuously? How much higher is this value than the value obtained with annual compounding for 10 years at 10%?

6. What is the present value of receiving $1,500 twenty-five years from now if the nominal interest rate is 6%, discounted continuously?

Fixed-Income Securities: Characteristics and Valuation

Learning Objectives

After studying this chapter you should be able to

1. Understand the principal characteristics of fixed-income (debt and preferred shares) securities, including

   a. The types of each form of security (bonds, debentures, notes, and preferred shares)

   b. The main features of each form of security

   c. The main users of each form of security

   d. The main advantages and disadvantages of each form of security

2. Read and interpret financial market data, including bond and preferred share price quotations. This is an essential skill for an effective financial manager

3. Understand that in the capitalization of cash flow method, the value of an asset is equal to the present value of the expected future cash flows discounted at the appropriate required rate of return

4. Understand that the required rate of return is a function of the risk or uncertainty associated with the cash flows from the asset, as well as the risk-free rate

5. Understand that the value of a bond with a finite maturity date is equal to the present value of the interest payments and principal payment (at maturity) discounted at the investor's required rate of return

6. Understand that the yield to maturity of a bond is equal to the rate of return that equates the price of the bond to the present value of the interest and principal payments

7. Understand that the value of a perpetual bond, or perpetuity, is determined by dividing the fixed interest payment per period by the required rate of return, since no calculation for payback of principal is needed in the valuation

8. Understand that preferred shares are often treated as *perpetuities* with a value equal to the annual dividend divided by the required rate of return

9. Understand that the market value or market price of an asset is the value placed on the asset by the marginally satisfied buyer and seller who exchange assets in the marketplace

10. Understand that market equilibrium occurs when the price of an asset is such that the expected rate of return is equal to the required rate of return

11. Understand that bond refunding involves the replacement of an expensive called bond issue with a lower interest cost issue

New Offering of BCE Debt and Preferred Share Issues

In the autumn of 2002, BCE Inc., Canada's largest telecommunications firm, raised $2 billion in three debt issues:

1. $300 million principal amount of 6.20% series A notes due in 2006

2. $1.05 billion principal amount of 6.75% series B notes due in 2007

3. $650 million principal amount of 7.35% series C notes due in 2009

These debt issues were offered to buyers around the world by a syndicate headed by TD Securities that included Merrill Lynch of the United States and Le Groupe Société Générale in Europe. BCE sold three issues with different interest rates and maturity dates to appeal to the various desires of the potential bond buyers. BCE relied on the advice of investment dealers in designing the appropriate package to obtain the funds it needed. The total package included preferred shares (also discussed in this chapter) and common shares (discussed in the next chapter). As part of the package, BCE sold 6 million cumulative redeemable first preferred shares, series AC, at a price of $25.50, through the same investment dealer/investment banker syndicate.

The net proceeds of the sale of these issues were used to pay part of the acquisition costs of buying back the minority interest in Bell Canada from SBC Communications. BCE now owns all of Bell Canada again.

Large companies like BCE are among the most frequent issuers of debt securities. Debt securities (e.g., bonds, debentures, and notes) issued by firms such as BCE are rated with respect to their riskiness by various debt rating agencies (i.e., private companies) such as the Dominion Bond Rating Service. Many investors use ratings information in their decisions to buy or sell a company's debt securities. The role that debt ratings agencies play in fixed-income financing is one of the topics examined in this chapter.

Introduction

Companies issue (offer for sale) various types of long-term securities to help meet their needs for funds. These include long-term debt (bonds, debentures, and notes), preferred shares, and common shares. Long-term debt and preferred shares are sometimes referred to as **fixed-income securities**, the focus of this chapter. Holders of these types of securities receive relatively constant distributions of interest or dividend payments over time and have a fixed claim on the assets of the firm in the event of bankruptcy.[1]

For example, Barrick Gold Corporation sold $500 million of bonds in 1997, at which time it agreed to pay its lenders an interest rate of 7.5 percent or $75 per year until 2007 for each $1,000 of debt outstanding. Since then, the company has continued to pay this interest rate, even though market interest rates have fluctuated.

Common shares, on the other hand, are **variable-income securities**, and are the focus of Chapter 6. Common shareholders are said to participate in a firm's earnings because they may receive a larger dividend if earnings increase in the future, or their dividend may be cut if earnings drop. Investors in common shares have a residual claim on the earnings (and assets) of the firm since they receive dividends only after the claims of bondholders and other creditors, as well as preferred shareholders, have been met.

Fixed-income securities—long-term debt and preferred shares—differ from each other in several ways. For example, the interest paid to bondholders is a tax-deductible expense for the borrowing company, whereas dividends paid to preferred shareholders are not. Legally, long-term debt holders are considered creditors, whereas preferred shareholders are considered owners. Thus, a firm is not legally required to pay dividends to its preferred shareholders, and the failure to do so has less serious consequences than the failure to meet interest payment and principal repayment obligations on long-term debt. In addition, long-term debt normally has a specific maturity, whereas preferred shares are often perpetual.

Knowledge of the characteristics of the various types of long-term securities is necessary in developing valuation models for these securities. The valuation of long-term securities is important to a firm's financial managers, as well as to current owners, prospective investors, and security analysts. For example, financial managers should understand how the price or value of the firm's securities (particularly common shares) is affected by its investment, financing, and dividend decisions. Similarly, both current owners and prospective investors should be able to compare their own valuations of the firm's securities with actual market prices to make rational security purchase and sale decisions. Likewise, security analysts use valuation techniques in evaluating long-term corporate securities when making investment recommendations.

Characteristics of Long-Term Debt

When a company borrows money in the capital markets, it issues long-term debt securities to investors. These securities are usually sold in denominations of $1,000 and constitute a promise by the issuing firm to repay a certain amount of money (the $1,000 principal) on a particular date (the maturity date) and to pay a specified amount of interest at fixed intervals (usually twice a year). Most debt securities have a *par value* of $1,000, and debt prices are often expressed as a percentage of that value. For example, a market price listing of "87" for a bond indicates that this $1,000 par value bond may be purchased for $870.

There are many different types of long-term debt. The type or types a firm chooses to use will depend on its own particular financial situation and the characteristics of the industry as a whole.

---

[1] While floating rate debt and adjustable rate preferred shares have interest and dividend distributions that can fluctuate over time (as described later in the chapter), they are still classified as fixed-income securities.

Types of Long-Term Debt

Long-term debt is generally classified according to whether it is secured by specific physical assets of the issuing company. Secured debt issues are usually called mortgage bonds, and issues not secured by specific assets are called **debentures** or, occasionally, *debenture bonds*. The term **bond** is often used generically to denote any type of long-term debt security (*long-term* is understood to be a term to maturity longer than one year). Sometimes the issuer of a debt security calls the security a note. This terminology typically applies to debt securities that have a term to maturity of greater than one year but usually less than 5 years. Occasionally, debt securities with longer terms to maturity are called notes by the issuer, although this rarely occurs if the maturity is longer than 10 years. Frequently, **notes** may be referred to as a form of intermediate-term financing, since their terms to maturity are at the lower end of the long-term financing range.

At the present time, utility companies are the largest users of mortgage bonds. In recent years, the use of mortgage bonds relative to other forms of long-term debt has declined, whereas the use of debentures has increased. Because debentures are unsecured, their quality depends on the general creditworthiness of the issuing company. As a result, they are usually issued by large, financially strong firms.

The yield differential between the mortgage bond and debenture alternatives is another example of the risk-return trade-off that occurs throughout finance. For example, suppose a firm could issue either mortgage bonds or debentures. If the mortgage bonds could be sold with a 10 percent interest rate, the debentures would have to be sold at a higher rate—for example, 10.25 percent—to attract investors. Investors require a higher return on debentures because they are backed only by the unmortgaged assets of the firm and the firm's earning power.

Debt issues are also classified according to whether they are **senior or junior**.[2] Senior debt has a higher priority claim to a firm's earnings and/or assets than junior debt. Occasionally, the actual name of the debt issue will contain a "junior" or "senior" qualifier. In most instances, however, identification of how a particular company's debt issues are ranked requires an analysis of the restrictions placed on the company by the purchasers of the issue.

Unsecured debt may also be classified according to whether it is **subordinated** to other types of debt. In the event of a liquidation or reorganization, the claims of *subordinated debenture holders* are considered only *after* the claims of *unsubordinated debenture holders*. In general, subordinated debentures are junior to other types of debt, including bank loans, and may even be junior to *all* of a firm's other debt.

Equipment trust certificates are used mainly by railway and trucking companies. The proceeds from these certificates are used to purchase specific assets, such as railway rolling stock. The certificate holders own the equipment and lease it to the company. Technically, equipment trust certificates are not true bonds, even though they are guaranteed by the issuing firm, because the interest and principal are paid by the trustee (the financial institution responsible for looking after the investors' interests). Even so, they are classified as debt because they have all of the characteristics of debt.

Collateral trust bonds are backed by shares or bonds of other corporations. This type of financing is principally of historic interest. It is used today primarily by holding companies. A holding company, for example, may raise needed funds by pledging the shares and/or bonds of its subsidiaries as collateral. In this arrangement, the holding company serves as the *parent* company. The *subsidiary* borrows from the parent, and the parent borrows from the capital markets. This makes good sense because the parent company can generally get more favourable terms for its debt in the capital markets than can the subsidiary.

---

[2] The senior-junior classification scheme is also used in connection with preferred and common shares. Preferred shares are junior to long-term debt and senior to common shares.

Debenture
A bond that is not secured by any specific asset but instead by the general credit and earning power of the issuing firm.

Bond
A long-term debt security that promises to pay the lender a series of periodic interest payments in addition to returning the principal at maturity. Most corporate bonds are offered in $1,000 principal amounts (par value).

Notes
Debt securities of intermediate term maturities (greater than one year but less than five years).

Senior Debt
Debt that has a higher claim on a firm's earnings and/or assets than junior debt.

Junior Debt
Debt that has a lower claim on a firm's earnings and/or assets than senior debt.

Subordinated Debenture
A bond with a claim on the issuing firm's assets that is junior to other forms of debt in the event of a liquidation. The claims of subordinated debenture holders can be met only after all the claims of senior creditors have been met.

Equipment Trust Certificate
A debt security that has transportation equipment as collateral.

Collateral Trust Bond
Debt securites that have other securities as collateral.

Income Bond
A bond that pays interest only if the firm earns sufficient income.

Income bonds are also largely of historic interest, although they are still used occasionally today. Income bonds promise to pay interest only if the issuing firm earns sufficient income. If it does not, no interest obligation exists. These securities are rarely issued directly. Instead, they are often created in reorganizations following bankruptcy and are normally issued in exchange for junior or subordinated issues. Thus, unsecured income bonds are generally considered to be "weak" securities.

Banks and finance companies often issue bonds backed by a stream of payments from consumer and commercial obligations, known as receivables. Credit card and automobile loan payments are the two primary types of receivables used in the market for *asset-backed securities.*

Features of Long-Term Debt

Long-term debt has a number of unique features. Several of these are discussed in the following paragraphs.[3]

Indenture
The contract between the issuing firm and the lenders in a debt obligation.

Indenture   An **indenture** is a contract between a firm that issues long-term debt securities and the lenders. In general, an indenture does the following:

- It thoroughly details the nature of the debt issue.

- It carefully specifies the manner in which the principal must be repaid.

- It lists any restrictions placed on the firm by the lenders. These restrictions are called *covenants,* and the firm must satisfy them to keep from defaulting on its obligations.[4] Typical restrictive covenants include the following:

    1. A minimum coverage, or times interest earned, ratio the firm must maintain

    2. A minimum level of working capital[5] the firm must maintain

    3. A maximum amount of dividends the firm can pay on its preferred and common shares

    4. Other restrictions that effectively limit how much leasing and issuing of additional debt the firm may do

Debt covenants are used to resolve agency problems among debt holders, shareholders, and managers.[6] Restrictive covenants, such as those listed above, can be used to protect debt holders by prohibiting certain actions by shareholders or managers that might be detrimental to the market value of the debt securities and the ability of the firm to repay the debt at maturity. Debt covenants can also be used to alter the terms of a debt issue if a future significant corporate event should lower the market value of the debt issue. One such example of "event risk language" is a poison put covenant,[7] which allows bondholders to sell their debt back to the company at par value in the event of a **leveraged buyout (LBO)** transaction[8] and a downgrade in the credit rating of the debt issue to below investment grade.[9]

Leveraged Buyout (LBO)
A transaction in which the buyer of a firm borrows a large portion of the purchase price, using the purchased assets as partial collateral for the loans.

---

[3] See Douglas R. Emery and John D. Finnerty, "A Review of Recent Research Concerning Corporate Debt Provisions," *Financial Markets, Institutions and Instruments* 1, no. 5 (December 1992): 23–39.

[4] A firm defaults on its debt when it does not pay interest or required principal on time or when it violates one or more of the bond's restrictive covenants. When default occurs, the debt is often said to be "triggered," meaning that the entire principal amount comes due immediately. This could result in bankruptcy.

[5] *Working capital,* defined as the firm's investment in current assets less its current liabilities, is discussed in Chapters 15 and 16.

[6] Agency problems were discussed in Chapter 1.

[7] A put option is an option to sell an asset at a set price. Put options are discussed in Chapter 17.

[8] In a leveraged buyout (LBO), the buyer of a firm borrows a large portion of the purchase price, using the purchased assets as collateral for the loan. This topic is further discussed in Chapter 20.

[9] Credit ratings are discussed later in this section.

See International Paper
Investor Information at
**www.internationalpaper.
com**

International Paper's 1992 issue of 7.625 percent notes, due 2007, contains a retraction feature allowing holders to redeem the bonds at par (plus accrued interest) in the event of a ratings decline to less than investment grade.

Strong debt covenants can reduce managerial flexibility and thus impose opportunity costs on the firm. At the same time, strong covenants can result in higher credit ratings and lower borrowing costs to the firm by limiting transfers of wealth from bondholders to shareholders and placing limits on the bargaining power of management in any future debt renegotiations. The optimal package of covenants minimizes the sum of these costs.

Trustee Because the holders of a large firm's long-term debt issue are likely to be widely scattered geographically, a trustee represents the debt holders in dealings with the issuing company. A trustee is usually a trust company that is responsible for ensuring that all the terms and covenants set forth in the indenture agreement are adhered to by the issuing company. The issuing company must pay the trustee's expenses.

Call Feature
A provision that permits an issuer of bonds (and sometimes preferred shares) to retire the obligation prior to its maturity.

Call Feature and Bond Refunding A **call feature** is an optional retirement provision that permits the issuing company to redeem, or *call*, a debt issue prior to its maturity date at a specified price termed the *redemption*, or call, price. Many firms use the call feature because it provides them with the potential flexibility to retire debt prior to maturity if, for example, interest rates decline.

The call price is greater than the par value of the debt, and the difference between the two is the **call premium**. During the early years of an issue, the call premium is usually equal to about one year's interest. Some debt issues specify *fixed* call premiums, whereas others specify *declining* call premiums. Many bonds are not callable at all for several years after the initial date. This situation is referred to as a *deferred call*.

Call Premium
The difference between a bond's call price and its par value.

Details of the call feature are worked out in the negotiations between the underwriters and the issuing company before the debt is sold. A call feature gives the company significant flexibility in its financing plans, while at the same time it potentially deprives the lenders of the advantages they would gain from holding the debt until maturity. Thus, the issuing company has to offer the investors compensation in the form of a call premium in exchange for the call privilege. In addition, the interest rate on a callable debt issue is usually slightly higher than the interest rate on a similar noncallable issue.

Because of the interest savings that can be achieved, a firm is most likely to call a debt issue when prevailing interest rates are appreciably lower than those that existed at the time of the original issue. When a company calls a relatively high interest rate issue and replaces it with a lower interest rate issue, the procedure is called bond refunding. This topic is discussed further in Appendix 10B of Chapter 10.

Sinking Fund Lenders often require that a borrowing company gradually reduce the outstanding balance of a debt issue over its life instead of having the entire principal amount come due on a particular date 20 or 30 years into the future. The usual method of providing for a gradual retirement is a sinking fund, so called because a certain amount of money is put aside annually, or "sunk," into a *sinking fund account*. In practice, however, a company can satisfy its sinking fund requirements either (1) by purchasing a portion of the debt each year in the open market or (2) if the debt is callable, by using a lottery technique to determine which actual numbered certificates will be called and retired within a given year. The alternative chosen depends on the current market price of the debt issue. In general, if current interest rates are above the issue's coupon rate, the current market price of the debt will be less than $1,000, and the company should meet its sinking fund obligation by purchasing the debt in the open market. Suppose, however, that market interest rates are lower than the issue's coupon rate and the market price of the debt is above the call price. Then the company should use the call procedure.

Conversion Feature
A feature of some debt securities that allows the holder to exchange the security for the issuing firm's common shares at the option of the holder.

See BCE at
www.bce.ca/en

Coupon Rate of Interest
The interest rate stated on a bond. The coupon rate of interest times the par, or principal, value of a bond determines the periodic dollar interest payment received by the bondholder.

See RBC Investor Relations at **www.rbc.com**

Maturity
The date when the principal of a loan must be repaid.

For more information see **www.bce.ca/en** and **www.cocacola.com**

Equity-Linked Debt   Some debt issues (and some preferred share issues) are linked to the equity (common shares) of the firm through a **conversion feature** that allows the holder to exchange the security for the company's common shares at the option of the holder. Interest costs of a convertible debt issue are usually less than a similar debt issue without the conversion option. That is, investors are willing to accept the value of the conversion privilege as part of their overall return. Another form of equity-linked debt is the issuance of *warrants* with debt securities. A warrant is an option to purchase shares of a company's common shares at a specified price during a given time period. Convertible securities and warrants are discussed in Chapter 17.

Typical Sizes of Debt Issues   Recall from the discussion in Chapter 2 that debt issues sold to the public through underwriters are usually for $25 million or more. During the past several years some large companies, such as BCE, have sold multibillion dollar bond issues to investors.

Because the use of an *underwriting syndicate* in a public offering involves considerable expense, it is usually uneconomical for a company to make a public offering of this nature for debt issues less than about $25 million. *Private placements,* however, frequently involve lesser amounts of money—for example, $5 to $10 million—because the entire debt issue is purchased by a single investor, such as an insurance company.

Coupon Rates   The **coupon rates** on new bonds are normally fixed and set equal to market interest rates on bonds of comparable quality and maturity so that the bonds sell at or near par value. However, during the inflationary period of the early 1980s, when interest rates reached record levels and bond prices were quite volatile, highly rated companies began issuing bonds with *floating coupon rates.*

An example of a floating rate debt security is Royal Bank of Canada's 2005 US-dollar denominated floating rate subordinated debentures. The interest rate paid on these securities is .0625 percent above the one-month US dollar London Interbank Offer Rate (LIBOR). Such a bond protects investors against a rise in interest rates because the market price of the bond does not fluctuate as much as for fixed interest rate bonds.

Original issue deep discount (OID) bonds have coupon rates below prevailing market interest rates at the time of issue and hence sell at a discount from par value. Some OID bond issues pay no interest and are known as *zero coupon* bonds. One of the advantages to the issuing firm of these types of bonds is the reduction in (or elimination of) interest payments (a cash outflow) during the life of the bonds. Another advantage is the slightly lower cost (yield to maturity) of these issues compared with bonds that are issued at or near par value. The primary disadvantage of these types of bonds is the large cash outflow required by the firm at maturity. OID bonds have decreased in popularity due to changes in the tax laws. These changes eliminated the tax advantages to companies of OID issues over debt issued at par. In addition, several brokerage firms have issued lower-risk substitutes. These securities, which pay no interest, are purchased at a discount from face value and can then be redeemed for the full face value at maturity.

Maturity   The typical **maturity** on long-term debt at the time of issue is about 20 to 30 years. Occasionally, companies borrow money for as long as 40 years. In 1953, Bell Canada sold 60-year bonds, and in 1993, Coca-Cola sold *100-year* bonds.

On the other end of the scale, companies in need of long-term financing are often willing to borrow for as few as five years. This is especially true if they feel that interest rates are temporarily high. In the environment of the early 1980s, with high rates of inflation and historically high interest rates, firms in need of long-term financing even borrowed for periods shorter than five years. In contrast, during the 1990s when generally low inflation and moderate interest rates prevailed, many large firms issued fixed-rate debt securities with 25- and 30-year maturities.

Chapter 5   Fixed-Income Securities: Characteristics and Valuation

Retractable Bond
A bond that allows the investor to reduce or shorten the maturity.

For more information see
www.tsx.ca and
www.nyse.com

See
www.globeinvestor.com
for more information

Yield to Maturity (*YTM*)
The discount rate that equates the present bond price with the present value of all expected interest payments and the repayment of principal at the maturity date from a bond.

For more information see
www.fin.gc.ca

Firms have also been issuing bonds that are *redeemable* at par *at the option of the holder*. These are known as **retractable bonds** or *put bonds*. Like the floating rate bonds described earlier, retractable bonds also protect investors against interest rate risk. If interest rates rise and the market price of the bond falls, the holder can redeem it at par and reinvest the proceeds in higher-yielding securities.

When performing bond valuation and yield-to-maturity calculations (described later in the chapter), bond investors should keep in mind that the realized maturity of a debt issue may differ from its stated maturity. This can occur for a variety of reasons. The bond indenture may include early repayment provisions through the exercise of a call option, required sinking fund payments, open market purchases, or tender offers. Also, maturity extensions or contractions may occur as the result of reorganization, merger, leveraged buyout (LBO), default, or liquidation.

Information on Debt Financing Activities

Every business day, financial newspapers contain information on debt financing activities, including announcements by underwriters concerning the characteristics of the new issues being offered. They also contain information on the secondary debt markets, including price quotations for the widely traded corporate debt issues. In this section we illustrate the information that can be obtained from bond quotations.

Corporate Bonds   The majority of existing debt issues (bonds) is traded in the over-the-counter market. The OTC market is a network of security dealers who buy and sell bonds and shares from each other, either for their own accounts or for their retail clients. However, some corporate bonds are listed and traded on the Toronto and New York stock exchanges.

Price quotations for these listed bonds are published daily in the financial press. Table 5.1 shows a selected list of Canadian bond quotations from *The Globe and Mail*.

Bond prices are quoted as a percentage of their par value (usually $1,000). For example, the closing price for the Bell Canada issue was $1,040.60. The Coupon column indicates the contractual interest rate of 6.5 percent. Thus, a holder of the issue receives $32.50 in interest every six months, for a total of $65 (.065 × $1,000) each year. This debt issue matures on May 9, 2005. The Yield column indicates the **yield to maturity (*YTM*)**, which is discussed later in this chapter.

Government Debt Securities   The Canadian federal, provincial, territorial, and municipal governments, as well as Crown corporations, raise funds by selling debt securities. These securities take the form of short-term bills, intermediate-term notes, and long-term bonds. Treasury bills (T-bills) usually have an initial maturity of 3, 6, or 12 months. Treasury bills are sold periodically at auctions in denominations ranging from $1,000 to $1,000,000. Treasury bills pay no explicit interest. Instead, they are sold at a discount from maturity value. An investor who buys a T-bill and holds it to maturity will receive as interest the difference between par value and the price paid.

Table 5.1	Selected Canadian Bond Quotations				
Issuer	**Coupon**	**Maturity**	**Price**	**Yield**	**Price Change**
Canada	8.750	Dec 01/05	114.77	3.80	0.02
CMHC	6.250	Dec 01/05	107.00	3.90	0.03
Quebec	6.500	Dec 01/05	107.54	3.97	0.03
Bell Canada	6.500	May 09/05	104.06	4.84	0.23
Ford Credit	6.650	Jun 20/05	100.75	6.34	0.03

Source: *The Globe and Mail* (September 14, 2002): B13.

Like corporate bonds, government bonds pay a stated coupon rate of interest semi-annually. They are issued in denominations of multiples of $1,000.

Bond Ratings

See the Dominion Bond Rating Service Web site at **www.dbrs.com** For Moody's Investors Service see **www.mergent.com** For Standard & Poor's Web site see **www. standardandpoors.com**

Debt issues are rated according to their relative degree of risk by various financial rating companies, including the Dominion Bond Rating Service (DBRS), Moody's Investors Service and Standard & Poor's (S&P) Corporation. These agencies consider a variety of factors when rating a firm's securities, including earnings stability, coverage ratios, the relative amount of debt in the firm's capital structure, and the degree of subordination, as well as past experience.

According to DBRS's rating scale, the highest-quality, lowest-risk issues are rated AAA, and the scale continues down through AA (superior quality), A (satisfactory quality), BBB (adequate quality), BB (speculative quality), B (highly speculative quality), CCC, CC, and C (all very highly speculative quality). D-rated securities are in default. Only the first four rating categories are considered investment-grade quality. The other rating services use similar but slightly different ratings scales to categorize bonds into the various categories.

In general, firms with the most favourable profitability and leverage ratios tend to have the highest credit ratings, and the firms with the highest credit ratings tend to pay the lowest interest costs. Normally, for any given maturity, the lower a bond's credit rating, the higher the yield, reflecting an increasing risk of default. As a risky bond's maturity increases, the chance for default tends to increase because there is more time for something to go wrong at a firm.

Companies with weak financial positions (e.g., highly leveraged balance sheets or low earnings) often issue high-yield debt securities to obtain capital needed for internal expansion or for corporate acquisitions and buyouts. Such debt, also known as junk bonds, or speculative debt, is rated BB or lower and typically yields three percentage points or more over the highest-quality corporate debt. For example, the Canadian firm Campeau Corporation had to pay over 17 percent in November 1988 to obtain some of the funds it needed to pay for the acquisition of Federated Department Stores in the United States. These bonds were rated CCC. At the time, the highest-quality (AAA) corporate debt was yielding less than 10 percent. Two years later Federated filed for bankruptcy when it was unable to meet the required debt payments. Junk bonds constitute an important segment of all corporate debt outstanding.

Users of Long-Term Debt

Most large and medium-sized companies finance some portion of their fixed assets with long-term debt. This debt may be in the form of either secured bonds or unsecured debentures. Utilities rely on debt capital to a large degree and, as a group, are the largest users of secured bonds. The *first mortgage bonds* of a utility are typically a safe, low-risk investment. Manufacturing companies, in contrast, rely on debt capital to varying degrees and generally use unsecured debt more often than secured debt.

Many large companies have virtually continuous capital expenditure programs. Usually, a company will plan to finance any new assets at least partially with long-term debt. Because it is generally uneconomical to borrow small amounts of long-term capital, however, companies that have ongoing construction programs often gradually "draw down" on their short-term revolving credit agreements. Then, once every couple of years or so, a firm of this type will enter the capital markets and sell long-term debt. At that time, a portion of the proceeds is used to repay the short-term borrowings, and the cycle begins again. This procedure is called *funding* short-term debt. As a result, long-term debt is sometimes referred to as *funded debt*.

Most established companies attempt to maintain reasonably constant proportions of long-term debt and common equity in their capital structures. During the course of

The International Bond Market

In addition to raising capital in the North American financial markets, many Canadian firms go to other countries to raise capital. International bonds are sold initially to investors outside the home country of the borrower. There are two major types of long-term instruments in the international bond market—Eurobonds and foreign bonds.

Eurobonds are bonds denominated in US dollars sold to investors outside the United States. The bond offering is often underwritten by an international syndicate of investment bankers. For example, Magna sold US dollar-denominated bonds to investors in Europe. The Eurobond market has been used because there is less stringent regulation than in the issuing country and, in some cases, less stringent disclosure requirements. Eurobonds are also bearer bonds (the name of the bond owner is not on the bond), providing the bondholder with tax anonymity and an opportunity, perhaps, to avoid the payment of taxes. Thus, the cost of Eurobond financing may be below that of domestic financing.

Foreign bonds, in contrast, are underwritten by an investment banking syndicate from a single country. Foreign bonds are normally denominated in the currency of the country of sale. The bond issuer, however, is from a country other than the country in which the bonds are being issued. For example, Magna also sold bonds in Europe denominated in euros.

The international bond market grew rapidly during the 1980s, and it continues to provide firms with additional alternative sources of funds that are, in some cases, lower in cost than purely domestic financing.

For more information, see Jeff Madura, *International Financial Management,* 7th ed. (Mason, OH: South-Western, 2003), Chapter 3.

NAFTA Note

Although foreign investors in Mexico are subject to currency risk if the value of the peso declines, many Canadian and US investors invest in Mexico to diversify their portfolios. They also want to take advantage of the higher rates of return on Mexican securities, especially Mexican government Treasury bills, called Cetes. For example, at the end of September 2002, the T-bill yield in the United States was only 1.63%, in Canada it was 2.81%, but in Mexico it was 6.69%. It is also possible to invest in Mexican government and corporate bonds and common shares.

a company's normal profitable operations, though, long-term debt is gradually retired as it matures, and the retained earnings portion of common equity is increased. This in turn decreases the debt-to-equity ratio. Thus, to maintain their desired capital structures, companies have to raise long-term debt capital periodically. This process, along with the tax deductibility of interest, accounts for the fact that most of the external long-term capital is raised in the form of debt.

Advantages and Disadvantages of Long-Term Debt Financing

From the issuing firm's perspective, the major advantages of long-term debt include the following:

■ Its relatively low after-tax cost due to the tax deductibility of interest

■ The increased earnings per share possible through financial leverage

- The ability of the firm's owners to maintain greater control over the firm

The following are the major disadvantages of long-term debt financing, from the firm's perspective:

- The increased financial risk of the firm resulting from the use of debt
- The restrictions placed on the firm by the lenders

From the investors' viewpoint, in general, debt securities offer stable returns and therefore are considered relatively low-risk investments compared with investments in common shares. Because debt holders are creditors, however, they do not participate in any increased earnings the firm may experience. In fact, during periods of relatively high inflation, holders of existing debt find that their *real* interest payments decrease because the nominal interest payments remain constant.

Valuation of Assets

The value of any asset is based on the *expected future benefits*, or *cash flows*, the owner will receive over the life of the asset. For example, the value of a *physical asset*, such as a new piece of equipment or production plant, is based on the expected cash flows the asset will generate for the firm over its useful life. These cash flows are derived from increased revenues and/or reduced costs plus any salvage value received from the sale of the asset.[10]

Similarly, the value of a *financial asset*, such as a bond or shares of stock, is based on the expected cash flows the asset will generate for the owner during the **holding period**. These cash flows take the form of interest or dividend payments over the holding period plus the amount the owner receives when the security is sold at the end of the holding period.

It is assumed throughout this and the following chapter that the firms under discussion are *going concerns*, that is, that their organization and assets will remain intact and be used to generate future cash flows. Techniques other than the ones described here must be used to value long-term securities of firms faced with the possibility of bankruptcy. In such cases, the liquidation value of the firm's assets is the primary determinant of the value of the various types of long-term securities.[11]

Capitalization of Cash Flow Method

One way of determining the value of an asset is to calculate the present value of the stream of expected future cash flows discounted at an appropriate *required rate of return*. This is known as the capitalization of cash flow method of valuation and is represented algebraically as follows:

(5.1)
$$V_0 = \sum_{t=1}^{n} \frac{CF_t}{(1 + k)^t}$$

where V_0 is the value of the asset at time zero, CF_t the expected cash flow in period t, k the required rate of return or discount rate, and n the length of the holding period.

For example, assume that the cash flows, CF_t, of an investment are expected to be an annuity of $1,000 per year for $n = 6$ years, and the required rate of return, k, is 8 percent. Using the **capitalization of cash flow method**, the value of this investment is

$$V_0 = \sum_{t=1}^{6} \frac{\$1,000}{(1 + 0.08)^t}$$

Holding Period
The period of time during which the investor holds a security.

---

[10] Chapters 9 through 11 contain a detailed discussion of capital budgeting.
[11] This topic is discussed in Chapter 20.

Recognizing this expression as the present value of an annuity ($PVAN_0$), the value of the investment is computed using Equation 4.24 of Chapter 4:

$$(5.2) \qquad \begin{aligned} V_0 &= \$1,000(PVIFA_{0.08,\,6}) \\ &= \$1,000(4.623) \\ &= \$4,623 \end{aligned}$$

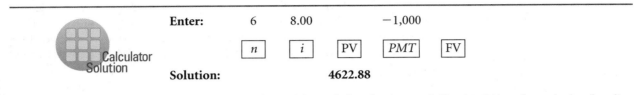

Calculator Solution

Enter: 6   8.00   −1,000

| n | i | PV | *PMT* | FV |

Solution: 4622.88

This solution is identical (rounded to the nearest dollar, $4,623) to that calculated earlier.

The solution can also be computed with a spreadsheet as follows:

Spreadsheet Solution

	A	B	C	
1	TVM	INPUTS	SOLUTION	
2	Periods, n	6		
3	Rate, i	8.00%		
4	PV		$4,622.88	
5	PMT	−1000		
6	FV			

Enter the appropriate data inputs in column B and choose the PV function for cell C4.

The *required rate of return, k,* on an asset is a function of the uncertainty, or risk, associated with the returns from the asset as well as the risk-free interest rate. This function is upward sloping, indicating that the higher the risk, the greater the investor's required rate of return. Risk is usually defined as the possibility that actual future returns will deviate from expected returns, This topic is discussed further in Chapter 7.

Market Value of Assets and Market Equilibrium

From Equation 5.1, it can be seen that the value of an asset depends on both the expected cash flows, CF_t, and the owner's (or prospective buyer's) required rate of return, k. However, potential buyers and sellers can have different opinions of an asset's value based on their individual assessments of the potential cash flows from the asset and individual required rates of return.

The *market price,* or *market value,* of an asset (such as bonds, preferred shares, and common shares) is determined in much the same way as the price of most goods and services in a market-oriented economy, namely, by the interaction of supply and demand. This interaction is shown in Figure 5.1. Potential buyers are represented by a *demand* schedule showing the maximum prices they are willing to pay for given quantities of an asset, and potential sellers are represented by a *supply* schedule showing the minimum prices at which they are willing to sell given quantities of the asset. The transaction price, the price at which an asset is sold, occurs at the intersection of the demand

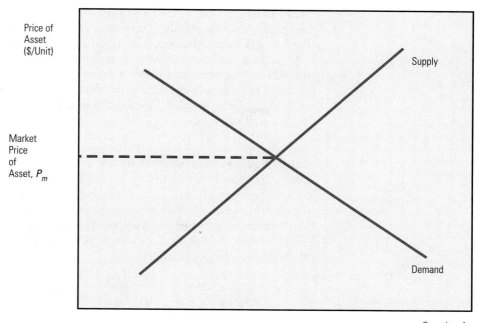

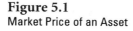

Figure 5.1
Market Price of an Asset

and supply schedules. The intersection represents the *market value,* or *market price,* of the asset, P_m, in Figure 5.1.

The market price of an asset is the value placed on the asset by the *marginally satisfied buyer and seller* who exchange assets in the marketplace. A marginally satisfied buyer is one who paid his or her maximum acceptable price for the asset, and a marginally satisfied seller is one who received his or her minimum acceptable price for the asset. Clearly, many owners (potential sellers) will place a higher value on the asset than the current market price. Likewise, many investors (potential buyers) will place a lower value on the asset than the current market price.

Market equilibrium exists whenever there is no tendency for the price of the asset to move higher or lower. At this point, the *expected* rate of return on the asset is equal to the marginal investor's *required* rate of return. *Market disequilibrium* occurs when investors' required rates of return, k, and/or the expected cash flows, CF_t, from the asset change. The market price adjusts over time—that is, it moves upward or downward—to reflect changing conditions, and a new market equilibrium is established.

Most financial assets are bought and sold in organized markets. The bonds, preferred shares, and common shares of many small, as well as most medium and large, firms are traded in one or more security exchanges, formal virtual markets such as NASDAQ, or in the over-the-counter markets. Because large numbers of competing buyers and sellers operate in the markets, the market price of a security represents a *consensus* judgement as to the security's value or worth. Although no such market-determined measure of value exists for securities of firms that are not publicly traded, their market values can be approximated using the market price of publicly traded securities of firms having similar operating and financial characteristics.

Bond Valuation

The valuation of bonds is a relatively straightforward process because future cash flows to the bondholder are always specified ahead of time in a contract. The firm issuing the bonds must meet the interest and principal payments as they come due or the bonds will go into default. Defaulting on bond payments can have disastrous consequences for the firm and its shareholders, such as possible bankruptcy, reorganization, or both.

Due to default risk, investors normally require a higher rate of return than the risk-free rate before agreeing to hold a firm's bonds. The required rate of return varies among bond issues of different firms, depending on their relative risks of default. All other things being equal, the greater the default risk on a given bond issue, the higher the required rate of return.

Bonds Having Finite Maturity Dates

Bonds that mature within finite periods of time pay the investor two types of returns: interest payments $(I_1, I_2, \ldots, I_n)$ during each of the next n periods and a principal payment (M) in period n. Period n is defined as the bond's *maturity date,* or the time at which the principal must be repaid and the bond issue retired.

The value of a bond can be computed by applying the capitalization of cash flow method to the series of cash flows:

$$(5.3) \quad P_0 = \frac{I_1}{(1 + k_d)^1} + \frac{I_2}{(1 + k_d)^2} + \ldots + \frac{I_{n-1}}{(1 + k_d)^{n-1}} + \frac{I_n + M}{(1 + k_d)^n}$$

where P_0 is the present value of the bond at time zero, or its purchase date, and k_d is the investor's required rate of return on this particular bond issue.

Because all of the interest payments on a bond are normally equal (that is $I_1 = I_2 = \ldots = I_{n-1} = I_n = I$), Equation 5.3 can be simplified as follows:

$$(5.4) \quad P_0 = \sum_{t=1}^{n} \frac{I}{(1 + k_d)^t} + \frac{M}{(1 + k_d)^n}$$

The first term in Equation 5.4 represents the present value of an *annuity* of I per period for n periods. The second term represents the present value of a *single payment* of M in period n. Equation 5.4 can be further simplified as follows:

$$(5.5) \quad P_0 = I(\text{PVIFA}_{k_d, n}) + M(\text{PVIF}_{k_d, n})$$

To illustrate the use of Equation 5.5, consider the following example. ABC issued $3 billion of 6 percent bonds maturing on March 15, 2009. The bonds were issued in $1,000 denominations (par value). For purposes of simplifying this example, assume that the bonds pay interest only on March 15 each year.[12]

An investor who wishes to purchase one of these ABC bonds on March 15, 2002, and requires an 8 percent rate of return on this particular bond issue would compute the value of the bond as follows. These calculations assume that the investor will hold the bond until maturity and receive seven annual $(n = 7)$ interest payments of $60 each ($I = $1,000 \times 0.06$) plus a principal payment, M, of $1,000 at the end of the seventh year, March 15, 2009. The expected cash flows from this bond are shown in Figure 5.2. Substituting these values along with $k_d = 8\%$ (0.08) into Equation 5.5 gives the following value for the bond:

$$P_0 = \$60(\text{PVIFA}_{0.08, 7}) + \$1,000(\text{PVIF}_{0.08, 7})$$
$$= \$60(5.206) + \$1,000(0.583)$$
$$= \$895.36 \text{ (or } \$895)$$

---

[12] This bond issue actually pays interest *semiannually* on March 15 and September 15 each year.

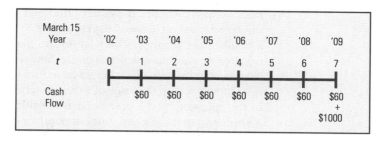

Figure 5.2
Cash Flows from an ABC Bond

In other words, an investor requiring an 8 percent return on this ABC bond would be willing to pay approximately $895 for it on March 15, 2002.

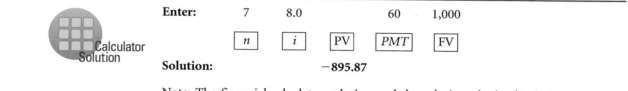

Enter: 7   8.0   60   1,000

         n i PV   PMT   FV

Calculator Solution

Solution: −**895.87**

Note: The financial calculator solution and the solution obtained using Equation 6.5 and the interest tables differ slightly due to the use of interest tables with three decimal places of accuracy. Using more accurate interest tables gives an answer closer to $895.87, the true answer to this problem.

The solution can also be computed with a spreadsheet as follows:

Spreadsheet Solution

	A	B	C	
1	TVM	INPUTS	SOLUTION	
2	Periods, n	7		
3	Rate, i	8.00%		
4	PV		−$895.87	
5	PMT	60		
6	FV	1000		

Enter the appropriate data inputs in column B and choose the PV function for cell C4.

A question often arises as to why investors would require an 8 percent rate of return on bonds that pay only 6 percent interest. The answer is that the required rate of return has increased since the bonds were originally issued. At the time of issue, the prevailing rate of interest (that is, the required rate of return) on bonds of this maturity and quality was approximately 6 percent. Hence, the coupon rate was set at 6 percent. Because of such factors as tight credit market conditions, higher inflation, increased firm risk, and so on, investors now require a higher rate of return to induce them to purchase these bonds.

An investor who desires more than an 8 percent rate of return on the ABC bond would value it at a price less than $895.87. Similarly, an investor who requires less than an 8 percent rate of return would value it at a price greater than $895.87. As the required rate of return increases, the value of the bond decreases, and vice versa. Thus, there is an *inverse relationship* between the required rate of return and the corresponding value of a bond to the investor. The relationship between a bond's value and the investor's required rate of return depends on the time remaining before maturity. All other things being equal, the value of a longer-term bond is affected more by changes in required rates of return than the value of a shorter-term bond. As Figure 5.3 shows, the variation in the value of the 15-year bond is considerably greater than the variation of the 3-year bond over the given range of required rates of return (2 to 10 percent).

Also, when the required rate of return (prevailing market interest rate) is less than the coupon rate, the bond is valued at a *premium* over its par value of $1,000. Conversely, when the required rate of return is greater than the coupon rate, the bond is valued at a *discount* under its par value.

Investors who purchase a bond at the price determined by Equation 5.5 and *hold it until maturity* will realize their required rate of return, regardless of any changes in the market price of the bond. However, if the market price of the bond declines due to a rise in prevailing interest rates and the bond is sold *prior to maturity,* the investors will earn less than their required rate of return and may even incur a loss on the bond. This variation in the market price (and hence in the realized rate of return) of a bond (or any fixed-income security) is known as **interest rate risk**.

In addition to interest rate risk, bond investors are subject to reinvestment rate risk. **Reinvestment rate risk** occurs when a bond issue matures (or is called) and, because of a decline in interest rates, the investor has to reinvest the principal at a lower coupon rate. For example, the owner of Barrick debentures, purchased at the time of issue in 1997, is receiving $75 annual interest per bond. However, as noted earlier, this bond issue was redeemable (callable). If Barrick decides to redeem the bonds because of a decline in interest rates since the time of issue, the bondholder will probably be unable

Interest Rate Risk
The variation in the market price (and hence in the realized rate of return or yield) of a security that arises from changes in interest rates.

Reinvestment Rate Risk
Risk that occurs when a bond issue matures (or is called) and because of a decline in interest rates, the owner has to reinvest the principal at a lower coupon rate.

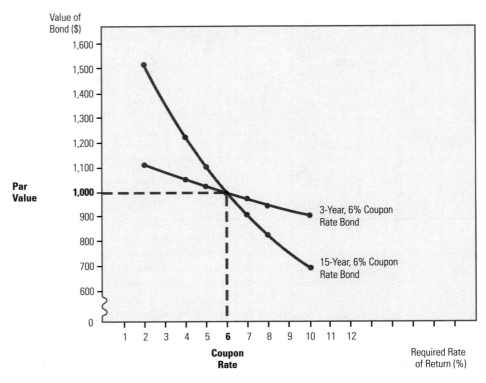

Figure 5.3
Relationship Between the Value of a Bond and the Required Rate of Return

to reinvest the principal in another bond, of comparable risk, that is yielding a 7.5 percent (or higher) rate of return. Reinvestment rate risk also refers to the rate at which interest cash flows can be reinvested over the life of the bond. When the reinvestment rate of interest cash flows is different from the yield to maturity on the bond, the return actually realized by a bond investor will be greater than (less than) the yield to maturity if the reinvestment rate is greater than (less than) the promised yield to maturity.

Semiannual Interest Payments   Most bonds, such as the ABC bonds, pay interest *semiannually*. Recall from the discussion of Effect of Compounding Periods on Present and Future Values in Chapter 4, the required rate of return (k_d) is divided by 2 and the number of periods (n) is multiplied by 2. Therefore, with semiannual interest payments and compounding, the bond valuation formula (Equation 5.4) becomes:

$$(5.6) \qquad P_0 = \sum_{t=1}^{2n} \frac{I/2}{(1 + k_d/2)^t} + \frac{M}{(1 + k_d/2)^{2n}}$$

With semiannual interest and compounding, the value for the ABC bond is calculated as follows:

$$P_0 = \$30(\text{PVIFA}_{0.04,\ 14}) + \$1,000(\text{PVIF}_{0.04,\ 14})$$
$$= \$30(10.563) + \$1,000(0.577)$$
$$= \$893.89 \ (\text{or } \$894)$$

In this problem, the annual required rate of return ($k_d = .08$) is divided by 2 ($.08/2 = .04$) and the number of periods ($n = 7$) is multiplied by 2 ($7 \times 2 = 14$).[13] These bond values differ only slightly from the solutions obtained above for annual interest payments and compounding.

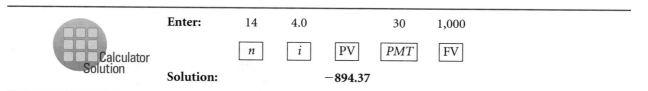

Enter: 14   4.0   30   1,000

                   [n]   [i]   [PV]   [PMT]   [FV]

Calculator Solution

Solution: −894.37

The solution can also be computed with a spreadsheet as follows:

Spreadsheet Solution

	A	B	C	
1	TVM	INPUTS	SOLUTION	
2	Periods, n	14		
3	Rate, i	4.00%		
4	PV		−$894.37	
5	PMT	30		
6	FV	1000		

Enter the appropriate data inputs in column B and choose the PV function for cell C4.

---

[13] Note that the use of a semiannual discount rate of 4% will result in a slightly greater than 8% effective annual discount rate. See the discussion of Effective Rate Calculations in Chapter 4, especially Equation 4.32.

Perpetual Bonds

Perpetual Bond
A bond that has no maturity date.

A **perpetual bond**, or perpetuity, is a bond issued without a finite maturity date.[14] Although not very popular with most firms, both Canadian Pacific and Canadian National have sold perpetual bonds. Perpetual bonds promise to pay interest indefinitely, and there is no contractual obligation to repay the principal, that is, $M = 0$.

The valuation of a perpetual bond is simpler than the valuation of a bond having a finite maturity date. Assuming that the bond pays a fixed amount of interest, I, per period forever, the value is as follows:

$$(5.7) \qquad P_0 = \sum_{t=1}^{\infty} \frac{I}{(1 + k_d)^t}$$

where k_d is the required rate of return. Equation 5.7 can be simplified to obtain the following expression:

$$(5.8) \qquad P_0 = \frac{I}{k_d}$$

Consider, for example, the Canadian Pacific Limited Railway's perpetual 4 percent debentures. What is the value of a $1,000 bond to an investor who requires an 8 percent rate of return on these Canadian Pacific bonds? Because $I = 0.04 \times \$1,000$, or $40, and $k_d = 8\%$, Equation 5.8 can be used to compute the answer as follows:

$$P_0 = \frac{\$40}{0.08} = \$500$$

Thus, the investor would be willing to pay up to $500 for this bond.

Yield to Maturity of a Bond

The yield to maturity (*YTM*) of a bond, which is the marginal investor's required rate of return in equilibrium, is the discount rate that equates the present bond price with the present value of all expected interest payments and the repayment of principal at the maturity date from a bond. (In contrast, the current yield, which is equal to the annual interest payment divided by the current price, ignores the repayment of the principal.) If the current price of a bond, P_0, the uniform annual interest payments, I, and the maturity value, or principal, M, are known, the yield to maturity of a bond having a finite maturity date n can be calculated by solving Equation 5.4 presented earlier for k_d:

$$P_0 = \sum_{t=1}^{n} \frac{I}{(1 + k_d)^t} + \frac{M}{(1 + k_d)^n}$$

Given values for any four of the five variables in this equation, one can solve for the value of the fifth variable. In the bond valuation calculation illustrated earlier in this section, this equation was used to determine the value of a bond (P_0) when the value of k_d is known (along with the values of n, I, and M). In the yield-to-maturity calculation that follows, the equation is used to determine k_d when the value of P_0 is known (along with the values of n, I, and M).

Yield to Call (*YTC*)
The discount rate that equates the present value of all expected interest payments and the repayment of principal at the call date from a bond with the present bond price.

For bonds with a call feature, the expected **yield to call (*YTC*)** can also be computed. This is done by replacing the maturity value (*M*) by the call price and the number of years until maturity (*n*) by the number of years until the company can call the bond. If present interest rates are significantly below the coupon rate on the (callable) bond, then it is likely that the bond will be called in the future. In such a case, the relevant expected rate of return on the bond is the yield to call rather than the yield to maturity.

---

14 Perpetual bonds are rare. Some countries, such as the United Kingdom, have issued perpetual bonds. The UK bonds are also referred to as *consols*.

There are a number of ways to compute the yield to maturity of a bond. Most financial calculators are programmed to compute the yield to maturity, given P_0, I, n, and M. Also, special bond tables can be used to identify the yield to maturity for any particular bond.

Consider again the ABC 6 percent bonds discussed earlier. Again, assume that interest is paid annually on March 15 each year. Suppose that the bonds are selling for $987.50 on March 15, 2002 (seven years prior to maturity). Determine the bond's exact yield to maturity. Given $n = 7$, $I = \$60$, $P_0 = \$987.50$, and $M = \$1,000$, we can compute k_d. Given these computations, the yield to maturity is 6.23 percent.[15]

Calculator Solution

Enter:	7		−987.50	60	1,000
	$\boxed{n}$	$\boxed{i}$	$\boxed{PV}$	$\boxed{PMT}$	$\boxed{FV}$
Solution:		6.23			

Spreadsheet Solution

The solution can also be computed with a spreadsheet as follows:

	A	B	C	
1	TVM	INPUTS	SOLUTION	
2	Periods, n	7		
3	Rate, i		6.23%	
4	PV	−987.50		
5	PMT	60		
6	FV	1000		

Enter the appropriate data inputs in column B and choose the RATE function for cell C3.

---

[15] If you do not have access to a computer or a financial calculator, you can use the following formula to find the approximate yield to maturity.

$$YTM = \frac{\left[I + \left(\frac{M - P_0}{n}\right)\right]}{\left[\frac{(P_0 + 2M)}{3}\right]} \quad \text{*TYPO} \quad 2P_0 + M$$

Substituting into this formula, you obtain

$$YTM = \frac{\left[\$60 + \left(\frac{\$1,000 - \$987.50}{7}\right)\right]}{\left[\frac{(\$987.50 + \$2,000)}{3}\right]} = \$61.79/\$995.83 = 6.20\%$$

An alternative approach is to find the present value of the stream of interest payments plus the principal payment using two different interest rates. Then one can use interpolation to find the approximate yield to maturity. In this example, 6% and 7% would be the appropriate rates to use, as the bond is selling at only a slight discount from par. That is, the coupon rate of 6% gives a present value of exactly the par value of $1,000. (If you actually do the calculation doing table values, this might not be true, but it would be an artifact of the rounded PVIF and PVIFA values.) The 7% rate will give a discount from par value.

Calculated $P_0 = \$60(PVIFA_{0.07,7}) + \$1,000(PVIF_{0.07,7})$
$= \$60(5.389) + \$1,000(0.623) = \$946.34$ (or $946)
$YTM \approx 6\% + [(\$1,000 - \$988)/(\$1,000 - \$946)]1\% = 6.22\%$

The interpolation method tends to result in a closer approximation to the actual YTM. (However, this need not be the case if the PVIF factor contains only two significant digits.) So, as a general rule of thumb, the first trial interest rate should be the table rate closest to the approximate formula YTM or 6% in this case.

The yield to maturity (or yield to call) can be used to compare the risk of two or more bonds that are similar *in all other respects,* including term (time) to maturity. The bond with the higher yield to maturity is the one perceived to be the riskier by investors. Also, the yield to maturity on existing bonds can be used as an estimate of the required returns of investors on any new (and similar) bonds the firm may issue.

Zero Coupon Bond

A bond that pays no annual interest but sells at a discount below par to provide compensation to investors in the form of a capital gain at the maturity date.

Zero Coupon Bonds For **zero coupon bonds** that pay no interest over their life, the only payment to holders is the principal payment at maturity. To illustrate the calculation of the yield to maturity for such a bond, suppose the zero coupon bonds (having a par value of $1,000) were purchased for $600 eight years prior to maturity. Determine the yield to maturity on these bonds.

Figure 5.4 shows cash flows from the purchase of a zero coupon bond. Because there are no interest payments, the yield-to-maturity equation (Equation 5.5) can be simplified to

(5.9)
$$P_0 = M(\text{PVIF}_{k_d, n})$$

Substituting $n = 8$, $P_0 = \$600$, and $M = \$1,000$ into this expression yields

$$\$600 = \$1,000(\text{PVIF}_{k_d, 8})$$

or
$$\text{PVIF}_{k_d, 8} = 0.600$$

From Table II at the back of the book, we find this present value interest factor in the eight-year row between the 6 percent (0.627) and 7 percent (0.582) interest rate columns. Hence, by interpolation, the yield to maturity (k_d) on this zero coupon bond is approximately[16]

$$k_d = 6\% + \frac{.627 - .600}{.627 - .582}(1\%) = 6.60\%$$

---

[16] Here, we interpolated on the PVIF factors. This can be done for zero coupon bonds because only the PVIF factor is needed to find the price (i.e., present value) of these bonds.

Contrast this with the interpolation (in Footnote 15) on the present values obtained by using different trial table interest rates. Of course, the interpolation procedure of Footnote 15 also applies to zero coupon bonds. It is a general procedure applicable to any type of bond with known price, interest payment I, maturity value M, and term to maturity n. First, using the formula for the approximate *YTM* gives

$$YTM = \frac{[(\$1,000 - \$600)/8]}{[(\$600 + \$2,000)/3]} = \$50.00/\$866.67 = 5.77\%$$

Note that this formula does not work very well for zero coupon bonds. Nevertheless, it does suggest 6% as a first trial table interest rate.

$$\text{Calculated } P_0 = \$1,000 \text{ PVIF}_{6\%, 8} = \$1,000(0.627) = \$627$$

Since this value is above the actual value of $600, the second trial table interest rate should be larger, say 7%.

$$\text{Calculated } P_0 = \$1,000 \text{ PVIF}_{7\%, 8} = \$1,000(0.582) = \$582$$

The interpolated *YTM* is

$$YTM \approx 6\% + [(\$627 - \$600)/(\$627 - \$582)]1\% = 6.60\%$$

This is exactly the interpolated *YTM* that we obtained before. Hence, the interpolation method used for generic bonds also can be used for zero coupon bonds. However, it is much more work than the special interpolation method applicable only to zero coupon bonds.

Note: A better approximation formula for zero coupon or other deep discount bonds is

$$YTM \approx \frac{\left[I + \left(\frac{M - P_0}{n} \right) \right]}{\left[\frac{(P_0 + M)}{2} \right]} = \$50/\$800 = 6.25\%$$

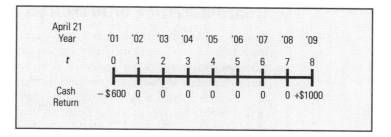

Figure 5.4
Cash Flows from the Purchase of a Zero Coupon Bond

Enter: 8   −600   0   1,000

| n | i | PV | PMT | FV |

Solution: 6.59

The solution can also be computed with a spreadsheet as follows:

	A	B	C	
1	TVM	INPUTS	SOLUTION	
2	Periods, n	8		
3	Rate, i		6.59%	
4	PV	−600		
5	PMT	0		
6	FV	1000		

Enter the appropriate data inputs in column B and choose the RATE function for cell C3.

Perpetual Bonds   The rate of return, or yield to maturity, on a *perpetual* bond can be found by solving the perpetual bond valuation equation presented earlier (Equation 5.8) for k_d:

$$P_0 = \frac{I}{k_d}$$

which gives

(5.10)
$$k_d = \frac{I}{P_0}$$

For example, recall the 4 percent Canadian Pacific Limited Railway debentures described earlier. If the current price of a bond is $640, what is the yield on the bond? Substituting P_0 = $640 and I = $40 (or 4 percent of $1,000) into Equation 5.10 gives the following:

$$k_d = \frac{\$40}{\$640} = 0.0625 \text{ (or 6.25 percent)}$$

Characteristics of Preferred Shares

As a source of capital for a firm, preferred shares occupy an intermediate position between long-term debt and common shares. Like common shares, preferred shares are part of the shareholders' equity. Like long-term debt, it is considered a fixed-income security, although preferred shareholders receive dividends instead of interest payments. Because the issuing firm often does not promise repayment at a specific date, preferred shares tend to be a more permanent form of financing than long-term debt. Dividends on preferred shares, like interest payments on long-term debt, normally remain constant over time.

Dividends cannot be deducted from income for corporate income tax purposes, whereas interest payments are tax-deductible. This means that for a firm typically paying about 40 percent of its income in taxes, the after-tax cost of preferred shares is greater than that of long-term debt, assuming that the pretax preferred shares and long-term debt rates are about the same and that the company makes no change in its capital structure.

Preferred shares usually have *preference*, or priority, over common shares with regard to the firm's dividends and assets (because of this preference, preferred shares are sometimes called preference shares). For example, if a firm's earnings in a given year are insufficient to pay dividends on preferred shares, the company is not permitted to pay dividends on its common shares. In the event of a liquidation following bankruptcy, the claims on the firm's assets by preferred shareholders are subordinate to those of creditors but have priority over those of common shareholders.

Features of Preferred Shares

Like long-term debt, preferred shares have their own unique distinguishing characteristics. A number are discussed here.

Selling Price and Par Value   The selling price, or issue price, is the per-share price at which preferred shares are sold to the public. Preferred shares are typically issued at prices of $25, $50, or $100 per share.

The par value is the value that may be assigned to the shares by the issuing firm in jurisdictions where this is permitted. Par value may be the same as the initial selling price. No relationship necessarily exists between the two, however.

Preferred shares are frequently designated by the dividend amount rather than the dividend percentage (the percentage is often based on the par value, if any). For example, suppose a company has a series of preferred shares that pays an annual dividend of $2.20, has a $1 par value, and was initially sold to the public at $25 per share. An investor would most likely refer to the shares as "$2.20 preferred."

Adjustable Rate Preferred Shares   This type of preferred shares became popular in the early 1980s. With these issues, dividends are reset periodically and offer returns that vary with interest rates.

Cumulative Feature   Most preferred shares are cumulative. This means that if a firm fails to pay its preferred dividend, it cannot pay dividends on its common shares until it has satisfied all or a prespecified amount of preferred dividends in arrears. The principal reason for this feature is that investors are generally unwilling to purchase preferred shares that are not cumulative.

Participation   Shares are said to be *participating* if the holders share in any increased earnings the company might experience. Virtually all preferred shares, however, are *nonparticipating*. That is, the preferred dividend remains constant, even if the company's earnings increase. Any dividend increases resulting from higher earnings accrue directly to the common shareholders.

Leveraged Buyouts and Bond Values

During the 1980s and early 1990s, many firms were acquired or financially restructured in a transaction called a *leveraged buyout* (LBO). In a typical LBO, the buyer of the firm borrows a large amount of the purchase price, using the purchased assets as collateral for a large portion of the borrowings. Debt ratios (debt to total capital) of 90 percent or more have not been uncommon in LBOs.

LBOs have led to enormous wealth increases for the common shareholders of the acquired firm. Bondholders generally have not fared quite so well. The impact of most LBOs has been a decline in the bond ratings of the acquired or restructured firm because of the substantial increase in perceived risk. Declines in the market value of bonds for firms acquired in LBO transactions have averaged about 7 percent.

What role do you think bond covenants should play in an analysis of the rights of bondholders and the obligations of management? How can bondholders protect themselves from losses arising out of LBOs?

Maturity   Preferred shares are technically part of a firm's equity capital. As such, some firms issue preferred shares that are intended to be *perpetual*. That is, these preferred shares are a permanent portion of the shareholders' equity, having no specific maturity date. Many preferred share investors, however, desire sinking fund provisions that guarantee that the issue will be retired over a specified time period.

Call Feature   Like long-term debt, preferred shares can sometimes be redeemed, or *called*, at the issuing firm's option at some specified price. Whereas the call feature allows the issuing company a measure of flexibility in its financing plans, the call feature is generally *not* attractive to investors. Thus, a firm usually must also provide investors with a *call premium*, should it decide to include a call feature for its preferred shares.

The probability that a firm will exercise the call privilege is likely to increase during times when market interest rates have decreased below those that existed at the time of issue. After calling the original issue, the firm can replace it with a lower-cost issue.

Voting Rights   As a general rule, preferred shareholders are not entitled to vote for the company's board of directors. However, special voting procedures frequently take effect if the company omits its preferred dividends or incurs losses for a period of time. In such a case, the preferred shareholders often vote as a separate group to elect one or more members of the company's board of directors. This ensures that the preferred holders will have direct representation on the board.

Trading of Preferred Shares

Following the initial sale of preferred shares by a firm, investors who purchase the shares may decide to sell them in the secondary markets. Large issues of actively traded preferred shares are listed on the major stock exchanges. However, a majority of preferred shares issues are traded rather thinly and these are traded over the counter.

Users of Preferred Shares

Many Canadian firms issue preferred shares. The following reasons may make such financing attractive:

- Firms may have relatively low marginal tax rates for various reasons. This makes the after-tax cost of preferred shares not appreciably different from the after-tax cost of debt.

- Protective covenants in the indentures of outstanding bond issues may prevent the judicious use of additional long-term debt.

- Depressed common share prices and the potential dilution of per-share earnings may cause a firm to decide against external common equity financing.

- Acquiring firms often issue preferred shares in exchange for the common shares of acquired companies. The shareholders of the acquired firms typically want some form of equity so the transaction is not deemed to be a current sale of their shares for tax purposes, thus triggering capital gains. From the acquiring firm's viewpoint, issuing preferred shares usually leads to an increase in earnings per share compared to the dilution that would occur if new common shares were issued.[17]

Buyers of Preferred Shares

Preferred share dividends received from one Canadian corporation by another Canadian corporation qualify for the intercompany dividend exclusion discussed in the corporate tax section of Chapter 2. Thus, Canadian corporations that have excess funds to invest but who desire current income may also find preferred shares more attractive than bonds.

Individuals who desire current income may also find preferred shares more attractive than bonds. This is because the dividend gross-up and tax credit system discussed in the personal tax section of Chapter 2 means that the effective tax rate on dividends is less than the tax rate on interest income for most individuals.

Advantages and Disadvantages of Preferred Shares Financing

From the issuing firm's perspective, the principal advantage of preferred shares is that preferred dividend payments are potentially flexible. Omitting a preferred dividend in difficult times usually results in less severe consequences than omitting an interest payment on long-term debt. In addition, preferred share financing can increase a firm's degree of financial leverage, thereby increasing earnings per share.

However, financial analysts may regard the issuance of preferred shares as equivalent to debt. In this case, the firm is viewed as having used up a portion of its "debt capacity." In effect, the firm has leveraged with preferred shares rather than long-term debt. Many Canadian firms face a marginal corporate tax rate of approximately 40 percent. Thus, the principal disadvantage of preferred share financing for such firms is its high after-tax cost compared with long-term debt because dividends cannot be deducted for income tax purposes. A more complete discussion of the cost of debt and preferred shares is in Chapter 8.

Valuation of Preferred Shares

Most preferred shares pay regular, fixed quarterly dividends. However, some preferred shares pay dividends only semiannually and some older issues pay only annual dividends. Preferred dividends per share are normally not increased when the earnings of a firm increase, nor are they cut or suspended unless the firm faces serious financial problems. If preferred share dividends are cut or suspended for a period of time for

---

[17] Chapter 20 contains a more detailed discussion of the use of preferred shares in mergers.

whatever reason, the firm is usually required to make up the past-due payments before paying any common share dividends. Thus, the investor's expected cash return from holding most preferred shares can be treated as a fixed, constant amount per period.

The investor's required rate of return on a preferred share issue is a function of the risk that the firm will be unable to meet its dividend payments. The higher the risk, the higher the required rate of return. Because bondholders have a prior claim over preferred shareholders on the income and assets of a firm, it is more risky to hold a firm's preferred shares than to hold its bonds. As a result, investors normally require a higher after-tax rate of return on preferred shares than on bonds. Because of differences in how dividends and interest are taxed, however, it is possible that the investor's pretax required rate of return k_p on preferred shares is lower than their pretax required rate of return k_d on bonds.

Since many preferred share issues do not have maturity dates, the cash flows from holding no-maturity preferred shares can be treated as a perpetual stream of payments, or perpetuity. Capitalizing the perpetual stream of dividend payments gives the following valuation expression:

$$(5.11) \qquad P_0 = \sum_{t=1}^{\infty} \frac{D_p}{(1 + k_p)^t}$$

where D_p is the dividend per period, and k_p is the investor's required rate of return.[18]

Equation 5.11 is similar to Equation 5.7 for a perpetual bond. Like the perpetual bond valuation model, this equation can be simplified into the following valuation model:

$$(5.12) \qquad P_0 = \frac{D_p}{k_p}$$

To illustrate the use of Equation 5.12, assume that a firm pays annual end-of-year dividends on its $4.50 series B cumulative preferred shares (issue price $100, no par value). What is the value of this share to an investor who requires an 8 percent annual rate of return on the investment? Assume that the issue will not be called for the foreseeable future. Substituting $4.50 (0.045 × $100) for D_p and 0.08 for k_p yields the following:

$$P_0 = \frac{\$4.50}{0.08} = \$56.25$$

Financial Challenge Revisited

As mentioned in Chapter 1, the goal of management is to maximize the value of the firm to its common shareholders. Thus, raising funds as BCE did by issuing long-term debt and preferred shares should have resulted in an increase in the market price of the BCE common shares.

Six months after the financing is perhaps too early, but already at that time, BCE common shares were trading at a higher price than the price at the time of the debt issue, in spite of the general decline in the stock market that occurred in early 2003. Thus, it seems that the debt issue was a success!

---

[18] If an investor is considering purchasing a preferred share issue that is expected to be called in the future, its value is calculated by capitalizing (that is, discounting) the call price plus the dividend payments to be received before the issue is called.

Summary

- The *capitalization of cash flow* method of valuation can be used to determine the value of a security to an investor. This involves calculating the present value of the stream of expected future cash flows discounted at the investor's required rate of return. The *required rate of return* is a function of the *risk* associated with the cash flows from the asset, as well as the risk-free rate.

- Long-term debt is generally classified according to whether it is *secured* by specific physical assets of the issuing company. Secured debt issues are *mortgage bonds,* whereas debt issues backed only by unmortgaged assets and the company's earning power are *debentures* and *notes. Notes* typically have shorter terms to maturity when issued than do debentures.

- Long-term debt usually has the following features:
  1. The *indenture,* or the contract between the issuing firm and the debt holders
  2. The *covenants,* which restrict the issuing firm
  3. The *trustee,* who represents the debt holders in dealings with the company
  4. The *call feature,* which gives the issuing company the option to retire the debt prior to maturity
  5. The *sinking fund requirement,* which means the company must gradually reduce the outstanding balance of the debt issue over its life

- *Bond refunding* occurs when a company redeems a callable issue and sells a lower-cost issue to take its place.

- The value of a *perpetual bond* is equal to the interest payment divided by the investor's required rate of return.

- The value of a *bond having a finite maturity date* is equal to the present value of the stream of interest and principal payments discounted at the investor's required rate of return.

- The *yield to maturity* on a bond is the rate of return the investor expects to earn if the bond is purchased at a given price and held until maturity. In equilibrium, the yield to maturity is the required rate of return of the marginal investor.

- Preferred shares usually have the following features:
  1. The *selling price,* or *issue price,* of a share is the price at which it was sold to the public.
  2. The *par value* is an arbitrary value that may be assigned to the shares by the issuing firm, where permitted by legislation.
  3. Most preferred shares are *cumulative.* That is, dividends on common shares cannot be paid as long as any past or present preferred dividends remain unpaid.
  4. Virtually all preferred shares are *nonparticipating.* That is, preferred shares do not share in any increased earnings of the firm.
  5. Some preferred shares are *perpetual,* whereas other preferred shares are gradually retired by the firm.
  6. Preferred shares are often *callable (redeemable).*

- From the issuing company's perspective, preferred share financing is advantageous due to the potential flexibility of preferred dividend payments.

- The principal disadvantage of preferred shares financing is that dividends are not tax-deductible, which causes the after-tax cost of preferred shares to the firm to be higher than the cost of long-term debt, all other things being equal.

Questions and Topics for Discussion

1. Define the following terms associated with long-term debt:
    a. Indenture
    b. Covenants
    c. Trustee
    d. Call feature
    e. Sinking fund
    f. Conversion feature
    g. Coupon rate
    h. Yield to maturity
    i. Yield to call

2. Describe the basic features of each of the following types of bonds:
    a. Mortgage bonds
    b. Debentures
    c. Subordinated debentures
    d. Equipment trust certificates
    e. Collateral trust bonds
    f. Income bonds

3. What is the relationship between par value, market value, and book value for the following?
    a. Long-term debt
    b. Preferred shares

4. Define the following terms associated with preferred shares:
    a. Cumulative feature
    b. Participation
    c. Call feature

5. What variables must be known (or estimated) in applying the capitalization of cash flow method of valuation to a physical or financial asset?

6. Define the following:
    a. The market value of an asset
    b. Market equilibrium

7. Describe the relationship between the coupon rate and the required rate of return that will result in a bond selling at
    a. A discount
    b. Par value
    c. A premium

8. How does the yield to maturity on a bond differ from the coupon yield or current yield?

9. Under what conditions will a bond's current yield be equal to its yield to maturity?

10. In what ways are preferred shares similar to long-term debt?

11. In what ways are preferred shares similar to common shares?

12. Explain why bondholders often prefer a sinking fund provision in a bond issue.

13. Explain what is meant by *interest rate risk*.

14. Explain how a bond can be classified as a fixed-income security when the yield to maturity can fluctuate significantly over time, depending on the market price of the bond.

15. Describe the basic features of each of the following types of bonds:
    a. Floating-rate bonds
    b. Original issue deep discount bonds
    c. Zero coupon bonds
    d. Retractable bonds (put bonds)
16. Explain what is meant by *reinvestment rate risk*.

Self-Test Problems

ST1. What is the current value of a $1,000 par value perpetual bond to an investor who requires a 10% annual rate of return? The perpetual bond pays interest at the rate of 8% per year.

ST2. A firm's zero coupon bonds (par value $1,000) mature on April 21, 2009. Calculate the yield to maturity if an investor purchases one of these bonds on April 21, 2003, at a price of $650.

ST3. A company has bonds outstanding ($1,000 par value) that mature 10 years from today and have a coupon interest rate of 9.375%. Calculate the maximum price an investor should be willing to pay if the investor desires a 10% yield to maturity.

ST4. What is the value of a series A $3.50 cumulative, perpetual preferred share to an investor who requires a 6% annual rate of return on this security? This preferred share was originally issued at $102 a share.

Problems*

BASIC

1. Determine the value of a $1,000 Canadian Pacific Limited perpetual 4% debenture (bond) at the following required rates of return:
   a. 4%
   b. 5%
   c. 6%

2. Recently the high and low market prices of Canadian Pacific Limited's debentures (see Problem 1) were $790 and $475, respectively. Determine the yield to maturity of one of these debentures if it was purchased under the following conditions:
   a. At the high market price
   b. At the low market price

 Excel

3. A firm has issued 8.125% debentures that will mature on July 15, 2024. Assume that interest is paid and compounded annually. If an investor purchases a $1,000 denomination bond for $1,025 on July 15, 2004, determine the bond's yield to maturity. Explain why an investor would be willing to pay $1,025 for a bond that it going to be worth only $1,000 at maturity.

 Excel

4. If you purchase a zero coupon bond today for $225 and it matures at $1,000 in 11 years, what rate of return will you earn on that bond (to the nearest 1/10 of 1%)?

5. Determine the value of a $3.50 cumulative preferred share to an investor who requires the following rates of return:
   a. 9%
   b. 10%
   c. 12%

*Coloured numbers and letters denote problems that have "check" answers provided at the back of the book.

Excel

6. Consider 8.75% bonds that mature on April 15, 2016. Assume that the interest on these bonds is paid and compounded annually. Determine the value of a $1,000 denomination bond as of April 15, 2004, to an investor who holds the bond until maturity and whose required rate of return is
   a. 7%
   b. 9%
   c. 11%
   d. What would be the value of the bonds at an 8% required rate of return if the interest were paid and compounded *semiannually?*

 Excel

7. A firm issued 7.375% bonds that mature on July 15, 2033. The bonds are callable at $1,037.08 on July 15, 2008. Assume that interest is paid and compounded annually. Determine the yield to maturity (to the nearest 10th of 1 percent) if an investor purchases a $1,000 denomination bond for $900 on July 15, 2001.

 Excel

8. Consider $1,000 zero coupon bonds of 2008. The bonds were issued in 1990 for $100. Determine the yield to maturity (to the nearest 1/10 of 1%) if the bonds are purchased at the
   a. Issue price in 1990. (Note: To avoid a fractional year holding period, assume that the issue and maturity dates are at the midpoint—July 1—of the respective years.)
   b. Market price as of July 1, 2004, of $750.
   c. Explain why the returns calculated in parts a and b are different.

 Excel

9. In 1991 a firm issued 8.625% debentures that will mature on December 1, 2031.
   a. If an investor purchased one of these bonds ($1,000 denomination) on December 1, 2001, for $1,050, determine the yield to maturity. Explain why an investor would be willing to pay $1,050 on December 1, 2001, for one of these bonds when he or she is going to receive only $1,000 when the bond matures in 2031.
   b. The 8.625% debentures are callable by the firm on December 1, 2006 at $1,044.50. Determine the *yield to call* as of December 1, 2006, assuming that the bonds are called on that date.

10. Determine the value of a $4.50 cumulative preferred share, no par, to an investor who requires a 9% rate of return on this security. The issue is callable at $120 per share plus accrued dividends. However, the issue is not expected to be called at any time in the foreseeable future.

11. Consider again the 8.125% debentures that mature on July 15, 2024 (see Problem 3). Determine the yield to call if the bonds are called on July 15, 2010, at $1,016.55.

12. Zaz Corporation bonds pay a coupon rate of interest of 12% annually and have a maturity value of $1,000. The bonds are scheduled to mature at the end of 14 years. The firm has the option to call the bonds in eight years at a premium of 12% above the maturity value. You believe the firm will exercise its option to call the bonds at that time. If you require a pretax return of 10% on bonds of this risk, how much would you pay for one of these bonds today?

13. Zhengco, a multinational company specializing in Chinese medicines, issued $100 million of bonds in January 1998, with a 15% annual coupon rate. The bonds had an initial maturity of 30 years. The bonds were sold at par and were callable in five years at 110 (i.e., 110% of par value). It is now January 2003, and interest rates have declined such that bonds of equivalent remaining maturity now sell to yield 11%. How much would you be willing to pay for one of these bonds today? Why?

14. Disney Enterprises issued 7.55% senior debentures (bonds) on July 15, 1993, with a 100-year maturity (i.e., due on July 15, 2093). Suppose an investor purchases one of these bonds on July 15, 2003, for $1,050.

   a. Determine the yield to maturity (nearest 1/100 of 1%) using the valuation formula for a bond with a finite maturity (Equation 5.5).

   b. Determine the yield to maturity (nearest 1/100 of 1%) using the valuation formula for a perpetual bond (Equation 5.8).

   c. Explain why the answers to parts a and b are the same.

CHALLENGE

15. A firm is planning to offer a $1,000 par value 15-year maturity bond with a coupon interest rate that changes every five years. The coupon rate for the first five years is 10%, 10.75% for the next five years, and 11.5% for the final five years. If you require an 11% rate of return on a bond of this quality and maturity, what is the maximum price you would pay for the bond? (Assume interest is paid annually at the end of each year.)

16. HB Company has outstanding preferred shares with a par value of $30 that pay a dividend of $2.50. The preferred shares are redeemable at the option of the shareholder in 10 years at a price equal to $30. The shares may be called for redemption by the firm in 15 years at a price of $32.50. (Any shares that are not redeemed at the end of 10 years can be expected to be called by the firm in 15 years.) If you know that investors require a 15% pretax rate of return on these preferred shares, what is the current market value of these preferred shares?

 Excel

17. Dooley has outstanding $100 million (par value) bonds that pay an annual coupon rate of interest of 10.5%. Par value of each bond is $1,000. The bonds are scheduled to mature in 20 years. Because of Dooley's increased risk, investors now require a 14% rate of return on bonds of similar quality with 20 years remaining until maturity. The bonds are callable at 110% of par at the end of 10 years.

   a. What price would the bonds sell for, assuming investors *do not expect* them to be called?

   b. What price would the bonds sell for, assuming investors *expect* them to be called at the end of 10 years?

 Excel

18. WalterCo has outstanding a $100 million (face value) issue of bonds. The bonds pay a coupon rate of interest of 8% per annum. At the time the bonds were first issued, they sold at face value of $1,000 per bond. The bonds have 12 years remaining until maturity. They are "puttable" at the option of the bondholder at face value in five years. The bonds are not callable by the firm. If you require a 9% return on bonds such as these with 5 years remaining until maturity and 8.2% on bonds such as these with 12 years remaining until maturity, how much would you pay for one of these bonds?

19. WT has issued preferred shares ($10 par value) that pay an annual dividend of $0.84. The preferred shares mature in five years. At that time, holders of the shares will receive, at their option, either $10 or one common share with a value up to $14. If the common share is trading at a price above $14, the preferred shareholders will receive a fractional common share worth $14. The current common share price is $8.875. The common shares pay a 10 cent per share dividend. This dividend is expected to grow at a 10% rate per year for the next five years. If you require a 12% rate of return on a share of this risk and maturity, what is the *maximum* value for which this share can be expected to trade?

20. Murphy's Brewhouse was a rapidly expanding chain of home-brew bars. The beer was not very good, but hopes were high when the company went public three years ago, because of founder/owner Kevin Murphy's promotional skills.

At the time the firm went public, Murphy's also issued $50 million of 20-year maturity debentures at an annual coupon rate of 9%. These debentures were sold at par ($1,000 per bond). Shortly after this debenture issue, Murphy's received some very negative reviews, both in the gourmet beer magazines and in the financial press. The firm is currently struggling. Its shares have plummeted from $40 three years ago to less than $5. Earnings remain positive but disappointing at $0.03 per share, and the firm is barely breaking even on a cash flow basis.

Murphy's debentures are currently selling at 40 cents on the dollar. The debentures are callable two years from now at $1,090. If you require a 20% rate of return on investments of this perceived risk level, should you buy these debentures?

Other Practice Materials and Resources

For interactive quizzes, Internet exercises, crossword puzzles, CTV videos, and more, go to the *Contemporary Financial Management* Web site at **http://cyr.nelson.com**

Common Shares: Characteristics and Valuation

Learning Objectives

After studying this chapter you should be able to

1. Understand the characteristics of variable income (common share) securities including

   a. Accounting aspects
   b. Shareholder rights
   c. Features
   d. Advantages and disadvantages

2. Understand that in the general dividend valuation model, the value of a common share is equal to the present value of all future dividend payments discounted at the investor's required rate of return

3. Understand that in the constant growth dividend valuation model, the value of a common share is equal to the next period's dividend divided by the difference between the investor's required rate of return and the dividend growth rate, as in a growth perpetuity

4. Understand that the zero growth dividend valuation model can be used when a firm's future dividend payments are expected to remain constant forever, as in a perpetuity

5. Understand that the nonconstant growth dividend valuation model uses the present value of yearly dividends plus the present value of the expected share price at the end of the period of nonconstant growth

6. Understand that the valuation of small firm shares requires an explicit consideration of their marketability, whether the shares represent minority or majority ownership, and whether the shares are voting or nonvoting

New Offering of BCE Equity

BCE is Canada's largest communications company. BCE shares are traded in Canada, the United States, and Europe. In 2002, BCE decided to raise $5 billion of new funds. In the previous chapter we discussed the company's debt issue. The equity issue that took place at the same time as the debt issue raised net proceeds of $2,078 million by the sale of 85 million BCE common shares at a price of $24.45 per share. The funds were used to pay part of the acquisition price of SBC Communications' minority interest in Bell Canada. As a result of the debt and equity issues, BCE was able to buy back the part of Bell Canada that it did not own. Thus, it again has full ownership of Bell Canada.

BCE has 24 million customer connections through the wireline, wireless, data/Internet, and satellite services that it provides. In addition, it has extensive content capabilities through Bell Globemedia, *The Globe and Mail* newspaper, CTV, and Sympatico, an Internet portal. It also has e-commerce capabilities under the BCE Emergis brand.

What is the value of this diversified company's common shares? The valuation of common shares is a challenging undertaking, not just for individual investors, but also for professional investment dealers/investment bankers who underwrite share offerings such as the BCE issue discussed above. In this chapter, the principles and tools used in the valuation of common shares are discussed.

© ALAN SCHEIN PHOTOGRAPHY/CORBIS/MAGMA

Introduction

Unlike long-term debt and preferred shares, which are normally fixed-income securities, common shares are variable-income securities. Common shareholders are said to participate in a firm's earnings because they may receive a larger dividend if earnings increase in the future or their dividends may be cut if earnings drop.

Common shares also differ from long-term debt and preferred shares in that the market price tends to fluctuate more than the price of bonds and preferred shares, thus causing returns on common share investments to vary more widely over time than returns on long-term debt or preferred shares.

This chapter describes the characteristics of common shares. In addition, this chapter discusses the valuation models for common shares.

For more information on the Toronto Stock Exchange see **www.tsx.ca**

Understanding Stock Quotations

Table 6.1 shows selected quotations for shares traded on the Toronto Stock Exchange as reported in the Saturday news. Beginning at the left-hand side, the table shows the share's *high* and *low* price range during the previous 365 days. For example, the common share price of Abitibi Consolidated ranged between $15.04 and $9.41. The *Stock* column provides an abbreviated name of the firm. The *Sym* column name shows the ticker symbol, A, used to identify this share on the exchange's ticker tape. The *div* column shows the current annual dividend rate. For A, it is 40 cents. Dividends are normally paid in four quarterly instalments throughout the year. The *close* column shows the closing price (other columns not shown here indicate the high and low prices during the week as well). The *chg* column indicates the change since the previous trading report, in this case a week ago. In the case of A shares, the closing price at the end of this week was up four cents from the previous week. The *Vol* column indicates the sales volume in hundreds of shares. In this particular week, 6,354,800 shares of A were traded. The *Yld* column shows the dividend (percentage) yield. For A, the figure is 3.77 (calculated as the annual dividend divided by the closing price, or $0.40/$10.60 = 3.77%). The *p/e* ratio column shows the price-to-earnings ratio (the closing price divided by the sum of the latest four quarters of earnings per share). The P/E ratio (20) indicates how much investors are willing to pay for $1 of current earnings from the firm. Generally, the greater the risk of the firm, the lower will be its P/E multiple. Similarly, the P/E ratio will tend to be higher the more rapid the expected growth rate in future earnings.

Characteristics of Common Shares

A firm's common shareholders are its true owners. Common shares are a *residual form of ownership* in that the claims of common shareholders on the firm's earnings and assets are considered only *after* the claims of governments, debt holders, and preferred shareholders have been met. Common shares are considered a *permanent* form of long-term financing because, unlike debt and some preferred shares, common shares have no maturity date.

Table 6.1		Selected Quotations from the Toronto Stock Exchange							
High	**Low**	**Stock**	**Sym**	**div**	**close**	**chg**	**Vol**	**Yld**	**p/e**
15.04	9.41	Abitibi	A	0.40	10.60	+0.04	63548	3.77	20.0
36.05	21.30	Barrick	ABX	0.35	27.55	+1.85	118512	1.27	39.9
58.04	38.75	CIBC	CM	1.64	43.26	+1.16	59414	3.76	18.5

Source: *The Globe and Mail* (September 14, 2002): B11.

Common Shares and Accounting

Common shares appear on the right-hand side of a firm's balance sheet as part of the shareholder's equity. This is shown for the St. Lawrence Company in Table 6.2.

Shareholders' equity includes both preferred shares (if any) and common shares. The total equity attributable to the common shares of the St. Lawrence Company is equal to the total shareholders' equity less the preferred shares: $117,820,000 − $37,500,000 = $80,320,000

In other words, the sum of the common shares and retained earnings accounts equals the total common shareholders' equity.

The book value per common share is calculated as follows:

$$(6.1) \qquad \text{Book value per share} = \frac{\text{Total common shareholders' equity}}{\text{Number of shares outstanding}}$$

In the case of the St. Lawrence Company,

$$\text{Book value per share} = \$80,320,000/6,675,000 = \$12.03$$

A common share's book value is calculated from balance sheet figures and does not necessarily have any relationship to the common share's *market value,* which is based primarily on expectations concerning general economic conditions and the firm's future earnings.

The amount shown in the common shares account is calculated by multiplying the number of shares actually outstanding by the price at which the shares were sold.[1] Since these shares may well have been sold at different times, the price that the firm received undoubtedly varied. Thus, if one divides the common share account of $42,063,000 by the number of shares outstanding, 6,675,000, one obtains $6.30 as the average selling price.

Additions to the retained earnings account occur when earnings are retained in the business, instead of earnings being paid out to the shareholders as dividends. Retained earnings, which are internally generated funds, are one of the most important sources of capital for business.

Shareholder Rights

Common shareholders have a number of general rights, including the following:

- **Dividend right** Shareholders have the right to share equally on a per-share basis in any distribution of corporate earnings in the form of dividends. Most firms that pay dividends make payments quarterly.

Table 6.2	St. Lawrence Company Shareholders' Equity December 31, 2003 (in Thousands of Dollars)
Shareholders' Equity	
Preferred shares; authorized, 2,000,000; issued and outstanding, 1,500,000	$ 37,500
Common shares; authorized, 10,000,000; issued and outstanding, 6,675,000	$ 42,063
Retained earnings	$ 38,257
Total shareholders' equity	$117,820

[1] Federal law *proscribes* par value for a corporation with a federal charter. However, par values are allowed by legislation in some provinces, although no Canadian jurisdiction requires firms to establish par values for their shares. Thus, most firms have "no par" shares. At one time, par value was considered important for any possible liquidation proceedings, but today it has little, if any, real significance. In the past, firms issued shares with par value and these firms may have a contributed capital account today, even though their shares no longer have a par value. Most firms now will have combined the contributed capital account with the common shares account, so they would now have only the common shares account plus retained earnings.

- **Asset right** In the event of liquidation, shareholders have the right to assets that remain after the obligations to the government (taxes), employees, debt holders, and preferred shareholders have been satisfied.

- **Preemptive right** If shareholders have the right to share proportionately in any new shares sold, then shareholders have the **preemptive right**. For example, a shareholder who owns 20 percent of a corporation's shares may be entitled to purchase 20 percent of any new issue.

- **Voting right** Shareholders have the right to vote on shareholder matters, such as the selection of the board of directors.

Whereas all shareholders have dividend and asset rights, in addition to the voting right (unless the shares are specifically nonvoting), the preemptive right exists in a relatively small minority of firms at the present time.

Shareholder Voting Right A firm's shareholders elect its board of directors by means of either a *majority* or a *cumulative* voting procedure. If two slates of people are running for the board, the one that receives more than 50 percent of the votes wins. With majority voting, it is possible that a group of shareholders with a minority viewpoint will have no representation on the board. Cumulative voting, in contrast, makes it easier for shareholders with minority views to elect sympathetic board members. Because of this, cumulative voting is rare among major corporations and is frequently opposed by management. In cumulative voting, each share represents as many votes as there are directors to be elected. For example, if a firm is electing seven directors, a particular holder of 100 shares would have 700 votes and could cast all of them for *one* candidate, thereby increasing that candidate's chance of being elected to the board. The following formula can be used to determine the number of shares necessary to elect a certain number of directors:

$$(6.2) \quad \text{Number of shares} = \frac{\text{Number of directors desired} \times \text{Number of shares outstanding}}{\text{Number of directors being elected} + 1} + 1$$

Of course, it is possible that not all of the shareholders will vote their shares. In this case, the calculation is based on the number of shares actually voting rather than the number of shares outstanding.

Consider the following example. The Markham Company has 11 members on its board and 1 million common shares outstanding. If seven members were up for reelection in a given year and all of the shares were voted, the number of shares necessary to elect one director would be as follows:

$$\frac{1 \times 1,000,000}{7 + 1} + 1 = 125,001$$

In addition to electing the board of directors, a firm's shareholders may vote from time to time on various other matters, such as whether to retain a particular auditing firm or to increase the number of shares authorized.

The election of directors and other voting normally occurs at the annual shareholders' meeting. Because it is usually not possible for all shareholders to attend, management—or anyone else—can solicit votes by *proxy*. Normally, a shareholder can expect to receive a single proxy statement from the firm's management requesting that shareholders follow management's recommendations. In the rather unlikely event that another group of shareholders sends out its own proxy statement, a *proxy fight* is said to occur. Proxy fights are most common when a company is performing poorly or is in the midst of a takeover attempt.

For information on Canadian companies see
www.sedar.com

Other Features of Common Shares

This section covers other topics related to the ownership of common shares, including *common share classes, stock splits, stock dividends,* and *stock repurchases.*

See Investor Information on the Canadian Tire Web site at **www.canadiantire.ca**

Common Share Classes   Occasionally, a firm may decide to create more than one class of common shares. The reason for this may be that the firm wishes to raise additional equity capital by selling a portion of the existing owners' shares while maintaining control of the firm. This can be accomplished by creating a separate class of *nonvoting shares.* Typically, so-called Class A common shares are nonvoting, whereas Class B has voting rights. Normally, the classes are otherwise equal. The Canadian Tire Corporation is an example of a large, well-known company that has more than one class of common shares. Canadian Tire common shares are the voting shares held by the family that founded the firm, while the Canadian Tire common shares Class A are the publicly held shares. Both classes of shares are listed on the TSX.

Stock Split
The issuance of a number of new shares in exchange for each old share held by a shareholder.

Stock Splits   If management feels that the firm's common shares should sell at a lower price to attract more purchasers, it can effect a **stock split**. There seems to be a feeling among some in the finance community that the optimum price range for a common share should be roughly $15 to $60. Consequently, if a share price rises above this range, management may decide on a stock split to get the price back to a more desirable trading level. Frequently, companies choose to raise their dividend levels at the time of a split. Many investors believe stock splits are an indication of good financial health. The mere splitting of a stock, however, should not be taken in and of itself as evidence that the shares will necessarily perform well in the future.

Reverse Stock Splits   *Reverse stock splits* are stock splits in which the number of shares is decreased. They are used to bring low-priced shares up to more desirable trading levels. Many investors feel reverse stock splits indicate poor corporate health. For this reason, such splits are relatively uncommon.

Stock Dividend
A payment of additional shares of common stock to shareholders

Stock Dividends   A **stock dividend** is a dividend to shareholders that consists of additional shares instead of cash. Normally, stock dividends are in the 2 to 10 percent range—that is, the number of shares outstanding is increased by 2 to 10 percent. From an accounting (but not a cash flow) standpoint, stock dividends involve a transfer from the retained earnings account to the common shares.[2]

Stock Repurchases   From time to time, companies repurchase some of their own shares of stock (known as treasury shares). In addition to undertaking stock repurchases as an alternative to the payment of cash dividends, which is discussed in Chapter 14, a company may have a number of other reasons for repurchasing its own shares. These include

- **Disposition of excess cash** The company may want to dispose of excess cash that it has accumulated from operations or the sale of assets. These funds are expendable because management may not feel that they can be invested profitably within the company in the foreseeable future.

- **Financial restructuring** By issuing debt and using the proceeds to repurchase its common shares, the firm can alter its capital structure to gain the benefits of increased financial leverage.

---

[2] Chapter 14 contains a more detailed discussion of stock dividends.

- **Future corporate needs** Shares can be repurchased for use in future acquisitions of other companies, stock option plans for executives, conversion of convertible securities, and the exercise of warrants.[3]

- **Reduction of takeover risk** Share repurchases reduce the number of shares outstanding. Thus, the outstanding shares controlled by management will become a larger percentage of the outstanding shares. Returning to the St. Lawrence example in Table 6.2, suppose that management controlled 3 million shares before the repurchase. This is somewhat less than half of the shares outstanding. However, if the firm repurchased 680,000 shares that management did not control, then management would control more than a majority of the shares that remain outstanding.

The reasons for repurchasing shares are not mutually exclusive—a firm may repurchase shares for a combination of reasons.

Advantages and Disadvantages of Common Share Financing

One of the major advantages of common share financing is that no fixed-dividend obligation exists, at least in principle. In practice, however, dividend cuts are relatively uncommon for companies paying a "regular" dividend, a fact that implies that corporate management generally views a firm's current level of dividends as a minimum for the future.[4] Nevertheless, common share financing does allow firms a greater degree of flexibility in their financing plans than fixed-income securities. Thus, common shares are less risky to the firm than fixed-income securities. Limits on additional debt and the maintenance of working capital levels are only two of the constraints imposed on a firm when fixed-income security financing is employed.

In addition, common share financing can be advantageous for a firm whose capital structure contains more than an optimal amount of debt. Under these circumstances, common share financing can lower the firm's weighted cost of capital.[5]

From the investors' perspective, however, buying common shares is a riskier investment than buying debt securities or preferred shares. Because of this, investors in common shares require relatively high rates of return, and this means that the firm's cost for common share financing is high compared with fixed-income securities.

From another perspective, external common share financing frequently results in an initial dilution of per-share earnings, particularly if the assets acquired with the proceeds of the financing do not produce earnings immediately. Table 6.3, which contains figures for Prairie Power Company for 20X6 and 20X5, illustrates this point.

Notice that whereas the firm's net income increased in 20X6 over 20X5, its earnings per share declined because of the new shares issued. Thus, the additional issue of common shares can dilute the original owners' claims on the firm's earnings. If, on the

Table 6.3	Example of Diluted Per-Share Earnings as a Result of Common Share Financing: Prairie Power Company	
	Year ended December 31	
	20X6	20X5
Net income available for common shares	$25,821,000	$20,673,000
Average number of common shares outstanding	15,600,000	12,122,007
Earnings per average common share	$1.66	$1.71

[3] Warrants and convertible securities are examined in Chapter 17.

[4] See Chapter 14 for a discussion of dividend policy.

[5] See Chapters 12–13 for a discussion of the measurement of and the effect of capital structure on the firm's weighted cost of capital.

Global Equity Markets

Large multinational corporations have increasingly been turning to international markets to raise both equity and debt capital. Large, non-US-domiciled corporations may sell equity in the United States because of the size and liquidity of the market for new issues there. For example, during 1993 Daimler-Benz, the large German conglomerate best known for its Mercedes-Benz automobiles, offered its equity in the US capital market. By selling its shares in multiple country capital markets, Daimler hoped to reach more potential investors and perhaps realize some capital cost savings. Later Daimler-Benz merged with Chrysler.

By dealing in global equity markets, multinational firms can take advantage of institutional differences from one country to another that may temporarily disadvantage a firm that is limited to selling its shares in a single capital market. Many multinational firms now have their shares trading on exchanges outside North America. For

example, Royal Bank of Canada shares are traded in Canada, the United States, and Switzerland; Thomson Corporation shares are traded in Toronto, New York, and London, while Barrick Gold Corporation is listed on the New York, Toronto, London, Paris, and Swiss stock exchanges. The existence of these markets permits nearly 24-hour-per-day trading in the shares of large multinational firms. Around-the-clock trading provides investors with opportunities to buy and sell shares at almost any time they wish. In addition, multinational firms can increase their name and product recognition abroad, to the benefit, it is hoped, of the firm's bottom-line performance.

As a truly global capital market emerges, it is clear that national borders will be less important in determining where, and in what form, capital will be acquired by a firm. Rather, firms can be expected to sell their shares in those markets with the greatest demand (and hence the lowest cost to the firm).

other hand, the new assets earn a higher rate of return than the existing assets, the original owners will benefit from the increased earnings. Also, the problem of diluted earnings should be only temporary if the firm is investing wisely and should have no adverse consequences in a well-informed market.

A final disadvantage of external equity financing involves the relatively high issuance costs associated with common shares sold to the public.[6]

Valuation of Common Shares

In principle, the valuation of common shares is no different from the valuation of other types of securities, such as bonds and preferred shares. The basic procedure involves capitalizing (that is, discounting) the expected stream of cash flows to be received from holding the common shares. This is complicated by several factors, however.

First, the expected cash flows from holding a common share take two forms: (1) the cash dividend payments made during the holding period and (2) changes in the price of the share (capital gains or losses) over the holding period. All of the cash flows

[6] Issuance costs for various sources of capital were discussed in Chapter 2.

received by the common shareholder are derived from the firm's earnings and can be either paid to shareholders in the current period as cash dividends or reinvested in the firm to (it is hoped) provide higher future dividends and a higher share price.

Second, because common share dividends are normally expected to grow rather than remain constant, the relatively simple annuity and perpetuity formulas used in the valuation of bonds and preferred shares are generally not applicable, and more complicated growth models must be used.

Finally, the expected cash flows from common shares are more uncertain than the cash flows from bonds and preferred shares. Common share dividend payments are related to the firm's earnings in some manner, and it can be difficult to forecast future long-term earnings and dividend payments with a high degree of accuracy.

To better understand the application of the capitalization of cash flow valuation method to common shares, it is best to begin by considering a *one*-period dividend valuation model and then move on to consider multiple-period valuation models.

One-Period Dividend Valuation Model

Assume that an investor plans to purchase a common share and hold it for *one* period. At the end of that period, the investor expects to receive a cash dividend, D_1, and sell the share for a price, P_1. What is the value of this share to the investor *today* (time 0), given a required rate of return on the investment, k_e?

In the capitalization of cash flow valuation method, the discounted present value of the expected cash flows from the share is calculated as follows:

(6.3)
$$P_0 = \frac{D_1}{1 + k_e} + \frac{P_1}{1 + k_e}$$

For example, if Ogopogo Engineering Company common shares are expected to pay a $1.00 dividend and sell for $27.50 at the end of one period, what is the value of this share to an investor who requires a 14 percent rate of return? The answer is computed as follows:

$$
\begin{aligned}
P_0 &= \frac{1.00}{(1 + 0.14)} + \frac{\$27.50}{(1 + 0.14)} \\
&= \$1.00(PVIF_{0.14,\,1}) + \$27.50(PVIF_{0.14,\,1}) \\
&= \$1.00(0.877) + \$27.50(0.877) \\
&= \$24.99 \text{ (or } \$25)
\end{aligned}
$$

Thus, the investor who purchases the share for $25, collects the $1 dividend, and sells the share for $27.50 at the end of one period will earn the 14 percent required rate of return.

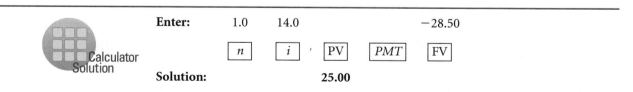

Enter:　　1.0　　14.0　　　　　　　　　　　　　−28.50

　　　　　　　n　　i　　PV　　PMT　　FV

Solution:　　　　　　　25.00

Note: The FV amount of $28.50 is equal to the sum of the dividend at the end of year 1 and the share price at the end of year 1.

The solution can also be computed with a spreadsheet as follows:

	A	B	C	
1	TVM	INPUTS	SOLUTION	
2	Periods, n	1		
3	Rate, i	14.00%		
4	PV		$25	
5	PMT			
6	FV	−28.50		

Enter the appropriate data inputs in column B and choose the PV function for cell C4.

Multiple-Period Dividend Valuation Model

The dividend valuation process just described can be generalized to a multiple-period case. The expected cash flows to the investor who purchases a common share and holds it for n periods consist of dividend payments during each of the next n periods (D_1, D_2, ..., D_n) plus an amount, P_n, from the sale of the share at the end of the nth period. Capitalizing these expected cash flows at the investor's required rate of return, k_e, gives the following valuation equation:

$$(6.4) \qquad P_0 = \frac{D_1}{(1 + k_e)^1} + \frac{D_2}{(1 + k_e)^2} + \ldots + \frac{D_n}{(1 + k_e)^n} + \frac{P_n}{(1 + k_e)^n}$$

Consider again the Ogopogo Engineering Company common shares. Suppose that the investor is considering purchasing a share and holding it for five years. Assume that the investor's required rate of return is still 14 percent. Dividends from the share are expected to be $1 in the first year, $1 in the second year, $1 in the third year, $1.25 in the fourth year, and $1.25 in the fifth year. The expected selling price of the share at the end of five years is $41.

Using Equation 6.4 and the appropriate present value interest factors (PVIFs), the value of the share to the investor is computed as follows:

$$P_0 = \$1.00(\text{PVIF}_{0.14,\,1}) + \$1.00(\text{PVIF}_{0.14,\,2})$$
$$+ \$1.00(\text{PVIF}_{0.14,\,3}) + \$1.25(\text{PVIF}_{0.14,\,4})$$
$$+ \$1.25(\text{PVIF}_{0.14,\,5}) + \$41.00(\text{PVIF}_{0.14,\,5})$$
$$= \$1.00(0.877) + \$1.00(0.769) + \$1.00(0.675)$$
$$+ \$1.25(0.592) + \$1.25(0.519) + \$41.00(0.519)$$
$$= \$24.99 \text{ (or } \$25)$$

Note that the *current* value of a share of Ogopogo Engineering common stock is the same (that is, $P_0 = \$25.00$) regardless of whether the investor plans to hold it for one, five, or any other number of years.[7]

---

[7] The value of a share at *any* point in time is simply the present value of all dividends expected to be paid from that time forward. Hence, the price P_5 of $41 reflects the present value at the end of year 5 of dividends expected in years 6 through infinity.

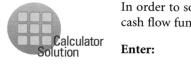
Calculator
Solution

In order to solve this problem with the aid of your calculator, it is necessary to use the cash flow function/keys (CF) on your calculator

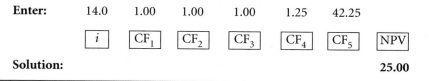

Enter: 14.0   1.00   1.00   1.00   1.25   42.25

| i | CF_1 | CF_2 | CF_3 | CF_4 | CF_5 | NPV |

Solution: **25.00**

Spreadsheet
Solution

The solution can also be computed with a spreadsheet as follows:

	A	B	C	D	E	F	G
1	Rate	14.00%					
2	Time	0	1	2	3	4	5
3	Cash Flows		1.00	1.00	1.00	1.25	42.25
4	NPV	$25.01					

A General Dividend Valuation Model

In each of the valuation models described, the current value of the share, P_0, is dependent on the expected price of the share at the end of the expected holding period. Although this seems straightforward, providing accurate forecasts of share prices when applying the models to specific shares can be difficult. A final generalization permits the elimination of P_n from the model, while showing that the dividend valuation models discussed are consistent with one another.

First, the value of the share at the end of the nth period, P_n, must be redefined. Using the capitalization of cash flow approach, it can be shown that P_n is a function of all expected *future* dividends that the investor will receive in periods $n + 1$, $n + 2$, and so on. Discounting the stream of dividends at the required rate of return, k_e, gives the value of the share at the end of the nth period:

$$(6.5) \qquad P_n = \sum_{t=n+1}^{\infty} \frac{D_t}{(1 + k_e)^{t-n}}$$

Substituting Equation 6.5 into Equation 6.4 and simplifying yields the following *general dividend valuation model:*

$$(6.6) \qquad P_0 = \sum_{t=1}^{\infty} \frac{D_t}{(1 + k_e)^t}$$

Thus, the value of a firm's common share to the investor is equal to the discounted present value of the expected future dividend stream. As was shown, the valuation of a firm's common share given by the multiple-period model (Equation 6.4) is equivalent to the valuation given by the general model (Equation 6.6). The general dividend valuation model is applicable regardless of whether the stream of dividends over time is fluctuating or constant, increasing or decreasing.

Note that the general dividend valuation model treats the stream of dividends as having no finite termination date. Whereas this assumption is reasonable for firms that are going concerns, shorter time horizons must be used when considering firms that might be either acquired by other firms or liquidated in the foreseeable future.

Some rapidly growing firms reinvest all of their earnings and do not pay current cash dividends. In fact, some profitable firms have *never* paid cash dividends for as long as they have been in existence and are not expected to do so in the near future. How can the general dividend valuation model be applied to the common share of a firm such as this? It must be assumed that the firm will be able to start making regular, periodic cash dividend payments to its shareholders *at some time in the future.* For example, Microsoft, which had a history of never paying dividends, announced in early 2003 that it would begin paying dividends. Alternatively, these returns could consist of the *proceeds from the sale of the firm's outstanding common shares,* should the firm be acquired by another company, or a final liquidating dividend (distribution), should the firm be liquidated.

As stated in Chapter 1, the primary goal of firms should be the *maximization of shareholder wealth.* The general dividend valuation model (Equation 6.6) indicates that shareholder wealth, as measured by the value of the firm's common shares, P_0, is a function of the expected stream of future dividend payments and the investor's required rate of return. Thus, when making financial decisions that are consistent with the goal of maximizing shareholder wealth, management should be concerned with how these decisions affect both the expected future dividend stream and the discount rate that investors apply to the dividend stream. The relationship between financial decision making and shareholder wealth is illustrated in Figure 6.1. A primary emphasis of the financial management function is attempting to define and measure this relationship.

Applications of the General Dividend Valuation Model

The general dividend valuation model can be simplified if a firm's dividend payments over time are expected to follow one of several different patterns, including *zero growth, constant growth,* and *nonconstant growth.*

Zero Growth Dividend Valuation Model

If a firm's future dividend payments are expected to remain constant *forever,* then D_t in Equation 6.6, the general dividend valuation model, can be replaced by a constant value D to yield the following:

$$(6.7) \qquad P_0 = \sum_{t=1}^{\infty} \frac{D}{(1 + k_e)^t}$$

This equation represents the value of a common share that is a perpetuity. It is analogous to those used for valuing a perpetual bond (Equation 5.7) and a preferred share (Equation 5.11) developed in the previous chapter, which in turn were based on the concept of a perpetuity (Equation 4.22) introduced in Chapter 4. It can be simplified to obtain

$$(6.8) \qquad P_0 = \frac{D}{k_e}$$

Figure 6.1
Relationship Between Financial Decisions and Shareholder Wealth

This model is valid only when a firm's dividend payments are expected to remain constant *forever*. Although few common shares strictly satisfy these conditions, the model can still be used to approximate the value of a share for which dividend payments are expected to remain constant for a relatively long period into the future. One of the patterns shown in Figure 6.2 is a zero growth dividend payment pattern.

To illustrate the zero growth dividend valuation model, assume that the Mountaineer Railway common share pays an annual dividend of $1.50 per share, which is expected to remain constant for the foreseeable future. What is the value of the share to an investor who requires a 12 percent rate of return? Substituting $1.50 for D and 12 percent (0.12) for k_e in Equation 6.8 yields the following:

$$P_0 = \frac{\$1.50}{0.12} = \$12.50$$

Constant Growth Dividend Valuation Model

If a firm's future dividend payments per share are expected to grow at a *constant* rate, g, per period forever, then the dividend at any future time period t can be forecast as follows:

(6.9)
$$D_t = D_0 (1 + g)^t$$

where D_0 is the dividend in the current period ($t = 0$). The expected dividend in period 1 is $D_1 = D_0(1 + g)^1$, the expected dividend in period 2 is $D_2 = D_0(1 + g)^2$, and so on. The constant-growth curve in Figure 6.2 illustrates such a dividend pattern.

Substituting Equation 6.9 for D_t in the general dividend valuation model (Equation 6.6) yields the following:

(6.10)
$$P_0 = \sum_{t=1}^{\infty} \frac{D_0(1 + g)^t}{(1 + k_e)^t}$$

Assuming that the required rate of return, k_e, is greater than the dividend growth rate,[8] g, Equation 6.10 can be transformed algebraically to obtain the following simplified common share valuation model:[9]

(6.11)
$$P_0 = \frac{D_1}{k_e - g}$$

Note that in the constant growth valuation model (Equation 6.11), the dividend value in the numerator is D_1, that is, the dividend expected to be received one year from now. The model assumes that D_0, the current dividend, has just been paid and does not enter the (forward-looking) valuation process. Equation 6.11 is an example of the concept of a growth perpetuity (Equation 4.29) introduced in Chapter 4.

The constant growth valuation model (Equation 6.11) assumes that a firm's *earnings, dividends and share price are expected to grow at a constant rate, g, into the future.* Hence, to apply this model to a specific common share, it is necessary to estimate the expected future growth rate, g. Considerable research evidence indicates that (1) the most accurate estimates of future growth are those provided by security analysts, and

---

[8] If this assumption is not satisfied—that is, if the growth rate (g) is greater than or equal to the required rate of return (k_e)—then the market price (P_0) would be infinite.

[9] Equation 6.11 is often referred to in finance literature as the *Gordon model*, for Myron J. Gordon, who pioneered its use. See Myron J. Gordon, *The Investment, Financing, and Valuation of the Corporation* (Homewood, IL: Irwin, 1962).

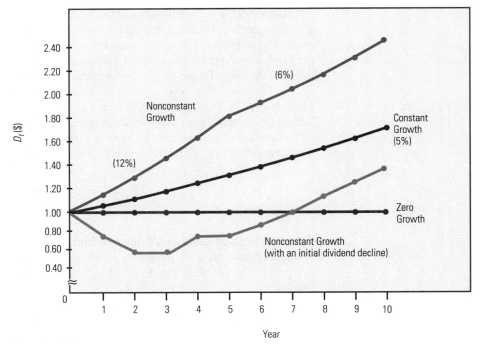

Figure 6.2
Dividend Growth Patterns

(2) consensus analyst forecasts of growth are an excellent proxy for growth expectations of investors. Sources of analyst growth rate forecasts include:

Visit **www.firstcall.com**

1. **Thomson Financial/First Call** This worldwide service includes the former Institutional Brokers Estimate System, Inc. (IBES) service for institutional investors and can be accessed through the Internet. It is primarily of interest for institutional investors and brokerage houses. Some brokers provide this information to their clients.

The Value Line Web site is located at **www.valueline. com**

2. **Value Line Investment Survey** Value Line reports, even though they represent only one analyst's forecast for each company, are readily available at most public and university libraries and have been shown to be reasonably accurate and closely related to investor expectations. They cover all of the Canadian firms that trade in the United States, which includes most of the larger firms.

Visit the Zacks Web Site at **www.zacks.com**

3. **Zacks Earnings Estimates** This service is probably the best one for individual investors and is very popular with daytraders (investors who buy and sell many times during each day). Forecasts from Zacks are available through the Internet.

The constant growth dividend valuation model can be used to illustrate the two forms of returns an investor can expect to receive from holding a common share. Solving Equation 6.11 for k_e yields the following:

$$(6.12) \qquad k_e = \frac{D_1}{P_0} + g$$

The investor's required rate of return is equal to the expected dividend yield, D_1/P_0, plus the price appreciation yield, g—the expected increase in dividends and, ultimately, in the price of the share.

To illustrate the application of the constant growth valuation model, consider Barrick Gold Corporation. In 2002 Barrick dividends were expected to be $0.35 per share *next year*. According to estimates from Zacks, earnings and dividends were expected to grow at about 4.8 percent annually. Let us determine the value of this share to an investor who requires a 12 percent rate of return. Substituting $0.35 for D_1, 4.8 percent (0.048) for g, and 12 percent (0.12) for k_e in Equation 6.11 yields the following value for a Barrick common share:

$$P_0 = \frac{\$0.35}{0.12 - 0.048} = \$4.86$$

Thus, the investor's 12 percent required return consists of a 7.2 percent dividend yield ($D_1/P_0 = \$0.35/\$4.86$) plus a price growth rate or price growth return of 4.8 percent annually. This price growth rate or percentage change in price is also called the **capital gains yield** or **price appreciation yield**. In the constant dividend growth model, the dividend growth rate and the price growth rate will be the same. However, in the nonconstant dividend growth model discussed next, the one-period dividend growth rate usually differs from the price growth rate for the same period.

Capital Gains Yield or Price Appreciation Yield
The expected percentage increase in the price of a capital asset.

Nonconstant Growth Dividend Valuation Model

Many firms experience growth rates in sales, earnings, and dividends that are *not* constant. Typically, many firms experience a period of above-normal growth as they exploit new technologies, new markets, or both. This generally occurs relatively early in a firm's life cycle. Following this period of rapid growth, earnings and dividends tend to stabilize or grow at a more normal rate comparable to the overall average rate of growth in the economy. The reduction in the growth rate occurs as the firm reaches maturity and has fewer sizable growth opportunities. The upper curve in Figure 6.2 illustrates such a nonconstant growth pattern.[10]

Nonconstant growth models can also be applied to the valuation of firms that are experiencing temporary periods of poor performance, after which a normal pattern of growth is expected to emerge. (The lower nonconstant growth line in Figure 6.2 illustrates this type of pattern.)

There is no single model or equation that can be universally applied when nonconstant growth is anticipated. However, the concept of a growth annuity factor (Equation 4.26) could be used to find the present value of dividends for the supernormal growth period (i.e., the period of 12 percent growth) in the upper curve of Figure 6.2. In general, the value of a share that is expected to experience a nonconstant growth rate pattern of dividends is equal to the present value of expected yearly dividends during the period of nonconstant growth plus the present value of the expected share price at the end of the nonconstant growth period.

The share price at the end of a nonconstant growth rate period can be estimated in a number of ways:

1. Security analysts usually provide an estimated (five-year) future price range for the shares they follow.

2. Thomson Financial/First Call, Value Line, and Zacks all provide earnings growth rate estimates for five years into the future. These growth rate estimates can be used to derive earnings per share (EPS) forecasts for five years in the future. The EPS forecasts can be multiplied by the expected price-to-earnings (P/E) multiple, estimated by looking at current P/E multiples for similar firms, to get an expected price in five years.

3. At the end of the period of nonconstant growth, an estimate of the value of the share can be derived by applying the constant growth rate valuation model (Equation 6.11). For example, consider a firm expected to experience dividend growth at a nonconstant

---

[10] The transition between the periods of above-normal and normal, or average, growth is usually not as pronounced as Figure 6.4 indicates. Typically, a firm's growth rate *declines gradually* over time from the above-normal rate to the normal rate. Growth models similar to Equation 6.13 can be developed to handle cases like this.

rate for m periods. Beginning in period $m + 1$, dividends are expected to grow at rate g_2 forever. The value of the share, P_m, at the end of period m is equal to

(6.13)
$$P_m = \frac{D_{m+1}}{k_e - g_2}$$

To demonstrate how this model works, suppose an investor expects the earnings and common share dividends of HILO to grow at a rate of 12 percent per annum for the next five years. Following the period of above-normal growth, dividends are expected to grow at the slower rate of 6 percent for the foreseeable future. The firm currently pays a dividend, D_0, of $2 per share. What is the value of a HILO common share to an investor who requires a 15 percent rate of return?

Table 6.4 illustrates the step-by-step solution to this problem.

- First, compute the sum of the present values of the dividends received during the nonconstant growth period (years 1 through 5 in this problem). According to Table 6.4, this equals $9.25. The present value of these first five dividends could also

Table 6.4 Value of HILO Common Shares

Year, t	Dividend $D_t = \$2.00(1 + 0.12)^t$	Present Value Interest Factor, $PVIF_{0.15,\,t}$	Present Value, D_t
Present Value of First 5 Years' Dividends			
1	$2.00 (1 + 0.12)^1 = \$2.24$	0.870	$1.95
2	$2.00 (1 + 0.12)^2 = 2.51$	0.756	$1.90
3	$2.00 (1 + 0.12)^3 = 2.81$	0.658	$1.85
4	$2.00 (1 + 0.12)^4 = 3.15$	0.572	$1.80
5	$2.00 (1 + 0.12)^5 = 3.53$	0.497	$1.75
			$9.25

Value of Share at End of Year 5:
$$P_5 = \frac{D_6}{k_e - g_2}$$

$$P_5 = \frac{D_6}{0.15 - 0.06}$$

$$D_6 = D_5(1 + g_2)$$

$$= \$3.53(1 + 0.06)$$

$$= \$3.74$$

$$P_5 = \frac{\$3.74}{0.15 - 0.06}$$

$$= \$41.56$$

Present Value of P_5, $PV(P_5)$:
$$= \frac{P_5}{(1 + k_e)^5}$$

$$= \frac{\$41.56}{(1 + 0.15)^5}$$

$$= \$41.56(PVIF_{0.15,5})$$

$$= \$41.56(0.497)$$

$$= \$20.66$$

Value of Common Share:
$$P_0 = PV \text{ (first 5 years' dividends)} + PV(P_5)$$
$$P_0 = \$9.25 + \$20.66$$
$$= \$29.91$$

be found by multiplying the first dividend of $2.24 by the growth annuity factor (Equation 4.26) with a 12 percent growth rate and a 15 percent discount rate, PV of first 5 years' dividends =

$$(\$2.24)\left[\dfrac{1 - \dfrac{(1.12)^5}{(1.15)^5}}{(.15 - .12)}\right] = (\$2.24)(4.1268) = \$9.24$$

- Second, use the constant growth model to determine the value of a HILO common share at the end of year 5; P_5 equals $41.56.

- Next, determine the present value of P_5, which is $20.66.

- Finally, add the present value of the dividends received during the first five years ($9.25) to the present value of P_5 ($20.66) to obtain the total value of the common share of $29.91.

A timeline showing the expected cash flows from the purchase of a HILO common share is given in Figure 6.3.

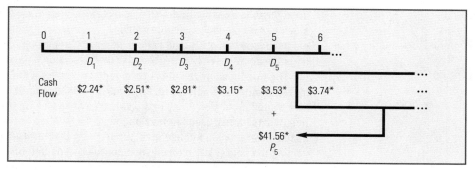

Figure 6.3
Cash Flows from a HILO Common Share
*Values as computed in Table 6.4

Calculator
Solution

This solution assumes that the reader has one of the financial calculators that has multiple storage registers as well as uneven cash flow registers. The dividends D_1 through D_5 are calculated by changing the value of n from 1 to 5 in the TVM menu. The solution for $n = 1$ is

Enter: 1   15.0   −2.00

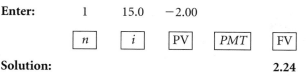

Solution: **2.24**

As each dividend is calculated, store the results in the registers 1 through 5, respectively, by using the [STO] [1] through [STO] [5] keys. Thus, 2.24 is stored in register 1, 2.51 in register 2, etc. Of course, the sixth dividend could be found by using the TVM menu with the new growth rate and the fifth dividend. However, it is faster to simply calculate $3.53(1.06) = 3.74$. (The astute reader may get $D_5 = 3.52$ and then want to use $3.52(1.06) = 3.73$ for D_6. However, to the nearest cent, $D_6 = 2.00(1.12)^5(1.06) = 3.74$. Whether one uses 3.52 or 3.53 for D_5 has no PV consequence (i.e., no change in P_0) as long as 3.74 is used for D_6.)

Next, calculate $P_5 = 3.74/(.15 - .06) = 41.56$. With 41.56 displayed in the calculator, use the [+] [RCL] [5] [=] keys to obtain the sum of $(P_5 + D_5) = 45.09$, and then store this result in register 5 by using the [STO] [5] keys.

ENTREPRENEURIAL ISSUES

Valuation of Closely Held Firms

The ownership of many small firms is closely held. An active market for shares of closely held companies normally does not exist. As a result, entrepreneurs occasionally need to have the value of their enterprises estimated by independent appraisers. The reasons for these valuations include mergers and acquisitions, divestitures and liquidations, initial public offerings, estate and gift tax returns, leveraged buyouts, recapitalizations, employee stock ownership plans, divorce settlements, estate valuation, and various other litigation matters.

The principles of valuation developed in this chapter and applied to large publicly traded firms also apply to the valuation of small firms. Small firm valuation poses several unique challenges. When valuing the shares of a closely held corporation, many factors are considered, including the nature and history of the business, the general economic outlook and the condition and outlook of the firm's industry, earnings capacity, dividend paying capacity, the book value of the company, the company's financial condition, whether the shares represent a

majority or minority (less than 50 percent) interest, and whether the shares are voting or nonvoting.

Specifically, however, in valuing a company that sells products and services, earnings capacity is usually the most important factor to be considered. Typically, the company as a whole is valued by determining a normal earnings level and multiplying that figure by an appropriate price-earnings multiple. This approach is known as the "capitalization of earnings" approach and results in a "going concern value." If the shares represent a minority interest in the corporation, a discount is taken for the lack of marketability of these shares.

Determination of Normal Earnings

The determination of an average, or "normal," earnings figure usually involves either a simple average or some type of weighted average of roughly the last five years of operations. For example, if the earnings of the company have been growing, some type of weighted average figure that places greater emphasis on more recent results is often used.

Then switch to the uneven cash flow menu and clear any previous work stored there. Enter the following data in the respective cash flow registers using the relevant [RCL] [1] through [RCL] [5] keys. Remember to enter 15 in the [i] register relevant for NPV calculations.

Enter:	2.24	2.51	2.81	3.15	45.09	15	
	CF1	CF2	CF3	CF4	CF5	i	NPV

Solution: 29.91

Spreadsheet Solution

The solution can also be computed with a spreadsheet as follows:

Enter the rate i as 15% in cell B1. Enter the five future cash flows in cells C3 through G3. In cell B4, type in the formula =**B3+NPV(B1,C3:G3)**. Although **B3+** is not really needed in this problem as we have no cash flow at $t = 0$, recall from Chapter 4 that it is

In some cases, the reported earnings of the company may not be an appropriate figure for valuation purposes. For example, suppose a portion of the salary paid to the president (and principal shareholder) really constitutes dividends paid as salary. In this situation, it is appropriate to adjust the reported earnings to account for these dividends.

Determination of an Appropriate Price–Earnings Multiple

The next step in the valuation process is to determine an appropriate rate at which to capitalize the normal earnings level. This is equivalent to multiplying the earnings by a price-earnings multiple. Had there been recent arms-length transactions in the shares, the price-earnings multiple would be known and observable in the financial marketplace. However, this situation rarely exists for closely held corporations. As a consequence, the analyst must examine the price-earnings multiple for widely held companies in the same industry as the firm being valued in an attempt to find firms that are similar to the firm of interest. The price-earnings multiple for these comparable firms is used to capitalize the normal earnings level.

Minority Interest Discount

The owner of a minority interest in a closely held corporation has an investment that lacks control and often marketability. There is usually either no market for the shares or the only buyer is either the other owners or the corporation itself. In addition, the owner of minority interest shares generally receives little, if any, dividends. The minority interest shareholder lacks control and is not able to change his or her inferior position. As a result of these problems, it is a widely practiced and accepted principle of valuation that the value of minority interest shares should be discounted.

The usual procedure in valuing minority interest shares is to value the corporation as a whole. Next, this value is divided by the number of shares outstanding to obtain a per-share value. Finally, a discount is applied to this per-share value to obtain the minority interest share value. These discounts have ranged from a low of 6 percent to more than 50 percent.

In conclusion, the basic valuation concepts are the same for small and large firms. However, the lack of marketability of shares for many small firms and the problem of minority interest positions pose special problems for the analyst.

	A	B	C	D	E	F	G
1	Rate	15%					
2	Time	0	1	2	3	4	5
3	Cash Flows		2.24	2.51	2.81	3.15	45.09
4	NPV	$29.91					

a term needed to transform the Excel NPV function into the finance definition of NPV. Note that the FV function could be used to calculate the first four cash flows in row C by using the cell B1 as the interest rate, while using −2.00 as the PV and varying the number of periods from 1 to 4. Then to find the fifth cash flow, use the formula =**FV(B1,−2,5)(1+(1.06/(.15−.06)))** in cell G3 to calculate the sum of (D_5+P_5). Your answer will differ somewhat from 45.09, and as a consequence, your NPV will differ by a few pennies.

Before its new share issue, BCE already was large and had many shares outstanding. Thus, the $24.45 per share price paid to BCE for its 85 million new shares by the underwriting syndicate of investment dealers/investment bankers most likely was linked in some fashion to the market price of existing shares. For example, it may be set at some percentage of the closing price on the day before the additional shares are issued. Nevertheless, the underwriting investment dealers/bankers would likely employ the valuation procedure of this chapter to estimate a share price for BCE by discounting the cash flow stream that shareholders expect to receive. This share price is often called a "**fair value**" or "**intrinsic value**" for the share. If this valuation were substantially less than the current share price, the underwriters may be somewhat reluctant to underwrite the new share issue because of concerns that they could not sell the issue. If this valuation were substantially above the current share price, the underwriters may counsel BCE to issue different securities now and wait for a more propitious time to issue common shares.

Fair Value or Intrinsic Value The value of a share determined by the discounted cash flow method.

Summary

- The *common shareholders* are the true owners of the firm. Thus, common shares are a permanent form of financing. Common shareholders participate in the firm's earnings, potentially receiving larger dividends if earnings rise or smaller dividends if earnings drop.

- Shareholder rights include the following:
  1. The right to dividends
  2. The right to any assets remaining after senior claims are satisfied in a liquidation
  3. Voting rights
  4. The *preemptive right,* or the right to share proportionately in any new shares sold. This right is available in some firms but not in others.

- *Common shares* permit a firm more flexibility in its financing plans than fixed-income securities because, in principle, no fixed-dividend obligation exists.

- The valuation of *common shares* is considerably more complicated than the valuation of either bonds or preferred shares for the following reasons:
  1. The cash flows can take two forms: cash dividend payments and price appreciation.
  2. Common share dividends are normally expected to grow and not remain constant.
  3. The cash flows from common shares are generally more uncertain than the cash flows from other types of securities.

- In the *general dividend valuation model,* the value of a common share is equal to the present value of all of the expected future dividends discounted at the investor's required rate of return. Simpler common share valuation models can be derived from assumptions concerning the expected growth of future dividend payments.

- The valuation of shares in small corporations poses special challenges because of its limited marketability, lack of liquidity, and the difference between minority interest and controlling interest shares.

Questions and Topics for Discussion

1. Define the following terms associated with common shares:
   a. Nonvoting shares
   b. Stock split
   c. Reverse stock split
   d. Stock dividend
   e. Book value
   f. Treasury shares

2. Does the retained earnings figure on a company's balance sheet indicate the amount of funds the company has available for current dividends or capital expenditures? Explain fully.

3. Discuss the reasons why a firm may repurchase its own common shares.

4. Explain the differences between par value, book value, and market value per share of common shares.

5. Discuss the various shareholder rights.

6. What factor or factors make the valuation of common shares more complicated than the valuation of bonds and preferred shares?

7. According to the general dividend valuation model, a firm that reinvests all of its earnings and pays no cash dividends can still have a common share value greater than zero. How is this possible?

8. Explain the relationship between financial decisions and shareholders' wealth.

9. Explain how *each* of the following factors would affect the valuation of a firm's common shares, assuming that all other factors remain constant:
   a. The general level of interest rates shifts upward, causing investors to require a higher rate of return on securities in general.
   b. Increased foreign competition reduces the future growth potential of the firm's earnings and dividends.
   c. Investors reevaluate upward their assessment of the risk of the firm's common shares as the result of increased South American investments by the firm.

10. In the context of the constant growth dividend valuation model, explain what is meant by
    a. Dividend yield
    b. Price appreciation yield

11. Explain why the valuation models for a perpetual bond, preferred shares, and common shares with constant dividend payments (zero growth) are virtually identical.

12. Explain how the book value of a common share can change over time.

13. What is the difference between majority voting and cumulative voting?

Self-Test Problems

ST1. What is the current value of a share of a company's common shares to an investor who requires a 12% annual rate of return, if *next* year's dividend (D_1) is expected to be $3 per share and dividends are expected to grow at an annual rate of 4% for the foreseeable future?

ST2. The EF Corporation currently pays a $2 per share dividend ($D_0$). This dividend is expected to grow at a 20% annual rate over the next three years and then to grow at 6% per year for the foreseeable future. What would you pay for this share if you demand a 20% rate of return?

Problems*

BASIC

Excel

1. GC common share dividends have been growing at an annual rate of 7% per year over the past 10 years. Current dividends (D_0) are $1.70 per share. What is the current value of a share of this firm to an investor who requires a 12% rate of return if the following conditions exist?
   a. Dividends are expected to continue growing at the historic rate for the foreseeable future.
   b. The dividend growth rate is expected to *increase* to 9% per year.
   c. The dividend growth rate is expected to *decrease* to 6.5% per year.

2. GLDC common shares are expected to pay a dividend (D_1) of $1.25 next year and currently sell for $25. Assume that the firm's future dividend payments are expected to grow at a constant rate for the foreseeable future. Determine the implied growth rate of GLDC's dividends (and earnings), assuming that the required rate of return of investors is 12%.

3. What is the current per-share value of JRM Corporation to an investor who requires a 16% annual rate of return, if JRM's current per-share dividend (D_0) is $2 and is expected to remain at $2 for the foreseeable future?

www.shareowner. com

4. The Canadian Share Owners Association has put together a list of share-picking techniques that "stand the test of time." Given what you learned in the previous chapters about valuation, coupled with what you now know about shares, do you agree or disagree with their techniques? Why or why not?

INTERMEDIATE

Excel

5. The Fondue Company's earnings and common share dividends have been growing at an annual rate of 6% over the past 10 years and are expected to continue growing at this rate for the foreseeable future. The firm currently (that is, as of year 0) pays an annual dividend of $5 per share. Determine the current value of a Fondue share to investors with each of the following required rates of return:
   a. 12%
   b. 14%
   c. 16%

Excel

6. Cascade Company expects its earnings and dividends to increase by 7% per year over the next six years and then to remain relatively constant thereafter. The firm currently (that is, as of year 0) pays a dividend of $5 per share. Determine the value of a Cascade share to an investor with a 12% required rate of return.

Excel

7. Over the past five years, the dividends of the Gamma Corporation have grown from $0.70 per share to the current level of $1.30 per share ($D_0$). This growth rate (computed to 1/10 of 1% accuracy) is expected to continue for the foreseeable future. What is the value of a Gamma Corporation common share to an investor who requires a 20% return on her investment?

Excel

8. Simtek currently pays a $2.50 dividend ($D_0$) per share. Next year's dividend is expected to be $3 per share. After next year, dividends are expected to increase at a 9% annual rate for three years and a 6% annual rate thereafter.
   a. What is the current value of a Simtek share to an investor who requires a 15% return on his or her investment?
   b. If the dividend in year 1 is expected to be $3 and the growth rate over the following three years is expected to be only 7% and then 6% thereafter, what will the new share price be?

*Coloured numbers and letters denote problems that have "check" answers provided at the back of the book.

Excel

9. The Seneca Company currently (that is, as of year 0) pays a common share dividend of $1.50. Dividends are expected to grow at a rate of 11% per year for the next four years and then to continue growing thereafter at a rate of 5% per year. What is the current value of a Seneca common share to an investor who requires a 14% rate of return?

 Excel

10. Ten years ago, Video Toys began manufacturing and selling coin-operated arcade games. Dividends are currently $1.50 per share, having grown at a 15% compound annual rate over the past five years. That growth rate is expected to be maintained for the next three years, after which dividends are expected to grow at half that rate for three years. Beyond that time, Video Toys's dividends are expected to grow at 5% per year. What is the current value of a Video Toys common share if your required rate of return is 18%?

11. Suppose you have accumulated a sizable investment (100,000 common shares) in ALD Company. You are dissatisfied with the performance of the present management and are considering running for the board of directors. The firm has a nine-member board and a total of 1.5 million common shares outstanding. Assume that all shares will be voted in the upcoming election and that four of the nine board members are up for reelection.

   a. If the voting procedure is cumulative, what number of shares is necessary to ensure your election to the board? Is it possible for you to be elected with fewer votes? Explain.

   b. Suppose a close friend of yours also owns a good deal of ALD and shares your feelings about the present management. If the voting procedure is cumulative, how many shares are necessary to elect both you and your friend to the board?

   c. If the voting procedure is majority, how many votes are necessary for election in parts a and b of this problem? Explain your answer.

12. CBE shares currently pay a dividend (D_0) of $3. This dividend is expected to grow at an annual rate of 15% for the next three years. The dividend is expected to increase by $1 in year 4 and to grow at a constant annual rate of 6% thereafter. If you require a 24% rate of return on an investment such as this, how much would you be willing to pay per share?

13. Blue Moon Corporation has one million common shares outstanding. In a typical annual election for the board of directors, shareholders representing 70% of the shares outstanding exercise their right to vote. The firm has nine members on its board of directors, all of whom are elected annually.

   a. If the firm uses a majority voting procedure to elect its board, how many votes are required to elect
      i. one director
      ii. two directors
      iii. a majority of the members of the board of directors

   b. If the firm uses a cumulative voting procedure, how many votes are required to elect
      i. one director
      ii. two directors
      iii. a majority of the members of the board of directors

CHALLENGE

14. The chairman of Heller Industries told a meeting of financial analysts that he expects the firm's earnings and dividends to double over the next six years. The firm's current (that is, as of year 0) earnings and dividends per share are $4 and $2, respectively.

a. Estimate the compound annual dividend growth rate over the six-year period (to the nearest whole percent).

b. Forecast Heller's earnings and dividends per share for each of the next six years, assuming that they grow at the rate determined in part a.

c. Based on the constant growth dividend valuation model, determine the current value of a Heller Industries common share to an investor who requires an 18% rate of return.

d. Why might the share price calculated in part c not represent an accurate valuation to an investor with an 18% required rate of return?

e. Determine the current value of a Heller Industries common share to an investor (with an 18% required rate of return) who plans to hold it for six years, assuming that earnings and dividends per share grow at the rate determined in part a for the next six years and then at 6% thereafter.

15. Kruger Associates is considering a substantial investment in the shares of McIntyre Enterprises. McIntyre currently (time 0) pays a dividend of $1.50 per share. This dividend is expected to grow at 15% per year for the next three years and 10% per year for the following three years. McIntyre's marginal tax rate is 40%. Kruger expects the value of the McIntyre shares to increase by 50% between now and the *beginning* of year 5. If Kruger requires a 12% rate of return on investments of this type, what value would Kruger place on the McIntyre shares?

16. Piedmont Enterprises currently pays a dividend (D_0) of $1 per share. This dividend is expected to grow at a 20% per year rate for the next two years, after which it is expected to grow at 6% per year for the foreseeable future. If you require a 15% rate of return on an investment of this type, what price do you expect the share to sell for *at the beginning of year 5*?

 Excel

17. Over the past 10 years, the dividends of Party Time, Inc. have grown at an annual rate of 15%. The current dividend (D_0) is $3 per share. This dividend is expected to grow to $3.40 next year, then grow at an annual rate of 10% for the following two years and 6% per year thereafter. You require a 15% rate of return on this share.

a. What would you be willing to pay for a Party Time share today?

b. What price would you anticipate the share selling for at the beginning of year 3?

c. If you anticipated selling the share at the end of two years, how much would you pay for it today?

Excel

18. Draveau Corporation currently pays a dividend (D_0) at the rate of $2 per share. This dividend is expected to increase at a 9% annual rate for the next three years, at a 7% annual rate for the following two years, and then at 4% per year thereafter. What is the value of a Draveau share to an investor who demands a 24% rate of return?

19. Excito Corporation has recently witnessed a period of depressed earnings performance. As a result, cash dividend payments have been suspended. Investors do not anticipate a resumption of dividends until two years from today, when a yearly dividend of $0.25 will be paid. That yearly dividend is expected to be increased to $0.75 in the following year and $1.50 in the year after that. Beyond the time when the $1.50 dividend is paid, investors expect the firm's dividends to grow at an annual rate of 5% into perpetuity. All dividends are assumed to be paid at the end of each year. If you require an 18% rate of return, what is the value of one Excito share to you today?

Excel

20. The Cremmins Coat Company has recently completed a period of extraordinary growth, due to the popularity of its yellow jackets. Earnings per share have grown at an average compound annual rate of 15%, while dividends have grown at a 20% annual rate over the past 10 years. The current dividend (D_0) rate is $2 per share. Current earnings are $3.25 per share. Earnings are expected to grow at an

annual rate of 15% for the next three years and 6% per annum thereafter. Dividends are expected to grow by 25% during the coming year, by 15% per annum for the following two years, and by 6% per annum thereafter.

    a. What price do you expect the share to sell for today, if your required rate of return on equity for a firm of this risk level is 16%?

    b. What price do you expect the share to sell for at the beginning of year 2?

21. The VSE Corporation currently pays no dividend because of depressed earnings. A recent change in management promises a brighter future. Investors expect VSE to pay a dividend of $1 next year (the end of year 1). This dividend is expected to increase to $2 the following year and to grow at a rate of 10% per annum for the following two years (years 3 and 4). Chuck Brown, a new investor, expects the price of the share to increase 50% in value between now (time zero) and the end of year 3. If Brown plans to hold the share for two years and requires a rate of return of 20% on his investment, what value would he place on the share today?

22. Sports Novelties, Inc. has experienced an explosion in demand for its products. The firm currently (time 0) pays a dividend of $0.25 per share. This dividend is expected to increase to $0.75 per share one year from now. It is expected to grow at a rate of 15% per year for the following seven years. Coley, a naive investor, seeks your advice regarding the current value of this share. Coley plans to purchase it today, if the price is right, and to hold it for three years. He believes that the share will increase in value to $30 at the end of four years. What is the current value of this share to Coley if he requires a 20% rate of return on shares of this risk level?

23. The Blinkelman Corporation has just announced that it plans to introduce a new solar panel that will greatly reduce the cost of solar energy. As a result, analysts now expect the firm's earnings, currently (year 0) $1 per share, to grow by 50% per year for the next three years, by 25% per year for the following three years, and by 8% per year thereafter. Blinkelman does not currently pay a dividend, but it expects to pay out 20% of its earnings beginning two years from now. The payout ratio is expected to become 50% in five years and to remain at that level. The firm's marginal tax rate is 40%. If you require a 20% rate of return on a share such as this, how much would you be willing to pay for it today?

24. Watkins, Inc. has experienced an explosion in demand for its products. The firm currently (time 0) pays a dividend of $0.50 per share. This dividend is expected to increase to $1.00 per share one year from now. It is expected to grow at a rate of 20% per year for the next seven years. Susan seeks your advice regarding the current value of this share. Susan plans to purchase this share today, if the price is right, and to hold it for three years. She believes that the share will increase in value to $40 at the end of five years. What is the current value of this share to Susan if she requires a 20% rate of return on shares of this risk level?

25. Whitehurst Associates is considering a substantial investment in the shares of Ivanhoe Enterprises. Ivanhoe currently (time 0) pays a dividend of $3 per share. This dividend is expected to grow at 15% per year for the next three years and 10% per year for the following three years. Ivanhoe's marginal tax rate is 40%. Whitehurst expects the value of the Ivanhoe shares to increase by 40% between now and the *beginning* of year 5. If Whitehurst requires a 12% rate of return on investments of this type, what value would Whitehurst place on the Ivanhoe shares?

26. The Alpha Corporation has never paid a dividend, but the new company president has announced that the firm would pay its first dividend exactly two years from now. That dividend is expected to be $2 per share. It is anticipated that this dividend will grow by 15% for the following three years, and by 10% for the two years after that. No explicit dividend forecast is available beyond that point in

time, although the firm is expected to continue to pay some dividends every year. The share's current price-to-earnings (P/E) multiple is 15 times. The firm (and investors) expect the P/E multiple to remain constant for the foreseeable future. Earnings per share at the end of year 6 are expected to be $7. If you require a 15% rate of return on this share, how much would you pay for one share today?

27. Konawalski's Kustom Erdapfel Chips, Inc. is the maker of gourmet German-style potato chips. The company began business three years ago in the Kitchener-Waterloo area, and grew quickly as the product became known. Konawalski is now poised for national growth. Some analysts call the firm the next Krispy Kreme. The firm pays a dividend of $0.10 per share. Earnings per share are currently $0.50, and analysts expect both earnings and dividends to grow at 20% per year for the next five years. The share price is expected to increase in value by 70% over the next three years. If you believe that investors require a 20% rate of return on a share of this risk class, what IPO price would you recommend for Konawalski?

Other Practice Materials and Resources

For interactive quizzes, Internet exercises, crossword puzzles, CTV videos, and more, go to the *Contemporary Financial Management* Web site at **http://cyr.nelson.com**

Analysis of Risk and Return

Learning Objectives

After studying this chapter you should be able to

1. Understand that *risk* represents the variability of possible future returns from an investment. Risk tends to increase as one looks further into the future

2. Understand that a probability distribution indicates the *percentage* chance of occurrence of each of the possible outcomes

   a. The expected value is a measure of mean or average value of the possible outcomes, each having an associated probability of occurrence

   b. The standard deviation is an important measure of the total risk or variability of possible outcomes, each having an associated probability of occurrence

   c. The coefficient of variation is a useful total risk measure when comparing two investments with different expected returns

3. Understand that the required rate of return on an investment—financial asset (security) or physical asset—is equal to the risk-free rate of return plus a risk premium. The risk premium is positively related to the risk that the investor faces

   a. The risk-free rate of return refers to the return available on a short-term investment with no risk of default

   b. The risk premium is a function of maturity risk, default risk, seniority risk, and marketability risk

4. Understand three theories about the term structure of interest rates and their impact on the yield curve

   a. According to the expectations theory, long-term interest rates are a function of expected future short-term rates

   b. According to the maturity risk premium theory, required returns on long-term securities tend to be greater the longer the term to maturity

   c. According to the market segmentation theory, the securities markets are segmented by maturity because various participants match the maturity structure of liabilities with the maturity structure of assets

5. Understand that portfolios are composed of two or more assets

   a. The risk of a portfolio of assets depends on the risk of the individual assets in the portfolio and the correlation of returns between the pairs of assets in the portfolio

   b. By combining assets that are less than perfectly positively correlated, portfolio risk can be reduced below the level of the weighted average risk of the individual assets

6. Understand that the capital asset pricing model (CAPM) can be used to determine required rates of return on investments in financial or physical assets

   a. The systematic risk of a security refers to that portion of the variability of an individual security's returns caused by factors affecting the security market as a whole

   b. Beta, measured as the slope of the characteristic (regression) line between market returns and a security's returns, is a measure of systematic risk

   c. The unsystematic risk of a security refers to the portion of the variability of a security's returns caused by factors unique to that security

   d. The security market line (SML) expresses the relationship between the required return from a security and the systematic risk of that security

   e. The capital market line (CML) expresses the relationship between the expected return of any efficient portfolio and total risk

   f. When there is a risk-free asset, an efficient portfolio is any combination of the risk-free asset and the market portfolio

7. Understand that holding period returns measure the actual or expected return from holding a security, including price changes and distributions, such as dividends or interest

8. Understand that in efficient capital markets, security prices represent an unbiased estimate of the true economic value of the cash flows expected to be generated for the benefit of that security holder

   a. With weak-form market efficiency, no investor can expect to earn excess returns based on an investment strategy using such information as historical price or return information

   b. With semistrong-form market efficiency, no investor can expect to earn excess returns based on an investment strategy using any publicly available information

   c. With strong-form market efficiency, security prices fully reflect all information, both public and private. Empirical evidence on North American markets tends to support both weak-form and semistrong-form market efficiency, but it does not support strong-form efficiency

9. Understand that the arbitrage pricing theory (APT) expresses the relationship between the required return of a security and its sensitivity to various economic factors. The APT is discussed in Appendix 7A.

Risk and Return on BCE Common Shares

BCE (Bell Canada Enterprises) is one of the most widely held stocks in Canada. For decades it was considered a very conservative, safe investment—a "widows and orphans" issue. It also paid cash dividends continuously. More recently, however, shareholders of BCE have seen their returns plummet. During the first half of the year 2002, the BCE share price declined by 31 percent, to $24.30 on July 26, 2002. Nortel Networks, a former BCE wholly owned subsidiary, was spun off to BCE shareholders on record on May 2, 2000. At the end of May 2000, Nortel shares traded at $79.75 each, and by the end of July 2000, they reached $109.75. However, just two years later, on July 26, 2002, Nortel shares traded at only $1.39 per share! Dividends declined as well; BCE paid less and Nortel stopped paying dividends.

BCE and Nortel are not alone. Many other blue-chip shares also suffered large declines. Likewise, dividend yields have been declining for many years. Two decades ago the dividend yield averaged almost 5 percent, but now it has dropped to less than 2 percent.

The buy-and-hold investment strategy has never been a sure thing. Large companies have been getting into financial difficulty (including bankruptcy) throughout the twentieth century. For example, Confederation Life, one of Canada's largest insurance companies, went bankrupt in 1994.

Recent data suggest that share prices have become much more volatile and that fewer investors are following a buy-and-hold strategy. The average individual investor now holds a share for only about one year compared with about five years in 1975.

This discussion illustrates the nature of investment risk. Even the best companies face unforeseen events that can have a significant impact on the market value of their shares. It is the existence of this type of risk that causes most prudent investors to hold well-diversified portfolios (groups) of shares, rather than concentrating their investments in just a few types of shares.

This chapter defines what is meant by risk and develops various techniques for measuring and managing risk that can be used by financial decision makers, such as corporate treasurers, money managers, and securities brokers. Individual investors can also use these techniques to assess the risks associated with personal investments (e.g., Registered Retirement Savings Plans).

Introduction

Chapter 1 provided a brief introduction to risk and the relationship between risk and return. Recall that the required rate of return on an investment—financial asset (security) or physical asset—was represented as an increasing function of that investment's perceived risk. That is, the greater the risk, the greater the required rate of return.[1]

This chapter develops the relationship between risk and return in more detail and presents methods for measuring risk. Later sections of the chapter focus on investment diversification and portfolio risk analysis. This leads to the development of the capital asset pricing model and the security and capital market lines. Then the concept of a holding period return is introduced to facilitate the estimation of relative systematic risk or the beta of the security market line. This chapter ends with the three forms of market efficiency. Arbitrage pricing theory is discussed in Appendix 7A.

Meaning and Measurement of Risk

Recall that in Chapter 1, risk was defined as the possibility that actual future returns will deviate from expected returns. In other words, it represents the variability of returns. Hence, risk implies that there is a chance for some unfavourable event to occur. From the perspective of security analysis or the analysis of an investment in some project (such as the development of a new product line), risk is the possibility that actual cash flows (returns) will be different from forecasted cash flows (returns).

An investment is said to be risk-free if the dollar returns from the initial investment are known with certainty. Some of the best examples of risk-free investments are government bonds and Treasury bills. There is virtually no chance that the government will fail to redeem these securities at maturity or that the government will default on any interest payments owed. As a last resort, the government can always print more money.[2]

In contrast, Nortel Networks (NT) bonds constitute a risky investment because it is possible that the company will default on one or more interest payments and will lack sufficient funds to redeem the bonds at face value at maturity. In other words, the possible returns from this investment are variable, and each potential outcome can be assigned a probability.

If, for example, you were considering investing in NT bonds, you might assign the probabilities shown in Table 7.1 to the three possible outcomes of this investment. These probabilities are interpreted to mean that an 80 percent chance exists that the bonds will not be in default over their life and will be redeemed at maturity, a 15 percent chance of interest default during the life of the bonds, and a 5 percent chance that the bonds will not be redeemed at maturity.

Enter "risk analysis" in the Google search engine and look at the vast wealth of Internet information available for analyzing risk. The results may surprise you.
www.google.ca

Table 7.1	Probability of Default on NT Bonds	
Outcome	**Probability**
No default, bonds redeemed at maturity	0.80
Default on interest for one or more periods	0.15
No interest default, but bonds not redeemed at maturity	0.05
	1.00

[1] The terms *asset* and *security* will be used interchangeably throughout the chapter to refer to investments in either financial assets (securities) or physical assets.

[2] Note that this discussion of risk deals with dollar returns and ignores other considerations, such as potential losses in purchasing power. In addition, it assumes that securities are held until maturity, which is not always the case. Sometimes a security must be sold prior to maturity for less than face value because of changes in the level of interest rates.

Hence, from an investment perspective, risk refers to the chance that returns from an investment will be different from those expected. We can define risk more precisely, however, by introducing some probability concepts.

Probability Distributions

The probability that a particular outcome will occur is defined as the percentage chance (or likelihood) of its occurrence. A probability distribution indicates the percentage chance of occurrence of each of the possible outcomes. Probabilities may be determined either objectively or subjectively. An objective determination is based on past occurrences of similar outcomes. A subjective one is merely the opinion of an individual about the likelihood that a given outcome will occur. In the case of projects that are frequently repeated—such as the drilling of developmental oil wells in an established oil field—reasonably good objective estimates can be made about the success of a new project. Similarly, good objective estimates can often be made about the expected returns of an NT bond. However, the expected returns from securities of new, small firms are often much more difficult to estimate objectively. Hence, highly subjective estimates regarding the likelihood of various returns are necessary. The fact that many probability estimates in business are at least partially subjective does not diminish their usefulness.

Summary of Notation

Before examining specific measures of risk and return, it is useful to summarize the basic elements of notation used throughout the chapter.

r = single rate of return on a given security; a subscript denotes the rate of return on a particular security (or portfolio of securities), such as r_p, described next, and a hat ($\wedge$) symbol denotes an expected rate of return.

r_f = riskless (risk-free) rate of return; the return offered on short-term Treasury bills

r_p = rate of return on a portfolio of securities

r_m = rate of return on the Market Portfolio; a broad-based security market index, such as the S&P/TSX Composite Index or the New York Stock Exchange Composite Index, is normally used as a measure of total market returns.

p = probability of occurrence of a specific rate of return

σ = standard deviation of the rate of return on a security (or portfolio of securities)

σ_p = standard deviation of the rate of return on a portfolio of securities

σ_m = standard deviation of the rate of return on the Market Portfolio

v = coefficient of variation

z = number of standard deviations that a particular value of a random variable (such as rate of return) is from its expected value

ρ = correlation coefficient between the returns on two securities

w = portion (weight) of funds invested in a given security within a portfolio

k_j = required rate of return on a given security

θ_j = risk premium required by investors on a given security

β_j = measure of the volatility (or risk) of a security's returns relative to the returns on the Market Portfolio

HPR = holding period return

β_p = measure of risk of a portfolio of securities

Expected Value

Suppose an investor is considering an investment of $100,000 in the shares of either Duke Energy (DX) or Telus Corporation (T), both listed on the TSX. By investing in the shares of either of these firms, an investor expects to receive dividend payments plus share price appreciation. We will assume that the investor plans to hold the stock for one year and then sell it. Over the coming year, the investor feels there is a 20 percent chance for an economic boom, a 60 percent chance for a normal economic environment, and a 20 percent chance for a recession. Given this assessment of the economic environment over the next year, the investor estimates the probability distribution of returns from the investment in DX and T as shown in Table 7.2.

From this information, the expected value of returns (or expected return) from investing in the stock of DX and T can be calculated. The **expected value** is a statistical measure of the mean or average value of the possible outcomes. Operationally, it is defined as the weighted average of possible outcomes, with the weights being the probabilities of occurrence.

Algebraically, the expected value of the returns from a security or project may be defined as follows:

$$(7.1) \qquad \hat{r} = \sum_{j=1}^{n} r_j p_j$$

where $\hat{r}$ is the expected return; r_j is the outcome for the jth case, where there are n possible outcomes; and p_j is the probability that the jth outcome will occur. The expected returns for DX and T are computed in Table 7.3. The expected return is 18 percent for both.

Standard Deviation: An Absolute Measure of Risk

The **standard deviation** is a statistical measure of the dispersion of possible outcomes about the expected value. It is defined as the square root of the weighted average squared deviations of possible outcomes from the expected value and is computed as follows:

$$(7.2) \qquad \sigma = \sqrt{\sum_{j=1}^{n} (r_j - \hat{r})^2 p_j}$$

where σ is the standard deviation.

The standard deviation can be used to measure the variability of returns from an investment. As such, it gives an indication of the risk involved in the asset or security. The larger the standard deviation, the more variable are an investment's returns and the riskier is the investment. A standard deviation of zero indicates no variability and thus no risk. Table 7.4 shows the calculation of the standard deviations for the investments in DX and T.

Expected Value
A statistical measure of the mean or average value of the possible outcomes. Operationally, it is defined as the weighted average of the possible outcomes, with the weights being the probability of occurrence.

Standard Deviation
A statistical measure of the dispersion, or variability, of possible outcomes around the expected value, or mean. Operationally, it is defined as the square root of the weighted average squared deviations of possible outcomes from the expected value. The standard deviation provides an absolute measure of risk.

Table 7.2   Probability Distribution of Returns from DX and T

State of the Economy	Probability	Rate of Return Anticipated under Each State of the Economy*	
		DX	T
Recession	0.2	10%	−4%
Normal year	0.6	18	18
Boom	0.2	26	40
	1.0		

*For example, a 10 percent rate of return for DX means that the stock value plus dividends total $110,000 at the end of one year. Working with a *discrete* probability distribution, as this example does, indicates that there is no probability of a loss by investing in DX. This, of course, is unrealistic. In the following text discussion of continuous distributions, this assumption is relaxed.

Table 7.3 Expected Return Calculation for Investment in DX and T

	DX			T		
r_j	p_j	$r_j \times p_j$	r_j	p_j	$r_j \times p_j$	
10%	0.2	2.0%	−4%	0.2	−0.8%	
18	0.6	10.8	18	0.6	10.8	
26	0.2	5.2	40	0.2	8.0	
	Expected return = $\hat{r}$ = 18.0%			Expected return = $\hat{r}$ = 18.0%		

As shown in the calculations in Table 7.4, T appears riskier than DX. T has a standard deviation of 13.91 percent. In contrast, DX has a standard deviation of only 5.06 percent.

This example deals with a discrete probability distribution of outcomes (returns) for each firm. That is, a limited number of possible outcomes are identified, and probabilities are assigned to them. In reality, however, many different outcomes are possible for the investment in the shares of each firm—ranging from losses during the year to returns in excess of T's 40 percent return. To indicate the probability of all possible outcomes for these investments, it is necessary to construct a continuous probability distribution. This is done by developing a table similar to Table 7.2, except that it would have many more possible outcomes and their associated probabilities. The detailed table of outcomes and probabilities can be used to develop the expected value of returns from DX and T, and a continuous curve would be constructed to approximate the probabilities associated with each outcome. Figure 7.1 illustrates continuous probability distributions of returns for investments in the stock of DX and T.

As seen in this figure, the possible returns for DX have a tighter probability distribution, indicating a lower variability of returns. The T possible returns have a flatter distribution, indicating higher variability and, by extension, more risk.

Normal Probability Distribution

The possible returns from many investments tend to follow a normal probability distribution. The normal probability distribution is characterized by a symmetrical, bell-like

Table 7.4 Computation of Standard Deviations of Return for DX and T

	j	r_j	$\hat{r}$	$r_j - \hat{r}$	$(r_j - \hat{r})^2$	p_j	$(r_j - \hat{r})^2 p_j$
DX	1 (Recession)	10%	18%	−8%	64	0.2	12.8
	2 (Normal)	18	18	0	0	0.6	0
	3 (Boom)	26	18	+8	64	0.2	12.8

$$\sum_{j=1}^{n}(r_j - \hat{r})^2 p_j = 25.6$$

$$\sigma = \sqrt{\sum_{j=1}^{n}(r_j - \hat{r})^2 p_j} = \sqrt{25.6} = 5.06\%$$

	j	r_j	$\hat{r}$	$r_j - \hat{r}$	$(r_j - \hat{r})^2$	p_j	$(r_j - \hat{r})^2 p_j$
T	1 (Recession)	−4%	18%	−22%	484	0.2	96.8
	2 (Normal)	18	18	0	0	0.6	0
	3 (Boom)	40	18	+22	484	0.2	96.8

$$\sum_{j=1}^{n}(r_j - \hat{r})^2 p_j = 193.6$$

$$\sigma = \sqrt{\sum_{j=1}^{n}(r_j - \hat{r})^2 p_j} = \sqrt{193.6} = 13.91\%$$

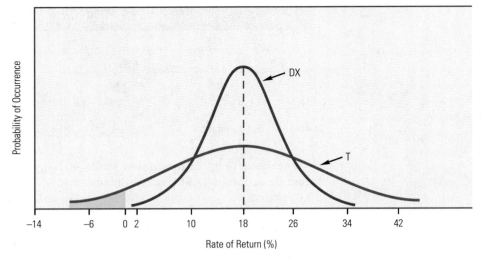

Figure 7.1
Continuous Probability Distributions for the Expected Returns from Investments in DX and T Stocks

curve. If the expected continuous probability distribution of returns is approximately normal, a table of the *standard normal probability distribution* (that is, a normal distribution with a mean equal to 0.0 and a standard deviation equal to 1.0, such as Table V at the back of the text) can be used to compute the probability of occurrence of any particular outcome. From this table, for example, it is apparent that the actual outcome should be between plus or minus 1 standard deviation from the expected value 68.26 percent of the time,[3] between plus or minus 2 standard deviations 95.44 percent of the time, and between plus or minus 3 standard deviations 99.74 percent of the time. This is illustrated in Figure 7.2.

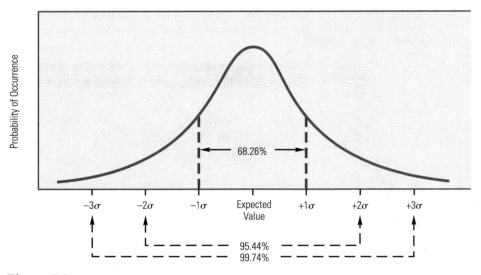

Figure 7.2
Areas under the Normal Probability Distribution

---

[3] For example, Table V indicates that there is a probability of 0.1587 of a value occurring that is greater than $+1\sigma$ from the mean and a probability of 0.1587 of a value occurring that is less than -1σ from the mean. Hence, the probability of a value between $+1\sigma$ and -1σ is 68.26 percent; that is, $1.00 - (2 \times 0.1587)$.

The number of standard deviations, z, that a particular value of r is from the expected value, $\hat{r}$, can be computed as follows:

$$(7.3) \qquad\qquad z = \frac{r - \hat{r}}{\sigma}$$

Equation 7.3, along with Table V, can be used to compute the probability of a return from an investment being less than (or greater than) some particular value.

For example, as part of the analysis of the risk of an investment in T's shares, suppose we are interested in determining the probability of earning a negative rate of return, that is, a return less than 0 percent. This probability is represented graphically in Figure 7.1 as the area to the left of 0 (that is, the shaded area) under T's probability distribution. The number of standard deviations that 0 percent is from the expected return (18 percent) must be calculated. Substituting the expected return and the standard deviation from Tables 7.3 and 7.4 into Equation 7.3 yields the following:

$$z = \frac{0\% - 18\%}{13.91\%} = -1.29$$

In other words, the return of 0 percent is 1.29 standard deviations below the mean. From Table V, the probability associated with 1.29 standard deviations is 0.0985. Therefore, there is a 9.85 percent chance that T will have returns below 0 percent. Conversely, there is a 90.15 percent (100 − 9.85) chance that the return will be greater than 0 percent.

Coefficient of Variation: A Relative Measure of Risk

The standard deviation is an appropriate measure of total risk when the investments being compared are approximately equal in expected returns and the returns are estimated to have symmetrical probability distributions. Because the standard deviation is an absolute measure of variability, it is generally not suitable for comparing investments with different expected returns. In these cases, the **coefficient of variation** provides a better measure of risk. It is defined as the ratio of the standard deviation, σ, to the expected return, $\hat{r}$:

$$(7.4) \qquad\qquad v = \frac{\sigma}{\hat{r}}$$

The coefficient of variation is a relative measure of variability, since it measures the risk per unit of expected return. As the coefficient of variation increases, so does the risk of an asset.

Consider, for example, two assets, R and S. Asset R has expected annual returns of 25 percent and a standard deviation of 20 percent. Asset S has expected annual returns of 10 percent and a standard deviation of 18 percent. Although Asset R has a higher standard deviation than Asset S, intuition tells us that Asset R is less risky because its relative variation is smaller. The coefficients of variation for Assets R and S are computed as follows using Equation 7.4:

$$\text{Asset R: } v = \frac{20\%}{25\%} = 0.8$$

$$\text{Asset S: } v = \frac{18\%}{10\%} = 1.8$$

Asset R's returns have a lower coefficient of variation than Asset S's. Therefore, Asset R is the less risky of the two investments.

Coefficient of Variation
The ratio of the standard deviation to the expected value. It provides a relative measure of risk.

In general, when comparing two investments with approximately equal expected returns, the standard deviation is an appropriate measure of total risk. When comparing two investments with different expected returns, the coefficient of variation is the more appropriate measure of total risk.[4]

Risk as an Increasing Function of Time

Most investment decisions require that returns be *forecasted* several years into the future. The riskiness of these forecasted returns may be thought of as an increasing function of time. Returns that are generated early can generally be predicted with more certainty than those that are anticipated further into the future.

Consider the risk facing the InterTAN Corporation in its decision to market a new line of stereo speakers through its Radio Shack stores. This project is expected to generate cash flows of $2 million per year over the seven-year life of the project. Even though the expected annual cash flows are equal for each year, it is reasonable to assume that the riskiness of these flows increases over time as more and more presently unknown variables have a chance to affect the project's cash flows. Figure 7.3 illustrates this situation.

The distribution is relatively tight in year 1, because the factors affecting that year's cash flows (e.g., demand and costs) are reasonably well known. By year 7, however, the distribution has become relatively flat, indicating a considerable increase in the standard deviation. This is caused by increased uncertainty about the factors that affect cash flows. For example, competitors may introduce similar (or improved) products that would cause demand to decline for the InterTAN speakers.

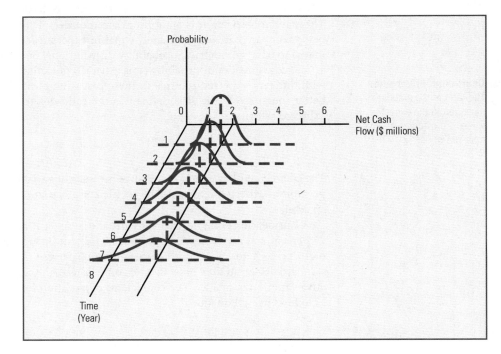

Figure 7.3
Risk of a Project over Time: InterTan

---

[4] The relationship between the coefficient of variation and several other measures of risk (including the standard deviation) is developed in John M. Wachowicz, Jr., and Ronald E. Shrieves, "An Argument for Generalized Mean-Coefficient of Variation Analysis," *Financial Management* (Winter 1980): 51–58.

Some types of cash flows are not subject to increasing variability. These include, for example, contractual arrangements, such as lease payments. Here the expected cash flows remain constant (or change at some predefined rate) over the life of the contract. In spite of the exceptions, it is reasonable to conclude that the riskiness of the cash flows from most investment projects gradually increases over time. Similarly, the riskiness of returns from most securities increases the further into the future these returns are being considered. For instance, the interest return from the purchase of GM bonds is nearly guaranteed for the next year. However, projecting the interest returns to be received 10 years in the future is much more difficult due to the potential impact of competition, new technology, and other factors.

Relationship Between Risk and Return

Foundation Concept

The trade-off between risk and return is a key element of effective financial decision making. This includes both decisions by individuals (and financial institutions) to invest in financial assets, such as common stocks, bonds, and other securities, and decisions by a firm's managers to invest in physical assets, such as new plants and equipment.

In Chapter 1 the relationship between risk and required return was introduced. The relationship between risk and *required rate of return* can be expressed as follows:

(7.5)   Required rate of return = Risk-free rate of return + Risk premium

A risk premium is a potential "reward" that an investor expects to receive when making a risky investment. Investors are generally considered to be *risk averse*. That is, they expect, on average, to be compensated for the risk they assume when making an investment. Thus, over the long term, expected returns and required returns from securities will tend to be equal.

The rate of return required by investors in financial assets is determined in the financial marketplace and depends on the supply of funds available as well as the demand for these funds. Investors who buy bonds receive interest payments and a return of principal as compensation for postponing consumption and accepting risk. Similarly, common equity investors expect to receive dividends and price appreciation from their shares. The rate of return required by these investors represents a cost of capital to the firm. This required rate of return is used by a firm's managers when computing the net present value of the cash flows expected to be generated from the company's investments. The **required rate of return** on a security is also an important determinant of the market value of financial securities, including common and preferred shares, and bonds.

The following sections focus on the two components of the required rate of return—the risk-free return and the risk premium—and also look at the historical relationship between risk and rates of return on various types of securities.

Required Rate of Return
The rate used to value a stream of expected cash flows from an asset (also called the discount rate). The riskier the expected cash flows from the asset, the higher the required rate of return.

Risk-Free Rate
The rate of return on securities that are free of default risk, such as T-bills.

Risk-Free Rate of Return

The concept of a **risk-free rate of return** refers to the return available on a security with no risk of default. In the case of debt securities, no default risk means that promised interest and principal payments are guaranteed to be made. Short-term government securities, such as Treasury bills, are generally considered to be risk-free investments.

The risk-free rate of return, r_f, is equal to the sum of a real rate of return and an expected inflation premium:

(7.6) r_f = Real rate of return + Expected inflation premium

The *real rate of return* is the return that investors would require from a security having no risk of default in a period of no expected inflation. It is the return necessary to convince investors to postpone current, real consumption opportunities. Historically, the real rate of return has been estimated to average in the range of 2 to 4 percent.

The second component of the risk-free rate of return is an *inflation premium* or *purchasing power loss premium*. Investors require compensation for expected losses in purchasing power when they postpone current consumption and lend funds. Consequently, a premium for expected inflation is included in the required return on any security. The inflation premium is normally equal to investors' expectations about future purchasing power changes. If, for example, inflation is expected to average 4 percent over some future period, the risk-free rate of return on Treasury bills (assuming a real rate of return of 3 percent) should be approximately equal to 3 percent + 4 percent = 7 percent by Equation 7.6. By extension, if inflation expectations suddenly increase from 4 to 6 percent, the risk-free rate should increase from 7 to 9 percent (3 percent real return plus 6 percent inflation premium).

At any point in time, the required risk-free rate of return on any security can be estimated from the yields on short-term government securities, such as Treasury bills.

When considering return requirements on all types of securities, it is important to remember *that increases in expected inflation rates normally lead to increases in the required rates of return on all securities.*

Risk Premium

The **risk premium** assigned by an investor to a given security in determining the required rate of return (Equation 7.5) is a function of several different risk elements. These risk elements (and premiums) include

- Maturity risk premium
- Default risk premium
- Seniority risk premium
- Marketability risk premium

Each of these risk elements is examined below.

Maturity Risk Premium   The return required on a security is influenced by the maturity of that security. The **term structure of interest rates** is the pattern of interest rate yields (required returns) for securities that differ only in the term (length of time) to maturity. Plotting interest rate yields (percent) on the vertical axis and the term to maturity (years) on the horizontal axis results in a **yield curve**. Two yield curves for government securities are shown in Figure 7.4. Note the different shapes of the two yield curves. The yield curve for December 1980 is downward sloping, indicating that the longer the term to maturity, the lower the required return on the security. The yield curve for July 1980 is upward sloping, indicating that the longer the term to maturity, the higher the required return on the security.[5]

In general, the yield curve has been upward sloping more often than it has been downward sloping. For example, at the end of September 2002, the yield on three-month Treasury bills was 2.84 percent. In contrast, the yield on 10-year government bonds was 4.95 percent, and the yield on 30-year government bonds was 5.45 percent.

---

[5] The primary reason for examining government securities is that we are able to hold many of the factors affecting yields, such as default risk, constant. Corporate debt security issues, even for the same company, often differ significantly with respect to their key provisions, including sinking fund, call, conversion, subordination, and mortgage features. Hence, these bond issues differ with respect to risk. Consequently, it is difficult to use corporate debt securities to make yield versus term-to-maturity comparisons. However, the same general conclusions concerning the term structure of interest rates apply to these securities.

Risk Premium
The difference between the required rate of return on a risky investment and the rate of return on a risk-free asset, such as T-bills. Components include maturity risk, default risk, seniority risk, and marketability risk.

Term Structure of Interest Rates
The pattern of interest rate yields for debt securities that are similar in all respects except for their length of time to maturity. The term structure of interest rates usually is represented by a graphic plot called a yield curve.

Yield Curve
A chart showing interest rate yields in percent on the vertical axis and term to maturity on the horizontal axis.

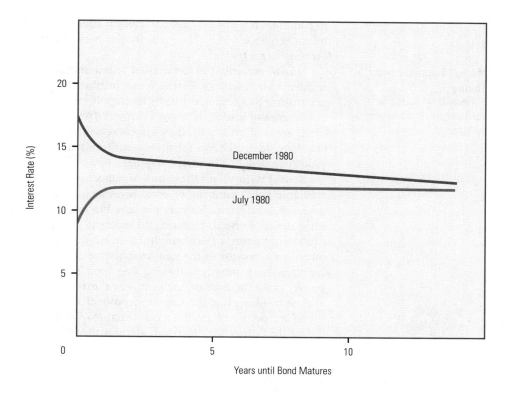

Figure 7.4
Yield Curves on Government of Canada Bonds

A number of theories have been advanced about the term structure interest rates that are useful in explaining the shape of the yield curve, including the expectations theory, maturity risk premium theory, and market segmentation theory.

According to the **expectations theory**, long-term interest rates are a function of expected future (that is, forward) short-term interest rates. If future short-term interest rates are expected to rise, the yield curve will tend to be upward sloping. In contrast, a downward-sloping yield curve reflects an expectation of declining future short-term interest rates. According to the expectations theory, current and expected future interest rates are dependent on expectations about future rates of inflation. Many economic and political conditions can cause expected future inflation and interest rates to rise or fall. These conditions include expected future government deficits or surpluses, changes in monetary policy (that is, the rate of growth of the money supply), and cyclical business conditions.

The **maturity risk premium theory** (called the *liquidity preference theory* by economists) about the term structure of interest rates holds that required returns on long-term securities tend to be greater the longer the term to maturity. The maturity risk premium reflects a preference by many lenders for shorter maturities because the *interest rate or price risk* associated with these securities is less than with longer-term securities. As we saw in Chapter 5, the value of a bond tends to vary more as interest rates change, the longer the term to maturity. Thus, if interest rates rise, the holder of a long-term bond will find that the value of the investment has declined substantially more than that of the holder of a short-term bond. In addition, the short-term bondholder has the option of holding the bond for the short time remaining to maturity and then reinvesting the proceeds from that bond at the new higher interest rate. The long-term bondholder must wait much longer before this opportunity is available.

Expectations Theory
A theory that posits that long-term interest rates are a function of expected short-term interest rates.

Maturity Risk Premium Theory
A theory that posits that required returns on long-term securities tend to be higher than returns on short-term securities.

Accordingly, it is argued that whatever the shape of the yield curve, a maturity risk premium is reflected in it. The maturity risk premium is larger for long-term bonds than for short-term bonds.

Finally, according to the **market segmentation theory**, the securities markets are segmented by maturity. Furthermore, interest rates within each maturity segment are determined to a certain extent by the supply and demand interactions of the segment's borrowers and lenders. If strong borrower demand exists for long-term funds and these funds are in short supply, the yield curve will be upward sloping. Conversely, if strong borrower demand exists for short-term funds and these funds are in short supply, the yield curve will be downward sloping.[6]

Several factors limit the choice of maturities by lenders. One such factor is the legal regulations that limit the types of investments that banks, insurance companies, and other financial institutions are permitted to make. Another limitation faced by lenders is the desire (or need) to match the maturity structure of their liabilities with assets of equivalent maturity. For example, life insurance companies and pension fund management firms, because of the long-term nature of their contractual obligations to clients, are interested primarily in making long-term investments. Chartered banks and money market funds, in contrast, are primarily short-term lenders because a large proportion of their liabilities is in the form of deposits that can be withdrawn on demand.

At any point in time, the term structure of interest rates is the result of the interaction of the factors just described. All three theories are useful in explaining the shape of the yield curve.

Default Risk Premium   Federal government securities are generally considered to be free of default risk—that is, the risk that interest and principal will not be paid as promised in the bond indenture. In contrast, corporate bonds are subject to varying degrees of default risk. Recall from Chapter 5 that bond rating agencies, such as DBRS, Moody's, and S&P, provide evaluations of the default risk of many corporate bonds in the form of bond ratings on a nine-point scale from AAA through C, where AAA-rated bonds have the lowest expected default risk. Investors require a higher **default risk premium** (and hence a higher rate of return) on any security subject to default risk, reflecting the positive relationship between risk and required return. Over time, the spread between the required returns on bonds having various levels of default risk varies, reflecting the economic prospects and the resulting probability of default.

Seniority Risk Premium   Corporations issue many different types of securities. These securities differ with respect to their claim on the cash flows generated by the company and the claim on the company's assets in the case of default. A partial listing of these securities, from the least senior (that is, from the security having the lowest priority claim on cash flows and assets) to the most senior, includes the following: common shares, preferred shares, income bonds, subordinated debentures, debentures, second mortgage bonds, and first mortgage bonds. Generally, the less senior the claims of the security holder, the greater the **seniority risk premium** (and hence the greater the required rate of return) demanded by investors in that security. For example, the holders of bonds issued by Nortel are assured that they will receive interest and principal payments on these bonds except in the highly unlikely event that the company faces bankruptcy. In contrast, Nortel common shareholders have no such assurance regarding dividend payments. Also, in the case of bankruptcy, all senior claim holders must be paid before common shareholders receive any proceeds from the liquidation of the firm.

Market Segmentation Theory
A theory that posits that capital markets are segmented by maturity.

Default Risk Premium
The premium over the risk-free rate that is due to the risk that the issuer may default and not pay interest and/or principal as promised in the indenture of the issue.

Seniority Risk Premium
The additional return that investors require on junior securities.

---

[6] Upward- and downward-sloping yield curves are not the only possible shapes. At various times in the past, the yield curve has been relatively flat and also has been hump-shaped, that is, with high intermediate-term yields and low short-term and long-term yields.

Accordingly, common shareholders require a higher rate of return on their investment in Nortel shares than do the company's bondholders.

Marketability Risk Premium **Marketability risk** refers to the ability of an investor to buy and sell a company's securities quickly and without a significant loss of value.[7] Listed securities tend to have relatively lower marketability risk premiums than unlisted securities because there is a more active market for them. The marketability risk premium can be significant for securities that are not regularly traded, such as the shares of many small- and medium-sized firms.

Business and Financial Risk[8]

Within individual security classes, one observes significant differences in required rates of return between firms. For example, the required rate of return on Air Canada common shares is considerably higher than the required rate of return on WestJet Airlines common shares. The difference in the required rate of return on the securities of these two companies reflects differences in their business and financial risk. The **business risk** of a firm refers to the variability in the firm's operating earnings over time. Business risk is influenced by many factors, including the variability in sales and operating costs over a business cycle, the diversity of a firm's product line, the market power of the firm, and the choice of production technology. From 1998 to 2002, the operating profit margin ratio for WestJet Airlines was consistently higher and also less variable from year to year than for any other Canadian airline. As a stronger and more efficient firm, WestJet Airlines can now be expected to have a lower perceived level of business risk and a resulting lower required return on its common shares (all other things held constant) than Air Canada.

Financial risk refers to the additional variability in a company's earnings per share that results from the use of fixed-cost sources of funds, such as debt and preferred shares. In addition, as debt financing increases, the risk of bankruptcy increases.

Business and financial risk are reflected in the default risk premium applied by investors to a firm's securities. The higher these risks are, the higher the risk premium and required rate of return on the firm's securities.

Systematic and Unsystematic Risk

As we will learn in more detail later in the chapter, much of the risk facing investors in a firm's securities can be decomposed into systematic (undiversifiable) and unsystematic (diversifiable) risk components. The *systematic risk* of a security refers to that portion of the return variability caused by factors affecting the security market as a whole, such as a change in the general business outlook. Systematic risk is often measured by a security's *beta*, a measure of the volatility of a security's returns relative to the returns of the overall security market. *Unsystematic risk* refers to the portion of the variability of an individual security's returns caused by factors unique to that security. Unsystematic risk can be greatly reduced or even totally eliminated by investors who hold a broad (diversified) collection (portfolio) of securities. Systematic risk cannot be diversified away. Business and financial risk are components of both systematic and unsystematic risk.

---

[7] In the literature on risk premiums, the marketability risk premium often is called the liquidity risk premium. In the past, we found that readers were easily confused between the liquidity preference theory, which is about maturity risk, and the liquidity risk premium. To avoid confusion between these concepts, we will use the terminology maturity risk premium theory instead of liquidity preference theory and marketability risk premium instead of liquidity risk premium.

[8] Business and financial risk are examined in more detail in Chapter 12.

Risk and Required Returns for Various Types of Securities

Figure 7.5 illustrates the relationship between required rates of return and risk, as represented by the various risk premiums just discussed. As shown in Figure 7.5, the lowest risk security is represented by short-term Treasury bills. All other securities have one or more elements of additional risk, resulting in increasing required returns by investors. The order illustrated in this figure is indicative of the general relationship between risk and required returns of various security types. There will be situations that result in differences in the ordering of risk and required returns. For example, it is possible that the risk of some junk (high-risk) bonds may be so great that investors require a higher rate of return on these bonds than they require on high-grade common shares.

The relationship between risk and return can be observed by examining the returns actually earned by investors in various types of securities over long periods of time. Finance professionals believe that investor expectations of the relative returns anticipated from various types of securities are heavily influenced by the returns that have been earned on these securities over long periods in the past. Over the period from 1976 to 2000, investors in Canadian common shares earned average returns of over 13 percent. However, their return on Canadian government bonds was only 11 percent. During the same period, Canadian investors in US common shares earned average returns of over 17 percent.[9] There is some evidence that investors in smaller company shares obtained even higher returns, but with substantially more variability in annual returns, as measured by the standard deviation. Returns on long-term corporate bonds have been lower than the returns on common shares, but their risk also has been lower. Short-term Treasury bills have offered the lowest average annual returns, but they have also had the lowest risk of all the securities examined.

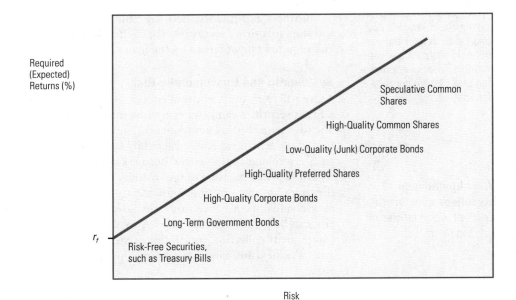

Figure 7.5
Conceptual Risk-Return Relationship

---

[9] Canadian Institute of Actuaries, *Report on Canadian Economic Statistics 1924–2000*, December 11, 2002, Table 1A.

Investment Diversification and Portfolio Risk Analysis[10]

Portfolio
A collection of two or more financial (securities) or physical assets.

The preceding sections examined the risk and returns associated with investments in single assets—either financial assets (securities) or physical assets. However, most individuals and institutions invest in a **portfolio** of assets, that is, a collection of two or more assets. Banks invest in many different types of financial assets when they make loans to consumers and businesses. Individuals invest in many different types of financial assets when they buy securities, such as bank guaranteed investment certificates and corporate bonds and shares. Corporations invest in many different kinds of physical assets when they acquire production and distribution facilities (i.e., plants and equipment). Consequently, it is important to know how the returns from portfolios of investments behave over time—not just how the returns from individual assets in the portfolio behave. Portfolio risk, the risk associated with collections of financial and physical assets, is considered in this and the following two sections. The questions of importance are as follows:

- What return can be expected to be earned from the portfolio?

- What is the risk of the portfolio?

Consider the following example. Suppose that Alcan is considering diversifying into gold mining and refining. During economic boom periods, aluminum sales tend to be brisk. Gold, on the other hand, tends to be most in demand during periods of economic uncertainty.[11] Therefore, let us assume that the returns from the aluminum business and the gold mining business are inversely, or negatively, related. If Alcan expands into gold mining and refining, its overall return will tend to be less variable than individual returns from these businesses.

This effect is illustrated in Figure 7.6. Panel (a) shows the variation of rates of return in the aluminum industry over time. Panel (b) shows the corresponding variation of returns from gold mining over the same time frame. Panel (c) shows the combined rate of return for both lines of business. As can be seen from this figure, when the return from aluminum operations is high, the return from gold mining tends to be low, and vice versa. The combined returns are more stable and therefore less risky.

This *portfolio effect* of reduced variability results because a negative correlation exists between the returns from aluminum operations and the returns from gold mining. The correlation between any two variables—such as rates of return or net cash flows—is a relative statistical measure of the degree to which these variables tend to move together. The **correlation coefficient** (ρ) measures the extent to which high (or low) values of one variable are associated with high (or low) values of another. Values of the correlation coefficient can range from +1.0 for *perfectly positively correlated* variables to –1.0 for *perfectly negatively correlated* variables. If two variables are unrelated (that is, uncorrelated), the correlation coefficient between these two variables will be 0.

Correlation Coefficient
A measure of the degree of relationship between two variables.

Figure 7.7 illustrates perfect positive correlation, perfect negative correlation, and zero correlation for different pairs of common share investments. For perfect positive

---

[10] Two economists, Harry M. Markowitz and William F. Sharpe, were corecipients (along with Merton H. Miller) of the 1990 Nobel Prize for Economics for their pioneering work in portfolio theory (discussed in this section of the text) and the capital asset pricing model (discussed in the following section). See Harry M. Markowitz, "Portfolio Selection," *Journal of Finance* 7 (March 1952): 77–91, and *Portfolio Selection: Efficient Diversification of Investments* (New York: John Wiley, 1959); William F. Sharpe, "A Simplified Model for Portfolio Analysis," *Management Science* (January 1963): 277–91, and "Capital Asset Prices: A Theory of Market Equilibrium under Conditions of Risk," *Journal of Finance* (September 1964): 425–42.

[11] As investors lose confidence in the economy's performance, many of them turn to gold as an investment. This drives the price of gold up and increases returns to gold mining firms, whose costs of operation are not directly related to the demand for gold.

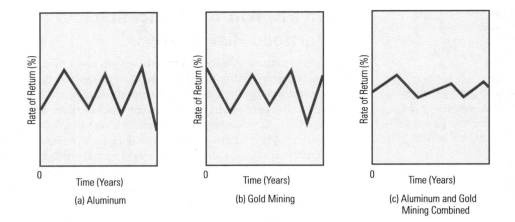

Figure 7.6
Illustration of Diversification and Risk Reduction: Alcan

correlation, panel (a), high rates of return from L shares are always associated with high rates of return from M shares. Conversely, low rates of return from L shares are always associated with low rates of return from M shares. For perfect negative correlation, panel (b), however, the opposite is true. High rates of return from P shares are associated with low rates of return from Q shares and vice versa. For zero correlation, panel (c), no perceptible pattern or relationship exists between the rates of return on V and W shares.

In practice, the returns from most investments a firm or individual considers are positively correlated with other investments held by the firm or individual. For example, returns from projects that are closely related to the firm's primary line of business have a high positive correlation with returns from projects already being carried out and thus provide limited opportunities to reduce risk. In the Alcan example, if Alcan were to build a new smelter, it would not realize the risk reduction possibilities that investing in gold mining and refining would produce. Similarly, the returns from most common shares are positively correlated because these returns are influenced by such common factors as the general state of the economy, the level of interest rates, and so on.

In order to explore further the concepts of diversification and portfolio risk, it is necessary to develop more precise measures of portfolio returns and risk.

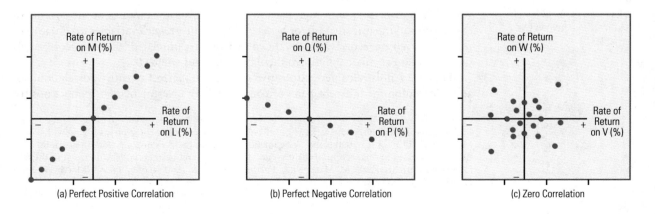

Figure 7.7
Illustration of (a) Perfect Positive, (b) Perfect Negative, and (c) Zero Correlation for Two Investments

Expected Returns from a Portfolio

When two or more securities are combined into a portfolio, the expected return of the portfolio is equal to the weighted average of the expected returns from the individual securities. If a portion, w_A, of the available funds (wealth) is invested in Security A, and the remaining portion, w_B, is invested in Security B, the expected return of the portfolio, $\hat{r}_p$, is as follows:

$$(7.7) \qquad \hat{r}_p = w_A\hat{r}_A + w_B\hat{r}_B$$

where $\hat{r}_A$ and $\hat{r}_B$ are the expected returns for Securities A and B, respectively. Furthermore, $w_A + w_B = 1$, indicating that all funds are invested in either Security A or Security B.

For example, consider a portfolio consisting of the A and B common shares. The expected returns on A and B are 12 percent ($\hat{r}_A$) and 16 percent ($\hat{r}_B$), respectively. A portfolio consisting of 75 percent (w_A) invested in A and the remainder, or 25 percent (w_B), invested in B would yield an expected return, by Equation 7.7, of

$$\hat{r}_p = 0.75(12\%) + 0.25(16\%) = 13.0\%$$

Table 7.5 (columns w_A and $\hat{r}_p$) and Figure 7.8 illustrate the relationship between the expected return for a portfolio containing Securities A and B and the proportion of the total portfolio invested in each security. For example, when $w_A = 1.0$ (100%) and $w_B = 0$ (because $w_A + w_B = 1.0$), the expected portfolio return is 12 percent, the same as the return for A. When $w_A = 0.5$ (50 percent) and $w_B = 0.5$ (50 percent), the expected portfolio return is 14 percent. As shown earlier, when $w_A = 0.75$ and $w_B = 0.25$, the expected portfolio return is 13 percent. Thus, it can be seen that the expected return from a portfolio of securities is simply equal to the weighted average of the individual security returns, where the weights represent the proportion of the total portfolio invested in each security. This results in the linear relationship shown in Figure 7.8.

In general, the expected return from any portfolio of n securities or assets is equal to the sum of the expected returns from each security times the proportion of the total portfolio invested in that security:

$$(7.8) \qquad \hat{r}_p = \sum_{t=1}^{n} w_i\hat{r}_i$$

where $\sum w_i = 1$ and $0 \le w_i \le 1$.

Table 7.5 Expected Returns and Portfolio Risk from a Portfolio of Securities A and B

Proportion Invested in Security A	Expected Return on Portfolio	Portfolio Risk σ_p (%)		
w_A(%)	$\hat{r}_p$(%)	$\rho_{AB} = +1.0$	$\rho_{AB} = 0.0$	$\rho_{AB} = -1.0$
0.0%	16.0%	20.0%	20.0%	20.0%
25.0	15.0	17.5	15.21	12.5
33.333	14.67	16.67	13.74	10.0
50.0	14.0	15.0	11.18	5.0
66.667	13.33	13.33	9.43	0.0
75.0	13.0	12.5	9.01	2.5
100.0	12.0	10.0	10.0	10.0

Note: $\hat{r}_A = 12\%$; $\hat{r}_B = 16\%$; $\sigma_A = 10\%$; $\sigma_B = 20\%$.

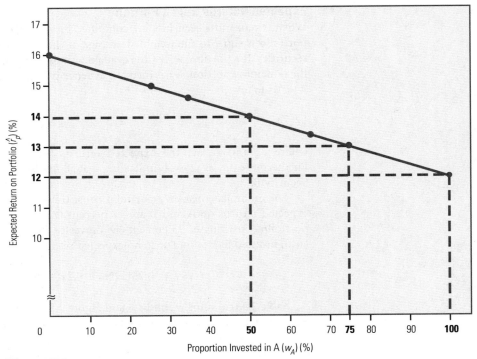

Figure 7.8

Expected Return from a Portfolio of Securities A and B

Note: $\hat{r}_A = 12\%$; $\hat{r}_B = 16\%$; $w_A + w_B = 1.0$ (100%). Data points in graph are from Table 7.5.

Portfolio Risk

Although the expected returns from a portfolio of two or more securities can be computed as a weighted average of the expected returns from the individual securities, it is generally not sufficient merely to calculate a weighted average of the risk of each individual security to arrive at a measure of the portfolio's risk. Whenever the returns from the individual securities are not perfectly positively correlated, the risk of any portfolio of these securities may be reduced through the effects of diversification. Thus, diversification can be achieved by investing in a set of securities that have different risk-return characteristics. The amount of risk reduction achieved through diversification depends on the degree of correlation between the returns of the individual securities in the portfolio. The lower the correlations among the individual securities, the greater the possibilities of risk reduction.

The risk for a two-security portfolio, measured by the standard deviation of portfolio returns, is computed as follows:

(7.9) $$\sigma_p = \sqrt{w_A^2 \sigma_A^2 + w_B^2 \sigma_B^2 + 2 w_A w_B \rho_{AB} \sigma_A \sigma_B}$$

where w_A is the proportion of funds invested in Security A; w_B is the proportion of funds invested in Security B; $w_A + w_B = 1$; σ_A^2 is the variance of returns from Security A (or the square of the standard deviation for Security A, σ_A); σ_B^2 is the variance of returns from Security B (or the square of the standard deviation for Security B, σ_B); and ρ_{AB} is the correlation coefficient of returns between Securities A and B.[12]

---

[12] In general, the risk of a portfolio containing n securities, as measured by the standard deviation of portfolio returns, is computed as follows:

$$\sigma_p = \sqrt{\sum_{i=1}^{n} \sum_{j=1}^{n} w_i w_j \rho_{ij} \sigma_i \sigma_j}$$

The double summation sign ($\sum\sum$) indicates that all possible combinations of i and j should be included in calculating the total value.

Consider, for example, the portfolio discussed earlier consisting of the common shares of A and B. The standard deviations of returns for these two securities are 10 percent (σ_A) and 20 percent (σ_B), respectively. Furthermore, suppose that the correlation coefficient (ρ_{AB}) between the returns on these securities is equal to +0.50. Using Equation 7.9, a portfolio consisting of 75 percent (w_A) invested in A and 25 percent (w_B) in B would yield a standard deviations of portfolio returns of

$$\sigma_p = \sqrt{(.75)^2(10)^2 + (.25)^2(20)^2 + 2(.75)(.25)(+.50)(10)(20)} = 10.90\%$$

With the techniques just described for calculating expected portfolio return and risk, we can now examine in more detail the risk versus return trade-offs associated with investment diversification. The following three special cases illustrate how the correlation coefficient can affect portfolio risk.

Case I: Perfect Positive Correlation ($r = +1.0$)   Table 7.5 (columns $\hat{r}_p$ and $\rho_{AB} = +1.0$) and panel (a) of Figure 7.9 illustrate the risk-return trade-offs associated with portfolios consisting of various combinations of A and B shares when $\rho_{AB} = +1.0$. *When the returns from the two securities are perfectly positively correlated, the risk of the portfolio is equal to the weighted average of the risk of the individual securities* (10 and 20 percent in this example). *Therefore, no risk reduction is achieved when perfectly positively correlated securities are combined in a portfolio.*

Case II: Zero Correlation ($r = 0.0$)   Table 7.5 (columns $\hat{r}_p$ and $\rho_{AB} = 0.0$) and panel (b) of Figure 7.9 illustrate the possible trade-offs when $\rho_{AB} = 0.0$. In this case, we see that diversification can reduce portfolio risk below the risk of either of the securities that make up the portfolio. For example, an investment consisting of 75 percent in A shares and 25 percent in B shares has a portfolio standard deviation of only 9.01 percent, which is less than the standard deviations of either of the two securities (10 and 20 percent, respectively) in the portfolio. In general, *when the correlation coefficient between the returns on two securities is less than 1.0, diversification can reduce the risk of a portfolio below the weighted average of the total risk of the individual securities. The less positively correlated the returns from two securities, the greater the portfolio effects of risk reduction.* For example, the expected returns from an investment in two firms in different industries, such as Nortel and WestJet, should generally be less positively correlated than the expected returns between two firms in the same industry, such as Nortel and JDS Uniphase.

Case III: Perfect Negative Correlation ($r = -1.0$)   Table 7.5 (columns $\hat{r}_p$ and $\rho_{AB} = -1.0$) and panel (c) of Figure 7.9 show the risk-return relationship when $\rho_{AB} = -1.0$. As illustrated, with perfectly negatively correlated returns, portfolio risk can be reduced to zero. In other words, *with a perfect negative correlation of returns between two securities, there will always be some proportion of the securities that will result in the complete elimination of portfolio risk.*

In summary, these three special cases serve to illustrate the effect that the correlation coefficient has on portfolio risk, as measured by the standard deviation. For any given pair of securities, the correlation coefficient is given (or can be estimated), and this number determines how much risk reduction can be achieved with various weighted combinations of the two securities.

Efficient Portfolios and the Capital Market Line

The risk-return relationships just discussed can be extended to analyze portfolios involving more than two securities. For example, consider the graph shown in Figure 7.10. Each dot within the shaded area represents the risk (standard deviation) and expected return for an individual security available for possible investment. The shaded

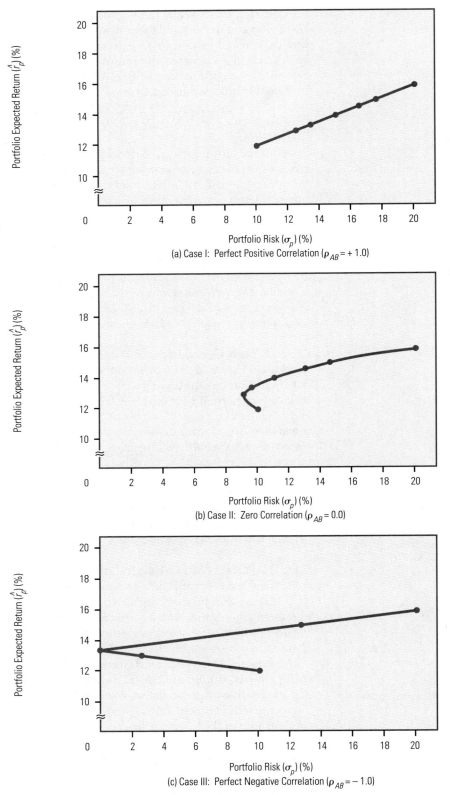

Figure 7.9

Relationship Between Portfolio Expected Return and Risk for Securities A and B

Note: $\hat{r}_A = 12\%$; $\hat{r}_B = 16\%$; $\sigma_A = 10\%$; $\sigma_B = 20\%$; $w_A + w_B = 1.0$ (100%). Data points in graphs are from Table 7.5.

area (or opportunity set) represents all of the possible portfolios found by combining the given securities in different proportions. The curved segment from A to B on the boundary of the shaded area represents the set of **efficient portfolios**, or the **efficient frontier**. A portfolio is efficient if, for a given standard deviation, there is no other portfolio with a higher expected return, or for a given expected return, there is no other portfolio with a lower standard deviation.

Risk-averse investors, in choosing their optimal portfolios, need only consider those portfolios on the efficient frontier. The choice of an optimal portfolio, whether portfolio A that minimizes risk or portfolio B that maximizes expected return or some other portfolio on the efficient frontier, depends on the investor's attitude toward risk (that is, risk aversion). More conservative investors will tend to choose lower-risk portfolios (closer to A). More aggressive investors will tend to select higher-risk portfolios (closer to B).

If investors are able to borrow and lend money at the risk-free rate (r_f), they can obtain any combination of risk and expected return on the straight line joining r_f and portfolio m as shown in Figure 7.11. When the market is in equilibrium, portfolio m represents the Market Portfolio, which consists of all available securities, weighted by their respective market values. The line joining r_f and m is known as the **capital market line (CML)**.[13] The capital market line has an *intercept* of r_f and a *slope* of $(\hat{r}_m - r_f)/\sigma_m$. The slope of the capital market line measures the equilibrium **market price of risk** or the additional expected return that can be obtained by incurring one additional unit of risk (one additional percentage point of standard deviation). Therefore, the equation of the CML is

$$(7.10) \qquad \hat{r}_p = r_f + \left(\frac{\hat{r}_m - r_f}{\sigma_m} \right) \sigma_p$$

Efficient Portfolio

A portfolio that, for a given standard deviation, has the highest expected return, or, for a given expected return, has the lowest standard deviation.

Efficient Frontier

The set of efficient portfolios.

Capital Market Line (CML)

The slope of the capital market line measures the equilibrium market price of risk.

Market Price of Risk

The additional expected return that can be obtained by incurring one additional unit of risk (one additional percentage point of standard deviation).

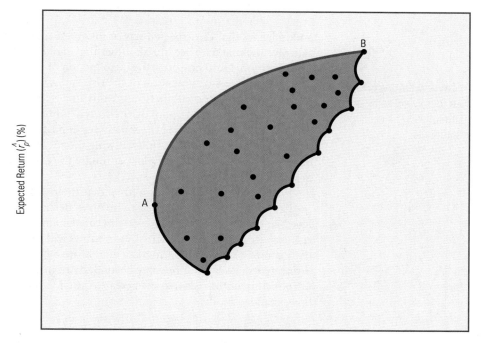

Figure 7.10
Portfolio Opportunity Set

---

[13] In constructing the capital market line, it is assumed that all investors have homogeneous (i.e., identical) expectations about the distributions of returns offered by securities. As a result of this assumption, all investors will perceive the same set of efficient portfolios.

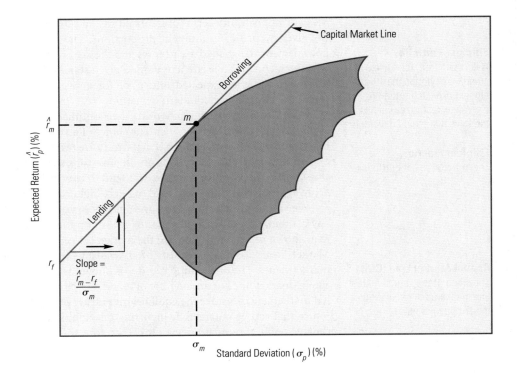

Figure 7.11
Capital Market Line

Visit **www.mathworks. com** to preview some of the quantitative tools used to evaluate risk.

and indicates that the expected return for an efficient portfolio is equal to the risk-free rate plus the market price of risk times the amount of risk (σ_p) of the portfolio under consideration. In other words, the introduction of the risk-free asset means that an efficient portfolio is a combination of the risk-free asset and the market portfolio.

Any risk-return combination on this line between r_f and m can be obtained by investing (i.e., lending) part of the initial funds in the risk-free security (such as Treasury bills) and investing the remainder in portfolio m. Any combination beyond m on this line can be obtained by borrowing money at the risk-free rate and investing the borrowed funds (as well as the initial funds) in portfolio m (that is, purchasing securities on margin).

With the ability to borrow and lend at the risk-free rate, the choice of an optimal portfolio for risk-averse investors involves determining the proportion of funds to invest in the Market Portfolio (m) with the remaining proportion being invested in the risk-free security. More conservative investors will tend to choose investments nearer to the r_f point on the capital market line. More aggressive investors will tend to select investments closer to, or possibly beyond, point m on the capital market line. Thus, the introduction of the risk-free asset creates the CML that becomes the efficient frontier in this expanded model.

Portfolio Risk and the Capital Asset Pricing Model

The preceding analysis illustrates the possibilities for portfolio risk reduction when two or more securities are combined to form a portfolio. Unfortunately, when more than two securities are involved—as is usually the case—the number of calculations required to compute the portfolio risk increases geometrically. For example, whereas 45 correlation coefficients are needed for a portfolio containing 10 securities, 4,950 correlation

Diversification and Multinational Corporations

As discussed in this chapter, the degree to which diversification can reduce risk depends on the correlation among security returns. The returns from domestic companies (DCs)—companies that are based and operate within a given country—tend to be positively related to the overall level of economic activity within the given country. Hence, these firms tend to have a relatively high degree of systematic risk. Since overall economic activity in different countries is not perfectly correlated, the returns from multinational companies (MNCs)—companies that operate in a number of different countries—may tend to have less systematic risk than those of DCs. This suggests that further risk reduction benefits may be achieved by either

1. Investing in MNCs, or
2. Investing directly in DCs located in countries in which the MNC would otherwise operate

If securities are traded in perfect financial markets, there should be no systematic advantage to holding shares in MNCs (Strategy 1) compared with owning shares directly in DCs located in different countries (Strategy 2). However, if market imperfections exist, such as controls on capital flows, differential trading costs, and different tax structures, then MNCs may be able to provide diversification benefits to investors.

The empirical evidence suggests that MNCs tend to have lower systematic risk (as measured by beta), as well as lower unsystematic risk, than DCs.[14] Overall, MNCs tend to have a lower total risk (as measured by the standard deviation of rates of return on equity) than DCs. Hence, MNCs appear to provide investors with substantial diversification benefits.

[14] Israel Shaked, "Are Multinational Corporations Safer?" *Journal of International Business Studies* (Spring 1986): 83–101.

coefficients must be computed for a portfolio containing 100 securities. In other words, a 10-fold increase in securities causes a greater than 100-fold increase in the required calculations.[15] In addition, a substantial computational undertaking is required to find the particular portfolio of securities that minimizes portfolio risk for a given level of return or maximizes return for a given level of risk, even for a portfolio that contains only a few securities. Obviously, a more workable method is needed to assess the effects of diversification on a portfolio of assets.

One method that has gained widespread use in analyzing the relationship between portfolio risk and return is the **capital asset pricing model (CAPM)**. This model provides a strong analytical basis for evaluating risk-return relationships—both in the context of financial management and securities investment decisions. The remainder of this section discusses the development and application of the CAPM.

Systematic and Unsystematic Risk

As illustrated in the previous section, whenever the individual securities in a portfolio are less than perfectly positively correlated, diversification can reduce the portfolio's risk below the weighted average of the total risk (measured by the standard deviation) of the

Capital Asset Pricing Model (CAPM)
A theory that formally describes the nature of the risk-required rate of return relationship on investments in assets.

[15] The number of correlation coefficients needed to evaluate an n-security portfolio is computed as $(n^2 - n)/2$.

individual securities. Because most securities are positively correlated with returns in the securities market in general, it is usually not possible to eliminate all risk in a portfolio of securities. As the economic outlook improves, returns on most individual securities tend to increase. As the economic outlook deteriorates, individual security returns tend to decline. In spite of this positive "comovement" among the returns of individual securities, each security experiences some "unique" variation in its returns that is unrelated to the underlying economic factors that influence all securities. In other words, there are two types of risk inherent in each security:

■ Systematic, or nondiversifiable, risk

■ Unsystematic, or diversifiable, risk

The sum of these two types of risk equals the total risk of the security:

$$(7.11) \qquad \text{Total risk} = \text{Systematic (Nondiversifiable) risk} + \text{Unsystematic (Diversifiable) risk}$$

Systematic risk refers to that portion of the variability of an individual security's returns caused by factors affecting the market as a whole. As such, it can be thought of as being nondiversifiable. Systematic risk accounts for 25 to 50 percent of the total risk of any security. Some of the sources of systematic risk, which cause the returns from all securities to vary more or less together, include the following:

■ Interest rate changes

■ Changes in purchasing power (inflation)

■ Changes in investor expectations about the overall performance of the economy

Because diversification cannot eliminate systematic risk, this type of risk is the predominant determinant of individual security risk premiums.

Unsystematic risk is risk that is unique to the firm. It is the variability in a security's returns caused by such factors as the following:

■ Management capabilities and decisions

■ Strikes

■ The availability of raw materials

■ The unique effects of government regulation, such as pollution control

■ The effects of foreign competition

■ The particular levels of financial and operating leverage the firm employs

Since unsystematic risk is unique to each firm, an efficiently diversified portfolio of securities can successfully eliminate most of the unsystematic risk inherent in individual securities, as is shown in Figure 7.12. To effectively eliminate the unsystematic risk inherent in a portfolio's individual securities, it is not necessary for the portfolio to include a large number of securities. In fact, randomly constructed portfolios of as few as 10 to 15 securities on average can successfully diversify away a large portion of the unsystematic risk of the individual securities.[16] The risk remaining after diversification

Systematic Risk
That portion of the variability of an individual security's returns that is caused by the factors affecting the market as a whole. This also is called nondiversifiable risk.

Unsystematic Risk
Risk that is unique to a firm. This is also called diversifiable risk.

---

[16] A recent study by John Y. Campbell, Martin Lettau, Burton G. Malkiel, Yexio Xu, "Have Individual Stocks Become More Volatile? An Empirical Exploration of Idiosyncratic Risk," *Journal of Finance*, vol. LVI, no. 1 (February 2001): 1–A3, of about 9,000 companies (including the Canadian interlisted firms) that are traded on the major U.S. stock exchanges suggests that the increased volatility (risk) of individual shares over the period from 1962 to 1997 may have increased the number of stocks required to successfully diversify away a large portion of the unsystematic risk in security returns. Their results indicate that as many as 50 stocks may be required today to achieve the same amount of risk reduction as 20 stocks did in the past.

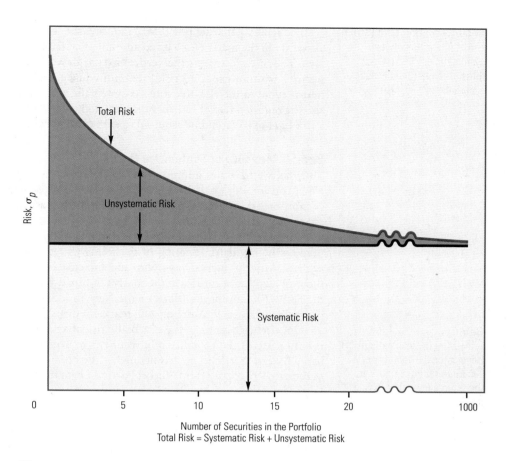

Figure 7.12
Unsystematic Risk and Portfolio Diversification

is market-related risk, or systematic risk, and it cannot be eliminated through diversification. Because unsystematic risk commonly accounts for 50 percent or more of the total risk of most individual securities, it should be obvious that the risk-reducing benefits of efficient diversification are well worth the effort.

Given the small number of securities required for efficient diversification by an individual investor, as well as the dominance of the securities markets by many large institutional investors who hold widely diversified portfolios, it is safe to conclude that the most relevant risk that must be considered for any widely traded individual security is its systematic risk. The unsystematic portion of total risk is relatively easy to diversify away.

Security Market Line (SML)

As discussed earlier (see Equation 7.5), the return required of any risky asset is determined by the prevailing level of risk-free interest rates plus a risk premium. The greater the level of risk an investor perceives about a security's return, the greater the required risk premium will be. In other words, investors require returns that are commensurate with the risk level they perceive. In algebraic terms, the required return from any Security j, k_j is equal to the following:

(7.12)
$$k_j = r_f + \theta_j$$

where r_f is the risk-free rate and θ_j is the risk premium required by investors.

The **security market line (SML)** indicates the "going" required rate of return (k_j) on a security in the market for a given amount of systematic risk and is illustrated in Figure 7.13. The SML intersects the vertical axis at the risk-free rate, r_f, indicating that any security with an expected risk premium equal to zero should be required to earn a return equal to the risk-free rate. As systematic risk increases, so do the risk premium and the required rate of return. According to Figure 7.13, for example, a security having a risk level of a' should be required to earn a 10 percent rate of return.

Beta: A Measure of Systematic Risk

Thus far, we have not addressed the question of the appropriate risk measure to use when considering the risk-return trade-offs illustrated by the SML. The previous discussion of risk in a portfolio context suggests that a measure of systematic risk is an appropriate starting point.

The systematic risk of a security is a function of the total risk of a security as measured by the standard deviation of the security's returns, the standard deviation of the returns from the market portfolio, and the correlation of the security's returns with those of all other securities in the market. A broad-based security market index, such as the S&P/TSX Composite Index or the New York Stock Exchange Composite Index, is normally used as a measure of total market returns.

One useful measure of the systematic risk of a Security j is the value called **beta**. Beta is a measure of the volatility of a security's returns relative to the returns of a broad-based Market Portfolio m. It is defined as the ratio of the covariance (or comovement) of returns on Security j and Market Portfolio m to the variance of returns on the Market Portfolio:

$$(7.13) \qquad \beta_j = \frac{\rho_{jm}\sigma_j\sigma_m}{\sigma_m^2}$$

where β_j is the measure of systematic risk for Security j; σ_j is the standard deviation of returns for Security j; σ_m is the standard deviation of returns for the Market Portfolio

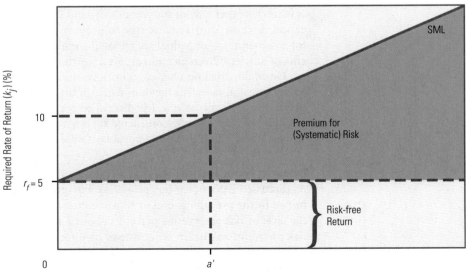

Figure 7.13
The Security Market Line (SML)

m; σ^2_m is the variance of returns for the Market Portfolio m; and ρ_{jm} is the correlation coefficient between returns for Security j and Market Portfolio m.

Estimating Beta Using Holding Period Returns

Holding Period Return (HPR)
The change in price from holding an asset (security) plus distributions received from the asset divided by the initial price at which the asset was acquired.

The return from holding an investment is called the *holding period return, holding period yield,* or *realized rate of return.* The **holding period return** (*HPR*) can be defined by the following equation:

(7.14)
$$HPR = \frac{EP - BP + DR}{BP} \times (100\%)$$

where

$$HPR = \text{Holding period return}$$
$$EP = \text{Ending price}$$
$$BP = \text{Beginning price}$$
$$DR = \text{Distributions received}$$

Distributions include the interest on debt or the dividends on equity. To illustrate, suppose you purchased one Bank of Montreal common share for $31 a year ago. During the year, you received $0.80 in dividends, and you now sell the share for $46. Your holding period return would be calculated as

$$HPR = \frac{\$46 - \$31 + 0.80}{\$31} \times 100\% = 50.97\%$$

Returns are expressed as a percentage or fraction and are frequently quoted on an annual basis. However, holding period returns can be calculated for any time period. But, in order for a calculated holding period return to be a meaningful number, it must be compared to other returns computed using equal time periods.

The return just computed is called a *realized,* or *ex post* (after the fact), return. Realized returns differ from *expected* or *ex ante* (before the fact) returns. Although ex ante returns are calculated in the same manner as ex post returns, ending prices and distributions for expected returns are *estimated* values, whereas ending prices and distributions for realized returns are *actual* values.

In practice, beta may be computed as the slope of a regression line between periodic (usually yearly, quarterly, or monthly) rates of return on the Market Portfolio and the periodic rates of return for Security j, as follows:

(7.15)
$$k_{jt} = a_j + b_j r_{mt} + e_{jt}, \, t = 1, 2, \ldots, n$$

Characteristic Line
A linear least-squares regression line that shows the relationship between a security's return and the returns on the "market." The slope, b, of this line is an estimate of the beta coefficient.

where k_{jt} is the periodic percentage holding period rate of return for Security j in period t; a_j is a constant term determined by the regression; b_j *is the computed historical beta for Security j*; r_{mt} is the periodic percentage holding period rate of return for the market index in period t; and e_{jt} is the residual error term about the regression line in period t. This equation describes a line called Security j's **characteristic line**.

Figure 7.14 shows the characteristic line for a sample common share. The slope (and intercept) of this line can be estimated using the least-squares technique of regression analysis. The slope of this line, or beta, is 0.97, indicating that the systematic returns from the sample common shares are slightly less variable than the returns for the market as a whole.

A beta of 1.0 for any security indicates that the security is of average systematic risk. That is, a security with a beta of 1.0 has the same risk characteristics as the market as a whole when only systematic risk is considered. When beta equals 1.0, a 1 percentage point increase (decline) in market returns indicates that the systematic returns for the individual security should increase (decline) by 1 percentage point. Of course, there will also be unsystematic components to a security's return at any point in time. We assume that these are diversified away in the portfolio. A beta greater than 1.0—for example, 2.0—indicates that the security has greater-than-average systematic risk. In this case, when market returns increase (decline) by 1 percentage point, the security's systematic returns can be expected to increase (decline) by 2 percentage points. A beta of less than 1.0—for example, 0.5—is indicative of a security of less-than-average systematic risk. In this case, a 1 percentage point increase (decline) in market returns implies a 0.5 percentage point increase (decline) in the security's systematic returns. Table 7.6 summarizes the interpretation of selected betas.

The beta for the Market Portfolio as measured by a broad-based market index equals 1.0. This can be seen in Equation 7.13. Because the correlation of the market with itself is 1.0, the beta of the Market Portfolio must also be 1.0.

Finally, the beta of any portfolio of n securities or assets is simply the weighted average of the individual security betas:

$$(7.16) \qquad \beta_p = \sum_{j=1}^{n} w_j \beta_j$$

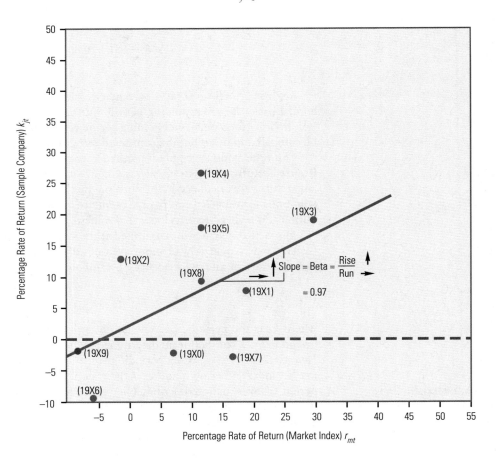

Figure 7.14
Characteristic Line for Sample Company

Table 7.6 Interpretation of Selected Beta Coefficients

Beta Value	Direction of Movement in Returns	Interpretation
2.0	Same as market	Twice as risky (responsive) as market
1.0	Same as market	Risk equal to that of market
0.5	Same as market	Half as risky as market
0	Uncorrelated with market movements	No market-related risk
−0.5	Opposite of market	Half as responsive as market but in the opposite direction

This concept is useful particularly when evaluating the effects of capital investment projects or mergers on a firm's systematic risk.

Fortunately for financial managers, it is not necessary to compute the beta for each security every time a security's systematic risk measure is needed. Some investment advisory services regularly compute and publish individual security beta estimates, and these are readily available. Table 7.7 presents some selected betas for Canadian shares.

Security Market Line and Beta

Given the information presented thus far, it is possible to compute risk premiums θ that are applicable to individual securities. The SML may also be defined in terms of beta. The risk premium for any Security j is equal to the difference between the investor's required return, k_j, and the risk-free rate, r_f:

$$(7.17) \qquad \theta_j = k_j - r_j$$

If we let r_m be the required rate of return on the overall Market Portfolio and r_f be the (short-term) risk-free rate (that is, the rate of return on Treasury bills), then the *market risk premium* or excess return on the market is equal to

$$\theta_m = r_m - r_f$$

Historic stock market data in North America over the time period from 1926 through 2000 indicate that the average market risk premium has been about 9.1 percent. More recent data indicate that it may now be lower than that. In addition, other

Table 7.7 Betas for Selected Canadian Shares

Company	Ticker Symbol	10-year FP Beta
Rothmans	ROC	−0.11
SNC-Lavalin	SNC	0.39
Magna	MG.A	0.50
Bank of Montreal	BMO	0.58
Domtar	DTC	0.69
Barrick	ABX	0.71
BCE	BCE	0.83
Alcan	AL	0.91
Canfor	CFP	0.98
Air Canada	AC	1.91
Nortel	NT	2.31

Source: *Financial Post Corporate Reports*, retrieved February 12, 2003.

estimates based on expected returns using security analyst data lead to somewhat lower equity risk premium estimates. For illustration, we use the long-term equity market risk premium of 9.1 percent.

For a security with average risk (β_j equal to 1.0), the risk premium should be equal to the market risk premium, or 9.1 percent. A security whose beta is 2.0, however, is twice as risky as the average security, so its risk premium should be twice the market risk premium:

$$\theta_j = \beta_j \, (r_m - r_f)$$
$$= 2.0 \, (9.1\%)$$
$$= 18.2\%$$

The required return for any Security j may be defined in terms of its systematic risk, β_j, the required market return, r_m, and the risk-free rate, r_f, as follows:

(7.18) $$k_j = r_f + \beta_j \, (r_m - r_f)$$

For example, if the risk-free rate is 6 percent and $(r_m - r_f)$ is 9.1 percent, then the required rate of return for any security j is given by

(7.19) $$k_j = 6 + 9.1\beta_j$$

The required return for Bombardier, which has a beta of 1.10, can be computed using Equation 7.19:

$$k_j = 6\% + 9.1\% \, (1.10)$$
$$= 16.01\%$$

Equation 7.18 provides an explicit definition of the SML in terms of the systematic risk of individual securities. The slope of the SML is constant throughout. When measured between a beta of 0 and a beta of 1.0, it is equal to $(r_m - r_f)/(1 - 0)$, or simply $r_m - r_f$. This slope represents the risk premium on an average risk security. Figure 7.15 illustrates the SML for Equation 7.19. Given a risk-free rate of 6 percent and a market risk premium of 9.1 percent, the return required on a low-risk share (for example, a security with a beta equal to 0.50) is 10.55 percent. The return required on a high-risk share (for example, a security with a beta equal to 1.50) is 19.65 percent, and the return required on an average risk share with a beta equal to 1.0 is 15.1 percent, the same as the market required return.

Also, from Figure 7.15 we can determine what securities (assets) are attractive investments by comparing the expected return from a security with the return required for that security, given its beta. For example, Security A with a beta of 1.0 and an expected return of 17 percent would be an attractive investment because the expected return exceeds the 15.1 percent required return. In contrast, Security B with a beta of 1.50 is not an acceptable investment because its expected return (18 percent) is less than its required return (19.65 percent).

Relationship Between the SML and the Characteristic Line

The SML expresses the one-period ex ante relationship between the required returns for a security and the market portfolio, given the systematic risk (beta) of the security and the known risk-free rate. The characteristic line is a regression line that expresses the relationship between realized returns for a security and the market portfolio.

Is there a relationship between the SML and the characteristic line? Yes, the SML is the principle that lies at the heart of the regression approach. For any regression line, the

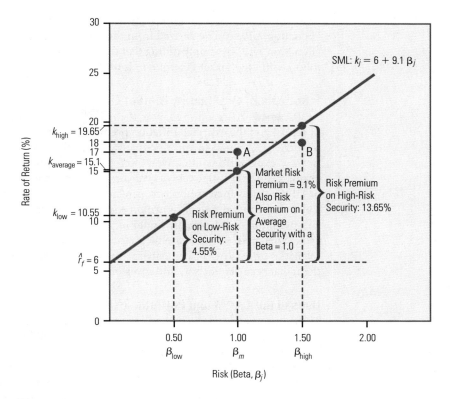

Figure 7.15
The Security Market Line in Terms of Beta

average value $\bar{e}_j$ of the residual errors is zero over the relevant time periods, and the pair of average holding period returns $\bar{k}_j$ and $\bar{r}_m$ lies on the characteristic line.

$$(7.20) \qquad \bar{k}_j = a_j + b_j r_m$$

Suppose that on average an investor in Security j received exactly the returns required for these time periods. Then the constant or intercept term can be expressed as

$$(7.21) \qquad a_j = \bar{r}_f(1 - b_j)$$

where $\bar{r}_f$ is the average risk-free rate.

Substituting for a_j in Equation 7.20 from Equation 7.21 and rearranging terms yields

$$(7.22) \qquad \bar{k}_j = \bar{r}_f + b_j(\bar{r}_m - \bar{r}_f)$$

The left-hand side of Equation 7.22 represents the average holding period return for Security j. The right-hand side of Equation 7.22 represents the average implied rate of return for Security j based on the calculated beta and the SML principle.

Relationship Between the SML and the CML

The SML expresses the relationship between the required rate of return from a security and the systematic risk (beta) of that security. The CML expresses the relationship between the expected return of any efficient portfolio and total risk.

Given that expected returns are in equilibrium, is there a relationship between the SML and the CML? Yes, in equilibrium the CML can be derived from the SML. Since the

SML holds for all securities, it also holds for efficient portfolios. Thus, the CML (Equation 7.10) can be derived from the SML (Equation 7.18) via the definition of beta (Equation 7.13) by simply noting that the correlation coefficient ρ_{jm} of an efficient portfolio j with the Market Portfolio m is one.

Inflation and the Security Market Line

As discussed earlier in the chapter, the risk-free rate of return, r_f, consists of the real rate of return and the expected inflation premium. Because the required return on any risky security, k_j, is equal to the risk-free rate plus the risk premium, an increase in inflationary expectations effectively increases the required return on all securities. For example, if the risk-free rate of return increases from 6 to 8 percent, the required returns of all securities increase by two percentage points—the change in expected inflation. Thus, the required rate of return on a security of average risk (beta equal to 1.0) with a risk premium of 9.1 percent would increase from 6 + 9.1 = 15.1 to 8 + 9.1 = 17.1 percent. When investors increase their required returns, they become unwilling to purchase securities at existing prices, causing prices to decline. It should come as no surprise, then, that security analysts and investors take a dim view of increased inflation.

Uses of the CAPM and Portfolio Risk Concepts

The concepts of portfolio risk, and the capital asset pricing model (CAPM), which relates required returns to systematic risk (beta), are powerful pedagogical tools to explain the nature of risk and its relationship to required returns on securities and physical assets. In Chapter 8, the CAPM is discussed as one technique that can be used to estimate the cost of equity capital. Chapter 8 also considers where the necessary data may be obtained to apply the model. Chapter 11 considers the use of CAPM-determined required rates of return as a technique to adjust for risk in the capital budgeting process.

Assumptions and Limitations of the CAPM

The theoretical CAPM and its applications are based on a number of crucial assumptions about the securities markets and investors' attitudes, including the following:

- Investors hold well-diversified portfolios of securities. Hence, their return requirements are influenced primarily by the systematic (rather than total) risk of each security.

- Securities are traded actively in a competitive market, where information about a given firm and its future prospects is freely available.

- Investors can borrow and lend at the risk-free rate, which remains constant over time.

- There are no brokerage charges for buying and selling securities.

- There are no taxes.

- All investors prefer the security that provides the highest expected return for a given level of risk or the lowest amount of risk for a given level of expected return.

- All investors have common (homogeneous) expectations regarding the expected returns, variances, and correlations of returns among all securities.

While these assumptions may seem fairly limiting at first glance, extensions of the basic theory presented in this chapter, which relax the assumptions, have generally yielded results consistent with the fundamental theory.

Empirical studies of the CAPM have produced mixed results. Some researchers have found positive relationships between systematic (beta) risk and return. However, depending on the time period under examination, the results sometimes do not meet the standard tests of statistical significance. Other investigators, using different share price data, have found that variables other than systematic risk are better predictors of the performance of common shares. Their results suggest that differences in company size and the ratio of book-to-market values explain the differences in share returns. Still other researchers have argued that the results of statistical tests of the relationship between systematic risk and return may be flawed because of the difficulty of obtaining accurate estimates of beta. Their studies suggest that the use of market indexes to measure returns on the true Market Portfolio can introduce significant errors into the process for estimating betas.

Despite the controversy concerning the validity of the CAPM, the model has been used extensively, both practically and conceptually, to consider the risk-return trade-off required by investors in the securities markets. For example, the CAPM (or a modification thereof) has been used in regulated public utility rate case testimony aimed at determining a reasonable allowed rate of return for the utility's investors.

However, users of this approach should also be aware of some of the major problems encountered in practical applications, which include the following:

- Estimating expected future market returns
- Determining the most appropriate estimate of the risk-free rate
- Determining the best estimate of an asset's future beta
- Reconciling the fact that some empirical tests have shown that investors do not totally ignore unsystematic risk, as the theory suggests
- Recognizing that measures of beta have been shown to be quite unstable over time, making it difficult to measure confidently the beta expected by investors
- Recognizing the growing body of evidence that suggests that required returns on most securities are determined by macroeconomic factors, such as interest rates and inflation, in addition to the risk-free rate of interest and the systematic risk of the security

An alternative model that is consistent with macroeconomic factors as determinants of required return is the arbitrage pricing theory discussed in Appendix 7A.

An even newer approach is the market-derived capital pricing model (MCPM) that is based on the traded prices of options on a firm's shares. A detailed discussion of this approach is beyond the scope of this introductory textbook. This approach requires the existence of long-lived options that do not yet exist.[17]

Other Dimensions of Risk

This chapter has focused on various measures of variability in returns—either total variability, measured by the standard deviation and the coefficient of variation, or systematic variability, measured by beta. Although variability of returns is very important, it does not adequately consider another important risk dimension, that is, the risk of failure. In the case of an individual investment project, failure is a situation in which a project generates a negative rate of return. In the case of the entire firm, failure is the situation in which a firm loses money and is ultimately forced into bankruptcy.

For risk-averse investors, the risk of failure may play a large role in determining the types of investments undertaken. For example, the management of a firm is not likely to be eager to invest in a project that has a high risk of failure and that may ultimately cause the firm to fail if it proves to be unsuccessful. After all, the continued survival of the firm is tied closely to the economic well-being of management.

From a shareholder wealth maximization perspective, failure is a particularly undesirable occurrence. The direct and indirect costs of bankruptcy can be very high. Consequently, this failure risk is often an important determinant of investment risk. The

---

[17] James J. McNulty, Tony D. Yeh, William S, Schulze and Michael H. Lubatkin, "What's Your Real Cost of Capital?" *Harvard Business Review* (October 2002): 117–121.

risk and cost of failure can explain, in large part, the desire of many firms to diversify. In addition to reducing the overall risk of a firm, diversification can result in a lower probability of bankruptcy and thus lower expected costs incurred during bankruptcy. These costs include the following:

- The loss of funds that occurs when assets are sold at distressed prices during liquidation
- The legal fees and selling costs incurred when a firm enters bankruptcy proceedings
- The opportunity costs of the funds that are unavailable to investors during the bankruptcy proceedings.

Lower expected bankruptcy costs should increase shareholder wealth, all other things being equal. This is examined in Chapter 12.

Diversification may also reduce a firm's cost of capital. (Cost of capital is the focus of the next chapter.) By reducing the overall risk of the firm, diversification will lower the default risk of the firm's debt securities, and the firm's bonds will receive higher ratings and require lower interest payments. In addition, the firm may be able to increase the proportion of low-cost debt relative to equity in its optimal capital structure (discussed in Chapter 12), further reducing the cost of capital and increasing shareholder wealth.

Although we will focus primarily on return variability as our measure of risk in this book, the risk and cost of failure should also be kept in mind.

Market Efficiency

A central theme of much of the academic finance and financial economics research since the 1960s has been the *efficiency* of the capital markets. The more efficient capital markets are, the more likely it is that resources will find their highest (risk-adjusted) return uses. Capital market efficiency is an implicit assumption in many decision models widely used in finance. Consequently, this concept is important to a full understanding of these decision models.

Efficient Capital Market
A financial market in which new information is quickly reflected in security prices in an unbiased manner.

In an **efficient capital market,** share prices provide an unbiased estimate of the true value of an enterprise. Share prices reflect a present value estimate of the firm's expected cash flows, evaluated at an appropriate required rate of return. The required rate of return is determined by conditions in the financial markets, including the supply of funds from savers, the investment demand for funds, and expectations regarding future inflation rates. The required rate of return on a security also depends on the seniority of the security, the maturity of that security, the business and financial risk of the firm issuing the security, the risk of default, and the marketability of the security. The efficiency of the capital markets is the important "glue" that binds the present value of a firm's net cash flows—discounted at the appropriate risk-adjusted required rate of return—to shareholder wealth as measured by the market value of a company's common shares. Hence, in this section of the chapter, the concept of market efficiency is defined, the evidence regarding the extent of capital market efficiency is reviewed briefly, and some important implications of market efficiency are identified.

Information and Capital Market Efficiency

Capital markets are efficient if security prices instantaneously reflect in an unbiased manner all economically relevant information about a security's prospective returns and the risk of those returns. What is meant by "all economically relevant information"? Information is a message about future events that may occur. Relevant information can be used by an individual to take actions that will change the welfare of that individual.

High-Risk Securities

The decade of the 1980s experienced a dramatic growth in high-risk, so-called junk bonds. These are bonds with credit ratings below investment grade (BBB from DBRS, as discussed in Chapter 5). The lure of these securities was their high returns relative to the returns available from investment-grade corporate and government-issued debt securities. Junk bonds appeared to offer an easy way to quickly increase the yield on the portfolios of assets held by many financial institutions. Financial institutions have frequently made conscious decisions to accept additional risk in the investment securities they purchase in exchange for additional expected return.

What standards of prudent business practice should be followed by firms when they attempt to improve their investment earnings performance? It is well known that, in the financial markets, higher returns can usually be achieved only by assuming greater risks. If this is true, should financial institutions completely avoid high-risk securities? How can these risks be managed effectively? What standards of voluntary disclosure of information to shareholders and customers about the risk and return characteristics of the assets held by the institution do you believe are appropriate?

Messages that you cannot act on to change your welfare have little value. For example, a wheat farmer who grows wheat on irrigated land might be willing to pay for accurate weekly rainfall forecasts, because these forecasts can be used to establish the most efficient irrigation schedule. In contrast, once a dry-land wheat farmer has planted his fields, weekly rainfall forecasts are of little use, because there are no actions the farmer can take on a day-to-day basis using this information.

In addition to being able to act on the information in a manner that will affect your welfare, you must be able to correlate the information with the future events when they occur. For example, if your broker always told you that a stock you had identified looked like a "good buy," this message would have little value to you, because you know that some of these stocks will perform well and others will not. In contrast, if your broker recommends stocks to buy and stocks to sell based on the broker's estimate of each security's return prospects and the broker is right more often than wrong, then this message constitutes economically relevant information.

In security markets, some messages are economically relevant to investors and others are not. If a message has no impact on the future return or risk prospects of a security, it is not relevant to investors and should not be correlated with security performance. That is, it does not constitute information. For example, the news that a company has changed the format of the presentation of its financial reports is not information because this cosmetic change has no impact on the return or risk of that company's securities. In contrast, if the company announces that it has adopted a new accounting convention that will result in significant tax savings, this news is information because it affects the return stream from that company's securities.

Degrees of Market Efficiency

Three levels of market efficiency have been identified based on the information set under consideration: weak-form efficiency, semistrong-form efficiency, and strong-form efficiency.

Weak-Form Efficiency   With **weak-form market efficiency**, no investor can expect to earn excess returns based on an investment strategy using such information as historical price or return information. All stock market information, including the record of past share price changes and share trading volume, is fully reflected in the current price of a share.

Tests of the weak-form market efficiency hypothesis have included statistical tests of independence of share price changes from various day-to-day periods. These studies have concluded that share price changes over time essentially are statistically independent and that a knowledge of past price changes cannot be used to predict future changes. Other tests have looked for the existence of longer-term cycles in share prices, such as monthly or seasonal cycles. In addition, numerous trading rules based solely on past market price and volume information have been tested. Pinches, in a review of much of this research, has concluded that "with some exceptions, the studies of mechanical trading rules do not indicate that profits can be generated by these rules."[18] In conclusion, the evidence indicates that US capital markets are efficient in a weak-form context. It is widely believed that this conclusion applies to Canada, as well.

Semistrong-Form Efficiency   With **semistrong-form market efficiency**, no investor can expect to earn excess returns based on an investment strategy using *any* publicly available information. Announcements of earnings changes, stock splits, dividend changes, interest rate changes, money supply levels, changes in accounting practices that affect a firm's cash flows, takeover announcements, and so on, are quickly and unbiasedly incorporated in the price of a security. A finding of semistrong-form market efficiency implies that the market is also weakly efficient because the information set considered in the weak-form case is also publicly available. Once information is made public in a semistrong-form efficient capital market, it is impossible for investors to earn excess returns (after considering trading costs) from transactions based on this information because the security price will already reflect the value of this information. Studies of stock splits, new issues, stock listing announcements, earnings and dividend announcements, stock acquisition announcements, and announcements of analyst recommendations support the notion of semistrong-form market efficiency, at least after the cost of commissions on transactions is considered. There have been a few apparent observed violations of semistrong-form market efficiency, but in many cases, alternative explanations for these exceptions have been found. Overall, the evidence on semistrong-form market efficiency tends to support this level of market efficiency.

Strong-Form Efficiency   With **strong-form market efficiency**, security prices fully reflect *all* information, both public and private. Thus, in a strong-form efficient capital market, no individual or group of individuals should be able to consistently earn above-normal profits, including insiders possessing information about the economic prospects of a firm. The existence of individuals, such as Ivan Boesky, who have traded illegally on the basis of inside information and have earned phenomenal profits until they were caught and prosecuted by the Securities and Exchange Commission, provides graphic evidence that strong-form efficiency does not hold.

---

[18] George Pinches, "The Random Walk Hypothesis and Technical Analysis," *Financial Analysts Journal* (March/April 1970): 104–110.

Implications of Market Efficiency for Financial Managers

In general, we can conclude that capital markets are quite efficient, both in an informational and an operational sense. The observed efficiency of capital markets has some very important implications for financial managers.

Timing or Gambling   In a weak-form efficient capital market, we know there are no detectable patterns in the movement of stock and bond prices. Companies often indicate that they have delayed a share or bond offering in anticipation of more favourable capital market conditions; that is, a higher share price or lower interest rates. Since there are no predictable patterns of share price and interest rate movements over time, financing decisions based on improved market timing are not likely to be productive, on average. If a share has traded as high as $30 recently but is now trading at only $28, management may delay a proposed new share issue in anticipation of a higher future price. If this delay is based on a market timing argument—such as "the market is now temporarily depressed"—rather than on some inside information known only to management that suggests that the share is currently undervalued, then the strategy is not likely to be successful. In some instances, the share price will increase in the direction of the target, while in others, it will decline even further. In weak-form efficient capital markets, financial decisions based on timing market cycles are not able to consistently lead to higher returns than are available to managers who do not attempt to time their financial decisions to take advantage of market cycles.[19]

An Expected NPV of Zero   In an efficient capital market, all securities are perfect substitutes for one another, in the sense that each security is priced so that its purchase represents a zero net present value investment. This is another way of saying that required returns equal expected returns in efficient capital markets. For example, if you buy one share of Agnico Eagle stock for $25, the present value of the market expectation of its cash flows is equal to $25. Hence, this purchase has a net present value of zero. If you buy for $35 one share of stock in Duke Energy Canada, a diversified energy firm with considerably less risk and lower earnings growth prospects, the present value of the market expectation of its cash flows is equal to $35. The difference between the risk and expected returns of the two companies' stocks is reflected in their market prices and the discount rate used by the market to evaluate the expected future cash flows. Only if an investor possesses information that is not known to the marketplace—for example, insider knowledge of a major new oil strike by an oil firm or of a pending takeover attempt—will the investment in a stock or bond have a positive net present value.

Expensive and Unnecessary Corporate Diversification   If capital markets are efficient and all securities are fairly priced, on average, investors can accomplish much on their own without the help of a firm's financial managers. In spite of this, financial managers of many firms continue to make acquisitions of other companies in order to

---

[19] Suppose one accepts that tests of the weak-form and semistrong-form of market efficiency are generally supportive of the "No Free Lunch" theorem in North American markets. That is, analysis of relevant publicly available information does not allow one to make abnormal returns. (Abnormal returns are returns in excess of required or risk-adjusted returns.)

Richard H. Thaler in a debate at the Wharton School of Business in October 2002 argued, however, that the "No Free Lunch" theorem does not imply the "Price is Right" theorem. (The "Price is Right" theorem is that in an efficient capital market, share prices provide an unbiased estimate of the true value of an enterprise.) For example, there can be periods of market euphoria, such as the "Internet Bubble" of the late 1990s, when stocks are overvalued and the "Price is Right" theorem does not hold. Yet, even during such a bubble, markets may still be efficient in the "No Free Lunch" sense.

Furthermore, if periods of euphoria can lead to overvaluation, then periods of despair can lead to undervaluation. Nevertheless, the "No Free Lunch" theorem could still be valid.

Hence, market timing of security issues by a firm's financial managers would still be ill-advised if it is not based on inside information and may cause serious legal problems if it is so based.

Market Efficiency Outside North America

Extensive testing of the efficiency of security markets in the United States and Canada has led researchers to conclude that the major capital markets in North America are quite efficient in their operation and in the way in which investors process new, economically relevant information. An important question facing the manager of a multinational firm that desires to raise capital outside of North America is: Are foreign capital markets also efficient with respect to security pricing and the processing of new information?

Extensive tests of the efficiency of capital markets outside North America have also been conducted, which concluded that the capital markets in the major industrialized countries, such as Japan, the United Kingdom, and most of Western Europe, are reasonably efficient.

Outside the major industrialized countries, capital markets function without the frequency of trading and liquidity (i.e., marketability) that are necessary for efficient markets. For example, one day in Cairo, the total number of trades on the Cairo Stock Exchange was eight! Transferring shares in Egypt is a complicated, bureaucratized process that requires many signatures, the payment of transfer taxes, and the reissue of stock certificates by the issuing company (a signature is required by two members of the company's board of directors). Overall, it can take between two and three months before the purchaser receives the shares. Brokers in Cairo have an unspoken agreement that prices will not be allowed to move more than 10 percent per day. When someone wants to buy shares from a broker in Egypt, the first question that is usually asked is "Why?" The broker always suspects that the buyer is privy to some inside information. Insider trading is not illegal in Egypt.[20] The inefficiency of the Cairo Exchange holds for the capital markets in many developing countries. Hence, most of the capital that is raised by multinational firms is acquired in countries with well-developed, efficiently functioning capital markets.

Even if the capital markets of the major industrialized countries are relatively efficient, it may still be true that international capital markets, in general, are not efficient. For example, to the extent that there are barriers to the free flow of capital among the major world capital markets, it is possible that a multinational firm can use these barriers to reduce the overall cost of raising capital. Some of the barriers that have been identified include the following:

1. *Legal restrictions* limit the amount of foreign investment by some institutional investors. Some countries limit the amount of foreign ownership of domestic industries in an attempt to prevent a loss of local control.

2. High *transactions costs* may also make the free flow of capital across country borders difficult. These high costs include the cost of gathering information, trading costs, fees for managing international investments, and security custodial service fees.

3. *Taxation policies* between nations sometimes discourage the flow of capital across borders.

4. International investments are subject to greater *political risks* than are domestic investments. These political risks range from expropriation to limits on the repatriation of profits and assets.

5. *Foreign exchange risks,* that is, the risks of unfavourable movements in the value of foreign currencies, also act as a deterrent to the flow of capital across national borders.

These factors may lead to somewhat segmented international capital markets. To the extent that international capital markets are not fully integrated, opportunities may exist for multinational firms that are willing to aggressively manage their investment and capital-raising functions to gain some advantage over less internationally integrated firms.

---

[20] G. Brooks, "To Play the Market in Egypt Requires a Lot of Patience," *The Wall Street Journal* (March 23, 1989): A1.

achieve "the benefits of diversification." In efficient capital markets, this type of activity is better left to individual investors.

Security Price Adjustments   In efficient capital markets, security prices reflect expected cash flows and the risk of those cash flows. If a transaction, such as an accounting change, does not impact the firm's expected *cash flows* or the *risk* of those cash flows, then the transaction should have no impact on security prices. Investors are not fooled by cosmetic accounting or other nonmaterial transactions.

Efficient capital markets research has shown that accounting format changes having no impact on a firm's cash flows do not result in changes in the firm's value. Actions such as including the capitalized value of financial leases on a firm's balance sheet, providing an inflation-adjusted income statement and balance sheet, company name changes, stock splits, and stock dividends unaccompanied by a rise in earnings and/or dividends have no significant impact on share prices. In contrast, any event impacting actual cash flows—such as a change in inventory valuation designed to reduce tax obligations—or the risk of these cash flows—such as an announcement by a publicly owned power company that it will sell all of its nuclear power plants—will be reflected quickly in the share price.

Prices in efficient capital markets have a story to tell. The response of the market to the proposed acquisition of Compaq Computer by Hewlett-Packard in 2001 suggests that this combination might not be value-enhancing.

Behavioural Finance Perspectives on the Financial Marketplace

In spite of an extensive body of literature that indicates that capital markets in financially sophisticated economies, such as Canada and the US, are highly efficient, these markets are not perfectly efficient. We continue to find anomalous events that are inconsistent with fully efficient markets. Some of these anomalies suggest that trading behaviour may not be consistent with fully rational investors.

These anomalies have led to the development of new financial models suggesting that investors sometimes behave irrationally. Behavioural finance seeks to explain how departures from totally rational decision making by investors and other market participants can help to explain otherwise curious market occurrences. There is growing evidence that these behavioural approaches to understanding market behaviour have some merit.[21]

Financial Challenge Revisited

In February 2003, BCE's ratings by Standard and Poor's were affirmed even though the firm had raised $5 billion of new capital during 2002. While the market had been going down in early 2003, BCE shares went up to $28.65 on February 14. The indicated dividend yield was 4.2% and some investment dealers were recommending their clients buy BCE as they expected the price to reach at least $34 within 12 months. (You should check to see whether they were correct.)

---

[21] An excellent collection of behavioural finance research can be found in Richard H. Thaler, ed., *Advances in Behavioral Finance* (New York: Russell Sage Foundation, 1993). In 2002, Daniel Kahneman and Vernon L. Smith shared the Nobel Prize in Economic Sciences for integrating insights from psychology into economics and establishing laboratory experiments as a tool for empirical economic analysis. Their work is the basis for behavioural research in financial economics.

Summary

- The *risk* of a security or an investment project is generally defined in terms of the potential *variability* of its returns. When only one return is possible—for example, as with Canadian government securities held to maturity—there is no risk. When more than one return is possible for a particular project, it is risky.

- The *expected rate of return* from a security reflects the distributions an investor *anticipates* receiving from an investment. The *required rate of return* reflects the return an investor *demands* as compensation for postponing consumption and assuming risk. In efficient financial markets, required rates of return and expected rates of return should be approximately equal.

- The required rate of return on a security is a function of the general level of interest rates, as reflected in the risk-free rate of return, the maturity risk of the security, the default risk of the security, the business and financial risk of the firm that issues the security, the seniority risk of the security, and the marketability risk of the security.

- Three theories of the *term structure of interest rates* and their impact on the *yield curve* were presented. In the *expectations theory*, long-term interest rates are a function of expected future short-term rates. In the *maturity risk premium theory*, required returns on long-term securities tend to be greater the longer the term to maturity. In the *market segmentation theory*, the securities markets are segmented by maturity because various participants match the maturity structure of liabilities with the maturity structure of assets.

- Risk is also influenced by the possibility of investment *diversification*. For example, if a proposed project's returns are not perfectly correlated with the returns from the firm's other investments; the total risk of the firm may be reduced by accepting the proposed project. This is known as the portfolio effect.

- The *expected return from a portfolio* of two or more securities is equal to the weighted average of the expected returns from the individual securities.

- The *risk of a portfolio* is a function of both the risk of the individual securities in the portfolio and the correlation among the individual securities' returns.

- The *capital asset pricing model (CAPM)* is a theory that can be used to determine required rates of return on financial and physical assets.

- The *unsystematic* portion of the total risk in a security's return is that portion of return variability unique to the firm. Efficient diversification of a portfolio of securities can eliminate most unsystematic risk.

- *Systematic risk* refers to the portion of total risk in a security's return caused by overall market forces. This risk cannot be diversified away in a portfolio. Systematic risk forms the basis for the risk premium required by investors in any risky security.

- The *security market line (SML)* provides an algebraic or graphic representation of the risk-return trade-off required in the marketplace for risky securities. It measures risk in terms of systematic risk.

- The *capital market line (CML)* provides an algebraic or graphic representation of the risk-return trade-off expected from efficient portfolios. It measures risk in terms of total risk.

- When there is a risk-free asset, an *efficient portfolio* is any combination of the risk-free asset and the market portfolio.

- Investment returns are normally measured using the *holding period return* concept.

- An indicator of systematic risk for a security is the security's *beta*. Beta is determined from the slope of a regression line (called the *characteristic line*) between the market return and the individual security's return. It is a measure of the volatility of a security's returns relative to the returns of the market as a whole.

■ In efficient capital markets, security prices represent an unbiased estimate of the true economic value of the cash flows expected to be generated for the benefit of that security holder. With *weak-form market efficiency*, no investor can expect to earn excess returns based on an investment strategy using such information as historical price or return information. With *semistrong-form market efficiency*, no investor can expect to earn excess returns based on an investment strategy using any publicly available information. With *strong-form market efficiency*, security prices fully reflect all information, both public and private. Empirical evidence on North American markets tends to support both weak-form and semistrong-form market efficiency, but it does not support strong-form market efficiency.

■ Arbitrage pricing theory, in Appendix 7A, expresses the relationship between the required return of a security and its sensitivity to various economic factors.

Questions and Topics for Discussion

1. Define the following terms:
   a. Risk
   b. Probability distribution
   c. Standard deviation
   d. Real rate
   e. Risk-free rate
   f. Inflation premium
   g. Required rate of return
   h. Maturity risk premium
   i. Default risk premium
   j. Seniority risk premium
   k. Marketability risk premium
   l. Term structure of interest rates
   m. Yield curve
   n. Expectations theory
   o. Maturity risk premium theory
   p. Market segmentation theory
   q. Coefficient of variation
   r. Financial risk
   s. Efficient portfolio
   t. Efficient frontier
   u. Capital market line
   v. Beta coefficient
   w. CAPM
   x. Correlation coefficient
   y. Portfolio
   z. Characteristic line
   aa. Security market line
   bb. Covariance
   cc. Systematic risk
   dd. Unsystematic risk
   ee. Weak-form efficiency
   ff. Semistrong-form efficiency
   gg. Strong-form efficiency

2. If the returns from a security were known with certainty, what shape would the probability distribution of returns graph have?

3. What is the nature of the risk associated with "risk-free" government bonds?

4. If inflation expectations increase, what would you expect to happen to the returns required by investors in bonds? What would happen to bond prices?

5. Under what circumstances will the coefficient of variation of a security's returns and the standard deviation of that security's returns give the same relative measure of risk when compared with the risk of another security?

6. Explain how diversification can reduce the risk of a portfolio of assets to below the weighted average of the risk of the individual assets.

7. What are the primary variables that influence the risk of a portfolio of assets?

8. Distinguish between unsystematic and systematic risk. Under what circumstances are investors likely to ignore the unsystematic risk characteristics of a security?

9. What effect do increasing inflation expectations have on the required returns of investors in common shares?

10. The shares of a firm have a beta value estimated to be 1.4. How would you interpret this beta value? How would you evaluate the firm's systematic risk?

11. How is a security's beta value computed?

12. Under what circumstances can the beta concept be used to estimate the rate of return required by investors in a stock? What problems are encountered when using the CAPM?

13. The enclosed area in the graph below shows all of the possible portfolios obtained by combining the given securities in different proportions (i.e., the opportunity set).

    a. Which of the portfolios (A, B, C, D, E, or F) is (are) on the efficient frontier?

    b. If an investor is interested in maximizing expected returns, which portfolio should be chosen?

    c. If an investor is interested in minimizing risk (as measured by standard deviation), which portfolio should be chosen?

14. How is risk defined in a financial sense?

15. Discuss the general relationship between risk and expected return.

16. What factors determine investors' required rates of return on corporate bonds? Common shares? Government bonds?

17. Why do yield curves sometimes have a downward slope and at other times have an upward slope?

18. What is the primary difference between 20-year bonds issued by the government and 20-year bonds issued by Nortel?

19. Is it possible for investors ever to require a lower rate of return on a company's equity than on its debt, assuming that the debt is in a junk-bond category of quality?

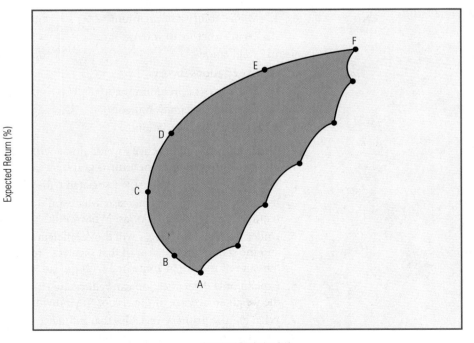

Standard Deviation (%)

20. What is a holding period return?

21. Describe the concept of market efficiency. In what sense is this concept an important part of the shareholder wealth maximization objective?

22. If a capital market is not efficient, what is the impact on a firm seeking to raise capital in that market? Why?

Self-Test Problems

ST1. The following are possible returns (dividends plus capital gains) over the coming year from a $10,000 investment in a firm's common shares:

State of the Economy	Probability	Return
Recession	0.20	−$1,000
Normal year	0.60	$1,500
Boom	0.20	$2,500

Determine the

a. Expected return

b. Standard deviation of returns

c. Coefficient of variation

ST2. Given that the rate of return on a firm's common shares over the coming year is normally distributed with an expected value of 15% and a standard deviation of 12%, determine the probability of earning a negative rate of return.

ST3. Two common shares, A and B, have the following expected return and standard deviation of return over the next year:

Common Share	Expected Rate of Return	Standard Deviation
A	12%	6%
B	20%	15%

Additionally, assume that the correlation coefficient of returns on the two securities is +0.50. For a portfolio consisting of 75% of the funds invested in A and the remainder in B, determine the

a. Expected rate of return on the portfolio

b. Standard deviation of the rate of return

ST4. Determine the beta of a portfolio consisting of equal investments in the following common shares:

Security	Beta
B	.95
DC	1.25
I	1.15
WM	1.05

ST5. The risk-free rate of return is 6%, based on an expected inflation premium of 3%. The expected rate of return on the market portfolio is 15%.

a. Determine the required rate of return on WPS common shares whose beta is 0.60.

b. Assume that the expected rate of return on the market portfolio remains constant but that the expected inflation premium increases from a current level of 3% to 4%. Determine the required rate of return on WPS common shares.

c. Assume that the expected inflation premium remains at 3% but that the expected return on the market portfolio increases to 16%. Determine the required rate of return on WPS common shares.

ST6. The yield to maturity on X Corp. bonds maturing in 2005 is 8.40%. The yield to maturity on a similar maturity government bond is 7.55%. The yield to maturity on 90-day Treasury bills is 6.11%.

a. What is the maturity risk premium between a Treasury bill and an X bond?

b. What is the default risk premium on an X bond?

ST7. Three months ago, you purchased 100 shares of ABC Enterprises for $11 per share. The stock has just paid a 10-cent-per-share dividend, and the current price per share is $8.75. What has been your holding period return on this investment?

Problems*

BASIC

1. You have estimated the following probability distributions of expected future returns for Shares X and Y:

	Share X		Share Y	
Probability	Return		Probability	Return
0.1	−10%		0.2	2%
0.2	10%		0.2	7%
0.4	15%		0.3	12%
0.2	20%		0.2	15%
0.1	40%		0.1	16%

a. What is the expected rate of return for Share X? Share Y?

b. What is the standard deviation of expected returns for Share X? For Share Y?

c. Which share would you consider to be riskier? Why?

2. The return expected from Project 542 is 22%. The standard deviation of these returns is 11%. If returns from the project are normally distributed, what is the chance that the project will result in a rate of return above 33%? What is the probability that the project will result in losses (negative rates of return)?

3. The expected rate of return for CE shares is 20%, with a standard deviation of 15%. The expected rate of return for MA shares is 10%, with a standard deviation of 9%.

a. Which share would you consider to be riskier? Why?

b. If you knew that the beta coefficient of CE is 1.5 and the beta of MA is 0.9, how would your answer to part a change?

4. PH shares have an estimated beta of 1.5. Calculate the required rate of return on PH's shares if the SML is estimated as follows:

$$k_j = 6 + 9.1\beta_j$$

based on

a. An initial inflation expectation of 4%

b. A new inflation expectation of 6%

---

*Coloured numbers and letters denote problems that have "check" answers provided at the back of the book.

5. An investor bought 100 shares of Venus Corporation common stock one year ago for $40 per share. She just sold the shares for $44 each, and during the year, she received four quarterly dividend cheques for $40 each. She expects the price of the Venus shares to fall to about $38 over the next year. Calculate the investor's realized percentage holding period return.

INTERMEDIATE

6. An investor currently has all of his wealth in Treasury bills. He is considering investing one-third of his funds in a firm whose beta is 1.30, with the remainder left in Treasury bills. The expected risk-free rate (Treasury bills) is 6% and the market risk premium is 8.8%. Determine the beta and the expected return on the proposed portfolio.

7. You are considering investing in two securities, X and Y. The following data are available for the two securities:

	Security X	Security Y
Expected return	0.10	0.07
Standard deviation of returns	0.08	0.04
Beta	1.10	0.75

a. If you invest 40% of your funds in Security X and 60% in Security Y and if the correlation of returns between X and Y is +0.5, compute the following:
  i. The expected return from the portfolio
  ii. The standard deviation of returns from the portfolio
b. What happens to the expected return and standard deviation of returns of the portfolio in part a if 70% of your funds are invested in Security X and 30% of your funds are invested in Security Y?
c. What happens to the expected return and standard deviation of returns of the portfolio in part a if the following conditions exist?
  i. The correlation of returns between Securities X and Y is +1.0.
  ii. The correlation of returns between Securities X and Y is 0.
  iii. The correlation of returns between Securities X and Y is –0.7.

8. You have the following information on two securities in which you have invested:

Security	Expected Return	Standard Deviation	Beta	Percent Invested (w)
X	15%	4.5%	1.20	35%
K	12%	3.8%	0.98	65%

a. Which share is riskier in a portfolio context? Which share is riskier if you are considering them as individual assets (not part of a portfolio)?
b. Compute the expected return on the portfolio.
c. If the securities have a correlation of +0.60, compute the standard deviation of the portfolio.
d. Compute the beta of the portfolio.

9. a. Suppose a Treasury bill, maturing in one year, can be purchased today for $92,500. Assuming that the security is held until maturity, the investor will receive $100,000 (face amount). Determine the rate of return on this investment.

  b. Suppose an NTT bond, maturing in one year, can be purchased today for $975. Assuming that the bond is held until maturity, the investor will receive

$1,000 (principal) plus 7% interest (that is, $0.07 \times \$1000 = \$70$). Determine the rate of return on this investment.

   c. Determine the implied risk premium on NTT bonds.

10. The real rate of interest has been estimated to be 3%, and the expected long-term annual inflation rate is 7%.

   a. What is the current risk-free rate of return on one-year Treasury bills?

   b. If the yield on 10-year government bonds is 12%, what is the maturity risk premium between a 10-year bond and a 1-year bill?

   c. If AA bonds, scheduled to mature in 10 years, currently sell to yield 13%, what is the default risk premium on these bonds?

   d. If investors in AA common shares require a 16% rate of return, what is the seniority risk premium on AA's common shares?

11. Using Equation 7.19, suppose you have computed the required rate of return for BT shares to be 16.6%. Given the current share price, the current dividend rate, and analysts' projections for future dividend growth, you expect to earn a rate of return of 18%.

   a. Would you recommend buying or selling this share? Why?

   b. If your expected rate of return from BT shares is 15%, what would you expect to happen to BT's share price?

12. KB shares are expected to return 14% with a standard deviation of 5%. PSW shares are expected to return 16% with a standard deviation of 9%.

   a. If you invest 30% of your funds in KB shares and 70% in PSW shares, what is the expected return on your portfolio?

   b. What is the expected risk of this portfolio if the returns for the two shares have

      i. A perfect positive correlation (+1.0)?

      ii. A slightly negative correlation (–0.2)?

13. Security A offers an expected return of 15% with a standard deviation of 7%. Security B offers an expected return of 9% with a standard deviation of 4%. The correlation between the returns of A and B is +0.6. If an investor puts one-fourth of his wealth in A and three-fourths in B, what is the expected return and risk (standard deviation) of this portfolio?

14. The return on T Corporation shares is expected to be 14% with a standard deviation of 8%. The beta of T is 0.8. The risk-free rate is 7%, and the expected return on the market portfolio is 15%. What is the probability that an investor in T will earn a rate of return less than the required rate of return? Assume that returns are normally distributed.

15. The Rivers Investment Company desires to construct a portfolio with a 20% expected return. The portfolio is to consist of some combination of Security X and Security Y, which have the following expected returns, standard deviations of returns, and betas:

	Security X	Security Y
Expected return	15%	26%
Standard deviation	10%	20%
Beta	0.94	1.33

Determine the expected beta of the portfolio.

16. a. Estimate beta for each of the following securities, assuming that the standard deviation of returns for the market portfolio (m) is 8.0%.

Security	Expected Return	Standard Deviation	Correlation Coefficient Between Returns for the Security and the Market Portfolio
P	12%	10%	.80
Q	18%	20%	.60
R	15%	15%	.40

b. Based on the capital asset pricing model, with a risk-free rate (r_f) of 7 percent and a market risk premium $(r_m - r_f)$ of 8.8%, which of the securities, P, Q, or R (if any) appear to be attractive investments?

17. Two securities have the following characteristics:

	Security A	Security B
Expected return	15%	12%
Standard deviation	4%	6%
Beta	0.90	−0.25

Furthermore, the correlation of returns between the securities is −1.0. Determine the risk (standard deviation) of a portfolio consisting of equal proportions of Securities A and B.

18. Consider again the SML given by Equation 7.19 and shown in Figure 7.15. Assume that the risk-free rate (r_f) of 6% is based on an expected inflation premium of 4%. Suppose expected inflation increases by two percentage points to 6%.

a. Write an equation for the SML given the increase in the expected inflation premium, assuming that all other factors remain constant.

b. Redraw the SML based on the new expected inflation premium.

c. Determine the required rate of return (k_j) on Amazon.com common shares before and after the expected increase in inflation. (Amazon's beta is 1.95.)

19. Six months ago, you purchased a tract of land in an area where a new industrial park was rumoured to be planned. This land cost you $110,000, and the seller offered you an interest-free loan for 70% of the land cost. Today, the industrial park project was formally announced, and a lawyer for the developer has just offered you $190,000 for your land. If you accept this offer, what will be your holding period return on this investment?

CHALLENGE

20. JTC shares are expected to return 13% annually with a standard deviation of 8%. BSM shares are expected to return 17% annually with a standard deviation of 14%. The correlation between the returns from the two securities has been estimated to be +0.3. The beta of the JTC shares is 0.9, and the beta of the BSM shares is 1.2. The risk-free rate of return is expected to be 8%, and the expected return on the market portfolio is 15%. The current dividend for JTC is $4. The current dividend for BSM is $6.

a. What is the expected return from a portfolio containing the two securities if 40% of your wealth is invested in JTC and 60% is invested in BSM?

b. What is the expected standard deviation of the portfolio of the two shares?

c. Which share is the better buy in the current market? Why?

21. The expected return and standard deviation of returns of a firm's common shares over the next year are estimated to be 20% and 12%, respectively. Assume that the returns are approximately normally distributed.

a. Determine the probability of incurring a loss (negative rate of return) from investing in this stock.

b. Determine the probability of earning a rate of return less than the risk-free rate of 6%.

22. The current (time zero) price of one F Corp. share is $25. The price is expected to increase by $5 over the coming year. The company is not expected to pay a dividend during the year. The standard deviation of the expected price change is $3. The distribution of the end-of-year possible prices is approximately normal. Determine the probability of earning a return greater than 30% over the coming year from your investment in F shares.

23. NC Company common shares have a beta of 1.50. The share currently pays a dividend of $3. The risk-free rate is 8%, and the market risk premium is expected to be 8.0%. The returns from NC shares are normally distributed with an expected value of 24% and a standard deviation of 12%.
    a. Determine the required rate of return for NC's common shares.
    b. Determine the probability that the NC shares are undervalued at the current market price of $25 per share.

24. The real rate of return has been estimated to be 2% under current economic conditions. The 30-day risk-free rate (annualized) is 5%. Twenty-year government bonds currently yield 8%. The yield on 20-year bonds issued by the F Company is 14%. Investors require an 18% return on F's common shares. The B Company common shares have a required return of 20%. Compute and identify all meaningful risk premiums. What might account for the difference in the required returns for B versus F?

25. BM.com shares have an estimated beta of 1.5. The share pays no dividend and is not expected to pay one for the foreseeable future. The current share price is $50. You expect this price to rise to $60 by the end of the coming year. You believe that the distribution of possible year-end prices is approximately normal with a standard deviation of $2.50. The risk-free rate of return is currently 4% and the market risk premium is 8.8%. What is the probability that BM.com's shares will earn less than their required rate of return?

26. Suppose that a portfolio consists of the following shares:

Share	Amount	Beta
T	$20,000	.70
G	$40,000	1.30
W	$40,000	1.10

The risk-free rate (r_f) is 5% and the market risk premium $(r_m - r_f)$ is 8.8%.
    a. Determine the beta for the portfolio.
    b. Determine how much G one must sell and reinvest in T in order to reduce the beta of the portfolio to 1.00.
    c. Determine the expected return on the portfolio in parts a and b.

27. IM's common shares have a beta of 0.9. The share does not currently pay a dividend, but is expected to appreciate in value from a current price of $15 to $25 in the next five years. The risk-free rate is 6% and the market risk premium is 7.4%. If the standard deviation of the expected return from this share is 2%, what is the probability that it will earn less than its required rate of return?

Other Practice Materials and Resources

For interactive quizzes, Internet exercises, crossword puzzles, CTV videos, and more, go to the *Contemporary Financial Management* Web site at **http://cyr.nelson.com**

APPENDIX 7A: ARBITRAGE PRICING THEORY (APT)

Like the capital asset pricing model (CAPM), the arbitrage pricing theory (APT) is a model that specifies a risk-return trade-off. The CAPM is a one-factor model with the factor being the required excess return or risk premium on the market portfolio. The APT contains one or more factors, but the theory does not specify what the factor(s) should be. In the APT, the required return k on an individual security is

$$(7A.1) \qquad k = r_f + \sum_{i=1}^{m} \beta_i (k_i - r_f)$$

where

β_i = the security's sensitivity to factor i

k_i = the required return on a portfolio with unit sensitivity to the ith economic factor ($\beta_i = 1$) and zero sensitivity to all other factors

$\sum_{i=1}^{m} \beta_i (k_i - r_f)$ = the risk premium on the security

In equilibrium in both the CAPM and APT, any required return on an asset would also be its expected return.

If the APT were to have only one factor and if this factor were the market portfolio, then Equation 7A.1 would become equivalent to the SML Equation 7.18 of the CAPM. However, unlike the CAPM, the single-factor version of the APT does not require the market portfolio to be this factor.

Like the CAPM, the APT separates total risk into nondiversifiable risk and diversifiable risk. The diversifiable risk is company specific.

The APT has two principal advantages over the CAPM:

- The APT permits any distribution of holding period returns. In contrast, the CAPM assumes that these returns are normally distributed, unless restrictive assumptions are made about the investor's preferences.

- The APT generally does not require the measurement of the return on the market portfolio.[22] (The only exception would be the case where the market portfolio is one of the factors.)

However, the APT also has two principal disadvantages:

- The APT assumes the possibility of unlimited short sales (borrowing a security and then selling it) and the ability to net short-sale proceeds against purchases of other securities.

- The factors are not actually specified in the APT.

Many argue that the limited usage of the APT to date is mainly because factors are unspecified. However, it is possible that additional empirical research will show which factors are likely to be significant in determining the required rate of return of an asset.[23] This may enhance the use of the APT.

---

[22] Because the market portfolio consists of all assets, not just assets comprising a market index such as the S&P/TSX Composite Index, the market portfolio is unmeasurable. See Richard Roll, "A Critique of the Asset Pricing Theory's Tests," *Journal of Financial Economics*, vol. 4 (March 1997): 129–176.

[23] L. Kryzanowski, S. Lalancette, and M.C. To, "Performance Attribution Using an APT with Prespecified Macrofactors and Time-Varying Risk Premia and Betas," *Journal of Financial and Quantitative Analysis*, vol. 32 (June 1997): 205–224.

Capital Investment Decisions

This part of the book looks at the financial management of the long-term asset portion of a firm's balance sheet. Investments in these assets (for example, property, plant, and equipment) have a major impact on a firm's future stream of cash flows and the risk of those cash flows. As such, the long-term investment (capital budgeting) decision has a significant effect on the value of the firm. Chapter 8 deals with the cost of capital, an important input in the capital budgeting process. Chapter 9 deals with the measurement of cash flows from long-term investments. Chapter 10 analyzes various investment decision criteria in light of the wealth maximization objective of the firm. Chapter 11 extends the analysis to consider techniques to account for differential levels of risk among projects.

The Cost of Capital

Learning Objectives

After studying this chapter you should be able to

1. Understand that the cost of capital is the rate of return required by investors in the firm's securities. The cost of capital determines the rate of return that the firm must earn on its new investments (of average risk) to maximize its value

2. Understand that the weighted cost of capital is equal to the after-tax cost of debt times its proportion in the optimal capital structure, plus the cost of preferred shares times their proportion in the optimal capital structure, plus the cost of common equity times its proportion in the optimal capital structure

3. Understand that the weighted cost of capital is appropriate for determining the return required on projects of average risk

4. Understand that for capital budgeting purposes, the marginal cost of each capital source needs to be calculated

   a. The after-tax cost of debt is equal to the pretax cost of new debt times one minus the firm's marginal tax rate

   b. The after-tax cost of perpetual preferred shares is equal to the annual dividend divided by the net proceeds to the firm from the sale of the preferred shares

   c. The cost of internal equity capital can be computed using a version of the dividend valuation model, the capital asset pricing model, or a risk-premium-on-debt approach

   d. The cost of external equity capital exceeds the cost of internal equity capital by the amount of the issuance costs

5. Understand that the beta concept can also be used to compute divisional costs of capital for firms with several operating divisions that differ substantially with respect to the risks of investments that are made

6. Understand that the cost of depreciation-generated funds is equal to the firm's weighted (marginal) cost of capital, before considering new stock issuance costs

Cost of Capital for Telus

Most firms rarely disclose in their annual reports or other public documents what they think is their cost of capital or what they consider to be their appropriate capital structure (proportions of debt and equity) that will minimize their cost of capital.

One significant exception is the Canadian telecommunications firm Telus. In 2002, Telus posted a FAQ (Frequently Asked Questions) document for investors on its Web site that indicated that the firm believes that its most efficient capital structure is made up of approximately 50 percent debt and 50 percent equity. Telus also indicated that this is a long-term guideline that may vary from time to time in any short-term period.

The cost of capital of any firm is a weighted average of the component costs of the debt, preferred shares, and common shares used to finance the firm. Some firms, like Telus, do not use preferred shares.

The cost of debt and preferred shares can be estimated rather easily. However, the cost of equity capital is the most difficult component cost to estimate. It can be considered to be an opportunity cost for the owners of the firm. If they invest in the firm, they forego alternative investments. The return they expect to get on their investments is the opportunity cost of capital for the firm.

What should the cost of equity capital be? The company should earn a return at least equal to that being earned by other firms with similar risks. In addition, the return should be sufficient to maintain the financial integrity of the company, maintain its credit, and give it access to the capital markets. The cost of capital changes, depending on business conditions and conditions in the financial markets. This chapter discusses how to calculate the cost of capital of a firm.

Visit **www.telus.com** and click on About Telus and Investors links.

PHOTODISC

Introduction

This chapter discusses the concept of the cost of capital and develops approaches that can be used to measure this important variable in capital expenditure analysis (discussed in Chapters 9 through 11). This chapter develops the principles and models that can be used to compute a firm's cost of debt, preferred shares, and common equity capital. All of the models require the use of some judgement by the analyst. This is particularly true in the case of the cost of common equity. The cost of common equity cannot be computed with the same precision as is possible with debt and preferred shares. There is normally some controversy regarding how the cost of common equity should be estimated. Some contend that the cost of equity capital should be determined by using a constant-growth dividend valuation model, with long-term growth rates provided from investment advisory services or consensus forecasts supplied by financial analysts. Others contend that the cost of equity capital can be estimated by using a risk premium over the cost of debt approach. Still others contend that only the capital asset pricing model approach should be used. However, an analyst who is knowledgeable of the basic principles contained in this chapter can make reasonable estimates of the cost of equity capital for any company.

The **cost of capital** is concerned with what a firm has to pay for the capital—that is, the debt, preferred shares, retained earnings, and common equity—it uses to finance new investments. It can also be thought of as the rate of return required by investors in the firm's securities. As such, the firm's cost of capital is determined in the capital markets and is closely related to the degree of risk associated with new investments, existing assets, and the firm's capital structure. In general, the greater the risk of a firm as perceived by investors, the greater the return investors will require and the greater will be the cost of capital.

The cost of capital can also be thought of as the minimum rate of return required on new investments undertaken by the firm.[1] If a new investment earns an internal rate of return (IRR) that is greater than the cost of capital, the value of the firm increases. Correspondingly, if a new investment earns an IRR less than the firm's cost of capital, the firm's value decreases.[2]

This chapter discusses the weighted cost of capital and its use in the capital budgeting process. The nature of the risk versus required return trade-off made by investors in a firm's securities and the measurement of the cost of individual capital components (debt, common equity, and preferred shares) is also presented.

Summary of Notation

Before beginning the discussion of the cost of capital, it is helpful to summarize the important elements of notation used throughout this chapter.

r_f = riskless (risk-free) rate of return; the return offered on short-term Treasury securities

k_d = pretax cost of debt

k_p = cost of preferred shares

k_e = cost of internal common equity

k_e' = cost of external common equity

k_a = weighted (marginal) cost of capital

Visit **http://finance. swcollege.com** for synopses of recent articles on the cost of capital.

Cost of Capital
The equilibrium rate of return demanded by investors in the securities issued by a firm.

---

[1] Technically, this statement assumes that the risk of the new investments is equal to the risk of the firm's existing assets. Also, when used in this context, the cost of capital refers to a weighted cost of the various sources of capital used by the firm. The computation of the weighted cost of capital is considered in this chapter.

[2] IRR is discussed in Chapter 10. (IRR is also equivalent to *YTM*, discussed in Chapter 5.)

P_0 = the current market price of a security

P_{net} = the net proceeds to the firm from the sale of a security

P_f = market value of a firm's preferred shares

E = market value of a firm's common equity

D = market value of a firm's debt in its capital structure

r_m = expected return on the market portfolio

β = the beta (systematic risk) of a company's common shares

Foundation
Concept

Weighted Cost of Capital
The weighted average of the marginal costs of debt, equity, and preferred shares, if any, in proportion to their inclusion in the firm's target capital structure.

Weighted Cost of Capital

The *weighted cost of capital* is an extremely important input in the capital budgeting decision process. The **weighted cost of capital** is the discount rate used when computing the net present value (NPV) of a project of average risk. Similarly, the weighted cost of capital is the hurdle rate used in conjunction with the internal rate of return (IRR) approach to project evaluation (for a project of average risk). NPV and IRR are discussed in Chapter 10.

Thus, the appropriate after-tax cost of capital figure to be used in capital budgeting not only is based on the next (marginal) capital to be raised, but also is weighted by the proportions of the capital components in the firm's long-range target capital structure. Therefore, this figure is called the *weighted*, or *overall*, *cost of capital*.

The general expression for calculating the weighted cost of capital, k_a, follows:[3]

$$(8.1) \quad k_a = \left(\frac{E}{E + D + P_f} \right)(k_e) + \left(\frac{D}{E + D + P_f} \right)(k_d)(1 - T) + \left(\frac{P_f}{E + D + P_f} \right)(k_p)$$

where D is debt, P_f is preferred shares, E is common equity in the target capital structure, k_e is the marginal cost of equity capital, k_d is the marginal pretax cost of debt capital, and k_p is the marginal cost of preferred share capital.

KR, Inc.'s Weighted Cost of Capital

KR, Inc. (KR) has a target capital structure consisting of 47 percent common equity, 51 percent debt, and 2 percent preferred shares. The company plans to finance future capital investments in these proportions. All common equity is expected to be derived internally from additions to retained earnings.

The marginal cost of internal common equity has been estimated to be 10.4 percent using the dividend valuation approach. The marginal cost of preferred shares is 8.1 percent and the pretax marginal cost of debt is 8 percent. The marginal tax rate is 40 percent. Using these figures, the weighted cost of capital for KR can be computed using Equation 8.1 as follows:

$$k_a = 0.47 \times 10.4\% + 0.51 \times 8.0\%(1 - 0.4) + 0.02 \times 8.1\%$$
$$= 7.5\%$$

Table 8.1	Weighted Cost of Capital for KR, Inc.		
Source of Capital	**After-Tax Cost**	**Target Proportion of Capital**	**Weighted Cost**
Internal common equity	10.4%	0.47	4.89%
Debt	4.8%	0.51	2.45%
Preferred Shares	8.1%	0.02	0.15%
		1.00	7.50%

[3] In the absence of preferred shares in a firm's capital structure, Equation 8.1 can be simplified to

$$k_a = \left(\frac{E}{E + D} \right)(k_e) + \left(\frac{D}{E + D} \right)(k_d)(1 - T)$$

This is the rate that KR should use to evaluate investment projects of average risk over the coming year. Table 8.1 illustrates the weighted cost of capital calculation for KR.

In the following sections, the techniques used to compute each of the component capital costs are presented and illustrated. Then more complex weighted cost of capital schedule calculations are presented.

The Problem of "Lumpy" Capital

Firms usually raise funds in "lumpy" amounts. For example, a firm may sell $50 million in bonds to finance capital expenditures at one point in time, and it may use retained earnings or proceeds from the sale of shares to finance capital expenditures later on. In spite of this tendency to raise funds in lumpy amounts from various sources at different points in time, the weighted (or composite) cost of funds, not the cost of any particular component of funds, is the cost we are interested in for capital budgeting purposes. Another way of saying this is that *it is generally incorrect to associate any particular source of financing with a particular project. That is, the investment and the financing decisions should be separate.*[4]

Consider, for example, the case of a firm that is financed 50 percent with debt and 50 percent with equity. The cost of equity is 16 percent, and the after-tax cost of debt is 10 percent. The firm has two plants, A and B, which are identical in every respect. The manager of Plant A proposes to acquire a new automated packaging machine costing $10 million. A bank has offered to loan the firm the needed $10 million at a rate that will give the firm a 10 percent after-tax cost. The internal rate of return for this project has been estimated to be 12 percent. Because the rate of return exceeds the cost of funds (debt) used to finance the machine, the manager of Plant A argues that the investment should be made.

The manager of Plant B now argues that she, too, should be allowed to make a similar investment. Unfortunately, she is reminded that the firm has a target capital structure of 50 percent debt and 50 percent equity and that her investment will have to be financed with equity in order for the firm to maintain its target capital structure. Because the cost of equity is 16 percent and the project offers only a 12 percent return, the investment is denied for Plant B.

The point of this illustration is that two economically identical projects were treated very differently, simply because the method of financing the projects was tied to the accept-reject decision. To avoid problems of this type, the capital expenditure decision is usually based on a composite capital cost—that is, each project is assumed to be financed with debt and equity in the proportion in which it appears in the target capital structure. In this example, the composite cost of capital is 13 percent, computed as follows:

Source of Capital	After-Tax Cost	Proportion	Composite Cost
Debt	10%	0.5	5%
Equity	16	0.5	8%
		Weighted cost of capital = 13%	

In this example, neither project should be accepted, because the company's weighted cost of capital exceeds the projects' expected rates of return.

Accordingly, as a firm evaluates proposed capital expenditure projects, it normally does not specify the proportions of debt, preferred share, and common equity financing for each individual project. Instead, each project is presumed to be financed with the same proportion of debt, preferred shares, and equity contained in the company's target capital structure.

---

[4] This statement is generally true. However, there are exceptions. For example, some projects may possess a higher "debt capacity" than is present for the firm as a whole. This may be due to a different level of business risk. The evaluation of mergers frequently considers the debt capacity of the to-be-acquired firm. Hence, the financing of the project may be considered along with the investment decision itself.

Relative Costs of Capital

As was noted in Chapter 7, the general risk-return trade-off between investors' required rates of return and various sources of funds indicates that as risk increases, investors expect higher rates of return. The risk-free rate, r_f, is usually measured as the rate of return on short-term Treasury bills. Longer-term government bonds normally command a higher rate than shorter-term debt because bond prices vary more than prices of shorter-term debt securities over time for equal changes in interest rates. Thus, if interest rates rise, the price of long-term bonds falls, resulting in losses for any investor who must sell the security prior to maturity. Investors normally require a premium to compensate for this interest rate risk.

Long-term debt securities of the Canadian government are always less risky than corporate long-term debt securities of the same maturity. The reason, of course, is the finite probability, however small, that a company will default on its obligation to pay interest and principal. Because the government controls the money supply, it can always meet its nominal financial obligations by printing more money. The actual difference in returns, or yields, between government debt and high-quality corporate debt (AAA-rated) is not often large and is sometimes less than 1.0 percent. In late 2002, the average yield on long-term AAA corporate bonds was 6.94 percent, and the average yield on long-term Government of Canada bonds was 5.46 percent. Firms with higher default risk must offer high coupon interest rates to investors in order to sell their debt issues because the market recognizes that these higher-default-risk companies are more likely to have difficulty meeting their obligations than lower-default-risk companies.

Preferred shares are normally riskier than debt. The claims of preferred shareholders on the firm's assets and earnings are junior to those of debt holders. Also, dividends on preferred shares are more likely to be cut or omitted than interest on debt. Consequently, investors usually demand a higher return after personal taxes on a firm's preferred shares than on its debt.

Common shares are the riskiest type of security considered here, because dividends paid to common shareholders are made from cash remaining after interest and preferred dividends have been paid. Thus, the common share dividends are the first to be cut when the firm encounters difficulties. Because there is a greater degree of uncertainty associated with common share dividends than with the interest on debt or preferred share dividends, common share dividends are judged to be riskier. In addition, the market price fluctuations of common shares tend to be wider than those of preferred shares or long-term debt.

So far, this section has shown that a particular security's risk affects the return required by investors. The analysis must be taken one important step further, however. If capital markets are to clear (that is, supply equals demand), the firm must offer returns consistent with investor requirements. Suppose, for example, that a firm offers a security for sale in the capital markets at a return that is less than investors generally require. Obviously, not enough buyers will come forth. Unless the firm increases the return (by dropping the price, raising the interest or dividend rate, and so on), the securities will remain unsold, and the firm will not be able to raise its capital. Therefore, *the cost of capital to the firm is equal to the equilibrium rate of return demanded by investors in the capital markets for securities with that degree of risk.*

Computing the Component Costs of Capital

This section develops and applies methods a firm can use to compute the cost of its major component sources of capital: debt, preferred shares, retained earnings, and new common equity. These are the component costs used in the calculation of the weighted cost of capital as shown in Equation 8.1.

Marginal Costs

Firms calculate their cost of capital in order to determine a discount rate to use for evaluating proposed capital expenditure projects. Therefore, it is logical that the capital whose cost is measured and compared with the expected benefits from the proposed projects should be the next or marginal capital the firm raises.

The capital budgeting process involves an extension of the marginal analysis principle from economics. The marginal revenue (internal rate of return) from a project is compared with the marginal cost of funds needed to finance the project. The marginal cost of funds is the cost of the next increment of capital raised by the firm. Hence, the costs of the various capital funding components (debt, preferred shares, and common equity) must be their marginal costs. Historic average capital costs are not relevant for making new (marginal) resource allocation decisions.

When computing the marginal cost of the various component capital sources, firms typically estimate the component costs they anticipate encountering (paying) during the coming year. If capital costs change significantly during the year, it may be necessary to recompute the new capital costs and use the new estimates when evaluating projects from that time forward. Under most circumstances, an annual computation of marginal capital costs is sufficient.

Cost of Debt

The cost of debt capital to the firm is the rate of return required by a firm's creditors. For a debt issue, this rate of return, k_d, equates the present value of all expected future receipts—interest, I, and principal repayment, M—with the net proceeds, P_{net}, of the debt security:

$$(8.2) \qquad P_{net} = \sum_{t=1}^{n} \frac{I}{(1 + k_d)^t} + \frac{M}{(1 + k_d)^n}$$

or

$$(8.3) \qquad P_{net} = I(\text{PVIFA}_{k_d,n}) + M(\text{PVIF}_{k_d,n})$$

The pretax cost of debt, k_d, is calculated in the same way as the yield to maturity, shown in Chapter 5. The only difference in the calculation is that when making yield-to-maturity calculations, the price of the bond is the current market price. When computing the pretax cost of debt to a firm, the price of the bond is the net proceeds the company receives after considering all issuance (i.e., flotation) costs.[5]

Interest payments made to investors are deductible from the firm's taxable income. Therefore, the after-tax cost of debt is computed by multiplying the pretax cost of debt, k_d, by 1 minus the firm's marginal tax rate, T:[6]

$$(8.4) \qquad \text{After-tax cost of debt} = k_d(1 - T)$$

To illustrate the cost-of-debt calculation for KR, assume that the firm sells $100 million of 20-year 7.8 percent coupon rate bonds. The net proceeds to KR after issuance costs are $980 for each $1,000 bond. To compute the pretax cost, k_d, of this debt offering, the relationship in Equation 8.3 can be used as follows:

$$\text{Net proceeds} = P_{net} = \$78(\text{PVIFA}_{k_d,20}) + \$1,000(\text{PVIF}_{k_d,20})$$

---

[5] Recall that issuance (flotation) costs were discussed in Chapter 2.

[6] The conversion from a pretax to an after-tax cost of debt is accurate when there are no bond issuance costs. When a bond offering entails issuance costs and the bond is sold either at a discount or premium over face value, there will be a small, insignificant error when using Equation 8.4.

The calculation of k_d can be done either by trial and error using Tables IV and II at the back of the book or with the aid of a financial calculator.

By trial and error, try 8 percent:

$$\$980 = \$78(9.818) + \$1000(0.215)$$
$$\approx \$980$$

Therefore, the pretax cost of debt is 8 percent.

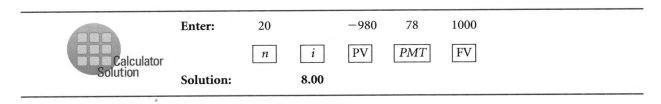

Enter: 20 -980 78   1000

$\boxed{n}$ $\boxed{i}$ $\boxed{PV}$ $\boxed{PMT}$ $\boxed{FV}$

Solution: 8.00

Calculator Solution

The solution can also be computed with a spreadsheet as follows:

Spreadsheet Solution

	A	B	C	
1	TVM	INPUTS	SOLUTION	
2	Periods, n	20		
3	Rate, i		8.00%	
4	PV	-980		
5	PMT	78		
6	FV	1000		

Enter the appropriate data inputs in column B and choose the RATE function for cell C3.

Assuming a 40 percent marginal tax rate, the after-tax cost of debt is computed using Equation 8.4:

$$k_d(1 - T) = 8\%(1 - 0.4)$$
$$= 4.80\%$$

The tax benefits of interest deductibility are available only to firms that are making profits. For a firm losing money, the tax rate in Equation 8.4 is zero, and the after-tax cost is the same as the pretax cost, k_d.

This procedure works well when a firm is in the process of selling, or has just sold, bonds at the time the cost of capital is being computed. However, in most instances, trips to the capital markets are sporadic. How can the marginal cost of debt be computed in these cases? That is, how can one determine what it would cost a firm to sell debt today (at the time of the cost of capital calculation)? This problem has two solutions:

1. If a firm has bonds that are currently outstanding and are being traded in the marketplace, the firm can observe the current market price for those bonds. Given a current price, the maturity of the bonds, and the coupon rate of interest, the yield to maturity on the bond can be computed. This yield to maturity may be used as an estimate of the marginal pretax cost of debt, k_d, for the firm.[7]

---

[7] This computed yield to maturity likely will understate slightly the pretax marginal cost of debt because it does not consider issuance costs.

2. If a firm's outstanding bonds are not traded frequently or are privately held, then the best estimate of the marginal pretax cost of debt can be derived by looking at the pretax cost of debt recently sold by other firms having risk similar to the firm under consideration. For these purposes, having similar risk is normally interpreted to mean that firms have equivalent bond ratings (i.e., DBRS or S&P).

Cost of Preferred Shares

Because many preferred shares are perpetuities, it is possible to use a modification of the simplified preferred share valuation model developed in Chapter 5:

$$(8.5) \qquad P_{net} = \frac{D_p}{k_p}$$

where P_{net} is the net proceeds per share from the sale of new preferred shares; D_p, the annual preferred dividend; and k_p, the investors' required rate of return. Solving for the cost of preferred shares, k_p, yields the following equation:

$$(8.6) \qquad k_p = \frac{D_p}{P_{net}}$$

Note that P_{net} is the preferred share price P_0 net of issuance costs. Thus, the cost of preferred shares would be essentially the same as the rate of return required by investors on preferred shares if issuance costs were negligible.

To illustrate, KR has just issued 3 million preferred shares that pay an annual dividend of $4.05. These preferred shares were sold to the public at a price of $52 per share. With issuance costs of $2 per share, the marginal cost of preferred shares is calculated as follows:

$$k_p = \frac{\$4.05}{\$52 - \$2} = 0.081 \text{ or } 8.1\%$$

Because payments by the firm to preferred shareholders are in the form of dividends, they are not tax-deductible. Therefore, the marginal cost of preferred shares, k_p, is already an after-tax cost.

Some preferred share issues are callable, have a sinking fund redemption provision, or have a fixed maturity. In these cases, the computation of the cost of preferred share financing is similar to that for bonds. For example, PE Inc. plans an offering of $50 par value preferred shares that will pay a $5.00 dividend per year. Each preferred share is expected to yield PE net proceeds of $46.40 after all issue costs. The preferred shares must be retired at par value in 15 years. The cost of this preferred share issue can be computed by solving for k_p in the following valuation model:

$$P_{net} = \$46.40 = \$5(PVIFA_{k_p,15}) + \$50(PVIF_{k_p,15})$$

Try:

$$k_p = 11 \text{ percent}$$

$$\$46.40 = \$5(7.191) + \$50(0.209)$$

$$= \$35.95 + \$10.45$$

$$\$46.40 = \$46.40$$

Therefore, k_p equals 11 percent for PE's anticipated preferred share offering.

Enter: 15   −46.50   5   50

[n]   [i]   [PV]   [PMT]   [FV]

Solution: **11.00**

The solution can also be computed with a spreadsheet as follows:

	A	B	C
1	TVM	INPUTS	SOLUTION
2	Periods, n	15	
3	Rate, i		11.00%
4	PV	−46.50	
5	PMT	5	
6	FV	50	

Enter the appropriate data inputs in column B and choose the RATE function for cell C3.

Cost of Internal Equity Capital

Like the cost of debt and preferred shares, the cost of equity capital to the firm is the equilibrium rate of return required by the firm's common share investors.

Firms raise equity capital in two primary ways:

■ Internally, through retained earnings

■ Externally, through the sale of new common shares

Some analysts and managers incorrectly assume that the cost of internal equity is zero. The opportunity cost concept makes it clear that this is an erroneous assumption. When funds are generated through the earnings of the firm, either managers can pay out these funds as dividends to common shareholders, or the funds can be retained and reinvested in the firm. If the funds were paid out to shareholders, the shareholders could reinvest the funds elsewhere to earn an appropriate return, given the risk of the investment. Therefore, if managers decide to retain earnings and reinvest them in the firm, there must be investment opportunities in the firm offering a return equivalent to the returns available to common shareholders, on a risk-adjusted basis, in alternative investments.

The cost of internal equity to the firm is less than the cost of new common shares because the sale of new shares requires the payment of issuance costs. The concept of the cost of internal equity (or simply equity, as it is commonly called) can be developed using several different approaches. The first considered here is based on the dividend valuation model.

Dividend Valuation Model Approach

Briefly reviewing from Chapter 6, the general dividend valuation model (or the dividend capitalization model, as it is often referred to) for common share valuation is as follows:

$$(8.7) \qquad P_0 = \sum_{t=1}^{n} \frac{D_t}{(1 + k_e)^t}$$

where P_0 is the share's present value or current market price; D_t, the dividend received in period t; and k_e, the return required by investors. This equation shows that in efficient capital markets, k_e, the required return and thus the cost of equity capital, equates the present value of all expected future dividends with the current market price of the share. In principle, the cost of equity capital can be calculated by solving Equation 8.7 for k_e. In practice, however, the expected future dividends are not known and cannot be estimated with the same degree of confidence as preferred share dividends and debt interest. As a result, the general form of the dividend valuation model is not directly useful in calculating the cost of equity capital.

As shown in Chapter 6, if the firm's future per-share dividends are expected to grow each period perpetually at a constant rate, g, the dividend valuation model can be written as follows:

$$(8.8) \qquad P_0 = \frac{D_1}{k_e - g}$$

where $D_1 = D_0(1 + g)$ and D_0 is the current period dividend ($t = 0$). Note that in Equation 8.8, k_e must be greater than g, the expected growth rate. As discussed in Chapter 6, the constant growth valuation model assumes that a firm's earnings, dividends, and share price will grow at rate g. Thus, g equates to the yearly price appreciation (capital gain). But the total return to shareholders, k_e, is composed of both the price appreciation and the dividend yield. Therefore, g cannot be greater than or equal to k_e because it is only one of two components making up k_e.

Equation 8.8 can be rearranged to obtain an expression for calculating the cost of equity, assuming that dividends are expected to grow perpetually at a rate g per year:[8]

$$(8.9) \qquad k_e = \frac{D_1}{P_0} + g$$

To illustrate the use of Equation 8.9, suppose KR's common share price is currently $56. Its present dividend, D_0, is $0.20 per share, and the expected long-term earnings and dividend growth rate is 10.0 percent. The cost of internal equity capital, k_e, is calculated as follows:

$$k_e = \frac{\$0.20(1 + 0.10)}{\$56} + 0.10 = 0.104 \text{ or } 10.4\%$$

Nonconstant Dividend Growth and the Cost of Common Equity The dividend valuation model can also be used to compute the cost of equity for common shares expected to pay dividends that grow at variable rates in the future. An approach similar to the nonconstant growth dividend valuation model illustrated in Chapter 6 (Equation 6.13) can be used.

For example, Avtec Corporation is a rapidly growing producer of microcircuit boards used in the aerospace industry. Its shares are currently selling for $10.95. Current dividends, D_0, are $1.00 per share and are expected to grow at a rate of 10 percent per year over the next four years and 6 percent annually thereafter. Avtec's cost of internal equity, k_e, can be found as follows:

$$\$10.95 = \frac{\$1.10}{(1 + k_e)^1} + \frac{\$1.21}{(1 + k_e)^2} + \frac{\$1.33}{(1 + k_e)^3} + \frac{\$1.46}{(1 + k_e)^4} + \frac{1}{(1 + k_e)^4} \times \frac{\$1.55}{k_e - 0.06}$$

$$= \$1.10(\text{PVIF}_{k_e,1}) + \$1.21(\text{PVIF}_{k_e,2}) + \$1.33(\text{PVIF}_{k_e,3})$$

$$+ \$1.46(\text{PVIF}_{k_e,4}) + (\text{PVIF}_{k_e,4})[\$1.55/(k_e - 0.06)]$$

---

[8] The relevant growth rate is the rate expected by investors. This is normally estimated by examining projected future growth rates provided by security analysts.

Note that the last term in this expression, $\$1.55/(k_e - 0.06)$, is equal to the expected share price at the beginning of year 5 (which is the same as the end of year 4 in time-value terms). Hence it must be discounted back four periods.

The valuation expression above must be solved for k_e, the cost of equity capital, using a trial-and-error procedure. A trial value of 17 percent for k_e yields the following:

$$\$10.95 = \$1.10(0.855) + \$1.21(0.731) + \$1.33(0.624)$$
$$+ \$1.46(0.534) + (0.534)[\$1.55/(0.17 - .06)]$$
$$= \$10.95$$

Thus, Avtec's cost of equity is 17 percent.

In principle, the general dividend valuation model approach can be used to estimate the cost of equity capital for any expected dividend pattern. In practice, many shares not only have exhibited rather constant growth rates in the past but look as though they will continue to do so in the future. For these shares, the constant growth form of the dividend capitalization model is appropriate, and the expected growth rate often can be estimated in the manner discussed in the next section.

Issues in Implementation

Dividend valuation models (sometimes also referred to as DCF models) are frequently used in the calculation of a firm's cost of equity capital. In implementing these models, the analyst must obtain an estimate of the growth rate(s) in earnings and dividends (and share price) expected by investors. Where can these investor expectations be obtained?

Investors form expectations about future growth rates based on past realized growth, current earnings and retention rates, expected future earnings rates (such as the return on equity), and conditions in the markets that the firm serves. These factors are often well summarized in the form of analysts' estimates of future growth rates. Analysts' forecasts may be viewed as the best market- and investor-available summary of all of the factors that determine future growth rates. There are two reasons for this. First, a growing body of research supports the conclusion that analysts' estimates of future earnings growth rates are very accurate—consistently more accurate than estimates provided from any other forecasting model. Second, another body of research has confirmed that analysts' forecasts outperform extrapolative forecasts in explaining share prices.

Analyst forecasts are available from a number of sources. As discussed in more detail in Chapter 6, they can be obtained from individual brokerage houses and investment advisory services.

Capital Asset Pricing Model (CAPM) Approach

Many firms use the capital asset pricing model (CAPM), discussed in Chapter 7, to compute their cost of common equity. The CAPM formally describes the risk-required return trade-off for securities. The rate of return required by investors consists of a risk-free return, r_f, plus a premium compensating the investor for bearing the risk. This risk premium varies from share to share.

Less risk is associated with an investment in a stable share, such as DX, than in a more volatile share, such as W. As a result, an investor in W's shares requires a higher return than the DX investor. Figure 8.1 illustrates the difference in required rates of return (or the cost of internal equity) for the two securities. The relationship illustrated in this figure is the security market line (SML). The SML depicts the risk-required return relationship in the market for all securities.

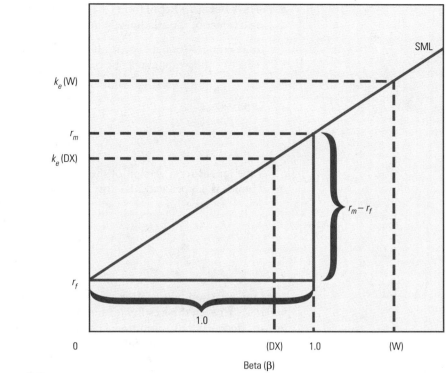

Figure 8.1
Security Market Line (SML)

Recall from Chapter 7 that the security market line is defined as follows:

$$(8.10) \qquad k_j = r_f + \beta_j(r_m - r_f)$$

where k_j = the required rate of return on any security j; r_f = the risk-free rate; β_j = the beta (systematic risk) measure for security j; and r_m = the required return on the market portfolio. Hence, the value $(r_m - r_f)$ equals the market risk premium or excess return on the market (the slope of the SML). It is also the risk premium applicable to a share of average (beta = 1.0) risk.

The SML concept is based on a security's risk and return characteristics. Required returns for any individual security are also dependent on the relevant risk-free interest rate and the required return on the market as a whole. These values are determined as follows:

- **Risk-Free Rate (r_f)** The value for r_f that is most frequently used in computing the required return for a security is the three- or six-month Treasury bill rate. (Some practitioners prefer to use a long-term government bond rate instead.)

- **Required Market Return (r_m)** The required market return is the return investors want to earn in the future on shares with an average beta of 1.0. Recall from Chapter 7 that the average long-term market risk premium in North America measured relative to short-term Treasury bill rates has been 9.1 percent. The average market risk premium measured relative to long-term government bond returns has been 7.8 percent. These risk premiums may be used for the market risk premium $(r_m - r_f)$ in Equation 8.10. Remember that if the 9.1 percent market risk premium is used, then the risk-free rate (the first term on the right-hand side of Equation 8.10) must be the short-term Treasury bill rate. When the 7.8 percent market risk premium is used, then the risk-free rate must be the long-term government bond rate.

- **Firm's Beta** (β_j) Recall from Chapter 7 that beta is normally estimated by using historic values of the relationship between a security's returns and the market returns.

To illustrate, KR's beta is 0.70. If short-term Treasury bills are yielding 3.0 percent, KR's cost of equity capital may be computed using the short-term SML as follows:

$$k_e = r_f + \beta_j(r_m - r_f)$$
$$= 3.0\% + 0.7(9.1\%)$$
$$= 9.4\%$$

If the longer-term version of the SML is used and the yield on long-term government bonds is 4.5 percent, KR's cost of equity capital may be computed as

$$k_e = r_f + \beta_j(r_m - r_f)$$
$$= 4.5\% + 0.7(7.8\%)$$
$$= 10.0\%$$

Note the variation between the two SML estimates of KR's cost of equity and also the variation between these estimates and the 10.4 percent figure derived using the constant growth dividend valuation model earlier in the chapter. Such variation is normal and highlights the fact that estimates of the cost of equity capital are subject to some error.

The SML concept is one more tool that may be used in computing the firm's cost of equity capital, k_e. If all of the parameters required of the model are correctly estimated (r_f, $r_m - r_f$, and β_j), the model should give a reasonably accurate estimate of k_e. Many analysts find it useful to compute k_e in more than one way to arrive at a consensus about the rate of return investors require on a security.

Recall from Chapter 7 that the beta measure of risk considers only the systematic risk or market risk of a share. Poorly diversified investors may be more interested in total risk than in systematic risk. When this is true, the CAPM may understate returns required by those investors.

Risk Premium on Debt and Other Approaches for Estimating the Cost of Equity Capital

This section begins by considering a shortcut method of estimating the cost of equity capital based on actual historic returns and ends by discussing nondividend-paying shares.

Studies analyzing the historical returns earned by common share investors have found that the holding period returns from average risk common share investments over very long time periods have averaged approximately 6.0 percentage points higher than holding period returns on corporate debt issues. Therefore, the cost of equity capital for an average risk company (a firm with a beta of about 1.0) can be estimated by adding approximately 6.0 percentage points to the company's current cost of debt. For companies with a less-than-average level of systematic risk, a risk premium over the company's current cost of long-term debt of 3 to 5 percentage points has been found to be approximately correct. For companies with a higher-than-average level of systematic risk, a risk premium in excess of 6.0 percentage points is warranted. Studies have shown that equity risk premiums over a company's debt yields tend to be higher when interest rates are relatively low and lower when interest rates are relatively high. Many analysts use this shortcut method as a reference. Whenever possible, however, the other more precise methods should be used.

For shares that do not pay dividends, the dividend capitalization model is obviously an inappropriate valuation model and therefore cannot be used to determine an accurate cost of equity capital. Investors in nondividend-paying shares expect to sell the shares in the future at a higher price than the present price, realizing a capital gain. Investors' expectations about the future price are incorporated into the following valuation model:[9]

$$(8.11) \qquad P_0 = \frac{P_t}{(1 + k_e)^t}$$

where P_t is the expected share price at time t. In principle, a firm could use this valuation model to determine its cost of equity capital. In practice, however, this would be difficult to do, because the company probably has no way of confidently determining the P_t expectations of investors. Instead, the cost of equity capital for nondividend-paying shares normally is determined either by using the capital asset pricing model, the risk premium on debt approach, or by estimating k_e for comparable dividend-paying shares in their industry.

Cost of External Equity Capital

The cost of external equity is greater than the cost of internal equity for the following reasons:

- Issuance (flotation) costs associated with new shares are usually high enough that they cannot realistically be ignored.

- The selling price of the new shares to the public is normally set less than the market price of the share before the announcement of the new issue. Before any announcement, the current market price of a share usually represents an equilibrium between supply and demand. If supply is increased (all other things being equal), the new equilibrium price will be lower.

In addition, retained earnings are a cheaper source of funds than the sale of new equity because retention defers the payment of taxable dividends to shareholders. Therefore, the present value of taxes that they must pay is reduced.

When a firm's future dividend payments are expected to grow at a constant rate of g per period forever, the cost of external equity, k_e', is defined as follows:

$$(8.12) \qquad k_e' = \frac{D_1}{P_{net}} + g$$

where P_{net} is the net proceeds to the firm on a per-share basis.[10] To illustrate, consider Adoin Corporation. Its current share price is $39. Adoin pays a current annual dividend of $1.68 per share. The consensus forecast from security analysts is that earnings and dividends will grow at an annual rate of 6.5 percent per annum for the foreseeable future.

The cost of internal equity capital for Adoin using a constant growth dividend valuation model is:

$$k_e = \frac{\$1.68(1 + 0.065)}{\$39} + 0.065 = 0.111 \text{ or } 11.1\%$$

The cost of external equity capital, assuming that new shares could be sold to net the company $37 per share, is:

$$k_e' = \frac{\$1.68(1 + 0.065)}{\$37} + 0.065 = 0.113 \text{ or } 11.3\%$$

---

[9] If investors in a nondividend-paying stock expected the company to begin paying dividends at some future date, a form of the dividend capitalization model could be constructed to reflect these expectations.

[10] An alternative approach to the treatment of issuance costs is to allocate the dollar amount of these costs to individual projects, thus increasing the project cost. When this procedure is used, no adjustment to capital costs is required. This procedure may be superior (from a theoretical perspective) to the cost of capital adjustment procedure, but it is difficult to implement and not widely used.

Because of the relatively high cost of newly issued equity, many companies try to avoid this means of raising capital. The question of whether a firm should raise capital with newly issued common shares depends on its investment opportunities.

Table 8.2 summarizes the cost of capital formulas developed in the preceding sections.

Divisional Costs of Capital

The approaches already discussed provide an estimate of the return required by equity investors on investment projects of "average" risk. When some divisions of a company have lower (higher) systematic risk than others, the discount rates for projects adopted by these divisions should be lower (higher) than the discount rate for the firm as a whole.

Conglomerate firms that compete in many different product and geographical markets often estimate separate divisional costs of capital. These divisional costs of capital reflect both the differential required returns of equity investors, estimated from the security market line, and the differential debt-carrying capacity of each division. For example, the parent company may have a debt-to-total-assets ratio of 60 percent. Individual divisions within the firm may compete against other firms that typically have higher or lower debt-to-total-assets ratios. In computing each divisional cost of capital, many firms try to reflect both the differential divisional risks and the differential normal debt ratios for each division.

Table 8.2	Formulas for Computing Component Costs
Cost of Debt	$k_i = k_d(1 - T)$ where: k_d = pretax cost of debt = yield to maturity on a new bond issue when the current price of the bond is set equal to the net proceeds to the issuing company
Cost of Preferred Shares	$k_p = \dfrac{\text{Annual preferred dividend}}{\text{Net proceeds to the company}}$ (for perpetual preferred shares) $= \dfrac{D_p}{P_{net}}$
Cost of Internal Common Equity	1. Dividend capitalization model approach, used when dividends grow at a perpetual constant rate: $k_e = \dfrac{\text{Next year's expected dividend}}{\text{Common share price}} + \text{Expected dividend growth rate}$ $= \dfrac{D_1}{P_0} + g$ 2. Capital asset pricing model approach: k_e = Risk-free return + Risk premium $= r_f + \beta_j(r_m - r_f)$
Cost of External Shares	$k_e = \dfrac{\text{Next year's expected dividend}}{\substack{\text{Net proceeds per share} \\ \text{to the company}}} + \text{Expected dividend growth rate}$ $= \dfrac{D_1}{P_{net}} + g$

Determining the Weighted (Marginal) Cost of Capital Schedule

In the beginning of the chapter, the computation of the weighted (marginal) cost of capital was based on the assumption that the firm would get equity funds only from internal sources, that all debt had a single cost, and that all preferred shares had a single cost. The procedure illustrated in that earlier discussion must be modified if the firm anticipates selling new common shares (having a higher component cost) or issuing additional increments of debt securities at successively higher costs to finance its capital budget.

To illustrate, suppose the Major Foods Corporation is developing its capital expenditure plans for the coming year. The company's schedule of potential capital expenditure projects for next year is as follows:

Project	Amount (in $Millions)	Internal Rate of Return
A	$4.0	13.8%
B	8.0	13.5
C	6.0	12.5
D	5.0	12.0
E	8.0	11.0
F	4.0	10.0

These projects are closely related to the company's present business and have the same degree of risk as its existing assets.

The firm's current capital structure (as well as its targeted future capital structure) consists of 40 percent debt, 10 percent preferred shares, and 50 percent common equity measured on the basis of the current market value of debt, preferred shares, and equity in the capital structure. Table 8.3 on page 313 shows the current balance sheet for Major Foods. The firm can raise up to $5 million in debt funds at a pretax cost of 9 percent; debt amounts exceeding $5 million will cost 10 percent. Preferred shares can be sold at an after-tax cost of 10 percent. The firm's marginal tax rate is 40 percent.

Major Foods expects to generate $10 million of retained earnings over the coming year. Its present dividend rate, D_0, is $2 per share. The firm's common share price is $25 per share, and new common shares can be sold to net the firm $24 per share.[11]

Over the past several years, Major Foods' earnings and dividends have grown at an average of 7 percent per year, and this growth rate is expected to continue for the foreseeable future. The company's dividend payout ratio has been, and is expected to remain, more or less constant.

Given this information, Major Foods' weighted (marginal) cost of capital can be calculated for the coming year:

- **Step 1:** *Calculate the cost of capital for each individual component*—the cost of debt, the cost of preferred shares, and the cost of equity.

  Cost of debt:

  $$k_d(1 - T) = 9.0 \times 0.6 = 5.4\% \text{ for the first \$5 million of debt}$$

  $$k_d(1 - T) = 10.0 \times 0.6 = 6.0\% \text{ for debt exceeding \$5 million}$$

  Cost of preferred shares:

  $$k_p = 10\% \text{ (given)}$$

---

[11] The net proceeds per share depend on the number of shares sold. As a very general rule, underwriters are reluctant to sell new shares in an amount that exceeds 10% to 15% of a firm's existing shares.

The Cost of Capital for Multinational Companies

Multinational companies (MNC) face a more complex cost of capital problem than purely domestic firms. However, the increased complexity of the problem also offers opportunities to reduce capital costs.

MNC have an opportunity to raise capital in other countries' capital markets, as well as at home, whenever these firms have major operations in foreign countries. One opportunity open to multinational firms is that a host country's government may offer preferential (subsidized) financing terms as an incentive for a firm to locate some of its operations in that country.

Evidence also indicates significant, persistent real differences in the cost of capital between countries. For example, studies of the relative real costs of capital for Canadian, US, and Japanese firms have concluded that the cost of capital for Canadian and US firms was about the same and averaged about 3 percentage points higher than for Japanese firms. However, as global capital markets become more integrated and barriers to international capital flows are reduced, opportunities to take advantage of country-to-country differences in capital costs have diminished. Evidence now suggests that differences in

capital costs between North American and Japanese firms have all but disappeared.

Most multinational companies raise all or the vast majority of their equity capital in their home country. However, multinational firms commonly raise a substantial portion of their debt capital in the countries in which they maintain significant operations. By doing so, a multinational firm effectively hedges much of the balance sheet risk associated with changes in the value of assets in place due to changes in exchange rates. For example, if Bombardier builds a plant in France, the accounting value of this investment will decline with decreases in the value of the euro against the dollar. Offsetting this decline in the accounting value of the French subsidiary's assets is a decline in the value of the debt obligations (when converted to dollars) of the subsidiary. Another advantage of raising a significant portion of a multinational firm's capital in the countries in which it operates is the fact that this insulates the firm from much of the risk of expropriation.

In summary, multinational firms have an opportunity to shop the world for the lowest available capital costs.

Cost of common equity:

Internal (for amounts of retained earnings up to $10 million):

$$k_e = \frac{\$2(1 + 0.07)}{\$25} + 0.07 = 0.156, \text{ or } 15.6\%$$

External (for amounts of new common shares greater than $10 million):

$$k_e' = \frac{\$2(1 + 0.07)}{\$24} + 0.07 = 0.159, \text{ or } 15.9\%$$

- **Step 2:** *Compute the weighted (marginal) cost of capital for each increment of capital raised.*

Major Foods should raise funds in proportion to its target capital structure from its lowest-cost sources first. In this case, these sources are retained earnings (15.6 percent after-tax cost), preferred shares (10 percent after-tax cost), and the first $5 million in debt (5.4 percent after-tax cost). When these sources are exhausted, the

Table 8.3 Balance Sheet for Major Foods (in $Millions)

Current assets	$100	Current liabilities	$50
Fixed assets	30	Long-term debt	32 (40%)
Total assets	$130	Preferred shares	8 (10%)
		Common equity	40 (50%)
		Total liabilities and equity	$130

company should consider using the higher-cost sources—external equity (15.9 percent after-tax cost) and additional debt (6.0 percent after-tax cost)—together with preferred shares.

How much total financing through combining retained earnings, preferred shares, and debt can be done before the $5 million in low-cost debt is exhausted and the firm must acquire additional debt funds at the higher cost? Because we know that the target capital structure consists of 40 percent debt, the total financing, X, that this will support is equal to the amount of low-cost debt available divided by the debt fraction in the capital structure:

$$X = \frac{\text{Amount of low-cost debt available}}{\text{Debt fraction of capital structure}}$$

$$= \frac{\$5 \text{ million}}{0.40}$$

$$= \$12.5 \text{ million}$$

This $12.5 million level represents a break point in the marginal cost of capital schedule. Break points delineate the levels of financing where the weighted cost of capital increases due to an increase in the cost of one component source of capital; that is, debt, preferred shares, or common equity.

Break points can be determined by dividing the amount of funds available from each financing source at a fixed cost by the target capital structure proportion for that financing source. Thus, we saw in the Major Foods example that the $5 million of debt, with an after-tax cost of 5.4 percent, would support total financing of $12.5 million. Beyond $12.5 million in total financing, the weighted (marginal) cost of capital will rise because higher-cost debt (6.0 percent) must now be used. Of this $12.5 million in total financing, $5 million will be debt, $1.25 million (10 percent of the total) will be preferred shares, and $6.25 million will be retained earnings. The cost of this first block of funds using Equation 8.1 is as follows:

$$k_a = 0.50 \times 15.6\% + 0.40 \times 5.4\% + 0.10 \times 10\%$$

$$= 10.96\%$$

The amount of available retained earnings also determines a break point. The $10 million of retained earnings will support total financing of $20 million ($10 million/0.5). Therefore, a new break point occurs at a total financing level of $20 million. Beyond that point, the weighted cost of capital increases due to the higher cost (15.9 percent) of external equity. Thus, the second block of financing totals $7.5 million ($20 million equity break point minus $12.5 million debt financing break point).

This $7.5 million block of funds represents the size of the second lowest-cost block of funds. Of this $7.5 million in financing, $3.75 million will be retained earnings, $0.75 million will be preferred shares, and $3 million will be debt. The cost of this second block of funds will be as follows:

$$k_a = 0.50 \times 15.6\% + 0.40 \times 6.0\% + 0.10 \times 10\%$$

$$= 11.20\%$$

The Cost of Capital

Small firms have a difficult time attracting capital to support their investment programs. Owners of small firms are reluctant to sell common shares because they do not want to lose voting control in the company. When shares are sold, many small firms create two classes of shares, such as Class A and Class B. The Class A shares are traded most extensively in the capital markets. Class A shares usually receive a higher dividend than Class B. In contrast, Class B shares, often held by the firm's founders, have greater voting power than Class A shares. In this way, capital can be raised without losing voting control.

Many firms are so small that it is nearly impossible to raise funds by selling common shares. If shares can be sold, investors will often pay much less for these shares than they would for similar firms that are larger and have their shares traded regularly on an organized exchange or over the counter. Issuance costs for common share sales of small firms may exceed 20 percent of the issue size. As a consequence, the cost of equity capital tends to be significantly higher for small firms than it is for larger firms. Because of the limited access to the capital markets for new equity, small firms tend to retain a much larger portion of their earnings to fund future growth than larger firms.

Similarly, the sources of debt capital to small firms are also limited. Bonds and debentures cannot be sold publicly until a firm has grown to a relatively large size. Before reaching a size that will permit it to sell securities publicly, the small firm will have to rely on the following sources for debt funds:

- The owners' own funds and loans from friends
- Loans from chartered banks and/or other financial institutions
- Small-business loans
- Leasing companies

Beyond the second block, all additional funds raised will be with high-cost debt, new common shares, and preferred shares. The weighted cost of these funds is as follows:

$$k_a = 0.50 \times 15.9\% + 0.40 \times 6.0\% + 0.10 \times 10\%$$

$$= 11.35\%$$

Figure 8.2 provides a graph of the weighted (marginal) cost of capital schedule for Major Foods.

The weighted (marginal) cost of capital schedule can be used to determine the optimal capital budget for Major Foods. This procedure will be discussed in Chapter 10.

Cost of Depreciation-Generated Funds

One large source of funds for many firms is funds generated from depreciation. Of course, depreciation per se does not generate cash. Rather, depreciation is simply a noncash expense charged against income. Therefore, a firm's reported net income will normally understate the amount of cash flow generated by the firm during a given time period. To adjust net income for the cash flow effect of depreciation, the amount of depreciation must be added to net income after taxes. It is in this sense that depreciation

- Venture capital firms that normally demand some equity interest in the firm through conversion features or warrants (discussed in Chapter 17)
- Private placements of debt issues with insurance companies and large corporations, often with a conversion feature or warrants

Generally, the cost of both debt and equity capital is significantly higher for small firms than for larger firms. The high cost of capital puts small firms at a competitive disadvantage relative to large firms in raising funds needed for expansion.

Conceptually, computing the cost of capital for a small, closely held firm is no different than for a large, publicly traded firm. The same models of valuation apply to small firms as to large firms. In practice, however, there are often serious difficulties in developing confident estimates of the cost of capital for small firms. Computing the cost of straight debt and preferred shares (nonconvertible and without attached warrants) is relatively easy. However, when debt and preferred shares are convertible or have attached warrants, an analyst must make an estimate about the time and conditions under which these securities will be converted into common shares or when the warrants to purchase common shares will be exercised.

In the case of common shares, there is often no ready market for them. Hence, it may not be possible to make confident estimates of the share price when computing the cost of equity. Also, because many small firms pay little or no dividends, applying the dividend valuation model is more difficult. As a consequence, when computing the cost of equity for small firms, analysts must often first compute the cost of equity for a group of larger, publicly traded firms in the same line of business that have similar financial risk (as measured by the capital structure). Then the analysts must add an additional risk premium reflective of the perceived increased risk due to reduced marketability (liquidity) of the small firm's shares and any differential in business and financial risk.

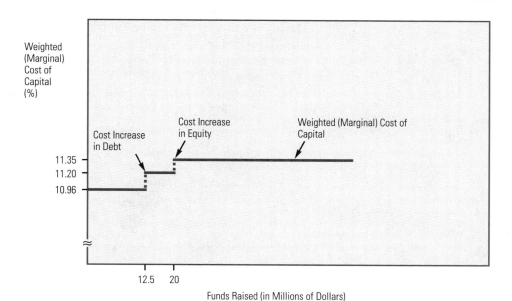

Figure 8.2
Weighted (Marginal) Cost of Capital Schedule for Major Foods

represents a source of funds. Also, some firms may generate funds from the sale of assets from time to time. What is the cost of these funds? Because the firm always has the option to either reinvest these funds in the firm or to return them to the shareholders as dividends and to retire outstanding debt, the appropriate opportunity cost of these funds is the firm's weighted (marginal) cost of capital, before considering new share issuance costs.

With respect to the marginal cost of capital schedule in Figure 8.2, it is generally agreed that these funds have an opportunity cost equal to the first "block" of funds, that is, 10.96 percent. If $10 million in depreciation-generated funds were available, the first block of funds would increase from $12.5 million to $22.5 million, and all other blocks would also be shifted to the right by $10 million.

Financial Challenge Revisited

The cost of capital of any firm is a weighted sum of the marginal component costs of the debt, preferred shares and common shares used to finance the firm. Some firms, like Telus, do not use preferred shares. The Telus target capital structure is 50% debt and 50% equity. Thus, we need to estimate the cost of each of these components.

According to recent newspaper quotations, Telus bonds were selling in February 2003 to yield 7.67%. If it were to issue additional debt in the first quarter of 2003, it might be able to do so at a cost of 8%. Since Telus is profitable, its after-tax cost of debt would be 8% $\times$ (1 − .4) = 4.8%.

The firm's cost of equity can be estimated with the CAPM. Since the cost of capital will be used in capital budgeting decisions concerning long-term investments, the most appropriate risk-free rate is the rate on long-term government bonds, which was 5.5% in early 2003. The market risk premium of 7.8% used earlier in the chapter is the appropriate one for this purpose. The Telus beta is 2.16.

Thus, $k_e = r_f + \beta_j(r_m - r_f)$

$$= 5.5\% + 2.16(7.8\%)$$

$$= 22.35\% \text{ or } 22.4\%$$

Source of Capital	After-Tax Cost	Proportion	Composite Cost
Debt	4.8%	0.5	2.4%
Equity	22.4%	0.5	11.2%
		Weighted cost of capital =	13.6%

Thus, the approximate weighted cost of capital for Telus is 14%. This rate should be used as the discount rate for calculating the NPV of potential investments or as the hurdle rate to be compared with the IRR of potential investments. This will be discussed in Chapter 10.

Summary

- A firm's *cost of capital* is defined as the rate the firm has to pay for the debt, preferred shares, common shares, and/or retained earnings it uses to finance its new investments in assets. The cost of capital is the rate of return required by investors in the firm's securities. Cost of capital can also be thought of as the minimum rate of return required on new investments of average risk undertaken by the firm.

- The higher the risk of a security, the higher the return required by investors. In general, common shares are more risky than preferred shares. Preferred shares are more risky than corporate debt securities. Corporate debt securities are more risky than government debt securities. Investors' required returns generally decrease in the same order.

- Firms normally use an after-tax *weighted cost of capital* to evaluate proposed capital expenditure projects. Each project is presumed to be financed with the same proportion of debt, preferred shares, and common equity contained in the company's target capital structure.

- A firm's pretax *cost of debt capital*, k_d, is the rate of return that satisfies Equation 8.2. The after-tax cost of debt is calculated as: $k_d(1 - T)$, where T is the firm's marginal tax rate.

- In the case of perpetual preferred shares, a firm's *cost of preferred shares*, k_p, is calculated as:

$$k_p = \frac{D_p}{P_{\text{net}}}$$

  where D_p is the annual preferred dividend and P_{net} is the preferred share price net of issuance costs on new issues. Since dividends are not tax-deductible, k_p already is after-tax. If a preferred share issue is not perpetual, then the computation of the cost of preferred share financing is similar to that for bonds. Preferred shares typically are used less frequently than debt as a source of capital because its after-tax cost, k_p, is normally significantly greater than that of debt. This is because interest on debt is a tax-deductible expense for the firm, whereas dividends on shares are not.

- A firm's *cost of equity capital* depends on the source of equity, as equity capital can be raised internally through retained earnings and externally through the sale of new common shares.

- A firm's *cost of internal equity*, k_e, is defined as the rate of return required by its common share investors. It can be determined by the dividend valuation model, the capital asset pricing model (CAPM) via the security market line (SML), or the risk premium on debt approach.

- A firm's *cost of external equity*, k_e', is greater than the cost of internal equity because of issuance (flotation) expenses.

Questions and Topics For Discussion

1. How do retained earnings differ from other sources of financing?
2. Does the retained earnings figure shown on a firm's balance sheet necessarily have any relationship to the amount of retained earnings the firm can generate in the coming year? Explain.
3. Why is corporate long-term debt riskier than government long-term debt?
4. Why do investors generally consider common shares to be riskier than preferred shares?

5. Should a firm pay cash dividends in a year in which it raises external common equity?

6. Evaluate the statement "Depreciation-generated funds have no explicit cost and therefore should be assigned a zero cost in computing a firm's cost of capital."

7. Describe how to derive the break points in the marginal cost of capital schedule.

8. Discuss the pros and cons of various sources of estimates of future earnings and dividend growth rates for a company.

9. What market risk premium should be used when applying the CAPM to compute the cost of equity capital for a firm in the following cases.

   a. The risk-free rate is the short-term Treasury bill rate.

   b. The risk-free rate is the long-term government bond rate.

10. What factors determine the required rate of return for any security?

11. What are the similarities and differences in preferred shares and debt as sources of financing for a firm?

12. Why is the marginal cost of capital the relevant concept for evaluating investment projects rather than a firm's actual, historic cost of capital?

Self-Test Problems

ST1. SE Inc. has a series of 8% coupon bonds outstanding with a $1,000 par value. The bonds mature in 10 years and currently sell for $946. If new bonds are issued, the issuance cost is expected to be $11 per bond. SE's marginal tax rate is 40%. What is the marginal after-tax cost of SE's debt? (Assume annual interest payments.)

ST2. CE Inc. currently pays a common share dividend, D_0, of $3.50. The common share price is $60. Analysts have forecast that earnings and dividends will grow at an average annual rate of 6.8% for the foreseeable future.

   a. What is the marginal cost of retained earnings?

   b. What is the marginal cost of new equity if the issuance costs per share are $3?

ST3. VI Inc. has an estimated beta of 1.3. The current risk-free rate (short term) is 7.5% and the market risk premium is 8.6%. What is the firm's cost of equity capital?

ST4. WE, Inc. has a capital structure target of 60% common equity, 15% preferred shares, and 25% long-term debt. WE's financial analysts have estimated the marginal, after-tax cost of debt, preferred shares, and common equity to be 9%, 15%, and 18%, respectively. What is WE's weighted marginal cost of capital?

Problems*

BASIC

Excel

1. Calculate the after-tax cost of a $25 million debt issue that PMC (40% marginal tax rate) is planning to place privately with a large insurance company. This long-term issue will yield 9.375% to the insurance company.

2. HE Inc. recently sold an issue of 10-year maturity bonds. The bonds were sold at a deep discount price of $615 each. After flotation costs, HE received $604.50 each. The bonds have a $1,000 maturity value and pay $50 interest at the end of

*Coloured numbers and letters denote problems that have "check" answers provided at the back of the book.

each year. Compute the after-tax cost of debt for these bonds if HE's marginal tax rate is 40%.

3. BWA Inc. is planning to sell $10 million of $6.50 cumulative preferred shares to the public at a price of $50 a share. Issuance costs are estimated to be $2 a share. The firm has a marginal tax rate of 40%. Calculate the after-tax cost of the preferred shares.

4. The HH Corporation is planning a major expansion. HH is financed 100% with equity and intends to maintain this capital structure after the expansion. HH's beta is 0.9. The required market return is 16% and the risk-free rate is 10%. If the expansion is expected to produce an internal rate of return of 17%, should HH make the investment?

INTERMEDIATE

 Excel

5. SJT Inc has sold an issue of $6 cumulative preferred shares to the public at a price of $60 per share. After issuance costs, SJT netted $57 per share. The company has a marginal tax rate of 40%.

   a. Calculate the after-tax cost of this preferred share offering assuming that it is a perpetuity.

   b. If the shares are callable in five years at $66 per share and investors expect it to be called at that time, what is the after-tax cost of this preferred share offering? (Compute to the nearest whole percent.)

6. The AT share price is $10.25. Its current dividend rate, D_0, is $1 per share. Analysts and investors expect AT to increase its dividends at a 10% rate for each of the next two years. This annual dividend growth rate is expected to decline to 8% for years 3 and 4 and then to settle down to 4% per year forever. Calculate AT's cost of internal equity.

7. The ED Company is planning a $100 million expansion of its chain of discount service stations. This expansion will be financed, in part, with debt issued with a coupon interest rate of 15%. The bonds have a 10-year maturity and a $1,000 face value, and they will be sold to net ED $990 after issue costs. ED's marginal tax rate is 40%.

   Preferred shares will cost ED 14% after taxes. ED's common shares pay a dividend, D_0, of $2 per share. The current market price per share is $15, and new shares can be sold to net $14 per share. ED's dividends are expected to increase at an annual rate of 5% for the foreseeable future. ED expects to have $20 million of retained earnings available to finance the expansion. ED's target capital structure is as follows:

Debt	20%
Preferred shares	5%
Common equity	75%

   Calculate the weighted cost of capital that is appropriate to use in evaluating this expansion program.

8. PIU Company has a present capital structure (which the company feels is optimal) of 50% long-term debt, 10% preferred shares, and 40% common equity. For the coming year, the firm has determined that its optimal capital budget can be externally financed with $70 million of 10% first-mortgage bonds sold at par and $14 million of preferred shares costing the company 11%. The remainder of the capital budget will be financed with retained earnings. The firm's common share price is $25, and next year's common dividend, D_1, is expected to be $2 per share. The company has 25 million common shares outstanding. Next year's net income available to common equity (including net income from next year's capital budget) is expected to be $106 million. The firm's past annual growth rate in dividends and earnings has been 6%. However, a 5% annual growth in earnings

and dividends is expected for the foreseeable future. The firm's marginal tax rate is 40%. Calculate the firm's weighted cost of capital for the coming year.

9. JR Inc. has the following capital structure:

Financing Source	Proportion of Capital Structure
Debentures (9% coupon, $1,000 par value, 12 year maturity)	27%
Preferred shares ($2 dividend, $25 par value)	8%
Common equity	65%
Total	100%

JR expects to raise future capital in the proportions currently indicated on the balance sheet. The current market price for JR debentures is $1,075. If new debentures were sold, the issuance cost would be $20 per bond. The current preferred share price is $19. Issuance costs on new preferred shares would be $1 per share for a $25 par value issue. Issuance costs on new equity would be $2.50 per share. The current common share price is $40. The share pays a current dividend, D_0, of $3. This dividend is expected to grow at an annual rate of 7%.

What is the weighted (marginal) cost of capital for JR, assuming new capital is raised in the proportions shown in the table above and that all new equity comes from the sale of new shares, new debt comes from the sale of debentures, and new preferred comes from the sale of preferred shares? The firm's marginal tax rate is 40%.

10. GS has decided to diversify into the home improvement field. As a result of this expansion, GS's beta value drops from 1.3 to 0.9, and the expected future long-term growth rate in the firm's dividends drops from 8% to 7%. The required market return is 14%, the risk-free rate is 7%, and the current dividends per share, D_0, are $3. Should GS undertake the planned diversification?

11. TMC has a beta estimated at 1.0. The risk-free rate is 6% and the required market return is 12%. TMC expects to pay a $4 dividend, D_1, next year. This dividend is expected to grow at 3% per year for the foreseeable future. The current market price for TMC is $40.

    a. Is the current share price an equilibrium price, based on the SML calculation of k_e for TMC?

    b. What do you think the appropriate equilibrium price is? How will that price be achieved?

12. WI Ltd. is 100% equity financed. Its current beta is 0.9. The expected market rate of return is 14% and the risk-free rate is 8%.

    a. Calculate WI's cost of equity.

    b. If WI changes its capital structure to 30% debt, it estimates that its beta will increase to 1.1. The after-tax cost of debt will be 7%. Should WI make the capital structure change?

 Excel

13. PI Inc. currently pays an annual common share dividend, D_0, of $2.20. The firm's dividend has grown steadily over the past nine years from $1.10 to its present level. This growth trend is expected to continue. The firm's present dividend payout ratio, also expected to continue, is 40%. In addition, the share presently sells at 8 times current earnings (that is, its P/E multiple is 8).

    PI shares have a beta of 1.15, as computed by a leading investment service. The present risk-free rate is 7.0%, and the required return on the stock market is 13.0%.

Calculate the firm's cost of equity capital using both the dividend capitalization model approach and the capital asset pricing model approach.

14. Colbyco Inc. has a target capital structure of 60% common equity, 30% debt, and 10% preferred shares. The cost of retained earnings is 15%, and the cost of new equity (external) is 16%. The firm anticipates having $20 million of new retained earnings available over the coming year. The firm can sell $15 million of first-mortgage bonds with an after-tax cost of 9%. Its investment dealers feel the company could sell $10 million of debentures with a 9.5% after-tax cost. Additional debt would cost 10% after tax and be in the form of subordinated debentures. The after-tax cost of preferred share financing is estimated to be 14%.

Compute the marginal cost of capital schedule for Colbyco, and determine the break points in the schedule.

15. The W Corp.'s capital structure consists of 60% common equity, 10% preferred shares, and 30% long-term debt. This capital structure is believed to be optimal. The firm is planning to raise funds over the coming year to finance expansion plans. The firm expects to have $40 million of retained earnings available. The cost of retained earnings is 18%. Additional common equity can be obtained by selling new common shares at a cost of 19.6%. The firm can sell a maximum amount of $20 million of preferred shares at a cost of 15%. First-mortgage bonds totalling $25 million can be sold at a pretax cost of 14%. Beyond $25 million, the firm would have to sell debentures at a pretax cost of 15%. The firm's marginal tax rate is 40%.

Identify the size of each block of funds and the cost of the funds in each block. Be sure to identify the maximum amount of funds that the firm can acquire.

16. OE Ltee is in the process of determining its capital budget for the next fiscal year. The firm's current capital structure based on market values is 30% debt and 70% equity. The firm considers this to be optimal.

The firm expects net income from this year to total $80 million. The firm intends to maintain its dividend policy of paying 42.25% of earnings to shareholders. The firm can borrow $18 million from its bank at a 13% annual rate. Any additional debt can be obtained through the issuance of debentures (at par) that carry a 15% coupon rate. The firm currently pays $4.40 per share in dividends, D_0. Dividends have grown at a 5% rate in the past. This growth is expected to continue. The firm's common share price is $44. If the firm were to raise any external equity, the newly issued shares would net the company $40 per share. The firm is in the 40% marginal tax bracket.

Compute the firm's marginal cost of capital schedule.

17. ML, a large conglomerate firm, has a capital structure that currently consists of 20% long-term debt, 10% preferred shares, and 70% common equity. ML has determined that it will raise funds in the future using 40% long-term debt, 10% preferred shares, and 50% common equity.

ML can raise up to $50 million in the long-term debt market at a pretax cost of 18%. Beyond $50 million, the pretax cost of long-term debt is expected to increase to 20%. Preferred shares can be sold at a cost of 19%. The limited demand for this security permits ML to sell only $20 million of preferred shares. ML's marginal tax rate is 40%.

ML's current share price is $40 and its beta is 1.5. ML pays no dividends and is not expected to pay any dividends for the foreseeable future. Investment advisory services expect the share price to increase from its current level of $40 to $99.50 per share at the end of five years. New shares can be sold to net the company $38.35. ML expects earnings after taxes and available for common shareholders to be $60 million.

Compute the marginal cost of capital schedule for ML, and determine the break points in the schedule.

18. The current SDC dividend, D_0, is $3 per share. Under present conditions, this dividend is expected to grow at a rate of 6% annually for the foreseeable future. The SDC beta is 1.5. The risk-free rate of return is 7% and the required market rate of return is 14%.

a. Estimate SDC's common share price.

b. If the risk-free rate of return declines to 6%, estimate what will happen to SDC's share price. (Assume that the required market rate of return remains at 14%.)

c. SDC's management is considering acquisitions in the machine tool industry. Management expects the firm's beta to increase to 1.6 as a result of these acquisitions. The dividend growth rate is expected to increase to 7% annually. Would you recommend this acquisition program to management? (Assume the same initial conditions that existed in part a.)

19. CM has an estimated beta of 1.6. The company is considering the acquisition of another firm that has a beta of 1.2. Both companies are exactly the same size and have the same capital structure.

a. What is the expected new beta value for the combined firm?

b. The risk-free rate of return is estimated at 7% and the market return is estimated as 12%. What is your estimate of the required return of investors in CM before and after the merger?

CM is expected to pay a $1 dividend, D_1, next year. This dividend is expected to grow at a rate of 6% per year for the foreseeable future if the merger is not completed. The merger is not expected to change the dividend, D_1, but future dividends are expected to grow at a 7% rate as a result of the merger.

c. What is the value of a CM share prior to the merger?

d. What is the new value of a CM share, assuming that the merger is completed?

e. Would you recommend that CM go ahead with the merger?

20. DSMN expects its earnings to grow from a current (time 0) level of $2 per share to $4 per share over the coming year. After that, earnings are expected to grow at 10% per year for five years. The current share price is $20. The share is expected to increase in value by 50% over the next three years. DSMN's dividend policy is to pay out 50% of each year's earnings as dividends. DSMN's marginal tax rate is 40% and its average tax rate is 35%. Compute DSMN's cost of internal equity capital.

Other Practice Materials and Resources

For interactive quizzes, Internet exercises, crossword puzzles, CTV videos, and more, go to the *Contemporary Financial Management* Web site at **http://cyr.nelson.com**

Capital Budgeting and Cash Flow Analysis

Learning Objectives

After studying this chapter you should be able to

1. Understand that *capital budgeting* is the process of planning for purchases of assets whose cash flows are expected to continue beyond one year

2. Understand that investment projects may be classified in different ways for different purposes

   a. Projects may be independent, mutually exclusive, or contingent. The acceptance of an *independent* project does not directly eliminate other projects from consideration. The acceptance of a *mutually exclusive* project precludes other alternatives. The acceptance of a *contingent* project depends on the adoption of one or more other projects

   b. Projects may be grouped into those generated by *growth opportunities*, those generated by *cost reduction opportunities*, and those generated by *legal requirements* and *health and safety standards*

   c. Projects may be categorized as asset expansions or asset replacements. An *asset expansion* project requires a firm to invest funds in additional assets to increase sales and/or reduce costs. An *asset replacement*

   project involves retiring one asset and replacing it with a more efficient one

3. Understand that there are key steps in the capital budgeting process

   a. Generating investment project proposals

   b. Estimating cash flows

   c. Evaluating alternatives and selecting projects to be implemented

   d. Reviewing a project's performance after it has been implemented and post-auditing its performance after termination

4. Understand that the optimal capital budget represents the level of investment in selected projects where the *marginal cost of capital (MCC) curve* intersects the *investment opportunity curve (IOC)*

5. Understand the concepts of opportunity cost and sunk costs

   a. An *opportunity cost* is based on the cash flows that a resource used in an investment project could generate in its next-best alternative use

   b. *Sunk costs* represent outlays that have already been made or committed to and cannot be recovered

6. Develop a deeper understanding of the capital cost allowance (CCA) system that was introduced in Chapter 2

   a. *Capital cost allowance (CCA)* is depreciation for tax purposes in Canada. All assets are assigned to a CCA class. Most asset classes are declining balance classes with specified CCA rates

   b. *Undepreciated capital cost (UCC)* is the remaining balance in an asset class. The CCA rate is applied to the UCC to determine the annual CCA amount

   c. The CCA system assumes that all assets acquired and placed into service during a taxation year are put in use at midyear of the first year. This *half-year convention* is required by law

7. Understand the concepts of net installed cost or incremental depreciable base (ΔDB) and net investment (NINV)

   a. The *net installed cost* or *incremental depreciable base (ΔDB)* for a project increases the firm's UCC. The ΔDB is the new project cost (less the net salvage value of the old assets, if applicable) *plus* installation and shipping costs

   b. The *net investment (NINV)* in a project is the net cash outlay required to place the project in service. It includes the ΔDB plus any necessary increases in net working capital.

8. Understand the *net operating cash flow* from a project

   a. A project's *net operating cash flow* is equal to the change in net operating earnings after tax *plus* the change in depreciation (CCA) for tax purposes *minus* the change in net working capital associated with the adoption of a project

   b. In the last year of a project's life, this net cash flow definition may have to be modified to reflect the *incremental salvage value* received and its related tax effects

   c. All project cash flows should be measured on an *incremental after-tax basis* and should include all of the *indirect effects* the project will have on the firm

   d. Project cash flows also are affected by special tax considerations, such as the use of scientific research and development tax credits, investment tax credits, and/or grants from the federal and/or provincial governments

Capital Investment Opportunities During a Business Downturn

When the economy enters a period of low or negative economic growth, many firms cut back on the capital investments they had planned to make. With low or no growth in demand for their products, many firms postpone expansions. During business downturns, other firms become strapped for cash and look to sell off surplus assets so they can acquire the cash that will be needed to survive the downturn. Still others are forced to enter bankruptcy proceedings and often liquidate assets as part of that process. It is in times like these, such as late 2001 and early 2002, that opportunities present themselves to firms that are well positioned with strong balance sheets and ample cash balances.

In some cases, the acquisition of another firm's assets may be driven by the fact that the assets being acquired may be a better *strategic* fit for the acquiring firm than for the seller. In other cases, the acquisitions represent moves of desperation by firms that are short of cash. Under these circumstances, "fire-sale" prices can be found by those with abundant liquid resources.

Other companies have used the weak business climate as an opportunity to acquire strategic resources at bargain prices. For example, Canada's Barrick Gold Corporation, which has the strongest financial position in the industry, was able to purchase the 125-year old US firm, Homestake Mining Company, in 2001. Another Canadian company, SNC-Lavalin, bought the engineering and construction part of Enron, including 5,000 employees and US$1 billion in contracts. In early 2003, another Canadian firm, Moore Corporation, finally succeeded in taking over the US firm Wallace Computer Services seven years after its first attempt failed. Acquisitions such as these offer some important lessons. First, liquidity provides a firm with opportunities to acquire assets at very favourable prices during times of weak business conditions. Strong firms set the stage for further growth by making bargain purchases during business downturns. Second, there is usually a price at which the assets in even the weakest industries can make good economic sense.

Regardless of the economic conditions, financial managers need to scrutinize all major capital investments to determine whether they are likely to contribute to the creation of shareholder value. The analysis of capital investments (that is, projects having economic lives extending beyond one year in time) is a key financial management function. Each year, large and small firms spend hundreds of billions of dollars on capital investments. These investments chart the course of a company's future for many years to come. Therefore, it is imperative that capital investment analysis be performed correctly. This chapter develops the principles of capital investment analysis—with an emphasis on the estimation of cash flows from a project. Chapter 10 considers appropriate decision criteria in the capital budgeting process that will maximize shareholder wealth.

LONNIE DUKA/INDEX STOCK

W W W

Visit **http://finance. swcollege.com** for synopses of recent articles on capital budgeting topics.

Introduction

This is the first of several chapters that explicitly deal with the financial management of the assets on a firm's balance sheet. In this and the following two chapters we consider the management of long-term assets. Later in the book (Chapters 15 and 16) the emphasis shifts to the management of short-term assets—that is, working capital decisions.

Capital budgeting is the process of planning for purchases of assets whose returns are expected to continue beyond one year. A **capital expenditure** is a cash outlay that is expected to generate a flow of future cash benefits lasting longer than one year. It is distinguished from a normal operating expenditure, which is expected to result in cash benefits during the coming one-year period. (The choice of a one-year period is arbitrary, but it does serve as a useful guideline.)

Several different types of outlays may be classified as capital expenditures and evaluated using the framework of capital budgeting models, including the following:

- The purchase of a new piece of equipment, real estate, or a building in order to expand an existing product or service line or enter a new line of business
- The replacement of an existing capital asset, such as a drill press
- Expenditures for an advertising campaign
- Expenditures for a research and development program
- Investments in permanent increases of target inventory levels or levels of accounts receivable
- Investments in employee education and training
- The refunding of an old bond issue with a new, lower-interest issue
- Lease-versus-buy analysis
- Merger and acquisition evaluation

Capital expenditures are important to a firm both because they require sizable cash outlays and because they have a long-range impact on the firm's performance. In the second quarter of 2002, a recessionary year, business gross fixed capital formation was 17.3 percent of Canada's gross domestic product (GDP). Thus, these capital expenditures are extremely important, both at the overall level of the economy and for individual firms.

A firm's capital expenditures affect its future profitability. Collectively, these expenditures essentially plot the company's future direction by determining which products will be produced, which markets will be entered, where production facilities will be located, and what type of technology will be used. Capital expenditure decision making is important for another reason as well. Specifically, it is often difficult, if not impossible, to reverse a major capital expenditure without incurring considerable additional expense. For example, if a firm acquires highly specialized production facilities and equipment, it must recognize that there may be no ready used-equipment market in which to dispose of them if they do not generate the desired future cash flows. For these reasons, a firm's management should establish a number of definite procedures to follow when analyzing capital expenditure projects. Choosing from among such projects is the objective of capital budgeting models.

Corporate Strategy and Capital Budgeting

Most firms have a vision of what they wish to become at some future time. They also have a mission statement that identifies the business they are in now. Most firms have a strategy that spells out how they intend to get from where they are now to the goal that represents their vision. Corporate strategies fall into three generic categories: focussing on niche markets, becoming the lowest-cost producer, or differentiating a firm and its products from all the others. Each of these possible strategies involves investment decisions to build the productive capacity to implement the strategy.

Key Terms and Concepts in Capital Budgeting

Before proceeding with the discussion of the capital budgeting process, it is necessary to introduce a number of terms and concepts encountered in subsequent chapters.

Cost of Capital

A firm's *cost of capital* is defined as the cost of the funds supplied to it. It is also termed the *required rate of return* because it specifies the minimum necessary rate of return required by the firm's investors. In this context, the cost of capital provides the firm with a basis for choosing among various capital investment projects. In this and the following two chapters, it is assumed that the cost of capital is a known value. Chapter 8 explored the methods used to determine the cost of capital.

How Projects Are Classified

A firm usually encounters several different types of projects when making capital expenditure decisions, including *independent projects, mutually exclusive projects,* and *contingent projects.* As is demonstrated in Chapter 10, project classification can influence the investment decision process.

Independent Project
A project whose acceptance or rejection does not result directly in the elimination of other projects from consideration.

Independent Projects   An **independent project** is one whose acceptance or rejection does not directly eliminate other projects from consideration. For example, a firm may want to install a new telephone communications system in its headquarters and replace a drill press during approximately the same time. In the absence of a constraint on the availability of funds, both projects could be adopted if they meet minimum investment criteria.

Mutually Exclusive Project
A project whose acceptance precludes the acceptance of one or more alternative projects.

Mutually Exclusive Projects   A **mutually exclusive project** is one whose acceptance precludes the acceptance of one or more alternative proposals. Because two mutually exclusive projects have the capacity to perform the same function for a firm, only one should be chosen. For example, Toyota was faced with deciding whether it should locate its new North American manufacturing capacity in Cambridge, Ontario, or at one of several competing North American sites. It chose the Cambridge site. This precluded other alternatives.

Contingent Project
A project whose acceptance depends on the adoption of one or more other projects.

Contingent Projects   A **contingent project** is one whose acceptance is dependent on the adoption of one or more other projects. When a firm is considering contingent projects, it is best to consider together all projects that are dependent on one another and treat them as a single project for purposes of evaluation.

Capital Rationing
The limiting of capital expenditure projects that meet the firm's criteria for acceptability. Capital rationing may be self-imposed (soft) because of a lack of sufficient managerial resources or externally imposed (hard) by the capital markets that make borrowing too expensive or impossible.

Availability of Funds

When a firm has adequate funds to invest in all projects that meet some capital budgeting selection criterion, the firm is said to be operating without a *funds constraint.* Frequently, however, the total initial cost of the acceptable projects in the absence of a funds constraint is greater than the total funds the firm has available to invest in capital projects.[1] This necessitates **capital rationing**, or setting limits on capital expenditures, and results in some special capital budgeting problems.[2]

---

[1] Many times, firms limit their capital expenditures, not because of a funds constraint but because of limited managerial resources needed to manage the project effectively.

[2] These are treated in Chapter 10.

Determining the Optimal Capital Budget

According to economic theory, a firm should operate at the point where the marginal cost of an additional unit of output just equals the marginal revenue derived from the output. Following this rule leads to *profit maximization*. This principle may also be applied to capital budgeting decisions. In this context, a firm's marginal revenue is the rates of return earned on succeeding investments, and marginal cost may be defined as the firm's *marginal cost of capital* (MCC), that is, the cost of successive increments of capital acquired by the firm.

Figure 9.1 illustrates a simplified capital budgeting model. This model assumes that all projects have the same risk and are consistent with the firm's strategy. The projects under consideration are indicated by lettered bars on the graph.

Project A requires an investment of $2 million and is expected to generate a 24 percent rate of return. Project B will cost $1 million ($3 million minus $2 million on the horizontal axis) and is expected to generate a 22 percent rate of return, and so on. The projects are arranged in descending order according to their expected rates of return, in recognition of the fact that no firm has an inexhaustible supply of projects offering high expected rates of return. This schedule of projects is often called the firm's *investment opportunity curve* (IOC). Typically, a firm will invest in its best projects first—such as Project A—before moving on to less attractive alternatives.

The MCC schedule (curve) represents the marginal cost of capital to the firm. Note that the schedule increases as more funds are sought in the capital markets. The reasons for this include the following:

- Investors' expectations about the firm's ability to successfully undertake a large number of new projects

- The business risk to which the firm is exposed because of its particular line of business

- The firm's financial risk, which is due to its capital structure

- The supply and demand for investment capital in the capital market

- The cost of selling new shares, which is greater than the cost of retained earnings

The basic capital budgeting model indicates that, in principle, the firm should undertake Projects A, B, C, D, and E, because the expected returns from each project

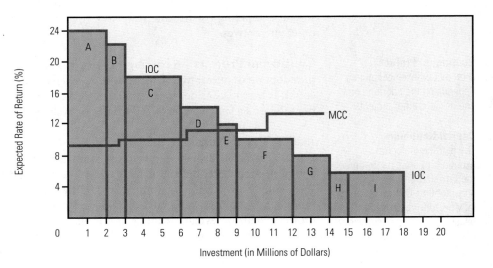

Figure 9.1
Simplified Capital Budgeting Model

exceed the firm's marginal cost of capital. Unfortunately, however, in practice, financial decision making is not this simple. Some practical problems are encountered in trying to apply this model, including the following:

- At any point in time, a firm probably will not know all of the capital projects available to it. In most firms, capital expenditures are proposed continually, based on results of research and development programs, changing market conditions, new technologies, corporate planning efforts, and so on. Thus, a schedule of projects similar to Figure 9.1 will probably be incomplete at the time the firm makes its capital expenditure decisions.

- The shape of the MCC schedule itself may be difficult to determine. (The problems and techniques involved in estimating a firm's cost of capital were discussed in Chapter 8.)

In most cases, a firm can make only uncertain estimates of a project's future costs and revenues (and, consequently, its rate of return). Some projects will be more risky than others. The riskier a project is, the greater the rate of return that is required before it will be acceptable. (This concept is considered in more detail in Chapter 11.)

In spite of these and other problems, all firms make capital investment decisions. This chapter and the following two chapters provide tools that may be applied to the capital budgeting decision-making process.

Briefly, that process consists of four important steps:

1. Generating capital investment project proposals
2. Estimating cash flows
3. Evaluating alternatives and selecting projects to be implemented
4. Reviewing a project's performance after it has been implemented, and post-auditing its performance after its termination

The remainder of this chapter is devoted to a discussion of the first two steps.

For more on the cash flow industry see **http://acfi-online.com** and **http://acfa-cashflow.com**

Generating Capital Investment Project Proposals

Ideas for new capital investments can come from many sources, both inside and outside a firm, from the top down or the bottom up. Investments relating to the vision usually come from the top down. Investments relating to the mission usually come from the bottom up. Thus, investment proposals may originate at all levels of the organization—from factory workers up to the board of directors. Most large and medium-sized firms allocate the responsibility for identifying and analyzing capital expenditures to specific staff groups. These groups can include cost accounting, industrial engineering, marketing research, research and development, and corporate planning. In most firms, systematic procedures are established to assist in the search and analysis steps. For example, many firms provide detailed forms that the originator of a capital expenditure proposal must complete. These forms normally request information on the project's initial cost, the revenues it is expected to generate, and how it will affect the firm's overall operating expenses. These data are then channelled to a reviewer or group of reviewers at a higher level in the firm for analysis and possible acceptance or rejection.

Where a proposal goes for review often depends on how the particular project is *classified*.

Classifying Investment Projects

As noted earlier, there are several types of capital expenditures. These can be grouped into *projects generated by growth opportunities, projects generated by cost reduction opportunities,* and *projects generated to meet legal requirements and health and safety standards.*

Investment proposals of the first two types are accepted if and only if they are compatible with the firm's strategy. The third type of project is imposed on the firm.

Projects Generated by Growth Opportunities

Assume that a firm produces a particular product that is expected to experience increased demand during the upcoming years. If the firm's existing facilities are inadequate to handle the demand, proposals should be developed for expanding the firm's capacity. These proposals may come from the corporate planning staff group, from a divisional staff group, or from some other source.

Because most existing products eventually become obsolete, a firm's growth is also dependent on the development and marketing of new products. This involves the generation of research and development investment proposals, marketing research investments, test marketing investments, and perhaps even investments in new plants, property, and equipment. For example, in order for the mineral extraction industries to keep growing, they must continually make investments in exploration and development. Similarly, firms in high-technology industries—such as electronics and pharmaceuticals—must undertake continuing programs of research and development to compete successfully.

Projects Generated by Cost Reduction Opportunities

Just as products become obsolete over time, so do plants, property, equipment, and production processes. Normal use makes older plants more expensive to operate because of the higher cost of maintenance and downtime (idle time). In addition, new technological developments may render existing equipment economically obsolete. These factors create opportunities for cost reduction investments, which include replacing old, obsolete capital equipment with newer, more efficient equipment.

Projects Generated to Meet Legal Requirements and Health and Safety Standards

These projects include investment proposals for such things as pollution control, ventilation, and fire protection equipment. In terms of analysis, this group of projects is best considered as contingent on other projects.

To illustrate, suppose Inco wishes to build a new smelter in Voisey's Bay, Labrador. The decision will be contingent on the investment in the amount of pollution abatement equipment required by federal, provincial, and local laws. Thus, the decision to invest in the new plant must be based on the *total* cost of the plant, including the pollution abatement equipment, and not just the operating equipment alone. In the case of existing facilities, this type of decision making is sometimes more complex. For example, suppose a firm is told it must install new pollution abatement equipment in a plant that has been in operation for some time. The firm first needs to determine the lowest-cost alternative that will meet these legal requirements. "Lowest cost" is normally measured by the smallest present value of net cash outflows from the project. Then management must decide whether the remaining stream of cash flows from the plant is sufficient to justify the expenditure. If it appears as though it will not be, the firm may consider building a new facility, or it may decide simply to close down the original plant.

Project Size and the Decision-Making Process

The classification of a proposed project influences the capital investment decision-making process. However, there are other factors to consider—in particular, the size of the expenditure required to carry out the project.

Most firms *decentralize* the decision-making function. For example, whereas the approval of the president and the board of directors may be needed for especially large outlays, a divisional vice president may be the final decision maker in the case of medium-sized outlays. A plant manager may have responsibility for deciding on smaller outlays, and a department head in a particular plant may be authorized to approve small outlays. This chain of command varies with individual companies. In large firms, however, it is impossible for any one person to make every decision regarding proposed capital expenditures, and a decentralized system is usually employed.

Principles of Estimating Cash Flows

Net Investment (NINV)
The net cash outlay required at the beginning of an investment project.

Normal or Conventional Project
A project whose cash flow stream requires an initial outlay of funds followed by a series of positive net cash inflows.

The capital budgeting process is concerned primarily with the estimation of the *cash flows* associated with a project, not just the project's contribution to accounting profits. Typically, a capital expenditure requires an initial *cash outflow,* termed the **net investment (NINV).** Thus it is important to measure a project's performance in terms of the *net (operating) cash flows* it is expected to generate over a number of future years.

Figure 9.2 shows the estimated cash flows for a particular project. After an initial net investment of $100,000, the project is expected to generate a stream of net cash inflows over its anticipated five-year life of $50,000 in year 1, $40,000 in year 2, $30,000 in year 3, $25,000 in year 4, and $5,000 in year 5. This type of project is called a **normal** or **conventional project**.

Nonnormal or nonconventional projects have cash flow patterns with either more than one or no sign change. Table 9.1 illustrates the cash flow patterns for three sample projects. Projects X and Y can cause some analytical problems, as we shall see in the discussion of the internal rate of return criterion in the following chapter. Project X might require that certain equipment be shut down and rebuilt in year 3, and Project Y could be an investment in a mining property, with the negative cash flow in year 5 representing abandonment costs associated with closing down the mine after its mineral wealth has been depleted. Finally, Project Z, which generates negative cash flows over the entire life of the investment, such as an investment in pollution control equipment, can be difficult to evaluate using the decision-making criteria developed in the next chapter.

Regardless of whether a project's cash flows are expected to be normal or nonnormal, certain basic principles should be applied during their estimation, including the following:

■ **Cash flows should be measured on an incremental basis** In other words, the cash flow stream for a particular project should be estimated from the perspective of how

Table 9.1	Sample Cash Flow Patterns for Nonnormal Projects					
	Year					
Project	**0**	**1**	**2**	**3**	**4**	**5**
X	−100,000	+80,000	+60,000	−50,000	+75,000	+60,000
Y	−200,000	+150,000	+50,000	+40,000	+30,000	−20,000
Z	−150,000	−20,000	−20,000	−25,000	−25,000	−30,000

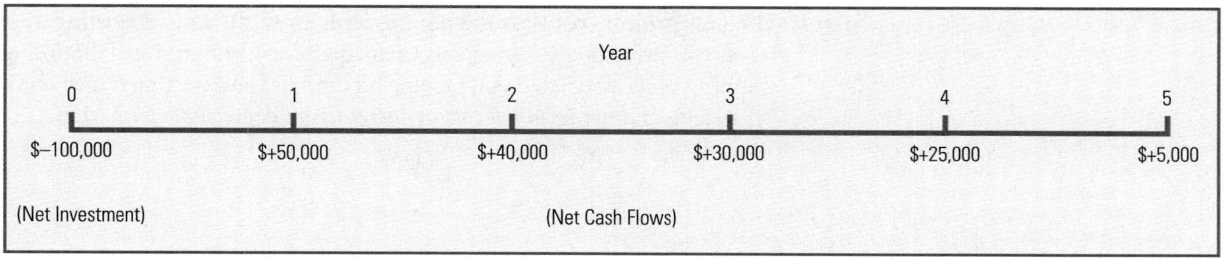

Figure 9.2
Illustration of Estimated Cash Flows for a Normal Capital Investment Project

the entire cash flow stream of the firm will be affected if the project is adopted as compared with how the stream will be affected if the project is not adopted. Therefore, *all* changes in the firm's revenue stream, cost stream, and tax stream that would result from the acceptance of the project should be included in the analysis. In contrast, cash flows that would not be changed by the investment should be disregarded.

- **Cash flows should be measured on an after-tax basis** Because the initial investment made on a project requires the outlay of after-tax cash dollars, the returns from the project should be measured in the same units, namely, after-tax cash flows.

- **All of the indirect effects of a project should be included in the cash flow calculations** For example, if a proposed plant expansion requires that working capital be increased for the firm as a whole—perhaps in the form of larger cash balances, inventories, or accounts receivable—the increase in working capital should be included in the *net investment* required for the project. As another example, assume that one division of a firm introduces a new product that competes directly with a product produced by another division. The first division may consider this product desirable, but when the impact on the second division's sales is considered, the project may be much less attractive.

- **Sunk costs should not be considered when evaluating a project** A *sunk cost* is an outlay that has already been made (or committed to be made). Hence, sunk costs should not be considered in the decision to accept or reject a project. Suppose, for example, that a firm had hired a consulting firm two years ago to conduct an environmental impact study at a cost of $500,000. This cost represents money already spent whether the project is undertaken or not. Thus, it should not be considered in the decision-making process today. The only relevant costs are the incremental outlays that will be made from this point forward if a project is undertaken.

- **The value of resources used in a project should be measured in terms of their opportunity costs** *Opportunity costs* of resources (assets) are the cash flows those resources could generate if they are not used in the project under consideration. For example, suppose a firm owns a parcel of land that it is considering to use for the construction of a new factory. The property originally cost $50,000, but a recent appraisal indicates that it could be sold for $1 million. Because the firm must forego the receipt of $1 million from the sale of the site if the factory is constructed there, the appropriate opportunity cost of this parcel of land is $1 million, not the original cost of $50,000.

These five principles of cash flow estimation may be applied to the specific problem of defining and calculating a project's *net investment* and *net cash flows*.

Net Investment (NINV)

The *net investment* (NINV) in a project is defined as the project's initial net cash outlay, that is, the outlay at time (period) 0. It is calculated using the following steps:

Step 1. The new project cost (less the net proceeds from the sale of existing assets[3] when the investment is a replacement decision) *plus* any installation and shipping costs associated with acquiring the asset and putting it into service. This yields the *net installed cost* or *incremental depreciable base* ΔDB.

PLUS

---

[3] This is normally computed as the actual salvage value of the asset being replaced less any costs associated with physically removing or selling it.

Step 2. Any increases in net working capital *initially* required as a result of the new investment

EQUALS

The net investment (NINV).

The calculation of the net investment for two example projects is illustrated in later sections of the chapter dealing with asset expansion and asset replacement projects. Also discussed are some of the tax consequences that can influence the net investment of a project.

If a project generates additional revenues and the company extends credit to its customers, an additional initial investment in accounts receivable is required. Moreover, if additional inventories are necessary to generate the increased revenues, then an additional initial investment in inventory is required, too. This increase in initial working capital—that is, cash, accounts receivable, and inventories—should be calculated *net* of any automatic increases in current liabilities, such as accounts payable or accrued wages and taxes payable, that occur because of the project. As a general rule, replacement projects require little or no net working capital increase. Expansion projects, on the other hand, normally require investments in additional net working capital.

Some projects require outlays over more than one year before positive cash inflows are generated. It may take several years to design and construct a new production facility, such as an automobile assembly plant. In these cases, the NINV for that project will be equal to the present value (at time 0) of this series of outlays, discounted at the firm's cost of capital if the project is of average risk for the firm. For example, consider a project requiring outlays of $100,000 in year 0, $30,000 in year 1, and $20,000 in year 2, with a cost of capital equal to 10 percent. The NINV or present value of the cash outlays is calculated as follows:[4]

Year t	Cash Outlay	PVIF $_{0.10,t}$	Present Value of Cash Outlay
0	$100,000	1.000	$100,000
1	$30,000	0.909	27,270
2	$20,000	0.826	16,520
			NINV = $143,790

Figure 9.3 illustrates this concept.

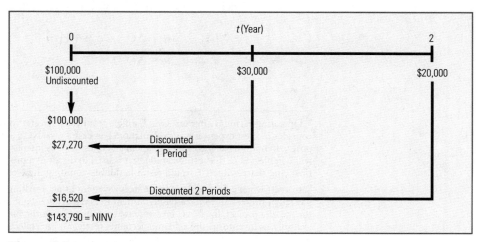

Figure 9.3
Timeline of NINV for a Project with Multiple Period Outlays

---

[4] For tax purposes, the installed cost of this asset would be $150,000—the actual cash outlays required to put the plant or equipment in service.

Net (Operating) Cash Flows

Capital investment projects are expected to generate after-tax cash flow streams after the initial net investment has been made. The process of estimating incremental cash flows associated with a specific project is an important part of the capital budgeting process.

Net (Operating) Cash Flow
Cash inflow minus cash outflow. It is measured as the change in net operating earnings after taxes plus the change in depreciation minus the change in net working capital requirements associated with a particular investment project.

Capital budgeting is concerned primarily with the after-tax **net (operating) cash flows** (NCF) of a particular project, or change in cash inflows *minus* change in cash outflows. For any year during the life of a project, these may be defined as the change in operating earnings after taxes, ΔOEAT,[5] *plus* the change in capital cost allowance, ΔCCA, *minus* the change in the net working capital investment required by the firm to support the project, ΔNWC:[6]

$$(9.1) \qquad NCF = \Delta OEAT + \Delta CCA - \Delta NWC$$

The term *change* (Δ) refers to the difference in cash (and noncash) flows *with* and *without* adoption of the investment project.

In Canada, capital cost allowance (CCA) is the systematic allocation for tax purposes of the cost of an asset with an economic life in excess of one year.[7] Although CCA is not a cash flow, it does affect a firm's after-tax cash flows by reducing reported earnings and thereby reducing taxes paid by a firm. If a firm's CCA increases in a particular year as a result of adopting a project, after-tax net cash flow in that year will increase, all other things being equal.

After-tax net cash flow also considers changes in a firm's investment in net working capital.[8] If a firm increases its accounts receivable, for example, in a particular year without increasing its current liabilities as a result of adopting a specific project, after-tax net cash flow in that year will decrease, all other things being equal. On the other hand, a reduction in a firm's investment in net working capital during a given year results in an increase in the firm's NCF for that year.

From basic accounting definitions, the change in operating earnings after taxes (ΔOEAT) in Equation 9.1 is equal to the change in operating earnings before taxes (ΔOEBT) times $(1 - T)$, where T is the marginal corporate income tax rate. Furthermore, ΔOEBT is equal to the change in revenues (ΔR) minus the change in operating costs (ΔO) minus the change in CCA (ΔCCA). Substituting these terms in Equation 9.1 yields the following definition of net cash flow:

$$(9.2) \qquad NCF = (\Delta R - \Delta O - \Delta CCA)(1 - T) + \Delta CCA - \Delta NWC$$

$$= (\Delta R - \Delta O)(1 - T) + T\Delta CCA - \Delta NWC$$

---

[5] Operating earnings after tax, OEAT, differs from earnings after tax, EAT, because OEAT *does not* consider interest expenses in its calculation. Net cash flows, NCF, as used for capital budgeting purposes, do not normally consider financing charges, such as interest, because these financing charges will be reflected in the cost of capital that is used to discount a project's cash flows. To include financing charges in NCF would result in double-counting these costs.

[6] In years when a firm must increase its investment in net working capital (NWC) associated with a particular project, this increased investment in NWC *reduces* NCF. Normally, however, at the end of the life of a project, the NWC investment accumulated over the life of the project is recovered (for example, as inventories are sold and accounts receivable are collected). Thus, ΔNWC is negative (a reduction). Because of the minus sign before ΔNWC in Equation 9.1, the effect of a decline in the net working capital investments is an *increase* in NCF.

[7] Equation 9.1 provides an easy procedure for reflecting the cash flow impact of capital cost allowance.

[8] Changes in net working capital can occur as part of the net investment at time 0 or at any time during the life of the project.

In the final year n of a project's economic life, Equation 9.2 must be modified to reflect recovery of the incremental salvage value of the asset(s) and the present value at time n of any tax effects from CCA beyond the asset's economic life, including the impact of the incremental salvage value.

The following two sections illustrate the calculation of net cash flows using Equation 9.2.

Recovery of Salvage Value and Capital Cost Allowance Effects

In Canada, most tangible assets are assigned to declining balance asset classes for tax purposes by the capital cost allowance system. Table 9.2 summarizes the major asset classes.

The CCA system assumes that all assets acquired and placed into service during a taxation year are placed into service at midyear. That is, this **half-year convention** is required by law. Thus, an asset generates only half of the normal depreciation for tax purposes in its first year of service, irrespective of when during the year it is actually put into use. Table 9.3 illustrates the CCA generated in years 1 to 4 for a class 8 asset with an initial cost of $100,000.

Because of the half-year convention, note that in Table 9.3 only $10,000 (i.e., 10% × $100,000) of CCA can be taken in year 1 instead of the normal annual depreciation for tax purposes of $20,000 (i.e., 20% × $100,000) that would apply without the half-year convention. The **undepreciated capital cost** (UCC) of $90,000 at the end of year 1 represents the initial cost of $100,000 less the CCA of $10,000 for year 1. For year 2, the CCA of $18,000 represents 20 percent times the UCC of $90,000 at the end of year 1. The CCA for each successive year is then generated by applying the class 8 CCA rate of 20 percent to the UCC at the end of each previous year. This is the essence of a declining balance system.

Consider a project that consists of investing in the $100,000 class 8 asset with an economic life of 4 years. The asset will be sold for $40,000 net of removal costs on the *first* day of year 5.

How do we adjust the net cash flow at time 4 for this salvage value and its related CCA effects? The salvage value ΔS_n should simply be added to the components of the net cash flow specified by the right-hand side of Equation 9.2. In addition, the present

Half-Year Convention
Canadian law assumes that all assets placed into service during a taxation year are placed into service at midyear for CCA purposes, so only half of the normal amount of CCA is allowed in the first year of service.

Undepreciated Capital Cost (UCC)
The cost of a fixed asset that still remains on the books to be written off in the future. The CCA rate is applied each year to this declining balance.

Table 9.2	Selected Declining Balance Capital Cost Allowance Classes and Rates	
Class	CCA Rate	Assets in Class
1	4%	Most buildings acquired after 1987, including components
3	5%	Most buildings acquired after 1978 and before 1988
6	10%	Other buildings that do not have footings below ground
7	15%	Ships, scows, vessels, etc., and their equipment
8	20%	Property not included in any other class
9	25%	Aircraft, including components, and spare parts
10	30%	Automobiles, vans, trucks, etc., and EDP equipment
12	100%	Computer applications software, dies, jigs, small tools, etc.

Source: Canada Customs and Revenue Agency, 2001: *Business and Professional Tax Guide*

Table 9.3	CCA for a Class 8 Asset with Initial Cost = $100,000	
Year	Capital Cost Allowance (CCA)	Undepreciated Capital Cost (UCC)
1	$10,000	$90,000
2	$18,000	$72,000
3	$14,400	$57,600
4	$11,520	$46,080

Depreciation for Tax Purposes

Other countries, of course, have different methods for calculating depreciation for tax purposes. In the United States, where many Canadian firms have subsidiaries, the modified accelerated cost recovery system (MACRS) is used. MACRS also has a half-year convention just like the CCA system in Canada. However, MACRS differs in one important aspect because MACRS allows for the complete write-off of the cost of the asset. In Canada, the CCA rate is applied to declining balance of the asset class, so the declining balance becomes smaller as time passes but never reaches zero. In the US system, it does go to zero. Under MACRS, assets are also placed into classes, as shown in the table below.

MACRS Classes

Class	Type of Property in Class
3-year	Certain types of manufacturing tools
5-year	Vehicles, computers, and special equipment
7-year	Most industrial equipment
10-year	Certain types of longer-lived equipment
39-year	Nonresidential real property and buildings

When the MACRS went into force in 1993, it shortened the depreciable lives of assets, thus giving US businesses larger tax deductions than the previous system. Instead of a constant rate applied to a declining balance, the US system each year applies different rates, called cost recovery allowances, to the original cost of the asset, as shown in the table below.

MACRS Recovery Allowance Percentages
Class of Investment

Year	3-year	5-year	7-year	10-year
1	33%	20%	14%	10%
2	45%	32%	25%	18%
3	15%	19%	17%	14%
4	7%	12%	13%	12%
5		11%	9%	9%
6		6%	9%	7%
7			9%	7%
8			4%	7%
9				7%
10				6%
11				3%
	100%	100%	100%	100%

The Mexican system differs somewhat from both the Canadian and the US systems. Some other countries allow 100% write-off in the year of acquisition to encourage firms to invest.

value at time 4 of future tax savings due to CCA must be included. The present value of these future tax savings is given by Equation 9.3, where d is the capital cost allowance rate and k is the project's cost of capital. If the project is one of average risk, k will simply be the firm's weighted cost of capital. In Chapter 11, we will discuss how to estimate a project's cost of capital when a project is *not* of average risk.

$$(9.3) \qquad \text{PV of CCA tax savings} = \frac{Td(\Delta UCC_n - \Delta S_n)}{(k + d)}$$

Equation 9.3 is another example of the growth perpetuity Equation 4.29 developed in Chapter 4. The tax savings from incremental CCA in year $n + 1$ of $Td(\Delta UCC_n - \Delta S_n)$ represents the "first payment" of the growth perpetuity. This payment is declining at the rate d. That is, it is "growing" at the negative rate $g = -d$.

Note that Equation 9.3 would give a *negative* value when the salvage value ΔS_n is greater than the ΔUCC_n. Equation 9.3 still gives the correct CCA effect as long as ΔS_n is less than or equal to the initial cost of the asset (i.e., there are no capital gains) and as long as ΔS_n is less than the undepreciated capital cost of *all* the assets in the class (i.e., the asset class *remains open*).

Let us now apply Equation 9.3 to our project. Assume that the project's cost of capital is 10 percent and firm's marginal income tax rate is 40 percent. Then the present value at time 4 of the CCA tax savings generated beyond year 4 is

$$(9.4) \qquad \text{PV of CCA tax savings} = \frac{(.40)(.20)(\$46{,}080 - \$40{,}000)}{(.10 + .20)}$$

$$= \$1{,}621$$

Thus, we must add the $1,621 present value of tax savings as well as the salvage value of $40,000 to the net cash flow components for year 4 specified by Equation 9.2.

Half-Year Convention, Capital Gains, Closing the Asset Class, Disposal Date

Equation 9.3 represents the PV of CCA tax savings at the end of the economic life of the asset under analysis. This equation was derived under the following assumptions:

1. No assets in the same class will be purchased in the year in which this asset will be disposed.

2. The salvage value of this asset (net of any removal costs) will be less than its original cost (including any installation and shipping costs).

3. The salvage value of this asset (net of any removal costs) will be less than the undepreciated capital cost of the entire class, and it is *not* the last asset in the class.

4. The asset will be disposed of on the first day of the year following the end of its economic life.

In this section, we will examine the effect on Equation 9.3 of individually relaxing these assumptions.

Assumption 1 means that Equation 9.3 does not incorporate the half-year convention on the salvage value ΔS_n. Suppose one feels certain that the firm's purchases will exceed the salvage value of all assets disposed of in the class during this asset's disposal year. In this case, Equation 9.3 should be replaced by Equation 9.3a:

$$(9.3a) \qquad \text{PV of CCA tax savings} = \frac{Td\Delta UCC_n}{(k + d)} - \left[\frac{(1 + .5k)}{(1 + k)}\right]\left[\frac{\Delta S_n}{(k + d)}\right]$$

Note that this half-year convention factor $(1 + .5k)/(1 + k)$ applies only to ΔS_n. This is because the value of ΔUCC_n already incorporates the effect of the half-year convention.[9]

---

[9] The half-year convention factor also appears in Equation 10.3a in the next chapter. See footnote 1 of Chapter 10 if you are interested in its derivation.

Since the salvage value ΔS_n appears in Equation 9.3 with a negative sign, the impact of the half-year convention in Equation 9.3a for any positive salvage value combined with a positive discount rate will be to raise the PV of CCA tax savings.

For our project, the PV of CCA tax savings will rise from $1,621 to $2,106. This is a substantial percentage increase in the PV of CCA tax savings. Nevertheless, it is a small dollar amount compared with the salvage value of $40,000 and with the project's other cash flows.

Now let us examine the effect on Equation 9.3 when assumptions 1, 3, and 4 hold, but the firm sells this asset for more than its initial cost (including any installation and shipping costs). In the case of a new project, this is the incremental depreciable base ΔDB. Even though the firm has partially depreciated this base ΔDB, Canadian tax law permits ΔDB to be written off from the class when $\Delta S_n > \Delta DB$, as long as assumption 3 holds.

The difference $(\Delta S_n - \Delta DB)$ is subject to the capital gains tax, which in 2003 is half the rate of tax on ordinary income. Since by assumption 4 we are still assuming that the asset is disposed of on the first day of the year after its economic life ends, these capital gains taxes will be due at the end of the disposal year. Hence, in Equation 9.3b these taxes are discounted for one year:

$$(9.3b) \quad \text{PV of CCA tax savings} = \frac{Td(\Delta UCC_n - \Delta DB)}{(k + d)} - \frac{(\Delta S_n - \Delta DB)(0.5T)}{(1 + k)}$$

For our class 8 asset with an initial cost of $100,000, suppose that its salvage value is now $150,000 instead of $40,000. Then the PV of CCA tax savings becomes

$$\text{PV of CCA tax savings} =$$

$$\frac{(.40)(.20)(\$46,080 - \$100,000)}{(.10 + .20)} - \left[\frac{(\$150,000 - \$100,000)(0.5 \times .40)}{(1.10)} \right]$$

$$= -\$14,379 - \$9,091 = -\$23,470$$

This represents quite a change from the value of $1,621 that we found in Equation 9.4. Remember, however, that the salvage value itself has increased from $40,000 to $150,000, which represents a net increase in cash flow of $110,000 for this item.

Now let us consider what happens when the asset class is closed but assumptions 1, 2, and 4 hold.

To simplify this discussion, we will assume that this asset is the only asset that was ever in the class. (This is the most likely case for an asset class being closed, as asset classes are rarely closed for a growing firm with many assets in a class.) Then the PV of CCA tax savings becomes Equation 9.3c:

$$(9.3c) \quad \text{PV of CCA tax savings} = \frac{T(\Delta UCC_n - \Delta S_n)}{(1 + k)}$$

The tax savings is positive if $\Delta UCC_n > \Delta S_n$, because $(\Delta UCC_n - \Delta S_n)$ is treated as an ordinary loss for tax purposes in this case. Similarly, taxes are owing (i.e., a negative tax savings) if $(\Delta UCC_n - \Delta S_n)$ is negative and is considered a recapture of CCA taxable as ordinary income in this case. (The discount factor $1/(1 + k)$ would not be needed if the asset were sold on the last day of its economic life instead of on the first day of the next year.)

Returning to our numerical example with salvage value of $40,000, the PV of CCA tax savings would now be

$$\text{PV of CCA tax savings} = \frac{(.40)(\$46,080 - \$40,000)}{1.10}$$

$$= \$2,211$$

If this asset were sold on the last day of the last year of its economic life, then PV of CCA tax savings = (.40)($46,080 − $40,000) = $2,432.

Finally, let's sell this asset on the last day of its economic life but the asset class remains open (assumption 3 holds) and assumptions 1 and 2 also hold. Then the CCA tax shields lost due to the salvage value ΔS_n all move toward the end of the asset's economic life by one year. This simply requires ΔS_n to be multiplied by $(1 + k)$ to undo the discounting by one year. Equation 9.3d now gives the correct PV of CCA tax savings:

$$(9.3d) \qquad \text{PV of CCA tax savings} = \frac{Td\Delta UCC_n}{(k + d)} - \left[\frac{(1 + k)Td\Delta S_n}{(k + d)} \right]$$

The PV of CCA tax savings for our numerical example then becomes

$$\text{PV of CCA tax savings} = \frac{(.40)(.20)($46,080)}{(.10 + .20)} - \left[\frac{(1.10)(.40)(.20)($40,000)}{(.10 + .20)} \right]$$

$$= $12,288 - $11,733 = $555$$

Recovery of Net Working Capital

At the end of a project's life, all net working capital additions required over the project's life are recovered—not just the initial net working capital outlay occurring at time 0. Hence, the total accumulated net working capital is normally recovered in the last year of the project. This *decrease* in net working capital in the last year of the project *increases* the net cash flow for that year, all other things being equal. Of course, no tax consequences are associated with the recovery of NWC.

Interest Charges and Net Cash Flows

Often the purchase of a particular asset is tied closely to the creation of some debt obligation, such as the sale of mortgage bonds or a bank loan. Nevertheless, it is generally considered *incorrect* to deduct the interest charges associated with a particular project from the estimated cash flows. This is true for two reasons.

First, the decision about how a firm should be financed can—and should—be made independently of the decision to accept or reject one or more projects. Instead, the firm should seek some combination of debt, equity (common shares), and preferred shares that is consistent with management's wishes concerning the trade-off between financial risk and the cost of capital. In many cases, this will result in a capital structure with the cost of capital at or near its minimum. Because investment and financing decisions should normally be made independently of one another, each new project can be viewed as being financed with the same proportions of the various sources of capital funds used to finance the firm as a whole.

Second, when a discounting framework is used for project evaluation, the discount rate, or cost of capital, already incorporates the cost of funds used to finance a project. Thus, including interest charges in cash flow calculations essentially would result in a double counting of costs.

Asset Expansion Projects

A project that requires a firm to invest funds in additional assets in order to increase sales (or reduce costs) is called an *asset expansion project*. For example, suppose the TLC Yogurt Company has decided to capitalize on the exercise fad and plans to open an exercise facility in conjunction with its main yogurt and health foods store. To get the project under way, the company will rent additional space adjacent to its current store. The equipment required for the facility will cost $95,000. Shipping and installation charges for the equipment are expected to total $5,000. This equipment will be placed in class 8 with a CCA rate of 20 percent. The estimated net salvage value is $40,000 at the end of its economic life of 4 years. In order to open the exercise facility, TLC estimates that it will have to add about $7,000 initially to its net working capital in the form of additional inventories of exercise supplies, cash, and accounts receivable for its exercise customers (less accounts payable). TLC estimates this project's cost of capital is 10 percent.

During the first year of operations, TLC expects its total revenues (from yogurt sales and exercise services) to increase by $50,000 above the level that would have prevailed without the exercise facility addition. These incremental revenues are expected to grow to $60,000 in year 2, $75,000 in year 3, and decline to $60,000 in year 4. The company's incremental operating costs associated with the exercise facility, including the rental of the facility, are expected to total $25,000 during the first year and increase at a rate of 6 percent per year over the four-year project life. Since the installed cost of the project is $100,000 ($95,000 for the equipment and $5,000 for installation and shipping), the relevant yearly capital cost allowances are given in Table 9.3, and the present value at time 4 of the CCA tax savings beyond year 4 is given by Equation 9.4 as $1,621. TLC has a marginal tax rate of 40 percent. In addition, TLC expects that it will have to add about $5,000 per year to its net working capital in years 1, 2, and 3 and nothing in year 4. At the end of the project, the total accumulated net working capital required by the project will be recovered.

Calculating the Net Investment

First, we determine the net investment required for the exercise facility expansion. TLC must make a cash outlay of $95,000 to pay for the facility equipment. In addition, it must pay $5,000 in cash to cover the costs of shipping and installation of the equipment. Finally, TLC must invest $7,000 in initial net working capital to get the project under way.

The two-step procedure discussed earlier for first calculating the net installed cost and then the net investment yields the NINV required at time 0:

Purchase price of exercise equipment	$ 95,000
Plus Shipping and installation	5,000
Equals Net installed cost	100,000
Plus Initial net working capital required	7,000
Equals Net investment	$107,000

Calculating Annual Net Cash Flows

Next, we need to calculate the annual net cash flows associated with the project. Using Equation 9.2, these cash flows can be computed as shown in Table 9.4.

Table 9.4 Calculation of TLC Annual Net Cash Flows

	Year 1	Year 2	Year 3	Year 4
Change in revenues (ΔR)	$50,000	$60,000	$75,000	$60,000
Minus Change in operating costs (ΔO)	−25,000	−26,500	−28,090	−29,775
Equals Net operating revenues ($\Delta R - \Delta O$)	$25,000	$33,500	$46,910	$30,225
Minus Taxes ignoring CCA tax savings $T(\Delta R - \Delta O)$	−10,000	−13,400	−18,764	−12,090
Equals After tax net operating revenues $(1 - T)(\Delta R - \Delta O)$	$15,000	$20,100	$28,146	$18,135
Plus CCA tax savings ($T\Delta CCA$)	4,000	7,200	5,760	4,608
Minus Change in net working capital (ΔNWC)	−5,000	−5,000	−5,000	22,000
Plus Net salvage value (ΔS)	0	0	0	40,000
Plus PV of future CCA savings $Td(\Delta UCC - \Delta S)/(k + d)$	0	0	0	1,621
Equals Net cash flow (NCF)	$14,000	$22,300	$28,906	$86,364

The cash flows associated with the exercise facility project can be summarized as follows:

Year	Net Investment and Net Cash Flows
0	−$107,000
1	14,000
2	22,300
3	28,906
4	86,364

In Chapter 10, several different capital budgeting decision models are applied to cash flows such as these to determine the desirability of capital investment projects.

Asset Replacement Projects

The previous example of an asset expansion project illustrated the key elements of the calculation of a project's net investment and its annual net cash flows. In this section, we consider an *asset replacement* project. Asset replacements involve retiring one asset and replacing it with a more efficient asset.

Suppose Howie's Machine Shop Corporation purchased an automated drill press 10 years ago that had an estimated economic life of 20 years. The drill press originally cost $150,000, was placed in class 8 with a CCA rate of 20 percent, and has a current undepreciated capital cost of $18,120. The actual market value of this drill press is $40,000. The firm is considering replacing the drill press with a new one costing $190,000. Shipping and installation charges will add an additional $10,000 to the cost. The new machine will also be placed in class 8. The new machine is expected to have a 10-year economic life. The net salvage value of the new machine in 10 years is estimated to be $25,000. If kept, the old machine has an estimated net salvage value of $1,000 in 10 years. The firm's current marginal tax rate is 40 percent. The firm's project cost of capital for this replacement decision is 15 percent. Assume also that the company's initial incremental net working capital increases by $1,500 as a result of replacing the drill press.

Calculating the Net Investment

Steps 1 and 2 of the net investment calculation are easy and are summarized in Table 9.5. The new project cost ($190,000) plus shipping and installation ($10,000) minus the net salvage value ($40,000) of the old asset equals a net installed cost (i.e., an incremental depreciable base) of $160,000. The original cost of the old asset is irrelevant for this replacement decision because the asset will be sold for less than its original cost. The undepreciated capital cost (UCC) of the old asset is also irrelevant for this replacement decision. This is because class 8 will remain open and the UCC of the old asset makes no *incremental* contribution to the depreciable base of the class and hence to the CCAs generated by the replacement decision. In effect, this old UCC remains on the books irrespective of the replacement decision. Hence, deducting the salvage value of $40,000 for the old asset is all that is required to obtain the incremental depreciable base of

Table 9.5 Net Investment Calculation	
Cost of new drill press	$190,000
Plus Shipping and installation costs	10,000
Equals Gross installed cost	$200,000
Minus Salvage value of old machine	40,000
Equals Net installed cost	$160,000
Plus Increase in initial working capital	1,500
Equals Net investment	$161,500

$160,000 shown in Table 9.5. Since the initial incremental net working capital increases by $1,500 in this example, the NINV is $161,500.

Calculating Annual Net Cash Flows

Suppose Howie's Machine Shop Corporation expects annual revenues during the project's first year to increase from $70,000 to $85,000 if the new drill press is purchased. (This might occur because the new press is faster than the old one and can meet the increasing demands for more work.) After the first year, revenues from the new project are expected to increase at a rate of $2,000 a year for the remainder of the project life.[10] The required incremental net working capital will be $200 at the end of each year for years 1 through 9. The cumulative increase in incremental net working capital of $3,300 ($1,500 initial increase + [9][$200]) will be returned at the end of year 10. Assume further that while the old drill press required two operators, the new drill press is more automated and needs only one, thereby reducing annual operating costs from $40,000 to $20,000 during the project's first year. After the first year, annual operating costs of the new drill press are expected to increase by $1,000 a year over the remaining life of the project.[11]

The first-year net cash flow from replacing the old drill press is computed by substituting into Equation 9.2:

Year 1:

$$
\begin{aligned}
NCF_1 &= [(\$85,000 - \$70,000) - (\$20,000 - \$40,000)](1 - 0.4) \\
&\quad + (0.4)(\$16,000) - \$200 \\
&= \$21,000 + \$6,400 - \$200 \\
&= \$27,200
\end{aligned}
$$

Using the different expected values for new revenues of $87,000 and new operating costs of $21,000 in the second year, the second-year net cash flows can be computed as follows:

Year 2:

$$
\begin{aligned}
NCF_2 &= [(\$87,000 - \$70,000) - (\$21,000 - \$40,000)](1 - 0.4) \\
&\quad + (0.4)(\$28,800) - \$200 \\
&= \$21,600 + \$11,520 - \$200 \\
&= \$32,920
\end{aligned}
$$

Similar calculations are used to obtain the net cash flows in years 3 through 9.

Finally, in year 10, the $24,000 *incremental* net salvage value ($25,000 − $1,000) must be added, along with the present value at time 10 of the future tax savings from *incremental* CCA. Note that the UCC of the old machine plays no role. Incremental UCC at time 10 arises solely from the incremental depreciable base or net installed cost of $160,000. This incremental UCC is $19,327. In other words, this UCC of $19,327 is the incremental depreciable base of $160,000 *less* the sum of the incremental CCA for years 1 through 10 of $140,673. Now substitute into Equation 9.3 to obtain the present value at time 10 of future incremental CCA tax savings of −$1,068:

$$
\text{PV of future CCA tax savings} = \frac{(.40)(.20)(\$19,327 - \$24,000)}{(.15 + .20)} = -\$1,068
$$

How can we write off an incremental salvage value of $24,000 if the incremental UCC at time 10 is only $19,327? The only assumption required is that the firm is a going

---

[10] For simplicity, we have assumed that the revenue figure of $70,000 without the project remains constant over the life of the project.

[11] For simplicity, we have assumed that the operating cost figure of $40,000 without the project remains constant over the life of the project.

concern that has more than $24,000 *in total* on its books for class 8 at time 10. Now let us combine our incremental salvage value of $24,000 and present value at time 10 of the future value of incremental CCA tax savings of $-\$1,068$ with the net cash flow components of Equation 9.2 to obtain the net cash flow for period 10:

$$
\begin{aligned}
\text{NCF}_{10} &= [(\$103,000 - \$70,000) - (\$29,000 - \$40,000)](1 - 0.4) \\
&\quad + (0.4)(\$4,832) + \$3,300 + \$24,000 - \$1,068 \\
&= \$26,400 + \$1,933 + \$3,300 + \$24,000 - \$1,068 \\
&= \$54,565
\end{aligned}
$$

Table 9.6 is a summary worksheet for computing the net cash flows for this replacement decision.

Table 9.7 summarizes the net cash flows for the entire project. The cash flows developed in this chapter are an essential input in the capital budgeting decision process.

Problems in Cash Flow Estimation

Because project cash flows occur in the future, there are varying degrees of *uncertainty* about the value of these flows. Therefore, it is difficult to predict the actual cash flows of a project. The capital budgeting process assumes that the decision maker is able to estimate cash flows accurately enough that these estimates can be used in project evaluation

Table 9.6   Annual Net Cash Flow Worksheet for Howie's Project

	Year 1	Year 2	Year 3	Year 4	Year 5	Year 6	Year 7	Year 8	Year 9	Year 10
ΔR	15,000	17,000	19,000	21,000	23,000	25,000	27,000	29,000	31,000	33,000
$-\Delta O$*	20,000	19,000	18,000	17,000	16,000	15,000	14,000	13,000	12,000	11,000
$= (\Delta R - \Delta O)$	35,000	36,000	37,000	38,000	39,000	40,000	41,000	42,000	43,000	44,000
$- T(\Delta R - \Delta O)$	$-14,000$	$-14,400$	$-14,800$	$-15,200$	$-15,600$	$-16,000$	$-16,400$	$-16,800$	$-17,200$	$-17,600$
$= (1 - T)(\Delta R - \Delta O)$	21,000	21,600	22,200	22,800	23,400	24,000	24,600	25,200	25,800	26,400
$+ T\Delta CCA$	6,400	11,520	9,216	7,373	5,898	4,718	3,775	3,020	2,416	1,933
$- \Delta NWC$	-200	-200	-200	-200	-200	-200	-200	-200	-200	$-3,300$
$+ \Delta S$	0	0	0	0	0	0	0	0	0	24,000
$+ Td(\Delta UCC - \Delta S)/(k + d)$	0	0	0	0	0	0	0	0	0	$-1,068$
$= \text{NCF}$	$27,200	$32,920	$31,216	$29,973	$29,098	$28,518	$28,175	$28,020	$28,016	$54,565

*In this particular example, ΔO each year is negative. Hence, $-\Delta O$ is positive.

Table 9.7   Summary Project Cash Flows for Howie's Project

Year	Net Investment and Net Cash Flows
0	$-\$161,500$
1	$27,200
2	$32,920
3	$31,216
4	$29,973
5	$29,098
6	$28,518
7	$28,175
8	$28,020
9	$28,016
10	$54,565

ETHICAL ISSUES

Cash Flow Estimation Biases

The estimation of the cash flows associated with an investment project is the most important step in the capital expenditure evaluation process. If the cash flow estimates associated with a project are intentionally or unintentionally biased, a firm's resources are unlikely to be allocated to the set of investment projects that will maximize shareholder wealth.

There are several reasons why managers might produce biased cash flow estimates when preparing capital expenditure project proposals. First, a manager might be tempted to overestimate the revenues or underestimate the costs associated with a project if the manager is attempting to expand the resource base over which the manager has control. By biasing the estimates of a project's cash flows upward, a manager is likely to receive a larger share of the investment resources of the firm. Because managerial compensation is sometimes tied to the span of job responsibilities, managers may be tempted to expand this span of control at the expense of other areas in the firm.

Second, some firms tie employee compensation to performance relative to stated objectives—a compensation scheme often called *management by objectives*. If a manager is confident that the best estimate of the cash flows from a proposed project is sufficiently large to guarantee project acceptance, the manager may be tempted to reduce these cash flow estimates to a level below the "most likely outcome" level, confident that the project will continue to be viewed as an acceptable investment and that it will be funded. However, once the project is under way, the project manager will feel less pressure to meet projected performance standards. The downward bias in the cash flow estimates provides a cushion that permits suboptimal management of the project while achieving the objectives enunciated when the project was first proposed.

What impact does intentionally biasing cash flow estimates for investment projects have on achieving the goal of shareholder wealth maximization?

and selection. For this assumption to be realistic, a project proposal should be based on inputs from marketing managers regarding revenue estimates and inputs from the production and engineering staffs regarding costs and achievable levels of performance. Objective inputs from these sources can help reduce the uncertainty associated with cash flow estimation.

In addition, cash flow estimates for different projects may have varying degrees of uncertainty. For example, the returns from asset replacement projects are generally easier to forecast than the returns from new product introduction projects. Chapter 11 discusses some of the techniques used to incorporate risk analysis into capital budgeting decision models.

The Practice of Cash Flow Estimation for Capital Budgeting

The analysis presented in this chapter and throughout the book suggests that generating accurate estimates of the cash flows from investment projects is extremely important to the success of the firm. A survey supports this conclusion and provides considerable insight regarding the cash flow estimation procedures used by larger firms.[12]

The majority of the firms responding to the survey had annual capital budgets of more than $100 million. Nearly 67 percent of the firms prepared formal cash flow estimates for over 60 percent of their annual capital outlays, and a majority produced detailed cash flow projections for capital investments requiring an initial outlay of $40,000 or more. Firms with high capital intensity and high leverage were more likely to have one or more persons, such as a financial analyst, treasurer, controller, or department manager, designated to oversee the process of cash flow estimation. This reflects the larger number of projects associated with capital-intensive firms and the need to effectively manage the risk associated with high leverage.

When asked about the type of cash flow estimates that were generated, 56 percent indicated that they used single-dollar estimates, 8 percent used a range of estimates, and 36 percent used both single-dollar estimates and a range of estimates. There was a significant positive correlation between firms that use both types of estimates and measures of operating and financial risk, suggesting that the use of a range of estimates is one procedure for managing high risk.

Forecasting methods employed by the respondent firms included subjective estimates from management, sensitivity analysis, consensus analysis of expert opinions, and computer simulation. Many firms used multiple cash flow forecasting techniques. The longer the forecasting horizon—that is, the longer the economic life of the project—the more likely a firm is to use multiple methods for forecasting future cash flows.

Financial factors considered to be important in generating cash flow estimates include working capital requirements, project risk, tax considerations, the project's impact on the firm's liquidity, the anticipated rate of inflation, and expected salvage value. Important marketing factors considered include sales forecasts, the competitive advantages and disadvantages of the product, and product life. Important production factors include operating expenses, material and supply costs, overhead and expenses for manufacturing, capacity utilization, and start-up costs.

Three-fourths of the companies surveyed make comparisons between actual and projected cash flows, with nearly all of the firms comparing actual versus projected initial outlays and operating cash flows over the project life. About two-thirds of these firms make comparisons of actual versus projected salvage values. The most accurate cash flow estimates are reported to be the initial outlay estimates, and the least accurate element of cash flow estimates is the annual operating cash flows. Cash flow forecasts were more accurate for equipment replacement investments than for expansion and modernization investments or for acquisitions of ongoing businesses. Firms with the information system in place to generate cash flow forecasts tend to produce more accurate forecasts than firms with less sophisticated capital project evaluation procedures.

---

[12] Janet D. Payne, Will Carrington Heath, and Lewis R. Gale, "Comparative Financial Practice in the US and Canada: Capital Budgeting and Risk Assessment Techniques." *Financial Practice and Education* (Spring/Summer 1999): 16–24.

Chapter 9 Capital Budgeting and Cash Flow Analysis **345**

Although this chapter focused on the cash flows that are expected to be obtained from an investment, it must be kept in mind that every investment must fit into the firm's strategy. Most firms have a vision about what they wish to become and a mission statement that indicates what business they are in at the present time. There is usually a gap between where the firm is now and where it wants to be in, say, five years. Firms usually need to invest to reach their objectives. They can buy another firm or just some of its assets, for example, thus growing externally. They can invest by building new factories and/or installing new equipment, thus growing internally. In either case they make the decision by comparing the expected incremental net cash flows to the net investment to see if the investment project adds value to the firm. If it adds value, then the firm should invest. If it does not add value, then the firm should not invest. The next chapter will consider this topic in more detail.

Summary

- *Capital budgeting* is the process of planning for purchases of assets whose returns are expected to continue beyond one year.

- Projects may be classified as *independent, mutually exclusive,* or *contingent.* The acceptance of an independent project does not directly eliminate other projects from consideration. The acceptance of a mutually exclusive project precludes other alternatives. The acceptance of a contingent project depends on the adoption of one or more other projects.

- Projects also may be grouped into projects *generated by growth opportunities*, projects *generated by cost reduction opportunities*, and projects *generated to meet legal requirements and health and safety standards.*

- Projects may be categorized as *asset expansions* or *asset replacements.* An asset expansion project requires a firm to invest funds in additional assets to increase sales or reduce costs. Asset replacements, in contrast, involve retiring one asset and replacing it with a more efficient one.

- There are four basic steps in the capital budgeting process: *the generation of proposals, the estimation of cash flows, the evaluation and selection of alternatives,* and *the post-audit or review.*

- The optimal capital budget represents the level of investment in selected projects where the *marginal cost of capital* (MCC) curve intersects the *investment opportunity curve* (IOC).

- Resources of a firm used in an investment project should be valued at their *opportunity cost* based on the cash flows these resources could generate in their next-best alternative use.

- *Sunk costs* represent outlays that have already been made or committed and that cannot be recovered. Sunk costs should not be considered when evaluating an investment project.

- *Capital cost allowance* (CCA) is depreciation for tax purposes in Canada. Most asset classes in the CCA system are declining balance classes.

- *Undepreciated capital cost* (UCC) is the remaining balance in an asset class. The CCA rate is applied to the UCC to determine the annual capital cost allowance.

- The CCA system assumes that all assets acquired and placed into service during a taxation year are put in use at midyear of the first year. This *half-year convention* is required by law.

- The *net installed cost* or *incremental depreciable base* (ΔDB) for a project increases the firm's UCC. The incremental depreciable base is the new project cost (less the net salvage value of the old assets, if applicable) *plus* installation and shipping costs.

- The *net investment* (NINV) in a project is the net cash outlay required to place the project in service. It includes the incremental depreciable base *plus* any necessary increases in initial net working capital.

- The *net (operating) cash flows* (NCF) from a project are the incremental changes in a firm's operating cash flows that result from investing in the project. These flows include the changes in the firm's revenues, operating costs, capital cost allowance (CCA), taxes, and net working capital with and without the project. In the last year of a project's life, this net cash flow definition typically must be modified to reflect incremental salvage value received and its related tax effects.

- Project cash flows should be measured on an *incremental after-tax* basis and should include all of the indirect effects the project will have on the firm. The economic viability of a project as well as its cash flows can be affected by special tax considerations, such as the use of scientific research and development tax credits, investment tax credits, and/or grants from the federal and/or provincial governments.

Questions and Topics for Discussion

1. Discuss how capital budgeting procedures might be used by each of the following:
   a. Personnel managers
   b. Research and development staffs
   c. Advertising executives
2. What is a mutually exclusive investment project? An independent project? A contingent project? Give an example of each.
3. What effect does capital rationing have on a firm's ability to maximize shareholder wealth?
4. What are the primary types of capital investment projects? Does a project's type influence how it is analyzed?
5. Cash flows for a particular project should be measured on an incremental basis and should consider all the indirect effects of the project. What does this involve?
6. What factors should be considered when estimating a project's NINV?
7. Capital cost allowance (CCA) is a noncash expense. Why is it considered when estimating a project's net cash flows?
8. What are the potential tax consequences of selling an old asset in an asset replacement investment decision?
9. Why is it generally incorrect to consider interest charges when computing a project's net cash flows?
10. Distinguish between asset expansion and asset replacement projects. How does this distinction affect the capital expenditure analysis process?
11. How is the opportunity cost concept used in the capital budgeting process?

Self-Test Problems

ST1. The F Company, a food distributor, is considering replacing a filling line at its warehouse. The existing line was purchased several years ago for $600,000. The line's UCC is $200,000, and management feels it could be sold at this time for $150,000. A new, increased-capacity line can be purchased for $1,200,000. Delivery and installation of the new line are expected to cost an additional $100,000. Both filling lines are included in class 8 with a CCA rate of 20%. The firm's marginal tax rate is 40%. Calculate the net investment for the new line.

ST2. IFC currently processes seafood with a computer-controlled unit it purchased several years ago. The unit, which originally cost $500,000, currently has a UCC of $250,000. IFC is considering replacing the existing unit with a newer, more efficient one. The new unit will cost $700,000 and will require an additional $50,000 for delivery and installation. The new unit will also require IFC to increase its investment in initial net working capital by $40,000. Both units are class 10 assets with a CCA rate of 30%. IFC expects to sell the existing unit for $275,000. IFC's marginal tax rate is 40% and this project's cost of capital is 10%.

If IFC purchases the new unit, annual revenues are expected to increase by $100,000 (due to increased processing capacity), and annual operating costs (exclusive of CCA) are expected to decrease by $20,000. Annual revenues and operating costs are expected to remain constant at this new level over the five-year life of the project. IFC estimates that its net working capital investment will increase by $10,000 per year over the life of the project, except that in the last year it will recover all of its additions to net working capital. After five years, the salvage value of the new unit is expected to be $70,000. If the firm continues to use the old unit, its expected net salvage value is $20,000.

a. Calculate the project's net investment (NINV).

b. Calculate the annual net cash flows for the project.

Problems*

BASIC

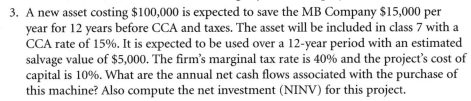

1. Calculate the annual CCA for an asset in class 10 with a CCA rate of 30% that costs $50,000, has installation and shipping costs that total $1,000, and has an economic life of 10 years. The firm's marginal tax rate is 40%.

2. JP Company is considering purchasing a new asset in class 16 (with a CCA rate of 40%) that costs $100,000. The asset's installation and shipping costs will total $2,500. If accepted, the project will require an initial net working capital investment of $20,000. JP plans to use the asset over a period of eight years. About a year ago, JP paid $10,000 to a consulting firm to conduct a feasibility study of the new asset. JP's marginal tax rate is 40%.

   a. Calculate the project's net investment (NINV).

   b. Calculate the CCA for each of the eight years of the project.

3. A new asset costing $100,000 is expected to save the MB Company $15,000 per year for 12 years before CCA and taxes. The asset will be included in class 7 with a CCA rate of 15%. It is expected to be used over a 12-year period with an estimated salvage value of $5,000. The firm's marginal tax rate is 40% and the project's cost of capital is 10%. What are the annual net cash flows associated with the purchase of this machine? Also compute the net investment (NINV) for this project.

---

*Coloured numbers and letters denote problems that have "check" answers provided at the back of the book.

4. The JC Company is considering building a new potassium sulphate plant. The following cash outlays are required to complete the plant:

Year	Cash Outlay
0	$4,000,000
1	$2,000,000
2	$500,000

JC's cost of capital is 12%, and its marginal tax rate is 40%.
   a. Calculate the plant's net investment (NINV).
   b. What is the installed cost of the plant for tax purposes?

 Excel

5. The TMU Company currently has annual cash revenues of $1.2 million and annual cash expenses of $700,000. These figures are expected to remain constant for the foreseeable future (at least 10 years). The firm's marginal tax rate is 40% and the project's cost of capital is 10%.

   A new high-speed processing unit costing $1.2 million is being considered as a potential investment designed to increase the firm's output capacity. This new piece of class 8 equipment with a CCA rate of 20% will have an estimated usable life of 10 years and a $100,000 estimated salvage value. If the processing unit is bought, Taylor's annual revenues are expected to increase to $1.6 million and annual expenses will increase to $900,000. Assume that no increase in net working capital will be required as a result of this project. Compute the project's annual net cash flows for the next 10 years, assuming that the new processing unit is purchased. Also compute the net investment (NINV) for this project.

INTERMEDIATE

6. The CE Company has developed the following schedule of potential investment projects that may be undertaken during the next six months:

Project	Cost in $Millions	Expected Rate of Return
A	$3.0	20%
B	$1.5	22%
C	$7.0	7%
D	$14.0	10%
E	$50.0	12%
F	$12.0	9%
G	$1.0	44%

   a. If CE requires a minimum rate of return of 10% on all investments, which projects should be adopted?
   b. In general, how would a capital budgeting constraint on the available amount of investment funds influence these decisions?
   c. How would differing levels of project risk influence these decisions?

7. A firm has an opportunity to invest in a new device that will replace two of the firm's older machines. The new device costs $570,000 and requires an additional outlay of $30,000 to cover installation and shipping. The new device will cause the firm to increase its net working capital by $20,000. Both of the old machines can be sold—the first for $100,000 (UCC equals $95,000) and the second for $150,000 (UCC equals $75,000). The original cost of the first machine was $200,000, and the original cost of the second machine was $160,000. The firm's marginal tax rate is 40%. Compute the net investment for this project.

Excel

8. N Inc. is considering the purchase of a new ICX computer system for $130,000. The system will require an additional $30,000 for installation. If the new computer is purchased, it will replace an old system that has a UCC of $19,681. Both systems are included in class 10 with a CCA rate of 30%. If the ICX is purchased, the old system will be sold for $20,000. The ICX system, which has a useful life of 10 years, is expected to increase revenues by $32,000 *per year* over its useful life. Operating costs are expected to decrease by $2,000 *per year* over the life of the system. The firm is taxed at a 40% marginal rate and it uses a 12% discount rate to evaluate replacement projects. The salvage value of the new computer will be $5,000 after 10 years, whereas the salvage value of the old computer will be $1,000 after 10 years if it is not replaced.

   a. What net investment is required to acquire the ICX system and replace the old system?

   b. Compute the annual net cash flows associated with the purchase of the ICX system.

9. HSI, which operates a chain of retail warehouse-type stores, is considering opening a new store in the Toronto area. The store itself will cost $7,000,000 to build and will be included in class 1. In addition, fixtures for the store are expected to cost $700,000, and installation of the fixtures is estimated to cost another $50,000. These assets will be included in class 8, which has a CCA rate of 20%. Initial net working capital (primarily due to inventory) is expected to be $600,000. HSI plans to build the Toronto store on land it purchased five years ago for $200,000. The land is presently worth $500,000 and is expected to remain at $500,000 while the store is being built. Calculate the net investment for the proposed Toronto store.

Excel

10. Hay Enterprises, a successful imaging products firm, is considering expanding into the lucrative laser-engraved self-portrait business. It is expected that this new business will generate first-year revenues of $2 million. These revenues are expected to grow at 10% per year for the next eight years. Year 1 incremental operating costs of this new business are expected to total $800,000 and to grow at 6% per year for the next eight years. The firm's marginal tax rate is 40%. CCA expenses are expected to be $100,000 during year 1, $200,000 during year 2, and $150,000 during year 3. Capital outlays required at time 0 total $2 million, and another $500,000 will be required at the end of year 1. Net working capital investments of $50,000, $75,000, and $85,000 are expected at the end of years 1, 2, and 3 respectively. Calculate the expected net cash flows for year 3.

CHALLENGE

Excel

11. B Inc. is planning to open a new sporting goods store in a suburban mall. The firm will lease the needed space in the mall. Equipment and fixtures for the store will cost $200,000 and be included in class 8, with a CCA rate of 20%. The new store will require B Inc. to increase its net working capital by $200,000 at time 0. First-year sales are expected to be $1 million and to increase at an annual rate of 8% over the expected 10-year life of the store. Operating expenses (including lease payments and excluding CCA) are projected to be $700,000 during the first year and increase at a 7% annual rate. The salvage value of the store's equipment and fixtures is anticipated to be $10,000 at the end of 10 years. B Inc.'s marginal tax rate is 40% and its cost of capital is 15%.

   a. Compute the required net investment (NINV).

   b. Compute the annual net cash flows for the 10-year projected life of the store.

Excel

12. AM Company is evaluating the possibility of expanding its operations. This expansion will require the purchase of land at a cost of $100,000. A new building will cost $100,000 and will be included in class 6 with a CCA rate of 10%. At the end of 20 years, its expected salvage value is $10,000. Actual land salvage at the

end of 20 years is expected to be $200,000. Equipment for the facility is expected to cost $250,000. Installation costs will be an additional $40,000 and shipping costs will be $10,000. This equipment will be included in class 8 with a CCA rate of 20%. Actual estimated salvage at the end of 20 years is $5,000. The project will require net working capital of $70,000 initially (year 0), an additional $40,000 at the end of year 1, and an additional $40,000 at the end of year 2. The project is expected to generate increased EBIT (operating income) for the firm of $100,000 during year 1. Annual EBIT is expected to grow at a rate of 4% per year until the project terminates at the end of year 20. The marginal tax rate is 40% and the cost of capital is 14%. Compute the initial net investment and the annual net cash flow from the project in year 20.

 Excel

13. RBW is planning to add a new product line that will require the acquisition of a new class 8 machine with CCA rate of 20%. The machine will cost $1,000,000. Interest costs associated with financing the equipment purchase are estimated to be $50,000 per year. The expected salvage value of the machine at the end of 10 years is $50,000. The decision to add the new product line will require additional net working capital of $50,000 immediately, $25,000 at the end of year 1, and $10,000 at the end of year 2. RBW expects to sell $300,000 worth of the new product during each of the 10 years of product life. RBW expects the sales of its other products to decline by $25,000 (in year 1) as a result of adding this new line. The lost sales level will remain constant at $25,000 over the 10-year life of the proposed project. The cost of producing and selling the new products is estimated to be $50,000 per year. RBW will realize savings of $5,000 each year because of lost sales on its other lines. The marginal tax rate is 40% and the cost of capital is 20%. Compute the net investment (year 0) and the net cash flows for years 1 and 10 for this project.

 Excel

14. BSW is considering an expansion proposal that will require an outlay of $1 million for land and $5 million for equipment. The equipment will be included in class 8 with a CCA rate of 20%. The salvage value of the equipment at the end of 10 years is expected to be $1 million. The actual life of the project is expected to be 10 years. At the end of 10 years, BSW hopes to sell the land for $1,800,000. Revenues from the project are expected to be $700,000 per year. Operating costs are expected to be $200,000 per year. The tax rate for BSW is 40% and the cost of capital is 16%. The project will require an additional investment in working capital of $250,000 in year 0 and $150,000 at the end of year 1. What net cash flow will this project produce in year 10?

 Excel

15. LQ Inc., a highly profitable maker of customized chariots, is planning to introduce a new model shortly. The firm must purchase equipment immediately at a cost of $900,000. Freight and installation costs for this equipment will be $100,000. The equipment will be included in class 8 with a CCA rate of 20%. During the first year, LQ will have incremental operating expenses of $300,000 that are attributable to this project. LQ expects to be able to sell 1,000 chariots during year 2 at an average price of $800 each and to incur operating expenses of $300,000. Also, LQ expects its net working capital investment will increase by $50,000 during year 2. (Assume all operating costs and revenues are incurred at the end of each year.) The marginal tax rate for LQ is 40%. What is the required net investment, and what are the year 1 and year 2 net cash flows?

Excel

16. CI wants to market its new Slammin Jammin Basketball Goal Set. To bring this product to the market will require the purchase of equipment costing $650,000. Shipping and installation expenses associated with the equipment are estimated to be $50,000. In addition, CI will incur incremental employee training and recruiting expenses of $100,000, all of which will be incurred at time 0. Additional net working capital investments of $50,000 will be required at time 0, $25,000 in

year 1, and $10,000 in year 2. Revenues are expected to be $250,000 in year 1 and grow at a rate of $25,000 per year through year 5, and then decline by $25,000 per year until the project is terminated at the end of year 10. Annual operating expenses are expected to be $80,000 in year 1 and to grow at a rate of $10,000 per year until the end of the project life. The asset will be included in class 8 with a CCA rate of 20%. The salvage value of the equipment at the end of 10 years is expected to be $50,000. The marginal tax rate is 40% and the cost of capital is 14%. Compute the expected net cash flow for year 10, the last year in the life of the project.

 Excel

17. HW is planning to acquire a new grape masher. The masher will cost $100,000 including shipping and installation and will be included in class 8 with a CCA rate of 20%. At the time the masher is purchased, HW will have to invest $5,000 in net working capital. Additional investments in net working capital are required at the end of year 1 ($3,000) and year 2 ($2,000). Net revenues attributable to the masher are expected to total $25,000 during year 1 and to grow by 5% per annum through the end of year 6. After that time, revenues are expected to decline by 10% per annum. Annual year 1 cash operating expenses are expected to total $10,000 and to grow at an annual rate of 10% per annum. HW expects to sell the masher at one second after midnight on the first day of year 8 for $10,000. The firm's marginal tax rate is 40% and its cost of capital is 16%. Compute the expected net cash flows for year 7. Include in your year 7 calculations the proceeds from the salvage value of the masher and recovery of net working capital at the beginning of year 8 as well as any PV of CCA tax benefits from beyond the project's life. For the purposes of present value calculations, you may assume that the end of year 7 is the same as the beginning of year 8.

Other Practice Materials and Resources

For interactive quizzes, Internet exercises, crossword puzzles, CTV videos, and more, go to the *Contemporary Financial Management* Web site at **http://cyr.nelson.com**

Capital Budgeting: Decision Criteria and Real Options

Learning Objectives

After studying this chapter you should be able to

1. Understand that the *net present value* of an investment project is defined as the present value of the stream of expected net cash flows from the project minus the project's net investment

   a. A project is acceptable if its NPV is greater than or equal to zero

   b. By maximizing the net present value of accepted projects, a firm will also maximize shareholder wealth

2. Understand that the *profitability index* (PI) is the ratio of the present value of expected net cash flows over the life of the project to the net investment

   a. If the project has a PI equal to or greater than 1.0, it is acceptable

   b. The PI can be used as a guide to resource allocation in capital rationing situations

3. Understand that the *internal rate of return* (IRR) is defined as the discount rate that equates the present value of the expected net cash flows from a project with the present value of the net investment

   a. A normal project is acceptable if it has an IRR greater than or equal to the firm's cost of capital. A *normal project* has an initial cash outlay or outlays followed by a stream of positive net cash flows

   b. The NPV and IRR approaches give the same accept-reject signals for independent normal projects

   c. The IRR approach can lead to multiple internal rates of return for nonnormal projects. When this occurs, none of these rates can be compared to the firm's cost of capital to determine the project's acceptability

4. Understand that the *payback period* of an investment is the period of time required for the cumulative cash inflows (net cash flows) from a project to equal the initial cash outlay

   a. Weaknesses of the payback method include that it ignores the timing of cash flows and cash flows beyond the payback period

   b. The payback technique can be used as a project liquidity measure and as a crude risk-screening technique

5. Understand that a firm may face a limit on the capital available (*capital rationing*) in some situations

   a. Soft rationing occurs when the constraint is self-imposed

b. Hard rationing occurs when the constraint is imposed by capital market conditions

6. Understand that when *mutually exclusive* projects have *unequal lives* and can be repeated, the NPV of replacement chains with common lives should be compared. If the repeatable projects are identical in all cash flows, then the *equivalent annual annuity* method can be used

7. Understand that project *post-audits* and reviews can assist management in uncovering biases in the project analysis procedure of a firm, and can assist management in making abandonment decisions

8. Understand that the use of conventional discounted cash flow techniques in capital budgeting without considering *real options* may result in a downward-biased estimate of the true value of a project's net present value

9. Understand that for international projects, the present value of a project's net cash flows to the parent company is equal to the present value of the project's net cash flows from the foreign subsidiary converted into the home country currency

Real Options and the Automobile Production Process

The car preferences of North American consumers have been changing rapidly. At one time the overwhelming top vehicle choice was the four-door family sedan. Each major automobile manufacturer had multiple entries in this large and lucrative market. Then Chrysler brought out the first minivan. It was an instant hit among the baby-boomer generation seeking to haul around a load of kids to soccer practice and other after-school events. Although the minivan remains popular, the sport utility vehicle, or SUV, has become the hot vehicle of choice. Manufacturers rushed to make SUVs in every size class, from the monster Ford Excursion to the compact Honda CR-V. Changing consumer preferences have been the result of growing consumer affluence, family life cycles, and the desire for individual self-expression. Consumer preferences have also fluctuated in response to volatility in the cost of gasoline.

PHOTODISC

Faced with a highly volatile demand function of consumers for vehicles, car manufacturers have often found themselves stuck with excess capacity in plants capable of making only one type of vehicle. When demand for that vehicle type declines, the manufacturers are forced to resort to costly incentives to sell their unpopular models. In many cases, expensive plants have been closed either temporarily or permanently.

It used to take two years or more to convert a plant from making cars to making small SUVs, for example. With the high volatility of demand for various vehicle types, automobile manufacturers have increasingly been developing flexible plant designs that give them the option to convert a plant from one vehicle type to another in less than six months. Toyota has refitted its assembly plants around the world, including its Canadian factory in Cambridge, Ontario, with common assembly equipment and plant layouts. Their goal is to be able to produce any vehicle type, from a car to a large SUV, without going through a major retooling of the plant.

Other auto manufacturers are pursuing similar goals. Honda claims that its plants, including the one in Alliston, Ontario, can produce a new model in as little as three months. Similar plant reengineering efforts are underway at General Motors and most other major car companies.

The value of this increased flexibility can be seen in the case of Honda's Swindon plant in the United Kingdom. Because of weak sales in Europe, Honda has found it difficult to operate this plant at anything close to its full capacity of 150,000 cars per year. During 2000, the plant produced only 76,500 vehicles. To complicate matters, the Swindon plant opened a second production line during the summer of 2001 with an additional capacity of 100,000 vehicles. At the same time, Honda found that it was running out of capacity at its Japanese and North American plants that produced their compact SUV.

By making investments in the manufacturing flexibility of the Swindon plant, Honda will be able to shift production of its compact SUV, the CR-V, and the hatchback version of the Honda Civic to Swindon, from Japan and North America. These vehicles will then be exported to the North American market.

As this example illustrates, manufacturing flexibility is an important and valuable real option for corporations. This chapter considers a number of techniques that are useful when evaluating the cash flows anticipated from capital expenditures, such as Honda's Swindon assembly plant. As we shall see in this chapter, in addition to estimating and evaluating the cash flows from a proposed investment, it is important to consider the value of real options that are inherent in an investment project.

Introduction

This chapter looks at some widely used capital budgeting decision models, discussing and illustrating their relative strengths and weaknesses. This chapter also examines project review and post-audit procedures and concludes by tracing a sample project through the capital budgeting analysis process.

Decision Models for Evaluating Alternatives

Four criteria are commonly used for evaluating and selecting investment projects:

- Net present value (NPV)

- Profitability index (PI)

- Internal rate of return (IRR)

- Payback (PB) period

Net Present Value

Recall from Chapter 1 that the net present value rule is the primary decision-making rule used throughout the practice of financial management. The net present value—that is, the present value of the expected future cash flows minus the initial outlay—of an investment made by a firm represents the contribution of that investment to the value of the firm and, accordingly, to the wealth of the firm's shareholders. In this chapter, we consider the net present value of capital expenditure projects.

Net Present Value (NPV)
The NPV is the present value of the stream of net cash flows from a project minus its net investment.

The **net present value (NPV)** of a capital expenditure project is defined as the present value of the stream of net (operating) cash flows from the project minus the project's net investment. The net present value method is also sometimes called the *discounted cash flow* (DCF) technique. The cash flows are discounted at the firm's required rate of return, that is, its *cost of capital*. A firm's cost of capital is defined as its minimum acceptable rate of return for projects of average risk.

The net present value of a project may be expressed as

$$(10.1) \qquad \qquad NPV = PVNCF - NINV$$

where NPV is the net present value; PVNCF, the present value of net (operating) cash flows; and NINV, the net investment.

Assuming a cost of capital, k, the net present value for a project with a five-year expected life would be the following:

$$(10.2) \quad NPV = \frac{NCF_1}{(1 + k)^1} + \frac{NCF_2}{(1 + k)^2} + \frac{NCF_3}{(1 + k)^3} + \frac{NCF_4}{(1 + k)^4} + \frac{NCF_5}{(1 + k)^5} - NINV$$

where $NCF_1 \ldots NCF_5$ are the net (operating) cash flows occurring in years 1 through 5. NCF_5 may be assumed to include any net salvage value remaining at the end of the project's life.

The annual net cash flows for normal projects are usually positive after the initial net investment. Occasionally, however, one or more of the expected net cash flows over the life of a project may be negative. When this occurs, positive numbers are used for years having positive net cash flows (net inflows), and negative numbers are used for years having negative net cash flows (net outflows).

In general, the net present value of a project may be defined as follows:

$$(10.3) \qquad \text{NPV} = \sum_{t=1}^{n} \frac{\text{NCF}_t}{(1 + k)^t} - \text{NINV}$$

$$= \sum_{t=1}^{n} \text{NCF}_t \times \text{PVIF}_{k,t} - \text{NINV}$$

where n is the expected project life and $\sum_{t=1}^{n} [\text{NCF}_t/(1 + k)^t]$ is the arithmetic sum of the discounted net cash flows for each year t over the life of the project (n years); that is, the present value of the net cash flows.

Equation 9.2 in the previous chapter decomposed the net cash flow NCF for any year except the last year of a project into the incremental after-tax net revenue $(\Delta R - \Delta O)(1 - T)$ plus the tax benefit of incremental capital cost allowance (CCA) of $T\Delta\text{CCA}$ less the incremental increase in net working capital ΔNWC. In the last year n of a project the incremental salvage value ΔS_n must be added to the cash flow as well as the present value of future tax benefits from incremental CCA beyond the economic life of the project $Td(\Delta\text{UCC}_n - \Delta S_n)/(k + d)$, where d is the CCA rate and ΔUCC_n is the incremental undepreciated capital cost at time $t = n$. Replacing the net cash flow NCF_t in Equation 10.3 with the components yields

$$(10.3a) \qquad \text{NPV} = \sum_{t=1}^{n} \frac{(\Delta R_t - \Delta O_t)(1 - T)}{(1 + k)^t} + \left[\frac{(1 + .5k)}{(1 + k)} \right] \left[\frac{Td\Delta\text{DB}}{(k + d)} \right]$$

$$+ \frac{\Delta S_n}{(1 + k)^n} - \left[\frac{1}{(1 + k)^n} \right] \left[\frac{Td\Delta S_n}{(k + d)} \right] - \sum_{t=1}^{n} \frac{\Delta\text{NWC}_t}{(1 + k)^t} - \text{NINV}$$

where DB is the incremental depreciable base or net installed cost as defined in Chapter 9. The second term of Equation 10.3a represents not only the tax benefits of incremental capital cost allowance during the life of the project but also the present value at $t = 0$ of such benefits due to the incremental undepreciated capital cost ΔUCC_n.[1]

To illustrate net present value calculations, suppose a firm is considering two projects, A and B, having net investments and net cash flows as shown in Table 10.1. The net present value computations for the two projects are presented in Table 10.2. These calculations assume a 14 percent cost of capital. The calculations in these tables also

---

[1] The term $[(1 + .5k)/(1 + k)][Td\Delta\text{DB}/(k + d)]$ can be derived using the constant growth dividend valuation model as we did in Chapter 9 for finding the present value at time $t = n$ of the incremental CCA tax benefits beyond the economic life n of the project. The half-year convention is equivalent to putting half of the incremental base (ΔDB) on the books this year at the full CCA rate d and the other half on the books next year at the full CCA rate d. In fact, this is how it is done on the tax form for calculating CCA. The present value at time $t = 0$ for the tax benefits in perpetuity for the first half of the depreciable base is $(.5)(Td\Delta\text{DB})/(k + d)$, which is also the present value at time $t = 1$ for the tax benefits in perpetuity for the second half of the depreciable base. Combining these two terms after discounting the effects of the second half back to $t = 0$ yields

$$.5 \left[\frac{Td\Delta\text{DB}}{(k + d)} \right] + \frac{.5}{1 + k} \left[\frac{Td\Delta\text{DB}}{(k + d)} \right] = \left[.5 + \frac{.5}{1 + k} \right] \left[\frac{Td\Delta\text{DB}}{(k + d)} \right] =$$

$$\left[\frac{(.5)(1 + k)}{1 + k} + \frac{.5}{1 + k} \right] \left[\frac{Td\Delta\text{DB}}{(k + d)} \right] = \left[\frac{(1 + .5k)}{(1 + k)} \right] \left[\frac{Td\Delta\text{DB}}{(k + d)} \right]$$

Table 10.1 Sample Project Cash Flows

Year	Project A Net Cash Flow After Taxes	Project B Net Cash Flow After Taxes
1	$12,500	$ 5,000
2	12,500	10,000
3	12,500	15,000
4	12,500	15,000
5	12,500	25,000
6	12,500	30,000
	Net investment = $50,000	Net investment = $50,000

Table 10.2 Sample Net Present Value Calculations

Project A		Project B			
		Year	NCF	$PVIF_{0.14,t}$*	PV of NCF
Present value of an annuity of $12,500 for 6 years at 14 percent:					
PV of NCF = $12,500(PVIFA_{0.14,6})		1	$ 5,000	0.877	$ 4,385
= $12,500(3.889)†		2	10,000	0.769	7,690
= $48,613		3	15,000	0.675	10,125
		4	15,000	0.592	8,880
		5	25,000	0.519	12,975
Less Net investment 50,000		6	30,000	0.456	13,680
					57,735
		Less Net investment			50,000
Net present value $–1,387		Net present value			$ 7,735

*From the PVIF table (Table II).
† From the PVIFA table (Table IV).

assume that cash flows are received at the end of each year, rather than as a flow during the year. This assumption, although a usual one, tends to slightly understate a project's net present value or internal rate of return. Project A is shown in Table 10.2 to have a negative net present value, and Project B has a positive net present value.

Calculator Solution

In order to calculate NPVs for these projects with the aid of your calculator, it is necessary to use the cash flow function/keys (CF) on your calculator.

Project A

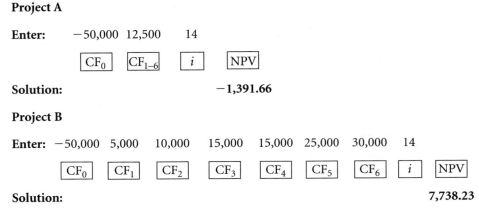

Enter: −50,000 12,500 14

$\boxed{CF_0}$ $\boxed{CF_{1-6}}$ $\boxed{i}$ $\boxed{NPV}$

Solution: −1,391.66

Project B

Enter: −50,000 5,000 10,000 15,000 15,000 25,000 30,000 14

$\boxed{CF_0}$ $\boxed{CF_1}$ $\boxed{CF_2}$ $\boxed{CF_3}$ $\boxed{CF_4}$ $\boxed{CF_5}$ $\boxed{CF_6}$ $\boxed{i}$ $\boxed{NPV}$

Solution: 7,738.23

Note: The calculator solutions and the solutions obtained using interest tables with three decimal places differ slightly. Using more accurate interest tables gives answers closer to the answers obtained using the calculator.

The solution can also be computed with a spreadsheet as follows:

Project A

Spreadsheet Solution

	A	B	C	D	E	F	G	H
1	Rate, i	14%						
2	Year	0	1	2	3	4	5	6
3	Cash Flows	−50000	12500	12500	12500	12500	12500	12500
4	NPV	−$1,391.66						

Project B

	A	B	C	D	E	F	G	H
1	Rate, i	14%						
2	Year	0	1	2	3	4	5	6
3	Cash Flows	−50000	5000	10000	15000	15000	25000	30000
4	NPV	$7,738.23						

Enter the appropriate data inputs in column B and row 3. For both projects, the formula entered in cell B4 is =B3+NPV(B1,C3:H3)

Decision Rule In general, a project should be accepted if its net present value is greater than or equal to zero and rejected if its net present value is less than zero. This is so because a positive net present value in principle translates directly into increases in share prices and increases in shareholders' wealth. In the previous example, Project A would be rejected because it has a negative net present value, and Project B would be accepted because it has a positive net present value.

If two or more *mutually exclusive* investments have positive net present values, the project having the largest net present value is the one selected. Assume, for example, that a firm has three mutually exclusive investment opportunities, G, H, and I, each requiring a net investment of $10,000 and each having a five-year expected economic life. Project G has a net present value of $2,000; H has a net present value of $4,000; and I has a net present value of $3,500. Of the three, H would be preferred over the other two because it has the highest net present value and therefore is expected to make the largest contribution to the objective of shareholder wealth maximization.

Howie's Asset Replacement Decision In Chapter 9, we introduced a drill press replacement project being considered by Howie's Machine Shop Corporation. In Table 9.5, we calculated the net installed cost or incremental depreciable base ΔDB to be $160,000 and the net investment NINV to be $161,500. In Table 9.6, we calculated the incremental net cash flows of this project for years 1 through 10. Now it is time for Howie to decide whether or not to replace the drill press.

Using Equation 10.3, the net present value for replacing the drill press, given Howie's 15 percent cost of capital, is

$$NPV = \frac{\$27{,}200}{1.15} + \frac{\$32{,}920}{(1.15)^2} + \frac{\$31{,}216}{(1.15)^3} + \frac{\$29{,}973}{(1.15)^4} + \frac{\$29{,}098}{(1.15)^5}$$

$$+ \frac{\$28{,}518}{(1.15)^6} + \frac{\$28{,}175}{(1.15)^7} + \frac{\$28{,}020}{(1.15)^8} + \frac{\$28{,}016}{(1.15)^9} + \frac{\$54{,}565}{(1.15)^{10}}$$

$$- \$161{,}500 = -\$7{,}294$$

Thus, Howie's should not replace the existing drill press because the net present value of replacement is negative. See Appendix 10A for a spreadsheet solution for this project.

When the incremental after-tax net operating revenues and incremental net working capital follow simple patterns, Equation 10.3a allows you to quickly calculate the NPV of a project without calculating the yearly cash flows. See Self-Test Problem ST4 for an example that is ideal for applying Equation 10.3a.

Sources of Positive Net Present Value Projects   What causes some projects to have a positive net present value and others to have a negative net present value? When product and factor markets are other than perfectly competitive, it is possible for a firm to earn above-normal profits (economic rents) that result in positive net present value projects. The reasons why these above-normal profits may be available arise from conditions that define each type of product and factor market and distinguish it from a perfectly competitive market. These reasons include the following barriers to entry and other factors:

1. Buyer preferences for established brand names
2. Ownership or control of favoured distribution systems (such as exclusive auto dealerships)
3. Patent control of superior product designs or production techniques
4. Exclusive ownership of superior natural resource deposits
5. Inability of new firms to acquire necessary factors of production (management, labour, equipment)
6. Superior access to financial resources at lower costs (economies of scale in attracting capital)
7. Economies of large-scale production and distribution arising from
   a. Capital-intensive production processes
   b. High initial start-up costs
8. Access to superior labour or managerial talents at costs that are not fully reflective of their value

These factors can permit a firm to identify positive net present value projects for internal investment. If barriers to entry are sufficiently high or if the start-up period for competitive ventures is sufficiently long, then it is possible that a project may have a positive net present value. However, in assessing the viability of such a project, it is important that the manager or analyst consider the likely period of time when above-normal returns can be earned before new competitors emerge and force cash flows back to a more normal level. It is generally unrealistic to expect to be able to earn above-normal returns over the entire life of an investment project.

Thus, it may be possible for a firm to identify investment projects with positive net present values. However, if capital markets are efficient, the securities of the firm making these investments will reflect the value of these projects. Recall that the net present value of a project can be thought of as the *contribution to the value of a firm*

Visit **http://finance. swcollege.com** and select a topic under Project Valuation.

resulting from undertaking that particular project. Therefore, even though a firm may be able to identify projects having expected positive net present values, efficient capital markets will quickly reflect these positive net present value projects in the market value of the firm's securities.

Suppose Project B in the preceding example is a new baby care product from Johnson & Johnson. Its positive net present value could be the result of buyer preferences due to Johnson & Johnson's established baby care business. Suppose Project A, on the other hand, involves a new soap product to compete with Procter & Gamble's Tide. Consumers' brand preferences for Tide, as well as Procter & Gamble's economies of scale for production and distribution, could easily cause Project A to have a negative net present value.

Advantages and Disadvantages of the Net Present Value Method   The net present value of a project is the expected number of dollars by which the present value of the firm is increased as a result of adopting the project. Therefore, as we have pointed out, the net present value method is consistent with the goal of shareholder wealth maximization. The net present value approach considers both the magnitude and the timing of cash flows over a project's entire expected life.

A firm can be thought of as a series of projects, and the firm's total value is the sum of the net present values of all of the independent projects that make it up. Therefore, when the firm undertakes a new project, the firm's value is increased by the net present value of the new project. The additivity of net present values of independent projects is referred to in finance as the *value additivity principle.*

The net present value approach also indicates whether a proposed project will yield the rate of return required by the firm's investors. The cost of capital represents this rate of return. When a project's net present value is greater than or equal to zero, the firm's investors can expect to earn at least their required rate of return.

The net present value criterion has a weakness in that many people find it difficult to work with a present value dollar return rather than a percentage return. As a result, many firms use another present value-based method that is interpreted more easily: the internal rate of return method. It is discussed later in the chapter. Also, the traditional NPV approach does not consider the value of real options that are part of a proposed project. Real options are discussed later in the chapter.

Profitability Index

Profitability Index (PI)
The ratio of the present value of net cash flows over the life of a project to the net investment. It is used to evaluate, rank, and select from among various investment projects. It is used frequently in capital rationing situations.

The **profitability index (PI)**, or benefit-cost ratio, is the ratio of the present value of expected net cash flows over the life of a project to the net investment. It is expressed as follows:

$$(10.4) \qquad \text{PI} = \frac{\sum_{t=1}^{n} \text{NCF}_t / (1 + k)^t}{\text{NINV}}$$

Assuming a 14 percent cost of capital, k, and using the data from Table 10.2, the profitability index for Projects A and B can be calculated as follows:

$$\text{PI}_A = \frac{\$48,613}{\$50,000} = 0.97$$

$$\text{PI}_B = \frac{\$57,735}{\$50,000} = 1.15$$

The profitability index is interpreted as the present value return *for each dollar of initial investment.* In comparison, the net present value approach measures the total present value dollar return.

Decision Rule A project whose profitability index is greater than or equal to 1 is considered acceptable. A project having a profitability index less than 1 is considered unacceptable.[2] In this case, Project B is acceptable, whereas Project A is not. When two or more *independent* projects with normal cash flows are considered, the profitability index, net present value, and internal rate of return approaches all will yield identical accept-reject signals. This is true, for example, with Projects A and B.

When dealing with mutually exclusive investments, conflicts may arise between the net present value and the profitability index criteria. This is most likely to occur if the alternative projects require significantly different net investments.

Consider, for example, the following information on Projects J and K. According to the net present value criterion, Project J would be preferred because of its larger net present value. According to the profitability index criterion, Project K would be preferred.

	Project J	Project K
Present value of net cash flows (PVNCF)	$25,000	$14,000
Less Net investment (NINV)	20,000	10,000
Net present value (NPV)	5,000	4,000
PI = PVNCF/NINV	**1.25**	**1.40**

When a conflict arises, the final decision must be made on the basis of other factors. For example, if a firm has no constraint on the funds available to it for capital investment—that is, no capital rationing—the net present value approach is preferred because it will select the projects that are expected to generate the largest *total dollar* increase in the firm's wealth and, by extension, maximize shareholder wealth. If, however, the firm is in a capital rationing situation and capital budgeting is being done for only one period, the profitability index approach may be preferred because it will indicate which projects will maximize the returns *per dollar of investment*—an appropriate objective when a funds constraint exists.

Internal Rate of Return

Internal Rate of Return (IRR)
The discount rate that equates the present value of net cash flows from a project with the present value of the net investment. It is the discount rate that gives the project a net present value equal to zero.

The **internal rate of return (IRR)** is defined as the discount rate that equates the present value of the net cash flows from a project with the present value of the net investment.[3] It is the discount rate that causes a project's net present value to equal zero. The internal rate of return for a capital expenditure project is identical to the yield to maturity for a bond investment.

A project's internal rate of return can be determined by means of the following equation:

$$(10.5) \qquad \sum_{t=1}^{n} \frac{\text{NCF}_t}{(1 + r)^t} = \text{NINV}$$

where $\text{NCF}_t/(1 + r)^t$ is the present value of net (operating) cash flows in period t discounted at the rate r, NINV is the net investment in the project, and r is the internal rate of return.

For a project having a five-year life, this basic formula can be rewritten as follows:

$$(10.6) \quad \frac{\text{NCF}_1}{(1 + r)^1} + \frac{\text{NCF}_2}{(1 + r)^2} + \frac{\text{NCF}_3}{(1 + r)^3} + \frac{\text{NCF}_4}{(1 + r)^4} + \frac{\text{NCF}_5}{(1 + r)^5} = \text{NINV}$$

[2] When a project has a profitability index equal to 1, the present value of the net cash flows is exactly equal to the net investment. Thus, the project has a net present value of zero, meaning that it is expected to earn the investors' required rate of return and nothing more.

[3] This also is called the *discounted cash flow (DCF)* rate of return in contrast to various types of "accounting rates of return" that are all nondiscounted cash flow returns. Since all nondiscounted cash flow returns have serious flaws when used in project evaluation, we omit them from this textbook.

Subtracting the net investment, NINV, from both sides of Equation 10.6 yields the following:

$$\frac{NCF_1}{(1+r)^1} + \frac{NCF_2}{(1+r)^2} + \frac{NCF_3}{(1+r)^3} + \frac{NCF_4}{(1+r)^4} + \frac{NCF_5}{(1+r)^5} - NINV = 0$$

This is essentially the same equation as that used in the net present value method. The only difference is that in the net present value approach, a discount rate, k, is specified and the net present value is computed. In the internal rate of return method the discount rate, r, which causes the project net present value to equal zero, is the unknown.

Figure 10.1 illustrates the relationship between net present value (NPV) and the discount rate for Projects A and B, whose net cash flows were given in Table 10.1. This relationship is called a *net present value profile*. Note from the NPV profile for Project B that at a 14 percent cost of capital, its NPV is $7,735. This is the same amount shown in Table 10.2.

The internal rate of return (IRR) for a project can be found from its NPV profile by simply noting the discount rate at which the NPV profile cuts the horizontal axis. At this discount rate, the NPV of a project is zero. From Figure 10.1 we note that the IRRs for Projects A and B are about 13 and 18.2 percent, respectively.

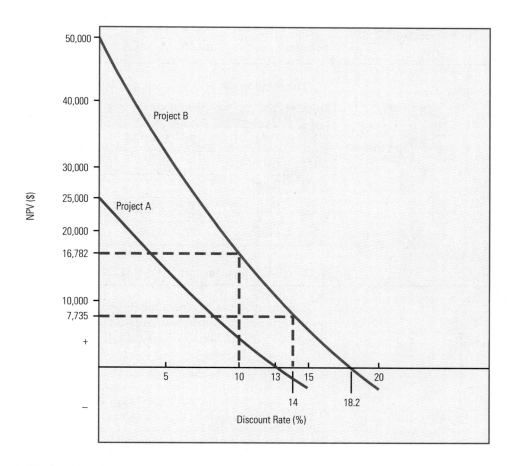

Figure 10.1
NPV Profiles: Relationship Between the Net Present Value and the Internal Rate of Return for Projects A and B

The NPV profile is an interesting pedagogical tool. Are there, however, more practical methods for calculating the IRR of a project? Yes, there are, and we shall demonstrate them by calculating the IRRs for Projects A and B.

Because Project A is an annuity of $12,500 for six years requiring a net investment of $50,000, its internal rate of return may be computed directly with the aid of a PVIFA table, such as Table IV, or with a financial calculator.

In this case, the present value of the annuity, $PVAN_0$, is $50,000, the annuity payment, PMT, is $12,500, and $n = 6$ years. The following equation

$$PVAN_0 = PMT(PVIFA_{r,n})$$

can be rewritten to solve for the PVIFA:

$$PVIFA_{r,n} = PVAN_0/PMT$$

In this case, PVIFA = $50,000/$12,500 = 4.000. Referring to Table IV and reading across the table for $n = 6$, it can be seen that the interest factor of 4.000 occurs near 13 percent, where it is 3.998. Thus, the internal rate of return for Project A is about 13 percent.[4]

Calculator Solution

Enter:	6		−50,000	12,500	
	n	i	PV	PMT	FV

Solution: 12.98

The solution can also be computed with a spreadsheet as follows:

Spreadsheet Solution

	A	B	C	
1	TVM	INPUTS	SOLUTION	
2	Periods, n	6		
3	Rate, i		12.98%	
4	PV	−50000		
5	PMT	12500		

In cell C3, enter the formula =**RATE(B2,B5,B4)**

The internal rate of return for Project B is more difficult to calculate because the project is expected to yield uneven cash flows. In this case, the internal rate of return is computed with the help of a financial calculator or by a spreadsheet program.

---

[4] This calculation of the IRR is typically only an approximation. It is exact only when the incremental undepreciated capital cost ΔUCC_n is equal to the incremental salvage value ΔS_n. Usually, the last cash flow actually contains a PV of CCA tax shields beyond the economic life of the project that is generated by the remaining incremental depreciable base $(\Delta UCC_n - \Delta S_n)$ at time n. This PV has been calculated using the project's cost of capital. To calculate the actual or true IRR, this PV must be calculated with the IRR. Thus, iterative (repetitive) techniques must be used to find the true IRR. This is demonstrated in Appendix 10A for Howie's drill press replacement decision. The same appendix also discusses the unusual case of closing an asset class.

In order to solve this problem with the aid of your calculator, it is necessary to use the cash flow function/keys (CF) on your calculator.

Calculator Solution

Enter: −50,000   5,000   10,000   15,000   15,000   25,000   30,000

CF_0 CF_1 CF_2 CF_3 CF_4 CF_5 CF_6 IRR

Solution: **18.19**

The solution can also be computed with a spreadsheet as follows:

Spreadsheet Solution

	A	B	C	D	E	F	G	H
1	Year	0	1	2	3	4	5	6
2	Cash Flows	−50000	5000	10000	15000	15000	25000	30000
3	IRR	18.19%						

In cell B3, enter the formula **=IRR(B2:H2)**

Decision Rule   Generally, the internal rate of return method indicates that a project whose internal rate of return is greater than or equal to the firm's cost of capital should be accepted, whereas a project whose internal rate of return is less than the firm's cost of capital should be rejected. In the case of Projects A and B, if the cost of capital were 14 percent, B would be acceptable and A would be unacceptable.

A **normal project** has an initial cash outlay or outlays followed by a stream of positive net cash flows (inflows). When two independent normal projects are considered under conditions of no capital rationing, the net present value and internal rate of return techniques result in the same accept-reject decision. This can be seen in Figure 10.1. For example, if the firm's cost of capital is 10 percent, Project B has a positive net present value of $16,782. Its internal rate of return is 18.19 percent, exceeding the cost of capital. When two or more mutually exclusive projects are being considered, it is *generally* preferable to accept the project having the highest internal rate of return as long as it is greater than or equal to the cost of capital. In this case, if A and B were mutually exclusive, B would be chosen over A, as can be seen in Figure 10.1. Exceptions to this general rule are considered later in the chapter.

Advantages and Disadvantages of the Internal Rate of Return Method   In Canada, the net present value method is slightly preferred to the internal rate of return method in practice. In the United States, the practice is reversed, although in both countries many firms employ both methods.[5] Some people may feel more comfortable dealing with the concept of a project's percentage rate of return than with its dollar amount of net present value. Like the net present value approach, the internal rate of return technique takes into account both the magnitude and the timing of cash flows over the entire life of a project in measuring the project's economic desirability.

However, some potential problems are involved in using the internal rate of return technique. The possible existence of **multiple internal rates of return** is one such problem. Whereas equating the net present value of a normal project to zero will yield only one internal rate of return, *r*, for *nonnormal* investments, there are times when two

Normal Project
A project that has an initial cash outlay followed by a stream of positive net cash inflows.

Multiple Internal Rates of Return
Two or more internal rates of return from the same project. This occurs only with nonnormal projects whose cash flow patterns contain more than one sign change.

---

5   J. D. Payne, W. C. Heath, and L.R. Gale, "Comparative Financial Practice in the US and Canada: Capital Budgeting and Risk Assessment Techniques," *Financial Practice and Education* 9 (Spring/ Summer 1999): 16–24.

or more rates may be obtained. If for some reason—such as large abandonment costs at the end of a project's life or a major shutdown and rebuilding of a facility sometime during its life—the initial net investment is followed by one or more positive net cash flows (inflows) that then are followed by a negative cash flow,[6] it is possible to obtain more than one internal rate of return.

Whenever a project has multiple internal rates of return, the pattern of cash flows over the project's life contains more than one sign change, for example, $- \uparrow + + \uparrow -$. In this case, there are two sign changes (indicated by the arrows)—from minus to plus and again from plus to minus.

Consider the following investment, which has three internal rates of return—0, 100, and 200 percent:

Year	Net Cash Flows
0	−$1,000
1	+$6,000
2	−$11,000
3	+$6,000

Unfortunately, none of these rates can be compared to the firm's cost of capital to determine the project's acceptability.

Although several techniques have been proposed for dealing with the multiple internal rate of return problem, none provide a simple, complete, and generally satisfactory solution.[7] The best approach is to use the net present value criterion. If a project's net present value is positive, it is acceptable. If it is negative, it is not acceptable. Many financial calculators and software packages are available that compute internal rates of return, and they usually will warn the user when a potential multiple internal rate of return problem exists. Whenever this is a possibility, the use of the net present value method is preferred.

Finally, just as is the case with the NPV approach, the traditional IRR approach does not consider the value of a project's real option characteristics.

NPV versus IRR: The Reinvestment Rate Assumption

As was indicated, both the net present value and the internal rate of return methods result in identical decisions to either accept or reject an *independent* normal project. This is true because the net present value is greater than (less than) zero if and only if the internal rate of return is greater than (less than) the required rate of return, k. In the case of *mutually exclusive* projects, however, the two methods may yield contradictory results. One project may have a *higher* internal rate of return than another and, at the same time, a *lower* net present value.

Consider, for example, *mutually exclusive* projects L and M described in the following table. Both require a net investment of $1,000. Using the internal rate of return approach, Project L is preferred, with an IRR of 21.6 percent compared with Project M's IRR of 18.3 percent. Using the net present value approach with a discount rate of 5 percent, Project M is preferred to Project L. Hence, it is necessary to determine which technique is the correct one to use in this situation.

---

[6] Table 9.2 in Chapter 9 illustrates two such projects, X and Y.

[7] The modified internal rate of return (MIRR) enjoys some popularity. In this method, all investment outlays and other net cash outflows for projects of average risk are discounted at the firm's cost of capital back to the start of the project. All net cash inflows are compounded at this rate to the end of the project's life to determine a terminal value. Then the discount rate that equates the terminal value to the previously calculated PV of net cash outflows is the MIRR.

	Project L	Project M
Net investment	$1,000	$1,000
Net cash flow in year 1	$667	$0
Net cash flow in year 2	$667	$1,400
Net present value at 5%	$240	$270
Internal rate of return	21.6%	18.3%

The outcome depends on what *assumptions* the decision maker chooses to make about the *implied reinvestment rate* for the net cash flows generated from each project. This can be seen in Figure 10.2. For discount (reinvestment) rates below 10 percent, Project M has a higher net present value than Project L and therefore is preferred. For discount rates greater than 10 percent, Project L is preferred using both the net present value and internal rate of return approaches. Hence, a conflict occurs in this case only for discount (cost-of-capital) rates below 10 percent. The net present value method assumes that cash flows are *reinvested at the firm's cost of capital*. The internal rate of return method assumes that these cash flows are *reinvested at the computed internal rate of return*. Generally, the cost of capital is considered to be a more realistic **reinvestment rate** than the computed internal rate of return because the cost of capital is the rate the next (marginal) investment project can be assumed to earn. This can be seen in Figure 9.1 in Chapter 9, where the last acceptable project, Project E, offers a rate of return nearly equal to the firm's marginal cost of capital.

Consequently, in the absence of capital rationing, the net present value approach is normally superior to both the profitability index and the internal rate of return when choosing among mutually exclusive investments.

Reinvestment Rate

The rate of return at which cash flows from an investment project are assumed to be reinvested from year to year. The reinvestment rate may vary, depending on the investment opportunities available to the firm.

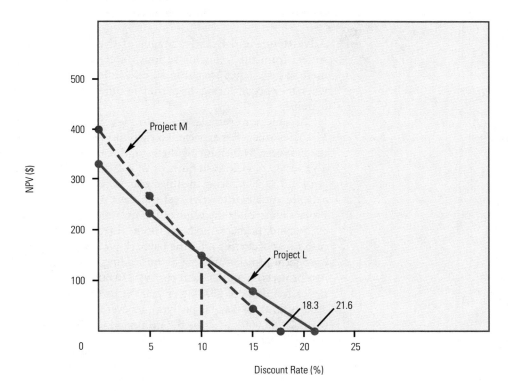

Figure 10.2
NPV Profiles: Net Present Value versus Internal Rate of Return for Mutually Exclusive Alternatives

Payback (PB) Period
The period of time required for
the cumulative cash inflows
from a project to equal the
initial cash outlay.

Payback (PB) Period

The **payback (PB) period** of an investment is the period of time required for the cumulative cash inflows (net cash flows) from a project to equal the initial cash outlay (net investment). If the expected net cash inflows are *equal* each year, then the payback period is equal to the ratio of the net investment to the annual net cash inflows of the project.[8]

$$PB = \text{Net Investment/Annual net cash inflows}$$

When the annual cash inflows are not equal each year, slightly more complex calculations are required to compute the payback period. In this case, the analyst must add up the yearly net cash flows until the cumulative total equals the net investment. The number of years it takes for this to occur is the project's payback period. One can also compute a *discounted* payback period, where the net cash inflows are discounted at the firm's cost of capital in determining the number of years required to recover the net investment in a project.

Table 10.3 illustrates the calculation of undiscounted and discounted (at a 14 percent required return) payback periods for projects A and B, which were presented earlier in this section. In panel (a) of the table we see that the *undiscounted* PB period is 4.0 years for Project A and 4.2 years for Project B. In panel (b) we see that the discounted PB period for Project A is undefined. This occurs because the NPV of the project is negative. That is, the discounted cash inflows are less than the net investment. For Project B the discounted PB period is 5.43 years.

Decision Rule   The decision criterion states that a project should be accepted if its payback period is less than or equal to a specified maximum period. Otherwise, it should be rejected. However, the payback method has a number of serious shortcomings, and it should not be used in deciding whether to accept or reject an investment project.

Advantages and Disadvantages of the Payback Method   The payback method suffers from the following serious disadvantages. First, the (undiscounted) payback method gives equal weight to all cash inflows within the payback period, regardless of when they occur during the period. In other words, the technique ignores the *time value of money*.

Assume, for example, that a firm is considering two projects, E and F, each costing $10,000. Project E is expected to yield cash flows over a three-year period: $6,000 during the first year, $4,000 during the second year, and $3,000 during the third year. Project F is expected to yield cash flows of $4,000 during the first year, $6,000 during the second year, and $3,000 during the third year. Viewed from the payback perspective, these projects are equally attractive, yet the net present value technique clearly indicates that Project E increases the value of the firm more than Project F.

Second, payback methods (both discounted and undiscounted) essentially ignore cash flows occurring after the payback period. Thus, payback figures are biased against long-term projects and can be misleading. For example, suppose a firm is considering two projects, C and D, each costing $10,000. It is expected that Project C will generate net cash inflows of $5,000 per year for three years and that Project D will generate net cash inflows of $4,500 per year forever. The PB period for Project C is two years ($10,000/$5,000), whereas the PB period for Project D is 2.2 years ($10,000/$4,500). If these projects were mutually exclusive, payback would favour C because it has the lower payback period. Yet Project D clearly has a higher net present value than Project C.

---

[8] The astute reader should note that there is a relationship between the payback period (PB) and the internal rate of return r when the net cash inflows are level: $PB = PVIFA_{r,n}$.

Table 10.3 Payback Period Calculations

	(a) Undiscounted		(b) Discounted (at 14%)	
Project A				
Year(t)	Cash Inflow	Cumulative Cash Inflow	Cash Inflow	Cumulative Cash Inflow
1	$12,500	$12,500	$10,962.50	$10,962.50
2	12,500	25,000	9,612.50	20,575.00
3	12,500	37,500	8,437.50	29,012.50
4	12,500	50,000	7,400.00	36,412.50
5	12,500	62,500	6,487.50	42,900.00
6	12,500	75,000	5,700.00	48,600.00

$$PB = \frac{\text{Net Investment}}{\text{Annual Cash Flow}}$$

$$PB = \frac{\text{Number of Full Years Before Recovery of Net Investment}}{} + \frac{\text{Unrecovered Initial Investment at Start of Year}}{\text{Discounted Cash Inflow During Year}}$$

$$= \frac{50,000}{12,500}$$

$$= \text{Undefined}$$

$$= 4.0 \text{ years}$$

	(a) Undiscounted		(b) Discounted (at 14%)	
Project B				
Year(t)	Cash Inflow	Cumulative Cash Inflow	Cash Inflow	Cumulative Cash Inflow
1	$5,000	$5,000	$4,385	$4,385
2	10,000	15,000	7,690	12,075
3	15,000	30,000	10,125	22,200
4	15,000	45,000	8,880	31,080
5	25,000	70,000	12,975	44,055
6	30,000	100,000	13,680	57,735

$$PB = \frac{\text{Number of Full Years Before Recovery of Net Investment}}{} + \frac{\text{Unrecovered Initial Investment at Start of Year}}{\text{Cash Inflow During Year}}$$

$$PB = \frac{\text{Number of Full Years Before Recovery of Net Investment}}{} + \frac{\text{Unrecovered Initial Investment at Start of Year}}{\text{Discounted Cash Inflow During Year}}$$

$$= 4 + \frac{(50,000 - 45,000)}{25,000}$$

$$= 5 + \frac{(50,000 - 44,055)}{13,680}$$

$$= 4.2 \text{ years}$$

$$= 5.43 \text{ years}$$

Third, payback provides no *objective* criterion for decision making that is consistent with shareholder wealth maximization. The payback methods (both discounted and undiscounted) may reject projects with positive net present values. The choice of an acceptable payback period is largely a *subjective* one, and different people using essentially identical data may make different accept-reject decisions about a project.

The payback method is sometimes justified on the basis that it provides a measure of the *risk* associated with a project. Although it is true that less risk may be associated with a shorter payback period than with a longer one, risk is best thought of in terms of the *variability* of project returns. Because payback ignores this dimension, it is at best a crude tool for risk analysis.

A more valid justification for the use of the payback method is that it gives some indication of a project's desirability from a *liquidity* perspective because it measures the time required for a firm to recover its initial investment in a project. A company that is very concerned about the early recovery of investment funds—such as one investing overseas in a politically unstable area or one expecting a cash shortage in the future—might find this method useful.

In summary, payback is not a satisfactory criterion for investment decision making because it may lead to a selection of projects that do not make the largest possible contribution to a firm's value. It can be useful as a supplementary decision-making tool, however.

Table 10.4 presents a summary of the four capital budgeting methods discussed in the chapter.

Capital Rationing and the Capital Budgeting Decision

For each of the selection criteria previously discussed, the decision rule is to undertake *all* independent investment projects that meet the acceptance standard. This rule places no restrictions on the total amount of acceptable capital projects a company may undertake in any particular period.

Capital Rationing
A constraint on the total amount the firm can invest in a given year.

However, many firms face **capital rationing**. Rather than letting the size of their capital budget be determined by the number of profitable investment opportunities available, many companies choose to place an upper limit, or *constraint*, on the amount of funds allocated to capital investments. This constraint may be either *self-imposed*

Table 10.4	Summary of the Capital Budgeting Methods		
Model	**Criterion**	**Project Acceptance Strengths**	**Weaknesses**
Net present value (NPV)	Accept project if project has a positive or zero NPV; that is, if the present value of net cash flows, evaluated at the firm's cost of capital, equals or exceeds the net investment required.	Considers the timing of cash flows. Provides an objective, return-based criterion for acceptance or rejection. Most conceptually correct approach.	Difficulty in working with a dollar return value, rather than percentage returns.
Profitability index (PI)	Accept project if PI is greater than or equal to 1.0.	Same benefits as the NPV. Useful to guide decisions in capital rationing problems.	Sometimes gives decision that conflicts with NPV.
Internal rate of return (IRR)	Accept project if IRR equals or exceeds the firm's cost of capital.	Same benefits as the NPV. Easy to interpret the meaning of IRR.	Multiple rates of return problem. Sometimes gives decision that conflicts with NPV.
Payback (PB)	PB should not be used in deciding whether to accept or reject an investment project.	Easy and inexpensive to use. Provides a crude measure of project risk. Provides a measure of project liquidity.	No objective decision criterion. Fails to consider timing of cash flows.

Soft Rationing
A self-imposed constraint.

Hard Rationing
An externally imposed
constraint.

(**soft rationing**) by the firm's management or *externally imposed* (**hard rationing**) by conditions in the capital markets.

For example, a very conservative firm may be reluctant to use debt or external equity to finance capital expenditures. Instead, it would limit capital expenditures to cash flows from continuing operations minus any dividends paid. Another firm may feel that it lacks the managerial resources to successfully undertake all acceptable projects in a given year and may choose to limit capital expenditures for this reason.

A number of externally imposed constraints might limit a firm's capital expenditures. For example, a firm's loan agreements may contain restrictive covenants that limit future borrowing. Similarly, a weak financial position, conditions in the securities markets, or both may make the flotation of a new bond or share issue by the firm impossible or prohibitively expensive. Examples of such market-imposed constraints include depressed share market prices, unusually high interest rates due to a "tight money" policy on the part of the Bank of Canada, and reluctance on the part of investors to purchase new securities if the firm has a large percentage of debt in its capital structure.

Several different methods can be used in making capital budgeting decisions under capital rationing. When the initial outlays occur in two (or more) periods, the methods are quite elaborate and require the use of linear, integer, or goal programming.[9] However, when there is a single-period capital budgeting constraint, a relatively simple approach employing the profitability index can be used. Briefly, the approach consists of the following steps:

Step 1: Calculate the profitability index for each of a series of investment projects.

Step 2: Rank the projects according to their profitability indexes (from highest to lowest).

Step 3: Beginning with the project having the highest profitability index, proceed down through the list, and accept projects having profitability indexes greater than or equal to 1 until the entire capital budget has been utilized.

At times, a firm may not be able to use its entire capital budget because the next acceptable project on its list is too large, given the remaining available funds. In this case, the firm's management should choose among the following three alternatives:

Alternative 1: Search for another combination of projects, perhaps including some smaller, less profitable ones that will allow for a more complete utilization of available funds *and* increase the net present value of the combination of projects.

Alternative 2: Attempt to relax the funds constraint so that sufficient resources are available to accept the last project for which funds were not fully available.

Alternative 3: Accept as many projects as possible and either invest any excess funds in short-term securities until the next period (if all available capital is not invested, an implicit opportunity cost of lost earnings is incurred), pay out the excess funds to shareholders as dividends, use the funds to reduce outstanding debt, or do a combination of the above.

The following example illustrates how these alternatives can be applied to an actual capital budgeting decision. Suppose that management of a firm has decided to limit next year's capital expenditures to $550,000. Eight capital expenditure projects have been proposed—P, R, S, U, T, V, Q, and W—and ranked according to their profitability indexes, as shown in Table 10.5. Given the $550,000 ceiling, the firm's management proceeds down the list of projects, selecting P, R, S, and U, in that order. Project T cannot

---

[9] See, for example J. R. McGuigan, R. C. Moyer, and F. H. de B. Harris, *Managerial Economics,* 9th ed. (Cincinnati: South-Western, 2002): Web Chapter B.

Table 10.5 Sample Ranking of Proposed Projects According to Their Profitability Indexes

Project (1)	Net Investment (2)	Net Present Value (3)	Present Value of Net Cash Flows (4)	PI = (4) ÷ (2)	Cumulative Net Investment	Cumulative Net Present Value
P	$100,000	$25,000	$125,000	1.25	$100,000	$ 25,000
R	150,000	33,000	183,000	1.22	250,000	58,000
S	175,000	36,750	211,750	1.21	425,000	94,750
U	100,000	20,000	120,000	1.20	525,000	114,750
T	50,000	9,000	59,000	1.18	575,000	123,750
V	75,000	12,500	87,500	1.17	650,000	136,250
Q	200,000	30,000	230,000	1.15	850,000	166,250
W	50,000	−10,000	40,000	0.80	900,000	156,250

be accepted because this would require a capital outlay of $25,000 in excess of the $550,000 limit. Projects P, R, S, and U together yield a net present value of $114,750 but require a total investment outlay of only $525,000, leaving $25,000 from the capital budget that is not invested in projects. Management is considering the following three alternatives:

Alternative 1: It could attempt to find another combination of projects, perhaps including some smaller ones that would allow for a more complete utilization of available funds and increase the cumulative net present value. In this case, a likely combination would be Projects P, R, S, T, and V. This combination would fully use the $550,000 available and create a net present value of $116,250—an increase of $1,500 over the net present value of $114,750 from Projects P, R, S, and U.

Alternative 2: It could attempt to increase the capital budget by another $25,000 to allow Project T to be added to the list of adopted projects. This would raise the net present value of accepted projects to $123,750.

Alternative 3: It could merely accept the first four projects—P, R, S, and U—and invest the remaining $25,000 in a short-term security until the next period. This alternative would result in an NPV of $114,750, assuming that the risk-adjusted required return on the short-term security is equal to its yield.

In this case, Alternative 2 seems to be the most desirable of the three if another $25,000 can be raised without increasing the firm's cost of capital.

Mutually Exclusive Investments Having Unequal Lives

Replacement Chains
When mutually exclusive investments are considered, it is assumed implicitly that the alternative projects have *equal lives*. In actual practice, however, this may not be the case. When two or more mutually exclusive alternatives have *unequal lives*, neither the net present value nor the internal rate of return method yields reliable accept-reject information unless the projects are evaluated for an equal period of time. If, for example, a firm adopts the longer-lived of two projects simply on the basis of net present value or

internal rate of return data, it essentially ignores any alternative investment opportunities that might have been available at the end of the shorter-lived project.

Suppose a firm is considering two mutually exclusive investments, I and II. Project I requires an initial outlay of $2,000 and is expected to generate a five-year stream of net cash flows of $600 per year. Project II also requires an initial outlay of $2,000 but is expected to generate a 10-year stream of net cash flows of $375 per year. The firm has a 10 percent cost of capital.

Table 10.6 shows that the net present value of Project I is $274.60 and the net present value of Project II is $304.37. Therefore, the net present value criterion suggests that Project II should be chosen over Project I.

The expected life of Project II is twice as long as that of Project I. Therefore, the two net present values calculated in Table 10.6 are not really comparable. At this point, the firm must also consider what might happen if Project I were replaced with a similar five-year life project at the end of five years. In other words, it would create a **replacement chain** for the shorter-lived project. Suppose, for example, the firm estimates that replacing Project I with a similar project at the end of five years would cost $2,100 and, like Project I, would generate annual net cash flows of $600. This results in a new stream of cash flows for Project I, as shown in Table 10.7. The new net present value for Project I is higher than that for Project II, thus indicating—correctly—that Project I should be chosen over Project II.

Many times it is not possible to get a series of projects (such as Project I with its replacement at the end of five years) that will have an identical time duration to that of the longer-lived project (II). For example, one project might have a life of 15 years, whereas an alternative requires replacement every eight years. Hence, the shorter-lived project together with its replacement has a 16-year life, whereas the longer-lived project has a 15-year life. Such a comparison will normally be acceptable because the discrepancy occurs for only one year that is 16 years in the future. In present value terms, this will not have much impact.

The importance of time discrepancies such as these depends on the following:

- The number of years of the discrepancy. The fewer the years of the discrepancy, the less important it is.

- The number of years into the future the discrepancy occurs. The further into the future, the less important the discrepancy is.

Replacement Chains
A method for making capital budgeting decisions involving projects that have different useful lives. It assumes that the original investment can be replicated indefinitely so as to match the useful life of an alternative project.

Table 10.6   Cash Flows for Projects I and II

	Project I		Project II	
Year	Net Investment	Net Cash Flow	Net Investment	Net Cash Flow
0	$2,000	—	$2,000	—
1		$600		$375
2		600		375
3		600		375
4		600		375
5		600		375
6		—		375
7		—		375
8		—		375
9		—		375
10		—		375
$\text{NPV}_\text{I} = -\$2,000 + \$600(3.791)$			$\text{NPV}_\text{II} = -\$2,000 + \$375(6.145)$	
$= \$274.60$			$= \$304.37$	

Table 10.7 Replacement Chain Cash Flows for Project I Compared with Project II

| | Project I | | Project II | |
| | Net Investment | Net Cash Flow | Net Investment | Net Cash Flow |
Year				
0	$2,000	—	$2,000	—
1		$600		$375
2		600		375
3		600		375
4		600		375
5	2,100	600		375
6		600		375
7		600		375
8		600		375
9		600		375
10		600		375

$$\text{NPV}_I = -\$2,000 + \$600(6.145) - \$2,100(0.621)$$
$$= \$382.80$$

$$\text{NPV}_{II} = -\$2,000 + \$375(6.145)$$
$$= \$304.37$$

- The relationship between the rate of return on future investments and the cost of capital. When the rate of return on future investments is equal to the cost of capital, these investments have an NPV = 0. Under these circumstances, the discrepancy can be ignored.

Equivalent Annual Annuities

An alternative approach for dealing with the problem of mutually exclusive investments having unequal lives is to use the equivalent annual annuity approach. This technique can solve the problem of time discrepancies often encountered when using the replacement chain approach.

For example, consider the case of a firm that needs to replace an ageing piece of machinery. One alternative would be to buy new Machine A having a nine-year life. Another alternative would be to buy new Machine B with a five-year life. In this case, the time discrepancy between A and B is significant—four years. Commonly, this problem is dealt with by developing a string of replacement chains out to a year when both machines would need replacement. The common denominator year in this case is 45 years—indicating nine investments in B and five investments in A.

In cases like this, the equivalent annual annuity approach is often easier to use. In our example, assume the new Machine A will require a net investment of $34,500 and generate net cash flows of $7,000 per year for nine years. Machine B will require a net investment of $25,000 and generate net cash flows of $8,000 per year for five years. The firm's cost of capital is 10 percent. To make our decision on the basis of the equivalent annual annuity criterion, we use the following three steps:

1. First, compute the net present value of each machine over its original expected economic life:

$$\text{NPV}_A = -\$34,500 + \$7,000(\text{PVIFA}_{0.10,9})$$
$$= -\$34,500 + \$7,000(5.759)$$
$$= \$5,813$$

$$\text{NPV}_B = -\$25,000 + \$8,000(\text{PVIFA}_{0.10,5})$$
$$= -\$25,000 + \$8,000(3.791)$$
$$= \$5,328$$

The Use of Shareholder Resources

Managers are employed by the owners of a firm with the objective of maximizing wealth for the shareholders. As we have learned, this objective can be accomplished by investing in the set of projects possessing the maximum expected net present value. As discussed in Chapter 1, the managers of some firms have focused intently on this objective and have had good success in achieving their objective. Other managers, however, seem to have strayed frequently from this objective.

Investing in projects with negative net present values is most likely to occur in firms possessing large discretionary cash flows. Usually these are firms in mature industries with few true growth opportunities. Mature firms tend to generate substantial cash flows over which managers have considerable control. Marginal projects may be accepted, often with little analysis, because of their "strategic"

importance to the firm. Managers may be reluctant to pay these "excess" cash flows out to shareholders as increased dividends because that will cause the firm to grow at a slower rate in the future.

As discussed in Chapter 3, Stern Stewart's performance measuring system is designed to consider how effective managers have been in adding to their shareholders' investment. Their "Market Value Added" (MVA) measure can be viewed as the "net present value of all of a company's past and projected capital investment projects."

What factors might cause managers to consistently adopt investment projects with negative net present values? What are the consequences of these decisions for shareholders? What are the consequences of these decisions for the North American economy?

As these calculations indicate, if the possibility of the replacement of Machine B at the end of five years is not considered, Machine A would appear to be the better alternative because of its greater net present value.

2. Next, divide the net present value for each machine computed in Step 1 by the PVIFA factor for the project's original life. This gives the **equivalent annual annuity:**[10]

Equivalent Annual Annuity
A method for making capital budgeting decisions involving projects having different useful lives.

$$\text{Equivalent annual annuity (A)} = \$5,813/\text{PVIFA}_{0.10,9}$$
$$= \$5,813/5.759 = \$1,009.38$$

$$\text{Equivalent annual annuity (B)} = \$5,328/\text{PVIFA}_{0.10,5}$$
$$= \$5,328/3.791 = \$1,405.43$$

3. The equivalent annual annuity method assumes that each machine will be replaced an infinite number of times into the future and therefore will provide these annual annuities in perpetuity. As perpetuities, these equivalent annual annuities can be valued (at present) by dividing the annuity amount by the cost of capital:

$$\text{NPV}_A(\text{assuming infinite replacement}) = \$1,009.38/0.10 = \$10,093.80$$
$$\text{NPV}_B(\text{assuming infinite replacement}) = \$1,405.43/0.10 = \$14,054.30$$

---

[10] Suppose a firm faces a situation where only the costs of the mutually exclusive alternatives differed. Then the firm should choose the alternative with the lowest *equivalent annual cost.*

A Framework for International Capital Expenditure Decisions

The capital budgeting decision criteria discussed earlier in this chapter can also be used to evaluate international capital expenditure projects. To illustrate, suppose Magna International Inc., Canada's premier auto parts company, is considering expanding its Magna Steyr operations in Austria.

The company plans to invest $10 million in additional facilities. Based on this level of investment, Magna estimates that its proposed Austrian expansion project will generate annual net cash inflows of 1.5 million euros for a period of 10 years and nothing thereafter. Also, based on its analysis of present Austrian capital market conditions, Magna has determined that the applicable local cost of capital, k, for the expansion project is 15 percent. The present value of the expected net cash flows from the project, denominated in the *foreign* currency, is calculated as follows:

$$(10.7) \quad \text{PVNCF}_f = \sum_{t=1}^{n} \frac{\text{NCF}_t}{(1+k)^t}$$

Using Equation 10.7, a present value of approximately 7.53 million euros is obtained for the net cash flows of Magna's proposed Austrian expansion:

$$\text{PVNCF}_f = \sum_{t=1}^{n} \frac{1,500,000}{(1.15)^t}$$
$$= 7.53 \text{ million euros}$$

The present value of the project's net cash flows from the foreign viewpoint (PVNCF_f) is used to calculate the present value of the project's net cash flows to the parent company in the *home* country (PVNCF_h) as follows:

$$(10.8) \quad \text{PVNCF}_h = \text{PVNCF}_f \times S_0$$

where S_0 is the spot exchange direct rate which is expressed in units of home country currency per unit of foreign currency. Using a spot exchange rate of $1.55 per euro, the present value of the net cash flows to the parent company for the proposed expansion project is approximately $11.67 million.

To see a "CBA Walk-Through," that is, a graphic walk-through cost–benefit analysis, go to the following Web site **www.gis.uiuc.edu/gems/cba/cba.html**

Post-Audit
A capital budgeting procedure that consists of comparing actual cash flows from a project with projected cash flows that were estimated at the time the project was adopted.

Machine B should be acquired because it has the higher net present value when evaluated over an infinite replacement horizon.

In general, the equivalent annual annuity method will give the same decision as the replacement chain technique. Its advantage is that it often is computationally simpler, and it simplifies the handling of the time discrepancies that frequently arise in the replacement chain method. However, if the links in the replacement chain are not identical, as was the case earlier for Project I where the initial outlay was $2,100 for the second link instead of $2,000 for the first link, the equivalent annual annuity method cannot be used.

Reviewing and Post-Auditing an Accepted Project

A final important step in the capital budgeting process is the review of investment projects after they have been implemented. This can provide useful information on the effectiveness of the company's selection process. The **post-audit** procedure consists of comparing *actual* cash flows from an accepted project with *projected* cash flows that were estimated when the project was adopted. Because projected cash flows contain an element of uncertainty, actual values would not be expected to match estimated values

$$PVNCF_h = 7.53 \text{ million euros} \times \$1.55/\text{euro}$$

$$= \$11.67 \text{ million}$$

The project's net present value is calculated by subtracting the parent company's net investment in the project from $PVNCF_h$, the parent company's present value of the net cash flows:

$$(10.9) \quad NPV = PVNCF_h - NINV$$

A net present value of approximately $1.67 million is obtained for the project.

$$NPV = \$11.67 \text{ million} - \$10.0 \text{ million}$$

$$= \$1.67 \text{ million}$$

Based on this analysis, the proposed Austrian expansion is an acceptable project.

The Magna example assumes that an efficient capital market exists in the foreign country, as it does in most developed countries. Assets can be bought and sold and the required rates of return for projects can be determined from prices of other comparable assets in the foreign market.

The Magna example also assumes that the amount and timing of the expected net cash flows to the foreign subsidiary are the same as for the parent company. If the amount and timing of the net cash inflows to the foreign subsidiary and the parent company are not the same, the evaluation of the capital expenditure project is more complex than the example presented in this section.

The example presented in this section shows that the present value of a project's net cash flows to the parent company is simply the present value of the project's net cash flows from the foreign viewpoint converted into the home country currency at the current spot exchange rate.

exactly. Instead, a project review should be concerned with identifying systematic biases or errors in cash flow estimation on the part of individuals, departments, plants, or divisions and attempting to determine *why* these biases or errors exist. This type of analysis, when properly performed, can help a company's decision makers better evaluate investment proposals submitted in the future.

The importance of the post-audit process has been highlighted in research by Brown and Miller.[11] They observed that in the common situation where bad projects outnumber good ones, the simple procedure of making unbiased cash flow estimates and choosing projects with positive net present values will result in an upwardly biased acceptance rate for proposed projects (and returns that are, on average, below those that are expected) if there is uncertainty regarding future cash flows. In a situation such as this, the firm needs to correct for this potential bias when projects are being reviewed.

[11] K. C. Brown, "A Note on the Apparent Bias of Net Revenue Estimates for Capital Investment Projects," *Journal of Finance* (September 1974): 1215–1216; K. C. Brown, "The Rate of Return on Selected Investment Projects," *Journal of Finance* (September 1978): 1250–1253; E. M. Miller, "Uncertainty Induced Bias in Capital Budgeting," *Financial Management* (Autumn 1978): 12–18; E. M. Miller, "The Competitive Market Assumption and Capital Budgeting Criteria," *Financial Management* (Winter 1987): 22–28.

ENTREPRENEURIAL ISSUES

Capital Budgeting

The capital budgeting techniques discussed in this chapter are appropriate for use when evaluating proposed investment projects in both small, or entrepreneurial, and large firms. Conceptually, there is no difference between the value-maximizing capital investment techniques used by large and entrepreneurial firms. In practice, however, there are often significant differences between the capital budgeting procedures used by entrepreneurial firms and larger firms.

As we have seen, larger firms tend to use the net present value and the internal rate of return approaches to evaluate proposed capital expenditures. A study by Runyon of firms with a net worth under $1 million found that nearly 70 percent used payback or another technically incorrect procedure, such as the accounting rate of return, to evaluate capital expenditures. Several of the firms surveyed reported that they performed no formal analysis of proposed capital expenditures.[12]

Several reasons have been advanced to explain the dramatic differences in the practice of capital expenditure analysis between large and entrepreneurial firms. First, many entrepreneurs may simply lack the expertise needed to implement formal analysis procedures. Or managerial talent may tend to be stretched to its limits in many entrepreneurial firms, such that the managers simply cannot find the time to implement better project evaluation techniques. Also, one must recognize that

The information needed to make this necessary bias-eliminating correction can be gathered from careful project post-audits.

The importance of a good project review and tracking system is illustrated in the following example from Nortel Networks's joint venture partner, Ameritech, a holding company consisting of five telephone companies in the US midwest and several other subsidiaries. Ameritech has a sophisticated tracking system that permits the company to identify the individual responsible for each estimate in a capital project proposal. When the tracking system was announced and initiated, budgets had already been submitted for the coming year. Divisions were permitted to take back their budgets and resubmit them in light of the new tracking system. Seven hundred projects disappeared from the new budgets, and many others had reduced estimates of benefits![13]

Another objective of the project review process involves determining whether a project that has not lived up to expectations should be continued or abandoned. The decision to abandon a project requires the company to compare the cost of abandonment with any future cash flows that are expected over the project's remaining life. These estimates of future cash flows will usually be more accurate after the project has been in service for a period of time.

---

[12] L. R. Runyon, "Capital Expenditure Decision Making in Small Firms," *Journal of Business Research* (September 1983): 389–397.

[13] "Capital Budgeting: A Panel Discussion," *Financial Management* (Spring 1989): 10–17.

378   *Part 3   Capital Investment Decisions*

NEL

implementing and maintaining a sophisticated capital budgeting system is expensive. Large fixed costs are associated with putting a formal system in place, and continuing costs are associated with collecting the data necessary for the system to function effectively. In entrepreneurial firms, investment projects tend to be small, and they may not justify the cost of a complete, formal analysis.

The emphasis on the use of payback techniques by entrepreneurial firms may also reflect the critical cash shortages that face many small and rapidly expanding firms. Because of their limited access to the capital markets for additional funds, these firms may be more concerned with the speed of cash generation from a project than with the profitability of the project.

Regardless of these impediments to the use of value-maximizing capital budgeting techniques, entrepreneurs have an excellent opportunity to improve their competitive position by implementing effective managerial control techniques. Entrepreneurs who rely on incorrect techniques, such as payback, to make their project accept-reject decisions are more likely to make poor investment decisions than managers who analyze their investment projects correctly.

Inflation and Capital Expenditures

During inflationary periods, the level of capital expenditures made by firms tends to decrease. For example, suppose a firm has an investment opportunity that is expected to generate 10 years of cash inflows of $300,000 per year. The net investment is $2,000,000. If the company's cost of capital is relatively low—say, 7 percent—the net present value is positive:

$$\text{NPV} = \text{PVNCF} - \text{NINV}$$
$$= \$300{,}000(\text{PVIFA}_{0.07,10}) - \$2{,}000{,}000$$
$$= \$300{,}000(7.024) - \$2{,}000{,}000$$
$$= \$107{,}200$$

According to the net present value decision rule, this project is acceptable.

Suppose, however, that inflation expectations increase and the overall cost of the firm's capital rises to say, 10 percent. The net present value of the project then would be negative:

$$\text{NPV} = \text{PVNCF} - \text{NINV}$$
$$= \$300{,}000(\text{PVIFA}_{0.10,10}) - \$2{,}000{,}000$$
$$= \$300{,}000(6.145) - \$2{,}000{,}000$$
$$= -\$156{,}500$$

Under these conditions, the project would *not* be acceptable.

The example assumes that expected cash inflows are not affected by inflation. Admittedly, project revenues usually will increase with rising inflation, but so will expenses. As a result, it is somewhat difficult to generalize about net cash inflows. Experience, however, seems to indicate that cash flow increases often are not sufficient to offset the increased cost of capital. Thus, capital expenditure levels tend to be lower (in real terms) during periods of relatively high inflation than during low inflation times.

Fortunately, it is quite easy to adjust the capital budgeting procedure to take inflationary effects into account. The cost of capital already includes the effects of expected inflation. As the expected future inflation rate increases, the cost of capital also tends to increase. Thus, the financial manager has to estimate future cash flows (revenues and expenses) that reflect the expected inflationary rate. For example, if prices are expected to increase at a rate of 5 percent per year over the life of a project, the revenue estimates made for the project should reflect this rising price trend. Cost or expense estimates also should be adjusted to reflect anticipated inflationary increases, such as labour wage rate increases and raw material price increases.

If these steps are taken, the capital budgeting procedure outlined in this and the preceding chapter will assist the financial manager even in an inflationary environment.

Real Options in Capital Budgeting

An excellent site providing links to extensive information dealing with the real options approach to capital budgeting is **www.rhsmith.umd. edu/finance/atriantis/ realoptionsportal.html** To download an Excel spreadsheet that can be used to value real options, go to **www.iur.ruhr-uni- bochum.de/forschung/ real_options.html** Additional resources on real options can be found at **www.real-options.com**

In our discussion of capital budgeting we have used so-called conventional discounted cash flow techniques. That is, we determine a project's net present value by discounting the expected net cash flows at an applicable cost of capital, minus the net investment. This type of analysis does not consider the value of any operating (real) options that may be embedded in the project or the value of any options, or flexibilities, that the firm may choose to incorporate into the project's design. An option gives its holder the right, but not the obligation, to buy, sell, or otherwise transform an asset at a set price during a specified time period.

To illustrate how an embedded option may influence the net present value of a project, consider a manufacturing firm that calculates a negative net present value on a proposed project to purchase a new lathe to make a series of industrial parts for a particular application. The project's negative net present value is based on a cash flow analysis that assumes that the lathe will produce the parts for the entire economic life of the project. This cash flow analysis does not take into consideration the option of the company to abandon the project and sell the lathe in the active secondary market that exists for lathes and other manufacturing equipment. Or the company could simply choose to switch from making the specific parts to another potentially more profitable product. The abandonment option is embedded in the project. Its existence may limit the downside risk of the project.

To illustrate a designed-in option, consider an electric power plant project that is evaluating whether to use a gas burner or an oil burner to fire the turbines. The designed-in option in this instance would be a flexible dual-fuel boiler that can switch back and forth between gas and oil, depending on which energy source is cheaper to acquire and use. It may be, under certain conditions, that the flexible boiler project has a higher net present value than either of the projects using the gas-fired boiler or the oil-fired boiler, even though the initial cost of the flexible boiler is higher than the cost of either of the two single-fuel boilers. In other words, the value of the designed-in option may be greater than the additional cost of the flexible boiler.[14]

---

[14] See N. Kulatilaka, "The Value of Flexibility: The Case of a Dual-Fuel Industrial Steam Boiler," *Financial Management* (Autumn 1993): 271–280 for a further discussion of the flexible boiler option.

To illustrate a growth option, suppose a company is evaluating an Internet investment project consisting of two stages. The first stage (today) is an investment in a Web site and the second stage (one year from today) is an investment in an electronic commerce venture. The investment in the Web site has an NPV of −$10 million. Setting up the Web site (first stage) gives the company the option, but not the obligation, to invest in the electronic commerce business (second stage) one year from today.

While the cash flows are highly uncertain, ranging from large losses to substantial profits, the best estimate today is that the electronic commerce business has an NPV of −$60 million. Based on the NPV decision rule, the Internet investment project would be unacceptable since it has an NPV of −$70 million [−$10 million + (−$60 million)]. However, one year from today, the company will have more information and be better able to estimate whether the electronic commerce business (second stage) is worth pursuing. At that time, suppose new information about the cash flows of the electronic commerce venture shows that it will be extremely profitable, yielding an overall NPV of +$50 million for the Internet project. Clearly, the project would be worth undertaking at that time.

Investing in the Web site today, even though it has a negative NPV, preserves the company's option to invest in a positive NPV project in the future. By investing only in the Web site initially, the company is able to limit its downside risk (−$10 million NPV) while preserving the upside potential (+$50 million NPV) for the Internet investment project.

While option valuation in actual capital budgeting projects is complicated, financial managers should recognize the presence of options in projects and should consider including designed-in options when possible in planning projects.

Real options in capital budgeting can be classified in the following manner:

1. **Investment Timing Options** Delaying investment in a project, say for a year or so, may allow a firm to evaluate additional information regarding demand for outputs and costs of inputs, for example. Investing in a project today or waiting one year to invest in the same project is an example of two mutually exclusive projects. In this example, the firm should select the project with the higher net present value, assuming at least one project has a positive net present value. The "waiting-to-invest" option is a common real option.

2. **Abandonment Option** The option to discontinue a project is an important real option in capital budgeting. A project may be discontinued either by shutting it down completely and selling the equipment or by switching its use to an alternative product. Generally, the existence of an abandonment option reduces the downside risk of a project and should be considered in project analysis.

3. **Shutdown Options** A firm may have the option of *temporarily* shutting down a project in order to avoid negative cash flows. Consider a mining or manufacturing operation characterized by relatively high variable costs. If output prices drop below variable costs, a business has the option to shut down until output prices recover and rise above variable costs. Thus, the shutdown option also reduces the downside risk of a project. Of course, the decision to temporarily shut down becomes more complicated if there are significant shutdown and restart costs. Nevertheless, even in this case, the shutdown option typically is valuable as it provides some reduction in downside risk.

4. **Growth Options** A firm may have an opportunity to undertake a research program, build a small manufacturing facility to serve a new market, or make a small strategic acquisition in a new line of business. Each of these examples may be a negative net present value project, but each project can be viewed as having generated a growth option for the company that, if exercised, may lead ultimately to a large positive net present value project.

Real Option

Managerial opportunities to make decisions that will impact the expected cash flows of a project, their timing, or the future acceptability of the project. Real options include abandonment options, investment timing (delay) options, shutdown options, growth options, and flexibility (designed-in) options.

5. **Designed-in Options** In addition to options that can occur naturally in projects, managers have the opportunity to include options in projects in order to increase net present value. These designed-in options are classified either as input flexibility options, output flexibility options, or expansion options.

- *Input flexibility options* allow a firm to design into a project the capability of switching between alternative inputs because of input cost differences. The dual-fuel boiler project discussed earlier in this section is an example of an input flexibility option.

- *Output flexibility options* allow a firm to design into a project the capability of shifting the product mix of the project if relative product prices dictate such a shift. Oil refineries normally have output flexibility options.

- *Expansion options* give project managers the ability to add future capacity to a project at a relatively low marginal cost. For example, consider a firm that presently needs a manufacturing facility totalling 4,645 square metres. If instead, it builds a facility now with 6,503 square metres of space, the cost to the company to expand by 1,858 square metres in the future may be less than if it has to build a separate 1,858 square-metre facility later. Even if the need for the additional capacity never materializes, the value of the expansion option may justify the cost of the larger initial facility beforehand, particularly if significant uncertainty about future product demand exists.

Using conventional discounted cash flow analyses in capital budgeting without considering real options often results in a downward-biased estimate of the true value of a project's net present value. Some operating options, such as an option to expand, may increase a project's upside potential, while other operating options, such as an option to abandon, may reduce a project's downside risk.

How Are Real Options Concepts Being Applied?

Real options analysis is being used in different ways by leading companies. Some firms use real options concepts to frame *a way of thinking* about decision analysis problems involving capital investments. This may be viewed as the foundation level of use of real options concepts. When used as a way of thinking about corporate investment problems, real options analysis increases awareness of the value of the various options that may exist within a project. It also helps managers to recognize that valuable options can be created or destroyed because of the decision actions taken by managers. When used in this way, real options thinking helps managers to think about risk and uncertainty as assets that can be exploited in a project, rather than negative factors that should be avoided. In addition, real options thinking helps to focus managers on the value of acquiring additional information before making irrevocable investment decisions.

Other firms use real options concepts as *an analytical tool.* These firms apply formal option pricing models, such as the Black-Scholes model and the binomial option pricing model, to formally value the option characteristics of investment projects.[15] More complex models are also being used by a growing number of firms to value the option characteristics of investment projects. Some firms that have used real options approaches when analyzing various investment project opportunities include:

- Genentech, which has used the real options approach to value drug development projects
- Intel, which has used the real options approach to value investments in flexible manufacturing facilities

---

[15] The Black-Scholes model is discussed in Appendix 17A.

A flexible manufacturing facility usually costs more to build than an ordinary plant of similar size. However, its flexibility typically provides the firm with a valuable real option that may exceed the extra construction costs. This option seems particularly valuable in the auto industry, where demand for different products can be volatile.

■ Chevron Texaco, which has used the real options approach to value oil and gas development projects

Much advanced work on real options has been done and more is being done. Financial managers should attempt to incorporate options analyses in project evaluations whenever possible.[16]

Summary

■ The *net present value* of an investment made by a firm represents the contribution of the investment to the value of the firm and, accordingly, to the wealth of shareholders.

■ The *net present value* is calculated by subtracting a project's net investment from the expected net cash flows discounted at the firm's cost of capital.

■ The *profitability index* is the ratio of the present value of net cash flows to the net investment. It gives a measure of the relative present value return per dollar of initial investment. The profitability index is useful when choosing among projects in a capital rationing situation.

■ The *internal rate of return* of a project is the discount rate that gives the project a net present value equal to zero.

■ The net present value and internal rate of return approaches normally yield the same accept-reject decisions for a particular project. However, conflicts may arise when dealing with *mutually exclusive* projects. The reinvestment rate assumption embodied in the net present value approach—namely, that cash flows from a project are re-invested at the cost of capital—generally is more realistic than that underlying the internal rate of return method. For this reason, the net present value method is preferred to the internal rate of return method because the NPV method maximizes shareholder wealth. When firms face single-period *capital rationing*, either *soft* or *hard*, then the profitability index can assist in maximizing the NPV of selected projects.

■ When mutually exclusive projects have unequal lives and the projects are repeatable, the NPV of *replacement chains* of identical length (number of years) should be compared. If the repeatable projects are identical in all cash flows, then the *equivalent annual annuity* method can be used.

---

[16] This discussion is based on A. Triantis and A. Borison, "Real Options: State of the Practice," *Journal of Applied Corporate Finance* (Summer 2001): 25–40. See also the Autumn 1993 issue of *Financial Management*, which contains a section of six articles devoted to "Topics in Real Options and Applications." In particular, see L. Trigeorgis, "Real Options and Interactions with Financial Flexibility," *Financial Management* (Autumn 1993): 202–224, for an extensive review of the real options literature. For a recent Canadian example, see Don Cyr, "An Application of Real Options Analysis to the Vineyard Replanting Decision," presented at the Northern Finance Association Conference, 2002.

- Post-audits can assist management in uncovering biases in the project analysis procedure of a firm. Such reviews can also assist management in making abandonment decisions.

- Financial managers must be aware that using conventional discounted cash flow techniques in capital budgeting without considering *real options* results in a downward-biased estimate of the true value of a project's net present value.

Questions and Topics for Discussion

1. How does the net present value model complement the objective of maximizing shareholder wealth?
2. When is it possible for the net present value and the internal rate of return approaches to give conflicting rankings of mutually exclusive investment projects?
3. When are multiple rates of return likely to occur in an internal rate of return computation? What should be done when a multiple rate of return problem arises?
4. Describe how the profitability index approach may be used by a firm faced with a capital rationing investment funds constraint.
5. What are the primary strengths and weaknesses of the payback approach in capital budgeting?
6. What are the primary objectives of the investment project post-audit review?
7. What is the likely effect of inflation on the level of capital expenditures made by private firms? What must the financial manager do to ensure that a firm's capital budgeting procedures will be effective in an inflationary environment?
8. What major problems can you foresee in applying capital budgeting techniques to investments made by public sector and not-for-profit enterprises or organizations?
9. What effect would you expect the consideration of real options to have on the acceptability of an investment project?

Self-Test Problems

ST1. Calculate the net present value of a project with a net investment of $20,000 for equipment and an additional net working capital investment of $5,000 at time 0. The project is expected to generate net cash flows of $7,000 per year over a 10-year estimated economic life. In addition, the net working capital will be recovered at the end of the project. The required return on the project is 11% and the firm has a marginal tax rate of 40%. What is the meaning of the computed net present value figure?

ST2. Calculate the internal rate of return and profitability index for a project that is expected to generate eight years of annual net cash flows of $75,000. The project has a net investment of $360,000 and the required return on the project is 12%.

ST3. Two mutually exclusive projects have the following expected cash flows:

Year	G	H
0	−$10,000	−$10,000
1	5,000	0
2	5,000	0
3	5,000	17,000

a. Calculate the internal rate of return for each project.

b. Calculate the net present value for each project, assuming the firm's weighted cost of capital is 12%.

c. Which project should be adopted? Why?

ST4. A junior executive is fed up with the operating policies of his boss. Before leaving the office of his angered superior, the young man suggests that a robot could handle the trivia assigned to him. Pausing a moment to consider the import of this closing statement, the boss is seized by the thought that this must have been in the back of her own mind ever since she hired the junior executive. She decides to consider replacing the executive with a Honda Asimo robot that is capable of recognizing faces and gestures, as well as being able to walk and even climb stairs. She figures that she could argue strongly to the board that such "capital deepening" is necessary for the cost-conscious firm. Two days later, a feasibility study is completed, and the following data are presented to the president:

- It would cost $12,000 to purchase a robot with a life expectancy of 20 years.
- Annual expenses of using the robot would be $4,000.
- The junior executive's annual salary is $7,000 (a potential saving if the robot is used).
- The cost of the robot will be placed in class 8 with a CCA rate of 20%.
- The firm's marginal tax rate is 40%.
- The firm's current cost of capital is estimated to be 11%.
- On the basis of the net present value criterion, should the robot be used (and the junior executive fired)?

Problems*

BASIC

1. Calculate the net present value and profitability index of a project with a net investment of $20,000 and expected net cash inflows of $3,000 a year for 10 years if the project's required return is 12%. Is the project acceptable?

2. A machine that costs $8,000 is expected to operate for 10 years. The estimated salvage value at the end of 10 years is $0. The machine is expected to save a non-profit organization $1,600 per year. What is the internal rate of return on this investment?

3. A hectare planted with walnut trees is estimated to be worth $12,000 in 25 years. If you want to realize a 15% rate of return on your investment, how much can you afford to invest per hectare? (Ignore all taxes and assume that annual cash outlays to maintain your stand of walnut trees are nil.)

4. A $1,230 investment has the following expected cash returns:

Year	Net Cash Flow
1	$800
2	$200
3	$400

Compute the internal rate of return for this project.

*Coloured numbers and letters denote problems that have "check" answers provided at the back of the book.

5. A firm wishes to bid on a contract that is expected to yield the following after-tax net cash flows at the end of each year:

Year	Net Cash Flow
1	$5,000
2	$8,000
3	$9,000
4	$8,000
5	$8,000
6	$5,000
7	$3,000
8	−$1,500

To secure the contract, the firm must spend $30,000 to retool its plant. This retooling will have no salvage value at the end of the eight years. Comparable investment alternatives are available to the firm that earn 12% compounded annually. The CCA tax benefits from the retooling are reflected in the net cash flows in the table.

a. Compute the project's net present value.

b. Should the project be adopted?

c. What is the meaning of the computed net present value figure?

Excel

6. JP Inc. is considering purchasing a new automatic press brake, which costs $300,000 including installation and shipping. The machine is expected to generate net cash inflows (including CCA tax benefits) of $80,000 per year for 10 years. At the end of 10 years, the salvage value of the machine will be $0. To simplify the calculations, assume that the undepreciated capital cost of this machine is also $0 after 10 years. If the press brake project is undertaken, JP will have to increase its net working capital by $75,000. When the project is terminated in 10 years, there will no longer be a need for this incremental working capital, and it can be liquidated and made available for other uses. JP requires a 12% annual return on this type of project and its marginal tax rate is 40%.

a. Calculate the press brake's net present value.

b. Is the project acceptable?

c. What is the meaning of the computed net present value figure?

d. What is the project's internal rate of return?

e. For the press brake project, at what annual rates of return do the net present value and internal rate of return methods assume that the net cash inflows are being reinvested?

7. A firm is planning to invest $100,000 (pretax) in a personnel training program. The $100,000 outlay will be charged off as an expense by the firm this year (year 0). The after-tax returns from the program in the form of greater productivity and a reduction in employee turnover are estimated as follows:

Years 1–10: $10,000 per year
Years 11–20: $22,000 per year

The firm has estimated its cost of capital to be 12%. Assume that the entire $100,000 is paid at time 0 (the beginning of the project). The marginal tax rate for the firm is 40%. Should the firm undertake the training program? Why or why not?

8. Two mutually exclusive investment projects have the following forecasted cash flows:

Year	Project A	Project B
0	−$20,000	−$20,000
1	+$10,000	0
2	+$10,000	0
3	+$10,000	0
4	+$10,000	+$60,000

a. Compute the internal rate of return for each project.
b. Compute the net present value for each project if the firm has a 10% cost of capital.
c. Which project should be adopted? Why?

9. Show that the internal rate of return of the following investment is 0, 100, and 200 percent:

Year 0	Net investment	−$1,000
Year 1	Net cash flow	+$6,000
Year 3	Net cash flow	−$11,000
Year 4	Net cash flow	+$6,000

10. Note the following information on two mutually exclusive projects under consideration by WFM Inc.

	Annual Cash Flows	
Year	Project A	Project B
0	−$30,000	−$60,000
1	$10,000	$20,000
2	$10,000	$20,000
3	$10,000	$20,000
4	$10,000	$20,000
5	$10,000	$20,000

WFM requires a 14% rate of return on projects of this nature.
a. Compute the NPV of both projects.
b. Compute the internal rate of return on both projects.
c. Compute the profitability index of both projects.
d. Compute the payback period on both projects.
e. Which of the two projects, if either, should WFM accept? Why?

11. Channel Tunnel Inc. plans to build a new 40-km-long tunnel under the English Channel for added train service. The cost (NINV) of the tunnel is expected to be $3.3 billion. Net cash inflows are expected to equal $651 million per year. How many years must the firm generate this cash inflow stream for investors to earn their required 19% rate of return?

12. Project Alpha requires an outlay of $10,000 immediately. Project Alpha has a one-year life and is expected to produce a net cash flow at the end of one year of $20,000. Project Beta, a mutually exclusive alternative to Alpha, requires an outlay of $20,000 immediately. It too is expected to have a one-year life and to produce a net cash flow at the end of one year of $35,000.
a. Compute the internal rate of return for both projects. Compute the NPV for both projects, using a cost of capital of 10%.
b. Which project should be undertaken?

13. IFC, a Canadian-based food company, is considering expanding its soup processing operations in Switzerland. The company plans a net investment of $8 million in the project. The current spot exchange rate is CHF6.25 per $ (CHF = Swiss francs). Net cash flows for the expansion project are estimated to be CHF5 million for 10 years and nothing thereafter. Based on its analysis of current conditions in Swiss capital markets, IFC has determined that the applicable cost of capital for the project is 16%. Calculate the net present value of the proposed project.

 Excel

14. You have just been named the chief financial officer of Fabco, a large metal fabricator located in Chama, Mexico. The company has long been a user of the net present value method for evaluating its investment projects. The firm undertakes all projects offering a positive net present value, based on data submitted by the proposer of the project. Fabco's weighted cost of capital has been estimated to be 15%. This capital cost has remained approximately constant over the past five years.

Over the past five years Fabco has earned a return on assets averaging 8%. You are concerned about the apparent disagreement between Fabco's cost of capital and its earned returns. The CEO has asked you to prepare a report on the situation. What factors (both within and outside of the firm) might account for this *apparent* discrepancy in performance?

CHALLENGE

15. Imperial Systems has $1 million available for capital investments during the current year. A list of possible investment projects, together with their net investments and net present values, is provided in the following table:

Project	Net Investment	Net Present Value
1	$200,000	$20,000
2	$500,000	$41,000
3	$275,000	$60,000
4	$150,000	$5,000
5	$250,000	$20,000
6	$100,000	$4,000
7	$275,000	$22,000
8	$200,000	-$18,000

a. Rank the various investment projects in terms of their profitability indexes (computed to three decimal places).
b. In the order of decreasing profitability index values and considering the capital constraints, which projects should be adopted? Are all capital funds expended?
c. Is there another combination that produces a higher aggregate net present value than the one developed in part b?
d. If less than the entire amount of available funds is invested, what is the opportunity cost of the unused funds?

16. The LSM Company is planning to open a new strip mine. The net investment required is $10 million. Net cash flows are expected to be +$20 million at the end of year 1 and +$5 million at the end of year 2. At the end of year 3, LSM will have a net cash *outflow* of $17 million to cover the cost of closing the mine and reclaiming the land.

a. Calculate the net present value of the strip mine if the cost of capital is 5, 10, 15, 30, 71, and 80%.
b. What is unique about this project?
c. Should the project be accepted if LSM's cost of capital is 10%? 20%?

17. Fred and Frieda have always wanted to enter the blueberry business. They locate a 50-hectare piece of hillside that is covered with blueberry bushes. They figure that the annual yield from the bushes will be 200 crates. Each crate is estimated to sell for $400 for the next 10 years. This price is expected to rise to $500 per crate for all sales from years 11 through 20.

In order to get started, Fred and Frieda must pay $150,000 for the land plus $20,000 for packing equipment. The packing equipment will be included in CCA class 8 and has a zero estimated salvage value at the end of 20 years. Fred and Frieda believe that at the end of 20 years, they will want to retire to Florida and sell their property.

Annual operating expenses, including salaries to Fred and Frieda and exclusive of CCA, are estimated to be $50,000 per year for the first 10 years and $60,000 thereafter. The land is expected to appreciate in value at a rate of 5% per year. The couple's marginal tax rate is 30% for both ordinary income and *taxable* capital gains and losses. (For individuals, *taxable* capital gains and losses are currently 50% of *actual* gains and losses. See Chapter 2.)

a. If the couple requires at least a 13% return on their investment, should they enter the blueberry business?

b. Assume that the land can be sold for only $50,000 at the end of 20 years (a capital loss of $100,000). Should the couple invest in the land and blueberry business? (Assume that the couple may claim the full amount of their capital loss in the year it occurs—year 20.)

18. The S Company is considering building a chili processing plant. The plant is expected to produce 50,000 kilograms of processed chili peppers each year for the next 10 years. During the first year, S expects to sell the processed peppers for $2 per kilogram. The price is expected to increase at a 7% rate per year over the 10-year economic life of the plant. The costs of operating the plant, exclusive of CCA, including the cost of fresh peppers, are estimated to be $50,000 during the first year. These costs are expected to increase at an 8% rate per year over the next 10 years.

The plant will cost $80,000 to build. It will be included in class 8 with a CCA rate of 20%. The estimated salvage at the end of 10 years is zero. The firm's marginal tax rate is 40%.

a. Calculate the net investment required to build the plant.

b. Calculate the annual net cash flows from the project.

c. If S uses a 20% cost of capital to evaluate projects of this type, should the plant be built?

d. Calculate the payback period for this project.

e. How many internal rates of return does this project have? Why?

19. CH is considering replacing one of its larger control devices. A new unit sells for $29,000 (delivered). An additional $3,000 will be needed to install the device. The new device has an estimated 20-year service life with an estimated salvage value of $2,000 at the end of 20 years. The new control device will be included in CCA class 8. The existing control device (original cost = $15,000) has been in use for 12 years, and has an estimated scrap value of $1,000. The existing device could be used indefinitely, assuming the firm is willing to pay for its very high maintenance costs. The new device requires lower maintenance costs and frees up personnel who normally would have to monitor the system. Estimated annual cash savings from the new device will be $9,000. The firm's cost of capital is 12% and its marginal tax rate is 40%. Evaluate the relative merits of replacing the old control device using the net present value approach.

20. BI Co. is planning to open a new sporting goods store in a suburban mall. BI will lease the needed space in the mall. Equipment and fixtures for the store will cost

$200,000 and will be placed in class 8 with a CCA rate of 20%. The new store will require BI to increase its net working capital by $200,000 at time 0.

First-year sales are expected to be $1 million and to increase at an annual rate of 8% over the expected 10-year life of the store. Operating expenses (including lease payments but excluding depreciation) are projected to be $700,000 during the first year and to increase at a 7% annual rate. The salvage value of the store's equipment and fixtures is anticipated to be $10,000 at the end of 10 years.

BI's marginal tax rate is 40%.

a. Calculate the store's net present value, using an 18% required return.
b. Should BI accept the project?
c. Calculate the store's internal rate of return.
d. Calculate the store's profitability index.

 Excel

21. SDE acquired a robotic saw six years ago at a cost of $10 million. The saw was placed in class 10 with a CCA rate of 30%. Actual salvage value today is estimated to be $2 million. The firm's average tax rate is 30%, its marginal tax rate is 40%, and its weighted cost of capital is 15%.

A new robotic saw will cost $15 million. It also will be included in class 10. If the new saw is acquired, the firm estimates that its net working capital investment will decline, due to the reduced need to carry inventories of spare parts for this more reliable machine. Net working capital should decline from a current level of $1 million to a new level of $500,000 as a result of this purchase.

a. Calculate the net investment required to acquire the new saw.
b. The new saw is expected to reduce operating costs (exclusive of CCA) by $800,000 per year over the asset's expected 10-year life. Also, the increased productivity of the new saw is expected to increase revenue by $2 million per year. Salvage value at the end of 10 years is expected to be $0 for either saw. Calculate the annual net cash flows for this replacement decision.
c. Compute the NPV for this project.

22. The Perth Pie Company is considering two mutually exclusive investments that would increase its capacity to make strawberry tarts. The firm uses a 12% cost of capital to evaluate potential investments. The two projects have the following costs and expected cash flow streams:

Year	Project A	Project B
0	−$30,000	−$30,000
1	$10,500	$6,500
2	$10,500	$6,500
3	$10,500	$6,500
4	$10,500	$6,500
5	—	$6,500
6	—	$6,500
7	—	$6,500
8	—	$6,500

a. Using these data, calculate the net present value for Projects A and B.
b. Create a replacement chain for Alternative A. Assume that the cost of replacing A will be $30,000 and that the replacement project will generate cash flows of $10,500 for years 5 through 8. Using these figures, recompute the net present value for Alternative A.
c. Which of the two alternatives should be chosen, A or B? Why?
d. Use the equivalent annual annuity method to solve this problem. How does your answer compare with the one obtained in part b?

23. BC Minerals is considering a new production process. Two alternative pieces of equipment are available. Alternative P costs $100,000, has a 10-year life, and is expected to generate annual cash inflows of $22,000 in each of the 10 years. Alternative R costs $85,000, has an eight-year life, and is expected to generate annual cash inflows of $18,000 in each of the eight years. BC Minerals' weighted cost of capital is 12%. Using the equivalent annual annuity method, which alternative should be chosen?

24. Germania Corporation is considering replacing its plant cooling unit. The existing unit has recently "died" and has no salvage value. Of the two competing cooling units, B has a long life but a higher initial cost than the cheaper unit A. The following data are available:

Year	NCF_A	NCF_B
0	−$50,000	−$79,000
1	$25,000	$28,000
2	$25,000	$28,000
3	$25,000	$28,000
4	—	$28,000
5	—	$28,000

The marginal cost of capital is 19%. Which cooling unit should be purchased? Why?

25. Turbomachinery Parts, Inc. is considering two mutually exclusive equipment investments that would increase its production capacity. The firm uses a 14% required rate of return to evaluate capital expenditure projects. The two investments have the following costs and expected cash flow streams:

Year	Investment D	Investment E
0	−$50,000	−$50,000
1	24,000	15,000
2	24,000	15,000
3	24,000	15,000
4	—	15,000
5	—	15,000
6	—	15,000

a. Calculate the net present value for Investments D and E, using the above data.
b. Create a replacement chain for Investment D. Assume that the cost of replacing D remains at $50,000 and that the replacement project will generate cash inflows of $24,000 for years 4 through 6. Using these figures, recompute the net present value for Investment D.
c. Which of the two investments should be chosen, D or E? Why?
d. Use the equivalent annual annuity method to solve this problem. How does your answer compare with the one obtained in part b?

Other Practice Materials and Resources

For interactive quizzes, Internet exercises, crossword puzzles, CTV videos, and more, go to the *Contemporary Financial Management* Web site at **http://cyr.nelson.com**

Using a Spreadsheet to Calculate NPV

Table 10A.1 presents the results for Howie's drill press replacement project that were generated by the MS Excel spreadsheet Capital Budgeting.xls that is available on the Web site for this book. Howie's project was introduced in Chapter 9 to demonstrate the calculation of net cash flows. Then, in Chapter 10, Howie's project was used to illustrate the NPV decision rule. Recall that since NPV < 0 for this project, Howie's should not replace the drill press.

In Table 10A.1, column A describes or labels the items entered or calculated in the succeeding column or columns. Single-year inputs are entered in cells B4 through B12. In general, multi-year inputs are entered in the block of cells B16 through V20 for projects with an economic life no greater than 20 years. Since Howie's project is for 10 years, only the relevant block of cells B16 through L20 are shown in Table 10A.1.

Intermediate outputs for Howie's project appear in the block of cells B23 through L31. Cash flow outputs are shown in the block of cells B35 through L41, with the NPV and approximate IRR shown in cells B42 and B43, respectively.

Table 10A.2 shows the data and formulas used for Howie's project through year 2. Formulas for years 3 through 20 can be generated by copying the relevant cells for year 2. (Of course, for Howie's project, you need to copy only the cells through year 10.)

Some of the formulas for year 2 also can be generated by copying the relevant cells from year 1. There are, however, two exceptions:

1. Starting UCC for year 1 in cell C26 is the net installed cost that is calculated in cell B23.

2. Starting UCC in each succeeding year in row 26 is the ending UCC in row 28 for the preceding year. CCA for year 1 in cell C27 reflects the half-year convention required by law. Succeeding years, of course do not have the factor 0.5 in their respective CCA cells in row 27.

The NPV of −$7,294 for Howie's project is shown in cell B42, which agrees with the value previously obtained in Chapter 10.

Extending the Spreadsheet to Calculate IRR

An approximate IRR of 13.85% is shown in cell B43. Is this calculated IRR of 13.85% the actual IRR for Howie's drill press replacement project? Yes, it is if one of the following two conditions is met:

1. If $\Delta UCC_n = \Delta S_n$, then the PV at time n of the CCA tax shields beyond the economic life of the asset are zero, irrespective of the project's discount rate.

2. The calculated IRR is sufficiently close to the project's discount rate so that the PV of these tax shields changes by an immaterial amount when the calculated IRR instead of the project's discount rate is used in cell B8.

Clearly, for Howie's project, $\Delta UCC_n = \$19,327 \neq \$24,000 = \Delta S_n$. So, does the second condition hold for Howie's project? Yes, it does. To see this, enter .1385 in cell B8 for the discount rate. Then, in cell L41, the PV of these CCA tax shields changes slightly from −$1,068 to −$1,104, the NPV in cell B45 becomes $2 (which is approximately zero), and the calculated IRR remains at 13.85%.

Suppose, however, the project's discount rate had been 40% initially. The actual IRR of 13.85% does not depend on the project's discount rate. However, the calculated IRR does change slightly from 13.85% to 13.87%.

Table 10A.1 NPV for Howie's

	A	B	C	D	E	F	G	H	I	J	K	L
1	Capital Budgeting											
2												
3	**Single-Year Inputs**											
4	New asset price	$190,000										
5	Ship. & instal.	$10,000										
6	Old salvage, $t = 0$	$40,000										
7	Life, $n \leq 20$	10										
8	Discount rate	15.00%										
9	Tax rate	40.00%										
10	CCA rate	20.00%										
11	New salvage, $t = n$	$25,000										
12	Old salvage, $t = n$	$1,000										
13												
14	**Multi-Year Inputs**											
15	Year	0	1	2	3	4	5	6	7	8	9	10
16	ΔNWC	$1,500	$200	$200	$200	$200	$200	$200	$200	$200	$200	-$3,300
17	New revenues	$0	$85,000	$87,000	$89,000	$91,000	$93,000	$95,000	$97,000	$99,000	$101,000	$103,000
18	Old revenues	$0	$70,000	$70,000	$70,000	$70,000	$70,000	$70,000	$70,000	$70,000	$70,000	$70,000
19	New oper. costs	$0	$20,000	$21,000	$22,000	$23,000	$24,000	$25,000	$26,000	$27,000	$28,000	$29,000
20	Old oper. costs	$0	$40,000	$40,000	$40,000	$40,000	$40,000	$40,000	$40,000	$40,000	$40,000	$40,000
21												
22	**Intermediate Outputs**											
23	Net installed cost	$160,000										
24	ΔSalvage, $t = n$	$24,000										

continued

	A	B	C	D	E	F	G	H	I	J	K	L
	Table 10A.1 NPV for Howie's *continued*											
25	Year	0	1	2	3	4	5	6	7	8	9	10
26	Starting UCC	$0	$160,000	$144,000	$115,200	$92,160	$73,728	$58,982	$47,186	$37,749	$30,199	$24,159
27	CCA	$0	$16,000	$28,800	$23,040	$18,432	$14,746	$11,796	$9,437	$7,550	$6,040	$4,832
28	Ending UCC	$0	$144,000	$115,200	$92,160	$73,728	$58,982	$47,186	$37,749	$30,199	$24,159	$19,327
29	ΔRevenues	$0	$15,000	$17,000	$19,000	$21,000	$23,000	$25,000	$27,000	$29,000	$31,000	$33,000
30	ΔOperating costs	$0	-$20,000	-$19,000	-$18,000	-$17,000	-$16,000	-$15,000	-$14,000	-$13,000	-$12,000	-$11,000
31	ΔNet revenues	$0	$35,000	$36,000	$37,000	$38,000	$39,000	$40,000	$41,000	$42,000	$43,000	$44,000
32												
33	**Cash-Flow Outputs**											
34	Year	0	1	2	3	4	5	6	7	8	9	10
35	Net installed cost	$160,000	$0	$0	$0	$0	$0	$0	$0	$0	$0	$0
36	$A - T$ Δnet revenues	$0	$21,000	$21,600	$22,200	$22,800	$23,400	$24,000	$24,600	$25,200	$25,800	$26,400
37	CCA tax shield $t \leq n$	$0	$6,400	$11,520	$9,216	$7,373	$5,898	$4,718	$3,775	$3,020	$2,416	$1,933
38	ΔNWC	$1,500	$200	$200	$200	$200	$200	$200	$200	$200	$200	-$3,300
39	ΔSalvage, $t = n$	$0	$0	$0	$0	$0	$0	$0	$0	$0	$0	$24,000
40	PV tax shield $t > n$	$0	$0	$0	$0	$0	$0	$0	$0	$0	$0	-$1,068
41	Net cash flow	-$161,500	$27,200	$32,920	$31,216	$29,973	$29,098	$28,518	$28,175	$28,020	$28,016	$54,565
42	Net present value	-$7,294										
43	Approx. IRR	13.85%										

Table 10A.2 Capital Budgeting Formulas

	A	B	C	D
1	Capital Budgeting			
2				
3	**Single-Year Inputs**			
4	New asset price	190000		
5	Ship. & install.	10000		
6	Old salvage, $t = 0$	40000		
7	Life, $n \leq 20$	10		
8	Discount rate	0.15		
9	Tax rate	0.4		
10	CCA rate	0.2		
11	New salvage, $t = n$	25000		
12	Old salvage, $t = n$	1000		
13				
14	**Multi-Year Inputs**			
15	Year	0	1	2
16	ΔNWC	1500	200	200
17	New revenues	0	85000	87000
18	Old revenues	0	70000	70000
19	New oper. costs	0	20000	21000
20	Old oper. costs	0	40000	40000
21				
22	**Intermediate Outputs**			
23	Net installed cost	=SUM($B$4:$B$5)-$B$6		
24	ΔSalvage, $t = n$	=$B$11-$B$12		

continued

Table 10A.2 Capital Budgeting Formulas *continued*

	A	B	C	D
25	Year	0	1	2
26	Starting UCC	0	=$B$23	=C28
27	CCA	0	=ROUND(0.5*$B$10*C26,0)	=ROUND($B$10*D26,0)
28	Ending UCC	0	=C26-C27	=D26-D27
29	ΔRevenues	=B$17-B$18	=C$17-C$18	=D$17-D$18
30	ΔOperating costs	=B$19-B$20	=C$19-C$20	=D$19-D$20
31	ΔNet revenues	=B$29-B$30	=C$29-C$30	=D$29-D$30
32				
33	**Cash-Flow Outputs**			
34	Year	0	1	2
35	Net installed cost	=SUM($B$4:$B$5)-$B$6	0	0
36	A − T Δnet revenues	=ROUND(B$31*(1-$B$9),0)	=ROUND(C$31*(1-$B$9),0)	=ROUND(D$31*(1-$B$9),0)
37	CCA tax shield t ≤ n	=ROUND(IF($B$7>=B$34,$B$9*B$27,0),0)	=ROUND(IF($B$7>=C$34,$B$9*C$27,0),0)	=ROUND(IF($B$7>=D$34,$B$9*D$27,0),0)
38	ΔNWC	=B$16	=C$16	=D$16
39	ΔSalvage, t = n	=ROUND(IF($B$7=B$34,$B$24,0),0)	=ROUND(IF($B$7=C$34,$B$24,0),0)	=ROUND(IF($B$7=D$34,$B$24,0),0)
40	PV tax shield t > n	=ROUND(IF($B$7=B$34,($B$9*$B$10)* (B$28-$B$24)/($B$8+$B$10),0),0)	=ROUND(IF($B$7=C$34,($B$9*$B$10)* (C$28-$B$24)/($B$8+$B$10),0),0)	=ROUND(IF($B$7=D$34,($B$9*$B$10)* (D$28-$B$24)/($B$8+$B$10),0),0)
41	Net cash flow	=-B$35+B$36+B$37-B$38+B$39+B$40	=-C$35+C$36+C$37-C$38+C$39+C$40	=-D$35+D$36+D$37-D$38+D$39+D$40
42	Net present value	=$B$41+ROUND(NPV($B$8,$C$41:$V$41),0)		
43	Approx. IRR	=IRR($B$41:$V$41)		

Thus, even if neither of the two conditions is satisfied, the IRR procedure outlined above should give a good approximate IRR for normal projects. Then, by replacing the project's discount rate in cell B8 with the approximate IRR, you should obtain the actual IRR. If not, repeat this process of replacing the value in B8 with the latest approximate IRR until the NPV is approximately zero and the calculated IRR does not change.

Closing an Asset Class

In developing this spreadsheet, it was assumed that the following assumptions held for the new asset (or the old asset, if the new one were not purchased):

1. No assets in the same class will be purchased in the year in which this asset will be disposed.

2. The salvage value of this asset (net of any removal costs) will be less than its original cost (including any installation and shipping costs).

3. The salvage value of this asset (net of any removal costs) will be less than the UCC of the entire class. That is, the asset class will remain open.

4. The asset will be disposed on the first day of the year following the end of its economic life.

Each one of these assumptions has one alternative. This means that the total number of possible sets of assumptions is $2 \times 2 \times 2 \times 2 = 16$. The possible outcome that we have used is, in our opinion the most frequent outcome.

Nevertheless, it would be useful to illustrate how the formulas in row 40 would be changed when we simultaneously change assumptions 3 and 4. That is, the asset class will be closed and the asset will be sold on the last day of year n.

In this case, there is a realized loss of $(\Delta UCC_n - \Delta S_n)$ if $\Delta UCC_n > \Delta S_n$ that generates a tax savings of $T(\Delta UCC_n - \Delta S_n)$ at the firm's marginal income tax rate T. If $\Delta S_n > \Delta UCC_n$, then the tax savings is still $T(\Delta UCC_n - \Delta S_n)$, but the savings are negative![17] That is, there is a recapture of excess depreciation charges $(\Delta S_n - \Delta UCC_n)$ that are taxable at the firm's marginal tax rate T. Thus, the appropriate formula for cell B40 becomes

$$=\text{ROUND(IF(\$B\$7=B\$34,\$B\$9*(B\$28-\$B\$24),0),0)}$$

This formula is then copied into cells C40 through V40 for years 2 through 20.

The above four assumptions were first discussed in Chapter 9 under the heading Half-Year Convention, Capital Gains, Closing the Asset Class, Disposal Date. See that section as a starting point for other modifications of the formulas in row 40 based on alternative assumptions.

Self-Test Problems: Appendix 10A

ST1. The exercise facility project for the TLC Yogurt Company was introduced in the Asset Expansion Projects section of Chapter 9.

 a. Use the spreadsheet introduced in this appendix to calculate the NPV for TLC's exercise facility project. (Hint: Enter 0 for any items on the spreadsheet that concern the old asset.)

---

[17] The astute reader may raise the issue that CCA cannot be taken on the tax return in the year an asset class is closed. While this is true for the tax return, it makes no difference to the net cash flow for year n. The decrease to zero for the CCA in row 23 and for the CCA tax shield in row 38 for year n would be exactly offset by an increase in the tax savings in row 40. Thus, the approach suggested here gives the correct NPV and is easiest to implement.

b. Should TLC undertake this project?

c. Calculate the approximate IRR for this project.

d. Calculate the actual IRR for this project.

ST2. Refer to Self-Test Problem ST2 in Chapter 9.

a. Use the spreadsheet introduced in this appendix to calculate the NPV for IPC's replacement project.

b. Should IPC replace the computer-controlled processing unit?

c. Calculate the approximate IRR for this project.

d. Calculate the actual IRR for this project.

Problems: Appendix 10A

Excel

1. Refer to Self-Test Problem ST4 in Chapter 10.

a. Use the spreadsheet introduced in this appendix to calculate the NPV for replacing the junior executive with the robot.

b. Calculate the approximate IRR for this replacement project.

c. Calculate the actual IRR for this replacement project.

Excel

2. A machine that costs $8,000 is expected to operate for 10 years and is a class 8 asset with a CCA rate of 20%. The estimated salvage value at the end of 10 years will equal the asset's UCC. The machine is expected to save the firm $1,600 per year before taxes and CCA. The firm has a marginal tax rate of 40%, and the project's cost of capital is 10%.

a. Use the spreadsheet introduced in this appendix to calculate the NPV of this machine.

b. Should this machine be purchased?

c. Calculate the approximate IRR for this machine.

d. Why is this approximate IRR the actual IRR?

APPENDIX 10B: BOND REFUNDING ANALYSIS

The Bond Refunding Process

Bond refunding occurs when a company exercises its option to redeem a callable issue and sells a lower-cost issue to take its place.[18] The decision of whether to refund a particular debt issue is usually based on a capital budgeting (present value) analysis. The principal benefit, or cash inflow, is the present value of the after-tax interest savings over the life of the issue. The principal investment, or cash outflow at the time of refunding, consists primarily of the call premium and the issuance (flotation) cost of the new debt.

Bond refunding differs from other capital expenditure projects in one very important way: The cash inflows are known with considerably more certainty than the cash flows from a typical capital expenditure project and thus are less risky. As a result, the weighted cost of capital is *not* used. Instead, the *after-tax cost of the new debt* is believed to be a more appropriate discount rate for bond refunding analysis.

Bond refunding becomes an important decision facing many firms whenever interest rates decline substantially from earlier levels. For example, firms that had issued bonds with coupon rates of 13 percent or more during the period of high inflation and

---

[18] Callable preferred shares can also be refunded. The same consideration and analysis apply to both debt and preferred shares. However, preferred share dividends are not tax-deductible and the appropriate discount rate is the cost of new preferred shares.

high interest rates in the early 1980s found that they could refund these issues at rates under 9 percent during the early 2000s.

As an illustration of bond refunding, consider the following example. The AP Company issued $100 million of 30-year, 13 percent debt five years ago. In the meantime, interest rates have declined, and the firm's management feels the decline has bottomed out. The debt issue is now callable at 107 percent of par. The firm could refund the old issue with a new 25-year, 10 percent, $100 million issue. Issuance costs on the new issue would be 0.5 percent, or $500,000.

If AP decided to call the old issue and refund it, both issues would be outstanding for a three-week period, resulting in overlapping interest payments. The company's marginal tax rate is 40 percent. For purposes of discounting, the after-tax cost of new debt is $0.10 \times (1 - 0.4) = 0.06$.

To determine whether AP should refund the old issue, a bond refunding analysis is carried out.

■ **Step 1:** Calculate the interest savings (cash inflows).[19]

$(10B.1)$ Annual interest, after tax = Issue size $\times$ Interest rate $\times$ (1 − Tax rate)

Annual after-tax interest, old issue = $100 million $\times$ 13% $\times$ 0.6 = $7.8 million

Annual after-tax interest, new issue = $100 million $\times$ 10% $\times$ 0.6 = $6.0 million

Annual after-tax interest savings = $1.8 million

Present value of interest savings = Annual after-tax interest savings $\times$ $PVIFA_{0.06,25}$

$$= \$1.8 \text{ million} \times 12.783$$

$$= \$23.009 \text{ million}$$

■ **Step 2:** Calculate the net investment (net cash outflow at time 0). This involves computing the after-tax call premium, the present value of the after-tax issuance cost of the new issue, and the overlapping interest.

Since the call premium is not a tax-deductible expense in Canada, the after-tax call premium is calculated as follows:

$(10B.2)$ Call premium, after-tax = % Call premium $\times$ Issue size

$$= 7\% \times \$100 \text{ million}$$

$$= \$7 \text{ million}$$

The call premium is a cash outflow.

The issuance cost on the new issue is 0.5 percent, or $500,000. This amount cannot be deducted from AP's current-period income for tax purposes. Instead, it must be capitalized and amortized on a straight line basis over the lesser of the life of the debt issue or five years. Thus, the PV of the after-tax issuance cost for AP is

$$= \text{Issuance cost} - T \times (\text{Issuance cost}/5) \times PVIFA_{0.06,5}$$

$$= \$500,000 - (.4)(\$100,000)(4.212)$$

$$= \$500,000 - \$163,480$$

$$= \$331,520$$

---

[19] This calculation assumes that interest is received once a year at year-end. Actually, interest is paid every six months. However, the two results are not materially different.

The present value of the issuance cost of the *new* issue is a net cash outflow.

In most bond refundings, it is necessary for a firm to sell the new issue and receive the proceeds before paying off the old lenders. Both issues are usually outstanding for less than a month. Thus, the interest expense on the old issue during the overlapping period is considered a cost, or part of the refunding investment. In AP's case, this expense is calculated as follows:

$$\text{Overlap interest, after tax} = \text{Annual after-tax interest, old issue} \times (\text{overlap days}/365)$$

$$= \$7.8 \text{ million} \times (21/365)$$

$$= \$448,767$$

The overlapping interest is a cash outflow.[20]

In summary, the net investment is calculated as follows:

Call premium	$7,000,000
Present value of issuance cost, new issue	$331,520
Overlapping interest	$448,767
Net investment (cash outflow)	$7,780,287

■ **Step 3:** Finally, calculate the net present value of refunding:

$$= \$23.009 \text{ million} - \$7.780 \text{ million}$$

$$= \$15.229 \text{ million}$$

Thus, AP should call its old issue and refund it with the new one because the NPV is positive.

Self-Test Problems: Appendix 10B

ST1. The W Company is considering refunding its $150 million, 12% debt issue with a 10%, 20-year debt issue. The existing (old) issue also matures in 20 years and now is callable at 105% of par. The issuance cost of the new issue is 0.4%. Both the new and old debt issues will be outstanding for four weeks, resulting in overlapping interest. W's weighted cost of capital is 10% and its marginal tax rate is 40%. The firm's treasurer feels that the decline in interest rates has bottomed out. Determine the net present value of refunding the old bond issue.

ST2. The SGE Company is considering refunding $50 million of 11% debt with an 8%, 20-year debt issue. The existing, or old, issue also matures in 20 years and now is callable at 108% of par. The issuance cost of the new issue is 0.875%. The firm estimates that both issues will be outstanding for one month, resulting in overlapping interest. Proceeds from the new issue will be invested in one-month T-bills that have a 6% annual yield to maturity. The firm has a weighted cost of capital of 10% and a 40% marginal tax rate. In addition, the firm's financial management feels as though the present interest rate decline has nearly bottomed out. Calculate the net present value of the refunding and make a recommendation to management on whether to refund the bonds.

(Note: $\text{PVIFA}_{0.048, 20}$ can be determined using Equation 4.19 in Chapter 4.)

---

[20] Normally, during the period of the overlap, the proceeds from the sale of the new issue are temporarily invested in short-term securities. The interest earned will offset part of the overlapping interest expense. For simplification, this offset against the overlapping interest expense has not been considered in this example. See Self-Test Problem ST2 for an example of temporary investment in T-bills.

Problems: Appendix 10B

1. The PP Company is considering refunding its $250 million, 11.5% debt issue with a 10%, 15-year debt issue. The existing (old) issue also matures in 15 years and now is callable at 103.5% of par. The issuance cost of the new issue is 0.5%. Both the new and old debt issues will be outstanding for three weeks, resulting in overlapping interest. PP's weighted cost of capital is 10%, and its marginal tax rate is 40%. The firm's chief financial officer feels that the decline in interest rates has bottomed out. Determine the net present value of refunding the old bond issue.

2. The AE Company is considering refunding its $200 million, 12.5% debt issue with a 10%, 10-year debt issue. The existing (old) issue also matures in 10 years and now is callable at 104% of par. The issuance cost of the new issue is 0.4%. Both the new and old debt issues will be outstanding for 25 days, resulting in overlapping interest. Proceeds from the new issue will be invested in T-bills that mature in 25 days and have a 6% nominal annual yield to maturity. AE's weighted cost of capital is 10%, and its marginal tax rate is 40%. The firm's treasurer feels that the decline in interest rates has bottomed out. Determine the net present value of refunding the old bond issue.

Capital Budgeting and Risk

Learning Objectives

After studying this chapter you should be able to

1. Understand that *total project risk* refers to the chance that a project will not perform up to expectations. It is often measured by either the standard deviation or the coefficient of variation of cash flows from a project.

2. Understand that the *portfolio,* or *systematic, risk* of a project refers to the contribution a project makes to the risk of the firm when the interactions between the cash flows of the project are considered in conjunction with the other cash flows of the firm

3. Understand that a number of techniques can be used to analyze total project risk. These techniques include

   a. The net present value/payback approach

   b. The simulation analysis approach
   c. The sensitivity analysis approach
   d. The scenario analysis approach
   e. The risk-adjusted discount rate approach
   f. The certainty equivalent approach

4. Understand that when considering the systematic risk of individual projects, the *beta* concept can be used to determine risk-adjusted discount rates for individual projects

5. Understand that the decision to employ a risk analysis technique to evaluate an investment project depends on the additional cost of applying such a technique compared to the perceived benefits of doing so. Typically, the larger the project, the more likely it is to be worthwhile

Aircraft Makers "Bet the Company"

© LANDMANN PATRICK/CORBIS SYGMA/MAGMA

In 1992, executives of Airbus and Boeing discussed whether or not the world's airlines needed a huge new jumbo jet, and if so, whether the two companies should jointly design and build it. After looking at the same data, Boeing executives decided that the project was too risky and expensive. However, Airbus executives came to the opposite conclusion. Namely, that it was even more risky not to develop the plane.

Boeing decided to work on a $2 billion overhaul of its existing 747 jumbo jet. Airbus built a huge structure for a mock-up of its new four-engine jet, the A-3XX, to show to prospective buyers. Based on their feedback, the A-3XX became the A-380. It will be the world's largest jetliner when it starts flying in 2006. The new jumbo jet will be about 50 percent larger than the Boeing 747-400. Seating capacity will range from 500 to 700 passengers depending on the plane's configuration. Airports probably will need to be redesigned to accommodate passengers boarding and exiting from the plane's two levels, each of which has two aisles. The development cost for the A-380 is more than US$12 billion.

The two strategies are based on two very different visions of the future. Airbus believes that the number of passengers flying between the world's busiest airports will grow faster than airport capacity, thus increasing demand for a new generation of jumbo jets. Boeing sees a future with more point-to-point flights between smaller cities as passengers seek to bypass congested hubs.

Who is right? The risk for both companies is huge. If Airbus is right, it will steal some of Boeing's most lucrative customers and significantly boost its market share. If Airbus is wrong, the financial impact will be devastating. If Boeing is right, it will stem its loss of market share to Airbus. However, if Boeing is wrong, Airbus will capture a significant portion of the market for jumbo jets, a segment that Boeing now controls entirely.

Capital investments sometimes take many years to pay off. In this case, the biggest risk facing Airbus is that the market for super-sized jumbo jets will not develop. Instead of more flights to major hub cities, airlines and passengers may prefer more direct city-to-city flights.

Firms need capital budgeting rules to protect themselves against higher risk projects that have a significant probability of turning out worse than expected. Requiring a higher acceptance threshold for riskier projects puts a cushion between the firm and the consequences of a miss in predicting the project's outcome. This makes failure or loss less likely. Would you expect the discount rates used by each company to evaluate their respective new aircraft investments to differ? Yes, we would. Boeing currently sells jumbo jets, and it is essentially modifying an existing aircraft platform. Its project is unlikely to greatly increase the risk of its existing business. The uncertainty surrounding future cash flows and the technology involved in the Airbus A-380 are much higher than normal. Accordingly, Airbus should use a higher cost of capital. Boeing now controls the entire market for jumbo jets. How would this fact impact the incremental cash flows of both Boeing and Airbus as they evaluate the NPV of a new super-sized jumbo jet? The relevant cash flows in the capital budgeting process are a company's incremental cash flows. Since Boeing currently sells jumbo jets, it must take into account the potential lost sales on existing jumbo jets. Since Airbus does not currently have a jumbo jet, it does not have to factor in lost sales on existing aircraft.

Introduction

Although risk cannot be eliminated when considering investment projects, a capable financial manager should try to determine at the outset what risks are being assumed when an investment is undertaken. What is the worst-case outcome? How likely is that outcome? What actions can be taken to reduce this risk? How will investors react to this risk? Given answers to these questions, risky projects can be evaluated properly. This chapter examines these important questions.

In Chapter 7, we discussed the nature of risk and its influence on financial decision making. The greater the risk associated with an investment, the greater the return required. This basic principle also applies in capital budgeting.

In the previous chapter, investment projects were evaluated using the firm's weighted cost of capital (required rate of return). This approach implicitly assumes that all projects being considered are of equal risk and that this risk is the same as that for the firm as a whole. When a project has more or less than an average risk level, it is necessary to adjust the analysis to account for this risk level.

Total Project Risk versus Portfolio Risk

The Society for Risk Analysis (SRA) provides current information on risk assessment, communication, and management, and its official publication, *Risk Analysis*, deals with the social, psychological, and theoretical aspects of risk. SRA's Web site offers links to risk-related sites at
www.sra.org

When analyzing the risk associated with a capital expenditure, it is important to distinguish between the *total project risk* and the *portfolio*, or *systematic, risk* of that investment. By total project risk, we mean the chance that a project will perform below expectations—possibly resulting in losses from the project and for the firm. In the worst case, these losses could be so severe as to cause the firm to fail.

In contrast, a project that has a high level of total project risk may not affect the portfolio risk of the firm at all. Consider the case of oil and gas exploration companies. The firms know that any wildcat well they drill will cost about $2 million and have only a 10 percent chance of success. Successful wells produce profits of $24 million. Unsuccessful wells produce no profits at all, and the entire investment will be a loss. If each firm drilled only one well, there would be a 90 percent chance the firm would fail (the total project risk would be very high). In contrast, if one firm drilled 100 wildcat wells, the risk of failure from all wells would be very low because of the portfolio risk reduction that results from drilling many wells. In this case, the expected return of the firm would be as follows:

$$\text{Expected return} = \frac{\text{Expected profit per well}}{\text{Investment required per well}}$$

$$= \frac{[(\text{Probability of success})(\text{Profit}) + (\text{Probability of failure})(\text{Profit})]}{\text{Investment required per well}}$$

$$= \frac{[(0.10)(\$24 \text{ million}) + (0.90)(-\$2 \text{ million})]}{\$2 \text{ million}}$$

$$= \frac{(\$2.4 \text{ million} - \$1.8 \text{ million})}{\$2 \text{ million}}$$

$$= 0.30, \text{ or } 30\%$$

This return is achieved with very little risk relative to that facing a firm drilling a single well. As this example illustrates, the risk of drilling any individual well can be diversified away very effectively. Consequently, these risks are not market-related, and they should have little, if any, impact on the systematic risk of the firm. That risk remains unchanged and approximately equal to the market risk facing other oil and gas exploration companies.

This example has shown that an investment with high total project risk does not necessarily have to possess high systematic risk. Of course, it is possible for a project to have both high total project risk and high systematic risk. For example, a grocery store chain (which typically has low systematic risk) might decide to develop and market a new line of small business computers. Because of the large number of competitors in this business and because of the grocery chain's lack of expertise, this investment can be expected to have a high level of total project risk. At the same time, the systematic risk of this investment is likely to be high relative to that of the grocery chain, because business computer sales expand rapidly during boom periods and slow down dramatically during recessions.

From a capital budgeting perspective, the systematic risk of a project is certainly important. It may affect the beta of the firm and thereby influence the returns required by investors in that firm. Hence, the value of the firm's shares would be affected.

Total project risk is also important to consider in most cases for several reasons. There are a number of relatively undiversified investors, including the owners of small firms, for whom total project and total firm risk are important. Also, the total risk of the firm—not just the systematic risk—determines the risk of firm failure and potential bankruptcy. Shareholders, creditors, managers, and other employees all are interested in preventing the tragedy (and avoiding the costs) of total firm failure.

Consequently, in the evaluation of an investment project, it is important to consider both the total project risk and the impact of the project on the systematic risk of the firm. We continue the chapter with a discussion of a number of techniques that can be used to account for total project risk in the capital budgeting process. In the final section, we examine techniques to use when evaluating the systematic risk of a project.

Adjusting for Total Project Risk

The risk adjustment procedures discussed in this section are appropriate when the firm believes that a project's total risk is the relevant risk to consider in evaluating the project and when it is assumed that the returns from the project being considered are highly positively correlated with the returns from the firm as a whole. Therefore, these methods are appropriate only in the absence of internal firm diversification benefits, which might change the firm's total risk (or the systematic portion of total risk).

Several different techniques are used to analyze total project risk. These include the net present value/payback approach, simulation analysis, sensitivity analysis, scenario analysis, the risk-adjusted discount rate approach, and the certainty equivalent approach. In addition, total project risk can be measured by calculating the standard deviation and coefficient of variation. These calculations are discussed in Chapter 7.

Visit **http://finance. swcollege.com** for more on risk and project valuation.

Net Present Value/Payback Approach

Many firms combine net present value (NPV) with payback (PB) when analyzing project risk. As noted in Chapter 10, the project payback period is the length of time required to recover the net investment. Because cash flow estimates tend to become more uncertain further into the future, applying a payback cutoff point can help reduce this degree of uncertainty. For example, a firm may decide not to accept projects unless they have positive net present values *and* paybacks of less than some stated number of years.

The net present value/payback method is both simple and inexpensive but it suffers from some notable weaknesses. First, the choice of which payback criterion should be applied is purely subjective and not directly related to the variability of returns from a project. Some investments may have relatively certain cash flows far into the future, whereas others may not. The use of a single payback cutoff point fails to allow for this. Second, some projects are more risky than others are during their start-up periods. The payback criterion also fails to recognize this. Finally, this approach may cause a firm to reject some actually acceptable projects. In spite of these weaknesses, however, some firms feel this approach is helpful when screening investment alternatives, particularly international investments in politically unstable countries and investments in products characterized by rapid technological advances. Also, firms that have difficulty raising external capital and thus are concerned about the timing of internally generated cash flows often find a consideration of a project's payback period to be useful.

Simulation Analysis

Computers have made it both feasible and relatively inexpensive to apply simulation techniques to capital budgeting decisions. The simulation approach is generally more appropriate for analyzing larger projects. A **simulation** is a financial planning tool that models some event. When simulation is used in capital budgeting, it requires that estimates be made of the probability distribution of each cash flow element (revenues, expenses, and so on). If, for example, a firm is considering introducing a new product, the elements of a simulation might include the number of units sold, market price, unit production costs, unit selling costs, the purchase price of the machinery needed to produce the new product, and the cost of capital. These probability distributions are then entered into the simulation model to compute the project's net present value probability distribution.

Recall from Chapter 10 that net present value is defined as follows:

$$(11.1) \qquad NPV = \sum_{t=1}^{n} \frac{NCF_t}{(1 + k)^t} - NINV$$

where NCF_t is the net cash flow in period t, NINV is the net investment, and k is the cost of capital. In any period, NCF_t may be computed as follows:

$$NCF_t = [q(p) - q(c + s)](1 - T) + T\Delta CCA - \Delta NWC$$

where q is the number of units sold; p, the price per unit; c, the unit production cost (excluding depreciation); s, the unit selling cost; ΔCCA, the annual incremental capital cost allowance; ΔNWC, the change in net working capital; and T, the firm's marginal tax rate.[1] Using Equation 11.1, it is possible to simulate the net present value of the project. Based on the probability distribution of each of the elements that influence the net present value, one value for each element is selected at random.

Assume, for example, that the following values for the input variables are randomly chosen: $q = 2{,}000$; $p = \$10$; $c = \$2$; $s = \$1$; $\Delta CCA = \$2{,}000$; $\Delta NWC = \$1{,}200$; and $T = 40\%$, or 0.40. Inserting these values into Equation 11.1 gives the following calculations:

$$NCF_t = [2{,}000(\$10) - 2{,}000 (\$2 + \$1)](1 - 0.40) + (0.4)(\$2{,}000) - \$1{,}200$$

$$= (\$20{,}000 - \$6{,}000)0.60 + \$800 - \$1{,}200$$

$$= \$8{,}000$$

Assuming that the net investment is equal to the purchase price of the machinery ($10,000, in this example) plus an initial increase of $1,200 in NWC; that the net cash flows in each year of the project's life are identical, except for year 5 when $6,000 of NWC is recovered; that $k = 10\%$; and that the project has a five-year life; the net present value of this particular iteration of the simulation can be computed as follows:

$$NPV = \frac{\$8{,}000}{(1 + 0.10)^1} + \frac{\$8{,}000}{(1 + 0.10)^2} + \frac{\$8{,}000}{(1 + 0.10)^3} + \frac{\$8{,}000}{(1 + 0.10)^4}$$

$$+ \frac{\$15{,}200}{(1 + 0.10)^5} - \$11{,}200$$

$$= \$8{,}000 \times 3.170 + \$15{,}200 \times 0.621 - \$11{,}200$$

$$= \$23{,}599$$

---

[1] We wish to focus on simulation here and deliberately simplify the calculation of ΔCCA in the example below by using straight-line depreciation with no half-year convention so that the ΔCCA is the same amount in each year. We also assume that the salvage value is zero. However, this too could be simulated and would change the net cash flow in the final year of the project.

In an actual simulation, the computer program is run typically 100 or more times, using different randomly selected input variables in each instance. Thus, the program can be said to be repeated, or iterated, and each run is termed an *iteration*. In each iteration, the net present value for the project would be computed accordingly. Figure 11.1 illustrates a typical simulation approach.

The results of these iterations are then used to plot a probability distribution of the project's net present values and to compute a mean and a standard deviation of returns. This information provides the decision maker with an estimate of a project's expected returns, as well as its risk. Given this information, it is possible to compute the probability of achieving a net present value that is greater or less than any particular value.

For example, assume that the simulation for the project previously illustrated results in an expected net present value $(\widehat{NPV})$ of $12,000, with a standard deviation (σ) of $6,000. The probability of the project's having a net present value of $0 or less now can be found using the standard normal probability distribution (Table V) and Equation 7.3 in Chapter 7 (substituting NPV for r as the variable of interest).[2] A value of $0 corresponds to

$$z = \frac{NPV - \widehat{NPV}}{\sigma}$$

$$= \frac{\$0 - \$12,000}{\$6,000}$$

$$z = -2.0$$

or, 2.0 standard deviations *below* the mean on the standard normal probability distribution.

It can be seen from Table V at the back of the book that the probability of a value less than -2.0 standard deviations from the mean is 2.28 percent. Thus, there is a

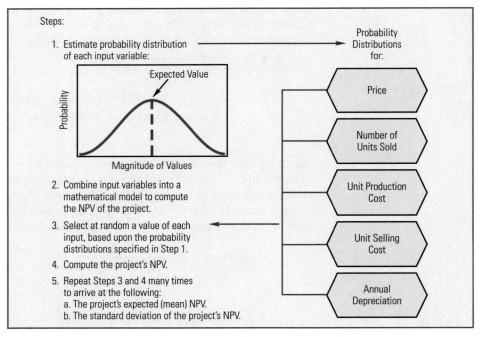

Figure 11.1
An Illustration of the Simulation Approach

***

[2] Regardless of the shape of the probability distribution for the individual variables used in the simulation, the net present value probability distribution will often be normally, or near normally, distributed.

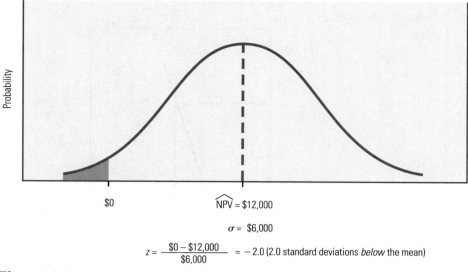

$$z = \frac{\$0 - \$12,000}{\$6,000} = -2.0 \ (2.0 \text{ standard deviations } below \text{ the mean})$$

Figure 11.2

A Sample Illustration of the Probability That a Project's Returns Will Be Less than $0

2.28 percent chance that the actual net present value for this project will be negative. Figure 11.2 shows the probability distribution of this project's net present value. The shaded area under the curve represents the probability that the project will have a net present value of $0 or less.

The simulation approach is a powerful one because it explicitly recognizes all of the interactions among the variables that influence a project's net present value. It provides both a mean net present value and a standard deviation that can help the decision maker analyze trade-offs between risk and expected return.[3] Unfortunately, it can take considerable time and effort to gather the information necessary for each of the input variables and to correctly formulate the model. This limits the feasibility of simulation to very large projects. In addition, the simulation examples illustrated assume that the values of the input variables are independent of one another. If this is not true—if, for example, the price of a product has a large influence on the number sold—then this interaction must be incorporated into the model, introducing even more complexity.

Sensitivity Analysis

Sensitivity analysis is a procedure that calculates the change in net present value given a change in one of the cash flow elements, such as product price. In other words, a decision maker can determine *how sensitive* a project's return is to changes in a particular variable.

Sensitivity analysis, like the simulation approach, also requires the definition of all relevant variables that influence the net present value of a project. The appropriate mathematical relationships between these variables must be defined, too, in order to estimate the cash flow from the project and compute the net present value. Rather than dealing with the entire probability distribution for each of the input variables, however, sensitivity analysis allows the decision maker to use only the "best estimate" of each variable to compute the net present value.

The decision maker can then ask various "what if" questions in which the project's net present value is recomputed under various conditions. For example, the best estimate of a product's price might be $10. The net present value of the project could be computed

How do you analyze cash flow sensitivity? Examine the sensitivity of cash flow in a new business at **www.toolkit.cch.com/ tools/tools.asp**

Sensitivity Analysis
A procedure that calculates the change in NPV given a change in one of the cash flow elements.

---

[3] Simulation may also be applied to other decision models, such as the internal rate of return or payback approaches.

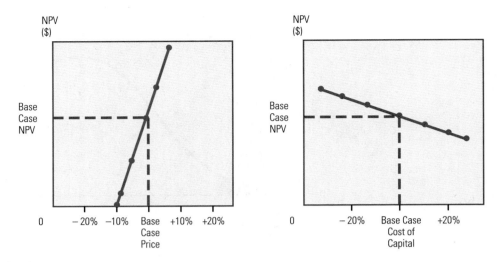

Figure 11.3
Illustrative Sensitivity Curves

using this input together with best estimates of all of the other variables. The next step would involve asking a question like "What if we cannot charge more than $8 per unit?" The net present value could be recomputed using the $8 price and the best estimates for each of the other input variables to determine the effect of the $8 price on the NPV.

Sensitivity analysis can be applied to any variable to determine the effect of changes in one or more of the inputs on a project's net present value.

It is often useful to construct sensitivity curves to summarize the impact of changes in different variables on the net present value of a project. A sensitivity curve has the project's net present value on the vertical axis and the variable of interest on the horizontal axis. For example, Figure 11.3 shows the sensitivity curves for two variables: sales price and cost of capital for a project.

The steep slope of the price–NPV curve indicates that the net present value is very sensitive to changes in the price for which the product can be sold. If the product price is approximately 10 percent below the base case (or initial analysis) estimate, the net present value of the project drops to $0, and the project becomes unacceptable for further price declines. In contrast, the relatively flat cost-of-capital–NPV curve indicates that the net present value is not very sensitive to changes in the firm's cost of capital. Similar curves could be constructed for project life, salvage value, units sold, operating costs, and other important variables.

Using Spreadsheets for Sensitivity Analysis   Spreadsheets, such as Excel, have made the application of sensitivity analysis techniques simple and inexpensive. Once the base case has been defined and entered in the spreadsheet, it is easy to ask hundreds of "what if" questions. For example, assume that revenues from a project are expected to be $20,000 in year 1 and to grow by 10 percent annually over the five-year life of the project. This relationship would be entered into the spreadsheet along with similar relationships for all other factors that go into the determination of the annual net cash flows from the project. The net present value of the base case is computed by the spreadsheet. Now, what if the revenues are estimated to grow only 5 percent annually, instead of 10 percent? Only one change must be made on the spreadsheet (redefine the growth rate to 5 percent), and it automatically recomputes each period's net cash flows and the net present value of the project. This process can be repeated rapidly, literally hundreds of times, to develop a profile of how sensitive the project is to changes in the individual components of the project's cash flows. This allows the decision maker to focus the analysis on the key variables that are critical to the project's success.

Scenario Analysis

Scenario Analysis
A technique that considers the simultaneous impact on NPV of changes in key variables.

Scenario analysis is another technique that has been used to assess the risk of an investment project. Sensitivity analysis considers the impact of changes in key variables, one at a time, on the desirability of an investment project. In contrast, **scenario analysis** considers the impact of simultaneous changes in key variables on the desirability of an investment project.

For example, consider the case of Bombardier's decision to invest in new, larger, longer-range versions of its Challenger airplane. The success of this proposed investment project depends on many factors, including the price of the plane, the number of units likely to be demanded, the cost of development, the time period required for development, and the cost of production. When using the scenario analysis technique, the financial analyst might ask the project director to provide various estimates of the project's expected net present value. In addition to what is perceived to be the most likely scenario, the project director might be asked to provide both optimistic and pessimistic estimates. An *optimistic scenario* might be defined by the most optimistic values of each of the most input variables—for example, low development costs, low production costs, high prices, and strong demand. A *pessimistic scenario* would be defined by low prices, soft demand, high development costs, and high production costs. The project manager could also be asked to provide estimates of the probability that the optimistic scenario will result and the probability that the pessimistic scenario will result. With these probability estimates, the financial manager can compute an estimate of the standard deviation of the NPV of the project.

Assume, for example, that the following estimates of the NPV of the Bombardier Challenger project have been developed using scenario analysis:

Outcome (j)	NPV_j	Probability (p_j)
Pessimistic	−$11.4 billion	0.20
Most likely	$1.3 billion	0.60
Optimistic	$10.1 billion	0.20

Recall from Chapter 7 that the expected value of a variable, such as net present value, is

$$\widehat{NPV} = \sum_{t=1}^{n} NPV \times p_j$$

The expected NPV of this project would be

$$\widehat{NPV} = 0.20(-\$11.4) + 0.60(\$1.3) + 0.20(\$10.1) = \$0.52 \text{ billion}$$

Recall also from Chapter 7 that the standard deviation of a variable, such as net present value, is

$$\sigma = \sqrt{\sum_{t=1}^{n}(NPV_j - NPV)^2 p_j}$$

Thus, the standard deviation of net present value can be computed as

$$\sigma = [(-\$11.4 - \$0.52)^2 0.20 + (\$1.3 - \$0.52)^2 0.60 + (\$10.1 - \$0.52)^2 0.20]^{0.5}$$

$$= \$6.87 \text{ billion}$$

Given the expected NPV of $0.52 billion and the expected standard deviation of $6.87 billion (and assuming that the probability distribution is approximately normally distributed), it is now possible to compute the probability that the project will have a negative net present value:

$$z = 0 - \frac{\widehat{NPV}}{\sigma}$$

$$z = \frac{0 - \$0.52}{\$6.87}$$

$$= -0.08$$

From Table V it can be seen that the probability of a value less than -0.08 standard deviations from the mean ($\$0.52$ billion) is about 46.8 percent. This means that there is a 46.8 percent chance that this project will have a negative NPV.

This example illustrates both the value of scenario analysis and some of its short-comings. With the aid of spreadsheet programs such as Excel, it is possible to easily estimate the impact of various scenarios on the expected performance of a project. However, scenario analysis techniques normally look at only a limited number of alternative scenarios. Furthermore, the process of assigning probabilities to the outcomes expected from alternative scenarios is difficult and largely subjective.

Risk-Adjusted Discount Rate Approach

The **risk-adjusted discount rate** approach (RADR) adjusts for risk by varying the rate at which the expected net cash flows are discounted when determining a project's net present value. The RADR approach can also be used in the analysis of projects for which total project risk is the applicable risk measure, as well as systematic risk.

In the risk-adjusted discount rate approach, net cash flows for each project are discounted at a risk-adjusted rate, k_a^* to obtain the NPV:

$$(11.2) \qquad NPV = \sum_{t=1}^{n} \frac{NCF_t}{(1 + k_a^*)^t} - NINV$$

where NCF_t is the net cash flow in period t and NINV is the net investment. The magnitude of k_a^* depends on the relationship between the total risk of the individual project and the overall risk of the firm. To compute k_a^*, the *risk-free rate*, r_f—that is, a required rate of return associated with investment projects characterized by certain cash flow streams—is used. Federal government securities are good examples of risk-free investments because there is no chance that investors will not get the dollar amount of interest and the principal repayment on schedule. Thus, the yield on government securities is usually used as the risk-free rate.

Most companies are not in business to invest in risk-free securities, as individual investors can do that just as well. Instead, companies assume some amount of risk, expecting to earn higher returns than those available on risk-free securities. The difference between the risk-free rate and the firm's required rate of return (cost of capital) is an *average risk premium* to compensate investors for the fact that the company's assets are risky. This relationship is expressed algebraically as follows:

$$(11.3) \qquad \theta = k_a - r_f$$

where θ is the average risk premium for the firm; r_f, the risk-free rate; and k_a, the required rate of return for projects of average risk, that is, the firm's cost of capital.

The cash flows from a project having greater than average risk are discounted at a higher rate, k_a^*—that is, a risk-adjusted discount rate—to reflect the increased riskiness. Total project risk premiums applied to individual projects are commonly established *subjectively*. For example, some firms establish a small number of *risk classes* and then apply a different *risk premium* to each class. Below-average-risk projects, such as straightforward equipment replacement decisions, might be evaluated at 2 percent *below* the firm's cost of capital (a risk discount). Average-risk projects, such as equipment modification decisions, might be evaluated at the firm's cost of capital. Above-average-risk projects, such as facility expansions, might be assigned a risk premium of 3 percent *above* the firm's cost of capital. High-risk projects, such as investments in totally new lines of business or the introduction of new products, might be assigned a risk premium of 8 percent *above* the firm's cost of capital.

Although the risk-class approach saves time in the analysis stage, it can lead to suboptimal decisions, because the risk premiums themselves are usually determined subjectively and no explicit consideration is given to the variation in returns of the projects assigned to individual classes. In short, the risk-class approach is most useful when evaluating relatively small projects that are repeated frequently. In these cases, much is known about the projects' potential returns, and it is probably not worth the effort to try to compute more "precise" risk premiums.

Certainty Equivalent Approach

Certainty Equivalent
The amount of cash someone would require with certainty in order to make him or her indifferent between that certain amount and an amount expected to be received with risk at the same point in time.

Another approach that can be used to deal with total project risk uses certainty equivalents. The **certainty equivalent** approach adjusts the net cash flows in the *numerator* of the NPV equation, in contrast to the RADR approach, which involves adjustments to the *denominator* of the NPV equation. A certainty equivalent factor is the ratio of the amount of cash someone would require with certainty at a point in time in order to make that person indifferent between that certain amount and an amount expected to be received with risk at the same point in time. The project is adjusted for risk by converting the expected risky cash flows to their certainty equivalents and then computing the net present value of the project. The risk-free rate, r_f—not the firm's cost of capital, k—is used as the discount rate for computing the net present value. This is done because the cost of capital is a *risky* rate, reflecting the firm's average risk, and using it would result in a double-counting of risk.

Certainty equivalent factors range from 0 to 1.0. The higher the factor, the more certain the expected cash flow. For example, one project might offer expected cash flows over its five-year life as follows:

Year	Expected NCF	Certainty Equivalent Factor (α)	Certainty Equivalent Cash Flows
0	−$10,000	1.0	−$10,000
1	+5,000	0.9	+4,500
2	+6,000	0.8	+4,800
3	+7,000	0.7	+4,900
4	+4,000	0.6	+2,400
5	+3,000	0.4	+1,200

The initial outlay of $10,000 is known with certainty. It might be for the purchase price of a piece of equipment. Hence, the certainty equivalent factor for year 0 is 1.0, and the certainty equivalent cash flow is −$10,000 (−$10,000 × 1.0). The $5,000 cash inflow in year 1 is viewed as being somewhat risky. Consequently, the decision maker has assigned a certainty equivalent factor of 0.9 to the net cash flow in year 1. Multiplying $5,000 times the 0.9 certainty equivalent factor yields a certainty equivalent cash flow of $4,500. This means that the decision maker would be indifferent between receiving the expected, risky $5,000 a year from now or receiving $4,500 with certainty at the same time. A similar interpretation is given to the certainty equivalent factors and certainty equivalent cash flows for years 2 through 5.

INTERNATIONAL ISSUES

Special Elements of Capital Budgeting Risk

The techniques of risk analysis presented in this chapter will serve a firm well whether it operates domestically or multi-nationally. However, managers of multinational firms need to be aware of special elements of risk when investing abroad.

When evaluating a capital expenditure to be made in another country, the parent firm must be concerned with the cash flows that can be expected to be received by the parent—not the cash flows that will accrue to the overseas subsidiary making the investment. There are several reasons for focusing on cash flows to the parent. First, the host country might block the subsidiary from remitting funds back to the parent. Hence, these "captive" funds are not available to the parent for reinvestment in projects offering the highest rate of return. Second, the parent needs to be concerned with the prospect that its assets in foreign subsidiaries could be taken by the host government with little or no compensation. Third, the parent must consider exchange rate risk between the host country's currency and the dollar.

(Exchange rate risk and procedures for managing it are discussed in detail in Chapters 2 and 18.) Related to exchange rate risk is the higher risk of inflation in many countries, particularly developing countries. The risk of highly volatile inflation and the ability of a firm to protect itself from this risk adds additional uncertainty to investments made abroad. Finally, more uncertainty may be associated with tax rates in the host country than is typical in North America.

Each of these factors affects the risk of the cash flows that can be expected from investments in other countries. Although multinational firms predominantly use standard capital budgeting procedures, such as NPV and IRR, to evaluate their investments abroad, there is evidence that many multinational firms also use the risk analysis techniques discussed in this chapter. In addition, some multinational financial managers rely more heavily on their own personal feelings about political and economic events in the host country than on quantitative methods to evaluate project risk.

Algebraically, the certainty equivalent factors, α_t, for the cash flows expected to be received during each time period, t, are expressed as follows:

$$(11.4) \qquad \alpha_t = \frac{\text{Certain return}}{\text{Expected return}}$$

The certainty equivalent factors are used to compute a certainty equivalent net present value as follows:

$$(11.5) \qquad \text{NPV} = -\text{NINV}(\alpha_0) + \sum_{t=1}^{n} \frac{\text{NCF}_t \alpha_t}{(1 + r_f)^t}$$

where

α_0 = Certainty equivalent factor associated with the net investment (NINV) at time 0

n = Expected economic life of the project

α_t = Certainty equivalent factor associated with the expected net cash flows (NCF) in each period, t

r_f = Risk-free rate

Note in this example that the certainty equivalent factors decline into the future. This reflects the fact that *most* cash flows are viewed as being more risky the further into the future they are projected to occur.[4] This point was discussed in more detail in Chapter 7. (See Figure 7.3.) In Table 11.1, we have computed the certainty equivalent net present value for this project assuming an 8 percent risk-free rate. It equals $4,753, and the project therefore is acceptable.

The certainty equivalent approach permits the decision maker to separately adjust each period's cash flows to account for their specific risk. This could be especially important if some later cash flows were more certain than some early cash flows. For example, a nuclear power plant may take several years to build, and there may be great uncertainty about construction cost overruns. Once the plant is built, however, estimates of net cash flows from operations may be less risky.

For any individual decision maker, the certainty equivalent net present value provides an unambiguous basis for making a decision once the appropriate certainty equivalent factors are chosen. A positive net present value means the project is acceptable to that decision maker, and a negative net present value indicates it should be rejected. However, different decision makers could have difficulty reaching a consensus over the choice of the subjective certainty equivalent factors. That is, there typically is no market basis for determining these factors. Perhaps as a consequence, the certainty equivalent approach is not widely used. Nevertheless, for large projects with unusual risk profiles, the certainty equivalent approach deserves consideration.

Adjusting for Systematic Risk in Capital Budgeting

The *beta* concept introduced in Chapter 7 for security risk analysis can also be used to determine risk-adjusted discount rates (RADR) for individual capital budgeting projects. This approach is appropriate for a firm whose shares are widely traded and for which there is very little chance of bankruptcy. (The probability of bankruptcy is a function of total risk, not just systematic risk.)

Just as the beta (systematic risk) of a portfolio of securities can be computed as the weighted average of the individual security betas, a firm may be considered as a portfolio of assets, each having its own beta. From this perspective, the systematic risk of the firm is simply the weighted average of the systematic risk of the individual assets.

You have probably heard about beta, arbitrage, CAPM, systematic risk, and the efficient frontier. But do you know what deltas, collars, leptokurtosis, swaptions, and inverse floaters are? Visit **www. contingencyanalysis.com** for a great glossary of risk terms.

Table 11.1	Calculation of Certainty Equivalent Net Present Value				
Year	Expected NCF	Certainty Equivalent Factor (α)	Certainty Equivalent Cash Flow	PVIF$_{0.08,\,t}$	Present Value of Cash Flows
0	$-10,000	1.0	$-10,000	1.000	$-10,000
1	+5,000	0.9	+4,500	0.926	+4,167
2	+6,000	0.8	+4,800	0.857	+4,114
3	+7,000	0.7	+4,900	0.794	+3,891
4	+4,000	0.6	+2,400	0.735	+1,764
5	+3,000	0.4	+1,200	0.681	+817
				Certainty Equivalent NPV =	+$4,753

---

[4] Different individuals may have different certainty equivalent factors, depending on each individual's relative risk aversion. Risk aversion is a function of many factors, including wealth, age, and the nature of a firm's reward structure.

The All-Equity Case

For example, consider the security market line shown in Figure 11.4. The firm has a beta of 1.2 and is financed exclusively with internally generated equity capital. The market risk premium is 7 percent. When considering projects of average risk—that is, projects that are highly correlated with the firm's returns on its existing assets and that have a beta similar to the firm's beta (1.2)—the firm should use the computed 13.4 percent cost of equity, or 5% + 1.2 (7%), from Figure 11.4. When considering projects having estimated betas different from 1.2, it should use an equity discount rate equal to the required return calculated from the security market line. For example, if a project's estimated beta is 1.7 and the risk-free rate is 5 percent, the project's required equity return would be 16.9 percent, or 5% + 1.7 (7%), and this would be used as the risk-adjusted discount rate for that project, assuming the project is financed with 100 percent equity.

The Equity and Debt Case

Next, we develop a procedure for computing the risk-adjusted discount rate for projects financed with both debt and equity. Recall that the concept of a weighted cost of capital was discussed in Chapter 8. At this point, recognize that the required return on the project discussed in this section reflects the project's equity return requirement and the debt return requirement for the funds expected to be used to finance the project.

Consider the example of Vulcan Industries, with a current capital structure consisting of 50 percent debt and 50 percent equity. Vulcan is considering expanding into a new line of business and wants to compute the rate of return that will be required on projects in this area. Vulcan has determined that the debt capacity associated with projects in its new business line is such that a capital structure consisting of 40 percent debt and 60 percent common equity is appropriate to finance these new projects. Vulcan's company beta has been estimated to be 1.3, but the Vulcan management does not believe that this systematic risk is appropriate for the new business line. Vulcan's man-

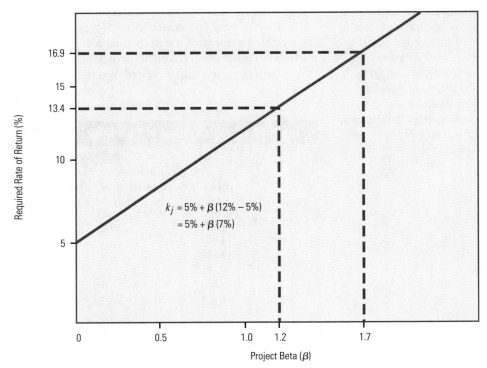

Figure 11.4
Risk-Adjusted Discount Rates and the SML

agers must estimate the systematic risk appropriate for projects in this new line of business and then determine the risk-adjusted return requirement on these projects.

Because the systematic risk of projects in this new business line is not directly observable, Vulcan's managers have decided to rely on surrogate market information. They have identified a firm, Olympic Materials, which competes exclusively in the line of business into which Vulcan proposes expanding. Finding such a firm is called the **pure play** approach. The beta of Olympic has been estimated to be 1.50.

Pure Play
An approach to evaluating risk based on surrogate market information of a benchmark firm.

Recall from Chapter 7 that a firm's beta is computed as the slope of its characteristic line and that actual security returns are used in the computations. Accordingly, a firm's computed beta is a measure of both its business risk *and* its financial risk. When a beta is computed for a firm such as Olympic, it reflects both the business and financial risk of that firm. To determine the beta associated with Vulcan's proposed new line of business using the observed beta from another firm (Olympic) that competes exclusively in that business line, it is necessary to convert the observed beta, often called a *leveraged beta*, β_p into an *unleveraged*, or pure project beta, β_u. This unleveraged beta can then be releveraged to reflect the amount of debt capacity appropriate for this type of project and that will be used by Vulcan to finance it. The following equation can be used to convert a leveraged beta into an unleveraged, or pure project, beta:[5]

$$(11.6) \qquad \beta_u = \frac{\beta_l}{1 + (1 - T)(D/E)}$$

where β_u is the unleveraged beta for a project or firm, β_l is the leveraged beta for a project or firm, D is the market value of the firm's debt, E is the market value of the firm's equity, and T is the firm's marginal tax rate.

The use of this equation can be illustrated for the Vulcan Materials example. The beta, β_l, for Olympic has been computed to be 1.50. Olympic has a capital structure consisting of 20 percent debt and 80 percent common equity and a tax rate of 35 percent. Substituting these values into Equation 11.6 yields

$$\beta_u = \frac{1.50}{1 + (1 - 0.35)(0.25)} = 1.29$$

The unleveraged, or pure project, beta for the proposed new line of business of Vulcan is estimated to be 1.29. Vulcan intends to finance this new line of business with a capital structure consisting of 40 percent debt and 60 percent common equity. In addition, Vulcan's tax rate is 40 percent. Equation 11.6 can be rearranged to compute the leveraged beta associated with this new line of business, given Vulcan's proposed target capital structure for the project:

$$(11.7) \qquad \beta_l = \beta_u [1 + (1 - T)(D/E)]$$
$$= 1.29[1 + (1 - 0.4)(0.667)]$$
$$= 1.81$$

With a risk-free rate of 5 percent and a market risk premium of 7 percent, the required return on the equity portion of the proposed new line of business is computed from the security market line as

$$k_e = 5\% + 1.81(7\%)$$
$$= 17.7\%$$

If the pretax cost of debt, k_d, used to finance the new line of business is 8 percent, the risk-adjusted required return, k_a^*, on the new line of business, given the proposed

[5] Robert Hamada, "The Effect of the Firm's Capital Structure on the Systematic Risk of Common Stocks," *Journal of Finance* (May 1972): 435–452.

capital structure of 40 percent debt and 60 percent equity, is a weighted average of the marginal, after-tax debt and equity costs, or

$$k_a^* = 0.4(8\%)(1-0.4) + 0.6(17.7\%)$$

$$= 12.5\%$$

Therefore, the risk-adjusted required rate of return on the proposed new line of business for Vulcan is 12.5 percent. This number reflects both the pure project risk and the financial risk associated with the project as Vulcan anticipates financing it.

Equations 11.6 and 11.7 provide only an approximation of the effect of leverage on beta. Capital market imperfections, such as the existence of risky debt and uncertainty regarding future levels of debt, introduce error into the beta adjustments just presented. Hence, this procedure should be used with caution. However, this general procedure is used by many different types of firms.

Computing the Risk-Adjusted Net Present Value

Suppose a company is considering a project whose net investment is $50,000 with expected cash inflows of $10,000 per year for 10 years. Using Equation 11.2, as shown in Table 11.2, the project's NPV is −$1,670 when evaluated at a risk-adjusted discount rate (k_a^*) and $6,500 when evaluated at the weighted average cost of capital (k_a). Assuming that the 16 percent RADR figure has been determined correctly by using the security market line with an accurate beta value, the project should *not* be accepted even though its NPV, calculated using the company's weighted cost of capital, is positive. This new product project is similar to Project 4 in Figure 11.5.

The new product project discussed in the previous paragraph has an internal rate of return of about 15 percent, compared to its 16 percent required return. Therefore, the project should be rejected, according to the IRR decision rule. When the IRR technique is used, the RADR given by the SML frequently is called the **hurdle rate**. Some finance practitioners use the term *hurdle rate* to describe any risk-adjusted discount rate.

Figure 11.5 illustrates the difference between the use of a single discount rate, the weighted cost of capital,[6] for all projects regardless of risk level and a discount rate based on the security market line for each project. In the example shown in Figure 11.5, Projects 1, 2, 3, and 4 are being evaluated by the firm. Using the weighted cost of capital approach, the firm would adopt Projects 3 and 4. However, if the firm considered the differential levels of systematic risk for the four alternatives, it would accept Projects 1

Hurdle Rate

The minimum acceptable rate of return from an investment project. For projects of average risk, it usually is equal to the firm's cost of capital.

Table 11.2 Calculation of NPV at Weighted Average Cost of Capital and Risk-Adjusted Discount Rate

Year t	Net Cash Flow	Weighted Average Cost of Capital ($k_a = .12$)		Risk-Adjusted Discount Rate ($k_a^* = .16$)	
		Interest Factor	Present Value	Interest Factor	Present Value
0	$−50,000	1.000	$−50,000	1.000	$−50,000
1–10	10,000	5.650	56,500	4.833	48,330
NPV			$ +6,500		$ −1,670

[6] The weighted cost of capital for a firm was defined in more detail in Chapter 8. It is equal to the marginal cost of equity times the proportion of common equity in the firm's target capital structure, plus the after-tax marginal cost of debt times the debt proportion in the firm's target capital structure, plus the after-tax marginal cost of preferred share capital times its proportion in the firm's target capital structure. In general, the weighted cost of capital is the appropriate discount rate to use when evaluating projects of average risk for a given firm.

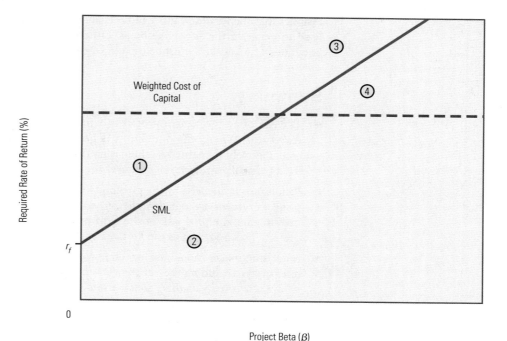

Figure 11.5
Risk-Adjusted Discount Rate versus Weighted Cost of Capital

and 3 and reject Projects 2 and 4. In general, *the risk-adjusted discount rate approach is considered preferable to the weighted cost of capital approach when the projects under consideration differ significantly in their risk characteristics.*

The one problem remaining with this suggested procedure involves the determination of beta values for individual projects. Thus far, the most workable approach available is the pure play approach which uses *surrogate market information,* as illustrated in the Vulcan Industries example. For example, if an aluminum firm is considering investing in the leisure-time product industry, the beta for this new project could be computed using the average beta for a sample of firms engaged principally in the leisure product industry. Although the beta for the aluminum firm might be 1.3—resulting in a required equity return on projects of average risk of 14.1 percent, or 5% + (1.3 × 7%), according to Figure 11.4—this would not be the appropriate rate for leisure product projects. Assuming a beta of 0.9 for leisure product firms, the leisure product projects would be required to earn an equity return of only 11.3 percent, or 5% + (0.9 × 7%), because of the lower average level of systematic risk associated with leisure product projects. This

Financial Challenge Revisited

Visit **www.airbus.com** and **www.boeing.com** or use **www.google.ca** to search for information.

Firms often face situations where they have to "bet the company" by investing in a new project that has a high cost and uncertain benefits. This chapter presented some techniques that can be used to help reduce the risks of such investments. In the Airbus and Boeing example what has happened since this book was written? We do not have a crystal ball to tell us, but you may be able to find out by researching the Internet.

assumes that the leisure product projects are financed in the same manner as the firms used to generate the surrogate betas. Otherwise, the beta adjustment procedure in Equations 11.6 and 11.7 must be used.

Summary

- The *risk* of an investment project is defined in terms of the potential *variability* of its returns. When only one return is possible—for example, as with government securities held to maturity—there is no risk. When more than one return is possible for a particular project, it is risky.

- Risk is also influenced by the possibility of investment *diversification*. If a proposed project's returns are not *perfectly correlated* with the returns from the firm's other investments, the total risk of the firm may be reduced by accepting the proposed project. This is known as the *portfolio effect*.

- A decision maker can adjust for total project risk in capital budgeting in several different ways, including the *net present value/payback approach (NPV/PB), simulation analysis, sensitivity analysis, scenario analysis,* the *risk-adjusted discount rate (RADR) approach,* and the *certainty equivalent (CE) approach.* The table below summarizes the advantages and disadvantages of these risk-adjustment approaches.

Approach	Advantages	Disadvantages
NPV/PB	• Simple • Inexpensive	• Choice of PB cut-off purely subjective • PB not necessarily a good proxy for risk
Simulation	• Explicitly recognizes interactions among variables • Provides mean and standard deviation of NPV	• Considerable time and effort necessary to gather required information • Expensive and thus suitable only for large projects
Sensitivity	• Determines how sensitive a project's NPV is to changes in individual variables • Calculations easily performed by spreadsheet	• No indication of likelihood of changes in individual variables • Not easy to interpret results in terms of accept/reject
Scenario	• Considers impact of simultaneous changes in key variables • Provides mean and standard deviation of NPV	• Typically examines a small number of scenarios • Assigned probabilities are largely subjective
RADR	• Often simply applied by assigning high, average, or low risk categories • Uses NPV decision rule	• Risk premiums usually must be subjectively determined • RADR is approximate
CE	• Separately adjusts each period's cash flows to account for their specific risk • Uses NPV decision rule	• CE adjustment factors are not market-determined • Decision makers can have difficulty reaching consensus on CE adjustment factors

- When a project differs significantly in its systematic risk profile (as measured by *beta*) from the systematic risk of the total firm, a risk-adjusted discount rate appropriate for that project can be computed using the security market line relationship between risk and required return from the capital asset pricing model.

- The decision to employ a risk analysis technique to evaluate an investment project depends on the project's size and the additional cost of applying such a technique compared with the perceived benefits of doing so. For small projects, only the simpler risk adjustment techniques should be used. For major projects that have above- or below-normal risk, it is worthwhile to analyze the project's risk as precisely as possible. Failure to fully analyze the risk of a large project could result in bad investment decisions and even substantial losses.

Questions and Topics for Discussion

1. How does the basic net present value model of capital budgeting deal with the problem of project risk? What are the shortcomings of this approach?

2. How would you define *risk* as it is used in a capital budgeting analysis context?

3. Recalling the meaning and measurement of risk discussion in Chapter 7, when is the standard deviation of a project's cash flows an appropriate measure of project risk? When is the coefficient of variation an appropriate measure?

4. How does the basic net present value capital budgeting model deal with the phenomenon of increasing risk of project cash flows over time?

5. When should a firm consider the portfolio effects of a new project?

6. What are the primary advantages and disadvantages of applying *simulation* to capital budgeting risk analysis?

7. Computer simulation is used to generate a large number of possible outcomes for an investment project. Most firms invest in a particular project only once, however. How can a computer simulation model be helpful to the typical decision maker who is making a one-time-only investment decision?

8. On average, the expected value of returns from each $1 of premiums paid on an insurance policy is less than $1. This is due to the insurance company's administrative costs and profits. In spite of this fact, why do so many individuals and organizations purchase insurance policies?

9. Describe how certainty equivalent cash flow estimates can be derived for individual project cash flows.

10. Will all individuals apply the same certainty equivalent estimates to the cash flows from a project? Why or why not?

Self-Test Problems

ST1. A firm is considering the purchase of new automated equipment. The project has an expected net present value of $250,000 with a standard deviation of $100,000. What is the probability that the project will have a net present value less than $50,000, assuming that net present value is normally distributed?

ST2. A firm is financed entirely with equity. Its beta has been estimated to be 1.0. The current risk-free rate is 10% and the expected market return is 15%.

   a. What rate of return should the firm require on a project of average risk?

   b. If a new venture is expected to have a beta of 1.6, what rate of return should the firm demand on this project?

c. The project in question requires an initial outlay of $9 million and is expected to generate a 10-year stream of annual net cash flows of $1.9 million. Calculate the NPV of the project using the firm's required return for projects of average risk.

d. Calculate the NPV of the project using the risk-adjusted rate computed in part b.

ST3. A firm is considering a new store that is expected to yield the following net cash flows following an initial (year 0), certain outlay (NINV) of $75,000:

Year	Net Cash Flows	Certainty Equivalent Factor
1	$30,000	0.90
2	30,000	0.80
3	30,000	0.65
4	20,000	0.50

a. Compute the NPV of this project at a 15% cost of capital.

b. If the risk-free rate is 8%, what is the certainty equivalent NPV for the new store?

Problems*

BASIC

1. MAP Inc. has estimated the probability distribution of its annual net cash flows as follows:

Probability	Cash Flow (in Thousands of Dollars)
0.10	$1,000
0.20	1,500
0.40	2,000
0.20	2,500
0.10	3,000

a. Compute the expected annual cash flow.

b. Compute the standard deviation of annual cash flows.

c. Compute the coefficient of variation of annual cash flows.

2. A proposed factory expansion project has an expected net present value of $100,000 with a standard deviation of $50,000. What is the probability that the project will have a negative net present value, assuming that net present value is normally distributed?

3. A firm is financed entirely with equity. Its beta is 1.5, and its price–earnings ratio is 16. The current risk-free rate is 8%, and the expected return on the market is 14%.

a. What rate of return should the company require on projects of average risk?

b. If a new project has a beta of 2.0, what rate of return should the company require?

4. Fox Enterprises is considering expanding into the growing laser copier business. Fox estimates that this expansion will cost $1.8 million and will generate a 20-year

---

*Coloured numbers and letters denote problems that have "check" answers provided at the back of the book.

stream of expected net cash flows amounting to $400,000 per year. The company's weighted cost of capital is 15%.

   a. Compute the net present value of the laser copier project using the firm's weighted cost of capital and the expected cash flows from the project.

   b. Using the risk-adjusted discount rate approach, management has decided that this project has substantially more risk than average and has decided that it requires a 24% expected rate of return. Recompute the risk-adjusted net present value of this project.

5. A simulation model similar to the one described in this chapter has been constructed by a firm to evaluate the largest of its new investment proposals. After many iterations of the model, management has arrived at an expected net present value for Project A of $1.0 million. The standard deviation of the net present value has been estimated from the simulation model results to be $0.8 million.

   a. What is the probability that the project will have a negative net present value?

   b. What is the probability that the project will have a net present value greater than $2.2 million?

6. You have estimated the expected NPV from a project to be $3,000,000 with a standard deviation of $4,000,000. The distribution of the possible NPVs is approximately normal. If you are willing to accept a 25% chance of incurring a negative NPV on the project, should it be undertaken?

7. The CS Corporation is evaluating a possible investment in a new regional distribution warehouse. A careful evaluation of the anticipated net cash flows and net investment expected from the project indicates that the expected net present value (NPV) of this project is $4.5 million. The anticipated standard deviation of this expected NPV is $3 million, and the distribution of the project's NPV is approximately normal. What is the chance that this project will have a positive NPV at least equal to $1,000,000?

INTERMEDIATE

8. A new project has expected annual net cash flows of $400,000 with a standard deviation of $250,000. The distribution of annual net cash flows is approximately normal.

   a. What is the probability of the project having negative annual net cash flows?

   b. What is the probability that annual net cash flows will be greater than $575,000?

9. Two projects have the following expected net present values and standard deviations of net present values:

Project	Expected Net Present Value	Standard Deviation
A	$50,000	$20,000
B	10,000	7,000

   a. Using the standard deviation criterion, which project is riskier?

   b. Using the coefficient of variation criterion, which project is riskier?

   c. Which criterion do you think is appropriate to use in this case? Why?

10. A firm is considering two investments. One is the purchase of a new continuous caster costing $100 million. The expected net present value of this project is $20 million. The other alternative is the purchase of a supermarket chain, also costing $100 million. It, too, has an expected net present value of $20 million. The firm's management is interested in reducing the variability of its earnings.

a. Which project should the company invest in?

b. What assumptions did you make to arrive at this decision?

11. VP Inc. is considering two independent investments having the following cash flow streams:

Year	Project A	Project B
0	−$50,000	−$40,000
1	+20,000	+20,000
2	+20,000	+10,000
3	+10,000	+5,000
4	+5,000	+5,000
5	+5,000	+40,000

VP uses a combination of the net present value approach and the payback approach to evaluate investment alternatives. It requires that all projects have a positive net present value when cash flows are discounted at 10% and that all projects have a payback no longer than three years. Which project or projects should the firm accept? Why?

12. AJ Inc. produces wine. The firm is considering expanding into the snack food business. This expansion will require an initial investment in new equipment of $200,000. The new equipment will be placed in class 8 with a CCA rate of 20%. At the end of the project, the equipment is estimated to have a salvage value of $50,000. The expansion will also require an increase in working capital for the firm of $40,000. Revenues from the new venture are forecasted at $200,000 per year for the first five years and $210,000 per year for years 6 through 10. Operating costs of the new venture are estimated at $90,000 for the first five years and $105,000 for years 6 through 10. It is assumed that at the end of year 10, the snack food equipment will be sold for its estimated salvage value. The firm's marginal tax rate is 40%. The required return for projects of average risk has been estimated at 15%.

a. Compute the project's net present value, assuming that it is an average-risk investment.

b. If management decides that all product line expansions have above-average risk and therefore should be evaluated at a 24% required rate of return, what will be the risk-adjusted net present value of the project?

13. The SP Company is analyzing the investment in a new line of business machines. The initial outlay required is $35 million. The firm's cost of capital (used for projects of average risk) is 15%. The net cash flows expected from the investment are as follows:

Year	Net Cash Flow (Million)
1	$5
2	8
3	15
4	20
5	15
6	10
7	4

a. Compute the net present value of this project assuming it possesses average risk.

b. Because of the risk inherent in this type of investment, the firm has decided to employ the certainty equivalent approach. After considerable discussion, management has agreed to apply the following certainty equivalents to the project's cash flows:

Year	α_t
0	1.00
1	0.95
2	0.90
3	0.80
4	0.60
5	0.40
6	0.35
7	0.30

If the risk-free rate is 9%, compute the project's certainty equivalent net present value.

c. On the basis of the certainty equivalent analysis, should the project be accepted?

 Excel

14. The BSS Company is considering manufacturing radial snowshoes, which are more durable and offer better traction. BSS also estimates that the investment in new equipment will cost $250,000 and will have a 10-year economic life with no salvage value. The new equipment will be placed in class 8 with a CCA rate of 20%. The estimated selling price of each pair of shoes will be $50. BSS anticipates that it can sell 5,000 pairs per year at this price. Unit production and selling costs will be about $25. The firm's marginal tax rate is 40%. A cost of capital of 12% is thought to be appropriate to analyze a project of this type. BSS has decided to perform a sensitivity analysis of the project before making a decision.

a. Compute the expected net present value of this project.

b. BSS's president does not believe that 5,000 pairs of the new snowshoes can be sold at a $50 price. He estimates that a maximum of 3,000 pairs will be sold at this price. How does the change in the estimated sales volume influence the net present value of the project?

15. Project Alpha offers the following net cash flows following an initial (year 0), certain outlay (NINV) of $70,000:

Year	Net Cash Flow	Certainty Equivalent Factor
1	$30,000	0.91
2	30,000	0.79
3	30,000	0.65
4	20,000	0.52
5	20,000	0.40
6	10,000	0.30

a. Compute the NPV of this project at a 17% cost of capital.

b. If the risk-free rate is 8%, what is the certainty equivalent NPV for Project Alpha?

16. The managers of ASR have analyzed a proposed investment project. The expected net present value (NPV) of the project, evaluated at the firm's weighted cost of capital of 18%, has been estimated to be $100,000. The firm's managers have determined that the most optimistic NPV estimate of the project is $175,000 and the most pessimistic estimate is $25,000. The most optimistic estimate is a value that is not expected to be exceeded more than 10% of the time. The most

pessimistic estimate represents a value that the project's NPV is not expected to fall below more than 10% of the time. What is the probability that this project will have a negative NPV?

17. EC Company is considering an expansion into a new product line that is more risky than its existing product mix. The new product line requires an investment, NINV, of $10 million and is expected to generate annual net cash inflows of $2.0 million over a 10-year estimated economic life. EC's weighted cost of capital is 12%, and the new product line requires an estimated risk-adjusted discount rate of 17%, based on the security market line and betas for comparable companies engaged in the contemplated new line of business.
    a. What is the project's NPV, using the company's weighted cost of capital?
    b. What is the project's NPV, using the risk-adjusted discount rate?
    c. Should EC adopt the project?

18. The ZZZ Company has estimated that a major project has an expected internal rate of return (IRR) of 18%. The most optimistic estimate of the project's IRR is 24%, and the most pessimistic estimate is 12%. The firm expects that its most optimistic estimate of the project's achieved IRR will not be exceeded more than 10% of the time. Similarly, the firm's managers do not expect an achieved IRR that is below 12% more than 10% of the time. The weighted cost of capital is 14%. What is the probability that this project will generate returns less than the firm's weighted cost of capital?

19. The management of GP Company has been evaluating the risk of the cash flows associated with a proposed new project. The expected net cash flow for year 1 is $50,000. The most optimistic estimate (not expected to be exceeded more than 10% of the time) of the year 1 net cash flow is $110,000, and the most pessimistic net cash flow estimate for year 1 is –$10,000 (no greater than a 10% chance of a value this low or lower). What is the probability that year 1 net cash flows will be negative?

20. WW Inc. is considering a new venture that would produce golden commemorative coins. WW has estimated that the net investment required will be $15,000, including a $2,000 investment in net working capital. The project is expected to have a four-year life. Annual net operating cash flows are estimated to be $10,000 in year 1, $8,000 in year 2, $7,000 in year 3, and $6,000 in year 4. The firm's cost of capital is 12% and its marginal tax rate is 40%. The standard deviation of the project's *net present value* is $3,000.
    What is the probability that this project will be an acceptable investment?

CHALLENGE

21. A firm is financed one-third with debt and two-thirds with equity. Its market beta has been estimated to be 1.5. The current risk-free rate is 8%, and the expected market return is 15%. The firm's tax rate is 40%. The firm is planning a major research and development (R&D) investment program. Management believes that these types of projects should be financed conservatively. Specifically, the company plans to finance all R&D investments with 90% equity and 10% debt.
    a. If the pure project beta for the R&D investment is the same as the pure project beta for the firm's other assets, what rate of return is required on the equity-financed portion of the R&D investment, assuming it is financed 90% with equity and 10% with debt?
    b. The firm's managers believe this project may have more risk than their other investments. Another firm that invests very heavily in similar R&D has been identified. Its capital structure is 80% equity and 20% debt. Its tax rate is 35%, and its market beta is 1.6. Using this information, determine the required return on the equity-financed portion of the R&D project, assuming it is financed 90% with equity and 10% with debt.

Excel

22. A new project is expected to have an eight-year economic life. The project will have an initial cost of $100,000. Installation and shipping charges for the equipment are estimated at $10,000. The assets will be placed in class 10 with a CCA rate of 30%. A working capital investment of $15,000 is required to undertake the project. The revenues from the project in year 1 are expected to be $60,000. These are expected to increase at a compound annual rate of 6%. Operating costs are $15,000. These costs are expected to increase at an 8% compound annual rate. The firm's marginal tax rate is 40%. The expected salvage value of the equipment at the end of year 8 is $20,000.

   a. Compute the project's net investment.
   b. Compute the annual net cash flows for the project.
   c. If the firm's cost of capital is 19%, should the project be undertaken?
   d. The managers of the firm have also decided to evaluate this project using the certainty equivalent approach. They have established the following certainty equivalent factors for the cash flows forecasted in each year:

Year	α_t
0	1.00
1	0.95
2	0.90
3	0.80
4	0.60
5	0.50
6	0.45
7	0.40
8	0.35

   The risk-free rate is 8%. Compute the certainty equivalent NPV for this project.

23. CSR has a current (and target) capital structure of 70% common equity and 30% debt. Its beta is 1.4. CSR is evaluating an investment in a totally new line of business. The new investment has an expected internal rate of return of 15%.

   CSR wishes to evaluate this investment proposal. If the investment is made, the firm intends to finance the project with the same capital structure as its current business. CSR's marginal tax rate is 34%. CSR has identified three firms that are primarily in the line of business into which CSR proposes expanding. Their average beta is 1.7, and their average capital structure is 40% common equity and 60% debt. The marginal tax rate for these three firms averages 40%. The risk-free rate is 8%, and the expected market risk premium is 8.3%. Should CSR undertake the project?

24. The SM Cookie Company is considering a diversification effort that would move it into small retail outlets at major malls around the country. Currently, the firm has a capital structure consisting of 30% debt and 70% equity. SMC believes that for the riskier retail outlet portion of its business, a more conservative capital structure of 20% debt and 80% equity is more appropriate. SMC's current pretax cost of debt is 12%. The firm's average tax rate is 30%, and its marginal tax rate is 40%.

   Another retail cookie company, D's Dessertery, has been identified. DD has a beta (leveraged) of 1.2. DD's current capital structure consists of 40% debt and 60% equity. DD's tax rate is 40%. The risk-free rate is 7% and the market risk premium is 7.4%.

   SMC wants to know what risk-adjusted rate of return is appropriate for investments in its retail outlets.

25. Jeff Himm has recently been hired as a financial analyst for the Bunich Corporation. Bunich has traditionally used the payback method in conjunction with NPV as a way to assess the risk of capital investments that the firm makes. Jeff is a new MBA graduate and is eager to put to work the tools he has learned.

    One project that the firm is considering has an expected NPV of $1.5 million. An analysis of the cash flows of the project suggests that the most optimistic estimate of the NPV is $4 million, and the most pessimistic estimate is a negative $1 million. By most optimistic, Jeff explains that it is a value not expected to be exceeded more than 10% of the time. By most pessimistic, Jeff explains that it is a value not expected to be less than negative $1 million more than 10% of the time. Cash flows are expected to be normally distributed.

    a. What is the probability that this project will be acceptable?

    b. What is the probability that this project will have an NPV in excess of $1 million?

26. BBW Inc. is the maker of new "easy spill" buckets. These buckets have quickly gained market share and now control 90% of the spillable bucket market. BBW is looking to do a product line expansion into the "spill-free" bucket market. The weighted cost of capital for BBW has been estimated to be 16%. The firm's beta is 1.3 and the risk-free rate is 6%. The firm has a capital structure composed of 40% debt and 60% equity. The marginal tax rate is 40%.

    Using pro forma statements prepared by BBW, the expected NPV of this project is −$5 million. The most optimistic estimate of the NPV is $10 million and the most pessimistic estimate is −$20 million. By most optimistic, BBW means a value not likely to be exceeded more than 5% of the time. By most pessimistic, BBW means a value not likely to fall below −$20 million more than 5% of the time. The distribution of NPV is assumed to be normally distributed.

    a. What is the probability that this project will be acceptable to BBW, if the goal is to maximize shareholder wealth?

    b. What other factors might be important in your analysis? Be specific.

Other Practice Materials and Resources

For interactive quizzes, Internet exercises, crossword puzzles, CTV videos, and more, go to the *Contemporary Financial Management* Web site at **http://cyr.nelson.com**

Part Four

Capital Structure and Dividend Policy Decisions

4

This part considers two closely related topics: capital structure (Chapters 12 and 13), and dividend policy (Chapter 14). The capital structure of a firm directly affects its cost of capital. A more debt-laden capital structure will at some point increase the risk of the firm's securities and increase the overall cost of capital in the firm. This results in a reduction in the value of the firm. Chapters 12 and 13 look at the determinants of an "optimal" capital structure—one that is consistent with the objective of shareholder wealth maximization. Finally, from the dividend policy of a firm discussed in Chapter 14, investors gain important information that may ultimately affect the firm's risk and cost of capital as perceived by those investors.

Capital Structure Concepts

Learning Objectives

After studying this chapter you should be able to

1. Understand that capital structure is defined as the relative amount of permanent short-term debt, long-term debt, preferred shares, and common equity used to finance a firm. The optimal capital structure occurs at the point at which the cost of capital is minimized and firm value is maximized

2. Understand that leverage involves the use of fixed operating costs or fixed capital costs by a firm

3. Understand that business risk is the inherent variability or uncertainty of a firm's operating income. Business risk is caused by many factors, including sales variability and the use of operating leverage

4. Understand that financial risk is the additional variability of earnings per share and the increased probability of insolvency resulting from the use of fixed cost sources of capital, such as debt and preferred shares

5. Understand that the value of the firm is independent of capital structure given perfect capital markets and no corporate income taxes

6. Understand that the optimal capital structure consists entirely of debt if a corporate income tax exists and there are no financial distress costs or agency costs

7. Understand that given a corporate income tax, financial distress costs, and agency costs, an optimal capital structure consists of some combination of both debt and equity

8. Understand that changes in the capital structure often serve as a signal to outside investors about management's expectations concerning future earnings prospects for the firm

9. Understand that according to the *pecking order theory*, firms prefer internal financing to external financing and, given that external financing is necessary, they prefer to issue debt securities first and then issue equity securities as a last resort

Optimal Capital Structure in the Airline Industry:
Air Canada versus WestJet Airlines

The commercial air transport industry has historically been a highly risky business from the perspective of investors. Veterans of the industry often tell the following story:

> Question: "Do you know how to get a million dollars by investing in the airline industry?"
>
> Answer: "Invest a billion dollars and wait a few years. By that time it will be worth only a million dollars."

The industry is extremely competitive, with many new carriers entering the business, often with a plan to offer low-cost service and attract customers from the larger airlines. Price wars are common and profits suffer. The bankruptcy rate among airlines is one of the highest of any industry.

AIR CANADA

In addition to the aggressive price competition in the industry, airline firms also have huge fixed costs and very low variable costs. In finance, this characteristic is called *high operating leverage*. It costs nearly the same to fly a plane half empty as it does to fly it full. Hence, very small changes in the load factor (percentage of seats filled on each flight) have a huge impact on profitability. As we will see in the following two chapters, when a firm has a high degree of business risk (due to volatility in prices, quantities sold, and operating costs, and to high operating leverage), it is prudent to use a capital structure with a low degree of financial leverage. *Low financial leverage* means that the firm uses relatively small amounts of debt to finance the assets of the firm.

Because of the high business risk of the airline industry, we would expect to see the best firms in the industry use relatively small amounts of debt to finance their assets. Arguably the best firm in the worldwide airline industry is Southwest Airlines. It has the lowest cost of operation per passenger mile of any of the major airlines. *It has made a profit every year since it was founded.* In 2001, Southwest's capital structure (based on book values) consisted of approximately 60 percent equity and 40 percent long-term debt.

The young Canadian airline, WestJet Airlines, based on the Southwest business model, was started in Calgary in 1996 to serve five cities with three aircraft. Since then, WestJet has steadily expanded its service to other Canadian cities from coast to coast, serving 23 cities in 2003 with more than 35 aircraft. WestJet (WJA) went public in 1999 and is listed on the Toronto Stock Exchange. Investors who paid $100 for WJA shares in July 1999 had an investment worth $363 at the end of 2002. In 2000, WJA was the second most profitable airline in North America, just behind the world leader, Southwest Airlines. At the end of 2002, WJA's capital structure (based on book values) consisted of approximately 58 percent equity and 42 percent long-term debt, not much different from Southwest's capital structure.

In contrast, Air Canada has struggled over the years to achieve profitability since it went public. By 2000, after a period of sustained losses and the merger with Canadian Airlines, the capital structure had slipped to barely 3 percent common equity and 97 percent long-term debt. The firm also had a substantial amount of fixed-cost lease obligations outstanding. The year 2001 was not a good one for the airlines, and it was unclear whether Air Canada would survive as an economically viable enterprise. At the end of 2001, Air Canada had a *negative* shareholders' equity (i.e., the book value of its liabilities exceeded the book value of its assets) of $938 million.

Although Air Canada may never have planned for the capital structure it experienced, its poor operating performance in a very risky industry resulted in a highly leveraged capital structure that has kept the airline in a precarious financial position during much of the past decade.

As this example illustrates, there is an important connection between the business risk that a firm faces and the choice of an optimal capital structure. The following two chapters discuss these concepts.

Introduction

Capital structure is defined as the amount of permanent short-term debt, long-term debt, preferred shares, and common equity used to finance a firm. In contrast, **financial structure** refers to the amount of total current liabilities (both *permanent* and *seasonal*), long-term debt, preferred shares, and common equity used to finance a firm. Thus, capital structure is part of the financial structure, representing the permanent sources of the firm's financing. This chapter deals only with the total permanent sources of a firm's financing. The decision about what proportions of debt should be long-term and permanent and seasonal short-term is considered in Chapter 15.

To illustrate the capital structure concept, suppose that Barrhead Oil Company currently has $10 million in permanent short-term debt, $40 million in long-term debt outstanding, $10 million in preferred shares, and $40 million in common equity (common shares and retained earnings). In this case, the firm's current capital structure is said to be "50 percent debt, 10 percent preferred shares, and 40 percent common equity." Thus, the capital structure pertains to the permanent debt, preferred shares, and common equity portion of the balance sheet.

The emphasis of capital structure analysis is on the firm's long-range **target capital structure**, that is, the capital structure at which the firm ultimately plans to operate. For most companies, the current and target capital structures are virtually identical, and calculating the target structure is a straightforward process. Occasionally, however, companies find it necessary to change from their current capital structure to a different target. The reasons for such a change may involve a change in the firm's asset mix (and a resulting change in its risk) or an increase in competition that may imply more risk.

This chapter examines some of the basic concepts used in determining a firm's optimal capital structure. The following chapter develops a number of tools of analysis that can assist managers in making actual capital structure decisions.

Capital Structure Decisions and Maximization of Shareholder Wealth

What is meant by a firm's optimal capital structure? The **optimal capital structure** is the mix of debt, preferred shares, and common equity that *minimizes* the *weighted cost* to the firm *of* its employed *capital*. At the capital structure where the weighted cost of capital is minimized, the total value of the firm's securities (and, hence, the value of the firm) is maximized. As a result, the minimum-cost capital structure is called the *optimal* capital structure.

The amount of debt contained in a firm's optimal capital structure is often referred to as the firm's **debt capacity**. The optimal capital structure and, accordingly, the debt

Capital Structure
The amount of permanent short-term debt, long-term debt, preferred shares, and common equity used to finance a firm.

Financial Structure
The amount of current liabilities, long-term debt, preferred shares, and common equity used to finance a firm.

Click on the Finance in the News button at **http:// finance.swcollege.com** for synopses of recent articles on capital structure topics.

Target Capital Structure
The proportions of permanent short-term debt, long-term debt, preferred shares, and common equity that a firm desires to have in its capital structure.

Optimal Capital Structure
The capital structure that minimizes a firm's weighted cost of capital and, therefore, maximizes the value of the firm.

Debt Capacity
The amount of debt contained in a firm's optimal capital structure.

capacity of a firm are determined by factors including the business risk of the firm, the tax structure, the extent of potential financial distress (e.g., bankruptcy) and agency costs, and the role played by capital structure policy in providing signals to the capital markets regarding the firm's performance. Each of these factors is considered in the sections below.

Assumptions of Capital Structure Analysis

The analysis that follows is based on some important assumptions. First, it is assumed that a firm's investment policy is held constant when we examine the effects of capital structure changes on firm value and particularly on the value of common shares. This assumption means that the level and variability of operating income (EBIT) is not expected to change as changes in capital structure are contemplated. Therefore, capital structure changes affect only the distribution of the operating income between the claims of debt holders, preferred shareholders, and common shareholders.

By assuming a constant investment policy, we also assume that the investments undertaken by the firm do not materially change the debt capacity of the firm. This assumption does not always hold in practice, but for the overwhelming majority of investment projects, it is a realistic assumption that also helps us focus on the key determinants of an optimal capital structure.

Business Risk
The variability of a firm's operating income.

Business Risk

Two elements of risk are primary considerations in the capital structure decision: the business risk and the financial risk of a firm. Financial risk is discussed in the following section. **Business risk** refers to the variability or uncertainty of a firm's operating income (EBIT).

Many factors influence a firm's business risk (holding constant the effects of all other important factors) including the following:

1. **Variability of sales volumes over the business cycle** Firms whose sales tend to fluctuate greatly over the business cycle have more business risk than firms whose sales fluctuate much less.

2. **Variability of selling prices** In some industries, prices are quite stable from year to year, or the firm may be able to increase prices regularly over time. This is true for many consumer products, such as brand-name prepared food items. In contrast, in other industries, price stability is much less certain. For example, over the past two decades, the oil companies have learned important lessons about the instability of prices as the price of crude oil declined from more than US$30 a barrel to less than US$10 a barrel only to return to nearly US$30 a barrel. Generally, the more price-competitive an industry is, the greater is the business risk for firms in that industry.

3. **Variability of costs** The more variability there is in the cost of the inputs used to produce a firm's output, the greater is the business risk of that firm. For example, airline companies have been affected significantly by the volatility in the price of jet fuel.

4. **Existence of market power** Firms that have greater market power, because of their size or the structure of the industries in which they compete, often have a greater ability to control their costs and the price of their outputs than firms operating in a more competitive market environment. Therefore, the greater a firm's market power, the less its business risk. When evaluating a firm's market power, it is often useful to consider not only the current competition facing the firm but also potential future competition, especially competition that might develop from abroad.

5. **Extent of product diversification** All other things held constant, the more diversified a firm's product line, the less variable its operating income is likely to be. For example, IBM offers a broad array of products and services, including computer chips, personal computers, mid-range computers, large mainframe computers,

computer software and systems, and financing. When demand falters for one of its products or services, this can be offset by sales in other areas. In contrast, AMD primarily produces integrated circuits for the computer industry. It has experienced great volatility in operating earnings over time as demand for its limited product line has fluctuated.

6. **Level and rate of growth** Rapidly growing firms, such as Amazon.com, often experience great variability in their operating earnings. Rapid growth causes many stresses on the operations of a firm. New facilities must be constructed, often possessing uncertain operating cost characteristics; internal control systems must be expanded and updated; the pool of managerial talent must be increased rapidly; and new products require expensive research and development outlays. These factors often combine to result in high variability of operating income.

7. **Degree of operating leverage (DOL)** Operating leverage involves the use of assets having fixed costs. The more a firm makes use of operating leverage, the more sensitive EBIT will be to changes in sales. The degree of operating leverage is the multiplier effect resulting from a firm's use of fixed operating costs. The DOL is defined as the *percentage change in EBIT* resulting from (divided by) a given *percentage change in sales (output)* and is discussed in greater detail in the next chapter. Thus, if a firm is subject to considerable sales volatility over the business cycle, the variability of EBIT (business risk) can be reduced by limiting the use of assets having fixed costs in the production process. Similarly, if a firm's sales tend to be stable over the business cycle, using a high percentage of fixed-cost assets in the production process will have little impact on the variability of EBIT.

In a sense, the business risk of a firm is determined by the accumulated investments the firm makes over time. These investments determine the industries in which a firm will compete, the amount of market power the firm will possess, and the extent of fixed costs in the production process. Firms in consumer products industries, such as grocery retailing, brewing, and food processing, tend to have low levels of business risk. In contrast, firms in durable goods manufacturing, industrial goods manufacturing, and airlines tend to have higher levels of business risk.

Business Risk: Systematic or Unsystematic Risk?

Business risk possesses elements of both systematic risk and unsystematic risk. Some of the variability in operating income that results from business risk cannot be diversified away by investors who hold a broad-based portfolio of securities. For example, variability attributable to business cycle behaviour is clearly systematic. In contrast, the variability attributable to specific managerial decisions, such as product line diversity, is primarily unsystematic. When analysts attempt to assess the specific total risk of a firm, they must consider both systematic and unsystematic components of that risk. A firm may encounter operating (and financial) difficulty both because of economy-wide factors that impact its operations and because of unique decisions made by its management.

Financial Risk and Financial Leverage

Foundation Concept

Financial Risk
The additional variability of earnings per share and the increased probability of insolvency that arises when a firm uses fixed-cost sources of funds in its capital structure.

Financial risk refers to the additional variability of earnings per share *and* the increased probability of insolvency that arises when a firm uses fixed-cost sources of funds, such as debt and preferred shares, in its capital structure.[1] (Insolvency occurs when a firm is unable to meet contractual financial obligations—such as interest and principal

---

[1] Long-term, noncancellable leases (often called *financial leases*) also represent a significant source of fixed-cost financing for many firms. They are not discussed in this chapter in order to simplify the analysis. See Chapter 19 for a discussion of lease financing.

payments on debt, payments on accounts payable, and income taxes—as they come due.) Fixed capital costs represent contractual obligations a firm must meet regardless of the EBIT level.[2] The use of increasing amounts of debt and preferred shares raises the firm's fixed financial costs. This, in turn, increases the level of EBIT that the firm must earn in order to meet its financial obligations and remain in business. The reason a firm accepts the risk of fixed-cost financing is to increase the possible returns to shareholders.

Financial Leverage
The extent to which a firm is financed by securities having fixed costs or charges, such as debt and preferred shares.

The use of fixed-cost financing sources is referred to as the use of **financial leverage**. Financial leverage causes a firm's earnings per share (EPS) to change at a rate greater than the change in operating income (EBIT). For example, if a firm is 100 percent equity financed and EBIT increases (decreases) by 10 percent, EPS will also increase (decrease) by 10 percent. When financial leverage, such as long-term debt, is used, a 10 percent change in EBIT will result in a greater than 10 percent change in EPS. Figure 12.1 illustrates the concept of financial leverage. Line A represents the financial leverage used by a firm financed *entirely with common shares*. A given percentage change in EBIT results in the *same* percentage change in EPS.

Line B represents a firm that uses debt (or other sources of fixed-cost funds) in its capital structure. As a result, the *slope* of the EPS-EBIT line is increased, thus increasing the responsiveness of EPS to changes in EBIT. As can be seen in Figure 12.1, a given

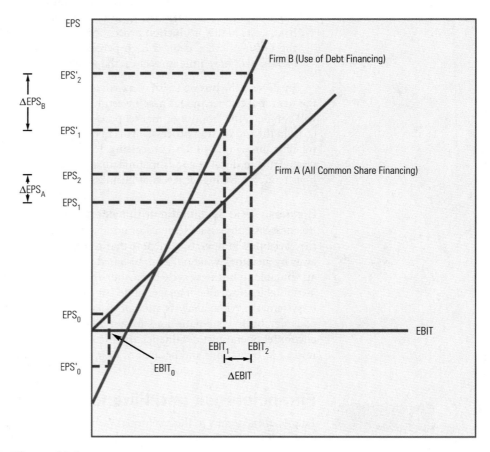

Figure 12.1
Illustration of Financial Leverage

---

[2] In financial emergencies, firms are able to omit preferred dividends. Omitting preferred dividends has many undesirable consequences for the firm, however (see Chapter 5). Therefore, the payment of preferred dividends is treated here as if it were a contractual obligation similar to interest.

change in EBIT yields a larger change in EPS if the firm is using debt financing (ΔEPS_B) than if the firm is financed entirely with common shares (ΔEPS_A).

It is also clear from Figure 12.1 that the use of financial leverage magnifies the returns—both positive and negative—to the shareholder. When EBIT is at a relatively high level, such as $EBIT_2$, Firm B's use of financial leverage *increases* EPS above the level attained by Firm A, which is not using financial leverage. On the other hand, when EBIT is relatively low—for example, at $EBIT_0$—the use of financial leverage *decreases* EPS below the level that would be obtained otherwise; that is, $EPS'_0 < EPS_0$. At $EBIT_0$, the use of financial leverage results in negative EPS for Firm B.

Financial Risk: Systematic or Unsystematic Risk?
Financial risk, like business risk, contributes to both the systematic and unsystematic risk of a firm's securities. To the extent that the use of *financial leverage* magnifies variations in operating income that come about because of unsystematic risk factors, financial leverage contributes to the unsystematic risk of a firm's securities.

Financial researchers have also studied the contribution that financial leverage makes to the systematic risk of a firm's securities.[3] It is well established that systematic risk is a function both of financial risk *and* operating risk. For example, recall Hamada's Equation 11.7 from the previous chapter that shows that the beta for a levered firm is the firm's unlevered beta adjusted upward by a factor that depends on the firm's marginal tax rate, T, and its debt-to-equity ratio, (D/E). Thus, $\beta_l = \beta_u [1 + (1 - T)(D/E)]$. Hence, security analysts and investors find the measurement of a firm's financial risk to be an important element of good financial analysis.

Effect of Financial Leverage on Shareholder Returns and Risk
Firms employ financial leverage to increase the returns to common shareholders. These increased returns are achieved at the expense of increased risk. The objective of capital structure management is to find the capital mix that leads to shareholder wealth maximization.

To illustrate the effects of financial leverage on shareholder returns and risk, consider the following example of KMI Technology, Inc. As can be seen in Table 12.1, KMI has total assets of $1 million. Suppose KMI expects an operating income (EBIT) of $200,000. If KMI uses debt in its capital structure, the pretax cost of this debt will be 10 percent per annum.[4] Table 12.1 shows the effect of an increase in the debt to total assets ratio (debt ratio) from 0 percent to 40 percent and to 80 percent on the return on shareholders' equity. With an all-equity capital structure, the return on equity is 12 percent. At a debt ratio of 40 percent, the return on equity increases to 16 percent, and at a debt ratio of 80 percent, the return on equity is 36 percent. KMI is earning 20 percent (pretax) on its assets. Thus, when KMI uses debt in its capital structure, the difference between the return on its assets and the cost of debt accrues to the benefit of equity holders.

However, this increased equity return is achieved only at the cost of higher risk. For example, if EBIT declines by 25 percent to $150,000, the return on equity for the all-equity capital structure also declines by 25 percent to 9.0 percent. In contrast, at a 40 percent debt ratio, the return on equity declines by 31.25 percent to 11 percent. At an 80 percent debt ratio, the return on equity declines by 41.67 percent to 21 percent. The

---

[3] An excellent review of the relationship between business risk and financial risk on one hand and systematic risk on the other can be found in C. M. Callahan and R. M. Mohr, "The Determinants of Systematic Risk: A Synthesis," *The Financial Review* (May 1989): 157–181. See also J. M. Gahlon and J. A. Gentry, "On the Relationship between Systematic Risk and the Degrees of Operating and Financial Leverage," *Financial Management* (Summer 1982): 15–23.

[4] In this simplified example, we hold the cost of debt constant as the ratio of debt to total assets increases from 0 percent to 80 percent. In reality, as the debt ratio increases, the cost of debt can also be expected to increase.

Table 12.1 Effect of Financial Leverage on Shareholder Returns and Risk at KMI Technology, Inc.

Leverage Factor (Debt/Total Assets)	0%	40%	80%
Total assets	$1,000,000	$1,000,000	$1,000,000
Debt (at 10% interest)	$ 0	$ 400,000	$ 800,000
Equity	1,000,000	600,000	200,000
Total liabilities and equity	$1,000,000	$1,000,000	$1,000,000
Expected operating income (EBIT)	$ 200,000	$ 200,000	$ 200,000
Interest (at 10%)	0	40,000	80,000
Earnings before tax	$ 200,000	$ 160,000	$ 120,000
Income tax at 40%	80,000	64,000	48,000
Earnings after tax	$ 120,000	$96,000	$ 72,000
Return on equity	12.0%	16.0%	36.0%
Effect of a 25% Reduction in EBIT to $150,000			
Expected operating income (EBIT)	$ 150,000	$ 150,000	$ 150,000
Interest (at 10%)	0	40,000	80,000
Earnings before tax	$ 150,000	$ 110,000	$ 70,000
Income tax at 40%	60,000	44,000	28,000
Earnings after tax	$ 90,000	$ 66,000	$ 42,000
Return on equity	9.0%	11.0%	21.0%
Effect of a 60% Reduction in EBIT to $80,000			
Expected operating income (EBIT)	$ 80,000	$ 80,000	$ 80,000
Interest (at 10%)	0	40,000	80,000
Earnings before tax	$ 80,000	$ 40,000	$ 0
Income tax at 40%	32,000	16,000	0
Earnings after tax	$ 48,000	$ 24,000	$ 0
Return on equity	4.8%	4.0%	0.0%

effects of a 60 percent reduction in EBIT to $80,000 are even more dramatic. In this case, the pretax return on assets is *less than* the pretax cost of debt. To pay the prior claims of the debt holders, the equity returns are reduced to a level below those that prevail under the all-equity capital structure. In the case of a 40 percent debt ratio, the return on equity is only 4.0 percent, and in the case of an 80 percent debt ratio, the return on equity is 0 percent. Thus, it can be seen that the use of financial leverage both increases the potential returns to common shareholders and the risk, or variability, of those returns.

Generally, *the greater a firm's business risk, the less the amount of financial leverage that will be used in the optimal capital structure,* holding constant all other relevant factors.

Capital Structure Theory

In this section, we develop some simplified models of the relationship between capital structure, as measured by the ratio of debt to total assets, and the cost of capital (and therefore the value of the firm). These models help isolate the impact of personal and corporate taxes, financial distress costs, and agency costs on the determination of an optimal capital structure. In this section we also consider some other factors that influence the choice of long-term financing instruments, including the impact of signalling and information asymmetries. We conclude with a brief review of the market reaction to various capital structure altering transactions that firms undertake.

Capital Structure Without a Corporate Income Tax

In 1958, two prominent financial researchers, Franco Modigliani and Merton Miller (MM), showed that, under certain assumptions, a firm's overall cost of capital, and therefore its value, is *independent* of capital structure.[5] In particular; assume that the following *perfect* capital market conditions exist:

- There are no transaction costs for buying and selling securities.

- A sufficient number of buyers and sellers exists in the market, so no single investor can have a significant influence on security prices.

- Relevant information is readily available to all investors and is costless to obtain.

- All investors can borrow or lend at the same rate.

- All investors are rational and have homogeneous (i.e., the same) expectations of a firm's earnings.

- Firms operating under similar conditions are assumed to face the same degree of business risk (*homogeneous risk class assumption*).

- The cost of debt does not vary with capital structure.

- There are no income taxes.

In this no-tax MM case, the overall cost of capital is constant regardless of a firm's financial leverage position, measured as the firm's debt-to-equity ratio, D/E. As a firm increases its relative debt level, the cost of equity capital, k_e, linearly increases, reflecting the higher return requirement of shareholders due to the increased risk imposed by the additional debt. (This is *MM Proposition II.*) The increased cost of equity capital exactly offsets the benefit of the lower cost of debt, k_d, so that the overall cost of capital does not change with changes in capital structure. This is illustrated in Figure 12.2. Because the firm's market value is calculated by discounting its expected future operating income by the weighted (marginal) cost of capital, k_a, the market value of the firm is independent of capital structure. (This is *MM Proposition I.*)

MM support their theory by arguing that a process of arbitrage will prevent otherwise equivalent firms from having different market values simply because of capital structure differences. **Arbitrage** is the process of simultaneously buying and selling the same or equivalent securities in different markets to take advantage of price differences and make a profit. Arbitrage transactions are risk-free. For example, suppose two firms in the same industry differed only in that one was *levered* (that is, it had some debt in its capital structure) and the other was *unlevered* (that is, it had no debt in its capital structure). If the MM theory did not hold, the unlevered firm could increase its market value by simply adding debt to its capital structure. However, in a perfect capital market without transactions costs, MM argue that investors would not reward the firm for increasing its debt. Shareholders could change *their own* financial debt-equity structure without cost to receive an equal return. Therefore, shareholders would not increase their opinion of the market value of an unlevered firm just because it took on some debt.

The MM argument is based on the *arbitrage* process. If one of two unlevered firms with identical business risk took on some debt and the MM theory did not hold, its value should increase and, therefore, so would the value of its shares. MM suggest that under these circumstances, investors will sell the overpriced shares of the levered firm. They then can use an arbitrage process of borrowing, buying the unlevered firm's shares, and investing the excess funds elsewhere. Through these costless transactions, investors

Arbitrage
The process of simultaneously buying and selling the same or equivalent securities in different markets to take advantage of temporary price differences.

---

[5] See Franco Modigliani and Merton Miller, "The Cost of Capital, Corporation Finance, and the Theory of Investment," *American Economic Review* 48 (June 1958): 261–296. Both of the authors are winners of the Nobel Prize for Economics.

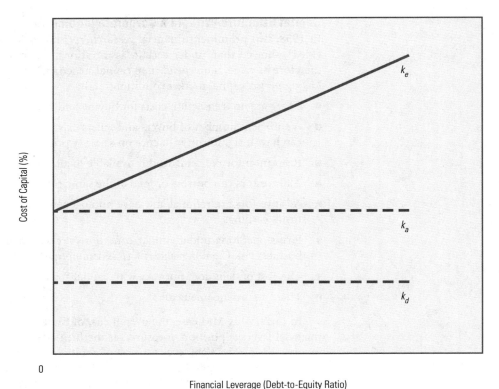

Figure 12.2
Weighted Cost of Capital: Miller and Modigliani (No Taxes)

can increase their return without increasing their risk. Hence, they have substituted their own personal financial leverage (*i.e., homemade leverage*) for corporate leverage. MM argue that this arbitrage process will continue until the selling of the levered firm's shares drives down its price to the point where it is equal to the unlevered firm's share price, which has been driven up due to increased buying.

The arbitrage process occurs so rapidly that the market values of the levered and unlevered firms are equal. Therefore, MM conclude that *the market value of a firm is independent of its capital structure in perfect capital markets with no income taxes. (MM Proposition I.)*

The MM no-tax theory is illustrated in the example shown in Table 12.2. The table contains financial data on two firms, U and L, that have equal levels of net operating

Table 12.2	Capital Structure Without a Corporate Income Tax: Financial Data of Firms U and L		
		Firm U	**Firm L**
Net operating income (EBIT)		$ 1,000	$ 1,000
Less: Interest payments to debt holders, I		–	100
Income available to shareholder (dividends), *Div*		$ 1,000	$ 900
Total income available to security holders ($I + Div$)		$ 1,000	$ 1,000
Required rate of return on debt, k_d		–	5%
Market value of debt, ($D = I/k_d$)		–	$ 2,000
Required rate of return on equity, k_e		10%	11.25%
Market value of equity, ($E = Div/k_e$)		$10,000	$ 8,000
Market value of firm, ($E + Div$)		$10,000	$10,000

income (EBIT = $1,000) and operating risk and differ only in their capital structure. Firm U is unlevered, and firm L is levered, with a perpetual debt of $2,000 having a coupon rate (i) of 5 percent in its capital structure. For simplicity, we assume that the income of both firms available for shareholders is paid out as dividends. As a result, the expected growth rate of both firms is zero, because no income is available for the firms to reinvest.

The present value of both firms is calculated using the following perpetuity valuation equation:

$$(12.1) \quad \text{Market value of firm} = \text{Market value of equity} + \text{Market value of debt}$$

$$= E + D$$

$$= \frac{Div}{k_e} + \frac{I}{k_d}$$

where E and D are the respective market values of equity and debt in the firm's capital structure; Div is the annual amount of dividends paid to the firm's shareholders; I is the interest paid on the firm's debt; k_e is the return required on common equity; and k_d is the return required on debt. The required rate of return on the common equity for the unlevered firm (U) is 10 percent. Because of the increased financial risk associated with the $2,000 in debt financing, the required rate of return on the common equity of the levered firm (L) is 11.25 percent. The required return on debt, k_d, is assumed to equal the coupon rate on the debt, i. For firm U, the present value of the expected future cash flows is $10,000, calculated as follows:

$$\text{Market value of firm U} = \$1,00/0.10 = \$10,000$$

For firm L, the present value is also $10,000, calculated as follows:

$$\text{Market value of firm L} = [\$900/0.1125] + [\$100/0.05]$$

$$= \$8,000 + \$2,000$$

$$= \$10,000$$

Thus, the market values of firms U and L are equal. This example shows that the market value of the firm is independent of capital structure, assuming that the MM theory holds and no corporate income tax exists.

Capital Structure with a Corporate Income Tax

Next, the relationship between capital structure and firm market value is considered, assuming that a corporate income tax exists. Table 12.3 shows financial data for an unlevered firm, U, and a levered firm, L, assuming the firm's marginal corporate income tax rate, T, is 40 percent. The total income available to the security holders of firm U is $600, and assuming a cost of equity capital equal to 10 percent, the value of firm U is calculated using Equation 12.1:

$$\text{Market value of firm U} = \$600/.10 = \$6,000$$

Tax Shield
The amount of tax savings from the deductibility of interest payments on debt or CCA in computing corporate income taxes.

Because interest paid to debt holders is a tax-deductible expense, the total income available to the debt and equity security holders of firm L, shown in Table 12.3, is $640. This amount is greater than the $600 available to the firm U equity security holders by $40. The $40 amount is the **tax shield** caused by the tax deductibility of the interest payments. The annual tax shield amount is calculated using the following equation:

$$(12.2) \quad \text{Tax shield amount} = i \times D \times T$$

$$= (0.05) \times (\$2,000) \times (0.40) = \$40$$

Table 12.3 Capital Structure with a Corporate Income Tax: Financial Data on Firms U and L

	Firm U	Firm L
Net operating income (EBIT)	$1,000	$ 1,000
Less: Interest payments to debt holders, *I*	–	100
Income before taxes	$1,000	$ 900
Less: Corporate taxes (*T* = 40%)	400	360
Income available to shareholders (dividends), *Div*	$ 600	$ 540
Total income available to security holders (*I* + *Div*)	$ 600	$ 640
Required rate of return on debt, k_d	–	5%
Market value of debt, ($D = I/k_d$)	–	$ 2,000
Required rate of return on equity, k_e	10%	11.25%
Market value of equity, ($E = Div/k_e$)	$6,000	$ 4,800
Market value of firm, ($E + D$)	$6,000	$ 6,800

The total market value of firm L is obtained using Equation 12.1:

$$\text{Market value of firm L} = (Div/k_e) + (I/k_d)$$
$$= (\$540/0.1125) + (\$100/0.05)$$
$$= \$4,800 + \$2,000$$
$$= \$6,800$$

In this example, the value of firm L is greater than firm U's value by an amount equal to $800. This difference in value is caused by the tax shield. In fact, the difference in value between the levered and unlevered firm is equal to the present value of the tax shield from the perpetual debt:

(12.3) $$\text{Present value of tax shield} = \frac{i \times D \times T}{i} = D \times T$$

In this equation, the annual tax shield amount, *iDT*, is discounted at a rate, *i* ($i = k_d$). In the case of firm L, the present value of the tax shield is $800, calculated as follows:

$$\text{Present value of tax shield} = \$2,000 \times 0.40 = \$800$$

We can now state that the market value of the levered firm is equal to the market value of the unlevered firm plus the present value of the tax shield:[6]

(12.4)

  Market value of levered firm = Market value of unlevered firm + PV of tax shield

---

[6] A similar approach to valuing a project is the *adjusted present value* (APV) method. See Stewart C. Myers, "Interactions of Corporate Financing and Investment Decisions—Implications for Capital Budgeting," *Journal of Finance* (March 1974): 1–25. The APV of a project is the net present value (NPV) of the project calculated at the project's cost of capital if it were all equity financed plus the present value (PV) of tax shield discounted at the rate, *i* ($I = k_d$).

  APV = NPV + PV of tax shield

Estimating each project's cost of capital as if it were all equity financed and then trying to estimate the amount of debt each project could support is cumbersome and, hence, impractical. For an in-depth discussion of difficulties in using APV, see Laurence Booth, "Finding Value Where None Exists: Pitfalls in Using Adjusted Present Value," *Journal of Applied Corporate Finance* (Spring 2002): 8–17.

Booth also discusses the flows to equity (FTE) method to directly value the equity of a firm by discounting the cash flows to equity holders at the equity holders' required rate of return. His general conclusion is that the weighted cost of capital approach used in Chapters 10 and 11 for capital budgeting analysis is the appropriate valuation framework, as long as the debt ratio is constant. In contrast, both the APV and FTE methods require relatively complex adjustments by sophisticated users.

From this equation, we can conclude that the value of the firm increases linearly as the amount of debt in the capital structure increases, as shown in panel (a) of Figure 12.3. This result implies that a firm should increase its level of debt to the point at which the capital structure consists entirely of debt. In other words, the market value of the firm is maximized and its optimal capital structure is achieved when capital structure is all debt. As shown in panel (b) of Figure 12.3, the weighted cost of capital k_a declines with increases in financial leverage.

In practice, we do not *normally* observe companies with extremely high levels of debt in their capital structures. (The large volume of financial restructurings and leveraged buyouts during the 1980s suggest that many managers are paying closer attention to the advantages of debt financing.) Even in the face of leveraged buyouts, however, we still do not observe many companies that approach a 100 percent debt financed capital structure. Hence, other factors must be influencing the determination of an optimal capital structure. Two of the most important factors are financial distress costs and agency costs. These are considered in the following section.

Capital Structure with Corporate Income Tax, Financial Distress Costs, and Agency Costs

This section examines the effect of capital structure on the market value of the firm given the existence of a corporate income tax and financial distress and agency costs.

Financial Distress Costs From a practical viewpoint, a firm cannot expect to gain the benefits associated with the tax deductibility of interest payments without also increasing certain costs. One significant cost category is the costs of financial distress. **Financial distress costs** include the costs incurred to avoid bankruptcy as well as the direct and indirect costs incurred if the firm files for bankruptcy protection. (Bankruptcy is discussed in more detail in Chapter 20.) As a firm increases its debt level, lenders may demand higher interest rates to compensate for the increased financial risk taken on by the firm. The higher interest payments constitute a cost to the firm. In the extreme, lenders may choose not to lend at all. Under these conditions, the firm may have to forego acceptable projects. Thus, the firm incurs an opportunity cost. In addition, some customers and potential customers may lose confidence in the firm's ability to continue in existence and instead buy from other companies more likely to remain in business. This loss of customer confidence is another financial distress cost. A firm that experiences cash flow, or insolvency, problems that lead to bankruptcy must incur legal and accounting costs as it attempts to restructure itself financially. Finally, if the firm is forced to liquidate, assets may have to be sold at less than their market values. These costs are also bankruptcy costs.

Altman has measured the size of bankruptcy costs for industrial firms.[7] He defines *bankruptcy costs* as those that consist of direct costs (costs paid by debtors in the bankruptcy and restructuring process) and indirect costs (costs associated with the loss of customers, suppliers, and key employees plus the managerial effort expended to manage the firm in its distressed condition). Altman found evidence that the direct costs of bankruptcy average about 6 percent of firm value at the time of filing for bankruptcy. Direct plus indirect costs as a percentage of firm value averaged 12.1 percent three years prior to filing and 16.7 percent at the time of filing. Thus, it appears that bankruptcy costs are significant, even if one adjusts for the expected time of occurrence and the probability of occurrence. Castanias offers evidence that supports this conclusion when

Financial Distress Costs
The costs incurred to avoid bankruptcy plus the direct and indirect costs incurred if a firm files for bankruptcy protection.

---

[7] E. I. Altman, "A Further Empirical Investigation of the Bankruptcy Cost Question," *Journal of Finance* 39 (1984): 1067–1089. See also E. I. Altman, *Corporate Financial Distress and Bankruptcy*, 2nd. ed. (New York: Wiley, 1993).

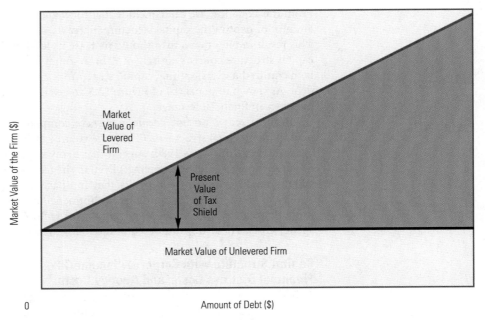

(a) **Market Value of the Firm as a Function of Capital Structure**

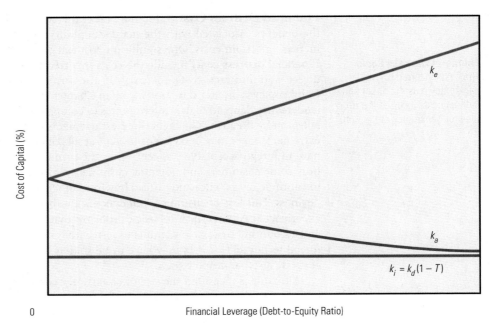

(b) **Cost of Capital as a Function of Capital Structure**

Figure 12.3
Market Value of the Firm and Cost of Capital as a Function of Capital Structure (with Corporate Income Tax)

he finds that small firms in industries with high failure rates tend to use less financial leverage.[8]

---

[8] R. Castanias, "Bankruptcy Risk and Optimal Capital Structure," *Journal of Finance* 38 (1983): 1617–1635.

The likelihood of bankruptcy is not a linear function of a firm's debt ratio. Rather, there is evidence that it increases at an increasing rate beyond some threshold level. Accordingly, bankruptcy costs also become more important beyond this threshold debt ratio.

Agency Costs   As discussed in Chapter 1, in most large firms, the security holders (often referred to as the *principals*), both debt holders and common shareholders, are not in a position to actively manage the firm's investment, financing, and daily operational activities. Security holders employ "agents" to carry out these important activities. Under these circumstances, conflicts can develop between the interests of the principal and those of the agent. In the case of the choice between debt and common equity financing, the debt holders can be viewed as the principals and the common shareholders can be viewed as the agents. The common shareholders are in a position to direct the investment and financing decisions of the firm through the elected board of directors and the managers hired by the board.

When debt is used in the capital structure of a firm, common shareholders have incentives to undertake actions that may be detrimental to the interests of the debt holders. These actions include investing in extremely risky projects. The higher expected returns from risky investments accrue to the benefit of shareholders. Also, in the absence of restraints, shareholders are inclined to increase the proportions of debt in the capital structure, thus diminishing the protection afforded the earlier bondholders. The higher risk resulting from these actions may lead to a reduction in a firm's bond ratings. Lower bond ratings translate into lower bond values in the marketplace and thus a loss in wealth to the bondholders.

Not surprisingly, bondholders will want to take actions that reduce the prospect of this wealth transfer to shareholders. Agency theory argues that expected agency costs will be borne by the agent. Therefore, debt holders can be expected to demand a higher interest rate on the bonds they purchase in order to compensate them for the expected wealth losses. As an alternative, monitoring and bonding expenses can be incurred to reduce the incidence of these agency problems and thereby reduce the interest rate that will be demanded by bondholders. In the case of bonds, monitoring and bonding expenses take the form of protective covenants in the bond indenture.

Typical protective covenants place restrictions on the payment of dividends, limit the issuance of additional debt, limit the sale of assets, and limit the type of assets that may be acquired. (Protective covenants are discussed in greater detail in Chapters 5 and 15.) However, the more extensive the protective covenants are, the more costly it is to monitor compliance. In addition, increasingly extensive covenants may restrict the operating freedom and efficiency of managers, to the detriment of both shareholders and bondholders.

Thus, the firm can be viewed as having a choice along a continuum. At one extreme, there would be no protective covenants, resulting in high interest rates, low or no monitoring costs, and no restrictions placed on the operating freedom of managers. At the other extreme, all decisions of the firm would be subject to review by the debt holders. This is obviously not feasible. *Monitoring and bonding activities should be carried out by the firm up to the point that the reduction in the interest rate charged by debt holders is balanced against the cost of additional monitoring and bonding activities.*

At low debt levels, bondholders do not demand extensive protective covenants and monitoring arrangements, because the risk exposure for the bondholders is viewed as being quite limited.[9] Also, at low debt levels, the interest cost of debt financing will be

---

[9] The takeover of RJR Nabisco by KKR appears to have altered this market perception somewhat. RJR's bondholders experienced a wealth loss of 20 percent or more as a result of the high leverage used in the takeover by KKR. This transaction had a significant impact on the corporate bond market as investors in the bonds of the most creditworthy US firms demanded higher returns to compensate them for this heretofore unexpected risk.

low. As the amount of debt increases as a proportion of the total capital structure, bondholders find themselves subject to increased risk that managers (acting on behalf of shareholders) may make investments or take financing actions that could harm the current bondholders. Accordingly, monitoring costs are assumed to increase with increases in a firm's financial leverage, resulting in an increase in the *implicit* cost of debt, including the cost of monitoring and lost operating efficiency. This increase in the cost of debt has the effect of reducing the total value of the firm's securities.

In summary, the agency costs of debt are an increasing function of the proportion of debt in the capital structure of a firm. Because of this, agency costs represent another powerful reason why, in addition to the increased probability of financial distress or bankruptcy at higher debt ratios, a firm will choose a value-maximizing capital structure that is less than the 100 percent debt corner solution implied by the MM analysis.

Value-Maximizing Capital Structure   The preceding discussion of the impact of taxes, bankruptcy costs, and agency costs indicates that the market value of a levered firm can be represented by the following equation:

(12.5)

$$
\begin{pmatrix} \text{Market value} \\ \text{of levered} \\ \text{firm} \end{pmatrix} = \begin{pmatrix} \text{Market value} \\ \text{of unlevered} \\ \text{firm} \end{pmatrix} + \begin{pmatrix} \text{PV of tax} \\ \text{shield} \end{pmatrix} - \begin{pmatrix} \text{PV of} \\ \text{financial} \\ \text{distress costs} \end{pmatrix} - \begin{pmatrix} \text{PV of} \\ \text{agency costs} \end{pmatrix}
$$

Figure 12.4 illustrates this relationship graphically. As indicated in this figure and in Equation 12.5, the present value of expected financial distress costs and the agency costs associated with debt financing offset the present value of the tax shield accruing from debt—resulting in an optimal (value-maximizing) amount of debt, D^*, and an optimal

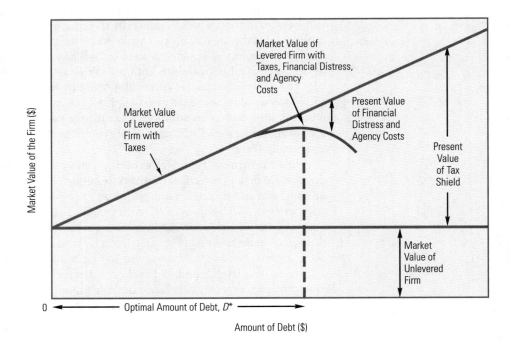

Figure 12.4
Value of the Firm as a Function of Capital Structure (with Corporate Income Tax, Financial Distress Costs, and Agency Costs)

capital structure, D^*/E^*. This approach to determining the optimal capital structure is sometimes referred to as the *static trade-off theory*.[10]

The Cost of Capital and the Optimal Capital Structure

In this section, we examine the relationship between the cost of capital and the firm's capital structure when corporate taxes, financial distress costs, and agency costs are considered. In the following analysis, we assume that capital structure contains only permanent debt and common equity. That is, we assume, for simplicity, that no preferred share financing is used.

The first step in the analysis considers the relationship between the cost of debt and capital structure. All other things being equal, investors in debt consider the debt less risky if the firm has a low, rather than high, proportion of debt in its capital structure. As the proportion of debt in the capital structure increases, bond investors require a higher return on the more risky debt. Since the firm's pretax cost of debt is the bond investor's required return, the cost of debt increases as the proportion of debt increases.

The precise relationship between the cost of debt and the debt ratio is difficult to determine, because it is impossible to observe the cost of debt at two different capital structures (at the same time) for a single firm. Nevertheless, as discussed earlier, evidence suggests that the cost of debt increases rather slowly for moderate amounts of debt. There is a point at which the capital markets begin to consider any new debt "excessive" and therefore much more risky. The after-tax cost of debt curve, $k_d(1-T)$ in Figure 12.5 illustrates such a relationship. The actual region where the cost of debt begins to increase more rapidly varies by firm and industry, depending on the firm's level of business risk.

The next step in this analysis focuses on the relationship between the cost of equity and capital structure. When a firm has low financial leverage, that is, a low debt-to-equity ratio, any equity employed is less risky than equity used when the firm is financed with a relatively high proportion of debt. Earlier in this chapter it was shown that the greater the fraction of debt used, the greater is the variability in earnings per common share. In addition, the greater the fraction of debt used, the greater is the risk of financial distress. Because the returns expected by shareholders in the form of present and future dividends depend partly on current earnings, it can be concluded that variability in earnings per common share can result in variability of the returns to investors, that is, greater risk. Therefore, it can be stated that investors' required returns and the cost of equity increase as the relative amount of debt used to finance the firm increases.

Once again, the exact nature of the relationship between the cost of equity and financial leverage is difficult to determine in practice. However, there is agreement that the cost of equity increases at a relatively slow rate as the debt proportion increases up to moderate amounts. Then, in the range where additional debt begins to be viewed as excessive and more risky, the cost of equity increases more rapidly. This is shown in Figure 12.5. As is true in the debt illustration, the region where the cost of equity capital, k_e, begins to increase more rapidly varies by firm and industry.

The relationship between the weighted cost of capital, k_a, and financial leverage can now be considered. The following equation (which is a modified version, without preferred shares in the capital structure, of Equation 8.1 from Chapter 8) can be used to calculate k_a for any level of financial leverage, provided that the values of k_e and k_d at the level of financial leverage are known:

$$(12.6) \qquad k_a = \left(\frac{E}{D+E} \right)(k_e) + \left(\frac{D}{D+E} \right)(k_d)(1-T)$$

---

[10] S.C. Myers, "The Capital Structure Puzzle," *Journal of Finance* 39 (July 1984): 575–592; and S. C. Myers, "Still Searching for Optimal Capital Structure," *Journal of Applied Corporate Finance* 6 (Spring 1993): 4–14.

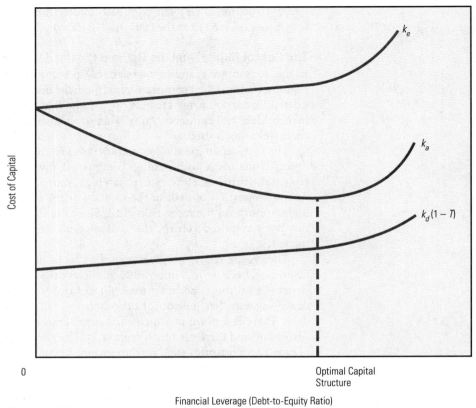

Figure 12.5
Overall Cost of Capital as a Function of Capital Structure

(D is the market value of debt, and E is the market value of equity in the firm's capital structure.) Because the relationships between financial leverage and k_d and k_e have been developed, the relationship between k_a and financial leverage follows accordingly. The k_a curve, shown in Figure 12.5, begins at $k_a = k_e$ because, by definition, the weighted cost of capital for an all-equity firm equals the cost of equity. As even small increments of debt are used, k_a becomes lower. As the debt proportion continues to increase from moderate to excessive, k_a "bottoms out" and then begins to increase. The resulting saucer-shaped curve contains a point at which the firm's overall cost of capital is minimized and its value maximized. This point is the firm's *optimal capital structure*. If the firm is thought of as a cash flow generator, then the lower the discount rate (the weighted cost of capital), the higher the firm's value.

Figure 12.6 ties together the relationship between the optimal capital structure (with taxes, financial distress costs, and agency costs) and the market value of a firm and its weighted cost of capital. Note that at the optimal capital structure, D^*/E^*, the market value of the firm is maximized and its weighted cost of capital is minimized.

Other Considerations in the Capital Structure Decision
In this section, we briefly discuss some other factors that have an impact on the determination of an optimal capital structure. These factors include personal tax effects, industry effects, signalling effects, and managerial preference effects.

Personal Tax Effects   The MM tax case led to the conclusion that, in the absence of financial distress costs and agency costs, the firm should attempt to minimize its taxes by employing the maximum amount of debt. The MM tax case did not consider the effect of personal income taxes, however. Miller has extended the tax case analysis to

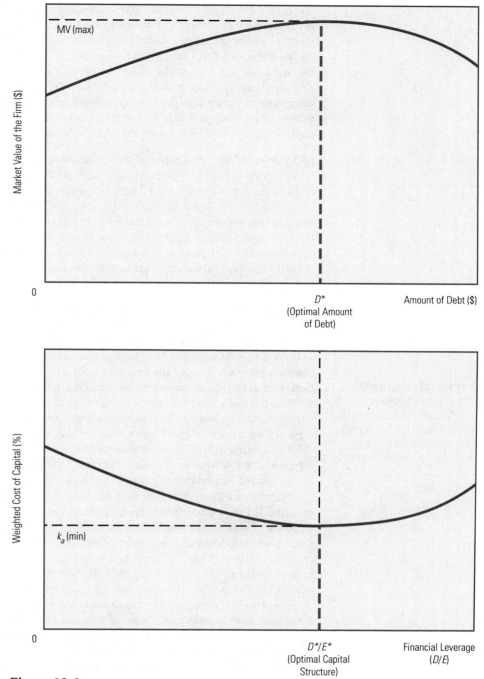

Figure 12.6
Relationship Between the Optimal Capital Structure and the Market Value of a Firm and Its Weighted Cost of Capital

include both corporate and personal income taxes.[11] Miller argued that although a firm can save taxes by increasing its debt ratio, individual investors would pay greater taxes on their returns from the firm if these returns were predominantly interest, rather than dividends and capital appreciation on common shares. Historically, the tax code has

---

[11] M. H. Miller, "Debt and Taxes," *Journal of Finance* 32 (May 1977): 261–276.

favoured capital gains income from shares over interest income because capital gains generally have been taxed at a lower rate than ordinary income (including interest income) and because taxes on capital gains are deferred until the capital gain is realized.

Miller concluded that in the United States, when both personal and corporate income taxes are considered, there is no optimal debt ratio for an individual firm, although there is an optimal amount of total debt in the marketplace, reflecting the difference in corporate and personal tax rates. Under the current tax law in Canada, corporate borrowing probably has some associated tax advantage as long as a firm is confident it can use the full amount of the interest tax shield.

Industry Effects   A number of studies have found significant capital structure differences among industries. For example, a study by Kester shows a debt-to-equity ratio for firms in the paper industry of 1.36 times, compared with 0.079 for firms in the pharmaceutical industry.[12] Kester found that the more profitable firms are, the less debt they tend to use. Other studies have found that leverage ratios are negatively related to the frequency of bankruptcy in the industry. Also, some evidence indicates that firms generating stable cash flows over the business cycle tend to have higher debt ratios. In general, the studies of industry effects in capital structure tend to conclude that there is an optimal capital structure for individual firms. The market rewards firms that achieve this capital structure.

Signalling Effects   The preceding discussion assumed that all investors have access to relevant information concerning a firm's future earnings prospects. However, this assumption may not be valid in many cases. Instead one can argue that the officers and managers of a firm, as insiders, have access to information about the expected future earnings and cash flows of the firm that is not available to outside investors. This situation is referred to as **asymmetric information**. Given that managers know more about the firm than do outside investors, changes in a firm's investment, financing, or dividend decisions can represent a *signal* to investors concerning management's assessment of the expected future returns, and hence market value, of the firm.

Thus, when a firm issues new securities, this event can be viewed as providing a signal to the financial marketplace regarding the future prospects of the firm or the future actions planned by the firm's managers.[13] Ross argues that signals provided by capital structure changes are credible because of the potential bankruptcy cost penalty incurred if the implied future cash flows do not occur. In general, studies of capital structure changes have found that new common equity offerings tend to yield *negative* share price responses and new debt offerings tend to yield no significant share price responses.[14] Repurchases of common shares have led to large *positive* announcement returns on the firm's common shares. Actions that *increase* leverage have generally been associated with *positive* stock returns, and actions that *decrease* leverage are associated with *negative* stock returns. The results of many studies of capital structure changes are consistent both with direct effects of the change, such as the benefits of greater tax shields, and with indirect information effects. Therefore, when a firm makes capital structure changes it must be mindful of the potential signal that the proposed transaction will transmit to the marketplace regarding the firm's current and future earnings prospects and the intentions of its managers.[15]

Asymmetric Information
The information that managers of a firm, as insiders, have about expected future earnings and cash flows that is not available to outside investors.

---

[12] W. C. Kester, "Capital and Ownership Structure: A Comparison of United States and Japanese Manufacturing Corporations," *Financial Management* (Spring 1986): 5–16

[13] S. A. Ross, "The Determination of Financial Structure: The Incentive-Signaling Approach," *Bell Journal of Economics* 8 (1977): 23–40.

[14] See T. E. Copeland and J. F. Weston, *Financial Theory and Corporate Policy*, 3rd ed. (Reading, MA: Addison-Wesley, 1988): 519–523, for a summary of empirical evidence concerning the effects of capital structure changes on security prices.

[15] See R. W. Masulis, *The Debt/Equity Choice* (Cambridge, MA: Ballinger Publishing, 1988), for an excellent discussion and review of the signalling literature as it relates to capital structure decisions.

INTERNATIONAL ISSUES

Capital Structure

Multinational firms have a more complex capital structure decision than purely domestic firms. Should each foreign subsidiary maintain the same capital structure as the parent's consolidated structure, or should separate capital structures be established for each foreign subsidiary? Most firms tend to pay relatively little attention to establishing uniquely optimal capital structures for their foreign subsidiaries. Rather, the approach normally is one of establishing an optimal capital structure for the multinational firm as a whole and then adjusting foreign subsidiary capital structures to take advantage of local financing opportunities. The object is to minimize the multinational firm's overall cost of capital.

Factors that determine the specific capital structure that will prevail for each subsidiary include the following:

1. **Exchange rate risk in the host country** When exchange rate risk is high, there will be a preference to raise more of the subsidiary's capital in the financial markets of the host country.
2. **Local industry standards** In some countries, it may be common for firms to have higher debt ratios than in others. Subsidiary capital structures normally reflect these traditions.[16]

3. **Host country requirements** Some governments place restrictions on the capital structure of multinational firms operating in their countries.
4. **Risk of expropriation** The greater the risk that a multinational firm's subsidiary assets may be expropriated without adequate compensation, the greater will be the incentive for the multinational firm to finance that subsidiary with debt capital, especially debt capital raised in the host country and not guaranteed by the parent firm.
5. **Availability of special, low-cost financing in a host country** Some host countries make low-cost financing available to multinational firms to stimulate additional investment. When this low-cost financing is available, firms normally take advantage of it.

Other factors that determine the optimal capital structure for a multinational firm as a whole include the increased capital market access for firms operating in several different countries and the extent to which political and economic country risk is diversified by the firm. The diversification of political and economic country risk is largely a function of the number and location of foreign subsidiaries of the multinational firm.

Pecking Order Theory

A capital structure theory indicating that firms prefer internal financing (retained earnings) to external financing (new security issues) and that, if external financing is required, debt is preferred to new common share issues.

Managerial Preference Effects: The Pecking Order Theory   According to the **pecking order theory,** as developed by Myers, a firm may not have a particular target or optimal capital structure.[17] Instead, a firm's capital structure changes when an imbalance between internal cash flows, net of cash dividend payments, and acceptable (i.e., NPV > 0) investment opportunities occurs. Firms whose investment opportunities exceed internally generated funds tend to issue more debt securities and hence have higher debt ratios. Conversely, highly profitable firms with limited needs for investment funds will tend to have lower debt ratios. In this situation, the firm builds up

---

[16] J. M. Collins and W. S. Sekely, "The Relationship of Headquarters Country and Industry Classification to Financial Structure," *Financial Management* (Autumn 1983): 45–51.

[17] S. C. Myers, "The Capital Structure Puzzle," *Journal of Finance* 39 (July 1984): 575–592; and S. C. Myers, "Still Searching for Optimal Capital Structure," *Journal of Applied Corporate Finance* 6 (Spring 1993): 4–14.

ETHICAL ISSUES

LBO Stakeholder Impacts

The rapid pace of mergers and acquisitions during the 1980s raised many interesting issues regarding the rights of the various corporate stakeholders in these transactions. Leveraged buyouts (LBOs) result in dramatic increases in the amount of debt used to finance a firm—up to 95 percent of the capital structure in some cases. The use of this large amount of debt permits a small group of investors to acquire ownership and control of a large firm with a relatively small equity investment. By concentrating ownership and control, the equity agency problems associated with separation of ownership from control are largely eliminated. Also, the heavy burden of fixed charges from the debt financing forces managers to dramatically increase the efficiency of operations of the acquired firm. These benefits from LBOs are well documented.[18]

However, these benefits do not come without significant costs. For example, increased operating efficiency is often achieved by eliminating jobs, reducing other payroll expenses, and closing inefficient plants. Bondholders of acquired firms typically experience a loss in the value of their bonds when an LBO is announced.[19]

LBOs raise important ethical questions. How are the competing interests of stakeholders to be resolved in LBOs and other significant financial transactions? These questions rarely have simple answers, however. Some issues to consider when debating the ethics of LBOs are

1. Is it in the long-run interest of employees to maintain staffing levels and operate facilities that are inefficient and reduce the firm's ability to compete with other enterprises?

2. Are bondholders truly harmed in LBO transactions, considering the bond covenants for which they contracted when they purchased the bonds and the relationship between bond yields and covenant protection?

Financial Slack
Highly liquid assets (i.e., cash and marketable securities) plus unused debt capacity that allow a firm to take advantage of any attractive investment opportunities.

financial slack in the form of highly liquid assets (i.e., cash and marketable securities) and unused debt capacity. Financial slack allows a firm to take advantage of any attractive investment opportunities that may occur in the future.

The pecking order theory indicates that firms prefer internal financing (retained earnings) to external financing (new security issues). This preference for internal financing is based on two considerations. First, because of flotation costs of new security issues, internal financing is less costly than external financing. Second, internal financing avoids the discipline and monitoring that occurs when new securities are sold publicly. Also, according to the pecking order theory, dividends are "sticky." That is, many firms are reluctant to make major changes in dividend payments and only gradually adjust dividend payout ratios to reflect their investment opportunities and thereby avoid the issuance of new securities. This is referred to as the *stable dollar dividend policy* and is discussed in more detail in Chapter 14.

If external financing is required, the "safest" securities, namely debt, are issued first. As discussed in Chapter 2, the flotation costs of debt securities are generally lower than

[18] See, for example, G. P. Baker and K. H. Wruck, "Organization Changes and Value Creation in Leveraged Buyouts: The Case of O. M. Scott & Sons Company," *Journal of Financial Economics* 25 (1989): 163–190.

[19] For example, see P. Asquith and T. A. Wizman, "Event Risk, Wealth Redistribution and the Return to Existing Bondholders in Corporate Buyouts," *Journal of Financial Economics* (September 1990): 195–214.

the costs of equity securities. Also, as noted in the discussion of asymmetric information above, the stock market tends to react negatively to announcements of new common share offerings, whereas debt security announcements tend to have little impact on share prices. As additional external financing is needed, the firm will work down the pecking order—from safe to more risky debt, then possibly to convertible debt, and finally to common equity as a last resort.

A survey of large firms suggests that the pecking order theory is more descriptive of how financing decisions are made in practice compared with optimal capital structure theories based on financial distress costs or agency costs.[20] Furthermore, among the respondents expressing a preference for the pecking order theory, approximately 85 percent ranked internal equity (retained earnings) as their first choice for financing new investments. Among external financing sources, straight (i.e., nonconvertible) debt was ranked highest (most preferred) and external equity (i.e., new common shares) was ranked lowest (least preferred) by the respondents. Given a list of principles that govern their financing decisions, maintaining financial flexibility and ensuring long-term survivability ranked highest among respondents. Of lesser importance were such considerations as maintaining a predictable source of funds, maximizing security prices, and maintaining financial independence. Finally, principles such as maintaining a high debt rating and maintaining comparability with other firms in the industry were ranked as relatively unimportant by the respondents.

Managerial Implications of Capital Structure Theory

The rich body of theoretical and empirical capital structure studies provides important insights for financial managers. First, it is clear that the capital structure decision is one of the centrally important decisions facing financial managers. There is little doubt that changes in capital structure result in changes in the market value of the firm. Second, the benefits of the tax shield from debt lead to increased firm value, at least up to the point that increased financial distress and agency costs begin to offset the debt advantage. Third, the optimal capital structure is heavily influenced by the business risk facing the firm. Fourth, when managers make explicit changes in a firm's capital structure, these actions transmit important information to investors about expected future returns and the market value of a firm.

Financial Challenge Revisited

Clearly, Air Canada has made excessive use of financial leverage. In fact, on a book value basis, the firm was more than 100 percent debt financed at the end of 2001! The capital structure theories discussed in this chapter, however, are based on market values. In March 2003, the market price of an Air Canada common share was $2.90. (Air Canada's share price was $13.70 at the end of 2000.) Thus, Air Canada is somewhat less than 100 percent debt financed on a market value basis. Nevertheless, companies in Air Canada's situation usually either get reorganized or eventually go out of business. In early 2003, Air Canada had to seek protection from its creditors.

---

[20] J. M. Pinegar and L. Wilbricht, "What Managers Think of Capital Structure Theory: A Survey," *Financial Management* 18, no. 4 (Winter 1989): 82–91.

Summary

- *Capital structure* is defined as the relative amount of permanent short-term debt, long-term debt, preferred shares, and common equity used to finance a firm. The capital structure decision is important to the firm because there exists in practice a capital structure at which the *cost of capital* is minimized. This minimum-cost capital structure is the *optimal* capital structure, because the value of the firm is maximized at this point.

- The *business risk* of a firm refers to the variability of a firm's operating income. It is influenced by the variability of sales volumes, prices, and costs over the business cycle. Business risk is also influenced by a firm's market power and its use of operating leverage.

- The *financial risk* of a firm is the additional variability of earnings per share and the increased probability of insolvency that arises when a firm uses fixed-cost sources of funds, such as debt and preferred shares, in its capital structure.

- The use of financial leverage results in an increase in perceived risk to the suppliers of a firm's capital. To offset this increased risk, higher returns are required.

- Modigliani and Miller show that the value of the firm is *independent* of capital structure given perfect capital markets and no corporate income taxes. MM also show that the optimal capital structure consists entirely of debt if a corporate income tax exists.

- Given a corporate income tax, financial distress costs, and agency costs, an optimal capital structure consisting of both debt and equity is shown to exist. Determination of the optimal capital structure involves balancing the present value of the tax shield accruing from debt financing against the present value of the expected financial distress costs and the agency costs associated with debt financing.

- Given that managers have access to better information about a firm's future prospects than do outside investors (*asymmetric information*), capital structure changes often *signal* important information to investors about a firm's future prospects.

- According to the *pecking order theory,* a firm may not have a particular target or optimal capital structure. Firms prefer internal financing to external financing and, given that external financing is necessary, they prefer to issue debt securities first and then equity securities only as a last resort.

Questions and Topics for Discussion

1. Explain the research results of Modigliani and Miller in the area of capital structure.
2. What is the relationship between the value of a firm and its capital structure without a corporate income tax? With a corporate income tax?
3. What is the relationship between the value of a firm and its capital structure, given the existence of a corporate income tax, bankruptcy costs, and agency costs?
4. What is the *asymmetric information* concept? What role does this concept play in a firm's decision to change its financial structure or issue new securities?
5. According to the pecking order theory, if additional external financing is required, what type of securities should a firm issue first? Last?
6. Explain why, according to the pecking order theory, firms prefer internal financing to external financing.
7. What assumptions are required in deriving the proposition that a firm's cost of capital is independent of its capital structure?
8. What role does *signalling* play in the establishment of a firm's capital structure?

9. What is arbitrage? How is it used in deriving the proposition that the value of a firm is independent of its capital structure?

10. Explain the difference between business risk and financial risk.

11. What other factors besides operating leverage can affect a firm's business risk?

Self-Test Problem

ST1. OO Company has estimated the following costs of debt and equity capital (with bankruptcy and agency costs) for various proportions of debt in its capital structure:

Proportion of Debt	Cost of Debt, $k_d(1-T)$	Cost of Equity, k_e
0.00	–	10.0%
0.10	4.0%	10.1
0.20	4.2	10.3
0.30	4.4	10.8
0.40	4.8	11.4
0.50	5.5	12.5
0.60	6.6	14.5
0.70	8.0	18.0

Determine the firm's optimal capital structure.

Problems*

BASIC

1. Using Table 12.2, calculate the market value of firm L (without a corporate income tax) if the equity amount in its capital structure decreases to $5,000 and the debt amount increases to $5,000. At this capital structure, the cost of equity is 15%.

2. a. Using Table 12.3, calculate the market value of firm L (with a corporate income tax) if the equity amount in its capital structure decreases to $3,000 and the debt amount increases to $3,000.

   b. For firm L (with equity = $3,000 and debt = $3,000), calculate (i) the income available to the shareholders and (ii) the cost of equity.

INTERMEDIATE

3. Two firms, NoLev Inc. and HiLev Inc., have equal levels of operating risk and differ only in their capital structure. NoLev is unlevered and HiLev has $500,000 of perpetual debt in its capital structure. Assume that the perpetual annual income of both firms available for shareholders is paid out as dividends. Hence, the growth rate for both firms is zero. The income tax rate for both firms is 40%. Assume that there are no financial distress costs or agency costs. Given the following data:

	NoLev Inc.	HiLev Inc.
Equity in capital structure	$1,000,000	$500,000
Cost of equity, k_e	10%	13%
Debt in capital structure	—	$500,000
Pretax cost of debt, k_d	—	7%
Net operating income (EBIT)	$ 100,000	$100,000

*Coloured numbers and letters denote problems that have "check" answers provided at the back of the book.

determine the

a. Market value of NoLev Inc.
b. Market value of HiLev Inc.
c. Present value of the tax shield to HiLev Inc.

4. JC Company has estimated the costs of debt and equity capital (with bankruptcy and agency costs) for various proportions of debt in its capital structure:

Proportion of Debt	After-Tax Cost of Debt, $k_d(1-T)$	Cost of Equity, k_e
0.00	—	12.0%
0.10	4.7%	12.1
0.20	4.9	12.5
0.30	5.1	13.0
0.40	5.5	13.9
0.50	6.1	15.0
0.60	7.5	17.0

a. Determine the firm's optimal capital structure, assuming a marginal income tax rate (T) of 40%.
b. Suppose that the firm's current capital structure consists of 30% debt (and 70% equity). How much higher is its weighted cost of capital than at the optimal capital structure?

5. PI Corporation has estimated the following costs of debt and equity capital for various fractions of debt in its capital structure.

Debt Fraction	$k_d(1-T)$	k_e with Financial Distress Costs without Agency Costs	k_e with Financial Distress Costs and Agency Costs
0.00	—	12.00%	12.00%
0.10	4.8%	12.05	12.05
0.30	4.9	12.10	12.20
0.40	5.0	12.20	12.60
0.45	5.2	12.40	13.40
0.50	5.7	12.80	14.80
0.60	7.0	15.00	18.00

a. Based on these data, determine the firm's optimal capital structure
   (i) with financial distress costs and without agency costs
   (ii) with financial distress and agency costs
b. Suppose the firm's actual capital structure is 50% debt and 50% equity. How much higher is k_a at this capital structure than at the optimal value of k_a, with financial distress and agency costs?
c. Is it necessary in practice for the firm to know precisely its optimal capital structure? Why?

6. CC Company has estimated the costs of debt and equity capital (with bankruptcy and agency costs) for various proportions of debt in its capital structure as shown in the following table.

Debt Ratio [$D/(D + E)$]	Pretax Cost of Debt (k_d)	Cost of Equity (k_e)	Weighted Average Cost of Capital k_a
0.00	—		12.0%
0.15		13.0	11.68
0.30	8.0	14.5	
0.45		16.5	11.775
	14.0	19.0	12.64

The firm's income tax rate is 40%.

    a. Fill in the missing entries in the table.

    b. Determine the capital structure (i.e., debt ratio) that minimizes the firm's weighted cost of capital.

7. WP Company has estimated the costs of debt and equity capital (with bankruptcy and agency costs) for various proportions of debt in its capital structure as follows:

Debt Ratio [$D/(D + E)$]	Pretax Cost of Debt (k_d)	Cost of Equity (k_e)
0.00	—	14.0%
0.10	7.0%	14.2
0.20	7.2	14.6
0.30	7.6	15.4
0.40	8.2	17.0
0.50	9.0	20.0
0.60	10.0	26.0

The firm's marginal (and average) income tax rate is 40%.
Determine the firm's optimal capital structure.

CHALLENGE

8. OQ Inc. has $12,000,000 in assets. Its expected operating income (EBIT) is $2,000,000 and its income tax rate is 40%. If OQ finances 20% of its total assets with debt capital, the pretax cost of funds is 10%. If the firm finances 40% of its total assets with debt capital, the pretax cost of funds is 15%.

    a. Determine the expected rate of return on equity (ROE) under the three different capital structures, i.e., 0%, 20%, and 40% debt ratios.

    b. Which capital structure yields the highest expected ROE?

    c. Determine the ROE under each of the three capital structures (0, 20, and 40% debt ratios) if expected EBIT decreases by 20%.

    d. Which capital structure yields the highest ROE calculated in part c?

    e. Determine the percentage change in ROE under each of the three capital structures (i.e., debt ratios) as the result of a 20% increase in EBIT.

    f. Based on the results in part e, which capital structure yields the highest variability (i.e., risk) in ROE?

Other Practice Materials and Resources

For interactive quizzes, Internet exercises, crossword puzzles, CTV videos, and more, go to the *Contemporary Financial Management* Web site at **http://cyr.nelson.com**

Capital Structure Management

Learning Objectives

After studying this chapter you should be able to

1. Understand that the degree of operating leverage (DOL) is defined as the percentage change in EBIT resulting from a 1 percent change in sales

   a. The degree of operating leverage approaches a maximum as the firm comes closer to operating at its break-even level of output

   b. All other things being equal, the higher a firm's DOL, the greater is its business risk

   c. Business risk, the inherent variability of a firm's EBIT, is also influenced by the variability of sales and operating costs over time

2. Understand that the degree of financial leverage (DFL) is defined as the percentage change in earnings per share (EPS) resulting from a 1 percent change in EBIT

   a. The degree of financial leverage approaches a maximum as the firm comes closer to operating at its loss level, the level where EPS = $0

   b. All other things being equal, the higher a firm's DFL, the greater is its financial risk

   c. Financial risk, the additional variability of a firm's EPS that results from the use of financial leverage, can also be measured by various financial ratios, such as the debt to total assets ratio and the times interest earned ratio

3. Understand that the degree of combined leverage (DCL) is defined as the percentage change in earnings per share resulting from a 1 percent change in sales. It is also equal to the DOL for a firm times that firm's DFL. The degree of combined leverage used by a firm is a measure of the overall variability of EPS due to the use of fixed operating and capital costs, as sales levels change

4. Understand that EBIT-EPS analysis is an analytical technique that can be used to help determine the circumstances under which a firm should employ financial leverage. The indifference point in EBIT-EPS analysis is that level of EBIT where earnings per share are the same regardless of which of two alternative capital structures is used

5. Understand that cash insolvency analysis can be used to evaluate the impact of a proposed capital structure on the cash position of a firm during a major business downturn

6. Understand that other factors that should be considered when establishing a capital structure policy are industry standards, profitability and need for funds, lender requirements, managerial risk aversion, and the desire of owners to retain control of the firm

A Significant Deleveraging of Doman Industries Ltd. Balance Sheet

Doman Industries Ltd., a lumber producer, announced in November 2002 that it had agreed with its bondholders to swap debt for equity. This agreement will reduce the firm's outstanding debt by $600 million and increase its equity by $100 million. The firm expects to continue operating and serving its customers. The firm is a major exporter of high-cost, high-priced cedar, mainly to the United States.

Doman had been experiencing declining sales revenues because of the lumber dispute with the United States and was in danger of going out of business. It was not able to pay the interest on its outstanding debt. The bondholders accepted the exchange of their bonds for shares to protect their investment and also because they felt that the firm's long-run prospects would improve following settlement of the lumber dispute.

Investors and financial analysts are concerned about the effect of high levels of debt on the riskiness of a firm's securities. Credit ratings, which reflect the riskiness of these securities, are important for a firm, especially one with a large amount of debt, because they affect both the availability and cost of credit.

If the credit ratings of any firm's long-term debts (bonds) were lowered, these securities would be less attractive to bond investors and the firm would have to pay higher interest rates on new issues of debt. This would result in an increase in the firm's weighted cost of capital and a decrease in the market value of the firm.

In order to avoid the costs associated with an excessive reliance on debt financing, some firms engage in major deleveraging efforts such as selling some nonstrategic assets. By swapping debt for equity, Doman Industries avoided such extreme measures.

This chapter focuses on the practical aspects of capital structure decisions, such as those faced by Doman.

w W w

For more information on
Doman Industries see
www.domans.com

Introduction

This chapter focuses on various tools of analysis that can assist managers in making capital structure decisions that will lead to a maximization of shareholder wealth. The following section develops techniques, derived from accounting data, for measuring operating and financial leverage. As discussed in the previous chapter, operating leverage and financial leverage are important components of a firm's business risk and financial risk. Other techniques, namely, *EBIT-EPS analysis* and *cash insolvency analysis,* can aid management in assessing the risk versus return trade-offs associated with the use of debt in a firm's capital structure.

Operating and Financial Leverage

The concepts of operating and financial leverage were introduced in the previous chapter. In finance, *leverage* is defined as a firm's use of assets and liabilities having fixed costs in an attempt to increase potential returns to shareholders. Specifically, operating leverage involves the use of *assets* having fixed costs, whereas financial leverage involves the use of *liabilities* (and *preferred shares*) having fixed costs.

A firm uses operating and financial leverage in the hope of earning returns in excess of the fixed costs of its assets and liabilities, thereby increasing the returns to common shareholders. Leverage is a double-edged sword, however, because it also increases the *variability* or risk of these returns. If, for example, a firm earns returns that are *less* than the fixed costs of its assets and liabilities, then the use of leverage can actually *decrease* the returns to common shareholders. Thus, leverage magnifies shareholders' potential losses as well as potential gains. Leverage concepts are particularly revealing to the financial analyst in that they highlight the *risk-return trade-offs* of various types of financial decisions, such as those involving the capital structure of the firm.

Leverage and the Income Statement

Financial statements of the Allegan Manufacturing Company are referred to throughout this section for purposes of illustration. Table 13.1 contains two types of statements for the firm—a traditional format and a revised format. The traditional format shows various categories of costs as separate entries. *Operating costs* include such items as the cost of sales and general, administrative, and selling expenses. Interest charges and preferred dividends, which represent *capital costs,* are listed separately, as are income taxes.

The revised format is more useful in leverage analysis because it divides the firm's operating costs into two categories: *variable* and *fixed*.

Short-Run Costs   Over the short run, certain operating costs within a firm vary directly with the level of sales whereas other costs remain constant, regardless of changes in the sales level. Costs that move in close relationship to changes in sales are called **variable costs.** They are tied to the number of units produced and sold by the firm, rather than to the passage of time. They include raw material and direct labour costs, as well as sales commissions.

Over the short run, certain other operating costs are independent of sales or output levels. These, termed **fixed costs**, are primarily related to the passage of time. Depreciation on property, plant, and equipment; rent; insurance; lighting and heating bills; property taxes; and the salaries of management are all usually considered fixed costs. If a firm expects to keep functioning, it must continue to pay these costs, regardless of the sales level.

A third category, *semivariable costs,* can also be considered. Semivariable costs are costs that increase in a *stepwise* manner as output is increased. One cost that sometimes behaves in a stepwise manner is management salaries. Whereas these costs are generally

Variable Costs
Costs that vary in close relationship with changes in a firm's output level.

Fixed Costs
Costs that do not vary as the level of a firm's output changes.

Table 13.1 Traditional and Revised Income Statements, Allegan Manufacturing Company, Year Ending December 31, 20X1

Traditional Income Statement Format

- - - - - - - - -	Sales		$5,000,000
Operating	*Less* Cost of sales	$2,500,000	
leverage	Selling, administrative, and general expenses	1,500,000	
	Total operating costs		4,000,000
- - - - - - - - -	Earnings before interest and taxes (EBIT)		1,000,000
	Less Interest expense		250,000
	Earnings before taxes (EBT)		750,000
Financial	*Less* Income taxes (40% rate)		300,000
leverage	Earnings after taxes (EAT)		450,000
	Less Preferred share dividends		150,000
	Earnings available to common shareholders		$ 300,000
- - - - - - - - -	Earnings per share (EPS)—100,000 shares		$ 3.00

Revised Income Statement Format

- - - - - - - - -	Sales		$5,000,000
Operating	*Less Variable* operating costs	$3,000,000	
leverage	*Fixed* operating costs	1,000,000	
	Total operating costs		4,000,000
- - - - - - - - -	Earnings before interest and taxes (EBIT)		1,000,000
	Less Fixed capital costs (interest)		250,000
	Earnings before taxes (EBT)		750,000
Financial	*Less* Income taxes (*variable*), 40% rate		300,000
leverage	Earnings after taxes (EAT)		450,000
	Less Fixed capital costs (preferred share dividends)		150,000
	Earnings available to common shareholders		$ 300,000
- - - - - - - - -	Earnings per share (EPS)—100,000 shares		$ 3.00

considered fixed, this assumption is not always valid. A firm faced with declining sales and profits during an economic downturn may often cut the size of its managerial staff.

Panels (a), (b), and (c) of Figure 13.1 show the behaviour of variable, fixed, and semivariable costs, respectively, over the firm's output range.

Not all costs can be classified as either completely fixed or variable; some have both fixed and variable components. Costs for utilities, such as water and electricity, frequently fall into this category. Whereas part of a firm's utility costs (such as electricity) is fixed and must be paid regardless of the level of sales or output, another part is variable in that

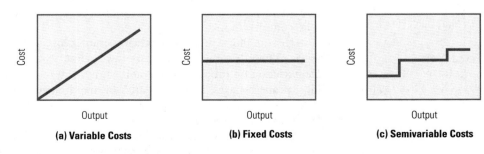

(a) Variable Costs   (b) Fixed Costs   (c) Semivariable Costs

Figure 13.1
Behaviour of (a) Variable, (b) Fixed, and (c) Semivariable Costs

it is tied directly to sales or production levels. In the revised format of Allegan's income statement, these are divided into their fixed and variable components and are included in their respective categories of operating costs.

Note that in the revised income statement format, both interest charges and preferred dividends represent fixed capital costs. These costs are contractual in nature and thus are independent of a firm's level of sales or earnings. Also note that income taxes represent a variable cost that is a function of earnings before taxes.

Long-Run Costs   Over the *long run,* all costs are variable. In time, a firm can change the size of its physical facilities and number of management personnel in response to changes in the level of sales. Fixed capital costs also can be changed in the long run.

Measurement of Operating and Financial Leverage

Fixed obligations allow a firm to magnify small changes into larger ones—just as a small push on one end of an actual lever results in a large "lift" at the other end.

Operating leverage has fixed operating costs for its "fulcrum." When a firm incurs fixed operating costs, a change in sales revenue is magnified into a relatively larger change in earnings before interest and taxes (EBIT). The multiplier effect resulting from the use of fixed operating costs is known as the **degree of operating leverage (DOL)**.

Financial leverage has fixed capital costs for its "fulcrum." When a firm incurs fixed capital costs, a change in EBIT is magnified into a larger change in earnings per share (EPS). The multiplier effect resulting from the use of fixed capital costs is known as the **degree of financial leverage (DFL)**.

Degree of Operating Leverage

A firm's *degree of operating leverage* (DOL) is defined as the multiplier effect resulting from the firm's use of fixed operating costs. More specifically, DOL can be computed as the *percentage change* in earnings before interest and taxes (EBIT) resulting from a given *percentage change* in sales (output):

$$\text{DOL at } X = \text{Percentage change in EBIT/Percentage change in sales}$$

This can be rewritten as follows:

(13.1)
$$\text{DOL at } X = \frac{\dfrac{\Delta\text{EBIT}}{\text{EBIT}}}{\dfrac{\Delta\text{Sales}}{\text{Sales}}}$$

where ΔEBIT and ΔSales are the changes in the firm's EBIT and sales, respectively. Because a firm's DOL differs at each sales (output) level, it is necessary to indicate the sales (units of output or dollar sales) point X, at which operating leverage is measured. The degree of operating leverage is analogous to the elasticity concept of economics (for example, price and income elasticity) in that it relates percentage changes in one variable (EBIT) to percentage changes in another variable (sales).

The calculation of the DOL can be illustrated using the Allegan Manufacturing Company example discussed earlier. From Table 13.1, recall that Allegan's variable operating costs were $3 million at the current sales level of $5 million. Therefore, the firm's *variable operating cost ratio* is $3 million/$5 million = 0.60, or 60 percent.

Suppose the firm increased sales by 10 percent to $5.5 million while keeping fixed operating costs constant at $1 million and the variable (operating) cost ratio at 60 percent. As can be seen in Table 13.2, this would increase the firm's earnings before interest and taxes (EBIT) to $1.2 million. Substituting the two sales figures ($5 million and

Degree of Operating Leverage (DOL)

The percentage change in a firm's EBIT resulting from a 1 percent change in sales or output.

Degree of Financial Leverage (DFL)

The percentage change in a firm's EPS resulting from a 1 percent change in EBIT.

Visit **www. infotrac-college.com** and enter the following key words: degree of operating leverage, degree of financial leverage

Table 13.2 Effect on Earnings per Share of a 10 Percent Increase in Sales, Allegan Manufacturing Company, Year Ending December 31, 20X1

		(1)		(2)	% Change [(2) − (1)] ÷ (1)
Sales		$5,000,000		$5,500,000	+10%
Less Variable operating costs (0.60 × Sales)	$3,000,000		$3,300,000		+10%
Fixed operating costs	1,000,000		1,000,000		0%
Total operating costs		4,000,000		4,300,000	+8%
Earnings before interest and taxes		$1,000,000		$1,200,000	+20%
Less Interest payments (fixed capital cost)		250,000		250,000	0%
Earnings before taxes		$ 750,000		$ 950,000	+27%
Less Income taxes (variable), 40%		300,000		380,000	+27%
Earnings after taxes		$ 450,000		$ 570,000	+27%
Less Preferred dividends (fixed capital cost)		150,000		150,000	0%
Earnings available to common shareholders		$ 300,000		$ 420,000	+40%
Earnings per share (100,000 shares)		$ 3.00		$ 4.20	+40%

$5.5 million) and associated EBIT figures ($1 million and $1.2 million) into Equation 13.1 yields the following:

$$\text{DOL at } \$500,000 = \frac{\dfrac{(\$1,200,000 - \$1,000,000)}{\$1,000,000}}{\dfrac{(\$5,500,000 - \$5,000,000)}{\$5,000,000}}$$

$$= \frac{\$200,000}{\$1,000,000} \times \frac{\$5,000,000}{\$500,000}$$

$$= 2.0$$

A DOL of 2.0 is interpreted to mean that each 1 percent change in sales from a base sales level of $5 million results in a 2 percent change in EBIT *in the same direction as the sales change.* In other words, a sales *increase* of 10 percent results in a 10% × 2.0 = 20% *increase* in EBIT. Similarly, a 10 percent *decrease* in sales produces a 10% × 2.0 = 20% *decrease* in EBIT. The greater a firm's DOL, the greater the magnification of sales changes into EBIT changes.

Equation 13.1 requires the use of two different values of sales and EBIT. Another equation that can be used to compute a firm's DOL more easily is:

(13.2)
$$\text{DOL at } X = \frac{\text{Sales} - \text{Variable costs}}{\text{EBIT}}$$

Inserting data from Table 13.1 on the Allegan Manufacturing Company into Equation 13.2 gives the following:

$$\text{DOL at } \$5 \text{ million} = (\$5 \text{ million} - \$3 \text{ million})/\$1 \text{ million} = 2.0$$

This result is the same as that obtained using the more complex Equation 13.1.

Table 13.3 shows the DOL at various sales levels for Allegan. Note that the firm's DOL is largest (in absolute value terms) when the firm is operating at the break-even sales point [that is, where Sales = $2,500,000 and EBIT = Sales − Variable Operating Costs − Fixed Operating Costs = $2,500,000 − 0.60($2,500,000) − $1,000,000 = $0].

Table 13.3 DOL at Various Sales Levels, Allegan Manufacturing Company

Sales, TR = $P \times Q^*$	Degree of Operating Leverage, DOL
$ 500,000	−0.25
1,000,000	−0.67
1,500,000	−1.50
2,000,000	−4.00
2,500,000**	(Undefined)
3,000,000	+6.00
3,500,000	+3.50
4,000,000	+2.67
4,500,000	+2.25
5,000,000	+2.00
5,500,000	+1.83
6,000,000	+1.71

*Total revenue = Price × quantity.
**Break-even sales level.

Note also that the firm's DOL is negative below the break-even sales level. A negative DOL indicates the percentage *reduction* in operating *losses* that occurs as the result of a 1 percent increase in output. For example, the DOL of −1.50 at a sales level of $1,500,000 indicates that, from a base sales level of $1,500,000, the firm's operating *losses* are *reduced* by 1.5 percent for each 1 percent *increase* in output.

A firm's DOL is a function of the nature of the production process. If the firm employs large amounts of labour-saving equipment in its operations, it tends to have relatively high fixed operating costs and relatively low variable operating costs. Such a cost structure yields a high DOL, which results in large operating profits (positive EBIT) if sales are high and large operating losses (negative EBIT) if sales are depressed.

Degree of Financial Leverage

A firm's degree of financial leverage (DFL) is computed as the *percentage change* in earnings per share (EPS) resulting from a given *percentage change* in earnings before interest and taxes (EBIT):

$$\text{DFL at } X = \text{Percentage change in EPS/Percentage change in EBIT}$$

This can also be written as:

$$(13.3) \qquad \text{DFL at } X = \frac{\dfrac{\Delta \text{EPS}}{\text{EPS}}}{\dfrac{\Delta \text{EBIT}}{\text{EBIT}}}$$

where ΔEPS and ΔEBIT are the changes in EPS and EBIT, respectively. Because a firm's DFL is different at each EBIT level, it is necessary to indicate the EBIT point, X, at which financial leverage is being measured.

Using the information contained in Table 13.4 and shown in Figure 13.2, the degree of financial leverage used by the Allegan Manufacturing Company can be calculated. The

EBIT	$ 400,000	$800,000	$1,000,000	$1,200,000	$1,600,000
Less Interest expenses	250,000	250,000	250,000	250,000	250,000
Earnings before taxes	$ 150,000	$550,000	$ 750,000	$ 950,000	$1,350,000
Less Income taxes	60,000	220,000	300,000	380,000	540,000
Earnings after taxes	$ 90,000	$330,000	$ 450,000	$ 570,000	$ 810,000
Less Preferred dividends	150,000	150,000	150,000	150,000	150,000
Earnings available to common shareholders	$−60,000	$180,000	$ 300,000	$ 420,000	$ 660,000
Earnings per share (EPS)	$ −0.60	$ 1.80	$ 3.00	$ 4.20	$ 6.60

firm's EPS level is $3.00 at an EBIT level of $1 million. At an EBIT level of $1.2 million, EPS equals $4.20. Substituting these quantities into Equation 13.3 yields

$$\text{DFL at } \$1,000,000 = \frac{\dfrac{(4.20 - \$3.00)}{3.00}}{\dfrac{(\$1,200,000 - \$1,000,000)}{\$1,000,000}}$$

$$= \frac{\$1.20}{\$3.00} \times \frac{\$1,000,000}{\$200,000}$$

$$= 2.0$$

A DFL of 2.0 indicates that each 1 percent change in EBIT from a base EBIT level of $1 million results in a 2 percent change in EPS *in the same direction as the EBIT*

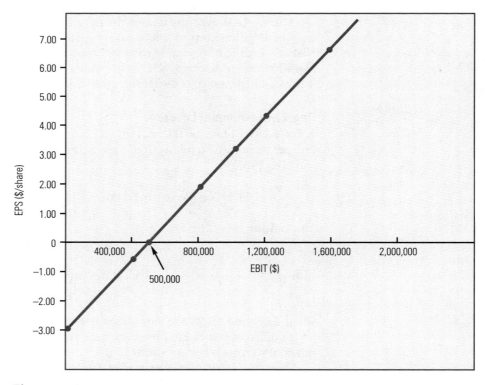

Figure 13.2
EPS-EBIT Graph for the Allegan Manufacturing Company

change. In other words, a 10 percent *increase* in EBIT results in a 10% × 2.0 = 20% *increase* in EPS. Similarly, a 10 percent *decrease* in EBIT produces a 20 percent *decrease* in EPS. The larger the firm's DFL, the greater the magnification of EBIT changes into EPS changes.

Measuring a firm's DFL using Equation 13.3 is somewhat cumbersome, because it necessitates using two EBIT and EPS projections. Computation is simplified when Equation 13.3 is rewritten as[1]

$$(13.4) \qquad \text{DFL at } X = \frac{\text{EBIT}}{\text{EBIT} - I - D_p/(1 - T)}$$

where I is the firm's interest payments, D_p the firm's preferred dividend payments, T the firm's marginal income tax rate, and X the level of EBIT at which the firm's DFL is being measured.

Unlike interest payments, preferred dividend payments are not tax-deductible. Therefore, on a comparable tax basis, a dollar of preferred dividends costs the firm more than a dollar of interest payments. Dividing preferred dividends in Equation 13.4 by $(1 - T)$ puts interest and preferred dividends on an equivalent, *pretax* basis.

As shown in Figure 13.2, Allegan will have EPS = $0 at an EBIT level of $500,000. With this level of EBIT, there is just enough operating earnings to pay interest ($250,000) and preferred dividends (after-tax). Using Equation 13.4, it can be seen that DFL will be maximized at that level of EBIT where EPS = $0.

Consider again the data presented in Table 13.1 on the Allegan Manufacturing Company. According to that table, EBIT = $1 million, I = $250,000, D_p = $150,000, and T = 40 percent, or 0.40. Substituting these values into Equation 13.4 yields

$$\text{DFL at } \$1,000,000 = \frac{\$1,000,000}{\$1,000,000 - \$250,000 - \$150,000/(1 - 0.40)} = 2.0$$

This result is the same as that obtained using Equation 13.3.

Just as a firm can change its DOL by raising or lowering fixed operating costs, it can also change its DFL by increasing or decreasing fixed capital costs. The amount of fixed capital costs incurred by a firm depends primarily on the mix of debt, preferred shares, and common equity in the firm's capital structure. Thus, a firm that has a relatively large proportion of debt and preferred shares in its capital structure will have relatively large fixed capital costs and a high DFL.

Degree of Combined Leverage

Combined leverage occurs whenever a firm employs *both* operating leverage and financial leverage in an effort to increase the returns to common shareholders. It represents the magnification of sales increases (or decreases) into relatively larger earnings per share increases (or decreases), resulting from the firm's use of both types of leverage. The joint multiplier effect is known as the **degree of combined leverage (DCL)**.

A firm's degree of combined leverage is computed as the percentage change in earnings per share resulting from a given percentage change in sales:

$$\text{DCL at } X = \text{Percentage change in EPS/Percentage change in sales}$$

Degree of Combined Leverage (DCL)
The percentage change in a firm's earnings per share (EPS) resulting from a 1 percent change in sales or output. This also is equal to the degree of operating leverage times the degree of financial leverage used by the firm.

---

[1] For the firm with no preferred shares, Equation 13.4 becomes the following:

$$\text{DFL at } X = \frac{\text{EBIT}}{\text{EBIT} - I} = \frac{\text{EBIT}}{\text{EBT}}$$

where EBT represents earnings before taxes.

This can be rewritten as:

$$(13.5) \qquad \text{DCL at } X = \frac{\dfrac{\Delta EPS}{EPS}}{\dfrac{\Delta Sales}{Sales}}$$

where ΔEPS and $\Delta Sales$ are the changes in a firm's EPS and sales, respectively, and X represents the level of sales at which the firm's combined leverage is measured. The degree of combined leverage is also equal to the product of the degree of operating leverage and the degree of financial leverage.

$$(13.6) \qquad \text{DCL at } X = \text{DOL} \times \text{DFL}$$

To simplify matters, Equations 13.2 and 13.4 can be substituted into Equation 13.6 to obtain a new formula for determining the DCL in terms of basic income statement quantities:

$$\text{DCL at } X = \frac{Sales - Variable\ costs}{EBIT} \times \frac{EBIT}{EBIT - I - D_p/(1 - T)}$$

or

$$(13.7) \qquad \text{DCL at } X = \frac{Sales - Variable\ costs}{EBIT - I - D_p/(1 - T)}$$

These three formulas for calculating DCL can be illustrated using the Allegan Manufacturing Company example. Equation 13.5 can be used to calculate Allegan's DCL with the data from Tables 13.1 and 13.2. The EPS level was $3.00 at a sales level of $5 million and $4.20 at a sales level of $5.5 million. Substituting these values into Equation 13.5 yields

$$\text{DCL at } \$5,000,000 = \frac{\dfrac{(\$4.20 - \$3.00)}{\$3.00}}{\dfrac{(\$5,500,000 - \$5,000,000)}{\$5,000,000}}$$

$$= \frac{\$1.20}{\$3.00} \times \frac{\$5,000,000}{\$500,000}$$

$$= 4.0$$

Substituting Sales = $5,000,000; Variable costs = $3,000,000; EBIT = $1,000,000; I = $250,000; D_p = $150,000; and T = 40% (0.40) into Equation 13.7 gives the same value for Allegan's DCL:

$$\text{DCL at } \$5,000,000 = \frac{\$5,000,000 - \$3,000,000}{\$1,000,000 - \$250,000 - \$150,000/(1 - 0.40)}$$

$$= 4.0$$

Also, recall from the earlier discussion of operating and financial leverage for Allegan that DOL = 2.0 and DFL = 2.0. Substituting these values into Equation 13.6 yields a DCL value identical to that just calculated:

$$\text{DCL at } \$5,000,000 = 2.0 \times 2.0 = 4.0$$

This DCL is interpreted to mean that each 1 percent change in sales from a base sales level of $5 million results in a 4 percent change in Allegan's EPS.

The degree of combined leverage used by a firm is a measure of the overall variability of EPS due to fixed operating and capital costs as sales levels vary. Fixed operating and capital costs can be combined in many different ways to achieve a desired DCL. In other words, a number of possible trade-offs can be made between operating and financial leverage.

Equation 13.6 shows that DCL is a function of DOL and DFL. If a firm has a relatively high DOL, for example, and wishes to achieve a certain DCL, it can offset this high DOL with a lower DFL. Or it may have a high DFL, in which case it would aim for a lower DOL. To illustrate, assume that a firm is considering purchasing assets that will increase fixed operating costs. To offset this high DOL, the firm may want to decrease the proportion of debt in its capital structure, thereby reducing fixed financial costs and the DFL.

Effect of Leverage on Shareholder Wealth and the Cost of Capital

Firms are limited in the amount of combined (i.e., operating and financial) leverage that can be used in seeking to increase EPS and shareholder wealth. Recall from Chapter 12 (see Figures 12.4, 12.5, and 12.6) that the use of "excessive" amounts of *financial* leverage caused the market value of the firm (i.e., shareholder wealth) to decline and the cost of capital to rise. Like financial leverage, the use of increasing amounts of combined leverage increases the risk of financial distress. As this risk increases, investors will require higher rates of return on the funds supplied to the firm in the form of preferred and common equity and debt. In other words, because of the financial distress costs and agency costs associated with "excessive" combined leverage, the firm will have to pay higher costs for its funds. These higher costs will tend to offset the returns gained from the combined leverage, resulting in a decline in the market value of the firm and a rise in its cost of capital.

Other Financial Risk Measures

In addition to using various financial ratios and the degree of combined leverage as measures of the financial risk facing a firm, it is possible to make more formal statements about the financial risk facing a firm if the probability distribution of future operating income (EBIT) is approximately normal and the mean and standard deviation can be estimated. The number of standard deviations, z, that a particular value of EBIT is from the expected value, $\widehat{\text{EBIT}}$, can be computed using an expression similar to Equation 7.3 in Chapter 7:

$$(13.8) \qquad z = \frac{\text{EBIT} - \widehat{\text{EBIT}}}{\sigma}$$

where σ is the standard deviation of EBIT. Equation 13.8, along with the probability values from Table V in the back of the book, can be used to compute the probability that EBIT will be less than (or greater than) some particular value.

For example, consider the case of the Travco Manufacturing Corporation. Given the current capital structure of Travco, the firm has interest payment obligations of $500,000 for the coming year. The firm has no preferred shares. The $500,000 in interest represents the *loss level* for Travco. If EBIT falls below $500,000, losses will be incurred (EPS will be negative). At EBIT levels above $500,000, Travco will have positive earnings per share. Based on past experience, Travco's managers have estimated that the expected value of EBIT over the coming year is $700,000 with a standard deviation of $200,000 and that the distribution of operating income is approximately normal, as illustrated in Figure 13.3. With this information, it is possible to compute the probability of Travco having negative earnings per share over the coming year (or, conversely, the probability of having positive earnings per share).

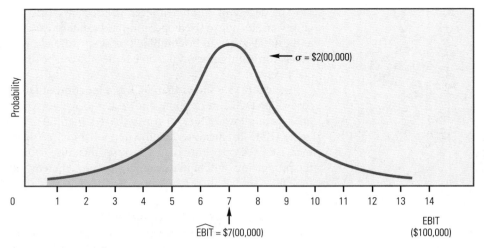

Figure 13.3
Probability Distribution of EBIT, Travco Manufacturing Company

Using Equation 13.8, the probability of Travco having negative EPS is equal to the probability of having EBIT below the loss level of $500,000, or

$$z = \frac{\$500,000 - \$700,000}{\$200,000} = -1.0$$

In other words, a level of EBIT of $500,000 is 1.0 standard deviation below the mean. From Table V, it can be seen that the probability associated with a value that is less than or equal to 1.0 standard deviation below the mean is 15.87 percent. Thus, there is a 15.87 percent chance that Travco will have negative earnings per share (i.e., the shaded area in Figure 13.3) with its current capital structure. Conversely, there is an 84.13 percent chance (100 percent less 15.87 percent chance of losses) of having positive earnings per share.

This type of analysis can give a financial manager a better feel for the level of financial risk facing a firm. As we shall see later in the chapter, when a financial manager is considering two or more alternative capital structures, this same kind of analysis can be used to help select the most desirable capital structure.

EBIT-EPS Analysis

An analytical technique called *EBIT-EPS analysis* can be used to help determine when debt financing is advantageous and when equity financing is advantageous.

Consider the Yoho Corporation with a present capital structure consisting only of common stock (35 million shares). Assume that Yoho is considering an expansion and evaluating two alternative financing plans. Plan 1, equity financing, would involve the sale of an additional 15 million common shares at $20 each. Plan 2, debt financing, would involve the sale of $300 million of 10 percent long-term debt.

If the firm adopts Plan 1, it remains totally equity financed. If, however, the firm adopts Plan 2, it becomes partially debt financed. Because Plan 2 involves the use of financial leverage, this financing issue is basically one of whether it is in the best interests of the firm's existing shareholders to employ financial leverage.

Table 13.5 illustrates the calculation of EPS at two different assumed levels of EBIT for both financing plans. Because the relationship between EBIT and EPS is linear, the two points calculated in Table 13.5 can be used to graph the relationship for each financing plan, as shown in Figure 13.4.

Table 13.5 EBIT-EPS Analysis, Yoho Corporation (All Dollar Figures Except Per-Share Amounts Are in Millions of Dollars)*

	EBIT = $75	EBIT = $125
Equity Financing (Plan 1)		
EBIT	$ 75	$ 125
Interest	—	—
EBT	$ 75	$ 125
Taxes @ 40%	30	50
EAT	$ 45	$ 75
Shares outstanding	50	50
EPS	$0.90	$1.50
% change in EBIT		+66.67%
% change in EPS		+66.67%
DFL		1.00
Debt Financing (Plan 2)		
EBIT	$ 75	$ 125
Interest	30	30
EBT	$ 45	$ 95
Taxes @ 40%	18	38
EAT	$ 27	$ 57
Shares outstanding	35	35
EPS	$0.77	$1.63
% change in EBIT		+66.67%
% change in EPS		+111.69%
DFL		1.68

*EBIT = earnings before interest and taxes; EBT = earnings before taxes; EAT = earnings after taxes; EPS = earnings per share.

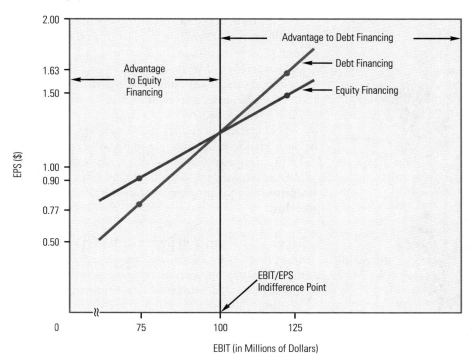

Figure 13.4
EBIT-EPS Analysis, Yoho Corporation

In this example, earnings per share at EBIT levels less than $100 million are higher using the equity financing alternative. Correspondingly, at EBIT levels greater than $100 million, earnings per share are higher with debt financing. The $100 million figure is called the **EBIT-EPS indifference point**. By definition, the earnings per share for the debt and equity financing alternatives are equal at the EBIT-EPS indifference point:

EBIT-EPS Indifference Point

EBIT-EPS Indifference Point
That level of EBIT where the earnings per share of a firm are the same, regardless of which of two alternative capital structures is employed.

$$(13.9) \qquad \text{EPS (debt financing)} = \text{EPS (equity financing)}$$

This equation may be rewritten as follows:

$$(13.10) \qquad \frac{(\text{EBIT} - I_d)(1 - T) - D_p}{N_d} = \frac{(\text{EBIT} - I_e)(1 - T) - D_p}{N_e}$$

where EBIT is earnings before interest and taxes; I_d is the firm's total interest payments if the debt alternative is chosen; I_e is the firm's total interest payments if the equity alternative is chosen; and N_d and N_e represent the number of common shares outstanding for the debt and equity alternatives, respectively. The firm's effective tax rate is indicated as T, and D_p is the amount of preferred dividends for the firm. This equation may be used to calculate directly the EBIT level at which earnings per share for the two alternatives are equal. The data from the example shown in Table 13.5 yield the EBIT-EPS indifference point:

$$\frac{(\text{EBIT} - \$30)(1 - 0.4) - 0}{35} = \frac{(\text{EBIT} - \$0)(1 - 0.4) - 0}{50}$$

$$50(0.6 \text{ EBIT} - \$18) = 35(0.6 \text{ EBIT})$$

$$30 \text{ EBIT} - \$900 = 21 \text{ EBIT}$$

$$9 \text{ EBIT} = \$900$$

$$\text{EBIT} = \$100 \text{ (million)}$$

Note that in the equity financing alternative, a 66.67 percent increase in EBIT (from $75 million to $125 million) results in a 66.67 percent increase in earnings per share (from $0.90 to $1.50), or, by Equation 13.3, a degree of financial leverage of DFL = 66.67%/66.67% = 1.00

Similarly, in the debt financing alternative, a 66.67 percent increase in EBIT results in a 111.69 percent increase in earnings per share, or a degree of financial leverage of DFL = 111.69%/66.67% = 1.68

A comparable magnification of earnings per share will occur if EBIT declines. This wider variation in earnings per share, which occurs with the debt financing alternative, is an illustration of *financial risk*, because *financial risk* is defined as the increased variability in earnings per share due to the firm's use of debt. All other things being equal, an increase in the proportion of debt financing is said to increase the financial risk of the firm.

EBIT-EPS Analysis and Capital Structure Decisions

The tools of EBIT-EPS analysis and the theory of an optimal capital structure can help a firm choose an appropriate capital structure. This section uses an example to develop a five-step procedure designed to assist financial managers in making capital structure decisions.

Balboa Tile Company has been 100 percent financed with equity funds since the firm was founded. While analyzing a major expansion program, the firm has decided to consider alternative capital structures. In particular, it has been suggested that the firm should use this expansion program as an opportunity to increase the long-term debt ratio from the current level of 0 percent to a new level of 30 percent. Interest on the proposed new debt will amount to $100,000 per year.

- **Step 1: Compute the expected level of EBIT after the expansion** Based on the firm's past operating experience and a projection of the impact of the expansion, it estimates its expected EBIT to be $500,000 per year under normal operating circumstances.

- **Step 2: Estimate the variability of this level of operating earnings** Based on the past performance of the firm over several business cycles, the standard deviation of operating earnings is estimated to be $200,000 per year. (Operating earnings are assumed to be normally distributed, or at least approximately so.)

- **Step 3: Compute the indifference point between the two financing alternatives** This calculation will determine whether it is preferable to add new debt or to maintain the all-equity capital structure. Using the techniques of EBIT-EPS analysis previously discussed, the indifference point is computed to be $300,000.

- **Step 4: Analyze these estimates in the context of the risk the firm is willing to assume** After considerable discussion, it has been decided that the firm is willing to accept a 25 percent chance that operating earnings in any year will be below the indifference point and a 5 percent chance that the firm will have to report a loss in any year. To complete this analysis, it is necessary to compute the probability that operating earnings will be below the indifference point, that is, the probability that EBIT will be less than $300,000. This is equivalent on the standard normal curve (using Equation 13.8) to the following:

$$z = \frac{\$300,000 - \$500,000}{\$200,000} = -1.0$$

or 1.0 standard deviation below the mean. The probability that EBIT will be less than 1.0 standard deviation below the mean is 15.87 percent. This is determined from Table V at the end of the book. Therefore, on the basis of the indifference point criterion, the proposed new capital structure appears acceptable. The probability of incurring losses must now be analyzed. This is the probability that EBIT will be less than the required interest payments of $100,000. On the standard normal curve, this corresponds to the following:

$$z = \frac{\$100,000 - \$500,000}{\$200,000} = -2.0$$

or 2.0 standard deviations below the mean. The probability that EBIT will be less than 2.0 standard deviations below the mean is 2.28 percent, as shown in Table V. According to this criterion, the proposed capital structure also seems acceptable.

If either or both of these tests had shown the proposed capital structure to have an unacceptable level of risk, the analysis would have been repeated for lower levels of debt than the proposed 30 percent rate. Similarly, because the proposed capital structure has exceeded the standards set by the firm, management might want to consider even higher levels of debt than the proposed 30 percent.

- **Step 5: Examine the market evidence to determine whether the proposed capital structure is too risky** This evaluation should be made in relation to the following: the firm's level of business risk, industry norms for leverage ratios and coverage ratios, and the recommendations of the firm's investment dealers/bankers.

This step is undertaken only after a proposed capital structure has met the "internal" tests for acceptability. Financial leverage is a double-edged sword: it enhances expected returns, but it also increases risk. If the increase in perceived risk is greater than the increase in expected returns, the firm's weighted cost of capital may rise instead of fall, and the firm's share price and market value will decline.

It is important to note that a firm need not feel constrained by industry standards in setting its own capital structure. If, for example, a firm has traditionally been more profitable than the average firm in the industry, or if a firm's operating income is more stable than the operating income of the average firm, a higher level of financial leverage can probably be tolerated. The final choice of a capital structure involves a careful analysis of expected future returns and risks relative to other firms in the industry.

EBIT-EPS Analysis and Share Prices

An important question arising from EBIT-EPS analysis is the impact of financial leverage on the firm's common share price. Specifically, which financing alternative results in the higher share price? Returning to the Yoho Corporation example discussed earlier (see Table 13.5), suppose the firm is able to operate at the $125 million EBIT level. Then, if the firm chooses the debt financing alternative, its EPS will equal $1.63, and if it chooses the equity alternative, its EPS will be $1.50. But the share price depends on the price-earnings (P/E) ratio that the market assigns to each alternative. Suppose the market assigns a P/E ratio of 16.0 to the firm's common shares if the equity alternative is chosen and a P/E ratio of 15.4 if the debt alternative is chosen. Recalling from Chapter 3 that the P/E ratio (Equation 3.15) was defined as the market price per common share (P_0) divided by the current earnings per share (EPS), the common share price can be calculated for both alternatives as follows:

$$(13.11) \qquad\qquad P_0 = (\text{P/E ratio})(\text{EPS})$$

Equity alternative:

$$P_0 = (16.0)(\$1.50) = \$24.00$$

Debt alternative:

$$P_0 = (15.4)(\$1.63) = \$25.10$$

These calculations show that in this case the market places a higher value on the firm's shares if the debt alternative is chosen rather than the equity alternative. Note that the market assigned a slightly lower P/E ratio to the debt alternative. The market recognized the increased financial risk associated with the debt alternative, but this increased risk was more than offset by the increased EPS possible with the use of debt.

To carry the Yoho Corporation example one important step further, suppose the firm, while operating at the $125 million EBIT level, chooses an even higher debt capital structure, which causes its EPS to increase to $2.25. Suppose further that the market feels that this high-debt capital structure significantly increases the firm's financial risk—to the point where bankruptcy could occur if EBIT levels turned downward in a recession. If the market assigns a P/E ratio of 10.0, for example, the share price would be $22.50 (= $2.25 × 10.0), and it would be clear that this change in capital structure is not desirable.

It is important to emphasize that the P/E ratios in the preceding example are simply assumptions. As an analytical technique, EBIT-EPS analysis does not provide a complete solution to the optimal capital structure question.

In summary, the firm potentially can show increased earnings to its shareholders by increasing its level of financial risk. However, because increases in risk tend to increase the cost of capital (which is analogous to a decrease in the P/E ratio), the firm's management has to assess the trade-off between the higher earnings per share for its shareholders and the higher costs of capital.

Cash Insolvency Analysis

In Chapter 3, the *times interest earned* and *fixed-charge coverage* ratios were introduced. These ratios provide an indicator of the ability of a firm to meet its interest and other fixed charge obligations (including lease payments, sinking fund payments, and preferred dividends) out of current operating income. Also, in that chapter, liquidity ratios, such as the *current ratio* and the *quick ratio,* were introduced. Liquidity ratios provide a simple measure of a firm's ability to meet its obligations, especially in the near term. In that chapter, we also prepared a detailed cash budget and indicated that it was the best measure of a firm's cash adequacy.

Coverage ratios and liquidity ratios do not provide an adequate picture of a firm's solvency position. A firm is said to be technically insolvent if it is unable to meet its current obligations. We need a more comprehensive measure of the ability of a firm to meet its obligations if this information is to be used to assist in capital structure planning. This measure must consider both the cash on hand and the cash expected to be generated in the future. Donaldson has suggested that a firm's level of fixed financial charges (including interest, preferred dividends, sinking fund obligations, and lease payments), and thus its debt-carrying capacity, should depend on the cash balances and net cash flows that can be expected to be available in a worst-case (recessionary environment) scenario.[2] This **cash insolvency analysis** requires the preparation of a detailed cash budget under assumed recessionary conditions.

Donaldson defines a firm's net cash balance in a recession, CB_R, to be

$$(13.12) \qquad CB_R = CB_0 + FCF_R$$

where CB_0 is the cash (and marketable securities) balance at the beginning of the recession, and FCF_R is the free cash flows expected to be generated during the recession. *Free cash flow* represents the portion of a firm's total cash flow available to service additional debt, to make dividend payments to common shareholders, and to invest in other projects.

For example, suppose MINECO, a natural resource firm, reported a cash (and marketable securities) balance of approximately $154 million. Suppose also that management anticipates free cash flows of $210 million during a projected one-year recession. These free cash flows reflect both operating cash flows during the recession and current required fixed financial charges. Under the current capital structure, consisting of approximately 32 percent debt, the cash balance at the end of the recession would be $364 million ($154 million plus $210 million). Assume that the management of MINECO is considering a change in its capital structure that would add an additional $280 million of annual after-tax interest and sinking fund payments (i.e., fixed financial charges). The effect would be a cash balance at the end of the recession of

$$CB_R = \$154 \text{ million} + \$210 \text{ million} - \$280 \text{ million} = \$84 \text{ million}$$

The managers of MINECO must decide if this projected cash balance of $84 million leaves them enough of a cushion in a recession.

This analysis can be enhanced if it is possible to specify the probability distribution of expected free cash flows during a recession. For example, if the MINECO managers believe, based on past experience, that free cash flows are approximately normally

Cash Insolvency Analysis
A method of financial forecasting that requires the preparation of a detailed cash budget under assumed recessionary conditions.

---

[2] See G. Donaldson, "New Framework for Corporate Debt Policy," *Harvard Business Review* 40 (March–April 1962): 117–131; and G. Donaldson, "Strategy for Financial Emergencies," *Harvard Business Review* 47 (November–December 1969): 67–79. For a discussion of debt policy in Canada, see Pauline M. Shum, "Taxes and Corporate Debt Policy in Canada: An Empirical Investigation," *Canadian Journal of Economics* (August 1996): 556–572 and M. Zyblock, "Corporate Financial Leverage: A Canada-US Comparison, 1961–1996," *Statistics Canada,* Paper #111 (December 1997).

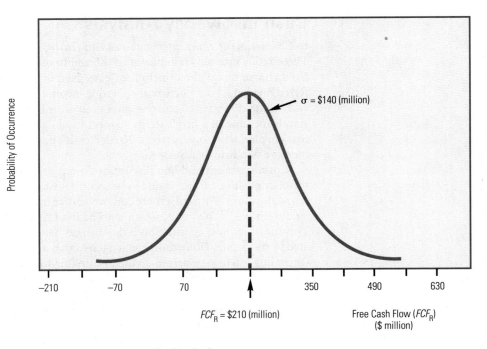

σ = $140 (million)

−210   −70   70   350   490   630

$FCF_R = \$210$ (million)

Free Cash Flow (FCF_R)
($ million)

(a) Free Cash Flow Probability Distribution

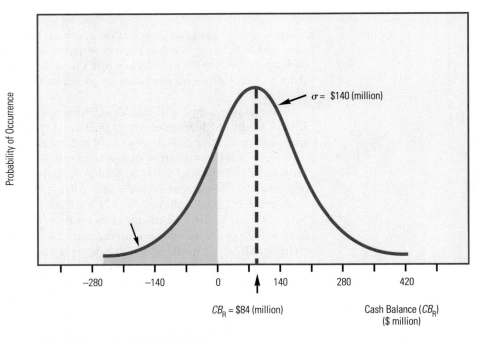

σ = $140 (million)

−280   −140   0   140   280   420

$CB_R = \$84$ (million)

Cash Balance (CB_R)
($ million)

(b) Cash Balance Probability Distribution

Figure 13.5
Cash Flows and Cash Balance Probability Distributions, MINECO

distributed [see panel (a) of Figure 13.5] with an expected value during a one-year recession (FCF_R) of $210 million and a standard deviation of $140 million, they can compute the probability of running out of cash if the new debt is added. The probability of running out of cash is equal to the probability of ending the recession with a cash balance of less than $0. The probability distribution of MINECO's *cash balance* [panel (b) of Figure 13.5] will have the same shape (i.e., approximately normal with a standard deviation, σ, of $140 million) as the probability distribution of *free cash flows* [panel (a) of Figure 13.5], except that it will be shifted to the left from a mean (FCF_R) of $210 million to a mean ($CB_R$) of $84 million [i.e., by the beginning cash balance ($154 million) plus expected free cash flows ($210 million) less additional fixed financial charges ($280 million)]. Employing an expression similar to Equation 13.8, where cash balance (CB_R) is the variable of interest rather than EBIT, a cash balance of $0 is equivalent on the standard normal curve to the following:

$$z = \frac{(\$0 - \$84 \text{ million})}{\$140 \text{ million}} = -0.60$$

From Table V, the probability of a z value of -0.60 or less is 27.43 percent. Thus, with an additional $280 million in fixed financial charges, the probability of MINECO running out of cash during a one-year recession is about 27 percent [i.e., shaded area in panel (b) of Figure 13.5].

The MINECO managers may feel that this is too much risk to assume. If they want to assume only a 5 percent risk of running out of cash during a one-year recession, they can determine the amount of additional interest and sinking fund payments (i.e., fixed financial charges) that can be safely added. First, find the number of standard deviations (z) to the left of the mean that gives a 5 percent probability of occurrence in the lower tail of the distribution (i.e., the shaded area in Figure 13.6). From Table V, this value of z is found to be approximately -1.65. Next, we calculate the expected cash balance (CB_R) needed at the end of a one-year recession if the risk of running out of cash is to be held to 5 percent:

$$z = -1.65 = \frac{(\$0 - CB_R)}{\$140 \text{ million}}$$

$$CB_R = \$231 \text{ million}$$

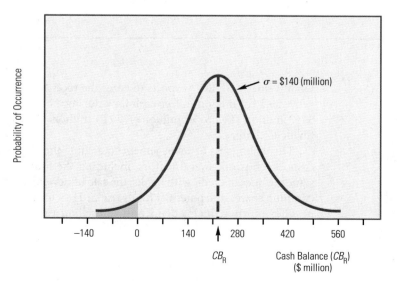

Figure 13.6
Cash Balance Probability Distribution, MINECO

Balancing Operating and Financial Risks at Nestlé

Nestlé is a huge, multinational Swiss foods corporation with operations in at least 150 countries. The overwhelming majority of its sales occur outside Switzerland. Nestlé's various foreign operating subsidiaries enjoy considerable decentralized operational flexibility. Local division managers handle all marketing and production decisions.

In contrast to its decentralized operating policy, Nestlé uses a highly centralized financing strategy. All financing decisions are handled at corporate headquarters. The small corporate finance staff makes all funding decisions for the subsidiaries, establishes the firm's worldwide consolidated capital structure, sets individual subsidiary capital structures, manages worldwide currency exposure risk, and mandates the dividend policy for subsidiaries.

When a subsidiary is first formed, about one-half of the needed financing— the funds used to acquire fixed assets— comes from equity contributions by the parent. The balance of the needed funds, primarily to support working capital investments, is acquired in the host country through the banking system or the sale of commercial paper. In some countries, where there is little or no risk of capital expropriation, the parent company may finance working capital needs, depending on the relative cost of funds for the parent compared to the local cost of funds for the subsidiary.

Each subsidiary normally pays a dividend of 100 percent of its profits back to the parent. This guarantees central control over the capital structure of each subsidiary. If additional funds are needed for investment, the parent provides them using the lowest-cost source of capital available. Nestlé manages its overall sources of capital with the objective of maintaining a top credit rating and thereby minimizing its capital costs.

Why does Nestlé follow such a conservative financing strategy? Senior vice president of finance Daniel Regolatti states, "Our basic strategy is that we are an industrial company. We have a lot of risks in a lot of countries, so we should not add high financial risks."[3] This strategy recognizes the trade-offs between business risk and financial risk that have been discussed in this chapter.

Finally, since MINECO expects to enter the recession with $154 million in cash and to generate $210 million in free cash flow during a one-year recession, it can take on just $133 million (i.e., $154 million + $210 million − $231 million) in additional fixed financial charges.

The willingness of management to assume the risk associated with running out of cash depends on several factors, including the following: funds available from outstanding lines of credit with banks; the sale of new long-term debt, preferred shares, and common shares; the potential funds realized by cutting back on expenses during a business downturn; reducing dividends; and selling assets.

---

[3] "The Nestlé Approach to Capital Markets and Innovation," *Business International Money Report* (October 27, 1986): 337.

Other Factors to Consider in Making Capital Structure Decisions

In addition to a consideration of tax effects, financial distress costs, agency costs, the business risk facing the firm, EBIT-EPS analysis, and cash insolvency analysis, there are additional factors normally considered as a firm makes its capital structure decisions. These factors are discussed briefly in this section.

Industry Standards

Financial analysts, investment dealers, bond rating agencies, common share investors, and bankers normally compare the financial risk for a firm, as measured by its interest and fixed-charge coverage ratios and its long-term debt ratio, with industry standards or norms. There is considerable evidence that the capital structure of an average firm varies significantly from industry to industry. While firms tend to cluster around the industry average debt ratio, there are exceptions. A firm adopting a capital structure that differs significantly from the industry norms will have to convince the financial markets that its business risk is sufficiently different from the risk facing the average firm in the industry to warrant this divergent capital structure.

Profitability and Need for Funds

As noted in the previous chapter, highly profitable firms, with limited needs for funds, tend to have lower debt ratios when compared with less profitable firms.

Lender and Bond-Rater Requirements

Lenders and bond-rating agencies often impose restrictions on a firm's capital structure choices as a condition for extending credit or maintaining a bond or preferred share rating. These are not the only factors considered when establishing a firm's bond rating, but they are very important guidelines that a firm must follow if it wishes to retain or improve its credit rating. A more complete discussion of the factors considered by bond rating agencies is contained in Chapter 5.

Managerial Risk Aversion

Management's willingness to assume risk often has a major impact on the capital structure chosen by the firm, although the relative risk aversion of management *does not* influence the firm's optimal capital structure. Some managers adopt unusually risky or unusually low-risk capital structures. When a suboptimal capital structure is chosen, the financial marketplace will normally penalize a firm for this action.

Retention of Control

Some firms use debt or preferred share financing rather than common share financing to avoid selling new common shares. When new voting common shares are sold, the relative control position of existing shareholders is diluted.

Like Air Canada, Doman Industries was using excessive leverage. Why were Doman's bondholders willing to swap debt for equity? Presumably they felt that the going-concern value of the equity that they received exceeded the funds that they could get by forcing Doman into liquidation. Is Air Canada headed for a similar debt-for-equity swap?

Summary

- *Leverage* refers to a firm's use of assets and liabilities having fixed costs. A firm uses leverage in an attempt to earn returns in excess of the fixed costs of these assets and liabilities, thus increasing the returns to common shareholders.

- *Operating leverage* occurs when a firm uses assets having fixed operating costs. The *degree of operating leverage* (DOL) measures the percentage change in a firm's EBIT resulting from a 1 percent change in sales (or units of output). As a firm's fixed operating costs rise, its DOL increases.

- *Financial leverage* occurs when a firm makes use of funds (primarily from debt and preferred shares) having fixed capital costs. The *degree of financial leverage* (DFL) measures the percentage change in the firm's EPS resulting from a 1 percent change in EBIT. As a firm's fixed capital costs rise, its DFL increases.

- The *combined leverage* of a firm is equal to the *product* of the degrees of operating and financial leverage. These two types of leverage can be combined in many different ways to achieve a given degree of combined leverage (DCL). The total variability of the firm's EPS is a combination of business risk and financial risk.

- *EBIT-EPS analysis* is an analytical technique that can be used to help determine the circumstances under which a firm should employ financial leverage. Basically, it involves calculating earnings per share at different levels of EBIT for debt and equity financing plans. This information may then be used to graph earnings per share versus EBIT to determine the EBIT levels at which financial leverage is advantageous to the firm.

- The *indifference point* in EBIT-EPS analysis is that level of EBIT where earnings per share are the same, regardless of which of two alternative capital structures is used. At EBIT levels greater than the indifference level, a more financially levered capital structure will produce a higher level of earnings per share. At EBIT levels less than the indifference point, a less financially levered capital structure will produce a higher level of earnings per share.

- *Cash insolvency analysis* can provide additional insights about the appropriate capital structure. Cash insolvency analysis evaluates the adequacy of a firm's cash position in a worst-case (recession) scenario.

- *Other factors* that should be considered when establishing a capital structure policy are industry standards, profitability and need for funds, lender requirements, and the desire of owners to retain control of the firm.

Questions and Topics for Discussion

1. Define *leverage* as it is used in finance.
2. Define and give examples of the following:
   a. Fixed costs
   b. Variable costs
3. Define the following:
   a. Operating leverage
   b. Financial leverage
4. How is a firm's degree of combined leverage (DCL) related to its degrees of operating and financial leverage?
5. Is it possible for a firm to have a high degree of operating leverage and a low level of business risk? Explain.
6. Is it possible for a firm to have a high degree of combined leverage and a low level of total risk? Explain.
7. What are the major limitations of EBIT-EPS analysis as a technique to determine the optimal capital structure?
8. In practice, how can a firm determine whether it is operating at (or near) its optimal capital structure?
9. Under what circumstances should a firm use *more* debt in its capital structure than is used by the "average" firm in the industry? When should it use *less* debt than the "average" firm?
10. Why do public utilities typically have capital structures with about 50 percent debt, whereas major oil companies average about 25 percent debt in their capital structures?
11. What is *cash insolvency analysis,* and how can it help in the establishment of an optimal capital structure?

Self-Test Problems

ST1. Pinches Salt Company has the following income statement for 20X1:

Sales	$5,000,000
Variable operating costs	1,000,000
Fixed operating costs	2,000,000
EBIT	$2,000,000
Interest	500,000
EBT	$1,500,000
Tax (at 40%)	600,000
EBT	$900,000
Preferred dividends	100,000
Earnings available to common shareholders	$ 800,000
Shares outstanding	400,000

   a. Compute the firm's DOL, DFL, and DCL.
   b. If sales increase to $5,500,000, what is your forecast of EPS?

ST2. FI estimates that its EBIT for the coming year is approximately normally distributed with an expected value of $1.75 million and a standard deviation of $1.2 million. Given its current capital structure, FI has $250,000 in interest obligations due during the coming year. Determine the probability that FI will have negative EPS.

ST3. The E Corporation has a present capital structure consisting of 100 million common shares. The firm is considering two alternative financial plans for expansion:

- **Plan 1: Equity financing** Sale of 10 million additional common shares at $15 per share
- **Plan 2: Debt financing** Sale of $150 million of 12% long-term debt

The firm's marginal tax rate is 40%.

a. Determine the indifference level of EBIT between the two financing plans.

b. Suppose that the firm's EBIT is normally distributed with an expected value of $250 million and a standard deviation of $200 million. If the debt alternative is chosen, determine the probability that the firm will have negative EPS.

c. Determine the probability that the debt financing alternative will produce higher earnings than the equity alternative.

ST4. BLD has a cash (and marketable securities) balance of $20 million. Free cash flows during a projected one-year recession are expected to be $60 million with a standard deviation of $60 million. (Assume the firm's free cash flows are approximately normally distributed.)

a. Determine the probability that the firm will run out of cash during the recession.

b. The firm is considering a change in its capital structure that would increase its annual fixed charges by $10 million. Determine the probability of running out of cash during the recession if the change in capital structure is undertaken.

Problems*

BASIC

 Excel

1. FAA's fixed operating costs are $5.8 million, and its variable cost ratio is 0.20. The firm has $2 million in bonds outstanding with a coupon interest rate of 8%. The firm has 30,000 preferred shares outstanding, which pay a $2.00 annual dividend. There are 100,000 common shares outstanding. Revenues for the firm are $8 million, and its tax rate is 40%.

a. Compute its degree of operating leverage.

b. Compute its degree of financial leverage.

c. Compute its degree of combined leverage and interpret this value.

2. Given the following information for C Company, compute the firm's degree of combined leverage (dollars are in thousands except EPS):

	20X1	20X2
Sales	$500,000	$570,000
Fixed costs	120,000	120,000
Variable costs	300,000	342,000
EBIT	80,000	108,000
Interest	30,000	30,000
EPS	$1.00	$1.56

3. A firm has earnings per share of $2.60 at a sales level of $5 million. If the firm has a degree of operating leverage of 3.0 and a degree of financial leverage of 5.5 (both at a sales level of $5 million), forecast earnings per share for a 2% sales decline.

*Coloured numbers and letters denote problems that have "check" answers provided at the back of the book.

Excel

4. The HL Company forecasts that next year's sales will be $6 million. Fixed operating costs are estimated to be $800,000, and the variable cost ratio (that is, variable costs as a fraction of sales) is estimated to be 0.75. The firm has a $600,000 loan at 10% interest. It has 20,000 of $3 preferred shares and 60,000 common shares outstanding. The firm's corporate tax rate is 40%.

 a. Forecast the firm's earnings per share (EPS) for next year. Develop a complete income statement using the revised format illustrated in Table 13.1. Then determine what the firm's EPS would be if sales were 10% above the projected $6 million level.

 b. Calculate the firm's degree of operating leverage (DOL) at a sales level of $6 million using the following:
   i. The definitional formula (Equation 13.1)
   ii. The simpler, computational formula (Equation 13.2)
   iii. What is the economic interpretation of this value?

 c. Calculate the firm's degree of financial leverage (DFL) at the EBIT level corresponding to sales of $6 million using the following:
   i. The definitional formula (Equation 13.3)
   ii. The simpler computational formula (Equation 13.4)
   iii. What is the economic interpretation of this value?

 d. Calculate the firm's degree of combined leverage (DCL) using the following:
   i. The definitional formula (Equation 13.5)
   ii. The simpler computational formula (Equation 13.7)
   iii. The degree of operating and financial leverage calculated in parts b and c
   iv. What is the economic interpretation of this value?

Excel

5. The A Company reported the following income statement for 20X1:

Sales		$15,000,000
Less Operating expenses		
Wages, salaries, benefits	$6,000,000	
Raw materials	3,000,000	
Depreciation	1,500,000	
General, administrative, and selling expenses	1,500,000	
Total operating expenses		12,000,000
EBIT		$3,000,000
Less Interest expense		750,000
EBT		$2,250,000
Less Taxes		1,000,000
EAT		$1,250,000
Less Preferred dividends		250,000
Earnings available to common shareholders		$1,000,000
EPS (250,000 shares outstanding)		$4.00

 Assume that all depreciation and 75% of the firm's general, administrative, and selling expenses are *fixed costs* and that the remainder of the firm's operating expenses are *variable costs*.

 a. Determine the firm's fixed costs, variable costs, and variable cost ratio.

 b. Based on its 20X1 sales, calculate the following:
   i. The firm's DOL
   ii. The firm's DFL
   iii. The firm's DCL

 c. Assuming that next year's sales increase by 15%, fixed operating and financial costs remain constant, and the variable cost ratio and tax rate also remain constant, use the leverage figures just calculated to forecast next year's EPS.

d. Show the validity of this forecast by constructing the firm's income statement for next year according to the revised format.

e. Construct an EPS-EBIT graph based on the firm's 20X1 income statement.

6. MG Corporation has fixed operating costs of $10 million and a variable cost ratio of 0.65. The firm has a $20 million, 10% bank loan and a $6 million, 12% bond issue outstanding. The firm has 1 million preferred shares that pay a $5 dividend and 2 million common shares. The firm's marginal tax rate is 40%. Sales are expected to be $80 million.

a. Compute the firm's degree of operating leverage at an $80 million sales level.

b. Compute the firm's degree of financial leverage at an $80 million sales level.

c. If sales decline to $76 million, forecast the firm's earnings per share.

7. B Company expects its operating income over the coming year to equal $1.5 million, with a standard deviation of $300,000. Its coefficient of variation is equal to 0.20. The firm must pay interest charges of $700,000 next year and preferred share dividends of $240,000. The firm's marginal tax rate is 40%. What is the probability that the firm will have negative earnings per share next year? (Assume that operating income is normally distributed.)

8. A firm has sales of $10 million, variable costs of $5 million, EBIT of $2 million, and a degree of combined leverage of 3.0.

a. If the firm has no preferred shares, what are its annual interest charges?

b. If the firm wishes to reduce its degree of combined leverage to 2.5 by reducing interest charges, what will be the new level of annual interest charges?

9. CBE has a degree of financial leverage of 2.0 and a degree of combined leverage of 6.0. The breakeven sales level has been estimated to be $500,000. Fixed costs total $250,000. What effect will a 15% increase in sales have on EBIT?

10. C Ltd. expects sales to be $30 million this year. Because this is a very capital-intensive business, fixed operating costs are $10 million. The variable cost ratio is 40%. The firm's debt obligations consist of a $2 million, 10% bank loan and a $10 million bond issue with a 12% coupon rate. The firm has 100,000 preferred shares outstanding that pay a $9.60 dividend. The firm has 1 million common shares outstanding and its marginal tax rate is 40%.

a. Compute the firm's degree of operating leverage.

b. Compute the firm's degree of financial leverage.

c. Compute the firm's degree of combined leverage.

d. Compute the firm's EPS if sales decline by 5%.

11. MGI has expected sales of $40 million. Fixed operating costs are $5 million, and the variable cost ratio is 65%. The firm has outstanding a $10 million, 10% bank loan and $3 million in 12% coupon-rate bonds. The firm also has 250,000 preferred shares outstanding that have a $10 dividend and 1 million common shares. The firm's average tax rate is 35%, and its marginal rate is 40%.

a. What is the firm's degree of operating leverage at a sales level of $40 million?

b. What is the firm's current degree of financial leverage?

c. Forecast the firm's EPS if sales drop to $38 million.

12. Earnings per share (EPS) for Valcor are $3 at a sales level of $2 million. If the firm's degree of operating leverage is 2.0 and its degree of combined leverage is 8.0, what will happen to EPS if operating income increases by 3%?

13. Two capital goods manufacturing companies, R and D, are virtually identical in all aspects of their operations—product lines, amount of sales, total size, and so on. The two companies differ only in their capital structures, as shown here:

	R	D
Debt (8%)	$400,000,000	$100,000,000
Common equity	$600,000,000	$900,000,000
Number of common shares outstanding	30,000,000	45,000,000

Each firm has $1,000 million ($1 billion) in total assets.

Capital goods manufacturers typically are subject to cyclical trends in the economy. Suppose that the EBIT level for both companies is $100 million during an expansion and $60 million during a recession. (Assume a 40% tax rate for both companies.)

a. Calculate the earnings per share for both firms during expansion and recession.

b. Which share is riskier? Why?

c. At what EBIT level are the earnings per share of the two companies identical?

d. Calculate the common share price for both companies during an expansion if the market assigns a price-earnings ratio of 10 to D and 9 to R.

14. The BC Corporation has computed the indifference point between a debt and common equity financing alternatives to be $4 million of EBIT. The EBIT is approximately normally distributed with an expected value of $4.5 million and a standard deviation of $600,000. The coefficient of variation is equal to 0.13.

a. What is the probability that the equity financing alternative will be superior to the debt alternative?

b. Under the debt alternative, the firm will incur $3 million in interest expenses. What is the chance of the firm losing money under the debt alternative?

15. Next year's EBIT for the L Company is approximately normally distributed with an expected value of $8 million and a standard deviation of $5 million. The firm's marginal tax rate is 40%. Fixed financial charges (interest payments) next year are $1.5 million. Determine the probability that the firm will have

a. Negative EPS

b. Positive EPS

 Excel

16. UTI has a current capital structure consisting of 10 million common shares, $200 million of first-mortgage bonds with a coupon interest rate of 13%, and $40 million of 5% dividend preferred shares. In order to expand into Asia, UTI will have to undertake an aggressive capital outlay campaign, expected to cost $200 million. This expansion can be financed either by selling 4 million new common shares at a price of $50 per share or by the sale of $200 million of subordinated debentures at a pretax interest rate of 15%. The firm's tax rate is 40%.

a. Compute the EBIT-EPS indifference point between the equity and debt financing alternatives.

b. If UTI expects next year's EBIT to be $150 million with a standard deviation of $20 million, what is the probability that the equity financing alternative will produce higher earnings per share than the debt financing alternative? (Assume that EBIT is normally distributed.)

CHALLENGE

17. G Company sales for the year 20X1 were $3 million. The firm's variable operating cost ratio was 0.50, and fixed costs (that is, overhead and depreciation) were $900,000. Its average (and marginal) income tax rate is 40%. Currently, the firm has $2.4 million of long-term bank loans outstanding at an average interest rate of 12.5%. The remainder of the firm's capital structure consists of 100,000 common shares outstanding at the present time.

a. Calculate the firm's degree of combined leverage for 20X1.

b. The firm is forecasting a 10% increase in sales for next year (20X2). Furthermore, the firm is planning to purchase additional labour-saving equipment, which will increase fixed costs by $150,000 and reduce the variable cost ratio to 0.475. Financing this equipment with debt will require additional bank loans of $500,000 at an interest rate of 12.5%. Calculate the firm's expected degree of combined leverage for 20X2.

c. Determine how much the firm must reduce its debt in 20X2 (for example, through the sale of common shares) to maintain its DCL at the 20X1 level.

18. W Company, a small-arms manufacturer, has current sales of $10 million and operating income (EBIT) of $450,000. The firm's degree of operating leverage is 2.5. Next year's sales are expected to increase by 5%. The firm has found that, over time, the standard deviation of operating income is $300,000 and operating income is approximately normally distributed about its expected value in any year. The firm's current financial structure contains both debt and preferred shares. Interest payments total $200,000, and preferred share dividends total $60,000. The firm's marginal tax rate is 40%. What is the probability that the firm will report negative earnings per share during the coming year?

19. S Corporation's current EPS is $5.00 at a sales level of $10,000,000. At this sales level, EBIT is $2,000,000. The firm's DCL has been estimated to be 2.0 at the current level of sales. Sales are forecast to have an expected value of $11,000,000 next year, with a standard deviation of $500,000. The coefficient of variation of sales is equal to 0.045. What is the probability that EPS will be less than $5.00 per share next year, assuming that sales are normally distributed?

20. K Industries expects next year's operating income (EBIT) to equal $4 million, with a standard deviation of $2 million. The coefficient of variation of operating income is equal to 0.50. Interest expenses will be $1 million, and preferred dividends will be $600,000. Debt retirement will require principal payments of $1 million. The firm's marginal tax rate is 40%. If EBIT is normally distributed, what is the probability that the firm will have negative EPS next year?

[Excel] 21. Emco has a present capital structure consisting only of 10 million common shares. The firm is planning a major expansion. At this time, the firm is undecided between the following two financing plans (assume a 40% marginal tax rate):

- **Plan 1: Equity Financing** Sell an additional 5 million common shares at $10 each.
- **Plan 2: Debt Financing** Sell $50 million of 10% long-term debt.

One piece of information the firm desires for its decision analysis is an EBIT-EPS analysis.

a. Calculate the EBIT-EPS indifference point.

b. Graphically determine the EBIT-EPS indifference point. *Hint:* Use EBIT = $10 million and $25 million.

c. What happens to the indifference point if the interest rate on debt increases and the common share sales price remains constant?

d. What happens to the indifference point if the interest rate on debt remains constant and the common share sales price increases?

[Excel] 22. M Industries is considering opening a new subsidiary in Barbados, to be operated as a separate company. The firm's financial analysts expect the new facility's average EBIT level to be $6 million per year. At this time, the firm is considering the following two financing plans (use a 40% marginal tax rate in your analysis):

- **Plan 1: Equity financing** Sell 2 million common shares at $10 each.
- **Plan 2: Debt-equity financing** Sell $10 million of 12% long-term debt and 1 million common shares at $10 each.

a. Calculate the EBIT-EPS indifference point.

b. Calculate the expected EPS for both financing plans.

c. What factors should the firm consider in deciding which financing plan to adopt?

d. Which plan do you recommend the firm adopt?

e. Suppose the firm adopts Plan 2, and the new facility initially operates at an annual EBIT level of $6 million. What is the times interest earned ratio?

f. If the lenders require that the new company maintain a times interest earned ratio equal to 3.5 or greater, by how much could the EBIT level drop and the firm still be in compliance with the loan agreement if Plan 2 is adopted?

g. Suppose the expected annual EBIT level of $6 million is normally distributed with a standard deviation of $3 million. What is the probability that the EPS will be negative in any given year if Plan 1 is selected?

 Excel

23. High Sky, Inc., a hot-air balloon manufacturing firm, currently has the following simplified balance sheet:

Assets		Liabilities and Capital	
Total assets	$1,100,000	Bonds (10% interest)	$600,000
		Common shares (100,000 shares outstanding)	400,000
		Retained earnings	100,000
		Total liabilities and capital	$1,100,000

The firm is planning an expansion that is expected to cost $600,000. The expansion can be financed with new equity (sold to net the firm $4 per share) or with the sale of new bonds at an interest rate of 11%. (The firm's marginal tax rate is 40%.)

a. Compute the indifference point between the two financing alternatives.

b. If the expected level of EBIT for the firm is $240,000 with a standard deviation of $50,000, what is the probability that the debt financing alternative will produce higher earnings than the equity alternative? (EBIT is normally distributed.)

c. If the debt alternative is chosen, what is the probability that the firm will have negative earnings per share in any period?

24. The Anaya Corporation is a leader in artificial intelligence research. The firm's present capital structure consists of 30 million common shares) and $250 million of debt with an interest rate of 15%. The firm is planning an expansion and wishes to examine alternative financing plans. The firm's marginal tax rate is 40%. Two alternatives under consideration are:

 Excel

- **Plan 1: Common Equity Financing** Sell an additional 3 million common shares at $20 each.

- **Plan 2: Debt Financing** Sell $30 million of first-mortgage bonds with a pretax cost of 14% and $30 million of debentures with a pretax cost of 15%.

a. Compute the indifference point between these two alternatives.

b. One of the firm's artificially intelligent financial managers has suggested that the firm might be better off to finance with preferred shares rather than common shares. He suggested that the indifference point be computed between the debt financing alternative and a preferred share financing alternative. Preferred shares ($60 million) will cost 16% after tax. Which option should be selected on an EPS basis? (No calculations are necessary if you set the problem up and think about the implications.)

25. JCP has a current capital structure that consists of $50 million in long-term debt at an interest rate of 10% and $40 million in common equity (10 million shares).

The firm is considering an expansion program that will cost $10 million. This program can be financed with additional long-term debt at a 13% rate of interest, preferred shares at a cost of 14%, or the sale of new common shares at $10 per share. The firm's marginal tax rate is 40%.

   a. Compute the indifference point level of EBIT between the debt financing alternative and the common share alternative.

   b. Compute the indifference point level of EBIT between the common share and the preferred share alternatives.

   c. Is there an indifference point between the debt and preferred share alternatives? Why or why not?

26. OSC has computed its indifference level of EBIT to be $500,000 between an equity financing alternative and a debt financing alternative. Interest expense under the debt alternative is $200,000 and interest expense under the equity alternative is $100,000. The EBIT for the firm is approximately normally distributed with an expected value of $620,000 and a standard deviation of $190,000.

   a. What is the probability that the equity financing alternative will be preferred to the debt financing alternative?

   b. What is the probability that the firm will incur losses under the debt alternative?

27. LB currently has 3 million common shares outstanding that sell at a price of $25 per share. LB also has $10 million of bank debt outstanding at a pretax interest rate of 12% and a private placement of $20 million in bonds at a pretax interest rate of 14%. LB's marginal tax rate is 40%.

   LB is planning entry into a new market area. This project will require the firm to raise $30 million. Two alternatives have been proposed:

   ■ **Plan 1: Common Equity Financing** Sell new shares at a net proceeds price of $20 per share.

   ■ **Plan 2: Debt-Equity Financing** Sell a combination of shares at a net proceeds price of $20 per share and $10 million of long-term debt at a pretax interest rate of 15%.

   a. Compute the indifference level of EBIT between these two alternatives.

   b. If LB's EBIT next year is approximately normally distributed with an expected value of $20 million and a standard deviation of $5 million, what is the probability that Plan 2 will result in higher earnings per share than Plan 1?

28. BM has a current cash and marketable securities balance of $50 million. The firm's economist is forecasting a two-year recession. Free cash flows during the recession, which are normally distributed, are expected to total $70 million, with a standard deviation of $60 million. The firm's marginal tax rate is 40%.

   a. Under these conditions, what is the probability that BM will run out of cash during the recession?

   b. BM is considering a major capital expansion project. If the project is undertaken it will be financed initially with debt totalling $200 million. This debt financing will require after-tax cash outflows for debt service during the two-year recession of $60 million. If BM is willing to accept a 10% chance of running out of cash, should the expansion (with debt financing) be undertaken?

29. WMC has a cash (and marketable securities) balance of $150 million. Free cash flows during a projected one-year recession are expected to be $200 million with a standard deviation of $200 million. (Assume that free cash flows are approximately normally distributed.)

   a. Determine the probability that the firm will run out of cash during the recession.

   b. WMC is considering a change in its capital structure that would add $50 million (after-tax) to its fixed financial charges. Determine the probability of running out of cash if the change in capital structure is undertaken.

c. Determine the maximum additional fixed financial charges that the firm can incur if it is willing to tolerate only a 5% chance of running out of cash during the recession.

30. EDA is considering the purchase of a fleet of new BMWs for the CEO and other senior managers. Currently the firm has a capital structure that consists of 60% debt, 30% common equity, and 10% preferred shares. The pretax interest rate on currently outstanding debt is 9%. The dividend yield on the firm's preferred shares is 12%. Total capitalization is $20 million. This fleet of new cars will cost $1,000,000 and the firm plans to finance the entire purchase with debt at a pretax interest rate of 10%. The firm's marginal tax rate is 40%. The expected level of EBIT for the firm over the coming year is $1.7 million with a standard deviation of $200,000. (Assume that EBIT is normally distributed.)

    If the firm acquires the cars and finances them with debt as proposed, what is the *increase* in the probability of the firm generating losses during the coming year?

31. E Company is planning a major expansion that will require $95 million of new financing. The firm currently has a capital structure consisting of $400 million of common equity (with a cost of 14% and 4 million shares outstanding), $50 million of preferred shares ($50 par, $5 dividend), and $200 million of long-term debt (with a coupon interest rate of 9%). The marginal tax rate is 40% and the average tax rate is 30%.

    In order to finance the expansion, the firm is considering two possible sources of funding: (1) the sale of new common shares at a net price of $95 per share; or (2) the sale of debentures at a coupon rate of interest of 10%.

    a. What is the level of EBIT at the indifference point between these two alternatives? What are the earnings per share at this level?

    b. If the expected level of EBIT is $100 million with a standard deviation of $20 million, what is the probability of having unfavourable financial leverage if the debt financing alternative is chosen? (Assume that EBIT is normally distributed.)

32. RR Company has traditionally been financed in a most conservative way. The CEO and founder, Rebecca, just does not believe in debt. However, after hearing a consultant discuss the concept of an optimal capital structure, she began to consider new financing options for the firm.

    The firm has an expected level of EBIT of $1.5 million, with an estimated standard deviation of $1 million.

    a. Given the current capital structure with no debt, what is the probability that the firm will have negative earnings per share during the coming year?

    b. The firm is considering a large share repurchase program to be funded with $10 million of 10% debentures. The current price per common share is $50. If this repurchase is undertaken, what is the probability of negative earnings per share during the coming year?

33. NVF Company is considering opening a new wholly owned subsidiary. To finance this investment, the firm is considering two financing plans. The first alternative is to sell 600,000 common shares at $20 each. The second plan is to sell 200,000 common shares at $20 each and $8 million of 10% long-term debt.

    a. If the firm has a marginal tax rate of 40%, what is the EBIT-EPS indifference point for this investment?

    b. The firm's expected level of EBIT from this subsidiary is $1.0 million with a standard deviation of $400,000. If the firm uses the second financing plan, what is the chance of having unfavourable financial leverage?

Other Practice Materials and Resources

For interactive quizzes, Internet exercises, crossword puzzles, CTV videos, and more, go to the *Contemporary Financial Management* Web site at **http://cyr.nelson.com**

Dividend Policy

Learning Objectives

After studying this chapter you should be able to

1. Understand that dividend policy determines the ultimate distribution of the firm's earnings between retention (that is, reinvestment) and cash dividend payments to shareholders

2. Understand that the major factors influencing the firm's choice of a dividend policy are

   a. Legal constraints
   b. Restrictive covenants
   c. Tax considerations
   d. Liquidity considerations
   e. Borrowing capacity and access to the capital markets
   f. Earnings stability
   g. Growth prospects
   h. Inflation
   i. Shareholder preferences
   j. Protection against dilution
   k. Potential liability lawsuits

3. Understand the informational content or signalling effects of dividend policies

4. Understand that the major alternative dividend policies include

   a. Passive residual approach
   b. Stable dollar dividend approach
   c. Constant payout ratio approach
   d. Policy of paying a small, regular dividend plus year-end extras

5. Understand that other important considerations in dividend policy making include

   a. How dividends are paid
   b. Dividend reinvestment plans
   c. Stock dividends
   d. Stock splits
   e. Share repurchase as a dividend decision

Financial Challenge

Rothmans Inc. Dividend Policy

For more information
on Rothmans see
www.rothmansinc.ca

Rothmans Inc. (ROC) is the only Canadian-owned and publicly traded tobacco company. It owns 60 percent of Rothmans, Benson & Hedges Inc. Phillip Morris Inc. owns the other 40 percent. Rothmans began operations in 1899 in Quebec City.

The company has a history of profitable operations, even in economic downturns. Rothmans continues to generate significant cash flows and it shares them with its shareholders, increasing the dividend by 50 percent over the period 2000–2002 up to approximately 50 percent of net earnings while some other firms were not able to even continue paying dividends at the previous rate. Despite the high dividend payout, Rothmans' share price went down during this period because of economic uncertainty, bad publicity for the tobacco industry, and increasing concern about the health risks of smoking.

Many financial analysts continue to recommend that their clients buy Rothmans shares because of the continued high profitability of the firm and its high dividend yield to investors. Some potential investors are reluctant to invest because they fear the firm may be subject to law suits.

This potential liability, indeed, may explain why Rothmans has a high dividend yield. Dividends already paid out to shareholders are not available to potential claimants.

This chapter illustrates some of the important dividend policy issues that must be considered by management, including shareholder preferences, signalling effects of changes in dividends, tax, earnings stability, and growth prospects.

Introduction

The value of a firm is influenced by three types of financial decisions:

- Investment decisions
- Financing decisions
- Dividend decisions

Although each is presented as a separate topic in this and most financial management textbooks,[1] these three types of financial decisions are interdependent in a number of ways. For example, the investments made by a firm determine the level of future earnings and future potential dividends; capital structure influences the cost of capital, which determines, in part, the number of acceptable investment opportunities; and dividend policy influences the amount of equity capital in a firm's capital structure (via retained earnings) and, by extension, influences the cost of capital. In making these interrelated decisions, the goal is to maximize shareholder wealth.

Consider the following dividend decisions:

1. During 2002, Cognos (a multinational software firm headquartered in Ottawa) had earnings of US$0.59 per share. The firm does *not* pay dividends. The firm's share price at the end of 2002 was $23.45.

2. During the fiscal year ending January 31, 2001, Bombardier repurchased 15,866,300 common shares for an aggregate price of $303.8 million while paying common dividends of approximately $186 million ($0.135 per share on the 347.4 million Class A common shares and $0.136563 per share on its 1,018.6 million Class B common shares). The dividend payout ratio on the Class A common shares was approximately 28 percent in 2001.

3. During 2002, BCE paid out approximately $1 billion ($1.18 per share) in common share dividends (a *decrease* in shareholders' equity). During the same year, the firm sold $2.078 billion (85 million new shares at $24.45 gross per share) in new common shares (an *increase* in shareholders' equity). The BCE payout ratio in 2002 was approximately 38 percent.

These dividend decisions raise a number of important questions, such as

For more information see the company Web sites:
www.cognos.com
www.bombardier.com
www.bce.ca

1. Is Bombardier's dividend policy more consistent with shareholder wealth maximization than the dividend policy of Cognos? Is one dividend policy necessarily optimal for all firms?

2. Why did BCE pay common share dividends *and* incur the issuance costs of selling new common shares during the same time period? As an alternative to issuing new common shares, why didn't BCE reduce its common share dividend temporarily until it accumulated the amount of equity funds it planned to raise externally?

3. Why do some firms pay stock dividends when the net effect of these transactions is that total shareholders' equity remains unchanged and each shareholder's proportionate claim on the firm's total earnings remains constant?

4. What are the advantages to Bombardier and its shareholders of the $303.8 million share repurchase program compared with paying shareholders $186 million in cash dividends?

5. Finally, on a more fundamental level, does it really matter, with respect to the maximization of shareholder wealth, what amount (or percentage of earnings) a firm pays out in dividends?

Visit **www.
infotrac-college.com** and
enter the keyword "dividend
policy."

In this chapter, we seek to answer dividend policy questions such as these.

---

[1] In this text, investment decisions are dealt with in Chapters 8 through 11, and financing decisions are discussed in Chapters 5, 6, 12, 13, 19, and 20.

This chapter begins by examining the factors that influence a firm's choice of dividend policy. Next, it considers the pros and cons of a number of different dividend policies. And, finally, it discusses the mechanics of dividend payments, along with stock dividends and share repurchase plans.

Determinants of Dividend Policy

Dividend policy determines how the earnings of a company are distributed. Earnings are either retained and reinvested in the firm or are paid out to shareholders. In recent years, the retention of earnings has been a major source of equity financing for private industry. On average, for the period 1960 to 1994, the proportion of total financial requirements provided by retained earnings for Canadian firms was 49 percent of available free cash flows.[2] Retained earnings are the most important source of equity. Retained earnings can be used to stimulate growth in future earnings and as a result can influence future share values. On the other hand, dividends provide shareholders with tangible current returns.

Industry and Company Variations in Dividend Payout Ratios

Dividend payout policies vary among different industries. There is a wide variation in dividend payout ratios among different industries. Likewise, within a given industry, while many firms may have similar dividend payout ratios, there can still be considerable variation. This section examines some of the more important factors that combine to determine the dividend policy of a firm.

Legal Constraints

Most jurisdictions have laws that regulate the dividend payments a firm chartered in that jurisdiction (federal or provincial) can make. These laws basically state the following:

- A firm's capital cannot be used to make dividend payments.
- Dividends must be paid out of a firm's present and past *net* earnings.
- Dividends cannot be paid when the firm is insolvent.

The first restriction is termed the *capital impairment restriction*.

The second restriction, called the *net earnings restriction*, requires that a firm have generated earnings *before* it is permitted to pay any cash dividends. This prevents the equity owners from withdrawing their initial investment in the firm and impairing the security position of any of the firm's creditors.

The third restriction, termed the *insolvency restriction*, states that an insolvent company may not pay cash dividends. When a company is insolvent, its liabilities exceed its assets. Payment of dividends would interfere with the creditors' prior claims on the firm's assets and therefore is prohibited.

These three restrictions affect different types of companies in different ways. New firms, or small firms with a minimum of accumulated retained earnings, are most likely to feel the weight of these legal constraints when determining their dividend policies, whereas well-established firms with histories of profitable performance and large retained earnings accounts are less likely to be influenced by them.

Restrictive Covenants

Restrictive covenants generally have more impact on dividend policy than the legal constraints just discussed. These covenants are contained in bond indentures, term loans, short-term borrowing agreements, lease contracts, and preferred share agreements.

---

[2] J-M Suret and J-F L'Her, "The Evolving Capital Structure of Large Canadian Firms," in Paul Halpern (ed.), *Financing Growth in Canada* (University of Calgary Press, 1997): 457–514.

Is Legal Behaviour Ethical?

Over a decade ago, a Canadian firm realized that its US subsidiary was headed for bankruptcy. The subsidiary, however, had been profitable in the past. Not all of the previous earnings of the subsidiary had been repatriated to the Canadian parent. So, the parent decided that a special dividend should be declared by the subsidiary to fully repatriate these profits. Shortly after the payment of this dividend, the subsidiary declared bankruptcy. Was this ethical behaviour?

The credit officer at a major US energy company that was owed a substantial sum by the bankrupt subsidiary did not think so. The credit officer immediately called all credit officers of firms that were owed $1,000 or more with a strategy for collection in mind. The strategy was to have the Canadian subsidiaries of these creditors put the offending Canadian firm on a cash-before-delivery basis for all of its supplies. This strategy was implemented and the offending firm was told why creditors no longer trusted it. Miraculously, the special dividend was returned to the bankruptcy court. Although the Canadian firm is no longer on a cash-before-delivery basis, it took many years to fully restore creditor confidence in the firm. Unethical behaviour can have brutal market consequences.

These restrictions limit the total amount of dividends a firm can pay. Sometimes they may state that dividends cannot be paid at all until a firm's earnings have reached a specified level. For example, many bond and preferred share issues limit the amount of common share dividends that can be paid if the firm's net income falls below a certain level. In a dividend policy study of 80 troubled firms that cut dividends, researchers found that more than half of the firms apparently faced binding debt covenants in the years managers reduced dividends.[3]

In addition, *sinking fund requirements,* which state that a certain portion of a firm's cash flow must be set aside for the retirement of debt, sometimes limit dividend payments. Also, dividends may be prohibited if a firm's net working capital (current assets less current liabilities) or its current ratio does not exceed a certain predetermined level.

Tax Considerations

At various times the top personal marginal tax rates on dividend income and capital gains have been changed. Some years they were almost the same, while in other years one or the other has been lower. More recently, the top effective marginal tax rate on capital gains has been lower.

Thus, there is a tax benefit for many individuals to receive distributions in the form of capital gains income (that arises when a firm retains and reinvests earnings in the company) rather than as cash dividends. (*See Chapter 2 for more information on the taxation of capital gains and the dividend gross-up and tax credit system.*)

Another tax disadvantage of dividends versus capital gains is that dividend income is taxed immediately (in the year it is received), but capital gains income (and corresponding taxes) can be deferred into the future. If a corporation decides to retain its

---

[3] Harry DeAngelo and Linda DeAngelo, "Dividend Policy and Financial Distress: An Empirical Investigation of Troubled NYSE Firms," *Journal of Finance* (December 1990): 1415–1431.

earnings in anticipation of providing growth and future capital appreciation for its investors, the investors are not taxed until their shares are sold. Consequently, for most investors, the *present value* of the taxes on future capital gains income is less than the taxes on an equivalent amount of current dividend income.[4] The deferral of taxes on capital gains can be viewed as an interest-free loan to the investor from the government.

Liquidity and Cash Flow Considerations

Recall from previous chapters that free cash flow represents the portion of a firm's cash flows available to service new debt, *make dividend payments* to shareholders, and invest in other projects. Since dividend payments represent cash outflows, the more liquid a firm is, the more able it is to pay dividends. Even if a firm has a past record of high earnings that have been reinvested, resulting in a large retained earnings balance, it may not be able to pay dividends unless it has sufficient liquid assets, primarily cash.[5] Liquidity is likely to be a problem during a long business downturn, when both earnings and cash flows often decline. Rapidly growing firms with many profitable investment opportunities also often find it difficult to maintain adequate liquidity and pay dividends at the same time.

Borrowing Capacity and Access to the Capital Markets

Liquidity is desirable for a number of reasons. Specifically, it provides protection in the event of a financial crisis. It also provides the flexibility needed to take advantage of unusual financial and investment opportunities. There are other ways of achieving this flexibility and security, however. For example, companies frequently establish lines of credit and revolving credit agreements with banks, allowing them to borrow on short notice. (This topic is discussed in more detail in Chapter 15.) Large well-established firms are usually able to go directly to credit markets with either a bond issue or a sale of commercial paper. The more access a firm has to these external sources of funds, the better able it will be to make dividend payments.

A small firm whose shares are closely held and infrequently traded often finds it difficult (or undesirable) to sell new equity shares in the markets. As a result, retained earnings are the only source of new equity. When a firm of this type is faced with desirable investment opportunities, the payment of dividends is often inconsistent with the objective of maximizing the value of the firm.

Earnings Stability

Most large widely held firms are reluctant to lower their dividend payments, even in times of financial stress. Therefore, a firm with a history of stable earnings is usually more willing to pay a higher dividend than a firm with erratic earnings.

A firm whose cash flows have been more or less constant over the years can be fairly confident about its future and frequently reflects this confidence in higher dividend payments.

Growth Prospects

A rapidly growing firm usually has a substantial need for funds to finance the abundance of attractive investment opportunities. Instead of paying large dividends and then attempting to sell new shares to raise the equity investment capital it needs, this type of

---

[4] The exceptions to this rule are institutional investors (such as pension funds) that pay no income taxes. For a recent discussion of the effect of taxation on dividend policy in Canada, see Fodil Adjaoud and Daniel Zeghal, "Taxation and Dividend Policy in Canada: New Evidence," *Finance Economie Comptabilité* (Second Semester 1999): 141–154.

[5] For example, John A. Brittain found that corporate dividend payments are positively related to a firm's liquidity. See John A. Brittain, *Corporate Dividend Policy* (Washington, DC: Brookings, 1966): 184–187.

firm usually retains larger portions of its earnings and avoids the expense and inconvenience of public share offerings. Firms with the highest dividend payout ratios tend to have the lowest growth rates and vice versa.

Inflation

In an inflationary environment, funds generated by depreciation often are not sufficient to replace a firm's assets as they become obsolete. Under these circumstances, a firm may be forced to retain a higher percentage of earnings to maintain the earning power of its asset base.

Inflation also has an impact on a firm's working capital needs. In an atmosphere of rising prices, *actual* dollars invested in inventories and accounts receivable tend to increase to support the same *physical* volume of business. In addition, because the dollar amounts of accounts payable and other payables requiring cash outlays are higher with rising prices, transaction cash balances normally have to be increased. Thus, inflation can force a firm to retain more earnings as it attempts to maintain its same relative pre-inflation working capital position.

Shareholder Preferences

In a closely held corporation with relatively few shareholders, management may be able to set dividends according to the preferences of its shareholders. For example, assume that the majority of a firm's shareholders are in high marginal tax brackets. They probably favour a policy of high earnings retention, resulting in eventual price appreciation, over a high payout dividend policy. However, high earnings retention implies that the firm has enough acceptable capital investment opportunities to justify the low payout dividend policy. A policy of high retention when investment opportunities are not available is inconsistent with the objective of maximizing shareholder wealth.

In a large corporation whose shares are widely held, it is nearly impossible for a financial manager to take individual shareholders' preferences into account when setting dividend policy. Some wealthy shareholders who are in high marginal income tax brackets may prefer that a company reinvest its earnings (i.e., low payout ratio) to generate long-term capital gains. Other shareholders, such as retired individuals and those living on fixed incomes (sometimes referred to as "widows and orphans"), may prefer a high dividend rate. These shareholders may be willing to pay a premium for shares in a firm that provides a higher dividend yield. Large institutional investors that are in a zero income tax bracket, such as pension funds, university endowment funds, philanthropic organizations (e.g., Canadian Legacy Foundation), and trust funds, may prefer a high dividend yield for reasons different from those of private individual shareholders. First, endowment and trust funds are sometimes prohibited from spending the principal and must limit expenditures to the dividend (and/or interest) income generated by their investments. Second, pension and trust funds have a legal obligation to follow conservative investment strategies, which have been interpreted by the courts to mean investments in firms that have a record of regular dividend payments.

It has been argued that firms tend to develop their own "clientele" of investors. This **clientele effect**, originally articulated by Merton Miller and Franco Modigliani, indicates that investors will tend to be attracted to firms that have dividend policies consistent with the investors' objectives.[6] Some firms that pay out a large percentage (typically 70 percent or more) of their earnings as dividends have traditionally attracted investors who desire a high dividend yield. In contrast, growth-oriented firms, which pay no (or very low) dividends, have tended to attract investors who prefer earnings retention and greater price appreciation.

Clientele Effect
The concept that investors will tend to be attracted to firms that have dividend policies consistent with the investors' objectives.

---

[6] Merton Miller and Franco Modigliani, "Dividend Policy, Growth, and the Valuation of Shares," *Journal of Business* 34 (October 1961): 411–433.

Protection Against Dilution

If a firm adopts a policy of paying out a large percentage of its annual earnings as dividends, it may need to sell new shares from time to time to raise the equity capital needed to invest in potentially profitable projects. If existing investors do not or cannot acquire a proportionate share of the new issue, their percentage ownership interest in the firm is *diluted.* Some firms choose to retain more of their earnings and pay out lower dividends rather than risk dilution.

One of the alternatives to high earnings retention, however, involves raising external capital in the form of debt. This increases the financial risk of the firm, ultimately raising the cost of equity capital and at some point lowering share prices. If the firm feels that it already has an optimal capital structure, a policy of obtaining all external capital in the form of debt is likely to be counterproductive, unless sufficient new equity capital is retained or acquired in the capital markets to offset the increased debt.

Potential Liability Lawsuits

In the Financial Challenge for this chapter, we noted that Rothmans may be paying high dividends to shareholders to keep these funds from potential claimants in product liability lawsuits. The tobacco industry is not the only industry to face such lawsuits. Fore example, the Canadian asbestos industry has already been devastated by such suits.

See **http://finance. swcollege.com** for articles on capital structure and dividend policy.

Dividend Policy and Firm Value

There are two major schools of thought among finance scholars regarding the effect dividend policy has on a firm's value. Although Miller and Modigliani argue that dividend policy does not have a significant effect on a firm's value,[7] Myron Gordon (Professor emeritus at the University of Toronto), among others, has argued that it does.[8] Each viewpoint is discussed in this section.

Arguments for the Irrelevance of Dividends

The group led by Miller and Modigliani (MM) contends that a firm's value is determined solely by its investment decisions and that the dividend payout ratio is a mere detail. They maintain that the effect of any particular dividend policy can be exactly offset by other forms of financing, such as the sale of new common shares. This argument depends on a number of key assumptions, however, including the following:

■ **No Taxes** Under this assumption, investors are indifferent about whether they receive either dividend income or capital gains income.

■ **No Transaction Costs** This assumption implies that investors in the securities of firms paying small or no dividends can sell at no cost any number of shares they wish in order to convert capital gains into current income.

■ **No Issuance Costs** If firms did not have to pay issuance costs on the issue of new securities, they could acquire needed equity capital at the same cost, regardless of whether they retained their past earnings or paid them out as dividends. The payment of dividends sometimes results in the need for periodic sales of new shares.

■ **Existence of a Fixed Investment Policy** According to MM, the firm's investment policy is not affected by its dividend policy. Furthermore, MM claim that it is investment policy, *not* dividend policy that really determines a firm's value.

---

[7] Merton Miller and Franco Modigliani, "Dividend Policy, Growth, and the Valuation of Shares."

[8] See Myron Gordon, "The Savings, Investment and Valuation of a Corporation," *Review of Economics and Statistics* (February 1962): 37–51.

Informational Content   MM realize that there is considerable empirical evidence indicating that changes in dividend policy influence share prices. As discussed later in this chapter, many firms favour a policy of reasonably stable dividends. An increase in dividends conveys a certain type of *information* to the shareholders, such as an expectation of higher future earnings. Similarly, a cut in dividends may be viewed as conveying unfavourable information about the firm's earnings prospects. MM argue that this **informational content** of dividend policy influences share prices, *not* the pattern of dividend payments per se.

Signalling Effects   In effect, changes in dividend payments represent a *signal* to investors concerning management's assessment of the future earnings and cash flows of the firm.[9] Management, as an insider, is perceived as having access to more complete information about future profitability than is available to investors outside the company. Dividend changes are thought to provide unambiguous signals about the firm's future prospects—information that cannot be conveyed fully through other methods, such as annual reports and management presentations before security analysts. The *signalling effect* of changes in dividends is similar to the signalling effect of changes in capital structure discussed in Chapter 12.

Clientele Effect   MM also claim that the existence of clienteles of investors favouring a particular firm's dividend policy should have no effect on share value. They recognize that a firm that changes its dividend policy could lose some shareholders to other firms with a more appealing dividend policy. This, in turn, may cause a temporary reduction in the firm's share price. Other investors, however, who prefer the newly adopted dividend policy, will view the firm as being undervalued and will purchase more shares. In the MM world, these transactions occur instantaneously and at no cost to the investor, the net result being that a share's value remains unchanged.

Arguments for the Relevance of Dividends

Scholars belonging to the second school of thought argue that share values are indeed influenced by the division of earnings between dividends and retention. Basically, they contend that the MM propositions are reasonable—given MM's restrictive assumptions—but that dividend policy becomes important once these assumptions are removed.

Risk Aversion   Specifically, Gordon asserts that shareholders who are risk-averse may prefer some dividends over the promise of future capital gains because dividends are regular, certain returns, whereas future capital gains are less certain. This is sometimes referred to as the "bird-in-the-hand theory" (or "bird-in-the-hand fallacy" by its critics). According to Gordon, dividends reduce investors' uncertainty, causing them to discount a firm's future earnings at a lower rate, thereby increasing the firm's value. In contrast, failure to pay dividends increases investors' uncertainty, which raises the discount rate and lowers share prices. Although there is some empirical evidence to support this argument, it is difficult to decide which is more valid—the MM informational content (or signalling effect) of dividends approach or the Gordon uncertainty resolution approach.

Transaction Costs   If the assumption of no transaction costs for investors is removed, then investors care whether they are paid cash dividends or receive capital gains. In the MM world, investors who own shares paying low or no dividends could

---

[9]   Shreesh D. Deshpande and Vijay M. Jog, "Further Evidence on Dividend Resumption, Initiation and Information Asymmetry," *Canadian Journal of Administrative Sciences* (June 1989): 25–36, and Richard D. Arnott and Clifford S. Asness, "Surprise! Higher Dividends = Higher Growth," *Financial Analysts Journal* 59 (January/February 2003): 70–87.

Dividend Policy

Small firms typically differ significantly from larger, more mature firms in terms of the dividend policies they follow. For example, one study of the financial differences between small and large firms found that the average dividend payout ratio for large firms was in excess of 40 percent, whereas the average dividend payout ratio for small firms was less than 3 percent.[10] The study found that the majority of small firms that were planning an initial public stock offering paid no dividends at all in the year prior to their offering.

What are the reasons for this dramatic difference in dividend policies between large and small firms? First, it is likely that many small firms are in the rapid growth phase of their business development. During this early phase, the firm is often short of funds needed to finance planned investments and increases in working capital. Another aspect related to the growth phase argument is that small firms typically have restricted access to capital markets, relative to larger firms. A small, closely held firm has no easy way to raise equity capital other than the retention of earnings. If new shares can be sold, the owners risk a loss of control. In addition, stock offerings for small firms are extremely expensive, both in terms of transactions costs and minority interest discounts (as well as

periodically sell a portion of their holdings to satisfy current income requirements. In actuality, however, brokerage charges and odd-lot differentials make such liquidations expensive and imperfect substitutes for regular dividend payments.

Taxes   Removal of the no-tax assumption also makes a difference to shareholders. As discussed earlier, shareholders in high income tax brackets may prefer low (or no) dividends and reinvestment of earnings within the firm because of the lower (marginal) tax rates on capital gains income and the ability to defer taxes into the future (when the shares are sold) on such income. Booth and Johnson showed that in Canada ex-dividend share prices drop from pre-dividend share prices by less than the dividend.[11] This suggests that collectively Canadian investors prefer capital gains.

In 1985, the Canadian government introduced a lifetime exemption from taxes for the first $100,000 of capital gains. Amoako-adu, Rashid, and Stebbins found that investors bid up the prices of stocks with low dividend yields in anticipation of this tax proposal becoming law. Firms also responded by lowering dividend yields.[12]

This lifetime exemption ended in 1994, but in 2000 the portion of capital gains subject to tax was first reduced from 75 percent to 66.667 percent and then to 50 percent. Thus, current tax law still gives Canadian investors an incentive to prefer capital gains to dividends.

---

[10]   Ernest W. Walker and J. W. Petty, II, "Financial Differences Between Large and Small Firms," *Financial Management* (Winter 1978): 61–68.

[11]   L. Booth and D.J. Johnson, "The Ex-Dividend Day Behavior of Canadian Stock Prices: Tax Changes and Clientele Effects," *Journal of Finance* (June 1984): 457–476.

[12]   B. Amoako-adu, M. Rashid, and M. Stebbins, "Capital Gains Tax and Equity Values: Empirical Test of Stock Price Reaction to the Introduction and Reduction of Capital Gains Tax Exemption," *Journal of Banking and Finance* 16 (1992): 275–287.

marketability) that investors demand.

Another reason dividend policies differ between small and large firms is because many small firms are closely held by only one or a few owners, and the dividend policy of these firms frequently reflects the income preferences of these individuals. If funds are retained in the firm, taxes are postponed until a distribution is made at some time in the future or until the firm is sold.

As firms mature, their need for funds to support rapid growth declines, and their access to capital markets improves. At this point, they show a tendency to begin or increase dividend payouts. For example,

Intel, which was founded in 1968, paid no cash dividends until 1982. Since then, the company has been steadily increasing its annual cash dividend payments. Intel's dividend payout ratio remains fairly low, reflecting the fact that, despite its large size (sales of $26 billion in 2001), the company still has significant growth opportunities.

Clearly, the dividend policies of small and large firms differ significantly. Small firms often pay out a smaller percentage of their earnings than larger firms because small firms tend to be growing rapidly and have limited access to the capital markets for other sources of funds to support their growth.

Issuance (Floatation) Costs   The existence of issuance costs on new equity sales also tends to make earnings retention more desirable. Given a firm's investment policy, the payout of earnings the firm needs for investments requires it to raise external equity. External equity is more expensive, however, because of issuance costs. Therefore, the use of external equity will raise the firm's cost of capital and reduce the value of the firm. In addition, the cost of selling small issues of equity to meet investment needs is likely to be prohibitively high for most firms. Therefore, firms that have sufficient investment opportunities to profitably use their retained funds tend to favour retention. This argument provides the basis for the passive residual or marginal theory of dividends discussed later in this chapter.

Agency Costs   It has also been argued that the payment of dividends can reduce *agency costs* between shareholders and management.[13] The payment of dividends reduces the amount of retained earnings available for reinvestment and requires the use of more external equity funds to finance growth. Raising external equity funds in the capital markets subjects the firm to the scrutiny of regulators and potential investors, thereby serving as a monitoring function of managerial performance.

Conclusions Regarding Dividend Relevance   The empirical evidence as to whether dividend policy affects firm valuation is mixed. Some studies have found that, because of tax effects, investors require higher pretax returns on high-dividend payout

---

[13] Agency costs were discussed in Chapter 1. See M. Rozeff, "Growth, Beta and Agency Costs as Determinants of Dividend Payout Ratios," *Journal of Financial Research* (Fall 1982): 249–259.

shares than on low-dividend payout shares.[14] Other studies have found that share prices are unaffected by dividend payout policy.[15]

Many practitioners believe that dividends are important, both for their informational content and because external equity capital is more expensive than retained equity.[16] Thus, when establishing an optimal dividend policy, a firm should consider shareholder preferences along with investment opportunities and the relative cost of retained equity versus externally raised equity.

Dividend Policies

The previous sections examined a number of practical considerations that influence a firm's board of directors in determining an "optimal" dividend policy. In this section, several alternative dividend strategies are discussed.

Passive Residual Dividend Policy

The **passive residual dividend policy** suggests that a firm should retain its earnings as long as it has investment opportunities that promise higher rates of return than the required rate. For example, assume that a firm's shareholders could invest their dividends in shares of similar risk with an expected rate of return (dividends plus capital gains) of 18 percent. This 18 percent figure, then, would constitute the required rate of return on the firm's retained earnings. As long as the firm can invest these earnings to earn this required rate or more, it should not pay dividends (according to the passive residual policy) because such payments would require either that the firm forego some acceptable investment opportunities or raise necessary equity capital in the more expensive external capital markets.

Interpreted literally, the residual theory implies that dividend payments will vary from year to year, depending on available investment opportunities. There is strong evidence, however, that most firms try to maintain a rather stable dividend payment record over time. Of course, this does not mean that firms ignore the principles of the residual theory in making their dividend decisions because dividends can be smoothed out from year to year in two ways.[17] First, a firm can choose to retain a larger percentage of earnings during years when funding needs are large. If the firm continues to grow, it can manage to do this without reducing the dollar amount of the dividend. Second, a firm can borrow the funds it needs, to temporarily raise its debt-to-equity ratio, and avoid a dividend cut in this way. Because issue costs are lower for large offerings of long-term debt, long-term debt capital tends to be raised in large, lumpy sums. If many good investment opportunities are available to a firm during a particular year, this type of borrowing is preferable to cutting back on dividends. The firm will need to retain earnings in future years to bring its debt-to-equity ratio back in line. A firm that has many good investment opportunities for a

---

[14] L. Booth and D.J. Johnson, "The Ex-Dividend Day Behavior of Canadian Stock Prices: Tax Changes and Clientele Effects," *Journal of Finance* (June 1984): 457–476, and B. Amoako-adu, M. Rashid, and M. Stebbins, "Capital Gains Tax and Equity Values: Empirical Test of Stock Price Reaction to the Introduction and Reduction of Capital Gains Tax Exemption," *Journal of Banking and Finance* 16 (1992): 275–587.

[15] I. G. Morgan found this to be true for the period 1972–1977, although prior to 1972, shares that paid dividends had higher pretax returns. See I. G. Morgan, "Dividends and Stock Price Behaviour in Canada," *Journal of Business Administration* 12 (Fall 1986): 91–106.

[16] For a survey of chief financial officers' attitudes on dividend policy, see H. Kent Baker, Gail E. Farrelly, and Richard B. Edelman, "A Survey of Management Views on Dividend Policy," *Financial Management* (Autumn 1985): 78–84. Although this is a US study, it seems that Canadian CFOs feel that dividends matter because dividend payout ratios are higher in Canada than in the United States.

[17] Robert C. Higgins, "The Corporate Dividend-Saving Decision," *Journal of Financial and Quantitative Analysis* (March 1972): 1531–1538, provides empirical support for the view that each period's dividends are a function of longer-term trends.

Dividend Policies for Multinational Firms

Dividend payments from foreign subsidiaries represent the primary means of transferring funds to the parent company. Many factors determine the dividend payments that are made back to the parent, including tax effects, exchange risk, political risk, the availability of funds, the financing requirements of the foreign subsidiary, and the existence of exchange controls.[18]

Taxes in the host country play a significant role in determining a multinational firm subsidiary's dividend policy. For example, in Germany, the tax rate on earnings paid out as dividends is much lower than the tax rate on retained earnings. When the parent is located in a country with a strong currency and the subsidiary is located in a country with a weak currency, there will be a tendency to rapidly transfer a greater portion of the subsidiary's earnings to the parent to minimize the exchange rate risk. In the face of high political risk, the parent may require the subsidiary to transfer all locally generated funds to the parent except for those funds necessary to meet the working capital and planned capital expenditure needs of the subsidiary. As is true for domestic enterprises, large and more mature foreign subsidiaries tend to remit a greater proportion of their earnings to the parent, reflecting the reduced growth opportunities and needs for funds that exist in larger firms. Also, when the foreign subsidiary has good access to capital within the host country, it tends to pay larger dividends to the parent because funds needed for future expansion can be obtained locally. Finally, some countries with balance-of-payments problems often restrict the payment of dividends from the subsidiary back to the parent.

Many firms require that the payout ratio for foreign subsidiaries be set equal to the payout ratio of the parent. The argument in favour of this strategy is that it requires each subsidiary to bear an equal proportionate burden of the parent's dividend policy. However, even when this strategy is adopted, it often is modified on a country-by-country basis to reflect the considerations just identified. As shown below, there is considerable variability in dividend yields in different countries, with Venezuela at the top and the United States at the bottom of the 40 countries covered by Wren Research Investment Advisors.

Country	Dividend yield in 2002
Venezuela	8.5%
Italy	3.9
Netherlands	3.8
United Kingdom	3.3
Germany	2.3
Canada	2.0
Switzerland	1.7
United States	1.4

Source: Wren Research. **www.wrenresearch. com.au** (March 4, 2003).

---

[18] A more thorough discussion of these issues is found in Alan C. Shapiro, *Multinational Financial Management*, 7th ed. (New York: Wiley, 2003). For a discussion of agency problems in an international context, see R. LaPorta, F. Lopez-de-Silanes, A. Schleifer, and R. W. Vishny, "Agency Problems and Dividend Policies Around the World," *Journal of Finance* 55 (February 2000): 1–33.

number of years may eventually be forced to cut its dividend and/or sell new equity shares to meet financing requirements and maintain an optimal capital structure.

The residual theory also suggests that "growth" firms will normally have lower dividend payout ratios than firms in mature, low-growth industries. As mentioned earlier, firms with low growth rates tend to have rather high payout ratios, whereas firms with high growth rates tend to have rather low payout ratios.

Stable Dollar Dividend Policy

Stable Dollar Dividend Policy
A dividend policy that aims to pay out a constant dollar dividend to shareholders.

Evidence indicates that most firms—and shareholders—prefer a reasonably **stable dollar dividend policy**. This stability is characterized by a rather strong reluctance to reduce the dollar amount of dividends from one period to the next. Similarly, increases in the dollar dividend rate normally are not made until the firm's management is satisfied that future earnings will be high enough to justify the larger dividend. Thus, although dividend rates tend to follow increases in earnings, they also tend to lag behind them to a certain degree.

Investors prefer stable dividends for a variety of reasons. For instance, many investors feel that dividend changes possess *informational content*. They equate changes in a firm's dividend levels with profitability. A cut in dividends may be interpreted as a signal that the firm's long-run profit potential has declined. Similarly, a dividend increase is seen as a verification of the expectation that future profits will increase. Of course, for some firms, an increase in the dividend payout ratio may signal that the firm no longer has as many available high-return opportunities.

In addition, many shareholders need and depend on a constant stream of dividends for their cash income requirements. Although they can sell off some of their shares as an alternative source of current income, associated transaction costs and odd-lot charges make this an imperfect substitute for steady dividend income.

Some managers feel that a stable and growing dividend policy tends to reduce investor uncertainty concerning future dividend streams. They believe investors will pay a higher price for the shares of a firm that pays stable dividends, thereby reducing the firm's cost of equity.

And, finally, stable dividends are legally desirable. Many regulated financial institutions—such as pension fund and insurance companies—are limited as to the types of common shares they are allowed to own. To qualify for inclusion in these "legal lists," a firm must have a record of continuous and stable dividends. The failure to pay a dividend or the reduction of a dividend amount can result in removal from these lists. This, in turn, reduces the potential market for the firm's shares and may lead to price declines.

Other Dividend Payment Policies

Constant Payout Ratio Dividend Policy
A dividend policy that aims to pay out a constant percentage of a firm's earnings to shareholders.

Some firms have adopted a **constant payout ratio dividend policy**. A firm that uses this approach pays out a certain percentage of each year's earnings—for example, 40 percent—as dividends. If the firm's earnings vary substantially from year to year, dividends also will fluctuate.

Because of the reluctance to reduce dividends, payout ratios tend to increase when profits are depressed and decrease as profits increase.

Small Quarterly Dividend plus Year-End Extras Dividend Policy
A dividend policy that aims to pay a small regular dividend plus occasional extra payments when profits are larger than expected.

Other firms choose a **small quarterly dividend plus year-end extras dividend policy**. This policy is especially well suited for a firm with a volatile earnings record, volatile year-to-year cash needs, or both. Even when earnings are low, the firm's investors can count on their regular dividend payments. When earnings are high and no immediate need for these excess funds exists, the firm declares a year-end extra dividend. This policy gives management the flexibility to retain funds as needed and still satisfy investors who desire to receive some "guaranteed" level of dividend payments.

How Dividends Are Paid

In most firms, the board of directors holds quarterly meetings to evaluate the firm's performance and decide the level of dividends to be paid during the next period. Changes in the amount of dividends paid tend to be made rather infrequently—especially in firms that follow a stable dividend policy—and only after there is clear evidence that the firm's future earnings are likely to be either permanently higher or permanently lower than previously reported levels.

Most firms follow a dividend declaration and payment procedure similar to that outlined in the following paragraphs. This procedure usually revolves around a *declaration date,* an *ex-dividend date,* a *record date,* and a *payment date.*

Figure 14.1 is a timeline that illustrates the dividend payment procedure. The firm's board of directors meets on the **declaration date**—January 15—to consider future dividends. They *declare* a dividend on that date, which will be payable to *shareholders of record* on the **record date**, January 31. On that date, the firm makes a list from its stock transfer books of those shareholders who are eligible to receive the declared dividend.

The major stock exchanges require two *business days* prior to the record date for recording ownership changes. The day that begins this two-day period is called the **ex-dividend date**—in this case, January 29. Investors who purchase shares prior to January 29 are eligible for the January 29 dividend; investors who purchase shares on or after January 29 are not entitled to the dividend. On January 29, the ex-dividend date, one would expect the share price to decline by the amount of the dividend because this much value has been removed from the firm. Empirical evidence indicates that, on average, share prices decline by less than the amount of the dividend on the ex-dividend day.[19]

The **payment date** is normally about four weeks or so after the record date; in this case, March 1. On this date, the firm makes dividend payments to the holders of record.

Dividend Reinvestment Plans

Many Canadian firms, including Alcan, BCE, Canadian Tire, Dofasco, Inco, Magna, Moore, Noranda, Telus, and TransCanada Pipelines as well as many others, have **dividend reinvestment plans** (**DRPs** or **DRIPs**). Under these plans, shareholders can have their dividends automatically reinvested in additional common shares. There are two types of dividend reinvestment plans. One type involves the purchase of *existing* shares, and the other type involves the purchase of *newly issued* shares. The first type of plan is executed through a bank that, acting as a trustee, purchases the shares on the open market and then allocates them on a pro rata basis to the participating shareholders. In the second type of plan, the cash dividends of the participants are used to purchase newly issued shares, often at a small discount (up to 5 percent) from the market price.

Declaration Date
The day on which the directors of a company declare a dividend.

Record Date
The date on which a firm makes a list from its stock transfer books of those shareholders who are eligible to receive the declared dividend.

Ex-Dividend Date
The date on which the right to the most recently declared dividend no longer goes along with the sale of the shares.

Payment Date
The date on which the firm actually pays the dividend to shareholders.

Dividend Reinvestment Plan (DRP or DRIP)
A plan that allows shareholders to have their cash dividends automatically reinvested in additional shares.

See **www.ndir.com/ si/drps.shtml** for information on Canadian firms that have dividend reinvestment plans.

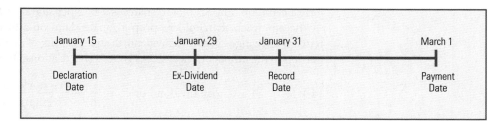

Figure 14.1
Key Dates in the Dividend Payment Procedure

---

[19] L. Booth and D.J. Johnson, "The Ex-Dividend Day Behavior of Canadian Stock Prices: Tax Changes and Clientele Effects," *Journal of Finance* (June 1984): 457–476.

This second type of plan enables the firm to raise substantial amounts of new equity capital over time as well as reduce the cash outflows required by dividend payments. The advantage of a dividend reinvestment plan to shareholders is that it represents a convenient method for them to purchase additional shares while saving brokerage commissions. The primary disadvantage is that shareholders must pay taxes on the cash dividends reinvested in the firm, even though they never receive any cash.

Stock Dividends and Stock Splits

A **stock dividend** is the payment of additional shares to common shareholders. It involves making a transfer from the retained earnings account to the other shareholders' equity accounts.

For example, the Colonial Copies Company has the following common shareholders' equity:

Pre-Stock Dividend: Common Shareholders' Equity	
Common shares (100,000 shares outstanding)	$1,500,000
Retained earnings	$5,000,000
Total common shareholders' equity	$6,500,000

Suppose the firm declares a 10 percent stock dividend and existing shareholders receive 10,000 (10% × 100,000) new shares. Because stock dividend accounting is usually based on the pre-dividend market price, a total of $200,000 (10,000 shares × a predividend market price of $20 per share) is transferred from the firm's retained earnings account to the common share account. Following the stock dividend, Colonial has the following common shareholders' equity:

Post-Stock Dividend: Common Shareholders' Equity	
Common shares (110,000 shares outstanding)	$1,700,000
Retained earnings	$4,800,000
Total common shareholders' equity	$6,500,000

The net effect of this transaction is to increase the number of outstanding shares and to redistribute funds among the firm's capital accounts. The firm's total shareholders' equity remains unchanged, and each shareholder's proportionate claim to the firm's earnings remains constant. For example, if Colonial has 100,000 shares outstanding prior to a 10 percent stock dividend and its total earnings are $200,000 ($2 per share), a shareholder who owns 100 shares has a claim on $200 of the firm's earnings. Following the 10 percent stock dividend, earnings per share decline to $1.82 ($200,000/110,000 shares). The shareholder who originally owned 100 shares now has 110 shares but continues to have a claim on only $200 (110 shares × $1.82 per share) of the firm's earnings.

Because each shareholder's proportionate claim on a firm's net worth and earnings remains unchanged in a stock dividend, the market price of each share should decline in proportion to the number of new shares issued. This relationship can be expressed as follows:

$$(14.1) \qquad \text{Post-stock dividend price} = \frac{\text{Pre-stock dividend price}}{1 + \text{Percentage stock dividend rate}}$$

In the Colonial example, a $20 pre-stock dividend price should result in a post-stock dividend price of $20/(1 + 0.10) = $18.18.

If a shareholder's wealth prior to the dividend is $2,000 (100 shares × $20 per share), post-dividend wealth should also remain at $2,000 (110 shares × $18.18 per share).

In essence, all a stock dividend does is increase the number of pieces of paper in the shareholders' hands. Nevertheless, there are a number of reasons why firms declare stock dividends. First, a stock dividend may have the effect of broadening the ownership of a firm's shares because existing shareholders often sell their stock dividends. Second, in the case of a firm that already pays a cash dividend, a stock dividend results in an effective increase in cash dividends, providing that the per-share dividend rate is not reduced. (It is rare for a firm to declare a stock dividend and reduce its cash dividend rate at the same time.) Finally, the declaration of stock dividends effectively lowers the price of a share, thereby possibly broadening its investment appeal. Investors seem to prefer shares selling in approximately the $15 to $70 price range because more investors will be financially able to purchase 100-share board (round) lots. Board lots of 100 shares are more desirable for investors to own because lower transactions costs are associated with their purchase and sale.

Stock splits are similar to stock dividends in that they have the effect of increasing the number of shares outstanding and reducing the price of each outstanding share. In a two-for-one stock split, the number of shares would be doubled. Although stock splits have an impact similar to stock dividends, they normally are not considered an element of a firm's dividend policy. They were discussed in greater detail in Chapter 6.

Masse, Hanrahan, and Kushner found a positive Canadian stock market response to regular stock splits and to stock dividends that is consistent with previous US findings.[20] They also found a positive market response for reverse stock splits in Canada. (A reverse split occurs when the number of shares outstanding is reduced by the split.) This result contrasts sharply with the US studies that have consistently shown a negative response to a reverse split.

Share Repurchases as Dividend Decisions

In addition to the reasons discussed in Chapter 6 for repurchasing shares, share repurchases can be undertaken as part of the firm's dividend decision. According to the passive residual dividend policy, a firm that has more funds than it needs for investments should pay a cash dividend to shareholders. In lieu of, or in addition to, cash dividends, some firms also repurchase outstanding shares from time to time.

Since the 1980s, share repurchases have become increasingly popular. A recent study found that aggregate repurchases in Canada rose from approximately $500 million in 1988 to $5.3 billion in 2000.[21]

Firms engaging in large buyback programs typically have large cash flows and an insufficient number of positive NPV investments in which to invest.[22]

Firms that are under threat of a hostile takeover sometimes announce large share repurchase programs designed to drain "excess" cash from the firm, thereby making it a less desirable takeover target.

Visit **www.google.ca** and search for stock splits. You will get a large number of hits. As you will see, stock splits are a very common corporate practice.

See **www. infotrac-college.com** and use the keywords share repurchasing, treasury stock.

---

[20] Isadore Masse, Robert Hanrahan, and Joseph Kushner, "The Effect of Canadian Stock Splits, Stock Dividends, and Reverse Splits on the Value of the Firm," *Quarterly Journal of Economics and Business* 36 #4 (Autumn 1997): 51–62.

[21] William J. McNally, "Open Market Share Repurchases in Canada," *Canadian Investment Review* (Winter 2002): 24–31.

[22] There is also evidence that firms that repurchase shares experience an increase in shareholder return. See: D. Ikenberry, J. Lakonishok, and T. Vermaelen, "Stock Repurchases in Canada: Performance and Strategic Trading," *Journal of Finance* 55 (October 2000): 2373–2397. William J. McNally, "Open Market Share Repurchases in Canada," *Canadian Investment Review* (Winter 2002): 24–31, found a similar result.

Procedures for Repurchasing Shares

Firms carry out share repurchase programs in a number of ways. For example, a company may buy directly from its shareholders in what is termed a **tender offer**. It may purchase the shares in the open market, or it may privately negotiate purchases from large holders, such as institutions. When a firm initiates a share repurchase program through a tender offer, it is, in effect, giving shareholders a *put option*—an option to sell their shares at a fixed price above the current market price for a limited period of time.

Repurchased shares become known as **treasury shares**. Treasury shares are often used to facilitate mergers and acquisitions; to satisfy the conversion provisions of some preferred shares and debentures, as well as the exercise of warrants; and to meet the need for new shares in executive stock options and employee stock purchase plans. From the shareholders' perspective, share repurchases increase earnings per share for the remaining outstanding shares and also increase share prices, assuming that investors continue to apply the same *price-to-earnings (P/E) ratio* to the earnings per share before and after repurchase. The P/E multiple indicates the value placed by investors on a dollar of a firm's earnings. It is influenced by a number of factors, including earnings prospects and investors' perceptions regarding a firm's risk. If a stock repurchase results in a substantial increase in the debt-to-equity ratio, the new P/E ratio could well be lower than before because of increased financial risk.

Normally, a firm will announce its intent to buy back some of its own shares so that investors will know why there is sudden additional trading in the shares. An announcement of repurchase is also useful to current shareholders, who may not want to sell their shares before they have had an opportunity to receive any price appreciation expected to result from the repurchase program.

Financial Flexibility

Substituting discretionary share repurchases for all or part of regular cash dividends (i.e., stable dollar dividend policy) provides a firm with greater financial flexibility. Under such a strategy, when the company has profitable uses for its funds, it can defer the buyback of its shares (and the corresponding cash outflows) until a more appropriate time in the future. The firm thus avoids incurring the costs associated with raising the external equity capital needed to finance investments. Likewise, when the firm accumulates excess funds, it can undertake periodic share repurchases.

Signalling Effects

Like the signalling effects of cash dividend increases, share repurchases can also have a positive impact on shareholder wealth. A share repurchase may represent a signal to investors that management expects the firm to have higher earnings and cash flows in the future.[23]

Advantages and Disadvantages

Let us summarize the advantages and disadvantages of share repurchases as an addition to, or as a substitute for, cash dividends.

Advantages   Share repurchases effectively convert dividend income into capital gains income. Shareholders in high (marginal) income tax brackets may prefer capital gains income because of the lower (marginal) tax rates on such income and because of the ability to defer taxes into the future (when the shares are sold). Also, share repurchases provide the firm with greater financial flexibility in timing the payment of returns to

---

Tender Offer
A public announcement by a firm or individual indicating that it will pay a price above the current market price for the shares "tendered" of a firm it wishes to acquire.

Treasury Shares
Common shares that have been reacquired by the issuing company.

---

[23] See Theo Vermaelen, "Common Stock Repurchases and Market Signalling: An Empirical Study," *Journal of Financial Economics* 9 (1981): 139–183.

Financial Challenge Revisited

Has Rothmans followed the dividend policy that maximized shareholder wealth, given that share price declined over the period 2000–2002 while dividends increased by 50 percent? At first glance, it appears it did not. However, if shareholders believe that the firm may well face a major lawsuit in the future, then shareholders would not want earnings reinvested and exposed to loss. Instead, distributing as much earnings as possible without jeopardizing the future earnings capability of the firm is a perfectly logical strategy for the firm to pursue. The market has clearly signalled the firm that investing in a tobacco company is an extremely risky investment because of potential liability issues.

shareholders. Finally, share repurchases can represent a signal to investors that the firm expects to have higher earnings and cash flows in the future.

Disadvantages   A firm may overpay for the shares that it repurchases. If the share price declines, the share repurchase represents an unprofitable use of the company's resources. Finally, some current shareholders may be unaware of the share repurchase program and may sell their shares before the expected benefits (i.e., price appreciation) occur.

Summary

- *Dividend policy* determines the ultimate distribution of a firm's earnings between retention (reinvestment) and cash dividend payments to shareholders. Retained earnings provide investors with a source of potential future earnings growth, whereas dividends provide them with a current distribution.

- A number of factors influence a firm's choice of dividend policy. These include the following:
  1. Legal constraints prohibiting dividends that impair capital
  2. Restrictive covenants in bond indentures and other financing agreements
  3. Tax considerations
  4. The need for liquidity
  5. Borrowing capacity and access to the capital markets
  6. Earnings stability
  7. Capital expansion (growth) opportunities
  8. Inflation
  9. Shareholder preferences (clientele effect)
  10. Protection against dilution
  11. Potential liability lawsuits

  Some of these factors favour high dividends, whereas others imply a lower payout policy. The board of directors should weigh these factors in each instance and arrive at the best possible dividend policy.

- Under a restrictive set of assumptions articulated by Miller and Modigliani (MM), the value of the firm is dependent solely on its investment decisions. They claim that any observed changes in firm value as a result of dividend decisions are due only to the *informational content* or *signalling effects* of dividend policy. Under these conditions, dividend policy does not affect the value of the firm. After the MM assumptions are removed, dividend policy may affect firm value because of

1. Risk-averse behaviour of investors
2. Shareholder transaction costs
3. Personal taxes
4. Issuance costs
5. Agency costs

- A firm may employ any one of a number of alternative dividend policies, including the following:

  1. The passive residual approach
  2. The stable dollar dividend approach
  3. The constant payout ratio approach
  4. The policy of paying a small, regular dividend plus year-end extras

  Ample evidence indicates that many firms favour a stable dollar dividend policy.

  Dividends are declared by the board of directors and are normally paid quarterly to shareholders of record.

- Many Canadian firms employ *dividend reinvestment plans*.

- *Stock dividends* are sometimes used in lieu of (and in conjunction with) cash dividends. The net effect of stock dividends is to leave the total book value of the firm unchanged while increasing the number of shares outstanding and broadening the ownership base.

- *Stock splits* are similar to stock dividends in that they have the effect of increasing the number of shares outstanding and reducing the price of each outstanding share.

- Some firms employ *share repurchase plans* in lieu of (or in addition to) cash dividends. Share repurchases convert shareholder benefits from dividend income to capital gains income. Theoretically, ignoring taxes, transaction costs, and other market imperfections, share repurchases should have the same effect on shareholder wealth as the payment of cash dividends. However, possibly due to tax considerations (the ability to defer taxes on capital gains income) and signalling effects, share repurchases (via tender offers) are observed to have a positive effect on shareholder wealth.

Questions and Topics for Discussion

1. What legal constraints limit the amount of cash dividends that may be paid by a firm?
2. What aspects of tax laws tend to (a) encourage and (b) discourage large dividend payments by corporations? Explain how.
3. What other "external" factors limit a firm's ability to pay cash dividends?
4. What is the likely impact of a highly inflationary economy on a firm's ability to pay dividends? Would you expect this impact to be greater or smaller for a rapidly expanding firm? Why?
5. Explain what is meant by the *clientele effect*.
6. Explain what is meant by the *informational content* or *signalling effects* of dividend policy.

7. In the theoretical world of Miller and Modigliani, what role does dividend policy play in the determination of share values?

8. What role do most practitioners think dividend policy plays in determining share values?

9. How can the "passive residual" view of dividend policy be reconciled with the tendency of most firms to maintain a constant or steadily growing dividend payment record?

10. Why do many managers prefer a stable dollar dividend policy to a policy of paying out a constant percentage of each year's earnings as dividends?

11. Under what circumstances would it make sense for a firm to borrow money to make its dividend payments?

12. Some people have suggested that it is irrational for a firm to pay dividends and sell new shares in the same year because the cost of newly issued equity is greater than the cost of retained earnings. Do you agree? Why or why not?

13. What is a *dividend reinvestment plan*? Explain the advantages of a dividend reinvestment plan to the firm and to shareholders.

14. Why do many firms choose to issue stock dividends? What is the value of a stock dividend to a shareholder?

15. What effect do share repurchases (undertaken as part of the firm's dividend decision) have on the value of the firm?

16. Suppose you are the holder of common shares in the GLA Company. Historically, the firm has paid generous cash dividends. The firm has recently announced that it would replace its cash dividend with a 20 percent annual stock dividend. Is this good news, bad news, or is it impossible to tell from the information provided? Explain the reason for your answer.

17. What issues of business ethics may be involved in the establishment of a firm's dividend payment amounts?

Self-Test Problems

ST1. The board of directors of Complex Computers has decided to declare a 20% stock dividend. The firm's common shareholders' equity is as follows:

Pre-Stock Dividend: Common Shareholders' Equity	
Common shares (100,000 shares outstanding)	$1,000,000
Retained earnings	$5,000,000
Total common shareholders' equity	$6,000,000

The common shares of Complex Computers are currently trading at $80 per share. The firm is growing rapidly and has never paid a cash dividend.

a. Show the firm's common shares, retained earnings, and common shareholders' equity accounts after the stock dividend.

b. Calculate the post-stock dividend share price assuming no other changes occur.

ST2. Sanchez Supermarkets, Inc. (50,000 common shares outstanding) currently has annual earnings before interest and taxes of $1,000,000. Its interest expenses are $200,000 per year, and it pays $100,000 in annual dividends to its shareholders. The firm's tax rate is 40%, and its common share's current dividend yield is 2.0%.

a. Calculate the firm's earnings per share.

b. Calculate the firm's dividend payout ratio.

c. Calculate the firm's current common share price.

d. If the firm declares and pays a 100% stock dividend and then pays an annual cash dividend of $1.10 per share, what is the effective rate by which the dividend has been increased?

Problems*

BASIC

1. JC earned $2 million after tax. The firm has 1.6 million outstanding common shares.

    a. Compute the firm's earnings per share.

    b. If the firm has a 40% payout ratio dividend policy, what are the dividends per share?

2. WB has just announced a 100% stock dividend. The annual cash dividend per share was $2.40 before the stock dividend. WB intends to pay $1.40 per share on each of the new shares. Compute the percentage increase in the cash dividend rate that will accompany the stock dividend.

3. TD pays a $2.50 cash dividend and earns $5 per share. The cash dividend has recently been increased to $2.65 per share, *and* a 3% stock dividend has been declared. What is the effective rate of increase in the dividends for TD as a result of this action?

4. On Friday, August 6, the board of directors of CI declares a $0.22 quarterly dividend payable on September 15 to shareholders of record on August 24. When is the ex-dividend date? If you purchase shares on this date are you entitled to receive the dividend?

INTERMEDIATE

5. DFA currently pays a quarterly dividend of 50 cents per share. This quarter's dividend will be paid to shareholders of record on Friday, February 22, 20X1. DFA has 200,000 common shares outstanding. The retained earnings account has a balance of $15 million before the dividend, and DFA holds $2.5 million in cash.

    a. What is the ex-dividend date for this quarter?

    b. The DFA share price was $22 on the day prior to the ex-dividend date. What would you expect the opening share price to be on the ex-dividend date? Give some reasons why this might not occur.

    c. What is the effect of the dividend payment on DFA's cash, retained earnings, and total assets?

6. WC plans to pay a $3 dividend per share on each of its 300,000 shares next year. WC anticipates earnings of $6.25 per share over the year. If the firm has a capital budget requiring an investment of $4 million over the year and it desires to maintain its present debt to total assets (debt) ratio of 0.40, how much external equity must it raise? Assume that WC's capital structure includes only common equity and debt, and that debt and equity will be the only sources of funds to finance capital projects over the year.

*Coloured numbers and letters denote problems that have "check" answers provided at the back of the book.

7. The MEN Company has the following equity accounts on its balance sheet:

Common shares (300,000 shares outstanding)	$4,500,000
Retained earnings	$6,000,000
Total common shareholders' equity	$10,500,000

a. What is the maximum amount of dividends that may be paid by the firm without impairing its capital?

b. What other factors may limit the firm's ability to pay dividends?

8. Champoux Inc. has earnings before interest and taxes of $200,000. Annual interest amounts to $80,000, and annual depreciation is $80,000. Taxes are computed at a 40% rate. Existing bond obligations require the payment of $40,000 per year into a sinking fund.

The firm wishes to pay a $2 per-share dividend on the existing 20,000 shares. The firm's bond indenture prohibits the payment of dividends unless the cash flow (before dividends and sinking fund payments) is greater than the total of dividends, interest, and sinking fund obligations.

a. Can the firm pay the proposed dividend?

b. What is the maximum dividend per share that may be paid?

9. LL Company believes in the "dividends as a residual" philosophy of dividend policy. This year's earnings are expected to total $10 million. A very conservative company, LL is financed solely with common shares. The required rate of return on retained earnings is 12%, whereas the cost of newly raised capital is 14% because of issuance costs.

a. If LL has $6 million of investment projects having expected returns greater than 12%, what total amount of dividends should the firm pay?

b. If LL has $12 million of investment projects having expected returns greater than 14%, what total amount of dividends should the firm pay?

c. What factors, other than its belief in the residual theory of dividends, should LL consider in setting its dividend policy in part b?

10. The STC Company has the following equity accounts on its balance sheet:

Common shares (500,000 shares outstanding)	$2,500,000
Retained earnings	$13,000,000
Total common shareholders' equity	$15,500,000

The current market price of the firm's shares is $50.

a. If the firm declares a 10% stock dividend, what will be the impact on the firm's common shares, retained earnings, and common shareholders' equity accounts?

b. If the firm currently pays no cash dividend, what is the impact of a 10% stock dividend on the wealth position of the firm's existing shareholders?

c. If the firm currently pays a cash dividend of $1 per share and this per-share dividend rate does not change after the 10% stock dividend, what impact would you expect the stock dividend to have on the wealth position of existing shareholders?

11. SMC reports the following financial data:

Net earnings	$3,000,000
Shares outstanding	1,000,000
Earnings per share	$3
Market price per share (ex-dividend)	$40
Expected dividend per share	$2

SMC is considering distributing $2 million to existing shareholders, either as cash dividends or through the repurchase of outstanding shares. The repurchase plan is favoured by some of the company's wealthiest and most influential shareholders. If the shares are repurchased, the firm would make a tender offer for 47,619 shares at a price of $42. Alternatively, the firm could pay a $2 dividend, after the payment of which each share would sell for $40.

    a. Ignoring taxes, what impact does the choice of a dividend payment or share repurchase plan have on the wealth position of the firm's shareholders?

    b. If most shareholders are in a very high marginal tax bracket, which alternative is favoured?

12. CS presently has earnings before interest and taxes of $3,000,000. Its interest expenses are $500,000 per year, and it pays $600,000 in annual dividends to its shareholders. CS has 300,000 common shares outstanding, and its tax rate is 40%. Its annual capital expenditures are $900,000. CS's present price-earnings ratio is 12.

    a. Calculate the firm's earnings per share.

    b. Calculate the firm's dividend payout ratio.

    c. Calculate the firm's dividend yield.

CHALLENGE

13. PTC and DTC have had a very similar record of earnings performance over the past eight years. Both firms are in the same industry and, in fact, compete directly with each other. The two firms have nearly identical capital structures. PTC has a policy of usually paying a constant 50% of each year's earnings as dividends, whereas DTC has sought to maintain a stable dollar dividend policy, with changes in the dollar dividend payment occurring infrequently. The record of the two firms follows:

	PTC			DTC		
Year	EPS	Dividend	Average Market Price	EPS	Dividend	Average Market Price
20X1	$2.00	$1.00	$20	$2.10	$0.75	$18
20X2	2.50	1.25	24	2.40	0.75	22
20X3	1.50	1.25	15	1.60	0.75	17
20X4	1.00	0.50	10	0.90	0.75	14
20X5	0.50	0.25	8	0.50	0.50	10
20X6	−1.25	Nil	8	−1.10	0.50	10
20X7	1.00	0.50	10	1.10	0.75	14
20X8	1.50	0.75	14	1.45	0.75	17

    The president of PTC wonders what accounts for DTC's current (20X8) higher share price, in spite of the fact that PTC currently earns more per share than DTC and frequently has paid a higher dividend.

    a. What factors can you cite that might account for this phenomenon?

    b. What do you suggest as an optimal dividend policy for both PTC and DTC that might lead to increases in both of their share prices? What are the limitations of your suggestions?

14. ESC has experienced a slow (3% per year) but steady increase in earnings per share. The firm has consistently paid out an average of 75% of each year's earnings as dividends. The stock market evaluates ESC primarily on the basis of its dividend payout because growth prospects are modest.

    ESC's management presents a proposal to the board of directors that would require the outlay of $50 million to build a new plant in a rapidly expanding market. The expected annual return on the investment in this plant is estimated to be in excess of 30%, more than twice the current firm average. To finance this investment, a number of alternatives are being considered. They include the following:

a. Finance the expansion with externally raised equity.

b. Finance the expansion with 50% externally generated equity and 50% internally generated equity. This alternative would necessitate a dividend cut for this year only.

c. Finance the expansion with a mix of debt and equity similar to their current relative proportions in the capital structure. Under this alternative, dividends would not be cut. Rather, any equity needs in excess of that which could be provided internally would be raised through a sale of new common shares.

Evaluate these various financing alternatives with reference to their effects on the dividend policy and common share values of the company.

15. CR expects earnings this year to be $2 per share. CR plans to pay a dividend of $0.70 for the year. During the year CR expects to borrow $10 million in addition to its already outstanding loan balances. CR has 10 million common shares outstanding.

a. If all capital outlays are funded from retained earnings and new borrowings and if CR follows a residual dividend policy, what capital outlays are planned for the coming year?

b. What is CR's target capital structure given these assumptions?

Other Practice Materials and Resources

For interactive quizzes, Internet exercises, crossword puzzles, CTV videos, and more, go to the *Contemporary Financial Management* Web site at **http://cyr.nelson.com**

Part Five

Working Capital Management Decisions

5

15 Working Capital Policy and Short-Term Financing

16 Current Asset Management

This part of the book considers the financial management of a firm's current assets and current liabilities, called *working capital management*. Chapter 15 deals with working capital policy, with emphasis on the risk–return trade-offs that are implied and the sources of short-term and intermediate term credit. Chapter 16 covers the management of the current assets: cash, marketable securities, accounts receivable and inventories. Working capital management influences both the risk of a firm and its expected returns. As such, it is an important determinant of firm value.

Working Capital Policy and Short-Term Financing

Learning Objectives

After studying this chapter you should be able to

1. Analyze a firm's operating cycle and cash conversion cycle, which is important in analyzing its liquidity

2. Understand that working capital policy decisions include

   a. Investment—level of working capital
   b. Financing—proportions of short-term and long-term debt

3. Understand that determining the optimal level of working capital investment involves profitability versus risk trade-off analysis:

   a. Higher levels of working capital generally reduce profitability
   b. Higher levels of working capital reduce the risk of financial difficulties

4. Determine the optimal proportions of short- and long-term debt that involves profitability versus risk trade-off analysis:

   a. Higher proportions of short-term debt increase profitability because of generally lower interest costs
   b. Higher proportions of short-term debt increase the risk of financial difficulties

5. Understand that overall working capital policy involves analyzing the joint impact of the working capital investment decision and the working capital financing decision on the firm's risk and profitability

6. Understand that *trade credit,* or *accounts payable,* is the principal source of *spontaneous* short-term credit. The cost of trade credit is dependent on the size of any cash discount offered and the lengths of the credit and discount periods

7. Understand that *bank loans, commercial paper, accounts receivable loans,* and *inventory loans* are the major sources of *negotiated* short-term credit. The types of short-term bank credit include *single loans, lines of credit,* and *revolving credit agreements*

8. Understand that commercial paper is a short-term unsecured credit instrument issued by major corporations with good credit ratings

9. Understand that a company can use its accounts receivable and/or inventory to obtain short-term financing. It can either *pledge* the accounts

receivable as collateral for a loan or sell *(factor)* the receivables to obtain cash. It can use its inventory as collateral for a short-term loan. The lender can either allow the borrower to hold the collateral (under a *floating lien* or *trust receipts* arrangement) or require that a third party hold the collateral (under a *terminal warehouse* or *field warehouse arrangement*)

10. Understand that term loans are debt obligations having an initial maturity between 1 and 10 years

    a. The major suppliers of term loans are banks, insurance companies, pension fund management firms, and equipment suppliers

    b. Term loans are usually amortized over the life of the loan

    c. The interest rate on term loans obtained from chartered banks is normally greater than the bank's prime rate

    d. Most term loans are secured. The loan agreement contains affirmative, negative, and restrictive covenants. In addition, the conditions that determine when a default on the loan has occurred are detailed in the loan agreement

Allstream: Accounts Receivable Securitization[1]

AT&T Canada (now know as Allstream) is one of the largest national broadband and business services providers and local exchange carriers, with over 18,500 route kilometres of local and long-haul broadband fibre optic network and world-class data, Internet, Web hosting, and e-commerce enabling capabilities.

On July 20, 2001, AT&T Canada announced that it had closed an accounts receivable securitization deal that involved the sale of certain of its accounts receivables to a special-purpose trust and had received cash proceeds of approximately CDN$100 million as a result of the transaction. The funds would be used for AT&T Canada's operating and working capital needs. AT&T Canada indicated that the proceeds from the sale would be increased over time up to a maximum of $150 million, depending on the growth in customer receivables.

Securitization or structured financing typically involves a company converting an income-producing asset, such as accounts receivable, into cash today by selling the asset to a trust that then issues short-term debt, such as commercial paper, to investors. The debt issued by the trust is backed by the accounts receivable purchased and is generally less risky than if the debt was issued directly by the company. As a result, companies like AT&T Canada can potentially benefit by reducing their effective interest cost through this process.

Securitization started to be used as an alternative to debt financing in the early 1980s and is now widely employed in Canada. One of the benefits of a securitization transaction such as the one carried out by AT&T Canada is that the accounts receivable are effectively removed from the company's balance sheet and replaced with the cash that it receives. This process results in a source of financing without issuance of additional debt or equity. As a result, the company's capital structure is not changed, allowing the company to preserve its borrowing capacity.

[1] Based on "AT&T Canada Announces Accounts Receivable Securitization," *Canadian News Wire*, July 21, 2001.

Introduction

The first half of this chapter deals with the management of working capital, which involves decisions about the optimal overall level of current assets and the optimal mix of short-term and long-term funds used to finance the company's assets. These decisions require an analysis of the risk and expected return trade-offs associated with the various alternative policies.

The second half of this chapter deals with the financing of the current assets that make up the working capital. A company normally employs a combination of short- and intermediate-term credit and long-term debt and equity in financing its current and fixed assets. The various sources of long-term financing have already been discussed. This chapter focuses on the major sources of short- and intermediate-term credit.

Short-term credit includes all of a firm's debt obligations that originally were scheduled for repayment within one year.[2] Short-term credit may be either *unsecured* or *secured*.[3] In the case of unsecured short-term debt, a firm obtains credit from the lender without having to pledge any specific assets as collateral, and the lender depends primarily on the cash-generating ability of the firm to repay the debt. If the firm becomes insolvent and declares bankruptcy, the unsecured lender usually stands little chance of recovering all or even a significant portion of the amount owed.

In the case of secured short-term debt, the borrower pledges certain specified assets—such as accounts receivable, inventory, or fixed assets—as collateral.[4] The law outlines the procedures that must be followed in order for a lender to establish a valid claim on a firm's collateral.

The first step in this process involves the execution of a *security agreement,* which is a contract between the lender and the firm specifying the collateral held against the loan. The security agreement is then filed at the appropriate provincial office in which the collateral is located. Future potential lenders can check with this office to determine which assets the firm has pledged and which are still free to be used as collateral. Filing this security agreement legally establishes the lender's security interest in the collateral. If the borrower defaults on the loan or otherwise fails to honour the terms of the agreement, the lender can seize and sell the collateral to recover the amount owed. Thus, the lender in a secured short-term debt agreement has *two* potential sources of loan repayment: the firm's cash-generating ability and the collateral value of the pledged assets.

In general, companies prefer to borrow funds on an unsecured basis because the added administrative costs involved in pledging assets as security raise the cost of the loan to the borrower. In addition, secured borrowing agreements can restrict a firm's future borrowing. Many companies, particularly small ones, are not able to obtain unsecured credit, however. For example, a firm may be financially weak or too new to justify an unsecured loan, or it may want more credit than the lender is willing to give on an unsecured basis. In any of these circumstances, either the firm must provide collateral or it will not receive the loan.

The short-term credit sources available to a company can be either *spontaneous* or *negotiated.* Spontaneous sources, the main one of which is *trade credit*, are discussed in upcoming sections. Later sections of this chapter consider the various negotiated sources, such as *bank credit, commercial paper, receivables loans,* and *inventory loans.*

Click on Finance in the News at **http://finance. swcollege.com** and select Short-Term Financial Management for articles on this topic.

---

[2] Short-term credit *does not* always correspond exactly to the current liabilities shown on the firm's balance sheet. Current liabilities also include that portion of long-term debt (such as term loans and mortgages) scheduled for repayment during the next year.

[3] Intermediate- and long-term debt may also be either unsecured or secured.

[4] As an alternative to pledging specific assets as collateral for a loan, a company may get a third party to *cosign,* or *guarantee,* the loan. If the borrower defaults, the third party becomes responsible for repayment. Lenders will usually accept only financially sound third parties, such as a shareholder, supplier, or customer who has a vested interest in the company's success.

The primary sources of intermediate-term funding for companies are term loans and leases. Term loans are examined later in the chapter and lease financing is examined in Chapter 19.

Working Capital Policy

Working capital policy involves decisions about a company's current assets and current liabilities—what they consist of, how they are used, and how their mix affects the risk versus return characteristics of the company. The term **working capital** (sometimes called gross working capital) means current assets. The term **net working capital** is defined as the difference between the firm's current assets and current liabilities. Unfortunately, the two terms are sometimes used interchangeably in practice and this may cause confusion.

Working capital policies, through their effect on the firm's expected future returns and the risk associated with these returns, ultimately have an impact on shareholder wealth.[5] Effective working capital policies are crucial to a firm's long-run growth and survival. If, for example, a company lacks the working capital needed to expand production and sales, it may lose revenues and profits. Working capital is used by firms to maintain **liquidity**, that is, the ability to meet their cash obligations as they come due. Otherwise, firms may incur the costs associated with a deteriorating credit rating, a potential forced liquidation of assets, and possible bankruptcy.

Working capital management is a continuing process that involves a number of day-to-day operations and decisions that determine the following:

- The firm's level of current assets
- The proportions of short-term and long-term debt the firm will use to finance its assets
- The level of investment in each type of current asset
- The specific sources and mix of short-term credit (current liabilities) the firm should employ

Working capital differs from *fixed* capital in terms of the time required to recover the investment in a given asset. In the case of fixed capital or long-term assets (such as land, buildings, and equipment), a company usually needs several years or more to recover the initial investment. In contrast, working capital is turned over, or circulated, at a relatively rapid rate. Investments in inventories and accounts receivable are usually recovered during a firm's normal operating cycle, when inventories are sold and receivables are collected.

Importance of Working Capital

It has already been noted that a firm must have working capital to operate and survive. In many industries, working capital (current assets) constitutes a relatively large percentage of total assets. In the manufacturing sector, for example, current assets comprise about 40 percent of the total assets of all manufacturing corporations. Among the wholesaling and retailing sectors, the percentages are even higher—in the 50 to 60 percent range. Because current assets constitute a relatively high percentage of total assets in most businesses, it is important to have effective working capital policies.

A firm's net working capital position is not only important from an internal standpoint; it is also widely used as one measure of the firm's risk. *Risk*, as used in this context, deals with the probability that a firm will encounter financial difficulties, such as the

Working Capital
The difference between a firm's current assets and current liabilities. The term *working capital* is used interchangeably with *net working capital*.

Net Working Capital
The difference between a firm's current assets and current liabilities. The term *net working capital* is frequently used interchangeably with *working capital*.

Liquidity
The ability of a firm to meet its cash obligations as they come due.

---

[5] See James A. Gentry, "State of the Art of Short-Run Financial Management," *Financial Management* 17 (Summer 1988): 41–57, for a review of the literature concerning the management of short-run assets and liabilities.

inability to pay bills on time. All other things being equal, the more net working capital a firm has, the more likely it is to be able to meet current financial obligations. Because net working capital is one measure of risk, a company's net working capital position affects its ability to obtain debt financing. Many loan agreements with chartered banks and other lending institutions contain a provision requiring the firm to maintain a minimum net working capital position. Likewise, bond indentures also often contain such provisions.

Operating Cycle Analysis

The activities of a firm typically create cash flows that are both unsynchronized and uncertain. They are unsynchronized because cash disbursements (for example, payments for resource purchases) usually take place before cash receipts (for example, collection of receivables). They are uncertain because future sales and costs, which generate the respective receipts and disbursements, cannot be forecasted with complete accuracy. If the firm is to maintain liquidity and function properly, it has to invest funds in various short-term assets (working capital). It has to maintain a cash balance to pay the bills as they come due. In addition, the firm must invest in inventories to fill customer orders promptly. And, finally, the company invests in accounts receivable to extend credit to its customers.

Figure 15.1 illustrates the operating cycle of a typical firm.[6] The **operating cycle** is equal to the length of the inventory and receivables conversion periods:

$$(15.1) \qquad \text{Operating cycle} = \text{Inventory conversion period} \\ + \text{Receivables conversion period}$$

The **inventory conversion period** is the length of time required to produce and sell the product. It is defined as follows:

$$(15.2) \qquad \text{Inventory conversion period} = \text{Average inventory}/(\text{Cost of sales}/365)$$

The **receivables conversion period**, or average collection period, represents the length of time required to collect the sales receipts. It is calculated as follows:

$$(15.3) \qquad \text{Receivables conversion period} = \frac{\text{Average accounts receivable}}{\text{Annual credit sales}/365}$$

Operating Cycle
Includes the three primary activities of purchasing resources, producing the product, and distributing (selling) the product. The operating cycle is calculated by summing the inventory conversion period and the receivables conversion period.

Inventory Conversion Period
The length of time required to produce and sell the product.

Receivables Conversion Period
The length of time required to collect sales receipts. *Receivables conversion period* is another name for the average collection period.

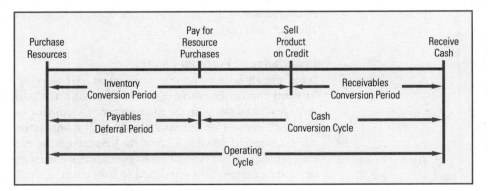

Figure 15.1
Operating Cycle of a Typical Company

---

[6] The following discussion in the text is based on Verlyn D. Richards and Eugene J. Laughlin, "A Cash Conversion Cycle Approach to Liquidity Analysis," *Financial Management* 9 (Spring 1980): 32–38.

The **payables deferral period** is the length of time the firm is able to defer payment on its various resource purchases (e.g., materials). The following equation is used to calculate the payables deferral period:[7]

(15.4)   Payables deferral period = Average accounts payable/(Cost of sales/365)

Finally, the **cash conversion cycle** represents the net time interval between the collection of cash receipts from product sales and the cash payments for the company's various resource purchases. It is calculated as follows:

(15.5)   Cash conversion cycle = Operating cycle − Payables deferral period

The cash conversion cycle shows the time interval over which additional *nonspontaneous* sources of working capital financing must be obtained to carry out the firm's activities.[8] An increase in the length of the operating cycle, without a corresponding increase in the payables deferral period, lengthens the cash conversion cycle and creates further working capital financing needs for the company.

Table 15.1 shows an actual cash conversion cycle analysis for SYSCO Corporation, a North American distributor of food service products. SYSCO's liquidity, as measured by the current and quick ratios, appears to have deteriorated slightly in 2000 compared to 1999. The reduction of SYSCO's cash conversion cycle from 24 days in 1999 to 22 days in 2000 indicates a more efficient utilization of its working capital. While the inventory conversion period and receivables conversion period remained constant from 1999 to 2000, its payables deferral period increased by two days, indicating that the firm was able to defer payments for its purchases for a slightly longer period of time.

Levels of Working Capital Investment

Overall working capital policy considers both a firm's level of working capital investment and its financing. In practice, the firm has to determine the joint impact of these

Table 15.1 Cash Conversion Cycle Analysis for SYSCO Corporation		
	2000	**1999**
Liquidity ratios:		
Current ratio	1.53	1.69
Quick ratio	1.01	1.09
Cash conversion cycle:		
Inventory conversion period	21 days	21 days
Receivables conversion period	27 days	27 days
Operating cycle	48 days	48 days
Less Payables deferral period	26 days	24 days
Cash conversion cycle	22 days	24 days

Source: *Mergent Industrial Manual,* 2001.

---

[7] A more precise estimate of the payables deferral period would include other resource purchases, such as wages and taxes, for which payment can be deferred. However, accounting information on such items as salaries, benefits, and payroll taxes payable and selling, general, and administrative expenses frequently is not shown as separate entries on a firm's balance sheet and income statement.

[8] Spontaneous sources of financing (such as trade credit offered by suppliers) automatically expand (contract) as the company's volume of purchases increases (decreases). Nonspontaneous (or negotiated) sources of financing (such as bank loans), in contrast, do not automatically expand or contract with the volume of purchases.

two decisions on its profitability and risk. However, to permit a better understanding of working capital policy, the working capital investment decision is discussed in this section, and the working capital financing decision is discussed in the following section. The two decisions are then considered together.

The size and nature of a firm's investment in current assets is a function of a number of different factors, including the following:

- The type of products manufactured
- The length of the operating cycle
- The sales level (because higher sales require more investment in inventories and receivables)
- Inventory policies (for example, the amount of safety stocks maintained; that is, inventories needed to meet higher than expected demand or unanticipated delays in obtaining new inventories)
- Credit policies
- How efficiently the firm manages current assets (Obviously, the more effectively management economizes on the amount of cash, marketable securities, inventories, and receivables employed, the smaller the working capital requirements.)

For the purposes of discussion and analysis, these factors are held constant for the remainder of this section. Instead of focusing on these factors, this section examines the risk-return trade-offs associated with alternative levels of working capital investment.

Profitability versus Risk Trade-off for Alternative Levels of Working Capital Investment

Before deciding on an appropriate level of working capital investment, a firm's management has to evaluate the trade-off between expected profitability and the risk that it may be unable to meet its financial obligations. Profitability is measured by the rate of (operating) return on total assets; that is, EBIT/total assets. As mentioned earlier in this chapter, the risk that a firm will encounter financial difficulties is related to the firm's net working capital position.

Figure 15.2 illustrates three alternative working capital policies.[9] Each curve in the figure demonstrates the relationship between the firm's investment in current assets and sales for that particular policy.

Policy C represents a *conservative* approach to working capital management. Under this policy, the company holds a relatively large proportion of its total assets in the form of current assets. The rate of return on current assets is normally assumed to be less than the rate of return on fixed assets.[10] Thus, this policy results in a *lower expected profitability* as measured by the rate of return on the company's total assets. Assuming that current liabilities remain constant, this type of policy also increases the company's net working capital position, resulting in a *lower risk* that the firm will encounter financial difficulties.

In contrast to Policy C, Policy A represents an *aggressive* approach. Under this policy, the company holds a relatively small proportion of its total assets in the form of lower-yielding current assets and thus has relatively less net working capital. As a result, this

---

[9] The relationship between current assets and sales is drawn as a concave, *curvilinear* function because it is assumed that economies of scale exist in the holding of current assets. In other words, increases in sales should normally require less than proportionate increases in current assets, particularly for cash and inventories. The amount of the company's *fixed* assets is held constant in the following discussion in the text.

[10] This assumption is based on the principle that the lower an asset's risk, the lower its expected return. Current assets are normally less risky than fixed assets because they can be converted into cash more easily and with less potential loss in value. Therefore, current assets should have lower expected returns.

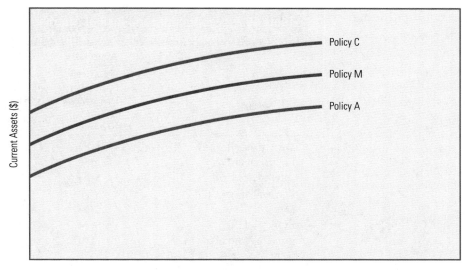

Figure 15.2
Three Alternative Working Capital Investment Policies

policy yields a *higher expected profitability* and a *higher risk* that the company will encounter financial difficulties.

Finally, Policy M represents a *moderate* approach. With this policy, expected profitability and risk levels fall between those of Policy C and Policy A.

These three approaches may be illustrated with the following example. Suppose Burlington Resources has forecasted sales next year to be $100 million and EBIT to be $10 million. The company has fixed assets of $30 million and current liabilities totalling $20 million.

The firm is considering three alternative working capital investment policies:

■ An *aggressive* policy consisting of $35 million in current assets

■ A *moderate* policy consisting of $40 million in current assets

■ A *conservative* policy consisting of $45 million in current assets

Assume that sales and EBIT remain constant under each policy.[11] Table 15.2 contains the results of the three proposed policies.

The aggressive policy would yield the highest expected rate of return on total assets, 15.38 percent, whereas the conservative policy would yield the lowest rate of return, 13.33 percent. The aggressive policy would also result in a lower net working capital position ($15 million) than would the conservative policy ($25 million).

Using net working capital as a measure of risk, the aggressive policy is the riskiest and the conservative policy is the least risky. The current ratio is another measure of a firm's ability to meet financial obligations as they come due. The aggressive policy would yield the lowest current ratio, and the conservative policy would yield the highest current ratio.

---

[11] In practice, however, this assumption may not be completely realistic because a firm's sales are usually a function of its inventory and credit policies. Higher levels of finished goods inventories and a more liberal credit extension policy—both of which increase a firm's investment in current assets—may also lead to higher sales. This effect can be incorporated into the analysis by modifying the sales and EBIT projections under the various alternative working capital policies. Although changing these projections would affect the numerical values contained in Table 15.2, it does not affect the general conclusions concerning the profitability versus risk trade-offs.

Table 15.2 Profitability and Risk of Alternative Working Capital Investment Policies for Burlington Resources (in Millions of Dollars)

	Aggressive	Moderate	Conservative
	Relatively Small Investment in Current Assets	Moderate Investment in Current Assets	Relatively Large Investment in Current Assets
Current assets (C/A)	$ 35	$ 40	$ 45
Fixed assets (F/A)	30	30	30
Total assets (T/A)	$ 65	$ 70	$ 75
Current liabilities (C/L)	$ 20	$ 20	$ 20
Forecasted sales	$100	$100	$100
Expected EBIT	$ 10	$ 10	$ 10
Expected rate of return on total assets (EBIT ÷ T/A)	15.38%	14.29%	13.33%
Net working capital position (C/A − C/L)	$ 15	$ 20	$ 25
Current ratio (C/A ÷ C/L)	1.75	2.0	2.25

Optimal Level of Working Capital Investment

The optimal level of working capital investment is the level expected to maximize shareholder wealth. It is a function of several factors, including the variability of sales and cash flows and the degree of operating and financial leverage employed by the firm. Therefore, no single working capital investment policy is necessarily optimal for all firms.

Proportions of Short-Term and Long-Term Financing

Not only does a firm have to be concerned about the level of current assets; it also has to determine the proportions of short- and long-term debt to use in financing these assets. This decision also involves trade-offs between profitability and risk.

Sources of debt financing are classified according to their *maturities*. Specifically, they can be categorized as being either *short-term* or *long-term,* with short-term sources having maturities of one year or less and long-term sources having maturities of greater than one year.[12]

Cost of Short-Term versus Long-Term Debt

Recall from Chapter 7 that the term structure of interest rates is defined as the relationship among interest rates of debt securities that differ in their length of time to maturity. Historically, long-term interest rates have normally exceeded short-term rates.

Also, because of the reduced flexibility of long-term borrowing relative to short-term borrowing, the *effective* cost of long-term debt may be higher than the cost of short-term debt, even when short-term interest rates are equal to or greater than long-term rates. With long-term debt, a firm incurs the interest expense even during times when it has no immediate need for the funds, such as during seasonal or cyclical downturns. With short-term debt, in contrast, the firm can avoid the interest costs on unneeded funds by paying off (or not renewing) the debt. In summary, the cost of long-term debt is generally higher than the cost of short-term debt.

---

[12] In this discussion, the term *long-term financing* includes any *intermediate-term financing.*

Risk of Long-Term versus Short-Term Debt

Borrowing companies have different attitudes toward the relative risk of long-term versus short-term debt than do lenders. Whereas lenders normally feel that risk increases with maturity, borrowers feel that there is more risk associated with short-term debt. The reasons for this are twofold.

First, there is always the chance that a firm will not be able to refinance its short-term debt. When a firm's debt matures, it either pays off the debt as part of a debt reduction program or arranges new financing. At the time of maturity, however, the firm could be faced with financial problems resulting from such events as strikes, natural disasters, or recessions that cause sales and cash inflows to decline. Under these circumstances the firm may find it very difficult or even impossible to obtain the needed funds. This could lead to operating and financial difficulties. The more frequently a firm must refinance debt, the greater is the risk of its not being able to obtain the necessary financing.

Second, short-term interest rates tend to fluctuate more over time than long-term interest rates. As a result, a firm's interest expenses and expected earnings after interest and taxes are subject to more variation over time with short-term debt than with long-term debt.

Profitability versus Risk Trade-Off for Alternative Financing Plans

A company's need for financing is equal to the sum of its fixed and current assets.[13] Current assets can be divided into the following two categories:

- *Permanent* current assets
- *Fluctuating* current assets

Fluctuating Current Assets
Current assets affected by the seasonal or cyclical nature of the firm's sales.

Permanent Current Assets
Current assets held to meet the firm's long-term minimum needs.

Matching Approach
A financing plan in which the maturity structure of a firm's liabilities is made to correspond exactly to the life of its assets.

Fluctuating current assets are those affected by the seasonal or cyclical nature of company sales. For example, a firm must make larger investments in inventories and receivables during peak selling periods than during other periods of the year. **Permanent current assets** are those held to meet the company's minimum long-term needs (for example, "safety stocks" of cash and inventories). Figure 15.3 illustrates a typical firm's financing needs over time. The fixed assets and permanent current assets lines are upward sloping, indicating that the investment in these assets and, by extension, financing needs tend to increase over time for a firm whose sales are increasing.

One way in which a firm can meet its financing needs is by using a **matching approach** in which the maturity structure of the firm's liabilities is made to correspond exactly to the life of its assets, as illustrated in Figure 15.4. Fixed and permanent current assets are financed with long-term debt and equity funds, whereas fluctuating current assets are financed with short-term debt.[14] Application of this approach is not as simple as it appears, however. In practice, the uncertainty associated with the lives of individual assets makes the matching approach difficult to implement.

Figures 15.5 and 15.6 illustrate two other financing plans. Figure 15.5 shows a *conservative* approach, which uses a relatively high proportion of long-term debt. The relatively low proportion of short-term debt in this approach reduces the risk that the company will be unable to refund its debt, and it also reduces the risk associated with interest rate fluctuations. At the same time, however, this approach cuts down on the expected returns available to shareholders because the cost of long-term debt is generally greater than the cost of short-term debt.

---

[13] The following discussion assumes a constant amount of equity financing.

[14] This analysis does not consider "spontaneous" sources of short-term credit, such as accounts payable. Since spontaneous short-term credit is virtually cost-free when used within reasonable limits, a company will normally employ this type of credit to the fullest extent possible before using "negotiated" sources of short-term credit, such as bank loans. Because none of the conclusions concerning the trade-off between profitability and risk are affected by ignoring spontaneous sources of short-term credit, it need not be considered here.

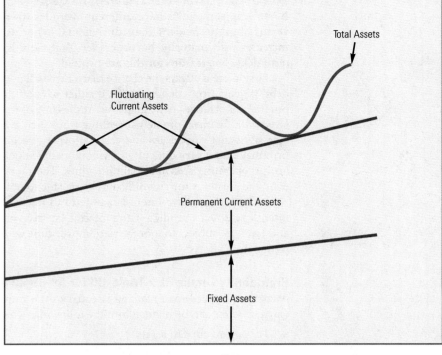

Figure 15.3
Financing Needs Over Time

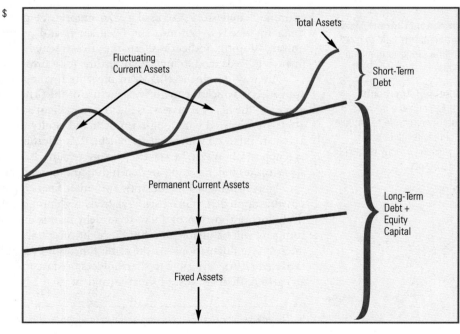

Figure 15.4
Matching Approach to Asset Financing

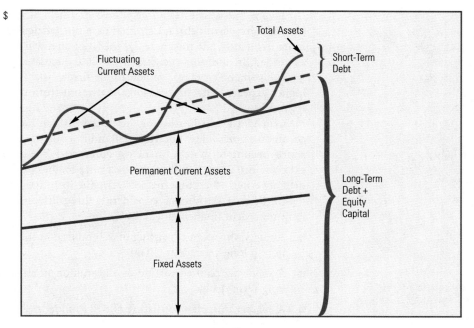

Figure 15.5
Conservative Approach to Asset Financing

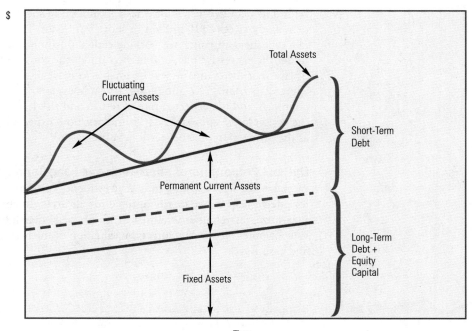

Figure 15.6
Aggressive Approach to Asset Financing

Figure 15.6 illustrates an *aggressive* approach, which uses a relatively high proportion of short-term debt. A firm that uses this particular approach must refinance debt more frequently, and this increases the risk that it will be unable to obtain new financing as needed. In addition, the greater possible fluctuations in interest expenses associated with this financing plan also add to the firm's risk. These higher risks are offset by the higher expected after-tax earnings that result from the normally lower costs of short-term debt.

Consider again Burlington Resources, which has total assets of $70 million and common shareholders' equity of $28 million on its books, thus requiring $42 million in short- or long-term debt financing. Forecasted sales for next year are $100 million and expected EBIT is $10 million. Interest rates on the company's short-term and long-term debt are 8 and 10 percent, respectively, due to an upward-sloping yield curve.

Burlington Resources is considering three different combinations of short-term and long-term debt financing:

- An *aggressive* plan consisting of $30 million in short-term debt (STD) and $12 million in long-term debt (LTD)

- A *moderate* plan consisting of $20 million in short-term debt and $22 million in long-term debt

- A *conservative* plan consisting of $10 million in short-term debt and $32 million in long-term debt

Table 15.3 shows the data for each of these alternative proposed financing plans. From the standpoint of profitability, the aggressive financing plan would yield the highest expected rate of return to the shareholders—13.6 percent—whereas the conservative plan would yield the lowest rate of return—12.9 percent. In contrast, the aggressive plan would involve a greater degree of risk that the company will be unable to refund its debt because it assumes $30 million in short-term debt and the conservative plan assumes only $10 million in short-term debt. This is substantiated further by the fact that the company's net working capital position and current ratio would be lowest under the aggressive plan and highest under the conservative plan—making the degree of risk that the company will be unable to meet financial obligations greater with the aggressive plan. The moderate financing plan represents a middle-of-the-road approach, and the expected rate of return and risk level are between the aggressive and the conservative approaches. In summary, both expected profitability and risk increase as the proportion of short-term debt increases.[15]

Optimal Proportions of Short-Term and Long-Term Debt

As is the case with working capital investment policy, no one combination of short- and long-term debt is necessarily optimal for all firms. In choosing a financing policy that maximizes shareholder wealth, a firm's financial manager must also take into account various other factors that affect the valuation of the firm, such as the variability of sales and cash flows.

---

[15] This example assumes that the costs of short-term and long-term debt of 8 percent and 10 percent, respectively, would be the same for each of the three financing policies. In practice, however, this would probably not be the case because lenders generally require higher interest rates before making loans involving higher risks. Thus, a company following an aggressive financing policy will probably have to pay slightly higher interest rates on debt than a company following a conservative policy. This effect can be incorporated into the analysis by modifying the interest rates on short-term and long-term debt under the various financing policies. This would affect the numerical values in the example, but it should not affect the general conclusions concerning the profitability versus risk trade-offs.

Table 15.3 Profitability and Risk of Alternative Financing Policies for Burlington Resources (in Millions of Dollars)

	Aggressive	Moderate	Conservative
	Relatively Large Amount of Short-Term Debt	Moderate Amount of Short-Term Debt	Relatively Small Amount of Short-Term Debt
Current assets (C/A)	$ 40	$ 40	$ 40
Fixed assets (F/A)	30	30	30
Total assets (T/A)	$ 70	$ 70	$ 70
Current liabilities (STD)(C/L) (interest rate, 8%)	$ 30	$ 20	$ 10
Long-term liabilities (LTD) (interest rate, 10%)	12	22	32
Total liabilities (60% of T/A)	$ 42	$ 42	$ 42
Common equity	28	28	28
Total liabilities and common equity	$ 70	$ 70	$ 70
Forecasted sales	$100	$100	$100
Expected EBIT	10	10	10
Less Interest:			
STD, 8%	2.4 ⎤	1.6 ⎤	0.8 ⎤
LTD, 10%	1.2 ⎦ 3.6	2.2 ⎦ 3.8	3.2 ⎦ 4.0
Taxable income	$ 6.4	$ 6.2	$ 6.0
Less Taxes (40%)	2.6	2.5	2.4
Net income after taxes	$ 3.8	$ 3.7	$ 3.6
Expected rate of return on common equity	13.6%	13.2%	12.9%
Net working capital position (C/A − C/L)	$10	$20	$30
Current ratio (C/A ÷ C/L)	1.33	2.0	4.0

Overall Working Capital Policy

Until now, this chapter has analyzed the working capital investment and financing decisions independent of one another in order to examine the profitability-risk trade-offs associated with each, assuming that all other factors are held constant. Effective working capital policy, however, also requires the consideration of the joint impact of these decisions on the firm's profitability and risk.

Referring to Burlington Resources again, assume that the company is 60 percent debt financed (both short-term and long-term) and 40 percent financed with common stock. Also, it is evaluating three alternative working capital investment and financing policies. The *aggressive* policy would require a relatively *small* investment in current assets, $35 million, and a relatively *large* amount of short-term debt, $30 million. The *conservative* policy would require a relatively *large* investment in current assets, $45 million, and a relatively *small* amount of short-term debt, $10 million. The firm is also considering a middle-of-the-road approach, which would involve a *moderate* investment in current assets, $40 million, and a *moderate* amount of short-term debt, $20 million.

Table 15.4 shows the data for each approach. The aggressive working capital policy is expected to yield the highest return on shareholders' equity, 15.4 percent, whereas the conservative policy is expected to yield the lowest return, 11.3 percent. The net working capital and current ratio are lowest under the aggressive policy and highest under the conservative policy, indicating that the aggressive policy is the riskiest. The moderate policy yields an expected return and risk level somewhere between the aggressive and the conservative policies.

Whereas this type of analysis will not directly yield the optimal working capital investment and financing policies a company should choose, it can give the financial

Table 15.4 Alternative Working Capital Investment and Financing Policies for Burlington Resources (in Millions of Dollars)

	Aggressive — Relatively Small Investment in Current Assets; Relatively Large Amount of Short-Term Debt	Moderate — Moderate Investment in Current Assets; Moderate Amount of Short-Term Debt	Conservative — Relatively Large Investment in Current Assets; Relatively Small Amount of Short-Term Debt
Current assets (C/A)	$ 35	$ 40	$ 45
Fixed assets (F/A)	30	30	30
Total assets (T/A)	$ 65	$ 70	$ 75
Current liabilities (STD)(C/L) (interest rate, 8%)	$ 30	$ 20	$ 10
Long-term liabilities (LTD) (interest rate, 10%)	9	22	35
Total liabilities (60% of T/A)	$ 39	$ 42	$ 45
Common equity	26	28	30
Total liabilities and common equity	$ 65	$ 70	$ 75
Forecasted sales	$100	$100	$100
Expected EBIT	10	10	10
Less Interest:			
STD, 8%	2.4 ⎫	1.6 ⎫	0.8 ⎫
LTD, 10%	0.9 ⎭ 3.3	2.2 ⎭ 3.8	3.5 ⎭ 4.3
Taxable income	$ 6.7	$ 6.2	$ 5.7
Less Taxes (40%)	2.7	2.5	2.3
Net income after taxes	$ 4.0	$ 3.7	$ 3.4
Expected rate of return on common equity	15.4%	13.2%	11.3%
Net working capital position (C/A − C/L)	$ 5	$ 20	$ 35
Current ratio (C/A ÷ C/L)	1.17	2.0	4.5

manager some insight into the profitability-risk trade-offs of alternative policies. With an understanding of these trade-offs, the financial manager should be able to make better decisions concerning the working capital policy that will lead to a maximization of shareholder wealth.

Cost of Short-Term Funds

Managers need a method to calculate the financing cost for the various sources of short-term financing available to a firm. Equation 4.1 from Chapter 4 gives the amount of interest paid, I, on borrowed money:

$$(15.6) \qquad I = PV_0 \times i \times n$$

where I = the interest amount in dollars; PV_0 = the principal amount at time 0, or the present value; i = the interest rate per time period; and n = the number of time periods. Solving for i, we obtain

$$(15.7) \qquad i = \frac{I}{PV} \times \frac{1}{n}$$

The interest rate, i, is equal to the fractional interest cost per period, I/PV_0, times 1 divided by the number of time periods, or $1/n$.

Annual Percentage Rate
The simple, annual percentage interest rate for a loan.

The equation we use to calculate the **annual percentage rate**, APR, for short-term financing sources is a variation of Equation 15.7:

$$(15.8) \qquad \text{APR} = \frac{\text{Interest costs} + \text{fees}}{\text{Usable funds}} \times \frac{365}{\text{Maturity(days)}}$$

Short-term financing sources may involve fees in addition to the interest costs. Also, the term *usable funds* is used in place of *present value* because some of the money from a particular short-term financing source may not actually be available for a company to use. The term, 365/maturity (days), converts the financing cost to an annual rate.

Effective Annual Rate
The effective annual rate of interest paid by the borrower or earned by the lender.

The annual percentage rate calculated using Equation 15.8 is only an approximation to the **effective annual rate**, or EAR, of a loan. Equation 15.8 does not consider compounding and understates the EAR. Also, Equation 15.8 is normally used for financing sources of one year or less. The following equation gives the EAR for a short-term financing source:

$$(15.9) \qquad \text{EAR} = \left(1 + \frac{\text{Interest costs} + \text{fees}}{\text{Usable funds}}\right)^m - 1$$

where m is the number of times per year compounding occurs. Equation 15.9 is a variation of Equation 4.28 from Chapter 4. In addition, the EAR of a loan is the internal rate of return between the funds received and the funds paid back.

To illustrate the use of Equations 15.8 and 15.9, consider a six-month, $10,000 loan that has $500 of interest. If we assume that principal is paid only at maturity and there are 182 days in the six-month period, the annual percentage rate is calculated, using Equation 15.8, as follows:

$$\text{APR} = \$500/\$10,000 \times 365/182 = 0.1003 \text{ or } 10.03\%$$

The loan's EAR is determined as follows, using Equation 15.9:

$$\text{EAR} = \left(1 + \frac{\$500}{\$10,000}\right)^{365/182} - 1$$
$$= 0.1028 \text{ or } 10.28\%$$

The APR closely approximates the EAR, unless the number of compounding periods is large.

Equation 15.8 is used throughout this chapter to calculate the annual percentage rate of the various short-term financing sources available to a firm.

Trade Credit

Whenever a business receives merchandise ordered from a supplier and is then permitted to wait a specified period of time before having to pay, it is receiving trade credit.[16] In the aggregate, trade credit is the most important source of short-term financing for business firms. Smaller businesses in particular usually rely heavily on trade credit to finance their operations because they are often unable to obtain funds from banks or other lenders in the financial markets.

Most trade credit is extended on an *open account* basis. A firm sends a purchase order to a supplier, who then evaluates the firm's creditworthiness using various information sources and decision criteria.[17] If the supplier decides to extend the firm credit, it ships the ordered merchandise to the firm, along with an invoice describing the

---

[16] If the supplier does not feel the firm is creditworthy, it can require that payment be made either before the goods are shipped (cash before delivery, or CBD) or on delivery of the merchandise (cash on delivery, or COD). These are cash sales and do not involve an extension of credit.

[17] These sources and criteria are discussed in Chapter 16.

contents of the shipment, the total amount due, and the terms of sale. When the firm accepts the merchandise shipped by the supplier, it in effect agrees to pay the amount due as specified by the terms of sale on the invoice. Once it has been established, trade credit becomes almost automatic and is subject to only periodic reviews by the supplier. Open account trade credit appears on the balance sheet as *accounts payable*.

Promissory notes are sometimes used as an alternative to the open account arrangement. When a company signs a **promissory note**, which specifies the amount to be paid and the due date, it is formally recognizing an obligation to repay the credit. A supplier may require a company to sign a promissory note if it questions the company's creditworthiness. Promissory notes usually appear on the balance sheet as *notes payable*.

Credit Terms

Credit terms, or terms of sale, specify the conditions under which a business is required to repay the credit that a supplier has extended to it. These conditions include the length and the beginning date of the credit period, the cash discount (if any) given for prompt repayment, and any special terms, such as seasonal datings.[18]

Cost of Trade Credit

Trade credit is considered a spontaneous source of financing because it normally expands as the volume of a company's purchases increases. For example, suppose a company experiences increased demand for its products. As a result, the company increases purchases from suppliers by 20 percent from an average of $10,000 per day to an average of $12,000 per day. Assuming that these purchases are made on credit terms of "net 30" and that the company waits until the last day of the credit period to make payment, its average accounts payable outstanding (trade credit) will automatically increase by 20 percent from $300,000 ($10,000 × 30) to $360,000 ($12,000 × 30).

Because trade credit is flexible, informal, and relatively easy to obtain, it is an attractive source of financing for virtually all firms, especially new and smaller firms. To make intelligent use of trade credit, however, a firm should consider the associated costs. Unlike other sources of financing, such as bank loans and bonds, which include explicit interest charges, the cost of trade credit is not always readily apparent. It may appear to be "cost-free" because of the lack of interest charges, but this reasoning can lead to incorrect financing decisions.

Obviously, someone has to bear the cost of trade credit. In extending trade credit, the supplier incurs the cost of the funds invested in accounts receivable, plus the cost of any cash discounts that are taken. Normally, the supplier passes on all or part of these costs to its customers implicitly as part of the purchase price of the merchandise, depending on market supply and demand conditions. If a company is in a position to pay cash for purchases, it may consider trying to avoid these implicit costs by negotiating lower prices with suppliers.

If the terms of sale include a cash discount, the firm must decide whether or not to take it. If the firm *takes the cash discount,* it foregoes the credit offered by the supplier beyond the end of the discount period. Assuming that the firm takes the cash discount and wants to make maximum use of the credit offered by suppliers, it should pay its bills on the last day of the discount period. Under these conditions, trade credit does represent a "cost-free" source of financing to the firm (assuming that no additional discounts are available if the firm pays cash on delivery or cash before delivery).

If a company *foregoes the cash discount* and pays bills after the end of the discount period, a definite opportunity cost of trade credit is incurred. In calculating the cost of not taking the cash discount, it is assumed that the company will make maximum use of extended trade credit by paying on the last day of the credit period. Paying after the

---

[18] This topic is discussed in Chapter 16.

end of the credit period, or *stretching accounts payable,* subjects the company to certain other costs.

The annual percentage rate of foregoing a cash discount is calculated using Equation 15.10. In this application, the APR is equal to the fractional interest cost per period times the number of borrowing periods per year:

$$(15.10) \quad \text{APR} = \frac{\text{Percentage discount}}{100 - \text{Percentage discount}} + \frac{365}{\text{Credit period} - \text{Discount period}}$$

For example, suppose the Benson Company has been extended $1,500 of trade credit from a supplier on terms of "2/10, net 30." As shown in Figure 15.7, the firm can either pay the discounted amount ($1,470) by the end of the discount period (day 10) or pay the full amount of the invoice ($1,500) by the end of the credit period (day 30).

By *not* paying on the tenth day—that is, by foregoing the cash discount—the company has the use of $1,470 (98 percent of the invoice amount) for an additional 20 days and effectively pays $30 in interest.[19] Substituting this information into Equation 15.10 yields the following:

$$\text{APR} = \frac{2}{100 - 2} \times \frac{365}{30 - 10}$$

$$= (2/98) \times (365/20)$$

$$= 37.2\%$$

As this example shows, the annual cost of foregoing cash discounts can be quite high. Therefore, when making financing decisions, a firm should compare this cost to the costs of other sources of credit.

Also, the company that offers credit terms of "2/10, net 30" should consider the annual percentage rate of having the use of funds for an additional 20 days. As the preceding calculation illustrates, the annual percentage rate of offering cash discounts when the credit terms are "2/10, net 30" is about 37 percent. Accordingly, a firm may want to consider other less-expensive methods of encouraging prompt payment of trade credit. However, other benefits may accrue to a firm that offers cash discounts. For

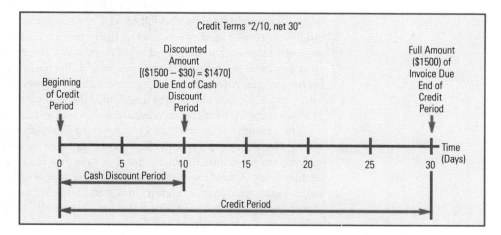

Figure 15.7
Benson Company's Cost of Foregoing the Cash Discount

---

[19] If a firm does not pay by the cash discount date, it should not pay the invoice until the final date. If the invoice is paid before the final due date, the cost of this financing increases dramatically. For example, assume Benson Company pays on day 11 and does not take the cash discount. The cost of this financing is nearly 745 percent.

example, a company may actually increase its sales by offering cash discounts. Or, a firm may find that its bad-debt loss ratio is lowered if it offers a discount.

Abuses of cash discounts also exist. For example, a purchaser may deduct the discount amount even when payment is made after the discount period has passed. As a result, the seller has to decide whether to simply accept the lower payment or attempt to collect the unearned cash discount amount. With either alternative, the seller incurs costs.

Stretching Accounts Payable

Rather than pay suppliers within the credit period specified in the terms of sale, a firm can postpone payment of the amount due to beyond the end of the credit period. Stretching payments in this manner generates additional short-term financing for the firm, but this credit is not cost-free. Not only does the firm incur the costs of foregoing any cash discounts, but its credit rating may also deteriorate, along with its ability to obtain future credit. Late payment penalties or interest charges may also be added to these costs, depending on specific industry practices. Although occasional stretching of payables—for example, to meet a seasonal need for funds—might be tolerated by suppliers and involve little or no cost to the firm, a firm that persistently stretches accounts payable well beyond their due dates may find its trade credit cut off by suppliers, who may adopt a cash before delivery (CBD) or a cash on delivery (COD) policy when dealing with the firm in the future. Finally, when a firm develops a reputation for being consistently slow in meeting financial obligations, banks and other lenders may refuse to loan funds on reasonable terms.

Accrued Expenses and Deferred Income

Accrued expenses and deferred income are additional spontaneous sources of un-secured short-term credit.

Accrued Expenses

Accrued expenses—such as accrued wages, taxes, and interest—represent liabilities for services rendered to the firm that have not yet been paid for by the firm. As such, they constitute an interest-free source of financing.

Accrued wages represent the money a business owes to its employees. Accrued wages build up between paydays and fall to zero again at the end of the pay period, when the employees receive their paycheques. A firm can increase the average amount of accrued wages by lengthening the period between paydays. For example, changing from a two-week pay cycle to a four-week pay cycle would effectively double a firm's average level of accrued wages. Also, a firm can increase accrued expenses by delaying the payment of sales commissions and bonuses. Legal and practical considerations, however, limit the extent to which a firm can increase accrued wages in this way.

The amounts of *accrued taxes* and *interest* a firm may accumulate is also determined by the frequency with which these expenses must be paid. For example, corporate income tax payments normally are due monthly for larger firms and quarterly for smaller firms. A firm can use accrued taxes as a source of funds between these payment dates. Similarly, accrued interest on a bond issue requiring semiannual interest payments can be used as a source of financing for periods as long as six months. Of course, a firm has no control over the frequency of these tax and interest payments, so the amount of financing provided by these sources depends solely on the amounts of the payments themselves.

Deferred Income

Deferred income consists of payments received for goods and services that the firm has agreed to deliver at some future date. Because these payments increase the firm's liquidity and assets—namely, cash—they constitute a source of funds.

Advance payments made by customers are the primary sources of deferred income. These payments are common on large, expensive products, such as jet aircraft. Because these payments are not "earned" by the firm until delivery of the goods or services to the customers, they are recognized on the balance sheet as a liability called *deferred income*.

Short-Term Bank Credit

Chartered banks are an important source of both secured and unsecured short-term credit. In terms of the aggregate amount of short-term financing they provide to business firms, they rank second behind trade credit. Although trade credit is a primary source of spontaneous short-term financing, bank loans represent the major source of negotiated short-term funds.

A major purpose of short-term bank loans is to meet the firm's seasonal needs for funds—such as financing the buildup of inventories and receivables. Bank loans used for this purpose are regarded as self-liquidating, because sale of the inventories and collection of the receivables are expected to generate sufficient cash flows to permit the firm to repay the loan prior to the next seasonal buildup.

When a firm obtains a short-term bank loan, it normally signs a promissory note specifying the amount of the loan, the interest rate being charged, and the due date. The loan agreement may also contain various protective covenants.[20] Short-term bank loans appear on the balance sheet under *notes payable*.

Prime Rate
The lowest rate normally charged by banks on loans made to their most creditworthy business customers.

The interest rate charged on a bank loan is usually related to the **prime rate**, which is the rate banks historically have charged on loans made to their most creditworthy, or *prime,* business customers. The prime rate fluctuates over time with changes in the supply of and demand for loanable funds. During the past 25 years, for instance, the prime rate ranged from as low as 4.5 percent to as high as 21.5 percent. In recent years many large, highly profitable companies have been able to borrow at less than the prime rate. Subprime borrowing is partially the result of increased competition among large banks and other suppliers of short-term financing for especially creditworthy borrowers.

As an alternative to borrowing funds in North America, large, well-established multinational firms can borrow short-term funds in the Eurodollar market.[21] The interest rate in the Eurodollar market is usually related to the **London Interbank Offer Rate**, or LIBOR. LIBOR is the interest rate at which banks in the Eurocurrency market lend to each other. For example, large, well-established multinational corporations usually can borrow at about 0.5 percentage points over LIBOR. Because LIBOR is frequently about 1.5 to 2.5 percentage points below Canadian bank prime rates, large firms can often borrow in the Eurodollar market at subprime rates. For example, in late 2001, the LIBOR rate was 1.9 percent, compared to an average Canadian prime rate of 4.00 percent. However, the LIBOR rate tends to be more volatile over time than the prime rate.

London Interbank Offer Rate (LIBOR)
The interest rate at which banks in the Eurocurrency market lend to each other.

Short-term bank financing is available under three different arrangements:

- Single loans (notes)
- Lines of credit
- Revolving credit agreements

Single Loans (Notes)

Businesses frequently need funds for short time periods to finance a particular undertaking. In such a case, they may request a bank loan. This type of loan is often referred to as a *note.* The length of this type of loan can range from 30 days to one year, with most being for 30 to 90 days.

---

[20] The section on term loans later in this chapter discusses these protective covenants.

[21] The Eurocurrency market is discussed in Chapter 2.

The interest rate a bank charges on an individual loan at a given point in time depends on a number of factors, including the borrower's creditworthiness relative to prime (lowest) credit risks. The interest rate often includes a premium of 1 to 2 or more percentage points above the prime rate, depending on how the bank officer perceives the borrower's overall business and financial risk. If the borrower is in a weak financial position and has overall risk that is thought to be too high, the bank may refuse to make an unsecured loan, regardless of the interest rate. When making the loan decision, the loan officer also considers the size of the chequing account balance the company maintains at the bank, the amount of other business it does with the bank, and the rates that competitive banks are charging on similar loans.

The stated interest rate of a bank loan is also a function of when the borrower must pay the interest.

Discounted Loan
A loan in which the bank deducts the interest in advance at the time the loan is made.

Interest Payments If the interest on a note is paid at *maturity*, the annual percentage rate is equal to the stated interest rate. In the case of a **discounted loan**, however, the interest is deducted at the time the loan is made, and thus the borrower does not receive the full loan amount. In other words, the borrower pays interest on funds it does not receive, and the annual percentage rate of the loan is greater than the stated interest rate.[22]

For example, suppose the Edge Gift Shop receives a six-month (183 day) $5,000 discounted loan at a stated interest rate of 8 percent. The firm pays $201 interest in advance ($0.08 \times \$5,000 \times 183/365$) and receives only $4,799 ($5,000 − $201). Using Equation 15.8, the annual percentage rate is calculated as follows:

$$APR = (\$201/\$4,799) \times (365/183) = 8.4\%$$

Discounted bank loans today are relatively uncommon. However, other securities—commercial paper and Treasury bills, for example—are sold on a discount basis.

Compensating Balance
A minimum (absolute or average) balance that a bank customer agrees to keep in its chequing account. This balance, which the bank can invest in interest-earning assets, compensates the bank for the services rendered to the customer.

Compensating Balances A **compensating balance** is a certain percentage, normally in the range of 5 to 20 percent, of a loan balance that the borrower keeps on deposit with a bank. Under the Bank Act, banks operating in Canada cannot require a compensating balance. However, the Bank Act permits a borrower to voluntarily suggest such a loan provision. For example, if a borrower felt that such a balance was needed for some other purpose anyway, then suggesting such a balance may lead to a lower stated annual percentage rate on a loan. Firms that borrow in the United States should be aware that banks operating there are permitted to require a compensating balance.

The compensating balance is stated either in terms of an *absolute minimum* balance or an *average* balance over some stipulated period. Borrowers prefer average balances to minimum balances. A compensating balance increases the return the bank earns on the loan and also provides the bank with a small measure of protection ("right of offset") in the event that the borrower defaults. Compensating balances tend to diminish in importance during periods of slack loan demand.

If the compensating balance is *in excess* of the amount of funds that normally would be maintained in the firm's chequing account, the actual annual percentage rate of the loan is greater than the stated annual percentage rate. It can be calculated using Equation 15.8. When the borrower maintains a compensating balance, the *usable funds* amount in the denominator is the *net* amount of the loan that the firm can spend after taking into account the amount borrowed, any compensating balance, and the balance normally maintained in the bank account.

---

[22] The process for determining the APR (sometimes called the annual financing cost or AFC) of a bank loan is a function of when the loan principal is repaid. The calculations in this section assume that the principal is repaid at maturity. In the case of *instalment* loans, principal payments are made periodically (e.g., monthly) over the term of the loan.

For example, suppose the Cutler Company obtains a one-year (365-day) $200,000 bank loan at 9 percent interest but agrees to maintain a 20 percent average compensating balance. In other words, the firm must maintain a $40,000 (0.20 × $200,000) average compensating balance to obtain the loan. If the firm currently maintains a $30,000 average balance that can be used to meet the compensating balance requirement, it needs to keep an additional $10,000 in the account, and thus the loan generates $190,000 in usable funds. The interest charges on the loan are $18,000 ($200,000 × 0.09). Substituting these values into Equation 15.8 yields the following:

$$APR = (\$18{,}000/\$190{,}000) \times (365/365) = 9.5\%$$

However, if Cutler currently has no balances in its bank account that can be used to meet the average compensating balance agreement, it has to keep $40,000 of the $200,000 loan in the chequing account, and the amount of usable funds is reduced to $160,000. In this case, the actual annual percentage rate becomes significantly higher:

$$APR = (\$18{,}000/\$160{,}000) \times (365/365) = 11.3\%$$

Lines of Credit

A firm that needs funds periodically throughout the year for a variety of purposes may find it useful to negotiate a line of credit with its bank. A **line of credit** is an agreement that permits the firm to borrow funds up to a predetermined limit at any time during the life of the agreement. The major advantage of this type of borrowing agreement, as compared with single loans, is that the firm does not have to renegotiate with the bank every time funds are required. Instead, it can obtain funds on short notice with little or no additional justification. Another advantage to establishing a line of credit is that the firm can plan for its future short-term financing requirements without having to anticipate exactly how much it will have to borrow each month.

A line of credit is usually negotiated for a one-year period, with renewals being subject to renegotiation each year. In determining the size of a credit line, a bank will consider a company's creditworthiness, along with its projected financing needs. As part of the application for a line of credit, the company is normally required to provide the bank with a cash budget for the next year, along with current and projected income statements and balance sheets. The interest rate on a line of credit is usually determined by adding to the prime rate a premium based on the borrower's creditworthiness. Because the prime rate normally fluctuates over time, the interest rate charged varies during the life of the agreement.

To illustrate, suppose the Bellevue Company has a $500,000 line of credit at 1 percentage point above the bank's prime rate.[23] During the year, the firm borrows, or "draws down," $200,000 on the line. The bank's prime rate is 8.0 percent from January 1 to March 31, and on April 1, the bank raises its prime rate to 8.25 percent, where it remains for the rest of the year. The annual interest costs are calculated as follows:

Interest costs (January 1–March 31):

$$I = \$200{,}000 \times 0.09 \times (90/365) = \$4{,}438.36$$

Interest costs (April 1–December 31):

$$I = \$200{,}000 \times 0.0925 \times (275/365) = \$13{,}938.36$$

Annual interest costs = $4,438.36 + $13,938.36 = $18,376.72

---

[23] Finance professionals often refer to this rate as "prime plus one," or "one over prime." In addition, they often write it as "P + 1."

A line of credit agreement normally includes certain protective covenants. The loan agreement may contain an annual "clean-up" provision requiring that the firm have no loans outstanding under the line of credit for a certain period of time each year, usually 30 to 90 days. This type of policy helps reassure the bank that the firm is using the line of credit to finance seasonal needs for funds and not to finance permanent capital requirements. Finally, a line of credit agreement may also contain provisions (similar to those in a term loan agreement) that require the firm to maintain a minimum working capital position, limit total debt and lease financing, and restrict dividend payments.

The KBK Capital Corporation provides information about working capital financing at **www.kbkcapital.com**

Revolving Credit Agreement
A binding agreement that commits a bank to make loans to a firm up to a predetermined credit limit. To obtain this type of commitment from a bank, a firm usually pays a commitment fee based on the unused portion of the pledged funds.

Revolving Credit Agreements

Although a line of credit agreement does not legally commit the bank to making loans to the firm under any and all conditions, the bank normally will feel morally obligated to honour the line of credit. Some banks, however, have chosen not to provide financing to a firm when the firm's financial position has deteriorated significantly or when the bank lacks sufficient loanable funds to satisfy all its commitments. If the firm desires a guaranteed line of credit, it must negotiate a committed revolving credit agreement.

Under a **revolving credit agreement**, or "revolver," the bank is *legally committed* to making loans to a company up to the predetermined credit limit specified in the agreement. Revolving credit agreements differ from line of credit agreements in that they often require the borrower to pay a *commitment fee* on the unused portion of the funds. This fee is typically in the range of 0.25 to 0.50 percent. Revolving credit agreements are frequently made for periods up to five years. For example, at the end of 2001, Bombardier had revolving credit agreements with various banks in the United States and Canada that permitted the firm to borrow up to US1.9 billion through at least mid-2005.[24]

Calculating the annual percentage rate of funds borrowed under a revolving credit agreement is slightly more complex than with either a single loan or a line of credit. In addition to the stated interest rate, commitment fee, compensating balance, and the firm's normal account balance, the annual percentage rate of a revolving credit loan also depends on the amount borrowed and the credit limit of the agreement. Thus, the annual percentage rate of the revolving credit agreement is usually higher than the stated interest rate.

Many financially sound companies view revolving credit agreements as a form of financial insurance, and, as a result, these companies frequently have little or no borrowings outstanding against the agreements. For example, in the case of Bombardier's revolving credit agreement mentioned earlier, the firm had only about half of it outstanding at the end of 2001.

Commercial Paper

Commercial Paper
Short-term unsecured promissory notes issued by major corporations with good credit ratings.

Commercial paper consists of short-term unsecured promissory notes issued by major corporations. Only companies with good credit ratings are able to borrow funds through the sale of commercial paper. Purchasers of commercial paper include corporations with excess funds to invest, banks, insurance companies, pension fund and money market mutual fund management firms, and other types of financial institutions.

Large finance companies, such as General Motors Acceptance Corporation (GMAC), issue sizable amounts of commercial paper on a regular basis, selling it directly to investors like those just mentioned. Large industrial, utility, and transportation firms, as well as smaller finance companies, issue commercial paper less frequently and in smaller amounts. They sell it to dealers who, in turn, sell the commercial paper to investors.

Maturities on commercial paper at the time of issue range from several days to a maximum of 365 days, although typical issues range from one month to three months.

---

24 Bombardier, *Annual Report* (2002): 89.

The size of an issue of commercial paper can range up to several hundred million dollars. It is usually sold to investors in multiples of $100,000 or more. Large issuers of commercial paper normally attempt to tailor the maturity and amounts of an issue to the needs of investors.

Commercial paper represents an attractive financing source for large, financially sound firms, because interest rates on commercial paper issues tend to be below the prime lending rate. To successfully market commercial paper, however, the firm normally must have unused bank lines of credit equal to the amount of the issue, as was the case in the Bombardier example discussed previously.

The primary disadvantage of this type of financing is that it is not always a reliable source of funds. The commercial paper market is impersonal. A firm that is suddenly faced with temporary financial difficulties may find that investors are unwilling to purchase new issues of commercial paper to replace maturing issues. In addition, the amount of loanable funds available in the commercial paper market is limited to the amount of excess liquidity of the various purchasers of commercial paper. During tight money periods, enough funds may not be available to meet the aggregate needs of corporate issuers of commercial paper at reasonable rates. As a result, a company should maintain adequate lines of bank credit and recognize the risks of relying too heavily on commercial paper. Finally, a commercial paper issue usually cannot be paid off until maturity. Even if a company no longer needs the funds from a commercial paper issue, it must still pay the interest costs.

Commercial paper is sold on a discount basis. This means that the firm receives less than the stated amount of the note at issue and then pays the investor the full face amount at maturity. The annual percentage rate of commercial paper depends on the maturity date of the issue and the prevailing short-term interest rates. In addition to the interest costs, borrowers also must pay a *placement fee* to the commercial paper dealer for arranging the sale of the issue. The actual annual percentage rate can be computed as follows, based on Equation 15.8:

$$(15.11) \qquad APR = [(\text{Interest costs} + \text{Placement fee})/\text{Usable funds}] \\ \times (365/\text{Maturity in days})$$

The usable funds are equal to the face amount of the issue less the interest costs and placement fee.

For example, suppose Hamilton Steel Company is considering issuing $10 million of commercial paper. A commercial paper dealer has indicated that the firm could sell a 90-day issue at a stated annual interest rate of 9.5 percent. The placement fee would be $25,000. Using Equation 15.11, the annual percentage rate of this commercial paper issue is calculated as follows:

$$\text{Interest costs} = \$10,000,000 \times 0.095 \times (90/365)$$

$$= \$234,247$$

$$APR = [(\$234,247 + \$25,000)/(\$10,000,000 - \$234,247 \\ - \$25,000)] \times [365/90]$$

$$= 10.79\%$$

Accounts Receivable Loans

Accounts receivable are one of the most commonly used forms of collateral for secured short-term borrowing. From the lender's standpoint, accounts receivable represent a desirable form of collateral, because they are relatively liquid and their value is relatively easy to recover if the borrower becomes insolvent. In addition, accounts receivable involve documents representing customer obligations rather than cumbersome physical assets. Offsetting these advantages, however, are potential difficulties. One disadvantage is that the borrower may attempt to defraud the lender by pledging nonexistent accounts. Also, the recovery process in the event of insolvency may be hampered if the customer who owes the receivables returns the merchandise or files a claim alleging that the merchandise is defective. Finally, the administrative costs of processing the receivables can be high, particularly when a firm has a large number of invoices involving small dollar amounts. Nevertheless, many companies use accounts receivable as collateral for short-term financing by either pledging their receivables or factoring them.

Pledging Accounts Receivable

The pledging process begins with a loan agreement specifying the procedures and terms under which the lender will advance funds to the firm. When **pledging accounts receivable**, the firm retains title to the receivables and continues to carry them on its balance sheet. However, the pledged status of the firm's receivables should be disclosed in a footnote to the financial statements. (Pledging is an accepted business practice, particularly with smaller businesses.) A firm that has pledged receivables as collateral is required to repay the loan, even if it is unable to collect the pledged receivables. In other words, the borrower assumes the default risk, and the lender has recourse back to the borrower. Both chartered banks and finance companies make loans secured by accounts receivable.

Once the pledging agreement has been established, the firm periodically sends the lender a group of invoices along with the loan request. On receipt of the customer invoices, the lender investigates the creditworthiness of the accounts to determine which are acceptable as collateral. The percentage of funds that the lender will advance against the collateral depends on the quality of the receivables and the company's financial position. The percentage normally ranges from 50 to 80 percent of the face amount of the receivables pledged. The company is then required to sign a promissory note and a security agreement, after which it receives the funds from the lender.

Most receivables loans are made on a *nonnotification basis*, which means the customer is not notified that the receivable has been pledged by the firm. The customer continues to make payments directly to the firm. To protect itself against possible fraud, the lender usually requires the firm to forward all customer payments in the form in which they are received. In addition, the borrower is usually subject to a periodic audit to ensure the integrity of its receivables and payments. Receivables that remain unpaid for 60 days or so must usually be replaced by the borrower.

The customer payments are used to reduce the loan balance and eventually repay the loan. Receivables loans can be a continuous source of financing for a company, however, provided that new receivables are pledged to the lender as existing accounts are collected. By periodically sending the lender new receivables, the company can maintain its collateral base and obtain a relatively constant amount of financing.

Receivables loans can be an attractive source of financing for a company that does not have access to unsecured credit. As the company grows and its level of receivables increases, it can normally obtain larger receivables loans fairly easily. Furthermore, unlike line of credit agreements, receivables loans usually do not have compensating balance or "clean-up" provisions.

The annual percentage rate of a loan in which receivables are pledged as collateral includes both the interest expense on the unpaid balance of the loan and the service fees charged for processing the receivables. Typically, the interest rate ranges from 2 to 5 percentage points over the prime rate, and service fees are approximately 1 to 2 percent of the amount of the pledged receivables. The services performed by the lender under a pledging agreement can include credit checking, keeping records of the pledged accounts and collections, and monitoring the agreement. This type of financing can be quite expensive for the firm.

Pledging of Accounts Receivable
A short-term borrowing arrangement with a financial institution in which a loan is secured by the borrower's accounts receivable.

The following example illustrates the calculation of the annual percentage rate of an accounts receivable loan: Suppose the PCP Corporation is considering pledging its receivables to finance a needed increase in working capital. Its bank will lend 75 percent of the pledged receivables at 2 percentage points above the prime rate, which is currently 10 percent. In addition, the bank charges a service fee equal to 1 percent of the pledged receivables. Both interest payments and the service fee are payable at the end of each borrowing period. PCP's average collection period is 45 days, and it has receivables totalling $2 million that the bank has indicated are acceptable as collateral. As shown in Table 15.5, the annual percentage rate for the pledged receivables is 22.8 percent.

Factoring Accounts Receivable

Factoring receivables involves the outright sale of the firm's receivables to a financial institution known as a factor. A number of so-called old-line factors, in addition to some finance companies (asset-based lenders), are engaged in factoring receivables. When receivables are factored, title to them is transferred to the factor, and the receivables no longer appear on the firm's balance sheet.

Traditionally, the use of factoring was confined primarily to the apparel, furniture, and textile industries. In other industries, the factoring of receivables was considered an indication of poor financial health. Today, factoring seems to be gaining increased acceptance in other industries.

The factoring process begins with an agreement that specifies the procedures for factoring the receivables and the terms under which the factor will advance funds to the firm. Under the normal factoring arrangement, the firm sends the customer order to the factor for credit checking and approval *before* filling it. The factor maintains a credit department to perform the credit checking and collection functions. Once the factor decides that the customer is an acceptable risk and agrees to purchase the receivable, the firm ships the order to the customer. The customer is usually notified that its account has been sold and is instructed to make payments directly to the factor.

Most factoring of receivables is done on a *nonrecourse* basis. In other words, the factor assumes the risk of default.[25] If the factor refuses to purchase a given receivable, the firm still can ship the order to the customer and assume the default risk itself, but this receivable does not provide any collateral for additional credit.

In the typical factoring agreement, the firm receives payment from the factor at the normal collection or due date of the factored accounts. This is called *maturity factoring*. If the firm wants to receive the funds prior to this date, it can usually obtain an advance from the factor. This is referred to as *advance factoring*. Therefore, in addition to credit checking,

Factoring
The sale of a firm's accounts receivable to a financial institution known as a factor.

Table 15.5 Cost of Pledging Receivables for PCP Corporation

$$\text{Usable funds} = 0.75 \times \text{Pledgeable receivables}$$
$$= 0.75 \times \$2,000,000$$
$$= \$1,500,000$$
$$\text{Interests costs} = \$1,500,000 \times 0.12 \times \frac{45}{365}$$
$$= \$22,192$$
$$\text{Service fee} = \$2,000,000 \times 0.01$$
$$= \$20,000$$
$$\text{APR} = \frac{\$22,192 + \$20,000}{\$1,500,000} \times \frac{45}{365}$$
$$= 22.8\%$$

---

[25] If the receivables are sold to the factor on a *recourse* basis, the firm is liable for losses on any receivables that are not collected by the factor.

collecting receivables, and bearing default risk, the factor also performs a lending function and assesses specific charges for each service provided. The maximum advance the firm can obtain from the factor is limited to the amount of factored receivables *less* the factoring commission, interest expense, and reserve that the factor withholds to cover any returns or allowances by customers. The reserve is usually 5 to 10 percent of the factored receivables and is paid to the firm after the factor collects the receivables.

The factor charges a factoring commission, or service fee, of 1 to 3 percent of the factored receivables to cover the costs of credit checking, collection, and bad-debt losses. The rate charged depends on the total volume of the receivables, the size of the individual receivables, and the default risk involved. The factor normally charges an interest rate of 2 to 5 percentage points over the prime rate on advances to the firm. These costs are somewhat offset by a number of internal savings that a business can realize through factoring its receivables. A company that factors all its receivables does not need a credit department and does not have to incur the administrative and clerical costs of credit investigation and collection or the losses on uncollected accounts. In addition, the factor may be able to control losses better than a credit department in a small- or medium-sized company due to its greater experience in credit evaluation. Thus, although factoring receivables may be a more costly form of credit than unsecured borrowing, the net cost may be below the stated factoring commission and interest rates because of credit department and bad-debt loss savings.

For example, the Masterson Apparel Company is considering an advance factoring agreement because of its weak financial position and because of the large degree of credit risk inherent in its business. The company primarily sells large quantities of apparel to a relatively small number of retailers, and if even one retailer does not pay, the company could experience severe cash flow problems. By factoring, Masterson transfers the credit risk to the factor, Partners Credit Corporation, an asset-based lender. Partners requires a 10 percent reserve for returns and allowances, charges a 2 percent factoring commission, and will advance Masterson funds at an annual interest rate of 4 percentage points over prime.[26] Assume the prime rate is 10 percent. Factoring receivables will allow the company to eliminate its credit department and save about $2,000 per month in administrative and clerical costs. Factoring will also eliminate bad-debt losses, which average about $6,000 per month. Masterson's average collection period is 60 days, and its average level of receivables is $1 million.

In Table 15.6, the amount of funds Masterson can borrow from the factor and the annual percentage rate of these funds are calculated. As the table shows, Masterson can obtain an advance of $859,748, and the annual percentage rate is 28.5 percent *before* considering cost savings and elimination of bad-debt losses. *After* considering credit department savings and reductions in bad-debt losses, the annual percentage rate drops to 17.2 percent. Masterson can compare the cost of this factoring arrangement with the cost of other sources of funds in deciding whether or not to factor its receivables. This example calculates the factoring cost for a single 60-day period. In practice, if Masterson did enter into a factoring agreement, the agreement would most likely become a continuous procedure.

Inventory Loans

Inventories are another commonly used form of collateral for secured short-term loans. They represent a flexible source of financing since additional funds can be obtained as the firm's sales and inventories expand. Like receivables, many types of inventories are fairly liquid. Therefore, lenders consider them a desirable form of collateral. When

---

[26] Although the reserve for returns is deducted when figuring the amount of usable funds advanced by the factor, it is not part of the cost of factoring, because the factor will return it to Masterson provided that the firm's customers make no returns or adjustments.

Table 15.6 Cost of Factoring Receivables for Masterson Apparel Company

Calculation of usable funds:

Average level of receivables		$1,000,000
Less Factoring commission	0.02 × $1,000,000	−20,000
Less Reserve for returns	0.10 × $1,000,000	−100,000
Amount available for advance before interest is deducted		$ 880,000
Less Interest on advance	(0.14 × $880,000 × 60/365)	−20,252
Amount of funds advanced by factor, or *usable funds*		$ 859,748

Interest costs and fees:

Interest costs	$ 20,252
Fee, or factoring commission	20,000
Total	$ 40,252

Calculation of annual percentage rate, *before* considering cost savings and bad-debt losses:

$$\text{APR} = \frac{\$40,252}{\$859,748} \times \frac{365}{60}$$

$$= 28.5\%$$

Calculation of annual percentage rate, *after* considering cost savings and bad-debt losses:

Credit department savings, per 60-day period	$ 4,000
Average bad-debt losses, per 60-day period	12,000
Total	$ 16,000

$$\text{APR} = \frac{\$40,252 - \$16,000}{\$859,748} \times \frac{365}{60}$$

$$= 17.2\%$$

judging whether a firm's inventory would be suitable collateral for a loan, the primary considerations of the lender are the type, physical characteristics, identifiability, liquidity, and marketability of the inventory.

Firms hold three types of inventories: *raw materials, work-in-process,* and *finished goods.* Normally, only raw materials and finished goods are considered acceptable as security for a loan. The physical characteristic with which lenders are most concerned is the item's *perishability.* Inventory subject to significant physical deterioration over time is usually not suitable as collateral.

Inventory items also should be *easily identifiable* by means of serial numbers or inventory control numbers. This helps protect the lender against possible fraud and also aids the lender in establishing a valid title claim to the collateral if the borrower becomes insolvent and defaults on the loan. The ease with which the inventory can be *liquidated* and the stability of its *market price* are other important considerations. In the event that the borrower defaults, the lender wants to be able to take possession, sell the collateral, and recover the full amount owed with minimal expense and difficulty.

Both banks and asset-based lenders make inventory loans. The percentage of funds that the lender will advance against the inventory's book value ranges from about 50 to 80 percent and depends on the inventory's characteristics. Advances near the upper end of this range are normally made only for inventories that are standardized, nonperishable, easily identified, and readily marketable. To receive an inventory loan, the borrower must sign both a promissory note and a security agreement describing the inventory that will serve as collateral.

In making a loan secured with inventories, the lender can either allow the borrower to hold the collateral or require that it be held by a third party. If the borrower holds the collateral, the loan may be made under a *floating lien* or *trust receipt* arrangement. If a third party is employed to hold the collateral, either a *terminal warehouse* or a *field warehouse* financing arrangement can be used.

Floating Liens

Floating Lien
An inventory loan in which the lender receives a security interest or general claim on all of a company's inventory.

Under a **floating lien** arrangement, the lender receives a security interest or general claim on the firm's entire inventory. This may include both present and future inventory. This type of agreement is often employed when the average value of the inventory items is small, the inventory turns over frequently, or both. Specific items are not identified. Thus, a floating lien does not offer the lender much protection against losses from fraud or bankruptcy. As a result, most lenders will not advance a very high percentage of funds against the book value of the borrower's inventory.

Trust Receipts

Trust Receipt
A security agreement under which the borrower holds the inventory and proceeds from the sale of the inventory in trust for the lender. This is also known as *floor planning*.

A **trust receipt** is a security agreement under which the firm holds the inventory and proceeds from the sale in trust for the lender. Whenever a portion of the inventory is sold, the firm is required to immediately forward the proceeds to the lender. These are then used to reduce the loan balance.

Some companies engage in inventory financing on a continuing basis. In these cases, a new security agreement is drawn up periodically, and the lender advances the company additional funds using recently purchased inventories as collateral.

All inventory items under a trust receipt arrangement must be readily identified by serial number or inventory code number. The lender makes periodic, unannounced inspections of the inventory to make sure that the firm has the collateral and has not withheld payment for inventory that has been sold.

Businesses that must have their inventories available for sale on their premises, such as automobile and appliance dealers, frequently engage in trust receipt financing, also known as *floor planning*. Many "captive" finance companies that are subsidiaries of manufacturers, such as General Motors Acceptance Corporation (GMAC), engage in floor planning for their dealers.

Terminal Warehouse and Field Warehouse Financing Arrangements

Terminal Warehouse Financing Agreement
A loan agreement in which the inventory being pledged as collateral is stored in a bonded warehouse operated by a public warehousing firm.

Under a **terminal warehouse financing arrangement**, the inventory being used as loan collateral is stored in a bonded warehouse operated by a public warehousing company. When the inventory is delivered to the warehouse, the warehouse company issues a warehouse receipt listing the specific items received by serial or lot number. The warehouse receipt is forwarded to the lender, who then advances funds to the borrower.

Holding the warehouse receipt gives the lender a security interest in the inventory. Because the warehouse company will release the stored inventory to the firm only when authorized to do so by the holder of the warehouse receipt, the lender is able to exercise control over the collateral. As the firm repays the loan, the lender authorizes the warehouse company to release appropriate amounts of the inventory to the firm.

Field Warehouse Financing Agreement
A loan agreement in which the inventory being pledged as collateral is segregated from the firm's other inventories and stored on its premises under the control of a field warehouse company.

Under a **field warehouse financing agreement**, the inventory that serves as collateral for a loan is segregated from the firm's other inventory and stored on its premises under the control of a field warehouse company. The field warehouse company issues a warehouse receipt, and the lender advances funds to the firm. The field warehouse releases inventory to the firm only when authorized to do so by the lender.

Although terminal warehouse and field warehouse financing arrangements provide the lender with more control over the collateral than it has when the borrower holds the inventory, fraud or negligence on the part of the warehouse company can result in losses for the lender. The fees charged by the warehouse company make this type of financing more expensive than floating lien or trust receipt loans. In a terminal warehouse arrangement, the firm incurs storage charges, in addition to fees for transporting the inventory to and from the public warehouse. In a field warehouse arrangement, the firm normally has to pay an installation charge, a fixed operating charge based on the overall size of the warehousing operation, and a monthly storage charge based on the value of the inventory in the field warehouse.

Overall warehousing fees are generally 1 to 3 percent of the inventory value. The total cost of an inventory loan includes the service fee charged by the lender and the warehousing fee charged by the warehousing company, plus the interest on the funds advanced by the lender. Any internal savings in inventory handling and storage costs that result when the inventory is held by a warehouse company are deducted in computing the cost of the loan.

Term Loans

A **term loan**, or intermediate-term credit, is defined as any debt obligation having an initial maturity between 1 and 10 years. It lacks the permanency characteristic of long-term debt. Term loans are well suited for financing small additions to plant facilities and equipment, such as a new piece of machinery. These loans can also be used to finance a moderate increase in working capital when

■ The cost of a public offering of bonds or shares is too high

■ The firm intends to use the term debt only until its earnings are sufficient to amortize the loan

■ The desired increase is relatively long term but not permanent

Term loans are often preferable to short-term loans because they provide the borrower with a certain degree of security. Rather than having to be concerned about whether a short-term loan will be renewed, the borrower can have a term loan structured in such a way that the maturity coincides with the economic life of the asset being financed. Thus, the cash flows generated by the asset can service the loan without putting any additional financial strain on the borrower.

Term loans also offer potential cost advantages over long-term sources of financing. Because term loans are privately negotiated between the borrowing firm and the lending institution, they are less expensive than public offerings of common shares or bonds. The issuing firm in a public offering must pay the registration and issue expenses necessary to sell the securities. For small- to moderate-sized offerings, these expenses can be large in relation to the funds raised.

Repayment Provisions

A term loan agreement usually requires that the principal be amortized over the life of the loan, which means that the firm is required to pay off the loan in instalments, rather than in one lump sum. Amortizing has the effect of reducing the risk to the lender that the borrower will be unable to retire the loan in one lump sum when it comes due. Amortization of principal is also consistent with the idea that term loans are not a permanent part of a firm's capital structure.

The **amortization schedule** of a term loan might require the firm to make equal quarterly, semiannual, or annual payments of principal and interest. For example, assume that Arrow Envelope Company borrows $250,000 payable over five years, with an interest rate of 10 percent per annum on the unpaid balance. The repayment schedule calls for five equal annual payments, the first occurring at the end of year 1.

Recall from Chapter 4 that the annual payment (PMT) required to pay off a loan can be computed using Equation 4.20:

$$(15.12) \qquad \text{PVAN}_0 = PMT(\text{PVIFA}_{i,n})$$

or

$$(15.12a) \qquad PMT = \text{PVAN}_0/\text{PVIFA}_{i,n}$$

In this example, substituting the present value of the annuity (PVAN_0) = \$250,000, the number of time periods (n) = 5, the interest rate (i) = 10 percent, and the $\text{PVIFA}_{0.10, 5}$ = 3.791 from Table IV into this equation yields an approximate annual payment of \$65,945.66. A more accurate solution, obtained with a financial calculator, is \$65,949.37.[27]

By making five annual payments of \$65,949.37 to the lender, Arrow will just pay off the loan and provide the lender with a 10 percent return. Part (a) of Table 15.7 shows the amortization schedule for this term loan.

Over the life of this loan, Arrow will make total payments of \$329,746.85. Of this amount, \$250,000 is the repayment of the principal, and the other \$79,746.85 is interest. It is important to know what proportions of a loan payment are principal and interest because interest payments are tax-deductible.

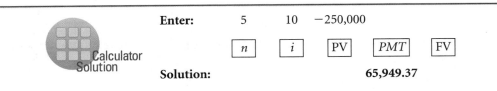

Enter: 5   10   −250,000

| n | i | PV | PMT | FV |

Solution: 65,949.37

Note: The solution obtained from Table IV differs slightly from the true payment because of rounding errors—the table is accurate to only three decimal places.

In this example, the repayment schedule calls for equal periodic payments to the lender consisting of both principal and interest. Other types of repayment schedules are also possible, including the following:

■ The borrower might be required to make equal reductions in the principal outstanding each period, with the interest being computed on the remaining balance for each period. Part (b) of Table 15.7 illustrates such a repayment schedule, where Arrow is required to repay \$50,000 of the principal each year.

■ The borrower might be required to make equal periodic payments over the life of the loan that only partially amortize the loan, leaving a lump sum payment that falls due at the termination of the loan period, called a **balloon loan**. Part (c) of Table 15.7 shows a repayment schedule requiring Arrow to repay one-half (\$125,000) of the term loan over the first four years, with the balance (\$125,000) due at the end of the fifth year.

■ The borrower might be required to make a single principal payment at maturity while making periodic (usually quarterly) interest payments only over the life of the loan, called a **bullet loan**. Part (d) of Table 15.7 lists the payments required to pay off this loan, given that Arrow is required to make only annual interest payments over the first four years of the loan with the principal (\$250,000) plus an annual interest payment due at maturity.

Balloon Loan
A loan that requires a large final payment greater than each of the periodic (principal and interest) payments.

Bullet Loan
A loan that requires only the periodic payment of interest during the term of the loan, with a final single repayment of principal at maturity.

---

[27] Chapter 4 provides an example of the calculation involved in an amortization schedule using a spreadsheet.

Table 15.7 Loan Amortization Schedules for Arrow Envelope Company

	End of Year (1)	Annual Payment (2)	Interest* (3)	Principal Reduction** (4)	Remaining Balance† (5)
(a) Equal Annual Payments	0	$ —	$ —	$ —	$250,000.00
	1	65,949.37††	25,000.00	40,949.37	209,050.63
	2	65,949.37	20,905.06	45,044.31	164,006.32
	3	65,949.37	16,400.63	49,548.74	114,457.58
	4	65,949.37	11,445.76	54,503.61	59,953.97
	5	65,949.37	5,995.40	59,953.47	0.00
	Total	$329,746.85	$ 79,746.85	$250,000.00	
(b) Equal Annual Reductions in Principal ($50,000 each year)	0	$ —	$ —	$ —	$250,000
	1	75,000	25,000	50,000	200,000
	2	70,000	20,000	50,000	150,000
	3	65,000	15,000	50,000	100,000
	4	60,000	10,000	50,000	50,000
	5	55,000	5,000	50,000	0
	Total	$325,000	$ 75,000	$250,000	
(c) Balloon Loan ($125,000 due at maturity)	0	$ —	$ —	$ —	$250,000.00
	1	51,933.85‡	25,000.00	26,933.85	223,066.15
	2	51,933.85	22,306.62	29,627.23	193,438.91
	3	51,933.85	19,343.89	32,589.96	160,848.95
	4	51,933.85	16,084.90	35,848.95	125,000.00
	5	137,500.00	12,500.00	125,000.00	0.00
	Total	$345,235.40	$ 95,235.41	$249,999.99‡‡	
(d) Bullet Loan ($250,000 due at maturity)	0	$ —	$ —	$ 0	$250,000
	1	25,000	25,000	0	250,000
	2	25,000	25,000	0	250,000
	3	25,000	25,000	0	250,000
	4	25,000	25,000	0	250,000
	5	275,000	25,000	250,000	0
	Total	$375,000	$125,000	$250,000	

*Interest each year is equal to 0.10 times the remaining balance from the previous year.
**Principal reduction each year equals the annual payment minus interest.
†Remaining balance each year is equal to the previous year's remaining balance minus principal reduction.
††$PMT = \$250,000/3.790786769 = \$65,949.37$.
‡$PMT = \$125,000/3.169865446 + \$125,000 \times 0.10 = \$51,933.85$.
‡‡Differs from $250,000 because of rounding error. If fractional cents were used, no rounding would be necessary.

Interest Costs

The interest rate charged on a term loan depends on a number of factors, including the general level of interest rates in the economy, the size of the loan, the maturity of the loan, and the borrower's credit standing. Generally, interest rates on intermediate-term loans tend to be slightly higher than interest rates on short-term loans because of the higher risk assumed by the lender. Also, large term loans tend to have lower rates than small term loans because the fixed costs associated with granting and administering a loan do not vary proportionately with the size of the loan. In addition, large borrowers often have better credit standings than small borrowers. An interest rate between 0.25 and 2.5 percentage points above the prime rate is common for term loans obtained from banks.

The interest rate on a small term loan is sometimes the same throughout the loan's lifetime. In contrast, most larger term loans specify a *variable* interest rate, which depends on the bank's prime lending rate. For example, if a loan is initially made at 0.5 percentage points above the prime rate, the loan agreement might specify that the interest charged on the remaining balance will continue to be 0.5 percentage points above the prevailing rate. Thus, whenever the prime rate is increased, the loan rate also increases. If the prime rate declines, so does the interest rate on the loan.

Security Provisions and Protective Covenants

The security provisions and protective covenants specified by a term loan agreement are often determined by the borrower's credit standing: The weaker the credit standing, the more restrictive the protective covenants.

Security Provisions

In general, security requirements apply more often to intermediate-term loans than to short-term loans, due to the fact that longer-term loan contracts tend to have more default risk. Security provisions are also dependent on the size of the borrowing firm. For example, term loans to small firms tend to be secured more often than term loans to large firms, although there is an increasing tendency for all bank-oriented term loans to be secured.

The sources of security for a term loan include the following:

- An assignment of payments due under a specific contract
- An assignment of a portion of the receivables or inventories
- The use of a floating lien on inventories and receivables
- A pledge of marketable securities held by the borrower
- A mortgage on property, plant, or equipment held by the borrower
- An assignment of the cash surrender value of a life insurance policy held by the borrower for its key executives

Affirmative Covenants

Affirmative Loan Covenant
A portion of a loan agreement that outlines actions a firm's management agrees to take as conditions for receiving the loan.

An **affirmative loan covenant** is a portion of a loan agreement that outlines actions the borrowing firm *agrees to take* during the term of the loan. Typical affirmative covenants include the following:

- The borrower agrees to furnish periodic financial statements to the lender, including a balance sheet, income statement, and a statement of cash flows. These may be furnished monthly, quarterly, or annually and frequently are required to be audited. Pro forma cash budgets and projections of the costs needed to complete contracts on hand may also be required.
- The borrower agrees to carry sufficient insurance to cover insurable business risk.
- The borrower agrees to maintain a minimum amount of net working capital (current assets less current liabilities).
- The borrower agrees to maintain management personnel who are acceptable to the financing institution.

Negative Covenants

Negative Loan Covenant
A portion of a loan agreement that outlines actions a firm's management agrees not to take during the term of the loan.

A **negative loan covenant** outlines actions that the borrowing firm's management agrees *not to take* without prior written consent of the lender. Typical negative covenants include the following:

- The borrowing firm agrees not to pledge any of its assets as security to other lenders, as well as not to factor (sell) its receivables. This type of agreement, called a *negative pledge clause,* is found in nearly all unsecured loans. It is designed to keep other lenders from interfering with the immediate lender's claims on the assets of the firm.

■ The borrower is prohibited from making mergers or consolidations without the lender's approval. In addition, the borrower may not sell or lease a major portion of its assets without written approval of the lender.

■ The borrower is prohibited from making or guaranteeing loans to others that would impair the lender's security.

Restrictive Covenants

Rather than requiring or prohibiting certain actions on the part of the borrower, **restrictive loan covenants** merely limit their scope. These are typical restrictive covenants:

■ Limitations on the amount of dividends a firm may pay

■ Limitations on the level of salaries, bonuses, and advances a firm may give to employees

These restrictions, in essence, force the firm to increase its equity capital base, thereby increasing the security for the loan.

Other restrictive covenants might include the following:

■ Limitations on the total amount of short- and long-term borrowing the firm may engage in during the period of the term loan

■ Limitations on the amount of funds the firm may invest in new property, plant, and equipment. (This restriction usually applies only to those investments that cannot be financed from internally generated funds.)

And, finally, a firm that has outstanding long-term debt may be restricted as to the amount of debt it can retire without also retiring a portion of the term loan.

These restrictions are quite common, but the list is not all-inclusive. For example, a standard loan agreement checklist published by a large bank lists 34 commonly used covenants. In general, covenants included in a loan agreement are determined by the particular conditions surrounding the granting of the term loan, including the credit record of the borrower and the maturity and security provisions of the loan.

Default Provisions

All term loans have default provisions that permit the lender to insist that the borrower repay the entire loan immediately under certain conditions. The following are examples:

■ The borrower fails to pay interest, principal, or both as specified by the terms of the loan.

■ The borrower materially misrepresents any information on the financial statements required under the loan's affirmative covenants.

■ The borrower fails to observe any of the affirmative, negative, or restrictive covenants specified within the loan.

A borrower who commits any of these common acts of default will not necessarily be called on to repay a loan immediately, however. Basically, a lender will use a default provision only as a last resort, seeking in the meantime to make some agreement with the borrower, such as working out an acceptable modified lending plan with which the borrower is more able to comply. Normally, a lender will call a loan due only if no reasonable alternative is available or if the borrower is facing near-certain failure.

Restrictive Loan Covenant
A portion of a loan agreement that limits the scope of certain actions a firm may take during the term of the loan.

Suppliers of Term Loans

There are numerous sources of term loans, including chartered banks, insurance companies, pension fund management firms, commercial finance companies, government agencies, and equipment suppliers. Many of these sources are discussed in the following subsections.

Chartered Banks

Most chartered banks are actively involved in term lending. For example, about one-third of all commercial and industrial loans made by chartered banks are term loans. However, the market share of the banks has declined as more firms have issued "junk" bonds, either publicly or in private placements.

In spite of this level of activity, banks generally tend to favour loans having relatively short maturities—that is, less than five years. Often banks will form *syndicates* to share larger term loans. This not only limits the risk exposure for any one bank but also complies with regulations that limit the size of *unsecured* loans made to single customers.

Life Insurance Companies and Pension Fund Management Firms

Whereas chartered banks tend to prefer shorter-term loans, insurance companies and pension fund management firms are more interested in longer-term commitments, for example, 10 to 20 years. As a result, it is common for a bank and an insurance company to share a term loan commitment. Under this type of arrangement, the bank might agree to finance the first five years of a loan, with the insurance company financing the loan for the remaining years. This arrangement also can be advantageous to the borrower because banks generally can charge a lower rate of interest for loans having shorter maturities.

From the borrowing firm's perspective, term loan agreements with pension fund and insurance companies have one significant limitation. If a firm decides to retire a term loan with a bank, it usually may do so without penalty. Because insurance companies are interested in having their funds invested for longer periods of time, however, prepayment of an insurance company term loan may involve some penalties.

Term loans from insurance companies and pension fund firms usually are secured, often with a mortgage on an asset, such as a building. These mortgage-secured loans are rarely made for amounts greater than 65 to 75 percent of the value of the collateral, however.

And, finally, term loans from life insurance companies and pension fund firms tend to have slightly higher stated rates of interest than bank term loans. This is because they are generally made for longer maturities.

Roughly seven months after securitizing its accounts receivables by selling them to investors, AT&T Canada was forced to buy the receivables back for the $100 million it received at the time of the sale. Unfortunately for AT&T Canada a clause that was part of the securitization agreement required that AT&T Canada repurchase the receivables if its debt experienced a significant downgrading. Such clauses, known as debt or rating triggers are often demanded by corporate lenders in order to lessen their risk should a company's credit quality deteriorate below investment grade. By March of 2002 both Moody's and Standard and Poor's gave AT&T Canada's bonds a Junk rating. Interest costs continued to rise for the firm at the same time as it was forced to refinance the receivables. AT&T Canada's troubles continued until it filed for protection from creditors in October 2002. Much of AT&T Canada's problems were the result of a CRTC commission decision that required the country's large established phone companies to cut the network access fees they charged smaller competitors. In April 2003, the firm was restructured as an independent company and renamed Allstream.

Summary

- *Net working capital* is the difference between current assets and current liabilities. The term *working capital* means current assets.

- A firm's *operating cycle* is equal to the sum of the inventory and receivables conversion periods. The *cash conversion cycle* is equal to the operating cycle less the payables deferral period.

- *Working capital policy* is concerned with determining the *aggregate amount* and *composition* of a firm's current assets and current liabilities.

- When the level of working capital is increased, both the expected profitability and the risk are lowered. Similarly, when the level of working capital is decreased, both the expected profitability and the risk are increased.

- When the proportion of short-term debt used is increased, both the expected profitability and the risk are increased. Similarly, when the proportion of short-term debt used is decreased, both the expected profitability and the risk are lowered.

- No single working capital investment and financing policy is necessarily *optimal* for all firms. To select the working capital policy that maximizes shareholder wealth, a financial manager should consider additional factors, including the inherent variability in sales and cash flows and the degree of operating and financial leverage employed.

- Short-term credit may be either *secured* or *unsecured*. In the case of secured credit, the borrower pledges certain assets (such as inventory, receivables, or fixed assets) as collateral for the loan. In general, firms prefer to borrow on an unsecured basis, because pledging assets as security generally raises the overall cost of the loan and also can reduce the firm's flexibility by restricting future borrowing.

- *Trade credit, accrued expenses,* and *deferred income* are the primary sources of spontaneous short-term credit. *Bank loans, commercial paper, accounts receivable loans,* and *inventory loans* represent the major sources of *negotiated* short-term credit.

- The *annual percentage rate, APR,* for a short-term credit source is calculated as follows:

$$APR = \frac{\text{Interest costs} + \text{fees}}{\text{Usable funds}} \times \frac{365}{\text{Maturity(days)}}$$

- Trade credit is extended to a firm when it makes purchases from a supplier and is permitted to wait a specified period of time before paying for them. It is normally extended on an *open-account* basis, which means that once a firm accepts merchandise from a supplier, it agrees to pay the amount due as specified by the terms of sale on the invoice.

- Short-term *bank credit* can be extended to the firm under a *single loan,* a *line of credit,* or a *revolving credit agreement.* A line of credit permits the firm to borrow funds up to a predetermined limit at any time during the life of the agreement. A revolving credit agreement legally commits the bank to provide the funds when the firm requests them.

- *Commercial paper* consists of short-term unsecured promissory notes issued by major corporations with good credit ratings.

- *Accounts receivable loans* can be obtained by either *pledging* or *factoring* receivables. In the case of a pledging arrangement, the firm retains title to the receivables, and the lender advances funds to the firm based on the amount and quality of the receivables. With factoring, receivables are sold to a factor, which takes the responsibility for credit checking and collection of the accounts. With pledging, the lender does not assume credit risk and has *recourse* back to the borrower if payment is not made, whereas factoring is normally a nonrecourse form of financing.

- Several types of *inventory loans* are available. In a *floating lien* or *trust receipt* arrangement, the borrower holds the collateral. In a floating lien arrangement, the lender has a general claim on all of the firm's inventory. In a trust receipt arrangement, the inventory being used as collateral is specifically identified by serial or inventory code numbers. In a *terminal warehouse* and a *field warehouse* arrangement, a third party holds the collateral. In the case of a terminal warehouse arrangement, collateral is stored in a public warehouse, whereas in a field warehouse arrangement, collateral is stored in a field warehouse located on the borrower's premises.

- No one source (or combination of sources) of short-term financing is necessarily optimal for all firms. Many other factors, in addition to the cost of financing, need to be considered when choosing the optimal source or sources of short-term financing. Some of these factors include the availability of funds during periods of financial crisis or tight money, restrictive covenants imposed on the firm, and the nature of the firm's operations and funds requirements.

- *Term loans,* or *intermediate-term credit,* include any debt obligation having an initial maturity between 1 and 10 years. Term loans are usually amortized by a series of instalments. The interest rate normally ranges between 0.25 and 2.5 percent above the prime rate. Many term loan agreements require that some specific asset be pledged as *security.* In addition, the borrowing firm may have to agree to certain *affirmative, negative,* and *restrictive covenants* governing its actions during the loan period.

Questions and Topics for Discussion

1. Why does the typical firm need to make investments in working capital?
2. Define and describe the difference between the operating cycle and cash conversion cycle for a typical manufacturing company.

3. Discuss the profitability versus risk trade-offs associated with alternative levels of working capital investment.

4. Describe the difference between permanent current assets and fluctuating current assets.

5. Why is it possible for the effective cost of long-term debt to exceed the cost of short-term debt, even when short-term interest rates are higher than long-term rates?

6. Describe the matching approach for meeting the financing needs of a company. What is the primary difficulty in implementing this approach?

7. Discuss the profitability versus risk trade-offs associated with alternative combinations of short-term and long-term debt used in financing a company's assets.

8. As the difference between the costs of short- and long-term debt becomes smaller, which financing plan, aggressive or conservative, becomes more attractive?

9. Why is no single working capital investment and financing policy necessarily optimal for all firms? What additional factors need to be considered in establishing a working capital policy?

10. a. Which of the following working capital financing policies subjects the firm to a greater risk?
    i. Financing permanent current assets with short-term debt
    ii. Financing fluctuating current assets with long-term debt
    b. Which policy will produce the higher expected profitability?

11. Define and discuss the function of *collateral* in short-term credit arrangements.

12. How is the annual percentage rate for a short-term financing source calculated? How does the annual percentage rate differ from the effective annual rate?

13. Under what condition or conditions is trade credit *not* a "cost-free" source of funds to the firm?

14. Explain the differences between a line of credit and a revolving credit agreement.

15. What are some of the disadvantages of relying too heavily on commercial paper as a source of short-term credit?

16. Explain the differences between pledging and factoring receivables.

17. Explain why the annual percentage rate of secured credit is frequently higher than that of unsecured credit.

18. What savings are realized when accounts receivable are factored rather than pledged?

19. Determine the effect of each of the following conditions on the annual percentage rate for a line of credit arrangement (assuming that all other factors remain constant):
    a. The bank raises the prime rate
    b. The bank lowers its compensating balance requirements
    c. The firm's average bank balance increases as the result of its instituting more stringent credit and collection policies

20. Under what condition or conditions, if any, might a firm find it desirable to borrow funds from a bank or other lending institution in order to take a cash discount?

21. Under what circumstances might a firm prefer intermediate-term borrowing to either long- or short-term borrowing?

22. Discuss the advantages and disadvantages of the following types of term loans:
    a. Those that require equal periodic payments
    b. Those that require equal periodic reductions in outstanding principal
    c. Balloon loans
    d. Bullet loans

23. What are the major factors that influence the effective cost of a term loan?
24. Define the following and give an example of each:
    a. Affirmative covenants
    b. Negative covenants
    c. Restrictive covenants
25. What institutions are the primary suppliers of business term loans?
26. Under what conditions would a firm prefer the following?
    a. A "fixed-rate" term loan from a bank
    b. A "floating-rate" term loan, with the rate tied to the bank's prime rate

Self-Test Problems

ST1. The Stowe Manufacturing Company's balance sheet and income statement for last year are as follows:

Balance Sheet (in Millions of Dollars)

Assets		Liabilities and Equity	
Cash and marketable securities	$ 887	Accounts payable	$ 724
Accounts receivable	2,075	Accrued liabilities	
Inventories*	2,120	(salaries and benefits)	332
Other current assets	300	Other current liabilities	1,665
Total current assets	$5,382	Total current liabilities	$2,721
Plant and equipment (net)	3,707	Long-term debt and other	
Other assets	687	liabilities	1,677
Total assets	$9,766	Common shares	296
		Retained earnings	5,082
		Total shareholders' equity	$5,378
		Total liabilities and equity	$9,776

*Assume that average inventory over the year was $2,120 million, that is, the same as ending inventory.

Income Statement (in Millions of Dollars)

Net sales*	$11,990
Cost of sales	6,946
Selling, general, and administrative expenses	2,394
Other expenses	581
Total expenses	$ 9,921
Earnings before taxes	2,069
Taxes	825
Earnings after taxes (net income)	$ 1,244

*All sales are credit sales.

Determine the length of Stowe's:
a. Inventory conversion period
b. Receivables conversion period
c. Operating cycle
d. Payables deferral period
e. Cash conversion cycle

ST2. Cranberry Company is considering the following two alternative working capital investment and financing policies:

	Policy A	Policy B
Current assets ÷ Sales	60%	40%
Short-term debt ÷ Total debt	30%	60%

Forecasted sales next year are $150 million. EBIT is projected to be 20% of sales. The firm's income tax rate is 40%. Fixed assets are $100 million. The firm wishes to maintain its current capital structure, which consists of 60% debt and 40% equity. Interest rates on the company's short-term and long-term debt are 10% and 14%, respectively.

a. Determine the expected rate of return on equity under each of the working capital policies.

b. Which working capital policy is riskier? Explain.

Note: Assume that there are 365 days per year when converting from annual to daily amounts or vice versa.

ST3. Determine the annual percentage rate of foregoing the cash discount under each of the following credit terms:

a. 2/10, net 120

b. 2/30, net four months (assume 122 days)

ST4. Determine the annual percentage rate of a nine-month (274-day), $25,000 discounted bank loan at a stated interest rate of 10.5%, assuming that no compensating balance is required.

ST5. The Chalfant Company is considering the use of commercial paper to finance a seasonal need for funds. A commercial paper dealer will sell a $25 million issue maturing in 91 days at a stated interest rate of 8.5% (deducted in advance). The fee to the dealer for selling the issue is $75,000. Determine the firm's annual percentage rate of this commercial paper issue.

ST6. The Bedford Furniture Company is considering factoring its receivables. Its average level of receivables is $4 million, and its average collection period is 70 days. Bedford's bad-debt losses average $9,000 per month. (Assume 30 days per month.) Factoring receivables will save the company $3,000 per month through the elimination of its credit department. The factor charges a 2% commission and requires a 10% reserve for returns and allowances. Bedford can borrow funds from the factor at 3 percentage points over the prime rate, which is currently 9%.

a. Determine the amount of usable funds Bedford can obtain by factoring its receivables.

b. Calculate the annual percentage rate associated with this arrangement.

ST7. Deseret Resources has received approval for a five-year term loan from a bank for $2 million at a stated interest rate of 8%. The loan requires that interest be paid at the end of each year on the balance remaining at the beginning of each year. In addition, a principal payment of $250,000 must be paid at the end of each of the first four years, with the remaining balance being paid off at the end of five years. The bank will charge Deseret a $50,000 loan-processing fee.

a. What payments are required at the end of each of the five years?

b. What is the effective, pretax cost of this loan?

Problems*

Note: Assume that there are 365 days per year when converting from annual to daily amounts or vice versa.

1. The Fisher Apparel Company balance sheet for the year ended 2006 is as follows:

December 31, 2006
(in Thousands of Dollars)

Assets		
Cash		$ 3,810
Marketable securities		2,700
Accounts receivable		27,480
Inventories		41,295
Plant and equipment	$64,650	
Less Accumulated depreciation	17,100	
Net plant and equipment		47,550
Total assets		$122,835
Liabilities and Shareholders' Equity		
Accounts payable		$ 14,582
Current portion of long-term debt		3,000
Accrued wages		1,200
Accrued taxes		3,600
Other current liabilities		2,200
Long-term debt		33,000
Common shares ($10 par)		19,500
Capital contributed in excess of par		15,000
Retained earnings		30,753
Total liabilities and shareholders' equity		$122,835

   a. What is Fisher's investment in current assets?

   b. Determine Fisher's working capital investment.

   c. Determine Fisher's current ratio.

   d. Determine Fisher's return on shareholders' equity if its 2006 earnings after tax are $10,000(000).

2. The Milton Company currently purchases an average of $22,000 per day in raw materials on credit terms of "net 30." The firm expects sales to increase substantially next year and anticipates that its raw material purchases will increase to an average of $25,000 per day. Milton feels that it may need to finance part of this sales expansion by *stretching* accounts payable.

   a. Assuming that Milton currently waits until the end of the credit period to pay its raw material suppliers, what is its current level of trade credit?

   b. If Milton stretches its accounts payable an extra 10 days beyond the due date next year, how much *additional* short-term funds (that is, trade credit) will be generated?

3. Determine the *annual percentage rate* of foregoing the cash discount under each of the following credit terms:

   a. 2/10, net 60

   b. 1.5/10, net 60

---

*Coloured numbers and letters denote problems that have "check" answers provided at the back of the book.

c. 2/30, net 60

d. 5/30, net four months (assume 122 days)

e. 1/10, net 30

4. Calculate the *effective annual rate* of foregoing the cash discount under each of the following credit terms:

a. 2/10, net 60

b. 2/10, net 30

5. Determine the *annual percentage rate* of foregoing the cash discount if the credit terms are "1/10, net 30" and the invoice is not paid until it is 20 days past due.

6. Determine the *annual percentage rate* of a one-year (365-day), $10,000 discounted bank loan at a stated annual interest rate of 9.5%. Assume that no compensating balance is needed.

INTERMEDIATE

7. Consider again the comprehensive example involving Burlington Resources (see Table 15.4). In this example, it was assumed that forecasted sales and expected EBIT, as well as the interest rates on short-term and long-term debt, were independent of the firm's working capital investment and financing policies. However, these assumptions are not always completely realistic in practice. Sales and EBIT are generally a function of the firm's inventory and receivables policies. Both of these policies, in turn, affect the firm's level of investment in working capital. Likewise, the interest rates on short-term and long-term debt are normally a function of the riskiness of the firm's debt as perceived by lenders and, hence, are affected by the firm's working capital investment and financing decisions. Recompute Burlington's rate of return on common equity under the following set of assumptions concerning sales, EBIT, and interest rates for each of the three different working capital investment and financing policies.

Policy	Forecasted Sales (in Millions of Dollars)	Expected EBIT (in Millions of Dollars)	Interest Rate STD(%)	LTD(%)
Aggressive	$ 98	$ 9.8	8.5	10.5
Moderate	100	10.0	8.0	10.0
Conservative	102	10.2	7.5	9.5

8. The Garcia Industries balance sheet and income statement for the year ended 2005 are as follows:

Balance Sheet
(in Millions of Dollars)

Assets		Liabilities and Shareholders' Equity	
Cash	$6.0	Accounts payable	$10.0
Accounts receivable	14.0	Salaries, benefits, and payroll taxes payable	2.0
Inventories*	12.0	Other current liabilities	10.0
Fixed assets, net	40.0	Long-term debt	12.0
	$72.0	Shareholders' equity	38.0
			$72.0

*The average inventory over the past two years also equals $12.0 million.

Income Statement (in Millions of Dollars)	
Net sales	$100.0
Cost of sales	60.0
Selling, general, and administrative expenses	20.0
Other expenses	15.0
Earnings after tax	$ 5.0

a. Determine the length of the inventory conversion period.
b. Determine the length of the receivables conversion period.
c. Determine the length of the operating cycle.
d. Determine the length of the payables deferral period.
e. Determine the length of the cash conversion cycle.
f. What is the meaning of the number you calculated in part e?

9. Wilson Company, a manufacturer of various types of electrical equipment, is examining its working capital investment policy for next year. Projected fixed assets and current liabilities are $20 million and $18 million, respectively. Sales and EBIT are partially a function of the company's investment in working capital—particularly its investment in inventories and receivables. Wilson is considering the following three different working capital investment policies:

Working Capital Investment Policy	Investment in Current Assets (in Millions of Dollars)	Projected Sales (in Millions of Dollars)	EBIT (in Millions of Dollars)
Aggressive (small investment in current assets)	$28	$59	$5.9
Moderate (moderate investment in current assets)	30	60	6.0
Conservative (large investment in current assets)	32	61	6.1

a. Determine the following for each of the working capital investment policies:
   i. Rate of return on total assets (that is, EBIT/total assets)
   ii. Net working capital position
   iii. Current ratio
b. Describe the profitability versus risk trade-offs of these three policies.

10. Reynolds Company is investigating the use of various combinations of short-term and long-term debt in financing its assets. Assume that the firm has decided to employ $30 million in current assets, along with $35 million in fixed assets, in its operations next year. Given this level of current assets, anticipated sales and EBIT for next year are $60 million and $6 million, respectively. The company's income tax rate is 40%. Shareholders' equity will be used to finance $40 million of its assets, with the remainder being financed by short-term and long-term debt. Reynolds is considering implementing one of the following financing policies:

Financing Policy	Amount of Short-Term Debt (in Millions of Dollars)	Interest Rate LTD(%)	STD(%)
Aggressive (large amount of short-term debt)	$24	8.5	5.5
Moderate (moderate amount of short-term debt)	18	8.0	5.0
Conservative (small amount of short-term debt)	12	7.5	4.5

    a. Determine the following for each of the financing policies:

       i. Expected rate of return on shareholders' equity

       ii. Net working capital position

       iii. Current ratio

    b. Evaluate the profitability versus risk trade-offs of these three policies.

11. Superior Brands, Inc. wishes to analyze the *joint impact* of its working capital investment and financing policies on shareholder return and risk. The firm has $40 million in fixed assets. Also, the firm's financial structure consists of short-term and long-term debt and common equity. Superior wishes to maintain a debt-to-total assets ratio of 50%, where debt consists of both short-term and long-term sources. The company's tax rate is 40%. The following information was developed for three different policies under consideration:

Working Capital Investment and Financing Policy	Investment in Current Assets (in Millions of Dollars)	Amount of STD (in Millions of Dollars)	Projected Sales (in Millions of Dollars)	EBIT (in Millions of Dollars)	Interest Rate LTD (%)	STD (%)
Aggressive	$56	$48	$118	$11.8	9.5	6.5
Moderate	60	36	120	12.0	9.0	6.0
Conservative	64	24	122	12.2	8.5	5.5

    a. Determine the following for each of the three working capital investment and financing policies:

       i. Expected rate of return on shareholders' equity

       ii. Net working capital position

       iii. Current ratio

    b. Evaluate the profitability versus risk trade-offs associated with these three policies.

12. Brakenridge Industries is considering the following two alternative working capital investment and financing policies:

	Policy A	Policy B
Current assets ÷ Sales	50%	40%
Short-term debt ÷ Total debt	40%	50%

    Forecasted sales next year are $30 million. EBIT is projected at 25% of sales. Fixed assets are $30 million. The firm's income tax rate is 40%. The firm desires to maintain its current capital structure, which consists of 50% debt and 50% equity. Interest rates on the firm's short-term and long-term debt are 9% and 12%, respectively.

    a. Determine the expected rate of return on equity capital under each of the working capital policies.

    b. Which working capital policy is riskier? Explain.

13. Van Buren Resources, Inc. is considering borrowing $100,000 for 182 days from its bank. Van Buren will pay $6,000 of interest at maturity, and it will repay the $100,000 of principal at maturity.
    a. Calculate the loan's effective annual rate.
    b. Calculate the loan's annual percentage rate.
    c. What is the reason for the difference in your answers to parts a and b?

14. The Pulaski Company has a line of credit with a bank under which it can borrow funds at an 8% interest rate. The firm plans to borrow $100,000 and has agreed with the bank to maintain a 15% compensating balance. Determine the annual percentage rate of the loan under each of the following conditions:
    a. The firm currently maintains $7,000 in its account at the bank that can be used as a compensating balance.
    b. The firm currently has no funds in its account at the bank that can be used as a compensating balance.

15. Wellsley Company has been approached by an investment dealer offering to sell an issue of commercial paper for the firm. The dealer indicates that the firm could sell a $5 million issue maturing in 182 days at an interest rate of 8.5% per annum (deducted in advance). The fee to the dealer for selling the issue would be $8,000. Determine the firm's annual percentage rate of this commercial paper financing.

16. Ranger Enterprises is considering pledging its receivables to finance a needed increase in working capital. Its bank will lend 75% of the pledged receivables at 1.5 percentage points above the prime rate, which is currently 12%. In addition, the bank charges a service fee equal to 1% of the pledged receivables. Both interest and the service fee are payable at the end of the borrowing period. Ranger's average collection period is 50 days, and it has receivables totalling $5 million that the bank has indicated are acceptable as collateral. Calculate the annual percentage rate for the pledged receivables.

17. The Eaton Company needs to raise $250,000 to expand its working capital and has been unsuccessful in attempting to obtain an unsecured line of credit with its bank. The firm is considering *stretching* its accounts payable. Eaton's suppliers extend credit on terms of "2/10, net 30." Payments beyond the credit period are subject to a 1.5% per month penalty. Eaton purchases $100,000 per month from its suppliers and currently takes cash discounts. For this problem, assume that a year consists of twelve 30-day months. Assuming that Eaton is able to raise the $250,000 it needs by stretching its accounts payable, determine the following:
    a. The firm's annual lost cash discounts
    b. Annual penalties
    c. The annual percentage rate of this source of financing

18. Which of the following credit terms would you prefer as a customer?
    a. 2/10, net 30
    b. 1/10, net 40
    c. 2/10, net 40
    d. 1/10, net 25
    e. Indifferent among all options
    Explain your choice.

19. The Odessa Supply Company is considering obtaining a loan from a sales finance company secured by inventories under a field warehousing arrangement. The firm would be permitted to borrow up to $300,000 under such an arrangement at an annual interest rate of 10%. The additional cost of maintaining a field warehouse is $16,000 per year. Determine the annual percentage rate of a loan under this arrangement if the firm borrows the following amounts:

a. $300,000

b. $250,000

20. Harpo Music Mart needs to raise $300,000 to increase its working capital. The bank, mindful of the firm's strained financial condition, has refused to loan the firm the needed funds. Harpo is considering *stretching* its accounts payable in order to raise the funds. Current credit terms are "3/10, net 30." Payments beyond the credit period are subject to a 1% per month penalty. Harpo purchases $125,000 per month from its suppliers and currently takes cash discounts. If Harpo is able to raise the $300,000 it needs by stretching its accounts payable, determine the annual percentage rate of this source of financing. For this problem, assume that a year consists of twelve 30-day months.

21. The Kittanning Company has a $2 million line of credit with its bank under which it can borrow funds at 1.5 percentage points above the prime rate (currently 9%). The company plans to borrow $1.5 million and has agreed with the bank to maintain a 10% compensating balance. Determine the annual percentage rate of the loan under each of the following conditions:

a. The firm currently maintains $100,000 in its account at the bank that can be used as a compensating balance.

b. The firm currently has no funds in its account at the bank that can be used as a compensating balance.

22. The Vandergrift Company has a revolving credit agreement with its bank under which the firm can borrow up to $5 million at an annual interest rate of 1 percentage point above the prime rate (currently 9%). The firm has agreed to maintain a 10% compensating balance on any funds borrowed under the agreement and to pay a 0.4% commitment fee on the unused portion of the credit line. Assume that Vandergrift has no funds in its account at the bank that can be used as a compensating balance. Determine the annual percentage rate of borrowing each of the following amounts under the credit agreement:

a. $1 million

b. $4 million

23. Titusville Petroleum Company is considering pledging its receivables to finance an increase in working capital. Its bank will lend the company 80% of the pledged receivables at 2 percentage points above the prime rate (currently 10%). The bank charges a service fee equal to 1.5% of the pledged receivables. The interest costs and the service fee are payable at the end of the borrowing period. Titusville has $2 million in receivables that can be pledged as collateral. The average collection period is 45 days. Determine the annual percentage rate of this receivables-backed loan.

24. NaftaFax has been granted a loan from a commercial finance company for $1 million at a stated interest rate of 10%. The loan requires that interest payments be made at the end of each of the next five years. At the end of five years, the entire loan balance must be repaid. The finance company requires NaftaFax to pay a $25,000 loan-processing fee at the time the loan is approved. What is the *effective* annual rate of this loan?

25. Greenwich Industries has forecasted its monthly needs for working capital (net of spontaneous sources, such as accounts payable) for 2003 as follows:

Month	Amount	Month	Amount
January	$7,500,000	July	$6,000,000
February	6,000,000	August	7,500,000
March	3,000,000	September	8,500,000
April	2,500,000	October	9,000,000
May	3,500,000	November	9,500,000
June	4,500,000	December	9,000,000

Short-term borrowing (that is, a bank line of credit) costs the firm 10% and long-term borrowing (that is, term loans) costs the company 12%. Any funds in excess of its monthly needs can be invested in interest-bearing marketable securities to yield 8% per annum.

a. Suppose the firm follows a *conservative* policy by financing the *maximum* amount of its working capital requirements for the coming year with long-term borrowing and investing any excess funds in short-term marketable securities. Determine Greenwich's *net* interest costs during 2003 under this policy.

b. Suppose the firm follows an *aggressive* policy by financing *all* of its working capital requirements for the coming year with short-term borrowing. Determine Greenwich's interest costs during 2003 under this policy.

c. Discuss the profitability versus risk trade-offs associated with these conservative and aggressive working capital financing policies.

26. Nguyen Enterprises is considering two alternative working capital investment and financing policies. *Policy A* requires the firm to keep its current assets at 65% of forecasted sales and to finance 70% of its debt requirements with long-term debt (and 30% with short-term debt). *Policy B,* on the other hand, requires the firm to keep its current assets at 40% of forecasted sales and to finance 40% of its debt requirements with long-term debt (and 60% with short-term debt). Forecasted sales for next year are $20 million. Earnings before interest and taxes are projected to be 15% of sales. The firm's corporate income tax rate is 40%. Its fixed assets total $10 million. The firm desires to maintain its existing financial structure, which consists of 50% debt and 50% equity. Interest rates on short- and long-term debt are 12% and 15%, respectively.

a. Determine the expected rate of return on equity next year for Nguyen under each of the working capital policies.

b. Which policy is riskier? Cite specific evidence to support this contention.

27. The Butler-Huron Company's balance sheet and income statement for last year are as follows:

Balance Sheet (in Millions of Dollars)

Assets		Liabilities and Equity	
Cash and marketable securities	$ 103	Accounts payable***	$1,166
Accounts receivable*	1,138	Accrued liabilities	
Inventories**	1,827	(salaries and benefits)	536
Other current assets	39	Other current liabilities	493
Total current assets	$3,107	Total current liabilities	$2,195
Plant and equipment (net)	3,523	Long-term debt and other	
Other assets	54	liabilities	2,736
Total assets	$6,684	Common shares	105
		Retained earnings	1,648
		Total shareholders' equity	$1,753
		Total liabilities and equity	$6,684

*Assume that all sales are credit sales and that average accounts receivable are the same as ending accounts receivable.
**Assume that average inventory over the year was the same as ending inventory.
***Assume that average acounts payable are the same as ending accounts payable.

Income Statement (in Millions of Dollars)

Net sales	$13,644
Cost of sales	9,890
Selling, general, and administrative expenses	2,264
Other expenses	812
Total expenses	$12,966
Earnings before taxes	678
Taxes	268
Earnings after taxes (net income)	$ 410

a. Determine Butler-Huron's cash conversion cycle.

b. Determine Butler-Huron's cash conversion cycle assuming that 75% of annual sales are credit sales (i.e., 25% represent cash sales).

c. Determine Butler-Huron's cash conversion cycle assuming that 50% of annual sales are credit sales.

28. Designer Textiles, Inc. is considering factoring its receivables. The firm's average collection period is 60 days, and its average level of receivables is $2.5 million. The firm's bad-debt losses average $15,000 per month. If the company factors its receivables, it will save $4,000 per month by eliminating its credit department. The factor has indicated that it requires a 10% reserve for returns and allowances and charges a 2.5% factoring commission. The factor will advance funds at 4 percentage points over prime, which is currently 8%.

a. Determine the annual percentage rate, *before* considering cost savings and bad-debt losses.

b. Determine the annual percentage rate, *after* considering cost savings and bad-debt losses.

29. DuBois Apparel Company is considering factoring its receivables. The firm's average level of receivables is $1.5 million, and its average collection period is 45 days. The firm's bad-debt losses average $8,000 per month, which it would not incur if it factored its receivables. (Assume 30 days per month.) Also, the company would save $4,000 per month in credit department costs if it factored its receivables. The factor requires a 10% reserve for returns and allowances and charges a

2% factoring commission. The firm can borrow funds from the factor at 3 percentage points over the prime rate (currently 9%). Determine the *net* annual percentage rate of this factoring arrangement.

30. Set up the amortization schedule for a five-year, $1 million, 9% loan that requires equal annual end-of-year *principal* payments plus interest on the unamortized loan balance. What is the *effective* annual rate of this loan?

31. Set up the amortization schedule for a five-year, $1 million, 9% bullet loan. How is the principal repaid in this type of loan? What is the *effective* annual rate of this loan?

32. A firm receives a $1 million, five-year loan at a 10% interest rate. The loan requires annual payments of $125,000 per year (at the end of each year) for years 1 to 4.
    a. What payment is required at the end of year 5?
    b. What would you call this type of loan?
    c. What is the *effective* annual rate of this loan?

33. A $10 million, five-year loan bears an interest rate of 7%. The loan repayment plan calls for five annual end-of-year payments. Each payment is to include an equal amount of principal repayment ($2 million per year) plus accrued interest. Set up the amortization schedule for this loan. Be sure to distinguish between the *interest* and the *principal* portions of each annual payment. What is the *effective* annual rate of this loan?

34. Mucklup Manufacturing Company has a two-year term loan for $200,000 at a stated annual rate of interest of 10%. Interest for the entire two-year period must be prepaid. That is, the loan's total interest payments must be made at the same time the loan is granted. Mucklup is required to repay the entire $200,000 principal balance at the end of the two-year period. Compute the *effective* annual rate of the loan.

35. The James Company has been offered a four-year loan from its bank in the amount of $100,000 at a stated interest rate of 10% per year. The loan will require four equal end-of-year payments of principal and interest plus a $30,000 balloon payment at the end of the fourth year.
    a. Compute the amount of each of the end-of-year payments.
    b. Prepare a loan amortization schedule detailing the amount of principal and interest in each year's payment.
    c. What is the *effective* interest rate on this loan? Prove your answer.

36. A $1 million loan requires five end-of-year equal payments of $284,333.
    a. Calculate the *effective* annual rate on this loan.
    b. How much interest (in dollars) is paid over the life of this loan?

37. A $10 million principal amount, three-year term loan carries an interest rate of 10%. All interest payments (which would normally be due at the end of each year) are deferred until the end of three years. The unpaid interest amount compounds at a 10% annual rate during the period(s) it remains unpaid. At the end of three years, the borrower must repay the principal amount, the deferred interest, plus interest on the deferred interest. The lender also charges a front-end loan origination fee on this loan of $100,000. Compute the *effective* annual rate of this loan.

Other Practice Materials and Resources

For interactive quizzes, Internet exercises, crossword puzzles, CTV videos, and more, go to the *Contemporary Financial Management* Web site at **http://cyr.nelson.com**

Current Asset Management

16

Learning Objectives

After studying this chapter you should be able to

1. Understand that companies hold liquid asset balances for several reasons, including

   a. To conduct transactions
   b. For precautionary reasons
   c. To meet future requirements
   d. For speculative reasons

2. Understand that the optimal liquid asset balance reflects risk and return trade-offs and is a function of the following:

   a. Holding costs, which are the opportunity returns the company could earn on these funds in their next best alternative use
   b. Shortage costs, which include possible lost cash discounts, deterioration of the company's credit rating, higher interest expenses, and financial insolvency

3. Understand that the primary objective in controlling cash collections is to reduce the delay between when the customer mails the payment and when it becomes a collected balance in the firm's bank account

4. Understand that the major methods for reducing collection time include

   a. Decentralized collection centres and concentration banking
   b. Special handling of large remittances

5. Understand that the primary objective in controlling cash disbursements is to slow payments and keep the firm's funds in the bank as long as possible

6. Understand that the major methods of slowing disbursements include

   a. Scheduling and centralizing payments (zero-balance systems)
   b. Maximizing cheque-clearing float
   c. Stretching payables
   d. Use of drafts rather than cheques

7. Understand that electronic funds transfer systems, including customer-directed computer movements of funds from one account to another, have the potential to greatly reduce the float in financial transactions

8. Understand that financial managers need to avoid overstepping the bounds of legal and ethical behaviour in making cash collection and disbursement decisions

9. Understand that the primary criteria the firm should use in selecting marketable securities include default risk, marketability (or liquidity), maturity date, and rate of return

10. Understand that *accounts receivable management* refers to the decisions

a business makes regarding its overall credit and collection policies and the evaluation of individual credit applicants

11. Understand that in formulating an optimal credit policy, a firm's financial managers must analyze the marginal benefits and costs associated with changes in each of the following:

    a. Credit standards
    b. Credit terms
    c. Collection effort

12. Understand that the evaluation of individual credit applicants consists of the following three principal steps:

    a. Gathering relevant information on the credit applicant
    b. Analyzing the information obtained to determine the applicant's creditworthiness
    c. Deciding whether to extend credit to the applicant and, if so, determining the amount of the line of credit

13. Understand that the determination of the optimal level of inventory investment requires that the benefits and costs associated with alternative levels be measured and compared

14. Understand that the use of inventory control models can aid in efficiently managing a company's level of inventory investment

15. Understand that the economic order quantity model permits determination of the quantity of an inventory item that should be ordered to minimize total inventory costs

How Canada's Banks Stack Up in Terms of Cash[1]

COURTESY OF RBC ROYAL BANK

In June 2002, the Bank of Nova Scotia listed its shares on the New York Stock Exchange, one of the last of Canada's Big Six banks to do so. Over the past few years, Canada's largest banks have become very eager acquirers of US-based financial services and assets as they look for opportunities for increased growth and diversification. Indeed, the banking industry in Canada is fairly competitive and hence Canada's Big Six banks have been pressured by increased global market competition to diversify south. The United States' far-larger population and relatively fragmented banking industry is very appealing as an area of potential growth.

In 1998, CIBC bought Oppenheimer & Co. for $525 million for an entry into mutual funds and full services brokerage. More recently, the Royal Bank of Canada picked up Barclays Bank's $2.9 billion of private banking assets in the United States and Latin America. For these, and purchases made by other Canadian banks, cash has been the primary currency.

The table below shows the relative size of Canada's six major banks as of June 2002 and in particular the size of cash holdings both in dollar value and as a percentage of total assets. It would appear that the Bank of Montreal, the Bank of Nova Scotia, and the National Bank of Canada were all maintaining relatively large cash balances as of that time, perhaps in anticipation of potential purchases of US and other international banking assets.

Size of Canada's Major Banks and Cash Balances as of June 2002						
Company	Market Value ($Bil)	Assets ($Bil)	Income ($Mil)	Cash ($Bil)	Cash/Total Assets	Employees
Royal Bank of Canada	38.9	362.5	2,421.8	1.8	0.51%	49,232
Bank of Montreal	18.4	239.4	1,051.5	17.9	7.49%	33,200
Canadian Imperial Bank of Commerce	18.2	287.6	1,198.7	1.4	0.48%	44,793
Toronto-Dominion Bank	23.3	287.9	1,011.6	6.4	2.24%	32,000
Bank of Nova Scotia	27.0	297.1	1,768.9	20.8	7.02%	46,804
National Bank of Canada	6.2	74.6	429.4	6.9	9.55%	17,235

As we saw in the discussion of dividend policy (Chapter 14), one theory (i.e., the passive residual policy) suggests that if a firm has more funds than it needs for investments in its business, it should either pay out these funds as cash dividends to shareholders or use the funds to buy back its common shares from time to time. Rather than return these funds to its shareholders, Canada's banks have been using their cash hoards for investment in US companies. In addition to buying entire companies, they have also been purchasing specific lines of business in the US financial services industry, buying their way into new markets and diversifying away risks associated with their domestic market. Whether these investments will be beneficial to the banks' shareholders over the long term remains to be seen.

---

[1] Based on A. Weinberg, "A Maple Leaf for Finance," June 10, 2002, www.Forbes.com

Some analysts have suggested that the prices that Canadian banks have paid for their US assets have been too high.

Determining a firm's appropriate liquid asset balance involves risk versus return trade-offs. The factors that must be considered in determining a firm's optimal cash and marketable securities balance are examined in this chapter.

Introduction

Cash and marketable securities are the most liquid of a company's assets. *Cash* is the sum of the currency a company has on hand and the funds on deposit in bank chequing accounts. Cash is the medium of exchange that permits management to carry on the various functions of the business organization. In fact, the survival of a firm can depend on the availability of cash to meet financial obligations on time. *Marketable securities* consist of short-term investments a firm makes with its temporarily idle cash. Marketable securities can be sold quickly and converted into cash when needed. Unlike cash, however, marketable securities provide a firm with interest income.

Effective cash and marketable securities management is important in contemporary companies, government agencies, and not-for-profit enterprises. Corporate treasurers continually seek ways to increase the yields on their liquid cash and marketable security reserves. Traditionally, these liquid reserves were invested almost exclusively in Treasury bills, commercial paper, and repurchase agreements (short-term loans backed by Treasury securities). However, in recent years many treasurers have shown a willingness to take some additional risks to increase the return on liquid assets. Financial managers constantly face these types of risk-return trade-offs.

Many firms hold significant cash and marketable securities balances. These cash balances give the firm a cushion to handle economic downturns and the ability to make investments in other firms when the price is attractive. Large cash balances can make firms attractive takeover targets for corporate raiders, who seek to redeploy these surplus funds in more productive ways.

In addition to managing the cash and marketable securities already in the firm's possession, financial managers also aggressively seek to speed up cash collections from customers and to slow down disbursements to suppliers.

Cash management involves much more than simply paying bills and receiving payments for goods and services. In addition to the process of cash budgeting covered in Chapter 3, the cash management function is also concerned with determining

- The optimal size of a firm's liquid asset balance
- The most efficient methods of controlling the collection and disbursement of cash
- The appropriate types and amounts of short-term investments a firm should make

Cash management decisions require a firm's managers to consider explicitly the risk versus expected return trade-offs from alternative policies. Because cash and marketable securities generally earn low rates of return relative to a firm's other assets, a firm can increase its expected return on assets and common equity by minimizing its investment in cash and marketable securities. However, a firm that carries a bare minimum of liquid assets exposes itself to the risk that it will run out of cash needed to keep the business operating. Also, a firm with extremely low cash balances may not be able to take advantage of unique investment opportunities when they arise.

In the first half of this chapter, we review the various cash management decisions that must be made by financial managers.[2] Our analysis considers the risk versus expected return trade-offs characteristic of these decisions. In the second half of this chapter, we consider other important investments for most companies: accounts receivable and inventories.

Liquid Asset Balance

Firms hold liquid asset balances for a number of reasons, including the following:

- First, because cash inflows and outflows of the day-to-day operations of a firm are not perfectly synchronized, liquid asset balances are necessary to serve as a buffer between these flows. This reason is the *transactions motive*. Liquid asset balances help a firm handle seasonal fluctuations in cash flows. For example, a firm may wish to hold a large amount of liquid assets during surplus months and "draw down" on them during deficit months.

- Second, because future cash flows and the ability to borrow additional funds on short notice are often uncertain, liquid asset balances are necessary to meet unexpected requirements for cash. This is the *precautionary motive*.

- Third, liquid asset balances are held to meet *future requirements*, which include fixed outlays required on specific dates, such as quarterly dividend and tax payments, capital expenditures, and repayments of loans or bond issues. A firm also may hold as liquid assets the proceeds from a new debt or equity securities offering prior to using these funds for expansion.

- Fourth, firms often hold liquid assets for *speculative reasons*. Some firms build up large cash balances in preparation for major acquisitions. Large cash balances give firms timing flexibility in pursuing acquisitions.

Optimal Liquid Asset Balance

When a firm holds liquid asset balances, whether in the form of currency, bank demand deposits, or marketable securities, in effect it is investing these funds. To determine the optimal investment in liquid assets, a firm must weigh the benefits and costs of holding these various balances. The determination of an optimal liquid asset balance reflects the classic *risk versus return* trade-off facing financial managers. Because liquid assets earn relatively low rates of return, a firm can increase its profitability in relation to its asset base by minimizing liquid asset balances. However, low liquid asset balances expose a firm to the risk of not being able to meet its obligations as they come due. Effective cash management calls for a careful balancing of the risk and return aspects of cash management.

The opportunity cost of excess liquid assets, held in the form of bank deposits, is the return the firm could earn on these funds in their next best use, such as in the expansion of other current or fixed assets. The net opportunity cost of liquid asset balances, held in the form of marketable securities, is the income that could be earned on these funds in their next best alternative use less the interest income received on the marketable securities.

Given the opportunity cost of holding liquid asset balances, why would a firm ever maintain a positive bank balance? The answer is that these balances help the firm avoid the "shortage" costs associated with inadequate liquid asset balances.

Shortage costs can take many different forms, including the following:

- Foregone cash discounts
- Deterioration of the firm's credit rating

---

[2] Chapter 3 contains a discussion of how cash budgets are developed.

- Higher interest expenses
- Possible financial insolvency

Many suppliers offer customers a cash discount for prompt payment. Having to forego this cash discount can be quite costly to a firm. In addition, the creditworthiness of a firm is determined at least partially by the current and quick ratios—both of which can be affected by an inadequate liquid asset balance. This, in turn, can cause a firm's credit rating to deteriorate and make loans on favourable terms more difficult to secure in the future. The credit rating also can fall if a firm fails to pay bills on time because of inadequate cash. This can make future credit difficult to obtain from suppliers. If a firm has inadequate liquid asset reserves, it may have to meet unforeseen needs for cash by short-term borrowing, and it may be unable to negotiate for the best terms—including the lowest possible interest rate—if its credit rating is questionable. Inadequate liquid asset balances may cause a firm to incur high transactions costs when converting illiquid assets into cash. Finally, an inadequate liquid asset balance increases a firm's risk of insolvency, because a serious recession or natural disaster would be more likely to reduce the firm's cash inflows to the point where it could not meet contractual financial obligations.

An inverse relationship exists between a firm's liquid asset balance and these shortage costs: The larger a firm's liquid asset balance, the smaller its associated shortage costs. The opportunity holding costs, in contrast, increase as a firm's liquid asset balance is increased. As shown in Figure 16.1, the optimal liquid asset balance occurs at the point where the sum of the opportunity holding costs and the shortage costs is minimized. Admittedly, many of these shortage costs are difficult to measure. Nevertheless, a firm should attempt to evaluate the trade-offs among these costs in order to economize on cash holdings.

The Practice of Liquidity Management

In practice, a wide variety of liquidity policies are found to exist among firms. Liquidity, as measured by the ratio of cash and marketable securities to total assets, varies significantly among industries and among firms within an industry. Utility firms, retailers, and service industry establishments, such as restaurants, tend to hold relatively lower liquid asset balances as a proportion of total assets than do firms in the automotive and computer industries.

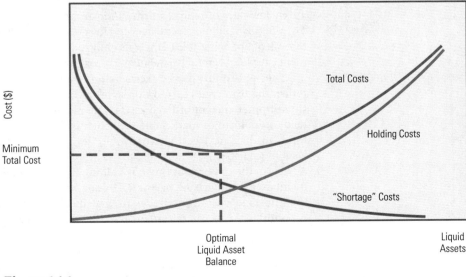

Figure 16.1
Optimal Liquid Asset Balance

In general, it can be observed that larger firms tend to hold lower liquid asset balances (relative to total assets) than smaller firms. This is because larger firms tend to have better access to "backup" short-term financing from banks or the commercial paper market. Because smaller firms have more limited credit access, they tend to hold greater liquid asset balances as a cushion against uncertain future needs for funds.

Controlling the Collection and Disbursement of Cash

The cash collection and disbursement processes provide a firm two areas in which it can economize on cash holdings. For example, the sales of Magna, the Canadian auto parts company, average about $5 million per business day. If the firm can speed up collections by only *one* day, the cash balance will increase by $5 million, and these released funds can be invested in other current assets or in fixed assets. If this additional cash can be invested to yield a 5 percent return, it will generate added income of $250,000 per year (5% × $5 million).

Cash collection and disbursement policies are designed to reduce a firm's liquid asset balances (cash and marketable securities) by exploiting imperfections in the collection and payment process. The objective is to speed up collections and slow down disbursements. Financial managers should be aware that policies designed to speed up collections and slow down disbursements are highly competitive. If all firms were to employ the same procedures, the net benefit would be zero. Thus, incremental benefits associated with procedures designed to control collections and disbursements will accrue only to the most aggressive and progressive firms. Similarly, cash managers who do not do at least as much as the average firm in speeding up collections and slowing disbursements will find their firms at a competitive disadvantage.

The primary objective of cash collection involves expediting collections by reducing the lag between the time customers pay their bills and the time the cheques are collected. In contrast, the primary objective of cash disbursement is to slow payments so that the firm can keep the funds invested or in the bank as long as possible. Expediting collections and slowing disbursements help increase a firm's cash balance and provide it with funds to use for other profitable investments. Policies designed to control collections and disbursements take advantage of the float present in the payment and disbursement system.

Float

Float

The difference between an account balance as shown on the bank's books and as shown on the firm's books. Float represents the net effect of the delays in the payment of cheques the firm writes and the collection of cheques the firm receives.

A firm's cash balance as shown on the bank's books generally differs from that shown on the firm's own books. This difference is known as **float** and represents the net effect of the delays in the payment of cheques a firm writes and the collection of cheques a firm receives. Cheques written by a firm result in *disbursement,* or *positive,* float. That is, an excess of bank net collected balances over the balances shown on a firm's books. In contrast, *collection float,* or *negative float,* arises from the delay between the time a customer writes a cheque to a supplier or other payee and the time the payee actually receives these funds as collected balances (which are spendable). Action being taken by the Bank of Canada and the rapid progress being made with electronic payment systems means that float will be less important over time. However, until these developments virtually eliminate float, financial managers must understand the sources of float so that they can take legal actions to benefit from it.

There are three primary components, or sources, of float:

1. *Mail float* is the delay between the time a payment is sent to the payee through the mail and the time that payment arrives at the payee's office.

2. *Processing float* represents the delay between receipt of payment from a payer and the deposit of that receipt in the payee's account.

3. *Availability (cheque-clearing) float* is the delay between the time a cheque is deposited in the payee's account and the time the funds are available to be spent. Cheques processed in the Canadian banking system normally "clear" in one day or less, although the depositor's bank may not make the funds available quite that fast, especially during weekends.

Expediting Collections

Figure 16.2 illustrates the main steps in the cash collection process. The total time involved in this process is a combination of mailing (float) time, processing (float) time, and availability (float) time, each of which may vary depending on where the firm's customers and their respective banks are located. Some methods available for reducing the collection float are discussed in the following paragraphs.

Decentralized Collection Centres and Concentrator Accounts   Cash collection systems can be either *centralized* or *decentralized*. In the centralized system, customers are instructed to send their payments to the firm's headquarters. In the *decentralized* system, customers mail their payments to a nearby collection centre, which is strategically located to minimize mail delay. The collection centre then deposits the cheques in a local branch of the firm's bank and reports this information to the firm's headquarters. Each business day, funds in excess of the desired balance are transferred to a **concentrator account,** where the firm maintains a disbursement account on which cheques are written.

A trade-off exists between the number of collection centres and the potential savings realized. The more collection centres used, the less time is required to convert customers' cheques into collected balances. However, these savings from faster collections are offset by costs involved in compensating the bank for these services. Financial managers must weigh the trade-offs involved in both savings and costs in deciding on the appropriate number and location of collection centres.

Lockboxes   A **lockbox** is a post office box maintained at a strategic location for the purpose of receiving a firm's remittances. Customers mail payments to this post office box, which is usually no more than a few hundred miles away. The local bank branch empties the box several times each working day, deposits the payments in the firm's account, puts the cheques into the clearing system, and sends the firm a list of the payments received each day. Not only does the lockbox reduce mailing time, it also eliminates company processing time because the cheques are deposited and begin the clearing process *before* the firm's accounting department processes the payments

Concentrator Accounts
The use of decentralized collection centres to collect customer payments and forward the funds to the concentrator account. This speeds up a firm's collections.

Lockbox
A post office box maintained by a firm's bank close to customers to speed up the collection of payments from customers.

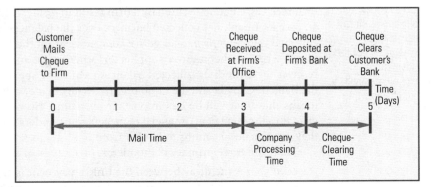

Figure 16.2
Cash Collection Process

received, rather than after processing them. The bank normally charges a fee for this service. Excess funds are usually transferred each day to a concentrator account.

The decision to establish a lockbox collection system requires a comparison of the associated benefits and costs. If the earnings on the funds released by the acceleration of collections exceed the costs of the lockbox service, the establishment of a lockbox collection system is profitable.

If the number of cheques handled is small and the dollar amount of each cheque is large, a lockbox arrangement is very beneficial to the firm. Under these conditions the bank's workload is light, and the associated costs are small. However, when large numbers of cheques with small dollar amounts are involved—for example, in the case of oil company credit cards—a lockbox system may not be profitable. Under these conditions, the costs may exceed the earnings the firm realizes from having the funds available a few days earlier.

Special Handling of Large Remittances Firms that receive individual remittances in the multimillion-dollar range may find it more profitable to use special courier services to pick up these cheques from customers (rather than having their customers mail the cheques) and present them to their bank for collection.

Slowing Disbursements

Several ways in which a firm can slow disbursements and keep funds in the bank for longer periods of time are discussed in the following paragraphs.

Scheduling and Centralizing Payments A firm should pay bills *on time*—not before or after they are due. There is no significant benefit to be received by paying bills before they are actually due, unless a cash discount is offered for early payment.[3] Payments made ahead of time lower the firm's average cash balance, whereas late payments can impair the firm's credit rating.

Centralizing payments from a master or concentrator account helps minimize the amount of idle funds a firm keeps in local field offices and divisional bank accounts. A number of firms have set up zero-balance systems to use disbursement float more effectively. In a **zero-balance system**, a master account is set up to receive all deposits coming into the zero-balance system. As cheques clear through the zero-balance accounts on which they are issued, funds are transferred to these accounts from the master account. These disbursement accounts are called zero-balance accounts because exactly enough funds are transferred into them daily to cover the cheques that have cleared, leaving a zero balance at the end of the day. In general, all disbursements for accounts payable, payroll, and whatever other purposes the firm desires are issued from these zero-balance accounts. For a zero-balance system to operate effectively, a firm must have a well-developed network for reporting deposits and disbursements, as well as a close working relationship with its bank. In making the decision to put into effect a more efficient cash disbursement system, such as a zero-balance system, a firm's financial managers need to compare the returns that can be earned on released funds to the cost of implementing the system.

Drafts A **draft** is similar to a cheque, except that it is not payable on demand. Instead, when a draft is transmitted to a firm's bank for collection, the bank must present the draft to the firm for acceptance before making payment. In practice, individual drafts are considered to be legally paid automatically by the bank on the business day following the day of presentation to the firm, unless the firm returns a draft and explicitly requests that it not be paid. Once the draft has been presented, the firm must immediately deposit the necessary funds to cover the payment.

Zero-Balance System
A payment system that uses a master disbursing account that services all other disbursing accounts. A zero balance is maintained in all but the master account until payments must be made.

Draft
A draft is similar to a cheque, except that it is not payable on demand.

---

[3] The cost of not taking cash discounts is discussed in Chapter 15.

ETHICAL ISSUES

Cash Management

Financial managers are confronted with legal and ethical issues as they make cash collection and disbursement decisions. For example, a large firm, such as General Motors (GM) might be tempted to systematically be a few days late in making payments to a small supplier. GM managers may be confident that the small firm will not risk damaging its supply relationship with GM over payment delays of a few days.

Similarly, a cash manager may take advantage of weak control mechanisms in its banks and make short-term investments using uncollected funds. E.F. Hutton's managers got into a lot of trouble with this type of activity. In 1985, E.F. Hutton & Company, a large securities brokerage firm (now part of Citigroup's Smith Barney securities brokerage subsidiary), pleaded guilty to federal fraud charges involving the operation of a massive cheque writing scheme to obtain money from many of its 400 banks without paying interest. The firm pleaded guilty to 2,000 counts of mail and wire fraud and agreed to pay more than $10 million in criminal fines and restitution to the banks.

According to the Justice Department, Hutton systematically overdrew hundreds of its own accounts in banks throughout the country and intentionally moved money between banks to artificially delay the collection of funds. The scheme involved cheques totalling more than $4 billion. By doing this, Hutton was able to use as much as $250 million in interest-free money on some days.

According to Justice Department documents, Hutton officials frequently misused bank accounts of its branches by writing cheques for amounts in excess of the volume of customer funds deposited in these accounts. Hutton also pleaded guilty to extending the float time during which cheques are cleared by setting up a chain of transfers between branch accounts. These transactions, according to the Justice Department, resembled a cheque-kiting scheme and were carried out illegally without the prior agreement or consent of the banks involved. Indeed, the banks generally did not realize they were victims until they were told by officials from the government.

A good financial manager should be mindful of the legal and ethical effects of the firm's actions. Legal violations can result in costly fines, embarrassment, and, in some cases, prison terms. Violations of business contracts and the trust built in business transactions may be very costly to a firm's reputation and its future business relationships. In the Hutton case, not only were key employees prosecuted, but also the firm's reputation was so damaged that it was forced to combine with another investment bank to avert failure.

The use of drafts rather than cheques permits a firm to keep smaller balances in its disbursement accounts because funds do not have to be deposited in them until the drafts are presented for payment. Normally, drafts are more expensive to use than cheques. The lower account balances and higher processing costs cause banks to impose service charges on firms using drafts. This cost must be included in the analysis of the benefits and costs of using drafts to pay bills.

Electronic Funds Transfer

The previous discussion of methods to speed up collections and slow disbursements assumes that most transactions involve the transfer of paper (cheques) between the payer and the payee. These methods to control collections and disbursements are designed to reduce the float involved in financial transactions. In a sense, the total float in the financial system can be viewed as a measure of inefficiency in the financial system. In an idealized world, the total float would be reduced to zero. Payments would be made and received as usable funds instantaneously. Although the financial system still has a way to go before this ideal is realized, in recent years, tremendous progress has been made in terms of electronic funds transfer (EFT).

Many consumers now have automatic teller cards that give them access to cash 24 hours a day, 7 days a week. In addition, banking customers can use automatic tellers to transfer funds between accounts. Debit cards are used by many consumers. When a debit card is used, funds are transferred from the consumer's bank account electronically to the account of the retailer. The retailer no longer must be concerned whether a cheque will be good when it is deposited. Increasingly, small and large businesses are using microcomputer links to manipulate funds between interest-bearing accounts and non-interest-bearing disbursement accounts.

In addition to ATM and debit card transactions, numerous other types of financial transactions are handled electronically. For example, many companies offer direct deposit of payroll cheques into their employees' bank accounts. Likewise, the government offers direct deposit of various types of transfer payments (e.g., Canada Pension Plan and Old Age Security) into recipients' bank accounts. Also, most major banks offer automatic bill payment services, whereby customers authorize the bank to periodically transfer funds electronically from their accounts to pay bills, such as mortgages, car loans, and utilities. Furthermore, both firms and individuals can now direct their banks to pay bills from their chequing accounts via the Internet.

EFT and electronic data interchange (EDI) mechanisms are profoundly changing the nature of the cash management function. Paper cheques, with their associated mail and processing float, will not disappear completely for some time (if ever). However, as increased volumes of payments are made electronically, the importance of developing elaborate mechanisms to manage float will be greatly reduced. Increased reliance on EFT as the mechanism for payment will free up some of the cash invested in accounts receivable for more productive uses in a firm. Contemporary financial managers will be challenged in the years ahead to stay current with a fast-changing, high-technology system of receiving payments and making disbursements.

Investing in Marketable Securities

Rather than let their cash reserves build up in excess of daily cash requirements, many firms invest in interest-bearing short-term marketable securities. Determining the level of liquid assets that should be invested in marketable securities depends on several factors, including:

■ The interest to be earned over the expected holding period

■ The transaction costs involved in buying and selling the securities

■ The variability of the firm's cash flows

Various quantitative models have been developed for determining the optimal division of a firm's liquid asset balance between cash and marketable securities.[4] These models vary in complexity, depending partly on the assumptions made about the firm's cash flows. The simpler deterministic models assume that cash payments occur at a

---

[4] Inventory models were first applied to cash management by William J. Baumol in "The Transactions Demand for Cash: An Inventory Theoretic Approach," *Quarterly Journal of Economics* 66 (November 1952): 545–556. See Terry S. Maness and John T. Zietlow, *Short-Term Financial Management*, 2nd ed. (Mason, OH: Thomson/South-Western, 2002), Chapter 15, for a discussion of the cash and marketable securities allocation decision.

ENTREPRENEURIAL ISSUES

Cash Management

Following efficient cash management policies is important for all firms, government agencies, and not-for-profit enterprises. However, effective cash management is particularly important for entrepreneurial firms for several reasons. First, entrepreneurial businesses do not have the same extensive access to the capital markets as do larger firms. A major source of capital funds to small firms is chartered banks. However, bankers require borrowers to present detailed analyses of their anticipated cash needs. To do this, a firm must have efficient cash management procedures in place. Second, because of an entrepreneurial firm's limited access to capital, a cash shortage problem is both more difficult and more costly for an entrepreneurial firm to rectify than for a large firm. Third, because many entrepreneurial firms are growing rapidly, they have a tendency to run out of cash. Growing sales require increases in inventories and accounts receivable, thereby using up cash resources. Finally, entrepreneurial firms frequently operate with only a bare minimum of cash resources because of the high cost of and limited access to capital. As a result, it is imperative that financial managers of entrepreneurial firms use their firm's scarce cash resources in the most efficient way possible.

uniform certain rate over time. The more complex probabilistic or stochastic models assume that cash balances fluctuate from day to day in a random or unpredictable manner. Although these models provide the financial manager with useful insights into the cost trade-offs involved in effective cash management, they have not been widely implemented in actual decision-making situations.

Choosing Marketable Securities

A firm may choose among many different types of securities when deciding where to invest excess cash reserves. In determining which securities to include in its portfolio, the firm should consider a number of criteria, including the following:

- Default risk
- Marketability
- Maturity date
- Rate of return

Notice that the first three criteria deal with risk and the last one deals with return.

Default Risk

The risk that a borrower will fail to make interest payments, principal payments, or both, on a loan.

Default Risk   Most firms invest only in marketable securities that have little or no **default risk** (the risk that a borrower will fail to make interest and/or principal payments on a loan). Canada securities, such as T-bills, have the lowest default risk, followed by securities of other governments and, finally, by corporate and municipal securities. Various rating agencies compile and publish information concerning the safety of the various securities. Given the positive relationship between a security's expected return and risk and the desire to select marketable securities having minimal default risk, a firm has to be willing to accept relatively low expected yields on its marketable securities investments.

Marketability A firm usually buys marketable securities that can be sold on short notice without a significant price concession. Thus, there are two dimensions to a security's marketability: the time required to sell the security and the price realized from the sale relative to the last quoted price. If a long period of time, a high transaction cost, or a significant price concession is required to dispose of a security, the security has poor marketability and generally is not considered suitable for inclusion in a marketable securities portfolio. Naturally, a trade-off is involved here between risk and return. Generally, a highly marketable security has a small degree of risk that the investor will incur a loss, and consequently, it usually has a lower expected yield than one with limited marketability.

Maturity Date Firms usually limit their marketable securities purchases to issues that have relatively short maturities. Recall that prices of debt securities decrease when interest rates rise and increase when interest rates fall. For a given change in interest rates, prices of long-term securities fluctuate more widely than prices of short-term securities with equal default risk. Thus, an investor who holds long-term securities is exposed to a greater risk of loss if the securities have to be sold prior to maturity. This is known as *interest rate risk*.[5] For this reason, most firms generally do not buy marketable securities that have more than six to nine months remaining until maturity, and many firms restrict most of their temporary investments to those maturing in less than three months. Because the yields on securities with short maturities are often lower than the yields on securities with longer maturities, a firm has to be willing to sacrifice yield to avoid interest rate risk.

Rate of Return Although the rate of return, or yield, is also given consideration in selecting securities for inclusion in a firm's portfolio, it is less important than the other three criteria just described. The desire to invest in securities that have minimum default and interest rate risk and that are readily marketable usually limits the selection to those having relatively low yields.

Types of Marketable Securities

Firms normally confine their marketable securities investments to "money market" instruments, that is, those high-grade (low default risk), short-term debt instruments having original maturities of one year or less. Money market instruments that are suitable for inclusion in a firm's marketable securities portfolio include Treasury bills, provincial government issues, municipal securities, commercial paper, repurchase agreements, bankers' acceptances, Eurodollar deposits, and money market mutual funds. (In some cases, firms will also use long-term bonds having one year or less remaining to maturity as "marketable" securities and treat them as money market instruments.)

Canada Issues Treasury bills are the most popular marketable securities. They are sold at auctions by the Bank of Canada and have standard maturities of three months, six months, and nine months. T-bills are issued at a discount and then redeemed for the full face amount at maturity. Once they are issued, T-bills can be bought and sold in the secondary markets through investment dealers. There is a large and active market for T-bills, which means that a firm can easily dispose of them when it needs cash.

  The advantages of T-bills include short maturities, a virtually default-free status, and ready marketability. Their primary disadvantage lies in the fact that their yields normally are the lowest of any marketable security.

---

[5] Interest rate risk is discussed in Chapter 5.

There are other Canada issues that have original maturities from 2 to 20 years. As these securities approach their maturity dates, they become, in effect, short-term instruments that are then suitable for inclusion in a firm's marketable securities portfolio.

Other Government Issues   Provincial and municipal governments and their agencies issue various types of interest-bearing securities. Short-term issues are suitable for inclusion in a firm's marketable securities portfolio. The yields on these securities vary with the creditworthiness of the issuer. The secondary market for provincial and municipal issues is not as strong as that for Canada issues.

Commercial Paper

Short-term unsecured promissory notes issued by major corporations with good credit ratings.

Commercial Paper   **Commercial paper** consists of short-term unsecured promissory notes issued by large, well-known corporations and finance companies with strong credit ratings. Some finance companies, such as General Motors Acceptance Corporation (GMAC), which issue large amounts of commercial paper regularly, sell it directly to investors. Industrial, utility, and transportation firms and smaller finance companies, which issue commercial paper less frequently and in smaller amounts, sell their commercial paper through dealers. Maturities on commercial paper at the time of issue range from 2 or 3 days to 365 days.

The secondary market for commercial paper is weak, although it is sometimes possible to make arrangements with the issuer or commercial paper dealer to repurchase the security prior to maturity. This weak secondary market combined with a somewhat higher default risk results in higher yields on commercial paper than on most other money market instruments.

Repurchase Agreement

An arrangement with a bank or securities dealer in which an investor acquires certain short-term securities subject to a commitment that the securities will be repurchased by the bank or securities dealer on a specified date.

Repurchase Agreements   A **repurchase agreement,** or "repo," is an arrangement with a bank or securities dealer in which the investor acquires certain short-term securities subject to a commitment from the bank or dealer to repurchase the securities on a specified date. Securities used in this agreement can be government securities or commercial paper. Their maturities tend to be relatively short, ranging from one day to several months, and are designed to meet the needs of the investor.

The yield on a repo is slightly less than the rate that can be obtained from outright purchase of the underlying security.

Banker's Acceptance

A short-term debt instrument issued by a firm as part of a commercial transaction. Payment is guaranteed by a bank that accepts it.

Bankers' Acceptances   A **bankers' acceptance** is a short-term debt instrument issued by a firm as part of a commercial transaction. Payment is guaranteed by a bank. Bankers' acceptances are commonly used financial instruments in international trade, as well as in certain lines of domestic trade.

These instruments vary in amount, depending on the size of the commercial transactions. A secondary market exists in which these acceptances can be traded should an investor choose not to hold them until maturity, which usually ranges between 30 and 180 days at the time of issue. Bankers' acceptances are relatively safe investments because both the bank and the borrower are liable for the amount due at maturity.

Contingency Analysis maintains a glossary that defines and then discusses such financial terms as repos, reverse repos, liquidity, payment netting, reinvestment risk, and much more. It's a handy reference source. **www. contingencyanalysis.com**

Eurodollar Deposits   Eurodollar deposits are US dollar-denominated deposits in banks or bank branches located outside the United States, usually in London, England. These deposits usually have slightly higher yields than on corresponding deposits in domestic banks because of the additional risks. Eurodollar certificates of deposit (CDs) issued by London banks are negotiable, and a secondary market is developing for them.

Money Market Mutual Funds   Many of the higher-yielding marketable securities described earlier are available only in relatively large denominations. As a result, a smaller firm that has limited funds to invest at any given time is often unable to obtain the higher yields offered on these securities. An alternative is a *money market mutual fund* that pools the investments of many other small investors and invests in large-denomination money market instruments.

Accounts Receivable Management

Accounts receivable consist of the credit a business grants its customers when selling goods or services.[6] They take the form of either trade credit, which the company extends to other companies, or consumer credit, which the company extends to its ultimate consumers.[7] The effectiveness of a company's credit policies can have a significant impact on its total performance. For example, a large firm's credit manager has estimated that a reduction of only one day in the average collection period for the firm's receivables increases its cash flow by $10 million and improves pretax profits by $1 million.

For a business to grant credit to its customers, it has to do the following:

- Establish credit and collection policies
- Evaluate individual credit applicants

In this section we develop the establishment of optimal credit and collection policies. In the following section we discuss procedures for evaluating individual credit applicants.

Shareholder Wealth and Optimal Investments in Accounts Receivable

When a company decides to extend credit to customers, it is making an investment decision, namely, an investment in accounts receivable, a current asset. As with the decision to invest in long-term assets, the primary goal is the maximization of shareholder wealth. Recall from the discussion of the basic framework for capital budgeting decisions in Chapter 10 that the optimal capital budget is determined by accepting all investment projects whose net present value is positive. Such a decision rule maximizes shareholder wealth because the projects accepted will increase the value of the firm. Following similar reasoning, a firm will maximize shareholder wealth by investing in accounts receivable as long as the expected marginal returns obtained from each additional dollar of receivables investment exceed the associated expected marginal costs of the investment, including the cost of the funds invested.

The establishment of an optimal credit extension policy requires the company to examine and attempt to measure the marginal costs and marginal returns (benefits) associated with alternative policies. What are the marginal returns and costs associated with a more liberal extension of credit to a firm's customers? With respect to returns, a more liberal extension presumably stimulates sales and leads to increased gross profits, assuming that all other factors (such as economic conditions, prices, production costs, and advertising expenses) remain constant. Offsetting these increased returns are several types of credit-related marginal costs, including the opportunity costs of the additional capital funds employed to support the higher level of receivables. Any increase in sales resulting from a more liberal credit extension policy may also result in increased inventory levels and associated inventory investment costs. Checking new credit accounts and collecting the higher level of receivables also results in additional costs. And finally, a more liberal credit policy frequently results in increased bad-debt expenses because a certain number of new accounts are likely to fail to repay the credit extended to them.

---

[6] From the customer's perspective, credit represents a form of short-term financing known as accounts payable. This is discussed in greater detail in Chapter 15.

[7] Some companies use their accounts receivable to obtain short-term financing. For example, a company that is somewhat weak financially might be unable to borrow short-term funds without putting up collateral for the loan. In such a case, the company might use its accounts receivable as the collateral by pledging them to the bank. Alternatively, the company might consider selling, or factoring, its accounts receivable to obtain cash. Accounts receivable pledging and factoring are discussed in Chapter 15.

Cash Management

Multilateral Netting
A process of international cash management designed to minimize the cost associated with misdirected funds.

Misdirected Funds
Funds that cross an international border unintentionally.

The goals of cash management in a multinational company (MNC) parallel the cash management goals of purely domestic corporations. That is, MNCs attempt to speed up collections, slow disbursements, and make the most efficient use of the firm's cash resources by minimizing excess balances and investing balances to earn the highest possible return, consistent with liquidity and safety constraints. However, there are some unique elements of cash management for an MNC.

First, cash management is complicated by difficulties and costs associated with moving funds from one country (and currency) to another. It is costly to convert cash from one currency to another. Second, there is a general lack of integrated international cash transfer facilities, such as exist in Canada and most other Western nations. The absence of this capability makes it difficult to move funds quickly from one country to another. Third, investment opportunities for temporary excess cash balances are much broader for an MNC than for a domestic firm. MNCs must consider short-term investment options in many different countries—a process further complicated by exchange rate risk. Fourth, the host government may place restrictions on the movement of cash out of the country.

Practicing MNC cash managers have developed a number of techniques designed to optimize the process of international cash management in the face of these difficulties. First, there is general agreement that the cash management function for an MNC should be centralized with respect to the information-gathering and decision-making process. The parent normally maintains an international cash manager who has the expertise and responsibility to keep track of the firm's cash balances around the world and to identify the best sources for short-term borrowing and lending.

Second, many MNCs have instituted a process called *multilateral netting*. **Multilateral netting** is designed to minimize the cost associated with misdirected funds. **Misdirected funds** are funds that cross an international border unnecessarily. It is costly to convert funds from one currency to another. Hence it is desirable to minimize unnecessary transactions. The greater the number of subsidiaries an MNC has, the more complex is the process of managing a multilateral netting system. At the same time, the potential cost savings are greatly increased.

In determining an optimal credit extension policy, a firm's financial managers must consider a number of major controllable variables that can be used to alter the level of receivables, including the following:

- Credit standards
- Credit terms
- Collection effort

The remainder of this section discusses each of these variables in more detail.

Credit Standards

Credit standards are the criteria a company uses to screen credit applicants in order to determine which of its customers should be offered credit and how much. The process of setting credit standards allows the firm to exercise a degree of control over the "quality" of accounts accepted.[8] The quality of credit extended to customers is a multidimensional concept involving the following:

- The time a customer takes to repay the credit obligation, given that it is repaid
- The probability that a customer will fail to repay the credit extended to it

Average Collection Period
The average number of days an account receivable remains outstanding.

The **average collection period** serves as one measure of the promptness with which customers repay their credit obligations. It indicates the average number of days a firm must wait after making a credit sale before receiving the customer's cash payment. Obviously, the longer the average collection period, the higher a company's receivables investment and its cost of extending credit to customers.

Bad-Debt Loss Ratio
The proportion of the total receivables volume that is never collected by a business.

The likelihood that a customer will fail to repay the credit extended to it is sometimes referred to as default risk. The **bad-debt loss ratio,** which is the proportion of the total receivables volume a firm never collects, serves as an overall, or aggregate, measure of this risk. A business can estimate its loss ratio by examining losses on credit that has been extended to similar types of customers in the past.[9] The higher a firm's loss ratio, the greater the cost of extending credit.

For example, suppose that Bassett Furniture Industries is considering making a change in its credit standards. Before reaching any decision, the company first must determine whether such a change would be profitable. The first step in making this decision involves an evaluation of the overall creditworthiness of the company's existing and potential customers (retailers) using various sources of information.[10] Table 16.1 illustrates the credit sales, average collection period, and loss ratio data for various credit risk groups of the company's customers in its western Canadian region.

Under its current credit policy, Bassett extends unlimited credit to all customers in Credit Risk Groups 1, 2, and 3, and no credit to customers in Groups 4 and 5, meaning that the customers in these latter two groups must submit payment along with their orders. As a result of this policy, Bassett estimates that it "loses" $300,000 per year in

Table 16.1 Credit Evaluation Data Compiled by Bassett Furniture Industries

Credit Risk Group	Credit Sales ($)	Average Collection Period (Days)	Bad-Debt Loss Ratio (%)
1	900,000	25	—
2	1,100,000	30	0.5
3	400,000	45	3
4	300,000*	60	7
5	100,000*	90	13

*Estimated lost sales due to the fact that no credit is extended to customers in these risk categories.

---

[8] Complete control over the quality of accounts accepted is generally impossible due to uncertainty about future events (for example, a recession or a strike) that could make it difficult or even impossible for a customer to repay its account.

[9] This estimation procedure assumes that the loss ratio does not change significantly over time because of changing economic conditions. Otherwise, the loss ratio should be adjusted to take account of expected future economic changes. This procedure also assumes that credit extension and repayment information is available on a sufficiently large sample of accounts to provide a company with a reliable estimate of its loss ratio. Without this information, the financial manager simply has to make an "educated guess" as to the size of the loss ratio.

[10] Some of these sources of information are described later in this chapter.

sales from Group 4 customers and $100,000 per year in sales from Group 5 customers.[11]

Bassett also estimates that its variable production, administrative, and marketing costs (including credit department costs) are approximately 75 percent of total sales. That is, the **variable cost ratio** is 0.75.[12] Thus, the profit contribution ratio per dollar of sales is $1.0 - 0.75 = 0.25$ or 25 percent. The company's required pretax rate of return (that is, the opportunity cost) on its current assets investment is 20 percent.

Variable Cost Ratio
Variable production, administrative, and marketing costs per dollar of sales.

One alternative Bassett is considering is to relax credit standards by extending full credit to Group 4 customers. Bassett estimates that an additional inventory investment (i.e., raw materials, work-in-process, and finished goods) of $120,000 is required to expand sales by $300,000. In evaluating this alternative, the financial manager has to analyze how this policy would affect pretax profits. If the marginal returns of this change in credit standards exceed the marginal costs, pretax profits would increase, and the decision to extend full credit to the Group 4 customers would increase shareholder wealth.

Table 16.2 contains the results of this analysis. In Step A, the marginal profitability of the additional sales, $75,000, is calculated. Next, the cost of the additional investment in receivables, $9,863, is calculated in Step B.[13] In Step C, the additional bad-debt loss, $21,000, is computed. Then, the cost of the additional investment in inventory, $24,000, is calculated in Step D. Finally, in Step E, the net change in pretax profits is determined by deducting the marginal costs computed in Steps B, C, and D from the marginal returns found in Step A. Because this expected net change is a positive $20,137, the analysis indicates that Bassett should relax its credit standards by extending full credit to the Group 4 customers.

This analysis contains a number of explicit and implicit assumptions of which the financial manager must be aware. One assumption is that the firm has excess capacity and thus could produce the additional output at a constant variable cost ratio of 0.75. If the firm is currently operating at or near full capacity, and additional output could be obtained only

---

[11] Throughout the chapter, estimates of variables, such as sales, the average collection period, and the bad-debt loss ratio, are used in the analysis of credit policy decisions. These estimates are subject to uncertainty. Sensitivity analysis (described in Chapter 11) can be performed to determine the effect on profitability of different estimates of one (or more) of these variables.

[12] This analysis assumes that the collection costs for Credit Risk Group 4 customers are the same as for customers in the other groups and are included in credit department costs.

[13] Note that we have chosen to use sales value in determining the (opportunity) cost of the additional receivables investment. Disagreement exists in the finance literature concerning the measurement of the incremental investment in accounts receivable (and its associated opportunity cost) arising from a change in credit standards. Some authors contend that the relevant measure of investment is the dollar cost the firm has tied up in the new accounts receivable, rather than the total sales value. The rationale for this approach is that the "profit" on the sale—that is, the difference between the amount of the accounts receivable and their associated cost—would be nonexistent without the change in credit standards. Hence, no opportunity cost is incurred on this uncollected "profit." Advocates of this approach use variable cost or total cost as a measure of the amount of funds invested in accounts receivable. Other authors claim that the total sales value of the new accounts receivable is indeed the relevant measure of investment in accounts receivable because the opportunity cost of the increased level of accounts receivable is the return a company could earn if it reduced accounts receivable back to its original level. In other words, considerations of symmetry require that the opportunity cost of increasing accounts receivable by a given amount should be equal to the returns that could be earned on the funds released from decreasing accounts receivable by the same amount. The interested reader should consult the following references for a more complete discussion of the issues involved: John S. Oh, "Opportunity Cost in the Evaluation of Investment in Accounts Receivable," *Financial Management* 5 (Summer 1976): 32–35; Edward A. Dyl, "Another Look at the Evaluation of Investment in Accounts Receivable," *Financial Management* 6 (Winter 1977): 67–70; Joseph C. Atkins and Yong H. Kim, "Comment and Correction: Opportunity Cost in the Evaluation of Investment in Accounts Receivable," *Financial Management* 6 (Winter 1977): 71–74; Tirlochan S. Walia, "Explicit and Implicit Cost of Changes in the Level of Accounts Receivable and the Credit Policy Decision of the Firm," *Financial Management* 6 (Winter 1977): 75–80; and J. Fred Weston and Pham D. Tuan, "Comment on Analysis of Credit Policy Changes," *Financial Management* 9 (Winter 1980): 59–63.

Table 16.2   Bassett Furniture Industries' Analysis of the Decision to Relax Credit Standards by Extending Full Credit to Customers in Credit Risk Group 4

Step A: Additional sales $300,000

Marginal profitability of additional sales

= Profit contribution ratio × Additional sales

= 0.25 × $300,000 $75,000

Step B: Additional investment in receivables

= Additional average daily sales*

   × Average collection period

$$= \frac{\text{Additional annual sales}}{365} \times 60 \qquad \$49{,}315$$

$$= \frac{\$300{,}000}{365} \times 60$$

Cost of the additional investment in receivables

= Additional investment in receivables

   × Required pretax rate of return

= $49,315 × 0.20 $9,863

Step C: Additional bad-debt loss

= Bad-debt loss ratio × Additional sales

= 0.07 × $300,000 $21,000

Step D: Additional investment in inventory $120,000

Cost of the additional investment in inventory

= Additional investment in inventory

   × Required pretax rate of return

= $120,000 × 0.20 $24,000

Step E: Net change in pretax profits

= Marginal returns − Marginal costs

= A − (B + C + D)

= $75,000 − ($9,863 + $21,000 + $24,000)   +$20,137

*Standard practice is to assume that there are 365 days per year.

by paying more costly overtime rates and/or investing in new facilities, this analysis would have to be modified to take account of these incremental costs. This analysis also assumes that the average collection period of the customers in Groups 1, 2, and 3 would not increase once the company began extending credit to Group 4 customers. If it became known that the Group 4 customers had 60 days or more to pay their bills with no penalty involved, the Group 1, 2, and 3 customers, who normally pay their bills promptly, might also start delaying their payments. If this occurred, the analysis would have to be modified to account for such shifts. It was also assumed that the required rate of return on the investment in receivables and inventories for Group 4 does not change as a result of extending credit to these more risky accounts. A case can be made for increasing the required rate of return to compensate for the increased risk of the new accounts. Finally, this example assumes that an increase in inventory investment is necessary as a result of changes in the firm's credit policy. In summary, for this type of analysis to be valid and to lead to the correct decision, it must include all of the marginal costs and benefits that result from the decision.

Credit Terms

A company's credit terms, or terms of sale, specify the conditions under which the customer is required to pay for the credit extended to it. These conditions include the length of the credit period and the cash discount (if any) given for prompt payment plus any special terms, such as seasonal datings. For example, credit terms of "net 30" mean that the customer has 30 days from the invoice date within which to pay the bill and that no discount is offered for early payment.

Credit Period
The length of time a credit customer has to pay the account in full.

Credit Period   The length of a company's **credit period** (the amount of time a credit customer has to pay the account in full) is frequently determined by industry customs, and thus it tends to vary among different industries. The credit period may be as short as seven days or as long as six months. Variation appears to be positively related to the length of time the merchandise is in the purchaser's inventory. For example, manufacturers of goods having relatively low inventory turnover periods, such as jewellery, tend to offer retailers longer credit periods than distributors of goods having higher inventory turnover periods, such as food products.

A company's credit terms can affect its sales. For example, if the demand for a particular product depends in part on its credit terms, the firm may consider lengthening the credit period to stimulate sales. In making this type of decision, however, a firm must also consider its closest competitors. If they lengthen their credit periods, too, every firm in the industry may end up having about the same level of sales, a much higher level of receivables investments and costs, and a lower rate of return.

Analyzing the possible effects of an increase in a firm's credit period involves comparing the profitability of the increased sales that are expected to occur with the required rate of return on the additional investment in receivables and inventories. Additional bad-debt losses must also be considered. If a company continues to accept the same quality of accounts under its lengthened credit terms, no significant change in the bad-debt loss ratio should occur.

For example, suppose that Nike, a distributor of athletic shoes and sportswear, is considering changing its credit terms from "net 30" to "net 60" in its western Canada sales territory. The company expects sales (all on credit) to increase by about 10 percent from a current level of $2.2 million, and it expects its average collection period to increase from 35 days to 65 days. The bad-debt loss ratio should remain at 3 percent of sales. The company also estimates that an additional inventory investment of $50,000 is required for the expected sales increase. The firm's variable cost ratio is 0.75, which means that its profit contribution ratio (per dollar of sales) is $1.00 - 0.75 = 0.25$. Nike's required pretax rate of return on investments in receivables and inventories is 20 percent.

Table 16.3 contains an analysis of Nike's decision. Many of the calculations in this table are similar to those in Table 16.2, which analyzed the effects of a change in credit standards. The marginal returns ($55,000) computed in Step A represent the marginal profitability of the additional sales generated by the longer credit period. The marginal costs (obtained in Steps B, C, and D) consist of the cost of the additional receivables investment ($44,000), the additional bad-debt losses ($6,600), and the cost of the additional inventory investment ($10,000). The net increase in pretax profits (Step E) that would result from the decision to lengthen the credit period is -$5,600. Therefore, the decision does not appear to be worthwhile.

Cash Discount
A price reduction offered for early payment of an invoice.

Cash Discounts   A **cash discount** is a discount offered on the condition that the customer will repay the credit extended within a specified period of time. A cash discount is normally expressed as a percentage discount on the net amount of the cost of goods purchased (usually excluding freight and taxes). The length of the discount period is also specified when discount terms are offered. For example, credit terms of "2/10, net 30" mean that the customer can deduct 2 percent of the invoice amount if payment is made within 10 days from the invoice date. If payment is not made by this time, the full invoice amount is due within 30 days from the invoice date. (In some cases, the discount period may begin with the date of shipment or the date of receipt by the customer.) Like the length of the credit period, the cash discount varies among different lines of business.

Table 16.3 Nike's Analysis of the Decision to Change Its Credit Terms from "Net 30" to "Net 60"

Step A: Additional sales
 = Percent increase × Present sales
 = 0.10 × $2,200,000 $220,000
 Marginal profitability of additional sales
 = Profit contribution ratio × Additional sales
 = 0.25 × $220,000 $55,000

Step B: Additional investment in receivables
 = New average balance − Present average balance

$$= \frac{\text{New annual sales}}{365} \times \text{New average collection period}$$

$$- \frac{\text{Present annual sales}}{365} \times \text{Present average collection period}$$

$$= \frac{\$2,420,000}{365} \times 65 - \frac{\$2,200,000}{365} \times 35$$

 = $430,959 − $210,959 $220,000
 Cost of the additional investment in receivables
 = Additional investment in receivables
    × Required pretax rate of return
 = $220,000 × 0.20 $44,000

Step C: Additional bad-debt loss
 = Bad-debt loss ratio × Additional sales
 = 0.03 × $220,000 $ 6,600

Step D: Additional investment in inventory $ 50,000
 Cost of the additional investment in inventory
 = Additional investment in inventory
    × Required pretax rate of return
 = $50,000 × 0.20 $10,000

Step E: Net change in pretax profits
 = Marginal returns − Marginal costs
 = A − (B + C + D)
 = $55,000 − ($44,000 + $6,600 + $10,000)   −$ 5,600

Cash discounts are offered (or increased) to speed up the collection of accounts receivable and, by extension, reduce a company's level of receivables investment and associated costs.[14] Offsetting these savings or benefits is the cost of the discounts that are taken, which is equal to the lost dollar revenues from the existing unit sales volume.

For example, suppose that Sony Music (a subsidiary of the Sony Corporation) is considering instituting a cash discount. The firm currently sells to record distributors on credit terms of "net 30" and wants to determine the effect on pretax profits of offering a 1 percent cash discount on terms of "1/10, net 30" to record distributors in its southwestern Ontario region. The firm's average collection period is now 50 days and is estimated to decrease to 28 days with the adoption of the 1 percent cash discount policy. It also is

---

[14] Offering a cash discount may also increase demand and sales because some potential customers may view it as a form of price cut and be willing to purchase the product at this new "lower" price. Throughout the ensuing analysis it is assumed that the cash discount is not perceived as a price cut and that there is no resulting increase in demand. It is also assumed that offering cash discounts will not reduce bad-debt losses by any measurable amount.

estimated that approximately 40 percent of the firm's customers will take advantage of the new cash discount. Sony's annual credit sales in the region are $2.5 million, and the company's required pretax rate of return on receivables investment is 20 percent.

Table 16.4 contains an analysis of Sony's proposed cash discount policy. The marginal returns ($30,137) computed in Step A represent the earnings Sony expects to realize on the funds released by the decrease in receivables. The marginal costs ($10,000) found in Step B represent the cost of the cash discount. Subtracting the marginal costs from the marginal returns (Step C) yields a net increase in pretax profits of $20,137, indicating that Sony should offer the proposed 1 percent cash discount, if it is confident about the accuracy of the estimates used in this analysis.

Seasonal Datings
Credit terms under which the buyer of seasonal merchandise is encouraged to take delivery well before the peak sales period. Payment on the purchase is deferred until after the peak sales period.

Seasonal Datings   **Seasonal datings** are special credit terms that are sometimes offered to retailers when sales are highly concentrated in one or more periods during the year. Under a seasonal dating credit arrangement, the retailer is encouraged to order and accept delivery of the product well ahead of the peak sales period and then to remit payment shortly after the peak sales period. The primary objective of seasonal dating is to increase sales to retailers who are unable to finance the buildup of inventories in advance of the peak selling period because of a weak working capital position, limited borrowing capacity, or both.

For example, O.M. Scott & Sons, manufacturers of lawn and garden products, has used a seasonal dating plan that is tied to the growing season. Payments for winter and early spring shipments are due at the end of April and May, depending on the geographical area, and payments for shipments during the summer months are due in October or November. Payments for purchases made outside the two main selling seasons are due on the 10th of the second month following shipment. A cash discount of 0.6 percent per month is offered to encourage payments in advance of these seasonal dates. The arrangement enables and encourages dealers of lawn and garden products to be fully stocked with Scott products in advance of the peak selling periods.

Table 16.4   Sony Music: Analysis of the Decision to Offer a 1 Percent Cash Discount

Step A: Decrease in average receivables balance

= Present average balance − New average balance

$$= \frac{\text{Annual sales}}{365} \times \text{Present average collection period}$$

$$= \frac{\$2,500,000}{365} \times 50 - \frac{\$2,500,000}{365} \times 28$$

= \$342,466 − \$191,781   **\$150,685**

Earnings on the funds released by the decrease in receivables

= Decrease in receivables × Required pretax rate of return

= \$150,685 × 0.20   **\$30,137**

Step B: Cost of cash discount

= Annual sales × Percentage taking discount

× Percentage discount

= \$2,500,000 × 0.40 × 0.01   **\$10,000**

Step C: Net change in pretax profits

= Marginal returns − Marginal costs

= A − B

= \$30,137 − \$10,000   **+\$20,137**

Collection Effort

The collection effort consists of the methods a business employs in attempting to collect payment on past-due accounts. Some commonly used methods include the following:

- Sending notices or letters informing the customer of the past-due status of the account and requesting payment

- Telephoning and/or visiting the customer in an effort to obtain payment

- Employing a collection agency

- Taking legal action against the customer

Another approach, which is also effective in some cases, is for the firm to refuse to make new shipments to the customer until the past-due bills are paid. Although the objectives of the collection effort are to speed up past-due payments and reduce bad-debt losses, a firm must also avoid antagonizing normally creditworthy customers who may be past due for some good reason—for example, because of temporary liquidity problems. A collection effort that is too aggressive may reduce future sales and profits if customers begin buying from other businesses whose collection policies are more lenient.

When determining which methods to use in its collection effort, a company has to consider the amount of funds it has available to spend for this purpose. If the firm has a relatively small amount of money available for collecting past-due accounts, it must confine itself to less costly (and less effective) methods, such as sending letters and making telephone calls. If it has a larger budget, the firm can employ more aggressive procedures, such as sending out representatives to personally contact past-due customers. In general, the larger the company's collection expenditures, the shorter its average collection period and the lower its level of bad-debt losses. The benefits of additional collection efforts, however, are likely to diminish rapidly at extremely high expenditure levels.

The marginal benefits of the decision to increase collection expenditures consist of the earnings on the funds released from the receivables investment as a result of the shorter average collection period, plus the reduction in bad-debt losses. A business should increase its collection expenditures only if these marginal benefits are expected to exceed the amount of the additional collection expenditures.

Monitoring Accounts Receivable

For a company to effectively control its receivables investment, the credit manager must monitor the status and composition of these accounts. An ageing of accounts is a useful monitoring technique. In an ageing analysis, a firm's accounts are classified into different categories based on the number of days they are past due. These classifications show both the aggregate amount of receivables and the percentage of the total receivables outstanding in each category. Ageing of accounts receivable provides more information than such summary ratios as, for example, the average collection period. Comparing ageing schedules at successive points in time (for example, monthly, quarterly, or semiannually) can help the credit manager monitor any changes in the "quality" of the company's accounts. An example of an ageing of accounts schedule is shown in Chapter 3.

Evaluating Individual Credit Applicants

Once a company has established its credit and collection policies, it can use them as a basis for evaluating individual credit applicants.[15] In general, the credit evaluation process consists of these main steps:

- Gathering relevant information on the credit applicant

---

[15] Once these policies are established, however, they do not have to remain static over time. The credit manager should review them periodically, making appropriate modifications as dictated by changing economic conditions (for example, rising interest rates) or other circumstances.

- Analyzing the information obtained to determine the applicant's creditworthiness
- Deciding whether to extend credit to the applicant and, if so, determining the amount of the line of credit

The credit evaluation process is limited by both time and cost. Often a business may have only a few days—or, in some cases, only a few hours—in which to evaluate a credit request. Delaying this decision too long may result in the loss of a potential customer's order.

The credit evaluation process is also limited by the amount of resources the credit department has available. The amount of time and money a firm spends on evaluating a customer's request for credit should depend on the size of the losses the firm would experience if it made an incorrect decision. These potential losses stem from either denying credit to a creditworthy customer or offering credit to a customer who is not creditworthy. The larger the potential losses, the more time and money a business should spend on evaluating the credit applicant.

Credit-Reporting Organizations A number of national and local organizations collect information on the financial position and credit standing of businesses. Other companies and lending institutions that are considering extending credit to a firm may obtain information about it from these organizations, usually for a fee.

The most widely known credit-reporting organization is Dun & Bradstreet Credit Services, which provides its subscribers with a credit reference book and written credit reports on individual businesses.

A D&B credit report provides far more detailed information about a company's financial position than the reference book does. A typical report contains a summary of trade credit payments to existing suppliers, which can be extremely valuable to firms that are considering extending credit to a particular company. Also included in a typical report are financial data from the firm's balance sheet and income statement, a review of its banking relationships, historical information about the owners, and a description of its operations, including the location of facilities and the kinds of products sold.[16]

Inventory Management

Inventories serve as a buffer between the various phases in the procurement-production-sales cycle of a manufacturing firm.[17] They uncouple the various phases by giving the firm flexibility with respect to timing the purchase of raw materials, scheduling production facilities and employees, and meeting fluctuating and uncertain demand for the finished product. Inventories also serve similar purposes in the procurement-sales cycle of a wholesaling or retailing firm.

The remainder of this chapter explores the various types of inventories and their functions, along with the different categories of inventory-related costs. It also develops some models and procedures that can be used in efficiently managing a firm's level of inventory investment. Although financial managers usually do not have primary responsibility for managing a company's inventories, they are responsible for seeing that funds are invested in a manner consistent with shareholder wealth maximization. (Normally, production and/or marketing management has primary responsibility for determining the specific quantities of the various types of inventories that the firm

---

[16] The reliability and comprehensiveness of this type of report depend in part on how willing a business is to supply D&B with pertinent information.

[17] Inventories are sometimes used as collateral for short-term loans. This topic is discussed in detail in Chapter 15.

holds.) To perform this function, financial managers must have a good working knowledge of inventory control techniques.

Like any other asset, the holding of inventories constitutes an investment of funds. Determining the optimal level of inventory investment requires that the benefits and costs, including the opportunity cost of the funds invested, associated with alternative levels be measured and compared. To do this, it is necessary to determine the specific benefits associated with holding the various types of inventories.

Benefits of Holding Inventories

Manufacturing firms generally hold three types of inventories:

- Raw materials inventories
- Work-in-process inventories
- Finished goods inventories

Raw Materials Inventories   Raw materials inventory consists of items a business purchases for use in its production process. It may consist of basic materials (for example, iron ore for a steel-making operation), manufactured goods (for example, memory chips for a computer assembly operation), or both. Maintaining adequate raw materials inventories provides a company with advantages in both purchasing and production. Specifically, the purchasing department benefits by being able to buy needed items in large quantities to take advantage of quantity discounts offered by suppliers. In addition, if rising prices, shortages of specific items, or both are forecasted for the future, maintaining a large stock of raw materials ensures that the company will have adequate supplies at reasonable costs.

Knowing that adequate stocks of raw materials will be available when needed permits the production department to meet production schedules and make the most efficient use of its personnel and facilities. Therefore, there are a number of valid reasons why a company's purchasing and production departments will want to maintain large inventories of raw materials.

Work-in-Process Inventories   Work-in-process inventory consists of all items that are presently in the production cycle at some intermediate stage of completion. For example, they may be currently undergoing some type of operation (such as assembly or painting); they may be in transit between operations; or they may be stored somewhere, awaiting the next step in the production cycle.

Work-in-process inventories are a necessary part of modern industrial production systems because they give each operation in the production cycle a certain degree of independence. This, in turn, aids in the efficient scheduling of the various operations and helps minimize costly delays and idle time. For these reasons, a firm's production department will want to maintain reasonable work-in-process inventories. In general, the longer a firm's production cycle, the larger its work-in-process inventory.

Finished Goods Inventories   Finished goods inventory consists of those items that have completed the production cycle and are available for sale. With the exception of large-scale, specialized types of equipment—such as industrial machinery, military armaments, jet airplanes, and nuclear reactors, which are normally contracted for before they are produced—most consumer and industrial products are manufactured and stored in inventory to meet forecasted future sales.

Keeping enough finished goods inventories on hand provides significant benefits for both the marketing and the production departments. From marketing's perspective, large finished goods inventories enable it to fill orders promptly, minimize lost sales, and avoid shipment delays due to stockouts. From production's standpoint, maintaining a large finished goods inventory permits items to be manufactured in large production runs, which helps keep unit production costs low by spreading fixed setup expenses over large volumes of output.

Inventory-Related Costs

At the same time that a number of benefits are to be realized from holding inventories, a number of costs also must be considered, including the following:

- Ordering costs
- Carrying costs
- Stockout costs

Ordering Costs Ordering costs represent all of the costs of placing and receiving an order. They are stated in dollars per order. When a company is ordering from an external source, these include the costs of preparing the purchase requisition, expediting the order (e.g., long-distance calls and follow-up letters), receiving and inspecting the shipment, and handling payment. Such factors as an item's price and engineering complexity also affect its ordering costs. When an order is placed for an item that is manufactured internally within a company, ordering costs consist primarily of production setup costs, which are the expenses incurred in getting the plant and equipment ready for a production run.

In practice, the cost per order generally contains both fixed and variable components because a portion of the cost—such as that of receiving and inspecting the order—normally varies with the quantity ordered. However, many simple inventory control models, such as the economic order quantity (EOQ) model (which is described later in this chapter), treat cost per order as fixed by assuming that these costs are independent of the number of units ordered.

Carrying Costs Carrying costs constitute all of the costs of holding items in inventory for a given period of time. They are expressed either in dollars per unit or as a percentage of the inventory value per period. Components of this cost include the following:

- Storage and handling costs
- Obsolescence and deterioration costs
- Insurance
- Taxes
- The cost of the funds invested in inventories

Storage and handling costs include the cost of warehouse space. If a firm leases warehouse space, this cost is equal to the rent paid. If a company owns the warehouse, this cost is equal to the value of the space in its next best alternative use (that is, the opportunity cost). These costs also include depreciation on the inventory handling equipment, such as conveyors and forklift trucks, and the wages and salaries paid to warehouse workers and supervisors.

Inventories are valuable only if they can be sold. Obsolescence costs represent the decline in inventory value caused by technological or style changes that make the existing product less saleable. Deterioration costs represent the decline in value caused by changes in the physical quality of the inventory, such as spoilage and breakage.

Another element of carrying cost is the cost of insuring the inventory against losses due to theft, fire, and natural disaster. In addition, a company must pay any personal property taxes and business taxes required by local and provincial governments on the value of its inventories.

Ordering Costs
All costs associated with placing and receiving an order.

Carrying Costs
All costs associated with holding items in inventory for a given period of time.

The cost of funds invested in inventories is measured by the required rate of return on these funds. Because inventory investments are likely to be of "average risk," the overall weighted cost of capital should be used to measure the cost of these funds. If it is felt that inventories constitute an investment with either an above-average or below-average risk, some adjustment in the weighted cost of capital may be necessary to account for this difference in risk.

Some firms incorrectly use the rate of interest on borrowed funds as a measure of this cost. This tends to understate the true cost because a given amount of lower-cost debt must be balanced with additional higher-cost equity financing. Inventory investment cost constitutes an opportunity cost in that it represents the return a firm foregoes as a result of deciding to invest its limited funds in inventories rather than in some other asset. Therefore, for most inventory decisions, the appropriate opportunity cost is the firm's weighted cost of capital.

The cost of carrying inventories can represent a significant cost of doing business. Like ordering costs, inventory carrying costs contain both fixed and variable components. Most carrying costs vary with the inventory level, but a certain portion of them—such as warehouse rent and depreciation on inventory handling equipment—are relatively fixed over the short run. Most of the simple inventory control models, such as the EOQ model, treat the entire carrying cost as variable.

Stockout Costs   **Stockout costs** are incurred whenever a business is unable to fill orders because the demand for an item is greater than the amount currently available in inventory. When a stockout in raw materials occurs, for example, stockout costs include the expenses of placing special orders (back ordering) and expediting incoming orders, in addition to the costs of any resulting production delays. A stockout in work-in-process inventory results in additional costs of rescheduling and speeding production within the plant, and it also may result in lost production costs if work stoppages occur. Finally, a stockout in finished goods inventory may result in the immediate loss of profits if customers decide to purchase the product from a competitor and in potential long-term losses if customers decide to order from other companies in the future.

Inventory Control Models

Given the significance of the benefits and costs associated with holding inventories, it is important that the firm efficiently control the level of inventory investments. A number of inventory control models are available that can help in determining the optimal inventory level of each item. These models range from the relatively simple to the extremely complex. Their degree of complexity depends primarily on the assumptions made about the demand or use for the particular item and the lead time required to secure additional stock.

A related question involves the extent of control and the type of inventory model that should be applied to different inventory items. A technique called ABC inventory classification can be helpful in this regard. The **ABC inventory classification** method divides a company's inventory items into three groups. Group A consists of those items with a relatively large dollar value but a relatively small percentage of the total items, whereas group C contains those items with a small dollar value but a large percentage of the total items. Group B contains the items that are in between groups A and C. A typical result of an ABC analysis is that group A contains roughly 1 to 10 percent of the total number of items carried in inventory, but these items may represent as high as 80 to 90 percent of the total dollar value of the inventory. On the other hand, group C may contain about 50 percent of the total number of items, but these items may constitute less than 10 percent of the inventory's total dollar value. Group B contains the remaining items. Even though the actual cut-off between the groups is somewhat arbitrary, the ABC method provides management with information that can be used to determine how closely different inventory items should be controlled.

As an example, consider the Toro Company, which manufactures lawn mowers. It purchases gasoline motors from another company for use in these mowers. Because of their cost, the motors might be classified as group A items. As a result, Toro management might determine the inventory costs associated with the motors and use a detailed model to calculate the economic order quantity. On the other hand, Toro might classify all nuts and bolts it uses as a group C item. As a result, the company's policy on nuts and bolts might consist of little more than simply keeping an ample supply on hand.

In the "classic" inventory models, which include both the simpler deterministic models and the more complex probabilistic models, it is assumed that demand is either uniform or dispersed and independent over time. In other words, demand is assumed either to be constant or to fluctuate over time due to random elements. These types of demand situations are common in retailing and some service operations.

The simpler deterministic inventory control models, such as the **economic order quantity (EOQ)** model, assume that both demand and lead times are constant and known with certainty. Thus, deterministic models eliminate the need to consider stock-outs. The more complex probabilistic inventory control models assume that demand, lead time, or both are random variables with known probability distributions.[18]

Economic Order Quantity (EOQ)
The quantity of an inventory item that should be ordered to minimize total inventory costs.

Basic Economic Order Quantity (EOQ) Model

In its simplest form, the EOQ model assumes that the annual demand or usage for a particular item is known with certainty. It also assumes that this demand is stationary or uniform throughout the year. In other words, seasonal fluctuations in the rate of demand are ruled out. Finally, the model assumes that orders to replenish the inventory of an item are filled instantaneously. Given a known demand and a zero lead time for replenishing inventories, there is no need for a firm to maintain additional inventories, or safety stocks, to protect itself against stockouts.

The assumptions of the EOQ model yield the saw-toothed inventory pattern shown in Figure 16.3. The vertical lines at the 0, T_1, T_2, and T_3 points in time represent the instantaneous replenishment of the item by the amount of the order quantity, Q, and the negatively sloped lines between the replenishment points represent the use of the item. Because the inventory level varies between 0 and the order quantity, average inventory is equal to one-half of the order quantity, or $Q/2$.

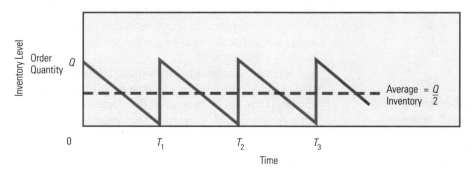

Figure 16.3
Certainty Case of the Inventory Cycle

---

[18] Rather than survey all the various inventory control models in depth, this chapter develops the deterministic EOQ model to illustrate the cost trade-offs involved in determining the optimal inventory level. It then examines the factors that must be considered and the cost trade-offs involved in developing a probabilistic model, without using mathematical analysis or formal solution techniques.

This model assumes that the costs of placing and receiving an order are the same for each order and independent of the number of units ordered. It also assumes that the annual cost of carrying one unit of the item in inventory is constant, regardless of the inventory level. Total annual inventory costs, then, are the sum of ordering costs and carrying costs.[19] The primary objective of the EOQ model is to find the order quantity, Q, that minimizes total annual inventory costs.

Algebraic Solution   In developing the algebraic form of the EOQ model, the following variables are defined:

Q = The order quantity, in units

D = The annual demand for the item, in units

S = The cost of placing and receiving an order, or setup cost

C = The annual cost of carrying one unit of the item in inventory

Ordering costs are equal to the number of orders per year multiplied by the cost per order, S. The number of orders per year is equal to annual demand, D, divided by the order quantity, Q. Carrying costs are equal to average inventory, $Q/2$, multiplied by the annual carrying cost per unit, C.

The total annual cost equation is as follows:

(16.1)   Total costs = Ordering costs + Carrying costs

By substituting the variables just defined into Equation 16.1, the following expression is obtained:

(16.2)   Total costs = (Number of orders per year $\times$ cost of order)

                    + (Average inventory $\times$ Annual carrying cost per unit)

or, in algebraic terms,

(16.3)   Total costs = $[(D/Q) \times S] + [(Q/2) \times C]$

The EOQ is the value of Q that minimizes the total costs given in Equation 16.3. The standard procedure for finding this value of Q involves calculus.[20] The optimal solution, or EOQ, is equal to the following:

(16.4) $$Q^* = \sqrt{\frac{2SD}{C}}$$

Another item of information that is sometimes useful for planning purposes is the optimal length of one inventory cycle, that is, the time between placements of orders for the item. The optimal length of one inventory cycle, T^*, measured in days, is equal to the economic order quantity, Q^*, divided by the average daily demand, $D/365$ (assuming 365 days per year), as follows:

(16.5) $$T^* = \frac{Q^*}{D/365}$$

---

[19] The actual cost of the item (that is, the price paid for items purchased externally or the production cost for items manufactured internally) is excluded from this analysis because it is assumed to be constant regardless of the order quantity. This assumption is relaxed when quantity discounts are considered, which are not discussed here.

[20] Specifically, Equation 16.3 can be written as: Total costs = $(DS/Q) + (C/2)Q$. Taking the first derivative of Equation 16.3 with respect to Q and setting the resulting equation equal to zero gives: $(2DS/Q^2) + (C/2) = 0$. Solving this equation for Q gives the optimal EOQ formula provided in Equation 16.4.

This equation can be rewritten as follows:

$$(16.6) \qquad T^\star = \frac{365 \times Q^\star}{D}$$

The following example illustrates the use of the EOQ model. Suppose that Sears sells Simmons mattresses through its department stores located in the Toronto metropolitan area. All inventories are maintained at the firm's centrally located warehouse. Annual demand for the Simmons standard-sized mattress is 3,600 units and is spread evenly throughout the year. The cost of placing and receiving an order is $31.25.

Suppose that the annual carrying costs are 20 percent of the inventory value. Based on a wholesale cost of $50 per mattress, the annual carrying cost per mattress is 0.20 × $50 = $10. Because Simmons maintains a large regional distribution centre in Toronto, Sears can replenish its inventory virtually instantaneously. The firm wishes to determine the number of standard-sized mattresses it should periodically order from Simmons in order to minimize the total annual inventory costs. Substituting $D = 3,600$, $S = \$31.25$, and $C = \$10$ into Equation 16.4 yields the following EOQ:

$$Q^\star = \sqrt{\frac{2 \times \$31.25 \times 3,600}{\$10}}$$

$$= 150 \text{ mattresses}$$

Using Equation 16.3, we can calculate the total annual inventory costs of this policy:

$$\text{Total costs} = (3,600/150) \times \$31.25 + (150/2) \times \$10 = \$1,500$$

Finally, Equation 16.6 can be used to determine Sears' optimal inventory cycle for these mattresses:

$$T^\star = (365 \times 150)/3,600 = 15.2 \text{ days}$$

Thus, the EOQ of 150 mattresses and the optimal inventory cycle of 15.2 days for this item indicate that Sears should place an order for 150 mattresses every 15.2 days.

Graphic Solution   The order quantity that minimizes total annual inventory costs can be determined graphically by plotting inventory costs (vertical axis) as a function of the order quantity (horizontal axis). As we can see in Figure 16.4, annual ordering costs, DS/Q, vary inversely with the order quantity, Q, because the number of orders placed per year, D/Q, decreases as the size of the order quantity increases. Carrying costs, $CQ/2$, vary directly with the order quantity, Q, because the average inventory, $Q/2$, increases as the size of the order quantity increases.

The total inventory cost curve is found by vertically summing the heights of the ordering cost and carrying cost functions. The order quantity corresponding to the lowest point on the total cost curve is the optimal solution—that is, the economic order quantity, $Q^\star$.

Extensions of the Basic EOQ Model

The basic EOQ model described above makes a number of simplifying assumptions, including those pertaining to replenishment lead time and demand for the item. In practical applications of inventory control models, however, some of these assumptions may not be valid. Thus, it is important to understand how different assumptions affect the analysis and the optimal order quantity. The following discussion examines what occurs when some of these assumptions are altered.

Nonzero Lead Time   The basic EOQ model assumes that orders to replenish the inventory of an item are filled instantaneously. That is, the lead time is zero. In practice,

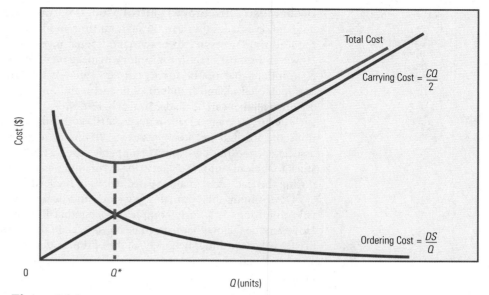

Figure 16.4
Graphic Solution of the EOQ Model

however, some time usually elapses between when a purchase order is placed and when the item actually is received in inventory. This lead time consists of the time it takes to manufacture the item, the time it takes to package and ship the item, or both.

If the lead time is constant and known with certainty, the optimal order quantity, Q^*, is not affected, although the time when an order should be placed is. Specifically, a company should not wait to reorder until the end of the inventory cycle, when the inventory level reaches zero—such as at points T_1, T_2, and T_3 in Figure 16.5. Instead, it should place an order n days prior to the end of each cycle, n being equal to the replenishment lead time measured in days. The **reorder point** is defined as the inventory level at which an order should be placed for replenishment of an item. Assuming that demand is constant over time, the reorder point, Q_r, is equal to the lead time, n (measured in days), multiplied by daily demand:

Reorder Point
The inventory level at which an order should be placed for replenishment of an item.

$$(16.7) \qquad Q_r = n \times (D/365)$$

where $D/365$ is daily demand (based on 365 days per year).

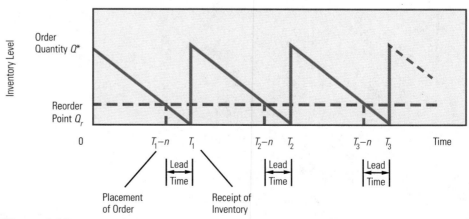

Figure 16.5
Nonzero Replenishment Lead Time Case of an Inventory Cycle

Chapter 16 Current Asset Management **599**

Probabilistic Inventory Control Models   Thus far, the analysis has assumed that demand or usage is uniform throughout time and known with certainty, as well as that the lead time necessary to procure additional inventory is also a fixed, known value. However, in most practical inventory management problems either (or both) of these assumptions may not be strictly correct. Typically, demand fluctuates over time due to seasonal, cyclical, and "random" influences, and imprecise forecasts of future demands are often all that can be made. Similarly, lead times are subject to uncertainty because of such factors as transportation delays, strikes, and natural disasters. Under these conditions, the possibility of stockouts exists. To minimize the possibility of stockouts and the associated stockout costs, most companies use a standard approach of adding a safety stock to their inventory. A safety stock is maintained to meet unexpectedly high demand during the lead time, unanticipated delays in the lead time, or both.

Determining the optimal safety stock and order quantities under these more realistic conditions is a fairly complex process that lies beyond the scope of this text.[21] However, the factors that have to be considered in this type of analysis can be identified briefly. All other things being equal, the optimal safety stock increases as the uncertainty associated with the demand forecasts and lead times increases. Likewise, all other things being equal, the optimal safety stock increases as the cost of stockouts increases. Determining the optimal safety stock involves balancing the expected costs of stockouts against the cost of carrying the additional inventory.

Just-in-Time Inventory Management Systems

Just-in-time (JIT) inventory management systems are part of a manufacturing approach that seeks to reduce the company's operating cycle and associated costs by eliminating wasteful procedures. Just-in-time inventory systems are based on the idea that all required inventory items should be supplied to the production process at exactly the right time and in exactly the right quantities. This approach was first developed by the Toyota Motor Corporation in the 1950s. In contrast, inventory models used in many plants, which rely on safety stocks, are sometimes referred to as "just-in-case" models.

The just-in-time approach works best for companies engaged in repetitive manufacturing operations. A key part of just-in-time techniques is the replacement of production in large batches with a continuous flow of smaller quantities. The use of a just-in-time inventory system requires close coordination between a company and its suppliers, because any disruption in the flow of parts and materials from the supplier can result in costly production delays and lost sales.

Just-in-Time (JIT) Inventory Management System
An approach to inventory and production management in which required inventory items are supplied exactly as needed by production.

---

[21] See N. Gaither and G. Frazier, *Production and Operations Management*, 8th ed. (Cincinnati: South-Western College Publishing, 1999), Chapter 10.

As we have seen, several factors are used to determine a firm's optimal liquid asset balances including the need to conduct transactions. In the case of the Canadian banking industry, deregulation and global competition resulted in the need for Canadian banks to increase their liquid asset balances in order to be able to expand their lines of business as well as to diversify internationally when suitable opportunities to do so arose. By the end July 2002, the Bank of Montreal had completed the acquisition of self-directed online client accounts of Morgan Stanley, which were then integrated with Harrisdirect, the Bank of Montreal's US direct investing business. In January 2003, National Bank acquired the $38.4 million deposit portfolio of the Standard Life Trust Company, thereby expanding its line of financial products.

The Bank of Nova Scotia ultimately did not engage in the purchase of other business assets, but, rather, early in 2003, it followed a strategy of aggressively buying back up to 5 percent of its outstanding common shares as well as redeeming a large number of its preferred share issues. The buying back of its own firm's shares is consistent with the passive residual dividend policy discussed in Chapter 14 and an alternative to increasing dividend payments. As we have seen, this is a strategy typically followed by firms that have large cash flows and an insufficient number of positive NPV investments in which to invest.

Summary

- A firm holds liquid asset balances for the following primary reasons:
    1. To conduct transactions
    2. For precautionary purposes
    3. To meet future requirements
    4. For speculative reasons

- A firm's optimal liquid asset balance reflects risk and return trade-offs and depends on both the opportunity cost of holding excess balances and the "shortage" costs associated with not having enough needed cash available.

- The primary objective in controlling cash collections is to reduce the delay between the time when the customer mails the payment and when it becomes a collected balance. Methods for reducing collection time include decentralized collection centres and concentration bank branches, lockboxes, electronic transfers, and special handling of large remittances.

- The primary objective in controlling cash disbursements is to slow payments and keep the firm's funds in the bank as long as possible. Techniques for slowing disbursements include scheduling and centralizing payments (zero-balance systems), using drafts rather than cheques, and stretching payables.

- Electronic funds transfer mechanisms increasingly will reduce the importance of float management techniques.

- The primary criteria a firm should use in selecting *marketable securities* include *default risk, marketability* (or *liquidity*), *maturity date,* and *rate of return.*

- A company should change its credit extension policy only if the expected marginal benefits of the change will exceed the expected marginal costs. A more liberal credit policy normally leads to increased sales and generates marginal benefits in the form of higher gross profits. The marginal costs of this type of policy, however, include the cost of the additional funds invested in accounts receivable and inventories, any additional credit checking and collection costs, and increased bad-debt expenses.

- A financial manager can exercise control over the company's level of receivables investment through three credit policy variables: credit standards, credit terms, and the collection effort. All three variables can be used to control the average collection period and bad-debt loss ratio.

  1. Credit standards are the criteria a business uses to screen its credit applicants.

  2. Credit terms are the conditions under which customers are required to repay the credit extended to them. Credit terms specify the length of the credit period and the cash discount (if any) given for early payment.

  3. The collection effort represents the methods used in attempting to collect payment from past-due accounts.

- Evaluating individual credit applicants involves gathering information about the applicant, analyzing this information to determine the applicant's creditworthiness, and then making the credit decision.

- Inventories serve as a buffer between the various stages of the manufacturing firm's procurement-production-sales cycle. By uncoupling the various phases of the firm's operations, inventories provide the firm with flexibility in timing purchases, scheduling production, and meeting fluctuating, uncertain demand for the finished product.

- Inventory-related costs include ordering costs, carrying costs, and stockout costs. Ordering costs include all of the costs of placing and receiving an order. Carrying costs include the various costs of holding items in inventory, including the cost of funds invested in inventory. Stockout costs are the costs incurred when demand exceeds available inventory, such as lost profits.

- Inventory control models are usually classified into two types: deterministic, if demand and lead time are known with certainty, and probabilistic, if demand and/or lead time are random variables with known probability distributions.

- The objective of the deterministic economic order quantity (EOQ) model is to find the order quantity that minimizes total inventory costs.

- The economic order quantity Q^* is equal to $\sqrt{2SD/C}$, where D is the annual demand; S, the fixed cost per order; and C, the annual carrying cost per unit.

- Probabilistic inventory control models require consideration of the possibility of stockouts. One approach used to handle this problem is to add a safety stock to the inventory.

- Just-in-time inventory models are based on the concept that required inventory items are supplied exactly as needed by production. Successful implementation of just-in-time models can reduce inventory investment.

Questions and Topics for Discussion

1. Define the following terms:
   a. Demand deposits
   b. Compensating balance
   c. Disbursement float

    d. Deposit float

    e. Lockbox

    f. Draft

2. What are the primary reasons a firm holds a liquid asset balance?

3. Describe the cost trade-offs associated with maintaining the following:

    a. Excessive liquid asset balances

    b. Inadequate liquid asset balances

4. Define *float* and describe the difference between *disbursement* float and *deposit* float.

5. Describe the primary services a bank provides to a firm. How is the bank compensated for these services?

6. Describe the methods available to a firm for expediting the collection of cash.

7. Describe the techniques available to a firm for slowing disbursements.

8. What are the primary criteria in selecting marketable securities for inclusion in a firm's portfolio?

9. What types of marketable securities are most suitable for inclusion in a firm's portfolio? What characteristics of these securities make them desirable investments for temporarily idle cash balances?

10. What are the marginal returns and costs associated with a more liberal extension of credit to a firm's customers?

11. What are the major credit policy variables a firm can use to control its level of receivables investment?

12. Describe the marginal costs and benefits associated with each of the following changes in a firm's credit and collection policies:

    a. Increasing the credit period from 7 to 30 days

    b. Increasing the cash discount from 1 to 2 percent

    c. Offering a seasonal dating credit plan

    d. Increasing collection expenditures (and effort)

13. How does a firm's required rate of return on investment enter into the analysis of changes in its credit and collection policies?

14. A firm is currently selling on credit terms of "net 30," and its accounts receivable average 30 days past due (i.e., the firm's average collection period is 60 days). What credit policy variables might the firm consider changing to reduce its average collection period?

15. "The objective of the firm's credit and collection policies should be to minimize its bad-debt losses." Do you agree or disagree with this statement? Explain.

16. Discuss how each of the following factors would tend to affect a firm's credit extension policies:

    a. A shortage of working capital

    b. An increase in output to the point where the firm is operating at full production capacity

    c. An increase in the firm's profit margin (i.e., its profit contribution ratio)

    d. An increase in interest rates (i.e., borrowing costs)

17. Describe the benefits of holding the following:

    a. Raw materials inventories

    b. Work-in-process inventories

    c. Finished goods inventories

18. Describe the components of carrying costs.

19. How do ordering costs for items purchased externally differ from ordering costs for items manufactured internally within the firm?

20. Describe the nature of stockout costs associated with a stockout in the following:
    a. Raw materials inventories
    b. Work-in-process inventories
    c. Finished goods inventories

21. What is ABC inventory classification? How can this method be useful to a business?

22. Describe the assumptions underlying the basic EOQ model.

23. In general terms, describe how to deal with each of the following conditions when determining the optimal inventory level:
    a. Constant (nonzero) replenishment lead time known with certainty
    b. Demand and replenishment lead time subject to uncertainty

24. How does the firm's required rate of return on investment enter into inventory decisions?

25. What are just-in-time inventory models?

Self-Test Problems

Note: When converting from annual data to daily data or vice versa, assume there are 365 days per year.

ST1. The White Oak Company's annual sales are $219 million. An average of nine days elapses between when a customer mails its payment and when the funds become usable by the firm.
    a. If the firm could speed up the collection of funds by two days, what would be the increase in the firm's average cash balance?
    b. Assuming that these additional funds can be invested in marketable securities that yield 7% per year, determine the increase in the firm's annual (pretax) earnings.

ST2. Builders Circle, a building supplies company, processes all of its customer credit card payments at its Toronto headquarters. A bank has offered to process the payments from the firm's customers located in the Atlantic region at its Halifax branch for $50,000 per year plus $0.20 per payment. Under this lockbox arrangement, the average mailing time for payments would be reduced from 3 days to 1.5 days. Cheque processing and clearing time would be reduced from 5 days to 2. Annual collections from the region are $292 million. The total number of payments received annually is 600,000 (an average of 50,000 credit cardholders × 12 payments per year). Assume that any funds released by this lockbox arrangement can be invested by Builders Circle to earn 10% per year before taxes. The establishment of a lockbox system for the Atlantic region will reduce payment processing costs at its Toronto headquarters by $40,000 per year. Using this information, determine
    a. The amount of funds released by this lockbox arrangement
    b. The annual (pretax) earnings on the released funds
    c. The annual fee that the firm must pay the bank for processing the payments
    d. The annual *net* (pretax) benefits the firm will receive by establishing this lockbox arrangement with the bank

ST3. TEC sells on terms of "net 30." Annual credit sales are $54.75 million, and its accounts receivable average 10 days overdue.

a. Determine TEC's investment in receivables.

b. Suppose that, as the result of a recession, annual credit sales decline by 15% and customers delay their payments to an average of 25 days past due. Determine the firm's new level of receivables investment.

ST4. PNI sells fertilizers and pesticides to various retail stores on terms of "2/10, net 30." The firm currently does not grant credit to retailers with a 3 (fair) or 4 (limited) Dun & Bradstreet Composite Credit Appraisal. An estimated $5,475,000 in additional sales per year could be generated if PNI extended credit to retailers in the "fair" category. The estimated average collection period for these customers is 75 days, and the expected bad-debt loss ratio is 5%. The firm also estimates that an additional inventory investment of $800,000 is required for the anticipated sales increase. Approximately 10% of these customers are expected to take the cash discount. PNI's variable cost ratio is 0.75, and its required pretax rate of return on investments in current assets is 18%. Determine the following:

a. Marginal profitability of additional sales
b. Cost of additional investment in receivables
c. Additional bad-debt loss
d. Cost of additional investment in inventory
e. Additional cash discounts
f. Net change in pretax profits

ST5. SportsMart, a chain of sporting goods stores, sells 360,000 baseballs per year. (Assume that sales are uniform throughout the year.) The baseballs cost SportsMart $15 per dozen ($1.25 each). Annual inventory carrying costs are 20% of inventory value. The costs of placing and receiving an order are $72. Assume that inventory replenishment occurs virtually instantaneously. Determine the following:

a. Economic order quantity
b. Total annual inventory costs of this policy
c. Optimal ordering frequency

Problems*

Note: When converting annual data to daily data or vice versa in these problems, assume there are 365 days per year.

BASIC

1. Dexter Instrument Company's sales average $3 million per day.
   a. If Dexter could reduce the time between customers' mailing their payments and the funds becoming collected balances by 2.5 days, what would be the increase in the firm's average cash balance?
   b. Assuming that these additional funds can be invested in marketable securities to yield 8.5% per annum, determine the annual increase in Dexter's (pretax) earnings.

2. Exman Company performed a study of its billing and collection procedures and found that an average of eight days elapses between the time when a customer's payment is received and when the funds become usable by the firm. The firm's *annual* sales are $540 million.

---

*Coloured numbers and letters denote problems that have "check" answers provided at the back of the book.

a. Assuming that Exman could reduce the time required to process customer payments by 1.5 days, determine the increase in the firm's average cash balance.

b. Assuming that these additional funds could be used to reduce the firm's outstanding bank loans (current interest rate is 8%) by an equivalent amount, determine the annual pretax savings in interest expenses.

3. Miranda Tool Company sells to retail hardware stores on credit terms of "net 30." Annual credit sales are $18 million and are spread evenly throughout the year. The firm's variable cost ratio is 0.70, and its accounts receivable average $1.9 million. Using this information, determine the following for the company:

a. Average daily credit sales

b. Average collection period

c. Average investment in receivables

4. Drake Paper Company sells on terms of "net 30." The firm's variable cost ratio is 0.80.

a. If annual credit sales are $20 million and its accounts receivable average 15 days overdue, what is Drake's investment in receivables?

b. Suppose that, as the result of a recession, annual credit sales decline by 10 percent to $18 million, and customers delay their payments to an average of 25 days past the due date. What will be Drake's new level of receivables investment?

INTERMEDIATE

5. Japanese Motors, an importer of foreign cars, has a subsidiary (Japanese Motor Credit Company, or JMCC) that finances dealer inventories, as well as retail instalment purchases of the firms' cars. With respect to the financing of retail purchases, JMCC currently employs a centralized billing and collection system. Once a customer's credit has been approved at one of the subsidiary's 50 local branch offices, the information is forwarded to JMCC headquarters (located in Vancouver) and the customer is issued a book of payment coupons. Each month during the life of the instalment contract, the customer mails a coupon stub along with the payment to the Vancouver office. The average mailing, processing, and cheque-clearing time with the present collection system is eight days.

In an effort to reduce this collection time, JMCC is considering establishing a decentralized collection system. Under this system, customers would be instructed to mail their payments to the nearest local branch office, which would then deposit the cheques in a local bank and report this information to JMCC headquarters in Vancouver. As the cheques clear in the local bank branches, funds would be sent each day to JMCC's central bank account in Vancouver. This decentralized collection system would reduce both mailing time and cheque-clearing time and reduce the average collection time to five days.

JMCC's annual instalment collections are $900 million. Implementation of the decentralized collection system is expected to reduce collection costs at the Vancouver headquarters by $100,000 a year compared with the currently employed centralized collection system. However, branch office collection costs are expected to rise by $225,000 if the decentralized system is implemented. Any funds released under the decentralized collections system would be used to reduce the firm's debt, which currently carries an interest rate of 7.5%.

Using this information, determine the annual net pretax benefits JMCC would realize by implementing a decentralized collection system.

6. Looking back at Tables 16.1 and 16.2, evaluate the impact on Bassett's pretax profits of extending full credit to the customers in Credit Risk Group 5. Assume that Bassett's pretax required rate of return on inventory investments is 20% and that an additional inventory investment of $40,000 is required due to the anticipated sales increase from customers in Credit Risk Group 5.

7. Once again, consider the Bassett Furniture Industries example (Tables 16.1 and 16.2). Assume that rising labour and interest costs have increased Bassett's variable cost ratio from 0.75 to 0.80 and its required pretax rate of return on receivables and inventory investments from 20 to 25%. Re-evaluate the effect of Bassett's pretax profits of extending full credit to the customers in Credit Risk Group 4.

 Excel

8. Epstein Company, a wholesale distributor of jewellery, sells to retail jewellery stores on terms of "net 120." Its average collection period is 150 days. The firm is considering the introduction of a 4% cash discount if customers pay within 30 days. Such a change in credit terms is expected to reduce the average collection period to 108 days. Epstein expects 30% of its customers to take the cash discount. Annual credit sales are $6 million. Epstein's variable cost ratio is 0.667, and its required pretax return on receivables investment is 15%. The firm does not expect its inventory level to change as a result of the change in credit terms. Determine the following:
   a. The funds released by the change in credit terms
   b. The net effect on Epstein's pretax profits

 Excel

9. In an effort to speed up the collection of receivables, Hill Publishing Company is considering increasing the size of its cash discount by changing its credit terms from "1/10, net 30" to "2/10, net 30." Currently, the company's collection period averages 43 days. Under the new credit terms, it is expected to decline to 28 days. Also, the percentage of customers who will take advantage of the cash discount is expected to increase from the current 50% to 70% with the new credit terms. Bad-debt losses currently average 4 percent of sales and are not expected to change significantly if Hill changes its credit policy. Annual credit sales are $3.5 million, the variable cost ratio is 60%, and the required pretax rate of return (i.e., the opportunity cost) on receivables investment is 14%. The company does not expect its inventory level to change as a result of its proposed change in credit terms. Assuming that Hill does decide to increase the size of its cash discount, determine the following:
   a. The earnings on the funds released by the change in credit terms
   b. The cost of the additional cash discounts taken
   c. The net effect on Hill's pretax profits

10. Allstar Shoe Company produces a wide variety of athletic-type shoes for tennis, basketball, and running. Although sales are somewhat seasonal, production is uniform throughout the year. Allstar's production and sales average 1.92 million pairs of shoes per year. The company purchases shoelaces for its entire product line. Shoelaces are bought in lots of 10,000 pairs at a price of $800 per lot. Ordering costs are $20, including the cost of preparing the purchase order and inspecting the shipment when it arrives at the company's warehouse. Annual inventory carrying costs average 15% of the inventory value. Assuming that the shoelace manufacturer is located nearby and that orders are filled on the same day they are placed (that is, virtually instantaneously), determine the following:
   a. The EOQ for shoelaces
   b. The total annual inventory costs of this policy
   c. The frequency with which Allstar should place its orders for shoelaces

11. Alberta Instruments uses integrated circuits (ICs) in its business calculators. Its annual demand for ICs is 120,000 units. The ICs cost the firm $10 each. The company has determined that the EOQ is 20,000 units. It takes 18 days between when an order is placed and when the delivery is received. Carrying costs are 20% of the inventory value. Determine the following:
   a. The optimal ordering frequency
   b. The average inventory and annual carrying costs
   c. The reorder point

12. Great Lakes Oil Company currently processes all of its credit card payments at its domestic headquarters in Calgary. The firm is considering establishing a lockbox arrangement with a Halifax bank to process its payments from the Atlantic region. Under the arrangement, the average mailing time for customer payments from the region would be reduced from 3 days to 1.5 days, whereas cheque processing and clearing time would be reduced from 6 days to 2.5 days. Annual collections from the region are $180 million. The total number of payments received annually is 4.8 million (an average of 400,000 credit card customers $\times$ 12 payments per year). The Halifax bank will process the payments for an annual fee of $75,000 plus $0.05 per payment. Assume that the funds released by the lockbox arrangement can be invested elsewhere in the firm to yield 10% before taxes. The establishment of a lockbox system for the Atlantic region will reduce payment-processing costs at the Calgary office by $50,000 per year. Using this information, determine the following:

    a. The amount of funds released by the lockbox arrangement
    b. The annual (pretax) earnings on the released funds
    c. The annual fee the firm must pay to the bank for processing the payments
    d. The annual *net* (pretax) benefits the firm will receive by establishing this lockbox arrangement with the bank

13. BC Paper Company is considering establishing a zero-balance system for its payroll account. The firm pays its employees every two weeks on Friday (that is, 26 pay periods per year). Currently, the firm deposits the necessary funds in the payroll account on Friday to cover the total amount of the cheques written each pay period, which averages $1 million. However, the firm has found that the majority of the cheques did not clear the payroll account until the following week. A typical distribution of when the cheques clear the payroll account is as follows:

Day	Amount of Funds Clearing Payroll Account
Friday	$ 300,000
Monday	450,000
Tuesday	150,000
Wednesday	100,000
Total	$1,000,000

    Assume that the firm can earn 6% on any funds released from its payroll account using a zero-balance system.

    a. Determine the annual pretax returns the firm would realize from the use of a zero-balance system for its payroll account.
    b. What additional information is necessary to make a decision concerning the desirability of establishing such a system?

14. NCFC manufactures upholstered furniture, which it sells to various small retailers on credit terms of "2/10, net 60." The firm currently does not grant credit to retailers with a 3 (fair) or 4 (limited) Dun & Bradstreet Composite Credit Appraisal. If NCFC were to extend credit to retailers in the "fair" category, an estimated additional $1.2 million per year in sales could be generated. The estimated average collection period for these customers is 90 days, and the expected bad-debt loss ratio is 6%. Approximately 20% of these customers are expected to take the cash discount. NCFC's variable cost ratio is 0.70, and its required pretax rate of return on current assets investments is 20%. The firm also estimates that an

additional investment in inventory of $350,000 is necessary for the anticipated sales increase. Determine the net change in NCFC's pretax profits from extending credit to retailers in the "fair" category.

15. Manitoba Pharmaceuticals, Inc., a wholesale distributor of ethical drugs, has been experiencing a relatively long average collection period because many of its customers face liquidity problems and delay their payments well beyond the due date. In addition, its bad-debt loss ratio is high because a number of pharmacies have closed due to financial difficulties. To avoid these problems in the future, Manitoba Pharmaceuticals is considering a plan to institute more stringent credit standards to keep the average collection period and bad-debt losses from rising beyond acceptable limits. Specifically, the firm plans to refuse to grant additional credit to any current customers more than 15 days past due on their payments. Such a change in credit policy is expected to reduce current annual sales of $6.5 million by 20%, reduce the average collection period from 110 days to 75 days, and lower bad-debt losses from 8 to 4%. Due to the expected decrease in sales, the company estimates that its inventories will decrease by $250,000. The firm's variable cost ratio is 0.75, and its required pretax return on investments in receivables and inventories is 15%. Determine the net effect of this plan on the pretax profits of Manitoba Pharmaceuticals.

16. Creole Industries, Inc. estimates that if it spent an additional $20,000 to hire another collection agent in its credit department, it could lower its bad-debt loss ratio to 3.5% from a current rate of 4% and also reduce its average collection period from 50 to 45 days. (Assume that sales and inventory remain unchanged if the agent is hired.) Creole's annual credit sales are $5 million, and its variable cost ratio is 0.75. The firm's required pretax rate of return on receivables investment (i.e., the opportunity cost) is 18%. Determine the net effect on the firm's pretax profits of hiring the additional collection agent.

 Excel

17. Jenkins Corporation sells $120 million of its products to wholesalers on terms of "net 50." Currently, the firm's average collection period is 65 days. In order to speed up the collection of receivables, Jenkins is considering offering a 1% cash discount if customers pay their bills within 15 days. The firm expects 40% of its customers to take the discount and its average collection period to decline to 40 days. The firm's required pretax return on receivables investments is 20%. Determine the net effect on Jenkins' pretax profits of offering a 1% cash discount.

 Excel

18. The Halifax Trading Corporation has been experiencing a decline in sales relative to its major competitors. Because the firm is confident about the quality of its products, it suspects that this sales loss may reflect its relatively stringent credit standards and terms. The firm currently has credit sales of $50 million annually. With current credit terms of "net 20," its average collection period is now 25 days. Bad-debt losses are 2% of credit sales. The firm's variable cost ratio is 0.80, and its required pretax return on receivables and inventory investments is 20%.

Halifax plans to change its credit terms to "2/10, net 30." It expects 20% of its customers to take advantage of the cash discount. Halifax also plans to relax credit standards and take on riskier accounts. This action is expected to increase credit sales by 30%. Bad-debt losses are expected to increase to 3% of credit sales, and the average collection period is expected to become 30 days. The company also estimates that an additional investment in inventory of $3 million is required because of the anticipated sales increase. Determine the net effect of this plan on the pretax profits of Halifax.

19. Saccomanno Industries, Inc. is considering whether to discontinue offering credit to customers who are more than 10 days overdue on repaying the credit extended to them. Current annual credit sales are $10 million on credit terms of "net 30." Such a change in policy is expected to reduce sales by 10%, cut the firm's bad-debt

losses from 5 to 3%, and reduce its average collection period from 72 days to 45 days. The firm's variable cost ratio is 0.70 and its required pretax return on receivables and inventory investments is 25%. Because of the anticipated decrease in sales, the company expects its inventories to decrease by $200,000. Determine the net effect of this credit-tightening policy on the pretax profits of the firm.

20. The Blawnox Company is concerned about its bad-debt losses and the length of time required to collect receivables. Current sales are $43.8 million per year. Bad-debt losses are currently 3.5% of sales, and the average collection period is 68 days (credit terms are "net 30"). One plan under consideration is to tighten credit standards by refusing to grant additional credit to any customers who are more than 15 days past due on their payments. This change in credit policy is expected to reduce sales by 10% but also reduce bad-debt losses to 2.5% of sales and reduce the average collection period to 40 days. The firm's variable cost ratio is 70%, and its required pretax rate of return on current assets investments is 18%. The company also expects its inventory investment to decrease by $1 million due to the anticipated decrease in sales. Determine the net effect of this plan on Blawnox's pretax profits.

21. Quick-Copy Company uses 110,000 reams of standard-sized paper per year at its various duplicating centres. Its current paper supplier charges $2.00 per ream. Annual inventory carrying costs are 15% of inventory value. The costs of placing and receiving an order of paper are $41.25. Assuming that inventory replenishment occurs virtually instantaneously, determine:
    a. The firm's EOQ
    b. The total annual inventory costs of this policy
    c. The optimal ordering frequency
    d. Compute and plot ordering costs, carrying costs, and total inventory costs for order quantities of 2,000, 4,000, 5,000, 5,500, 6,000, 7,000, and 9,000 reams. Connect the points on each function with a smooth curve, and determine the EOQ from the graph (and the table used in constructing the graph).

22. Books, etc., a nationwide chain of bookstores, anticipates that annual demand for the paperback version of a best-selling novel will be 150,000 copies. The books cost the firm $2 each. Books, etc. has determined that the optimal order quantity (EOQ) is 30,000 copies. It takes 20 days between when an order is placed and when the delivery is received. Carrying costs are 15% of the inventory value. Determine the following:
    a. Optimal ordering frequency
    b. Average inventory and annual carrying costs
    c. Reorder point
       Books, etc. decides that it wants to maintain a 60-day safety stock of the novel to meet unexpected demand and possible shipment delays from the publisher. Determine the following:
    d. Amount of safety stock, in units
    e. Average inventory and annual carrying costs
    f. Reorder point

Other Practice Materials and Resources

For interactive quizzes, Internet exercises, crossword puzzles, CTV videos, and more, go to the *Contemporary Financial Management* Web site at **http://cyr.nelson.com**

Part Six

Risk Management

6

Because every Canadian firm must disclose its risk management policies, Part Six looks at some advanced topics that are important for financial managers. Chapter 17 discusses *derivative* financial instruments including options and option-related financing instruments as well as interest rate swaps and some of the more important ways they can be used in domestic risk management strategies. Chapter 18 covers international risk management topics including parity conditions and international risk hedging. Each of the decision areas covered in this part offers significant opportunities for adding to shareholders' wealth.

Managing Domestic Risk

Learning Objectives

After studying this chapter you should be able to

1. Understand the different types of securities the firm can issue to manage long-term funding sources and risks effectively

2. Identify an *option* as one type of *derivative* security giving the right to the holder, but not the obligation, to buy or sell an asset at a set price during a specified time period

   a. A *call* option is an option to *buy* an asset at a set price

   b. A *put* option is an option to *sell* an asset at a set price

3. Understand that the value of a call option is dependent on six variables:

   a. The price of an underlying security

   b. The option's exercise price

   c. The time remaining until the option expires

   d. The level of interest rates

   e. The expected volatility of the underlying security's price

   f. The dividend (if any) on the underlying asset

4. Understand several formal option valuation models that are available to compute the value of options, including the Black-Scholes model, which is presented and illustrated in Appendix 17A

5. Understand that a convertible security is a fixed-income security, such as a debenture or a preferred share, which may be exchanged for the firm's common shares at the holder's option

6. Understand that a warrant is an option issued by a firm to purchase the firm's common shares for a particular price during a specified period of time

7. Understand that in a rights offering, common shareholders receive an option to purchase additional common shares of the firm, in proportion to the shares they currently own, at a price below the market value

8. Understand that *swaps* can be used to manage certain types of financial risk

Repricing "Underwater Options"

Options are financial instruments that give the holder the right to buy or sell something in the future at a price established today. Call options give the holder the right (but not the obligation) to buy something, such as a share, in the future at a price (called the *exercise* or *strike price*) established today. Corporations frequently use stock options as part of their compensation plan to provide a strong incentive for the firm's managers and employees to work hard to increase the value of the firm's shares. If the combined actions of managers increase shareholder wealth, this will be reflected in increased share prices. Since the value of a call option at the time of exercise is equal to the difference between the share price and the exercise price, the holders of these options also benefit from the share price increase.

CP PHOTO/AARON HARRIS

Stock options are used widely by corporations, both large and small, to provide a supplemental form of compensation to employees that more closely aligns the interests of managers with the interests of owners. Stock options, as incentives to managers, are a centrepiece of the economic value added (EVA) incentive systems proposed by Stern Stewart and discussed in Chapter 3.

Although there is growing evidence that the proper use of stock option plans can result in improved company performance, these compensation systems are not without problems. For example, consider the dilemma faced by the board of directors of Nortel in 2001. In the face of a slumping stock market, Nortel's share price had dropped from a high of over $109 in July 2000 to less than $10 in 2001. Employees of the company held options to purchase more than 93 million Nortel shares. With the exercise price of these options so far above the share price, the board of directors was concerned that these options no longer provided the incentives needed for high future performance.

Accordingly, the board approved a new stock option program that terminated the old options and substituted new options at more realistic exercise prices. Unfortunately, Nortel's share price continued to drop, so these new options are also underwater.

Nortel has not been alone in repricing the options it has granted to directors, managers, and employees. In recent years, almost all of the high-flying high-tech companies have repriced employee stock options to give them exercise prices much closer to the market share prices. Firms that have repriced their executive stock options argue that it is necessary in order to keep key employees. In addition, when an option is "deep out of the money," much of the positive incentive for improved performance is lost.

The ultimate value of executive stock options in improving corporate performance is still the subject of debate. As you might guess, the policy of repricing options after a company's share price has "tanked" is even more controversial.

In this chapter, we discuss the use of derivative financial instruments, including put and call options, their valuation, and their role in the financing plans of a company.

Introduction

For an excellent example of compliance with CICA *Handbook* Section 3860, see the 2002 Annual Report for the Swiss Water Decaffeinated Coffee Income Fund of Burnaby, BC, at **www.swisswater.com**

According to Section 3860 of the CICA *Handbook,* the annual report of every firm must disclose the firm's risk management policies for interest rate risk and foreign currency risk. Firms may also disclose how they manage commodity risk and credit risk.

This chapter discusses the management of interest rate risk, among other topics, and Chapter 18 discusses foreign currency risk management. Credit risk management has already been discussed in Chapter 16. Commodity risk management is not discussed in this introductory book. However, the principle of hedging risk that is developed in Chapters 17 and 18 also applies to commodities.

Options and option-related financing play an important role in the management of a firm's assets and liabilities. Options are one of an important type of derivative securities—that is, securities whose value is derived from another asset. Swaps are another type of derivative securities that are discussed in this chapter and are used to manage interest rate risk. Another important class of derivative securities is forward-type contracts, such as futures contracts and forward contracts. (These are discussed in Chapter 18.) A wide array of securities contain option features, including

1. *Short-term options* on common shares, stock market indexes, bonds (e.g., interest rate options), and foreign currencies (e.g., on the British pound and Japanese yen). These options are traded on organized exchanges, such as the Montreal Exchange, the Chicago Mercantile Exchange and the Chicago Board Options Exchange.[1]

2. *Convertible fixed-income securities,* such as debentures or preferred shares that may be exchanged for the firm's common shares at the holder's option. By giving the fixed-income security holder an opportunity to participate in any increase in the common share value, the firm is able to reduce potential conflicts between the fixed-income security holders and shareholders, resulting in lower agency costs.

3. *Warrants,* in contrast to short-term options, are options issued by a company to purchase common shares of the firm at a particular price during a specified period of time. Warrants are frequently sold to investors as part of a *unit* that consists of a fixed-income security with a warrant attached. As a result, warrants are issued by firms for similar reasons as convertible securities.

4. A *rights offering* occurs when common shareholders are given an option to purchase additional common shares, in proportion to the fraction they currently own, at a price below the market value.

Also, as we will see in the next section, a firm's common shares can be understood more fully using an options framework.

This chapter examines the characteristics and valuation of options and option-related financing. An understanding of these concepts is necessary to evaluate the impact that decisions to issue or purchase these types of securities have on shareholder wealth.

Options

Option
A contract that gives its holder the right but not the obligation to buy (call) or sell (put) an asset at a set price during a specified time period.

Call
A contract that gives the holder the right but not the obligation to *buy* an asset at a set price.

Put
A contract that gives the holder the right but not the obligation to *sell* an asset at a set price during a specified period of time.

An **option** *is a security that gives its holder the right, but not the obligation, to buy or sell an asset at a set price (the exercise price) during a specified time period.* Options are classified as either *call* or *put* options. A **call** is an option to *buy* a particular asset. A **put** is an option to *sell* it.

---

[1] Options were introduced in Chapter 2. For more information see Charles W. Smithson and Clifford W. Smith, *Managing Financial Risk* (NY: McGraw-Hill, 1998), for a discussion of many of these instruments. See also Robert Jarrow and Stuart Turnbull, *Derivative Securities,* 2nd ed. (Mason, OH: South-Western, 2000), and John C. Hull, *Options, Futures and Other Derivatives,* 5th ed. (Upper Saddle River, NJ: Prentice Hall, 2003).

Option Valuation Concepts

Suppose an investor is offered an opportunity to purchase a call option on one share of the Mackey Company. Consider the following sets of conditions:

1. The option's exercise price is $25. The Mackey share price is $30. The option's expiration date is today. Under these conditions, the investor is willing to pay $5 for the option. In other words, the value of a call option is equal to the share price minus the exercise price, or

(17.1)   Value of a call option at expiration = Share price − Exercise price

2. The option's exercise price is $25. The Mackey share price is $30. The option expires in six months. Given these conditions, the investor is willing to pay more than $5 for the option because of the chance that the share price will increase. This would also cause the option to increase in value. Therefore,

(17.2)   Value of a call option prior to expiration > Share price − Exercise price

3. The option's exercise price is $0.01. The Mackey share price is $30. The option expires in six months. Under these somewhat unusual conditions, the option investor is willing to pay *almost as much as the share price*. However, under no conditions should the investor be willing to pay more than the share price. Therefore,

(17.3)   Maximum value of a call option = Share price

4. The option's exercise price is $25. The Mackey share price is $0.01. The option expires today. The investor most likely is willing to pay nothing for the option given these conditions, but the investor also is not willing to pay someone to take the option "off his hands," because it is an option and can be allowed to expire with no additional cost. Therefore,

(17.4)   Minimum value of a call option = 0

The results of these sets of conditions are shown in Figure 17.1.[2]

Variables Affecting Call Option Valuation

The examples in the previous section illustrate that the value of a call option is dependent on the price of the underlying share, the option's exercise price, and the length of time before the option's expiration date. Three other variables that influence the value of a call option are the level of interest rates, the expected volatility of the underlying share's price, and the share's dividend. A discussion of these six variables follows.[3]

Relationship Between the Exercise Price and the Share Price   The effect of the exercise or strike price on option value is seen by examining Table 17.1, which lists some options quotations for Nortel. At the time, Nortel's shares were selling at $2.95. For options expiring in January, the call option with a $2.50 exercise price sold at a higher

---

[2] Figure 17.1 shows a $25 exercise price. Technically, Figure 17.1 shows only the results of conditions 1, 2, and 4.

[3] A model for determining the equilibrium value of an option as a function of these variables is developed in Fischer Black and Myron Scholes, "The Pricing of Options and Corporate Liabilities," *Journal of Political Economy* 81 (May–June 1973): 637–654. The Excel templates available at the text's Web site include a Black-Scholes option pricing model. The Black-Scholes option pricing model is presented and illustrated in Appendix 17A.

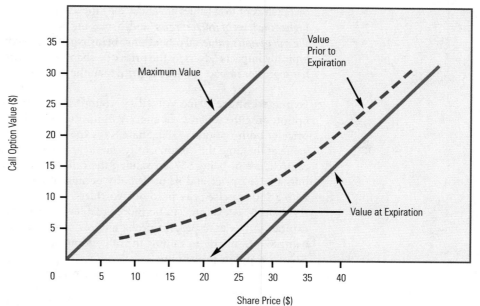

Figure 17.1
Call Option Valuation at Different Share Prices*
*Exercise price = $25.

price than the option with a $4 exercise price because buyers have to pay more money to exercise options with higher exercise prices. Thus, these options have less value to potential buyers. Therefore, *the higher the exercise price, given the share price, the lower the call option value,* all other things being equal. Of course, inspection of Equations 17.1 and 17.2 also show that *the higher the share price, given the exercise price, the higher the call option value,* all other things being equal.

Because an option's value (payoff) is dependent or *contingent* on the value of another security (in this case, the underlying share), an option is said to be a **contingent claim**.

Contingent Claim
A security whose payoffs depend on the value of another security.

Time Remaining Until Expiration Date   The figures in Table 17.1 show that an option expiring in March has a higher value than an option with a January expiration date because investors realize that Nortel's share has a greater chance to increase in value with three additional months before expiration. Thus, *the longer the time remaining before the option expires, the higher the option value,* all other things being equal. Because of this, an option is sometimes referred to as a "wasting asset."

Interest Rates   The buyer of common shares incurs either interest expense (explicit cost) if the purchase funds are borrowed or lost interest income (implicit cost) if existing funds are used for purchase. In either case, an interest cost is incurred.

Buying a call option is an alternative to buying shares. By buying an option, the interest cost associated with holding shares is avoided. Because options are an alternative to

Table 17.1 Selected Call Option Prices for Nortel		
	Expiration Month	
Exercise Price	**January 2003**	**March 2003**
2.50	0.60	1.10
4.00	0.03	0.20

Note: Nortel's share price was $2.95 on December 6, 2002

ownership, option values are affected by the share ownership interest costs. As a result, *the higher the level of interest rates* (and, hence, the interest cost of share ownership), *the higher the call option's value,* all other things being equal. However, in reality, a higher interest rate typically impacts adversely the price of a share. This indirect effect on share price usually has a greater impact on the call price than the direct effect of the interest rate.

Expected Share Price Volatility   Suppose an investor has a choice of buying a call option on either share S or share V. Both shares currently sell at $50, and the exercise price of both options is $50. Share S is expected to be the more stable of the two—its value at the time the option expires has a 50 percent chance of being $45 and a 50 percent chance of being $57. In valuing the call option on share S, the investor considers only the $57 price and its probability because if the share goes to $45, the call option with a $50 exercise price becomes worthless.

Share V is expected to be more volatile—its expected value at the time of option expiration has a 40 percent probability of being $30 and a 60 percent probability of being $70. Similarly, in valuing the call option on share V, the investor considers only the $70 price and its probability.

The investor now has sufficient information to conclude that the call option on share V is more valuable than the call option on share S because a greater return can be earned by investing in an option that has a 60 percent chance of being worth $20 (share price − exercise price = $70 − $50 = $20) at expiration than an option that has a 50 percent probability of being worth $7 (share price − exercise price = $57 − $50 = $7) at expiration. Therefore, the *greater the expected share price volatility, the higher the call option value,* all other things being equal.

Dividends (if any) on the Underlying Asset   If the underlying share pays dividends, this reduces the value of the option.

Option Valuation Models   Financial researchers have made considerable progress in developing formal models to value options. Appendix 17A illustrates the popular Black-Scholes option pricing model.

Common Shares in an Options Framework

Any firm with debt can be analyzed in an options framework.[4] Suppose a start-up firm raises equity capital and also borrows $7 million, due two years from now. Then, suppose further that the firm undertakes a risky project to develop new computer parts. In two years, the firm must decide whether or not to default on its debt repayment obligation.

Consider this example in an options context. The shareholders can be viewed as having sold this firm to the debt holders for $7 million when they borrowed the $7 million. However, the shareholders retained an option to buy back the firm. The shareholders have the right to exercise their option by paying off the debt claim at maturity. Whether they do depends on the value of the firm at the time the debt is due. If the value of the firm is greater than the debt claim, the shareholders will exercise their option by paying off the debt. If the value of the firm is less than the debt claim, the shareholders will let their option expire by not repaying the debt.

This simplified example has interesting implications. Earlier in the options discussion, we showed that the greater the expected share price volatility, the higher the call option value will be. Therefore, if the shareholders choose high-risk projects with a chance of very large payoffs, they increase the value of their option. However, at the

---

[4] The following discussion is based on Scott P. Mason and Robert C. Merton, "The Role of Contingent Claims Analysis in Corporate Finance," in *Recent Advances in Corporate Finance,* Edward I. Altman and Marti G. Subrahmanyam, eds. (Homewood, IL: Richard D. Irwin, 1985).

same time, they also increase the likelihood of defaulting on the debt, thereby decreasing its value. Thus, it is easy to see how potential conflicts between shareholders and debt holders can occur. These potential conflicts are discussed further in the next section on convertible securities. In fact, we shall see that giving the bondholders an equity stake in the firm decreases the potential for conflicts between shareholders and debt holders.

Convertible Securities

Both debentures and preferred shares can have convertibility or conversion features. When a firm issues convertible securities, its usual intention is the future issuance of common shares. To illustrate, suppose the Beloit Corporation issues two million convertible preferred shares at a price of $50. After the sale, the firm receives gross proceeds of $100 million. Because of the convertibility feature, the company can expect to issue common shares in exchange for the redemption of the convertible preferred shares over some future time period. As a result, convertibles are sometimes described as a *deferred equity offering.* In the case of Beloit's convertible preferred, each $50 preferred share can be exchanged for two common shares. That is, the holder has in effect a call option to buy two common shares at an exercise price with a PV of $25 a share ($50 preferred share price/2). Therefore, if all the preferred shares are converted, the firm in effect will have issued four million new common shares, and the preferred shares will no longer appear on Beloit's balance sheet. No additional funds are raised by the company at the time of conversion.

Features of Convertible Securities

Convertible Security
A fixed-income security that may be exchanged for a firm's common shares at the holder's option. The two most common types of convertible securities are *convertible preferred shares* and *convertible debentures.*

Conversion Price
The effective price an investor pays for common shares obtained by converting a convertible security.

Conversion Ratio
The number of common shares an investor obtains by converting a convertible security.

As an introduction to the terminology and features of convertible securities, consider the US$1,800 million, seven-year issue of 4.25 percent convertible senior notes sold by Nortel on August 15, 2001. The notes are due September 1, 2008. **Convertible securities** are exchangeable for common shares at a stated **conversion price**. In the case of the Nortel issue, the conversion price at the time of issue was $10. This means that each $1,000 note was convertible into common shares at $10 per share.

The number of common shares that can be obtained when a convertible security is exchanged is determined by the **conversion ratio**, which is calculated as follows:

(17.5)   Conversion ratio = Par or face value of security/Conversion price

In the case of Nortel's convertible senior notes, the conversion ratio at the time of issue was the following:

$$\text{Conversion ratio} = \$1,000/\$10 = 100$$

Thus, each $1,000 Nortel note could be exchanged for 100 common shares. Although the conversion ratio may change one or more times during the life of the conversion option, it is more usual for it to remain constant.

Normally, the conversion price is set about 15 to 30 percent above the common share's market price prevailing at the time of issue. Holders of convertible securities are protected against dilution by the company. For example, suppose Nortel were to split its common shares two for one. The conversion price (and therefore the conversion ratio) would be adjusted so that the holders would not be disadvantaged by the split. Specifically, in the Nortel case, the new conversion price would be $5, and the new conversion ratio would be 200.

Managing Long-Term Funding with Convertibles

As a general rule, relatively small, risky companies whose common shares are publicly traded are the principal issuers of convertibles. These firms, for the most part, are rapidly growing and in need of funds to finance their growth. Investors, on the other hand, are frequently reluctant to lend money to small, risky companies without promises of high interest payments and assurances from the company that it will properly manage the debt.

Recall that in Chapter 1, we introduced agency problems and discussed the conflicts that can occur between a firm's shareholders and its creditors. We said that creditors often insist on certain protective covenants in the company's bond indentures. The agency costs to properly implement and monitor the covenants can be high, particularly for small, risky firms. As a result, because of potential conflicts between shareholders and bondholders and the associated agency costs, it is usually easier and cheaper to offer the bondholders an equity stake in the company—that is, a convertible security. With an equity stake, bondholders are less concerned about any company attempts to increase the returns to the shareholders by means of risky projects.

In addition to agency costs, there are several other reasons for issuing convertibles. One is that cash flow benefits accrue to the issuing company in the form of lower interest payments or dividends. This occurs because investors are willing to accept the conversion privilege as part of their overall return. Typically, firms can issue convertible securities with interest rates or dividend yields about 3 or 4 percentage points below similar, nonconvertible issues, that is, issues without convertibility features.

Another reason that firms issue convertible securities is to sell common shares at a higher price than the prevailing market price at the time of issue. Suppose a company needs additional equity financing because of a relatively high proportion of fixed-income securities in its capital structure. If the firm's management feels the price of its common shares is temporarily depressed, one alternative is to consider issuing a convertible security. With the conversion price typically set about 15 to 30 percent above the market price at the time of issue, the use of a convertible security effectively gives the issuing company the potential for selling common shares above the existing market price. It may seem that issuing convertible securities is like having the proverbial free lunch. What is the catch?

Suppose a firm does poorly in the future and the price per common share falls. Then, the firm would be better off if it sold common shares at today's higher price instead of issuing convertibles today. This is because the dividends on the additional common shares are highly likely to be less than the interest payments or preferred dividend payments on the convertibles. Furthermore, if the convertibles were bonds, the firm may experience financial distress or even a bankruptcy that may have been avoided by selling common shares today.

On the other hand, suppose the firm does extremely well and the share price rises substantially above the conversion price. Then, assuming that the holders of the convertibles convert to common shares, the firm effectively sold these new shares at the conversion prices instead of the new higher price. In other words, the firm would be better off to issue straight (i.e., nonconvertible) debt or preferred shares today and then retire this issue in the future by issuing common shares then at the new higher price.

Thus, if the financial manager has perfect foresight, the manager can always find a funding strategy that outperforms the convertibles strategy. However, good financial managers realize that their foresight is less than perfect. Issuing convertibles is a better strategy than issuing straight debt or preferred shares today if the firm performs poorly in the future. Similarly, issuing convertibles is a better strategy than issuing common shares today if the firm performs superbly in the future.

A final reason for issuing convertible securities centres around the fact that the earnings resulting from projects funded by a particular external financing issue may not begin for some time after financing occurs. For example, the construction and start-up period for a major expansion may be several years. During this period, the firm may desire debt or preferred share financing. Eventually, once the expansion is fully operational and producing income, the firm may want to achieve its original goal of additional common share financing. The deferred issue of common shares minimizes the dilution in earnings per share that results from the immediate issuance of common shares.

There is, however, another potential drawback to issuing convertibles. A high percentage of convertibles is held by hedge funds that specialize in convertible arbitrage. One of the first steps such an arbitrageur takes after buying a firm's convertibles is to sell short the firm's common shares. That is, the arbitrageur borrows the firm's shares from other investors and promises to repay them later and then sells these shares today. Needless to say, this is not popular with the firm's management that is trying to maximize shareholder wealth because the action of the arbitrageur tends to depress the common share price.

Valuation of Convertible Securities

Because convertible securities possess certain characteristics of both common shares and fixed-income securities, their valuation is more complex than that of ordinary non-convertible securities. The actual market value of a convertible security depends on both the *common share value*, or *conversion value*, and the value of a fixed-income security, or *straight-bond* or *investment value*. Each of these is discussed here.[5]

Conversion Value

The value of a convertible security, based on the value of the underlying common shares.

Conversion Value The **conversion value**, or share value, of a convertible bond is defined as the conversion ratio times the common share's market price:

$$(17.6) \qquad \text{Conversion value} = \text{Conversion ratio} \times \text{Share price}$$

To illustrate, assume that a firm offers a convertible bond that can be exchanged for 40 common shares. If the market price of the firm's common share is $20, the conversion value is $800. If the market price of the common share rises to $25 per share, the conversion value becomes $1,000. If the share price rises to $30, the conversion value becomes $1,200.

Straight-Bond Value

The value a convertible debt security would have if it did not possess the conversion feature, also referred to as the *investment value*.

Straight-Bond Value The **straight-bond value**, or *investment value*, of a convertible debt issue is the value it would have if it did not possess the conversion feature (option). Thus, it is equal to the sum of the present value of the interest annuity plus the present value of the expected principal repayment:

$$(17.7) \qquad \text{Straight-bond value} = \sum_{t=1}^{n} \frac{\text{Interest}}{(1 + k_d)^t} + \frac{\text{Principal}}{(1 + k_d)^n}$$

where k_d is the current yield to maturity for *nonconvertible* debt issues of similar quality and maturity; t, the number of years; and n, the time to maturity.

Considering again Nortel's 4.25 percent, 7-year convertible senior notes, the bond value at the time of issue is calculated as follows, assuming that 9 percent is the appropriate discount rate (and that interest is paid annually):

$$\text{Straight-bond value} = \sum_{t=1}^{7} \frac{\$42.50}{(1.09)^t} + \frac{\$1,000}{(1.09)^7}$$

$$= \$42.50(\text{PVIFA}_{0.09, 7}) + \$1,000(\text{PVIF}_{0.09, 7})$$

$$= \$42.50(5.033) + \$1,000(0.547)$$

$$= \$760.90$$

Market Value The market value of a convertible debt issue is usually somewhat above the higher of the conversion or the straight-bond value. This is illustrated in Figure 17.2.

---

[5] For simplicity, only convertible debt is considered in this discussion, although the principles apply to convertible preferred shares as well.

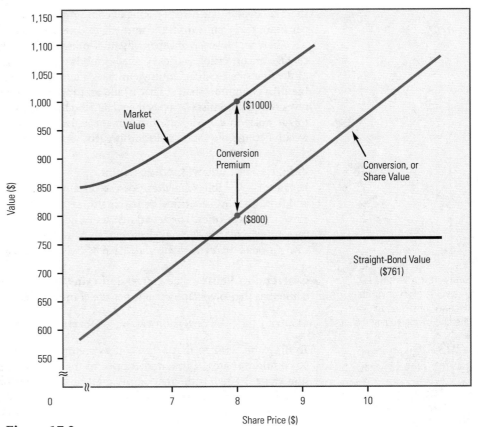

Figure 17.2
Nortel: Convertible Senior Notes Valuation at Different Share Prices*

*Conversion ratio = 100
Straight-bond value = $761

The difference between the market value and the higher of the conversion or the straight-bond value is the conversion premium for which the issue sells. This premium tends to be largest when the conversion value and the straight-bond value are nearly identical. This set of circumstances allows investors to participate in any common share appreciation while having some degree of downside protection because the straight-bond value can represent a "floor" below which the market value will not fall.[6] This premium can be thought of as the value of the implicit call option on a firm's common shares associated with this convertible security. In practice, convertible securities are valued by adding the straight-bond value to the value of the conversion options to buy common shares. These conversion options can be valued using a variant of the Black-Scholes option pricing model (see Appendix 17A).

Converting Convertible Securities

Conversion can occur in one of two ways:

■ It may be *voluntary* on the part of the investor.

■ It can be effectively *forced* by the issuing company.

Whereas voluntary conversions can occur at any time prior to the expiration of a conversion feature, forced conversions occur at specific points in time.

---

[6] The straight-bond value may fall if long-term interest rates rise or if the perceived risk of the firm increases.

The method most commonly used by companies to force conversion is the exercise of the *call* privilege on the convertible security. By calling the convertible securities, a firm can remove a large amount of long-term debt from its balance sheet, thus saving on interest expense.

Another way in which a company can encourage conversion is by raising its common share dividend to a high enough level that holders of convertible securities are better off converting them and receiving the higher dividend.

Note that the firm receives no new funds at the time of conversion.

Convertible Securities and Earnings Dilution

Valuing convertible securities and their embedded options is easy using the convertible bond calculator available at **www.numa.com** (Be sure to read the Web site instructions!)

If a convertible security (or warrant) issue is ultimately exchanged for common shares, the number of common shares will increase and earnings per share will be reduced (i.e., diluted), all other things being equal. Companies are required to disclose this potential dilution by reporting both basic and diluted earnings per share. Basic earnings per share are calculated based on the number of common shares outstanding plus common share equivalents. A common share equivalent must meet certain tests, but it usually includes any convertible security that derives its value primarily from the common share into which it can be converted. Diluted earnings per share are calculated based on the assumption that *all* dilutive securities are converted into common shares. In calculating basic or diluted earnings per share, earnings must be adjusted for the interest or preferred dividends saved as the result of conversion.

Warrants

Warrant
A company-issued long-term option to purchase a specified number of common shares at a particular price during a specified time period.

As mentioned earlier in this chapter, a **warrant** is a company-issued option to purchase a specific number of common shares of the issuing firm at a particular price during a specified time period. Warrants are frequently issued in conjunction with an offering of debentures or preferred shares. In these instances, like convertibles, warrants tend to lower agency costs.

In addition, during the 1980s, the various ways in which warrants were used as a financing device seemed to expand. For example, warrants were used in conjunction with bond swaps, equity offerings, and debt restructurings. Also, small, high-risk firms in need of additional financing may offer warrants to prospective lenders in order to give the potential for high expected returns as compensation for the loan's high risk.

Features of Warrants

For more information about Maxxcom see **www.maxxcom.com**

To illustrate some of the features of financing with warrants, consider Maxxcom (MXX), the largest full-service marketing communications organization based in Canada, which raised $40 million of mezzanine financing by selling 12.35 percent subordinated debentures with five-year warrants attached, in July of 2001 (mezzanine financing is discussed in more detail in Chapter 20). Each of the warrants gives debenture holders the right to purchase Maxxcom common shares at a price of $9.

The exercise price of a warrant is the price at which the holder can purchase a common share of the issuing firm. The exercise price is usually between 10 and 35 percent above the market price of the common share at the time of issue. The exercise price normally remains constant over the life of the warrant. One exception is the case of a stock split. When this occurs, the exercise price of the warrant is adjusted to reflect the new number of shares and share price. Typically, the life of a warrant is between 5 and 10 years, although on occasion the life can be longer or even perpetual.

When the management of Maxxcom issued the warrants, they hoped that the common share price would rise above the $9 level and remain there, especially until after the warrants expired. This would mean that the company could reasonably expect holders to exercise their warrants. If this happened, Maxxcom would realize its goal of raising additional capital. (Unlike the case of convertibles, the firm indeed does raise additional capital when warrants are exercised.)

If a warrant is issued as part of a "unit" with a fixed-income security, the warrant is usually *detachable* from the debenture or preferred share. This means that purchasers of the units have the option of selling the warrants separately and continuing to hold the debenture or preferred share. As a result, other investors can purchase and trade warrants.

Prior to 1970, warrants were not usually used as a financing vehicle by large, established firms. In April of that year, however, AT&T sold $1.6 billion of 30-year debentures with warrants to buy 31.4 million common shares at $52 each through May 15, 1975. The use of warrant financing by AT&T undoubtedly caused other large, established firms to consider warrants. Also, before 1970, the New York Stock Exchange would not list warrants. However, with the AT&T warrants, the NYSE changed its policy and began to list warrants of NYSE companies if the warrants met certain requirements, including a life greater than five years. The Canadian firm, Inco, for example, is among the many firms that have warrants traded on the NYSE.

Holders of warrants do not have the rights of common shareholders, such as the right to vote for directors or receive dividends, until they exercise their warrants.

Reasons for Issuing Warrants

The primary reason for issuing warrants with a fixed-income security offering is to lower agency costs. In addition, just as with convertible securities, warrants can permit a company to sell common shares at a price above the price prevailing at the time of original issue. Warrants also allow a firm to sell common shares in the future without incurring significant issuance costs at the time of sale.

Valuation of Warrants

In general, the value of a warrant depends on the same variables that affect call option valuation. Because a warrant's value depends on the price of the issuing firm's shares, it is a contingent claim, just like an option. In this connection, the formula or intrinsic value of a warrant (also called "the value at expiration") is defined by the following equation:

$$(17.8) \quad \begin{matrix} \text{Formula} \\ \text{value} \\ \text{of a} \\ \text{warrant} \end{matrix} = \text{Max} \left\{ \$0; \left(\begin{matrix} \text{Common share} \\ \text{market price} \end{matrix} - \begin{matrix} \text{Exercise} \\ \text{price} \\ \text{per share} \end{matrix} \right) \times \begin{matrix} \text{Number of shares} \\ \text{obtainable with} \\ \text{each warrant} \end{matrix} \right\}$$

Valuing warrants is easy using the warrant calculator available at **www.numa.com**

At the time of issue, a warrant's exercise price is normally greater than the common share price. Even though the calculated formula value may be negative, it is considered to be zero because securities cannot sell for negative amounts. Once the share price rises above the exercise price of the warrant, the formula value will be greater than zero. On the expiration date of a warrant, the market price of the warrant should be equal to the formula value, as was the case for options discussed earlier.

Comparison of Convertible Securities and Warrants

Having covered the characteristics and valuation of convertible securities and warrants, we now summarize the similarities of and differences between these types of securities. In this comparison, we are assuming that the warrants are issued as part of a fixed-income security offering, such as the Maxxcom warrants discussed above. The similarities include the following:

1. Both convertibles and warrants tend to lessen potential conflicts between fixed-income security holders and shareholders, thereby reducing agency costs.

2. The intention is the deferred issuance of common shares at a price higher than that prevailing at the time of the convertible or warrant issue.

3. Both the convertibility option and the inclusion of warrants result in interest expense or preferred dividend savings for the issuing company, thereby easing potential cash flow problems.

Some of the differences include the following:

1. The firm receives additional funds at the time warrants are exercised, whereas no additional funds are received at the time convertibles are converted.

2. The fixed-income security remains on the firm's books after the exercise of warrants. In the case of convertibles, the fixed-income security is exchanged for common shares and taken off the firm's books.

3. Because of the call feature, convertible securities potentially give the firm more control than warrants over when the common shares are issued.

Analysis of Rights Offerings

In addition to the sale of new common shares through underwriters, new equity capital can be raised using another option-based financing approach called a **rights offering**. In a rights offering, the firm's existing shareholders are given an *option* to purchase a fraction of the new shares equal to the fraction they currently own, thereby maintaining their original ownership percentage.

Hence, rights offerings are used in equity financing by companies whose charters contain the **preemptive right**. (The preemptive right gives existing shareholders the right to purchase on a pro rata basis new issues of common shares or securities convertible into common shares. This allows them to maintain their proportionate ownership status.) In addition, rights offerings *may* be used as a means of selling common shares in firms in which preemptive rights do not exist. The number of rights offerings has gradually declined over the years.

The following example illustrates what a rights offering involves. The Miller Company has 10 million shares outstanding and plans to sell an additional 1 million shares via a rights offering. In this case, each right entitles the holder to purchase 0.1 share, and it takes 10 rights to purchase one share. (The rights themselves really are the documents describing the offer. Each shareholder receives one right for each share currently held.) The firm has to decide on a **subscription price**, which is the price the right holder will have to pay per new share. The subscription price has to be less than the market price, or right holders will have no incentive to subscribe to the new issue. As a general rule, subscription prices are 5 to 20 percent below market prices. If the Miller shares are selling at $40, a reasonable subscription price might be $35 per share.

Valuation of Rights

Because a right represents an opportunity to purchase stock below its current market value, the right itself has a certain value, which is calculated under two sets of circumstances:

- The *rights-on* case
- The *ex-rights* case

A share is said to "trade with rights-on" when the purchasers receive the rights along with the shares they purchase. In contrast, a share is said to "trade ex-rights" when the share purchasers no longer receive the rights.

For example, suppose the Miller Company announced on May 15 that shareholders of record as of June 20 will receive the rights. This means that anyone who purchased shares on or before June 18 will receive the rights, and anyone who purchased shares on

---

Rights Offering
The sale of new shares by distributing rights to a firm's existing shareholders.

Preemptive Right
The right of shareholders to buy on a pro rata basis any new common share issues.

Subscription Price
The price a rights holder pays for a new share.

or later than June 19 will not.[7] The share trades with rights-on up to and including June 18 and goes ex-rights on June 19, the *ex-rights date*. On that date, the share's market value falls by the value of the right, all other things being equal.

The theoretical, or formula, value of a right for the rights-on case can be calculated using the following equation:

(17.9)
$$R = \frac{M_0 - S}{N + 1}$$

where R is the theoretical value for the right; M_0, the rights-on market price of the share; S, the subscription price of the right; and N, the number of rights necessary to purchase one new share. In the Miller Company example, the right's theoretical value is

$$R = \frac{\$40 - \$35}{10 + 1} = \$0.455$$

The theoretical value of a right when the share is trading ex-rights can be calculated by using the following equation:

(17.10)
$$R = \frac{M_e - S}{N}$$

where M_e is the ex-rights market price of the share; S, the subscription price of the right; and N, the number of rights necessary to purchase one new share. If the Miller shares were trading ex-rights, the theoretical value of a right would be as follows:

$$R = \frac{\$39.545 - \$35}{10} = \$0.455$$

(Note that M_e is lower than M_0 by the amount of the right; that is, $40 versus $39.545.)

Some shareholders may decide not to use their rights because of lack of funds or some other reason. These shareholders can sell their rights to other investors who wish to purchase them. Thus, a market exists for the rights, and a market price is established for them. Generally, the market price is higher than the theoretical value until the time of expiration. The same factors discussed previously, which determine the value of a call option, also determine the value of a right, since a right is simply a short-term call option on the share. As with call options, investors can earn a higher return by purchasing the rights than by purchasing the shares because of the leverage rights provide. In general, the premium of market value over theoretical value decreases as the rights expiration date approaches. A right is worthless after its expiration date.

You can demonstrate that there is no net gain or loss to shareholders either from exercising the right or from selling the right at the theoretical formula value.[8] For example, suppose an investor owns 100 Miller Company common shares discussed earlier. The investor is entitled to purchase 10 (0.1 × 100) additional shares at $35 each. Prior to the rights offering, the 100 shares of Miller Company are valued at $4,000 (100 shares × $40 each). *Exercise* of the rights will give the investor 10 additional shares at a cost of $35 per share, or a total of $350. These 110 shares will be valued at $4,350 (110 × $39.545). Deducting the cost of these additional shares ($350) from the total value of the shares ($4,350), one obtains the same value ($4,000) as before the rights offering. *Sale* of the rights will yield $45.50 (100 × $0.455) to the investor. Combining this value with the $3,954.50 (100 × $39.545) value of the 100 shares still owned, you also obtain the same value ($4,000) as before the rights offering.

Interest Rate Swaps

A **swap** is another type of financial derivative that can be used in the financing activities of a firm. A *financial swap* is a contractual agreement between two parties (financial

Swap
A contractual agreement between two parties to make periodic payments to each other. They can be interest rate or currency swaps. Fixed-rate interest can be swapped for floating-rate interest. Payments in one currency can be swapped for another currency.

---

[7] A share purchaser becomes a "shareholder of record" two *trading* days after purchase.

[8] This analysis ignores any brokerage fees incurred in the sale of the rights.

institutions or businesses) to make periodic payments to each other. There are two major types of swaps: *interest rate swaps* and *currency swaps.* This section focuses on interest rate swaps.[9] The over-the-counter swaps market is largely unregulated. Over $80 *trillion* worth of interest rate swaps are outstanding worldwide.

Interest rate swaps can be used to protect financial institutions and businesses against fluctuations in interest rates. Like futures contracts,[10] swaps can be used to hedge against interest rate risk. Even though futures contracts are more effective in hedging against short-term risks (less than one year), swaps are more effective in hedging against longer-term risks (up to 10 years or more).

Of the many and various types of interest rate swaps, the most basic is one in which a party is seeking to exchange floating rate interest payments for fixed rate interest payments, or vice versa. Consider the case of a finance company (e.g., GMAC) with floating rate debt (e.g., floating rate bonds) and fixed rate loans (e.g., automobile instalment loans) that wants to protect itself against an increase in interest rates. The finance company can enter into a swap contract with another party who agrees to pay the interest costs in excess of a specified rate (e.g., 7.5 percent) for a given period of time (e.g., three years). Should interest rates increase in the future, the finance company will receive rising payments from the other party to the swap agreement to cover its losses.

The other party to the swap agreement could be a bank, which borrows at fixed interest rates and lends money to corporations at floating rates. The bank may desire to protect itself against a decline in interest rates. Should interest rates decline in the future, the bank will continue receiving fixed interest payments from the other party to the swap agreement. This swap is illustrated in Figure 17.3. In most interest rate swaps, the floating rate used in computing the payments between the parties to the swap is tied to the London Interbank Offer Rate (LIBOR). (LIBOR was discussed in Chapter 2.) In this example, it is 2.5 percentage points above LIBOR. Generally, in a swap agreement, the parties exchange only the interest differential, not the principal or actual interest payments.

Many financial institutions, such as banks, and nonfinancial companies, act as intermediaries in arranging swaps. Some intermediaries act as brokers and receive commissions for finding parties with matching needs. Other intermediaries act as dealers or market makers by offering themselves as a party to the swap until such time as they can arrange a match with another party.

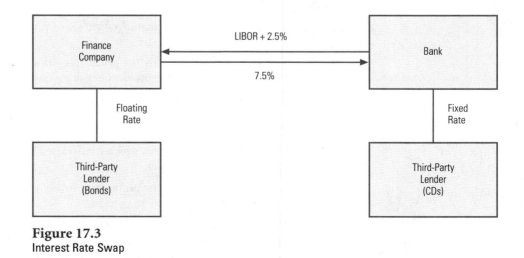

Figure 17.3
Interest Rate Swap

---

[9] See John F. Marshall and Kenneth R. Kapnes, *Understanding Swap Finance* (Mason, OH: South-Western, 1990), for a more detailed discussion of interest rate swaps.

[10] Futures contracts were introduced in Chapter 2 and are discussed in more detail in Chapter 18.

Options are one type of compensation that firms use to better align manager interests with shareholder interests. Unfortunately, if a firm's share price declines and leaves managerial stock options under water, then these options no longer provide the intended incentive. One action that a firm can take is to reprice these options as Nortel did. However, firms are reluctant to reprice options a second time as this makes management the likely target of the wrath of shareholders.

Summary

Options

- An *option* is a derivative security that gives its holder the right (but not the obligation) to buy or sell an asset at a set *exercise price* until a specified *expiration date*. A *call* is an option to *buy*. A *put* is an option to *sell*.

- The value of a call option is dependent on six variables:

  1. The price of the underlying share

  2. The exercise price of the option

  3. The time remaining until the option's expiration date

  4. The level of interest rates

  5. The expected share price volatility

  6. The dividend (if any) on the underlying asset

- An option is a *contingent claim*. That is, its value depends on the value of another security.

Convertible Securities

- *Convertible* debt or preferred share securities are exchangeable for a firm's common shares at the option of the holder.

- Convertible securities tend to reduce potential conflicts between fixed-income security holders and common shareholders, resulting in reduced agency costs.

- The price at which a convertible security is exchangeable for a common share is the *conversion price.*

- The number of common shares that can be obtained when a convertible security is exchanged is the *conversion ratio,* which is calculated by dividing the par value of the security by the conversion price.

- At the time of issue, the conversion price normally exceeds the market price of the common shares by about 15 to 30 percent.

- Convertible securities possess characteristics of both common shares and fixed-income securities. Their market value is a function of both their share or conversion value and their value as a fixed-income security. The *conversion value* is calculated by multiplying the conversion ratio by the current share price.

Warrants

- A *warrant* is an option issued by a company to purchase shares of the firm's common shares at a particular price during a specific time period. Warrants are frequently issued as part of a fixed-income security offering.

- The *exercise price* of a warrant is the price at which the holder can purchase common shares of the issuing company.

- The primary reason for issuing a warrant with a fixed-income security offering is that warrants tend to lower agency costs.

- The *formula value* of a warrant depends on the number of common shares each warrant is entitled to receive when exercised and the difference between the common share market price and the warrant exercise price. Warrants normally sell at a premium over their formula value.

Rights Offering

- In a *rights offering*, common shareholders receive share purchase rights. These rights entitle them to purchase additional shares of the firm in proportion to the shares they currently own. These additional shares can be purchased at a price that is below the market price.

- In a rights offering, there is no gain or loss to shareholders from either exercising the rights or selling the rights at the theoretical formula value.

Swaps

- A swap is another type of financial derivative that can be used in the financing activities of a firm. A *financial swap*, such as an interest rate swap, is a contractual agreement between two parties (financial institutions or businesses) to make periodic payments to each other.

Questions and Topics for Discussion

1. Define the following terms:
   a. Option
   b. Call
   c. Put
   d. Contingent claim
2. What are the similarities and differences between options and warrants?
3. What variables are important in determining call option prices?
4. Will call option values generally be higher at a time when interest rates are relatively high, compared with a time when interest rates are relatively low, all other things being equal?
5. How does a share's expected price volatility affect the value of a call option on it?
6. In what ways are convertible securities and warrants similar? Dissimilar?
7. Why do companies issue convertible securities?
8. What is the relationship between conversion value, bond value, and market value for a convertible security?
9. How can a company effectively force conversion of a convertible security?
10. What is the *preemptive right* of common shareholders? In what type of company is the preemptive right important? Unimportant?
11. Why would a firm use an interest rate swap as part of its financing strategy?

Self-Test Problems

ST1. The Bradford Company has debentures outstanding (par value $1,000) that are convertible into common shares at a price of $40. The convertible bonds have a coupon interest rate of 8% and mature in 20 years. The convertible bonds are callable at 102% of par value. The firm has a marginal tax rate of 40%.

    a. Calculate the conversion value of the bonds if the firm's common shares sell for $35.

    b. Calculate the straight-bond value, assuming that straight debt of equivalent risk and maturity is yielding 11%.

    c. Determine the conversion premium if the market value of the bonds is $925.

    d. Determine the conversion value of the bonds if the firm's common share price increases to $55.

    e. Given the information in part d, what is a realistic estimate of the market price of the convertible bond issue? (No numerical calculations are necessary for this part of the problem.)

ST2. The Somerset Company has warrants outstanding that expire in three years. Each warrant entitles the holder to purchase one common share at an exercise price of $40. Determine the formula value and premium over the formula value if the respective prices of common share and warrants are:

    a. $32 per share and $1.50 per warrant

    b. $40 per share and $3.50 per warrant

    c. $48 per share and $10 per warrant

ST3. The Seven Springs Company plans to sell an additional 2 million common shares through a rights offering. The firm currently has 20 million shares outstanding. Each shareholder will receive one right for each share currently held. Therefore, each right will enable shareholders to purchase 0.10 shares. The firm's common share currently sells for $25 per share and the subscription price of the rights will be $22 per share.

    a. Calculate the theoretical value of the right for both the *rights-on* and *ex-rights* cases.

    b. Determine the amount that the market price of the firm's shares are expected to drop on the ex-rights date, assuming all other things are equal.

    c. If the market price per share of the firm's common stock increases to $30, determine the theoretical value of the rights (*rights-on* case).

Problems*

BASIC

1. The BWS Corporation common shares are selling at $50 per share today.

    a. Calculate the value of a BWS call option if its exercise price is $40 and it expires today.

    b. What can you say about the value of a BWS call option if its exercise price is $40 and it expires in six months?

    c. Calculate the value of a BWS call option if its exercise price is $60 and it expires today.

    d. What can you say about the value of a BWS call option if its exercise price is $60 and it expires in six months?

*Coloured numbers and letters denote problems that have "check" answers provided at the back of the book.

2. The BWS Corporation common shares are selling at $60 per share today.
   a. Calculate the value of a BWS put option if its exercise price is $40 and it expires today.
   b. What can you say about the value of a BWS put option if its exercise price is $40 and it expires in six months?
   c. Calculate the value of a BWS put option if its exercise price is $60 and it expires today.
   d. What can you say about the value of a BWS put option if its exercise price is $60 and it expires in six months?

3. The Manchester Corporation has warrants presently outstanding, and each warrant entitles the holder to purchase one common share at an exercise price of $20. If the market price of the warrants is $8 and the common share price is $24, what is the premium over the formula value for the warrants?

4. Horizon Corporation has warrants to purchase common shares outstanding. Each warrant entitles the holder to purchase one common share at an exercise price of $20. Suppose the warrants expire on September 1, 2009. One month ago, when the company's common share was trading at about $21.50, the warrants were trading at $5 each.
   a. What was the formula value of the warrants one month ago?
   b. What was the premium over the formula value one month ago?
   c. What are the reasons investors were willing to pay more than the formula value for these warrants one month ago?
   d. Suppose that in August 2009, the Horizon common share is still trading at $21.50. What do you think the warrant price would be then? Why?
   e. Horizon paid an annual dividend of $1 per share, as of one month ago, to its common shareholders. Do warrant holders receive dividends?

INTERMEDIATE

5. The LeMonde Corporation has debentures outstanding (par value $1,000) that are convertible into the firm's common shares at a price of $25 per share. The convertibles have a coupon interest rate of 6% and mature 20 years from now. In addition, the convertible debenture is callable at 107% of par value. The firm has a marginal tax rate of 40%.
   a. Calculate the conversion value if the firm's common shares are selling at $25 per share.
   b. Calculate the bond value, assuming that straight debt of equivalent risk and maturity is yielding 9%.
   c. Using the answers from parts a and b, what is a realistic estimate of the market value of the convertible debentures? (No calculation is necessary for this part of the problem.)
   d. What is the conversion value if the firm's common share price increases to $35?
   e. Given the situation presented in part d, what is a realistic estimate of the market value of the convertible debenture? (No calculation is necessary for this part of the problem.)
   f. What is the minimum common share price that will allow the firm's management to use the call feature of the debentures to effectively force conversion?
   g. Suppose that increased expectations concerning inflation cause the yield on straight debt of equivalent risk and maturity to reach 10%. How will this affect the bond value of the convertible?

6. ADP recently issued $150 million of 6.5% convertible debentures maturing in 2011. The debentures are convertible into common shares at $83.45 a share. The

firm's common share was trading at about $67 when the convertibles were issued.

a. How many common shares can be obtained by converting one $1,000 par value debenture? That is, what is the conversion ratio?

b. What was the conversion value of this issue when these debentures were originally issued?

c. By what percentage was the conversion price above the share price when these debentures were originally issued?

7. Shaw Company, whose present balance sheet is summarized here, is considering issuing $100 million of 6% subordinated debentures (par value $1,000), which are convertible into common shares at a price of $40.

Shaw Company Balance Sheet (in Millions of Dollars)			
Current assets	$200	Current liabilities	$100
Fixed assets, net	300	Long-term debt	150
Total assets	$500	Common equity	250
		Total liabilities and equity	$500

a. Show the pro forma balance sheet for the issuance of the convertibles prior to conversion. Assume the proceeds are invested in new plant and equipment, and disregard issuance costs.

b. Show the pro forma balance sheet, assuming conversion of the entire issue.

c. How much additional money will the company raise at the time of conversion?

8. The capital structure of Whitefield Mills, Inc. is as follows:

Long-term debt	$250 million
Common shares	175 million
Retained earnings	350 million
Total capitalization	$775 million

The firm has decided to raise additional capital by selling $75 million of 8% debentures with warrants attached. Each $1,000 debenture will have 25 warrants attached, and each warrant will entitle the holder to purchase one common share at $30.

a. Show the firm's new capital structure after the sale of debentures and the exercise of all the warrants. Assume that no other changes in capital structure occur between now and the time the warrants are exercised.

b. What condition is necessary for the warrants to be exercised?

c. How much total money will the company raise as a result of this security issue, if all warrants are exercised?

9. You own 10 Bitterroot Industries, Inc. 8% convertible debentures maturing in 2020. The conversion ratio of the debentures is 30, and the debentures are callable at $1,070 each. You bought the debentures when they were originally issued in 1990 for $1,000 each. At that time, the firm's common share was selling at $28.50, and now it is up to $44. The convertible debentures are now selling at $1,320 each. Last week, you received a notice from the firm stating that the firm is calling the debentures.

a. What are your alternatives?

b. Which alternative should you choose?

10. The Oil City Company plans to sell an additional 1 million common shares through a rights offering. The firm currently has 12 million shares outstanding. Each shareholder will receive one right for each share currently held. Therefore, each right will enable shareholders to purchase 0.0833 shares. The firm's common

shares are currently selling for $30 per share, and the subscription price of the rights will be $25 per share.

   a. Calculate the theoretical value of the right for both the *rights-on* and *ex-rights* cases.

   b. Determine the amount that the market price of the firm's share is expected to drop on the ex-rights date, assuming that all other things are equal.

   c. If the market price of the firm's common shares increases to $40 per share, what is the theoretical value of the rights (rights-on case)?

11. The Munro Company has warrants outstanding that expire in five years. Each warrant entitles the holder to purchase 0.5 common shares at an exercise price of $32 per share. Determine the formula value and premium over the formula value if the respective prices of common shares and warrants are:

   a. $30 per share and $1 per warrant

   b. $32 per share and $2 per warrant

   c. $38 per share and $3.50 per warrant

12. The Wolverine Corporation has a convertible preferred share issue outstanding. The par value of this preferred share is $100, and it pays a $10 dividend. The preferred share is callable at 103% of par value. It has 10 years remaining until maturity and is convertible into 2.5 common shares. The current common share price is $42. Similar (quality and maturity) nonconvertible preferred shares sell at a price to yield 9%.

   a. What is the conversion value of this preferred share?

   b. What is the straight (nonconvertible) preferred share value of this security?

   c. If interest rates decline such that similar (quality and maturity) nonconvertible preferred shares sell at a price to yield 7% and the price of the firm's common shares increase to $44 per share, for how much will this convertible security sell?

CHALLENGE

13. Calculate the after-tax component cost of capital, k_c, for a 7.5% convertible debenture sold at par and due to mature in 25 years. The conversion ratio is 25, and conversion is expected to occur at the end of 10 years, when the common share price is expected to be $54 per share. The firm has a 40% marginal tax rate. Is there any reason for you to believe that this estimate may be biased up or down?

14. Ogilvie Manufacturing Company has decided to sell additional common shares through a rights offering. The firm has 50 million shares outstanding and plans to sell an additional 5 million shares through the rights offering. Each shareholder will receive one right for each share currently held, and thus each right will entitle shareholders to purchase 0.1 shares. The firm's common share is currently selling at $50, and the subscription price of the rights will be $45.

   a. Calculate the theoretical value of the right for both the *rights-on* and the *ex-rights* cases.

   b. How much is the market price of the company's share expected to drop on the ex-rights date, all other things being equal? Why?

   c. If the market price of the firm's common shares increases to $52 per share, what will be the theoretical value of the right (*rights-on* case)?

   d. Discuss the trend of the right's market price over its life, assuming the firm's common shares continue to trade in the $50 range. (No numerical calculations are necessary for this part of the problem.)

15. The Findlay Company has debentures outstanding (par value $1,000) that are convertible into common shares at a price of $50 per share. The convertible bonds have a coupon interest rate of 9% and mature in 18 years. The convertible bonds are callable at 103% of par value. The company has a marginal tax rate of 40%.

a. Calculate the conversion value of the bonds if the firm's common share is selling for $45.

b. Calculate the straight-bond value, assuming that straight debt of equivalent risk and maturity is yielding 12%.

c. Determine the conversion premium if the market value of the bonds is $935.

d. Determine the conversion value of the bonds if the company's common share price increases to $65.

e. Given the information in part d, what is a realistic estimate of the market price of the convertible bond issue? (No calculations are required for this part of the problem.)

16. Five years ago, in conjunction with a financial restructuring, Lunenburg Electric sold a $100 million issue of bonds at a coupon interest rate of 12%. Each bond came with 30 detachable warrants. Each warrant entitled the holder to purchase one common share at $15 per share. The warrants were set to expire 25 years from the date of issue. When the firm's share sold for $7, the value of a warrant in the marketplace was $0.50.

a. What is the theoretical value of each warrant under these conditions?

b. What factors influence this value?

At a share price of $15, the market price of each warrant was $3. At a share price of $20, the market price of each warrant was $6.50. At a share price of $25, the market price of each warrant was $10.50.

c. If an investor purchases the share and the warrant when the share price is $15, what rate of return will be earned on both, assuming that the share and the warrant are sold when the share price reaches $20?

d. If an investor purchases the share and the warrant when the share price is $20, what rate of return will be earned on both, assuming that the share and the warrant are sold when the share price reaches $25?

e. What happens to the rate of return from the warrant as the share price rises? Why do you think this happens?

17. Nullcom, Inc. has debentures (face value $1,000) outstanding that are convertible into common shares at a price of $40 per share. The debentures pay an interest rate of 9% per annum and have a remaining life of 10 years. Nonconvertible debentures of a similar credit rating and maturity are selling at a price to yield 11%. The current share price is $35.

a. Compute the straight-bond value of each of these debentures.

b. Compute the conversion value of each of these debentures.

c. What is the absolute minimum price for one of these debentures today? What price would you expect to pay for one of these debentures?

d. If the debentures are called at 105 today and you own 10 of these debentures, what action should you take?

Other Practice Materials and Resources

For interactive quizzes, Internet exercises, crossword puzzles, CTV videos, and more, go to the *Contemporary Financial Management* Web site at **http://cyr.nelson.com**

The Foundations of Option Valuation

In Chapter 17, the valuation of a call of option was determined to be a function of the following variables:

- The current price of the asset underlying the option. In the case of stock options, this is the price of the common share on which the option has been written.
- The exercise price of the option.
- The time remaining until the option expires.
- The risk-free rate of interest.
- The volatility of the underlying asset, e.g., the share on which the option was written.
- The dividend (if any) on the underlying asset.

Financial research has made large strides in the formal valuation of options. A path-breaking paper by Fischer Black and Myron Scholes[11] developed a formal model for option valuation that is widely used today. The Black-Scholes model was developed from the premise that a strategy of borrowing to buy shares can exactly equal the risk associated with the purchase of a call option. Because the price of a common share is readily observable, as is the borrowing rate, they showed that it is possible to derive the theoretically correct value for a call option.

The Black-Scholes model is based on the following assumptions:

1. The share pays no dividends during the life of the option. Although this might seem like a serious limitation of the model, other models have been developed that take dividends into account. A common way of adjusting the Black-Scholes model for the effect of dividends is to subtract the present value of expected dividend payments during the life of the option from the share price variable in the model.

2. The call option is a *European option*. European options can be exercised only at expiration, whereas *American options* can be exercised at any time up until the expiration date. This assumption is not important because few options are exercised prior to expiration. However, most of the exchange-traded options are American. When an option is exercised prior to expiration, the option holder loses the value of any premium that is contained in the option price. (The *premium* is the difference between the market value of the option and option's intrinsic value or value at expiration, where the value at expiration is defined as the difference between the share price and the exercise price.)

3. Share prices are assumed to follow a random walk. Investors are assumed not to be able to predict the direction of the overall market or of any particular share price.

4. There are no transaction costs in the buying and selling of options. This assumption is violated in reality, but transaction costs are low enough that this assumption is not a serious limitation of the model.

5. The probability distribution of share returns is log-normally distributed.

6. Short-term, risk-free interest rates are assumed to be known and constant over the life of the option contract. The discount rate on one-month Treasury bills is often used as the risk-free rate in the Black-Scholes model.

---

[11] Fischer Black and Myron Scholes, "The Pricing of Options and Corporate Liabilities," *Journal of Political Economy* (May–June 1973): 637–654.

7. The variance of returns on the underlying share is assumed to be constant and known to investors over the option's life.

With these assumptions, the "correct" market value of an option can be determined. If the price of an option differs from this theoretically "correct" value, it is possible for investors to set up a risk-free arbitrage position and earn a rate of return in excess of the risk-free rate. Hence, it can be said that there are powerful market forces at work to keep actual market values of options consistent with their theoretical values.

The Black-Scholes Option Pricing Model

The Black-Scholes model defines the equilibrium value of a call option to buy one common share as:

(17A.1)
$$C = S\,N(d_1) - \frac{X}{e^{rt}}\,N(d_2)$$

where

S = current share price

t = time in years until the expiration of the option

X = exercise price of the call option

r = short-term annual, continuously compounded, risk-free rate of interest

$N(d)$ = the value of a cumulative normal density function; the probability that a standardized, normally distributed random variable will be less than or equal to the value d

e = the exponential value (2.71828)

$$d_1 = \frac{\ln(S/X) + \left(\dfrac{r + \sigma^2}{2}\right)t}{\sigma\sqrt{t}}$$

$$d_2 = d_1 - \sigma\sqrt{t}$$

σ = the standard deviation per year in the continuous return on the stock

$\ln$ = natural logarithm

Equation 17A.1 is a rather intimidating-looking formula. Fortunately, applying this formula to actual data is relatively easy, as illustrated in the next section.

Applying the Black-Scholes Model

Consider the case of Queen Pharmaceuticals, Inc. Based on an analysis of past returns for the firm's common shares, the standard deviation of its share returns has been estimated to be 0.3 or 30 percent. As of January 14, the firm's share price was $S = \$30$. The exercise price of its call options was $X = \$29$. The short-term annual, continuously compounded interest rate was $r = 0.06$, and the time to expiration of the call option was $t = 0.5$ or one-half year. With this information, we can now compute the equilibrium value of one of these call options.

■ **Step 1:** Compute the values for d_1 and d_2.

$$d_1 = \frac{\ln(S/X) + \left(\frac{r + \sigma^2}{2}\right)t}{\sigma\sqrt{t}}$$

$$= \frac{\ln\left(\frac{30}{29}\right) + \left(0.06 + \frac{(0.3)^2}{2}\right)0.5}{0.3\sqrt{0.5}}$$

$$= \frac{0.0339 + .0525}{0.2121}$$

$$= 0.4074$$

$$d_2 = d_1 - \sigma\sqrt{t}$$

$$= 0.1953$$

■ **Step 2:** Compute $N(d_1)$ and $N(d_2)$.

To compute the values for $N(d_1)$ and $N(d_2)$ we need to answer the following type of question: What is the probability that a value from a standardized normal distribution will be below a specific value, such as d_1 or d_2?

This question can be easily answered using Table V at the back of the book. Recall that the values in Table V are the probabilities of having a value greater than z (for positive standard normalized values such as d_1 or d_2 in this example) or less than z (for negative standard normalized values). Because d_1 and d_2 are both positive, we can find the probability of a value greater than d_1 or d_2 directly from Table V and then subtract this probability from 1.0 to get the probability of a value less than d_1 or d_2, as is required in the Black-Scholes model.

From Table V, the probability of a value greater than d_1 (rounded to 0.41) is 0.3409. Hence the value for $N(d_1)$ will be $1.0 - 0.3409$ or 0.6591. Similarly the probability of a value greater than d_2 (rounded to 0.20) is 0.4207. Hence the value for $N(d_2)$, that is, the probability of a value less than d_2, will be $1.0 - 0.4207 = 0.5793$.

■ **Step 3:** Calculate the value of C, the call option for a Queen Pharmaceuticals share.

$$C = S\,N(d_1) - X/e^{rt}\,N(d_2)$$

$$= \$30(0.6591) - \frac{\$29}{e^{(0.06)(0.5)}}(0.5793)$$

$$= \$3.47$$

These calculations can be simplified by using one of the many free option price calculators available on the Web, such as **www.numa.com** or **www.freeoptionpricing.com** or **www.optionvue.com**

Therefore, the Black-Scholes model indicates that an option to purchase one Queen Pharmaceuticals share is worth approximately $3.47, given the assumptions presented above. Option values are especially sensitive to the estimates of share return volatility that are input in the model.

Put-Call Parity

Recall that the purchaser of a put option has the right but not the obligation to sell a share of stock at a specified price for a specified period of time. Is there a simple relationship between the price P of a European put option and the price C of a European call option for the same share? Under the seven assumptions of the Black-Scholes model, the answer is yes, provided both options have the same exercise price X and the same time to expiration t. This relationship is called **put-call parity**.

Put-Call Parity
The price of a share equals the price of the same share synthetically created. See Equation 17A.2.

Suppose today one buys the call option, sells the put option, and invests the present value of the strike price X/e^{rt} in the risk-free asset. You have just created a *synthetic share* of the stock. As we shall now show, this synthetic share has the same payoffs as the actual share.

Suppose the share price S_t at the expiry of the options is greater than the exercise price X. Then one uses the proceeds X from the maturing risk-free asset to pay the exercise price X on the call option to receive a share worth S_t. The purchaser of the put option that you previously sold will have a worthless option. This is because the holder of the put would rather sell the share for S_t (or, perhaps even keep it) than sell the share to you for the exercise price X.

Then suppose that the share price S_t at expiration is less than the exercise price X. Your call option will be worthless. (Why would anyone pay X for a share via the call option when it can be bought directly for S_t?) The put option, however, has value and will be exercised. As the seller of this put option, you are now obligated to buy the share for the exercise price X when the purchaser of the put chooses to sell the share. Thus, you must use the proceeds X from the maturing risk-free asset to purchase the share that is now worth S_t.

Now suppose the share price S_t equals the exercise price X at expiration of the options. Then both options are worthless. However, you can use the proceeds X of your maturing risk-free asset to directly buy the share.

Thus, irrespective of which state of the world occurs, the synthetic share becomes a share worth S_t at the expiration of the options. If you buy the share today for S_0, then you will also own a share worth S_t at expiration of the options. Thus, the price of the synthetic share today must equal the price of the actual share today. *Hence, put-call parity, as expressed in Equation 17A.2, is simply an application of the law of one price for identical goods selling in the same market.*

$$(17A.2) \qquad S_0 = C - P + \frac{X}{e^{rt}}$$

If this single price did not hold, then investors could make an arbitrage profit today by borrowing and selling the higher priced "share" and buying the lower priced "share." This price difference is a risk-free profit today because the lower priced "share" that is purchased will simply be an actual share that is delivered to the lender of the higher priced "share" at expiry of the options.

Now let us rearrange Equation 17A.2 to obtain an expression for the value of the European put.

$$(17A.3) \qquad P = C + \frac{X}{e^{rt}} - S_0$$

Given the assumptions previously made for Queen Pharmaceuticals, what is the value of its put?

$$P = \$3.47 + \frac{\$29}{e^{(0.06)(0.5)}} - \$30 = \$1.61$$

Problems: Appendix 17A

Excel

1. Targezept Bionics, Inc. common shares sell for $21 per share. A call option on the share has an exercise price of $20 and will expire in three months. Based on an analysis of the share's past volatility, you have estimated the standard deviation of returns to be 0.6. The short-term interest rate is now 5% and you expect that to remain constant over the next six months.

   Use the Black-Scholes option pricing model to estimate the value of this option.

Excel

2. Use the option price calculator that can be found at **www.numa.com**, or another option price calculator, to test the sensitivity of option values to changes in the key input variables. Use the data from Problem 1 as the base case and vary the values for the interest rate, time to maturity, and share return volatility to see what happens to the value of the call option on the Targezept share. Note: Be sure to read the instructions at the Web site you choose. Most option price calculators require the risk-free rate and volatility to be entered in percentage form without the percentage sign, just as you enter the interest rate on a financial calculator.

Managing International Risk

Learning Objectives

After studying this chapter you should be able to

1. Understand that the theory of *interest rate parity* states that the percentage differential between the spot and the forward rate for a currency is equal to the approximate difference in interest rates in the two countries over the same time horizon

2. Understand that the theory of *relative purchasing power parity* states that in comparison to a period when exchange rates between two countries are in equilibrium, changes in differential rates of inflation between the countries will be offset by equal but opposite changes in the future spot currency rate

3. Understand that the *forward rate* is often considered to be an *unbiased estimator* of the *future spot currency rate*

4. Understand that the *Fisher effect* states that nominal interest rates are approximately equal to the sum of the real interest rate and the expected inflation rate

5. Understand that the *international Fisher effect* theory states that differences in interest rates between two countries should be offset by equal but opposite changes in the future spot rate

6. Understand that the three important categories of foreign exchange risk are (1) transaction exposure, (2) economic exposure, and (3) translation exposure

7. Understand that a hedge is an offsetting transaction designed to reduce or avoid risk. Forward and futures exchange hedges and money market hedges are used to reduce transaction exposure. Financing with debt denominated in the same currency as foreign assets is a means of hedging against translation and economic exposure

Argentina Takes a Financial Dive[1]

© AFP PHOTO/FABIAN FREDILLAS

In 1991, Argentina's president, Carlos Menem, was faced with an economy suffering from hyperinflation and on the brink of collapse. In a bold attempt to reverse this situation, Menem decided to peg the value of the peso to the value of the US dollar. All pesos in circulation were to be backed with dollars held in the country's currency reserves.

This strategy initially halted Argentina's runaway inflation. The peso became Latin America's most stable currency and Argentina became one of the world's fastest-growing economies. There was a sudden boom in foreign investments in Argentina. However, the government continued to suffer deficits. The only way to fund these deficits was to attract dollars into the country in the form of loans or foreign investments, or by way of export earnings, because pegging the peso to the dollar eliminated the option of the government simply printing more money. In 1995, faced with a recession and slowing foreign investment, Argentina was forced to increase borrowings. In 1999, Brazil devalued its currency, thereby enhancing its export competitiveness, to the detriment of Argentina's important export markets. By early 2002, Argentina faced over $141 billion of public debt that it could no longer service. In addition, it became clear that Argentina could no longer maintain the one-to-one peg of its currency to the dollar.

Finally on January 6, 2002, Argentina abandoned its 10-year experiment in monetary policy. Overnight, the value of the peso plummeted from 1 peso per dollar to 1.55 pesos per dollar among money changers, and the official exchange rate was reset to 1.4 pesos per dollar.

Who are the losers in the Argentine currency meltdown?

- Because Argentines earn their salaries in pesos and more than 80 percent of the country's financial contracts and debts are quoted in dollars, devaluation could force large numbers of businesses and households into bankruptcy. At the new official exchange rate of 1.4 pesos per dollar, a monthly salary of 500 pesos, worth $500 in December 2001, would now be worth only about $360.

- Foreign banks operating in Argentina, including Scotiabank, will have large losses because the government plans to convert dollar loans of $100,000 or less into pesos at the old rate of one to one, rather than at the new exchange rate.

- Other creditors who hold Argentina's $132 billion in foreign debt will receive only a fraction of this amount.

- Privatized utility companies that are largely owned by European investors will suffer large losses as dollar-denominated revenues are restated into lower-valued pesos.

The lessons of the Argentine experiment will be important for other countries seeking a quick fix for hyperinflation that lack discipline in their fiscal policies. Eventually, the root problem will rise back to the surface, as it did in Argentina. Then the government is faced with making the tough choices that it avoided earlier. In Argentina's case, this means huge reductions in public spending. Other

Go to **http://finance. swcollege.com** and select International Financial Management for articles on international topics. For more on Argentina see the Global Macroeconomic and Financial Policy site at **www.stern.nyu.edu/ globalmacro**

---

[1] Based on "A Wrong Turn?" *Business Week* (January 21, 2002): 42–43.

painful measures include devaluation, controls on capital flows, restrictions on the use of private funds held in banks, and high taxes on oil exports.

This chapter looks at the determinants of foreign currency exchange rates and considers the alternatives open to multinational firms that must compete globally in a currency marketplace characterized by rapid changes in relative values.

Introduction

As the world economy has become more globally integrated, virtually every firm and individual is affected by developments in the economies of countries other than their own. The debate over the North American Free Trade Agreement (NAFTA) has brought many of these relationships to the fore. Individuals are affected by global economic conditions as multinational firms seek the cheapest place to produce their products—resulting in employment winners and losers. A textile firm may move to Mexico from Montreal at the same time that Toyota considers the construction of a new plant in Ontario or the United States. In making plant location decisions, managers consider wage costs, the quality of the workforce, transportation costs, the cost of raw materials, exchange rate levels and risks, and political risk (such as the risk of expropriation or the blocking of funds). In addition, firms may decide to locate in multiple countries to gain quicker access to new technologies as they develop. Some international plant location decisions are designed, at least in part, to avoid political and regulatory barriers. For example, Japanese auto firms, including Toyota and Honda, have built large North American assembly plants in both the United States and Canada to reduce the currency risk and labour cost risk associated with a one-country location strategy.

Financial managers willing to venture into the global financial marketplace may find lower-cost financing alternatives than are available in their home country. With trade barriers being lowered around the world, the managers of tomorrow cannot limit their knowledge to "Island North America." Rather, these managers will find that understanding the functioning of the global financial marketplace is a key element of their knowledge and skill base.

This chapter continues the discussion of international finance that was begun in Chapter 2, where we discussed the domestic and global financial marketplace, particularly foreign currency markets and exchange rates. Here we explore the factors that determine exchange rates, look at ways to forecast future exchange rates, and consider various aspects of foreign exchange risk and ways of managing that risk. Capital budgeting for a multinational firm was discussed in Chapter 10.

See **http://finance. swcollege.com** for links to global financial information.

Factors That Affect Exchange Rates

Exchange rates between currencies vary over time, reflecting supply and demand considerations for each currency.[2] For example, the demand for British pounds comes from a number of sources, which include foreign buyers of British exports who must pay for their purchases in pounds, foreign investors who desire to make investments in physical or financial assets in Britain, and speculators who expect British pounds to increase in value relative to other currencies. The British government may also be a source of demand if it attempts to keep the value of the pound (relative to other currencies) from falling by using its supply of foreign currencies or gold to purchase pounds in the market.

---

[2] See Jeff Madura, *International Financial Management*, 7th ed. (Mason, OH: South-Western College, 2003) for more on the relationships among inflation, interest rates, and exchange rates.

Sources of supply include British importers who need to convert their pounds into foreign currency to pay for purchases, British investors who desire to make investments in foreign countries, and speculators who expect British pounds to decrease in value relative to other currencies.

Exchange rates are also affected by economic and political conditions that influence the supply of or demand for a country's currency. Some of these conditions include differential inflation and interest rates among countries, the government's trade policies, and the government's political stability. A high rate of inflation within a country tends to lower the value of its currency with respect to the currencies of other countries experiencing lower rates of inflation. The exchange rate will tend to decline as holders sell or exchange the country's currency for other currencies whose purchasing power is not declining at as high a rate. In contrast, relatively high interest rates within a country tend to increase the exchange rate as foreign investors seek to convert their currencies and purchase these higher-yielding securities.

Government trade policies that limit imports—such as the imposition of tariffs, import quotas, and restrictions on foreign exchange transactions—reduce the supply of the country's currency in the foreign exchange market. This, in turn, tends to increase the value of the country's currency with respect to other currencies and thus to increase exchange rates.

Finally, the political stability of the government affects the risks perceived by foreign investors and companies doing business in the country. These risks include the possible expropriation of investments or restrictions on the amount of funds (such as returns from investments) that may be taken out of the country.

In the following sections we develop the important relationships among spot rates, forward rates, interest rates, and inflation rates as they impact foreign currency exchange rates.

Covered Interest Arbitrage and Interest Rate Parity

There is a close relationship between the interest rates in two countries and the forward exchange rate premium or discount. Consider a Canadian investor with CAD2.16 million to invest. Suppose that the interest rate on three-month deposits available at Swiss banks is 4 percent for three months. At the same time, the similar rate in Canada is only 2 percent. The **spot rate** of the Swiss franc (CHF) is CAD1.08/CHF and the three-month **forward rate** is also CAD1.08/CHF. As an investor, you know that you can immediately convert CAD2.16 million into CHF2 million at today's spot rate of CAD1.08/CHF with no risk.[3] You can also lock in the 4 percent Swiss interest rate for three months by making a deposit in a Swiss bank of your CHF2 million. However, there is risk regarding the exchange rate at which you will be able to convert CHF back to CAD at the end of 3 months. You can guarantee this rate by selling CHF2 million (plus the interest you will receive on your Swiss deposit) in the three-month forward market at today's forward rate of CAD1.08/CHF. This transaction will guarantee you a risk-free profit. Consider the following steps in this transaction:

1. Convert CAD2.16 million into CHF2 million at today's spot rate of CAD1.08/CHF.

2. Make a deposit for three months at a Swiss bank yielding 4 percent every three months.

3. Simultaneously sell CHF2.08 million forward (original CHF2 million plus CHF80,000 in interest) at CAD1.08/CHF to net you CAD2,246,400.

4. This compares favourably with the CAD2,203,200 (CAD2.16 million plus interest at 2 percent) you could have received from investing in Canada.

Spot Rate
The rate of exchange between two currencies being bought and sold for immediate delivery.

Forward Rate
The rate of exchange between two currencies being bought and sold for delivery at a future date.

---

[3] The notation used for exchange rates is the ISO 4217 standard, which has been adopted by most financial institutions worldwide (including the Bank of Canada). For more information see **www.xe.com/iso4217htm**

This risk-free transaction enabled you to earn an additional return of CAD43,200 over what would be available by investing in Canada. Because there are virtually no barriers to prevent individuals from engaging in this transaction called **covered interest arbitrage**, it can be expected that opportunities to earn risk-free additional returns such as these will not persist very long. The demand by Canadian investors for CHF will put upward pressure on the spot price of CHF, to a price greater than CAD1.08/CHF. At the same time, as Canadian investors sell CHF forward to cover their position, this will put downward pressure on the forward rate of the CHF to a price less than CAD1.08/CHF. Furthermore, as funds leave Canada for Switzerland, the reduced supply of funds will tend to increase Canadian interest rates. The increased supply of funds in Switzerland, on the other hand, will tend to lower Swiss interest rates.

The net effect of these transactions and market pressures will be an equilibrium condition where covered interest arbitrage transactions are not possible. This relationship is called **interest rate parity** (IRP). When IRP exists, the forward rate will differ from the spot rate by just enough to offset the interest rate differential between the two currencies. The IRP condition states that the home (or domestic) interest rate must be higher (lower) than the foreign interest rate by an amount equal to the forward discount (premium) on the home currency. In other words, the forward premium or discount for a currency quoted in terms of another currency is approximately equal to the difference in interest rates prevailing between the two countries. Thus, if interest rates in Switzerland are higher than interest rates in Canada, then the IRP condition indicates that the Canadian dollar can be expected to increase in value relative to the CHF. The exact IRP relationship is

$$(18.1) \qquad \text{IRP:} \left(\frac{F - S_0}{S_0} \right) = \left(\frac{i_h - i_f}{1 + i_f} \right)$$

where i_h is the home (Canadian) interest rate, i_f is the comparable foreign (Swiss) interest rate, F is the *direct quote* forward rate, and S_0 is the *direct quote* spot rate. Recall from Chapter 2 that a direct quote is the home currency price of a unit of foreign currency.

Note that the interest rates in Equation 18.1 are the interest rates for the same period of time as the number of days in the forward price. The relationship in Equation 18.1 can be simplified to

$$(18.2) \qquad \text{IRP:} \frac{F}{S_0} = \frac{1 + i_h}{1 + i_f}$$

An approximation of the IRP relationship is

$$(18.3) \qquad \text{Approximate IRP:} \left(\frac{F - S_0}{S_0} \right) \approx (i_h - i_f)$$

Equation 18.3 indicates that when interest rate parity exists, differences in interest rates between two countries will be (approximately) offset by changes in the relative value of the two currencies.

To illustrate, assume that the three-month interest rate is 2.465 percent in Canada and 3.5 percent in Switzerland, and the current spot exchange rate between Canadian dollars and CHF is CAD1.085/CHF. If IRP holds, what will be the three-month forward rate (using the exact relationship in Equation 18.2)?

$$F/(\text{CAD}1.085/\text{CHF}) = (1 + 0.02465)/(1 + 0.035)$$

$$F = \text{CAD}1.07415/\text{CHF}$$

In this case, the Canadian dollar is increasing in value over time relative to the CHF (i.e., it takes fewer Canadian dollars in three months to buy each CHF). Why do you think this should occur?

Purchasing Power Parity

Purchasing Power Parity (PPP)

A theory that posits that the law of one price for the same product in different countries will be the same in each country after making the appropriate conversion from one currency into the other.

When there are no significant costs or other barriers associated with moving goods or services between markets, then the price of each product should be the same in each market. In economics, this is known as the *law of one price*. When the different markets represent different countries, the law of one price says that prices will be the same in each country after making the appropriate conversion from one currency to another. Alternatively, one can say that exchange rates between two currencies will equal the ratio of the price indexes between the countries. In international finance and trade, this relationship is known as the absolute version of **purchasing power parity** (PPP).

In reality, we know that this relationship does not hold because of the costs of moving goods and services and the existence of tariffs and other trade barriers. For example, *The Economist*, a British publication, in a lighthearted look at the law of one price, regularly reports on the price of Big Mac hamburgers in various countries. When the price of a Big Mac was about USD2.55 in the United States, it cost (after converting currencies) about USD1.91 (CAD2.99) in Canada, USD1.18 in China, USD2.99 in Great Britain, USD3.52 in Israel, USD2.53 in Japan, and USD1.06 in the Philippines.[4] It is obviously not possible to buy Big Macs in Manila and ship them to Tel Aviv for sale, for example. Hence, the law of one price does not hold for Big Macs. On the other hand, for goods that are standardized and somewhat easier to move and store, such as gold or crude oil, one would expect only minor violations of the law of one price.

Relative Purchasing Power Parity

The theory that the spot exchange rate between two currencies should change by an amount approximately equal to the difference in expected inflation rates in the two countries.

A less restrictive form of the law of one price is known as **relative purchasing power parity**. The relative PPP principle states that in comparison to a period when exchange rates between two countries are in equilibrium, changes in the differential rates of inflation between two countries will be offset by equal but opposite changes in the future spot exchange rate. For example, if prices in Canada rise by 4 percent per year and prices in Switzerland rise by 6 percent per year, then relative PPP holds if the Swiss franc (CHF) weakens relative to the Canadian dollar by approximately 2 percent.

The exact relative purchasing power parity relationship is

$$(18.4) \qquad \text{Relative PPP:} \left(\frac{S_1 - S_0}{S_0} \right) = \left(\frac{\pi_h - \pi_f}{1 + \pi_f} \right)$$

where S_1 is the expected future (direct quote) spot rate at time period 1, S_0 is the current (direct quote) spot rate, π_h is the expected home country inflation rate, and π_f is the expected foreign country inflation rate.[5] This relationship can be simplified to

$$(18.5) \qquad \text{Relative PPP:} \left(\frac{S_1}{S_0} \right) = \left(\frac{1 + \pi_h}{1 + \pi_f} \right)$$

Using the previous example, if Canadian prices are expected to rise by 2.96 percent over the coming year, prices in Switzerland are expected to rise by 4 percent during the same time, and the current spot exchange rate (S_0), is CAD1.08/CHF, then the expected spot rate in one year (S_1), will be

$$S_1/(CAD1.08/CHF) = (1 + 0.0296)/(1 + 0.04)$$

$$S_1 = CAD1.0692/CHF$$

The higher Swiss inflation rate can be expected to result in a decline in the future spot value of the CHF relative to the dollar by 1.00 percent.

The market forces that support the relative PPP relationship operate in the following way. If one nation has a higher inflation rate than another, its goods and services will

---

[4] Retrieved December 15, 2002, from **www.economist.com** based on an article in *The Economist*, January 11, 2001.

[5] The relationship in Equation 18.4 can be approximated as $(S_i - S_0)/S_0 \approx \pi_h - \pi_f$.

become relatively more expensive, making its exports less price competitive and imports more price competitive. The resulting deficit in foreign trade will place downward pressure on the currency value of the high inflation country until a new, lower equilibrium value is established. The opposite will be true for the country with the lower inflation rate. For example, if Canada has a lower inflation rate than its major trading partners, relative PPP indicates that the value of the Canadian dollar can be expected to increase relative to the value of the currencies of these other trading partners.

Tests of relative PPP indicate that the relationship holds up reasonably well over long periods, but it is a less accurate indicator of short-term currency value changes.[6] Also, the relative PPP relationship is stronger for those countries experiencing high rates of inflation. Tests of the strength of the PPP relationship are hampered by the use of noncomparable price indexes between countries and government interference in commodity and currency markets. Nevertheless, the general relationship between inflation rates and currency values is widely accepted, even if it is difficult to measure properly.

Expectations Theory and Forward Exchange Rates

If foreign currency markets are efficient, the forward rate should reflect what market participants expect the future spot rate for a currency to be. For example, if market participants expected the one-year future spot rate (S_1) for CHF to be CAD1.0692/CHF, then what would the one-year forward rate (F_1) have to be? It would also have to be CAD1.0692/CHF. If the forward rate were lower than this amount, market participants would want to buy CHF forward, thereby placing upward price pressure on the CHF until equilibrium is reached where the forward rate equals the expected future spot rate.

If the expected future spot rate is equivalent to the forward rate, we can say that the forward rate is an *unbiased* estimator of the future spot rate. It is important to recognize that this does not mean that the forward rate will always be equal to the actual future spot rate. Rather, it means that the estimates of the future spot rate provided by the forward rate will not systematically overshoot or undershoot the actual future spot rate, but will equal it *on average*.

Evidence regarding the expectations theory of forward exchange rates indicates that, in general, the forward rate is an unbiased estimate of expected future spot rates, if risk in the currency markets is ignored.[7] There is some evidence, however, that when the forward rate implies a large change from the current spot rate, these forecasts tend to overshoot the actual future spot rate.

Forward rates as unbiased estimates of expected future spot rates have important implications for managers. First, managers should not spend the firm's resources to buy forecasts of future exchange rates since unbiased forecasts are provided free in the marketplace. Second, managers will find that hedging their future foreign currency risk by making use of the forward market should be a cost-effective way of limiting this risk exposure. In the following sections, some of these hedging techniques are considered.

The International Fisher Effect

The final piece in the international currency market puzzle is the relationship between interest rates and future spot currency rates. In his 1930 book, *The Theory of Interest*, Irving Fisher established that in equilibrium, lenders will receive a nominal rate of interest equal to a real interest rate plus an amount sufficient to offset the effects of

---

[6] James P. Lothian and Mark P. Taylor, "Real Exchange Rate Behavior: The Recent Float from the Perspective of the Last Two Centuries," *Journal of Political Economy*, vol. 104, no. 3 (June 1996): 488–509.

[7] Lars P. Hansen and Robert J. Hodrick, "Forward Exchange Rates as Optimal Predictors of Future Spot Rates: An Econometric Analysis," *Journal of Political Economy*, vol. 88, no. 5 (October 1980): 829–853.

expected inflation. *Nominal interest rates* are market rates stated in current, not real, terms, such as the rates quoted in financial publications like *The Globe and Mail* and the *National Post.* Real rates of return are not directly observable. The relationship between nominal (risk-free) rates of return, real rates of return, and expected inflation is

$$(1 + i) = (1 + i_R)(1 + \pi)$$

or

(18.6) $$i = i_R + \pi + i_R\pi$$

where i is the nominal (and risk-free) rate of interest, i_R is the real rate of return, and π is the expected inflation rate. This relationship is often referred to as the *Fisher effect.*[8] For example, if the annual real rate of return in Hong Kong was 3 percent and the expected annual inflation rate was 8 percent, the nominal interest rate would be

$$i = 0.03 + 0.08 + (0.03)(0.08) = 0.1124 \text{ or } 11.24\%$$

Fisher argues that in the absence of government interference and holding risk constant, real rates of return across countries will be equalized through a process of arbitrage. If real rates of return are higher in Canada than in Japan, for example, capital will flow to Canada from Japan until equilibrium is reached. The assumption of equal real rates of return across countries ignores differences in risk and attitudes toward risk that may exist in different cultures. Also, to the extent that there are barriers to the movement of capital between countries, real rates of return may be different between countries. In spite of these limitations, the assumption of equal real returns is useful because (1) it is a reasonable representation of reality among the major industrialized countries and (2) as capital markets become increasingly internationalized and barriers to capital flows fall, differences in real rates of return can be expected to decrease.

If real rates of return tend to be equalized across countries, it follows that differences in observed nominal rates between countries must be due primarily to different inflation expectations. Incorporating the equilibrium condition for real interest rates with relative PPP leads to what has been called the **international Fisher effect (IFE)**. The IFE states that differences in interest rates between two countries should be offset by equal but opposite changes in the future spot exchange rate. For example, if one-year nominal interest rates are 10 percent in Canada and 7 percent in Hong Kong, then IFE predicts that the Hong Kong dollar (HKD) should increase in value relative to the Canadian dollar by approximately 3 percent.

The exact IFE relationship is

(18.7) $$\text{IFE:} \left(\frac{S_1 - S_0}{S_0} \right) = \left(\frac{i_h - i_f}{1 + i_f} \right)$$

where S_1 is the expected future (direct quote) spot rate at time period 1, S_0 is the current (direct quote) spot rate, i_h is the home country nominal interest rate, and i_f is the foreign country nominal interest rate.[9] This relationship can be simplified to

(18.8) $$\text{IFE:} \left(\frac{S_1}{S_0} \right) = \left(\frac{1 + i_h}{1 + i_f} \right)$$

Using the previous example, if one-year Canadian nominal interest rates are 10 percent, one-year Hong Kong nominal interest rates are 7 percent, and the current spot exchange rate, S_0, is CAD0.20/HKD, then the expected spot rate in one year, S_1, will be

International Fisher Effect (IFE)

The theory that the difference in interest rates between two countries should be offset by equal but opposite changes in the future spot exchange rate.

---

[8] This relationship can be approximated as $i \approx i_R + \pi$.

[9] This relationship can be approximated as $(S_i - S_0)/S_0 \approx i_h - i_f$.

$$S_1/(CAD0.20/HKD) = (1 + 0.10)/(1 + 0.07)$$

$$S_1 = CAD0.2056/HKD$$

The lower nominal Hong Kong interest rate results in an expected increase in the value of the HKD (decrease in the value of the Canadian dollar) of 2.80 percent.

An Integrative Look at International Parity Relationships

Figure 18.1 provides an integrative look at international parity relationships. Beginning with the lower box in the figure, suppose one observes that the one-year nominal interest rate is 10 percent in Canada and 5 percent in Switzerland. This implies, according to the Fisher effect, that the difference in expected inflation rates between Canada and Switzerland is about 5 percent because real rates of return are assumed to be equal between Canada and Switzerland. The approximately 5 percent inflation differential means that the one-year future spot rate of exchange between dollars and CHF can be expected to change such that the dollar will weaken by about 5 percent relative to the CHF. This condition is expected from the purchasing power parity relationship.

The 5 percent differential in interest rates also implies that the dollar will sell at about 5 percent discount in the one-year forward market relative to the CHF. This expectation arises from the interest rate parity relationship. If the forward rate is an unbiased estimator of future spot rates, then the one-year future spot rate of exchange

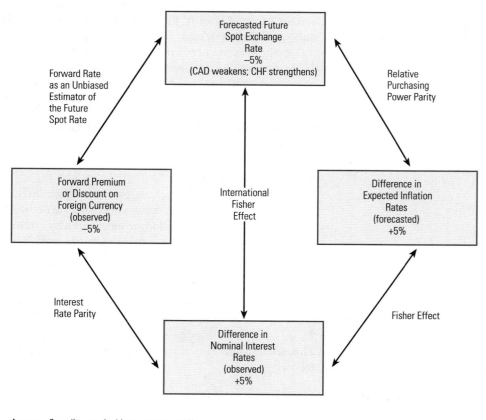

Assume: Canadian nominal interest rate = 10%
Swiss nominal interest rate = 5%
Time horizon = One year

Figure 18.1
International Parity Conditions: An Integrative Look

between dollars and CHF can be expected to change such that the Canadian dollar will weaken by about 5 percent relative to the CHF.

Finally, the international Fisher effect implies that if one-year nominal interest rates are about 5 percent higher in Canada than in Switzerland, then the one-year future spot rate of exchange between the Canadian dollar and the CHF will change such that the dollar will weaken by about 5 percent relative to the CHF.

Forecasting Future Exchange Rates

The equilibrium relationships discussed in the previous sections can be useful to managers who need forecasts of future spot exchange rates. Although empirical evidence indicates that these relationships are not perfect, the financial markets in developed countries operate in a way that efficiently incorporates the effect of interest rate differentials in the forward market and the future spot exchange market. Therefore, managers can use the information contained in forward rates and interest rates to make forecasts of the future spot exchange rates. These forecasts are useful, for example, when pricing products for sale in international markets, when making international capital investment decisions, and when deciding whether to hedge foreign currency risks.

Using Forward Rates

The simplest forecast of future spot exchange rates can be derived from current forward rates. If the one-year forward rate of exchange between Canadian dollars and Japanese yen is CAD0.013324/JPY, then this can be used as an unbiased estimate of the expected one-year future spot rate of exchange between Canadian dollars and yen. For example, if Bombardier were negotiating the sale of a Bombardier CRJ900 airliner to Air Nippon Airways (ANA) with delivery and payment to take place in one year, and if ANA insisted on a price quoted in yen, then Bombardier could use this forward rate to convert its desired Canadian dollar proceeds from the transaction into yen. As we will see in a later section, Bombardier may want to hedge against the risk of a change in this exchange rate between the time the contract is signed and the time the plane is delivered and payment is received.

Using Interest Rates

Forward rates provide a direct and convenient forecast of future spot currency exchange rates. Unfortunately, forward quotes normally are not readily available beyond one year. Hence, if a manager needs a longer-term currency exchange rate forecast, forward rates are of little help. Fortunately, one can use observed interest rate differentials between two countries and the general international Fisher effect (IFE) relationship to make longer-term exchange rate forecasts. Recall from Equation 18.8 that the IFE relationship is given as

$$\left(\frac{S_1}{S_0} \right) = \left(\frac{1 + i_h}{1 + i_f} \right)$$

This relationship can be modified to cover more than one period into the future as follows:

(18.9)
$$\left(\frac{S_n}{S_0} \right) = \left(\frac{(1 + i_h)^n}{(1 + i_f)^n} \right)$$

For example, assume that the annual nominal interest rate on five-year Government of Canada bonds is 6 percent and the annual nominal interest rate on five-year Swiss government bonds is 4.5 percent. Also, assume that the current spot exchange rate between Canadian dollars and Swiss francs (CHF) is CAD1.08/CHF. What is the expected future spot rate in five years? It can be calculated using Equation 18.9 as follows:

$$S_5/(CAD1.08/CHF) = (1 + 0.06)^5/(1 + 0.045)^5$$

$$S_5 = CAD1.1598/CHF$$

The IFE relationship predicts that the Canadian dollar will lose value relative to the CHF. The expected spot exchange rate in five years is CAD1.1598/CHF.

One could also use the PPP relationship to forecast future exchange rates. However, the advantage of the IFE relationship is that interest rates between two countries are readily observable for almost any maturity, whereas differential levels of future inflation are not. In order to use PPP to make exchange rate forecasts, one would first have to forecast the inflation rates in both countries. Hence it is normally desirable to use the IFE relationship when making longer-term exchange rate forecasts.

Foreign Exchange Risk

Foreign exchange risk is said to exist when a portion of the cash flows expected to be received by a firm are denominated in foreign currencies. As exchange rates change, there is uncertainty about the amount of domestic currency that will be received from a transaction denominated in a foreign currency.[10] There are three primary categories of foreign exchange risk that multinational firms must consider:

1. Transaction exposure (short-term)
2. Economic (operating) exposure (long-term)
3. Translation (accounting) exposure

Transaction Exposure

Most firms have contracts to buy and sell goods and services, with delivery and payment to occur at some time in the future. If payments under the contract involve the use of foreign currency, additional risk is involved. The potential for change in value of a foreign currency–denominated transaction due to an exchange rate change is called **transaction exposure**.

Transaction Exposure
The potential for a change in the value of a foreign currency–denominated transaction due to a change in the exchange rate after the transaction is entered into but before it is settled.

For example, Nortel, a Canadian firm, is a major worldwide producer of telecommunications equipment. Suppose that Nortel contracts with British Telecomm (BT) to sell network switching equipment for delivery one year from now. Nortel wants to realize USD155 million from this sale. (Nortel uses the US dollar as its functional currency and reports to shareholders in US dollars.) However, BT has indicated that it will enter into the contract only if the price is stated in British pounds (GBP). The one-year forward rate is USD1.55/GBP. Hence, Nortel quotes a price of GBP100 million. Once the contract has been signed, Nortel faces a significant transaction exposure. Unless Nortel takes actions to guarantee its future dollar proceeds from the sale—that is, unless it hedges its position, for example, by selling GBP100 million in the one-year forward market—it stands to lose on the transaction if the value of the GBP weakens. Suppose that over the coming year the inflation rate in GBP rises significantly beyond what was expected at the time the deal was signed. According to relative PPP, the value of the GBP can be expected to decline, say to USD1.40/GBP. If this happens, Nortel will receive only USD140 million (GBP100 million × USD1.40/GBP) rather than the USD155 million it was expecting.

---

[10] See Jeff Madura, *International Financial Management*, 7th ed. (Mason, OH: South-Western College Publishing, 2003), Chaps. 9–12 for more on the management of foreign exchange risk.

One well-documented example of the potential consequences of transaction exposure is the case of Laker Airlines. In the late 1970s, in the face of growing demand from British tourists travelling to the United States, Laker purchased several DC-10 aircraft and financed them in US dollars. This transaction ultimately led to Laker's bankruptcy because Laker's primary source of revenue was British pounds, whereas its debt costs were denominated in US dollars. Over the period from the late 1970s to 1982, when Laker failed, the US dollar strengthened relative to the British pound. This had a devastating effect because (1) the strong US dollar discouraged British travel to the United States, and (2) the British pound cost of principal and interest payments on the US dollar-denominated debt increased.

Managing Transaction Exposure   A number of alternatives are available to a firm faced with transaction exposure. First, the firm may choose to do nothing, and simply accept the risk associated with the transaction. Doing nothing works well for firms with extensive international transactions that may tend to cancel each other out. For example, if Nortel has purchased goods or services from British firms that require the payment in approximately the same number of GBP as it expects to receive from the sale of the network switching equipment, then it is not necessary to do anything to counter the risk arising from a loss in value of the GBP relative to the USD.

A second alternative is for Nortel to invoice all transactions in US dollars. This avoids any transaction risk for the firm, but shifts this risk to the other party. When a firm is considering this alternative, it needs to determine whether this strategy is competitively possible, or whether parties on the other side of the transaction may resist or perhaps insist on a lower price if they are forced to bear all of the transaction risk.

There are two hedging techniques that can be used by any firm to protect itself against transaction exposure:

■ Execute a contract in the forward exchange market or in the foreign exchange futures market.

■ Execute a *money market hedge.*

Consider the situation of Canadian-based NHL teams that must pay all of their players in US dollars (all hockey player contracts are in USD by league rule) but generate most of their revenues in Canadian dollars. Suppose, for example, the Ottawa Senators have a payroll of USD1.2 million for each week of the 25-week season. Further, suppose that the spot rate for the Canadian dollar suddenly rises (i.e., the Canadian dollar falls in value relative to the US dollar) from CAD1.56/USD to CAD1.60/USD. Then, the weekly payroll obligation rises from CAD1.872 million (USD1.2 million × CAD1.56/USD) to CAD1.920 million (USD1.2 million × CAD1.60/USD). This transaction exposure would cost the Senators CAD48,000 per week or CAD1.2 million per season. This is roughly equivalent to the salary of a decent third-line player. To stay within its self-mandated salary cap, the Senators would probably need to replace two veteran players with untested rookies. Such a player move could spell disaster at the box office if the team goes on a losing streak because of these roster moves. How might the Senators protect themselves?

First, the Senators could execute a series of contracts in the forward exchange market to buy USD1.2 million each week of the 25-week season. This is referred to as a *forward market hedge.* Such standard exchange-traded contracts are available for one month, two months, three months, six months, and one year. However, for other periods, the Senators would need to enter into a custom contract with a bank, an insurance company, or some other motivated party.

A second hedging technique, called a *money market hedge,* involves the Senators borrowing funds from its bank, exchanging them for US dollars at the spot rate, and investing these US dollars in interest-bearing US securities that will yield USD1.2 million every week of the season. By investing in securities that mature on the same date the payroll cheques are due, the Senators will have the necessary amount of US dollars on hand to meet the monthly payroll obligations. The net cost of this money market hedge to the Senators will depend on the interest rate on the funds it borrows from its bank relative to the interest rate on the funds it invests in securities. If the conditions of interest rate parity are satisfied, these two hedging techniques are equivalent.

Other transaction risk reduction strategies include the use of options on foreign currencies and negotiating a risk-sharing contract between the two parties to a transaction in which both parties agree in advance to share in some way the financial consequences of changes in value between the affected currencies.

For large multinational companies, there will be many international transactions involving many different currencies. Attempting to hedge separately the transaction exposure for each international transaction would be time-consuming and inefficient. For example, consider Alcatel, a French company that is a rival of Nortel in the telecommunications equipment business. Alcatel has operations in both Canada and the United States as well as elsewhere in the world. The Canadian subsidiary makes purchases in Canada. Some of these purchases in Canada may be denominated in US dollars, but some may be in Canadian dollars. To the extent that these US dollar and Canadian dollar purchases are offset by US dollar and Canadian dollar sales, no hedge is necessary. Multinational firms often make thousands of overlapping transactions using different currencies. Thus, it is a complex matter to keep track of *net* currency exposures and avoid hedging against risks that do not really exist when one takes the consolidated corporate view, rather than the narrow subsidiary view, of exchange risk.

Economic Exposure

Economic Exposure
The extent to which changes in real exchange rates lead to a change in the value of a firm's operating cash flows, and hence its value. Also known as operating exposure.

Economic (or operating) **exposure** refers to changes in a firm's operating cash flows (and hence the firm's value) that come about because of *real* rather than *nominal* changes in exchange rates. Real exchange rate changes occur when there are deviations from purchasing power parity (PPP). Under relative PPP, exchange rates should vary to reflect changes in the price level of goods and services in one country relative to another. For example, if the inflation rate in Mexico is 5 percent higher per year than in the United States, relative PPP says that the value of the Mexican peso can be expected to decline by about 5 percent relative to the US dollar. Thus, goods purchased in the United States from Mexico will cost the same as they did before the increase in Mexican inflation, after adjusting for the decline in the value of the peso.

Real exchange rate changes can affect the way competing companies in different countries do business and can impact the business conditions in the countries. The showcase example of these effects is the relative performance of the Japanese and North American automobile industries. In the mid-1980s, the Japanese yen was "weak" compared to either the US or Canadian dollar. The Japanese share of the North American auto market was growing, restrained only by voluntary import restrictions agreed to by the Japanese. By 1995, the value of the yen relative to North American dollars had reversed the fortunes of automakers in Japan and North America. Japanese autos were selling for several thousand dollars more in 1995 than comparable North American products. North American firms reported significant increases in market share at the expense of the Japanese. Japanese auto firms were experiencing significant financial difficulties at a time when North American auto firms were reporting substantial increases in profit. North American firms had also begun exporting vehicles to Japan.

In an attempt to offset the impact of their significant economic exposure in North America, Japanese firms have aggressively moved to establish manufacturing and assembly operations in the North America as well as in some European countries, so that many of their costs will be denominated in the same currency as their revenues. Also, by locating plants in many different countries, multinational firms have the flexibility to shift production from one location to another in order to offset unfavourable economic exposure.

Managing Economic Exposure   Economic exposure is much more difficult and expensive to manage than the shorter-term transaction exposure already discussed. Strategies to manage the impact of real changes in exchange rates in countries where a multinational firm operates include

1. *Shift production from high-cost (exchange-rate adjusted) plants to lower-cost plants*—for example, moving labour-intensive sewing operations from Canadian textile plants to plants in Mexico.

2. *Increase productivity*—adopt labour-saving technologies, implement flexible manufacturing systems, reduce product cycles, make use of benchmarking, that is, copy your strongest competitors.

3. *"Outsource" the supply of many of the components needed to produce a product to lower-cost locations*—for example, some North American publishing houses have outsourced typesetting to areas in the Far East with lower labour costs.

4. *Increase product differentiation to reduce the price sensitivity in the market*—for example, the Japanese have moved more to the luxury car market as the yen has strengthened because of the greater price flexibility the luxury market provides relative to the economy car market.

5. *Enter markets with strong currencies and reduce involvement in competitive markets with weak currencies*—North American firms have become increasingly aggressive in entering the Japanese market as the yen has increased in value relative to the dollar.

Translation Exposure

When a multinational firm has one or more foreign subsidiaries with assets and liabilities denominated in a foreign currency, it faces **translation exposure**. For example, if a Canadian-based multinational firm operates a subsidiary in Poland, the "zloty" value of the subsidiary's assets and liabilities must be translated into the home (CAD) currency when the parent firm prepares its consolidated financial statements. When the translation occurs, there can be gains or losses, which must be recognized in the financial statements of the parent.

Current accounting standards are set forth in Section 1650 of the CICA *Handbook*. The major provisions of this standard are

- Current assets, unless covered by forward exchange contracts, and fixed assets are translated into Canadian dollars at the rate of exchange prevailing on the date of the balance sheet.

- Current and long-term liabilities payable in foreign currency are translated into Canadian dollars at the rate of exchange prevailing on the date of the balance sheet.

- Income statement items are translated either at the rate on the date of a particular transaction or at a weighted average of the exchange rates for the period of the income statement.

- Dividends are translated at the exchange rate on the date the dividend is paid

- Equity accounts, including common shares and contributed capital, are translated at historical rates.

- Gains and losses to the parent from translation are not included in the parent's calculation of net income, nor are they included in the parent's retained earnings. Rather, they are reported in a separate equity account named "Cumulative translation adjustments" or a similar title. Gains or losses in this account are not recognized in the income statement until the parent's investment in the foreign subsidiary is sold or liquidated.

Translation Exposure

The change in owners' (accounting) equity because of a change in exchange rates that affects the "converted" value of foreign assets and liabilities.

A decline in the value of a foreign currency relative to the Canadian dollar reduces the conversion value of the foreign subsidiary's liabilities as well as its assets. Therefore, the parent company's risk exposure depends on the foreign subsidiary's net equity position (that is, assets minus liabilities). Thus, on the books of the parent company, the subsidiary's creditors in effect bear part of the decline in the value of the subsidiary's assets.

Obviously, if a foreign currency strengthens relative to the Canadian dollar, then a Canadian company would experience a currency exchange gain. For example, suppose that Canadian Products has a subsidiary, American Products, with total assets of USD12 million and total liabilities of USD8 million. Based on an exchange rate of CAD1.56/USD, the net equity position of the American subsidiary on Canadian Products' balance sheet, as shown in Table 18.1, is CAD6.24 million. Suppose now that the Canadian dollar weakens relative to the US dollar (i.e., the direct quote from the Canadian perspective rises) to CAD1.60/USD and all other things remain the same. As can be seen in the table, the net equity position of the American subsidiary on Canadian Products' balance sheet increases to CAD6.40 million, resulting in a CAD160,000 currency exchange gain.

Managing Translation Exposure   In general, when a foreign subsidiary's assets are greater than its liabilities, currency exchange losses will occur when the home currency strengthens (i.e., the direct quote in the home currency falls). As the above example illustrated, the opposite effects are true when the home currency weakens. A company can hedge and manage its balance sheet translation exposure by financing its foreign assets with debt denominated in the same currency.

For example, Bombardier has several debt issues outstanding in foreign currencies. One issue that totals EUR500 million has staggered maturities from 2004 to 2027 with an average coupon rate of 6.4 percent. Since Bombardier has operations in Germany and Austria, this issue helps hedge Bombardier against translation losses.

A multinational company can also minimize its exchange rate risk, as well as the risk of expropriation or nationalization of its assets by a foreign government, by developing a *portfolio* of foreign investments. Rather than making all its direct investments in foreign subsidiaries that are located in one particular country, the firm can spread its foreign investments among a number of different countries, thus limiting the risk of incurring large losses within any one country. Bombardier already has a diversified portfolio of factories in Canada, the United States, the United Kingdom, Germany, and Austria.

Table 18.1   Effect of a Weakening of the Canadian Dollar on Canadian Products' Balance Sheet

	Exchange Rate			
	CAD1.56/USD		CAD1.60/USD	
	USD	CAD	USD	CAD
Assets	12,000,000	18,720,000	12,000,000	19,200,000
Liabilities	8,000,000	12,480,000	8,000,000	12,800,000
Net equity position	4,000,000	6,240,000	4,000,000	6,400,000

International trade is facilitated when currency value differences are not too large and also not too volatile. Argentina has not yet found a stable solution. Ecuador decided to adopt the US dollar as its currency, joining Liberia in using the US dollar for its domestic transactions. Some other countries are also considering using the US dollar. In Canada, there are some who advocate adopting the US dollar. However, the majority of Canadians still believe that the Canadian dollar has advantages.

Summary

- The theory of *interest rate parity* states that the percentage differential between the spot and the forward rates for a currency quoted in terms of another currency is equal to the approximate difference in interest rates in the two countries over the same time horizon.

- The theory of *relative purchasing power parity* states that in comparison to a period when exchange rates between two countries are in equilibrium, changes in differential rates of inflation between two countries will be offset by equal but opposite changes in the future spot currency rate.

- The *forward rate* is often taken as an *unbiased estimator* of the *future spot currency rate*.

- The nominal rate of interest is approximately equal to the sum of the real rate of interest and the expected inflation rate. This relationship is known as the *Fisher effect*.

- The *international Fisher effect* theory states that differences in interest rates between two countries will be offset by equal but opposite changes in the future spot rate.

- Forecasts of future spot exchange rates can be derived from forward rates, if available, or from observed interest rates between two countries in conjunction with the international Fisher effect theory.

- Firms that compete in a global economy face three categories of foreign exchange risk:

  1. Transaction or short-term exposure
  2. Economic (operating) or long-term exposure
  3. Translation (accounting) exposure

- Many risk-reducing strategies are available to firms facing these risks, including the use of various hedges, such as a forward hedge and a money market hedge.

Questions and Topics for Discussion

1. What is the theory of interest rate parity?
2. What is covered interest arbitrage?
3. Describe two techniques that a company can use to hedge against transaction exchange risk.
4. Describe the factors that cause exchange rates to change over time.

5. What are the advantages to a Canadian firm of financing its foreign investments with funds raised abroad?

6. Describe how the concepts of relative purchasing power parity, interest rate parity, and the international Fisher effect are related.

Self-Test Problems

ST1. Assume that the annualized discount on forward Canadian dollars is 3%. The annualized US interest rate is 8%, and the comparable Canadian interest rate is 12%. How can a Canadian trader use covered interest arbitrage to take advantage of this situation?

ST2. Fording, a former subsidiary of Canadian Pacific, exports coal to Japan. Fording receives CAD45.00/tonne for coal sales in Canada and wants to get the same net proceeds from its export sales.

    a. If the exchange rate is JPY77.37/CAD, what price must Fording charge in Japan (in yen)?

    b. What price will Fording have to charge in Japan if the value of the Canadian dollar falls to JPY75.00/CAD?

ST3. The annualized yield on three-year maturity Government of Canada bonds is 4%, while the yield on similar maturity Swiss bonds is 5%. The current spot exchange rate between the Canadian dollar and the Swiss franc is CAD1.08/CHF. What is the expected future spot rate for the CHF in three years?

Problems*

BASIC

1. If the one-year Canadian Treasury bill rate is 3.0%, the spot rate between Canadian dollars and British pounds is CAD2.48/GBP, and the three-month forward rate is CAD2.47/GBP, what rate of interest is expected on Sterling Treasury bills, assuming that interest rate parity between the Canadian dollar and the pound exists?

2. Last year, the French marketing subsidiary of Multinational Pharmaceuticals Corporation (MPC), a Montreal-based drug manufacturer, earned 700,000 euros. This year, partly due to a weaker Canadian dollar, the French subsidiary will earn 900,000 euros. Last year, the exchange rate was CAD1.5/EUR, and this year, it is CAD1.6/EUR. Calculate how many Canadian dollars the French subsidiary contributes to MPC's earnings in each year.

3. Using the currency calculator at the **www.xe.com/ucc** Web site, calculate the foreign currency equivalent of CAD100 in terms of British pounds, Swiss francs, US dollars, and Japanese yen.

INTERMEDIATE

4. Suppose the British short-term interest rate is 9% and the corresponding Canadian rate is 4%. Suppose at the same time that the discount on forward pounds is 3% per year. Do these conditions present an opportunity for covered interest arbitrage? If so, what steps should a trader in Toronto take? What annual rate will the trader earn?

5. Mammouth Mutual Fund of Vancouver has CAD5 million to invest in short-term securities for the next six months. It can buy either a CIBC short-term security

---

*Coloured numbers and letters denote problems that have "check" answers provided at the back of the book.

with an annual yield of 4% or a Paribas (France) short-term security with a yield of 6%. Assume that the securities are of comparable default risk. The analysts of the mutual fund are concerned about exchange rate risk. They were quoted the following exchange rates by the international department of a Toronto bank:

Euro (EUR)	
Spot	CAD1.5956/EUR
One-month forward	CAD1.5953/EUR
Three-month forward	CAD1.5953/EUR
Six-month forward	CAD1.5954/EUR

   a. If the Paribas short-term security is purchased and held to maturity, determine the net gain (loss) in Canadian dollars relative to the CIBC security, assuming that the exchange rate in six months equals today's spot rate.

   b. Suppose the euro (EUR) declines in value by 5% relative to the Canadian dollar over the next six months. Determine the net gain (loss) of the Paribas short-term security in Canadian dollars relative to the CIBC short-term security for an uncovered position.

   c. Determine the net gain (loss) from a covered position.

   d. What other factor or factors should be considered in the decision to purchase the Paribas short-term security?

6. As of today, the following information is available:

	Canada	Israel
Real rate of interest required by investors	2.0%	2.0%
Nominal interest rate	4.0%	8.0%
Spot rate	CAD0.3354/ILS	
One-year forward rate	CAD0.3186/ILS	
Call option premium at a strike price of CAD0.3354/ILS	2.0%	

Using this information, make three *independent* forecasts of the one-year future spot rate for the Israeli shekel. (Use exact, not approximation, relationships.)

7. Shoesmith Wave, Inc., a new and largely unproven economic forecasting service, expects the inflation rate in South Korea to average 9% per year over the next five years. In comparison, Shoesmith expects a Canadian inflation rate over this same period to be 3% per year. The yield on five-year Government of Canada bonds is 6% per year. The yield on five-year Korean government bonds is 11% per year. One percentage point of this yield differential can be accounted for by political risk differences between Canada and South Korea, with Canada perceived as having the lower political risk. The current exchange rate is KRW2,000/CAD.

Forecast the future five-year spot rate for the South Korean won (versus the Canadian dollar) using the Shoesmith Wave forecast and the forecast from the financial markets.

8. On January 1, the cost of borrowing Hong Kong dollars (HKD) for one year was 18%. During the year the Canadian inflation rate was 2% and the Chinese inflation rate was 9%. The exchange rate on January 1 was HKD4.50/CAD. On December 31 the exchange rate was HKD5.00/CAD. If you borrowed HKD100,000 on January 1, converted this into Canadian dollars and used these funds for one year, and then paid off the HKD loan on December 31, what was the *actual* cost of borrowing HKD for one year?

9. The Swiss franc (CHF) is currently trading in the spot market at CAD1.08/CHF. The six-month forward rate is CAD1.07/CHF. The Canadian Treasury bill rate for six months is 3.1%. What do you expect is the six-month Swiss government security rate? Why?

CHALLENGE

10. The Jeannette Corporation, a firm based in Flin Flon, Manitoba, has an account payable with a British firm coming due in six months. The payable requires Jeannette to pay GBP200,000. Claudette Jeannette, the firm's founder and CEO, is an astute manager. She has asked her CFO, William Frank, to advise her on the various alternatives for dealing with the exchange risk inherent in this payable. She wishes to know the expected Canadian dollar cost of (1) a forward hedge, (2) a money market hedge, and (3) remaining unhedged.

    The following information is available to William. The spot rate today is CAD2.48/GBP. The current six-month forward rate is CAD2.47/GBP. Interest rates are as follows:

	Great Britain	Canada
Six-month deposit rate	4.5%	4.5%
Six-month borrowing rate	5.0%	5.0%

    a. What is the expected Canadian dollar cost of the forward hedge?
    b. What is the expected Canadian dollar cost of the money market hedge?
    c. What is the expected Canadian dollar cost of remaining unhedged?
    d. Which alternative do you recommend? What are the risks associated with this recommendation?

11. VFA sells a broad range of economic forecasting services to businesses and government agencies. One of its primary products is the VFA Exchange Rate Seer, a model that forecasts future spot exchange rates.

    Finley Inc., a maker and exporter of Fightin Blue Hen paraphernalia, has just received a large order from Kruse AG, a large Swiss retailing chain. Delivery of the merchandise would occur in two years and Finley wishes to determine the price in Swiss francs (CHF) to charge for the order. If the items were being sold for delivery today, Finley would want to receive CAD1.4 million, an amount that would recover all variable costs and make an acceptable contribution to overhead and profit. The current exchange rate is CAD1.08/CHF. Finley expects that its (CAD) costs will rise at about 3% per year over the coming two years and would like to recover these cost increases in proportional increases in the contract price. The annual yield on two-year Government of Canada bonds is 3.5%. Similar risk bonds sell to yield 4.5% annually in Switzerland. VFA forecasts that the spot rate of exchange will be CAD1.06/CHF.

    If you had to make a recommendation regarding the pricing of this order, what is the *best* estimate of the price (in CHF) you can recommend that management charge if it wants to just cover its costs and profit objectives?

Other Practice Materials and Resources

For interactive quizzes, Internet exercises, crossword puzzles, CTV videos, and more, go to the *Contemporary Financial Management* Web site at **http://cyr.nelson.com**

Advanced Capital Investment and Structure Decisions

7

Part Seven covers some advanced topics that are important for financial managers. Chapter 19 deals with some of the more important financial aspects of leasing. Chapter 20 focuses on corporate restructuring, with emphasis on mergers, liquidations, spinoffs, and failure and reorganization. Each of the decision areas covered in this part offers significant opportunities for adding to shareholders' wealth.

Leasing

Learning Objectives

After studying this chapter, you should be able to

1. Define a *lease* as a contract that allows an individual or a firm to make economic use of an asset for a stated period of time without obtaining an ownership interest in the asset

2. Identify the major parties to a lease as the *lessor* and the *lessee*:

   a. The lessor is the owner of the asset and the party who receives the lease payments

   b. The lessee is the user of the asset and the party who makes the lease payments

3. Identify the major different classifications of leases:

   a. *Operating leases* are cancellable, period-by-period leases

   b. *Financial* or *capital leases* are not cancellable. The lease payments under a financial lease are sufficient to fully amortize the cost of the asset plus provide a return to the lessor

   c. *Leveraged leases* are special financial leases involving three parties: the lessor, the lessee, and a group of lenders. Leveraged leases are especially important to firms that cannot take advantage of the tax benefits of ownership

4. Appreciate that leasing decisions are often influenced by the tax and accounting treatment of the transaction

5. Decide that an asset should be leased rather than owned if the present value cost of leasing is less than the present value cost of owning. In that case, there will be a net advantage to leasing. The decision to lease in such a case will increase shareholder wealth

Air Canada Becomes New SES Customer[1]

CP PHOTO/THE LEADER-POST/ROY ANTAL

On October 1, 2002, Air Canada announced a sale and leaseback agreement with Shannon Engine Support (SES) for five CFM56-5 spare engines. SES purchased the engines outright from Air Canada and will lease them back to the airline for 10 years. SES specializes in flexible, cost-effective engine leasing solutions tailored to the specific requirements of the airlines. SES has a portfolio of 140 CFM56 engines, used by 40 customers worldwide, mainly in Europe and China.

SES is a wholly owned subsidiary of CFM International. CFM International is a 50/50 joint venture of SNECMA Moteurs of France and General Electric. CFM produces the world's best-selling commercial airline engines product line, the CFM56 family.

The agreement with SES is part of a larger sale and leaseback transaction that also includes six spare engines that are being purchased by GE Engine Leasing. GE Engine Leasing is a joint services unit of GE Engine Services and GE Capital Aviation Services.

Air Canada announced that the total transaction would generate approximately US$67 million in new financing. Air Canada is one of the largest operators of CFM56-5-powered Airbus A320 aircraft, with approximately 75 airplanes in its fleet.

What is important for Air Canada is that it has some spare engines for its planes, should they be needed, because if they are needed, the need will be urgent. However, it is not really necessary for Air Canada to be the owner of these engines. By leasing the engines for regular payments, Air Canada has a sort of "insurance policy" that guarantees that the spare engines will be available whenever they may be needed. The sale and leaseback gives Air Canada some needed funds to invest in its business now. Air Canada could also lease some new engines if more should be needed. Likewise, Air Canada could lease airplanes rather than own them. This chapter discusses leasing as a method of obtaining the use of assets needed for business purposes. Specifically, we will examine the type of analysis that should go into a lease versus purchase decision if the firm wishes to maximize shareholder wealth.

[1] Air Canada news release, October 1, 2002 (retrieved from **www.sedar.com**).

Introduction

The value of a machine is in its use, not its ownership. This is true in the sense that a firm may wish to acquire the *use* of an asset needed in the production of goods and the providing of services, but finds it unnecessary to acquire legal title to the asset. **Leasing** is a means of obtaining economic use of an asset for a specific period of time without obtaining an ownership interest in the asset. In the lease contract, the property owner (**lessor**) agrees to permit the property user (**lessee**) to make use of the property for a stated time. In return, the lessee agrees to make a series of periodic payments to the lessor.

Leasing as a source of intermediate- and long-term financing has become increasingly popular since World War II. Prior to that time, most lease contracts were written for real estate and farm property. Today, few major firms are not involved in leasing. Leased assets range from transportation equipment (such as railway rolling stock, trucks, automobiles, airplanes, and ships) to computers, medical equipment, specialized industrial equipment, energy transmission equipment, and mining equipment. Some firms lease entire power-generating plants and aluminum reduction mills. In the hotel and motel industry, leases may even include bathroom fixtures, paintings, furniture, and bedding.

The volume of equipment-leasing activity worldwide expanded greatly during the latter half of the 1990s, to about US$474 billion at the end of the decade.[2] Many types of firms originate leases: banks, finance companies, insurance companies, equipment manufacturing companies (often through captive leasing subsidiaries), and independent leasing companies. Canada ranks seventh in the world in annual plant and equipment leasing.[3]

Because of the growing importance and widespread acceptance of lease financing, the contemporary financial manager should have a good understanding of this financing method. The following sections discuss the characteristics of various types of leases. Later sections consider the tax and accounting treatment of leases and the advantages and disadvantages of leases. Finally, a lease analysis model is developed from the perspective of the lessee.

Types of Leases

Leases are classified in a number of ways. "True leases," which are the primary focus of this chapter, are traditional leases in which the lessor holds the legal title to the leased asset. The asset user, the lessee, has no ownership interest in the asset. *Operating leases* and various types of *financial,* or *capital, leases* are subcategories of true leases.

Operating Leases

An **operating lease**, sometimes called a *service* or *maintenance lease,* is an agreement that provides the lessee with use of an asset on a period-by-period basis. Normally, the payments under an operating lease contract are insufficient to recover the full cost of the asset for the lessor. As a result, the contract period in an operating lease tends to be somewhat less than the usable economic life of the asset. The lessor expects to recover the costs (plus a return) from renewal rental payments, from the sale of the asset at the end of the lease period, or from both.

The most important characteristic of an operating lease is that it may be cancelled at the option of the lessee as long as the lessor is given sufficient notice. Even though the lessee may be required to pay a penalty to the lessor on cancellation, this is preferable to

---

Leasing
A procedure for obtaining the economic use of an asset for a stated period of time by agreeing to make periodic payments.

Lessor
The property owner who collects rental payments from the lessee in a lease transaction.

Lessee
The user and renter of the property in a lease transaction.

Operating Lease
A *cancellable* lease agreement that provides the lessee with the use of an asset on a period-by-period basis. This sometimes is called a *service* or *maintenance lease,* especially if the lessor provides maintenance services as part of the lease contract.

---

[2] "CFLA Backgrounder on the Asset-Based Financing, Equipment & Vehicle Leasing Industry in Canada" (Toronto: Canadian Finance & Leasing Association, 2001).

[3] Ibid., p. 3.

being compelled to keep an asset that is expected to become obsolete in the near future. For example, many firms lease their computers under an operating lease arrangement. (Of course, the lessor charges a rental fee that is consistent with expectations of the asset's economic life.)

Most operating leases require the lessor to maintain the leased asset. In addition, the lessor is normally responsible for any property taxes owed on the asset and for providing appropriate insurance coverage. The costs of these services are built into the lease rate.

Financial or Capital Leases

Financial Lease

A noncancellable agreement that obligates the lessee to make payments to the lessor for a predetermined period of time. These payments are usually sufficient to amortize the full cost of the asset plus provide the lessor with a reasonable rate of return on its investment in the asset.

A **financial lease**, also termed a *capital lease,* is a noncancellable agreement.[4] The lessee is required to make payments throughout the lease period, whether or not the asset continues to generate economic benefits. Failure to make payments has serious financial consequences and could eventually force the lessee into bankruptcy.

With financial leases, the lessee is generally responsible for maintenance of the asset. The lessee may also have to pay insurance and property taxes. The total payments over the lease period are sufficient to amortize the original cost of the asset and provide a return to the lessor. Some financial leases provide for a renewal or repurchase option at the end of the lease. These renewal and repurchase options are subject to tax regulations.

A financial lease may originate either as a *sale and leaseback* or as a *direct lease.*

Sale and Leaseback

A lease that is initiated when a firm sells an asset it owns to another firm and simultaneously leases the asset back for its own use.

Sale and Leaseback A **sale and leaseback** occurs when a firm sells an asset to another firm and immediately leases it back for its own use. In this transaction, the lessor normally pays a price close to the asset's fair market value. The lease payments are set at a level that will return the full purchase price of the asset to the lessor, plus provide a reasonable rate of return. The sale and leaseback is advantageous to the lessee for the following reasons:

■ The lessee receives cash from the sale of the asset, which may be reinvested elsewhere in the firm or used to increase the firm's liquidity.

■ The lessee can continue using the asset, even though it is owned by someone else.

Sale and leaseback financing has been popular among firms with weak capital positions. Firms have sold headquarters buildings for a price greater than their book value, recorded a gain on the sale, thereby bolstering the capital account, and leased back the building under a long-term, generally noncancellable lease. The resulting increase in the firm's capital accounts reduces pressure to increase capital via the sale of new equity (common shares).

These types of transactions do not change the fundamental value or risk of the firm. They are primarily accounting manipulations.

Direct Lease

A lease that is initiated when a firm acquires the use of an asset that it did not previously own.

Direct Lease A **direct lease** is initiated when a firm acquires the use of an asset that it previously did not own. The lessor may be the manufacturer of the asset or a financial institution. In the latter instance, the user-lessee first determines the following:

■ What equipment will be leased

■ Which manufacturer will supply the equipment

■ What warranties, terms of delivery, instalment agreements, and service agreements will have to be made

■ What price will be paid for the asset

---

[4] This chapter focuses primarily on financial leases, rather than operating leases, because financial leases represent more permanent obligations. The analysis techniques discussed later in this chapter, however, are equally applicable to both operating and financial leases.

The lessee then contacts a financial institution and works out the terms of the lease, after which the institution (which then becomes the lessor) acquires the asset for the lessee and the lessee starts making the lease payments. Under this arrangement, the lessee is usually responsible for taxes, insurance, and maintenance.

Leveraged Lease
A type of financial lease in which the lessor borrows up to 80 percent of the cost of the leased asset on a nonrecourse basis. The lessor receives the full tax benefits of ownership. This is also sometimes called a third-party equity lease or a tax lease.

Leveraged Leases   A **leveraged lease** is a three-sided agreement among the lessee, the lessor, and the lenders. The *lessee* selects the leased asset, receives all of the income generated from its use, and makes the periodic lease payments. The *lessor* (normally a leasing company) acts either for itself or as an agent for an individual or a group of individuals to provide the equity funds needed to purchase the asset. The *lenders* (usually banks, insurance companies, pension fund management firms, or foundations) lend the funds needed to make up the asset's full purchase price. Specifically, the lessor normally supplies 20 to 40 percent of the purchase price, and the lenders provide the remaining 60 to 80 percent.

Tax Motivation for Leasing

As the owner of the asset, the lessor reports the lease payments as gross income. Because the lessor also receives the permitted capital cost allowance (CCA) and interest tax shields although making a relatively small equity investment, the lessor may provide an attractive lease rate to the lessee.

A large proportion of all financial leases for expensive assets are leveraged leases. Also known as *third-party equity leases* and *tax leases,* leveraged leases are usually tax motivated because the asset user (lessee) is not in a tax position where it can make use of the CCA tax shields if the asset were owned instead of leased. These include lessee firms with low profit levels, large tax-loss carryforwards, or large amounts of tax-exempt income. In fact, *the majority of financial leases, whether leveraged or not, are tax motivated.* In essence, the lessee effectively gives up the tax benefits of ownership in exchange for more favourable lease rates.

Advantages and Disadvantages of Leasing

Leasing offers a number of potential advantages. However, the prudent financial manager should also be aware of the disadvantages.

Advantages

In addition to the tax motivation discussed above, perhaps the second major advantage of leasing is that it provides *flexible financing*. Most lease arrangements tend to have fewer restrictive covenants than loan agreements. In addition, leasing is well suited to piecemeal financing. A firm that is acquiring assets over time may find it more convenient to lease them than to negotiate term loans or sell securities each time it makes a new capital outlay.

In addition, it *may* be possible for the lessee to *avoid some of the risks of obsolescence* associated with ownership. The lessor will charge a lease rate intended to provide a specified return on the required net investment. If the actual salvage is less than originally expected, the lessor bears the loss.

For the small or marginally profitable firm, *leasing is often the only available source of financing* because the title to leased property remains with the lessor and reduces the lessor's risk in the event of failure. If the lessee does fail, the lessor can recover the leased property more quickly than a secured lender.[5]

---

[5] For a more complete discussion of the bankruptcy implications of leasing, see V. S. Krishnan and R. C. Moyer, "Bankruptcy Costs and the Financial Leasing Decision," *Financial Management* (Summer 1994): 31–42.

Leasing by Small Businesses

During business downturns, many small businesses find it difficult to get small business loans from banks. Many firms have sought lease financing as an alternative to traditional bank financing. In addition to its greater availability, firms that have made use of lease financing cite the following advantages:

1. Less cash required up-front
2. Better protection against obsolescence at the end of the lease term
3. Quicker approvals from lessors than from lenders
4. Fewer restrictive covenants from lessors than from lenders

However, these advantages do not come cheap. Lease financing often entails high effective interest costs relative to borrowing. Thus, while leasing has gained favour among small firms as a quick and flexible financing alternative, these benefits have typically come at a high cost.

In April 2002, the Canadian government launched a unique, five-year, pilot project to guarantee small business capital leases up to $250,000 for eligible small businesses. The pilot project guarantees up to 85 percent of a lessor's eligible losses on capital leases in the event of default. Thus, lessors will be encouraged to provide more leased assets to small businesses at more favourable rates. This program is the first of its kind in the world.

Leasing tends to *smooth out expenses* for the lessee. Because lease payments are a constant annual outlay, whereas CCA tax depreciation expenses are large in the early years of ownership and less in later years, earnings tend to appear more stable when assets are leased rather than owned.

Leasing is said to provide *100 percent financing,* whereas most borrowing requires a down payment. This is the major reason cited by lessees for why they choose lease financing. However, because lease payments are normally made in advance of each period, this 100 percent financing benefit is diminished by the amount of the first required lease payment.

From the lessee's perspective, leases can *increase a firm's liquidity.* For example, a sale and leaseback transforms some of a firm's fixed assets into cash in exchange for an obligation to make a series of fixed future payments. This has been the primary motivation for sale and leaseback transactions undertaken by several troubled airlines.

Finally, leasing gives some plant or divisional managers additional *flexibility in acquiring assets* if lease agreements are not subject to internal capital expenditure constraints. In recent years, the MUSH (municipalities, universities, school boards, and hospitals) sector has also used leasing to circumvent capital outlay restrictions.

Disadvantages

The primary disadvantage of leasing is *cost.* For a firm with a strong earnings record, good access to the credit markets, and the ability to take advantage of the tax benefits of ownership, leasing is often a more-expensive alternative. Of course, the actual cost difference between ownership and leasing depends on a number of factors and varies from case to case.

Another disadvantage of leasing is the *loss of the asset's salvage value.* In real estate, this loss can be substantial. A lessee may also have *difficulty getting approval to make property improvements* on leased real estate. If the improvements substantially alter the property or reduce its potential range of uses, the lessor may be reluctant to permit them.

In addition, if a leased asset (with a financial lease) becomes obsolete or if the capital project financed by the lease becomes uneconomical, the *lessee may not cancel the lease without paying a substantial penalty.*

Tax and Accounting Aspects of Leases

Leasing assets involves a number of tax and accounting considerations, which are examined in this section.

Tax Status of True Leases

For information see
www.ccra-adrc.gc.ca

Annual lease payments are tax-deductible for the lessee if one crucial criterion is met. The CCRA (Canada Customs and Revenue Agency) must agree that a contract truly is a lease and not just an instalment loan called a lease. Before embarking on a lease transaction, all involved parties should obtain an opinion from the CCRA regarding the tax status of the proposed lease.

If the CCRA does not agree that a contract is truly a lease, taxes are applied as if the property had been sold to the lessee and pledged to the lessor as security for a loan. The reason for the CCRA restrictions is to prohibit lease transactions set up purely to speed up tax deductions. In the past, CCRA has disallowed lease transactions if the lessee had the right during or after the lease to acquire the asset at a price that was less than the fair market value of the asset at that time, or if the lessee was required to buy the asset at the end of the lease, or if the lessee automatically became the owner of the asset at the end of the lease.

Leases and Accounting Practices

In recent years, firms have tended to disclose more information regarding lease obligations. Worldwide accounting standards are converging and becoming more and more similar. The Canadian accounting standards are contained in the Canadian Institute of Chartered Accountants (CICA) *Handbook*. The US accounting standards are promulgated by the Financial Accounting Standards Board (FASB). Most of the other countries in the world adhere to the International Accounting Standards promulgated by the International Accounting Standards Board (IASB), of which both Canada and the United States are members. The differences between and among the various generally accepted accounting principles (GAAP) concerning leasing are relatively minor.[6]

Firms are normally *required* to capitalize financial or capital leases. The capitalized value of a lease is determined by computing the present value of all required lease payments. In addition to making balance sheet adjustments, firms must show the following information for financial leases in the footnotes to the financial statements:[7]

1. The gross amount of assets by major classes according to nature or use reported under financial leases as of the date of the balance sheet

2. The amount of accumulated lease amortization

3. Future minimum lease payments as of the date of the latest balance sheet presented, in total and for each of the next five years

---

[6] For more information, see the *GAAP Guide 2001–2002*, Canadian Certified General Accountants Association.

[7] The requirements presented here are not inclusive. They merely summarize the most significant disclosures. See CICA *Handbook* Section 3065.

The effect of these disclosure requirements is to lower a firm's reported return on investment and to increase the reported debt-to-equity ratios of a firm that has acquired a portion of its assets through leasing. In the past, some analysts argued that one of the advantages of leasing was that it provided "off-balance sheet" financing and tended to increase a firm's capacity to borrow. Whether or not this was true, the lease-reporting requirements help to eliminate this distortion, facilitate clearer analysis of a firm's financial condition, and make it easier to make comparisons among firms.

Lease-Buy Analysis: The Lessee's Perspective

Financial theorists and model builders have devoted a substantial amount of time and effort to developing an analytical framework within which the differential costs associated with leasing versus buying can be compared. At least 15 different approaches to the problem have been suggested, and there is considerable disagreement as to which one is the best.[8] In spite of this abundance of models, the perplexed financial manager can take some comfort in the fact that the practical effects resulting from the differences in the models tend to be small because few real-world decisions are changed as a result of which lease-buy model is chosen.[9]

One of the most commonly used approaches to the analysis of a lease versus purchase decision assumes that the appropriate comparison should be between *leasing* and *borrowing to buy*. Advocates of this approach argue that a financial lease is much like a loan in that it requires a series of fixed payments. Failure to make lease payments, like failure to make loan payments, may result in bankruptcy.

The basic approach of the lease-buy model is an *incremental* analysis that computes the *net advantage to leasing* (NAL). The **net advantage to leasing** compares the *present value cost of leasing* with the *present value cost of owning* the asset. If the cost of owning the asset is greater than the cost of leasing the asset, the NAL is positive and the model indicates that the asset should be leased.

The *net advantage to leasing* calculation is as follows:

	Installed cost of the asset
Less	Present value of the after-tax lease payments
Less	Present value of CCA tax shields for the asset's economic life, if owned
Plus	Present value of after-tax operating costs incurred if owned but not if leased
Less	Present value of the salvage value
Less	Present value of CCA tax shields beyond the asset's economic life
Equals	Net advantage to leasing

The installed cost or depreciable base of the asset equals the purchase price plus installation and shipping charges. The installed cost forms the basis on which CCA is computed. We assume that any changes in the net working capital would occur whether the firm leases or buys the asset. Hence, these changes are irrelevant for computing NAL. The present value of the after-tax lease payments that are made if the asset is leased

---

Net Advantage to Leasing (NAL)

The NAL method compares the NPV cost of leasing with the NPV cost of owning the asset to see if it is advantageous (cheaper) for the firm to lease an asset rather than buy it. This is a financing decision that is made after the firm has completed the capital budgeting decision process and decided that the asset should be acquired.

---

[8] Basically, the various models differ as to which discount rate should be used to evaluate various components of the cash flows and which cash flows should be considered.

[9] Evidence of this is presented in a paper by Arthur Gudikunst and Gordon Roberts, "Empirical Analysis of Lease-Buy Decisions," presented at the 1975 Meeting of the Eastern Finance Association.

reduces the NAL. Hence, they are subtracted when computing the NAL. These lease payments are discounted at the firm's after-tax marginal cost of borrowing to reflect the fact that lease payments are contractually known in advance and thus are not subject to much uncertainty. The present value of the CCA tax shield is equal to the CCA claimed each year if the asset is owned times the firm's marginal tax rate. The CCA tax shields reduce the cost of ownership and hence are subtracted when computing the NAL. Because the CCA amounts are also known with relative certainty, they are also discounted at the firm's after-tax marginal cost of borrowing.[10]

Sometimes operating costs are incurred if the asset is owned but not if it is leased. These may include property tax payments, insurance, or some maintenance expenses. If these do exist, they represent a benefit of leasing and increase the NAL. Hence, the after-tax amount of these costs is added in the NAL calculation. These operating costs are also discounted at the after-tax marginal cost of borrowing, reflecting their relative certainty.

Next, if the asset is owned, the owner will receive the salvage value. This is lost if the asset is leased. Hence the salvage reduces the NAL and must be subtracted when calculating the NAL. Because the salvage value is generally subject to substantial uncertainty, one could justify discounting the salvage value at a rate equal to the firm's weighted (marginal) cost of capital. Nevertheless, we will simplify the analysis by also using the after-tax cost of debt to discount the salvage value, ΔS_n. We also assume that the lessee's asset class is and remains open.

Finally, the present value of the CCA tax shields beyond the economic life of the asset should be calculated using the after-tax cost of debt $k_d(1 - T)$ and deducted from the NAL as it is a benefit of owning. To simplify the formulas presented in this chapter, we shall use the symbol k_i to denote the after-tax cost of debt $k_d(1 - T)$. These tax shields are worth $Td(\Delta UCC_n - \Delta S_n)/(k_i + d)$ at the end of the asset's economic life and must then be discounted back to time zero.[11]

Recall from Chapter 10 that T is the firm's marginal tax rate, d is the CCA rate, and ΔUCC_n is the undepreciated capital cost at the end of the economic life of the asset.

Example of Lease-Buy Analysis

Consider the following example to illustrate the lease-buy analysis procedure just described. Suppose that the Alcan Corporation is trying to decide whether it should purchase or lease a new heavy-duty GMC truck. (The firm has already computed the net present value of this proposed asset acquisition and found the project to be acceptable.) The truck can be purchased for $50,000, including delivery. Alternatively, the truck can be leased from General Motors Acceptance Corporation (GMAC) for a six-year period at a beginning-of-the-year lease payment of $10,000. If purchased, Alcan could borrow the needed funds from the National Bank at an annual interest rate of 10 percent. If the truck is purchased, Alcan estimates that it will incur $750 per year of expenses to cover insurance and a maintenance contract. These expenses would not be incurred if the truck is leased. The truck is a class 10 asset with a CCA rate of 30 percent. Alcan expects the actual salvage value to be $2,000 at the end of six years. Alcan's marginal tax rate is 40 percent, and its weighted after-tax cost of capital is 15 percent. Which alternative—leasing or buying—should be chosen? In order to answer this question, we need to compute the NAL. This is shown in Table 19.1. The calculation in Table 19.1 indicates a net

---

[10] The CCA amounts are known with certainty, but the tax shield from CCA may not be certain because of potential future changes in the marginal corporate tax rate. Such changes may alter the present value of the tax shields. Also, there is always the chance that a firm will not have sufficient taxable income to take advantage of the CCA tax shields.

[11] If we had not previously simplified the analysis by using the after-tax cost of debt to discount the salvage value, then the appropriate treatment of this CCA tax shield is quite complex and, in our opinion, beyond the scope of an introductory course. The simplification introduces a relatively small bias against leasing as long as the salvage value is small relative to the installed cost.

Table 19.1 Calculation of the Net Advantage to Leasing for Alcan

End of Year [1]	Installed Asset Cost [2]	Lease Payment [3]	Lease Payment Tax Shields [4]	CCA [5]	[5]×.4 CCA Tax Shields [6]	Additional Operating Costs if Owned After-Tax [7]	Salvage Value [8]	CCA Tax Shields after Year 6 [9]	[2]−[3]+[4]−[6]+[7]−[8]−[9] NAL Cash Flows [10]	PVIF at 6% [11]	[10]×[11] NAL [12]
0	$50,000	$10,000	–	–	–	–	–	–	$40,000	1.000	$40,000
1	–	10,000	$4,000	$7,500	$3,000	$450	–	–	−8,550	0.943	−8,063
2	–	10,000	4,000	12,750	5,100	450	–	–	−10,650	0.890	−9,479
3	–	10,000	4,000	8,925	3,570	450	–	–	−9,120	0.840	−7,661
4	–	10,000	4,000	6,248	2,499	450	–	–	−8,049	0.792	−6,375
5	–	10,000	4,000	4,373	1,749	450	–	–	−7,299	0.747	−5,452
6	–		4,000	3,061	1,224	450	$2,000	1714*	−488	0.705	−344
				$42,857					Net Advantage to Leasing =		$2,626

* The present value at $t = 6$ of the CCA tax shields beyond the economic life of the asset is simply Equation 9.3 altered to reflect the usage of the after-tax cost of debt k_i. That is, $Td(\Delta UCC - \Delta S_n)/(k_i + d) = (.4)(.3)(\$7,143 - \$2,000)/(.06 + .30) = \$1,714$. ΔUCC_n = Installed cost − Accumulated capital cost allowance = $50,000 − $42,857, the total of column [5]

> The above NAL procedure can be used to evaluate any lease versus buy decision only after it has been determined by standard capital budgeting techniques that an asset should be acquired.

advantage to leasing of $2,626. Because the NAL is positive, the asset should be leased rather than bought.[12] It appears that GMAC, the captive finance company subsidiary of General Motors, is offering below-market leasing terms to attract customers.

Table 19.2 contains a lease-buy spreadsheet for Alcan. This spreadsheet is a modification of the capital budgeting spreadsheet in Appendix 10A. To calculate the NAL in this spreadsheet, the Excel NPV function discounts the yearly cash flows. This function calculates more accurately than the three-decimal-place factors in Table 19.1. Thus, it is not surprising that the spreadsheet NAL value of $2,624 differs somewhat from the NAL value of $2,626 in Table 19.1.

Note that the approximate IRR of 3.49 percent is in cell B35. This is the approximate after-tax cost of debt k_i^* where the NAL is zero. That is, the NPV of leasing is equivalent to the NPV of owning.

This rate k_i^* is approximate because the actual after-tax cost of debt k_i is used in cell H32 instead of k_i^* to calculate the PV of the tax shield beyond the economic life of the asset. Refer to Appendix 10A for a further discussion of this approximation in the context of capital budgeting.

Cell B36 contains the approximate before-tax "indifference" cost of debt of 5.81 percent, which is simply $k_i^*/(1 - T) = 3.49/(1 - .4)$. To find the actual before-tax "indifference" cost of debt, the result in cell B36 must be entered in the before-tax cost of debt

---

12 The lease-buy analysis procedure used here implicitly assumes that the leasing alternative and the borrowing-to-buy alternative have the same impact on the company's debt capacity. This is desirable because leasing and borrowing both represent fixed obligations that are treated by financial analysts as equivalent to debt. Note that a case can be made for moving the interest tax shields to the beginning of each year because a firm the size of Alcan must pay taxes in monthly instalments. However, one could also move the CCA tax shields forward by buying and placing the truck in service on the last day of the previous year. In our opinion, an analyst who moves forward the interest tax shields without moving forward the CCA tax shields creates a bias toward leasing. Furthermore, small businesses (which typically do not have access to capital markets) are more likely to lease. These businesses must make quarterly instalment tax payments. During the tax year 2002, these small businesses could defer their quarterly payments by six months without penalty. Thus, in our opinion, placing each interest tax shield at the end of the appropriate year is a realistic scenario for many lessees.

Table 19.2 Lease-Buy Analysis for Alcan

	A	B	C	D	E	F	G	H
1	Lease-Buy Analysis							
2								
3	**Single-Year Inputs**							
4	New asset price	$50,000						
5	Ship. & instal.	$0						
6	Life, n ≤ 20	6						
7	B−T cost of debt	10.00%						
8	Tax rate	40.00%						
9	CCA rate	30.00%						
10	Salvage	$2,000						
11								
12	**Multi-Year Inputs**							
13	Year	0	1	2	3	4	5	6
14	Lease payment	$10,000	$10,000	$10,000	$10,000	$10,000	$10,000	
15	ΔOperating costs		$750	$750	$750	$750	$750	$750
16								
17	**Intermediate Outputs**							
18	A−T cost of debt	6.00%						
19	Year	0	1	2	3	4	5	6
20	Starting UCC		$50,000	$42,500	$29,750	$20,825	$14,577	$10,204
21	CCA		$7,500	$12,750	$8,925	$6,248	$4,373	$3,061
22	Ending UCC		$42,500	$29,750	$20,825	$14,577	$10,204	$7,143
23								
24	**Cash-Flow Outputs**							
25	Year	0	1	2	3	4	5	6
26	Net installed cost	$50,000						
27	Lease payment	$10,000	$10,000	$10,000	$10,000	$10,000	$10,000	$0
28	Lease tax shield	$0	$4,000	$4,000	$4,000	$4,000	$4,000	$4,000
29	CCA tax shield t ≤ n	$0	$3,000	$5,100	$3,570	$2,499	$1,749	$1,224
30	A−T ΔOp. costs	$0	$450	$450	$450	$450	$450	$450
31	Salvage, t = n	$0	$0	$0	$0	$0	$0	$2,000
32	PV tax shield t > n	$0	$0	$0	$0	$0	$0	$1,714
33	Net cash flow	$40,000	−$8,550	−$10,650	−$9,120	−$8,049	−$7,299	−$488
34	NAL	$2,624						
35	Approximate IRR	3.49%						
36	Approximate B−T	5.81%						
37	"indifference"							
38	cost of debt							

cell B8. This process may have to be repeated a few times before cells B8 and B36 display the same value and the NAL cell B34 is close to zero. We did this twice to find the actual before-tax cost of debt of 5.96 percent with an NAL of −$2. *If Alcan could find a lender offering a rate lower than this, it would prefer buying to leasing.*

Recall that in Chapter 10 we presented in Equation 10.3a an alternative method for calculating the NPV of an investment. The NAL is, in essence, the NPV of leasing *minus* the NPV of owning. Thus, if Equation 10.3a is appropriately modified, it can be used as an alternative method of calculating NAL.

First, since the NPV of owning is subtracted in the NAL calculation, the signs of the terms in Equation 10.3a must be reversed. Furthermore, revenues and net working capital effects are assumed to be the same in leasing and buying. Hence, these terms net out and become irrelevant in calculating the NAL. Since the net investment NINV is the incremental installed cost or depreciable base ΔDB plus the initial increase in net working capital, only ΔDB will appear in the lease-buy formula. The incremental operating costs ΔO_t should be interpreted as only incremental operating costs from owning the asset instead of leasing it. Furthermore, the appropriate discount rate is the after-tax cost of debt $k_i = k_d(1 - T)$ in this analysis. This is a simplifying assumption with respect to the salvage value but is reasonable for the other cash flows. We also assumed that the lease payments L_t are made at the beginning of each year and the lease tax shields occur at the end of the year. Equation 19.1 gives the alternative method of calculating the NAL.

$$(19.1) \quad NAL = \Delta DB - \sum_{t=1}^{n} \frac{L_t}{(1 + k_i)^{t-1}} + \sum_{t=1}^{n} \frac{TL_t}{(1 + k_i)^t} + \sum_{t=1}^{n} \frac{\Delta O_t(1 - T)}{(1 + k_i)^t}$$

$$- \frac{[(1 + .5k_i)]}{[(1 + k_i)]}\left[\frac{Td\Delta DB}{(k_i + d)}\right] - \frac{\Delta S_n}{(1 + k_i)^n} + \left[\frac{1}{(1 + k_i)^n}\right]\left[\frac{Td\Delta S_n}{k_i + d}\right]$$

Note that the term multiplied by the half-year convention effect represents the tax shields from ΔDB during the asset's economic life and the tax shields from the undepreciated capital cost ΔUCC_n beyond the economic life. Now let's apply Equation 19.1 to Alcan's situation, noting that $(PVIFA_{6\%,6})(1.06)$ represents the present value of an annuity due.

$$NAL = \$50,000 - (\$10,000)(PVIFA_{6\%,6})(1.06) + (.4)(\$10,000)(PVIFA_{6\%,6})$$
$$+ (\$750)(1-.4)(PVIFA_{6\%,6}) - [1.03/1.06][(.4)(.3)(\$50,000)/(.06 +.30)]$$
$$- (\$2,000)(PVIF_{6\%,6}) + (PVIF_{6\%,6})[(.4)(.3)(\$2,000)/(.06 +.30)]$$

$$NAL = \$50,000 - (\$10,000)(4.917)(1.06) + (\$4,000)(4.917) + (\$450)(4.917)$$
$$- [1.03/1.06][(.12)(\$50,000)/(.36)] - (\$2,000)(0.705)$$
$$+ (0.705)[(.12)(\$2,000)/(.36)]$$

$$NAL = \$50,000 - \$52,120 + \$19,668 + \$2,213 - \$16,195 - \$1,410 + \$470$$
$$= \$2,626$$

This result agrees with the previous result for NAL in Table 19.1.

Again, we must emphasize that the NAL approach to lease-buy analysis assumes that the project is already acceptable to buy. The NAL analysis answers only the question of whether or not leasing is more attractive than buying.

Why did Air Canada sell some spare engines and lease them back? Air Canada was not profitable, so it could not take advantage of the CCA deductions for the engines. By selling them, it raised some much-needed cash to invest in its business. By leasing the spare engines, it assured itself that the engines would be available if they were needed at some time in the future. The lease payment is, therefore, a type of "insurance" for Air Canada.

Summary

- A *lease* is a written agreement that permits the *lessee* to use a piece of property owned by the *lessor* in exchange for a series of periodic lease or rental payments.

- An *operating lease* provides the lessee with the use of an asset on a period-by-period basis. An operating lease *may be cancelled* at the lessee's option. Most operating leases are written for a relatively short period of time, normally less than five years.

- A *financial lease* is a *noncancellable* agreement that obligates the lessee to make payments to the lessor for a predetermined period of time. There are two major types of financial leases: *sale and leaseback* agreements and *direct leases. Leveraged leases,* also called *tax leases,* have become increasingly common.

- Decisions by the Canadian Institute of Chartered Accountants (CICA) require that many financial leases be capitalized and shown on the lessee's balance sheet.

- Leasing offers a number of potential advantages, including tax benefits (in some cases), flexibility, and reducing the risks of obsolescence. It may also be the only source of financing available to many marginally profitable firms. It has a number of potential disadvantages, too. For example, leasing tends to be more costly than ownership for a firm with a good earnings record and good access to the capital markets.

- A model was presented to assist the lessee in determining which is the less expensive source of financing—leasing or borrowing to buy.

Questions and Topics for Discussion

1. What are the primary differences between operating leases and financial leases?
2. How does a leveraged lease differ from a nonleveraged financial lease? What type of firm or organization is most likely to take advantage of the leveraged lease financing option? What type of individual or organization is most likely to act as the lessor in a leveraged lease?
3. From a tax perspective, what primary requirements in a lease transaction must be met in order for the CCRA to consider the transaction a genuine lease? Why is a favourable CCRA ruling regarding the tax status of a lease important to both the lessor and the lessee?
4. One advantage that has often been claimed for lease financing is that it creates "off-balance sheet" financing. Evaluate this benefit in light of CICA reporting requirements for financial leases.
5. What effect does leasing have on the stability of a firm's reported earnings?

6. It has been argued that leasing is almost always more expensive than borrowing and owning. Do you think this is true? Why or why not? Under what circumstances is leasing likely to be more desirable than direct ownership?

7. Why do you think it is easier for firms with weak credit positions to obtain lease financing than bank loan financing?

Self-Test Problem

ST1. Medical Associates can lease a new server and four workstations for an annual payment of $6,000 at the *beginning* of each year for the next five years. Alternatively, the firm can purchase the computer system for $25,000. The system would be placed in class 10 with a CCA rate of 30%. Maintenance expenses will be the same under leasing or buying. The salvage value of the system at the end of five years is expected to be negligible. The firm can borrow from its bank at a cost of 12%, and its marginal tax rate is 25%. Assume that the firm feels that the computer system is a strategic asset that it needs to stay in business.

   a. Should the firm lease or buy?

   b. What is the approximate before-tax cost of debt that will make the firm indifferent between leasing and buying?

   c. What is the actual before-tax cost of debt that will make the firm indifferent between leasing and buying?

Problems*

BASIC

1. MacKenzie Corporation is considering leasing a new asset. The lease would run for eight years and require eight *beginning-of-year* payments of $100,000 each. If MacKenzie capitalizes this lease for financial reporting purposes at a 10% rate, what asset amount will be reported initially on its balance sheet? What liability amount will be reported on its balance sheet? (Remember, lease payments are made at the beginning of each year, making them an annuity due.)

INTERMEDIATE

 Excel

2. A local firm has approached Springer Leasing to arrange lease financing for $10 million in new machinery. The economic life of the machinery is estimated to be 20 years. The estimated salvage value at the end of the 20-year period is $0. The local firm has indicated a willingness to pay the leasing company $1 million per year at the *beginning* of each year for 20 years under the terms of a financial lease. If the firm bought the asset, it would place the asset in class 8 with a CCA rate of 20%. The estimated salvage value of the asset is $50,000. The firm's marginal tax rate is 40%. The firm can borrow at a rate of 15%. Assume that the asset satisfies normal capital budgeting criteria.

   a. Should the firm lease or buy the machinery?

   b. What is the approximate before-tax cost of debt that will make the firm indifferent between leasing and buying?

   c. What is the actual before-tax cost of debt that will make the firm indifferent between leasing and buying?

*Coloured numbers and letters denote problems that have "check" answers provided at the back of the book.

3. Jenkins Corporation wants to acquire a $200,000 computer. Jenkins has a 40% marginal tax rate. If owned, the computer would be placed in class 10 with a CCA rate of 30%. The actual cash salvage value is expected to be $20,000 at the end of 10 years. If the computer is purchased, Jenkins could borrow the needed funds at an annual pretax interest rate of 10%. If purchased, Jenkins will incur annual maintenance expenses of $1,000. These expenses will not be incurred if the computer is leased. The lease rate would be $28,000 per year, payable at the *beginning* of each year. Jenkins' weighted after-tax cost of capital is 12%.

   a. Compute the *net advantage* to leasing.

   b. What alternative, leasing or owning, should be chosen? Why?

   c. What is the approximate before-tax cost of debt that will make the firm indifferent between leasing and buying?

   d. What is the actual before-tax cost of debt that will make the firm indifferent between leasing and buying?

4. As a financial analyst for Muffin Construction, you have been asked to recommend the method of financing the acquisition of new equipment needed by the firm. The equipment has a useful life of eight years. If purchased, the equipment, which costs $700,000, will be placed in class 8 with a CCA rate of 20%. If purchased, the needed funds can be borrowed at a 10% pretax annual rate. Muffin's weighted cost of capital after-tax rate is 12%. The *actual* salvage value at the end of eight years is expected to be $50,000. Muffin's marginal ordinary tax rate is 40%. Annual, *beginning-of-year* lease payments would be $160,000.

   a. Compute the net advantage to leasing.

   b. Should Muffin lease or own the equipment? Why?

   c. What is the approximate before-tax cost of debt that will make the firm indifferent between leasing and buying?

   d. What is the actual before-tax cost of debt that will make the firm indifferent between leasing and buying?

CHALLENGE

5. Ajax Leasing Services has been approached by Gamma Tools to provide lease financing for a new automated screw machine. The machine will cost $220,000 and will be leased by Gamma for five years. Lease payments will be made at the *beginning* of each year. If Gamma were to buy the asset, it would place the machine in class 8 with a CCA rate of 20%. Gamma estimates that the salvage value of the machine will be $0 after five years. Gamma's marginal tax rate is 40% and its before-tax cost of borrowing is 10%. What are the annual *beginning-of-year* lease payments that would make Gamma indifferent between leasing and buying?

6. Suppose you are considering leasing or buying the vehicle of your dreams, the Amphibus Z-200. This vehicle is equally at home on the highway, on rugged terrain, or on the water. Since this vehicle is for personal use, there will be no tax shields if purchased or leased.

   The Z-200 sells for $200,000 and can be leased for $4,500 per month for 48 months. The lease payments will be at the *beginning* of each month, except that both the payment for the last month and the payment for the first month are due on signing of the lease.

   In addition, there is a security deposit of $2,000 due on signing. In talking to friends who have leased the vehicle, the dealer always finds a way to claim damage and keep the security deposit if you do not purchase the vehicle at the end of the lease for the specified residual value. According to your friends, the residual value has typically been a fair estimate of the selling price of a five-year old Z-200 and is $40,000 in your lease.

There is also a charge of $0.40/km for every kilometre over 24,000 km/year. You expect to drive the vehicle somewhat less than 24,000 km/year. This charge, if any, is waived if you purchase the vehicle for its residual value.

You can borrow at a 12% APR (annual percentage rate), compounded monthly. Pre-delivery charges, taxes, registration or filing fees, licence fees, and maintenance expenses are extra, but you may assume that they will be the same on a PV basis for leasing or buying.

   a. Calculate the NAL of leasing, assuming that you would buy the Z-200 for its residual value at the end of the lease.
   b. Should you lease or buy the Z-200 today?
   c. What is the approximate before-tax cost of debt that will make you indifferent between leasing and buying?
   d. What is the actual before-tax cost of debt that will make you indifferent between leasing and buying?

7. Visit **www.mercedes.ca** to compare leasing versus buying the C230 Kompressor Sport Coupe.

   a. Calculate the NAL of leasing, assuming that you would buy the car for its residual value at the end of the lease.
   b. Should you lease or buy the car today?
   c. What is the approximate before-tax cost of debt that will make you indifferent between leasing and buying?
   d. What is the actual before-tax cost of debt that will make you indifferent between leasing and buying?

Other Practice Materials and Resources

For interactive quizzes, Internet exercises, crossword puzzles, CTV videos, and more, go to the *Contemporary Financial Management* Web site at **http://cyr.nelson.com**

Corporate Restructuring

Learning Objectives

After studying this chapter you should be able to

1. Recognize that a firm may choose external growth by merger over internal growth for the following reasons:

   a. The availability of lower-cost assets

   b. Greater economies of scale

   c. The availability of more secure raw material supplies and/or additional end-product markets

   d. The possibility of more rapid growth

   e. Greater diversification

   f. Tax considerations

2. Understand that the valuation of merger candidates involves application of capital budgeting principles. A merger is an acceptable project if the present value of its expected free cash inflows exceeds the acquisition cost

3. Understand that the acquisition of a firm with a higher P/E ratio causes the earnings per share figure of the acquiring company to decrease if the exchange ratio is based on current share prices and no synergy exists. Similarly, the acquisition of a firm with a lower P/E ratio causes the earnings per share figure of the acquiring company to increase

4. Understand that in the *purchase method*, acquired assets are recorded at their fair market values, and any additional amount paid is listed as goodwill, which must then be amortized

5. Understand that in a financial context, a firm is

   a. *Technically insolvent* when it is unable to meet its current obligations as they come due, even though the value of the assets exceeds its liabilities

   b. *Legally insolvent* if the recorded value of its assets is less than the recorded value of its liabilities

   c. *Bankrupt* if it is unable to pay its debts

6. Understand that a failing company can either

   a. Attempt to resolve its difficulties with its creditors on a voluntary, or informal, basis or

   b. Petition the courts for assistance and formally declare bankruptcy

7. Understand that in a bankruptcy proceeding, if the going-concern value of the firm is greater than its liquidation value, it is reorganized. Otherwise, it is liquidated

8. Recognize other important topics including

   a. Leveraged buyouts

   b. Divestitures and restructuring

   c. Anti-takeover measures

The Swift Collapse of Canada 3000 Airlines

State-of-the-Art Airbus A320 (174-seat) Aircraft

CANADA NEWSWIRE/CANADA 3000 AIRLINES-110

Canada 3000 started in Toronto as a charter airline in 1988. It soon became Canada's largest charter airline by buying its rivals, Royal Aviation and CanJet. Unfortunately, it was difficult to combine the diverse operations and fleets of the three component airlines, so efficiency suffered for a time. Although Canada 3000 was successful in the charter business, the takeover of Canadian Airlines by Air Canada in 1999 provided an opportunity for Canada 3000 to become a scheduled airline. This change in strategy proved to be an error because scheduled flights can be cancelled only for safety reasons. Recreational travel, on which Canada 3000 relied, is discretionary. After the terrorist attacks of September 11, 2001, travellers no longer wanted to fly and North American airlines reduced their flights drastically. During its last weeks of operation, Canada 3000 lost $700,000 per day. On November 9, 2001, Canada 3000 suddenly ceased all operations and grounded its entire fleet, stranding thousands of travellers around the world. On November 10, Canada 3000 filed for bankruptcy protection. All of its 4,800 employees lost their jobs. Other airlines scrambled to add capacity to rescue the Canada 3000 customers, but many of them lost money. Some students from eastern Canada studying in universities in British Columbia were not able to fly home for Christmas for the cheap fares they had expected to pay on Canada 3000 but had to find alternative ways and means to get home. The bankruptcy of Canada 3000 was a catastrophe for the Cook Islands, one of the destinations that the airline served, as their tourism industry depended on the spending of many Canadian tourists.

What went wrong?

- When the number of vacation travellers declined, Canada 3000 could not cover its costs of operating nearly empty planes.

- Canada 3000 did not have a sufficient number of smaller aircraft that could be put on the routes that now had fewer passengers.

- The terrorist attacks of September 11, 2001, were an unforeseen event that the management of Canada 3000 had not considered when they changed their strategy to become a scheduled airline.

- Charter flights are obviously much easier to cancel if there are no passengers.

- Although managers of Canada 3000 had little experience with scheduled airline operations, they believed that they could handle the more complex tasks involved in implementing their new strategy.

The first part of this chapter discusses the external growth of firms by merger and acquisition. This was the way Canada 3000 grew. The second part of this chapter examines some of the causes of business failure (i.e., bankruptcy) and alternatives available to failing firms in resolving their problems. The rapid growth of Canada 3000 led it to "crash" into bankruptcy.

Introduction

Corporate restructuring encompasses a broad array of activities that include changes in the ownership, asset structure, and/or capital structure of a company. The goal of any corporate restructuring should be to maximize shareholder wealth. Some aspects of corporate restructuring have already been examined, such as share repurchases discussed in Chapters 6 and 14. This chapter focuses on a number of other forms of corporate restructuring, including external expansion (mergers) and business failure (bankruptcy). The next three sections examine mergers, and the final two sections discuss bankruptcy.

See **http://finance. swcollege.com** and select Mergers and Acquisitions for articles on this topic.

Mergers

Businesses grow *externally* by acquiring or combining with other ongoing businesses. This is in contrast to *internal* growth, which is achieved by purchasing individual assets, such as those evaluated in the discussion of capital expenditures in Chapters 9 through 11. When two companies combine, the acquiring company generally pays for the acquired business either with cash or with its own securities, and the acquired firm's liabilities and assets are transferred to the acquiring company.

Mergers Defined

Merger
The fusion of two or more firms into one of the constituent firms that becomes the surviving company.

Amalgamation
The fusion of two or more firms by transfer of their assets and liabilities to a new firm.

Acquisition
Any transaction whereby one firm obtains control of another.

Takeover
The purchase by one firm of the majority of another firm's shares.

A **merger** is technically a combination of two or more firms in which all but one of the combining firms legally cease to exist and the surviving firm continues in operation under its original name. An **amalgamation** (consolidation) is the fusion of two or more firms by transfer of their assets and liabilities to a new firm. An **acquisition** is any transaction wherein one firm obtains control of another. Such an acquisition is called a **takeover** when the acquiring firm purchases a majority of the other firm's shares. The term *merger* is generally used generically to describe all of these types of business combinations. In the following discussion, the term *merger* is used, and it is assumed that only two firms are involved—the acquiring company and the target merger candidate.[1]

Merger Activity

Merger activity expanded greatly during the late 1980s. Then, during the recession of the early 1990s, mergers declined. In the late 1990s, merger activity boomed again; however, in the early 2000s, merger activity hit new lows. During the first quarter of 2002, Canadian mergers and acquisitions activity was the lowest since 1993. Not all mergers that are announced end up being completed. The major transactions of 2002 were

- The creation of EnCana by combining Alberta Energy Company with Pan Canadian Energy

- The Petro-Canada acquisition of oil and gas properties from British Petroleum and Veba

See **www.crosbieco.com** for the latest information about Canadian mergers and acquisitions.

Horizontal Merger
A combination of two or more firms that compete directly with each other.

Types of Mergers

Mergers are generally classified according to whether they are *horizontal, vertical,* or *conglomerate.* A **horizontal merger** is a combination of two or more companies that compete directly with one another. For example, the 1999 acquisition of Alusuisse by Alcan—both large aluminum companies—was a horizontal merger. Some governments have enforced anticombines legislation in an attempt to stop large horizontal combinations. However, horizontal combinations in which one of the firms is failing are often

---

[1] In some instances, merger candidates may be referred to as takeover candidates, to-be-acquired companies, acquired companies, or target companies.

viewed more favourably. Also, mergers that allow the firms to compete effectively in world markets are viewed more favourably. For example, in 1999 the Canadian telecommunications equipment manufacturer JDS Fitel acquired the US firm Uniphase and is now called JDS Uniphase. Then, in the same industry, the French company Alcatel acquired the Canadian company Newbridge Networks in 2000.

A **vertical merger** is a combination of companies that may have a buyer-seller relationship with one another. For example, the Canadian telecommunications equipment manufacturer Nortel acquired its US suppliers Qtera and Alteon Websystems in 1999 and 2000, respectively.

A **conglomerate merger** is a combination of two or more companies in which neither competes directly with the other and no buyer-seller relationship exists. For example, in 1988 the Canadian real estate firm Campeau acquired Federated Department Stores, one of the largest US retailers. This was a conglomerate merger.

Form of Merger Transactions

A merger transaction may be a share purchase or an asset purchase. In a *share purchase,* the acquiring firm buys the shares of the to-be-acquired firm and assumes its liabilities. In an *asset purchase,* the acquiring firm buys only the assets (some or all) of the to-be-acquired firm and does not assume any of its liabilities.

Normally, the buyer of a business prefers an asset purchase rather than a share purchase, because unknown liabilities, such as any future lawsuits against the firm, are not incurred. In addition, an asset purchase frequently allows the acquiring firm to depreciate its new assets from a higher base than is possible in a share purchase. As a result of the unknown liability question, many large firms that acquire small firms refuse to negotiate on any terms other than an asset purchase.

Holding Companies

One form of business combination is the **holding company** in which the acquiring firm simply purchases all or a controlling block of another firm's common shares. The two companies then become *affiliated,* and the acquiring firm becomes the holding company in this *parent-subsidiary* relationship. BCE is one of Canada's best-known holding companies. It owns Bell Canada, Bell Globemedia, Bell Emergis, and BCE Ventures.

Joint Ventures

Another form of business combination is a **joint venture**, in which two (unaffiliated) companies contribute financial and/or physical assets, as well as personnel, to a new company formed to engage in some economic activity, such as the production or marketing of a product. Joint ventures are often international in scope, such as the agreement among IBM (United States), Toshiba (Japan), and Siemens (Germany) to form a company to develop and produce computer memory chips. This was necessary to reduce risk as well as to obtain enough capital to engage in this highly capital-intensive activity. The Canadian firm Nortel has joint ventures in the United States and China. Its partner in the United States provides marketing expertise. Its partner in China provides local manufacturing and marketing expertise.

Leveraged Buyouts

One frequently used method to buy a company or a division of a large company is a **leveraged buyout**, or LBO. In a typical LBO, the buyer borrows a large amount of the purchase price, using the purchased assets as collateral for a large portion of the borrowings. The buyers are frequently the managers of the division or firm being sold. It is anticipated that the earnings (and cash flows) of the new firm will be sufficient to service the debt and permit the new owners to earn a reasonable return on their investment. In some

---

Vertical Merger
A combination of two or more firms that have a buyer-seller relationship with one another.

Conglomerate Merger
A combination of two or more firms in which neither competes directly with the other and no buyer-seller relationship exists.

Holding Company
A corporation that controls the voting power of one or more other firms.

Joint Venture
A business combination in which two unaffiliated firms contribute financial, physical, and/or personnel assets to a new firm formed to engage in a specific economic activity.

Leveraged Buyout (LBO)
A transaction in which the buyer of a firm borrows a large portion of the purchase price, using the purchased assets as partial collateral for the loans.

cases, sales of assets are used to help pay off the debt. The LBO of a publicly held company is sometimes referred to as *going private* because the entire equity in the firm is purchased by a small group of investors and is no longer publicly traded.

The majority of LBOs involve relatively small companies. However, a number of LBOs involving large companies have occurred. By the early 1990s, the number of LBO transactions had declined sharply, partly because many existing LBOs were experiencing difficulties servicing their large debt loads.

In addition to LBOs undertaken by investment bankers and managers, workers sometimes take over their division or company through an employee stock ownership plan (ESOP). In the past, ESOPs were used to buy either larger companies faced with financial difficulties or smaller companies.

Divestitures and Restructurings

Divestitures and *restructurings* can be an important part of a company's merger and acquisition strategy. After an acquiring company completes an acquisition, it frequently examines the various assets and divisions of the recently acquired firm to determine whether all of the acquired firm's pieces "fit" into the acquiring company's future plans. If not, the acquiring company may sell off, or *divest*, a portion of the acquired firm. In so doing, the acquiring company is said to be **restructuring** itself.

Divestitures and restructurings, however, are frequently not associated directly with a firm's acquisitions. A company may divest itself of certain assets because of a change in overall corporate strategy. A firm may change, or restructure, the asset side of its balance sheet. This is called an **operational restructuring**. In addition, a firm may change its capital structure. This is called a **financial restructuring**.

Instead of selling a part of the firm for cash, divestitures can be accomplished through either a *spinoff* or an *equity carve-out*. In a **spinoff**, common shares in a division or subsidiary are distributed to shareholders of the parent company on a pro rata basis. The subsidiary or division becomes a separate company. Owners of the parent firm who receive common shares in the new company can keep the shares or sell them to other investors. An example was the 2001 spinoff of Canadian Pacific subsidiaries whereby each CP shareholder received shares in five companies: CP Railway, CP Ships, PanCanadian Energy, Fairmont Hotels, and Fording Coal. The aggregate value of the shareholders' investment increased almost immediately and the CP shareholders are still winners at the time this chapter was written. An earlier example was the 2000 spinoff of Nortel by Bell Canada.

In an *equity carve-out*, also called a *partial public offering* or *spin out*, common shares in the subsidiary or division are sold directly to the public, with the parent company usually retaining a controlling interest in the shares outstanding.

Spinoffs and equity carve-outs can be used by large, diversified companies to remove either an underperforming unit that is hurting the overall firm or a healthy subsidiary that is buried among underperforming units. In the 1990s and later, spinoffs may achieve the same results that leveraged buyouts did in the 1980s, namely, more focused and efficient companies.

Sometimes, though, it appears that the market has trouble with arithmetic. The US network systems company 3COM decided in 2000 to have a 5 percent spinout of the shares of its subsidiary Palm and a 95 percent spinoff. (Palm is a manufacturer of personal digital assistants or PDAs and is a major competitor of the Canadian firm Research in Motion (RIM) that makes the BlackBerry PDA.) 3COM arranged an initial public offering (IPO) for 5 percent of the shares of Palm and committed itself to distribute the remaining 95 percent of the Palm shares to 3COM shareholders on the basis of 1.5 Palm shares for each 3COM share.

On the day before the Palm IPO, the 3COM stock closed at US$104.13 per share. On the next day, the Palm stock closed at US$95.06 per share. This implied that the shares

See the ESOP Association Canada Web site for more information at **www. esop-canada.com**

Restructuring
A firm may reorganize itself and/or divest some of its assets.

Divestiture
A firm may divest, or sell off, a division that no longer fits its strategy.

Operational Restructuring
A change in the asset side of a firm's balance sheet

Financial Restructuring
A change in the capital structure of a firm.

Spinoff
A spinoff is effected by distributing shares in a subsidiary to shareholders of the parent firm.

of 3COM should have been worth at least US$142.59 (1.5 Palm shares/3COM share × US$95.06/Palm share). Amazingly, the shares of 3COM closed at only US$81.81! This mispricing was noted the next day in both *The Wall Street Journal* and *The New York Times*. In spite of this, the mispricing persisted for months.[2]

An alternative to either selling or spinning off a division is to issue a *tracking stock*. A tracking stock is a special type of stock issued by a publicly held company to track the value of one segment of the firm. The company keeps control over the subsidiary. The buyers of the stock have no voting rights. A tracking stock enables a large company that has a subsidiary in a high-growth business, which is buried within the organization, to capture the value of this business. The theory is that the sum of the values of the tracking stock of the high-growth business and the parent company's shares, which are traded separately, will be worth more than the single share of the parent company.

Tracking stocks were first issued in the mid-1980s when General Motors created separate stocks for two of its higher-growth subsidiaries—Electronic Data Services and Hughes Electronics. These were later spun off to become separate firms. During the boom for Internet stocks in the late 1990s, a number of firms with online subsidiaries issued tracking stocks.[3] However, the popularity of tracking stocks has declined drastically. In early 2003, only 10 tracking stocks of the 39 that had once existed were being traded.

Tender Offers

Although many mergers are the result of a friendly agreement between the two companies, a firm may wish to acquire another firm even when the combination is opposed by the management or board of directors of the merger candidate company. In such a case, the acquiring company makes a **tender offer** for common shares of the merger candidate. In a tender offer, the acquiring company effectively announces that it will pay a certain price above the then-existing market price for any of the merger candidate's shares that are "tendered" (that is, offered to it) before a particular date.

Rationale for Restructuring

A number of reasons have been suggested for the increased corporate restructuring activity during the 1980s and 1990s. According to Jensen, the most important reason was the failure of internal control mechanisms to prevent unproductive capital investment (that is, overinvestment) and organizational inefficiencies (overstaffing) by many large U.S. firms.[4] He claims that this control system—the internal management supervised by a board of directors—breaks down in mature companies with large cash flows and few good investment opportunities. These inefficiencies allow acquirers to pay a large premium over the pre-takeover market value of the firm and earn high returns on their investment by using the acquired firm's resources more efficiently.

A second reason cited is the emergence of active investors, such as the Canadian firm Onex, which holds large equity (and/or debt) positions in several companies. Unlike more passive institutional investors, such as pension funds, these investors take an active role in setting the strategic direction and monitoring the performance of their portfolio companies. Often these investors give managers significant equity positions in the companies as incentives to operate efficiently and increase shareholder value.

Tender Offer
A public announcement by a firm (or individual) indicating that it will pay a price above the current market price for the shares "tendered" of a firm it wishes to acquire.

---

[2] Owen A. Lamont and Richard H. Thaler, "Can the Market Add and Subtract?: Mispriced Stocks Break the Rules of Efficient Markets" *Capital Ideas*, vol. 3, no. 3 (Winter 2002): 1–5. Downloaded December 31, 2002, from http:gsbwww.uchicago.edu/news/capideas/win02/market.html The authors also give five more technology stock examples.

[3] "Are Two Stocks Better Than One?" *Business Week* (June 28, 1999): 98–99.

[4] Michael C. Jensen, "Corporate Control and the Politics of Finance," *Journal of Applied Corporate Finance* (Summer 1991): 13–33.

A third reason for the corporate restructuring boom of the 1980s was the ready availability of credit to finance these transactions. Junk bond financing, as well as financing provided by banks, insurance companies, and pension fund management firms, provided debt capital that permitted acquirers to leverage their purchases.

Finally, the inflationary environment and long economic expansion of the 1980s increased the revenues and asset values of the acquired companies. This allowed acquirers to sell off unwanted corporate assets and to meet their debt obligations.

Anti-Takeover Measures

In response to the merger and acquisitions boom of the late 1980s, many companies adopted various measures designed to discourage unfriendly takeover attempts. These *anti-takeover measures*, sometimes referred to as **shark repellents**, include

Shark Repellents
Anti-takeover measures to deter hostile takeovers.

1. **Staggered Board** Stagger the terms of the board of directors over several years instead of having the entire board come up for election at one time. Thus, the acquiring firm will have difficulty electing its own board of directors to gain control. Staggering the terms of the members of the board of directors also reduces the benefit of cumulative voting for the minority shareholders, thus making it more likely that management will remain in control.

2. **Golden Parachute Contracts** Give key executives employment contracts under which the executives will receive large benefits if they are terminated without sufficient cause after a merger. Corporate takeovers often raise serious agency problems between shareholders and managers. A takeover at a large premium over the firm's current market share price is beneficial to shareholders. At the same time, the offer may be detrimental to managers because they may lose their jobs if the takeover is successful and the new owners replace them. Golden parachute contracts are a type of shark repellent. However, if used appropriately, they can be used to encourage management to act in the interests of shareholders in any takeover attempt.

3. **Supermajority Voting Rules** Insert in the corporate charter voting rules that require a supermajority of shares (e.g., 80 percent) to approve any takeover proposals.

4. **Poison Pills** Issue securities that become valuable only when an unfriendly bidder obtains control of a certain percentage of a firm's shares. One example is a bond that contains a put option (called a "poison put") that can be exercised only if an unfriendly takeover occurs. The issuing firm hopes that the cashing in by bondholders of a portion of its debt will make the takeover unattractive.

Once an unfriendly takeover attempt has been initiated, the target company's management has various other anti-takeover measures that it can employ to deter a takeover, including

1. **White Knight** The target firm's management can try to find another, more friendly acquiring firm that is willing to enter into a bidding war with the company making the first offer.

2. **Standstill Agreement** The target firm's management can attempt to negotiate an agreement with the bidder whereby the bidder agrees to limit its holdings in the target firm.

3. **Pacman Defence** Named after the video game, the target firm can make a takeover bid for the shares of the bidder.

4. **Litigation** Legal action can be used to delay a takeover attempt.

5. **Asset and/or Liability Restructuring** A target firm can sell assets that the bidder wants to another firm, or it can issue larger amounts of debt and use the proceeds to repurchase its common shares. These actions make the target company less desirable to the bidder.

6. **Greenmail** The takeover candidate can attempt to buy back its shares, at a premium over the shares' market price, from the company or investor who initiated the unfriendly takeover attempt. The amount of the premium is referred to as "greenmail."

More recently, institutional investors, who often control a significant block of a firm's shares, have become increasingly active participants in battles for control in many firms. Some institutional investors have used what is called *boardmail* to fight anti-takeover devices, such as poison pills and staggered elections of board members. Boardmail consists of requiring the board of directors to adopt weaker anti-takeover measures in exchange for voting support from the institutional owners. In some cases, institutions have been successful in placing sympathetic members on boards of companies in which the institution has a significant ownership interest.

Reasons for Mergers

The following are some of the reasons why a firm might consider acquiring another firm, rather than choosing to grow internally:

- A firm may be able to acquire certain desirable assets at a lower cost by combining with another firm than it could if it purchased the assets directly. In this context, when the *market* value of a company's common shares are below *book* value (or, more importantly, below the replacement value of the firm's net assets), this firm is frequently considered a possible "takeover candidate."

- A firm may be able to achieve greater economies of scale by merging with another firm. This is particularly true in the case of a horizontal merger.

- A firm may be able to achieve greater economies of scope by merging with another firm. This is particularly true in the case of a vertical merger.

- A firm that is concerned about its sources of raw materials or end-product markets might acquire other firms at different stages of its production or distribution processes. These are vertical mergers.

- A firm may wish to grow more rapidly than is possible through internal expansion. Acquiring another firm may allow a growing firm to move more rapidly into a geographic or product area in which the acquired firm already has established markets, sales personnel, management capability, warehouse facilities, and so on, than would be possible by starting from scratch.

- A firm may desire to diversify its product lines and businesses in an attempt to reduce its business risk by smoothing out cyclical movements in its earnings. For example, a capital equipment manufacturer might achieve steadier earnings by expanding into the replacement parts business. During a recession, expenditures for capital equipment may slow down, but expenditures on maintenance and replacement parts may increase. This reason is of questionable benefit to the company's shareholders because most investors can diversify their holdings (through the securities markets) more easily and at a lower cost than the company can.

- A firm that has suffered losses and has a tax-loss carryforward may be a valuable merger candidate to a firm that is generating taxable income. If the two companies merge, the losses may be deductible from the profitable firm's taxable income and hence lower the combined company's income tax payments.

Synergy
A situation in which the whole is greater than the sum of its parts. In a synergistic merger, the post-merger earnings exceed the sum of the separate firms' pre-merger earnings.

- Whenever the net income for the combined firms after merger exceeds the sum of the net incomes prior to the merger, *synergy* is said to exist. This is frequently given by managers as the main reason for mergers. It is often said that in the case of a synergistic merger, 2 + 2 = 5. Sources of **synergy** can include strategic benefits in the form of competitive advantages, marketing advantages, lowered costs, and elimination of inefficient managers.

This list, although not exhaustive, does indicate the principal reasons why a firm may choose external expansion over internal growth.

If one firm wishes to acquire all or a portion of another firm, it is important to question whether the acquisition will be anything more than a zero net present value project in an efficient capital market. If it is, this excess value must result from the acquiring firm's access to superior managerial and labour talents at costs not fully reflective of their marginal value, access to raw material and other necessary inputs at lower costs, an ability to price the product in a more profitable way (perhaps because of an established brand name), operating synergies in the production and/or distribution areas, access to capital at a lower cost, generally more efficient operations due to lower agency costs in the acquiring firm compared to those in the acquired firm, or some other reason. Each of these possible reasons is suggestive of an inefficiency in a factor, product, or portion of the capital markets.

A number of empirical studies have examined the returns to the shareholders of the merger candidate and the acquiring firm in a takeover.[5] Because the acquiring company must pay a premium over the current market price to obtain the merger candidate, one would expect to see positive returns to the acquired firm's shareholders. This is the case, with average returns of 20 percent or more in successful mergers. For the acquiring company's shareholders, the returns are not as good—averaging 5 percent or less in successful mergers.

Accounting Aspects of Mergers

In Canada, Section 1581 of the CICA *Handbook* requires that all business combinations occurring after 2001 be accounted for under the **purchase method**. In the purchase method, the total value paid or exchanged for the acquired firm's assets is recorded on the acquiring company's books. The tangible assets acquired are recorded at their fair market values, which may or may not be more than the amount at which they were carried on the acquired firm's balance sheet prior to the merger. The excess of the total value paid over the fair market value of the acquired assets is an intangible asset termed **goodwill**.[6] The intangible asset of goodwill can be quite significant for many companies.

Suppose, for example, that the book value of Company T's *assets* is $10 million. Suppose that the market value of Company T's assets at the date of acquisition is $11 million. Company B paid $3 million above the book value of *shareholders' equity*. Of this $3 million, the $1 million difference between the assets' market value and book value is recorded on the balance sheet in the appropriate tangible assets accounts. The other $2 million is recorded as goodwill.

Before 2002, an alternative method, the *pooling of interests method* was available. In the pooling of interests method, the acquired firm's assets are recorded on the acquiring firm's books at their cost (net of depreciation) when originally acquired. Thus, any difference between the purchase price and the book value is not recorded on the acquiring firm's books, and no goodwill account is created. The pooling of interests method has certain advantages over the purchase method. All other things being equal, reported earnings will be higher under the pooling method, primarily because depreciation will not be more than the sum of the depreciation charges prior to the merger. In addition,

Purchase Method
A method of accounting for mergers in which the total value paid or exchanged for the acquired firm's assets is recorded on the acquiring firm's books. Any difference between the acquired assets' fair market value and their purchase price is recorded as goodwill.

Goodwill
An intangible asset equal to the premium over fair market value of the acquired assets that is paid for a target company in a merger.

---

[5] See J. Fred Weston, Juan A. Siu, and Brian A. Johnson, *Mergers, Restructuring, and Corporate Control*, 3rd ed. (Upper Saddle River, NJ: Prentice-Hall, 2001), Chapters 11–13, for a summary of the empirical studies relating to the returns associated with corporate restructuring. See also Steven Kaplan, "The Effects of Management Buyouts on Operating Performance and Value," *Journal of Financial Economics* (October 1989): 217–254, and C. Robinson versus W. Block (live debate), "Are Corporate Takeovers Good or Bad? A Debate," *Canadian Investment Review* (Spring 1990), 71–76.

[6] The expression *goodwill* is not always found on the balance sheet. Instead, there may be other terminology, such as "investment in consolidated subsidiaries in excess of net assets at date of acquisition, less amortization."

because goodwill is not created on the balance sheet in a pooling, it cannot appear as an amortization charge on the acquiring firm's income statement. The pooling of interests method is no longer allowed in Canada or in the United States, nor is it consistent with international accounting standards, which generally do not allow the pooling of interests method.

Tax Aspects of Mergers

Taxes can play an important role in determining how an acquired firm's shareholders receive compensation for their shares. Merger transactions that are effected through the use of equity securities (either common or preferred shares) are *generally* tax-free. For example, suppose an acquired firm's shareholders have a gain on the value of their shares at the time of the merger. The gain is not recognized for tax purposes if these shareholders receive equity securities of the acquiring firm. Any gains are not recognized until the newly acquired shares are sold.

In contrast, if the acquired company's shareholders receive cash or debt securities in exchange for their shares, any gains are *usually* taxable at the time of the merger. When a partial cash down payment is made, however, the exchange may be treated as an instalment purchase. In this case, the tax liability can be spread over the payment period. For the most up-to-date tax information, it is always a good idea to consult the Canada Customs and Revenue Agency.

Financial Aspects of Mergers: Valuation of Candidates

In principle, the valuation of merger candidates (targets) is an application of the capital budgeting techniques described in Chapters 9 through 11. The purchase price of a proposed acquisition is compared to the present value of the expected future cash inflows from the merger candidate. If the present value of the cash inflows exceeds the purchase price, the merger project has a positive net present value and is acceptable.

In the case of an acquisition candidate whose common shares are actively traded, the market price of the share is a key factor in the valuation process. To induce the shareholders of the acquisition candidate to give up their shares for the cash and/or securities of the acquiring firm, they have to be offered a premium over the market share prior to the merger announcement. Generally, a 10 to 20 percent premium is considered a minimum offer. Even then, in many situations, shareholders may hold out for much better offers—either from the firm making the initial offer or from other interested companies.

Valuation Techniques

Three major methods are typically used to value merger candidates: the comparative price-earnings ratio method, the adjusted book value method, and the discounted cash flow method.

The *comparative price-earnings ratio method* examines the recent prices and price-earnings (P/E) ratios paid for other merger candidates that are comparable to the firm being valued. For example, if two firms in a specific industry were recently acquired at P/E ratios of 10, the comparative P/E ratio method suggests that a P/E ratio of 10 may be reasonable for other, similar firms. Financial analysts who use this method should exercise caution and determine whether the companies being compared really are similar. This method, which focuses on the current income statement, may not be useful if the P/E ratios of recent, similar mergers vary widely.

The *adjusted book value method* involves determining the market value of the company's underlying assets. For example, suppose a company has equipment fully depreciated on its books but still in use. The market value of this equipment is determined, and the shareholders' equity (book value) of the firm is adjusted by the difference between the book value and market value of assets. Financial analysts who use this method should exercise caution because the determination of the market value of the merger candidate's assets may be difficult.

The *discounted cash flow method* for valuing merger candidates calculates the present value of the firm's expected future *free cash flows* and compares this figure to the proposed purchase price to determine the proposed acquisition's net present value. The free cash flow (FCF) concept is particularly important in long-range corporate financial planning and when evaluating the acquisition of a firm or a portion of a firm. FCF recognizes that part of the funds generated by an ongoing enterprise must be set aside for reinvestment in the firm. Therefore, these funds are not available for distribution to the firm's owners.

Free cash flow can be computed as

$$(20.1) \qquad FCF = CF - I(1 - T) - D_p - P_f - B - Y$$

where CF is the after-tax operating cash flow, I is the before-tax interest payments, D_p is the preferred share dividend payments, P_f is the required redemption of preferred shares, B is the required redemption of debt, and Y is the investment in property, plant, and equipment required to maintain cash flows at their current levels. (If a firm has interest income, this is netted out against interest expense. If interest income exceeds interest expense, FCF will increase by the amount of the net after-tax interest income.) FCF represents the portion of a firm's total cash flow available to service additional debt, to make dividend payments to common shareholders, and to invest in other projects.

When valuing a takeover prospect, it is important to recognize that explicit cash outlays are normally required to sustain or increase the current cash flows of the firm. For example, in considering the acquisition of an oil production company, it is not correct to project current cash flows into an indefinite future without explicitly recognizing that crude oil reserves are a depleting resource that requires continual, significant investment to ensure future cash flow streams. Also, the free cash flows from a merger should include any effects of synergy because the marginal impact of the merger on the acquiring firm is of interest to us.

Consider the following example. Suppose the annual after-tax free cash flow from a merger candidate is calculated to be $2 million and is expected to continue for 15 years, at which time the business can be sold for $10 million. If the appropriate risk-adjusted discount rate is 14 percent, for example, the present value of the expected cash inflows is as follows:

Present value of an annuity of $2 million for 15 years at 14%

+ Present value of $10 million in 15 years at 14%

$= \$2,000,000(PVIFA_{0.14,\ 15}) + \$10,000,000(PVIF_{0.14,\ 15})$

$= \$2,000,000(6.142) + \$10,000,000(0.140)$

$= \$13,684,000$

Therefore, if the merger candidate's purchase price is less than $13,684,000, the proposed merger has a positive net present value and is an acceptable "project."

In principle, the discounted cash flow method is the most correct of the three methods discussed in this section, because this method compares the present value of the cash flow benefits from the merger with the present value of the merger costs. However, in practice, the future cash inflows from a merger can be quite difficult to estimate.

Most financial analysts who work on proposed mergers use all of these methods to attempt to value merger candidates. In addition, they consider a large number of other factors in valuing merger candidates. These factors include the merger candidate's management, products, markets, distribution channels, production costs, expected growth rate, debt capacity, and reputation.

Analysis of a Merger

The following merger examples illustrate some of the steps and considerations involved in typical mergers. Diversified Industries, Inc. is considering acquiring either High-Tech Products, Inc. or Stable Products, Inc. High-Tech Products has a high expected growth rate and sells at a higher P/E ratio than Diversified. Stable Products, on the other hand, has a low expected growth rate and sells at a lower P/E ratio than Diversified. Table 20.1 contains financial statistics on Diversified and the two merger candidates.

The possible merger of Diversified with Stable Products is considered first. To entice Stable Products' present shareholders to tender their shares, Diversified would probably have to offer them a premium of at least 10 to 20 percent over Stable Products' present share price. Suppose Diversified decides to offer $24 per share and Stable Products accepts. The exchange is on a share-for-share basis. As a result, because Diversified's share price is $30, Stable Products' shareholders receive 0.8 Diversified common share for every share of Stable Products they hold. In other words, the **exchange ratio** is 0.8. The exchange ratio, ER, is the number of acquiring firm shares received per acquired company share owned.

Exchange Ratio
The number of shares an acquiring company must give, or exchange, for each share of an acquired company in a merger.

Next, the possible merger of Diversified with High-Tech Products is considered. If Diversified decides to offer $60 a share and High-Tech Products accepts, the High-Tech Products' shareholders would receive two Diversified common shares for every High-Tech Products share they hold. In other words, the exchange ratio would be 2.0.

Table 20.2 shows the pro forma financial statement summary for Diversified, assuming separate mergers with each of the merger candidates. The following equation is used to calculate the postmerger earnings per share for the combined companies, EPS_c:

$$(20.2) \qquad EPS_c = \frac{EAT_1 + EAT_2 + EAT_{1,2}}{NS_1 + NS_2(ER)}$$

where EAT_1 and EAT_2 are the earnings after taxes of the acquiring and acquired companies, respectively, $EAT_{1,2}$ is the immediate synergistic earnings from the merger, and NS_1 and NS_2 are the number of shares outstanding of the acquiring and acquired firm, respectively. For the acquisition of Stable Products by Diversified, EPS_c is calculated as follows:

$$EPS_c = \frac{\$120 \text{ million} + \$12 \text{ million} + 0}{40 \text{ million} + [(4 \text{million})(0.8)]} = \$3.06$$

Table 20.1	Selected Financial Data: Diversified Industries and Two Merger Candidates		
	Diversified Industries	Stable Products	High-Tech Products
Sales	$1,200 million	$130 million	$100 million
Earnings after taxes (EAT)	$120 million	$12 million	$16 million
Number of shares outstanding, NS	40 million	4 million	4 million
Earnings per share, EPS	$3.00	$3.00	$4.00
Dividends per share, D_0	$1.65	$1.50	$0.80
Common share market price, P_0	$30.00	$21.00	$52.00
Price-earnings (P/E) ratio	10.0	7.0	13.0
Expected annual growth rate, g	7%	5%	14%

Table 20.2 Diversified Industries: Pro Forma Financial Statement Summary Assuming Separate Mergers*

	Before Merger	After Merger with Stable Products	After Merger with High-Tech Products
Sales	$1,200 million	$1,330 million	$1,300 million
Earnings after taxes (EAT)	$120 million	$132 million	$136 million
Common shares outstanding, NS	40 million	43.2 million	48 million
Earnings per share, EPS	$3.00	$3.06	$2.83

*The exchange ratio is 0.8 share of Diversified for each 1.0 share of Stable Products and 2.0 shares of Diversified for each 1.0 share of High-Tech Products. The net income figure for Diversified Industries (after merger) assumes that no economies of scale or synergistic benefits are realized as a result of either proposed merger.

As a result of a merger with Stable Products, Diversified has earnings per share of $3.06, as compared with $3.00 without the merger. In other words, the merger transaction can cause Diversified's earnings to change, due to P/E differences between merging companies. Specifically, if the exchange ratio is based on current stock market prices and no synergy exists, *the acquisition of a company with a lower P/E ratio causes the earnings per share figure of the acquiring company to increase.* Similarly, *the acquisition of a company with a higher P/E ratio causes the earnings per share figure to decrease.* This short-term earnings per share change is caused solely by the merger transaction, and a rational stock market does not perceive this change to be *real* growth or *real* decline.

A more important question remains: What will happen to the price and the P/E ratio of Diversified's shares after a merger has been accomplished? Obviously, it can go up, stay the same, or go down. Normally, the stock market seems to view mergers rationally, recognizing that the postmerger P/E ratio is a weighted average of the two premerger P/E ratios. As a result, the postmerger share price of the acquiring company is usually in the same range as prior to the merger, unless significant economies of scale or synergistic benefits are achieved in the merger.

With regard to a possible merger with Stable Products, suppose Diversified's management is not willing to incur an initial dilution in its earnings per share. What is the maximum price and exchange ratio Diversified should agree to under this criterion? The maximum price is calculated using the following equation:

$$(20.3) \qquad P_{max} = (P/E)_1(EPS_2)$$

where P_{max} is the maximum offering price without incurring an initial EPS dilution, $(P/E)_1$ is the price-to-earnings ratio of the acquiring company, and EPS_2 is the earnings per share for the to-be-acquired company. Diversified can offer up to $30 a share for Stable Products without diluting its EPS:

$$P_{max} = (10)(\$3.00) = \$30$$

A price of $30 per share in this example results in an exchange ratio of 1.0, because Diversified's shares are also selling at $30.

Suppose Diversified Industries merges with High-Tech Products and initially dilutes its EPS to $2.83 from its present $3.00 level, assuming no immediate synergy. Diversified's managers may want to know how long it will take the expected EPS of the combined companies to equal the expected EPS of Diversified without the acquisition. To answer this question, we have to consider the expected growth rates of the individual companies given in Table 20.1. Without a merger, Diversified's earnings, dividends, and assets are expected to grow at an annual rate of 7 percent, and High-Tech Products' earnings are expected to grow at 14 percent per year. Assume that the combined companies grow at 9 percent per year. The expected EPS growth for Diversified with and without the merger is shown in Figure 20.1. Based on expected growth rates, the EPS of Diversified with the merger will be equal to its EPS without the merger in slightly over three years.[7] This information will be used by the Diversified management in its decision whether to acquire High-Tech Products.

Analysis of a Leveraged Buyout

The following example illustrates some of the steps and considerations involved in typical LBOs. Suppose that, as part of a corporate restructuring, Universal Industries, Inc. has recently decided to sell its Gray Manufacturing Division, a manufacturer of

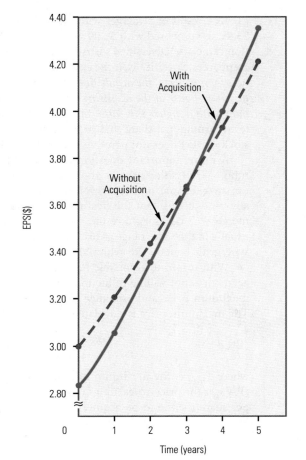

Figure 20.1
Diversified Industries' Expected EPS Growth With and Without the High-Tech Products Acquisition

---

[7] The number of years, n, for no-merger and merger alternatives (denoted a and b, respectively) to produce equal EPS levels is calculated using the following equation:

$$\text{EPS}_a (1 + g_a)^n = \text{EPS}_b (1 + g_b)^n$$

where EPS_a and EPS_b are the initial EPS values for each alternative, and g_a and g_b are the expected annual growth rates for each alternative.

industrial products. The Gray division's top management, together with several private investors, is considering buying Gray and operating it as a separate company. As is fairly typical of LBO candidates, Gray is in a mature industry and its products have a low probability of becoming obsolete. In addition, Gray's fixed assets have a present market value greater than their book value.

The Gray division's financial statements listed in Table 20.3 show that the division presently has an annual pretax loss of $1 million, and therefore its return on shareholders' equity is negative. The Gray management group intends to return Gray to profitability by various cost-cutting and other measures. Gray's parent company, Universal Industries, could also have initiated cost-cutting measures to attempt to return Gray to profitability. However, partly because of Universal's new corporate strategy to get out of the industrial products business, it has chosen instead to sell Gray. Following negotiations between the Gray management group and Universal Industries, the management group agreed to purchase all of the assets of the Gray division for $30 million.

The Gray management group plans to take the following steps to complete the LBO transaction:

1. The management group has put together equity totalling $5 million. In LBO terminology, equity is sometimes referred to as "*ground floor financing.*"

2. The management group has arranged for short-term bank financing, agreeing to pledge Gray's accounts receivable and inventory as collateral. This level of financing is called either "*second floor*" or "*top floor*" financing.

3. The management group has also arranged to finance the remaining portion of the buyout with subordinated long-term debt financing from an investment banking firm specializing in providing financing for LBOs. This subordinated debt is called "*mezzanine*" financing because of its position between the ground floor and the second floor financing. Mezzanine financing is high-risk capital because the company's fixed assets do not provide sufficient collateral for the debt. In addition, Gray's cash flow forecast for its early years as a separate entity indicates that it may experience some difficulty in servicing its debt obligations. As a result, the investment bankers providing the mezzanine financing have insisted that the debentures include attached warrants to provide additional opportunities for return other than

Table 20.3 Leveraged Buyout of Gray Manufacturing Division

Balance Sheet (in Millions of Dollars)

	Before LBO	Pro Forma After LBO
Current assets	$22	$22
Fixed assets, net	8	16
Total assets	$30	$38
Current liabilities	$15	$15
Long-term debt	—	18
Shareholders' equity	15	5
Total liabilities and equity	$30	$38

Annual Income Statement (in Millions of Dollars)

	Before LBO	Pro Forma After LBO
Revenues	$30	$30
Cash operating expenses	29	21
Interest expense	1	5
Depreciation	1	3
Earnings before tax	$–1	$ 1

the debt's interest payments. Because these debentures are highly risky, they are referred to as junk bonds. (Recall from Chapter 5 that the term *junk bond* is frequently applied to a debt issue rated BB or lower by the rating agencies.)[8]

4. The management group intends to initiate a major cost-cutting program as soon as Gray becomes a separate company. They plan to cut unnecessary personnel at all levels, and for the remaining employees, they plan to cut salaries and employee benefits. In return, however, they do plan to offer key employees stock options, and all employees will participate in a bonus plan. In addition, Gray personnel will no longer have to provide reports to Universal, which in turn reports to its shareholders and the appropriate securities commissions. Furthermore, the Gray managers themselves will no longer be spending time talking to security analysts.

5. The management group has determined that Gray's fixed assets (real estate and equipment) have a market value of approximately $16 million, or about twice their present book value. As a result of the LBO, the fixed assets will be written up to their market value and depreciated on the basis of the higher value. The increased depreciation charge will shelter a greater portion of Gray's cash flow from income taxes, all other things being equal.

This example illustrates many of the steps a buyer usually takes in an LBO.

The largest leveraged buyout in Canada occurred on November 29, 2002, when the Ontario Teachers' Pension Plan Board, Bell Canada, and the US investment banking firm Kohlberg, Kravis & Roberts joined forces to acquire the yellow and white pages directories and the e-directories businesses of Bell ActiMedia for $3 billion. The Bank of Nova Scotia (Scotiabank), the Canadian Imperial Bank of Commerce (CIBC) and Credit Suisse First Boston arranged $2.2 billion in senior secured financing and subordinated unsecured bridge financing to partially fund the purchase price.

Business Failure

For more information on bankruptcy in Canada see **www.bankruptcycanada. com** For more on the CCAA see **www.bdplaw.com/ articles/spring99/ccaa.htm** The Office of the Superintendent of Bankruptcy has a Web site at **http://strategis.ic.gc.ca/ sc_mrksv/bankrupt/ engdoc/superint.html**

The remainder of this chapter considers what happens when businesses experience severe and extended problems that might cause failure. The purpose is to present an overview of business failure and the alternatives available to the failing firm. In this section, we define business failure and discuss its frequency and causes. The following section examines the various alternatives available to failing firms, including the procedures involving the federal bankruptcy laws. There are two federal laws governing business failure: the Bankruptcy and Insolvency Act (BIA) and the lesser known Companies' Creditors Arrangement Act (CCAA). These two laws are administered by the Office of the Superintendent of Bankruptcy. In this chapter we focus on the Bankruptcy and Insolvency Act. The CCAA is a depression-era law that is much less often used than the BIA, is less well known, and is confined only to debt restructuring despite the fact that a business turnaround usually requires far more than just concessions from the creditors. Because it has not been used very often, there is not much case law to clarify its provisions that some lawyers claim to be too vague. The BIA, however, is periodically reviewed and new legislation is promulgated, so it is more up to date. There are also court cases that have been decided, so they can serve as precedent in interpreting the law.

Definitions of Business Failure

Business failure can be considered from both an *economic* and a *financial* viewpoint. In an economic sense, *business success* is associated with firms that earn an adequate return

---

[8] In the case of privately placed debt, a junk bond is a debt issue whose characteristics would cause it to be rated BB, or lower, if it were rated.

(equal to or greater than the cost of capital) on their investments. Similarly, *business failure* is associated with firms that earn an inadequate return on their investments. An important aspect of business failure involves the question of whether the failure is *permanent* or *temporary*. For example, suppose a company has $1 million invested in assets and generates operating earnings of only $10,000. Obviously, this 1 percent return on investment is inadequate. However, the appropriate course of action depends to some extent on whether this business failure is judged to be permanent or temporary. If it is permanent, the firm should probably be liquidated. If failure is temporary, the company should probably attempt to "ride out the storm," especially if steps can be taken to speed the firm's return to business success. From an economic standpoint, business failure is also said to exist when a firm's revenues are not sufficient to cover the costs of doing business.

It is more common, however, for business failure to be viewed in a *financial context,* as a *technical insolvency,* a *legal insolvency,* or a *bankruptcy.* A firm is said to be **technically insolvent** if it is unable to meet its current obligations as they come due, even though the value of its assets exceeds the value of its liabilities.[9] A firm is **legally insolvent** if the recorded value of its assets is less than the recorded value of its liabilities. A firm is **bankrupt** if it is unable to pay its debts and files a bankruptcy petition in accordance with the federal bankruptcy laws.

Causes of Business Failure

Although there are a number of reasons why businesses fail, most failures seem to be due at least in part to economic factors, financial causes, and lack of experience on the part of the owners of the businesses.

When businesses experience problems such as inadequate sales and heavy operating expenses, they frequently encounter cash flow problems as well. As a result of the cash flow problems, these businesses often increase their short-term borrowings. If the problems persist, the cash flow difficulties can become more acute, and the business may not be able to meet its obligations to its creditors on a timely basis.

Many of these characteristics of failing firms were measured by the financial ratios used in the Altman bankruptcy prediction model discussed in Chapter 3. Such financial variables as sales, operating expenses (through its effect on EBIT), short-term borrowings (debt), and cash flow (through its effect on net working capital) were all components of one or more of the ratios used to forecast failure.

Alternatives for Failing Businesses

Once a firm begins encountering these difficulties, the firm's owners and management have to consider the alternatives available to failing businesses. In general, a failing company has two alternatives:

1. It can attempt to resolve its difficulties with its creditors on a *voluntary,* or *informal,* basis.

2. It can petition the courts for assistance and *formally* declare *bankruptcy.*

   A company's creditors may also petition the courts and this may result in the company's being involuntarily declared bankrupt.

Regardless of whether a business chooses informal or formal methods to deal with its difficulties, eventually the decision has to be made whether to *reorganize* or *liquidate* the business. Before this decision can be made, both the business's liquidation value and its going-concern value have to be determined. *Liquidation value* equals the proceeds

Technical Insolvency
A situation in which a firm is unable to meet its current obligations as they come due, even though the value of its assets may exceed its liabilities.

Legal Insolvency
A situation in which the recorded value of a firm's assets is less than its liabilities.

Bankruptcy
A situation in which a firm is unable to pay its debts and its assets are turned over to the court for administration.

---

[9] A firm that is technically insolvent can also be said to be illiquid.

Bankruptcy in Other Countries

Since many Canadian companies have subsidiaries in other countries around the world, it may happen that a subsidiary firm becomes insolvent. It is likely that bankruptcy laws in other countries will differ from those in effect in Canada.

Fortunately, the Internet provides many sources of information that may be useful to Canadian managers who do business internationally.

The American Bankruptcy Institute maintains a Directory of International Bankruptcy Laws (in English) at its Web site:
www.abiworld.org/international/foreign.html

The InterNet Bankruptcy Library has a variety of resources at its Web site: **http://bankrupt.com**

that would be received from the sale of the business assets minus liabilities. *Going-concern value* equals the capitalized value of the company's operating earnings minus its liabilities. Basically, if the going-concern value exceeds the liquidation value, the business should be reorganized. Otherwise, it should be liquidated. However, in practice, the determination of the going-concern and liquidation values is not an easy matter. For example, problems may exist in estimating the price the firm's assets will bring at auction. In addition, the company's future operating earnings and the appropriate discount rate at which to capitalize the earnings may be difficult to determine. Also, management understandably is not in a position to be completely objective about these values.

Informal Alternatives for Failing Businesses

Regardless of the exact reasons why a business begins to experience difficulties, the result is often the same. Namely, there are cash flow problems.

Frequently, the first steps taken by the troubled firm involve stretching its payables. In some cases, this action can buy the troubled firm up to several weeks of needed time before creditors take action.

If the difficulties are more than just minor and temporary, the firm may next turn to its bankers and request additional working capital loans. In some situations, the bankers may make the additional loans, especially if they perceive the situation to be temporary. Another possible action the firm's bankers and creditors may take is to restructure the company's debt.

Debt restructuring by bankers and other creditors can be quite complex. However, debt restructuring basically involves either extension, composition, or a combination of the two. In an *extension*, the failing firm tries to reach an agreement with its creditors that will permit it to lengthen the time it has to meet its obligations. In a *composition*, the firm's creditors accept some percentage amount less than their actual original claims, and the firm is permitted to discharge its debt obligations by paying less than the full amounts owed. The percentage a firm's creditors will agree to in the event of a composition is usually greater than the percentage they could net if the firm had to sell its assets to satisfy their claims. If a company's creditors feel that the firm can overcome its financial difficulties and become a valuable customer over the long run, they may be willing to accept some form of composition.

Debt restructuring by lenders can involve deferment of both interest and principal payments for a time. Before lenders will agree to these deferments, they often require the troubled firm's suppliers and workers to make various concessions as well. In addition, the lenders frequently demand and receive *warrants* in return for making their deferment concessions.

Large companies that experience cash flow difficulties often sell off real estate, various operating divisions, or both to raise needed cash.

Another method often used by failing companies to raise needed cash involves the sale and leaseback of its land and buildings. Some companies also resort to more unusual methods of conserving cash, such as offering preferred shares to certain employees in exchange for a portion of their salary.

Frequently, failing companies voluntarily form a *creditors' committee* that meets regularly and attempts to help the firm out of its predicament. The creditors are usually requested to accept deferred payments, and in return, the creditors usually request that the firm cut various expenditures. If the firm and its creditors are able to reach an agreement on the appropriate actions to take, the legal and administrative expenses associated with formal bankruptcy procedures are not incurred. Accordingly, both the firm and creditors may be better off as a result.

Liquidation can also occur outside the bankruptcy courts. The process is called an *assignment*. Usually a trustee, who is probably one of the major creditors, is assigned the assets. The trustee then has the responsibility of selling the assets and distributing the proceeds in the best interest of the creditors.

Formal Alternatives for Failing Businesses under the Bankruptcy Law

The Bankruptcy and Insolvency Act states the basic mechanics of the bankruptcy procedure.[10] Either the failing company or its unsecured creditors may initiate bankruptcy procedures by filing a claim in bankruptcy court. When the debtor company files for bankruptcy, it is termed a *voluntary* petition. A bankruptcy proceeding may also be initiated by a group of three or more of the company's unsecured creditors. The unsecured creditors filing the claim must assert that the debtor company is not paying its present debts as they come due. Such a claim is termed an *involuntary* petition.

After the initial bankruptcy petition has been filed, both the failing company and its creditors receive protection from the courts. The firm itself is protected from any further actions on the part of the creditors while it attempts to work out a *plan of reorganization*. The debtor company has a limited time period to work out a plan of reorganization. After that, the creditors may file a plan of their own. The court has considerable latitude in a bankruptcy case. For example, depending on the nature of the case, it may decide to appoint a *trustee* who will be responsible for running the business and protecting the creditors' interests. Normally, the troubled firm is allowed to continue operations. If there is reason to believe that continuing operations will result in further deterioration of the creditors' position, however, the court can order the firm to cease operating.

An important aspect of the bankruptcy procedures involves what to do with the failing firm. Just as in the case of the informal alternatives, a decision has to be made about whether a firm's value as a *going concern* is greater than its *liquidation* value. Generally, if this is the case and a suitable plan of reorganization can be formulated, the firm is reorganized. Otherwise, it is liquidated.

Reorganization

During bankruptcy proceedings, the failing firm presents its current financial status and its proposed plan of reorganization. This plan of reorganization is normally similar to either composition or extension.

---

[10] For more details on the Bankruptcy and Insolvency Act see Lloyd W. Houldon and Geoffrey B. Morawetz, *The 2003 Annotated Bankruptcy and Insolvency Act* (Toronto: Carswell, 2002).

The bankruptcy court reviews the plan of reorganization for fairness and feasibility. The term *fairness* means that the claims are to be settled in the order of their priority. The priority of claims is discussed in detail in the next section on liquidation. A *feasible* plan of reorganization is one that gives the business a good chance of re-establishing successful operations. For example, the plan must provide an adequate level of working capital, a reasonable capital structure and debt-to-equity ratio, and an earning power sufficient to reasonably cover interest and dividend requirements. Often a recapitalization may result in fewer fixed charges for the reorganized company and thereby afford it a better chance of succeeding. The reorganization may also involve an extension of the debt maturities, which would help the firm's cash flow by causing the debt's principal retirement to occur at later dates.

Once the bankrupt company obtains approval from the bankruptcy court, the court-appointed trustee's task is to implement the plan.

Liquidation

If for some reason reorganization is judged unfeasible, a legally declared bankrupt company may be liquidated. A *trustee* is normally appointed to handle the administrative aspects of the bankruptcy procedure. The trustee then liquidates the business and pays the creditors' claims according to the priority of claims set forth in the Bankruptcy and Insolvency Act.

In general, secured debts are satisfied first from the sale of the secured assets and all claims of creditors must be satisfied before any claims by shareholders. The following list specifies the order of priority in which unsecured debts must be paid:

1. The expenses involved in the administration of the bankruptcy

2. Wages, salaries, commissions, etc., owed for services performed during the six months prior to the bankruptcy proceedings, not to exceed $2,000 per employee

3. Municipal taxes assessed or levied against the bankrupt firm within two years immediately preceding the bankruptcy

4. Rent due the landlord for a period of three months immediately preceding the bankruptcy

5. Claims of general or unsecured creditors, including taxes due the Crown (the holders of outstanding trade credit, unsecured loans, the unsatisfied portion of secured loans, and debenture bondholders are classed as general creditors)

6. Preferred shareholders—receive an amount up to the par value or stated value of their preferred shares

7. Common shareholders—share any remaining funds equally on a per-share basis

To illustrate the absolute priority rule in liquidation, consider the balance sheet prior to the liquidation of Failures Galore, Inc., shown in Table 20.4.[11] Suppose the total proceeds of the liquidation are $6.8 million. The distribution of these proceeds is shown in Table 20.5. The proceeds have been distributed in accordance with the absolute priority rule. Each general and unsecured creditor receives a settlement percentage of the funds owed after priority claims have been settled. As shown in Table 20.5, these priority claims are bankruptcy administration expenses, wages, and municipal taxes owed. In addition, mortgage bondholders receive $1.5 million from the sale of secured assets. This leaves the mortgage bondholders as general creditors for the balance of their claim ($500,000). After these priority claims have been met, there is $4.25 million in assets left to meet the remaining creditor claims of $8.5 million. Each general creditor receives 50 percent of the claim, except bank notes. Because the subordinated debentures are

---

[11] Assume that this liquidation is a voluntary petition.

Table 20.4 Balance Sheet, Failures Galore, Inc.*

Assets		Liabilities and Equity	
Current assets	$ 6,000,000	Accounts payable	$ 2,000,000
Fixed assets, net	6,500,000	Bank notes payable	2,000,000
		Accrued wages	200,000
		Accrued taxes	300,000
		Mortgage bonds	2,000,000
		Debentures	2,000,000
		Subordinated debentures	2,000,000
		Preferred shares	1,000,000
		Common equity	1,000,000
Total assets	$12,500,000	Liabilities and equity	$12,500,000

*The subordinated debentures are subordinate to the bank notes payable. Assume that all of the accrued wages can be paid out of the liquidation proceeds.

Table 20.5 Distribution of the Proceeds from the Liquidation of Failures Galore, Inc.

Total liquidation proceeds	$6,800,000
1. Bankruptcy administration expenses	$ 550,000
2. Wages owed to employees	200,000
3. Taxes owed to municipal governments	300,000
Total priority claims	$1,050,000
Funds available for claims of creditors	$5,750,000
4. Payment to mortgage bondholders (proceeds from sale of secured assets)	1,500,000
Funds available for claims of general and unsecured creditors	$4,250,000

$$\text{Settlement percentage for general and unsecured creditors} = \frac{\text{Funds available for general and unsecured creditors}}{\text{Total claims of general and unsecured creditors}}$$

$$= \frac{\$4,250,000}{\$8,500,000}$$

$$= 50\%$$

	Total Claim	Settlement, 50% of Claim (before Subordination Adjustment)	Settlement, 50% of Claim (after Subordination Adjustment)
Accounts payable	$2,000,000	$1,000,000	$1,000,000
Bank notes payable	2,000,000	1,000,000	2,000,000
Mortgage bonds	500,000	250,000	250,000
Debentures	2,000,000	1,000,000	1,000,000
Subordinated debentures	2,000,000	1,000,000	0
	$8,500,000	$4,250,000	$4,250,000

Funds available for preferred and common shareholders $0

subordinate to bank notes, the bank notes receive the proportionate claim of the subordinated holders ($1 million in this case) in addition to the $1 million directly due the bank notes. Hence, because of the subordination provision in the debentures, the bank notes are paid off in full.

Although Canada 3000 is still in bankruptcy as this chapter is being written, CanJet is flying again. The IMP Group re-launched CanJet on June 20, 2002, with service from Halifax, Moncton, St. John's, Ottawa, and Montreal. CanJet operates four Boeing 737 aircraft that seat 120 passengers. This small fleet of similar aircraft allows CanJet to be more efficient with pilot training and aircraft maintenance since pilots and mechanics can focus on the one type of plane. In western Canada, WestJet continues to provide similar service with similar aircraft. Thus, these two Canadian airlines both use the strategy created by Southwest Airlines in the United States—focus on what you do best and get even better at doing it.

The same priority rule may also be used in bankruptcy reorganizations. However, in some reorganization proceedings, deviations from the priority rule by the courts have been observed.

Two of the major reasons for the deviations are that the creditors may lack adequate information about the firm's value or that they may be willing to compromise because of the potential cost of a lengthy reorganization.

Summary

- There are a number of reasons companies choose external growth over internal growth, including the following:
  1. The availability of lower-cost assets
  2. Greater economies of scale
  3. The availability of more secure raw material supplies and/or additional end-product markets
  4. The possibility of more rapid growth
  5. Greater diversification
  6. Tax considerations

- Technically, a *merger* is a combination of two or more companies in which all but one of the firms legally cease to exist and the surviving company continues operation under its original name. An *amalgamation (consolidation)* is a combination in which all of the companies are dissolved and a new company is formed. The term *merger* is often used generically to describe both of these types of business combinations.

- Mergers are classified according to whether they are *horizontal, vertical,* or *conglomerate.* In a horizontal merger, the combining companies are direct competitors. In a vertical merger, the companies have a buyer-seller relationship. In a conglomerate merger, neither firm competes directly with the other, nor is there a buyer-seller relationship.

- Three major methods are used to value merger candidates: the *comparative price-earnings ratio method,* the *adjusted book value method,* and the *discounted cash flow method.* The discounted cash flow method, which is an application of capital budgeting techniques, is the most theoretically correct valuation method.

- The acquisition of a firm with *higher* (lower) P/E ratio causes the earnings per share of the acquiring firm to *decrease* (increase) if the exchange ratio is based on current share prices and *no* synergy exists.

- In the *purchase* method of accounting for mergers, acquired assets are recorded at their fair market values, and any additional amount paid is listed as *goodwill,* which must then be amortized.

- Various *anti-takeover measures* are available to firms. Some of these can be established before any takeover is attempted. Others are designed to thwart a takeover once an attempt is started.

- A *holding company* owns controlling interest in another legally separate company, and the relationship between these affiliated companies is called a *parent-subsidiary* relationship.

- A *joint venture* is formed by two (or more) unaffiliated companies that contribute financial and/or physical assets, as well as personnel, to a new company formed to engage in some economic activity that is not feasible for any one of the participants individually.

- In a *leveraged buyout,* the buyer of a company borrows a large portion of the purchase price, using the purchased assets as partial collateral for the loans.

- *Divestitures* can be accomplished through either a spinoff or an equity carve-out.
  1. In a *spinoff,* a division or subsidiary becomes a separate company and common shares in this new firm are distributed to the shareholders of the parent company on a pro rata basis.
  2. In an *equity carve-out,* common shares in the subsidiary or division are sold directly to the public, with the parent company usually retaining a controlling interest in the shares outstanding.

- A firm is *technically insolvent* if it cannot meet its current obligations as they come due, even though the value of its assets exceeds its liabilities. A firm is *legally insolvent* if its total liabilities exceed the value of its total assets. A firm is *bankrupt* if it is unable to pay its debts.

- Failing firms have two basic alternatives:
  1. They can attempt to resolve the difficulties with their creditors on an *informal,* voluntary basis.
  2. They can petition the courts for assistance and *formally* declare *bankruptcy.* In addition, the creditors may petition the courts, and the firm may be involuntarily declared bankrupt.

- Legal bankruptcy proceedings focus on the decision of whether the failing firm should be *reorganized* or *liquidated.* If its going-concern value is greater than its liquidation value, the business will usually be reorganized. Otherwise, it will be liquidated.

- The Bankruptcy and Insolvency Act governs bankruptcy procedures. A distressed company may seek court protection from its creditors while it works out a *reorganization plan.* If reorganization is judged not feasible, the bankrupt company is liquidated. The liquidation procedures are set forth in the act.

Questions and Topics for Discussion

1. Define the following terms:
   a. Merger
   b. Amalgamation
   c. Holding company

2. Describe some of the measures used by companies to discourage unfriendly takeover attempts.
3. What is the difference between an asset purchase and a share purchase?
4. What is the difference between an operational restructuring and a financial restructuring?
5. Discuss the differences between the following types of mergers:
    a. Horizontal mergers
    b. Vertical mergers
    c. Conglomerate mergers
6. What are some of the reasons why firms merge with other firms?
7. What methods do financial analysts use to value merger candidates? What are the limitations of each method?
8. Explain what happens to the postmerger earnings per share figure when a firm with a relatively high P/E ratio acquires a firm with a lower P/E ratio, assuming that the exchange ratio is based on current stock market prices and no synergy exists.
9. What is a *leveraged buyout?* What is *ground floor financing?* What is *mezzanine financing?* What is *second floor* or *top floor financing?*
10. What is a *tax-free merger?*
11. Explain the difference between the economic and financial definitions of business failure.
12. Explain the differences among the following terms related to financial failure:
    a. Technical insolvency
    b. Legal insolvency
    c. Bankruptcy
13. What alternatives are available to the failing firm?
14. Basically, what determines whether a bankrupt company is reorganized or liquidated?
15. In a debt reorganization, explain the difference between a *composition* and an *extension.*
16. Explain why an informal settlement may be preferable to declaring bankruptcy for both the failing firm and its creditors.
17. In connection with reorganization plans, what do *fairness* and *feasibility* mean?
18. Explain how a firm that has failed can be reorganized to operate successfully.
19. Rank in order of priority (highest to lowest) the following claims on the proceeds from the liquidation of a bankrupt firm:
    - Taxes owed to the municipal government
    - Preferred shareholders
    - Common shareholders
    - Expenses of administering the bankruptcy
    - Secured creditors
    - Unsecured creditors
    - Wages in the six months before bankruptcy (up to $2,000 per employee)

Self-Test Problem

ST1. Zenith Industries is considering the acquisition of the Nadir Corporation in a share-for-share exchange. (The expression *share-for-share exchange* means that the common shares of one company are exchanged for the common shares of another company.) Assume that no immediate synergistic benefits are expected. Selected financial data on the two companies are shown here:

	Zenith	Nadir
Sales (millions)	$500	$100
Earnings after taxes (millions)	$30	$12
Common shares outstanding (millions)	6	2
Earnings per share	$5	$6
Common share price	$50	$40
Dividends per share	$2	$1.50

    a. If Zenith is not willing to incur an initial dilution in its earnings per share—that is, not have the postmerger earnings per share be below $5—and if Zenith also feels that it will have to offer the Nadir shareholders a minimum of 25% over Nadir's current market price, what is the relevant range of Nadir per-share prices with which Zenith is working?

    b. Calculate Zenith's postmerger earnings per share if the Nadir shareholders accept an offer by Zenith of $50 per share in a share-for-share exchange.

Problems*

BASIC

1. Apex Corporation is considering the purchase of Pinnacle Company in a share-for-share exchange. Selected data on the two companies are shown in the following table:

	Apex	Pinnacle
Sales (millions)	$750	$175
Earnings after taxes (millions)	$100	$20
Common shares outstanding (millions)	50	20
Common share price	$40	$15
Earnings per share	$2.00	$1.00
Dividends per share	$1.00	$0.40
P/E ratio	20	15
Dividend payout ratio	50%	40%

    Assume that there are no synergistic benefits as the result of the merger. Determine EPS for the combined company if Apex offers a

    a. 20% premium for Pinnacle

    b. 40% premium for Pinnacle

    c. 50% premium for Pinnacle

2. Consider Problem 1 again. Assume that there are immediate synergistic benefits of $4 million if Apex and Pinnacle merge. Answer parts a, b, and c of Problem 1 under these conditions.

---

*Coloured numbers and letters denote problems that have "check" answers provided at the back of the book.

3. The BO Corporation and the GP Company have agreed to a merger. The GP shareholders will receive 0.75 BO shares for each share of GP held. Assume that no synergistic benefits are expected.

    a. Complete the following table:

	BO	GP	Combined Firms
Sales (millions)	$500	$125	
Earnings after taxes (millions)	$60	$13	
Common shares outstanding (millions)	16	4	
Common share price	$41.25	$26	
Earnings per share	$3.75	$3.25	
Dividends per share	$1.00	$ 0.40	
P/E ratio			10.0

    b. Calculate the premium percentage received by the GP shareholders. Assume *both* that immediate synergistic earnings of $3 million per year will occur as a result of the merger and that the P/E ratio of the combined companies is 10.5.

    c. Rework part a.

    d. Rework part b.

4. Ball Industries is considering acquiring the Keyes Corporation in a share-for-share exchange. Selected financial data on the two companies follow:

	Ball	Keyes
Sales (millions)	$600	$75
Earnings after taxes (millions)	$30	$10
Common shares outstanding (millions)	6	4
Common share price	$ 50	$20
Earnings per share	$5.00	$2.50

    Assume that no synergistic benefits are expected.

    a. What is the maximum exchange ratio Ball should agree to if one of its acquisition criteria is no initial dilution in earnings per share?

    b. Suppose an investor had purchased 100 common shares of Keyes five years ago at $12 per share. If the Keyes shareholders accept an offer of $24 per share in a share-for-share exchange, how much capital gains tax would this investor have to pay at the time the Keyes shares are exchanged for the Ball shares? (Assume a capital gains tax rate of 23% for this investor.) Assume that immediate synergistic earnings of $4 million will occur as a result of the acquisition.

    c. Calculate the postmerger earnings per share if the Keyes shareholders accept an offer by Ball of $24 per share in a share-for-share exchange.

5. Looking back at Tables 20.1 and 20.2, assume that Diversified Industries acquires High-Tech Products in a share-for-share transaction and no immediate synergistic benefits are expected. How long will it take the expected EPS of the combined companies to equal the expected EPS of Diversified without the merger if Diversified is expected to grow at an annual rate of 7% without the merger and the combined companies are expected to grow at 8% per year?

6. Consider Failures Galore, Inc. (Tables 20.4 and 20.5), discussed in this chapter.

    a. If total liquidation proceeds are $5.95 million, what is the distribution of these proceeds among the various creditors of Failures Galore?

b. If total liquidation proceeds are $7.65 million, what is the distribution of these proceeds among the various creditors of Failures Galore?

7. Wilso Industries is considering the acquisition of the Blanco Company in a share-for-share exchange. Selected financial data for the two firms are shown below. An immediate synergistic earnings benefit of $1 million is expected in this merger, due to cost savings.

	Wilso	Blanco
Sales (millions)	$150	$30
Earnings after taxes (millions)	$25	$3.5
Common shares outstanding (millions)	8	2
Common share price	$40	$19.50
Earnings per share	$3.125	$1.75
Dividends per share	$1.50	$0.75

Calculate the postmerger earnings per share if the Blanco shareholders accept an offer of $22 per share in a share-for-share exchange.

8. A financial analyst with MTC International has estimated the annual after-tax free cash flow from a proposed merger to be $1.5 million. This cash flow is expected to continue for 10 years. For the following five years, the free cash flow is estimated to be $0.7 million per year. MTC feels that the appropriate risk-adjusted discount rate is 16%. Calculate the present value of the expected free cash flows from the proposed merger through year 15.

CHALLENGE

9. The McPherson Company is considering acquiring the McAlester Company. Selected financial data for the two companies are shown here:

	McPherson	McAlester
Sales (millions)	$250	$30
Earnings after taxes (millions)	$20	$2.25
Common shares outstanding (millions)	5	1
Common share price	$40	$18
Earnings per share	$4.00	$2.25
Dividends per share	$1.20	$0.40

Both firms have 40% marginal tax rates. Assume that no synergistic benefits are expected.

a. Calculate the McPherson Company's postmerger earnings per share if the McAlester shareholders accept an offer of $20 per share in a share-for-share exchange.

b. Recalculate part a, assuming that the McPherson common share price is $42. (All other figures remain constant.)

c. Calculate McPherson's earnings per share if the McAlester shareholders accept one $6 convertible preferred share (stated value, $100) for each five McAlester shares held.

d. Calculate McPherson's earnings per share if each group of 50 McAlester shares is exchanged for one 8%, $1,000 debenture.

e. Compare the premerger expected dividend return on the McAlester shares with the expected postmerger dividends or interest available with the exchanges described in parts a, c, and d. (Undoubtedly, at the time of acquisition, McPherson would have pointed out these expected increases in yield to the McAlester share-holders.) Assume that an investor initially holds 100 McAlester shares.

f. What can be said about comparing the expected total postmerger return (dividends plus price appreciation) on the McAlester shares versus the expected total postmerger return on the McPherson securities?

10. Go-for-Broke Company is being liquidated. When it filed for bankruptcy, its balance sheet was as follows:

Assets		Liabilities and Equity	
Current assets	$14,500,000	Accounts payable	$12,145,000
Land & Buildings (net)	6,525,000	Accrued wages*	2,030,000
Equipment	7,975,000	Accrued taxes	1,160,000
Total assets	$29,000,000	Notes payable (bank)[†]	1,350,000
		Total current liabilities	$16,685,000
		Mortgage bonds[††]	4,775,000
		Debentures	2,450,000
		Shareholders' equity	5,090,000
		Total liabilities and equity	$29,000,000

* All accrued wages must be paid out of liquidation proceeds.

[†] The bank loan is unsecured.

[††] Mortgage bonds are secured by land and buildings.

Assume that the liquidation is a voluntary petition. The proceeds from the liquidation of the firm's assets are as follows:

Current assets	$9,425,000
Land and buildings	3,045,000
Equipment	4,130,000
Total	$16,600,000

Bankruptcy administration charges are $643,750.

a. Determine the distribution (dollar amount and percentage) of the liquidation proceeds among the various creditors of Go-for-Broke.

b. Assume that the debentures ($2.45 million) are subordinated to bank notes payable. Determine the distribution (dollar amount and percentage) of the liquidation proceeds among the various creditors of Go-for-Broke.

Other Practice Materials and Resources

For interactive quizzes, Internet exercises, crossword puzzles, CTV videos, and more, go to the *Contemporary Financial Management* Web site at **http://cyr.nelson.com**

Reference Materials

Table I — Future Value Interest Factor (FVIF) ($1 at i% per period for n periods); $FVIF = (1 + i)^n$; $FV_n = PV_0 (FVIF_{i,n})$

Period, n	1%	2%	3%	4%	5%	6%	7%	8%	9%	10%	11%	12%	13%
0	1.000	1.000	1.000	1.000	1.000	1.000	1.000	1.000	1.000	1.000	1.000	1.000	1.000
1	1.010	1.020	1.030	1.040	1.050	1.060	1.070	1.080	1.090	1.100	1.110	1.120	1.130
2	1.020	1.040	1.061	1.082	1.102	1.124	1.145	1.166	1.188	1.210	1.232	1.254	1.277
3	1.030	1.061	1.093	1.125	1.158	1.191	1.225	1.260	1.295	1.331	1.368	1.405	1.443
4	1.041	1.082	1.126	1.170	1.216	1.262	1.311	1.360	1.412	1.464	1.518	1.574	1.630
5	1.051	1.104	1.159	1.217	1.276	1.338	1.403	1.469	1.539	1.611	1.685	1.762	1.842
6	1.062	1.126	1.194	1.265	1.340	1.419	1.501	1.587	1.677	1.772	1.870	1.974	2.082
7	1.072	1.149	1.230	1.316	1.407	1.504	1.606	1.714	1.828	1.949	2.076	2.211	2.353
8	1.083	1.172	1.267	1.369	1.477	1.594	1.718	1.851	1.993	2.144	2.305	2.476	2.658
9	1.094	1.195	1.305	1.423	1.551	1.689	1.838	1.999	2.172	2.358	2.558	2.773	3.004
10	1.105	1.219	1.344	1.480	1.629	1.791	1.967	2.159	2.367	2.594	2.839	3.106	3.395
11	1.116	1.243	1.384	1.539	1.710	1.898	2.105	2.332	2.580	2.853	3.152	3.479	3.836
12	1.127	1.268	1.426	1.601	1.796	2.012	2.252	2.518	2.813	3.138	3.498	3.896	4.335
13	1.138	1.294	1.469	1.665	1.886	2.133	2.410	2.720	3.066	3.452	3.883	4.363	4.898
14	1.149	1.319	1.513	1.732	1.980	2.261	2.579	2.937	3.342	3.797	4.310	4.887	5.535
15	1.161	1.346	1.558	1.801	2.079	2.397	2.759	3.172	3.642	4.177	4.785	5.474	6.254
16	1.173	1.373	1.605	1.873	2.183	2.540	2.952	3.426	3.970	4.595	5.311	6.130	7.067
17	1.184	1.400	1.653	1.948	2.292	2.693	3.159	3.700	4.328	5.054	5.895	6.866	7.986
18	1.196	1.428	1.702	2.026	2.407	2.854	3.380	3.996	4.717	5.560	6.544	7.690	9.024
19	1.208	1.457	1.754	2.107	2.527	3.026	3.617	4.316	5.142	6.116	7.263	8.613	10.197
20	1.220	1.486	1.806	2.191	2.653	3.207	3.870	4.661	5.604	6.728	8.062	9.646	11.523
24	1.270	1.608	2.033	2.563	3.225	4.049	5.072	6.341	7.911	9.850	12.239	15.179	18.790
25	1.282	1.641	2.094	2.666	3.386	4.292	5.427	6.848	8.623	10.835	13.585	17.000	21.231
30	1.348	1.811	2.427	3.243	4.322	5.743	7.612	10.063	13.268	17.449	22.892	29.960	39.116
40	1.489	2.208	3.262	4.801	7.040	10.286	14.974	21.725	31.409	45.259	65.001	93.051	132.782
50	1.645	2.692	4.384	7.107	11.467	18.420	29.457	46.902	74.358	117.391	184.565	289.002	450.736
60	1.817	3.281	5.892	10.520	18.679	32.988	57.946	101.257	176.031	304.482	524.057	897.597	1,530.05

Period, n	14%	15%	16%	17%	18%	19%	20%	24%	28%	32%	36%	40%
0	1.000	1.000	1.000	1.000	1.000	1.000	1.000	1.000	1.000	1.000	1.000	1.000
1	1.140	1.150	1.160	1.170	1.180	1.190	1.200	1.240	1.280	1.320	1.360	1.400
2	1.300	1.322	1.346	1.369	1.392	1.416	1.440	1.538	1.638	1.742	1.850	1.960
3	1.482	1.521	1.561	1.602	1.643	1.685	1.728	1.907	2.067	2.300	2.515	2.744
4	1.689	1.749	1.811	1.874	1.939	2.005	2.074	2.364	2.684	3.036	3.421	3.842
5	1.925	2.011	2.100	2.192	2.288	2.386	2.488	2.932	3.436	4.007	4.653	5.378
6	2.195	2.313	2.436	2.565	2.700	2.840	2.986	3.635	4.398	5.290	6.328	7.530
7	2.502	2.660	2.826	3.001	3.185	3.379	3.583	4.508	5.629	6.983	8.605	10.541
8	2.853	3.059	3.278	3.511	3.759	4.021	4.300	5.590	7.206	9.217	11.703	14.758
9	3.252	3.518	3.803	4.108	4.435	4.785	5.160	6.931	9.223	12.166	15.917	20.661
10	3.707	4.046	4.411	4.807	5.234	5.695	6.192	8.594	11.806	16.060	21.647	28.925
11	4.226	4.652	5.117	5.624	6.176	6.777	7.430	10.657	15.112	21.199	29.439	40.496
12	4.818	5.350	5.926	6.580	7.288	8.064	8.916	13.215	19.343	27.983	40.037	56.694
13	5.492	6.153	6.886	7.699	8.599	9.596	10.699	16.386	24.759	36.937	54.451	79.372
14	6.261	7.076	7.988	9.007	10.147	11.420	12.839	20.319	31.961	48.757	74.053	111.120
15	7.138	8.137	9.266	10.539	11.974	13.590	15.407	25.196	40.565	64.359	100.712	155.568
16	8.137	9.358	10.748	12.330	14.129	16.172	18.488	31.243	51.923	84.954	136.969	217.795
17	9.276	10.761	12.468	14.426	16.672	19.244	22.186	38.741	66.461	112.139	186.278	304.914
18	10.575	12.375	14.463	16.879	19.673	22.901	26.623	48.039	85.071	148.023	253.338	426.879
19	12.056	14.232	16.777	19.748	23.214	27.252	31.948	59.568	108.890	195.391	344.540	597.630
20	13.743	16.367	19.461	23.106	27.393	32.429	38.338	73.864	139.380	257.916	468.574	836.683
24	23.212	28.625	35.236	43.297	53.109	65.032	79.497	174.631	374.144	783.023	1,603.00	3,214.20
25	26.462	32.919	40.874	50.658	62.669	77.388	95.396	216.542	478.905	1,033.59	2,180.08	4,499.88
30	50.950	66.212	85.850	111.065	143.371	184.675	237.376	634.820	1,645.50	4,142.07	10,143.0	24,201.4
40	188.884	267.864	378.721	533.869	750.378	1,051.67	1,469.77	5,455.91	19,426.7	66,520.8	219,562	700,038
50	700.233	1,083.66	1,670.70	2,566.22	3,927.36	5,988.91	9,100.44	46,890.4	229,350	*	*	*
60	2,595.92	4,384.00	7,370.20	12,335.4	20,555.1	34,105.0	56,347.5	402,996	*	*	*	*

*These interest factors exceed 1,000,000

Table II

Table II — Present Value Interest Factor (PVIF) ($1 at *i*% per period for *n* periods);

$$\text{PVIF} = \frac{1}{(1+i)^n} \; ; \; PV_0 = FV_n \, (\text{PVIF}_{i,n})$$

Period, *n*	1%	2%	3%	4%	5%	6%	7%	8%	9%	10%	11%	12%	13%
0	1.000	1.000	1.000	1.000	1.000	1.000	1.000	1.000	1.000	1.000	1.000	1.000	1.000
1	0.990	0.980	0.971	0.962	0.952	0.943	0.935	0.926	0.917	0.909	0.901	0.893	0.885
2	0.980	0.961	0.943	0.925	0.907	0.890	0.873	0.857	0.842	0.826	0.812	0.797	0.783
3	0.971	0.942	0.915	0.889	0.864	0.840	0.816	0.794	0.772	0.751	0.731	0.712	0.693
4	0.961	0.924	0.889	0.855	0.823	0.792	0.763	0.735	0.708	0.683	0.659	0.636	0.613
5	0.951	0.906	0.863	0.822	0.784	0.747	0.713	0.681	0.650	0.621	0.593	0.567	0.543
6	0.942	0.888	0.838	0.790	0.746	0.705	0.666	0.630	0.596	0.564	0.535	0.507	0.480
7	0.933	0.871	0.813	0.760	0.711	0.665	0.623	0.583	0.547	0.513	0.482	0.452	0.425
8	0.923	0.853	0.789	0.731	0.677	0.627	0.582	0.540	0.502	0.467	0.434	0.404	0.376
9	0.914	0.837	0.766	0.703	0.645	0.592	0.544	0.500	0.460	0.424	0.391	0.361	0.333
10	0.905	0.820	0.744	0.676	0.614	0.558	0.508	0.463	0.422	0.386	0.352	0.322	0.295
11	0.896	0.804	0.722	0.650	0.585	0.527	0.475	0.429	0.388	0.350	0.317	0.287	0.261
12	0.887	0.788	0.701	0.625	0.557	0.497	0.444	0.397	0.356	0.319	0.286	0.257	0.231
13	0.879	0.773	0.681	0.601	0.530	0.469	0.415	0.368	0.326	0.290	0.258	0.229	0.204
14	0.870	0.758	0.661	0.577	0.505	0.442	0.388	0.340	0.299	0.263	0.232	0.205	0.181
15	0.861	0.743	0.642	0.555	0.481	0.417	0.362	0.315	0.275	0.239	0.209	0.183	0.160
16	0.853	0.728	0.623	0.534	0.458	0.394	0.339	0.292	0.252	0.218	0.188	0.163	0.141
17	0.844	0.714	0.605	0.513	0.436	0.371	0.317	0.270	0.231	0.198	0.170	0.146	0.125
18	0.836	0.700	0.587	0.494	0.416	0.350	0.296	0.250	0.212	0.180	0.153	0.130	0.111
19	0.828	0.686	0.570	0.475	0.396	0.331	0.276	0.232	0.194	0.164	0.138	0.116	0.098
20	0.820	0.673	0.554	0.456	0.377	0.312	0.258	0.215	0.178	0.149	0.124	0.104	0.087
24	0.788	0.622	0.492	0.390	0.310	0.247	0.197	0.158	0.126	0.102	0.082	0.066	0.053
25	0.780	0.610	0.478	0.375	0.295	0.233	0.184	0.146	0.116	0.092	0.074	0.059	0.047
30	0.742	0.552	0.412	0.308	0.231	0.174	0.131	0.099	0.075	0.057	0.044	0.033	0.026
40	0.672	0.453	0.307	0.208	0.142	0.097	0.067	0.046	0.032	0.022	0.015	0.011	0.008
50	0.608	0.372	0.228	0.141	0.087	0.054	0.034	0.021	0.013	0.009	0.005	0.003	0.002
60	0.550	0.305	0.170	0.095	0.054	0.030	0.017	0.010	0.006	0.003	0.002	0.001	0.001

Period, *n*	14%	15%	16%	17%	18%	19%	20%	24%	28%	32%	36%	40%
0	1.000	1.000	1.000	1.000	1.000	1.000	1.000	1.000	1.000	1.000	1.000	1.000
1	0.877	0.870	0.862	0.855	0.847	0.840	0.833	0.806	0.781	0.758	0.735	0.714
2	0.769	0.756	0.743	0.731	0.718	0.706	0.694	0.650	0.610	0.574	0.541	0.510
3	0.675	0.658	0.641	0.624	0.609	0.593	0.579	0.524	0.477	0.435	0.398	0.364
4	0.592	0.572	0.552	0.534	0.516	0.499	0.482	0.423	0.373	0.329	0.292	0.260
5	0.519	0.497	0.476	0.456	0.437	0.419	0.402	0.341	0.291	0.250	0.215	0.186
6	0.456	0.432	0.410	0.390	0.370	0.352	0.335	0.275	0.227	0.189	0.158	0.133
7	0.400	0.376	0.354	0.333	0.314	0.296	0.279	0.222	0.178	0.143	0.116	0.095
8	0.351	0.327	0.305	0.285	0.266	0.249	0.233	0.179	0.139	0.108	0.085	0.068
9	0.308	0.284	0.263	0.243	0.225	0.209	0.194	0.144	0.108	0.082	0.063	0.048
10	0.270	0.247	0.227	0.208	0.191	0.176	0.162	0.116	0.085	0.062	0.046	0.035
11	0.237	0.215	0.195	0.178	0.162	0.148	0.135	0.094	0.066	0.047	0.034	0.025
12	0.208	0.187	0.168	0.152	0.137	0.124	0.112	0.076	0.052	0.036	0.025	0.018
13	0.182	0.163	0.145	0.130	0.116	0.104	0.093	0.061	0.040	0.027	0.018	0.013
14	0.160	0.141	0.125	0.111	0.099	0.088	0.078	0.049	0.032	0.021	0.014	0.009
15	0.140	0.123	0.108	0.095	0.084	0.074	0.065	0.040	0.025	0.016	0.010	0.006
16	0.123	0.107	0.093	0.081	0.071	0.062	0.054	0.032	0.019	0.012	0.007	0.005
17	0.108	0.093	0.080	0.069	0.060	0.052	0.045	0.026	0.015	0.009	0.005	0.003
18	0.095	0.081	0.069	0.059	0.051	0.044	0.038	0.021	0.012	0.007	0.004	0.002
19	0.083	0.070	0.060	0.051	0.043	0.037	0.031	0.017	0.009	0.005	0.003	0.002
20	0.073	0.061	0.051	0.043	0.037	0.031	0.026	0.014	0.007	0.004	0.002	0.001
24	0.043	0.035	0.028	0.023	0.019	0.015	0.013	0.006	0.003	0.001	0.001	0.000
25	0.038	0.030	0.024	0.020	0.016	0.013	0.010	0.005	0.002	0.001	0.000	0.000
30	0.020	0.015	0.012	0.009	0.007	0.005	0.004	0.002	0.001	0.000	0.000	0.000
40	0.005	0.004	0.003	0.002	0.001	0.001	0.001	0.000	0.000	0.000	0.000	0.000
50	0.001	0.001	0.001	0.000	0.000	0.000	0.000	0.000	0.000	0.000	0.000	0.000
60	0.000	0.000	0.000	0.000	0.000	0.000	0.000	0.000	0.000	0.000	0.000	0.000

Table III — Future Value of an Annuity Interest Factor (FVIFA) ($1 per period at i% per period for n periods); $FVIFA = \dfrac{(1+i)^n - 1}{i}$; $FVAN_n = PMT(FVIFA_{i,n})$

Period, n	1%	2%	3%	4%	5%	6%	7%	8%	9%	10%	11%	12%	13%
1	1.000	1.000	1.000	1.000	1.000	1.000	1.000	1.000	1.000	1.000	1.000	1.000	1.000
2	2.010	2.020	2.030	2.040	2.050	2.060	2.070	2.080	2.090	2.100	2.110	2.120	2.130
3	3.030	3.060	3.091	3.122	3.152	3.184	3.215	3.246	3.278	3.310	3.342	3.374	3.407
4	4.060	4.122	4.184	4.246	4.310	4.375	4.440	4.506	4.573	4.641	4.710	4.779	4.850
5	5.101	5.204	5.309	5.416	5.526	5.637	5.751	5.867	5.985	6.105	6.228	6.353	6.480
6	6.152	6.308	6.468	6.633	6.802	6.975	7.153	7.336	7.523	7.716	7.913	8.115	8.323
7	7.214	7.434	7.662	7.898	8.142	8.394	8.654	8.923	9.200	9.487	9.783	10.089	10.405
8	8.286	8.583	8.892	9.214	9.549	9.897	10.260	10.637	11.028	11.436	11.859	12.300	12.757
9	9.369	9.755	10.159	10.583	11.027	11.491	11.978	12.488	13.021	13.579	14.164	14.776	15.416
10	10.462	10.950	11.464	12.006	12.578	13.181	13.816	14.487	15.193	15.937	16.722	17.549	18.420
11	11.567	12.169	12.808	13.486	14.207	14.972	15.784	16.645	17.560	18.531	19.561	20.655	21.814
12	12.683	13.412	14.192	15.026	15.917	16.870	17.888	18.977	20.141	21.384	22.713	24.133	25.650
13	13.809	14.680	15.618	16.627	17.713	18.882	20.141	21.495	22.953	24.523	26.212	28.029	29.985
14	14.947	15.974	17.086	18.292	19.599	21.051	22.550	24.215	26.019	27.975	30.095	32.393	34.883
15	16.097	17.293	18.599	20.024	21.579	23.276	25.129	27.152	29.361	31.772	34.405	37.280	40.417
16	17.258	18.639	20.157	21.825	23.657	25.673	27.888	30.324	33.003	35.950	39.190	42.753	46.672
17	18.430	20.012	21.762	23.698	25.840	28.213	30.840	33.750	36.974	40.545	44.501	48.884	53.739
18	19.615	21.412	23.414	25.645	28.132	30.906	33.999	37.450	41.301	45.599	50.396	55.750	61.725
19	20.811	22.841	25.117	27.671	30.539	33.760	37.379	41.446	46.018	51.159	56.939	63.440	70.749
20	22.019	24.297	26.870	29.778	33.066	36.786	40.995	45.762	51.160	57.275	64.203	72.052	80.947
24	26.973	30.422	34.426	39.083	44.502	50.816	58.117	66.765	76.790	88.497	102.174	118.155	136.831
25	28.243	32.030	36.459	41.646	47.727	54.865	63.249	73.106	84.701	98.347	114.413	133.334	155.620
30	34.785	40.568	47.575	56.085	66.439	79.058	94.461	113.283	136.308	164.494	199.021	241.333	293.199
40	48.886	60.402	75.401	95.026	120.080	154.762	199.635	259.057	337.882	442.593	581.826	767.091	1,013.70
50	64.463	84.572	112.797	152.667	209.348	290.336	406.529	573.770	815.084	1,163.91	1,668.77	2,400.02	3,459.51
60	81.670	114.052	163.053	237.991	353.584	533.128	813.520	1,253.21	1,944.79	3,034.82	4,755.07	7,471.64	11,761.9

Period, n	14%	15%	16%	17%	18%	19%	20%	24%	28%	32%	36%	40%
1	1.000	1.000	1.000	1.000	1.000	1.000	1.000	1.000	1.000	1.000	1.000	1.000
2	2.140	2.150	2.160	2.170	2.180	2.190	2.200	2.240	2.280	2.320	2.360	2.400
3	3.440	3.473	3.506	3.539	3.572	3.606	3.640	3.778	3.918	4.062	4.210	4.360
4	4.921	4.993	5.066	5.141	5.215	5.291	5.368	5.684	6.016	6.362	6.725	7.104
5	6.610	6.742	6.877	7.014	7.154	7.297	7.442	8.048	8.700	9.398	10.146	10.846
6	8.536	8.754	8.977	9.207	9.442	9.683	9.930	10.980	12.136	13.406	14.799	16.324
7	10.730	11.067	11.414	11.772	12.142	12.523	12.916	14.615	16.534	18.696	21.126	23.853
8	13.233	13.727	14.240	14.773	15.327	15.902	16.499	19.123	22.163	25.678	29.732	34.395
9	16.085	16.786	17.518	18.285	19.086	19.923	20.799	24.712	29.369	34.895	41.435	49.153
10	19.337	20.304	21.321	22.393	23.521	24.709	25.959	31.643	38.592	47.062	57.352	69.814
11	23.044	24.349	25.733	27.200	28.755	30.404	32.150	40.238	50.399	63.122	78.998	98.739
12	27.271	29.002	30.850	32.824	34.931	37.180	39.580	50.985	65.510	84.320	108.437	139.235
13	32.089	34.352	36.786	39.404	42.219	45.244	48.497	64.110	84.853	112.303	148.475	195.929
14	37.581	40.505	43.672	47.103	50.818	54.841	59.196	80.496	109.612	149.240	202.926	275.300
15	43.842	47.580	51.660	56.110	60.965	66.261	72.035	100.815	141.303	197.997	276.979	386.420
16	50.980	55.717	60.925	66.649	72.939	79.850	87.442	126.011	181.868	262.356	377.692	541.988
17	59.118	65.075	71.673	78.979	87.068	96.022	105.931	157.253	233.791	347.310	514.661	759.784
18	68.394	75.836	84.141	93.406	103.740	115.266	128.117	195.994	300.252	459.449	700.939	1,064.70
19	78.969	88.212	98.603	110.285	123.414	138.166	154.740	244.033	385.323	607.472	954.277	1,491.58
20	91.025	102.444	115.380	130.033	146.628	165.418	186.688	303.601	494.213	802.863	1,298.82	2,089.21
24	158.659	184.168	213.978	248.808	289.494	337.010	392.484	723.461	1,322.66	2,443.82	4,450.00	8,033.00
25	181.871	212.793	249.214	292.105	342.603	402.042	471.981	898.092	1,706.80	3,226.84	6,053.00	11,247.2
30	356.787	434.745	530.321	647.439	790.948	966.712	1,181.88	2,640.92	5,873.23	12,940.9	28,172.3	60,501.1
40	1,342.03	1,779.09	2,360.76	3,134.52	4,163.21	5,529.83	7,343.86	22,728.8	69,377.5	207,874	609,890	*
50	4,994.52	7,217.72	10,435.6	15,089.5	21,813.1	31,515.3	45,497.2	195,373	819,103	*	*	*
60	18,535.1	29,220.0	46,057.5	72,555.0	114,190	179,495	281,733	*	*	*	*	*

*These interest factors exceed 1,000,000

Table IV — Present Value of an Annuity Interest Factor (PVIFA)

($1 per period at i% per period for n periods); $\text{PVIFA} = \dfrac{1 - \dfrac{1}{(1+i)^n}}{i}$; $\text{PVAN}_0 = PMT\,(\text{PVIFA}_{i,n})$

Period, n	1%	2%	3%	4%	5%	6%	7%	8%	9%	10%	11%	12%	13%
1	0.990	0.980	0.971	0.962	0.952	0.943	0.935	0.926	0.917	0.909	0.901	0.893	0.885
2	1.970	1.942	1.913	1.886	1.859	1.833	1.808	1.783	1.759	1.736	1.713	1.690	1.668
3	2.941	2.884	2.829	2.775	2.723	2.673	2.624	2.577	2.531	2.487	2.444	2.402	2.361
4	3.902	3.808	3.717	3.630	3.546	3.465	3.387	3.312	3.240	3.170	3.102	3.037	2.974
5	4.853	4.713	4.580	4.452	4.329	4.212	4.100	3.993	3.890	3.791	3.696	3.605	3.517
6	5.795	5.601	5.417	5.242	5.076	4.917	4.766	4.623	4.486	4.355	4.231	4.111	3.998
7	6.728	6.472	6.230	6.002	5.786	5.582	5.389	5.206	5.033	4.868	4.712	4.564	4.423
8	7.652	7.325	7.020	6.733	6.463	6.210	5.971	5.747	5.535	5.335	5.146	4.968	4.799
9	8.566	8.162	7.786	7.435	7.108	6.802	6.515	6.247	5.995	5.759	5.537	5.328	5.132
10	9.471	8.983	8.530	8.111	7.722	7.360	7.024	6.710	6.418	6.145	5.889	5.650	5.426
11	10.368	9.787	9.253	8.760	8.306	7.887	7.499	7.139	6.805	6.495	6.207	5.938	5.687
12	11.255	10.575	9.954	9.385	8.863	8.384	7.943	7.536	7.161	6.814	6.492	6.194	5.918
13	12.134	11.348	10.635	9.986	9.394	8.853	8.358	7.904	7.487	7.103	6.750	6.424	6.122
14	13.004	12.106	11.296	10.563	9.899	9.295	8.745	8.244	7.786	7.367	6.982	6.628	6.302
15	13.865	12.849	11.938	11.118	10.380	9.712	9.108	8.559	8.061	7.606	7.191	6.811	6.462
16	14.718	13.578	12.561	11.652	10.838	10.106	9.447	8.851	8.312	7.824	7.379	6.974	6.604
17	15.562	14.292	13.166	12.166	11.274	10.477	9.763	9.122	8.544	8.022	7.549	7.120	6.729
18	16.398	14.992	13.754	12.659	11.690	10.828	10.059	9.372	8.756	8.201	7.702	7.250	6.840
19	17.226	15.678	14.324	13.134	12.085	11.158	10.336	9.604	8.950	8.365	7.839	7.366	6.938
20	18.046	16.351	14.877	13.590	12.462	11.470	10.594	9.818	9.128	8.514	7.963	7.469	7.025
24	21.243	18.914	16.936	15.247	13.799	12.550	11.469	10.529	9.707	8.985	8.348	7.784	7.283
25	22.023	19.523	17.413	15.622	14.094	12.783	11.654	10.675	9.823	9.077	8.422	7.843	7.330
30	25.808	22.397	19.600	17.292	15.373	13.765	12.409	11.258	10.274	9.427	8.694	8.055	7.496
40	32.835	27.355	23.115	19.793	17.159	15.046	13.332	11.925	10.757	9.779	8.951	8.244	7.634
50	39.196	31.424	25.730	21.482	18.256	15.762	13.801	12.233	10.962	9.915	9.042	8.304	7.675
60	44.955	34.761	27.676	22.623	18.929	16.161	14.039	12.377	11.048	9.967	9.074	8.324	7.687

Period, n	14%	15%	16%	17%	18%	19%	20%	24%	28%	32%	36%	40%
1	0.877	0.870	0.862	0.855	0.847	0.840	0.833	0.806	0.781	0.758	0.735	0.714
2	1.647	1.626	1.605	1.585	1.566	1.547	1.528	1.457	1.392	1.332	1.276	1.224
3	2.322	2.283	2.246	2.210	2.174	2.140	2.106	1.981	1.868	1.766	1.674	1.589
4	2.914	2.855	2.798	2.743	2.690	2.639	2.589	2.404	2.241	2.096	1.966	1.849
5	3.433	3.352	3.274	3.199	3.127	3.058	2.991	2.745	2.532	2.345	2.181	2.035
6	3.889	3.784	3.685	3.589	3.498	3.410	3.326	3.020	2.759	2.534	2.399	2.168
7	4.288	4.160	4.039	3.922	3.812	3.706	3.605	3.242	2.937	2.678	2.455	2.263
8	4.639	4.487	4.344	4.207	4.078	3.954	3.837	3.421	3.076	2.786	2.540	2.331
9	4.946	4.772	4.607	4.451	4.303	4.163	4.031	3.566	3.184	2.868	2.603	2.379
10	5.216	5.019	4.833	4.659	4.494	4.339	4.193	3.682	3.269	2.930	2.650	2.414
11	5.453	5.234	5.029	4.836	4.656	4.486	4.327	3.776	3.335	2.978	2.683	2.438
12	5.660	5.421	5.197	4.988	4.793	4.611	4.439	3.851	3.387	3.013	2.708	2.456
13	5.842	5.583	5.342	5.118	4.910	4.715	4.533	3.912	3.427	3.040	2.727	2.469
14	6.002	5.724	5.468	5.229	5.008	4.802	4.611	3.962	3.459	3.061	2.740	2.478
15	6.142	5.847	5.575	5.324	5.092	4.876	4.675	4.001	3.483	3.076	2.750	2.484
16	6.265	5.954	5.669	5.405	5.162	4.938	4.730	4.033	3.503	3.088	2.758	2.489
17	6.373	6.047	5.749	5.475	5.222	4.990	4.775	4.059	3.518	3.097	2.763	2.492
18	6.467	6.128	5.818	5.534	5.273	5.033	4.812	4.080	3.529	3.104	2.767	2.494
19	6.550	6.198	5.877	5.584	5.316	5.070	4.844	4.097	3.539	3.109	2.770	2.496
20	6.623	6.259	5.929	5.628	5.353	5.101	4.870	4.110	3.546	3.113	2.772	2.497
24	6.835	6.434	6.073	5.746	5.451	5.182	4.937	4.143	3.562	3.121	2.776	2.499
25	6.873	6.464	6.097	5.766	5.467	5.195	4.948	4.147	3.564	3.122	2.776	2.499
30	7.003	6.566	6.177	5.829	5.517	5.235	4.979	4.160	3.569	3.124	2.778	2.500
40	7.105	6.642	6.233	5.871	5.548	5.258	4.997	4.166	3.571	3.125	2.778	2.500
50	7.133	6.661	6.246	5.880	5.554	5.262	4.999	4.167	3.571	3.125	2.778	2.500
60	7.140	6.665	6.249	5.882	5.555	5.263	5.000	4.167	3.571	3.125	2.778	2.500

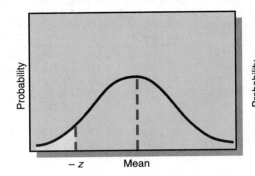

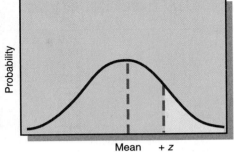

z*	.00	.01	.02	.03	.04	.05	.06	.07	.08	.09
0.0	.5000	.4960	.4920	.4880	.4840	.4801	.4761	.4721	.4681	.4641
.1	.4602	.4562	.4522	.4483	.4443	.4404	.4364	.4325	.4286	.4247
.2	.4207	.4168	.4129	.4090	.4052	.4013	.3974	.3936	.3897	.3859
.3	.3821	.3783	.3745	.3707	.3669	.3632	.3594	.3557	.3520	.3483
.4	.3446	.3409	.3372	.3336	.3300	.3264	.3228	.3192	.3156	.3121
.5	.3085	.3050	.3015	.2981	.2946	.2912	.2877	.2843	.2810	.2776
.6	.2743	.2709	.2676	.2643	.2611	.2578	.2546	.2514	.2483	.2451
.7	.2420	.2389	.2358	.2327	.2296	.2266	.2236	.2206	.2177	.2148
.8	.2119	.2090	.2061	.2033	.2005	.1977	.1949	.1922	.1894	.1867
.9	.1841	.1814	.1788	.1762	.1736	.1711	.1685	.1660	.1635	.1611
1.0	.1587	.1562	.1539	.1515	.1492	.1469	.1446	.1423	.1401	.1379
1.1	.1357	.1335	.1314	.1292	.1271	.1251	.1230	.1210	.1190	.1170
1.2	.1151	.1131	.1112	.1093	.1075	.1056	.1038	.1020	.1003	.0985
1.3	.0968	.0951	.0934	.0918	.0901	.0885	.0869	.0853	.0838	.0823
1.4	.0808	.0793	.0778	.0764	.0749	.0735	.0721	.0708	.0694	.0681
1.5	.0668	.0655	.0643	.0630	.0618	.0606	.0594	.0582	.0571	.0559
1.6	.0548	.0537	.0526	.0516	.0505	.0495	.0485	.0475	.0465	.0455
1.7	.0446	.0436	.0427	.0418	.0409	.0401	.0392	.0384	.0375	.0367
1.8	.0359	.0351	.0344	.0336	.0329	.0322	.0314	.0307	.0301	.0294
1.9	.0287	.0281	.0274	.0268	.0262	.0256	.0250	.0244	.0239	.0233
2.0	.0228	.0222	.0217	.0212	.0207	.0202	.0197	.0192	.0188	.0183
2.1	.0179	.0174	.0170	.0166	.0162	.0158	.0154	.0150	.0146	.0143
2.2	.0139	.0136	.0132	.0129	.0125	.0122	.0119	.0116	.0113	.0110
2.3	.0107	.0104	.0102	.0099	.0096	.0094	.0091	.0089	.0087	.0084
2.4	.0082	.0080	.0078	.0075	.0073	.0071	.0069	.0068	.0066	.0064
2.5	.0062	.0060	.0059	.0057	.0055	.0054	.0052	.0051	.0049	.0048
2.6	.0047	.0045	.0044	.0043	.0041	.0040	.0039	.0038	.0037	.0036
2.7	.0035	.0034	.0033	.0032	.0031	.0030	.0029	.0028	.0027	.0026
2.8	.0026	.0025	.0024	.0023	.0023	.0022	.0021	.0021	.0020	.0019
2.9	.0019	.0018	.0018	.0017	.0016	.0016	.0015	.0015	.0014	.0014
3.0	.0013									
3.05	.0011									
3.10	.0010									
3.25	.0006									
3.50	.00023									
4.00	.00003									
5.00	.0000003									

*Absolute values of z

A

ABC Inventory Classification A method of dividing inventory items into three groups—those with a relatively large dollar value but a small percentage of the total items, those with a small dollar value but a large percentage of the total items, and those items in between.

Absolute Priority A decision rule sometimes used in bankruptcy proceedings that states that the claims of creditors are satisfied before the claims of shareholders.

Accrued Expenses Expenses such as accrued wages, taxes, and interest, which represent liabilities for services rendered to the firm that have not yet been paid for by the firm. As such, they constitute an interest-free source of financing.

Acquisition Any transaction whereby one firm obtains control over another.

Advance Factoring The case where a firm obtains an advance on factored assets prior to the normal collection or due date of the factored accounts.

Affirmative Loan Covenant A portion of a loan agreement that outlines actions a firm's management *agrees to take* as conditions for receiving the loan.

After-Tax Cash Flow (ATCF) Earnings after tax plus noncash charges, such as depreciation and future tax liabilities.

Agency Costs Costs incurred by owners of a firm when the firm is managed by others, including monitoring costs, bonding costs, and any losses that cannot be eliminated economically by monitoring and bonding.

Agency Relationships Occur when one (or more) person (principal) hires another person (agent) to perform a service on the principal's behalf. Agency relationships often lead to agency problems and costs. Two of the most important agency relationships are those between owners (shareholders) and managers and between owners and creditors.

Agent The person who acts on behalf of the principal and has a legal responsibility to act in the best interests of the principal in an agency relationship.

Amalgamation The fusion of two or more firms by transfer of their assets and liabilities to a new firm.

Amortization Schedule A listing of the periodic payments of interest and principal owed on a debt obligation.

Annual Financing Cost (AFC) See *Annual Percentage Rate (APR)*.

Annual Percentage Rate (APR) The simple, annual percentage interest rate for a loan.

Annuity The payment or receipt of a series of equal cash flows per period for a specified amount of time. In an *ordinary annuity,* payments are made at the end of each period. In an *annuity due,* payments are made at the beginning of each period.

Arbitrage The process of simultaneously buying and selling the same or equivalent securities in different markets to take advantage of temporary price differences.

Asset Management Ratios Financial ratios that indicate how efficiently a firm is using its assets.

Assignment The process of informally liquidating a business. Assignment occurs outside the jurisdiction of the bankruptcy courts.

Asymmetric Information The information that managers of a firm, as insiders, have about expected future earnings and cash flows that is not available to outside investors.

Availability (Cheque-Clearing) Float The delay between the time a cheque is deposited in the payee's account and the time the funds are available to be spent.

Average Collection Period The average number of days between when a credit sale is made and when the customer's payment is received.

Average Tax Rate The average tax rate is calculated by dividing the total amount of taxes payable by the taxable income.

B

Bad-Debt Loss Ratio The proportion of the total receivables volume that is never collected by a business.

Balance Sheet A financial statement that lists a firm's assets, liabilities, and shareholders' equity at a point in time.

Balloon Loan A loan that requires a large final payment greater than each of the periodic (principal and interest) payments.

Bank Rate The rate of interest charged to banks that borrow from the Bank of Canada.

Banker's Acceptance A short-term debt instrument issued by a firm as part of a commercial transaction. Payment is guaranteed by a bank that accepts it.

Bankruptcy A situation in which a firm is unable to pay its debts and its assets are turned over to the court for administration.

Bankruptcy and Insolvency Act The federal law governing bankruptcies.

Best Efforts A transaction in which the investment dealers agree to do their best to sell the securities being issued. The issuing firm has no guarantee that the desired amount of money will be raised.

Beta A measure of systematic risk. It indicates the volatility of a security's returns relative to the returns of a broad-based market portfolio of securities.

Bond A long-term debt security that promises to pay the lender a series of periodic interest payments in addition to returning the principal at maturity. Most corporate bonds are offered in $1,000 principal amounts (par value).

Bond Rating An evaluation of a bond's probability of default. This is performed by an outside rating agency, such as DBRS or S&P.

Bond Refunding The redemption of a callable bond issue and replacement with a lower-interest cost issue.

Book Value The accounting value of an asset or a corporation. The book value per common share is equal to the total book value of the firm, or shareholders' equity, divided by the total number of common shares outstanding.

Bought Deal A firm commitment underwriting by investment dealers who agree to buy all of the securities issued by a firm. The underwriters then take the risk that they will be able to sell the securities.

Break-Even Analysis An analysis tool that considers the relationship between sales, fixed costs, variable operating costs, and operating income at various output levels.

Bullet Loan A loan that requires only the periodic payment of interest during the term of the loan, with a final single repayment of principal at maturity.

Business Risk The variability in a firm's operating earnings (EBIT).

C

Call Feature A provision that permits an issuer of bonds (and sometimes preferred shares) to retire the obligation prior to its maturity.

Call Option A contract that gives the holder the right but not the obligation to *buy* an asset at a set price. Also referred to as a *call*.

Call Premium The difference between a bond's call price and its par value.

Call Price The price at which a bond may be retired, or called, prior to its maturity.

Capital Asset Pricing Model (CAPM) A theory that formally describes the nature of the risk-required rate of return relationship on investments in assets.

Capital Budgeting The process of planning for purchases of assets whose cash flows are expected to continue beyond one year.

Capital Cost Allowance (CCA) The depreciation system that must be used for Canadian income tax purposes and capital budgeting decisions. Each depreciable asset is placed in an asset class and the appropriate CCA rate is applied each year to the declining balance in the class.

Capital Expenditure The amount of money spent to purchase a long-term asset, such as a piece of equipment. This cash outlay generally is expected to result in a flow of future cash benefits extending beyond one year in time. (Also called *capital investment.*)

Capital Gain Profit on the sale of a capital asset.

Capital Gains Yield The expected percentage increase in the price of a capital asset.

Capital Loss Loss on the sale of a capital asset.

Capital Markets Financial markets in which long-term securities are bought and sold.

Capital Market Line (CML) The slope of the capital market line measures the equilibrium market price of risk.

Capital Rationing The limiting of capital expenditure projects that meet the firm's criteria for acceptability. Capital rationing may be self-imposed (soft) because of a lack of sufficient managerial resources or externally imposed (hard) by the capital markets that make borrowing too expensive or impossible.

Capital Recovery An annuity amount necessary to recover a capital investment.

Capital Structure The amount of permanent short-term debt, long-term debt, preferred shares, and common equity used to finance a firm.

Capitalization of Cash Flow Valuation Method A method of determining the present value of an asset that is expected to produce a stream of future cash flows. This involves discounting the stream of expected cash flows at an appropriate rate.

Carrying Costs All costs associated with holding items in inventory for a given period of time.

Cash Break-Even Point The level of output (units) required to cover a firm's fixed cash operating outlays.

Cash Budget A projection of a firm's cash receipts and disbursements over some future time period.

Cash Conversion Cycle The net time interval between the collection of cash receipts from sales and the cash payments for the firm's various resources. The cash conversion cycle is calculated by subtracting the payables deferral period from the operating cycle.

Cash Discount A price reduction offered for early payment of an invoice.

Cash Flow The actual amount of cash collected and paid out by a firm.

Cash Flow Forecasting The projection and estimation of a firm's future cash flows.

Cash Flow Statement A financial statement showing the effects of a firm's operating, investing, and financing activities on its cash balance.

Cash Insolvency Analysis A method of financial forecasting that requires the preparation of a detailed cash budget under assumed recessionary conditions.

Certainty Equivalent The amount of cash someone would require with certainty in order to make him or her indifferent between that certain amount and an amount expected to be received with risk at the same point in time.

Characteristic Line A regression line relating the periodic returns for a specific security to the periodic returns on the market portfolio. The slope of this regression line is an estimate of the *beta* of the security—a measure of its systematic risk.

Chattel Mortgage A lien on personal property, such as machinery, as security for the repayment of a loan.

Clientele Effect The concept that investors will tend to be attracted to firms that have dividend policies consistent with the investors' objectives.

Coefficient of Variation The ratio of the standard deviation to the expected value. It provides a relative measure of risk.

Collection Effort The methods a business employs in attempting to collect payment on past-due accounts.

Commercial Paper Short-term unsecured promissory notes issued by major corporations with good credit ratings.

Common-Size Balance Sheet A balance sheet in which a firm's assets and liabilities are expressed as a percentage of total assets, rather than as dollar amounts.

Common-Size Income Statement An income statement in which a firm's income and expense items are expressed as a percentage of net sales, rather than as dollar amounts.

Common Shares A type of equity that represents a residual claim in that dividends are paid out only after more senior financial obligations are fulfilled, such as interest on debt and dividends on preferred shares.

Comparative Analysis An examination of a firm's performance based on one or more financial ratios, which are compared with the financial ratios of competitive firms or with an industry standard or benchmark.

Compensating Balance A minimum (absolute or average) balance that a bank customer agrees to keep in its chequing account. This balance, which the bank can invest in interest-earning assets, compensates the bank for the services rendered to the customer.

Competitive Bidding The process of selling a new security offering to the highest bidding underwriting syndicate of investment dealers.

Composition A situation in which a failing business is permitted to discharge its debt obligations by paying less than the full amounts owed to creditors.

Compound Interest Interest that is paid not only on the principal but also on any interest earned but not withdrawn during earlier periods.

Concentrator Accounts The use of decentralized collection centres to collect customer payments and forward the funds to the concentrator account. This speeds up a firm's collections.

Conditional Sales Contract A financing agreement in which the seller of a piece of equipment retains title until all payments have been made.

Conglomerate Merger A combination of two or more firms in which neither competes directly with the other and no buyer-seller relationship exists.

Consolidation A combination in which all of the combining firms are dissolved and a new firm is formed.

Constant Payout Dividend Policy A dividend policy that aims to pay out a constant percentage of a firm's earnings to shareholders.

Contingent Claim A security whose payoffs depend on the value of another security.

Contingent Project A project whose acceptance depends on the adoption of one or more other projects.

Contribution Margin In *break-even analysis,* the difference between the selling price per unit and the variable cost per unit.

Conversion Premium The amount by which the market value of a convertible security exceeds the higher of its conversion value or straight-bond (preferred) value.

Conversion Price The effective price an investor pays for common shares obtained by converting a convertible security.

Conversion Ratio The number of common shares an investor obtains by converting a convertible security.

Conversion Value The value of a convertible security, based on the value of the underlying common shares.

Convertible Bond A bond that may be exchanged for common shares at the holder's option.

Convertible Security A fixed-income security that may be exchanged for a firm's common shares at the holder's option. The two most common types of convertible securities are *convertible preferred shares* and *convertible debentures.*

Core Earnings A less volatile measure of a firm's earnings used by S&P.

Corporation A business organization that is created as a "legal person" separate and distinct from the individual or individuals who own the firm's shares. The primary characteristics and advantages of incorporating include limited liability for the firm's owners, permanency, and flexibility with respect to making changes in ownership.

Correlation A relative statistical measure of the degree to which two series of numbers, such as the returns from two assets, tend to move or vary together.

Cost of Capital The equilibrium rate of return demanded by investors in the securities issued by a firm.

Coupon Rate of Interest The interest rate stated on a bond. The coupon rate of interest times the par, or principal, value of a bond determines the periodic dollar interest payment received by the bondholder.

Covariance An absolute statistical measure of how closely two variables (such as securities' returns) move together. It measures the degree to which increases (decreases) in the level of one variable tend to be associated with increases (decreases) in the level of another variable over time.

Covered Interest Arbitrage A risk-free transaction in which short-term funds are moved between two currencies to take advantage of interest rate differentials. Exchange rate risk is eliminated through the use of forward contracts.

Credit Period The length of time a credit customer has to pay the account in full.

Credit Standard The criteria a firm uses to screen credit applicants to determine which of its customers should be offered credit and how much.

Creditor A lender to a firm.

Cumulative Dividends A typical feature of preferred shares that requires past-due dividends to be paid before any common share dividends can be paid.

Cumulative Voting A procedure by which shareholders may cast multiple votes for a single candidate for the board of directors. It makes it easier for shareholders with minority views to elect sympathetic board members.

Current Ratio A measure of liquidity that is calculated as current assets divided by current liabilities.

Current Yield The annual periodic payment divided by the current (market) price of a financial asset.

D

Debenture A bond that is not secured by any specific asset but instead by the general credit and earning power of the issuing firm.

Debt Capacity The amount of debt contained in a firm's optimal capital structure.

Debt Ratio A leverage ratio calculated by dividing total debt by total assets that indicates how much of the firm's assets were financed with debt.

Debt Securities Financial assets that represent debt transactions.

Debt-to-Equity Ratio A leverage ratio calculated by dividing total debt by total equity that indicates how much of the firm's capital comes from debt financing.

Declaration Date The day on which the directors of a company declare a dividend.

Default Provisions Permit the lender to insist that the borrower repay the entire loan immediately under certain conditions.

Default Risk The risk that a borrower will fail to make interest payments, principal payments, or both, on a loan.

Default Risk Premium The premium that investors require on securities that have default risk.

Deferred Income Payments received for goods and services that the firm has agreed to deliver at some future date.

Degree of Combined Leverage (DCL) The percentage change in a firm's earnings per share (EPS) resulting from a 1 percent change in sales or output. This also is equal to the degree of operating leverage times the degree of financial leverage used by the firm.

Degree of Financial Leverage (DFL) The percentage change in a firm's EPS resulting from a 1 percent change in EBIT.

Degree of Operating Leverage (DOL) The percentage change in a firm's EBIT resulting from a 1 percent change in sales or output.

Demand Deposits Money deposited in a chequing account.

Depreciation The systematic allocation of the cost of an asset over its expected economic life or some other period of time for financial reporting purposes.

Derivative Securities Financial assets that derive their value from some other security or asset, such as shares, bonds, currencies, commodities, or interest rates. The two broadest categories of derivative securities are options and forward contracts.

Deterministic Model A financial planning model that projects single number estimates of a financial variable or variables without specifying their probability of occurrence.

Direct Lease A lease that is initiated when a firm acquires the use of an asset that it did not previously own.

Direct Placement The sale of an entire security offering to one or more institutional investors rather than the general public. This also is termed a *private placement.*

Direct Quote The home currency price of one unit of a foreign currency.

Direct Transfer The transfer of funds directly from lenders to borrowers, usually facilitated by investment dealers.

Discount Period The length of time a credit customer has to pay the account and still be eligible to take any cash discount offered.

Discount Rate The rate of interest used in the process of finding present values, also called the *required rate of return.*

Discounted Loan A loan in which the bank deducts the interest in advance at the time the loan is made.

Discriminant Analysis A statistical technique designed to classify observations (firms) into two or more predetermined groups based on certain characteristics (such as financial ratios) of the observations.

Diversification The act of investing in a set of financial (securities) or physical assets having different risk-return characteristics.

Divestiture A firm may divest, or sell off, a division that no longer fits its strategy.

Dividend Gross-Up and Tax Credit A method used in Canada to partially compensate investors for the taxes already paid by the corporation. According to the tax rules in effect in 2003, the cash dividend received by the investor is grossed-up by 25% and the investor is allowed a tax credit (reduction) of 13.33% of the grossed-up amount.

Dividend Payout Ratio A ratio calculated by dividing the dividend per share by the earnings per share.

Dividend Reinvestment Plan (DRP or DRIP) A plan that allows shareholders to have their cash dividends automatically reinvested in additional shares.

Dividend Yield The annual dividend payment divided by the market price of the share.

Divisional Cost of Capital A risk-adjusted discount rate for investments being evaluated by a firm's various divisions. It reflects both the differential required returns of equity investors, estimated from the security market line, and a division's differential debt capacity.

Draft A financial instrument that is similar to a cheque except it is not payable on demand. Rather a draft must be presented to the issuer for approval before a payment is made.

E

Earnings after Taxes (EAT) A firm's earnings after taxes is the amount available for dividends to shareholders or for reinvestment in the firm.

Earnings before Interest and Taxes (EBIT) A firm's earnings before payment of interest and taxes (also called *operating earnings*).

Earnings per Share (EPS) A firm's earnings per share is calculated by dividing the earnings after tax by the number of shares outstanding.

EBIT-EPS Indifference Point That level of EBIT where the earnings per share of a firm are the same, regardless of which of two alternative capital structures is employed.

Economic Exposure The extent to which changes in *real* exchange rates lead to a change in the value of a firm's operating cash flows, and hence its value. Also known as *operating exposure.*

Economic Order Quantity (EOQ) The quantity of an inventory item that should be ordered to minimize total inventory costs.

Economic Value Added (EVA) The difference between operating profits after tax and the cost of capital that indicates a firm's success in creating value for shareholders.

Effective Annual Rate (EAR) The effective annual rate of interest paid by the borrower or earned by the lender.

Efficient Capital Market A financial market in which new information is quickly reflected in security prices in an unbiased manner.

Efficient Frontier The set of efficient portfolios.

Efficient Portfolio A portfolio that, for a given standard deviation, has the highest expected return, or, for a given expected return, has the lowest standard deviation.

Equity Multiplier A ratio calculated by dividing total assets by total equity.

Equity Securities Financial assets that represent ownership transactions.

Equivalent Annual Annuity A method for making capital budgeting decisions involving projects having different useful lives.

Euro The European single currency that went into circulation in 2002.

Eurobond An international bond issued outside the country in whose currency the bonds are denominated.

Eurocurrency A currency that is deposited in a bank outside of the country of origin.

Eurodollars US dollars deposited in banks outside the United States.

Exchange Rate The rate at which a currency can be converted into another currency.

Exchange Ratio The number of shares an acquiring company must give, or *exchange,* for each share of an acquired company in a merger.

Ex-Dividend Date The date on which the right to the most recently declared dividend no longer goes along with the sale of the shares.

Exercise Price The price at which an option holder can purchase or sell the underlying asset, such as common shares. This also is termed the *strike price.*

Expectations Theory A theory that posits that long-term interest rates are a function of expected short-term interest rates.

Expected Market Return The return investors expect to earn on shares with average risk, i.e., a beta of 1.0.

Expected Return The benefits (price appreciation and distributions) an investor anticipates receiving from an investment.

Expected Value A statistical measure of the mean or average value of the possible outcomes. Operationally, it is defined as the weighted average of the possible outcomes with the weights being the probability of occurrence.

Ex-Rights A share sells ex-rights when purchasers no longer receive the *rights* along with the shares purchased.

Extendible Bonds Bonds whose maturity may be extended by the investor.

Extension A situation in which a failing business is permitted to lengthen the amount of time it has to meet its obligations with creditors.

F

Factoring The sale of a firm's accounts receivable to a financial institution known as a *factor.*

Field Warehouse Financing Agreement A loan agreement in which the inventory being pledged as collateral is segregated from the firm's other inventories and stored on its premises under the control of a field warehouse company.

Fair Value The value of a share determined by the discounted cash flow method.

FIFO The acronym for the *first-in, first-out* inventory valuation method. The method assumes that a firm uses the oldest items in the inventory first. Thus, they are *priced out* of the inventory based on the oldest inventory acquisition costs rather than the most recent.

Financial Analysis The utilization of a group of analytical techniques, including financial ratio analysis, to determine the strengths, weaknesses, and direction of a firm's performance.

Financial Distress Costs The costs incurred to avoid bankruptcy plus the direct and indirect costs incurred if a firm files for bankruptcy protection.

Financial Forecasting The projection and estimation of a firm's future financial statements.

Financial Lease A *noncancellable* agreement that obligates the lessee to make payments to the lessor for a predetermined period of time. These payments are usually sufficient to amortize the full cost of the asset plus provide the lessor with a reasonable rate of return on its investment in the asset.

Financial Leverage The extent to which a firm is financed by securities having fixed costs or charges, such as debt and preferred shares.

Financial Leverage Management Ratios Financial ratios that measure the degree to which a firm is financing its assets with fixed-charge sources of funds such as debt, preferred shares, or leases.

Financial Planning Model A computerized representation of some aspect of a firm's financial planning process.

Financial Ratio A statistical yardstick that relates two numbers generally taken from a firm's income statement, balance sheet, or both at a specific point in time.

Financial Risk The additional variability of a firm's earnings per share and the increased probability of insolvency that result from the use of fixed-cost sources of funds, such as debt and preferred shares. In general, the more financial leverage a firm uses, the greater is its financial risk.

Financial Slack Highly liquid assets (i.e., cash and marketable securities) plus unused debt capacity that allow a firm to take advantage of any attractive investment opportunities.

Financial Structure The amount of current liabilities, long-term debt, preferred shares, and common equity used to finance a firm.

Finder's Fee A commission paid to an investment dealer who finds a buyer for a direct placement.

Fisher Effect A relationship indicating that nominal (and risk-free) interest rates are approximately equal to the sum of the real interest rate and the expected inflation rate.

Fixed-Asset Turnover Ratio An asset management ratio calculated by dividing sales by net fixed assets that shows how well a firm is using its fixed assets to generate sales.

Fixed Costs Costs that do not vary as the level of a firm's output changes.

Fixed-Income Securities Financial assets, such as bonds and preferred shares, that pay contractually fixed periodic payments to investors.

Float The difference between an account balance as shown on the bank's books and as shown on the firm's books. Float represents the net effect of the delays in the payment of cheques the firm writes and the collection of cheques the firm receives.

Floating Lien An inventory loan in which the lender receives a security interest or general claim on all of a company's inventory.

Flotation Cost The cost of issuing new securities. This includes both underwriting expenses and other issue expenses, such as printing and legal fees.

Fluctuating Current Assets Current assets affected by the seasonal or cyclical nature of the firm's sales.

Foreign Bond An international bond denominated in the currency of the country in which it is issued. The issuer, however, is from another country.

Formal Virtual Markets Secondary securities markets that have listing requirements but no physical place of business, such as NASDAQ.

Forward Contract A contract calling for the delivery of a specified amount of some item at a future point in time at a price set at the present time. Compared to *futures contracts*, forward contracts are not liquid, can be customized with regard to the date or amount, and carry performance risk.

Forward Rate The rate of exchange between two currencies being bought and sold for delivery at a *future* date.

Free Cash Flow That portion of a firm's total cash flow that is available to pay interest, pay dividends, or make capital investments.

Functional Currency The currency in which the majority of a firm's transactions are denominated. The US dollar is the functional currency for many Canadian firms.

Future Value The value at some future point in time of a present payment (or a series of payments) evaluated at the appropriate interest (growth) rate.

Futures Contract A contract calling for the delivery of a standardized quantity and quality of some item, such as a foreign currency, crude oil, or securities, at a future point in time at a price set at the present time.

G

Generally Accepted Accounting Principles (GAAP) A broad set of accounting rules followed in preparing financial statements.

Going-Concern Value The value of a firm, assuming that the firm's organization and assets remain intact and are used to generate future income and cash flows.

Golden Parachute A large top management bonus payable in case of early (involuntary) retirement.

Goodwill An intangible asset equal to the premium over fair market value of the acquired assets that is paid for a target company in a merger.

Greenmail An operation whereby a firm's management buys back a block of shares at a premium over the market price from another firm to stop it from making a takeover.

Green Shoe Option An overallotment of shares to the underwriters of new issues that gives them an incentive to work harder.

Gross Profit Margin Ratio A profitability ratio calculated by dividing sales minus cost of sales that indicates how efficiently the firm is managing the production process.

Growth Annuity In a growth annuity each succeeding payment grows by a constant percentage of the preceding payment.

Growth Perpetuity A growth annuity that lasts forever.

H

Half-Year Convention The income tax law assumes that all assets purchased during any tax year are actually placed into service in the middle of the year, regardless of the actual date.

Hedge A transaction in which a position is taken in another market, such as the forward or futures market, to offset the risk associated with a position in the current cash (spot) market.

Holding Company A corporation that controls the voting power of one or more other firms.

Holding Period Return (HPR) The change in price from holding an asset (security) plus distributions received from the asset divided by the initial price at which the asset was acquired.

Horizontal Merger A combination of two or more firms that compete directly with each other.

Hurdle Rate The minimum acceptable rate of return from an investment project. For projects of average risk, it usually is equal to the firm's cost of capital.

I

Income Bond A bond that pays interest only if the firm earns sufficient income.

Income Statement A financial statement that indicates how a firm performed during a period of time.

Indenture The contract between the issuing firm and the lenders in a debt obligation.

Independent Project A project whose acceptance or rejection does not result directly in the elimination of other projects from consideration.

Indirect Quote The foreign currency price of one unit of the home currency.

Indirect Transfers The transfer of funds from savers to investors through financial intermediaries, such as banks.

Informational Content The concept that, for a firm following a stable dividend policy, changes in dividend payments convey information (i.e., a signal) to investors concerning management's expectations about the firm's future profitability.

Initial Public Offering (IPO) The first public sale of a firm's shares to the public.

Insolvency A situation in which either a firm's liabilities exceed its assets or the firm is unable to pay its creditors as required.

Institutional Brokers Estimate System (IBES) A service providing summaries of the earnings growth rate forecasts of security analysts.

Interest The return earned by or the amount paid to an investor who foregoes current consumption or alternative investments and "rents" money to a business, a bank, an individual, the government.

Interest Rate Parity (IRP) The theory that the percentage differential between the spot and the forward rate for a currency quoted in terms of another currency is equal to the approximate difference in interest rates in the two countries over the same time horizon.

Interest Rate Risk The variation in the market price (and hence in the real-ized rate of return or yield) of a security that arises from changes in interest rates.

Interest Rate Swap The exchange of floating rate interest payments for fixed-rate interest payments, or vice versa.

Internal Rate of Return (IRR) The discount rate that equates the present value of net cash flows from a project with the present value of the net investment. It is the discount rate that gives the project a net present value equal to zero.

International Bond A bond issued outside the country of the borrower.

International Fisher Effect (IFE) The theory that the difference in interest rates between two countries should be offset by equal but opposite changes in the future spot exchange rate.

Intrinsic Value The value of a share determined by the discounted cash flow method.

Inventory Conversion Period The length of time required to produce and sell the product.

Inventory Cycle The time between placement of successive orders of an item.

Inventory Loan A short-term loan where the firm's inventory is used as collateral.

Inventory Turnover Ratio An asset management ratio calculated as cost of sales divided by average inventory that indicates how fast a firm is selling its products.

Investment Dealer/Banker A financial institution that underwrites and sells new securities. Investment dealers help firms to obtain new financing.

Investment Opportunity Curve A graph or listing showing a firm's investment opportunities (projects) ranked from highest to lowest expected rate of return.

J

Joint Venture A business combination in which two unaffiliated firms contribute financial, physical, and/or personnel assets to a new firm formed to engage in a specific economic activity.

Junk Bond A high-yield debt security issued by a company with a low credit rating.

Just-in-Time (JIT) Inventory Management System An approach to inventory and production management in which required inventory items are supplied exactly as needed by production.

L

Large Value Transfer System (LVTS) An electronic transfer method for settling transactions between and among Canadian chartered banks.

Lead Time The time between when an order is placed for an item and when the item actually is received in inventory.

Lease A contract that allows an individual or a firm to make economic use of an asset for a stated period of time without obtaining an ownership interest in it.

Legal Insolvency A situation in which the recorded value of a firm's assets is less than its liabilities.

Lessee The user and renter of the property in a lease transaction.

Lessor The property owner who collects rental payments from the lessee in a lease transaction.

Leveraged Buyout (LBO) A transaction in which the buyer of a firm borrows a large portion of the purchase price, using the purchased assets as partial collateral for the loans.

Leveraged Lease A type of financial lease in which the lessor borrows up to 80 percent of the cost of the leased asset on a nonrecourse basis. The lessor receives the full tax benefits of ownership. This is also sometimes called a *third-party equity lease* or a *tax lease.*

LIFO The acronym for the *last-in, first-out* inventory valuation method. The method assumes that a firm uses the most recently acquired items in the inventory first. Thus, they are *priced out* of the inventory based on the most recent inventory acquisition costs rather than the oldest.

Limited Liability Liability for the debts of a business venture that is limited to the amount invested.

Line of Credit An agreement that permits a firm to borrow funds up to a predetermined limit at any time during the life of the agreement.

Liquidation Value The value of a firm, assuming that it sells all its assets and stops using them to generate future income and cash flows.

Liquidity The ability of a firm to meet its cash obligations as they come due.

Liquidity Preference Theory See *Maturity Risk Premium Theory.*

Liquidity Ratios Financial ratios that indicate a firm's ability to meet short-term financial obligations.

Listed Security Exchanges Organized secondary security markets, such as the Toronto Stock Exchange (TSX) that operate at designated places of business.

Lockbox A post office box maintained by a firm's bank close to customers to speed up the collection of payments from customers.

London Interbank Offer Rate (LIBOR) The interest rate at which banks in the Eurocurrency market lend to each other.

M

Mail Float The delay between the time a payment is sent to the payee through the mail and the time that payment arrives at the payee's office.

Marginal Cost of Capital The weighted after-tax cost of the next dollar of capital the firm expects to raise to finance a new investment project.

Marginal Tax Rate The tax rate on the next dollar of taxable income earned by a taxpayer.

Market Portfolio The portfolio of securities consisting of all available securities weighted by their respective market values.

Market Segmentation Theory A theory that posits that capital markets are segmented by maturity.

Market Value (of a security) The price at which a security trades in the financial marketplace.

Market Value Added (MVA) The difference between the market value of a firm's debt and equity securities and the capital that has been invested in the firm.

Market Price-to-Book Value Ratio A ratio calculated by dividing the market price per share by the book value per share.

Marketability Risk The ability of an investor to buy and sell an asset (security) quickly and without a significant loss of value.

Marketability Risk Premium The additional return investors require because a security has marketability risk.

Marketable Securities Short-term investments in which firms often invest their temporarily idle cash.

Market-Based Ratios Financial ratios that measure the market's (investors') assessment of the risk and performance of a firm.

Matching Approach A financing plan in which the maturity structure of a firm's liabilities is made to correspond exactly to the life of its assets.

Maturity Risk Premium Theory A theory that posits that required returns on long-term securities tend to be higher than returns on short-term securities.

Merger The fusion of two or more firms into one of the constituent firms that becomes the surviving company.

Misdirected Funds Funds that cross an international border unintentionally.

Modified Accelerated Cost Recovery System (MACRS) The depreciation system that must be used in the United States for income tax purposes and capital budgeting decisions.

Modified Internal Rate of Return (MIRR) The modified IRR assumes reinvestment of the periodic cash flows at the cost of capital rather than the internal rate of return. It is calculated by equating the PV of the costs of a project with the PV of the terminal value of the cash flows at the end of the project's life.

Money Markets Financial markets in which short-term securities are bought and sold.

Mortgage Bond A bond secured by a pledge of a specific asset or group of assets.

Multijurisdictional Disclosure System (MJDS) A joint Canada-US system that allows issuing firms to use the registration statements and prospectuses of their home country for sales of their securities in the other country.

Multilateral Netting A process of international cash management designed to minimize the cost associated with misdirected funds.

Multinational Corporation A firm with direct investments in more than one country.

Multiple Internal Rates of Return Two or more internal rates of return from the same project. This occurs only with nonnormal projects whose cash flow patterns contain more than one sign change.

Mutually Exclusive Project A project whose acceptance precludes the acceptance of one or more alternative projects.

N

Negative Loan Covenant A portion of a loan agreement that outlines actions a firm's management *agrees not to take* during the term of the loan.

Negative Pledge Clause A clause found in nearly all unsecured loans. It is designed to keep other lenders from interfering with the immediate lender's claims on the assets of the firm.

Negotiated Underwriting A process whereby a firm wishing to sell new securities to the public negotiates the terms of the underwriting with the investment dealers.

Net Advantage to Leasing (NAL) The NAL method compares the NPV cost of leasing with the NPV cost of owning the asset to see if it is advantageous (cheaper) for the firm to lease an asset rather than buy it. This is a financing decision that is made after the firm has completed the capital budgeting decision process and decided that the asset should be acquired.

Net (Operating) Cash Flow Cash inflow minus cash outflow. It is measured as the change in net operating earnings after taxes plus the change in depreciation minus the change in net working capital requirements associated with a particular investment project.

Net Investment (NINV) The net cash outlay required at the beginning of an investment project.

Net Present Value (NPV) The present value of the stream of net cash flows resulting from a project, discounted at the appropriate discount rate (usually the firm's cost of capital), minus the project's net investment. It is used to evaluate, rank, and select from among various investment projects according to the contribution of an investment to shareholders' wealth.

Net Profit Margin Ratio A profitability ratio calculated by dividing earnings after tax by sales.

Net Working Capital The difference between a firm's current assets and current liabilities. The term *net working capital* is frequently used interchangeably with *working capital*.

Nexus of Contracts A view of the firm as a focal point of contracts among various stakeholders.

Nonnotification Basis The customer is not notified that the receivable has been pledged by the firm.

Normal Project A project whose cash flow stream requires an initial outlay of funds followed by a series of positive net cash inflows. This is sometimes called a *conventional project*.

O

Operating Cycle Includes the three primary activities of purchasing resources, producing the product, and distributing (selling) the product. The operating cycle is calculated by summing the inventory conversion period and the receivables conversion period.

Operating Lease A *cancellable* lease agreement that provides the lessee with the use of an asset on a period-by-period basis. This sometimes is called a *service* or *maintenance lease*, especially if the lessor provides maintenance services as part of the lease contract.

Operating Leverage The extent to which a firm uses assets having fixed costs.

Operational Cash Flow per Share (OPS) The operational cash flow per share is calculated by dividing cash flow from operations by the number of shares outstanding.

Opportunity Cost The rate of return that can be earned on funds if they are invested in the *next best* alternative investment.

Optimal Capital Budget The level of capital spending at which a firm's investment opportunity curve just intersects its marginal cost of capital curve.

Optimal Capital Structure The capital structure that minimizes a firm's weighted cost of capital and, therefore, maximizes the value of the firm.

Optimization Model A financial planning model that determines the values of financial decision variables that maximize (or minimize) some objective function such as profits (or costs).

Option A contract (often in the form of a security) that gives its holder the right but not the obligation to buy (call) or sell (put) an asset at a set price during a specified time period.

Ordering Costs All costs associated with placing and receiving an order.

Over-the-Counter (OTC) Securities Markets A network of security dealers connected by a communications system of telephones and computer terminals that provides price quotations on individual securities.

Overnight Rate The interest rate charged on loans from one chartered bank to another.

P

Par Value (Bond) The amount of principal borrowed (usually $1,000) and due at maturity.

Par Value (Preferred or Common Shares) An arbitrary value assigned by the issuing firm.

Partnership A business organization in which two or more persons form a business with the intention of making a profit. In a *general partnership,* each partner has unlimited liability for the debts of the firm. *Limited partnerships* allow one or more partners to have limited liability.

Passive Residual Dividend Policy A theory of dividend policy that suggests that a firm should retain its earnings as long as there are investment opportunities available promising a rate of return higher than the required rate of return.

Payables Deferral Period The length of time a firm is able to deter payment on its resource purchases.

Payback (PB) Period The period of time required for the cumulative cash inflows from a project to equal the initial cash outlay.

Pecking Order Theory A capital structure theory indicating that firms prefer internal financing (retained earnings) to external financing (new security issues) and that, if external financing is required, debt is preferred to new common share issues.

Percentage of Sales Forecasting Method A method of estimating the additional financing that will be needed to support a given future sales level.

Performance Shares Shares given to executives depending on their performance.

Permanent Current Assets Current assets held to meet the firm's long-term minimum needs.

Perpetual Bond A bond that has no maturity date.

Perpetuity A financial instrument that pays an equal cash flow per period into the indefinite future (that is, infinity).

Pledging of Accounts Receivable A short-term borrowing arrangement with a financial institution in which a loan is secured by the borrower's accounts receivable.

Poison Pill An action taken by a firm to make itself unattractive to potential takeovers.

Pooling of Interests Method A method of accounting for mergers in which the acquired firm's assets are recorded on the acquiring firm's books at their cost when originally acquired. No goodwill account is created under the pooling method.

Portfolio A collection of two or more financial (securities) or physical assets.

Post-Audit A capital budgeting procedure that consists of comparing *actual* cash flows from a project with *projected* cash flows that were estimated at the time the project was adopted.

Precautionary Motive The future cash flows and the ability to borrow additional funds on short notice are often uncertain. Hence, a motive to hold liquid asset balances necessary to meet unexpected requirements for cash.

Preemptive Right A provision contained in some corporate charters that gives common shareholders the right to buy on a pro rata basis any new common shares sold by the firm.

Preferred Shares A type of equity with a claim on earnings and assets of a firm—in the form of a (normally) fixed periodic dividend payment— that takes precedence over the claims of common shareholders.

Present Value The value today of a future payment (or a series of future payments) evaluated at the appropriate discount rate.

Price-to-Earnings Ratio A ratio calculated by dividing the market price per share by the earnings per share that serves as an indicator of the riskiness of the firm.

Primary Markets Financial markets in which *new* securities from an issuing firm are bought and sold for the first time. Investment dealers are active in the primary markets.

Prime Rate The lowest rate normally charged by banks on loans made to their most creditworthy business customers.

Principal (1) An amount of money that has been borrowed or invested.

Principal (2) In an agency relationship, the party who employs someone else, the agent, to perform service on behalf of the principal.

Pro Forma Financial Statements Financial statements that project the results of some *assumed* event, rather than an *actual* event.

Probabilistic Model A financial planning model that uses probability distributions as inputs and generates a probability distribution for financial variables as output.

Processing Float The delay between receipt of payment from a payer and the deposit of that receipt in the payee's account.

Profitability Index (PI) The ratio of the present value of net cash flows over the life of a project to the net investment. It is used to evaluate, rank, and select from among various investment projects. It is used frequently in capital rationing situations.

Profitability Ratios Financial ratios that measure the total effectiveness of a company's management in generating profits.

Promissory Note A formal short-term credit obligation that states the amount to be paid and the due date.

Prompt Offering Prospectus (POP) System A method whereby large firms can issue securities over a period of time with the same registration statement and prospectus.

Prospectus A document that contains information about a company's legal, operational, and financial position. It is prepared for the benefit of prospective investors in a new security issued by the firm.

Purchase Method A method of accounting for mergers in which the total value paid or exchanged for the acquired firm's assets is recorded on the acquiring firm's books. Any difference between the acquired assets' fair market value and their purchase price is recorded as goodwill.

Purchasing Power Parity (PPP) A theory that posits that the law of one price for the same product in different countries will be the same in each country after making the appropriate conversion from one currency into the other.

Purchasing Syndicate A *group* of investment dealers who agree to underwrite a new security issue in order to spread the risk of underwriting.

Put-Call Parity The price of a share equals the price of the same share synthetically created. (See Equation 17A.2.) The synthetic share consists of buying one European call, selling one European put with the same strike price and time to maturity, and buying a risk-free asset whose maturity value is the strike price.

Put Option A contract that gives the holder the right but not the obligation to *sell* an asset at a set price during a specified period of time. Also referred to as a *put*.

Q

Quick Ratio A liquidity ratio calculated as current assets minus inventories divided by current liabilities.

R

Rate of Interest The percentage on the principal that the borrower pays the lender per time period as compensation for foregoing other investment or consumption opportunities.

Real Interest Rate An interest rate adjusted for the effects of inflation.

Real Option Managerial opportunities to make decisions that will impact the expected cash flows of a project, their timing, or the future acceptability of the project. Real options include abandonment options, investment timing (delay) options, shutdown options, growth options, and flexibility (designed-in) options.

Receivables Conversion Period The length of time required to collect sales receipts. Receivables conversion period is another name for the *average collection period*.

Receivables Turnover Ratio An asset management ratio calculated by dividing 365 by the average collection period that indicates how fast a firm is collecting its accounts receivable.

Record Date The date on which a firm makes a list from its stock transfer books of those shareholders who are eligible to receive the declared dividend.

Reinvestment Rate The rate of return at which cash flows from an investment project are assumed to be reinvested from year to year. The reinvestment rate may vary, depending on the investment opportunities available to the firm.

Reinvestment Rate Risk Risk that occurs when a bond issue matures (or is called) and because of a decline in interest rates, the owner has to reinvest the principal at a lower coupon rate.

Registration Statement An information disclosure document required of firms that issue securities.

Relative Purchasing Power Parity The theory that the spot exchange rate between two currencies should change by an amount approximately equal to the difference in expected inflation rates in the two countries.

Reorder Point The inventory level at which an order should be placed for replenishment of an item.

Replacement Chains A method for making capital budgeting decisions involving projects that have different useful lives. It assumes that the original investment can be replicated indefinitely so as to match the useful life of an alternative project.

Repurchase Agreement An arrangement with a bank or securities dealer in which an investor acquires certain short-term securities subject to a commitment that the securities will be repurchased by the bank or securities dealer on a specified date.

Required Rate of Return The rate used to value a stream of expected cash flows from an asset (also called the *discount rate*). The riskier the expected cash flows from the asset, the higher the required rate of return.

Restrictive Loan Covenant A portion of a loan agreement that limits the scope of certain actions a firm may take during the term of the loan.

Retractable Bond A bond that allows the investor to reduce or shorten the maturity.

Return on Investment Ratio A profitability ratio calculated by dividing earnings after tax by total assets that indicates how profitably the firm uses its assets.

Return on Total Equity A profitability ratio calculated by dividing earnings after tax by total equity that indicates how profitably the firm uses its assets that were financed by equity.

Reverse Stock Split A stock split in which the number of outstanding shares is reduced.

Revolving Credit Agreement A binding agreement that commits a bank to make loans to a firm up to a predetermined credit limit. To obtain this type of commitment from a bank, a firm usually pays a *commitment fee* based on the unused portion of the pledged funds.

Right A short-term option issued by a firm that permits an existing shareholder to buy a specified number of shares at a specified price (the *subscription price*), which is below the current market price.

Rights Offering The sale of new common shares by distributing stock purchase rights to a firm's existing shareholders. This also is termed a *privileged subscription*.

Rights-On A share sells rights-on when purchasers receive the *rights* along with the shares purchased.

Risk The possibility that actual future returns will deviate from expected returns; the variability of returns.

Risk-Adjusted Discount Rate (RADR) A discount rate that reflects the risk associated with a particular project. In capital budgeting, a higher risk-adjusted rate is used to discount cash flows for riskier projects, whereas a lower risk-adjusted rate is used to discount cash flows for less risky projects.

Risk-Free Rate The rate of return on securities that are free of default risk, such as T-bills.

Risk Premium The difference between the required rate of return on a risky investment and the rate of return on a risk-free asset, such as T-bills. Components include maturity risk, default risk, seniority risk, and marketability risk.

S

Sale and Leaseback A lease that is initiated when a firm sells an asset it owns to another firm and simultaneously leases the asset back for its own use.

Scenario Analysis A procedure used to evaluate the change in some objective, such as net present value, to simultaneous changes in several variables influencing that objective, such as price, unit sales volume, and operating costs.

Seasonal Datings Credit terms under which the buyer of seasonal merchandise is encouraged to take delivery well before the peak sales period. Payment on the purchase is deferred until after the peak sales period.

Secondary Markets Financial markets in which *existing* securities are offered for resale. The Toronto Stock Exchange (TSX) is a secondary market.

Secured Short-Term Debt Short-term debt whereby a borrower pledges certain specified assets—such as accounts receivable, inventory, or fixed assets—as collateral.

Security Agreement A contract between the lender and the firm specifying the collateral held against the loan.

Security Market Line (SML) The relationship between systematic risk and required rates of return for individual securities.

Semistrong-Form Market Efficiency A situation in which no investor can expect to earn excess returns based on an investment strategy using any public information.

Senior Debt Debt that has a higher claim on a firm's earnings and/or assets than junior debt.

Seniority Risk Premium The additional return that investors require on junior securities.

Sensitivity Analysis A method of analysis in which a financial planning model is rerun to determine the effect on the output variable(s) (for example, profit) of given changes in the input variable(s) (for example, sales). Sensitivity analysis is sometimes called *what if* analysis.

Shareholder Wealth Present value of the expected future returns to the owners (that is, shareholders) of the firm. It is equal to the market value (price) per common share times the number of shares outstanding.

Shareholders' Equity The total of a firm's common shares, contributed capital (if any), and retained earnings (if any) accounts from the balance sheet. It sometimes is called the *book value* of the firm, *owners' equity, stockholders' equity,* or *net worth.*

Shark Repellents Anti-takeover measures to deter hostile takeovers.

Shelf Registration A method whereby large firms can issue securities over a period of time with the same registration statement and prospectus. (See also *Prompt Offering Prospectus.*)

Signal Changes in investment, financing or dividend policies that convey information to outside investors concerning management's assessment of the expected future returns of the company.

Simple Interest Interest paid or earned on the principal only.

Simulation A financial planning tool that models some event, such as the cash flows from an investment project. A computerized simulation is one technique used to assess the risk associated with a particular project.

Sinking Fund An annuity amount that must be invested each period (year) to produce a future value.

Sole Proprietorship A business owned by one person. The owner of a sole proprietorship has unlimited liability for debts incurred by the business.

Spinoff A spinoff is effected by distributing shares in a subsidiary to shareholders of the parent firm.

Spot Rate The rate of exchange between two currencies being bought and sold for *immediate* delivery.

Stable Dollar Dividend Policy A dividend policy that aims to pay out a constant dollar dividend to shareholders.

Stakeholders The constituent groups in a firm, including shareholders, bondholders, suppliers, customers, employees, community neighbours, and creditors, as well as governments.

Standard Deviation A statistical measure of the dispersion, or variability, of possible outcomes around the expected value, or mean. Operationally, it is defined as the square root of the weighted average squared deviations of possible outcomes from the expected value. The standard deviation provides an absolute measure of risk.

Standby Underwriting An agreement by an investment dealer to purchase all the shares that are not sold to rights holders. The investment dealer then resells the shares to the public and the firm receives the total amount of funds needed, even if the existing shareholders do not all exercise their rights.

Stock Dividend A payment of additional shares of common stock to shareholders.

Stock Split The issuance of a number of new shares in exchange for each old share held by a shareholder.

Stockout Cost The costs that occur when a business is unable to fill orders because the demand for an item is greater than the amount currently available in inventory.

Straight-Bond Value The value a convertible debt security would have if it did not possess the conversion feature, also referred to as the *investment value.*

Strong-Form Market Efficiency A situation in which no investor can expect to consistently earn excess returns because security prices reflect all information, both public and private.

Subordinated Debenture A bond with a claim on the issuing firm's assets that is junior to other forms of debt in the event of a liquidation. The claims

of subordinated debenture holders can be met only after all the claims of senior creditors have been met.

Swap A contractual agreement between two parties to make periodic payments to each other. They can be interest rate or currency swaps. Fixed-rate interest can be swapped for floating-rate interest. Payments in one currency can be swapped for another currency.

Systematic Risk That portion of the variability of an individual security's returns that is caused by the factors affecting the market as a whole. This also is called *nondiversifiable risk.*

Systematic Risk of a Project The risk contribution of a project to the systematic risk of the firm.

T

Takeover The purchase by one firm of the majority of another firm's shares.

Target Capital Structure The proportions of permanent short-term debt, long-term debt, preferred shares, and common equity that a firm desires to have in its capital structure.

Tax Deduction An amount subtracted from taxable income. For a corporation with a 40 percent marginal tax rate, a $100 tax deduction reduces taxable income by $100 and reduces taxes owed by $40.

Tax Shield The amount of tax savings from the deductibility of interest payments on debt or CCA in computing corporate income taxes.

Technical Insolvency A situation in which a firm is unable to meet its current obligations as they come due, even though the value of its assets may exceed its liabilities.

Tender Offer A public announcement by a firm or individual indicating that it will pay a price above the current market price for the shares "tendered" of a firm it wishes to acquire.

Term Loan A debt obligation having an initial maturity (i.e., maturity at the time of issue) between 1 and 10 years. Term loans are usually repaid in instalments over the life of the loan. This often is referred to as *intermediate-term credit.*

Term Structure of Interest Rates The pattern of interest rate yields for debt securities that are similar in all respects except for their length of time to maturity. The term structure of interest rates usually is represented by a graphic plot called a *yield curve*.

Terminal Value The future value of an uneven cash flow stream is found by compounding each payment to the end of the stream and then summing the future values. (See also *MIRR.*)

Terminal Value The free cash flow of a firm that grows at a constant rate beyond the end date of a forecast period. Also called the *horizon value* or *continuing value*.

Terminal Warehouse Financing Agreement A loan agreement in which the inventory being pledged as collateral is stored in a bonded warehouse operated by a public warehousing firm.

Times Interest Earned Ratio A leverage ratio calculated by dividing EBIT by interest charges that indicates the likelihood that a borrower can make required interest payments on time.

Total Asset Turnover Ratio An asset management ratio calculated by dividing sales by total assets that indicates how well a firm is using its assets to generate sales.

Trade Credit The short-term credit sources available to a firm can be either spontaneous or negotiated. The major spontaneous source of funds is trade credit.

Transaction Exposure The potential for a change in the value of a foreign currency–denominated transaction due to a change in the exchange rate after the transaction is entered into but before it is settled.

Translation Exposure The change in owners' (accounting) equity because of a change in exchange rates that affects the "converted" value of foreign assets and liabilities.

Treasury Shares Common shares that have been reacquired by the issuing company.

Trend Analysis An examination of a firm's performance over time. It is frequently based on one or more financial ratios.

Trust Receipt A security agreement under which the borrower holds the inventory and proceeds from the sale of the inventory in trust for the lender. This is also known as *floor planning*.

Trustee The bondholder's representative in a public debt offering. The trustee is responsible for monitoring the borrower's compliance with the terms of the indenture.

U

Undepreciated Capital Cost (UCC) The cost of a fixed asset that still remains on the books to be written off in the future. The CCA rate is applied each year to this declining balance.

Underwriting A process whereby a group of investment dealers agrees to purchase a new security issue at a set price and then offers it for sale to investors.

Underwriting Spread The difference between the selling price to the public of a new security offering and the proceeds received by the offering firm. This also is termed an *underwriting discount*.

Unsystematic Risk Risk that is unique to a firm. This is also called *diversifiable risk*.

V

Variable Cost Ratio Variable production, administrative, and marketing costs per dollar of sales.

Variable Costs Costs that vary in close relationship with changes in a firm's output level.

Variable-Income Securities Financial assets, such as common shares, that do not pay contractually fixed periodic payments to investors.

Vertical Merger A combination of two or more firms that have a buyer-seller relationship with one another.

W

Warrant A company-issued long-term option to purchase a specified number of common shares at a particular price during a specified time period.

Weak-Form Market Efficiency A situation in which no investor can expect to earn excess returns based on historical information.

Weighted Cost of Capital The weighted average of the marginal costs of debt, equity, and preferred shares, if any, in proportion to their inclusion in the firm's target capital structure.

Working Capital The difference between a firm's current assets and current liabilities. The term *working capital* is used interchangeably with *net working capital*.

Y

Yield Curve A chart showing interest rate yields in percent on the vertical axis and term to maturity on the horizontal axis.

Yield to Call (*YTC*) The discount rate that equates the present value of all expected interest payments and the repayment of principal at the call date from a bond with the present bond price.

Yield to Maturity (*YTM*) The discount rate that equates the present bond price with the present value of all expected interest payments and the repayment of principal at the maturity date from a bond.

Z

Zero-Balance System A payment system that uses a master disbursing account that services all other disbursing accounts. A zero balance is maintained in all but the master account until payments must be made.

Solutions to Self-Test Problems

CHAPTER 2

ST1. The firm can deduct the $30,000 interest payment from its gross income of $250,000 so its taxable income is $220,000 (dividend payments are not deductible). As you noted from the Entrepreneurial Issues feature, the firm is a small business, so it can use the lower rates shown in Table 2.3. Its federal tax rates are 13.12% on the first $200,000 of income and 22.12% on the remaining $20,000, so its federal tax liability is $200,000 × .1312 = $26,240 plus $20,000 × .2212 = 4,424 for a total of $30,664. Its Manitoba tax rates are 18.12% on the first $200,000 of income and 29.12% on the remaining $20,000, so its Manitoba tax liability is $200,000 × .1812 = $36,240 plus $20,000 × .2912 = 5,824 for a total of $42,064. Thus, the total tax bill is $30,664 + $42,064 = $72,728.

ST2. The firm had a combined federal and provincial tax bill in prior years of $200,000 × .3124 = $62,480 each year. It can carry back this 2003 loss for three years so it will get a cheque for $62,480 × 3 = $187,440. The remaining unused loss of $812,560 can be carried forward seven years.

ST3. The direct quote for the yen is given in Table 2.2 as 0.01178.

The indirect quote for the yen is 1/.01178 = 84.89

CHAPTER 3

ST1. **a.** Current ratio = Current assets/current liabilities = $52,000/$25,000 = 2.08

   b. Quick ratio = (Current assets – inventories)/Current liabilities

$$= (\$52,000 - \$33,000)/\$25,000 = 0.76$$

ST2. **a.** Average collection period = Accounts receivable/(Annual credit sales/365)

$$= \$15,000/(\$130,000/365) = 42.1 \text{ days}$$

   b. Inventory turnover = Cost of sales/Average Inventory

$$= \$103,000/\$33,000 = 3.12$$

   c. Fixed asset turnover = Sales/Net fixed assets = $130,000/$35,000 = 3.71
   d. Total asset turnover = Sales/Total assets = $130,000/$87,000 = 1.49

ST3. **a.** Debt ratio = Total debt/Total assets = $47,000/$87,000 = 0.54
   b. Debt-to-equity ratio = Total debt/Total equity = $47,000/$40,000 = 1.18
   c. Times interest earned = EBIT/Interest charges = $11,000/$3,000 = 3.67
   d. Fixed charge coverage = (EBIT + LP)/(I + LP + PDBT+SFBT)

$$= (\$11,000+\$200)/(\$3,000 +\$200) = 3.50$$

ST4. **a.** Gross profit margin = (Sales – Cost of sales)/Sales

$$= (\$130,000 -\$103,000)/\$130,000 = 20.8\%$$

   b. Net profit margin = EAT/Sales = $5,000/$130,000 = 3.85%
   c. Return on investment = EAT/Total assets = $5,000/$87,000 = 5.75%
   d. Return on total equity = EAT/Total equity

$$= \$5,000/\$40,000 = 12.5\%$$

ST5. **a.** Price to earnings ratio = Market price per share/EPS

$$= \$9.50/(\$5,000/5,000) = 9.5$$

   b. Market to book ratio = MPS/BVPS = $9.50/$8.00 = 1.19

ST6. Return on total equity = Net profit margin × Total asset turnover × Equity multiplier = ($5,000/$130,000) × ($130,000/$87,000) × ($87,000/$40,000) = 12.5%

ST7. **a.** Depreciation expense = Increase in accumulated depreciation

$$= \$575 - \$500 = \$75$$

b.

Sales	$500
Operating expenses	−125
Depreciation	−75
EBT	300
Taxes	−120
EAT	$180

c. ATCF = EAT + Depreciation = $180 + $75 = $255

d. Increase in net fixed assets:

$100	Increase in gross fixed assets (GFA)
− 75	Increase in accumulated depreciation
$ 25	Increase in net fixed assets (NFA)

EAT less increase in NFA = ATCF less increase in GFA

$180 − $25 = $255 − $100

$155 = $155

ST8. Rate of sales increase is one-third (33.33%) from $60 to $80 million

Accounts receivable	$9,000,000
Inventories	15,000,000
Net fixed assets	21,000,000
Assets that vary with sales	$45,000,000

Increased funds needed for these asset increases = 1/3 × $45,000,000 = $15,000,000

Funds provided by accounts payable increase = $4,000,000

Funds required for cash balance increase = $3,000,000

Increased retained earnings = $12,000,000 − $2,000,000 dividend = $10,000,000

AFN = $3,000,000 + $15,000,000 − $4,000,000 − $10,000,000 = $4,000,000

ST9. AFN = [($10,500,000/$20,000,000)($5,000,000) − ($3,000,000/$20,000,000)($5,000,000)] − [$1,000,000 − $300,000] = $1,175,000

Notes:		
	$10,500,000	assets that vary with sales
	$3,000,000	accounts payable
	$5,000,000	sales increase
	$20,000,000	current sales

CHAPTER 4

ST1. $FV_n = PV_0(1 + i)^n$

a. $FV_5 = \$1,000(1.08)^5 = \$1,000(FVIF_{0.08, 5}) = \$1,000(1.469)$

$$= \$1,469$$

Enter:	5	8	−1,000		
	n	i	PV	PMT	FV

Solution: 1,469.33

b. $FV_5 = \$1,000(1.02)^{20} = \$1,000(FVIF_{0.02, \, 20}) = \$1,000(1.486)$
$$= \$1,486$$

Enter: 20 2 −1,000

n	i	PV	PMT	FV

Solution: 1,485.95

ST2. $PVAN_0 = PMT(PVIFA_{0.12, \, 10})$
$$= \$1,000(5.650)$$
$$= \$5,650$$

Enter: 10 12 −1,000

n	i	PV	PMT	FV

Solution: 5,650.22

ST3. $FV_n = PV_0(FVIF_{i, \, n})$
$1.52 = 0.90(FVIF_{i, \, 5})$
$FVIF_{i,5} = 1.689$

Using Table I and reading across the five-year row, 1.685 is found in the 11% column. Thus, the growth rate is approximately 11% per year.

Enter: 5   −.90   1.52

n	i	PV	PMT	FV

Solution: 11.05

ST4. $PVAN_3 = \$2,000(PVIFA_{0.14, \, 5})$
$$= \$2,000(3.433)$$
$$= \$6,866$$

This step calculates the present value of the five-year *ordinary* annuity at the beginning of year four, i.e., the end of year three. Next, $PVAN_3$ must be discounted to the present:

$$PVAN_0 = PVAN_3(PVIF_{0.14, \, 3})$$
$$= \$6,866(0.675)$$
$$= \$4,635$$

Enter: 5 14 22,000

n	i	PV	PMT	FV

Solution: 6,866.16

Enter: 3 14   −6,866.16

n	i	PV	PMT	FV

Solution: 4,634.46

ST5. $PVAN_0 = \$50,000(PVIF_{0.10, \, 20})$
$$= \$50,000(8.514)$$
$$= \$425,700 \text{ (amount needed in account on 60th birthday)}$$
$FVAN_{25} = PMT(FVIFA_{0.10, \, 25})$
$\$425,700 = PMT(98.347)$
$PMT = \$4,329$

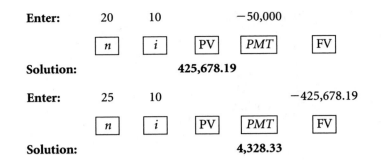

Enter: | 20 | 10 | | | −50,000 | |
| | $\boxed{n}$ | $\boxed{i}$ | $\boxed{PV}$ | $\boxed{PMT}$ | | $\boxed{FV}$ |

Solution: 425,678.19

Enter: | 25 | 10 | | | | −425,678.19 |
| | $\boxed{n}$ | $\boxed{i}$ | $\boxed{PV}$ | $\boxed{PMT}$ | | $\boxed{FV}$ |

Solution: 4,328.33

APPENDIX 4A

ST1. $FV_7 = \$1,000(e)^{0.10(7)}$
$= \$2,013.75$

ST2. $PV_0 = \$5,000(e)^{-0.09(8)}$
$= \$2,433.76$

ST3. $i_{eff} = e^{0.12} - 1.0$
$= 1.1275 - 1.0$
$= 0.1275$ or 12.75%

CHAPTER 5

ST1. $P_0 = \dfrac{I}{k_d} = \dfrac{\$80}{0.10} = \$800$

ST2. $P_0 = M(PVIF_{k_d,n})$
$n = 6 \quad M = \$1,000 \quad P_0 = \$650$
$\$650 = \$1,000\,(PVIF_{k_d,6})$
$(PVIF_{k_d,6}) = 0.650$

Using Table II and reading across the 6-year row, 0.650 is found between the 7% (0.666) and 8% (0.630) interest rate columns. Interpolation between these two values gives an approximate yield to maturity (k_d) of

$$k_d = 7\% + \frac{.666 - .650}{.666 - .630}(1\%)$$

$$= 7.44\%$$

Enter: | 6 | | | −650 | 0 | 1,000 |
| | $\boxed{n}$ | $\boxed{i}$ | $\boxed{PV}$ | $\boxed{PMT}$ | $\boxed{FV}$ |

Solution: 7.44

ST3. $P_0 = \displaystyle\sum_{t=1}^{n} \dfrac{I}{(1 + k_d)^t} + \dfrac{M}{(1 + k_d)^n}$

$n = 10 \quad I = .09375(\$1,000) = \$93.75 \quad M = \$1,000 \quad k_d = 0.10$

$= \$93.75(PVIFA_{0.10,\,10}) + \$1,000(PVIF_{0.10,\,10})$

$= \$93.75(6.145) + \$1,000(0.386)$

$= \$962.09$ (*or* \$962)

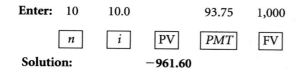

Enter: 10   10.0   93.75   1,000

$$\boxed{n} \quad \boxed{i} \quad \boxed{PV} \quad \boxed{PMT} \quad \boxed{FV}$$

Solution: −961.60

If the investor pays $961.60, the expected yield to maturity is 10%. If the investor pays more than $961.60, the expected yield to maturity is less than 10%. Therefore, the maximum price the investor should be willing to pay is $961.60.

ST4. $P_0 = \dfrac{D_p}{k_p} = \dfrac{\$3.50}{0.06} = \$58.33$

CHAPTER 6

ST1. $P_0 = \dfrac{\$3.00}{0.12 - 0.04} = \$37.50$

ST2. Present Value of First 3 Years' Dividends

$D_0 = \$2.00 \quad g_1 = 0.20 \quad k_e = 0.20$

Year	Dividend	PV Interest Factor	Present Value
t	$D_t = \$2.00(1 + 0.20)^t$	$PVIF_{0.20,\ t} = 1/(1 + 0.20)^t$	$D_t \times PVIF_{0.20,\ t}$
1	$\$2.00(1 + 0.20)^1 = \$2.400$	0.833	$2.00
2	$2.00(1 + 0.20)^2 = \$2.880$	0.694	2.00
3	$2.00(1 + 0.20)^3 = \$3.456$	0.579	2.00
PV (First 3 Years' Dividends)			$6.00

Value of Share at End of Year 3

$$P_3 = \dfrac{D_4}{(k_e - g_2)} \qquad g_2 = 0.06$$

$$D_4 = D_3 (1 + g_2) = \$3.456(1 + 0.06) = \$3.663$$

$$P_3 = \dfrac{\$3.663}{(0.20 - 0.06)} = \$26.164$$

Present Value of P_3

$$PV(P_3) = \dfrac{P_3}{(1 + k_e)^3} = \dfrac{\$26.164}{(1 + 0.20)^3}$$

$$= \$26.164(PVIF_{0.20,\ t}) = \$26.164(0.579) = \$15.15$$

Value of Common Share

$$P_0 = PV(\text{First 3 Years' Dividends}) + PV(P_3)$$

$$= \$6.00 + \$15.15 = \$21.15$$

CHAPTER 7

ST1. a. $\hat{r} = \sum_{j=1}^{n} r_j p_j$

$= -\$1,000(0.20) + \$1,500(0.60) + \$2,500(0.20)$

$= \$1,200$

b. $\sigma = \sqrt{\sum_{j=1}^{n} (r_j - \hat{r})^2 p_j}$

$= [(-\$1,000 - \$1,200)^2(0.20) + (\$1,500 - \$1,200)^2(0.60)$

$+ (\$2,500 - \$1,200)^2(0.20)]^{0.50} = \$1,166$

c. $v = \dfrac{\sigma}{\hat{r}}$

$= \dfrac{\$1166}{\$1200}$

$= 0.97$

ST2. $z = \dfrac{r - \hat{r}}{\sigma}$

$= \dfrac{0 - 15}{12} = -1.25$

$p = 0.1056 \text{ (or } 10.56\%)$

ST3. a. $\hat{r}_p = w_A \hat{r}_A + w_B \hat{r}_B$

$= 0.75(12) + 0.25(20)$

$= 14\%$

b. $\sigma_p = \sqrt{w_A^2 \sigma_A^2 + w_B^2 \sigma_B^2 + w_A^2 w_B^2 \rho_{AB} \sigma_A \, \sigma_B}$

$= [(0.75)^2(6)^2 + (0.25)^2(15)^2 + 2(0.75)(0.25)(.50)(6)(15)]^{0.50}$

$= 7.15\%$

ST4. $\beta_p = \sum_{j=1}^{n} w_j \beta_j$

$= 0.25(.95) + 0.25(1.25) + 0.25(1.15) + 0.25(1.05)$

$= 1.10$

ST5. a. $k_j = \hat{r}_f + \beta_j(\hat{r}_m - \hat{r}_f)$

$= 6 + 0.60 \, (15 - 6)$

$= 11.4\%$

b. $k_j = 7 + 0.60(15 - 7)$

$= 11.8\%$

c. $k_j = 6 + 0.60(16 - 6)$

$= 12.0\%$

ST6. a. Maturity risk premium: $7.55\% - 6.11\% = 1.44\%$. The maturity risk premium on the X bond will be the same as on the Treasury bonds.

b. Default risk premium: $8.40\% - 7.55\% = 0.85\%$

ST7. Holding Period Return (%) $= \dfrac{\$8.75 - \$11.00 + \$0.10}{\$11.00} \times 100\%$

$$= 19.55\%$$

CHAPTER 8

ST1. Net proceeds $= \$946 - \$11 = \$935$

$\$935 = \$80(\text{PVIFA}_{k_d,10}) + \$1,000(\text{PVIF}_{k_d,10})$

Try $k_d = 9\%$

$\$935 = \$80(6.418) + \$1,000(0.422)$

$\$935 \approx \$935.44$

Therefore, $k_i = 9\%(1 - 0.4) = 5.4\%$

ST2. a. $k_e = \dfrac{D_1}{P_0} + g$

$= \dfrac{\$3.50(1 + 0.068)}{\$60} + 0.068$

$= 0.13$ or 13%

b. $k'_e = \dfrac{\$3.50(1 + 0.068)}{\$60 - \$3} + 0.068$

$= 0.134$ or 13.4%

ST3. $k_e = r_f + \beta(r_m - r_f)$

$= 7.5\% + 1.3(8.6\%)$

$= 18.7\%$

ST4. $k_a = 0.60(k_e) + 0.15(k_p) + 0.25(k_i)$

$= 0.60(18\%) + 0.15(15\%) + 0.25(9\%)$

$= 15.3\%$

CHAPTER 9

ST1.

New asset price	$1,200,000
Plus Shipping and installation	100,000
Gross installed cost	$1,300,000
Less Salvage value of old asset	.150,000
Net installed cost	$1,150,000
Initial increase in NWC	0
Net investment	$1,150,000

ST2.

Annual Net Cash Flows

Single-Year Inputs

New asset price	$700,000
Ship. & instal.	$50,000
Old salvage, $t = 0$	$275,000
Life, $n \leq 20$	5
Discount rate	10.00%
Tax rate	40.00%
CCA rate	30.00%
New salvage, $t = n$	$70,000
Old salvage, $t = n$	$20,000

Multi-Year Inputs

Year	0	1	2	3	4	5
ΔNWC	$40,000	$10,000	$10,000	$10,000	$10,000	-$80,000
New revenues		$100,000	$100,000	$100,000	$100,000	$100,000
Old revenues						
New oper. costs						
Old oper. costs		$20,000	$20,000	$20,000	$20,000	$20,000

Intermediate Outputs

Net installed cost	$475,000					
ΔSalvage, $t = n$	$50,000					
Year	0	1	2	3	4	5
Starting UCC	$0	$475,000	$403,750	$282,625	$197,837	$138,486
CCA	$0	$71,250	$121,125	$84,788	$59,351	$41,546
Ending UCC	$0	$403,750	$282,625	$197,837	$138,486	$96,940
ΔRevenues	$0	$100,000	$100,000	$100,000	$100,000	$100,000
ΔOperating costs	$0	-$20,000	-$20,000	-$20,000	-$20,000	-$20,000
ΔNet revenues	$0	$120,000	$120,000	$120,000	$120,000	$120,000

Cash-Flow Outputs

Year	0	1	2	3	4	5
Net installed cost	$475,000	$0	$0	$0	$0	$0
A-T Δnet revenues	$0	$72,000	$72,000	$72,000	$72,000	$72,000
CCA tax shield $t \leq n$	$0	$28,500	$48,450	$33,915	$23,740	$16,618
ΔNWC	$40,000	$10,000	$10,000	$10,000	$10,000	-$80,000
ΔSalvage, $t = n$	$0	$0	$0	$0	$0	$50,000
PV tax shield $t > n$	$0	$0	$0	$0	$0	$14,082
Net cash flow	-$515,000	$90,500	$110,450	$95,915	$85,740	$232,700

a. The net investment $= -$ Net cash flow at time 0 $=$ $515,000.

b. The annual net cash flows are given in the bottom row of the above spreadsheet.

Note: This spreadsheet is explained and further developed in Appendix 10A.

CHAPTER 10

ST1. NPV $= -(\$20,000 + \$5,000) + \$7,000(\text{PVIFA}_{0.11,10}) + \$5,000(\text{PVIF}_{0.11,10})$
$= \$17,983$

The value of the firm, and therefore the shareholders' wealth, is increased by $17,983 as a result of undertaking the project. The project is acceptable because its NPV is positive.

ST2. $\text{NPV} = \text{PV cash inflows} - \text{Net investment}$

$$0 = \$75{,}000(\text{PVIFA}_{r,8}) - \$360{,}000$$

$$(\text{PVIFA}_{r,8}) = 4.80$$

$$r \approx 13 \text{ percent (from Table IV)}$$

$$PI = \frac{\$75{,}000(\text{PVIFA}_{0.12,8})}{\$360{,}000}$$

$$= 1.035$$

ST3. a.   Project G: $\$10{,}000 = \$5{,}000\,(\text{PVIFA}_{r,3})$

$$\text{PVIFA}_{r,3} = 2.0$$

$$r \approx 23.4 \text{ percent (from Table IV)}$$

Project H: $\$10{,}000 = \$17{,}000(\text{PVIF}_{r,3})$

$$\text{PVIF}_{r,3} = 0.588$$

$$r \approx 19.3 \text{ percent (from Table II)}$$

b. $\text{NPV}_G = -\$10{,}000 + \$5{,}000(\text{PVIFA}_{0.12,3})$

$$= \$2{,}010$$

$$\text{NPV}_H = -\$10{,}000 + \$17{,}000(\text{PVIF}_{0.12,3})$$

$$= \$2{,}104$$

c.   Project H should be adopted because it has the higher NPV. It is assumed that the firm's reinvestment opportunities are represented more accurately by the firm's cost of capital than by the unique internal rate of return of either project.

ST4.   This problem is ideal for using Equation 10.3a because ΔR_t and ΔO_t are the same for each year of the project. In particular, $\Delta R_t = \$0$ and $\Delta O_t = \$4{,}000 - \$7{,}000 = -\$3{,}000$, which means that $\Delta R_t - \Delta O_t = \$0 - (-\$3{,}000) = +\$3{,}000$. Thus, the first term of Equation 10.3a simplifies to an annuity of $(\$3{,}000)(1 - .4) = \$1{,}800$ for 20 years at an 11% discount rate. By financial calculator, this amount is $\$14{,}333.99$.

Furthermore, since there are no changes to net working capital, the PV of these changes is zero and the net investment will be the same as the incremental depreciable base of $\$12{,}000$. The two terms involving the salvage value are also zero. Substituting into Equation 10.3a yields

$$\text{NPV} = \$14{,}333.99 + \left[\frac{1.055}{1.11}\right]\left[\frac{(.4)(.2)(\$12{,}000)}{(0.11 + 0.20)}\right] - \$12{,}000$$

$$= \$14{,}333.99 + \$2{,}943.33 - \$12{,}000$$

$$= \$5{,}277.32$$

Based on this positive NPV, the robot should replace the junior executive.

APPENDIX 10A

ST1. a. NPV = $4,862 (see spreadsheet below)

b. Since the NPV is positive, TLC should undertake the project.

c. Approximate IRR = 11.57% (see spreadsheet below)

d. Replacing the 10.00% discount rate with the approximate IRR of 11.57% results in a new approximate IRR of 11.56%. Replacing 11.57% with 11.56% as the discount rate results in no further change in the IRR and an NPV = −$8 ≈ 0. Thus, 11.56% is the actual IRR.

Capital Budgeting

Single-Year Inputs

New asset price	$95,000
Ship. & install.	$5,000
Old salvage, $t = 0$	$0
Life, $n \leq 20$	4
Discount rate	10.00%
Tax rate	40.00%
CCA rate	20.00%
New salvage, $t = n$	$40,000
Old salvage, $t = n$	$0

Multi-Year Inputs

Year	0	1	2	3	4
ΔNWC	$7,000	$5,000	$5,000	$5,000	-$22,000
New revenues	$0	$50,000	$60,000	$75,000	$60,000
Old revenues	$0	$0	$0	$0	$0
New oper. costs	$0	$25,000	$26,500	$28,090	$29,775
Old oper. costs	$0	$0	$0	$0	$0

Intermediate Outputs

Net installed cost	$100,000
ΔSalvage, $t = n$	$40,000

Year	0	1	2	3	4
Starting UCC	$0	$100,000	$90,000	$72,000	$57,600
CCA	$0	$10,000	$18,000	$14,400	$11,520
Ending UCC	$0	$90,000	$72,000	$57,600	$46,080
ΔRevenues	$0	$50,000	$60,000	$75,000	$60,000
ΔOperating costs	$0	$25,000	$26,500	$28,090	$29,775
ΔNet revenues	$0	$25,000	$33,500	$46,910	$30,225

Cash-Flow Outputs

Year	0	1	2	3	4
Net installed cost	$100,000	$0	$0	$0	$0
A-T Δnet revenues	$0	$15,000	$20,100	$28,146	$18,135
CCA tax shield $t \leq n$	$0	$4,000	$7,200	$5,760	$4,608
ΔNWC	$7,000	$5,000	$5,000	$5,000	-$22,000
ΔSalvage, $t = n$	$0	$0	$0	$0	$40,000
PV tax shield $t > n$	$0	$0	$0	$0	$1,621
Net cash flow	-$107,000	$14,000	$22,300	$28,906	$86,364
Net present value (NPV)	$4,862				
Approx. IRR	11.57%				

ST2. The spreadsheet for this problem appears in the solution for ST2. in Chapter 9. The last two lines giving an NPV of −$66,334 and an approximate IRR of 5.44% were omitted, however. Thus, IFC should not replace the computer-controlled unit because the replacement project has negative NPV. Following the iterative process described above, actual IRR is 5.52% with an NPV = −$8 ≈ 0.

APPENDIX 10B

ST1. Information Concerning Original Issue

Issue size	$150,000,000
Coupon interest rate	12.000%
Call price ($ per bond)	$1,050

Information Concerning New Issue

Coupon interest rate	10.000%
Years to maturity	20
Flotation percentage	0.400%
Overlap period (number of days)	28
Annual rate of return (overlap period)	0.000%
Marginal tax rate	40.000%

Benefits of Refunding

After-tax annual interest savings	$1,800,000	
Present value of interest savings		$20,645,858

Less: Costs of Refunding

After-tax call premium		$7,500,000
Flotation cost	$600,000	
Present value flotation costs (new issue)		$397,807
Overlapping interest		$828,493
Total cost of refunding		$8,726,300
Net present value of refunding decision		$11,919,558

Assumptions:

(1) Years to maturity of new issue = Remaining years to maturity of old issue
(2) Both the old and new issues are annual pay.
(3) Size of old issue = Size of new issue
(4) Flotation costs of old issue are fully amortized.

ST2. **Information Concerning Original Issue**

Issue size	$50,000,000
Coupon interest rate	11.000%
Call price ($ per bond)	$1,080

Information Concerning New Issue

Coupon interest rate	8.000%
Years to maturity	20
Flotation percentage	0.875%
Overlap period (number of days)	30
Annual rate of return (overlap period)	6.000%
Marginal tax rate	40.000%

Benefits of Refunding

After-tax annual interest savings	$900,000	
Present value of interest savings		$11,408,655

Less: Costs of Refunding

After-tax call premium		$4,000,000
Flotation cost	$437,500	
Present value flotation costs (new issue)		$285,127
Overlapping interest		$123,288
Total cost of refunding		$4,408,415
Net present value of refunding decision		$7,000,240

Assumptions:

(1) Years to maturity of new issue = Remaining years to maturity of old issue

(2) Both the old and new issues are annual pay.

(3) Size of old issue = Size of new issue

(4) Flotation costs of old issue are fully amortized.

CHAPTER 11

ST1.
$$z = \frac{\$50{,}000 - \$250{,}000}{\$100{,}000}$$

$$= 22.0$$

It can be seen from Table V at the back of the book that the probability of a value less than -2.0 standard deviations from the mean is 2.28 percent. Thus, there is a 2.28% chance that the actual net present value for the project will be less than $50,000.

ST2. a. $k_e = 10\% + 1.0(15\% - 10\%) = 15\%$

b. $k_a^\star = 10\% + 1.6(15\% - 10\%) = 18\%$

c. NPV @ 15% $= -\$9 + \$1.9(5.019) = \$0.54$ million

d. NPV @ 18% $= -\$9 + \$1.9(4.494) = -\$0.46$ million

The project is acceptable using the required return for average risk projects, but it is unacceptable using the risk-adjusted rate.

ST3. a. NPV calculation:

$$\text{NPV} = -\$75{,}000 + \$30{,}000(0.870) + \$30{,}000(0.756)$$
$$+ \$30{,}000(0.658) + \$20{,}000(0.572)$$
$$= \$4{,}960$$

b. Certainty equivalent NPV:

$$\text{NPV} = -\$75{,}000 + \$30{,}000(0.90)(0.926) + \$30{,}000(0.80)(0.857)$$
$$+ \$30{,}000(0.65)(0.794) + \$20{,}000(0.5)(0.735)$$
$$= -\$6{,}597$$

CHAPTER 12

ST1.

Proportion of Debt $\left(\dfrac{D}{D+E}\right)$	Cost of Debt, $k_d(1-T)$	Cost of Equity, k_e	Weighted Cost of Capital, k_a
0.00	—	10.0%	10.00%
0.10	4.0%	10.1	9.49
0.20	4.2	10.3	9.08
0.30	4.4	10.8	8.88
0.40	4.8	11.4	8.76
0.50	5.5	12.5	9.00
0.60	6.6	14.5	9.76
0.70	8.0	18.0	11.00

Note: $k_a = \left(\dfrac{E}{D+E}\right)k_e + \left(\dfrac{D}{D+E}\right)k_d(1-T)$

The optimal capital structure consists of 40% debt and 60% equity since this minimizes the firm's cost of capital

CHAPTER 13

ST1. a.

$$\text{DOL} = \frac{\text{Sales} - \text{Variable Costs}}{\text{EBIT}}$$

$$= \frac{\$5,000,000 - \$1,000,000}{\$2,000,000}$$

$$= 2.0$$

$$\text{DFL} = \frac{\text{EBIT}}{\text{EBIT} - I - D_p/(1-T)}$$

$$= \frac{\$2,000,000}{\$2,000,000 - \$500,000 - \dfrac{\$100,000}{(1 - 0.4)}}$$

$$= \frac{\$2,000,000}{\$1,333,333}$$

$$= 1.5$$

$$\text{DCL} = \frac{\text{Sales} - \text{Variable Costs}}{\text{EBIT} - I - D_p/(1 - T)}$$

$$= \frac{\$5,000,000 - \$1,000,000}{\$2,000,000 - \$500,000 - \dfrac{\$100,000}{(1 - 0.4)}}$$

$$= 3.0$$

Check: $\text{DCL} = \text{DOL} \times \text{DFL}$

$$= 2.0 \times 1.5$$

$$= 3.0$$

b. Current EPS $= \dfrac{\$800,000}{400,000 \text{ shares}} = \$2.00$

A sales increase to \$5.5 million represents a 10% increase in sales. Hence, EPS should increase by 30% (10% × 3.0), to \$2.60.

ST2. $p(\text{EPS} < \$0) = p(\text{EBIT} < \$250,000)$

$$z = \frac{\text{EBIT} - \widehat{\text{EBIT}}}{\sigma}$$

$$= \frac{\$250,000 - \$1,750,000}{\$1,200,000}$$

$$= -1.25$$

$$p = 0.1056 \text{ (or } 10.56\%)$$

ST3. a.

$$\frac{(\text{EBIT} - I_d)(1 - T) - D_p}{N_d} = \frac{(\text{EBIT} - I_e)(1 - T) - D_p}{N_e}$$

$$\frac{(\text{EBIT} - \$18)(1 - 0.40)}{100} = \frac{(\text{EBIT} - \$0)(1 - 0.40)}{110}$$

$$\text{EBIT} = \$198 \text{ (million)}$$

b. $p(\text{EPS} < \$0) = p(\text{EBIT} < \$18.0)$

$$z = \frac{\text{EBIT} - \widehat{\text{EBIT}}}{\sigma}$$

$$= \frac{\$18.0 - \$250}{\$200}$$

$$= -1.16$$

$$p = 0.1230 \text{ (or 12.30\%)}$$

c. $p(\text{EBIT} > \$198)$

$$z = \frac{\$198 - \$250}{\$200}$$

$$= -0.26$$

$$p = 1 - 0.3974 = 0.6026 \text{ (or 60.26\%)}$$

ST4. a. $CB_0 = \$20$ million; $FCF_R = \$60$ million; $\sigma = \$60$ million

$$CB_R = CB_0 + FCF_R$$

$$= \$20 \text{ million} + \$60 \text{ million}$$

$$= \$80 \text{ million}$$

$$z = \frac{\$0 - CB_R}{\sigma}$$

$$= \frac{\$0 - \$80}{\$60}$$

$$= -1.33$$

$$p = 0.0918 \text{ (or 9.18\%)}$$

b. $CB_R = \$20$ million $+ \$60$ million $- \$10$ million

$$= \$70 \text{ million}$$

$$\sigma = \$60 \text{ million}$$

$$z = \frac{\$0 - \$70}{\$60} = -1.17$$

$$p = 0.1210 \text{ (or 12.10\%)}$$

CHAPTER 14

ST1. a. **Post-Stock Dividend Common Shareholders' Equity**

Common shares (120,000 shares)	$2,600,000
Retained earnings	3,400,000
Total common shareholders' equity	$6,000,000

A total of $1,600,000 (20,000 shares $\times$ an assumed market price of $80 per share) is transferred from retained earnings to the common shares account.

b. Post-stock dividend price $= \dfrac{\$80}{1 + 0.20}$

$$= \$66.67$$

ST2. a.

EBIT	$1,000,000
Interest	200,000
EBT	$ 800,000
Taxes	320,000
EAT	$ 480,000

Earnings per share $= \dfrac{\$480,000}{50,000 \text{ shares}}$

$$= \$9.60$$

b. Dividends per share $= \dfrac{\$100,000}{50,000 \text{ shares}}$

$$= \$2.00$$

Dividend payout ratio $= \dfrac{\$2.00}{\$9.60}$

$$= 20.8\%$$

c. Dividend yield $= \dfrac{\text{Dividend per share}}{\text{Price per share}}$

$$0.02 = \dfrac{\$2.00}{\text{Price per share}}$$

Price per share $= \$100.00$

d. Equivalent (pre-stock dividend)
dividend per share: $\$2.00 \div 2 = \$1.00$

Dividend rate increase $= \dfrac{\$1.10 - \$1.00}{\$1.00}$

$$= 0.10 \text{ or } 10\%$$

CHAPTER 15

ST1. a. Inventory conversion period $= \dfrac{\text{Average inventory}}{\text{Cost of sales}/365}$

$$= \dfrac{\$2,120}{\$6,946/365}$$

$$= 111.4 \text{ days}$$

b. Receivables conversion period $= \dfrac{\text{Accounts receivable}}{\text{Annual credit sales}/365}$

$$= \dfrac{\$2,075}{\$11,990/365}$$

$$= 63.2 \text{ days}$$

c. Operating cycle $=$ Inventory conversion period $+$ Receivables conversion period

$$= 111.4 + 63.2$$

$$= 174.6 \text{ days}$$

d.

$$\text{Payables deferral period} = \frac{\text{Average accounts payable}}{(\text{Cost of sales})/365}$$

$$= \frac{724}{(6{,}946)/365}$$

$$= 38.0 \text{ days}$$

e.

$$\text{Cash conversion cycle} = \text{Operating cycle} - \text{Payables deferral period}$$

$$= 174.6 - 38.0$$

$$= 136.6 \text{ days}$$

ST2. a.

	Policy A	Policy B
Current assets	$ 90,000,000	$ 60,000,000
Total assets	190,000,000	160,000,000
Total equity	76,000,000	64,000,000
Total debt	114,000,000	96,000,000
Short-term debt	34,200,000	57,600,000
Long-term debt	79,800,000	38,400,000
EBIT	30,000,000	30,000,000
Interest $\begin{cases} \text{STD (10\%)} \\ \text{LTD (14\%)} \end{cases}$	14,592,000	11,136,000
EBT	15,408,000	18,864,000
Taxes	6,163,200	7,545,600
EAT	9,244,800	11,318,400
Rate of return on equity	12.16%	17.69%

b. Policy B is riskier than policy A since it results in a lower net working capital position ($2,400,000 versus $55,800,000) and a lower current ratio (1.04 versus 2.63). (This answer assumes there are no current liabilities other than short-term debt. If there were, the numbers would differ but the relative magnitudes of both calculated measures of risk would be unchanged.)

ST3. a.

$$\text{APR} = \frac{\text{Percentage discount}}{100 - \text{Percentage discount}} \times \frac{365}{\text{Credit period} - \text{Discount period}}$$

$$= \frac{2}{100 - 2} \times \frac{365}{120 - 10}$$

$$= 6.77\%$$

b.

$$\text{APR} = \frac{2}{100 - 2} \times \frac{365}{122 - 30}$$

$$= 8.10\%$$

ST4.

$$\text{APR} = \frac{\text{Interest cost}}{\text{Usable funds}} \times \frac{365}{\text{Maturity (days)}}$$

$$\text{Interest cost} = 0.105\,(\$25{,}000) \times \frac{274}{365}$$

$$= \$1{,}971$$

$$\text{APR} = \frac{\$1{,}971}{\$25{,}000 - \$1{,}971} \times \frac{365}{274}$$

$$= 11.4\%$$

ST5. $$\text{APR} = \frac{\text{Interest costs} + \text{Placement fee}}{\text{Usable funds}} \times \frac{365}{\text{Maturity date (days)}}$$

Interest costs $= 0.085 \, (\$25,000,000) \left(\dfrac{91}{365} \right) = \$529,795$

Usable funds $= \$25,000,000 - \$529,795 - \$75,000 = \$24,395,205$

$$\text{APR} = \frac{\$529,795 + \$75,000}{\$24,395,205} \times \frac{365}{91} = 9.94\%$$

ST6. a.

Average level of receivables	$4,000,000
Less Factoring commission	
$\quad 0.02 \times \$4,000,000 =$	−80,000
Less Reserve for returns	
$\quad 0.10 \times \$4,000,000 =$	−400,000
Amount available for advance before interest is deducted	$3,520,000
Less Interest on advance	
$\quad 0.12 \times \$3,520,000 \times \dfrac{70}{365} =$	−81,008
Amount of funds advanced by factor (Usable funds)	$3,438,992

b.

Interest costs	$ 81,008
Factoring commission	80,000
Total interest and factoring costs	$ 161,008
Less Credit department savings per 70-day period	
$\quad \$3,000 \times \dfrac{70}{30} =$	−7,000
Less Average bad-debt losses per 70-day period	
$\quad \$9,000 \times \dfrac{70}{30} =$	−21,000
Net financing cost per 70 days	$ 133,008

$$\text{APR} = \frac{\$133,008}{\$3,438,992} \times \frac{365}{70}$$
$$= 20.2\%$$

ST7. a.

End of Year	Principal Payment	Interest Payment	Total Payment	Remaining Balance
0	—	—	—	$2,000,000
1	$ 250,000	$160,000	$ 410,000	1,750,000
2	250,000	140,000	390,000	1,500,000
3	250,000	120,000	370,000	1,250,000
4	250,000	100,000	350,000	1,000,000
5	1,000,000	80,000	1,080,000	0

b. Funds available for use:

$$\$2,000,000 - \$50,000 \text{ processing fee} = \$1,950,000$$

$$\$1,950,000 = \$410,000(\text{PVIF}_{i,\,1}) + \$390,000(\text{PVIF}_{i,\,2})$$
$$+ \$370,000(\text{PVIF}_{i,\,3}) + \$350,000(\text{PVIF}_{i,\,4})$$
$$+ \$1,080,000(\text{PVIF}_{i,\,5})$$
$$i = 8.83\% \text{ (by calculator)}$$

CHAPTER 16

ST1. a. Increase in average cash balance = Average daily sales × Decrease in payment processing time
$$= (\$219,000,000/365) \times 2 = \$1,200,000$$

b. Increase in (pretax) earnings = Increase in average cash balance × Interest rate
$$= \$1,200,000 \times 0.07 = \$84,000$$

ST2. a. Reduction in collection time = Reduction in mailing time + Reduction in processing and clearing time
$$= (3.0 - 1.5) + (5.0 - 2.0) = 4.5 \text{ days}$$

Average daily collections = Annual credit sales/365
$$= \$292,000,000/365 = \$800,000$$

Amount of funds released = Average daily collections × Reduction in collection time
$$= \$800,000 \times 4.5 = \$3,600,000$$

b. Annual (pretax) earnings on released funds = Amount of funds released × Interest rate
$$= \$3,600,000 \times 0.10 = \$360,000$$

c. Annual bank processing fee = Fixed cost + Number of payments per year × Variable cost per payment
$$= \$50,000 + (600,000 \times \$0.20) = \$170,000$$

d. Net (pretax) benefits = Annual (pretax) earnings on released funds + Reduction in firm's payment processing costs − Annual bank processing fee
$$= \$360,000 + \$40,000 - \$170,000 = \$230,000$$

ST3. a. Average collection period = 30 + 10 = 40 days

Average daily sales = Annual sales/365
$$= \$54,750,000/365$$
$$= \$150,000$$

Investment in receivables = Average daily sales × Average collection period
$$= \$150,000 \times 40 = \$6,000,000$$

b. Investment in receivables = $\{[\$54,750,000 \times (1 - 0.15)]/365\} \times (30 + 25)$
$$= \$7,012,500$$

ST4. a. Additional sales = $5,475,000

Marginal profitability of additional sales = Additional sales × Profit contribution ratio
$$= \$5,475,000 \times (1 - 0.75) = \$1,368,750$$

b. Additional investment in receivables = (Additional annual sales/365) × Average collection period
$$= (\$5,475,000/365) \times 75 = \$1,125,000$$

Cost of additional investment in receivables = Additional investment in receivables × Required rate of return
$$= \$1,125,000 \times 0.18 = \$202,500$$

c. Additional bad-debt loss = Additional sales × Bad-debt loss ratio
$$= \$5,475,000 \times 0.05 = \$273,750$$

d. Cost of additional investment in inventory = Additional investment in inventory × Required rate of return
$$= \$800,000 \times 0.18 = \$144,000$$

e. Additional cash discounts = Additional sales × Percent taking discount × Cash discount percent
$$= \$5,475,000 \times 0.10 \times 0.02 = \$10,950$$

f. Net change in pretax profits = Marginal returns − Marginal costs

$$= \$1,368,750 - (\$202,500 + \$273,750 + \$10,950 + \$144,000)$$

$$= \$737,550$$

ST5. a. $S = \$72$; $D = 360,000$ baseballs;

$C = 0.20 \times \$1.25 = \$0.25$/baseball

$$Q^* = \sqrt{\frac{2SD}{C}}$$

$$= \sqrt{\frac{2(\$72)(360,000)}{\$0.25}}$$

$$= 14,400 \text{ baseballs (1,200 dozen)}$$

b. $\text{TC} = \dfrac{D \times S}{Q^*} + \dfrac{Q^* \times C}{2}$

$$= \frac{360,000 \times \$72}{14,400} + \frac{14,400 \times \$0.25}{2}$$

$$= \$3,600$$

c. $\text{T}^* = \dfrac{365 \times Q^*}{D}$

$$= \frac{365 \times 14,400}{360,000}$$

$$= 14.6 \text{ days}$$

CHAPTER 17

ST1. a. Conversion value = Conversion ratio × Share price

$$= \left(\frac{\$1,000}{\$40}\right)(\$35)$$

$$= \$875$$

b. Straight-bond value $= \displaystyle\sum_{t=1}^{n} \frac{\text{Interest}}{(1 + k_d)^t} + \frac{\text{Principal}}{(1 + k_d)^n}$

$$= \sum_{t=1}^{20} \frac{\$80}{(1 + 0.11)^t} + \frac{\$1,000}{(1 + 0.11)^{20}}$$

$$= \$80(\text{PVIFA}_{0.11,\,20}) + \$1000(\text{PVIF}_{0.11,\,20})$$

$$= \$80(7.963) + \$1000(0.124)$$

$$= \$761$$

c. Conversion premium $= \$925 - \text{Max}\ \{\$875;\ \$761\}$

$$= \$50$$

d. Conversion value = Conversion ratio × Share price

$$= \left(\frac{\$1,000}{\$40}\right)(\$55)$$

$$= \$1,375$$

e. $1,375. At this price, the bond issue is likely to be called, effectively forcing conversion. Therefore, the debenture cannot be expected to sell at a premium above the conversion value.

ST2. a. Formula value = Max { $0; (Common share price − Exercise price)
                     × Number of shares per warrant}
= Max {$0; ($32 − $40)(1)}
= $0
Premium = $1.50 − $0 = $1.50

b. Formula value = Max {$0; ($40 − $40)(1)}
= $0
Premium = $3.50 − $0 = $3.50

c. Formula value = Max {$0; ($48 − $40)(1)}
= $8
Premium = $10.00 − $8.00 = $2.00

ST3. a. Rights-on case

$$R = \frac{M_0 - S}{N + 1}$$

$$= \frac{\$25 - \$22}{10 + 1}$$

$$= \$0.27$$

Ex-rights case

$$R = \frac{M_e - S}{N}$$

$$= \frac{\$24.73 - \$22}{10}$$

$$= \$0.27$$

b. $0.27

c. $$R = \frac{M_0 - S}{N + 1}$$

$$= \frac{\$30 - \$22}{10 + 1}$$

$$= \$0.73$$

CHAPTER 18

ST1. A Canadian trader could borrow US dollars, buy spot Canadian dollars, and invest in Canadian securities to earn 12%. Simultaneously, the trader could sell Canadian dollars forward at a 3% annual discount. At the end of the forward period, the trader could convert Canadian dollars back to US dollars. The net effect of these transactions is the trader earns 9% (12% interest less 3% depreciation in value) compared with the 8% return available in the US market.

If the Canadian trader wishes to keep the profit in Canadian dollars, the trader can sell forward only enough Canadian dollars to pay off the US loan.

ST2 a. Yen price = (JPY77.37/CAD)(CAD45.00/tonne) = JPY3481.65/tonne

b. Yen price = (JPY75.00/CAD)(CAD45.00/tonne) = JPY3375.00/tonne

A decline in the value of the Canadian dollar relative to the yen makes Canadian goods more attractive in Japan.

ST3.
$$\frac{S_n}{S_0} = \frac{(1 + i_h)^n}{(1 + i_f)^n}$$

$$\frac{S_3}{\text{CAD1.08/CHF}} = \frac{(1 + .04)^3}{(1 + .05)^3}$$

$$S_3 = \text{CAD1.0494/CHF}$$

The higher Swiss interest rate relative to the Canadian rate implies (using IFE) that the Swiss franc should decline in value relative to the Canadian dollar, as this computation verifies.

CHAPTER 19

ST1. Parts a and b

Lease-Buy Analysis

Single-Year Inputs

New asset price	$25,000
Ship. & instal.	$0
Life, $n \leq 20$	5
B-T cost of debt	12.00%
Tax rate	25.00%
CCA rate	30.00%
Salvage	$0

Multi-Year Inputs

Year	0	1	2	3	4
Lease payment	$6,000	$6,000	$6,000	$6,000	$6,000
ΔOperating costs					

Intermediate Outputs

A-T cost of debt: 9.00%

Year	0	1	2	3	4	5	6	7	8	9	10	11	12	13	14	15	16	17	18	19	20
Starting UCC		$25,000	$21,250	$14,875	$10,412	$7,288	$5,102	$3,571	$2,500	$1,750	$1,225	$857	$600	$420	$294	$206	$144	$101	$71	$50	$35
CCA		$3,750	$6,375	$4,463	$3,124	$2,186	$1,531	$1,071	$750	$525	$368	$257	$180	$126	$88	$62	$43	$30	$21	$15	$11
Ending UCC		$21,250	$14,875	$10,412	$7,288	$5,102	$3,571	$2,500	$1,750	$1,225	$857	$600	$420	$294	$206	$144	$101	$71	$50	$35	$24

Cash-Flow Outputs

Year	0	1	2	3	4	5	6	7	8	9	10	11	12	13	14	15	16	17	18	19	20
Net installed cost	$25,000																				
Lease payment	$6,000	$6,000	$6,000	$6,000	$6,000	$0	$0	$0	$0	$0	$0	$0	$0	$0	$0	$0	$0	$0	$0	$0	$0
Lease tax shield		$1,500	$1,500	$1,500	$1,500	$1,500	$0	$0	$0	$0	$0	$0	$0	$0	$0	$0	$0	$0	$0	$0	$0
CCA tax shield $t \leq n$		$938	$1,594	$1,116	$781	$547	$0	$0	$0	$0	$0	$0	$0	$0	$0	$0	$0	$0	$0	$0	$0
A-T ΔOp. costs		$0	$0	$0	$0	$0	$0	$0	$0	$0	$0	$0	$0	$0	$0	$0	$0	$0	$0	$0	$0
Salvage, $t = n$		$0	$0	$0	$0	$0	$0	$0	$0	$0	$0	$0	$0	$0	$0	$0	$0	$0	$0	$0	$0
PV tax shield $t > n$		$0	$0	$0	$0	$981	$0	$0	$0	$0	$0	$0	$0	$0	$0	$0	$0	$0	$0	$0	$0
Net cash flow	$19,000	−$5,438	−$6,094	−$5,616	−$5,281	−$28	$0	$0	$0	$0	$0	$0	$0	$0	$0	$0	$0	$0	$0	$0	$0

NAL	$786
Approximate IRR	7.09%
Approximate B-T "indifference" cost of debt	9.45%

a. Since NAL is positive, the firm should lease the computer system.

b. The approximate before-tax indifference cost of debt is 9.45%.

ST1. Part c

Lease-Buy Analysis

Single-Year Inputs

New asset price	$25,000
Ship. & instal.	$0
Life, $n \le 20$	5
B-T cost of debt	9.56%
Tax rate	25.00%
CCA rate	30.00%
Salvage	$0

Multi-Year Inputs

Year	0	1	2	3	4
Lease payment	$6,000	$6,000	$6,000	$6,000	$6,000
ΔOperating costs					

Intermediate Outputs

A-T cost of debt 7.17%

Year	0	1	2	3	4	5	6	7	8	9	10	11	12	13	14	15	16	17	18	19	20
Starting UCC		$25,000	$21,250	$14,875	$10,412	$7,288	$5,102	$3,571	$2,500	$1,750	$1,225	$857	$600	$420	$294	$206	$144	$101	$71	$50	$35
CCA		$3,750	$6,375	$4,463	$3,124	$2,186	$1,531	$1,071	$750	$525	$368	$257	$180	$126	$88	$62	$43	$30	$21	$15	$11
Ending UCC		$21,250	$14,875	$10,412	$7,288	$5,102	$3,571	$2,500	$1,750	$1,225	$857	$600	$420	$294	$206	$144	$101	$71	$50	$35	$24

Cash-Flow Outputs

Year	0	1	2	3	4	5	6	7	8	9	10	11	12	13	14	15	16	17	18	19	20
Net installed cost	$25,000																				
Lease payment	$6,000	$6,000	$6,000	$6,000	$6,000	$0	$0	$0	$0	$0	$0	$0	$0	$0	$0	$0	$0	$0	$0	$0	$0
Lease tax shield	$0	$1,500	$1,500	$1,500	$1,500	$1,500	$0	$0	$0	$0	$0	$0	$0	$0	$0	$0	$0	$0	$0	$0	$0
CCA tax shield $t \le n$	$0	$938	$1,594	$1,116	$781	$547	$0	$0	$0	$0	$0	$0	$0	$0	$0	$0	$0	$0	$0	$0	$0
A-T ΔOp. costs	$0	$0	$0	$0	$0	$0	$0	$0	$0	$0	$0	$0	$0	$0	$0	$0	$0	$0	$0	$0	$0
Salvage, $t = n$	$0	$0	$0	$0	$0	$0	$0	$0	$0	$0	$0	$0	$0	$0	$0	$0	$0	$0	$0	$0	$0
PV tax shield $t > n$	$0	$0	$0	$0	$0	$1,029	$0	$0	$0	$0	$0	$0	$0	$0	$0	$0	$0	$0	$0	$0	$0
Net cash flow	$19,000	-$5,438	-$6,094	-$5,616	-$5,281	-$76	$0	$0	$0	$0	$0	$0	$0	$0	$0	$0	$0	$0	$0	$0	$0

NAL	$0
Approximate IRR	7.17%
Approximate B-T "indifference" cost of debt	9.56%

c. The actual before-tax indifference cost of debt is 9.56% where NAL = 0.

CHAPTER 20

ST1. a. Low end of range:

$$\$40 \times 1.25 = \$50$$

High end of range:

$$P_{max} = (P/E)_1(EPS_2)$$
$$= (10)(\$6.00)$$
$$= \$60$$

b. $$EPS_c = \frac{EAT_1 + EAT_2 + EAT_{1,2}}{NS_1 + NS_2 \ (ER)}$$

$$= \frac{\$30 \text{ million} + \$12 \text{ million} + 0}{\$6 \text{ million} + \$2 \text{ million} \ (1.0)}$$

$$= \$5.25$$

Check Answers to Selected Problems

CHAPTER 2

1. $12,493,886
2. $35,378

CHAPTER 3

1. a. $219,178
2. a. 15%
3. $3,945,205
6. $1,150,000
7. $200(000)
11. b. Current ratio = 2.2X
     Quick ratio = 1.8X
12. a. ROE = 25%
14. a. ROE = 28.57%
22. a. Firm A: ROE = 30%
     Equity multiplier = 1.5
26. a. 5.0 times
27. c. $16
28. $66.7 million

CHAPTER 4

1. a. $1,191
3. $240,410.40
5. $1,343.72
6. 13%
9. 20%
13. $13,018.71
26. $51,980.44
27. $94,337
28. $21,879
33. $3,386
34. $51,354
35. $5,907.83
37. $3,890

APPENDIX 4A

2. $2,744
4. d. 22.14%
6. $123.13

CHAPTER 5

1. b. $P_0 = 800
5. a. $P_0 = 38.89
6. a. $P_0 = $1,139$

d. $P_0 = $1,057$
7. $YTM = 8.3\%$
15. $P_0 = 964
19. $10.97

CHAPTER 6

1. b. $61.77
2. 7%
3. $12.50
5. a. $88.33
6. $57.36
9. $21.34
10. $16.21
18. $12.10
22. $16.80
24. $20.25

CHAPTER 7

1. a. $r_x = 15\%$
    b. $\sigma_x = 11.62\%$
2. $p(\text{loss}) = 2.28\%$
7. a. i. $r_p = 8.2\%$
       ii. $\sigma_p = 4.87\%$
8. b. $r_p = 13.05\%$
    c. $\sigma_p = 3.64\%$
9. b. 9.74%
12. b. i. $\sigma_p = 7.8\%$
       ii. $\sigma_p = 6.18\%$
14. 47%
17. $p(\text{loss}) = 1.0\%$
23. b. 62.93%
27. 82.89%

CHAPTER 8

2. 7.2%
5. b. 13%
7. 17.3%
12. a. 13.4%
14. First break: $33.33 million
    $k_a = 13.1\%$ (for first block)
16. First break: $60 million
    $k_a = 13.19\%$ (for first block)
18. a. $27.65
19. a. 1.4

CHAPTER 9

1. a.
Year	CCA
1	$7,650
2	$13,005
3	$9,104
4	$6,372
5	$4,461
6	$3,122
7	$2,186
8	$1,530
9	$1,071
10	$750

8. a. $140,000
11. a. $200,000

CHAPTER 10

1. NPV = −$3,050, PI = 0.85
2. 9.11%
3. $364.53
5. a. $158
11. $n \approx 19$

CHAPTER 11

3. a. 17%
4. a. $703,600
8. a. 5.48%
13. b. −$0.1795 million
18. 19.8%

CHAPTER 12

1. $10,000
3. a. $600,000
5. a. i. 45% debt + 55% equity

CHAPTER 13

4. a. EPS = $5.40
    d. i. DCL = 2.778
5. b. i. DOL = 1.875
       ii. DFL = 1.67
       iii. DCL = 3.13
18. 24.51%
19. 2.28%
21. a. EBIT = $15 million
22. a. EBIT = $2.4 million
28. a. 2.28%

Chapter 14

1. b. $0.50
2. 16.7%
6. $1,425,000
8. b. $1.60

Chapter 15

1. b. $50,703,000
7. Aggressive ROE = 14.55%
8. c. 124.1 days
   e. 69.35 days
9. a. i. Aggressive ROA = 12.29%
10. a. iii. Aggressive CA/CL = 1.25
11. a. i. Aggressive: 10.85%
25. a. $889,890
27. a. 46.7 days

Chapter 16

1. a. $7,500,000
2. b. $177,534

3. b. 38.5 days
5. $411,044
9. c. −$11,363
12. d. −$18,424
15. $158,062
16. $17,329
17. $1,163,836
20. $104,700
22. d. 24,658

Chapter 17

1. c. $0
4. a. $1.50
   b. $3.50
5. a. $1,000
   b. $726
6. a. 11.98 shares
7. c. $0
8. c. $131,25 million
10. c. $1.15

15. b. $783
17. c. $882.11, higher

Chapter 18

1. 4.68%
7. 2654 and 2407

Chapter 19

1. $586,850 for both
2. Yes, NAL = $2,889.00

Chapter 20

3. b. 19%
4. a. 0.5 of B share for 1 of K
7. EPS_c = $3.24
9. a. EPS = $4.045
   d. EPS = $4.258

KEY NOTATION USED IN THE TEXT

α	Certainty equivalent factor
A	Assets
APR	Annual percentage rate
APT	Arbitrage pricing theory
ATCF	After-tax cash flow
b_j	Computed historical beta of a security
β_j	Beta of a security
β_l	Leveraged beta
β_p	Portfolio beta
β_u	Unleveraged beta
c	Unit production cost
C	Value of a call option
CA	Current assets
CAPM	Capital asset pricing model
CCA	Capital cost allowance
CE	Certainty equivalent
CF	Cash flow
CL	Current liabilities
D	(1) Debt in capital structure
	(2) Market value of a firm's debt
D_p	Preferred share dividends
D_t	Common share dividends
DB	Depreciable base
Dep	Depreciation
DCL	Degree of combined leverage
DFL	Degree of financial leverage
Div	Common share dividends
DOL	Degree of operating leverage
e	Exponential e; value ≈ 2.71828
E	(1) Common equity in capital structure
	(2) Market value of a firm's equity
EAR	Effective annual rate
EAT	Earnings after taxes
EBIT	Earnings before interest and taxes
EBT	Earnings before taxes
EPS	Earnings per share
ER	Exchange ratio
EVA	Economic value added
F	Forward foreign exchange rate
FCF	Free cash flow

FIFO	First in, first out inventory valuation
FV	Future value
FVAN	Future value of an annuity
FVAND	Future value of an annuity due
FVIF	Future value interest factor
FVIFA	Future value interest factor of an annuity
g	Expected annual growth rate in earnings, dividends, and/or share price
i	Interest rate per time period
i_{eff}	Effective annual interest rate
i_f	Interest rate in foreign currency country
i_h	Interest rate in home currency country
i_{nom}	Nominal annual interest rate
i_R	Real rate of return
I	Interest payments before taxes
IFE	International Fisher effect
IOC	Investment opportunity curve
IRP	Interest rate parity
IRR	Internal rate of return
k	A percentage required rate of return or cost of capital; discount rate
k_a	Weighted (marginal) cost of capital
k_a^*	Risk-adjusted weighted cost of capital or required return on an investment
k_d	Required return on a bond; pretax cost of debt; yield to maturity on a bond
k_e	Required return on a common share; cost of internal equity
k_e'	Cost of external equity
k_i	After-tax cost of debt
k_j	Required return from security j
k_p	Required return on preferred shares; cost of preferred share financing
L_t	Lease payment
LBO	Leveraged buyout
LIBOR	London interbank offer rate
LIFO	Last-in, first-out inventory valuation
m	Frequency of compounding per time period
M	Maturity value of a bond
M_e	Market price of a share ex-rights
M_o	Market price of a share rights-on